Lr Adobe Lightroom CC

Library | Develop | Map | B

the Adobe® Photoshop® Lightroom® CC book for digital photographers

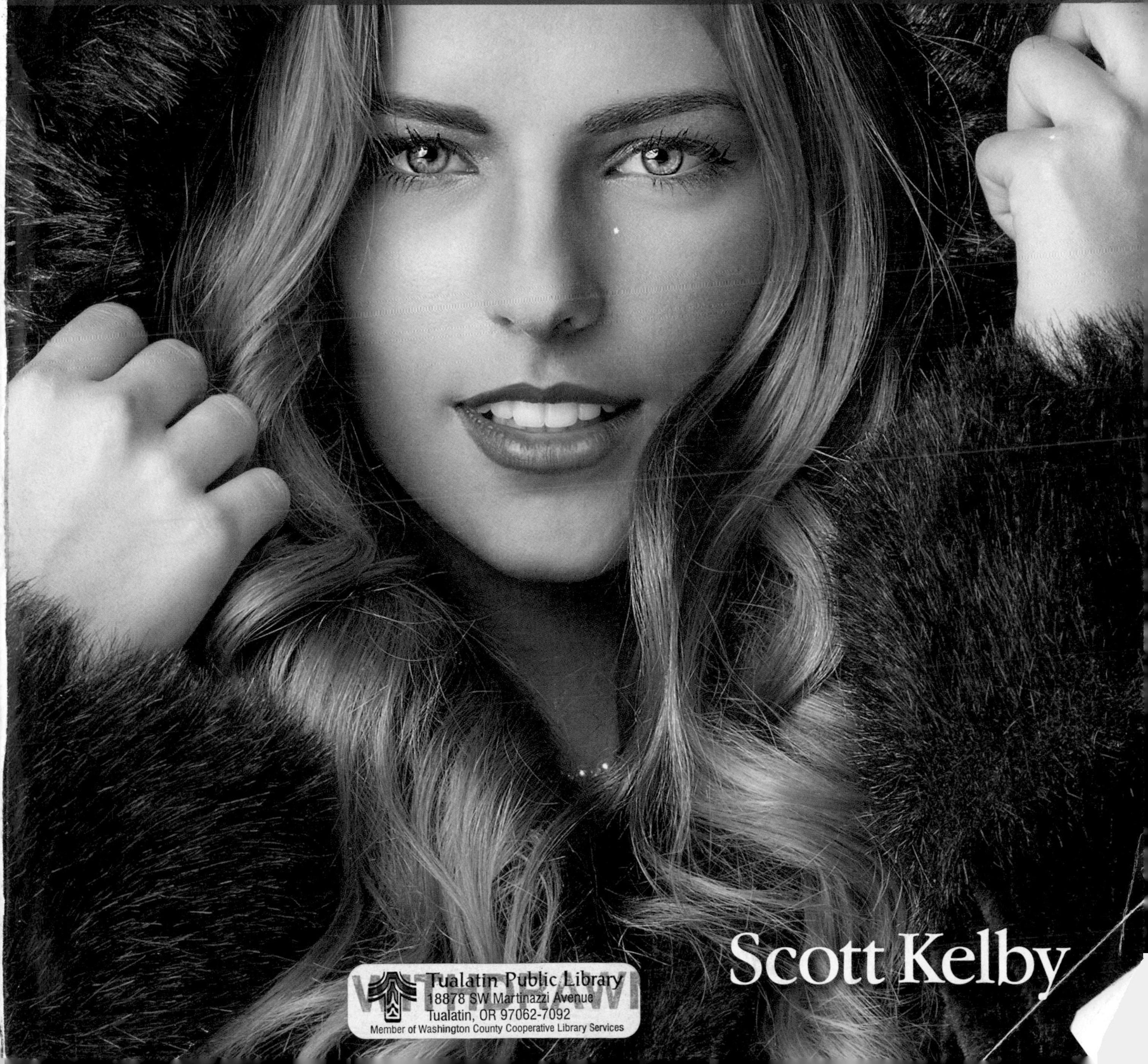

Scott Kelby

The Adobe Photoshop Lightroom CC Book for Digital Photographers Team

MANAGING EDITOR
Kim Doty

TECHNICAL EDITOR
Cindy Snyder

ART DIRECTOR
Jessica Maldonado

COVER PHOTO BY
Scott Kelby

Published by **New Riders**

Composed in Myriad Pro, Helvetica, and Blair ITC by Kelby Media Group, Inc.

Trademarks

All terms mentioned in this book that are known to be trademarks or service marks have been appropriately capitalized. New Riders cannot attest to the accuracy of this information. Use of a term in the book should not be regarded as affecting the validity of any trademark or service mark.

Photoshop, Photoshop Lightroom, and Photoshop Elements are registered trademarks of Adobe Systems, Inc.

Macintosh, Mac, and Mac OS X are registered trademarks of Apple Inc.

Windows is a registered trademark of Microsoft Corporation.

Warning and Disclaimer

This book is designed to provide information about Adobe Photoshop Lightroom for digital photographers. Every effort has been made to make this book as complete and as accurate as possible, but no warranty of fitness is implied.

The information is provided on an as-is basis. The author and New Riders shall have neither liability nor responsibility to any person or entity with respect to any loss or damages arising from the information contained in this book or from the use of the discs, electronic files, or programs that may accompany it.

THIS PRODUCT IS NOT ENDORSED OR SPONSORED BY ADOBE SYSTEMS INCORPORATED, PUBLISHER OF ADOBE PHOTOSHOP LIGHTROOM CC.

ISBN13: 978-0-13-397979-4
ISBN10: 0-13-397979-2

9 8 7 6 5 4 3 2 1

http://kelbyone.com
www.newriders.com

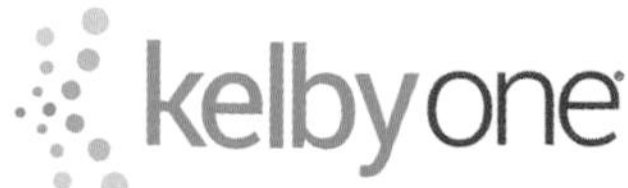

This book is dedicated to
my dear friend, Manny Steigman.
This world is a better place
because he's in it.

ACKNOWLEDGMENTS

I start the acknowledgments for every book I've ever written the same way—by thanking my amazing wife, Kalebra. If you knew what an incredible woman she is, you'd totally understand why.

This is going to sound silly, but if we go grocery shopping together, and she sends me off to a different aisle to get milk, when I return with the milk and she sees me coming back down the aisle, she gives me the warmest, most wonderful smile. It's not because she's happy that I found the milk; I get that same smile every time I see her, even if we've only been apart for 60 seconds. It's a smile that says, "There's the man I love."

If you got that smile, dozens of times a day, for nearly 26 years of marriage, you'd feel like the luckiest guy in the world, and believe me—I do. To this day, just seeing her puts a song in my heart and makes it skip a beat. When you go through life like this, it makes you one incredibly happy and grateful guy, and I truly am.

So, thank you, my love. Thanks for your kindness, your hugs, your understanding, your advice, your patience, your generosity, and for being such a caring and compassionate mother and wife. I love you.

Secondly, a big thanks to my son, Jordan. I wrote my first book when my wife was pregnant with him (19 years ago), and he has literally grown up around my writing. It has been a blast watching him grow up into such a wonderful young man, with his mother's tender and loving heart and compassion way beyond his years. As he heads off to college this year, out-of-state (sniff, sniff), he knows that his dad just could not be prouder or more excited for him, but he may not realize just how much I'll miss seeing his big smile every morning before school and at the dinner table every night. Throughout his life, he has touched so many people, in so many different ways, and even though he's so young, he has already inspired so many, and I just cannot wait to see the amazing adventure, and the love and laughter this life has in store for him. Hey, little buddy—this world needs more "yous!"

Thanks to our wonderful daughter, Kira, for being the answer to our prayers, for being such a blessing to your older brother, and for proving once again that miracles happen every day. You are a little clone of your mother, and believe me, there is no greater compliment I could give you. It is such a blessing to get to see such a happy, hilarious, clever, creative, and just awesome little force of nature running around the house each day—she just has no idea how happy and proud she makes us. She is awesomeness wrapped in a layer of chocolate with sprinkles. It doesn't get much better than that.

A special thanks to my big brother, Jeff. I have so much to be thankful for in my life, and having you as such a positive role model while I was growing up is one thing I'm particularly thankful for. You're the best brother any guy could ever have, and I've said it a million times before, but one more surely wouldn't hurt—I love you, man!

My heartfelt thanks go to my entire team at Kelby Media Group. I know everybody thinks their team is really special, but this one time—I'm right. I'm so proud to get to work with you all, and I'm still amazed at what you're able to accomplish day in, day out, and I'm constantly impressed with how much passion and pride you put into everything you do.

A warm word of thanks goes to my in-house Editor Kim Doty. It's her amazing attitude, passion, poise, and attention to detail that has kept me writing books. When you're writing a book like this, sometimes you can really feel like you're all alone, but she really makes me feel that I'm not alone—that we're a team. It often is her encouraging words or helpful ideas that keep me going when I've hit a wall, and I just can't thank her enough. Kim, you are "the best!"

http://kelbyone.com

I'm equally as lucky to have the immensely talented Jessica Maldonado working on the design of my books. I just love the way Jessica designs, and all the clever little things she adds to her layouts and cover designs. She's not just incredibly talented and a joy to work with, she's a very smart designer and thinks five steps ahead in every layout she builds. I feel very, very fortunate to have her on my team.

Also, a big thanks to my in-house tech editor Cindy Snyder, who helps test all the techniques in the book (and makes sure I didn't leave out that one little step that would take the train off the tracks), and she catches lots of little things others would have missed. Plus, her dedication, skill, and attitude really makes working with her a pleasure. Thank you, Cindy!

To my best buddy and book-publishing powerhouse, Dave Moser (also known as "the guiding light, force of nature, miracle birth, etc."), for always insisting that we raise the bar and make everything we do better than anything we've done before.

Thanks to my friend and business partner, Jean A. Kendra, for her support and friendship all these years. You mean a lot to me, to Kalebra, and to our company.

My heartfelt thanks to Jeff Gatt and Audra Carpenter for all their hard work and dedication in taking our company to the next level, and caring enough to always do the right thing.

A big thanks to my Executive Assistant, Lynn Miller, for wrangling a "kitten that's always trying to jump out of the box" each day, and for keeping me focused, organized, and on track, which has to be just an insanely challenging job, but she seems to do it pretty effortlessly, which is a testament to how good she is at it. Thank you, Lynn.

A high-five to the entire crew at Peachpit Press. Thanks for all your hard work and dedication to making the kind of books that make a difference. Also, a special thanks to my longtime Publisher at Peachpit, Nancy Aldrich-Ruenzel, who retired this year. It was an honor to get to work with you, and your wisdom, advice, direction, and insights will never be forgotten, and while we'll miss you terribly, we'll do our best to create the kind of book that would make you proud.

Thanks to Lightroom Product Manager Sharad Mangalick, and Adobe's Viceroy of Digital Happiness, Tom Hogarty, for answering lots of questions and late-night emails, and helping make this book better than it would have been. You guys are the best!

Thanks to my friends at Adobe Systems: Brian Hughes, Terry White, Scott Morris, Jim Heiser, Stephen Nielsen, Bryan Lamkin, Julieanne Kost, and Russell Preston Brown. Gone but not forgotten: Barbara Rice, Rye Livingston, John Loiacono, Kevin Connor, Deb Whitman, Addy Roff, Cari Gushiken, and Karen Gauthier.

I want to thank all the talented and gifted photographers who've taught me so much over the years, including: Moose Peterson, Joe McNally, Bill Fortney, George Lepp, Anne Cahill, Vincent Versace, David Ziser, Jim DiVitale, Cliff Mautner, Dave Black, Helene Glassman, and Monte Zucker.

Thanks to my mentors, whose wisdom and whip-cracking have helped me immeasurably, including John Graden, Jack Lee, Dave Gales, Judy Farmer, and Douglas Poole.

Most importantly, I want to thank God, and His Son Jesus Christ, for leading me to the woman of my dreams, for blessing us with two amazing children, for allowing me to make a living doing something I truly love, for always being there when I need Him, for blessing me with a wonderful, fulfilling, and happy life, and such a warm, loving family to share it with.

OTHER BOOKS BY SCOTT KELBY

Photoshop for Lightroom Users

Professional Portrait Retouching Techniques for Photographers Using Photoshop

The Digital Photography Book, parts 1, 2, 3, 4 & 5

Light It, Shoot It, Retouch It: Learn Step by Step How to Go from Empty Studio to Finished Image

The Adobe Photoshop CC Book for Digital Photographers

The Photoshop Elements Book for Digital Photographers

The iPhone Book

Professional Sports Photography Workflow

Photo Recipes Live: Behind the Scenes: Your Guide to Today's Most Popular Lighting Techniques, parts 1 & 2

It's a Jesus Thing: The Book for Wanna Be-lievers

ABOUT THE AUTHOR

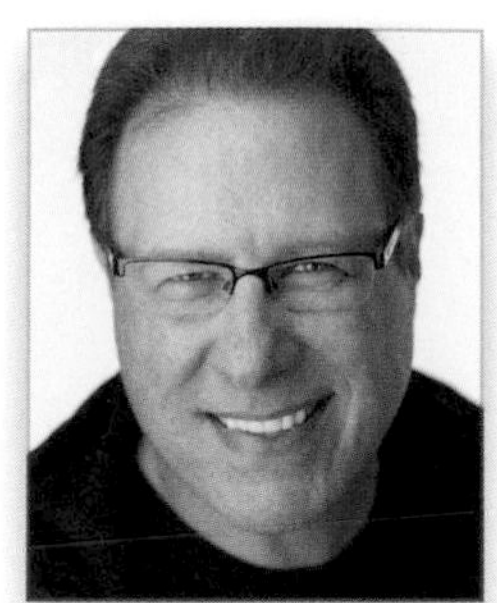

Scott Kelby

Scott is Editor, Publisher, and co-founder of *Photoshop User* magazine, co-host of *The Lightroom Show*, and co-host of *The Grid*, the weekly, live talk show for photographers, and Executive Producer of the top-rated weekly show *Photoshop User TV*.

He is President and CEO of KelbyOne, an online training and education firm dedicated to teaching Lightroom, Photoshop, and photography.

Scott is a photographer, designer, and award-winning author of more than 60 books, including *Photoshop for Lightroom Users, Professional Portrait Retouching Techniques for Photographers Using Photoshop, Light It, Shoot It, Retouch It: Learn Step by Step How to Go from Empty Studio to Finished Image, The Adobe Photoshop Book for Digital Photographers*, and *The Digital Photography Book*, parts 1, 2, 3, 4 & 5.

For the past five years, Scott has been honored with the distinction of being the world's #1 best-selling author of photography technique books. His book, *The Digital Photography Book*, part 1, is now the best-selling book on digital photography in history. And, he recently received the HIPA Award for his contributions to photography education worldwide.

His books have been translated into dozens of different languages, including Chinese, Russian, Spanish, Korean, Polish, Taiwanese, French, German, Italian, Japanese, Dutch, Arabic, Swedish, Turkish, Hebrew, and Portuguese, among others, and he is a recipient of the prestigious ASP International Award, presented annually by the American Society of Photographers for "...contributions in a special or significant way to the ideals of Professional Photography as an art and a science."

Scott is Training Director for the official Adobe Photoshop Seminar Tour and Conference Technical Chair for the Photoshop World Conference & Expo. He's a frequent speaker at conferences and trade shows around the world, is featured in a series of online learning courses at KelbyOne.com, and has been training Photoshop users and photographers since 1993.

For more information on Scott, visit him at:

His daily blog: **http://scottkelby.com**

Twitter: @**scottkelby**

Facebook: **www.facebook.com/skelby**

Google+: **Scottgplus.com**

TABLE OF CONTENTS

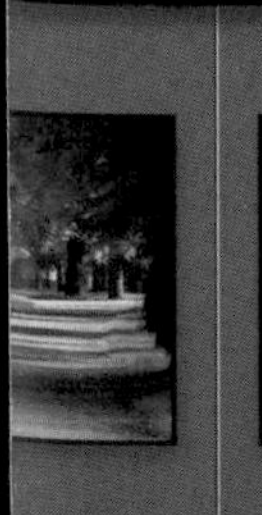
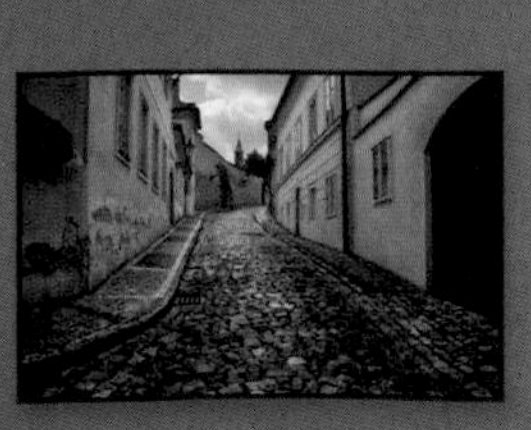
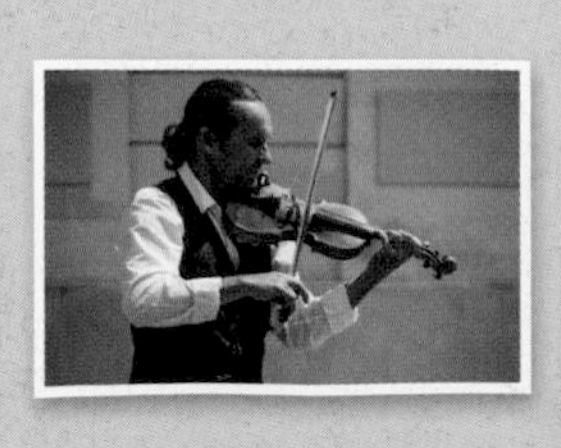
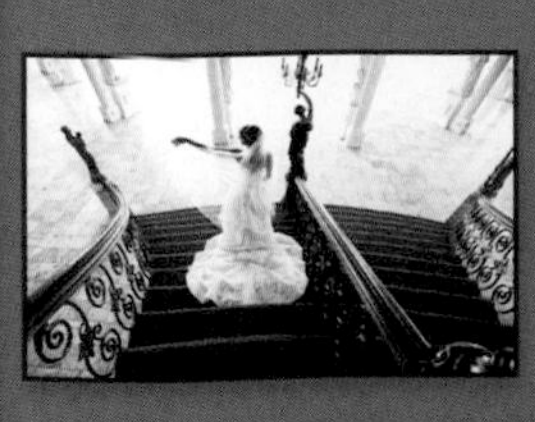
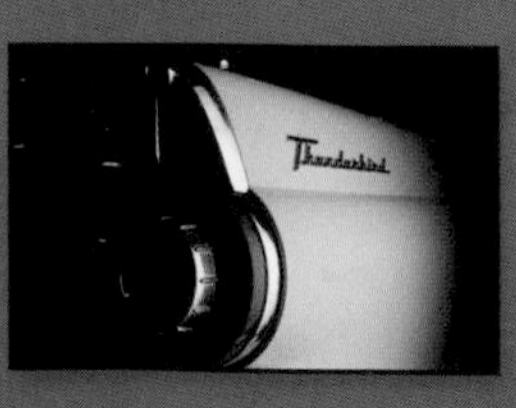
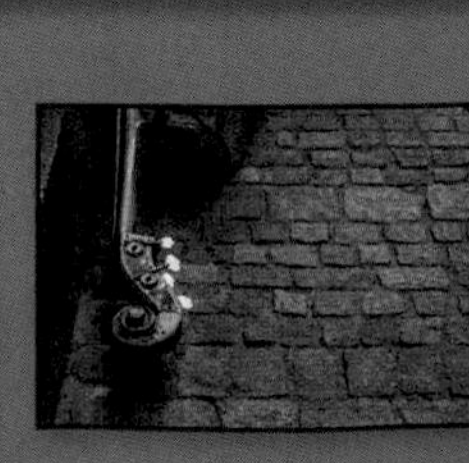

http://kelbyone.com

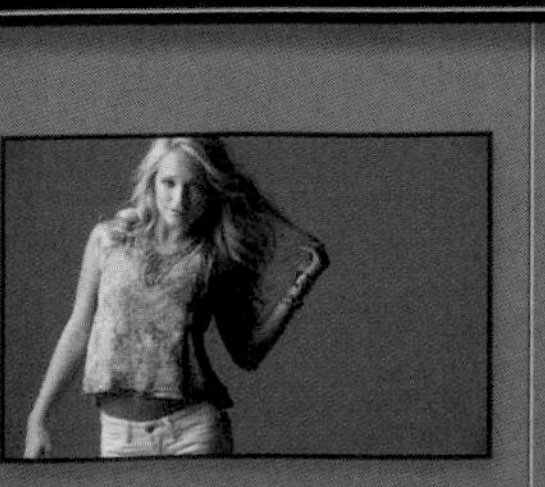
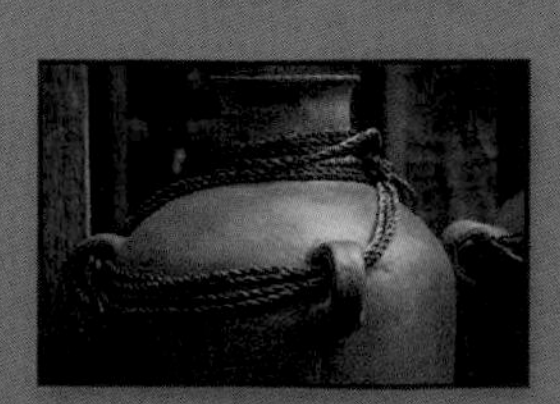
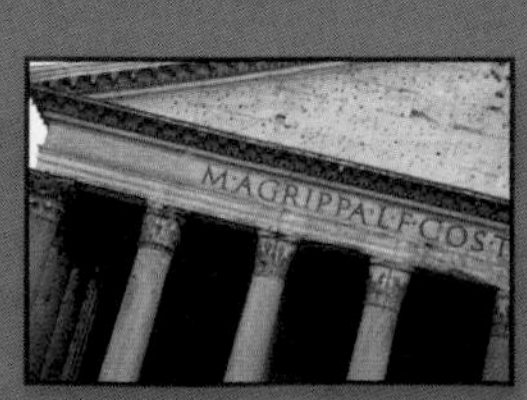

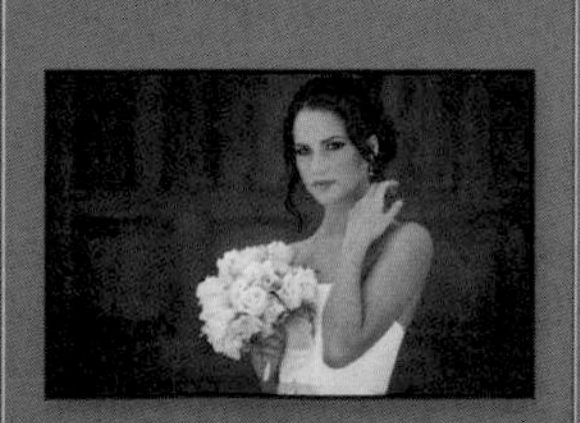
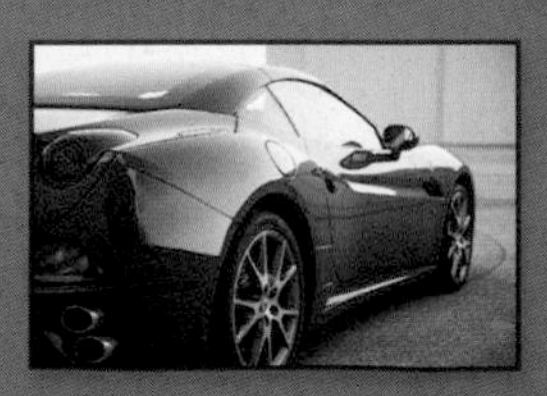
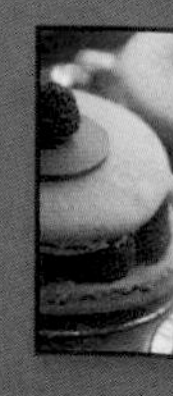

TABLE OF CONTENTS

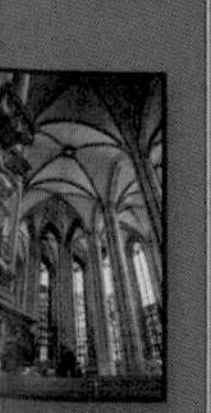
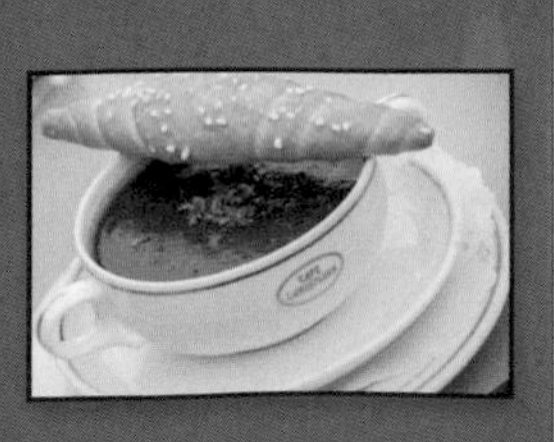

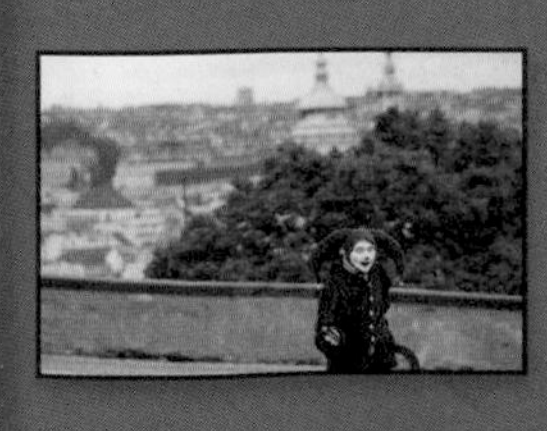
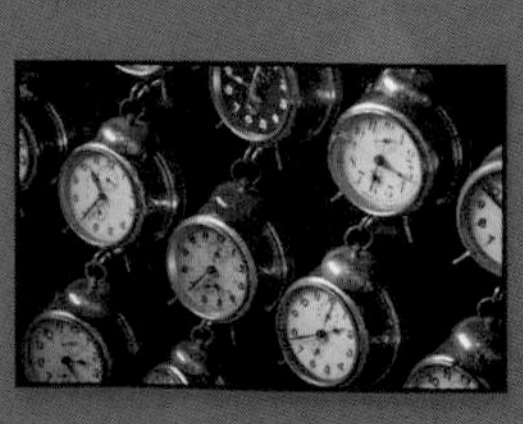
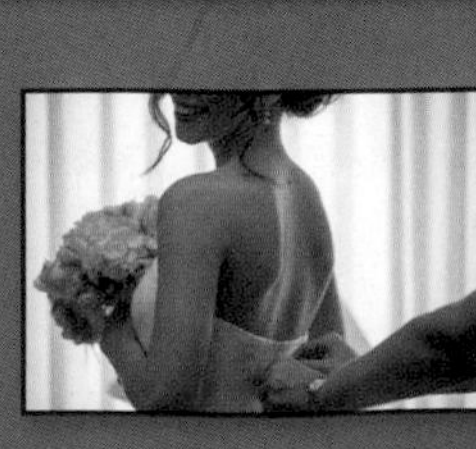

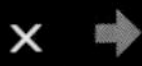

http://kelbyone.com

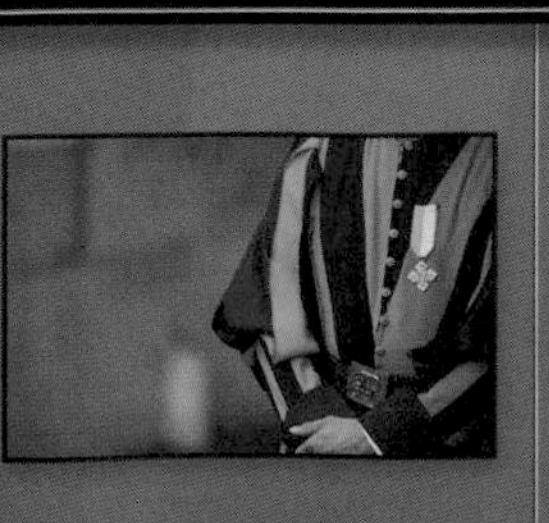
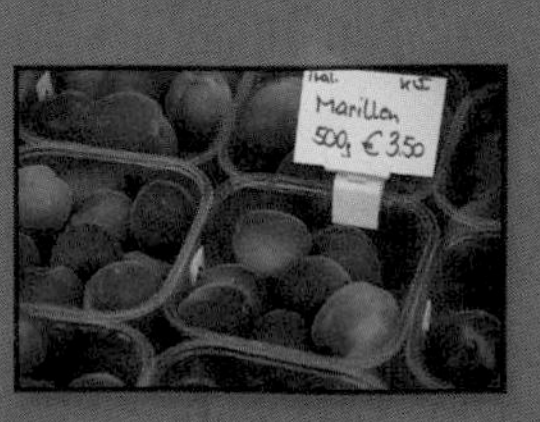

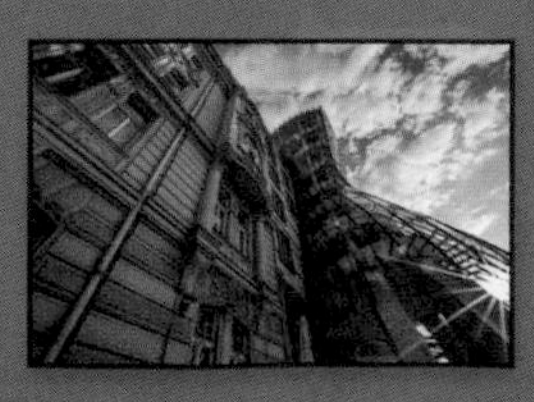
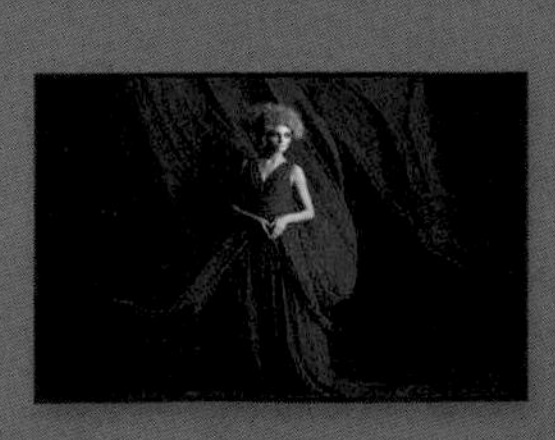
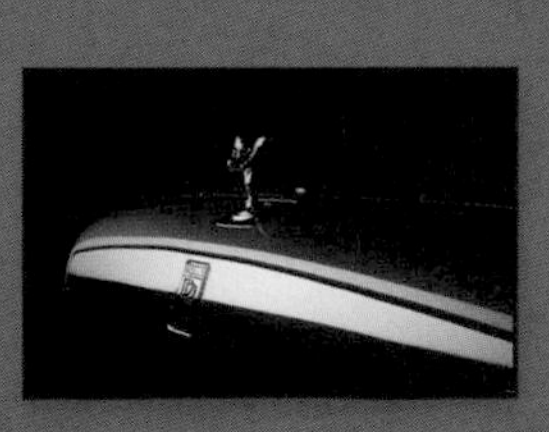
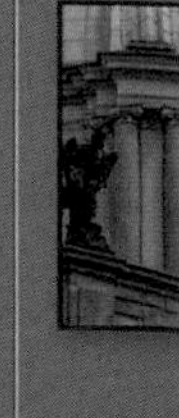

Seven (or So) Things You'll Wish You Had Known Before Reading This Book

I really want to make sure you get the absolute most out of reading this book, and if you take two minutes and read these seven (or so) things now, I promise it will make a big difference in your success with Lightroom, and with this book (plus, it will keep you from sending me an email asking something that everyone who skips this part will wind up doing). By the way, the captures shown below are just for looks. Hey, we're photographers—how things look really matters.

(1) This book is for Lightroom CC or Lightroom 6 users—either one (they both released with the exact same features). No matter which version you have, you're covered (so, if you bought Lightroom 6, and you see the words "Lightroom CC" in the book, you know not to let that freak you out). By the way, although the two were released with the exact same features, Lightroom CC users do get to use a free version of Lightroom for their mobile phone and tablet, so I included a bonus chapter for them. If you're a Lightroom 6 user, you can just skip over that mobile chapter.

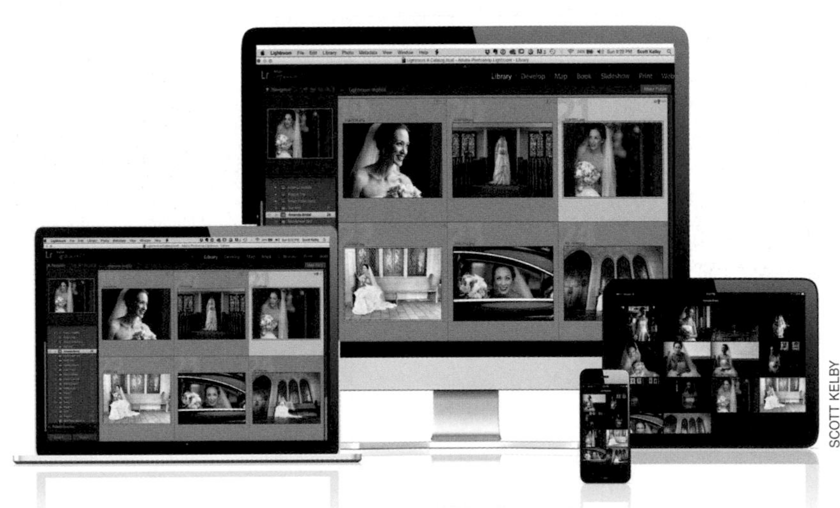

SCOTT KELBY

(2) You can download many of the key photos used here in the book, so you can follow along using many of the same images that I used, at **http://kelbyone.com/books/lrcc**. See, this is one of those things I was talking about that you'd miss if you skipped over this and jumped right to Chapter 1. Then you'd send me an angry email about how I didn't tell you where to download the photos. You wouldn't be the first.

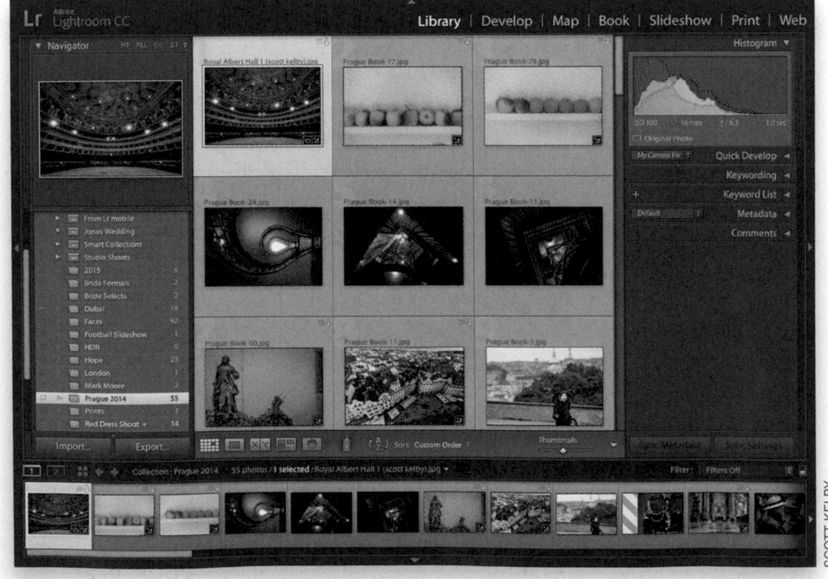

SCOTT KELBY

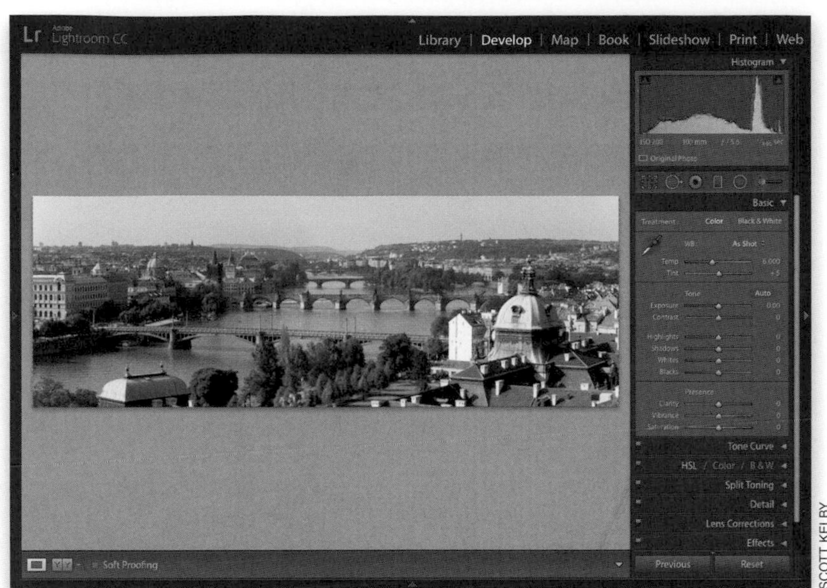

SCOTT KELBY

(3) If you've read my other books, you know they're usually "jump in anywhere" books, but with Lightroom, I wrote the book in the order you'll probably wind up using the program, so if you're new to Lightroom, I would really recommend you start with Chapter 1 and go through the book in order. But hey—it's your book—if you decide to just hollow out the insides and store your valuables in there, I'll never know. Also, make sure you read the opening to each project, up at the top of the page. Those actually have information you'll want to know, so don't skip over them.

(4) The official name of the software is "Adobe Photoshop Lightroom CC" because it's part of the Photoshop family, but if every time I referred to it throughout the book, I called it "Adobe Photoshop Lightroom CC," you'd eventually want to strangle me (or the person sitting nearest you), so from here on out, I usually just refer to it as "Lightroom" or "Lightroom CC." Just so you know.

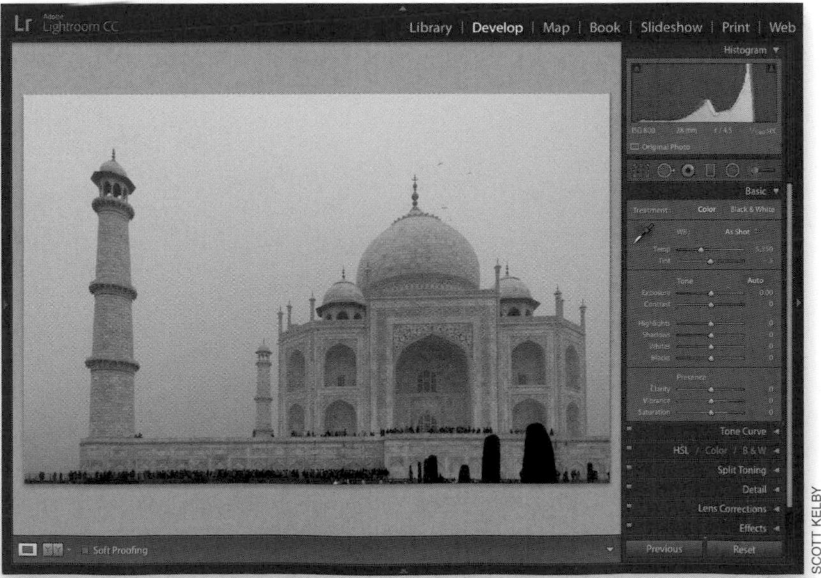

SCOTT KELBY

(5) The intro page at the beginning of each chapter is designed to give you a quick mental break, and honestly, they have little to do with the chapter. In fact, they have little to do with anything, but writing these quirky chapter intros is kind of a tradition of mine (I do this in all my books, and I even released a book of just the best chapter intros from all of my books. I am not making this up), but if you're one of those really "serious" types, you can skip them, because they'll just get on your nerves.

(6) At the end of the book is a special bonus chapter, where I share my own start-to-finish workflow. However, don't read it until you've read the entire book first, or you might not know how to do certain things that I'll be telling you to do (that's why I put it at the end of the book).

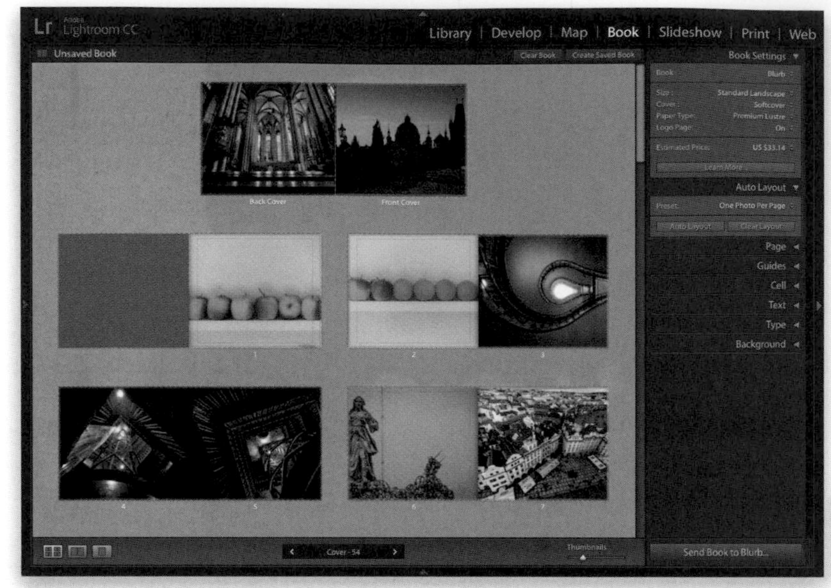

SCOTT KELBY

(7) Where's the chapter on the Web module? It's on the web (you'll find it at the address in #7.2). I put it there because Adobe has...well...they've kind of abandoned it (not officially mind you, but come on—they haven't really added any new features in the past three versions, even though they finally replaced the old Flash galleries with HTML 5 ones in this latest version, so I can't [with a straight face] recommend that you use it at all). But, just in case, I still updated it with the new HTML 5 gallery stuff (I took out the old stuff) and posted the chapter on the web for you (the link is on the download page), so just think of it as a bonus you won't ever use.

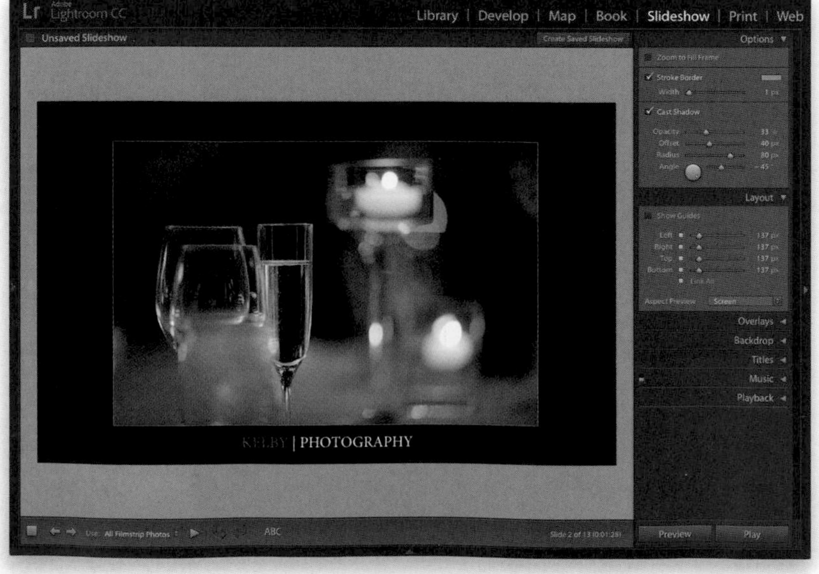

SCOTT KELBY

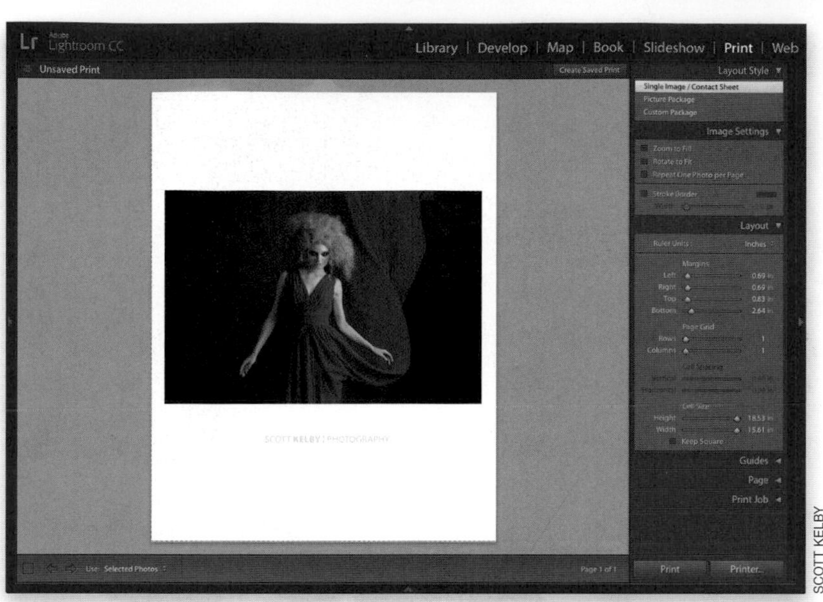

(7.1) Who's up for some cool, free Lightroom presets? I think you've earned 'em (well, at least you will have by the time you finish this book). Now, if you're a brand new user and you're not sure what presets are yet, they are basically "one-click wonders" that make your photos look awesome. There's a huge market for presets and people sell presets like these all day long (for bunches of money). But, because I dig you with the passion of a thousand burning suns (or because you bought this book—I'll let you decide which reason fits you best), I'm giving you a whole bunch of them we created here in-house. Anyway, the link to them, and samples of how they look, are found on the downloads page (mentioned below in #7.2). See, I care.

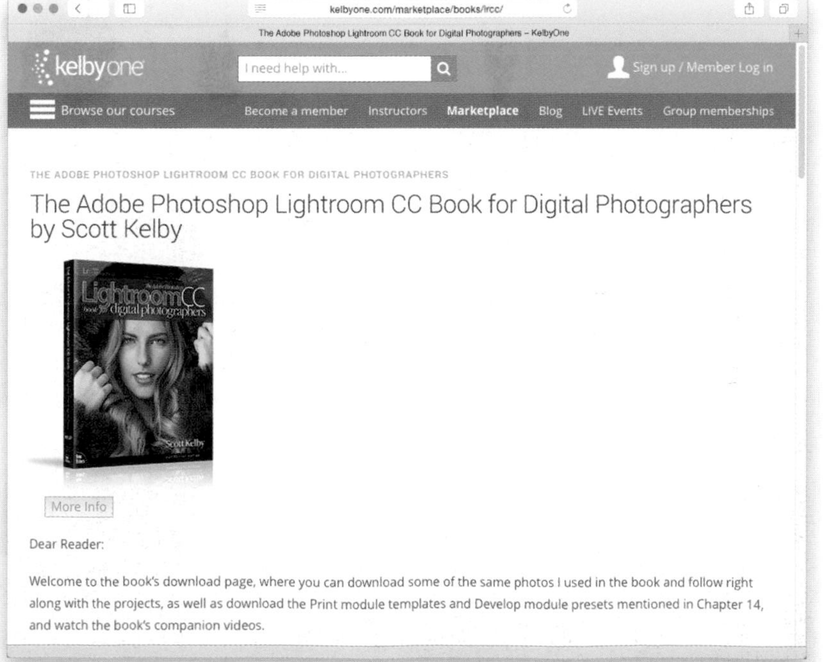

(7.2) I created a short bonus video. It shows you step by step how to create Identity Plate graphics with transparency (which you'll learn about in Chapters 12 and 13). You can find it at **http://kelbyone.com/books/lrcc**. Okay, now turn the page and let's get to work.

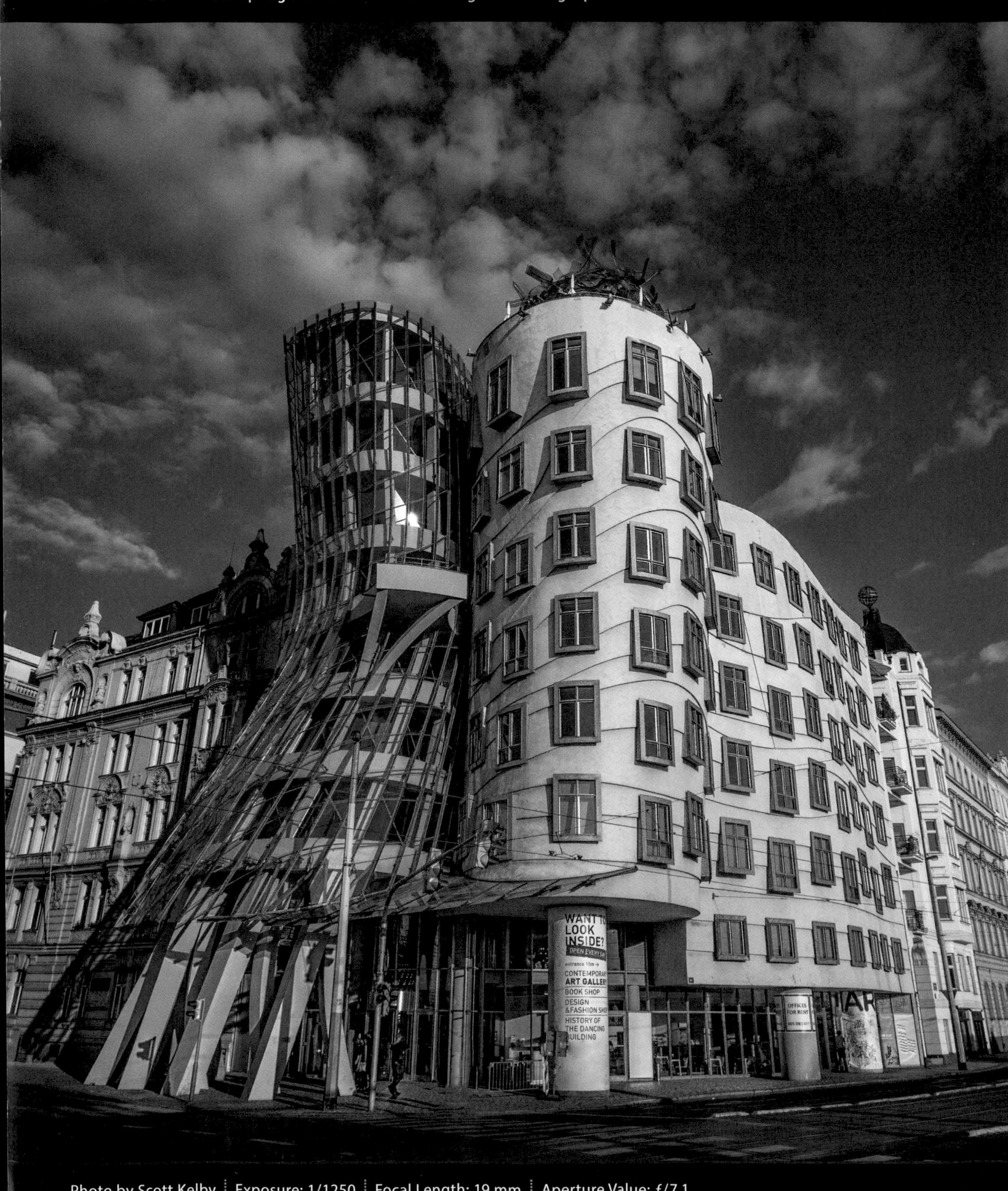

Photo by Scott Kelby | Exposure: 1/1250 | Focal Length: 19 mm | Aperture Value: ƒ/7.1

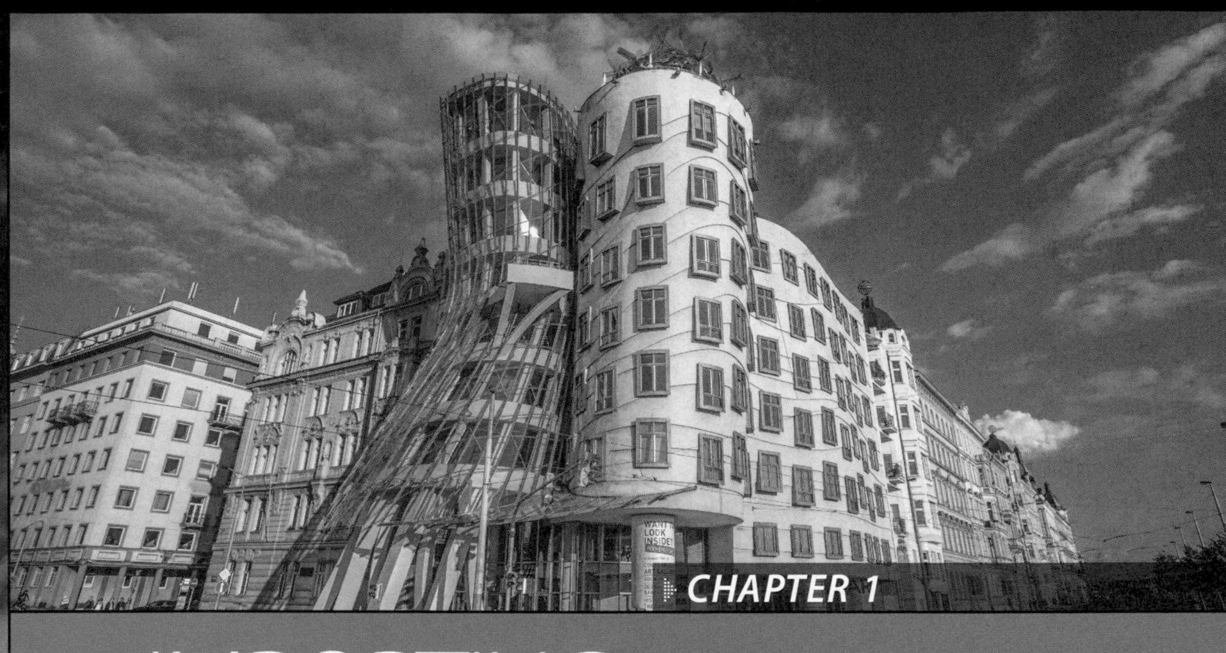

CHAPTER 1

IMPORTING
getting your photos into lightroom

Okay, if you're reading this chapter intro, then it's safe to assume that you read my brief warning (given just a page earlier), that these chapter intros have little, if anything, to do with what's actually in the chapter ahead. These are here strictly to give you a quick mental break from all the learning. Of course where it kind of falls apart is right here at the beginning of the book, because…well…you haven't really learned anything at this point, so you probably don't need a mental break quite yet. Of course, this concerns me, but clearly not enough to actually skip having a chapter intro for Chapter One, because then this page would be blank, and if there's one thing I've learned—people don't like blank pages. That's why in some books when you see a blank page, it says, "This page intentionally left blank." This fascinates me, partly because they never tell you why it's intentionally left blank and partly because, since they've printed the sentence "This page intentionally left blank," the page isn't actually blank anymore. So really, the whole thing's a big blank page scam, but if you call them on it, they start talking about "printers' spreads" and "pagination for press" and "propaganda spread by subversive anti-government organizations" and a dozen other technical reasons why sometimes a page has to be left blank. Well, I don't want you to think that this page was a part of their larger conspiracy, so even though you didn't actually need a mental break at this point (but probably do now), you're still getting one. In the publishing world, this is called "paying it forward." By the way, that's not what it's really called, but what it's really called can only be included on pages that were intentionally left blank. (Hey, I warned you these intros would be like this.)

Before You Do Anything, Choose Where to Store Your Photos

Before you dive into Lightroom, you need to make a decision about where you're going to store all your photos (and I mean *all* your photos—all the photos you've taken in the past, all the photos you'll take this year, and all the photos you'll take in the next few years—all of them). You're going to need a very large storage device to hold your entire photo library. The good news is storage has never been cheaper than it is today.

Go With an External Hard Drive: You can store all your photos right on your computer if you have enough empty hard drive space. However, if I were telling a friend, I would tell them to start by buying a very large external hard drive and to get one way larger than they think they'll need (at least 4 terabytes for starters). If you try to get away with storing your lifetime of images on your computer's internal hard drive, it will be full before you know it, and then you're going to have to buy an external hard drive anyway. So, to avoid this, just get a good, fast, large external drive from the start. By the way, don't worry, Lightroom is totally cool with you storing your images on a separate hard drive (you'll learn how to set this up shortly). Anyway, whichever external storage unit you choose (I use G-Technology external drives), it will fill up faster than you ever imagined, thanks to the high-megapixel cameras that are becoming standard these days. Luckily, hard drive storage space has never been cheaper. You can buy a 4-TB (4,000 gigabytes of space) drive for around $129. You're probably thinking, "I'll never fill 4 terabytes!" Well, consider this: if you shoot just once a week, and fill up nothing more than a single 16-GB card with each shoot, in one year alone, you'll eat up more than 400 GB of drive space. And, that's just new stuff; that doesn't count all the stuff you've shot before that's already on that drive. So, when it comes to hard drive storage space, think big!

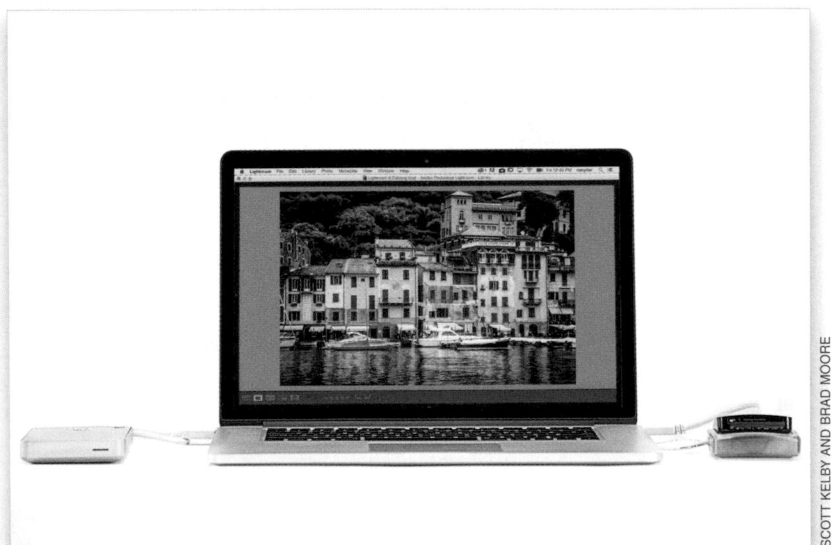

SCOTT KELBY AND BRAD MOORE

Now Choose Your Backup Strategy

Okay, once you've got your external hard drive—the one where your entire lifetime of shots will be stored—what happens when that hard drive dies? Notice, I didn't say, "*if* it dies," I said "*when* it dies." Eventually, they all die, with all your stuff lost forever inside. That is why you absolutely, positively *must* have at least one additional backup of your library. Notice I said "at least one." This is serious stuff.

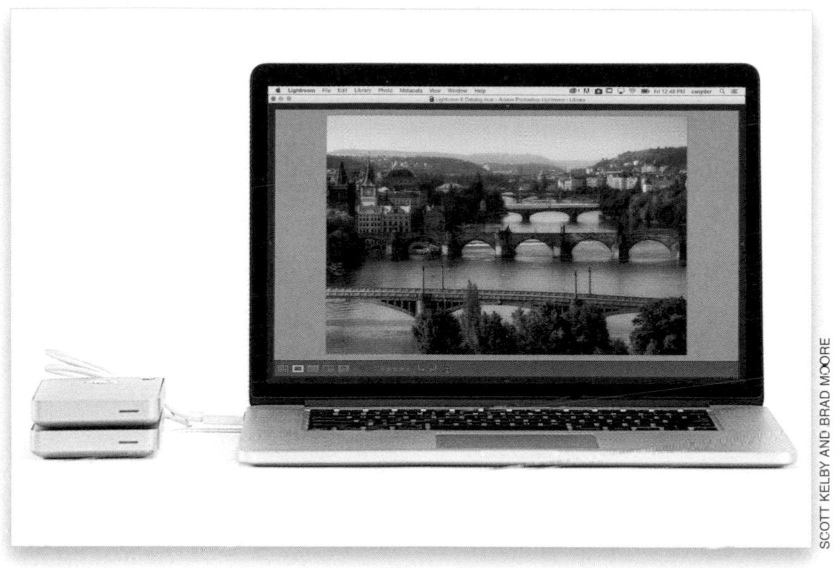

SCOTT KELBY AND BRAD MOORE

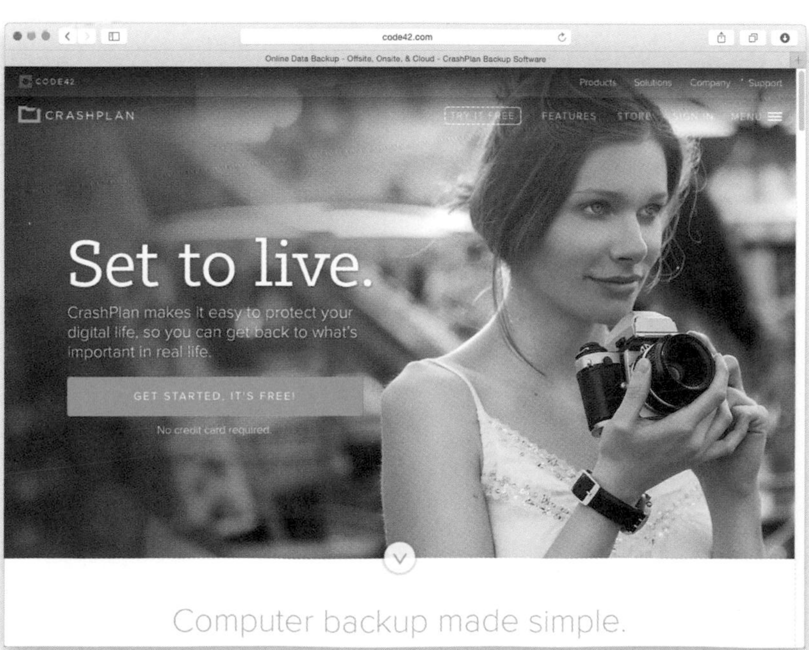

It Has to Be a Totally Separate Drive:
Your backup has to be a totally independent external hard drive from your main external hard drive (not just a partition or another folder on the same hard drive. I talk to photographers who actually do this not realizing that when your hard drive dies, both your original library and backup library will both die at the exact same time, and the result is the same—all your images are probably lost forever). You definitely need a second drive for your backup, so your images are copied to two distinct, separate hard drives. More on this in a moment.

A Second and Third Strategy:
If a hurricane, tornado, flood, or fire hits your home (or office), even if you have two external hard drives, chances are likely that they will both be destroyed and all your images will be lost forever. If your home or office gets broken into, they might grab your entire computer setup, including external hard drives. That's why you might consider having your backup external drive off-site at a different location. For example, I have one G-tech drive at home, and another one just like it at the office with the same stuff on it. My third strategy is to have another complete backup of your entire photo library "in the cloud." I use a service called Crash Plan that automatically backs up everything for me to their servers, for which I pay a monthly fee. It's worth it to me for the peace of mind.

My Method for Getting Your Photos Organized Before You Get Into Lightroom

I talk to photographers almost every day who are somewhat or totally confused about where their photos are located. They're frustrated and feel disorganized and all that has nothing to do with Lightroom. However, if you get organized *first* (I'm about to share a really simple way to do this), before you start using Lightroom, it will make your Lightroom life sooooooo much easier. Plus, not only will you know exactly where your photos are, you'll be able to tell someone else their exact location even when you're not in front of your computer.

Step One:

Go to your external hard drive (see page 2) and, on that drive, create a single new folder. This is your main photo library folder and creating this one folder, and putting all your images (old ones you've taken in years past and new ones you're about to take) inside this one folder is the key to staying fully organized before you ever even get to the Lightroom part of this. By the way, I name this one all-important folder "Lightroom Photos," but you can name yours anything you like. Whatever you name it, just know this is the new home for your entire photographic library. Also know that when you need to back up your entire library, you only have to back up this one folder. Pretty sweet already, right?

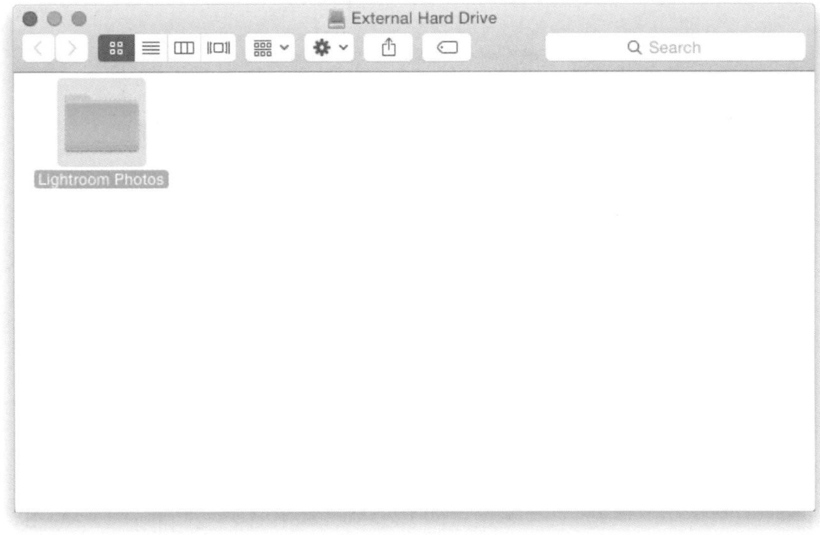

Step Two:

Inside that folder you're going to create more folders and name them with topics of things you shoot. For example, I have separate folders for travel, sports, family, automotive, people, landscapes, events, and misc. shoots—all separate folders. Now, since I shoot a lot of different sports, inside my Sports folder I have created separate folders for football, baseball, motorsports, basketball, hockey, soccer, and other sports. You don't have to do that last part; I just do it because, again, I shoot a lot of different sports and that makes it easier to find stuff when I'm not in Lightroom.

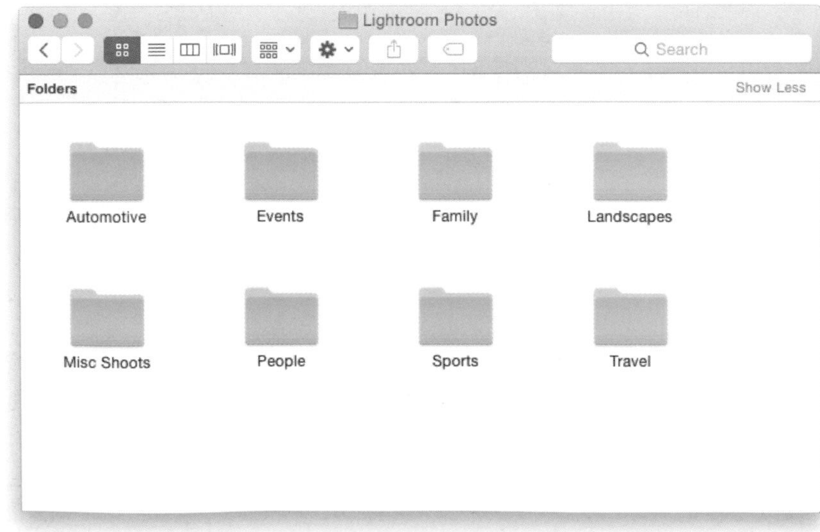

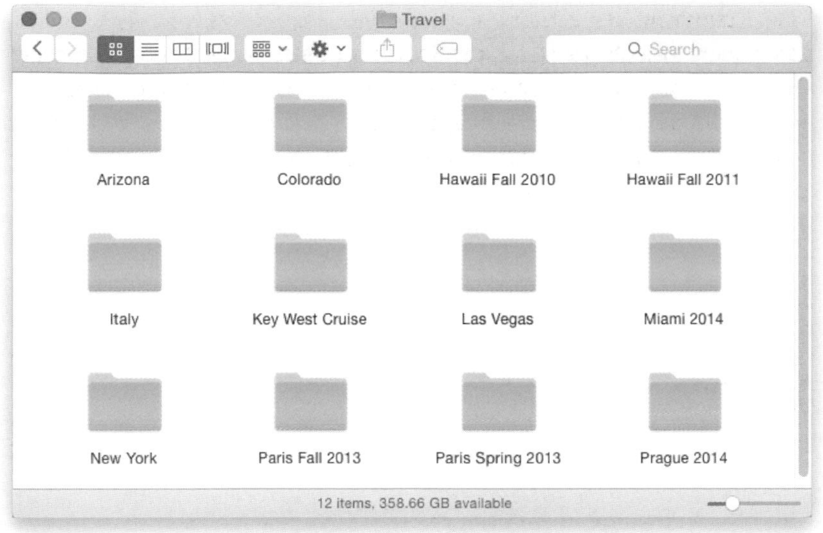

Step Three:

Now, you probably have lots of folders full of photos on your computer already. Your job (this is easier than it sounds) is to drag those folders directly into the topic folder that matches what they are. So, if you have a folder with photos from your trip to Hawaii, drag that folder into your Lightroom Photos folder, and into the Travel folder. By the way, if your folder of Hawaii vacation images isn't named something really easy, like "Maui Trip 2012," now would be the time to rename it. The simpler and more descriptive your folder names, the better. Let's continue: If you shot your daughter's softball championship game, drag that folder into your Lightroom Photos folder, and into the Sports folder. Now, you might decide, since the photos are of your daughter, to instead put them in your Family folder. No problem, that's your choice, but if you choose your Family folder, then from now on, all your kid's sports should go in that Family folder—not some in Sports and some in Family. Consistency is key.

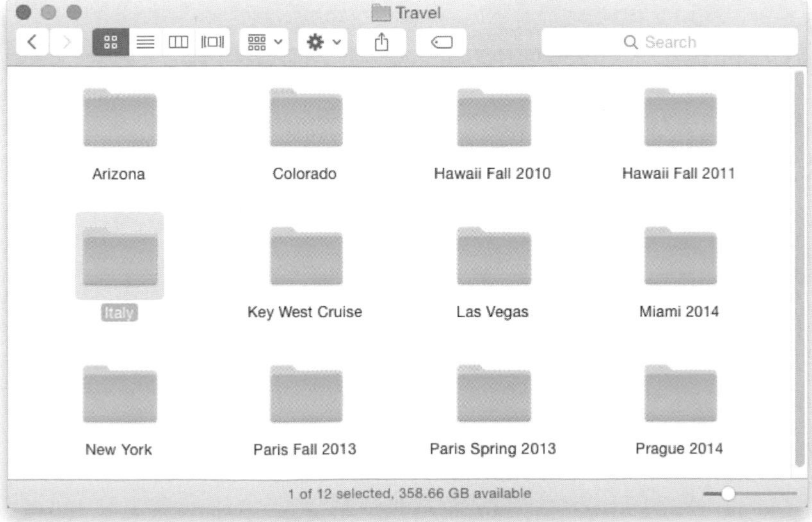

Step Four:

So, how long will it take to move all these images from your hard drive into the right folders? Not as long as you'd think. A couple of hours tops in most cases. What does this accomplish? Well, for starters, you'll know exactly where every photo you've taken is, without even being in front of your computer. For example, if I asked you, "Where are your photos from your trip to Italy?" You would already know they were in your Lightroom Photos folder, in your Travel folder, in a folder called "Italy." If you went to Italy more than once, maybe you'd see three folders there—Italy Winter 2014, Italy Spring 2012, and Italy Christmas 2011—and I'd be totally jealous that you got to go to Italy three times, so I probably wouldn't ask you this question in the first place. But, if I did, at least you'd know the answer. But there's more.

Continued

Step Five:
If you want a deeper level of organization (some folks do), you could add one more step to this process after you create your main Lightroom Photos folder: Instead of first creating topic folders like Travel, Sports, and Family, you'd create folders with year names, like 2015, 2014, 2013, and so on, for as far back as you want to go. Then, inside each year, you'd create those topic folders (so, inside each year folder you'd have folders for Travel, Sports, Family, etc.). That way, you're organizing your images in folders by the year they were taken. Let's try it out: If you went to London in 2012, drag that London folder inside your 2012 folder first, and then inside the Travel folder, and you're done. If you went to London again in 2014, put that folder in your 2014 folder, inside of Travel. So, why don't I do this extra step in my workflow? To me it just adds an extra step. Plus, I don't always remember which year I did everything off the top of my head (Did I go to Italy in 2012 or 2013?), so I wouldn't always know exactly where my photos are.

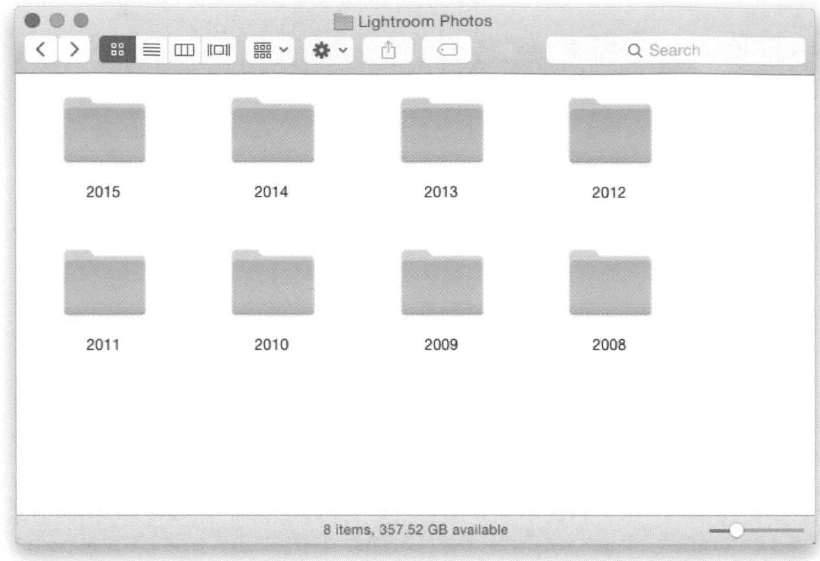

Step Six:
Now, if you told me you shoot a lot of concerts, and I asked, "Where are your Eric Clapton concert photos?" You'd say, "On my external hard drive, in my Lightroom Photos folder, inside my 2013 folder, inside my Concert Shots folder." End of story—that's where they are. That's where all your concert photos are from all the concerts you shot in 2013 in alphabetical order. How easy is that? As long as you use simple, easy names for all your folders, like "Travis Tritt" or "Rome" or "Family Reunion," you're in a happy place. By the way, where are your photos from your 2012 family reunion? Why they're in your Lightroom Photos folder, in your 2012 folder, in your Family folder, in a folder called "Family Reunion." Boom. Done! Yes, it can be that easy. Take the time now (just an hour or so) and reap glorious the benefits forever.

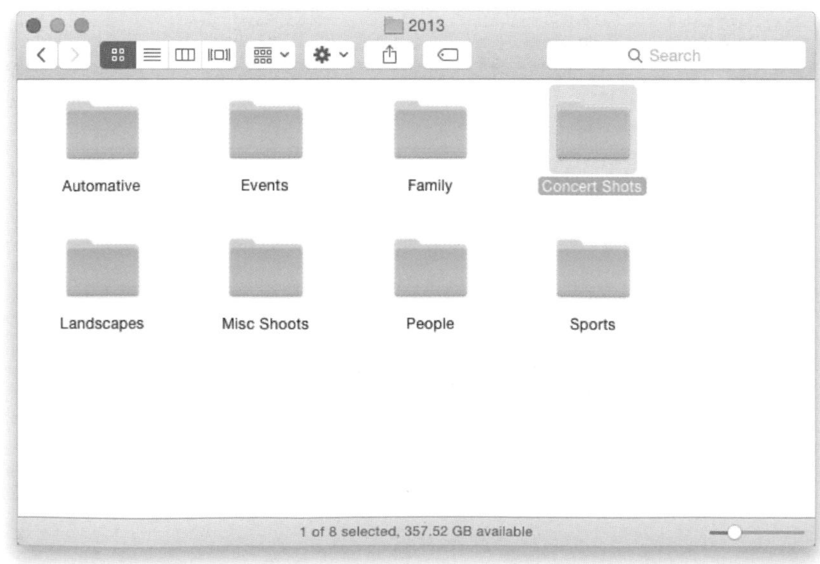

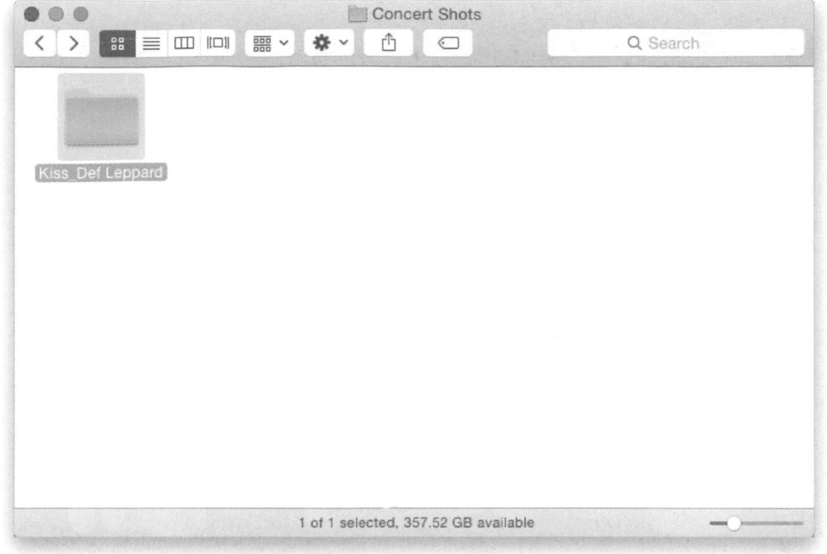

Step Seven:

What if you're importing new images from your camera's memory card? You do the same thing: import them directly into the right topic folder (more on this coming up), and then inside that folder you'd create a new folder with a simple name describing the shoot. So, let's say you took photos at a KISS and Def Leppard concert (they've been touring together. Awesome show, by the way). They would go on your external hard drive, inside your Lightroom Photos folder, inside your Concert Shots folder, and inside your Kiss_Def Leppard folder. (*Note:* If you're a serious event photographer, you might need a separate topic folder called "Events," and a bunch of other folders inside Events just to stay organized, like Concerts, and Celebrities, and Award Shows, and Political Events.)

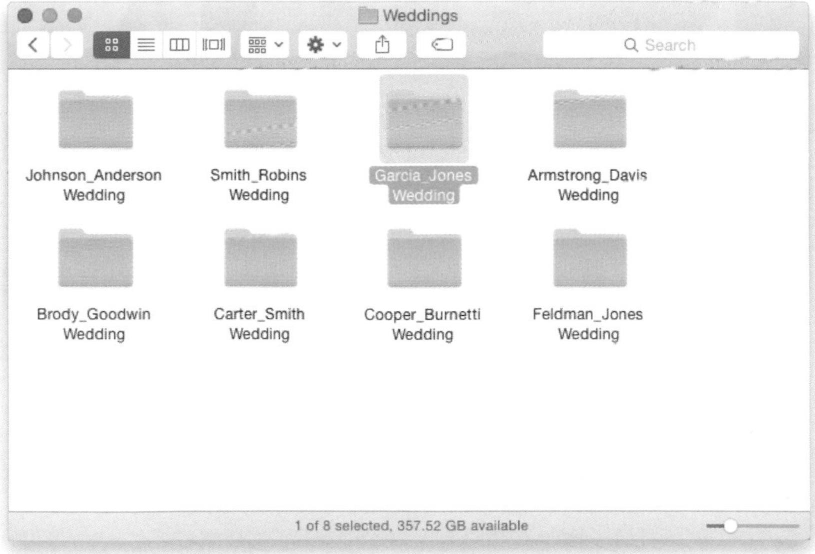

Step Eight:

Again, I prefer skipping the year folders and just doing categories. So, if you're a wedding photographer, you'd have a Weddings folder, and inside that you'd see other folders with simple names like Johnson_Anderson Wedding and Smith_Robins Wedding and so on. That way, if Mrs. Garcia calls and says, "I need another print from our wedding," you'd know exactly where their photos are: inside your Lightroom Photos folder, inside Weddings, inside the Garcia_Jones wedding folder! Couldn't be easier (well, it actually can be easier, in Lightroom, but that comes later because you do all this organizing *before* you ever even launch Lightroom). And, if you follow these steps, you'll be totally organized, in a simple way that will let you sleep you at night (and use Lightroom like a boss!). This is the secret. Now, while we're passing on secrets here's the secret to a happy marriage. It's simple, but it works. The secret is… (wait for it, wait for it…) separate bathrooms. There. I said it. Two secrets, both in one book. Whodathunkit?

Getting Photos from Your Camera Into Lightroom (for New Lightroom Users)

In this version of the book, I have a major change to how we import images from our cameras' memory cards that is designed for people who are brand new to Lightroom (if you've been using Lightroom for a while now, you can skip this and jump to page 12). In fact, I've totally changed how I teach this part of the process because I've talked to so many photographers who are confused and concerned about where their images actually are stored. This fixes all that by bypassing one part of Lightroom that confuses a lot of people, and once you do that, suddenly it all makes sense.

Step One:

This is where we bypass that Lightroom feature where a lot of folks get stuck (as mentioned above): Plug your memory card reader into your computer, put your memory card in the reader, and then skip Lightroom for now. That's right—just drag the images straight from the memory card right into the place they need to be on your external hard drive, based on what you learned on the previous pages. So, for example, for these images from Prague, I would go to my external drive, and go inside my Lightroom Photos folder. Then, inside my Travel folder I'd make a new folder named "Prague 2014," and I'd drag those images from the memory card straight into that folder. Now there is zero confusion or concern about where those photos are—you know right where they are because you put them there.

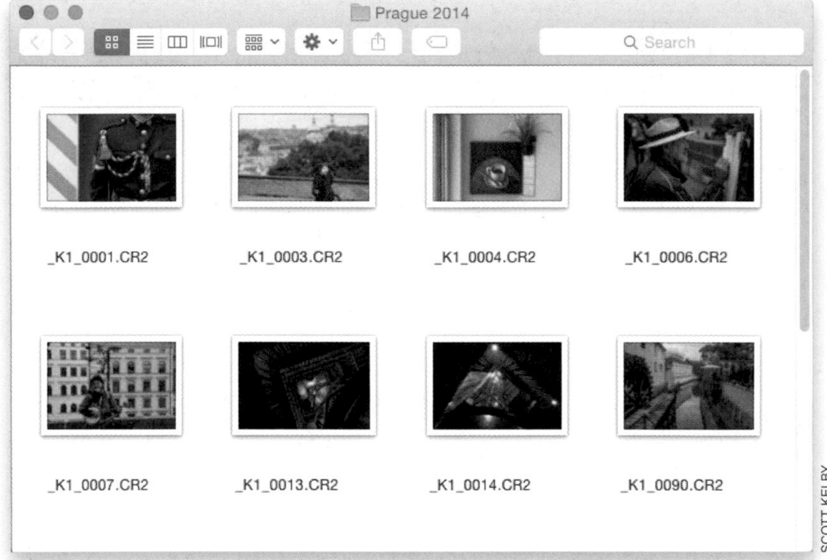

SCOTT KELBY

Step Two:

Okay, let's get those photos into Lightroom (we're not going to actually move them at all. We're just going to let Lightroom know where they are so we can start working with them in Lightroom). Luckily, since the photos are already on your external hard drive, this part goes really fast! Launch Lightroom and, in the bottom-left corner of the Library module, click the Import button (shown circled here in red) or use the keyboard shortcut **Command-Shift-I (PC: Ctrl-Shift-I)**.

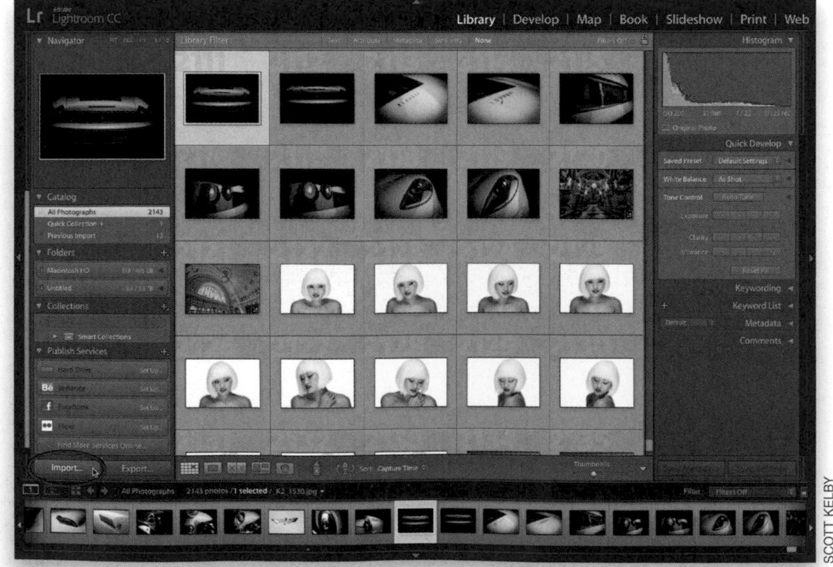

SCOTT KELBY

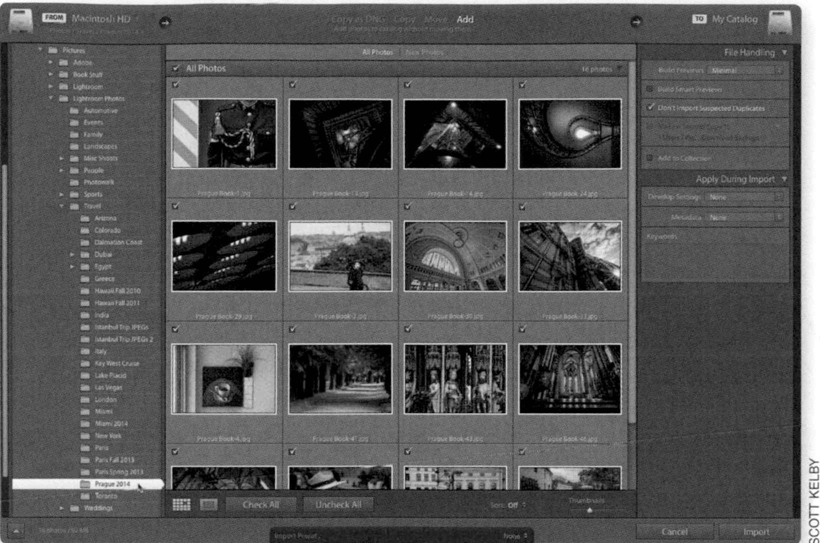

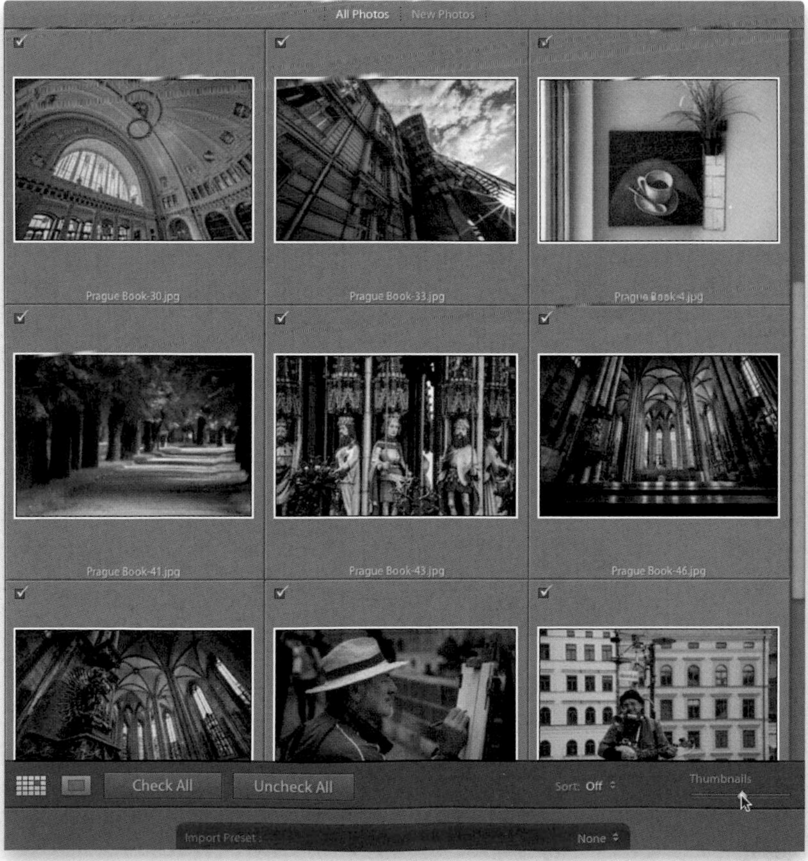

Step Three:

This brings up the Import window, seen here. We handle things a little differently depending on where you're storing your images. We handle it one way if you're storing all your images directly on your computer, and slightly differently if you're storing them on an external hard drive (in which case, jump directly to Step Five now). If you decided to store all your photos on your computer, in the Source panel, click on the arrow to the left of your hard drive to see a list of what's on it. Keep clicking those little arrows to navigate to your Lightroom Photos folder, then click to the left of your Travel folder to see a list of what's inside it, and then click on that Prague 2014 folder you made when you copied the photos onto your computer (as shown here). Now you should see thumbnails of all your Prague photos—ready for importing (if, for some reason, you see a much smaller version of the window, just click the Show More Options button [the down-facing arrow] in the bottom-left corner to expand it to what you see here, complete with thumbnails).

TIP: See How Many Images and How Much Room They'll Take

If you look in the bottom-left corner of the Import window, you'll see the total number of images you have checked to import, along with how much space they will take up on your hard drive.

Step Four:

To change the size of the thumbnails, click-and-drag the Thumbnails slider at the bottom right of the Preview area (as shown here). By default, all the photos in that folder will be imported, but if there are any you don't want imported, just turn off the checkbox at the top left of each of those photos.

Continued

Step Five:

If you stored your images on an external drive (highly recommended by the way—see page 2), then you need to let Lightroom know the images are coming from an external drive. You do this right in the Import window. Your external hard drive should appear below your hard drive in the Source panel, so click on the arrow to the left of it to see what's on it. Find your Lightroom Photos folder, click on the little arrow to its left, then find your Travel folder, and click on the arrow to the left of that. Finally, click on your Prague 2014 folder. Now, you'll see thumbnails of all your Prague photos (to change their size, click-and-drag the Thumbnails slider at the bottom right of the Preview area). By default, all the photos in that folder will be imported, but if there are any you don't want imported, just turn off the checkbox at the top left of each of those photos.

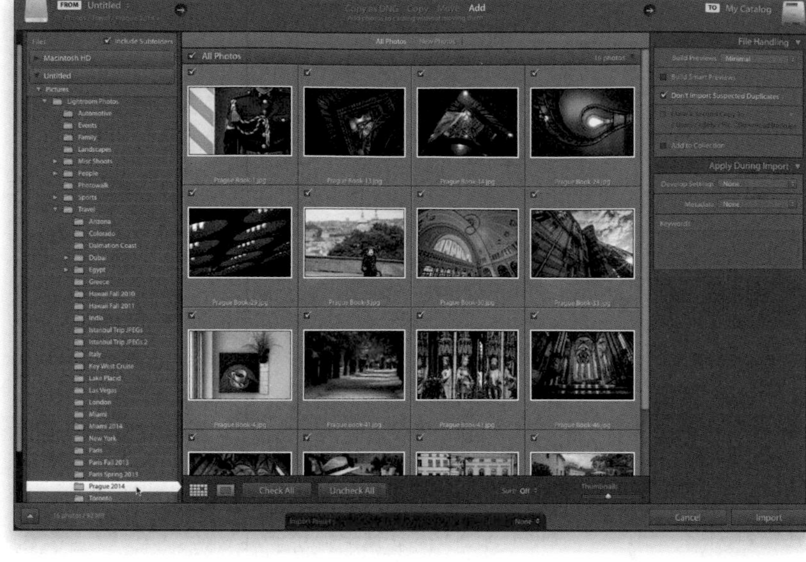

Step Six:

Since the photos are already on your external hard drive (or on your computer), there's very little you have to do in the rest of the Import window, but there are a few decisions you might want to consider. First, is deciding how quickly you want your images to appear once they're in Lightroom and you zoom in on them. You do this in the File Handling panel (up near the top right) from the Build Previews pop-up menu. If you jump to page 17, Step 11, I describe what these four Build Previews choices do, and how to choose the one that's right for you.

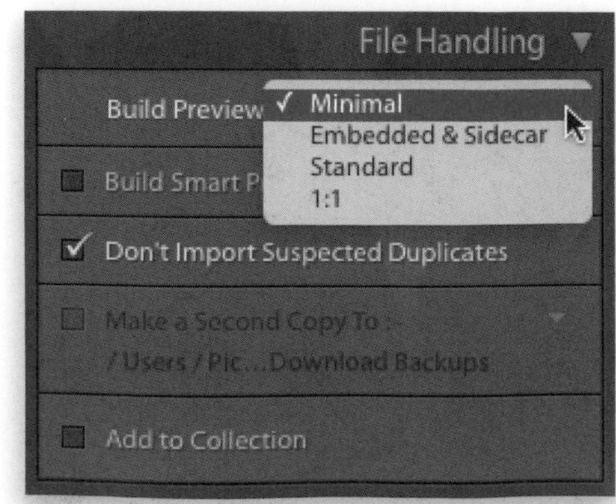

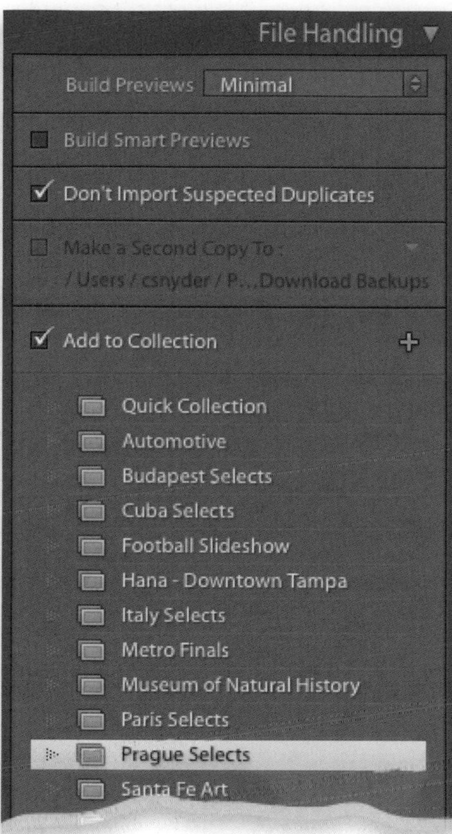

Step Seven:

Right below that is the Build Smart Previews checkbox. You turn this checkbox on only if you want the ability to edit these images in the Develop module (adjusting Exposure and Vibrance and stuff like that) when your external hard drive is *disconnected* from your computer (Smart Previews are for people working on a laptop. If you don't work on a laptop, you'd always leave this turned off. See page 23 for more about Smart Previews). Also, I recommend leaving the checkbox turned on for Don't Import Suspected Duplicates, just so you don't accidentally import two copies of the same image (this is probably only likely to happen when you import multiple times from the same memory card). You'll know they're duplicates because their thumbnails will be grayed out. If all the images are duplicate, the Import button will also be grayed out. If you want your imported images to appear inside a collection (this saves you a step if you were planning on doing it later anyway), then turn on the Add to Collection checkbox. That brings up a list of your existing collections. Just click on the one you want these images added to, or click on the plus sign icon to the right of the checkbox to create a new collection, and Lightroom will take care of the rest. Now, if you're new to Lightroom and you're asking yourself, "What's a collection?" just skip this whole Add to Collection thing for now. It will come in handy after you've read Chapter 2.

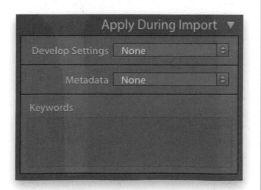

Step Eight:

There's one other set of options you need to know about: the Apply During Import panel settings (also on the right side of the window). I explain these on page 20, starting in Step 14, so jump over there, check those out, make your choices, and that's about it—you're ready to hit the Import button and start working with those images you took in Prague, in Lightroom.

Getting Photos from Your Camera Into Lightroom (for More Advanced Users)

If you've been using Lightroom for a while now, and you're totally comfortable with where your photos are stored—you know exactly where they are and have zero amount of stress over where your images reside—then this is for you. I'm going to make you a Ninja Master Fourth Level Mage (or something like that) on the importing process and the options you have in the Import window. However, if you are brand new to Lightroom or already have photos on your drive, I absolutely do not recommend this workflow—jump back to page 8. You'll thank me.

Step One:

If you have Lightroom open, and connect your camera or memory card reader to your computer, the Import window you see here appears over your Lightroom window. The top section of this Import window is important because it shows you what's about to happen. From left to right: (1) it shows where the photos are coming from (in this case, a camera); (2) what's going to happen to these images (in this case, they're getting copied from the camera); and (3) where they're going to (in this case, onto your external hard drive, into your Lightroom Photos folder). If you don't want to import the photos from your camera or memory card right now, just click the Cancel button and this window goes away. If you do this, you can always get back to the Import window by clicking on the Import button (at the bottom of the left side Panels area in the Library module).

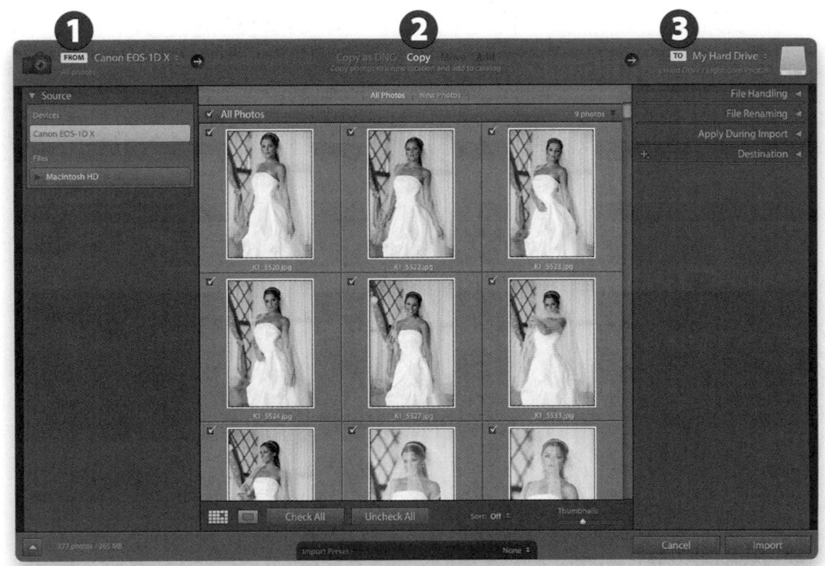

SCOTT KELBY

Step Two:

If your camera or memory card reader is connected, Lightroom assumes you want to import photos from that card, and you'll see it listed next to "From" in the top-left corner of the window (circled here). If you want to import from a different card (you could have two card readers connected to your computer), click on the From button, and a pop-up menu will appear (seen here) where you can choose the other card reader, or you can choose to import photos from somewhere else, like your desktop, or Pictures folder, or any recent folders you've imported from.

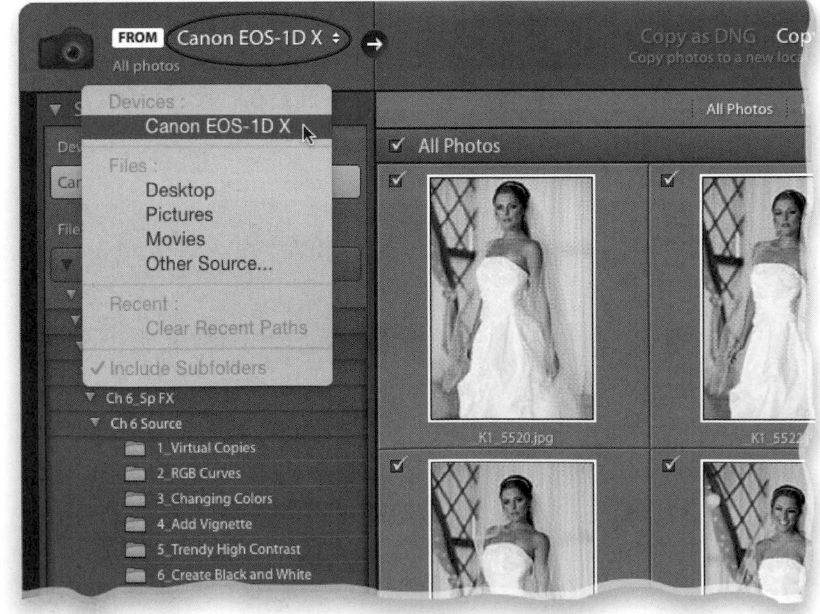

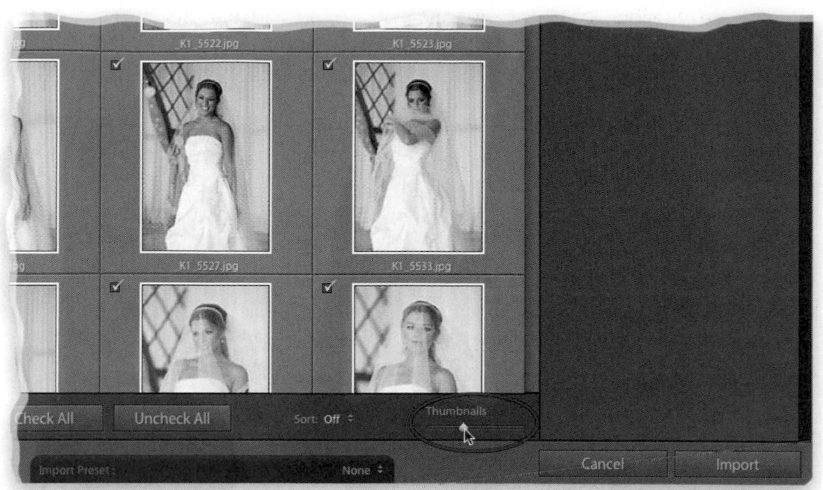

Step Three:

There is a Thumbnails size slider below the bottom-right corner of the center Preview area that controls the size of the thumbnail previews, so if you want to see them larger, just drag that slider to the right.

TIP: See a Photo Larger

If you want to see any photo you're about to import at a large, full-screen size, just double-click on it to zoom in, or click on it, then press the letter **E**. Double-click to zoom back out, or press the letter **G**. To see your thumbnails larger, use the **+ (plus sign) key** on your keyboard. Use the **– (minus sign) key** to make them smaller again. These work in both the Import window and the Library module's Grid view.

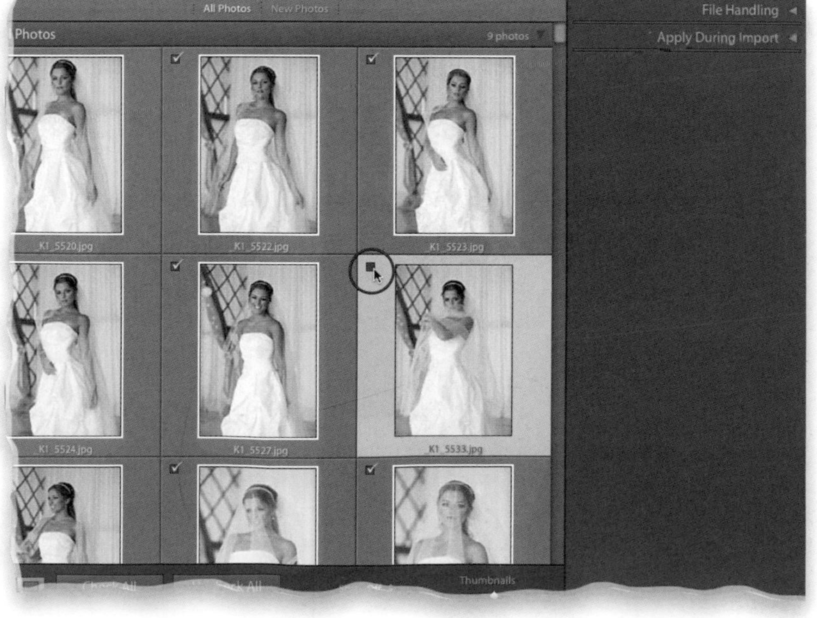

Step Four:

The big advantage of getting to see the thumbnail previews of the photos you're about to import is that you get to choose which ones actually get imported (after all, if you accidentally took a photo of the ground while you were walking, which for some inexplicable reason I seem to do on nearly every location shoot, there's no reason to even import that photo at all, right?). By default, all the photos have a checkmark at the top left of their grid cell (meaning they are all marked to be imported). If you see one or more photos you don't want imported, just turn off their checkboxes.

Continued

Step Five:

Now, what if you have 300+ photos on your memory card, but you only want a handful of them imported? Then you'd click the Uncheck All button at the bottom of the Preview area (which unchecks every photo), and Command-click (PC: Ctrl-click) on just the photos you want to import. Then, turn on the checkbox for any of these selected photos, and all the selected photos become checked and will be imported. Also, if you choose **Checked State** from the Sort pop-up menu (beneath the Preview area), all of the images you checked will appear together at the top of the Preview area.

TIP: Selecting Multiple Photos

If the photos you want are contiguous, then click on the first photo, press-and-hold the Shift key, scroll down to the last photo, and click on it to select all the photos in between at once.

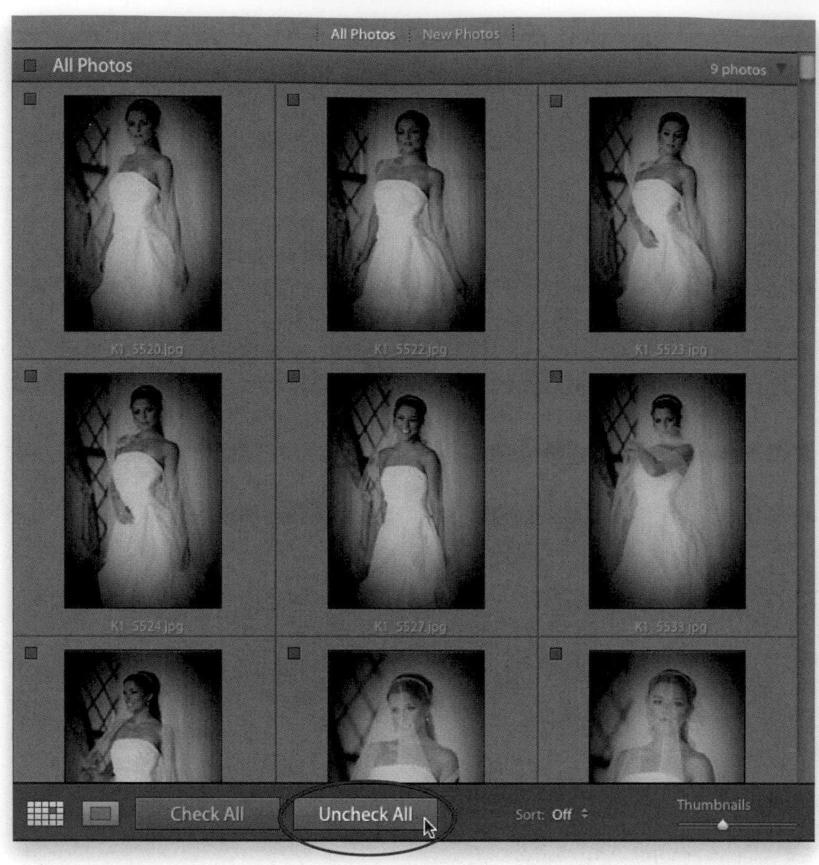

Step Six:

At the top center of the Import window, you get to choose whether you want to copy the files "as is" (Copy) or Copy as DNG to convert them to Adobe's DNG format as they're being imported (if you're not familiar with the advantages of Adobe's DNG [digital negative] file format, turn to page 44). Luckily, there's no wrong answer here, so if at this point you're unsure of what to do, for now just choose the default setting of Copy, which copies the images off the card onto your computer (or external drive) and imports them into Lightroom. Neither choice moves your originals off the card (you'll notice Move is grayed out), it only copies them, so if there's a serious problem during import (hey, it happens), you still have the originals on your memory card.

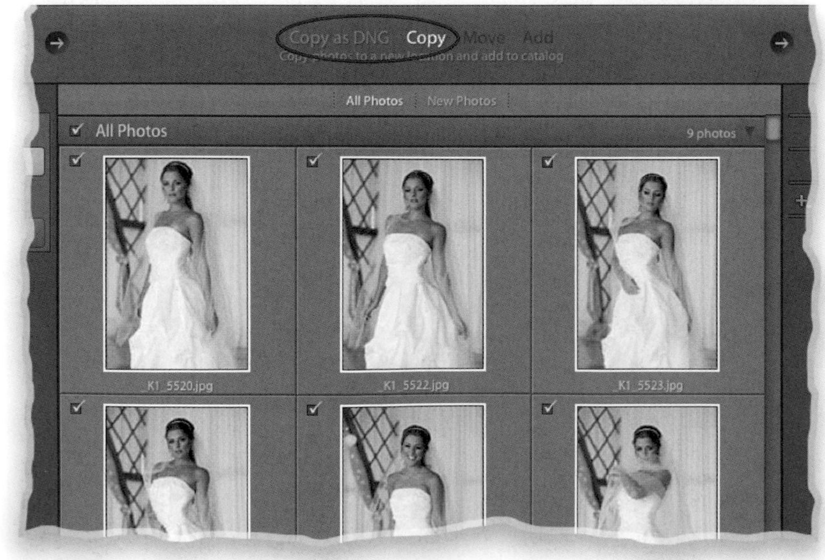

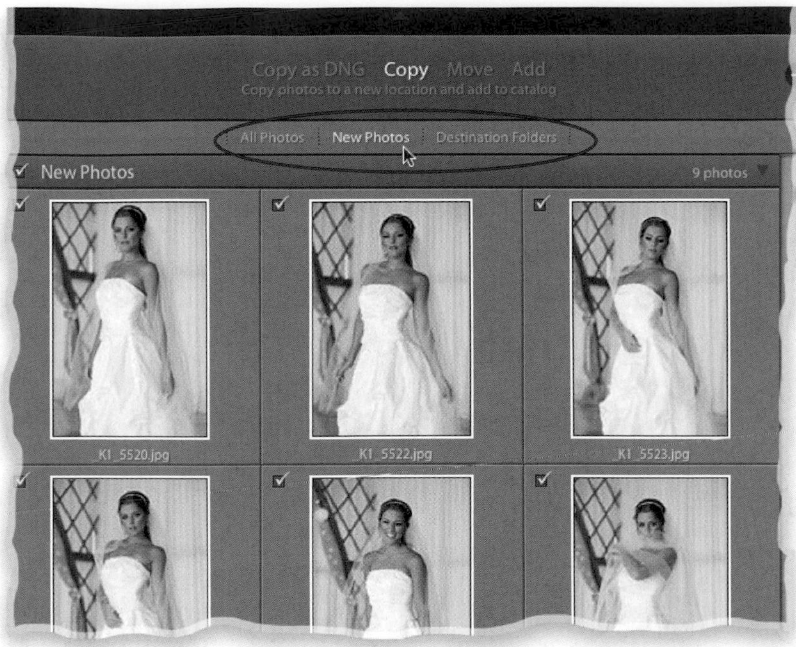

Step Seven:

Below the Copy as DNG and Copy buttons are three handy view options. By default, it displays all the photos on your card, but if you shoot to a card, then download those photos, pop the card back into the camera, shoot some more, then download again (which is pretty common), you can click New Photos, and now it only shows the photos on the card that you haven't imported yet, and hides the rest from view (sweet—I know). There's also a Destination Folders view, which hides any photos with the same name as photos that are already in the folder you're importing into. These last two buttons are just there to clear up the clutter and make it easier for you to see what's going on as you move files from one place to another, so you don't have to use them at all if you don't need them.

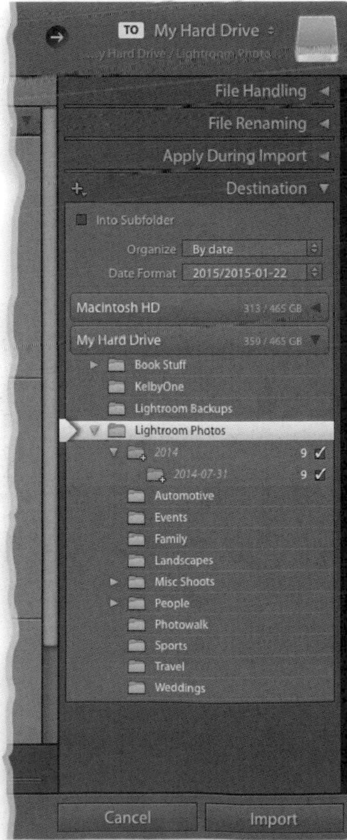

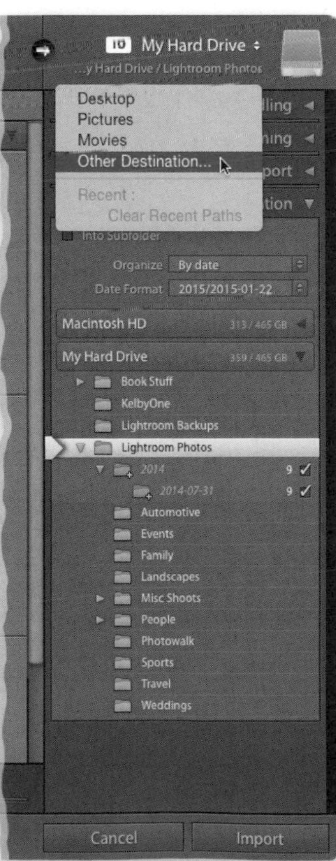

Step Eight:

Now we've come to the part where you tell Lightroom where to store the photos you're importing. If you look in the top-right corner of the window, you'll see the To section, which shows where they'll be stored on your computer (in my case here, on the left, they're going into my Lightroom Photos folder on my external hard drive). If you click-and-hold on To, a menu pops up (as seen far right) that lets you choose your default Pictures folder, or you can choose another location, plus you can choose any recent folders you've saved into. Whatever you choose, if you look in the Destination panel below, it now displays the path to that folder on your computer, just so you can see where your photos are going. So now, at this point, you know three things: (1) the photos are coming from your memory card; (2) they're being copied from that card, not just moved; and (3) they're going into a folder you just chose in the To section. So far, so good.

Continued

Step Nine:

Now, if you choose the Lightroom Photos folder we created earlier as the place to store your photos—don't worry—it's not going to just toss your images in there scattered all over the place. Instead, it will either put them in a folder organized by date, or you can have it create a folder for you, and name it whatever you like (which is what I do, so we'll start with that). Go to the Destination panel on the right side of the window, turn on the Into Subfolder checkbox (shown here), and a text field appears to the right where you can type in whatever name you want for your folder. So, in my case, I'd be importing my photos into a folder called "Weddings 2014" inside Lightroom Photos. Personally, it makes it easy for me to keep track of my images by just naming my shoots exactly what they are, but some folks prefer to have everything sorted by year, or by month, and that's cool, too (and we'll cover that option in the next step).

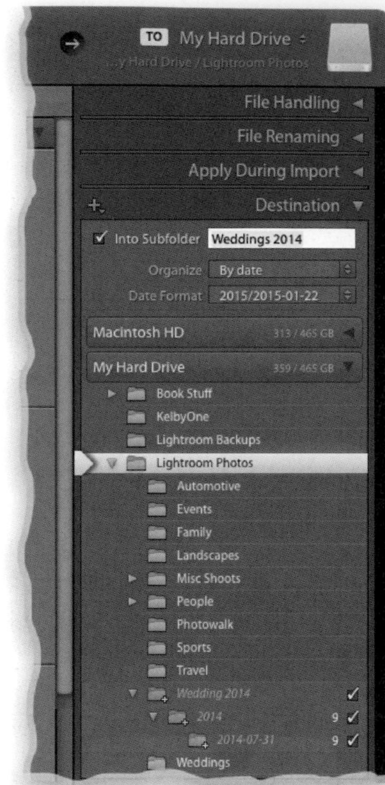

Step 10:

To have Lightroom organize your photos into folders by date, first make sure the Into Subfolder checkbox is turned off, set the Organize pop-up menu to **By Date**, then click on the Date Format pop-up menu, and choose the date format you like best (they all start with the year first, because that is the main subfolder. What appears after the slash [/] is what the folder inside the year folder will be named). So, if I chose the date format shown here, then my photos would be stored inside Lightroom Photos, where I'd find a 2014 folder, and inside of that there would be another folder named "July" (since I shot these in July 2014). So, what you're really choosing from this list is the name of the folder that appears inside your year folder. By the way, if you choose a date option with no slash, it doesn't create a year folder with another folder inside. Instead, it just creates one folder with that entire name.

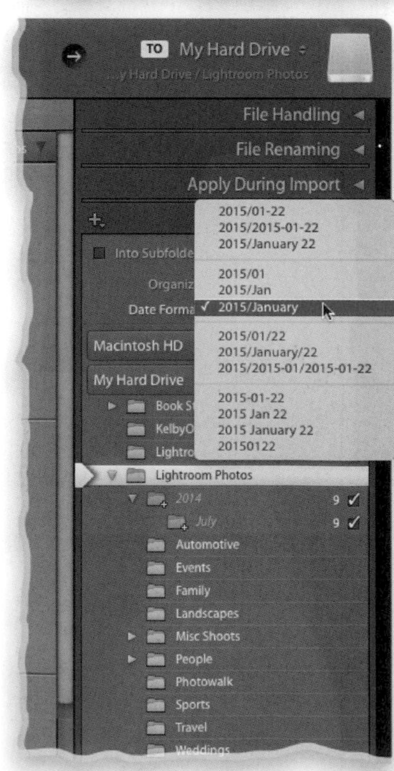

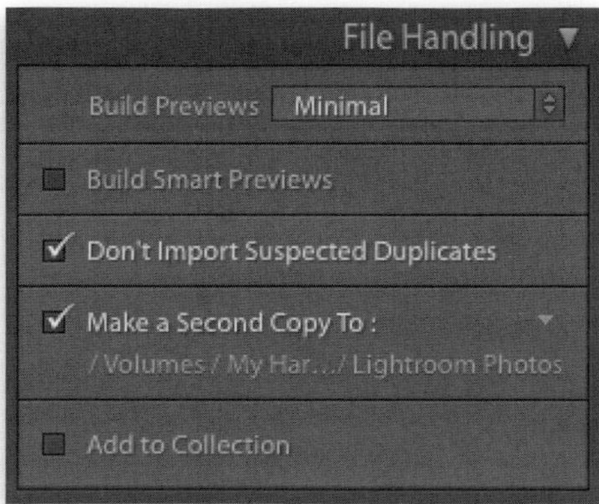

Step 11:
Okay, so now that you know where your files are coming from and going to, you can make a few important choices about what happens along the way in the File Handling panel (at the top right of the Import window). You choose, from the Build Previews pop-up menu, just how fast larger previews (larger sizes than just your thumbnails) will appear when you zoom in on a photo once it's in Lightroom. There are four choices:

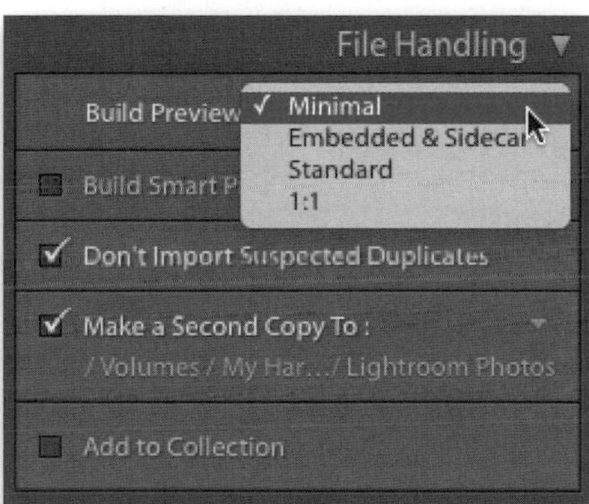

(1) Minimal
Minimal doesn't worry about rendering previews of your images, it just puts 'em in Lightroom as quickly as it can, and if you double-click on a photo to zoom in to Fit in Window view, it builds the preview right then, which is why you'll have to wait just a few moments before this larger, higher-quality preview appears onscreen (you'll literally see a message appear onscreen that says "Loading"). If you zoom in even closer, to a 100% view (called a 1:1 view), you'll have to wait a few moments more (the message will read "Loading" again). That's because it doesn't create a higher-quality preview until you try to zoom in.

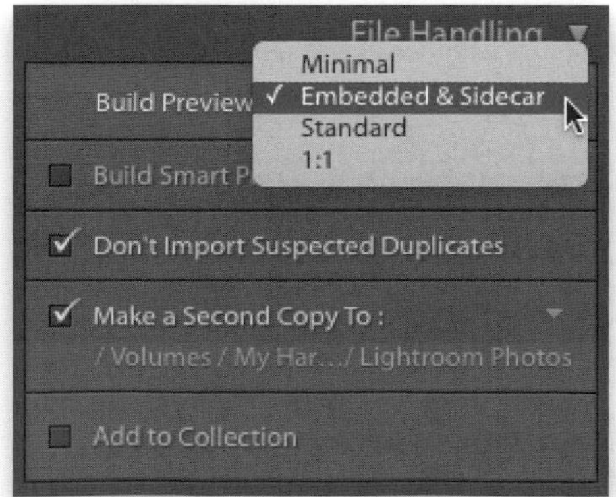

(2) Embedded & Sidecar
This method grabs the low-res JPEG thumbnails that are embedded in the files you're importing, too (the same ones you see on the back of your camera on the LCD screen), and once they load, it starts to load higher-resolution thumbnails that look more like what the higher-quality zoomed-in view will look like (even though the preview is still small).

Continued

(3) Standard

The Standard preview takes quite a bit longer, because it renders a higher-resolution preview as soon as the low-res JPEG previews are imported, so you don't have to wait for it to render the Fit in Window preview (if you double-click on one in the Grid view, it zooms up to a Fit in Window view without having to wait for rendering). However, if you zoom in even closer, to a 1:1 view or higher, you'll get that same rendering message, and you'll have to wait a few seconds more.

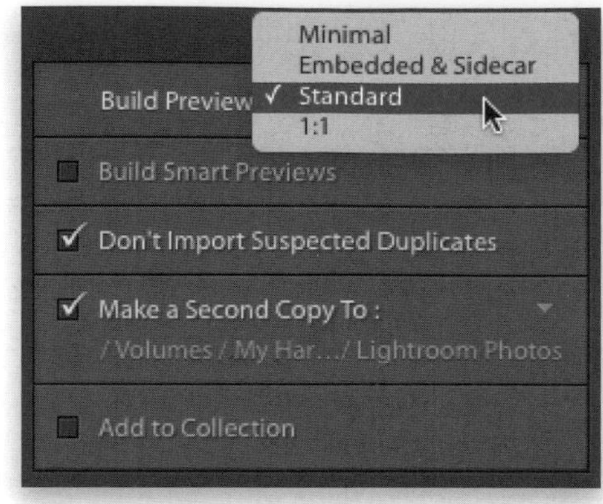

(4) 1:1

The 1:1 (one-to-one) preview displays the low-res thumbnails, then starts rendering the highest-quality previews, so you can zoom in as much as you want with no waiting. However, there are two downsides: (1) It's notoriously slow. Basically, you need to click the Import button, then get a cup of coffee (maybe two), but you can zoom in on any photo and never see a rendering message. (2) These large, high-quality previews get stored in your Lightroom database, so that file is going to get very large. So large that Lightroom lets you automatically delete these 1:1 previews after a period of time (up to 30 days). If you haven't looked at a particular set of photos for 30 days, you probably don't need the high-res previews, right? You set this in Lightroom by going under the Lightroom (PC: Edit) menu and choosing **Catalog Settings**, then clicking on the File Handling tab and choosing when to discard (as shown here).

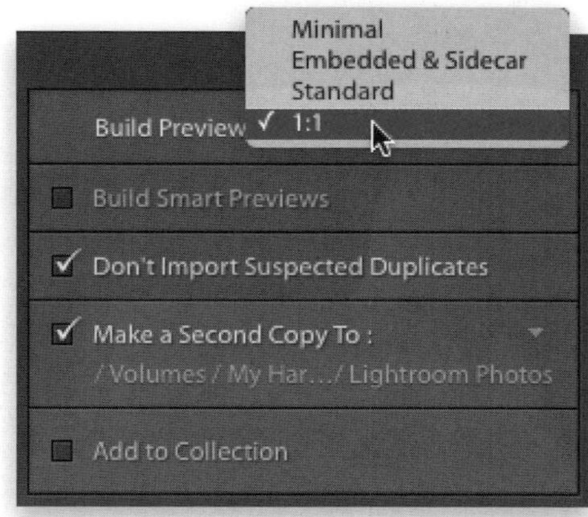

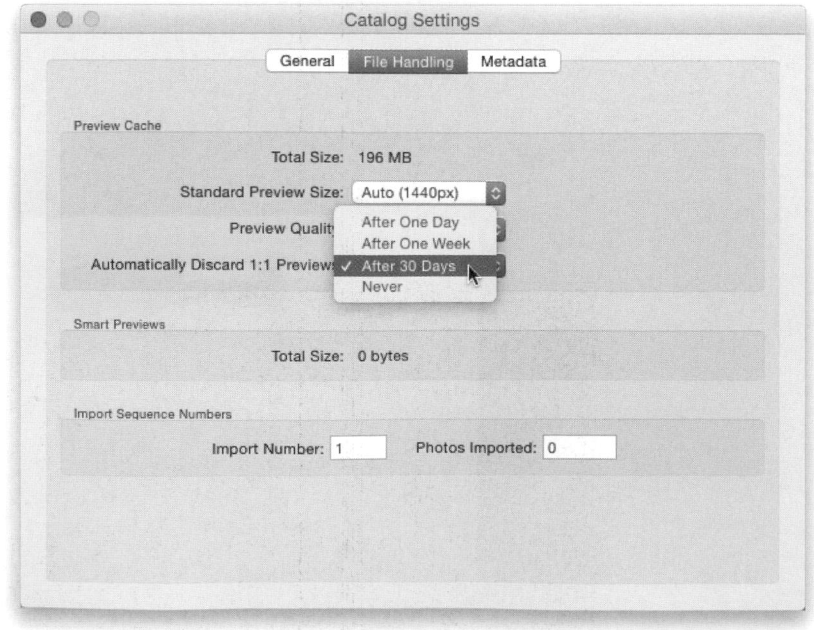

Note: Which one do I use? Minimal. I don't mind waiting a couple of seconds when I zoom in on an image. Besides, it only draws previews for the ones I double-click on, which are the ones I think might be good (an ideal workflow for people who want instant gratification, like me). But, if you charge by the hour, choose 1:1 previews—it will increase your billable hours. (You know I'm joking, right?)

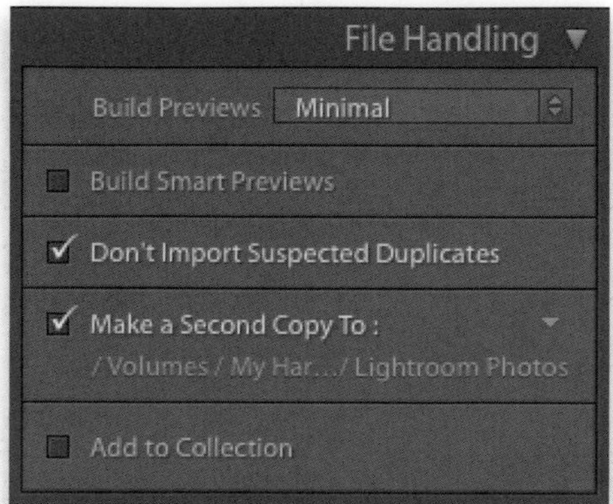

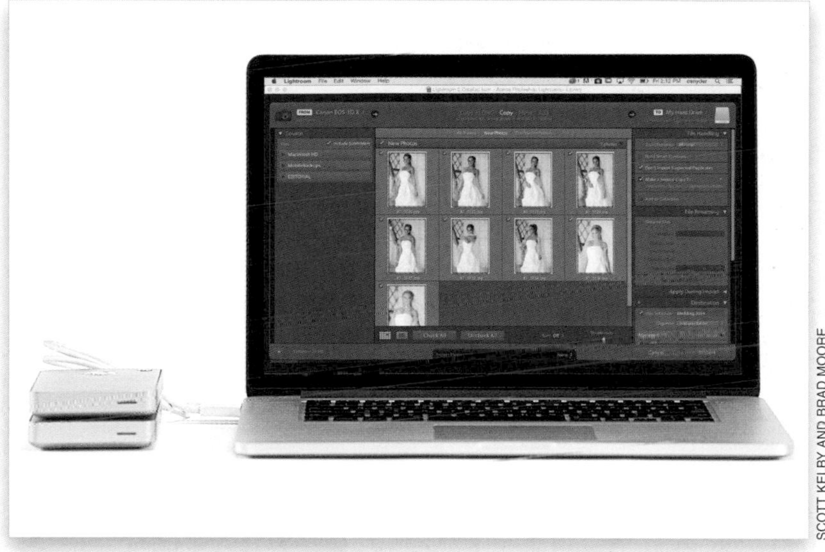

SCOTT KELBY AND BRAD MOORE

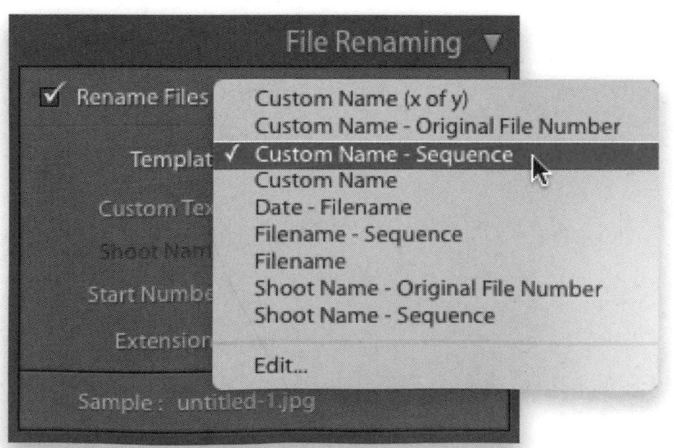

Step 12:

Below the Build Previews pop-up menu (and below Build Smart Previews; more on this coming up next) is a checkbox you should turn on to keep you from accidentally importing duplicates (files with the same name), but right below that is a checkbox that I feel is the most important one: Make a Second Copy To, which makes a backup copy of the photos you're importing on a separate hard drive. That way, you have a working set of photos on your computer (or external drive) that you can experiment with, change, and edit, knowing that you have the untouched originals (the digital negatives) backed up on a separate drive. I just can't tell you how important it is to have more than one copy of your photos. In fact, I won't erase my camera's memory card until I have at least two copies of my photos (one on my computer/external drive and one on my backup drive). Once you turn on the checkbox, click right below it and choose where you want your backup copies saved (or click the down-facing arrow on the right to choose a recent location).

Step 13:

The next panel down is File Renaming, which you use if you want to have your photos renamed automatically as they're imported. I always do this, giving my files a name that makes sense (in this case, something like Andrews Wedding, which makes more sense to me than _DSC0399 .NEF, especially if I have to search for them). If you turn on the Rename Files checkbox, there's a pop-up menu with lots of different choices. I like to give my files a name, followed by a sequence of numbers (like Andrews Wedding 001, Andrews Wedding 002, etc.), so I choose **Custom Name - Sequence**, as seen here. Just by looking at the list, you can see how it will rename your files, so choose whichever one you like best, or create your own by choosing **Edit** at the bottom of the menu (I take you through that whole process on page 37).

Continued

Step 14:
Right below that is a panel called Apply During Import, which is where you can apply three things to your images as they're imported. Let's start at the top. The Develop Settings pop-up menu lets you apply special effects or corrections automatically as your photos are imported. For example, you could have all your photos appear in Lightroom already converted to black and white, or they could all already be adjusted to be more red, or blue, or… whatever. If you click on the Develop Settings pop-up menu, you'll see a list of built-in presets that come with Lightroom and if you choose one, that look gets applied to your images as they're imported (you'll learn more about these, along with how to create your own custom Develop presets in Chapter 6, so for now, just leave the Develop Settings set to None, but at least you know what it does).

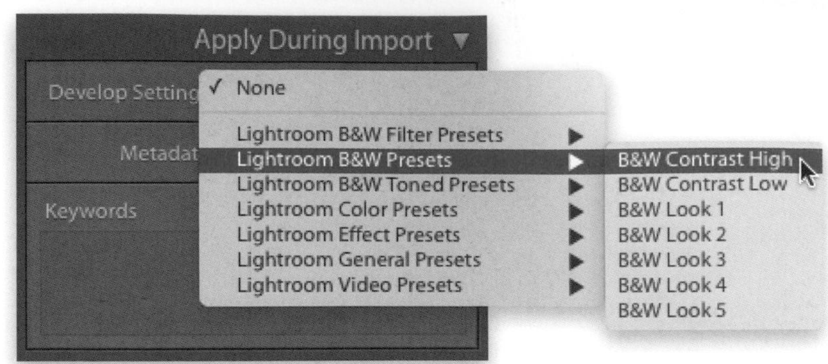

Step 15:
The next pop-up menu, Metadata, is where you can embed your own personal copyright and contact info, usage rights, captions, and loads of other information right into each file as it's imported. You do this by first entering all your info into a template (called a metadata template), and then when you save your template, it appears in the Metadata pop-up menu (as shown here). You're not limited to just one template—you can have different ones for different reasons if you like (like one of just your copyright info, and another with all your contact info, as well). I show you, step by step, how to create a metadata template on page 45 of this chapter, so go ahead and jump over there now and create your first metadata template, then come right back here and choose your copyright template from this pop-up menu. Go ahead. I'll wait for you. Really, it's no bother. (*Note:* I embed my copyright info into every photo [well, at least the ones I actually shot] using a metadata template like this while importing.)

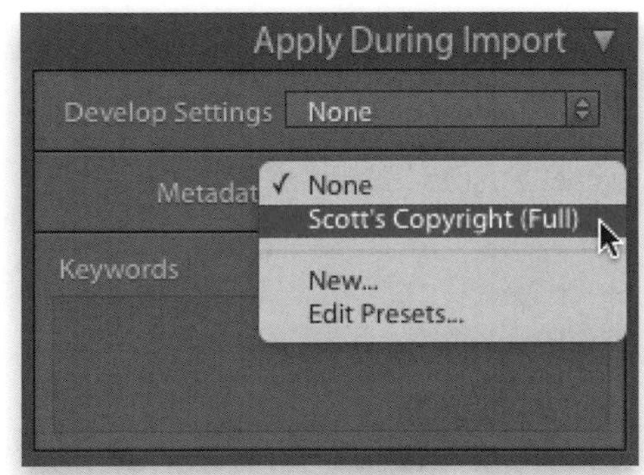

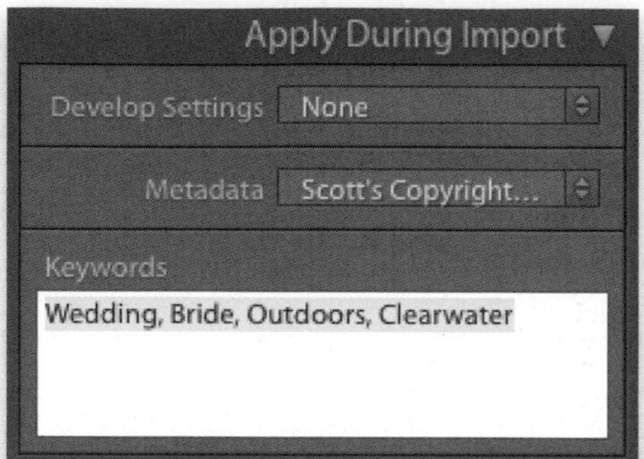

Step 16:
At the bottom of the Apply During Import panel is a field where you can type in keywords, which is just a fancy name for search terms (words you'd type in if, months later, you were searching for the photos you're now importing). Lightroom embeds these keywords right into your photos as they're imported, so later you can search for (and actually find) them by using any one of these keywords. At this stage of the game, you'll want to use very generic keywords—words that apply to every photo you're importing. For example, for these wedding photos, I clicked in the Keywords field, and typed in generic keywords like Wedding, Bride, Outdoors, and Clearwater (where the wedding was held). Put a comma between each search word or phrase, and just make sure the words you choose are generic enough to cover all the photos (in other words, don't use Smile, because she's not smiling in every photo).

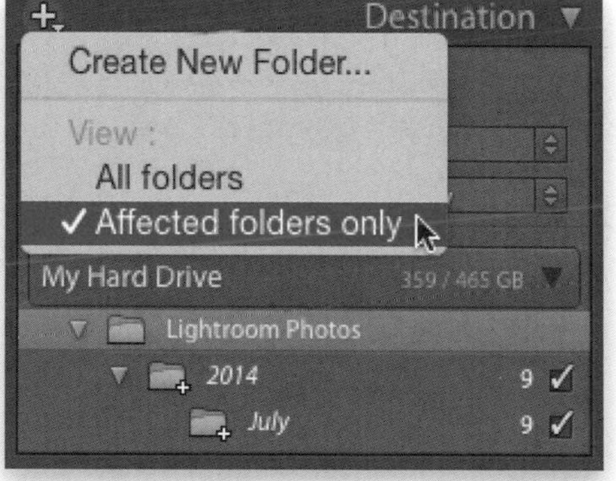

Step 17:
I mentioned this earlier, but at the bottom right of the Import window is the Destination panel, which just shows again exactly where your photos are going to be stored once they're imported from your memory card. At the top left of this panel is a + (plus sign) button and if you click on it, there's a pop-up menu (shown here) where you can choose to Create New Folder, which actually creates a new folder on your computer at whatever location you choose (you can click on any folder you see to jump there). While you're in that menu, try the Affected Folders Only command to see a much simpler view of the path to the folder you've chosen (as seen here—this is the view I use, since I always store my photos within the Lightroom Photos folder. I don't like to see all those other folders all the time, so this just hides them from view until I choose otherwise).

Continued

TIP: Organize Multiple Shoots by Date

If you're like me, you probably wind up having multiple shoots on the same memory card (for example, I often shoot one day and then shoot a few days later with the same memory card in my camera). If that's the case, then there's an advantage to using the Organize By Date feature in the Import window's Destination panel, and that is it shows each of the shoots on your memory card by their date. The folders will vary slightly, depending on the Date Format you choose, but you will have a folder for each day you shot. Only the shoots with a checkmark beside them will be imported into Lightroom, so if you only want to import shots from a particular date, you can turn off the checkbox beside the dates you don't want imported.

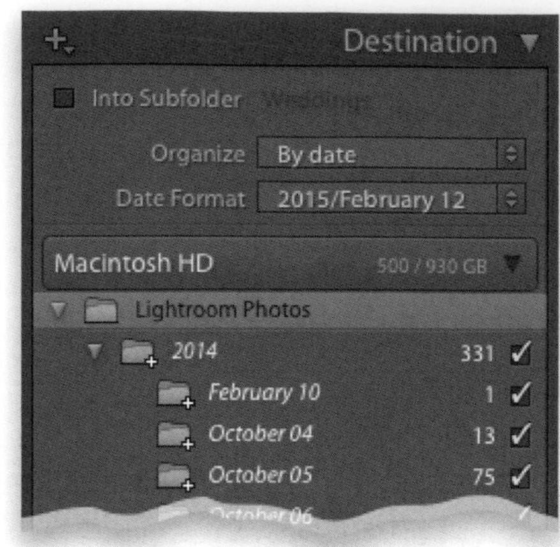

Step 18:

Now you're set—you've chosen where the images are coming from and where they're going, and how fast you'll be able to view larger previews when they appear in Lightroom. You've added your own custom name to the images, embedded your copyright info, and added some search terms. All that's left to do is click the Import button in the bottom-right corner of the Import window (as shown here) to get the images into Lightroom. If this seems like a lot of work to go through, don't worry—you've created custom file naming and metadata presets (templates), remember? (You'll be surprised at how many presets you can create in Lightroom to make your workflow faster and more efficient. You'll see as we go on. Presets rule! As a matter of fact, you can turn to page 25 before you click Import to learn how to save this as an Import preset.)

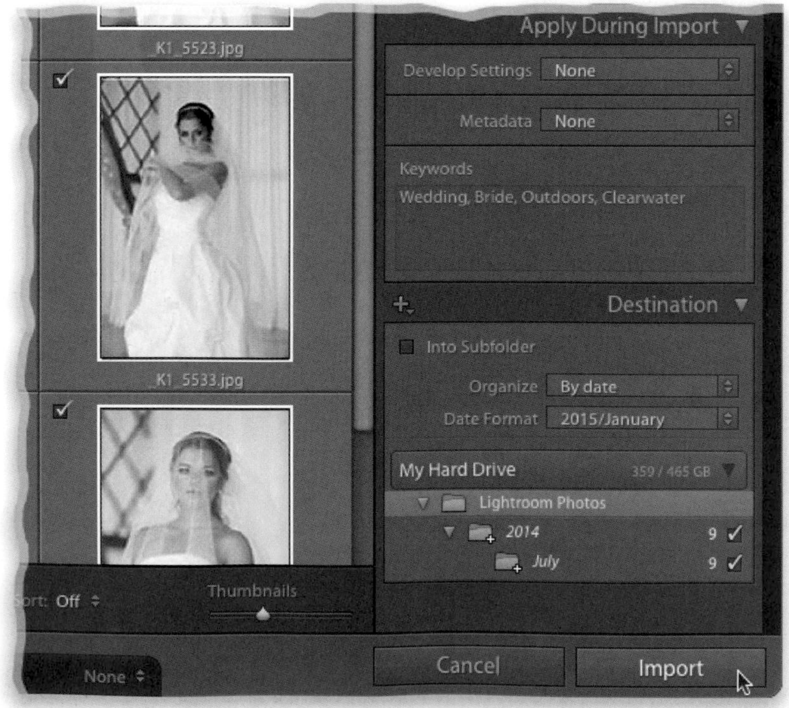

Using Lightroom with a Laptop? You'll Love Smart Previews

If you work on a laptop, you probably (hopefully) have stored your images on an external hard drive, but if you disconnect that drive, you can't change things like Exposure, or White Balance, and so on, because you don't have access to the original high-res files (which are on that external hard drive you disconnected). All you have now are thumbnails, which are handy for sorting and stuff, but you can't do any Develop module editing. Well, creating Smart Previews changes all that.

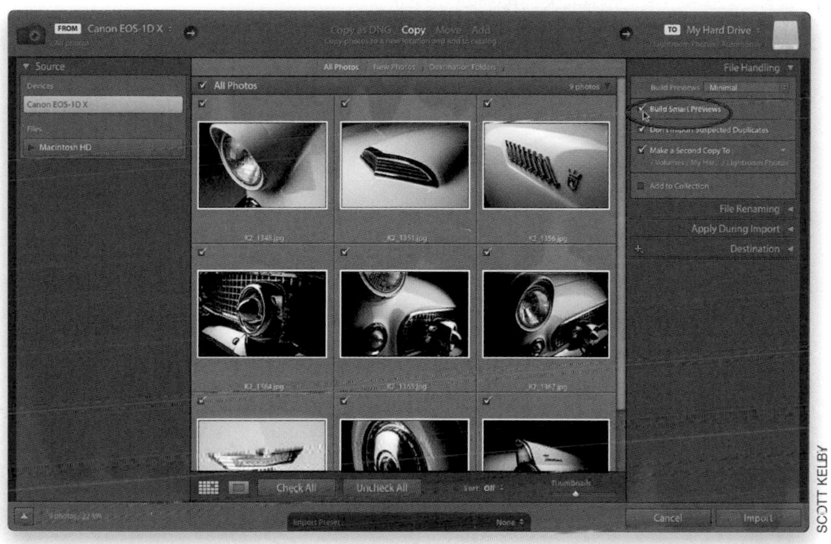

SCOTT KELBY

Step One:

To be able to still edit your images when they're "offline" (the external hard drive with your images is not currently attached to your laptop), you need to turn this feature on in the Import window. Just turn on the Build Smart Previews checkbox in the top-right corner (in the File Handling panel; it's shown circled here in red).This tells Lightroom to make a special larger preview that allows you to make edits in the Develop Module, and later, when you reconnect your laptop to your external hard drive, it applies to same edits to your high-resolution images. It's a beautiful thing.

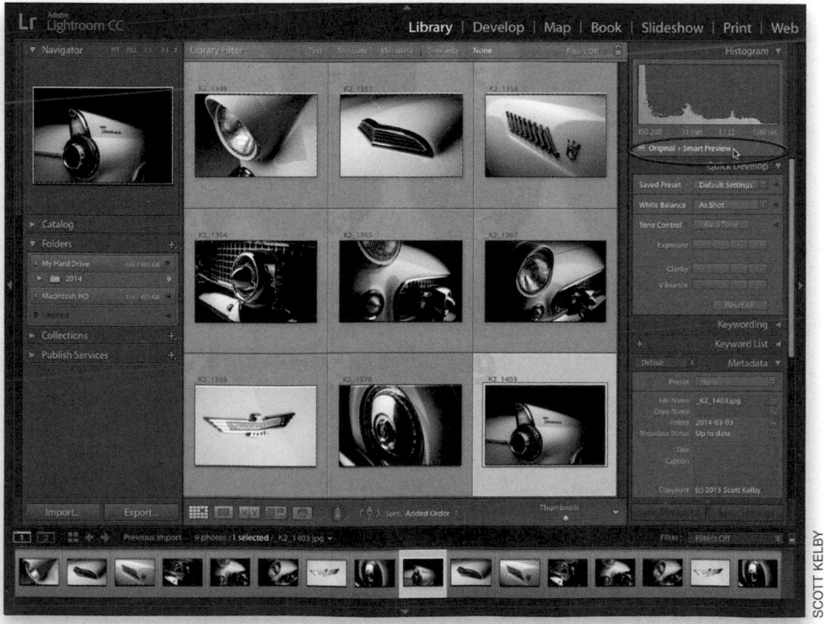

SCOTT KELBY

Step Two:

Once your images are imported, click on one of your images, then look right underneath the histogram at the top right and you'll see "Original + Smart Preview," which lets you know that you're seeing the real original image (since the hard drive with the real original file is connected—look over in the left side Panels area here, in the Folders panel, and you'll see "My Hard Drive" listed as one of my mounted drives), but that the image also has a Smart Preview.

TIP: Smart Previews After Importing

If you forgot to turn on the Build Smart Previews checkbox on import, no sweat. In the grid, just select the photos you want to have smart previews, then go under the Library menu, under Previews, and choose **Build Smart Previews**.

Continued

Step Three:

Now let's put this Smart Previews feature to work: Eject your external drive with these photos on it. Over in the Folders panel, your folder on your external hard drive is now grayed out (since the drive has been ejected, it's no longer available, right?), and you'll see a gray rectangle above the top-right corner of each thumbnail (instead of the question mark icon that used to appear there when your image was unavailable, although if you don't create Smart Previews, you'll now see an exclamation point icon). That rectangle is letting you know that what you're seeing is a smart preview. Also, take a look under the histogram now. Since the original image has been ejected, it just reads "Smart Preview."

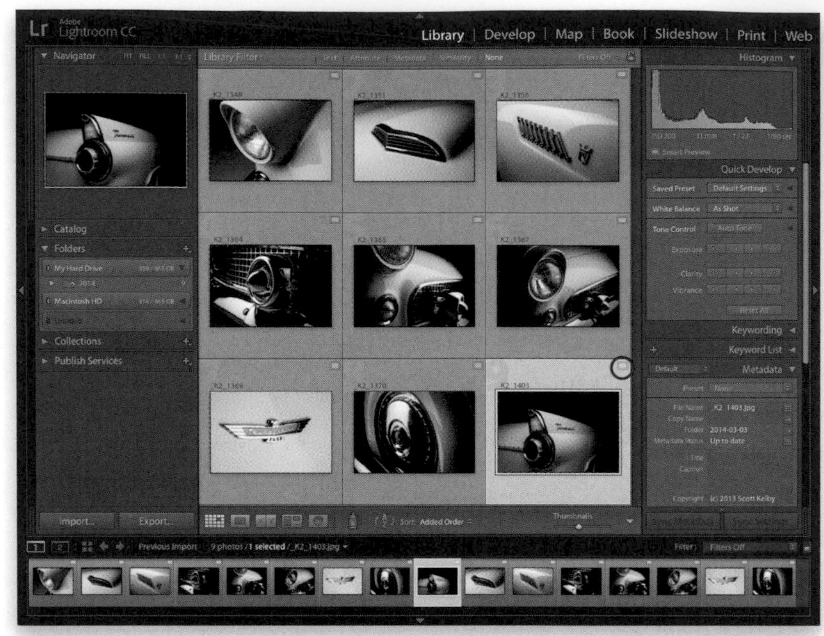

Step Four:

Press **D** to jump over to the Develop module and, check this out, even though your external drive is disconnected, you can still edit the photo—adjust the Exposure, White Balance, use the Adjustment Brush, you name it—just as if the original was connected (how handy is that?!). No more carrying a bunch of drives with you on the road. The nice thing about all this is that when you do plug that external drive back into your laptop, it automatically updates the real files with your changes. So, what's the downside to this? Why would you ever not make Smart Previews? Well, it stores those previews in your catalog, so it makes your catalog's file size a lot bigger. For example, by importing these 12 images with Smart Previews, it added 4 megabytes to my catalog (and to my hard drive). That doesn't sound like that much, but remember—that's just 12 images.

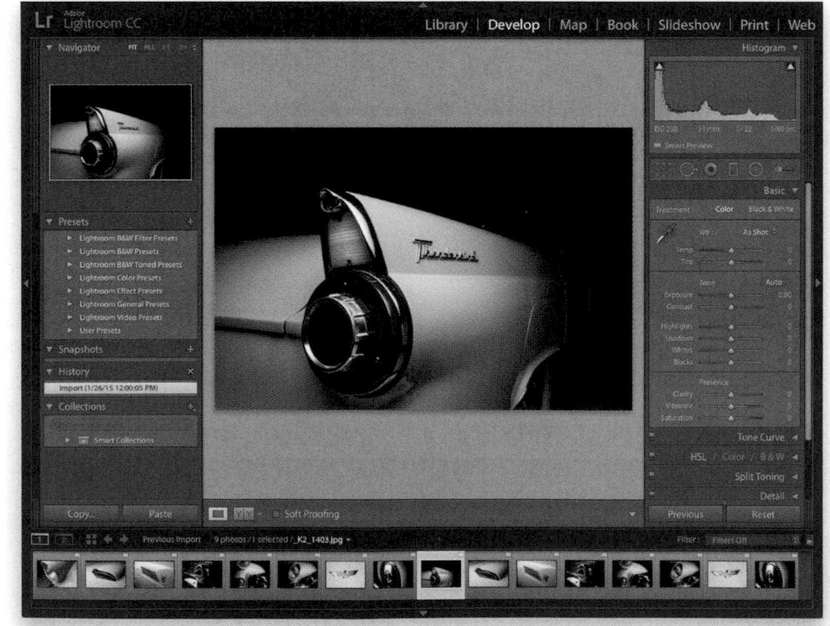

SCOTT KELBY

TIP: Deleting Smart Previews

If you don't need the Smart Previews for a particular group of images, just select them and then go under the Library menu, under Previews, and choose **Discard Smart Previews**.

Save Time Importing Using Import Presets (and a Compact View)

If you find yourself using the same settings when importing images, you're probably wondering, "Why do I have to enter this same info every time I import?" Luckily, you don't. You can just enter it once, and then turn those settings into an Import preset that remembers all that stuff. Then, you can choose the preset, add a few keywords, maybe choose a different name for the subfolder they're being saved into, and you're all set. In fact, once you create a few presets, you can skip the full-sized Import window altogether and save time by using a compact version instead. Here's how:

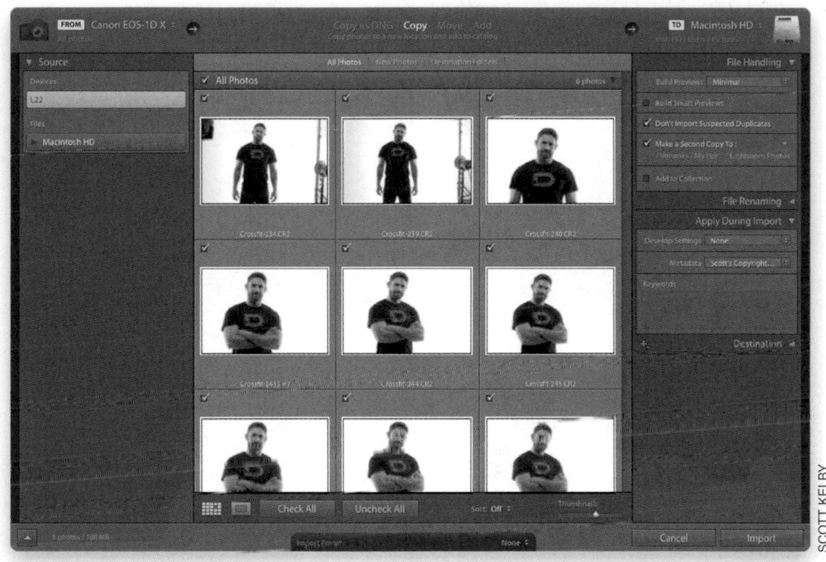

SCOTT KELBY

Step One:

We'll start by setting up your import settings, just like always. For this example, we'll assume you're importing images from a memory card attached to your computer, and you're going to copy them into a subfolder inside your Pictures folder, and then have it make a backup copy of the images to an external hard drive (a pretty common import setup, by the way). We'll have your copyright info added as they're imported, and we'll choose Minimal Render Previews, so the thumbnails show up fast. Go ahead and set that up now (or just set it up the way you actually would for your own workflow).

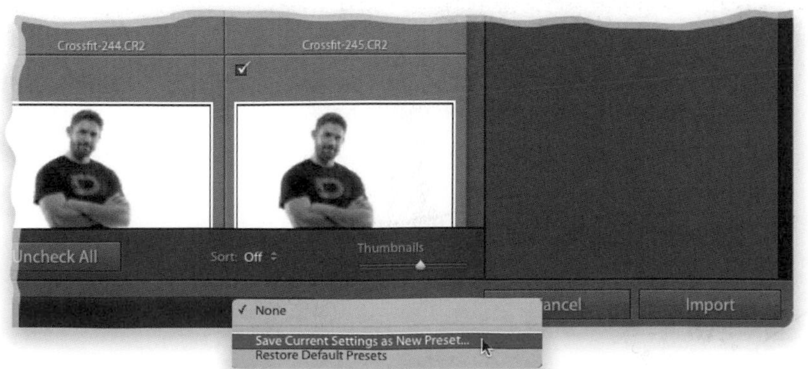

Step Two:

Now go to the bottom center of the Import window, where you'll see a thin black bar, and the words "Import Preset" on the far left. On the far right, click-and-hold on None and, from the pop-up menu that appears, choose **Save Current Settings as New Preset** (as shown here). You might want to save a second preset for importing images that are already on your hard drive, too. Okay, that's the hard part. Now let's put it to work.

Continued

Step Three:

Click the Show Fewer Options button (it's the up-facing arrow) in the bottom-left corner of the Import window, and it switches to the compact view (as seen here). The beauty of this smaller window is: you don't need to see all those panels, the grid, and all that other stuff, because you've already saved most of the info you'll need to import your photos as a preset. So, from now on, your Import window will appear like this (in the compact view), and all you have to do is choose your preset from the pop-up menu at the bottom (as shown here, where I'm choosing my From Memory Card preset), and then enter just the few bits of info that do change when you import a new set of photos (see the next step). *Note:* You can return to the full-size Import window anytime by clicking the Show More Options button (the down-facing arrow) in the bottom-left corner.

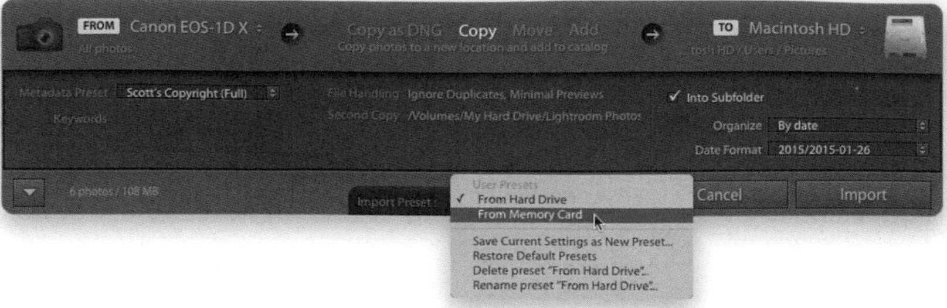

Step Four:

Across the top of the Minimal Import window, you can see that same visual 1-2-3 roadmap we saw in the full-size Import window on page 12 of where your images are coming from, what's going to happen to them, and where they're going, complete with arrows leading you from left to right. The images here are (1) coming from your card reader, (2) then they are being copied, and (3) these copies are being stored in a folder on your hard drive. In the middle section, you can add any keywords that would be specific to these images (which is why I leave this field blank when I save my Import presets. Otherwise, I'd see keywords here from the previous import). Then, it shows your preferences for file handing and backing up a second copy of your images. On the right, you can name the subfolder these images are going to be saved into. So, how does this save you time? Well, now you only have to type in a few keywords, give your subfolder a name, and click the Import button. That's fast and easy!

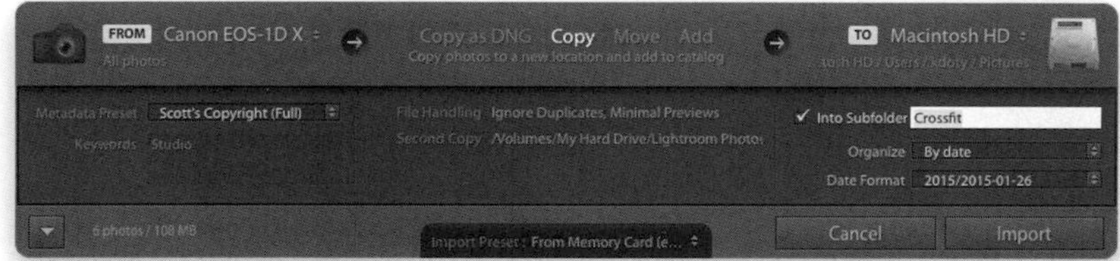

Importing Video from Your DSLR

You can hardly find a new DSLR these days that doesn't include the ability to shoot high-definition video, so we're lucky that Lightroom lets you import this video. Besides adding metadata, sorting them in collections, adding ratings, labels, Pick flags, and so on, you really can't do much video editing per se (see Chapter 15 for more on what you can do with them), but at least now these are no longer invisible files in our workflow (plus you can easily preview them). Here's how it works:

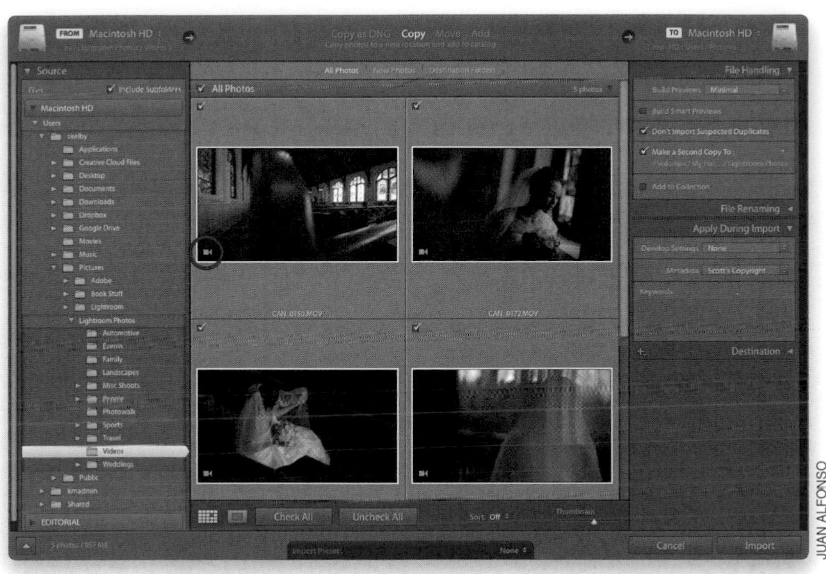

JUAN ALFONSO

Step One:

When you're in the Import window, you'll know which files are video files because they'll have a little movie camera icon in the bottom-left corner of the thumbnail (shown circled here in red). When you click the Import button, these video clips will import into Lightroom and appear right alongside your still images (of course, if you don't want these videos imported, turn off their checkboxes in the top-left corner of their thumbnail cell).

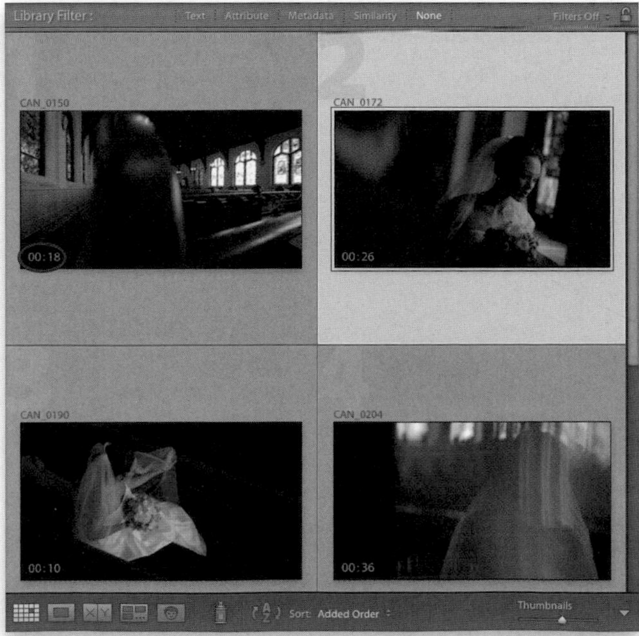

Step Two:

Once the video clip has been imported into Lightroom, in the Grid view, you'll no longer see the movie camera icon, but you'll see the length of the clip in the bottom-left corner of it (shown circled in red here). You can see a larger view of the first frame by just selecting the video, then pressing the **Spacebar** on your computer or clicking on that time stamp.

Continued

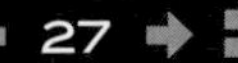

Step Three:

If you want to see a preview of the video, once you're in Loupe view, click the Play button beneath the video (it turns into a Pause button) and it plays the video clip. Also, you can export your video clips from Lightroom (just be sure to turn on the Include Video Files checkbox in the Video section of the Export dialog).

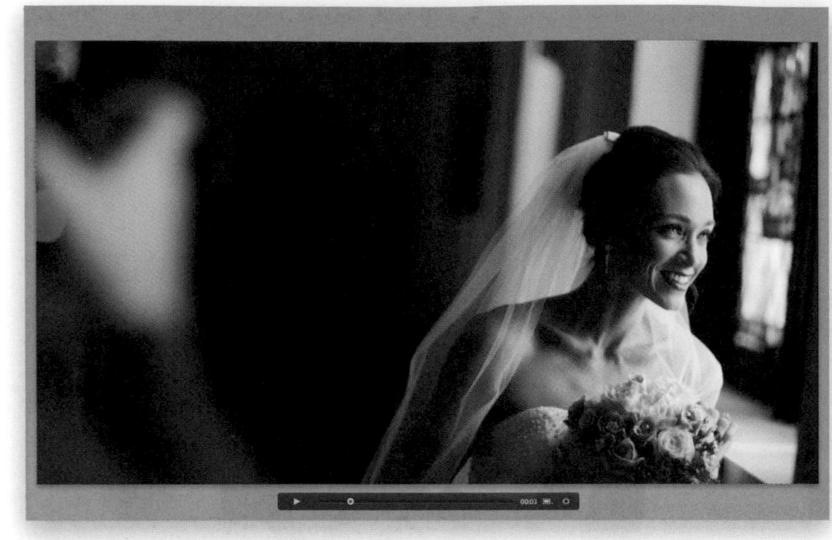

TIP: Program for Editing DSLR Video

Adobe's latest version of Premiere Pro has built-in support for editing DSLR video, so if you're really into this stuff, at least go download the free 30-day trial from www.adobe.com.

Step Four:

If you want to organize all your video clips into one central location, create a smart collection to do it for you. In the Collections panel, click on the + (plus sign) button on the right side of the panel header and choose **Create Smart Collection** from the pop-up menu. When the dialog appears, from the first pop-up menu on the left, under File Name/Type, choose File Type, from the second menu, choose Is, and from the third, choose Video. Name your smart collection and click the Create button, and it gathers all your video clips and puts them in a smart collection, but best of all, this collection updates live—anytime you import a video clip, it's also added to your new smart collection of video clips.

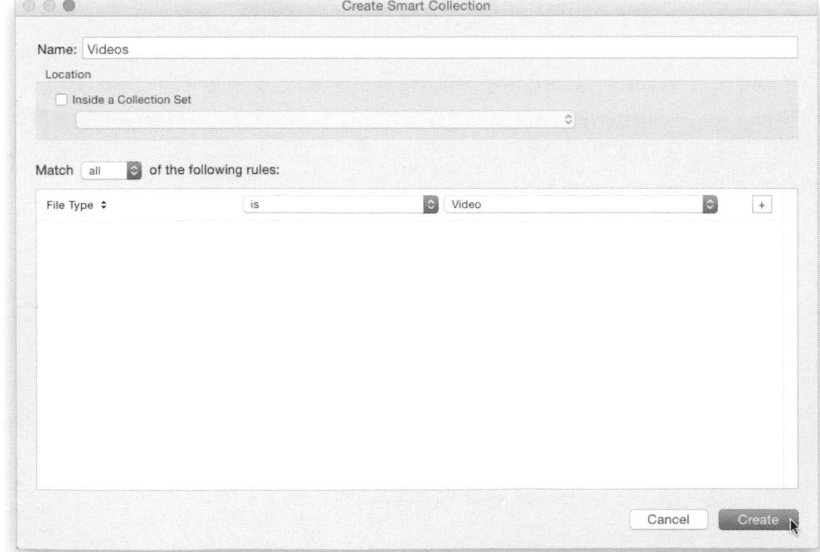

Shooting Tethered (Go Straight from Your Camera, Right Into Lightroom)

One of my favorite features in Lightroom is the built-in ability to shoot tethered (shooting directly from your camera into Lightroom), without using third-party software, which is what we used to do. The advantages are: (1) you can see your images much bigger on your computer's screen than on that tiny LCD on the back of the camera, so you'll make better images; and (2) you don't have to import after the shoot—the images are already there. Warning: Once you try this, you'll never want to shoot any other way.

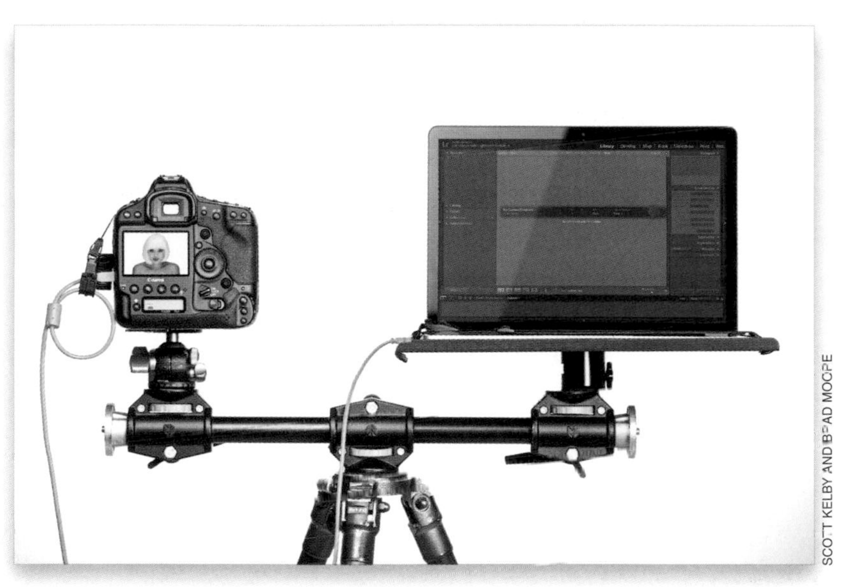

SCOTT KELBY AND BRAD MOORE

Step One:

The first step is to connect your camera to your computer using that little USB cable that came with your camera. (Don't worry, it's probably still in the box your camera came in, along with your manual and some other weird cables that come with digital cameras. So, go look there for it.) Go ahead and connect your camera now. In the studio, and on location, I use the tethered setup you see here (which I learned about from world-famous photographer Joe McNally). The bar is the Manfrotto 131DDB Tripod Accessory Arm, with a TetherTools Aero Traveler Tether Table attached.

Tethered Capture Settings

Session
Session Name: Studio Sessions
Segment Photos By Shots

Naming
Sample: White Wig-1.DNG
Template: Custom Name - Sequence
Custom Text: White Wig Start Number: 1

Destination
Location: /Users/Pictures/Lightroom Photos/People Choose...
Add to Collection

Information
Metadata: Scott's Copyright (Full)
Keywords: Fashion, head shot, wig

Cancel OK

Step Two:

Now go under Lightroom's File menu, under Tethered Capture, and choose **Start Tethered Capture**. This brings up the dialog you see here, where you enter pretty much the same info as you would in the Import window (you type in the name of your shoot at the top in the Session Name field, and you choose whether you want the images to have a custom name or not. You also choose where on your hard drive you want these images saved to, and if you want any metadata or keywords added—just like usual). However, there is one important feature here that's different—the Segment Photos By Shots checkbox (shown circled in red here)—which can be incredibly handy when you're shooting tethered (as you'll see).

Continued

Step Three:

The Segment Photos By Shots feature lets you organize your tethered shots as you go. So, let's say you're doing a fashion shoot, and you're using two lighting setups—one where your background is gray and one where it's white. You can separate each of these looks into different folders by clicking the Shot Name (this will make more sense in a moment). Try it out by turning on the Segment Photos By Shot checkbox and clicking OK. When you do this, a naming dialog appears (shown here), where you can type in a descriptive name for your shoot.

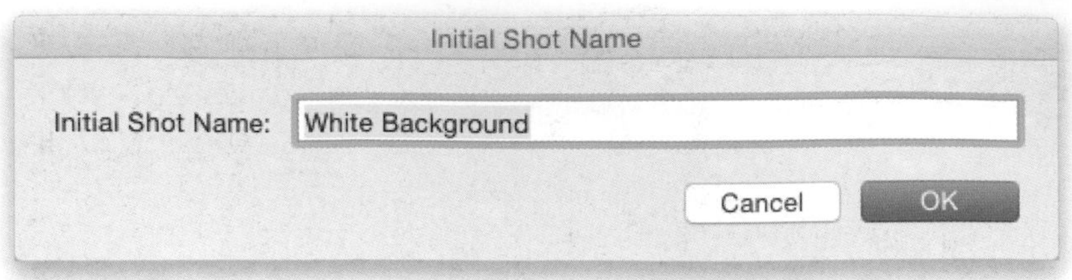

Step Four:

When you click OK, the Tethered Capture window appears (seen here). If Lightroom sees your camera, its model name will appear on the left (if you have more than one camera connected, you can choose which one to use by clicking on the camera's name and choosing from the pop-up menu). If Lightroom doesn't see your camera, it'll read "No Camera Detected," in which case you need to make sure your USB cable is connected correctly, and that Lightroom supports your camera's make and model. To the right of the camera's model, you'll see its current settings, including shutter speed, f-stop, and ISO. To the right of that, you can apply a Develop module preset (see Chapter 6 for more on those, but for now, leave it set at None).

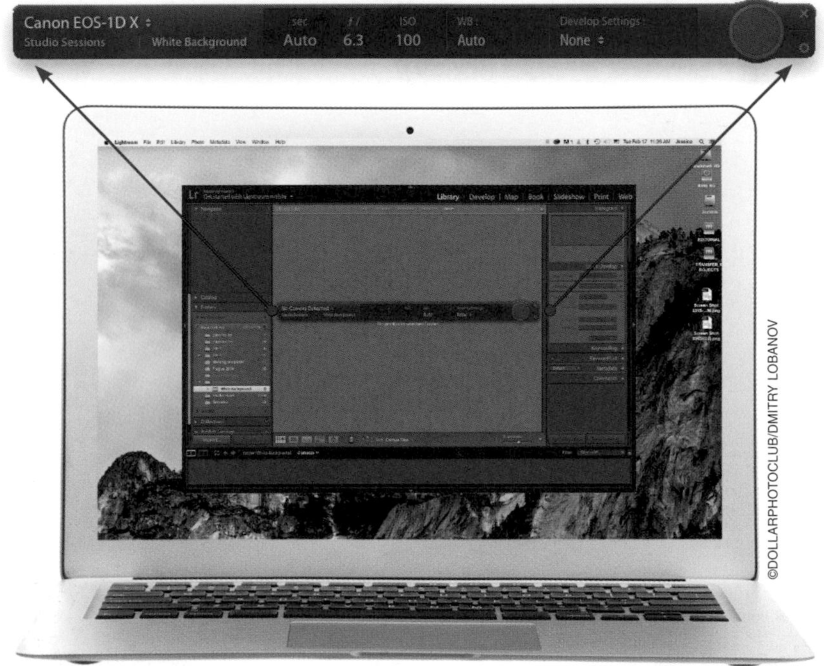

©DOLLARPHOTOCLUB/DMITRY LOBANOV

TIP: Hiding or Shrinking the Tethered Capture Window

Press **Command-T (PC: Ctrl-T)** to show/hide it. If you want to keep it onscreen, but you want it smaller (so you can tuck it to the side of your screen), press-and-hold the Option (PC: Alt) key and the little X in the top right that you'd click on to close the window changes into a – (minus sign). Click on that and the window shrinks down to just the shutter button. To bring it back full size, Option-click (PC: Alt-click) in the top right again.

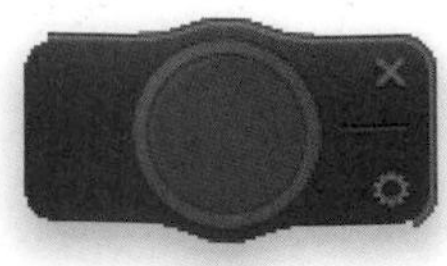

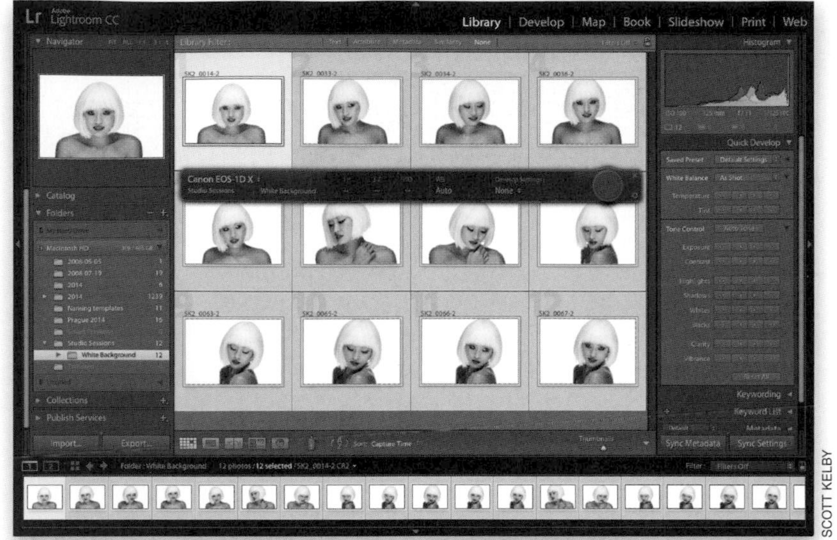

SCOTT KELBY

Step Five:

The round button on the right side of the Tethered Capture window is actually a shutter button, and if you click on it, it'll take a photo just as if you were pressing the shutter button on the camera itself (pretty slick). When you take a shot now, in just a few moments, the image will appear in Lightroom. The image doesn't appear quite as fast in Lightroom as it does on the back of the camera, because you're transferring the entire file from the camera to the computer over that USB cable (or wireless transmitter, if you have one connected to your camera), so it takes a second or two. Also, if you shoot in JPEG mode, the file sizes are much smaller, so your images appear in Lightroom much faster than RAW images. Here's a set of images taken during a tethered shoot. The problem is if you view them in the Library module's Grid view like this, they're not much bigger than the LCD on the back of your camera. *Note:* Canon and Nikon react to tethering differently. For example, if you shoot Canon, and you have a memory card in the camera while shooting tethered, it writes the images to your hard drive and the memory card, but Nikons write only to your hard drive.

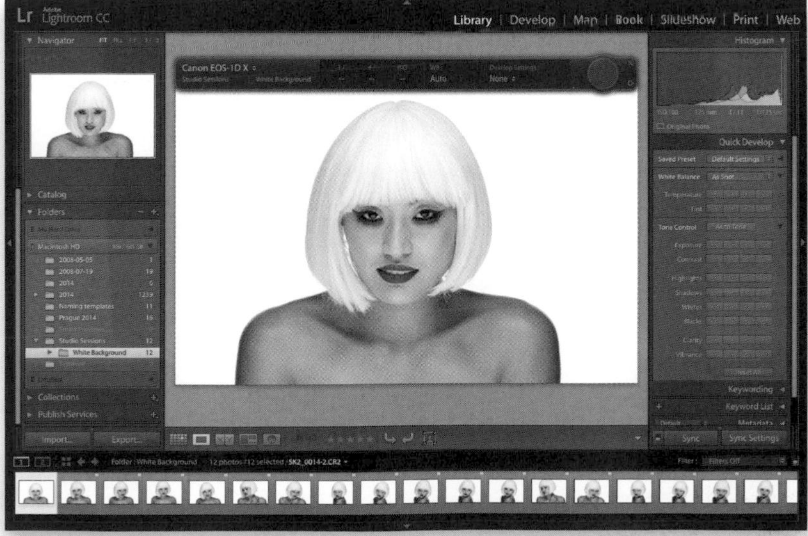

Step Six:

Of course, the big advantage of shooting tethered is seeing your images really large (you can check the lighting, focus, and overall result much easier at these larger sizes, and clients love it when you shoot tethered when they're in the studio, because they can see how it's going without looking over your shoulder and squinting to see a tiny screen). So, double-click on any of the images to jump up to Loupe view (as shown here), where you get a much bigger view as your images appear in Lightroom. (*Note:* If you do want to shoot in Grid view, and just make your thumbnails really big, then you'll probably want to go to the toolbar and, to the left of Sort Order, click on the A–Z button, so your most recent shot always appears at the top of the grid.

Continued

Step Seven:

Now let's put that Segment Photos By Shot feature to use. Let's say you finish this round of shots with your subject in the first lighting setup (the white background) and now you want to switch to the other. Just click directly on the words "White Background" in the Tethered Capture window (or press **Command-Shift-T [PC: Ctrl-Shift-T]**) and the Shot Name dialog appears. Give this new set of shots a name (I named mine "Gray Background") and then go back to shooting. Now these images will appear in their own separate folder, but all within my main Studio Sessions folder.

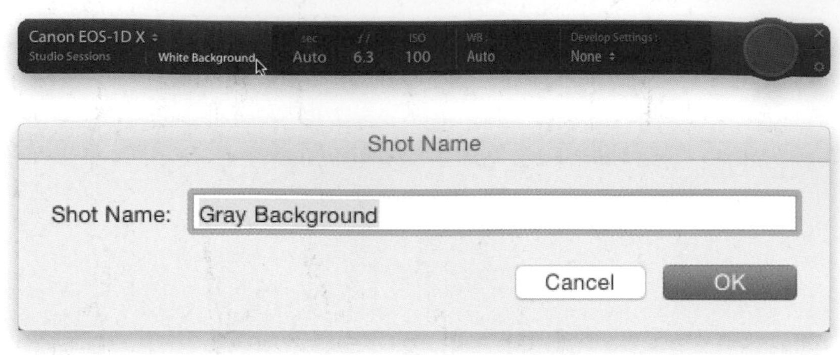

TIP: Shortcut for Triggering Tethered Capture

They added this back in Lightroom 5 and as somebody who uses tethering a lot, I was happy to see that you can trigger a tethered capture by pressing **F12** on your keyboard.

Step Eight:

When I'm shooting tethered (which I always do when I'm in the studio, and as often as I can on location), rather than looking at the Library module's Loupe view, I switch to the Develop module, so if I need to make a quick tweak to anything, I'm already in the right place. Also, when shooting tethered, my goal is to make the image as big as possible onscreen, so I hide Lightroom's panels by pressing **Shift-Tab**, which enlarges the size of your image to take up nearly the whole screen. Then lastly, I press the letter **L** twice to enter Lights Out mode, so all I see is the full-screen-sized image centered on a black background, with no distractions (as shown here). If I want to adjust something, I press L twice, then Shift-Tab to get the panels back.

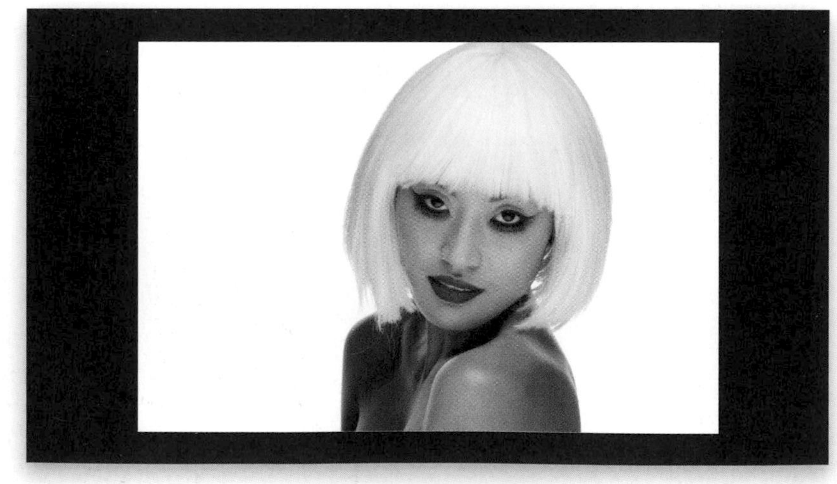

Using Image Overlay to See if Your Images Fit Your Layout

This is one of those features that once you try it, you fall in love with it, because it gives you the opportunity to make sure an image you're shooting for a specific project (like a magazine cover, brochure cover, inside layout, wedding book, etc.) looks and fits the way you want it to, because you get to see the artwork as an overlay in front of your image as you're shooting tethered. This is a big time and frustration saver, and it's simple to use (you just need a little tweaking in Photoshop to set up your artwork).

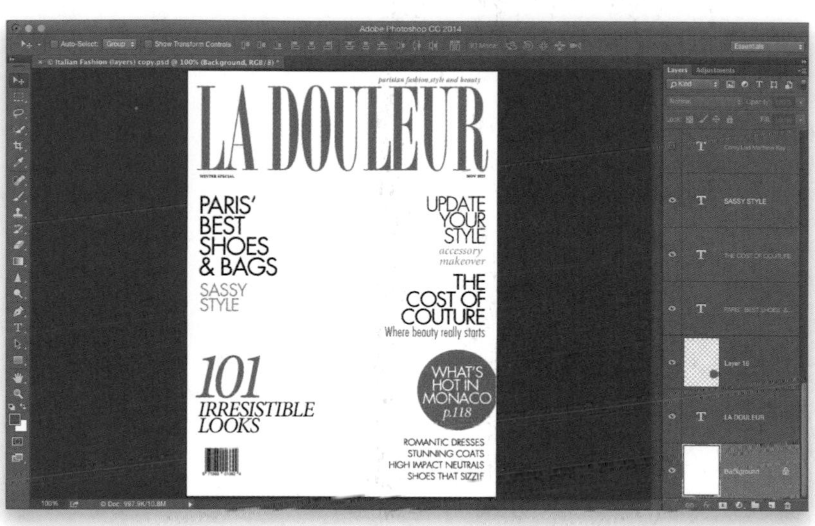

Step One:

You'll need to start in Photoshop by opening the layered version of the cover (or other artwork) you want to use as an overlay in Lightroom. The reason is this: you need to make the background for the entire file transparent, leaving just the type and graphics visible. In the cover mock-up we have here, the cover has a solid white background (of course, once you drag an image in there inside of Photoshop, it would simply cover that white background). We need to prep this file for use in Lightroom, which means: (a) we need to keep all our layers intact, and (b) we need to get rid of that solid white background.

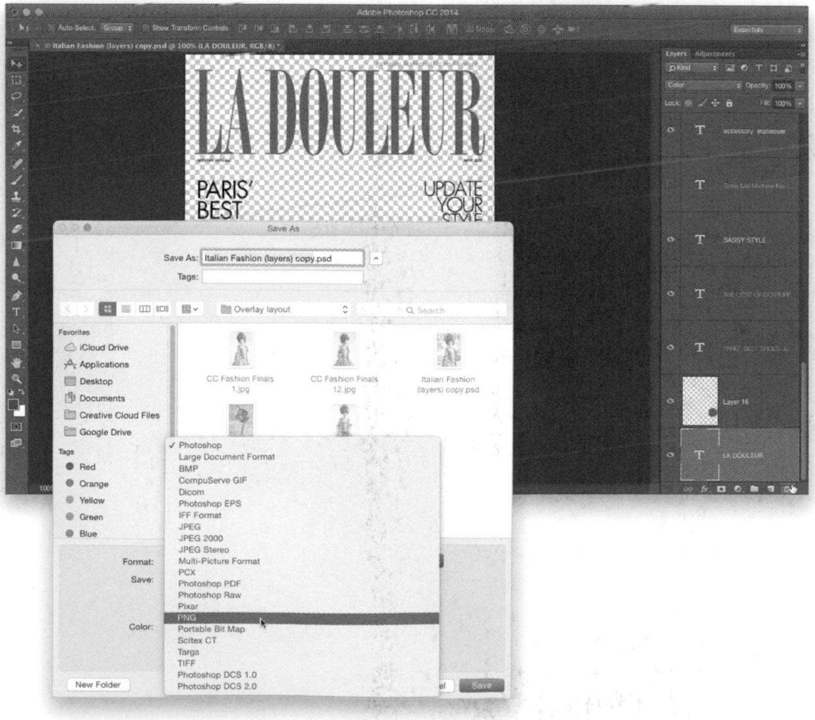

Step Two:

Luckily, prepping this for Lightroom couldn't be simpler: (1) Go to the Background layer (the solid white layer in this case), and delete that layer by dragging it onto the Trash icon at the bottom of the Layers panel (as shown here). Now, (2) all you have to do is go under the File menu, choose Save As, and when the Save As dialog appears, from the Format pop-up menu (where you choose the file type to save it in), choose **PNG**. This format lets you keep the layers intact and, since you deleted the solid white background layer, it makes the background transparent (as seen here). By the way, in the Save As dialog, it will tell you that it has to save a copy to save in PNG format, and that's fine by us, so don't sweat it.

Continued

Step Three:

That's all you have to do in Photoshop, so head back over to Lightroom and go to the Library module. Now, go under the View menu, under Loupe Overlay, and select **Choose Layout Image** (as shown here). Then, find that layered PNG file you just created in Photoshop and choose it.

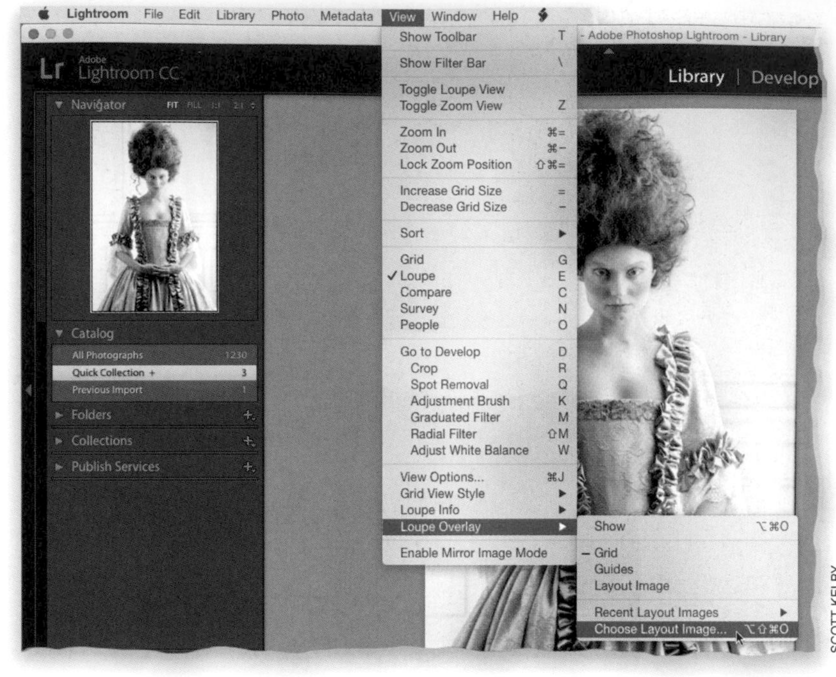

Step Four:

Once you select your layout overlay image, your cover appears over whichever image you currently have onscreen (as shown here). To hide the cover, go under the same Loupe Overlay menu, and you'll see that Layout Image has a checkmark by it, letting you know it's visible. Just choose Layout Image to hide it from view. To see it again, choose it again. Or press **Command-Option-O (PC: Ctrl-Alt-O)** to show/hide it. Remember, if you hadn't deleted the Background layer, what you'd be seeing here is a bunch of text over a white background (and your image would be hidden). That's why it's so important to delete that background layer and save in PNG format. Okay, let's roll on, because there are a few more features here you'll want to know about.

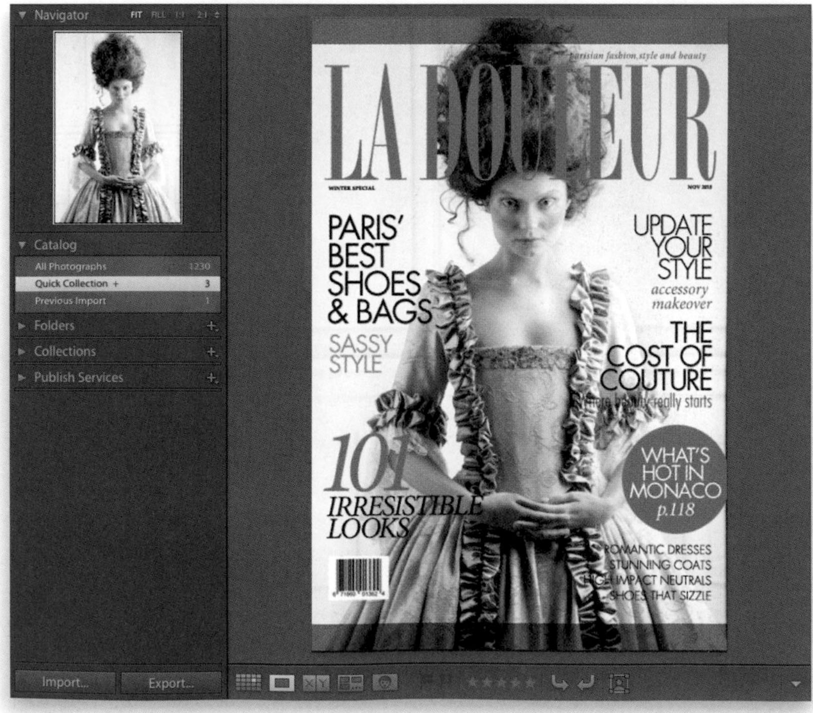

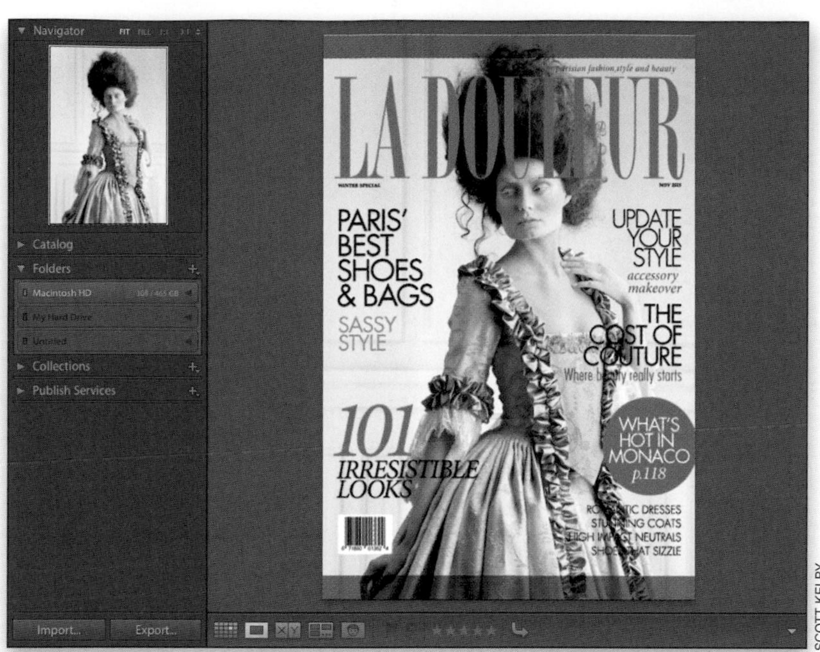

SCOTT KELBY

Step Five:

Now that your layout image overlay is in place, you can use the Left/Right Arrow keys on your keyboard to try different images on your cover (or whatever file you used). Here's what it would look like with a different shot.

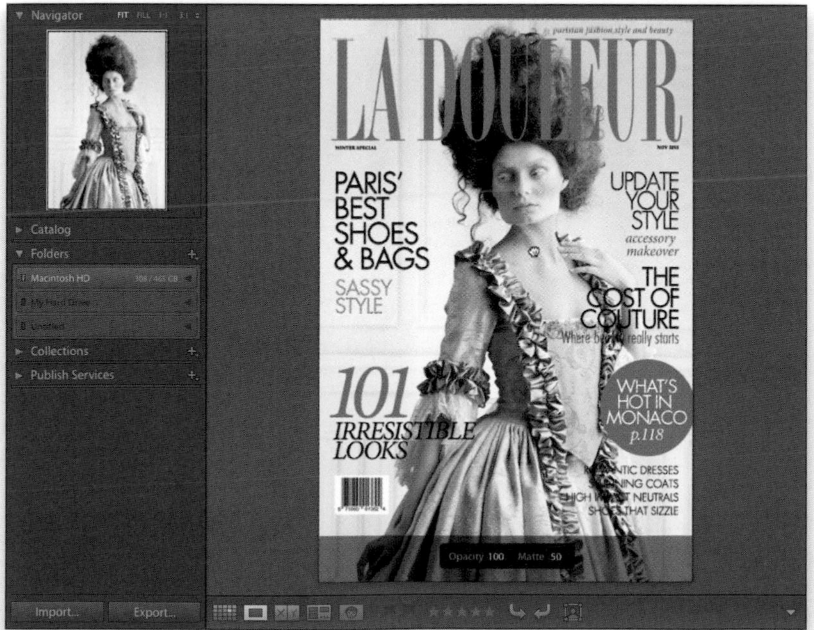

Step Six:

When you look at the image in the previous step, did you notice that she's positioned a little too high? Luckily, you can reposition the cover to see what it would look like with her a little lower. Just press-and-hold the Command (PC: Ctrl) key and your cursor changes into the grabber hand (shown circled here in red). Now, just click-and-drag on the cover and it moves left/right and up/down. What's kind of weird at first is that it doesn't move your image inside the cover. It actually moves the cover. It takes a little getting used to at first, but then it becomes second nature.

Continued

Step Seven:

You can control the Opacity level of your Overlay Image, as well (I switched to a different image here). When you press-and-hold the Command (PC: Ctrl) key, two little controls appear near the bottom of the overlay image. On the left is Opacity, and you just click-and-drag to the left directly on the word "Opacity" to lower the setting (as seen here, where I've lowered our cover image to 60%). To raise the Opacity back up, drag back to the right.

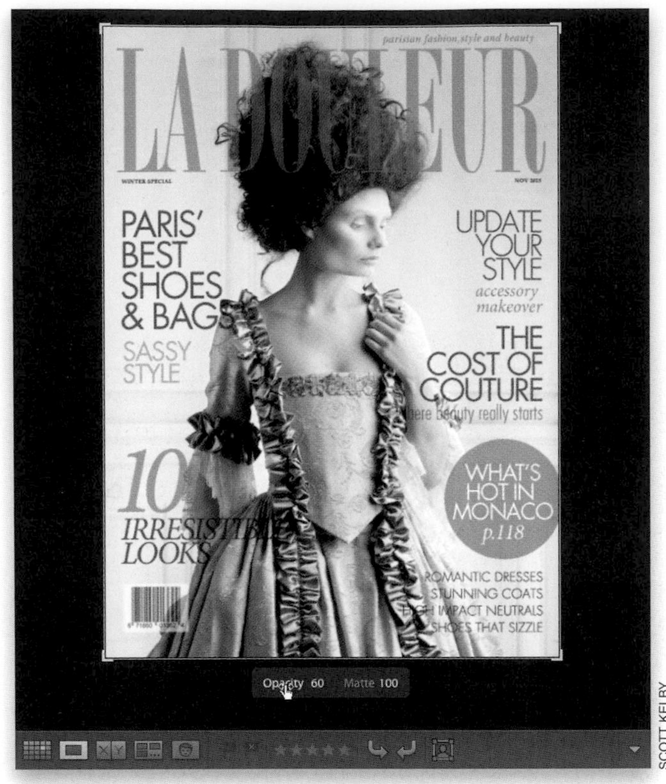

SCOTT KELBY

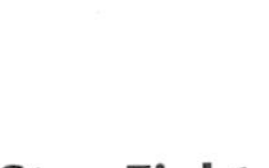

Step Eight:

The other control, which I actually think is more useful, is the Matte control. You see, in the previous step, how the area surrounding the cover is solid black? Well, if you lower the Matte amount, it lets you see through that black background, so you can see the rest of your image that doesn't appear inside the overlay area. Take a look at the image here. See how you can see the background outside the cover? Now I know that this image has room for me to move her either up or down, and parts of her are still there. Pretty handy, and it works the same as the Opacity control—press-and-hold the Command key and click-and-drag right on the word "Matte."

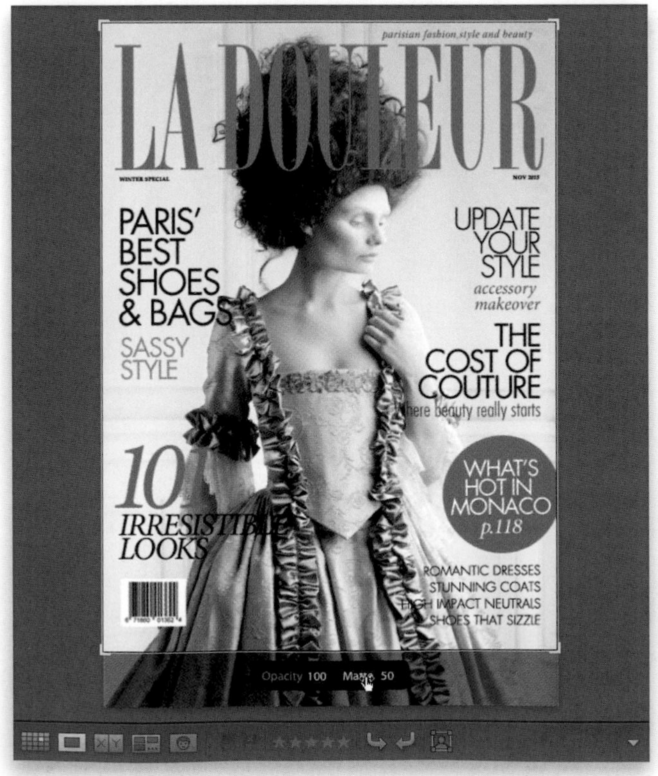

Staying organized is critical when you have thousands of photos, and because digital cameras generate the same set of names over and over, it's really important that you rename your photos with a unique name right during import. A popular strategy is to include the date of the shoot as part of the new name. Unfortunately, only one of Lightroom's import naming presets includes the date, and it makes you keep the camera's original filename along with it. Luckily, you can create your own custom file naming template just the way you want it. Here's how:

Creating Your Own Custom File Naming Templates

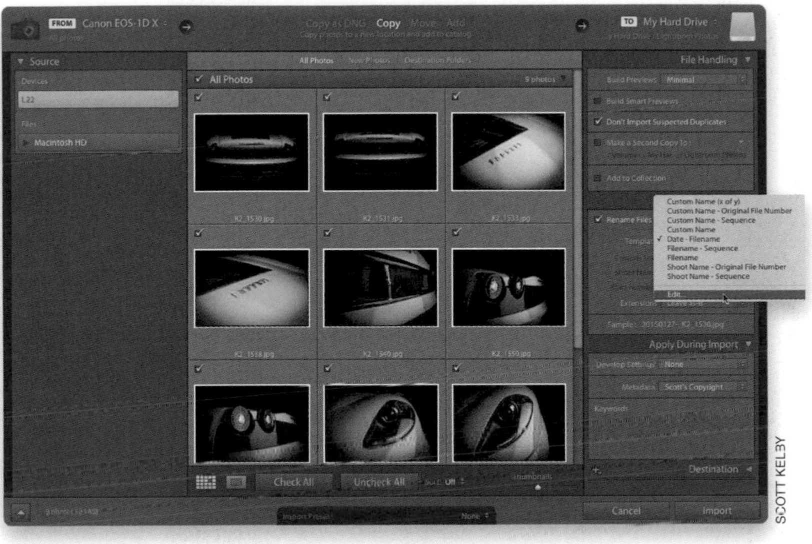

Step One:

Start in the Library module, and click on the Import button on the bottom-left side of the window (or use the keyboard shortcut **Command-Shift-I [PC: Ctrl-Shift-I])**. When the Import window appears, click on Copy as DNG or Copy at the top center, and the File Renaming panel will appear on the right side. In that panel, turn on the Rename Files checkbox, then click on the Template pop-up menu and choose **Edit** (as shown here) to bring up the Filename Template Editor (shown below in Step Two).

Filename Template Editor

Preset: Custom Name - Sequence

Example: untitled-1.jpg

Custom Text - Sequence # (1)

Image Name

Filename Insert

Numbering

Import # (1) Insert

Image # (1) Insert

Sequence # (1) Insert

Additional

Date (YYYY) Insert

Dimensions Insert

Custom

Shoot Name Insert

Custom Text Insert

Cancel Done

Step Two:

At the top of the dialog, there is a pop-up menu where you can choose any of the built-in naming presets as a starting place. For example, if you choose Custom Name – Sequence, the field below shows two blue tokens (that's what Adobe calls them; on a PC, the info appears within braces) that make up that preset: the first represents the text, the second represents the auto numbering. To remove either token, click on it, then press the Delete (PC: Backspace) key on your keyboard. If you want to just start from scratch (as I'm going to do), delete both tokens, choose the options you want from the pop-up menus below, then click the Insert buttons to add them to the field.

Continued

Step Three:

I'm going to show you the setup for a popular file naming system for photographers, but this is only an example—you can create a custom template later that fits your studio's needs. We'll start by adding the year first (this helps keep your filenames together when sorted by name). To keep your filenames from getting too long, I recommend using just the last two digits of the year. So go to the Additional section of the dialog, click on the pop-up menu, and choose **Date (YY)**, as shown here (the Y lets you know this is a year entry, the YY lets you know it's only going to display two digits). The Date (YY) token will appear in the naming field and if you look above the top-left side of it, you'll see a live example of the name template you're creating. At this point, my new filename is 15.jpg, as seen here.

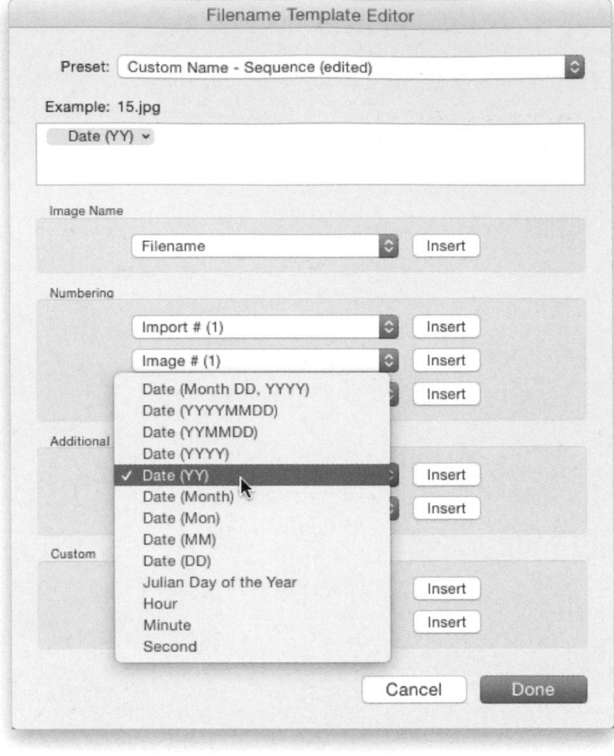

Step Four:

After the two-digit year, we add the two-digit month the photo was taken by going to the same pop-up menu, but this time choosing **Date (MM)**, as shown here. (Both of these dates are drawn automatically from the metadata embedded into your photo by your digital camera at the moment the shot was taken.) By the way, if you had chosen Date (Month), it would display the entire month name, so your filename would have looked like this: 15January, rather than what we want, which is 1501.

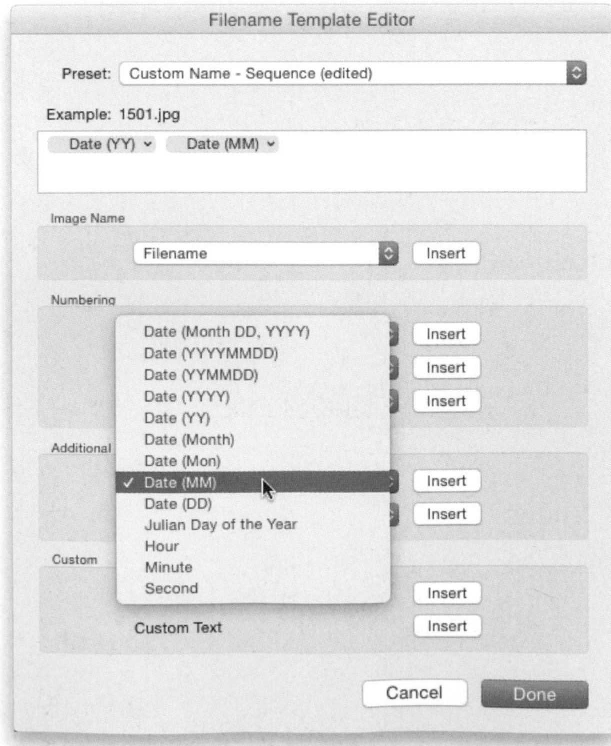

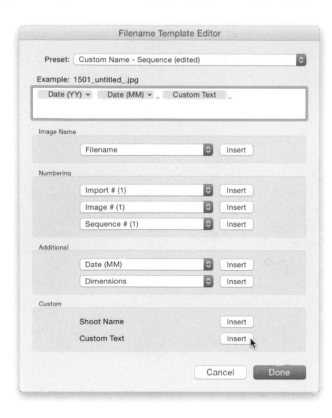

Step Five:

Before we go any further, you should know there's a rule for file naming, and that's no spaces between words. However, if everything just runs together, it's really hard to read. So, after the date, you're going to add a visual separator—a thin flat line called an underscore. To add one, just click your cursor right after the Date (MM) token, then press the Shift key and the Hyphen key to add an underscore (seen here). Now, here's where I differ from some of the other naming conventions: after the date, I include a custom name that describes what's in each shoot. This differs because some people choose to have the original camera-assigned filename appear there instead (personally, I like to have a name in there that makes sense to me without having to open the photo). So to do that, go to the Custom section of the dialog and to the right of Custom Text, click the Insert button (as shown here) to add a Custom Text token after your underscore (this lets you type in a one-word text description later), then add another underscore (so it looks like _Custom Text_. In your example up top, though, it will say "untitled" until you add your custom text).

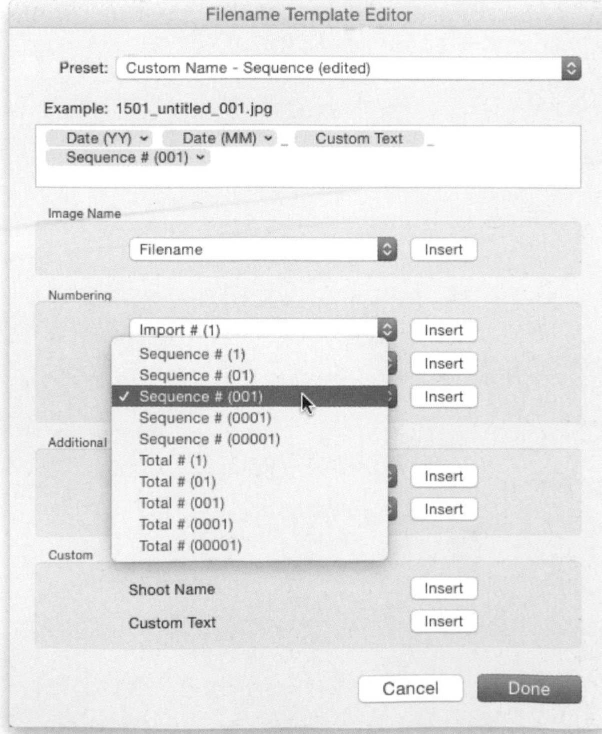

Step Six:

Now you're going to have Lightroom automatically number these photos sequentially. To do that, go to the Numbering section and choose your numbering sequence from the third pop-up menu down. Here I chose the Sequence # (001) token, which adds three-digit auto-numbering to the end of your filename (you can see the example above the naming field).

Continued

Step Seven:

Once the little naming example looks right to you, go under the Preset pop-up menu, and choose **Save Current Settings as New Preset**. A dialog will appear where you can name your preset. Type in a descriptive name (so you'll know what it will do the next time you want to apply it—I chose "Year, Month, Type in Name, Auto Nbr"), click Create, and then click Done in the Filename Template Editor. Now, when you go to the Import window and click on the File Renaming panel's Template pop-up menu, you'll see your custom template as one of the preset choices (as shown here).

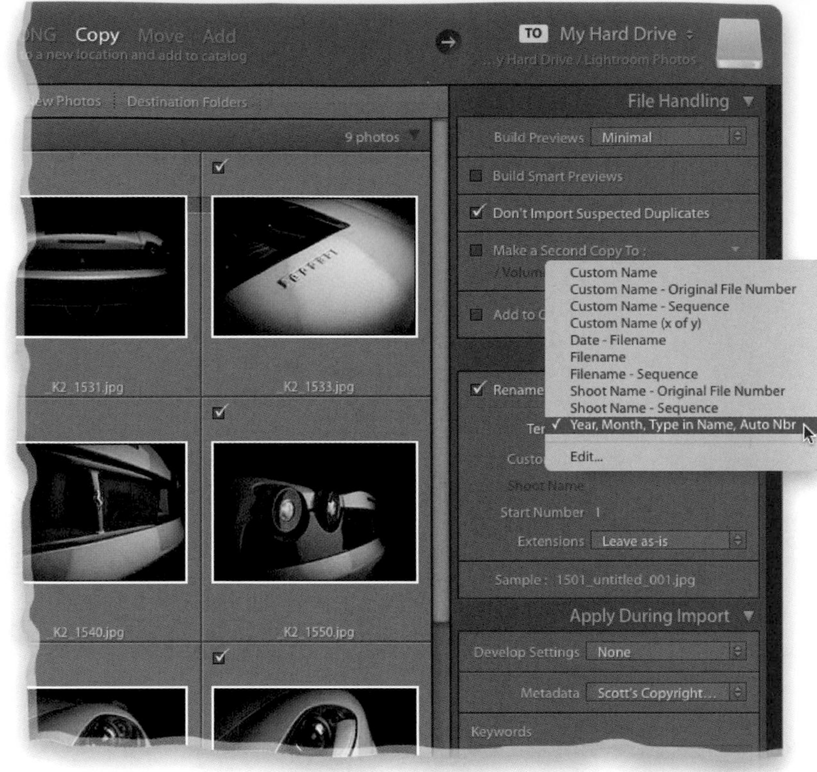

Step Eight:

After you choose this new naming template from the Template pop-up menu, click below it in the Custom Text field (this is where that Custom Text token we added earlier comes into play) and type in the descriptive part of the name (in this case, I typed in "FerrariShoot," all one word—no spaces between words). That custom text will appear between two underscores, giving you a visual separator so everything doesn't all run together (see, it all makes sense now). Once you type it in, if you look at the Sample at the bottom of the File Renaming panel, you'll see a preview of how the photos will be renamed. Once you've chosen all your Apply During Import and Destination panel settings, you can click the Import button.

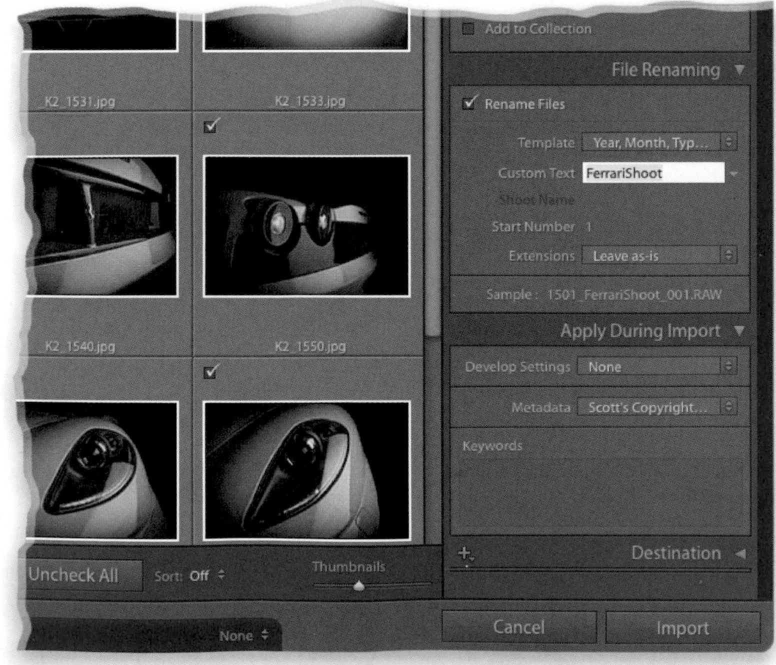

Choosing Your Preferences for Importing Photos

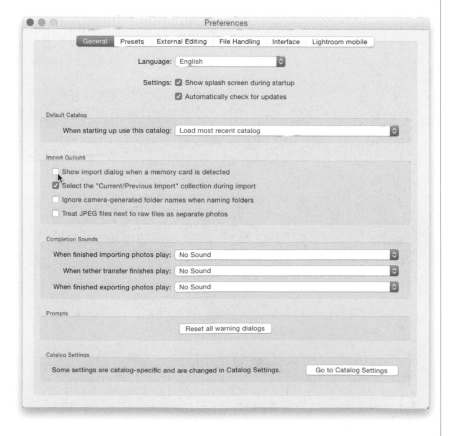

I put the import preferences toward the end of the Importing chapter because I figured that, by now, you've imported some photos and you know enough about the importing process to know what you wish was different. That's what preferences are all about (and Lightroom has preference controls because it gives you lots of control over the way you want to work).

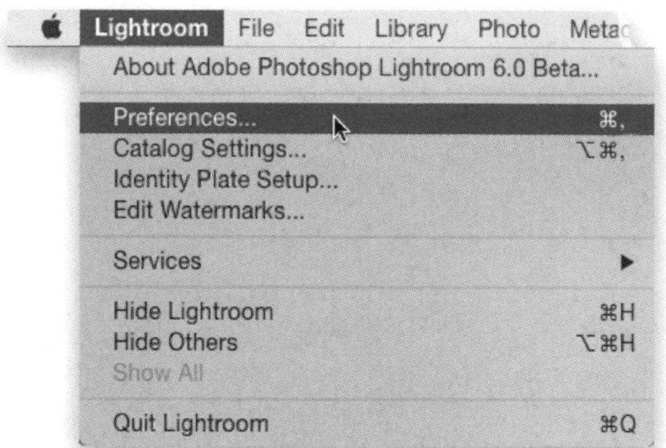

Step One:

The preferences for importing photos are found in a couple different places. First, to get to the Preferences dialog, go under the Lightroom menu on a Mac or the Edit menu on a PC, and choose **Preferences** (as shown here).

Step Two:

When the Preferences dialog appears, first click on the General tab up top (shown highlighted here). Under Import Options in the middle, the first preference lets you tell Lightroom how to react when you connect a memory card from your camera to your computer. By default, it opens the Import window. However, if you'd prefer it didn't automatically open that window each time you plug in a camera or card reader, just turn off its checkbox (as shown here). The second preference here was added back in Lightroom 5. In all previous versions, if you used the keyboard shortcut to start importing photos while in another module, Lightroom left whatever you were working on and jumped over to the Library module to show you the images as they were importing (basically, it assumed you wanted to stop working on whatever you were doing, and start working on these currently importing images). Now, you can choose to stay in the folder or collection you are in and just have those images import in the background by turning off the Select the "Current/Previous Import" Collection During Import checkbox.

Continued

Step Three:

There are two other importing preference settings I'd like to mention that are also found on the General tab. In the Completion Sounds section, you not only get to choose whether or not Lightroom plays an audible sound when it's done importing your photos, you also get to choose which sound (from the pop-up menu of system alert sounds already in your computer, as seen here).

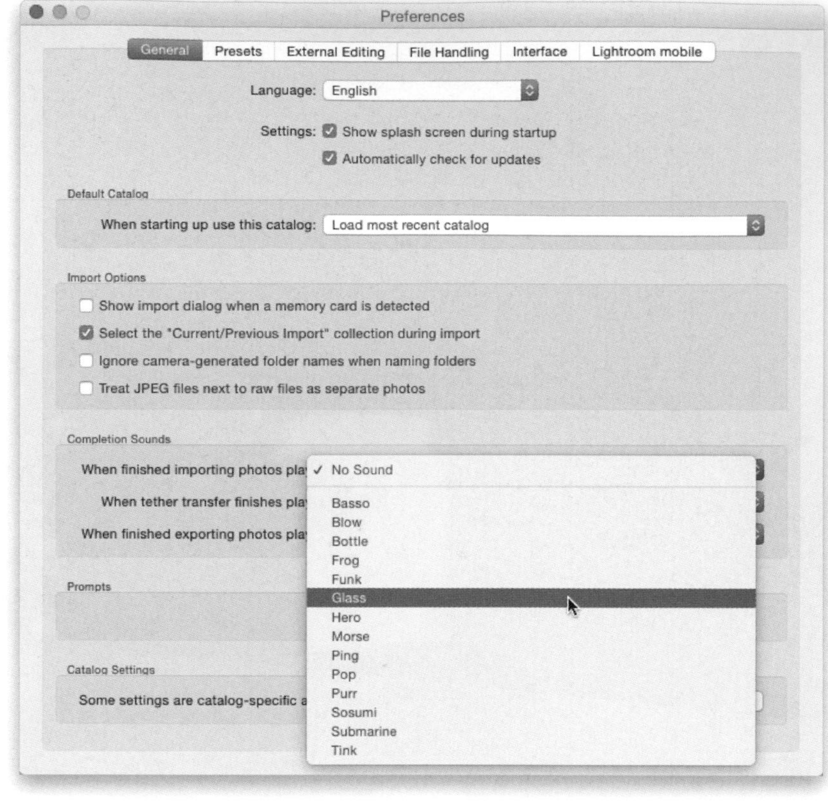

Step Four:

While you're right there, directly below the menu for choosing an "importing's done" sound are two other pop-up menus for choosing a sound for when your tether transfer finishes and for when your exporting is done. I know, the second one isn't an importing preference, but since we're right there, I thought… what the heck. I'll talk more about some of the other preferences later in the book, but since this chapter is on importing, I thought I'd better tackle these here.

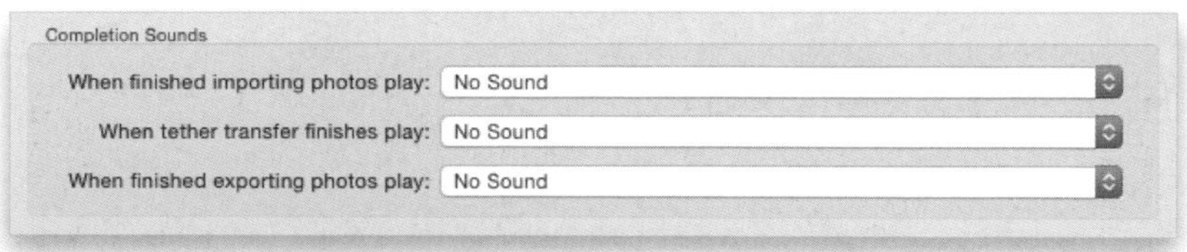

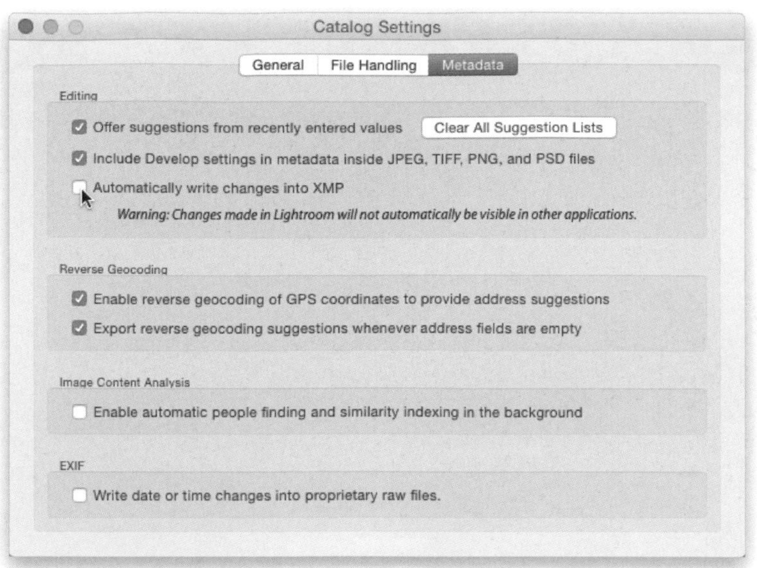

Step Five:

Now, at the bottom of the General tab, click the Go to Catalog Settings button (also found under the Lightroom [PC: Edit] menu). In the Catalog Settings dialog, click on the Metadata tab. Here you can determine whether you want to take the metadata you add to your RAW photos (copyright, keywords, etc.) and have it written to a totally separate file, so then for each photo you'll have two files—one that contains the photo itself and a separate file (called an XMP sidecar) that contains that photo's metadata. You do this by turning on the Automatically Write Changes into XMP checkbox, but why would you ever want to do this? Well, normally Lightroom keeps track of all this metadata you add in its database file—it doesn't actually embed the info until your photo leaves Lightroom (by exporting a copy over to Photoshop, or exporting the file as a JPEG, TIFF, or PSD—all of which support having this metadata embedded right into the photo itself). However, some programs can't read embedded metadata, so they need a separate XMP sidecar file.

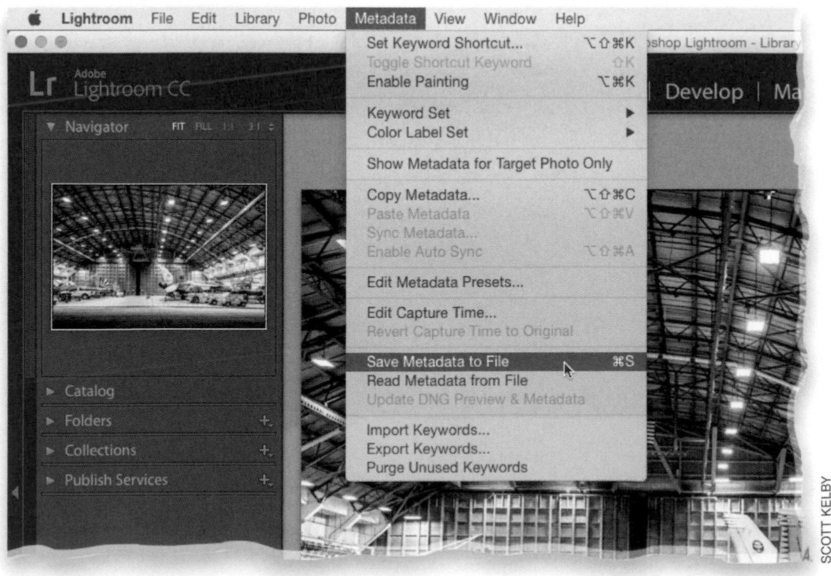

Step Six:

Now that I've shown you that Automatically Write Changes into XMP checkbox, I don't actually recommend you turn it on, because writing all those XMP sidecars takes time, which slows Lightroom down. Instead, if you want to send a file to a friend or client and you want the metadata written to an XMP sidecar file, first go to the Library module and click on an image to select it, then press **Command-S (PC: Ctrl-S)**, which is the shortcut for **Save Metadata to File** (which is found under the Metadata menu). This writes any existing metadata to a separate XMP file (so you'll need to send both the photo and the XMP sidecar together).

The Adobe DNG File Format Advantage

I mentioned that you have the option of having your photos converted to DNG (Digital Negative) format as they're imported. DNG was created by Adobe because today each camera manufacturer has its own proprietary RAW file format, and Adobe is concerned that, one day, one or more manufacturers might abandon an older format for something new. With DNG, it's not proprietary—Adobe made it an open format, so anyone can write to that specification. While ensuring that your negatives could be opened in the future was the main goal, DNG brings other advantages, as well.

Setting Your DNG Preferences:

Press **Command-,** (comma; **PC: Ctrl-,**) to bring up Lightroom's Preferences dialog, then click on the File Handling tab (as shown here). In the Import DNG Creation section at the top here, you can see the settings I use for DNG conversion. Although you can embed the original proprietary RAW file, I don't (it adds to the file size, and pretty much kills Advantage #1 below). By the way, you choose Copy as DNG at the top center of the Import window (as shown below).

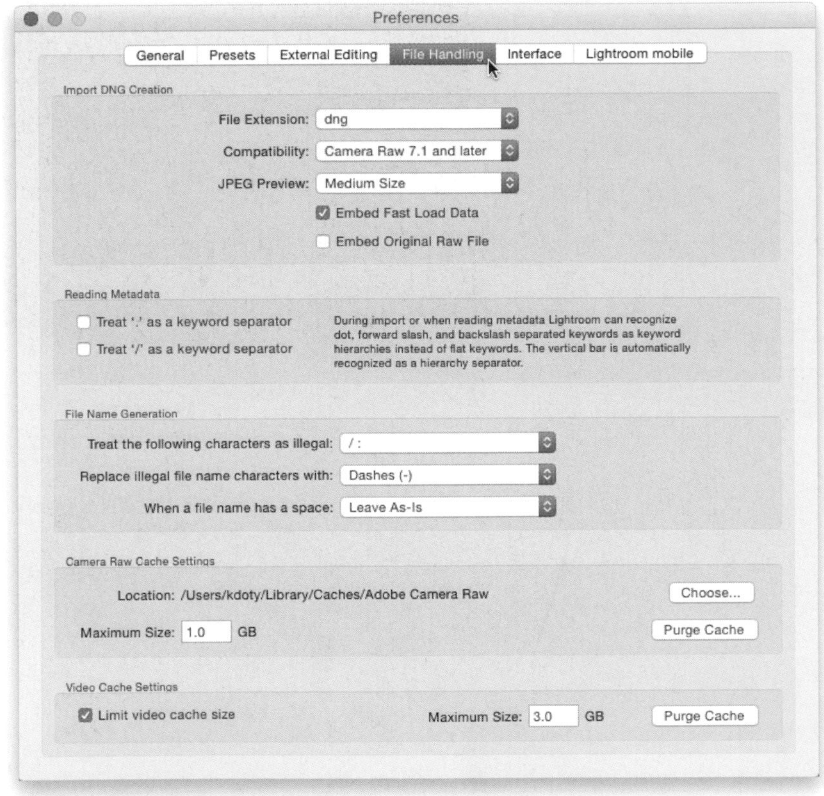

Advantage #1: DNG files are smaller

RAW files usually have a pretty large file size, so they eat up hard disk space pretty quickly, but when you convert a file to DNG, it's generally about 20% smaller.

Advantage #2: DNG files don't need a separate sidecar

When you edit a RAW file, that metadata is actually stored in a separate file called an XMP sidecar file. If you want to give someone your RAW file and have it include the metadata and changes you applied to it in Lightroom, you'd have to give them two files: (1) the RAW file itself, and (2) the XMP sidecar file, which holds the metadata and edit info. But with a DNG, if you press **Command-S (PC: Ctrl-S)**, that info is embedded right into the DNG file itself. So, before you give somebody your DNG file, just remember to use that shortcut so it writes the metadata to the file first.

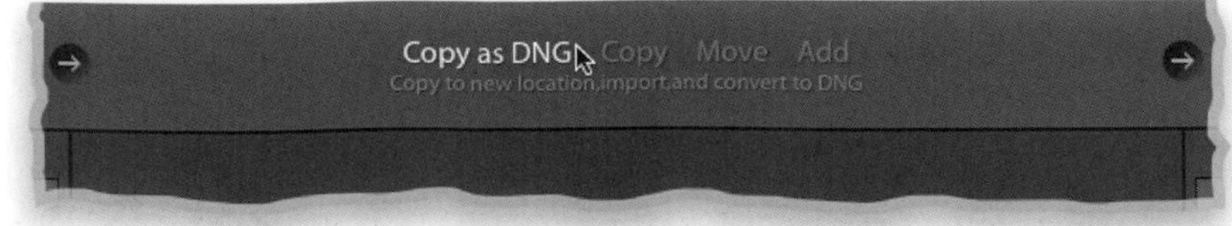

Creating Your Own Custom Metadata (Copyright) Templates

At the beginning of this chapter, I mentioned that you'll want to set up your own custom metadata template, so you can easily and automatically embed your own copyright and contact information right into your photos as they're imported into Lightroom. Well, here's how to do just that. Keep in mind that you can create more than one template, so if you create one with your full contact info (including your phone number), you might want to create one with just basic info, or one for when you're exporting images to be sent to a stock photo agency, etc.

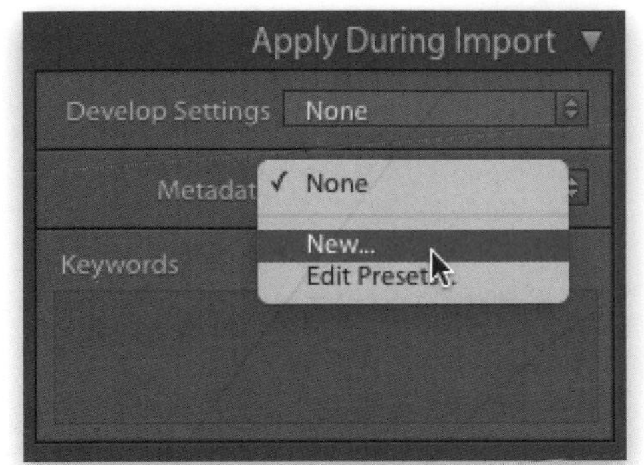

Step One:

You can create a metadata template from right within the Import window, so press **Command-Shift-I (PC: Ctrl-Shift-I)** to bring it up. Once the Import window appears, go to the Apply During Import panel, and from the Metadata pop-up menu, choose **New** (as shown here).

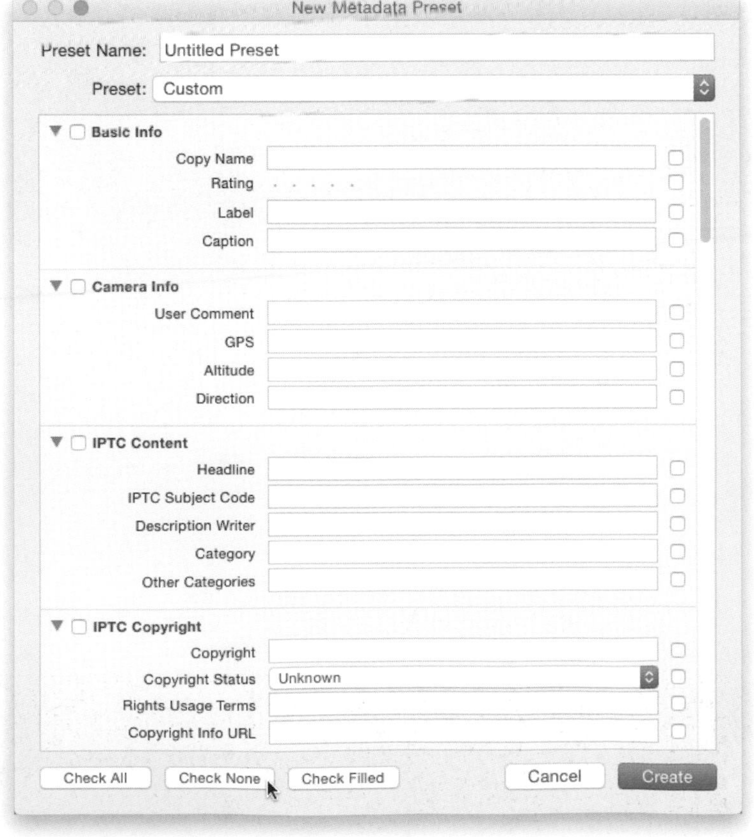

Step Two:

A blank New Metadata Preset dialog will appear. First, click the Check None button at the bottom of the dialog, as shown here (so no blank fields will appear when you view this metadata in Lightroom—only fields with data will be displayed).

Continued

Step Three:

In the IPTC Copyright section, type in your copyright information (as shown here). Next, go to the IPTC Creator section and enter your contact info (after all, if someone goes by your website and downloads some of your images, you might want them to be able to contact you to arrange to license your photo). Now, you may feel that the Copyright Info URL (web address) that you added in the previous section is enough contact info, and if that's the case, you can skip filling out the IPTC Creator info (after all, this metadata preset is to help make potential clients aware that your work is copyrighted, and tell them how to get in contact with you). Once all the metadata info you want embedded in your photos is complete, go up to the top of the dialog, give your preset a name—I chose "Scott's Copyright (Full)"—and then click the Create button.

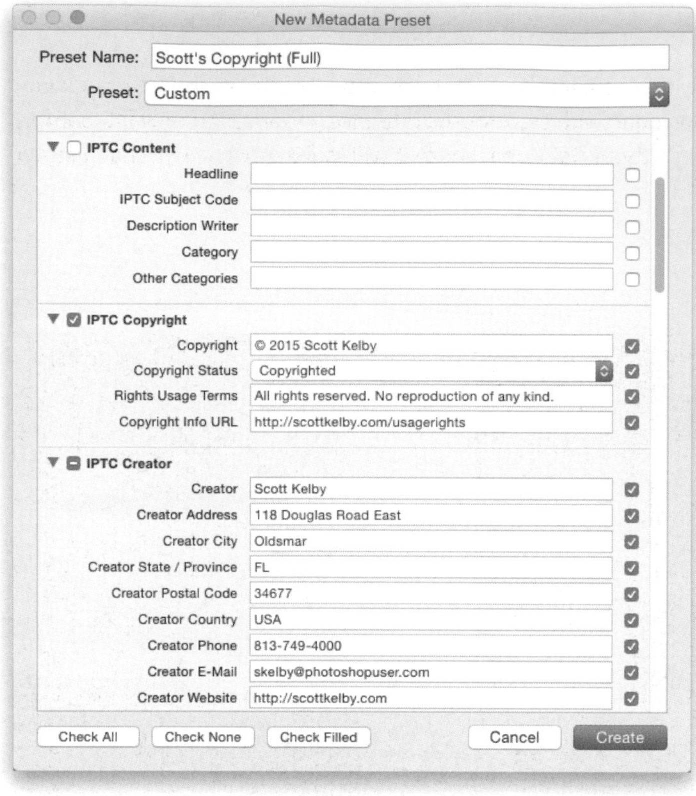

Step Four:

As easy as it is to create a metadata template, deleting one isn't much harder. Go back to the Apply During Import panel and, from the Metadata pop-up menu, choose **Edit Presets**. That brings up the Edit Metadata Presets dialog (which looks just like the New Metadata Preset dialog). From the Preset pop-up menu at the top, choose the preset you want to delete. Once all the metadata appears in the dialog, go back to that Preset pop-up menu, and now choose **Delete Preset [Name of Preset]**. A warning dialog will pop up, asking if you're sure you want to delete this preset. Click Delete, and it is gone forever.

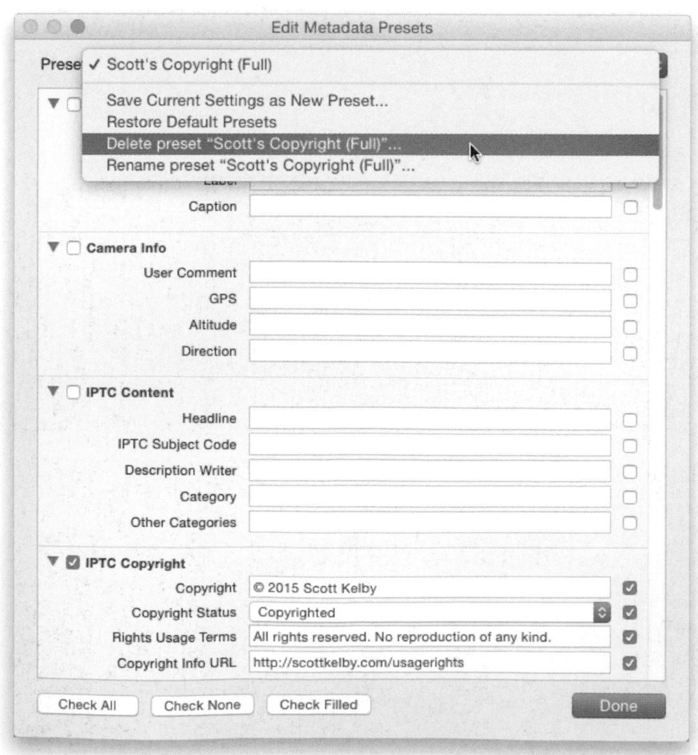

Four Things You'll Want to Know Now About Getting Around Lightroom

Now that your images have been imported, there are some tips about working with Lightroom's interface you're going to want to know about right up front that will make working in it much easier.

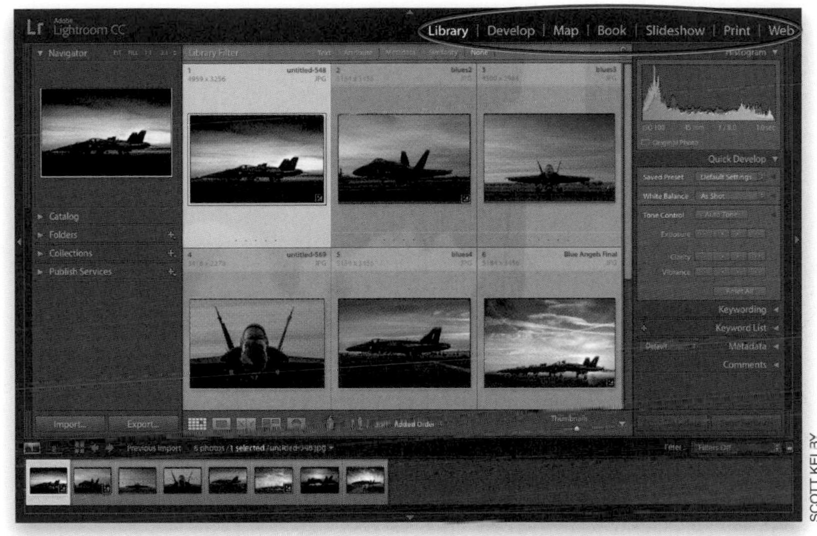

SCOTT KELBY

Step One:

There are seven different modules in Lightroom, and each does a different thing. When your imported photos appear in Lightroom, they always appear in the center of the Library module, which is where we do all our sorting, searching, keywording, etc. The Develop module is where you go to do your photo editing (like changing the exposure, white balance, tweaking colors, etc.), and it's pretty obvious what the other five do (I'll spare you). You move from module to module by clicking on the module's name up in the taskbar across the top, or you can use the shortcuts **Command-Option-1** for Library, **Command-Option-2** for Develop, and so on (on a PC, it would be **Ctrl-Alt-1, Ctrl-Alt-2**, and so on).

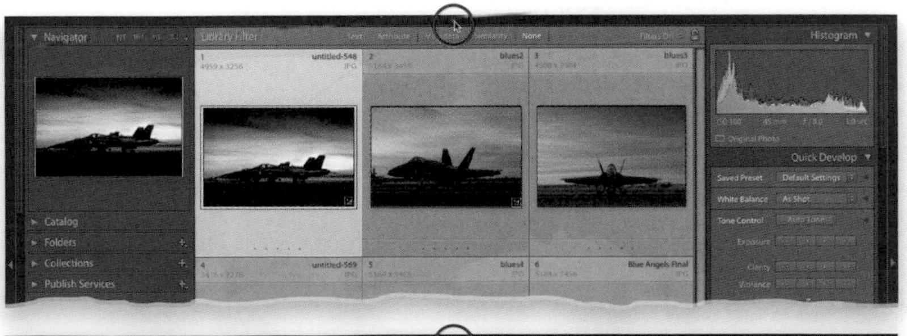

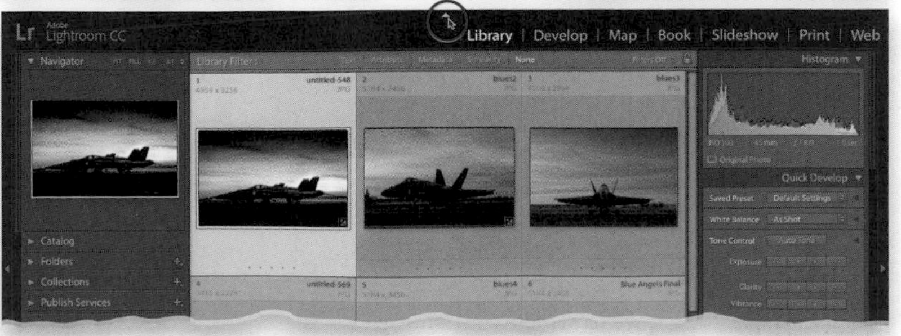

Step Two:

There are five areas in the Lightroom interface overall: that taskbar on the top, the left and right side Panels areas, a Filmstrip across the bottom, and your photos always appear in the center Preview area. You can hide any panel (which makes the Preview area, where your photos are displayed, larger) by clicking on the little gray triangle in the center edge of the panel. For example, go ahead and click on the little gray triangle at the top center of the interface, and you'll see it hides the taskbar. Click it again; it comes back.

Continued

Step Three:

The #1 complaint I hear from Lightroom users about working with panels is they hate the Auto Hide & Show feature (which is on by default). The idea behind it sounds great: if you've hidden a panel, and need it visible again to make an adjustment, you move your cursor over where the panel used to be, and it pops out. When you're done, you move your cursor away, and it automatically tucks back out of sight. Sounds great, right? The problem is one pops out anytime you move your cursor to the far right, left, top, or bottom of your screen. It really drives them nuts, and I've had people literally beg me to show them how to turn it off. You can turn Auto Hide & Show off by Right-clicking on the little gray triangle for any panel. A pop-up menu will appear (shown here) where you'll choose **Manual**, which turns the feature off. This works on a per-panel basis, so you'll have to do it to each of the four panels.

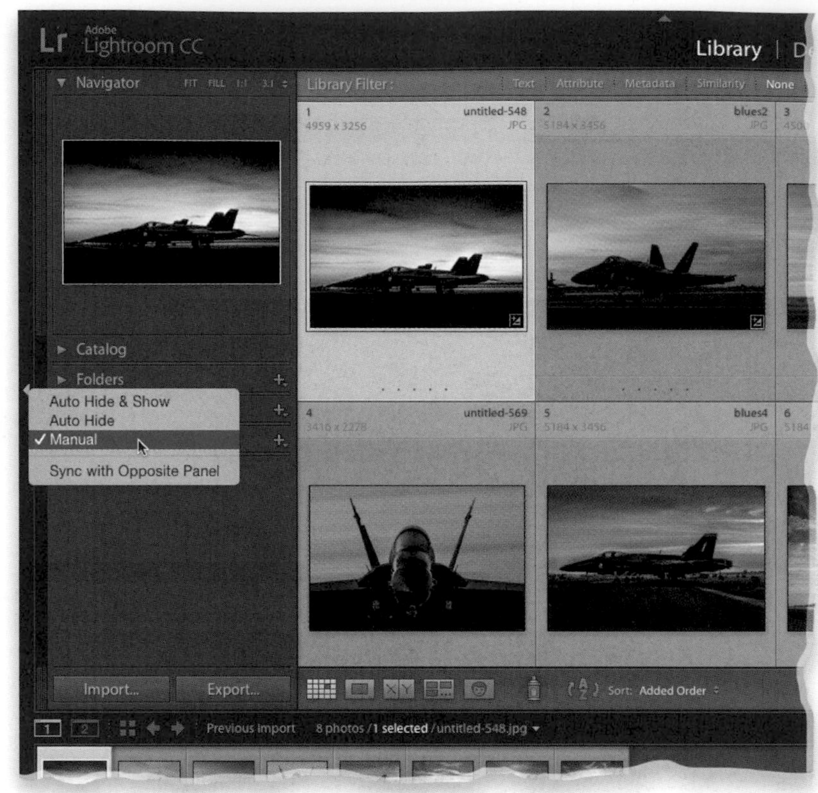

Step Four:

I use the Manual mode, so I can just open and close panels as I need them. You can also use the keyboard shortcuts: **F5** closes/opens the top taskbar, **F6** hides the Filmstrip, **F7** hides the left side Panels area, and **F8** hides the right side (on a newer Mac keyboard or a laptop, you may have to press the Fn key with these). You can hide both side Panels areas by pressing the **Tab key**, but the one shortcut I probably use the most is **Shift-Tab**, because it hides everything—all the panels—and leaves just your photos visible (as shown here). Also, here's an insight into what is found where: the left side Panels area is used primarily for applying presets and templates, and showing you a preview of the photo, preset, or template you're working with. Everything else (all adjustments) is found on the right side. Okay, on the next page: tips on viewing.

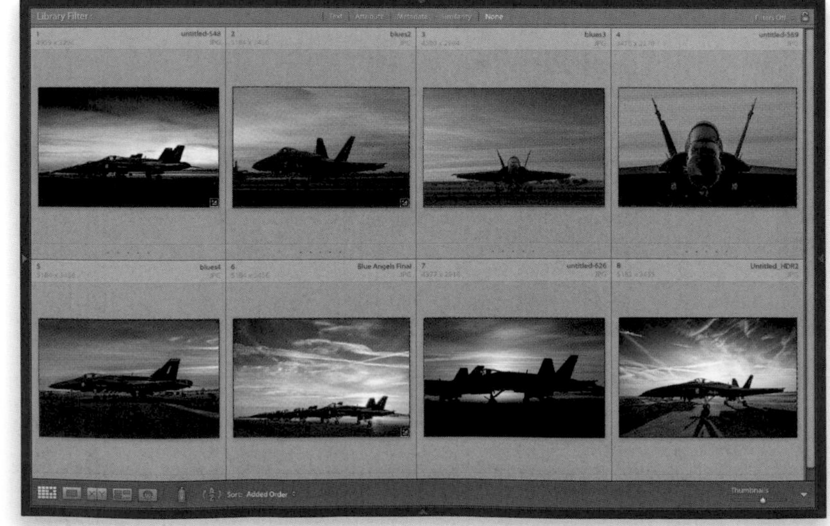

Before we get to sorting our photos and separating the winners from the losers (which we cover in the next chapter), taking a minute just to learn the ins and outs of how Lightroom lets you view your imported photos is important. Learning these viewing options now will really help you make the most informed decisions possible about which photos make it (and which ones don't).

Viewing Your Imported Photos

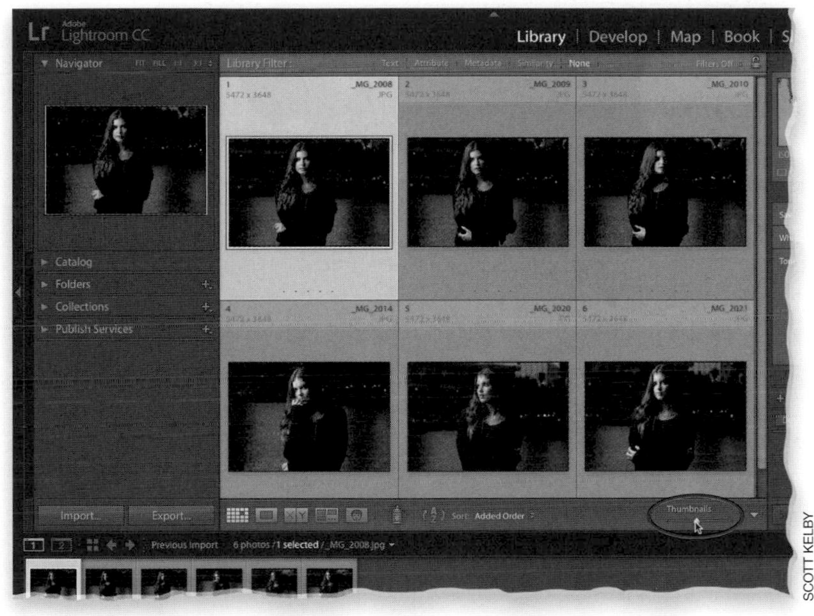

SCOTT KELBY

Step One:

When your imported photos appear in Lightroom, they are displayed as small thumbnails in the center Preview area (as seen here). You can change the size of these thumbnails using the Thumbnails slider that appears on the right side of the toolbar (the dark gray horizontal bar that appears directly below the center Preview area). Drag it to the right, and they get bigger; drag to the left, and they get smaller (the slider is circled here).

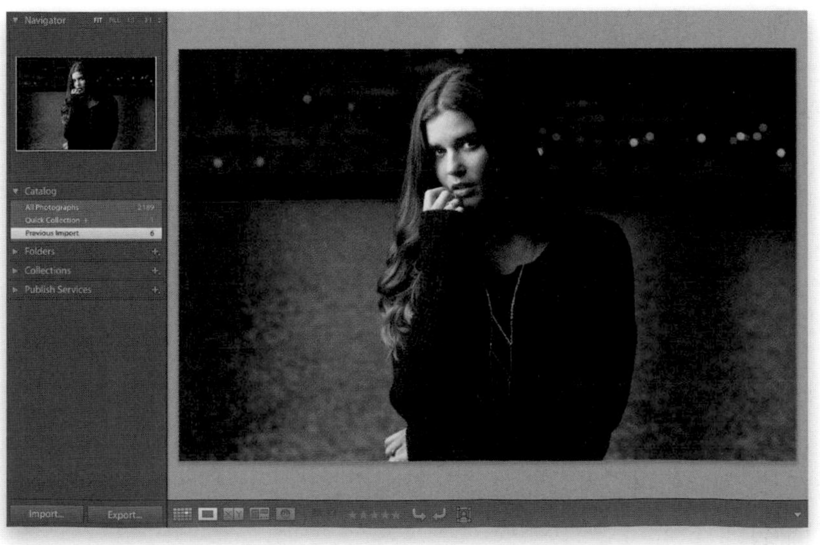

Step Two:

To see any thumbnail at a larger size, just double-click on it, press the letter **E** on your keyboard, or press the **Spacebar**. This larger size is called Loupe view (as if you were looking at the photo through a loupe), and by default it zooms in so you can see your entire photo in the Preview area. This is called a Fit in Window view, but if you'd prefer that it zoomed in tighter, you can go up to the Navigator panel at the top left, and click on a different size, like Fill, and now when you double-click, it will zoom in until your photo literally fills the Preview area. Choosing 1:1 will zoom your photo in to a 100% actual size view when it's double-clicked, but I have to tell you, it's kind of awkward to go from a tiny thumbnail to a huge, tight zoom like that.

Continued

Step Three:

I leave my Navigator panel setting at Fit, so when I double-click I can see the entire photo fitting in the center Preview area, but if you want to get in closer to check sharpness, you'll notice that when you're in Loupe view, your cursor has changed into a magnifying glass. If you click it once on your photo, it jumps to a 1:1 view of the area where you clicked. To zoom back out, just click it again. To return to the thumbnail view (called Grid view), just press the letter **G** on your keyboard. This is one of the most important keyboard shortcuts to memorize (so far, the ones you really need to know are: **Shift-Tab** to hide all the panels, and now G to return to Grid view). This is a particularly handy shortcut, because when you're in any other module, pressing G brings you right back here to the Library module and your thumbnail grid.

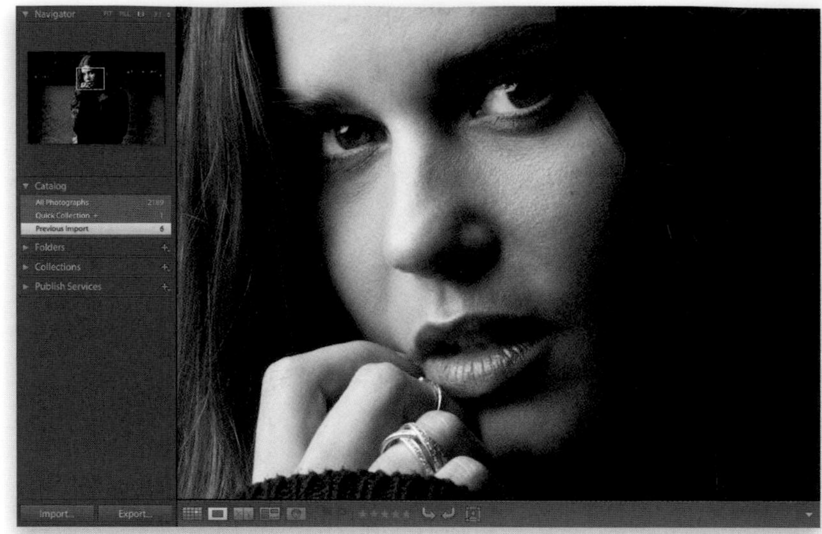

Step Four:

The area that surrounds your thumbnail is called a cell, and each cell displays information about the photo, from the filename, to the file format, dimensions, etc.—you get to customize how much or how little it displays, as you'll see in Chapter 3. But in the meantime, here's another keyboard shortcut you'll want to know about: press the letter **J**. Each time you press it, it toggles you through the three different cell views, each of which displays different groups of info—an expanded cell with lots of info, a compact cell with just a little info, and one that hides all that distracting stuff altogether (great for when you're showing thumbnails to clients). Also, you can hide (or show) the toolbar by pressing **T**. If you press-and-hold T, it only hides it for as long as you have the T key held down.

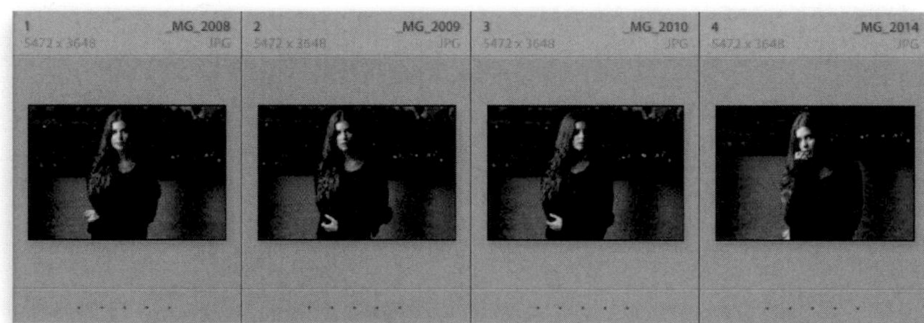

The default cell view is called Expanded and gives you the most info

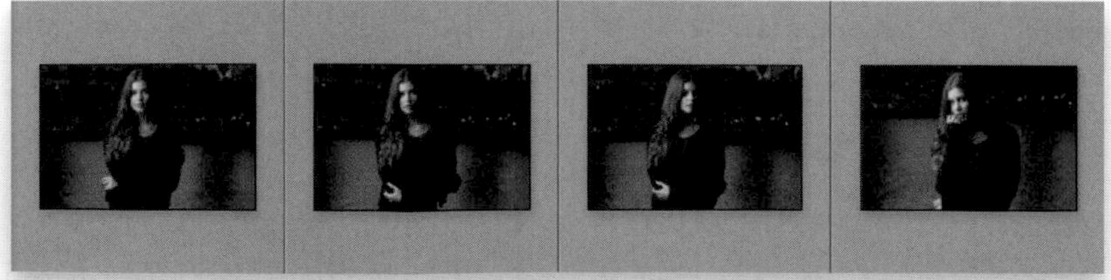

Press J to switch to Compact view, which shrinks the size of the cell, hides all the info, and just shows the photos

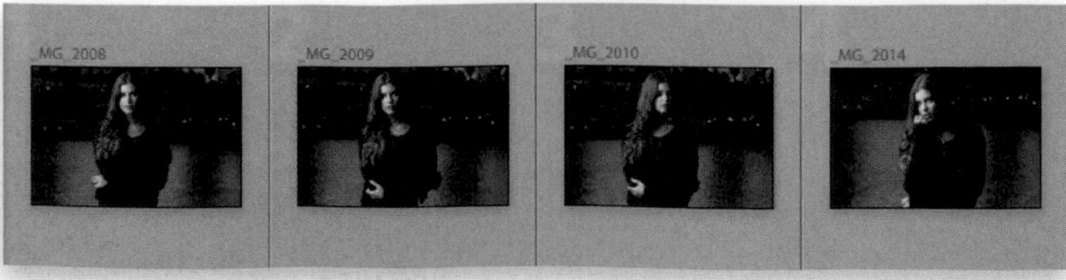

Press J one more time and it adds back some info and numbers to each cell

Using Lights Dim, Lights Out, and Other Viewing Modes

One of the things I love best about Lightroom is how it gets out of your way and lets your photos be the focus. That's why I love the Shift-Tab shortcut that hides all the panels. But if you want to really take things to the next level, after you hide those panels, you can dim everything around your photo, or literally "turn the lights out," so everything is blacked out but your photos. Here's how:

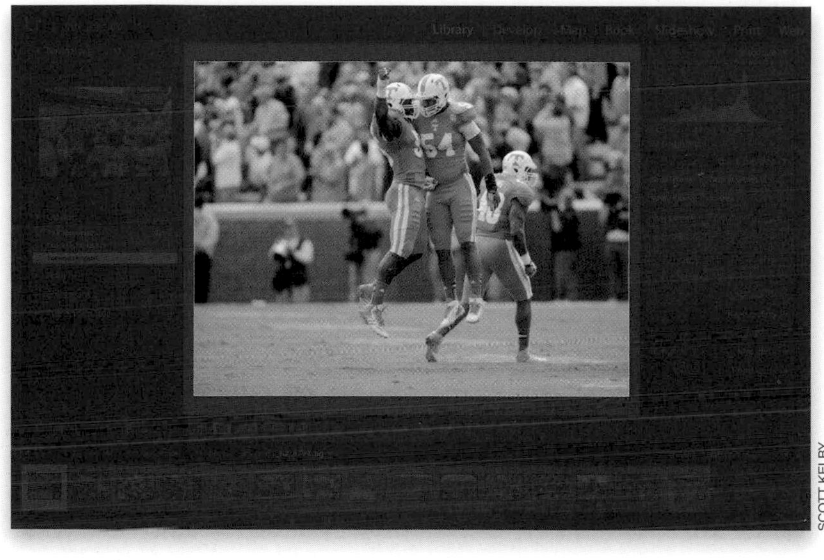

SCOTT KELBY

Step One:

Press the letter **L** on your keyboard to enter Lights Dim mode, in which everything but your photo(s) in the center Preview area is dimmed (kind of like you turned down a lighting dimmer). Perhaps the coolest thing about this dimmed mode is the fact that the Panels areas, taskbar, and Filmstrip all still work—you can still make adjustments, change photos, etc., just like when the "lights" are all on.

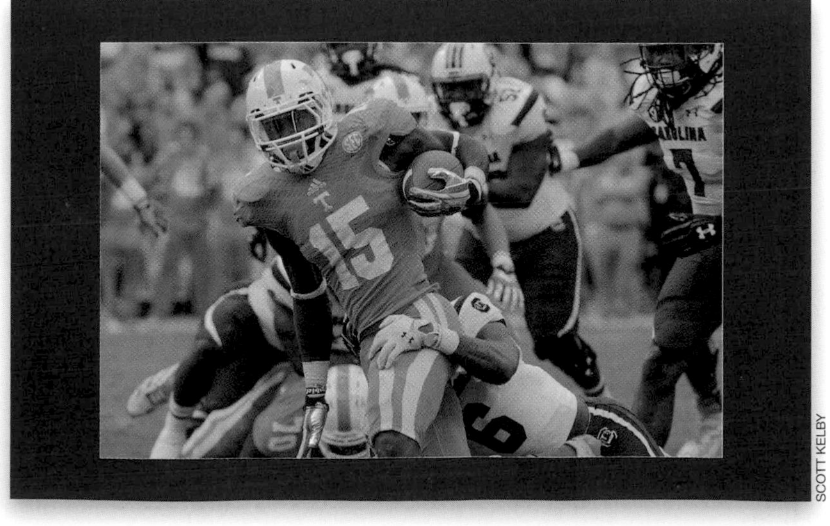

SCOTT KELBY

Step Two:

The next viewing mode is Lights Out (you get Lights Out by pressing **L** a second time), and this one really makes your photos the star of the show because everything else is totally blacked out, so there's nothing (and I mean nothing) but your photos onscreen (to return to regular Lights On mode, just press L again). To get your image as big onscreen as possible, right before you enter Lights Out mode, press **Shift-Tab** to hide all the panels on the sides, top, and bottom—that way you get the big image view you see here. Without the Shift-Tab, you'd have the smaller size image you see in Step One, with lots and lots of empty black space around it.

Continued

TIP: Controlling Lights Out Mode

You have more control over Lightroom's Lights Out mode than you might think: just go to Lightroom's preferences (under the Lightroom menu on a Mac or the Edit menu on a PC), click on the Interface tab, and you'll find pop-up menus that control both the Dim Level and the Screen Color when you're in full Lights Out mode.

Preferences
General | Presets | External Editing | File Handling | Interface | Lightroom mobile
Panels
End Marks: None (default) | Font Size: Small (default)
Lights Out
Screen Color: ✓ Black (default) | Dark Gray | Medium Gray | Light Gray | White
Dim Level: 80% (default)
Background
Secondary Window
Fill Color: Medium Gray (default) | Medium Gray (default)
Texture: None | None
Keyword Entry

Step Three:

If you want to view your grid of photos without distractions in the Lightroom window, press **Shift-F** on your keyboard twice. The first time you press Shift-F, it makes the Lightroom window fill your screen and hides the window's title bar (directly above the taskbar in Lightroom's interface). The second Shift-F actually hides the menu bar at the very top of your screen, so if you combine this with Shift-Tab to hide your panels, taskbar, and Filmstrip, and **T** to hide the toolbar (and **\ [backslash]** if your Filter bar is showing), you'll see just your photos on a solid top-to-bottom gray background. I know you might be thinking, "I don't know if I find those two thin bars at the top really that distracting." So, try hiding them once and see what you think. Luckily, there's an easy shortcut to jump to the "super-clean, distraction-free nirvana view" you see here: you press **Command-Shift-F (PC: Ctrl-Shift-F)**, ****, then **T**. To return to regular view, use the same shortcut. The image on top is the gray layout you just learned, and on bottom, I pressed L twice to enter Lights Out mode.

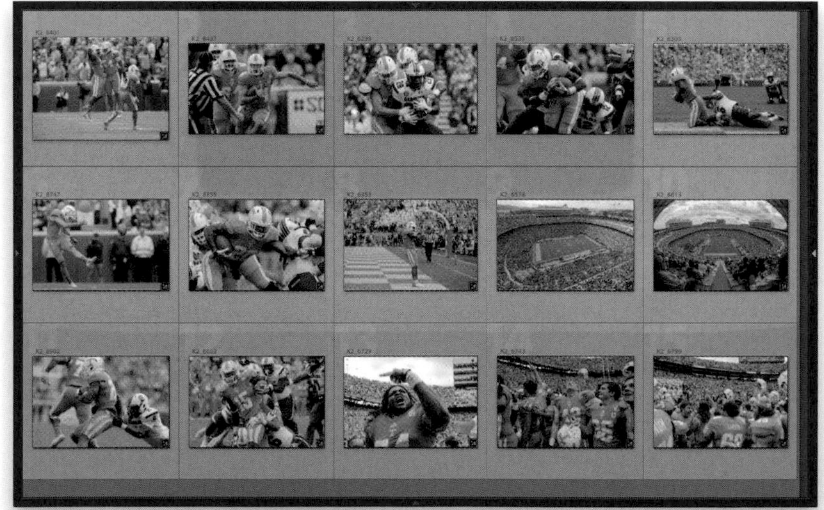

SCOTT KELBY

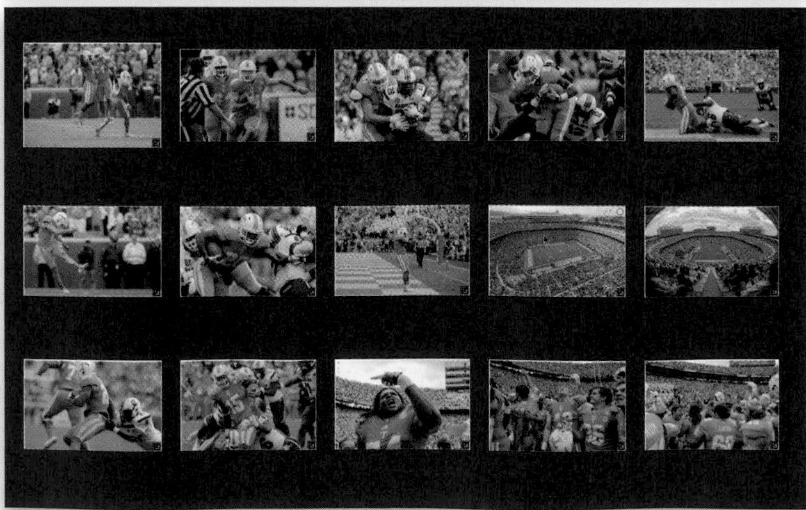

Seeing a Real Full-Screen View

In earlier versions of Lightroom, you could technically do what they called a "full-screen view," but sadly, your image never really filled the full screen—it filled most of it, but there were black bars around all four sides of your image. It was dramatic for sure, but it lacked the impact of a real full-screen view (and it took about four clicks to get to that "almost-full-screen" view and four clicks to get back out. Well, now we have the real deal, and it's just one key away.

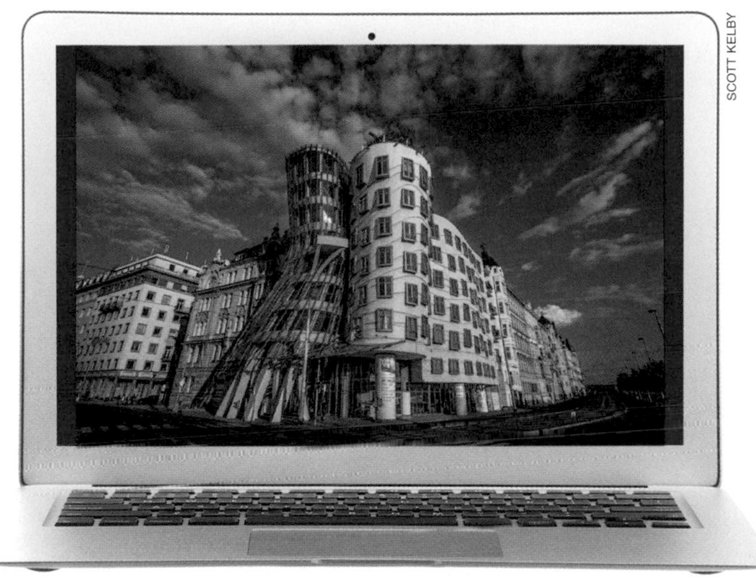
SCOTT KELBY

Step One:
Back in earlier versions of Lightroom, getting to "almost-full-screen" was a pain. You had to (1) press Shift-Tab to hide all the panels, (2) press F to switch to Full Screen mode, then (3) press L twice to enter Lights Out mode. When you were done, you had to undo all that, so basically it was an 8-click move. Now, to see your current image at full screen, you just press the letter F on your keyboard.

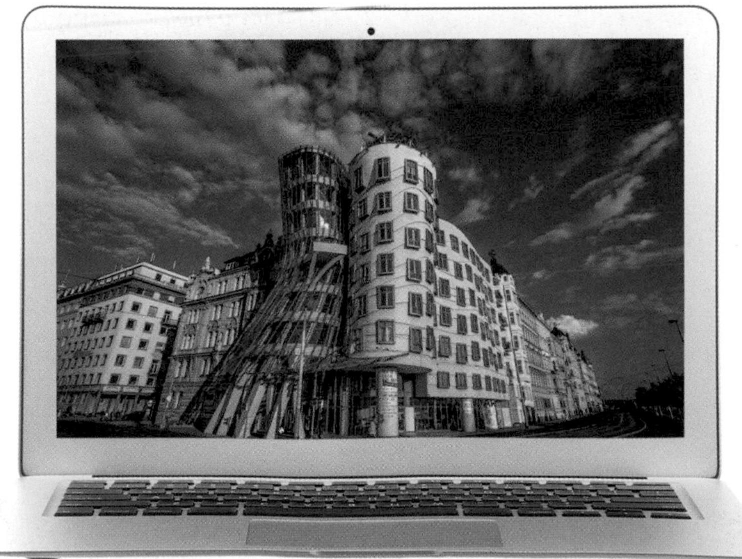

Step Two:
If you look at the image above, you'll see that it fills the screen top-to-bottom, but it does leave a tiny little black bar on the left and right sides of your image. It's really small, but it's there. If you want to zoom in a tiny bit to fill that area (and every inch of your entire screen), just press Command-+ (plus sign; PC: Ctrl-+). To return to regular view mode, just press F again (or the Esc key). Also, it's nice to note that if you use this "zoom-to-fill-that-tiny-space-on-the-sides" trick, it remembers that full-screen setting for the rest of your session (meaning, until you restart Lightroom again). I actually wish this was a preference setting, because I would always have it set at "zoom to fill" for full screen.

Using Guides and the Resizable Grid Overlays

Back in Lightroom 5, Adobe added moveable non-printing guides (like Photoshop's guides, only these may be better). Also, they added the ability to have a resizable, non-printing grid over your image, as well (helpful for lining things up or for straightening a part of your image), but it's not just a static grid, and it's not just resizable. We'll start with the guides.

Step One:

To make the non-printing guides visible, go under the View menu, under Loupe Overlay, and choose **Guides**. Two white guides will appear centered on your screen. To move either the horizontal or vertical guide by itself, press-and-hold the Command (PC: Ctrl) key, then move your cursor right over either guide, and your cursor will change to a double-sided arrow cursor. Just click-and-drag that guide where you want it. To move the two guides together (like they're one unit), press-and-hold the Command (PC: Ctrl) key, then click directly on the black circle where they intersect and drag. To clear the guides, press **Command-Option-O (PC: Ctrl-Alt-O)**.

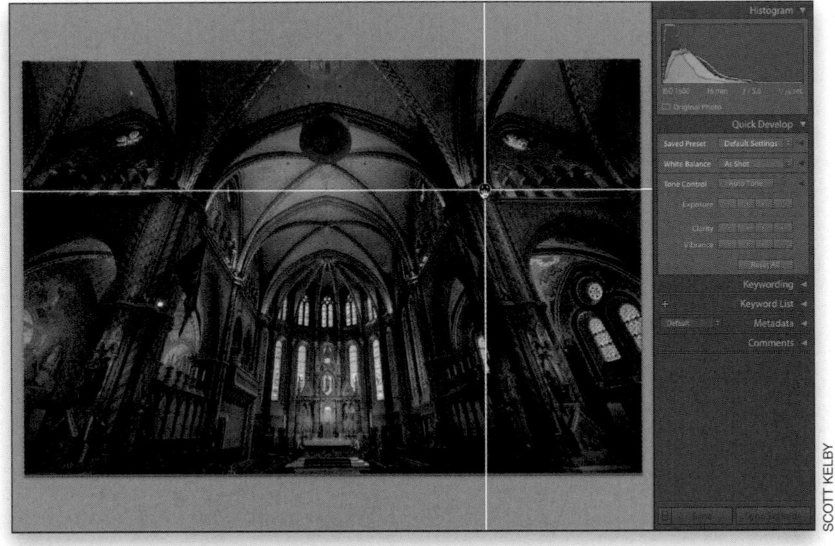

SCOTT KELBY

Step Two:

You also have a grid that pretty much works the same. Go under the View menu, under Loupe Overlay, and choose **Grid**. This puts a non-printing grid over your image, which you can use for alignment (or anything else you want). If you press-and-hold the Command (PC: Ctrl) key, a control bar appears at the top of the screen. Click directly on the word Opacity to change how visible the grid is (here, I cranked it up to 100%, so the lines are solid). Click directly on the word "Size," to change the size of the grid blocks themselves—drag left to make the grid smaller or right to make it larger. To clear the grid, press **Command-Option-O (PC: Ctrl-Alt-O)**. *Note:* You can have more than one overlay, so you can have both the guides and grid visible at the same time.

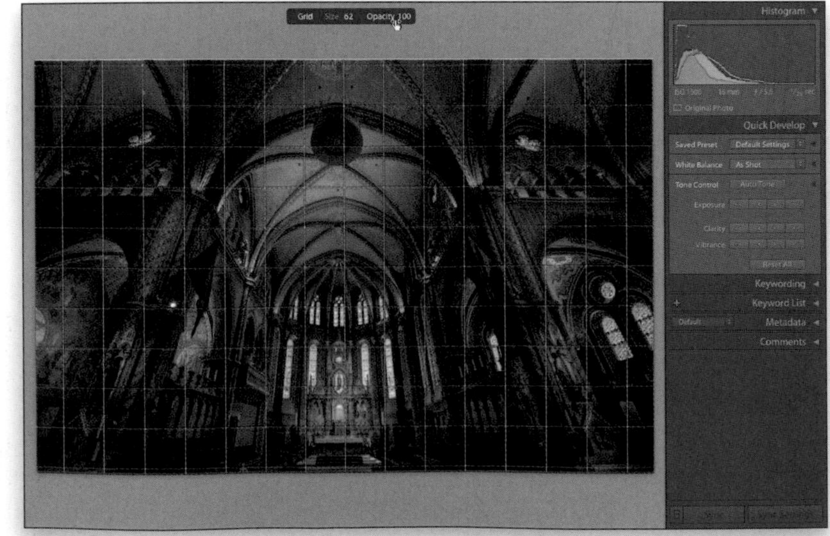

Lightroom Killer Tips > >

▼ Drag-and-Drop Straight Into Lightroom (It's Smarter Than You'd Think)

You can drag-and-drop an image (or a number of images for that matter) from your desktop, or from a folder on your computer, right onto the Lightroom icon (or the Dock icon if you're using a Mac)

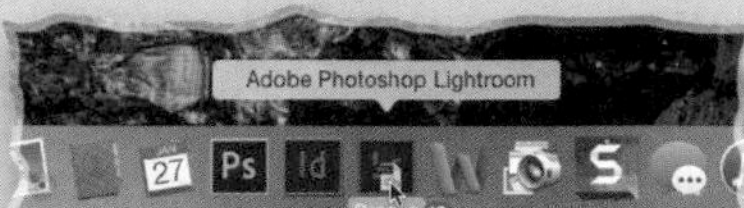

and it not only brings up the Import window, but it selects the folder (or desktop) where those images appear. And it's even smarter: if you have 20 or 30 images on your desktop (or in your folder), only the images you dragged onto that icon will have checkmarks by them for importing. That way, it ignores the other images on the desktop (or in that folder) and only imports the ones you selected.

▼ Changing Your Grid View Thumbnail Size

You don't have to have the toolbar at the bottom of the center Preview area visible to change your thumbnail size in the Library module's Grid view—just use the **+ (plus sign)** and **– (minus sign) keys** on your keyboard to change sizes. The cool thing is that this works in the Import window, too.

▼ Using Separate Catalogs to Make Lightroom Faster

Although I keep one single catalog for all the photos on my laptop, and just three catalogs for my entire collection in the studio, I have a friend who's a full-time wedding photographer who uses a different Lightroom catalog strategy that freaked me out when I first heard it, but really makes perfect sense (in fact, it may be just what you need). He creates a separate Lightroom catalog (go under the File menu and choose **New Catalog**)

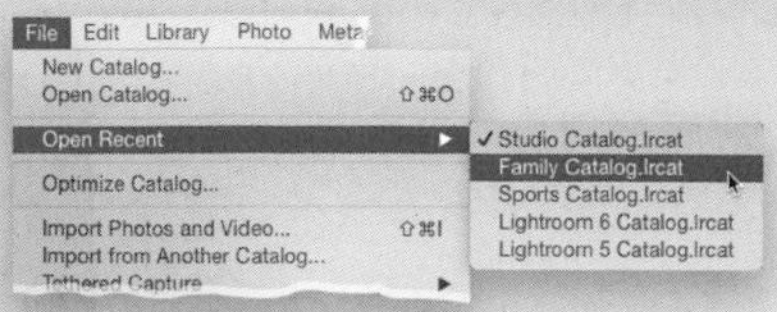

for every single wedding. At each wedding, he shoots more than a thousand shots, and often he has one to two other photographers shooting with him. His way, Lightroom really screams, because each catalog has only a thousand or so photos (where for many folks, it's not unusual to have 30,000 or 40,000 images, which tends to slow Lightroom down a bit). Hey, if you're a high-volume shooter, it's worth considering.

▼ Why You Might Want to Wait to Rename Your Files

As you saw in this chapter, you can rename your files as you import them into Lightroom (and I definitely think you should give your files descriptive names), but you might want to wait until after you've sorted your photos (and deleted any out-of-focus shots, or shots where the flash didn't fire, etc.), because Lightroom auto-numbers the files for you. Well, if you delete some of these files, then your numbering will be out of sequence (there will be numbers missing). This doesn't bother me at all, but I've learned that it drives some people crazy (you know who you are), so it's definitely something to consider.

▼ Getting Back to Your Last Imported Images

Lightroom keeps track of the last set of images you imported, and you can get back to those images anytime by going to the Catalog panel (in the Library module's left side Panels area) and clicking on Previous Import. However, I think it's faster (and more convenient) to go down to the Filmstrip, and on the left side, where you see the current image's name, click-and-hold, and from the pop-up menu that appears, choose **Previous Import**.

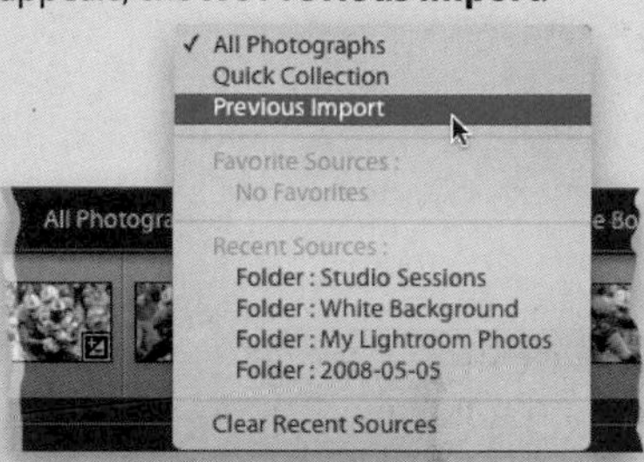

▼ Multiple Cards from One Shoot

If you shot two or three memory cards of the same subject, you'll want to choose **Custom Name - Sequence** from the File Renaming panel's Template pop-up menu, which adds a Start Number field, where you can type in which number you want to start with as you import each card (rather than always starting with the number 1, like the Custom Name template). For example, if you imported 236 photos from your first card, you'd want the second card to start numbering with 237, so these shots of the same subject stay sequential.

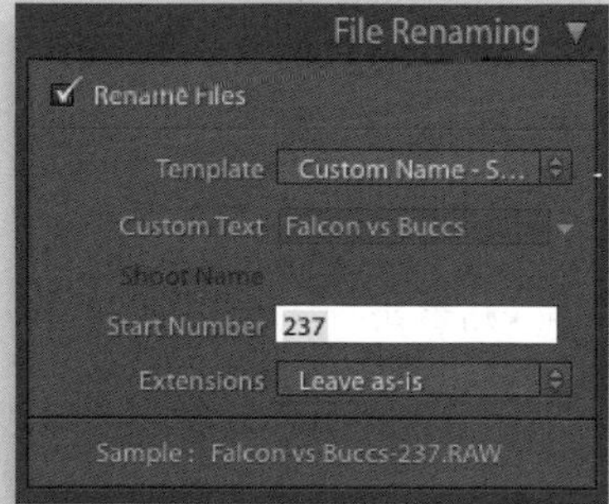

Once that card is imported (let's say you had 244 shots on that card), then you'd want the start number for the third card's photos to be 481. (By the way, I don't do the math, I just look at the file number of the last photo I imported, and then add one to it in the Start Number field.)

▼ Converting Photos to DNG

If you didn't choose Copy as DNG at the top center of the Import window,

Lightroom Killer Tips > >

and you want your imported photos saved in this file format, you can always convert any photo you've imported into Lightroom into a DNG by just clicking on the photo(s), going to Lightroom's Library menu, and choosing **Convert Photo to DNG** (although, technically, you can

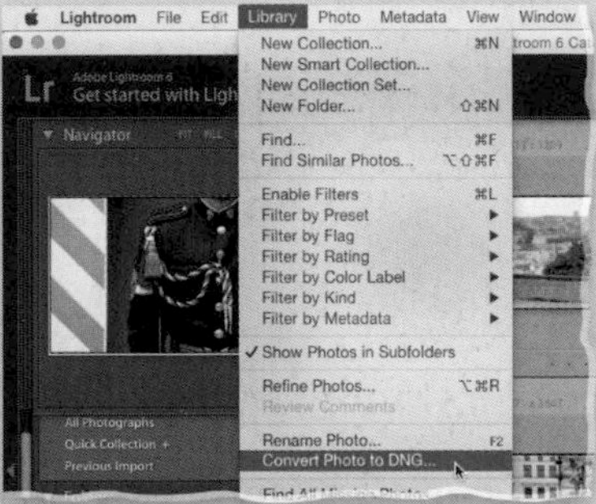

convert JPEGs and TIFFs into DNG format, converting them into DNG doesn't really offer any advantages, so I only convert RAW photos to DNG). This DNG replaces the RAW file you see in Lightroom, and the RAW file remains in the same folder on your computer (Lightroom, though, gives you the option of deleting the original RAW file when you make the conversion. This is what I choose, since the DNG can include the RAW photo within it).

▼ Hard Drive Space an Issue? Convert to DNG on Import

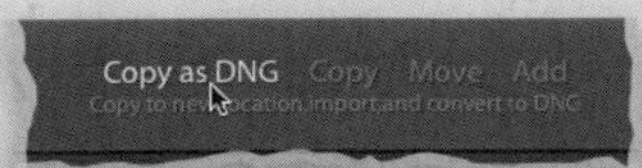

If you're working on a laptop, and you'd like to save between 15% and 20% (in most cases) of your hard drive space when importing RAW files, click on Copy as DNG at the top center of the Import window.

▼ Organizing Images in Folders

You get to choose how your images are organized, as they're imported, in the Destination panel. If you don't turn on the Into Subfolder checkbox and you

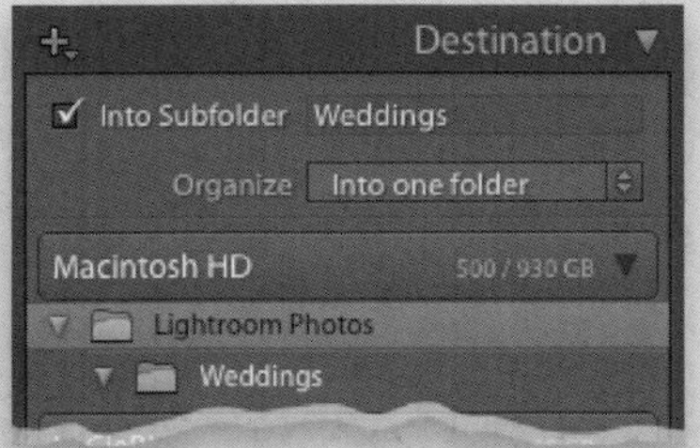

choose Into One Folder from the Organize pop-up menu, Lightroom tosses the loose photos into whichever folder you chose in the To section at the top right of the Import window, and they're not organized within their own separate folder. So, if you choose the Into One Folder option, I recommend that you turn on the Into Subfolder checkbox and then name the folder. That way, it imports them into their own separate folder inside your Pictures or Lightroom Photos folder. Otherwise, things will get very messy, very quickly.

▼ Save Time Importing into Existing Folders

If you're going to import some photos into a folder you've already created, just go to the Folders panel in the Library module, Right-click on the folder, and choose **Import to this Folder** from the

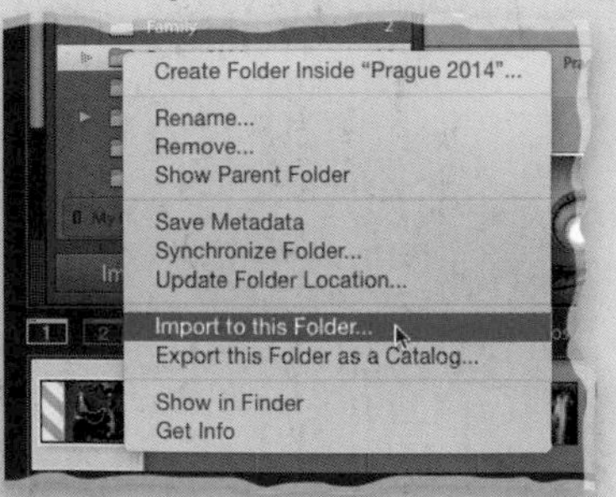

pop-up menu. This brings up the Import window with this folder already chosen as the destination for your imported photos.

▼ Choosing Your Preview Rendering

I ran a Lightroom preview time trial, importing just 14 RAW images off a memory card onto a laptop. Here's how long it took to import them and render their previews:

Embedded & Sidecar: 19 seconds
Minimal: 21 seconds
Standard: 1 minute, 15 seconds
1:1: 2 minutes, 14 seconds

You can see that the 1:1 preview took seven times as long as Embedded & Sidecar. That may not seem that bad with 14 photos, but what about 140 or 340 photos? Yikes! So, armed with that info, you can make a decision that fits your workflow. If you're the type of photographer that likes to zoom in tight on each and every photo to check focus and detail, then it might be worth it for you to wait for the 1:1 previews to render before working on your images. If you're like me, and want to quickly search through them, and just zoom in tight on the most likely keepers (maybe 15 or 20 images from an import), then Embedded & Sidecar makes sense. If you look at them mostly in full-screen view (but don't zoom in really tight that often), then Standard might work, and if you want thumbnails that more closely represent what your photo will look like when it is rendered at high quality, choose Minimal instead.

▼ You Can Import and Edit PSDs and More!

In earlier versions of Lightroom, you could only import and edit RAW images, TIFFs, and JPEGs, but in Lightroom 3, Adobe added the ability to import PSDs (Photoshop's native file format), along with images in CMYK mode or Grayscale mode.

▼ Using Smart Previews If You've Lost the Original File

The smaller version of your image created as a smart preview is actually pretty large (it's 2,540 px on the long edge), so if you get in a bind and lose the original image (hey, it happens), at least you can export

Lightroom Killer Tips > >

the smart preview as a DNG file so you'll have a physical file—it just won't have the full resolution of the original.

▼ Ejecting Your Memory Card

If you decide not to import anything and want to eject your camera's memory card, just Right-click directly on it in the Import window's Source panel, then choose **Eject** from the pop-up menu that appears. If you pop in a new card, click on the From button at the top left of the window, and choose it from the pop-up menu that appears.

▼ Seeing Just Your Video Clips

First choose **All Photographs** from the path pop-up menu at the top-left side of the Filmstrip. Then, in the Library module go up to the Library Filter at the top of the window (if it's not visible, press the **\ [backslash] key**), and click on Attribute.

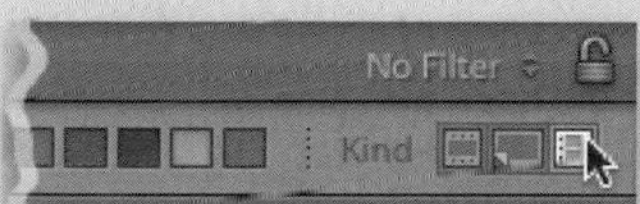

Over on the far-right side, to the right of Kind, click on the Videos button (its icon is a filmstrip and it's the third icon from the left) and now it displays nothing but all the video clips you have in Lightroom (pretty handy if you want to make a regular collection of just your video clips).

▼ To Advance or Not to Advance

When I'm shooting tethered, as each new image comes in, I like to see it onscreen at full size. If you'd prefer to control which image appears onscreen, and for how long (remember, if you see one onscreen

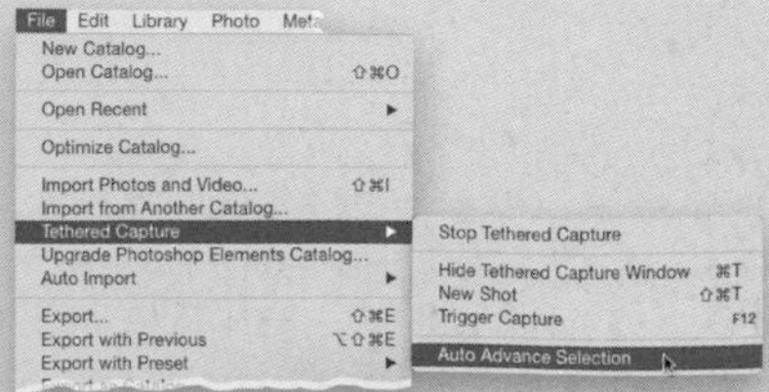

you like, it may only stay there a moment or two until the next shot comes in), go under the File menu, under Tethered Capture, and turn off **Auto Advance Selection.** Now, you'll use the Left/Right Arrow keys on your keyboard to move through your images, rather than always seeing the image you just took onscreen.

▼ Hiding Folders You Don't Need

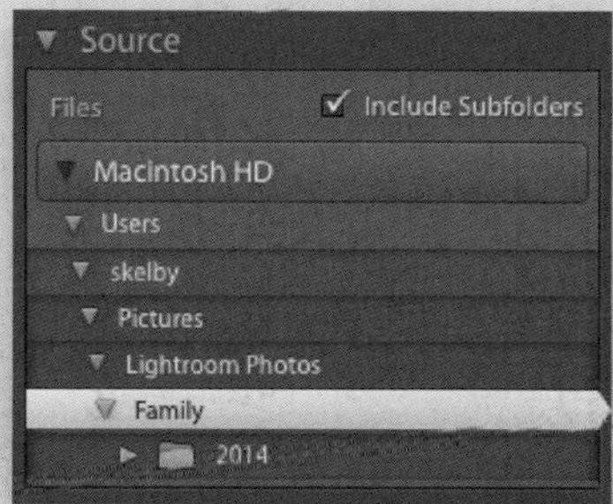

If you're importing photos that are already on your computer, that long list of folders in the Source panel can get really long and distracting, but now you can hide all those extra folders you don't need to see. Once you find the folder you're importing from, just double-click on it, and everything else tucks away leaving just that folder visible. Try this once and you'll use it all the time.

▼ If Your Nikon Won't Tether

If your Nikon camera is supported for tethered shooting in Lightroom (like the D90, D5200, D7000, D300, D300s, D600, D700, D3, and D3x), but it doesn't work, chances are your camera's USB settings aren't set up to work with tethering. Go to your camera's Setup menu, click on USB, and change the setting to MTP/PTP. (*Note*: Newer cameras, like Nikon's D4 and D7100, are set to this mode by default.)

▼ Tethering to a Collection

As you saw earlier in this chapter, you can now import directly into a collection. Well, for those of you who shoot tethered

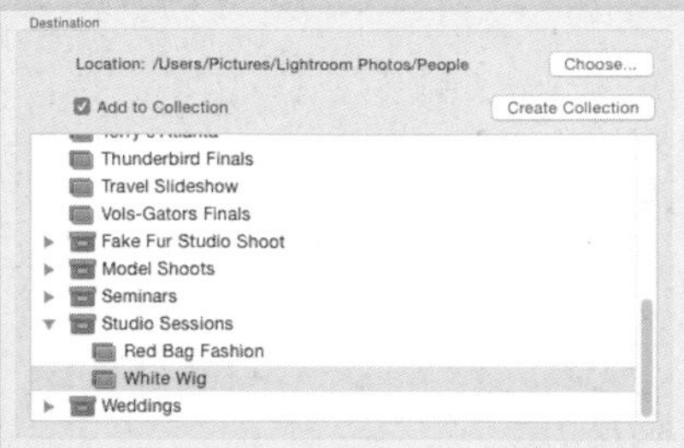

(and you know who you are), now you can also shoot tethered directly into a collection. To do this, in the Destination section of the Tethered Settings dialog, turn on the Add to Collection checkbox, and it displays a list of all your current collections. Click on the one you want, and now your tethered images will import straight into that collection. There's also a Create Collection button if you need to create a new collection for them.

▼ Shooting Tethered Battery Warning

To make sure you don't lose any images while you're shooting tethered, if Lightroom realizes that your camera battery is getting low, it now gives you an onscreen warning before it's too late, so you have time to change batteries and keep on shootin'.

▼ Your Elements Library

If you're moving to Lightroom from Elements 5 or later, you can have Lightroom import your Elements catalog. Just go under Lightroom's File menu, choose **Upgrade Photoshop Elements Catalog**, and then choose your Elements catalog from the dialog's pop-up menu. You may need to upgrade your Elements catalog for Lightroom, so just click Upgrade if prompted to. Lightroom will close and then reopen with your Elements catalog imported.

Photo by Scott Kelby | Exposure: 1/50 sec | Focal Length: 16mm | Aperture Value: f/13

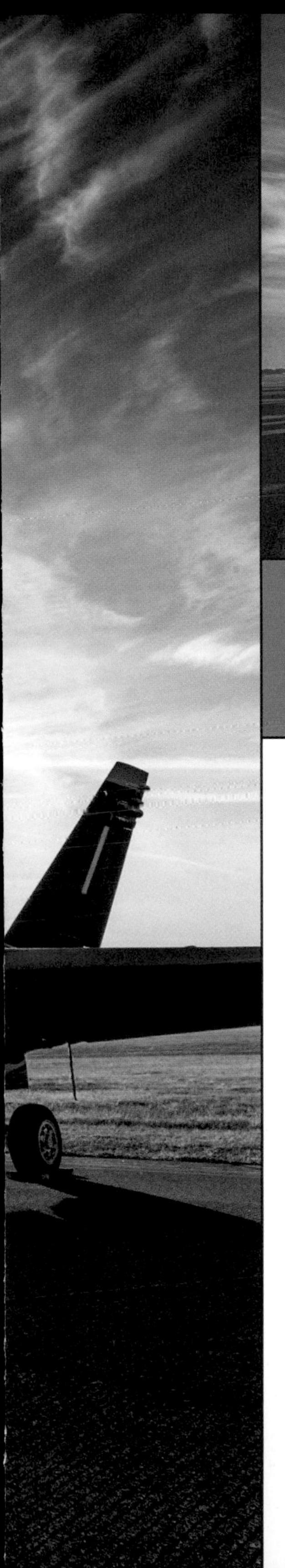

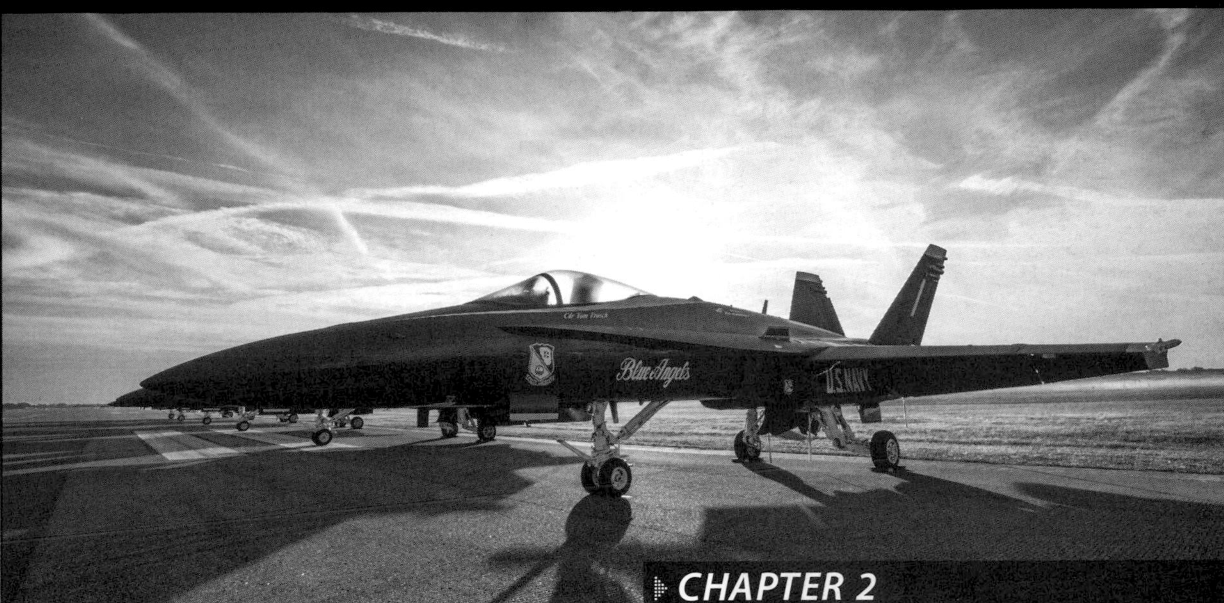

CHAPTER 2

LIBRARY
how to organize your photos

It's been a tradition in all my books to name each chapter with either a song title, TV show title, or movie title. For example, in one of my books on Photoshop, I have a chapter on sharpening, and I called it "Sharp Dressed Man" (a nod to the 1983 hit of the same name from the Texas-based rock band ZZ Top). Under the chapter name, I would put a subhead that explains what the chapter is actually about, because sometimes from the name it wasn't quite as obvious. For example, in another book, I have a chapter called "Super Size Me" (from the movie of the same name), about how to resize your images. But for the earlier editions of this book, I dispensed with those titles and just gave each chapter a regular boring ol' name, and now that I'm writing the Lightroom CC version, I'm kinda wishing I hadn't done away with it (even though I guess this way does make it easier). See, I was thinking that people who buy books on Lightroom are photographers, and that means they're creative people, which to me means that if I named the chapters after things that in themselves are creative (like songs, TV shows, and movies…well…songs and movies any-way), they'd totally dig it. Well, as luck would have it, I just checked on the iTunes Store and there actually is a song named "Library" by a band called Final Fantasy from their album *Has a Good Home*. Anyway, I listened to the song and I have to say, it was mind numbingly bad—bad on a level I haven't heard in years, yet the album has 12 five-star reviews, so either these people are criminally insane, or they were basing their review on their general love of one of Final Fantasy's other songs, titled "He Poos Clouds." Man, I wish I could have used that name for a chapter. My 18-year-old son would still be giggling.

Folders and Why I Don't Mess with Them (This Is Really Important!)

When you import photos, you have to choose a folder in which to store them on your hard drive. This is the only time I really do anything with folders because I think of them as where my negatives are stored, and like with traditional film negatives, I store them someplace safe, and I really don't touch them again. I use the same type of thinking in Lightroom. I don't really use the Folders panel (I use something safer—collections, which is covered next). So, here I'm only going to briefly explain folders, and show one instance where you might use them.

Step One:

If you quit Lightroom and on your computer look inside your Pictures folder, you'll see all the subfolders containing the files of your actual photos. Of course, you can move photos from folder to folder (as seen here), add photos, or delete photos, and so on, right? Well, you don't actually have to leave Lightroom to do stuff like that—you can do those things from within the Folders panel in Lightroom. You can see all those same folders, and move and delete real files just like you do on your computer.

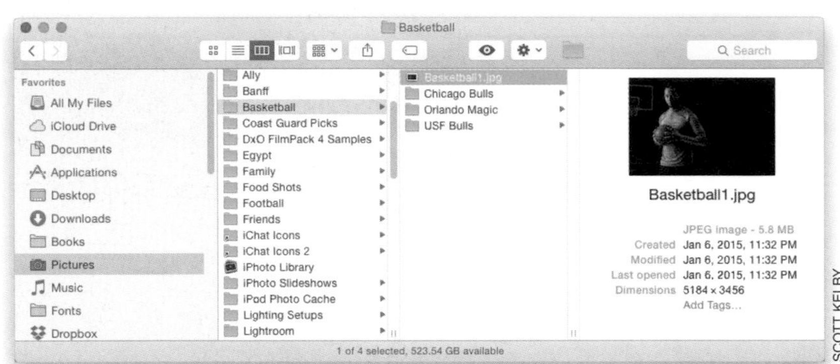

SCOTT KELBY

Step Two:

Go to the Library module, and you'll find the Folders panel (shown here) in the left side Panels area. What you're seeing here are all the folders of photos that you imported into Lightroom (by the way, they're not actually in Lightroom itself—Lightroom is just managing those photos—they're still sitting in the same folders you imported them into from your memory card).

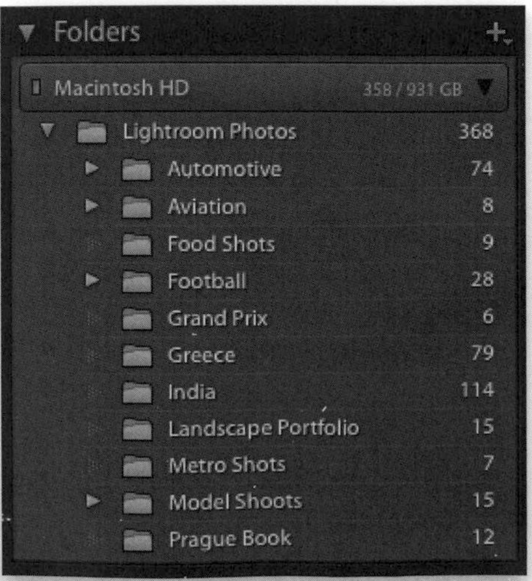

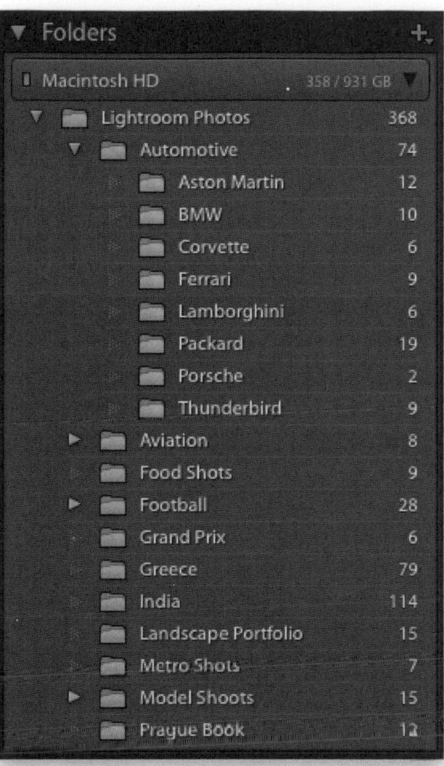

Step Three:

There's a little triangle to the left of each folder's name. If the triangle is solid gray, it means there are subfolders inside that folder, and you can just click on that triangle to see them. If it's not solid gray, it just means there are no subfolders inside. (*Note:* These little triangles are officially called "disclosure triangles," but the only people who actually use that term are...well...let's just say these people probably didn't have a date for the prom.)

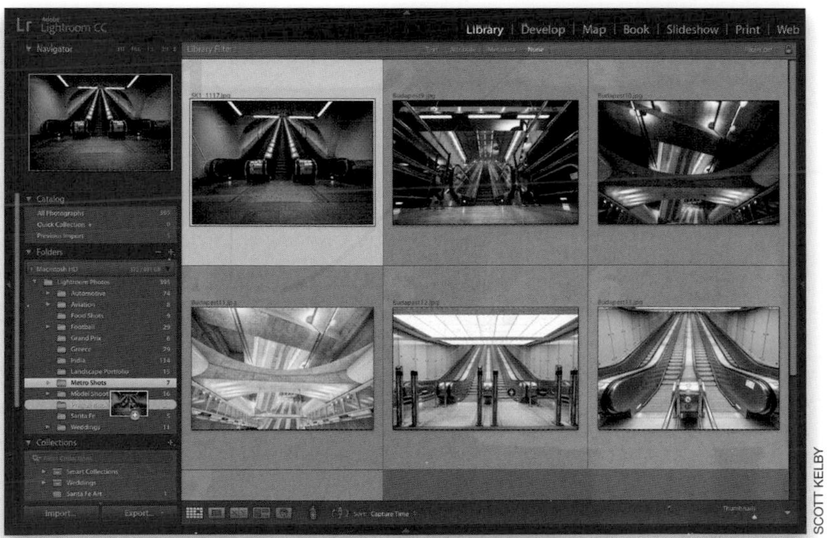

SCOTT KELBY

Moving a File on Disk

This will cause the corresponding file on disk to be moved. If you proceed, neither this move nor any change you've made prior to this can be undone.

Don't show again   Cancel   Move

Step Four:

When you click on a folder, it shows you the photos in that folder that have been imported into Lightroom. If you click on a thumbnail and drag it into another folder (like I'm doing here), it physically moves that photo on your computer from one folder to another, just as if you moved the file on your computer outside of Lightroom. Because you're actually moving the real file here, you get a "Hey, you're about to move the real file" warning from Lightroom (see here below). The warning sounds scarier than it is—especially the "This cannot be undone" part. What that means is, you can't just press **Command-Z (PC: Ctrl-Z)** to instantly undo the move if you change your mind. However, you could just click on the folder you moved it to (in this case, the Prague Book folder), find the photo you just moved, and drag it right back to the original folder (here, it's the Metro Shots folder), so the dialog's bark is worse than its bite.

Continued

Step Five:

If you see a grayed-out folder in the Folders panel with a question mark on it, that's Lightroom's way of letting you know it can't find this folder of photos (you either just moved them somewhere else on your computer, or you have them stored on an external hard drive, and that drive isn't connected to your computer right now). So, if it's the external drive thing, just reconnect your external drive and it will find that folder. If it's the old "moved them somewhere else" problem, then Right-click on the grayed-out folder and choose **Find Missing Folder** from the pop-up menu. This brings up a standard Open dialog, so you can show Lightroom where you moved the folder. When you click on the moved folder and click Choose, it relinks all the photos inside for you.

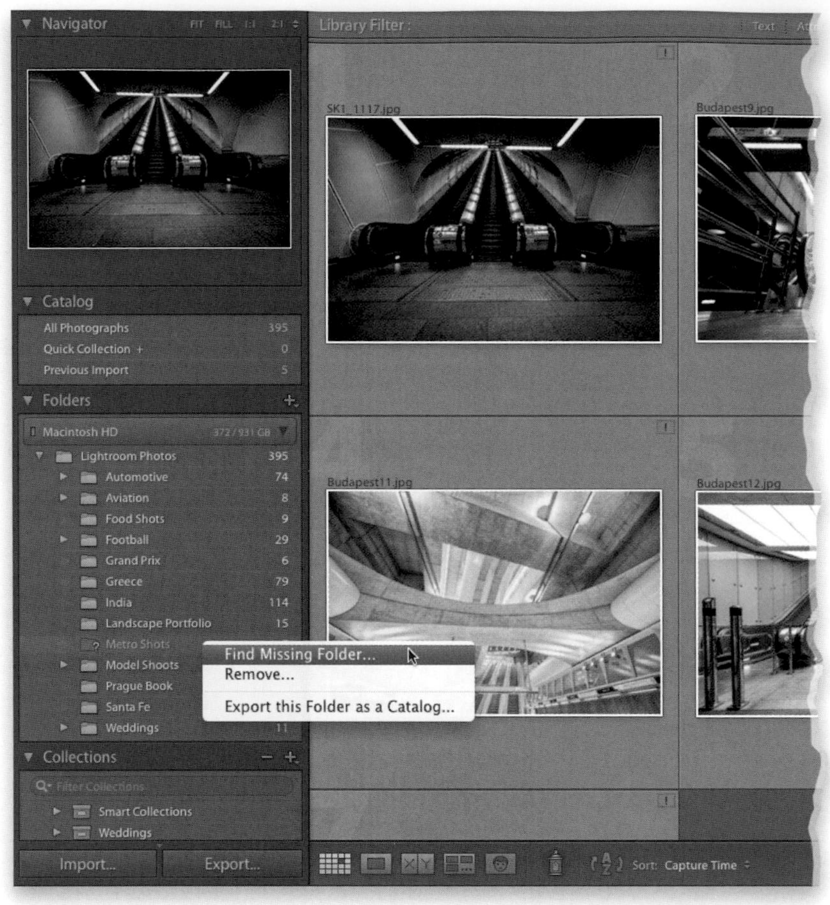

TIP: Moving Multiple Folders

In earlier versions of Lightroom, you could only move one folder at a time, but in Lightroom CC you can Command-click (PC: Ctrl-click) on multiple folders to select them, and then drag them all at the same time. A little time saver.

Step Six:

Now, there's one particular thing I sometimes use the Folders panel for, and that's when I add images to a folder on my computer after I've imported. For example, let's say I imported some photos from a trip to Budapest and then, later, my brother emails me some shots he took. If I drag his photos into my Budapest Finals folder on my computer, Lightroom doesn't automatically suck them right in. In fact, it ignores them unless I go to the Folders panel, Right-click on my Budapest Finals folder, and choose **Synchronize Folder**.

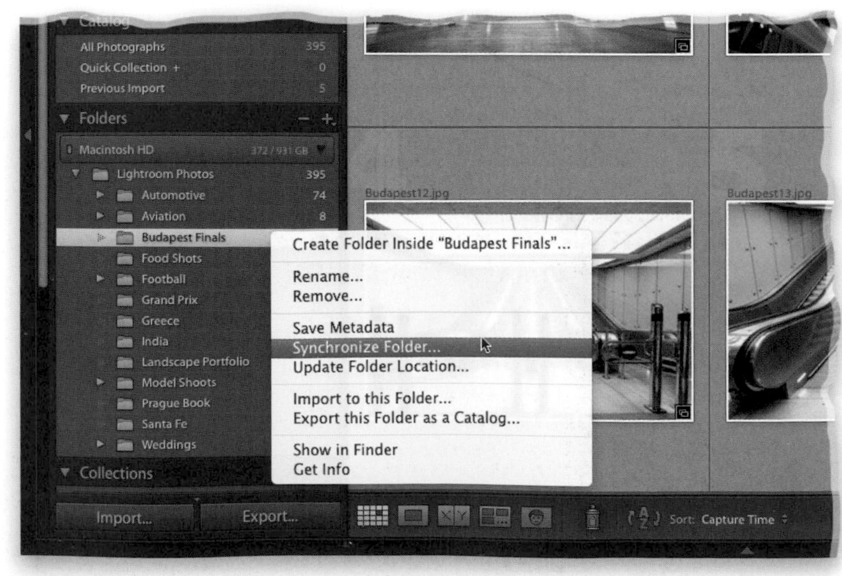

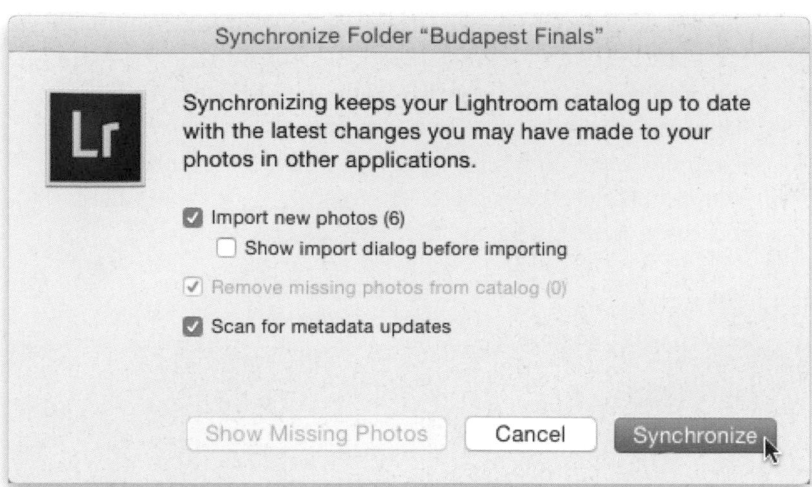

Step Seven:

Choosing Sychronize Folder brings up the Synchronize Folder dialog for that folder. I dragged the six new photos my brother sent me into my Budapest Finals folder, and you can see it's ready to import six new photos. There is a checkbox to have Lightroom bring up the standard Import window before you import the photos (so you can add your copyright, and metadata, and stuff like that if you like), or you just bring them in by clicking Synchronize and adding that stuff once the images are in Lightroom (if you even want to. Since my brother took these, I won't be adding my copyright info to them. At least, not while he's looking). So, that's pretty much the main instance where I use folders—when I drag new images into an existing folder. Other than that, I just leave that panel closed pretty much all the time, and just work in the Collections panel (as you'll learn about in the next tutorial).

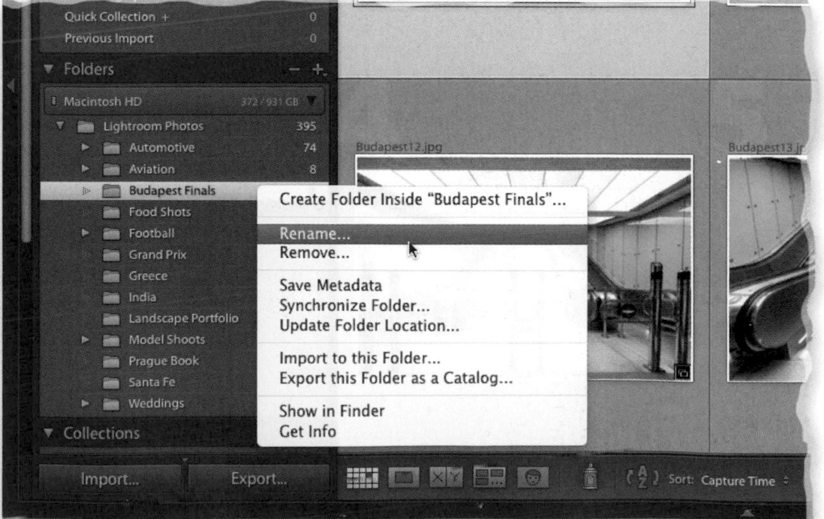

TIP: Other Folder Options

When you Right-click on a folder, and the pop-up menu appears, you can choose to do other things like rename your folder, create subfolders, etc. There's also a Remove option, but in Lightroom, choosing Remove just means "remove this folder of photos from Lightroom." However, this folder (and the photos inside it) will still be right there in your Pictures folder on your computer. Just so you know.

Sorting Your Photos Using Collections

Sorting your images can be one of the most fun, or one of the most frustrating, parts of the editing process—it just depends on how you go about it. Personally, this is one of the parts I enjoy the most, but I have to admit that I enjoy it more now than I used to, and that's mostly because I've come up with a workflow that's fast and efficient, and helps me get to the real goal of sorting, which is finding the best shots from your shoot—the "keepers"—the ones you'll actually show your client, or add to your portfolio, or print. Here's how I do it:

Step One:

When you boil it down, our real goal is to find the best photos from our shoot, but we also want to find the worst photos (those photos where the subject is totally out of focus, or you pressed the shutter by accident, or the flash didn't fire, etc.), because there's no sense in having photos that you'll never use taking up hard drive space, right? Lightroom gives you three ways to rate (or rank) your photos, the most popular being the 1-to-5-star rating system. To mark a photo with a star rating, just click on it and type the number on your keyboard. So, to mark a photo with a 3-star rating, you'd press the number **3**, and you'd see three stars appear under the photo (shown here at the top). To change a star rating, type in a new number. To remove it altogether, press **0** (zero). The idea is that once you've got your 5-star photos marked, you can turn on a filter that displays only your 5-star photos. You can also use that filter to see just your 4-star, 3-star, etc., photos. Besides stars, you can also use color labels, so you could mark the worst photos with a Red label, slightly better ones with Yellow, and so on. Or, you could use these in conjunction with the stars to mark your best 5-star photo with a Green label (as shown here at the bottom).

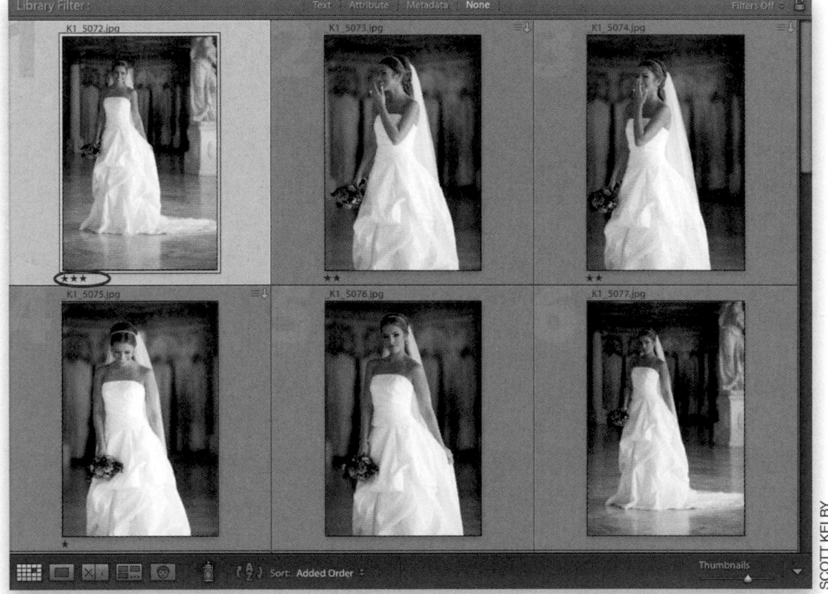

SCOTT KELBY

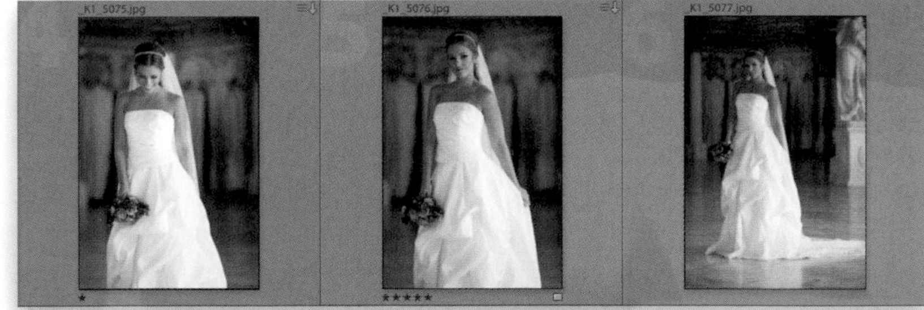

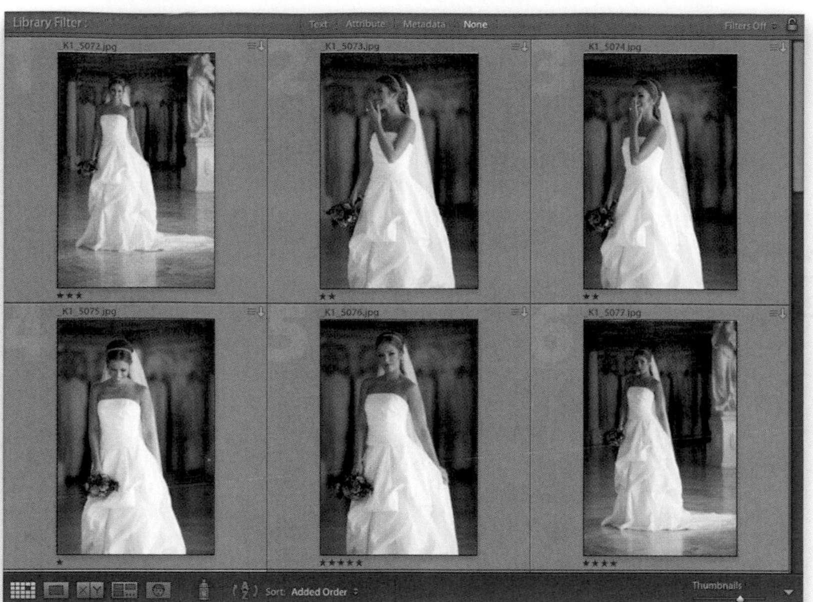

Step Two:

Now that I've mentioned star ratings and labels, I want to talk you out of using them. Here's why: they're way too slow. Think about it—your 5-star photos would be your very best shots, right? The only ones you'll show anybody. So your 4-star ones are good, but not good enough. Your 3-star ones are just so-so (nobody will ever see these). Your 2-star ones are bad shots—not so bad that you'll delete them, but bad—and your 1-star shots are out-of-focus, blurry, totally messed up shots you're going to delete. So what are you going to do with your 2- and 3-star photos? Nothing. What about your 4-star photos? Nothing. The 5-stars you keep, the 1-stars you delete, the rest you pretty much do nothing with, right? So, all we really care about are the best shots and the worst shots, right? The rest we ignore.

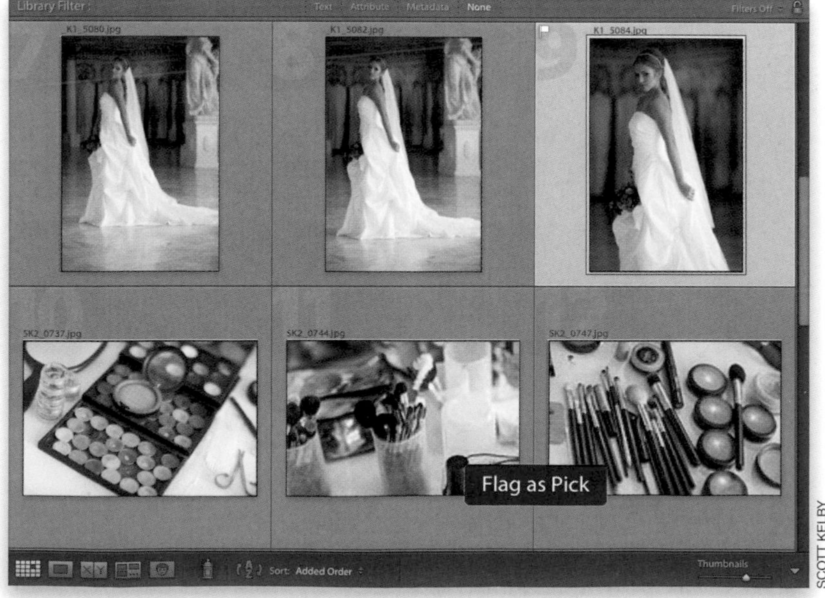

SCOTT KELBY

Step Three:

So instead, I hope you'll try flags. You mark the best shots as Picks and the really bad ones (the ones to be deleted) as Rejects. Lightroom will delete the Rejects for you when you're ready, leaving you with just your best shots and the ones you don't care about, but you don't waste time trying to decide if a particular photo you don't care about is a 3-star or a 2-star. I can't tell you how many times I've seen people sitting there saying out loud, "Now, is this a 2-star or a 3-star?" Who cares? It's not a 5-star; move on! To mark a photo as a Pick, just press the letter **P**. To mark a photo as a Reject, press the letter **X**. A little message will appear onscreen to tell you which flag you assigned to the photo, and a tiny flag icon will appear in that photo's grid cell. A white flag means it's marked as a Pick. A black flag means it's a Reject.

Continued

Step Four:

So here's how I go about the process: Once my photos are in Lightroom, and they appear in the Library module's Grid view, I double-click on the first photo to jump to Loupe view to get a closer look. If I think it's one of the better shots from the shoot, I press P to flag it as a Pick. If it's so bad that I want to delete it, I press X instead. If it's just okay, I don't do anything; I move on to the next photo by pressing the Right Arrow key on my keyboard. If I make a mistake and mis-flag a photo (for example, if I accidentally mark one as a Reject when I didn't mean to), I press the letter **U** to unflag it. That's it—that's the process. You'll be amazed at how quickly you can move through a few hundred photos and mark the keepers and rejects. If you want to go even faster, you can press **Shift-P** to flag a photo as a Pick and move to the next one at once. But you've still got some other things to do once you've done this first essential part.

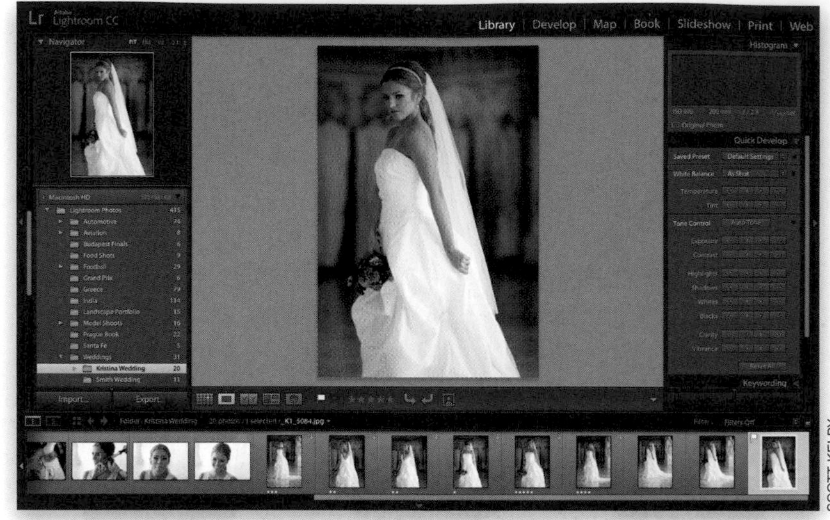

SCOTT KELBY

Step Five:

Once you've got your Picks and Rejects flagged, let's get rid of the Rejects and delete them from your hard drive. Go under the Photo menu and choose **Delete Rejected Photos**. This displays just the photos you've marked as Rejects, and a dialog appears asking if you want to delete them from your disk or just remove them from Lightroom. I always choose Delete from Disk, because if they were bad enough for me to mark them as Rejects, why would I want to keep them? What could I possibly use them for? So, if you feel the same way, click the Delete from Disk button and it returns you to the Grid view, and the rest of your photos. (*Note:* Because we just imported the photos into Lightroom, and they're not in a collection yet, it gives you the option to delete the images from the disk. Once they're actually in a collection, doing this just removes the photos from the collection, and not from your hard disk.)

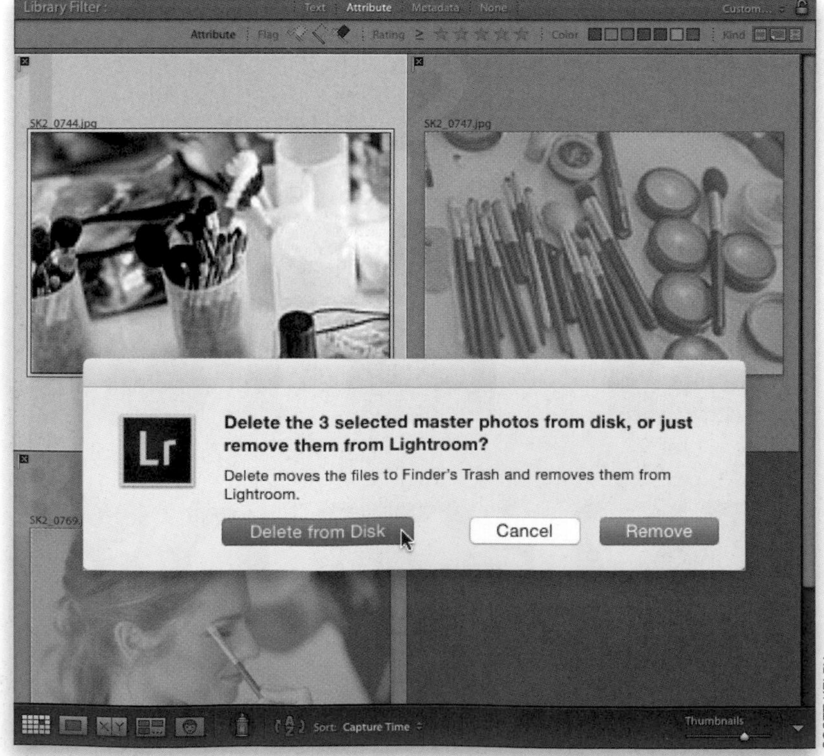

SCOTT KELBY

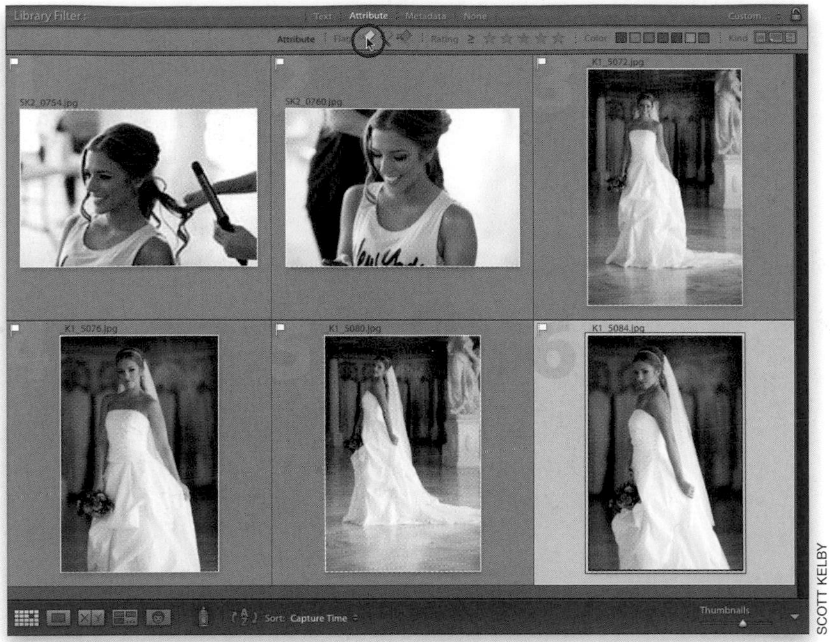

Step Six:

Now to see just your Picks, click on the word **Attribute** up in the Library Filter bar that appears at the top of the center Preview area (if you don't see it, just press the **\ [backslash] key** on your keyboard), and a little Attribute bar pops down. Click on the white Pick flag (shown circled here), and now just your Picks are visible.

TIP: Use the Other Library Filter

You can also choose to see just your Picks, Rejects, or your unflagged photos from down on the top-right side of the Filmstrip. There's a Library filter there too, but just for attributes like flags and star ratings, and some metadata.

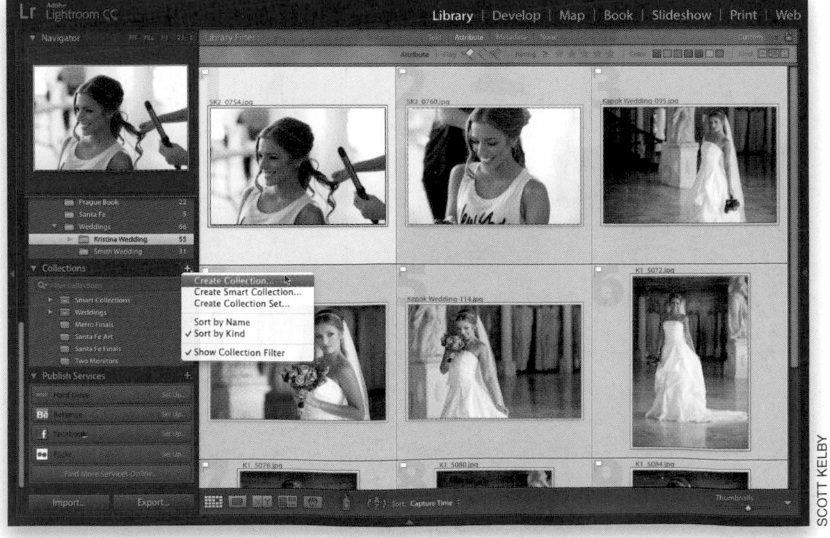

Step Seven:

What I do next is put these Picks into a collection. Collections are the key organizational tool we use, not just here in the sorting phase, but throughout the Lightroom workflow. You can think of a collection as an album of your favorite photos from a shoot, and once you put your Picks into their own collection, you'll always be just one click away from your keepers from the shoot. To get your Picks into a collection, press **Command-A (PC: Ctrl-A)** to select all the currently visible photos (your Picks), then go over to the Collections panel (in the left side Panels area), and click on the little + (plus sign) button on the right side of the panel header. A pop-up menu will appear, and from this menu, choose **Create Collection** (as shown here).

Continued

Step Eight:
This brings up the Create Collection dialog you see here, where you type in a name for this collection, and below that you can assign it to a set (we haven't talked about sets yet, or created any sets, or even admitted that they exist. So for now, leave this checkbox turned off, but don't worry, sets are coming soon enough). In the Options section, you want your collection to include the photos you selected (your Picks) in the previous step, and because you made a selection first, this checkbox is already turned on for you. For now, leave the Make New Virtual Copies and Set as Target Collection checkboxes turned off, then click the Create button.

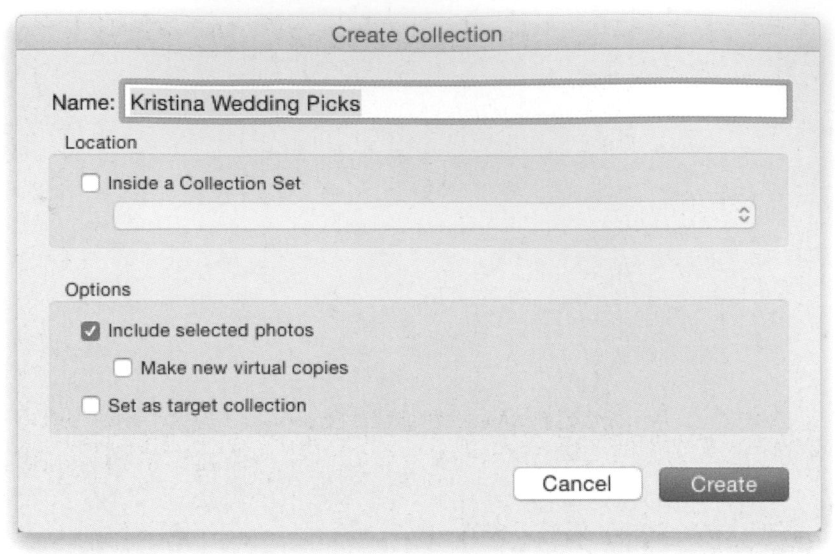

Step Nine:
Now you've got a collection of just your keepers from that shoot, and anytime you want to see these keepers, just go to the Collections panel and click on the collection named Kristina Wedding Picks (as seen here). Just in case you were wondering, collections don't affect the actual photos on your computer—these are just "working collections" for our convenience—so we can delete photos from our collections and it doesn't affect the real photos (they're still in their folder on your computer, except for the Rejects we deleted earlier, before we created this collection).

Note: If you're an Apple iPod, iPad, or iPhone owner, then you're familiar with Apple's iTunes software and how you create playlists of your favorite songs (like big hair bands of the '80s, or party music, or classic rock, etc.). When you remove a song from a playlist, it doesn't delete it from your hard disk (or your main iTunes Music Library), it just removes it from that particular playlist, right? Well, you can think of collections in Lightroom as kind of the same thing, but instead of songs, they're photos.

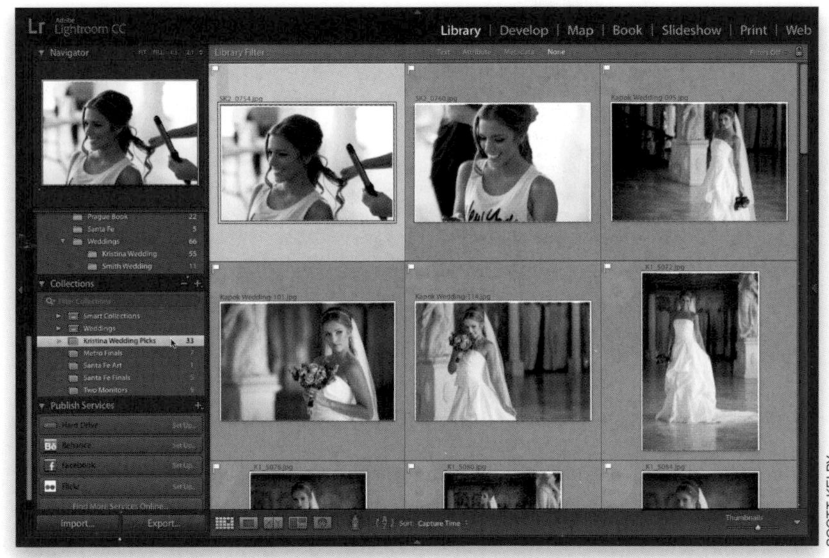

SCOTT KELBY

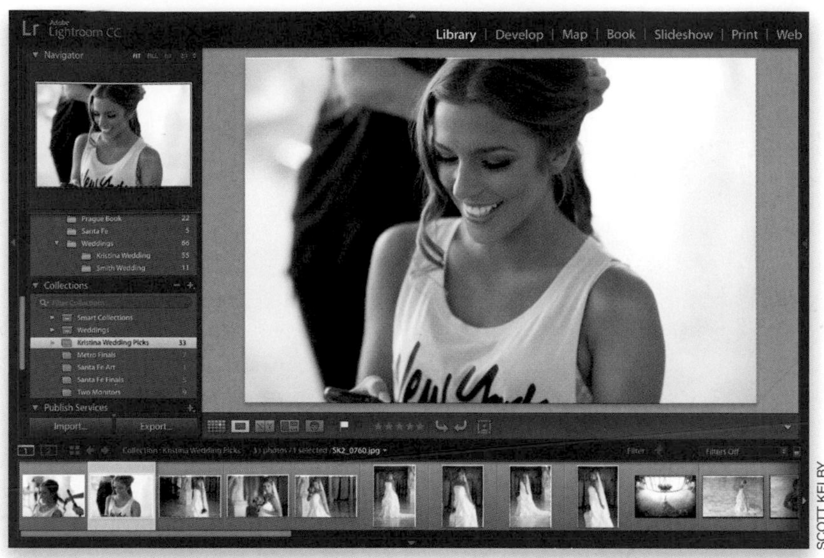

SCOTT KELBY

Step 10:

Now, from this point on, we'll just be working with the photos in our collection. Out of the 298 bridal shots that were taken that day, only 33 of them were flagged as good shots, and that's how many wound up in our Picks collection. But here are some questions: Are you going to print all 33 of these keepers? Are all 33 going in your portfolio, or are you going to email 33 shots of this one bridal shoot to the bride? Probably not, right? So, within our collection of keepers, there are some shots that really stand out—the best of the best, the ones you actually will want to email to the client, or print, or add to your portfolio. So, we need to refine our sorting process a little more to find our best shots from this group of keepers—our "Selects."

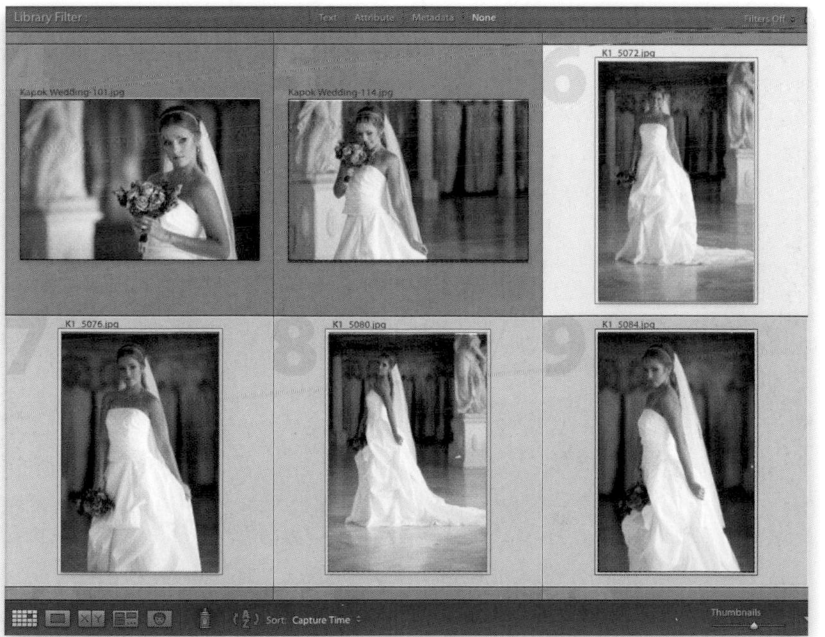

Step 11:

At this stage, there are three ways to go about viewing your photos to narrow things down. You already know the first method, which is the whole Pick flag thing, and you can do that same process again here in your collection, but first you'll need to remove the existing Pick flags (in earlier versions of Lightroom, when you added photos to a collection, it automatically removed the flags, but in Lightroom CC, it remembers them). To remove them press **Command-A (PC: Ctrl-A)** to select all of the photos in your collection, then press the letter **U** on your keyboard to remove all the Pick flags, so we can add new ones. The second view that you might find helpful is called Survey view, and I use this view quite a bit when I have a number of shots that are very similar (like a number of shots of the same pose) and I'm trying to find the best ones from that group. You enter this view by first selecting the similar photos, as seen here (click on one, then press-and-hold the Command [PC: Ctrl] key and click on the others).

Continued

Step 12:

Now press the letter **N** to jump to Survey view (I don't know which is worse, this view being named Survey or using the letter N as its shortcut. Don't get me started). This puts your selected photos all onscreen, side by side, so you can easily compare them (as shown here). Also, anytime I enter Survey view, I immediately press **Shift-Tab** to hide all the panels, which makes the photos as large as possible on my screen.

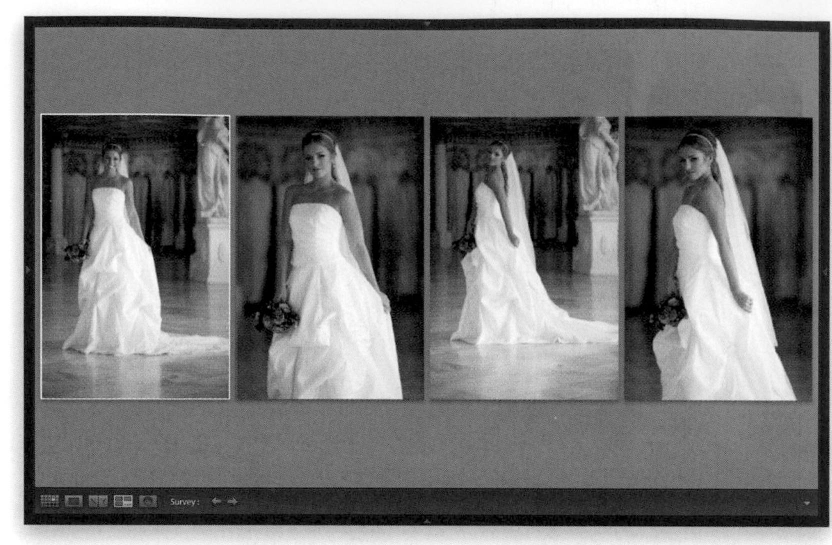

TIP: Try Lights Out Mode

Survey view is a perfect place to use the Lights Out feature that blacks out everything but your photos. Just press the letter **L** on your keyboard twice to enter Lights Out mode and you'll see what I mean. To return to the regular view, press L again.

Step 13:

Now that my photos are displayed in Survey view, I start the process of elimination: I look for the weakest photo of the bunch and get rid of it first, then the next weakest, and the next, until I'm left with just the best couple shots of that pose. To eliminate a photo, move your cursor over the photo you want to remove from contention (the weakest of the bunch) and click on the small X that appears in the bottom-right corner of the image (as seen here), and it's hidden from view. It isn't removed from your collection, it's just hidden to help with your process of elimination. Here, I removed one photo and the others automatically readjusted to fill in the free space. As you continue to eliminate images, the remaining images get larger and larger as they expand to take up the free space.

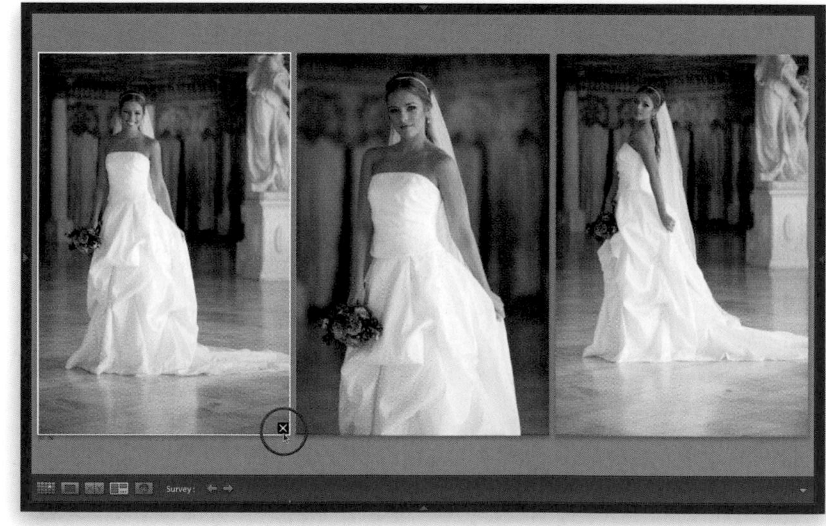

TIP: Changing Your Survey Order

While you're in Survey view, you can change the order of the images displayed onscreen by just dragging-and-dropping them into the order you want.

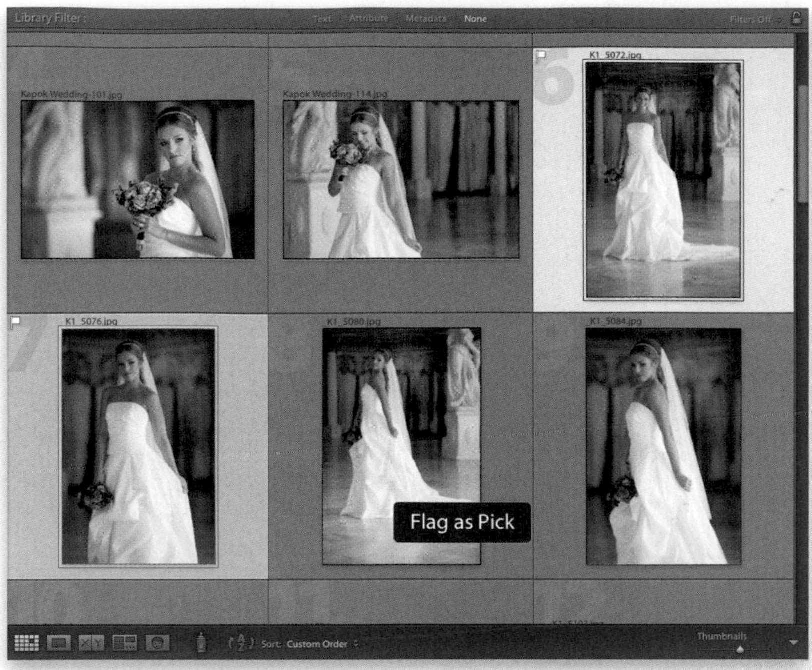

Step 14:

Once you narrow things down to just the ones you want to keep of this pose, press **G** to return to the thumbnail Grid view and those photos that were left onscreen will automatically be the only ones selected (see the two final photos I wound up leaving onscreen—they're the only ones selected). Now, just press the letter P to flag those as Picks. Once they're flagged, press **Command-D (PC: Ctrl-D)** to deselect those photos, then go and select another group of photos that are similar, press N to jump to Survey view, and start the process of elimination on that group. You can do this as many times as you need, until you've got the best shots from each set of similar shots or poses tagged as Picks.

Note: Remember, when you first made your collection from flagged Picks, we selected all the photos and removed the Pick flags by pressing the letter U. That's why you're able to use them again here.

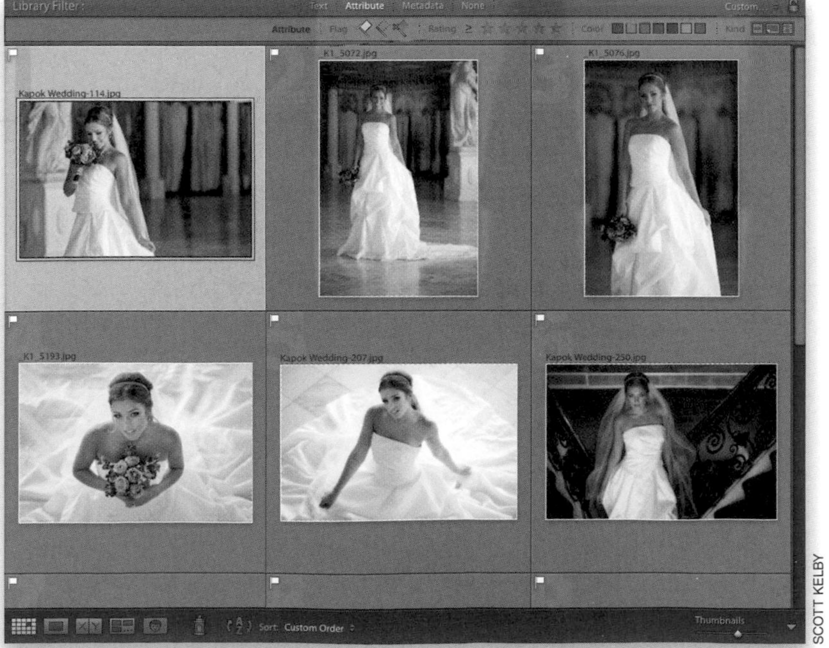

TIP: Removing Photos from Survey View

There's a little-known shortcut for removing a selected photo from contention when you're looking at them in Survey view: just press the **/ (forward slash) key** on your keyboard.

Step 15:

Now that you've gone through and marked the very best shots from your Picks collection, let's put just those "best of the best" in their own separate collection (this will make more sense in just a minute). At the top of the center Preview area, in the Library Filter bar, click on Attribute, and when the Attribute bar pops down, click on the white Pick flag to display just the Picks from your Picks collection (as seen here).

Continued

Step 16:

Now press **Command-A (PC: Ctrl-A)** to select all the Picks displayed onscreen, and then press **Command-N (PC: Ctrl-N)** to bring up the Create Collection dialog. Here's a tip: name this collection by starting with the name of your keepers collection, then add the word "Selects" (so in my case, I would name my new collection "Kristina Wedding Selects"). Collections appear listed in alphabetical order, so if you start with the same names, both collections will wind up together, which makes things easier for you in the next step (besides, you can always change the name later by Right-clicking on it in the Collections panel and choosing **Rename** from the pop-up menu).

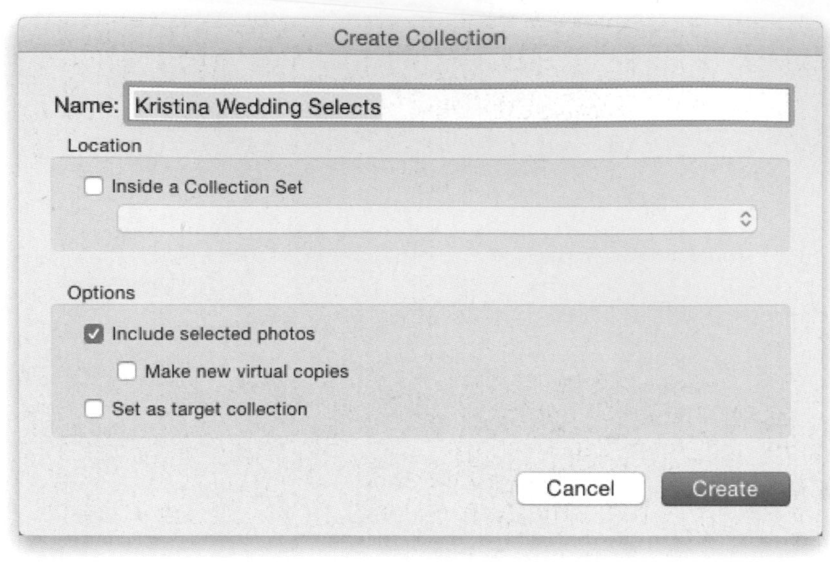

Step 17:

Just to recap, now you have two collections: one with your keepers from the shoot (the Picks), and a Selects collection with only the very best images from the shoot. When you look in the Collections panel, you'll see your keepers collection with the Selects one right below (as shown here).

Note: We still have one more method to cover for narrowing things down, but just so you know, after that you'll learn how to use collection sets, which make things easy when you have multiple collections from the same shoot—like we do here with a Picks collection and Selects collection.

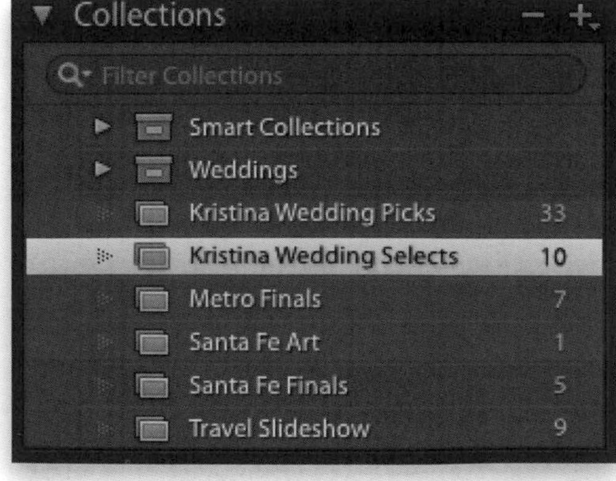

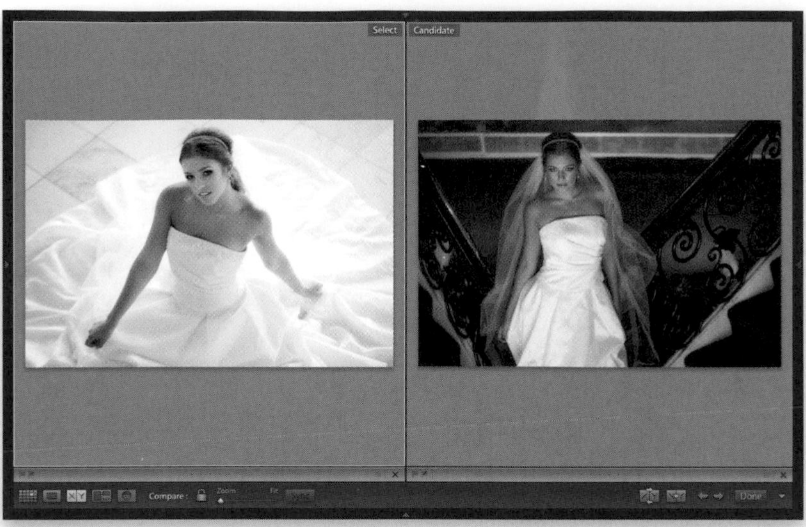

Step 18:

There's a third view you can use to view your images that can help you in situations where you need to find the one single, solitary, best shot from a shoot (for example, let's say you want to post one single shot from your bridal shoot on your studio's blog, so you need to find that one perfect shot to run with your post). That's when you use Compare view—it's designed to let you go through your photos and find that one, single, best shot. Here's how it works: First, select the first two photos in your Selects collection (click on the first photo, then Command-click [PC: Ctrl-click] on the second image, so they're both selected). Now, press the letter **C** to enter Compare view, where the two photos will appear side by side (as shown here), then press Shift-Tab to hide the panels and make the photos as large as possible. Also, you can enter Lights Out mode now, if you like (press the letter L twice).

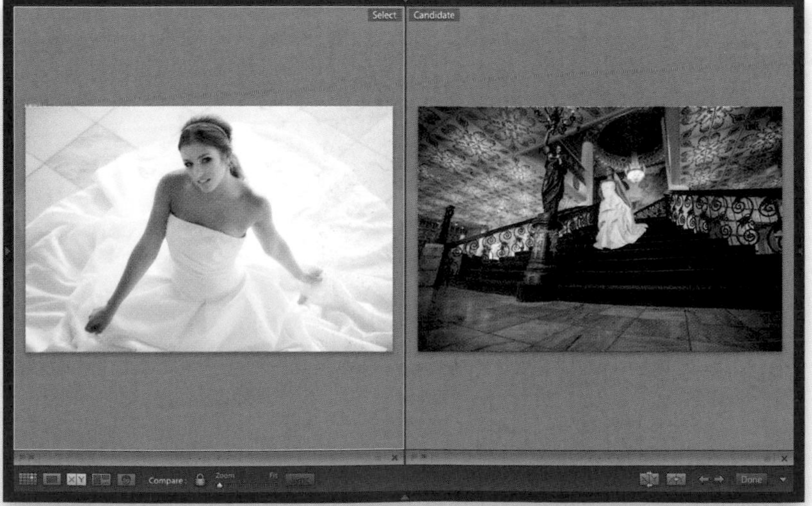

Step 19:

So, here's how this works, and this is a battle where only one photo can win: On the left is the current champion (called the Select), and on the right is the contender (called the Candidate). All you have to do is look at both photos, and then decide if the photo on the right is better than the photo on the left (in other words, does the photo on the right "beat the current champ?"). If it doesn't, then press the **Right Arrow key** on your keyboard and the next photo in your collection (the new contender) appears on the right to challenge the current champ on the left (as seen here, where a new photo has appeared on the right side).

Continued

Step 20:

If you press the Right Arrow key to bring up a new Candidate, and this new photo on the right actually does look better than the Select photo on the left, then click the Make Select button (the X|Y button with a single arrow, on the right side of the toolbar below the center Preview area, shown circled here in red). This makes the Candidate image become the Select image (it moves to the left side), and the battle starts again. So, to recap the process: You select two photos and press C to enter Compare view, then ask yourself the question, "Is the photo on the right better than the one on the left?" If it's not better, press the Right Arrow key on your keyboard. If it is better, click the Make Select button and continue the process. Once you've gone through all the photos in your Selects collection, whichever photo remains on the left (as the Select photo) is the best image from the shoot. When you're done, click the Done button on the right side of the toolbar.

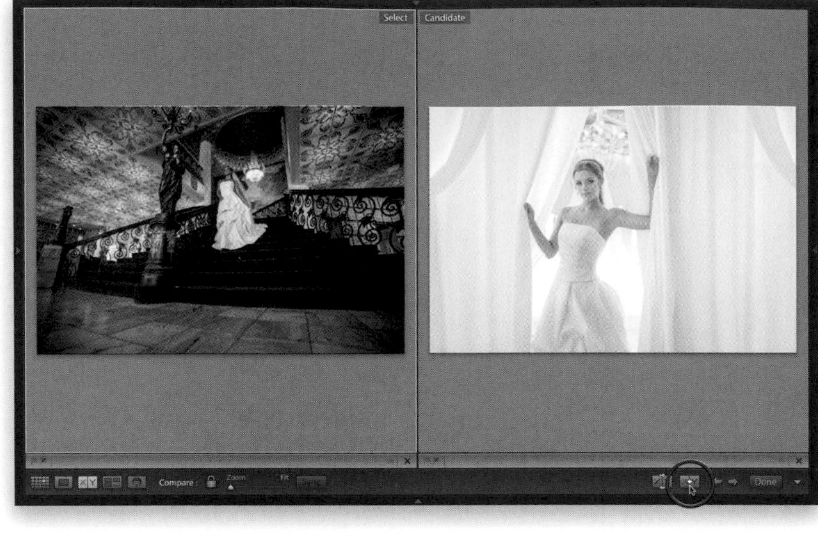

Step 21:

Although I always use the Arrow keys on my keyboard to "do battle" in Compare view, you can also use the Previous and Next buttons in the toolbar. To the left of the Make Select button is the Swap button, which just swaps the two photos (making the Candidate the Select, and vice versa), but I haven't found a good reason to use this Swap button, and just stick to the Make Select button. So, which of the three views do you use when? Here's what I do: (1) the Loupe view is my main view when making Picks, (2) I use Survey view only when comparing a number of shots of a similar pose or scene, and (3) I use Compare view when I'm trying to find a single "best" image.

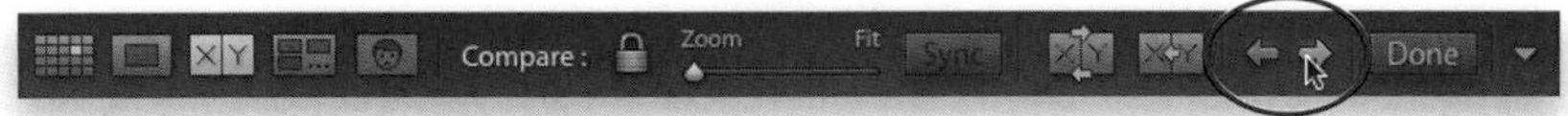

If you don't want to use the Left and Right Arrow keys on your keyboard, you can use the Previous and Next buttons in the toolbar to bring up the next Candidate or return to the previous one

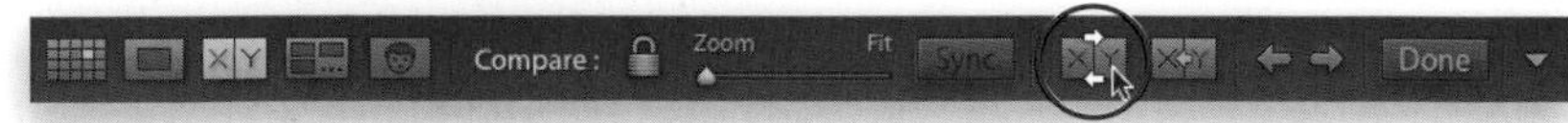

The Swap button lets you swap the Candidate and Select images. I honestly haven't found a lot of use for this button

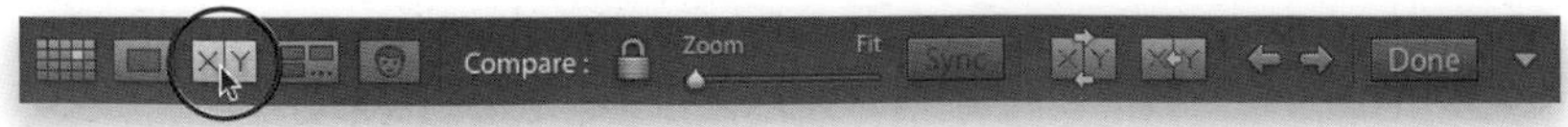

Besides pressing C to enter Compare view, you can also click the Compare View button. The button to the right of it is the button to enter Survey view

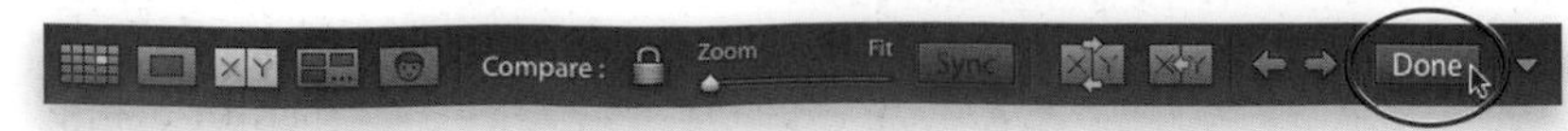

When you're finished using Compare view, either click the Done button to go to Loupe view, or click the Compare View button to return to the regular Grid view

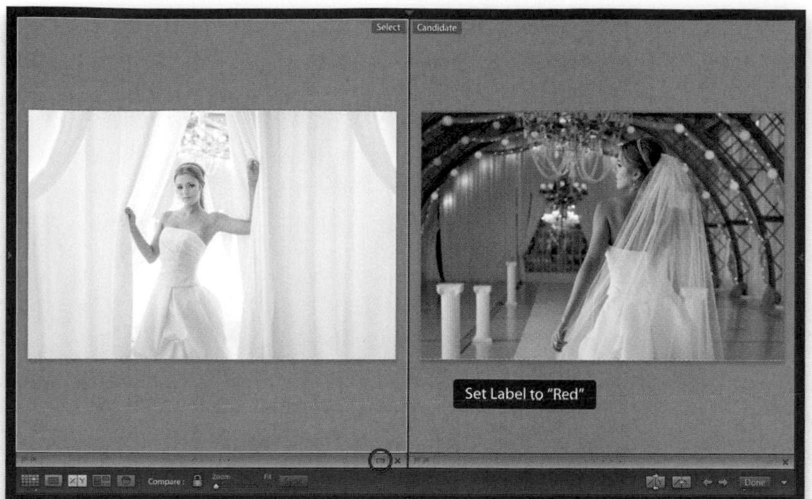

Step 22:
One last thing about Compare view: once I've determined which photo is the single best photo from the shoot (which should be the image on the left side when I get through all the images in my Selects collection—what I call "the last photo standing"), I don't make a whole new Selects collection for just this one photo. Instead, I mark this one photo on the left as the winner by pressing the number **6** on my keyboard. This assigns a Red label to this photo (as shown here).

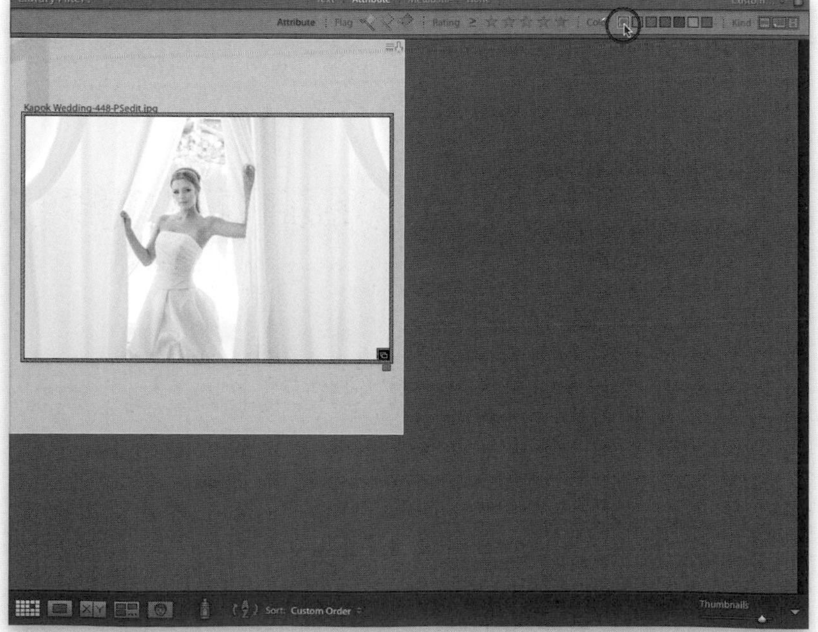

Step 23:
Now anytime I want to find the single best photo out of this shoot, I can go to the Library module's Grid view **(G)**, click on Attribute in the Library Filter bar, and then in the Attribute bar below it, I can click the Red label (as shown circled here), and bang—there's my "Best of Show." So, in this tutorial, you've just learned a key part of the organization process—creating collections—and using collections puts both "your keepers" and your very best photos from each shoot just one click away. Next, we'll look at how to organize related shoots that will have multiple collections (like a wedding or vacation).

Organizing Multiple Shoots Using Collection Sets

If you spent a week in New York and went out shooting every day, once you got all your shoots into Lightroom, you'd probably have collections with names like Times Square, Central Park, 5th Avenue, The Village, and so on. Because Lightroom automatically alphabetizes collections, these related shoots (they're all in New York, taken during the same trip) would be spread out throughout your list of collections. This is just one place where collection sets come in handy, because you could put all those shoots under one collection set: New York.

Step One:

To create a collection set (which just acts like a folder to keep related collections organized together), click on the little + (plus sign) button on the right side of the Collections panel header (in the left side Panels area), and choose **Create Collection Set**, as shown here. This brings up the Create Collection Set dialog where you can name your set. In this example, we're going to use it to organize all the different shoots from a wedding, so name it "Jones Wedding" and click the Create button.

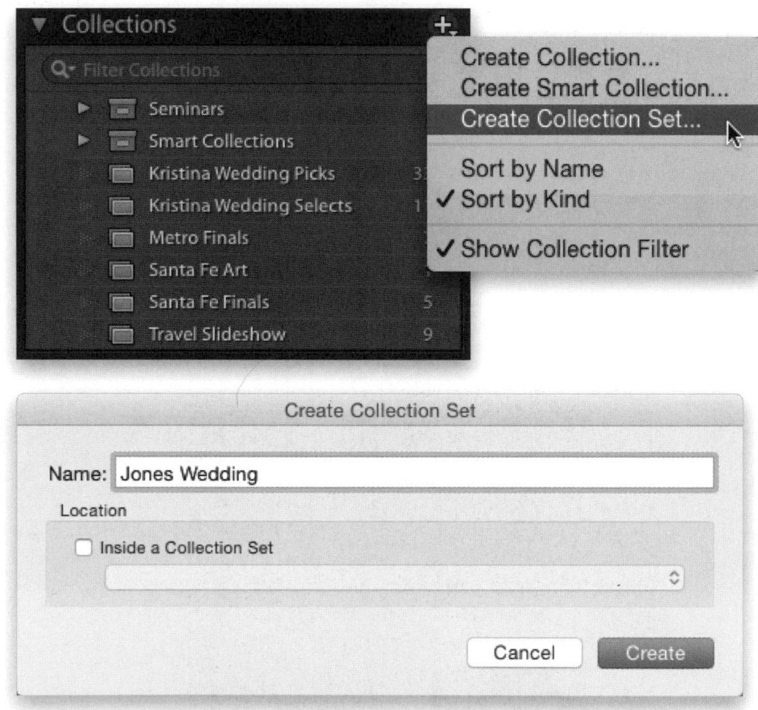

Step Two:

This empty collection set now appears in the Collections panel. When you go to create a new collection of shots from this wedding, Command-click (PC: Ctrl-click) on the images you want in the collection, then choose **Create Collection** from the little + (plus sign) button's pop-up menu. In the Create Collection dialog, name your new collection, then turn on the Inside a Collection Set checkbox, choose Jones Wedding from the pop-up menu, and click Create.

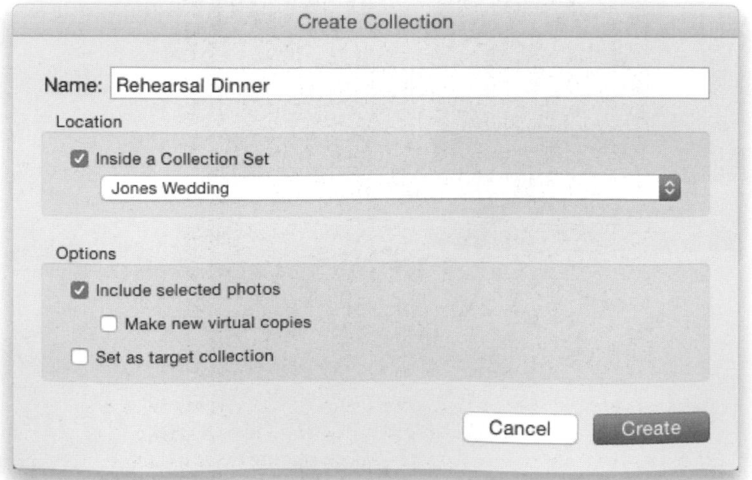

Here's the collection set expanded, so you can see all the collections you saved inside it

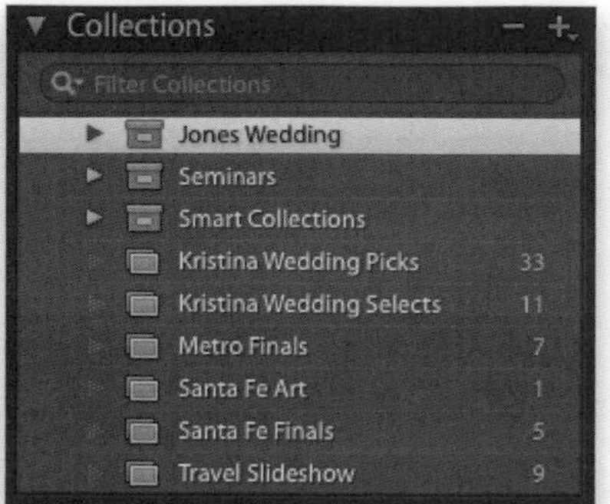

Here's the same collection set collapsed, and you can see how much shorter this makes your list of collections

Step Three:

When you look in the Collections panel, you'll see the collections you've added to the Jones Wedding collection set appearing directly under it (well, they actually are grouped with it). With something like a wedding, where you might wind up creating a lot of separate collections for different parts of the wedding, you can see how keeping everything organized under one header like this really makes sense. Also, here we created the collection set first, but you don't have to—you can create one whenever you want, and then just drag-and-drop existing collections right onto that set in the Collections panel.

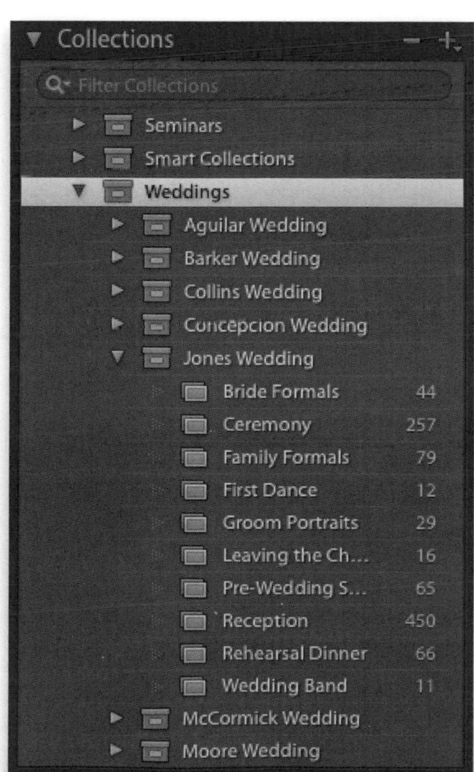

Here, all your weddings are contained within one main Weddings collection set. If you want to see the individual collections inside a particular wedding, then you click on the triangle that appears before its name to reveal its contents

Step Four:

If you want to take things a step further, you can even create a collection set inside another collection set (that's why, back in Step One, when you created your first collection set, the Inside a Collection Set pop-up menu appeared in that dialog—so you could put this new collection set inside an existing collection set). An example of why you might want to do this is so you can keep all your wedding shoots together. So, you'd have one collection set called Weddings (as shown here), and then inside of that you'd have separate collection sets for individual weddings. That way, anytime you want to see, or search through, all your wedding photos from all your weddings, you can click on that one Weddings collection set.

Using Smart Collections for Automatic Organization

Say you wanted to create a collection of your 5-star bridal portraits from the past three years. You could search through all your collections, or you could have smart collections find them all for you, and put them in a collection automatically. Just choose the criteria and Lightroom will do the gathering, and in seconds, it's done. Best of all, smart collections update live, so if you create one of just your red-labeled images, any time you rate a photo with a red label, it's automatically added to that smart collection. You can create as many of these as you'd like.

Step One:

To understand the power of smart collections, let's build one that creates a collection of all your best cathedral photos. In the Collections panel, click on the + (plus sign) button on the right side of the panel header, and choose **Create Smart Collection** from the pop-up menu. This brings up the Create Smart Collection dialog. In the Name field at the top, name your smart collection and from the Match pop-up menu, choose **All**. Then, from the pop-up menu beneath that, under Other Metadata, choose Keywords, choose Contains from the pop-up menu to the right, and in the text field, type "Cathedral." Now, if you just want your latest work included, create another line of criteria, by clicking on the little + (plus sign) button to the right of the text field, and another line of criteria appears. Under Date, choose Capture Date from the first pop-up menu, Is in the Last from the second, type "12" in the text field, and then choose Months from the last pop-up menu.

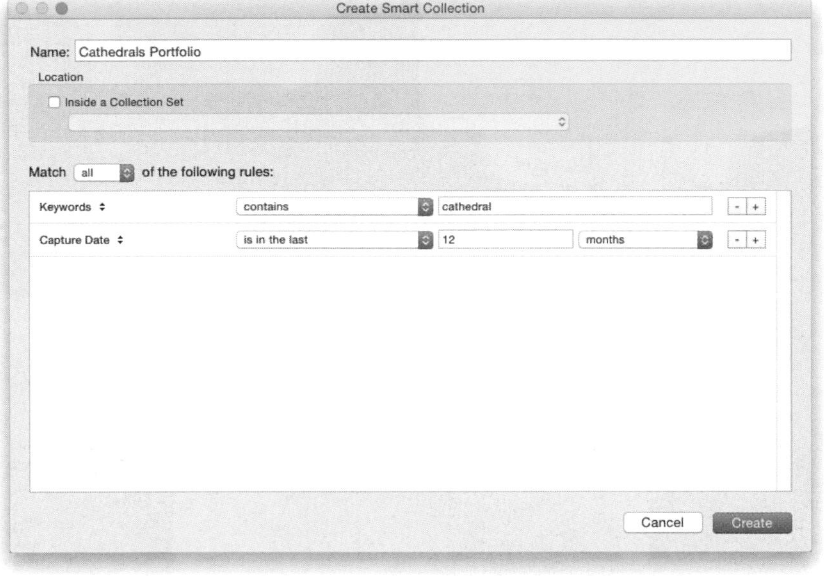

Step Two:

Now, let's narrow things down. Press-and-hold the Option (PC: Alt) key and the + buttons will turn into # (number sign) buttons. Click on the one to the right of your last line of criteria to get additional criteria choices. Leave the first pop-up menu set to Any of the Following Are True, then under Source, choose Collection from the first pop-up menu below, choose Contains from the one to the right, and in the text field, type "Selects." It's now set to gather all the photos in all your Selects collections.

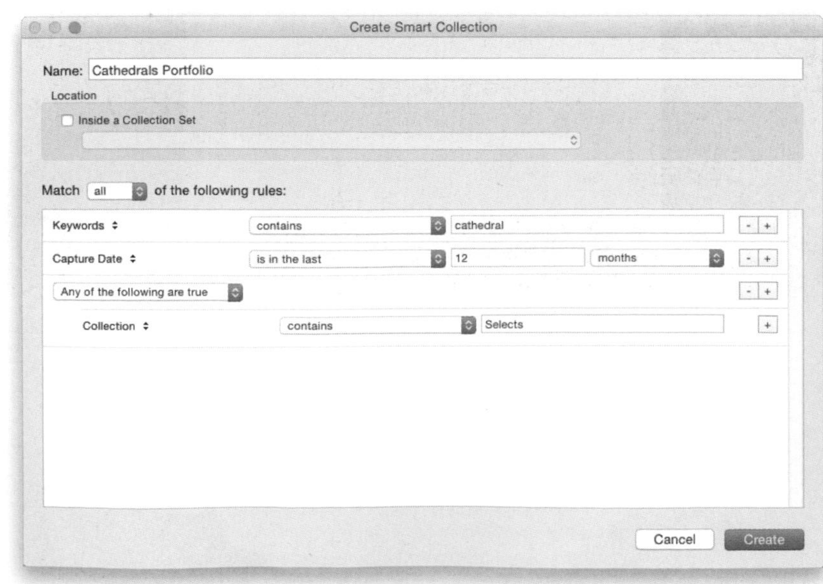

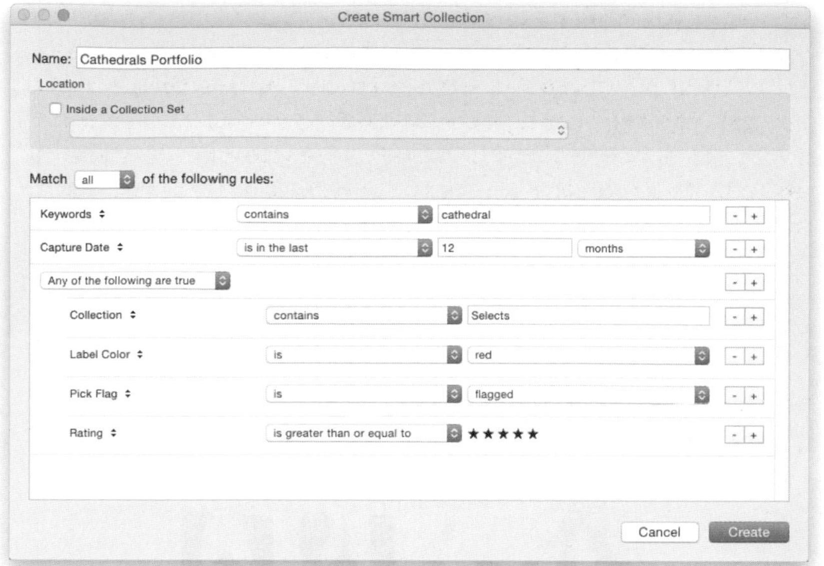

Step Three:

Let's add another criterion in case you labeled one Select photo red, rather than just putting it in a collection. From the first pop-up menu, choose Label Color, from the second choose Is, and choose Red from the third. Clicking the Create button now would make a smart collection of all the photos in any Selects collection, along with any photos labeled red that have the keyword "cathedral" and were taken in the last 12 months. If you've been using Pick flags or the 1-to-5-star rating system, you can also add additional lines of criteria for these, as well, to pick up any Picks or 5-star rated photos that you have. (*Note:* There are a lot of choices in Smart Collections: you can even create one based on image size, or color profile, or a particular bit depth, or number of color channels, or if the file type is PNG, or an image's Smart Preview status. Check out LightroomKillerTips.com for more on these.)

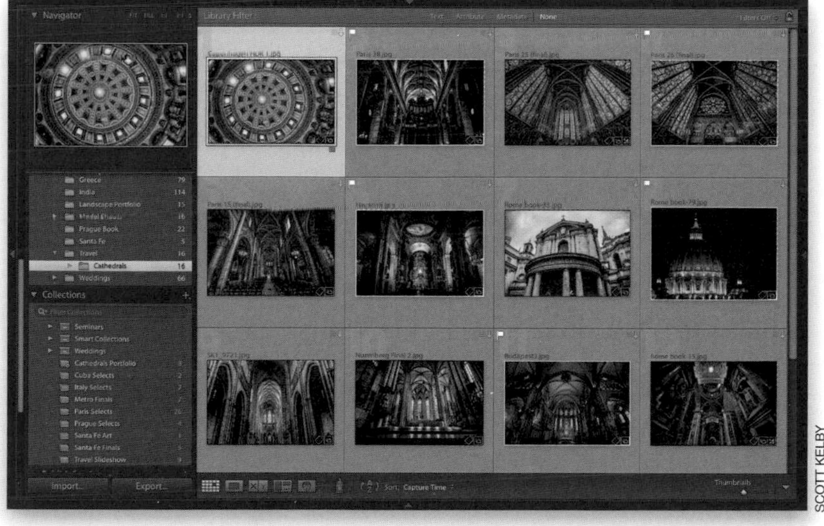

SCOTT KELBY

Step Four:

Now when you hit the Create button, it compiles all of this for you and best of all, it will constantly be updated. New photos with the cathedral keyword in any Selects collection, or labeled red, or 5 star, or flagged with a Pick flag, will automatically be added to this collection and any images older than 12 months will automatically be removed. Also, say you remove the red label from a recent cathedral photo that wasn't in a Selects collection and didn't have a Pick flag or a star rating, it gets removed from this smart collection without you having to do anything, because it no longer matches the criteria. You can edit the criteria for any existing smart collection anytime by just double-clicking directly on it in the Collections panel. This brings up the Edit Smart Collection dialog with all your current criteria in place, where you can add additional criteria (by clicking the + button), delete criteria (by clicking the – [minus sign] button), or change the criteria in the pop-up menus.

Keeping Things Tidy Using Stacks

Stacking images (which had been a feature in folders) has finally made its way to collections. With stacking, now we can group similar-looking images together within our collections, so we have less scrolling through the grid with big shoots. It works like this: Say you had 22 shots of the bride in pretty much the same pose. Do you really need to see those 22 shots all the time? Probably not. With stacks, you can tuck those 22 thumbnails behind just one thumbnail, which represents the rest. That way, you don't have to scroll through 22 nearly identical thumbnails to get to your other images.

Step One:

Here, we've imported images from a model shoot, and you can see what I was talking about above, where there are several shots that include the same pose. Seeing all these photos at once just adds clutter and makes finding your "keepers" that much more of a task. So, we're going to group similar poses into a stack with just one thumbnail showing. The rest of the photos are collapsed behind that photo. Start by clicking on the first photo of a similar pose (as seen highlighted here), then press-and-hold the Shift key and click on the last photo that has the same pose (as shown here) to select them all (you can also select photos in the Filmstrip, if you prefer).

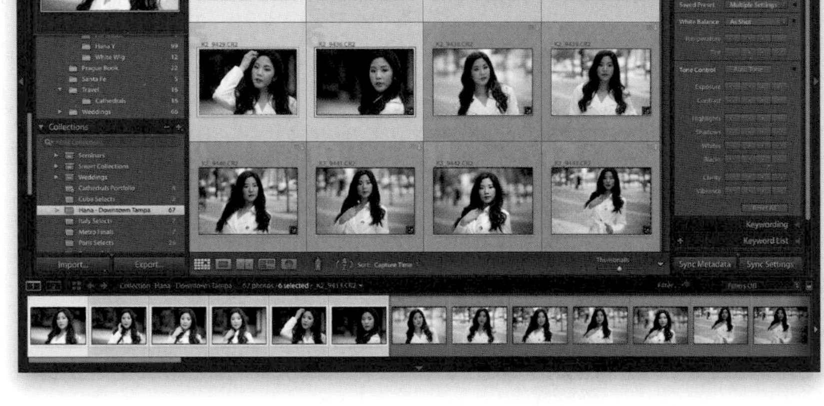

SCOTT KELBY

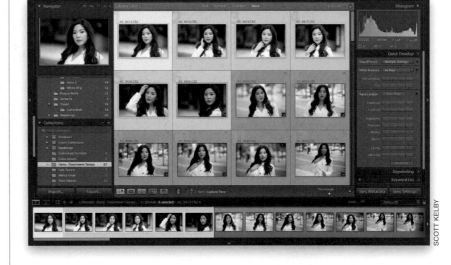

Step Two:

Now press **Command-G (PC: Ctrl-G)** to put all your selected photos into a stack (this keyboard shortcut is easy to remember, if you think of G for Group). If you look in the grid now, you can see there's just one thumbnail visible with that pose. It didn't delete or remove those other photos—they stacked behind that one thumbnail (in a computery, technical, you'll-just-have-to-trust-that's-what's-happening kind of way). Look how much more manageable things are now that those four photos are collapsed down to one.

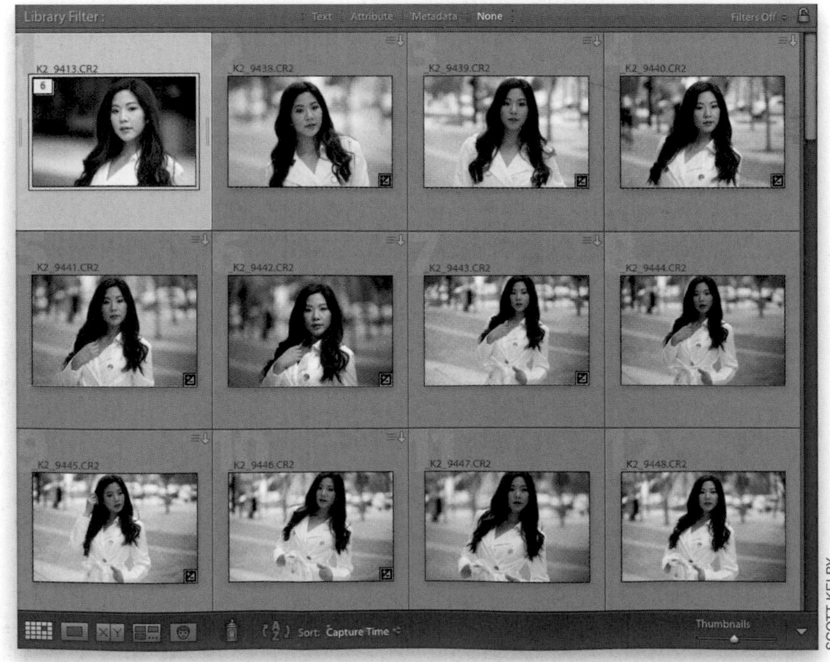

SCOTT KELBY

Step Three:

In the zoomed-in view here, you can see the number 6 in a rectangle in the top left of the thumbnail. That's to let you know two things: (1) this isn't just one photo, it's a stack of photos, and (2) how many photos are in this stack. The view you're seeing here is the stack's collapsed view (where five similar photos are collapsed behind the first one). To expand your stack and see all the photos in it, just click directly on that little number 6 (the expanded view is shown in the next step), press **S** on your keyboard, or click on one of the two little thin bars that appear on either side of the thumbnail. (To collapse the stack, just do any of these again.) By the way, to add a photo to an existing stack, just drag-and-drop the photo you want to add right onto the existing collapsed stack.

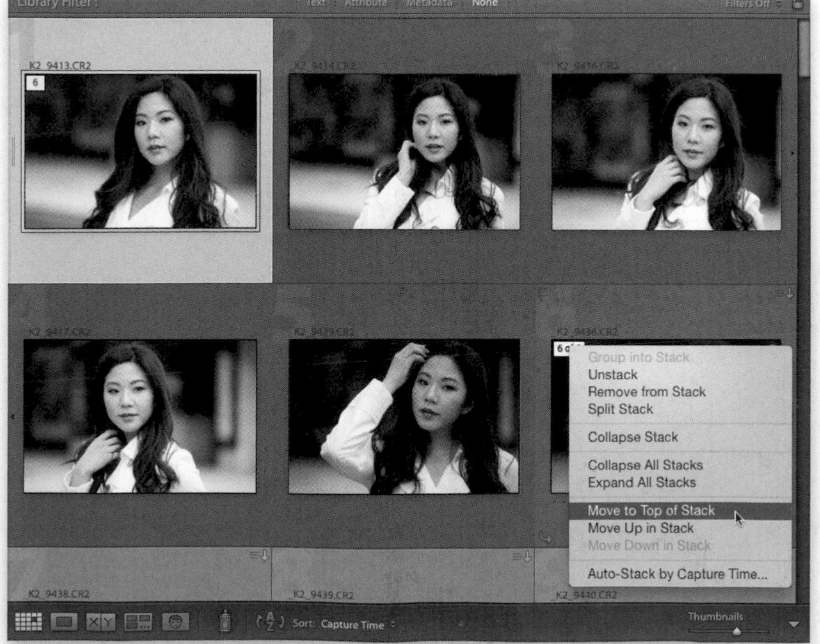

Step Four:

Here are a few things that will help you in managing your stacks. The first photo you select when creating a stack (the top photo) will be the one that remains visible when the stack is collapsed. If that's not the photo you want to represent your stack, you can make any photo in your stack the top photo. First, expand the stack, then Right-click directly on the little rectangle with the photo number in it, and choose **Move to Top of Stack** (as shown here).

Continued

Step Five:

To remove a photo from a stack, first expand the stack, then Right-click directly on that photo's photo number, and choose **Remove from Stack** from the pop-up menu (as shown here). This doesn't delete it, or remove it from a collection, etc., it just takes it out of this stack. So, for example, if you removed just one photo, when you collapsed the stack again, you'd see two thumbnails in the grid—one representing the three photos still stacked, and a second thumbnail of just that individual photo you removed. *Note:* If you want to remove more than one photo from your stack at the same time, Command-click (PC: Ctrl-click) on the ones you want removed to select them, Right-click on the photo number on one of them, and then choose Remove from Stack from the pop-up menu.

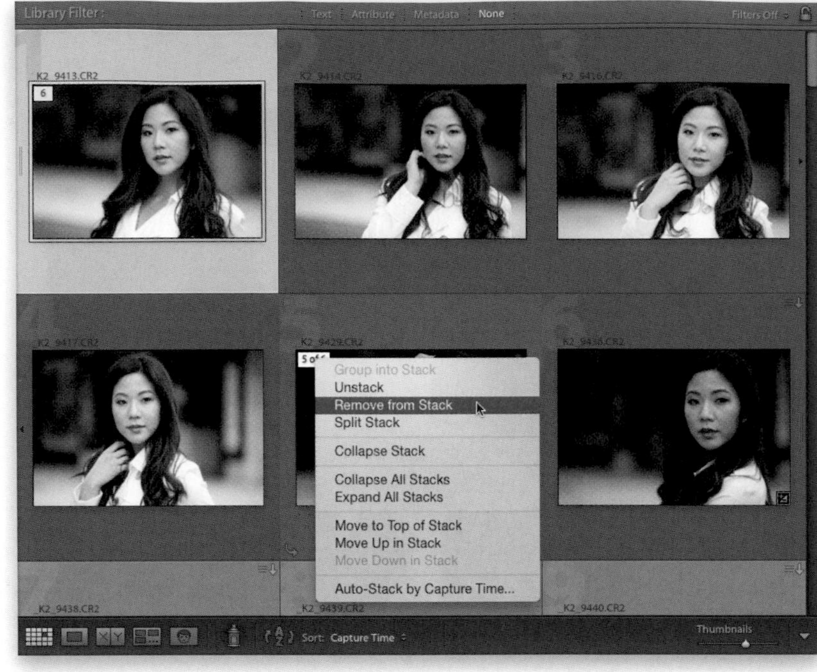

Step Six:

Before we move on, there's one more thing on the topic of removing photos from your stack. If you do want to actually delete a photo in your stack (not just remove it from your stack), just expand the stack, then click on the photo and press the Delete (PC: Backspace) key on your keyboard. Okay, here's another tip: if you want all your stacks expanded at once (so every thumbnail from the shoot is visible again), just Right-click on any thumbnail (not just a stack—any thumbnail), choose Stacking, and then choose **Expand All Stacks** (or Right-click on any stack's photo number rectangle and choose Expand All Stacks). If you want to collapse all your stacks, instead choose **Collapse All Stacks**, and now you'll see just one photo representing each pose.

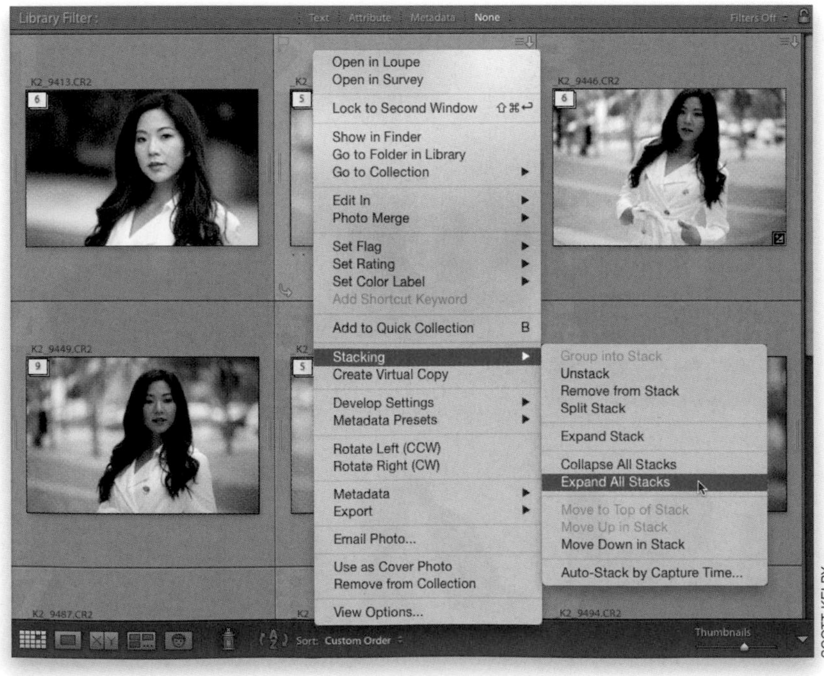

SCOTT KELBY

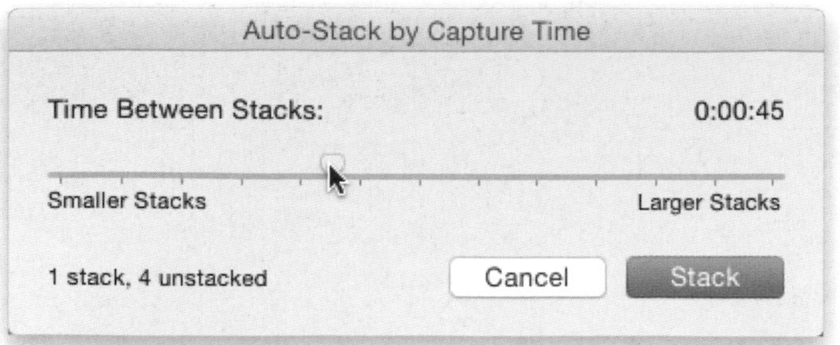

Step Seven:

Lightroom can automatically stack similar photos together based on how much time passed between shots. Let's say you're shooting in the studio where you're firing off shots pretty regularly, but when it's time for your subject to change outfits (or for you to change the lighting setup), it probably takes at least five minutes. So, you'd set the Auto-Stack feature to five minutes, and that way, when you stop shooting for five minutes or more, it takes everything you just shot and puts it in a stack for you (this works better than it sounds). To turn on this Auto-Stack feature, Right-click on any thumbnail, then from the pop-up menu, under Stacking, choose **Auto-Stack by Capture Time**. The dialog shown here appears, and as you drag the slider to the left or right, you'll see photos start jumping into stacks in real time. This is one of those you just have to try to see that it usually works pretty darn well.

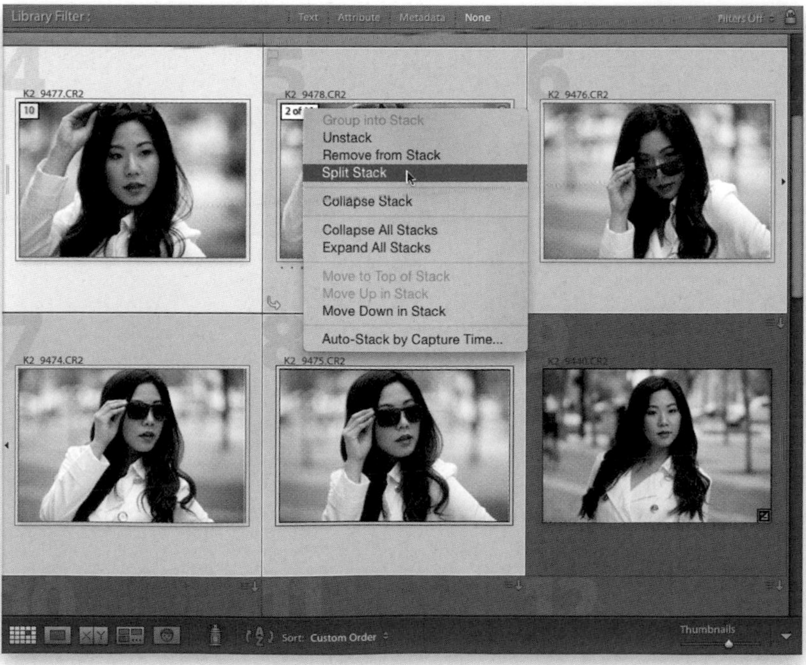

Step Eight:

By the way, if you use the Auto-Stack feature, it might stack some photos together that don't actually belong together. If that happens, it's easy to split a stack and have those other photos separated into their own stack. To split a stack, expand it, then just select the photos you want to split out into their own stack, Right-click on the photo number rectangle on any one of them, and in the pop-up menu that appears, choose **Split Stack** (as shown here). Now, you'll have two stacks—in our case, one with eight photos, and one with four. One last thing about stacks: once photos are in a stack, any edits you apply to your stack while it's collapsed are actually only applied to the top photo, not to the rest of the photos in the stack. Quick Develop settings, keywords, and any other edits can be applied to the entire stack if you expand the stack and select them all before you change your setting or add your keyword.

When to Use a Quick Collection Instead

When you create collections, they're a more permanent way of keeping your photos organized into separate albums (by permanent, I mean that when you relaunch Lightroom months later, your collections are still there—but of course, you can also choose to delete a collection, so they're never really that permanent). However, sometimes you want to just group a few photos temporarily, and you don't actually want to save these groupings long term. That's where Quick Collections can come in handy.

Step One:

There are a lot of reasons why you might want a temporary collection, but most of the time I use Quick Collections when I need to throw a quick slide show together, especially if I need to use images from a number of different collections. For example, let's say I get a call from a potential client, and they want to see some examples of football games I've shot. I'd go to a recent football game shoot, click on its Selects collection, and then double-click on an image to look at them in Loupe view. When I see one I want in my slide show, I just press the letter **B** to add it to my Quick Collection (you get a message onscreen to show you that it has been added).

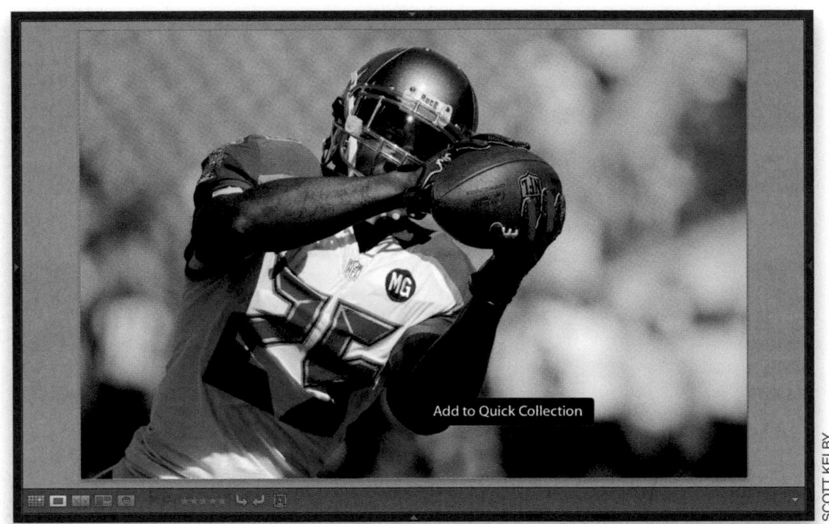

SCOTT KELBY

Step Two:

Now I go to another football game collection and do the same thing—each time I see an image that I want in my slide show, I press B and it's added, so in no time I can whip through 10 or 15 "Best of" collections and mark the ones I want in my slide show as I go. (You can also add photos to your Quick Collection by clicking on the little circle that appears in the top-right corner of each thumbnail in the Grid view when you move your cursor over the thumbnail—it'll turn gray with a thick black line around it when you click on it. You can hide the gray dot by pressing **Command-J [PC: Ctrl-J]**, clicking on the Grid View tab up top, then turning off the checkbox for Quick Collection Markers, as shown on the left here.)

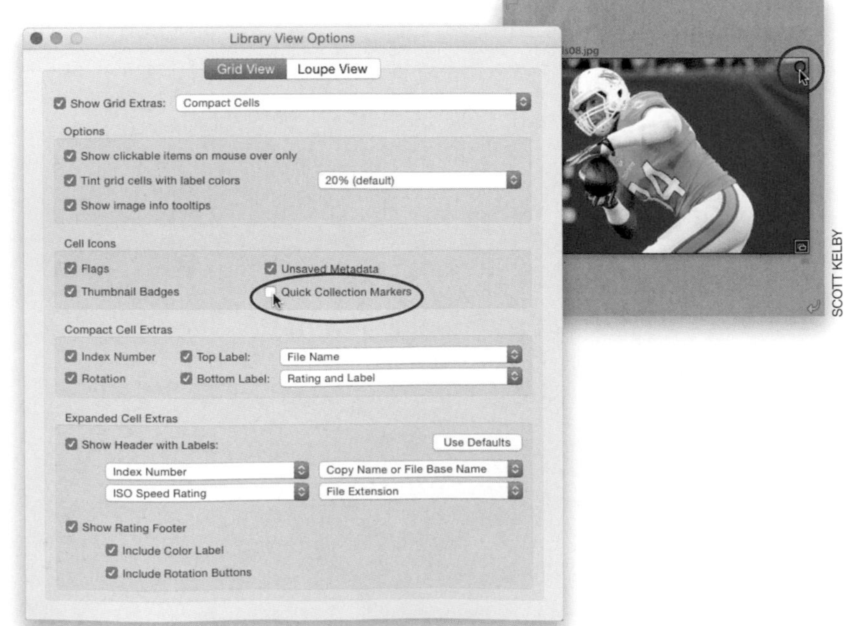

SCOTT KELBY

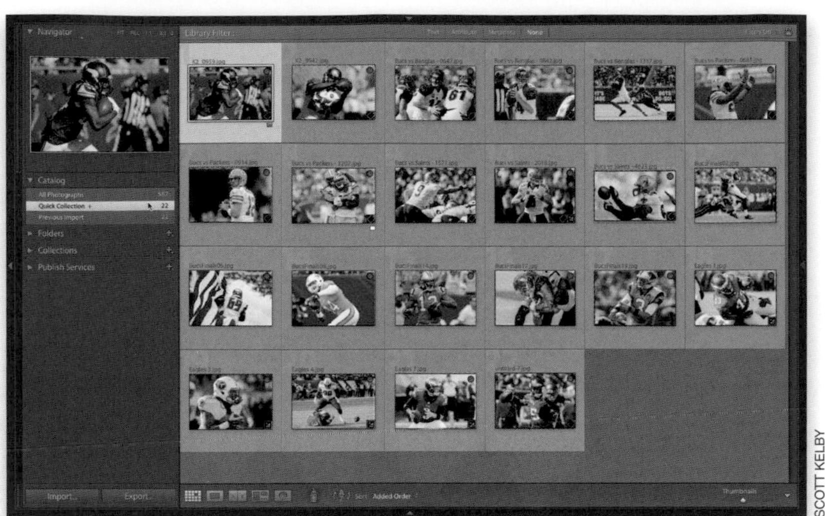
SCOTT KELBY

Step Three:

To see the photos you put in a Quick Collection, go to the Catalog panel (in the left side Panels area), click on Quick Collection (shown here), and now just those photos are visible. To remove a photo from your Quick Collection, just click on it and press the **Delete (PC: Backspace) key** on your keyboard (it doesn't delete the original, it just removes it from this temporary Quick Collection).

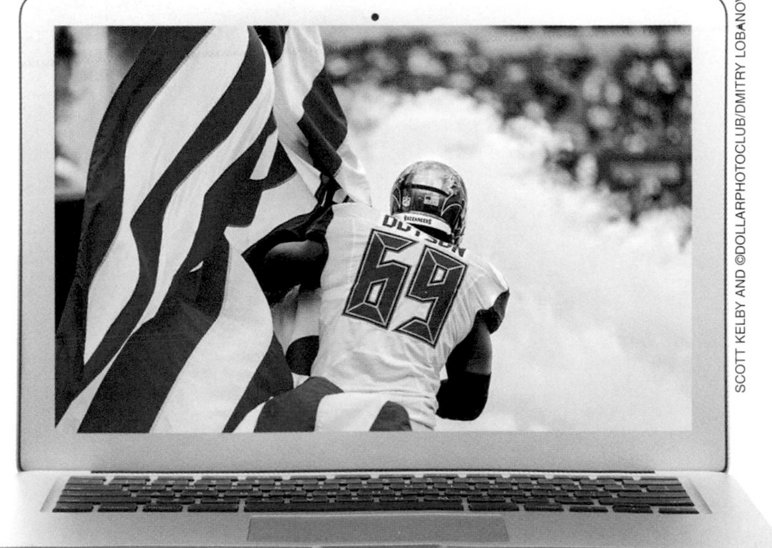
SCOTT KELBY AND ©DOLLARPHOTOCLUB/DMITRY LOBANOV

Step Four:

Now that your photos from all those different collections are in a Quick Collection, you can press **Command-Return (PC: Ctrl-Enter)** to start Lightroom's Impromptu Slideshow feature, which plays a full-screen slide show (as shown here) of the photos in your Quick Collection, using the Default preset in Lightroom's Slideshow module. To stop the slide show, just press the Esc key.

TIP: Saving Your Quick Collection

If you decide you want your Quick Collection to be saved as a regular collection, just go to the Catalog panel, Right-click on Quick Collection, choose **Save Quick Collection** from the pop-up menu, and a dialog appears where you can give your new collection a name.

Using Target Collections (and Why They're So Handy)

We just talked about Quick Collections and how you can temporarily toss things in there for an impromptu slide show, or until you figure out if you actually want to create a collection of those images, but something you might find more useful is to replace the Quick Collection with a target collection. You use the same keyboard shortcut, but instead of sending things to the Quick Collection, now they go to an existing collection. So, why would you want to do that? Read these two pages and you'll totally see why these are so handy (you are soooo going to dig this!).

Step One:

Let's say during the year you shoot a lot of photos of cars. Well, wouldn't it be handy to have one collection of all your favorite car shots, so they're all just one click away? If that sounds handy to you (it sure does to me), then create a new collection and name it "Cars." Once it appears, Right-click on it and, from the pop-up menu that appears, choose **Set as Target Collection** (as shown here). This adds a + (plus sign) to the end of the collection's name, so you know at a glance it's your target collection (as seen here).

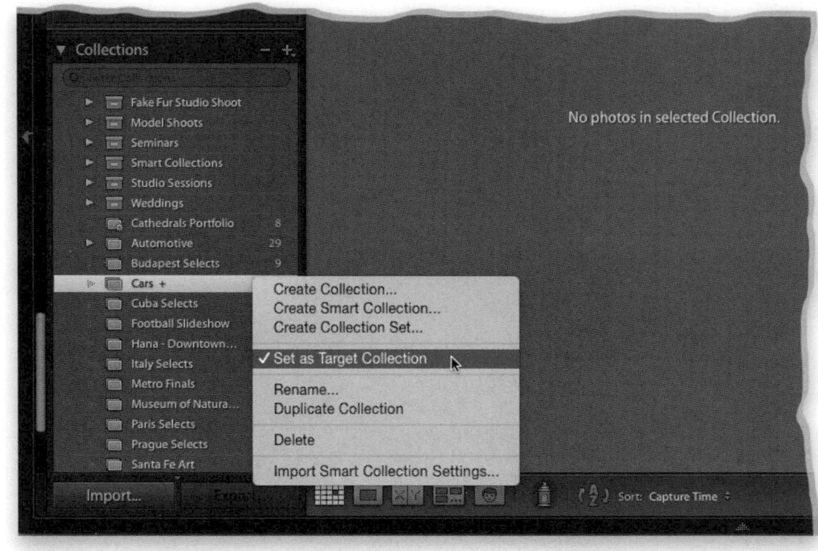

Step Two:

Now that you've created your target collection, adding images to it is easy—just click on any image, press the letter **B** on your keyboard (the same shortcut you used to use for Quick Collection), and that image is added to your Cars target collection. For example, here we're looking at the finals from a studio shoot I did of a Ford Thunderbird. I have them in a regular collection called, "Thunderbird Finals." I also want some of these final images added to my Cars target collection, so I selected them all and simply pressed B. I get a confirmation onscreen that reads, "Add to Target Collection 'Cars,'" so I know they were added. It doesn't remove them from my Thunderbird Finals collection; it just also adds them to the Cars target collection.

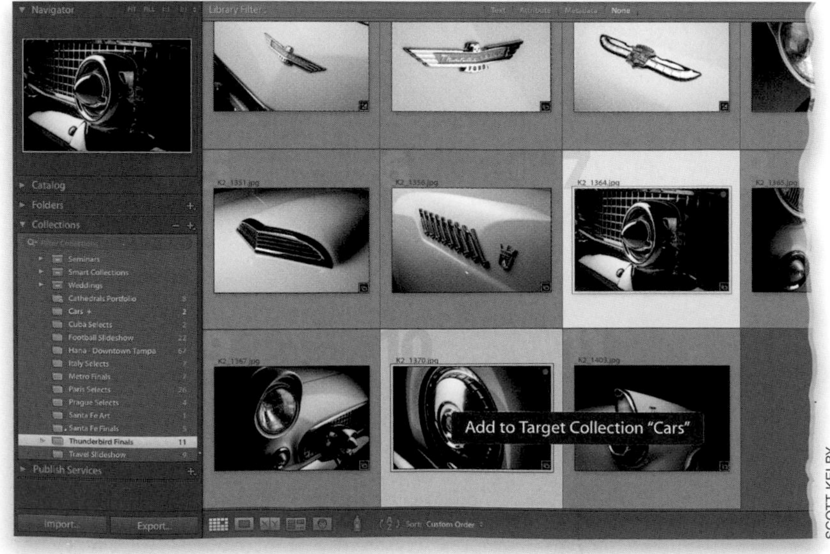

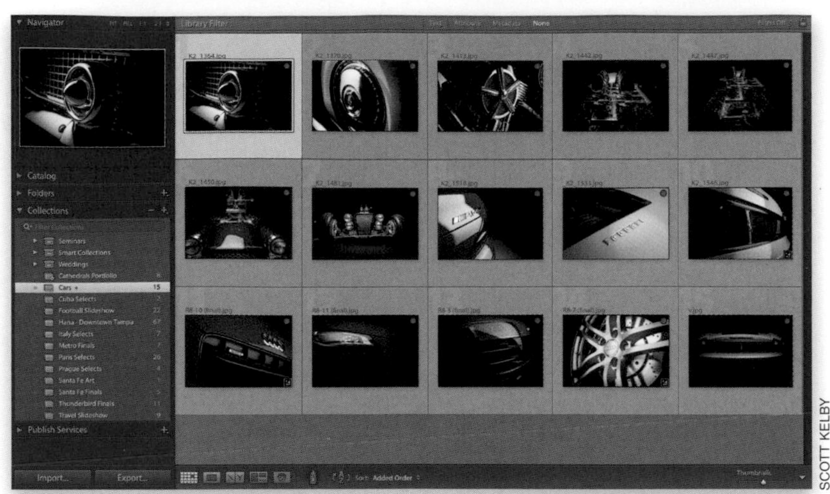

SCOTT KELBY

Step Three:

Now, if I click on that Cars target collection, I see those Thunderbird images, plus images from other car shoots, as well, because now all my car shoot finals are in one place (I told you this was pretty handy, right?).

Create Collection
Name: Ferarri F430 Spider Convertible
Location
Inside a Collection Set
Options
Include selected photos
Make new virtual copies
Set as target collection
Cancel Create

Step Four:

Back in Lightroom 5, Adobe made the process of creating target collections a little more convenient, because now when you create a collection, there's a checkbox in the Create Collection dialog that will make this new collection a target collection (just turn on the **Set as Target Collection** checkbox and this new collection is your new target collection). By the way, you can only have one target collection at a time, so when you choose a different collection to become the target collection, it removes the target from the previously selected collection (the collection is still there—it doesn't delete it. But, pressing B doesn't send images to that collection anymore—it sends them to the new collection you just designated as the target collection). Also, just keep in mind that if you want to go back to creating a Quick Collection (using the B keyboard shortcut), you'll need to turn off your target collection, by just Right-clicking on it and choosing **Set as Target Collection**.

Adding Specific Keywords for Advanced Searching

Most of the time, finding images you want in Lightroom will be easy. Want to look at photos from your vacation to New York? Just click on your New York collection. If you want to see all your photos from all your New York trips, then you could search by the keyword New York (remember those generic keywords you added when you first imported your photos?). But what if you want just photos of the Empire State Building, and just photos of it at night? If that sounds like something you'd wind up doing fairly regularly, then this is for you.

Step One:

Before we go into all this, I just want to say up front that most folks won't need to do the level of keywording I'm about to go into. But if you're a commercial photographer, or if you work with a stock photo agency, keywording all your images is pretty much what you have to do. Luckily, Lightroom makes the process fairly painless. There are a few ways to add specific keywords, and there are different reasons why you might choose one way over another. We'll start with the Keywording panel in the right side Panels area. When you click on a photo, it will list any keywords already assigned to that photo near the top of the Keywording panel (as shown here). By the way, we don't really use the word "assigned," we say a photo's been "tagged" with a keyword, as in, "It's tagged with the keyword NFL."

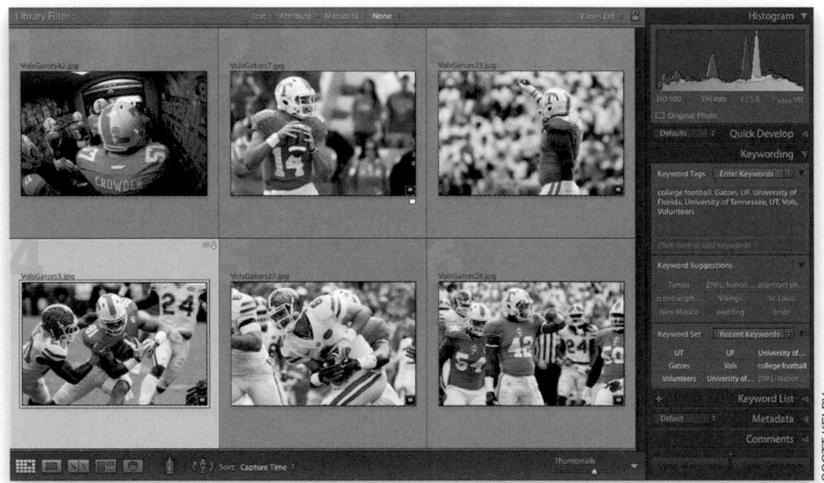

SCOTT KELBY

Step Two:

I tagged all the photos here with eight kinda generic keywords when I imported them, like UF, UT, Vols, and Gators. To add another keyword, you'll see a text field below the keyword field where it literally reads, "Click here to add keywords." Just click in that field, and type in the keyword you want to add (if you want to add more than one keyword, just put a comma between them), then press the **Return (PC: Enter) key**. For the selected photo in Step One, I added the keyword "Jonathon Johnson" Easy enough.

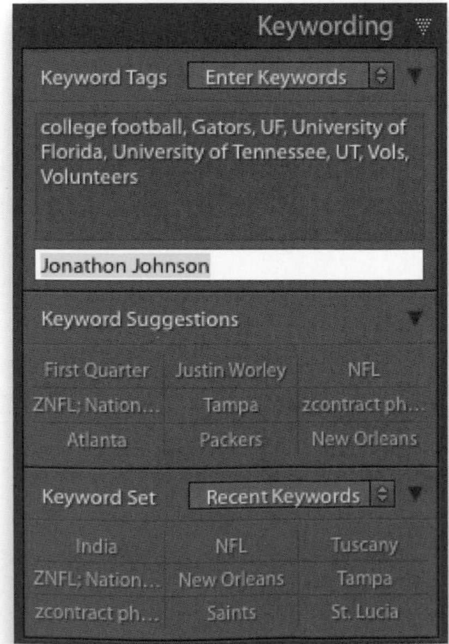

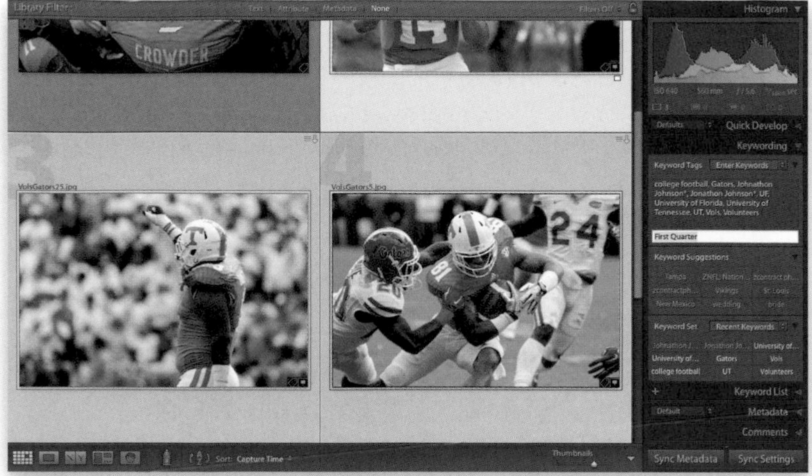

Step Three:

The Keywording panel is also ideal if you want to add the same keywords to a bunch of photos at once. For example, let's say that 71 photos from your full shoot were taken in the first quarter. You'd select those 71 photos first (click on the first one, press-and-hold the Shift key, then scroll down to the last one, and click on it—it'll select all the photos in between), then in the Keywording panel, add your keywords in the Keyword Tags text field. For example, here I typed "First Quarter" and it added "First Quarter" to all 71 selected photos. So, the Keywording panel is my first choice when I need to tag a number of photos from a shoot with the same keywords.

TIP: Choosing Keywords

Here's how I choose my keywords: I ask myself, "If, months from now, I was trying to find these same photos, what words would I most likely type in the Find field?" Then I use those words. It works better than you'd think.

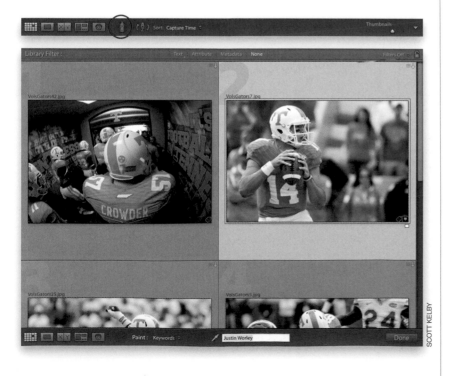

Step Four:

Say you wanted to add some specific keywords to just certain photos, like those of one particular player. If it's just three or four photos kind of near each other, you can use the Keywording panel technique I just showed you. But if it's 20 or 30 spread throughout a shoot, then try the Painter tool (in Grid view, it's found down in the toolbar—it looks like a spray paint can), which lets you "paint" on keywords as you scroll through your images. First, click on the Painter tool (or press **Command-Option-K [PC: Ctrl-Alt-K]**), then to the right, make sure Keywords appears after Paint, then in the field to the right, type in "Justin Worley" or any other specific keywords that relate to just those photos.

SCOTT KELBY

Continued

Step Five:

Scroll through your images and any time you see a Justin Worley photo, just click once on it and it "paints" that keyword onto your photo (you can add as many as you want—just remember to put a comma between them). As you click the Painter tool, a white highlight border will appear around the tagged photo, and a dark rectangular box appears with the keyword(s) you've just assigned (as seen here). If you see multiple photos in a row you want to tag, just press-and-hold your mouse button and paint right across them, and they'll all be tagged. When you're done with the Painter tool, just click back where you found it in the toolbar. The Painter tool is what I use when I have a lot of photos in a shoot, but just need to tag some individual photos with a particular keyword.

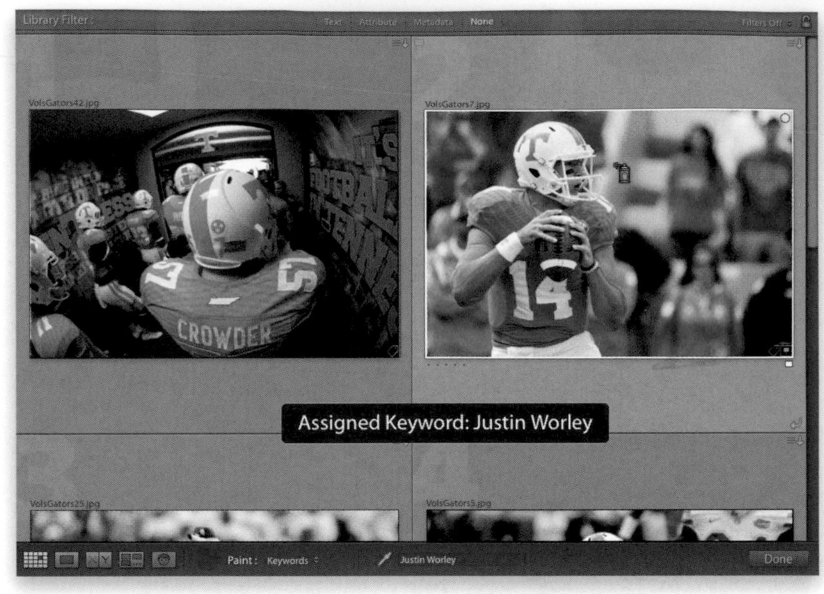

TIP: Create Keyword Sets

If you use the same keywords often, you can save them as a Keyword Set, so they're just one click away. To create a set, just type the keywords in the Keyword Tags text field, then click on the Keyword Set pop-up menu at the bottom of the panel. Choose **Save Current Settings as New Preset** and they're added to the list, along with built-in sets like Wedding, Portrait, etc.

Step Six:

The next panel down, Keyword List, lists all the keywords you've created or that were already embedded into the photos you've imported. The number to the right of each keyword tells you how many photos are tagged with that keyword. If you hover your cursor over a keyword in the list, a white arrow appears on the far right. Click on it and it displays just the photos with that keyword (in the example shown here, I clicked on the arrow for Matt Jones, and it brought up the only two photos in my entire catalog tagged with that keyword). This is why specific keywords are so powerful.

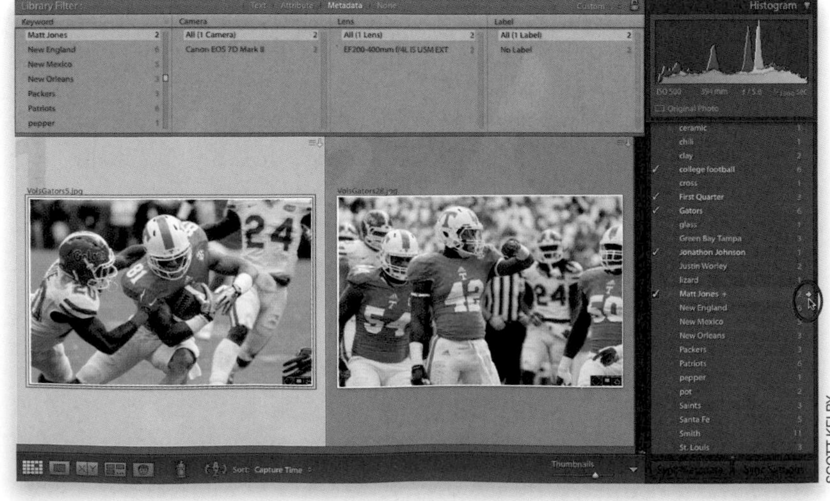

SCOTT KELBY

clay 2
college football 6
First Quarter 3
Gators 6
Jonathon Johnson 1
Justin Worley 2
Matt Jones + 2
UF 6
University of Florida 6
University of Tennessee 6
UT 6
Vols 6
Volunteers 6
cross 1
glass 1
Green Bay Tampa 3
India 114
lizard 1
New England 6
New Mexico 5
New Orleans 3
NFL 30
Packers 3
Patriots 6
pepper 1
pot 2
Saints 0
Santa Fe 5
Smith 11
St. Louis 3
Tampa 9

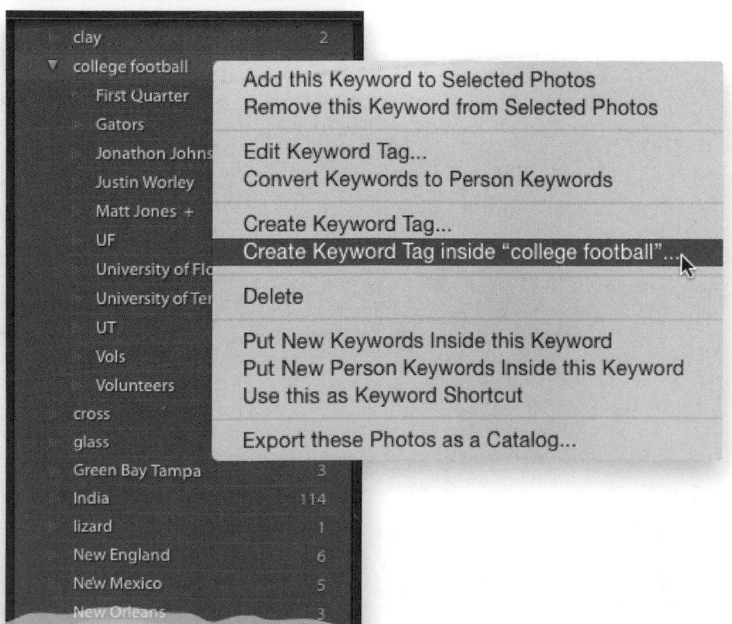

Step Seven:

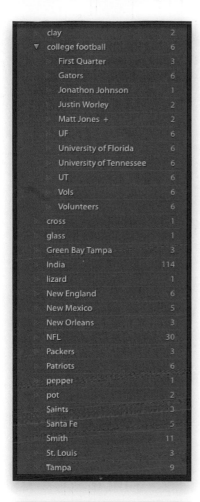

Now, it doesn't take very long for your list of keywords to get really long. So, to keep things organized, you can create a keyword that has sub-keywords (like College Football as the main keyword, then inside that is UF, UT, Vols, and so on). Besides having a shorter keyword list, it also gives you more sorting power. For example, if you click on College Football (the top-level keyword) in the Keyword List panel, it will show you every file in your catalog tagged with UF, UT, etc. But, if you click on UF, it will show you only the photos tagged with UF. This is a huge time saver and I'll show you how to set this up in the next step.

TIP: Drag-and-Drop and Delete Keywords

You can drag-and-drop keywords in the Keyword List panel right onto photos to tag them and vice-versa—you can drag-and-drop photos right onto keywords. To remove a keyword from a photo, in the Keywording panel, just delete it from the Keyword Tags field. To delete a keyword entirely (from all photos and the Keyword List panel itself), scroll down to the Keyword List panel, click on the keyword, then click the – (minus sign) button on the left side of the panel header.

Step Eight:

To make a keyword into a top-level one, just drag-and-drop other keywords directly onto it. That's all you have to do. If you haven't added the keywords you want as sub-keywords yet, do this instead: Right-click on the keyword you want as a top-level keyword, then from the pop-up menu, choose **Create Keyword Tag Inside** (as shown here) to bring up a dialog where you can create your new sub-keyword. Click the Create button, and this new keyword will appear under your main keyword. To hide the sub-keywords, click the triangle to the left of your main keyword.

Face Tagging to Find People Fast

Face tagging (automatic face recognition) is Lightroom's latest tool for helping you stay organized. What it basically does is it automatically recognizes when there's a face in an image. Once it does, you can assign a name to that face, and then it tries to automatically find other photos with that person in it and it assigns that name as a keyword for you. Now, to see all the pictures you have of a particular person, it's just one click in the Keywording panel.

Step One:

First, a heads-up: While we might refer to Lightroom's face tagging as "automatic," it's going to feel more semi-automatic because you do a lot of the initial work yourself. At first, it only recognizes that there's a face in the photo—it doesn't know who it is. That part is up to you, as is tagging ones it misses, or assigns to the wrong person, etc. So, if you have a decent sized catalog, and you want your entire catalog set up with face tagging, you might need to set aside an hour or two (or more) to initially set this up. Okay, now that you know that, to start face tagging, go to the Library module and click on the People icon in the toolbar (shown circled here; or choose **People** from the View menu, or just press the letter **O** to jump there fast).

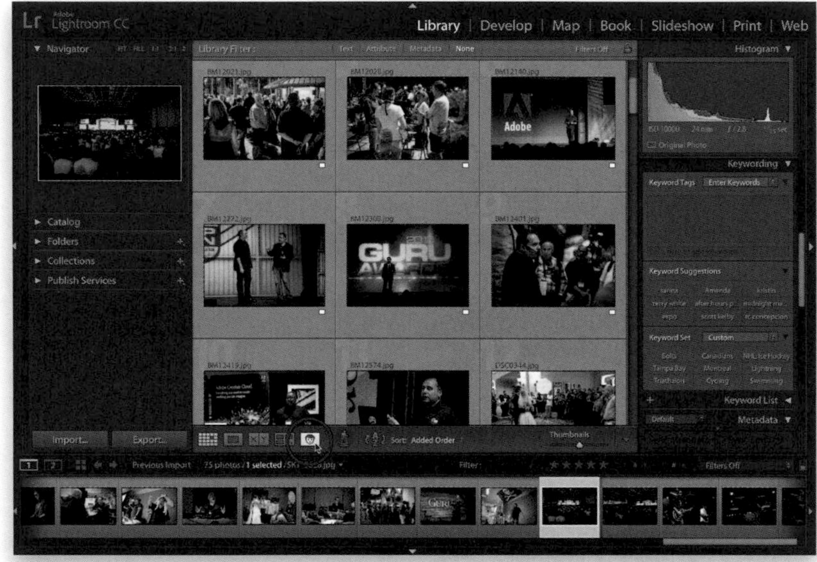

BRAD MOORE

Step Two:

The first time you launch this, you get a screen that lets you know that it takes a while for Lightroom to go through your catalog and search each image for faces (luckily, it does this in the background, so it doesn't stop you from working). But, it does give you a choice: start now and do your entire catalog in the background, or just do it when you actually click the People icon. You'll have to make this call based on how much you think you'll be using this feature (I went with Only Find Faces As-Needed, so it only does recognition on the collection I'm currently working in, and then only when I click on the People icon). When you make your choice, it sends you to People view (seen in the next step).

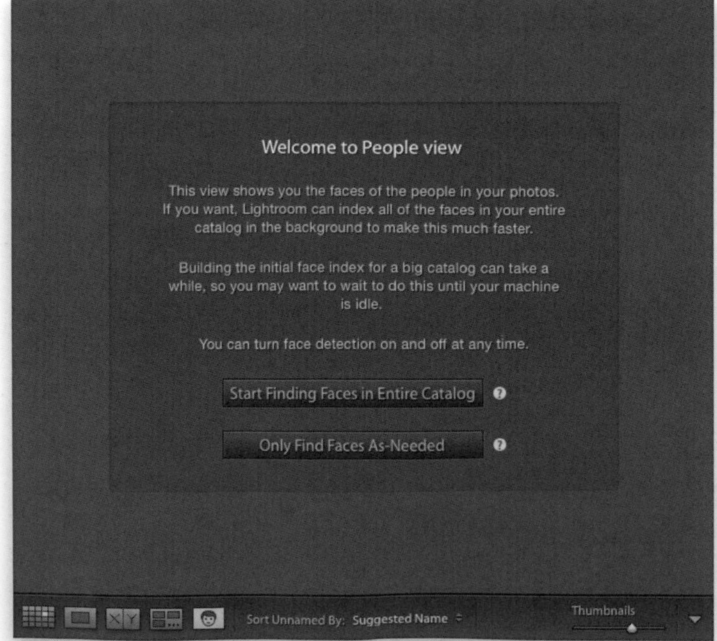

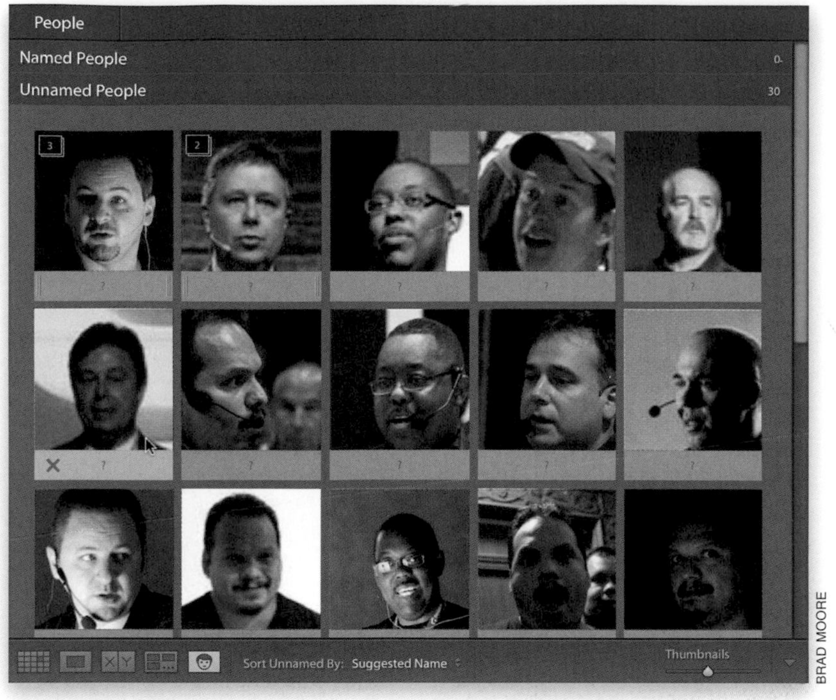

Step Three

Here's the People view of a collection of images taken at the Photoshop World Conference & Expo. It scanned the images and found these faces. The "?" below each thumbnail shows that it doesn't know who the face is (and, at this point, that makes sense—you haven't told Lightroom yet who's who.) It also found some blurry faces of people in the background in some of the photos, but since I don't know who those people are, I would just delete those. To delete faces you don't want tagged, just move your cursor over a thumbnail and an "X" icon will appear in the bottom-left corner of the thumbnail (as seen here in the first thumbnail in the second row). Just click on that "X" to remove that image from People view (it doesn't remove it from Lightroom, just from this People view).

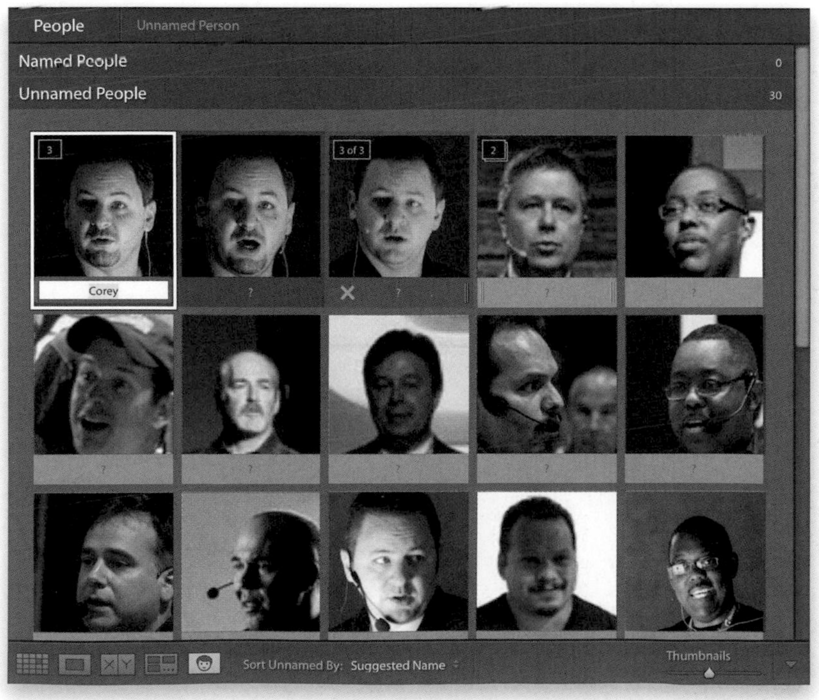

Step Four:

Lightroom not only finds which photos have faces, but if it finds similar faces, it groups them together in a stack to make the tagging process faster. Take a look in the top row here—it found three similar faces and it grouped them together (there's a "3" in the top left of the first thumbnail). The fourth thumbnail in the top row shows it found two similar faces and grouped them (there's a "2" in its top-left corner). To see which images are in a stack, click on a thumbnail with a stack icon, then press **S** on your keyboard and the stack expands (as seen here for the first stack). To collapse it, press S again. To take a peek inside the stack, press-and-hold the S key to see inside, then when you release that key, it collapses. To tag any one of those photos with a name, just move your cursor over the thumbnail and your cursor changes to a text cursor, so you can click and start typing (that's Corey Barker in the photo, so I tagged it "Corey"). To tag all three photos by just typing Corey once, select all three first, then type the name in one of the thumbnail's text fields, and it applies it to all three.

Continued

Step Five:

Once you tag a photo(s) with a name, those move to the Named People section at the top of the preview area (as seen here). Now, you might be thinking, "Hey, isn't that another photo of Corey in the bottom right? Why didn't it automatically tag that shot of Corey?" It's because facial recognition is kind of like voice recognition—it doesn't work 100% of the time (and that's being generous). There are lots of times where you'll need to kind of "help it along," which is why I mentioned that this isn't completely automatic, but that it's more like semi-automatic—you're going to be helping it out quite a bit, not just tagging the initial face, but removing a tag when it tags a person with a name that isn't theirs (just click and type in a new name), or adding a tag when it misses a face like it did here.

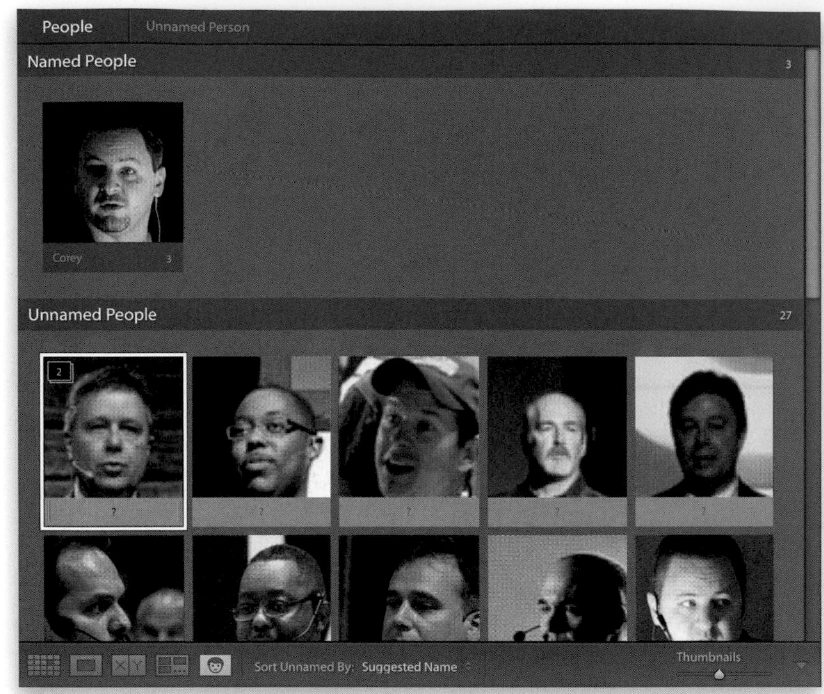

TIP: Faster Facial Indexing

Lightroom does the behind-the-scenes indexing faster if you create Smart Previews for your images because it doesn't have to search the full-size RAW images to find a face.

Step Six:

Even though it missed tagging Corey's face in that photo, it's pretty easy to fix since I've already got some photos of Corey in the Named People section—I just click on the thumbnail it missed down in the Unnamed People section and drag-and-drop it right onto Corey's thumbnail up in the Named People section (as shown here). You'll see a green plus sign appear, letting you know that you're adding the Corey tag to this face (and you'll see the number of images in the Corey stack increase by one, or however many you selected and dragged up there.

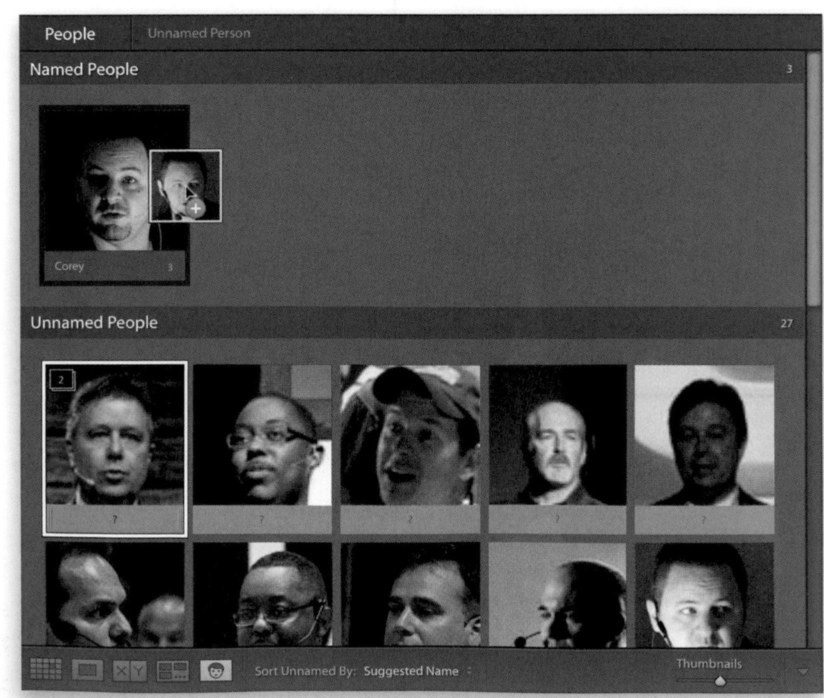

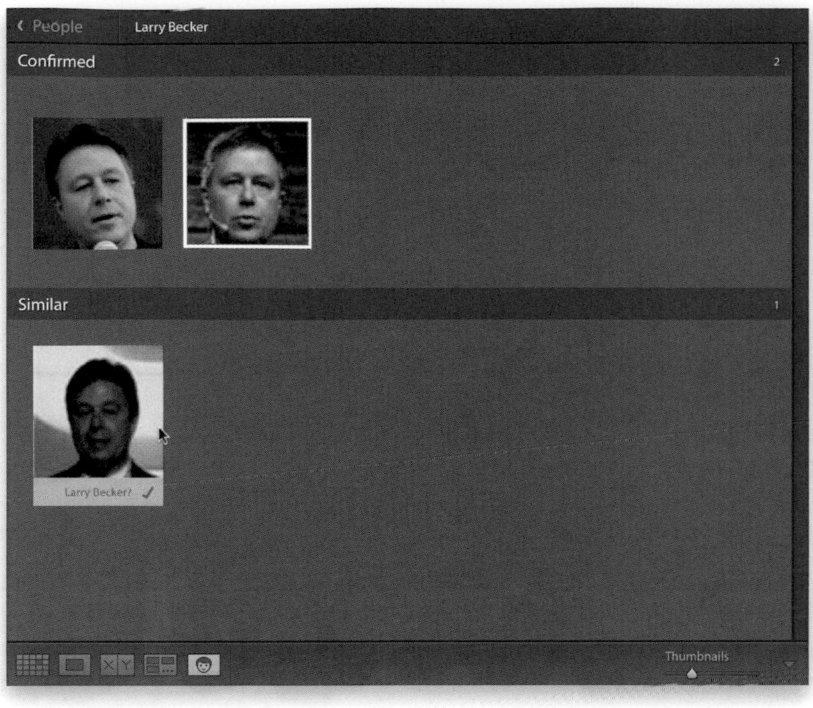

Step Seven:

If you double-click on a tagged photo in the Named People section (I recognized my buddy Larry Becker in a stack of two, so I tagged his name, and it moved up to that section) it takes you to the Confirmed section, which shows you which photos are confirmed to be that person. In the Similar section below, it shows you other photos it thinks may be Larry, but it's not certain, which is why when you move your cursor over a thumbnail, a question mark appears after Larry's name (as seen here. Expect this to happen pretty frequently). To confirm it's Larry, I'll click on the checkmark, and that image moves up to the Confirmed section.

TIP: Changing the Sort Order

By default, your Unnamed People images are sorted either alphabetically by who Lightroom thinks the person is or by the number of photos in each stack. But, you can change the sort order using the Sort Unnamed By pop-up menu in the toolbar at the bottom of the Preview area.

BRAD MOORE

Step Eight:

Once that one photo of Larry moved up to the Confirmed section, Lightroom took that information and then said, "How about these? These look similar, right?" Um. No. That's Winston, Tony, and Rich in the Similar section now. That's okay, though, because I can just return to People view by clicking on the word "People" in the top-left corner (shown circled here in red) and keep tagging other images. That's the basics, but let's dig in a little deeper.

Continued

Step Nine:

Okay, so we saw what happens when you double-click on a photo of someone that's already tagged—it takes you to Single Person view. Well, what if you double-click on someone that's untagged? Then, it'll take you to Loupe view, where it shows you the face region it mapped from, along with a text field with a question mark in it (basically asking you, "Who is this?"). This one's easy. That's my buddy RC (he's our Training Director at KelbyOne, so I see him every day), so I type in "RC," and then hit Return (PC: Enter) on my keyboard. If the face region is in the wrong place, just click-and-drag it to the right spot. And, if there are multiple people in a shot, you can delete regions you don't want tagged by clicking on the little "X" that appears when your cursor is over a face region. To return to People view, I'll just double-click on the image and RC's thumbnail will now appear under Named People. Once I did that, I now see some other thumbnails under Unnamed People asking, "Is this RC?" (as seen in the overlay).

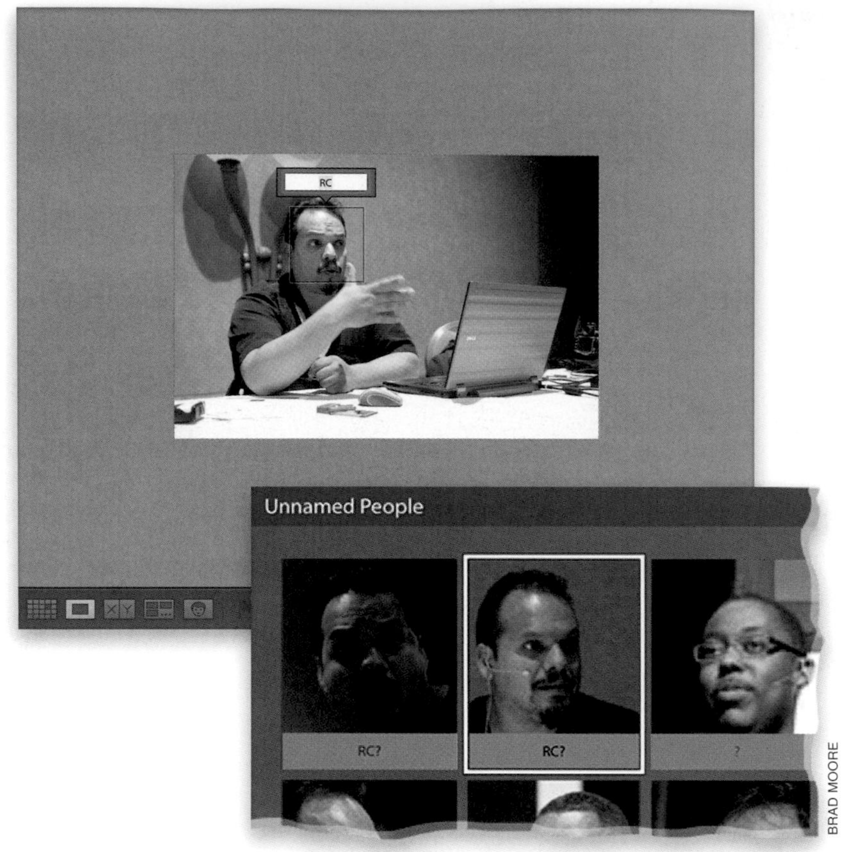

BRAD MOORE

Step 10:

Now, what do you do if Lightroom missed adding a face region to someone in a photo (without that region, it doesn't know anyone else is in the photo—like in this case, where it recognized the face on the projection screen, but missed my face and the real Amanda on stage)? Well, then, you just add a region yourself. When you double-click on a thumbnail and enter Loupe view, it automatically selects the Draw Face Region tool for you (it's down in the toolbar, just in case it didn't). Now, click-and-drag the tool out over a face it missed (like I did here, where I clicked-and-dragged over mine), and a name field appears, along with that selection. Type in a name and hit the Return (PC: Enter) key to lock it in.

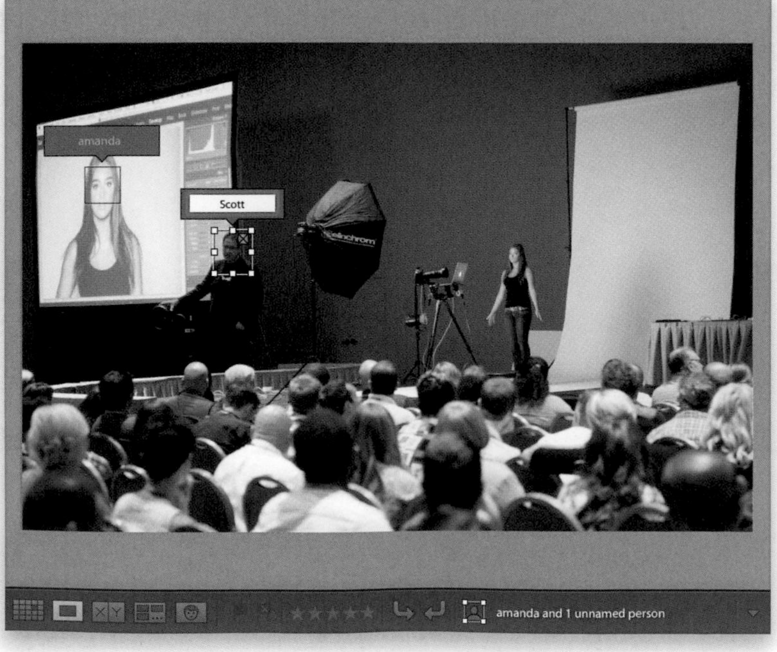

BRAD MOORE

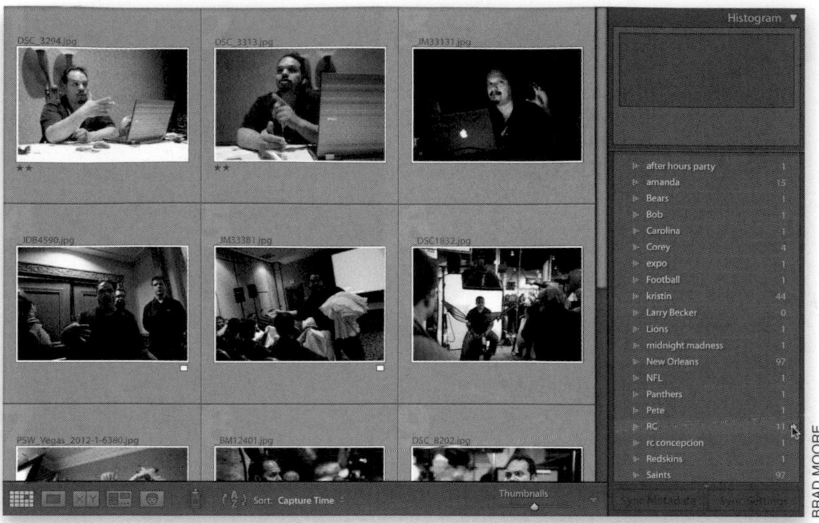

BRAD MOORE

Step 11:

Once you've got these People keywords applied, they work just like regular keywords to help you find tagged images fast. Just go the Keywording panel (in this case, we're looking for images I just tagged with "RC"), and when you move your cursor over the RC keyword, an arrow appears to its right. Click on that, and it now displays just those images that are tagged with RC.

TIP: It Only Indexes Linked Photos

The way the background indexing works for face tagging is that the images have to either be: (a) linked (meaning the hard drive with the original is connected to your computer, or the original is already on your computer and Lightroom's link to them is active), or (b) you're using Smart Previews, in which case the Smart Preview is enough for it to do its thing.

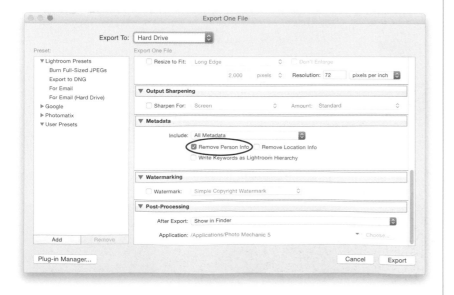

Step 12:

When you go to export an image (maybe you're saving a JPEG or TIFF), in the Export dialog, there's an option to remove the People keywords that were added during face tagging. Just go to the Metadata section and turn on the Remove Person Info checkbox (shown circled here in red).

TIP: Shortcut for Highlighting the Name Field

When you select an image in the Unnamed People section, you'll want to know this one: it's **Shift-O**.

Continued

ANOTHER TIP: Filter Keywords
Once you've assigned a People keyword to an image, of course you can use those just like regular keywords. But, you also have the added benefit of being able to see just your images tagged with People keywords in one click. You do this at the top of the Keyword List panel, right under the Filter Keywords search field—there are three choices: All (which shows all regular keywords and all People keywords), People (which shows just your People keywords—that's the having your People keywords "one click away" part), and Other (which shows everything but People keywords). By the way, if for some reason you don't see these three buttons, just click on the little left-facing arrow to the right of the Filter Keywords search field to reveal them.

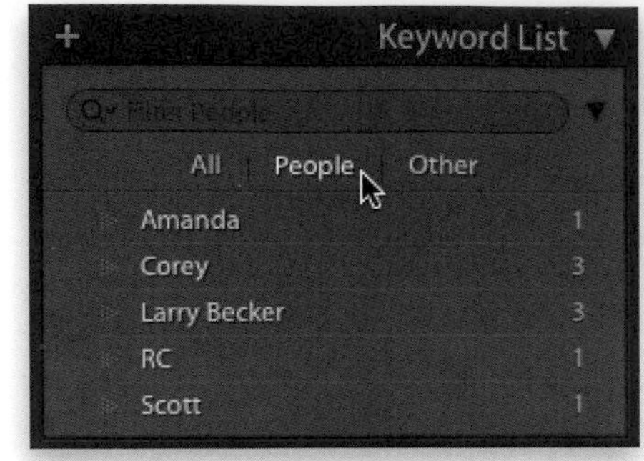

ONE MORE TIP: Finding the Location for a Face
If you're indexing your entire catalog, and an image appears in People view, and you'd like to know which folder or which collection that image appears within, just Right-click on the image's thumbnail and choose **Go to Folder in Library** or **Go to Collection** from the pop-up menu.

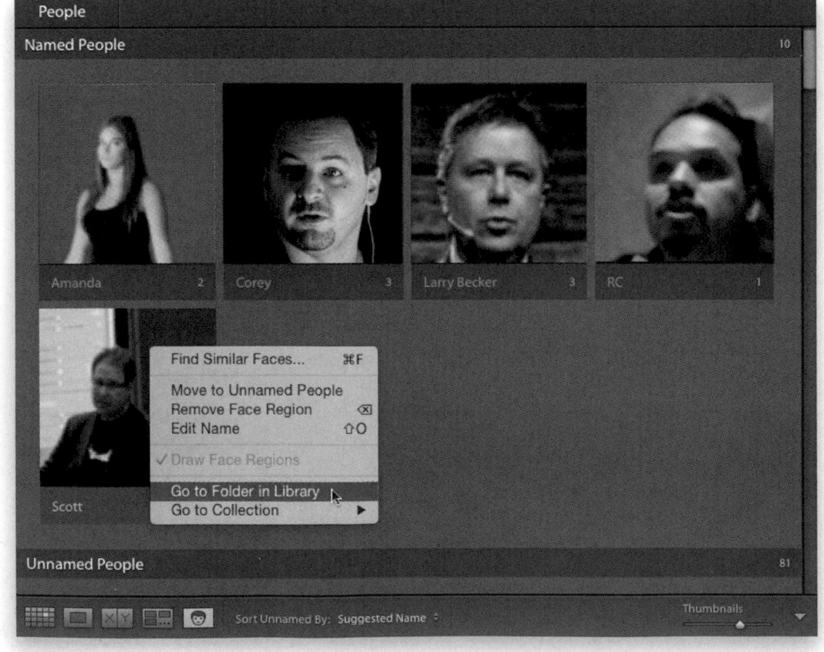

In Chapter 1, you learned how to rename photos as they're imported from your camera's memory card, but if you're importing photos that are already on your computer, they keep the same names they had (because you're just adding them to Lightroom). So, if they're still named with those cryptic names assigned by your digital camera, like "_DSC0035.jpg," here's how to rename them to something that makes sense.

Renaming Photos Already in Lightroom

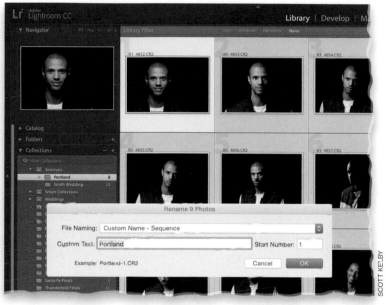

Step One:

Click on the collection of photos you want to rename, then press **Command-A (PC: Ctrl-A)** to select all of the photos in this collection. Go under the Library menu and choose **Rename Photos**, or press **F2** on your keyboard to bring up the Rename Photos dialog (shown here). Here, it gives you the same File Naming presets as the Import window does. Choose whichever File Naming preset you want to use. In this case, I chose the Custom Name – Sequence preset, which lets you enter a custom name, and then it starts the automatic numbering at 1.

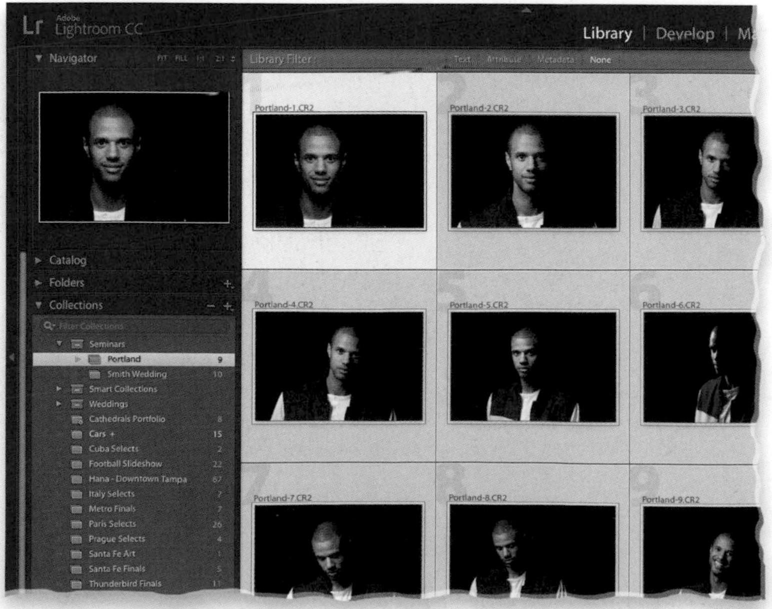

Step Two:

Now just click OK, and all the photos are renamed in an instant. This whole process takes just seconds, but makes a big difference when you're searching for photos—not only here in Lightroom, but especially outside of Lightroom in folders, in emails, etc., plus it's easier for clients to find photos you've sent them for approval.

Adding Copyright Info, Captions, and Other Metadata

Your digital camera automatically embeds all kinds of info right into the photo itself, including everything from the make and model of the camera it was taken with, to the type of lens you used, and even whether your flash fired or not. Lightroom can search for photos based on this embedded information, called EXIF data. Beyond that, you can embed your own info into the file, like your copyright info, or photo captions for uploading to news services.

Step One:

You can see the info embedded in a photo (called metadata) by going to the Metadata panel in the right side Panels area in the Library module. By default, it shows you some of the different kinds of data embedded in your photo, so you see a little bit of the stuff your camera embedded (called EXIF data—stuff like the make and model of camera you took the photo with, which kind of lens you used, etc.), and you see the photo's dimensions, any ratings or labels you've added in Lightroom, and so on, but again, this is just a small portion of what's there. To see all of just what your camera embedded into your photo, choose **EXIF** from the pop-up menu in the left side of the panel header (as shown here), or to see all the metadata fields (including where to add captions and your copyright info), choose **EXIF and IPTC**.

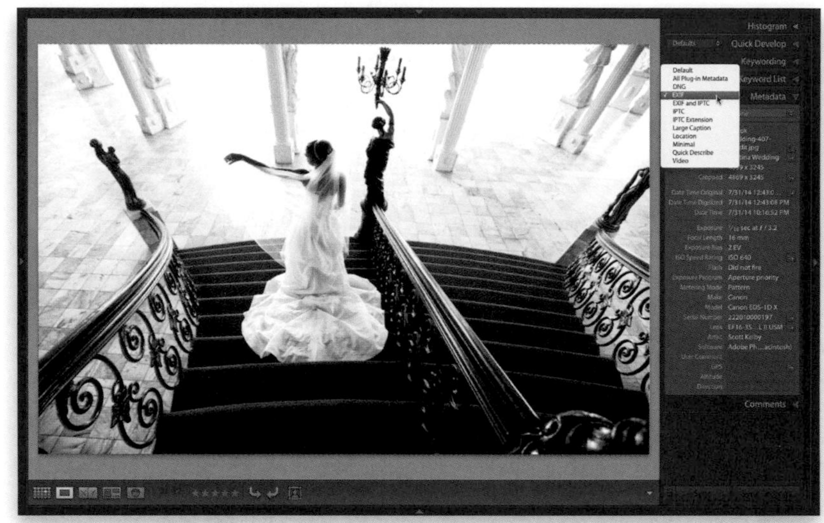

SCOTT KELBY

TIP: Get More Info or Search

While in Grid view, if you see an arrow to the right of any metadata field, that's a link to either more information or an instant search. For example, scroll down to the EXIF metadata (the info embedded by your camera). Now, hover your cursor over the arrow that appears to the right of ISO Speed Rating for a few seconds and a little message will appear telling you what that arrow does (in this case, clicking that arrow would show you all the photos in your catalog taken at 640 ISO).

Exposure 1/10 sec at f / 3.2
Focal Length 16 mm
Exposure Bias 2 EV
ISO Speed Rating ISO 640
Flash Did not fire
Exposure Program Aperture priority
Metering Mode Pattern
Make Canon
Model Canon EOS-1D X
Serial Number 222010000197
Lens EF16-35...L II USM
Artist Scott Kelby
Software Adobe Ph...acintosh)
User Comment
GPS
Altitude
Direction

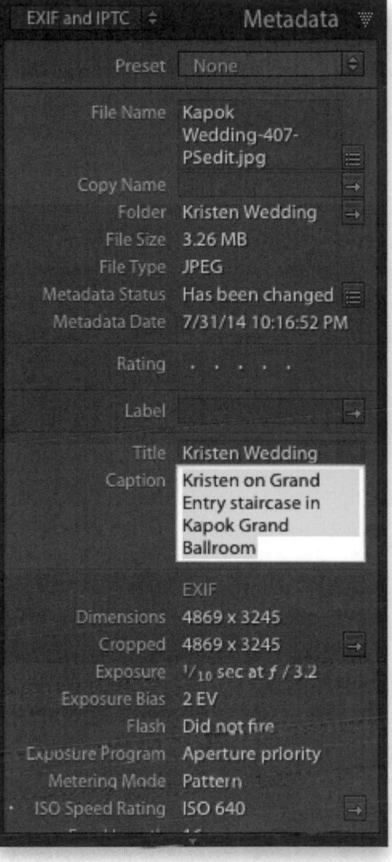

Step Two:

Although you can't change the EXIF data embedded by your camera, there are fields where you can add your own info. For example, if you need to add captions (maybe you're going to be uploading photos to a wire service), just go to the Caption field in the IPTC metadata, click your cursor inside the field, and start typing (as shown here). When you're done, just press the **Return (PC: Enter) key**. You can also add a star rating or label here in the Metadata panel, as well (though I usually don't do that here).

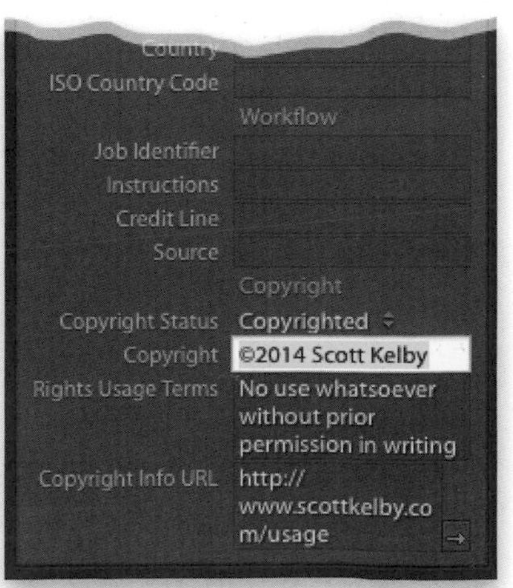

Step Three:

If you created a Copyright Metadata preset (see Chapter 1), but didn't apply it when you imported these photos, you can apply that now from the Preset menu at the top of the Metadata panel. Or if you didn't create a copyright template at all, you can add your copyright info manually. Scroll down to the bottom of the Metadata panel to the Copyright section, and just type in your copyright info (and make sure you choose Copyrighted from the Copyright Status pop-up menu). By the way, you can do this for more than one photo at a time. First, Command-click (PC: Ctrl-click) to select all the photos you want to add this copyright info to, then when you add the information in the Metadata panel, it's instantly added to every selected photo.

Note: This metadata you're adding is stored in Lightroom's database, and when you export your photos from Lightroom as either JPEGs, PSDs, or TIFFs, this metadata (along with all your color correction and image editing) gets embedded into the file itself at that moment. However, it's different when working with RAW photos (as you'll see in the next step).

Continued

Step Four:

If you want to give someone your original RAW file (maybe a client or co-worker) or if you want to use your original RAW file in another application that processes RAW images, the metadata you've added in Lightroom (including copyright info, keywords, and even color correction edits to your photo) won't be visible because you can't embed info directly into a RAW file. To get around that, all this information gets written into a separate file called an XMP sidecar file. These XMP sidecar files aren't created automatically—you create them by pressing **Command-S (PC: Ctrl-S)** before you give someone your RAW file. After you press this, if you look in the photo's folder on your computer, you'll see your RAW file, then next to it an XMP sidecar file with the same name, but with the .xmp file extension (the two files are circled here in red). These two files need to stay together, so if you move it, or give the RAW file to a co-worker or client, be sure to grab both files.

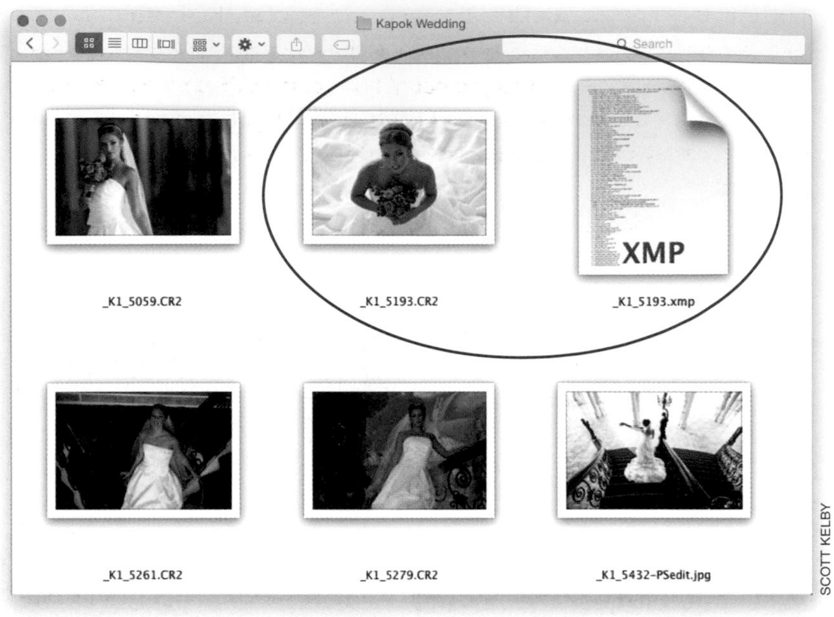

Step Five:

Now, if you converted your RAW file into a DNG file when you imported it, then when you press Command-S, it does embed the info into the single DNG file (a big advantage of DNG—see Chapter 1), so there will be no separate XMP file. There actually is a Lightroom catalog preference (choose **Catalog Settings** from the Lightroom menu on a Mac, or the Edit menu on a PC, then click on the Metadata tab, shown here) that automatically writes every change you make to a RAW file to the XMP sidecar, but the downside is a speed issue. Each time you make a change to a RAW file, Lightroom has to write that change into XMP, which slows things down a bit, so I leave the Automatically Write Changes into XMP checkbox turned off.

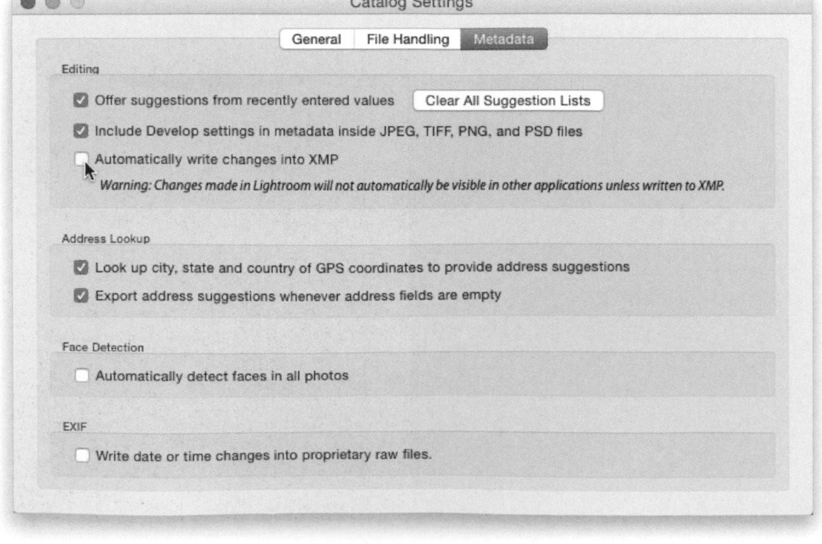

If Your Camera Supports GPS, Prepare to Amaze Your Friends

This is more of a "Wow, that's cool!" feature than an incredibly useful one, but if your camera has built-in GPS (which embeds the exact latitude and longitude of where the photo was shot), or if you bought one of the GPS units now available for digital cameras, then gather your friends around Lightroom and prepare to blow them away, because it not only displays this GPS information, but one click will actually bring up a map pinpointing the location where you took the photo. Amazing! Next thing you know they'll put a man on the moon.

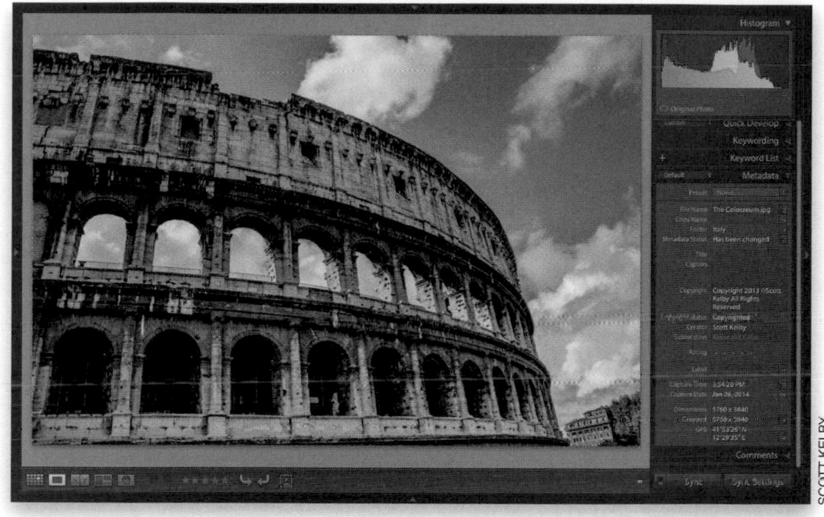

SCOTT KELBY

Step One:

Import a photo into Lightroom that was taken with a digital camera that has the built-in (or add-on) ability to record GPS data (camera companies like Ricoh, Canon, and Nikon make GPS-enabled digital cameras, and many Nikon and Canon DSLRs have a GPS-compatible connector port, which can make use of add-ons like Nikon's GP-1A unit, with a street price of around $250 [at the time of writing] or Canon's GP-E2 unit, with a street price of around $230).

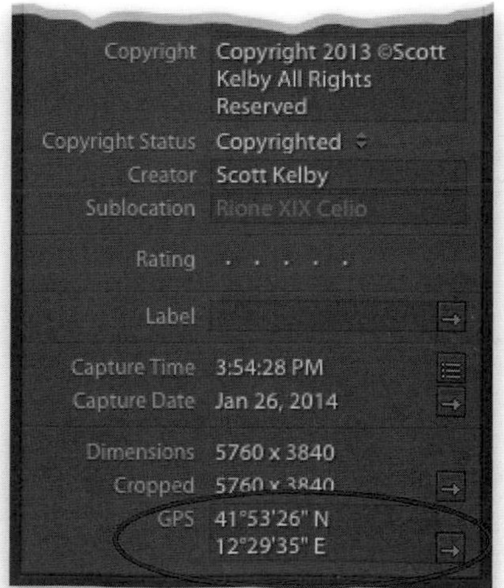

Step Two:

In the Library module, go to the Metadata panel in the right side Panels area. Near the bottom of the EXIF section, if your photo has GPS info encoded, you'll see a metadata field labeled GPS with the exact coordinates of where that shot was taken (shown circled here in red).

Continued

Step Three:

Just seeing that GPS info is amazing enough, but it's what comes next that always drops jaws whenever I show this feature live in front of a class. Click on the little arrow that appears to the far right of the GPS field (it's shown circled here in red).

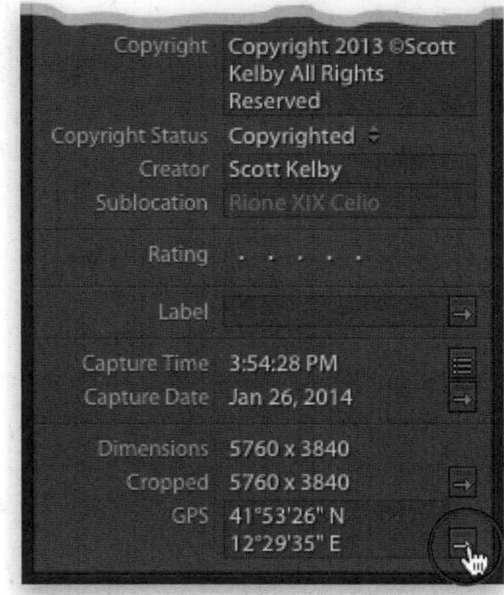

Step Four:

When you click on that little arrow, if you're connected to the Internet, Lightroom will automatically switch to the Map module and display a full-color photographic satellite image with the exact location the shot was taken pinpointed on the map (as shown here). Seriously, how cool is that!? Now, in all honesty, I've never had even a semi-legitimate use for this feature, but I've found that despite that fact, I still think it's just so darn cool. All guys do. We just can't explain why. If you want to learn more about the Map module, turn the page.

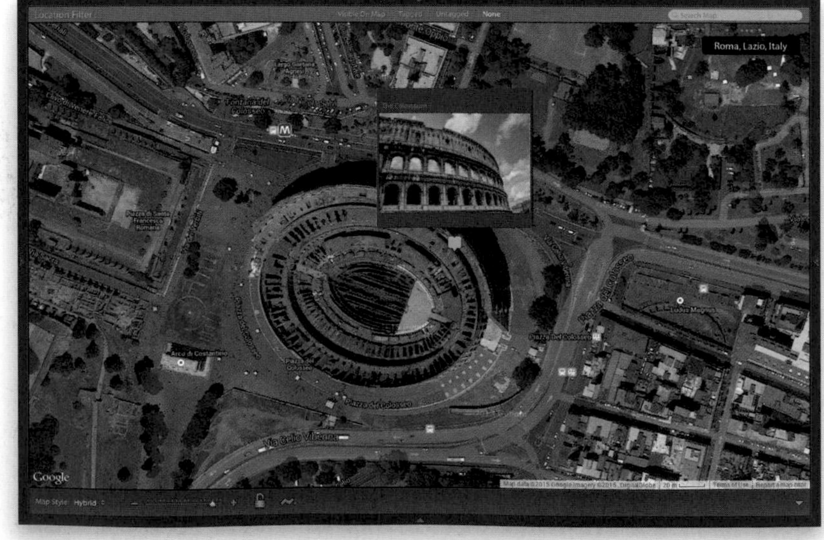

This is another feature in Lightroom that is yet another way to organize your images—a very visual one at that. Even if this doesn't sound like something you'd like to do, you've just gotta try it once, because it's so well done, it might surprise you. By the way, although this uses the Map module, I thought it belonged here in the Library chapter because it's really just another way to organize your images, which is what the Library is all about.

Organizing Your Photos on a World Map

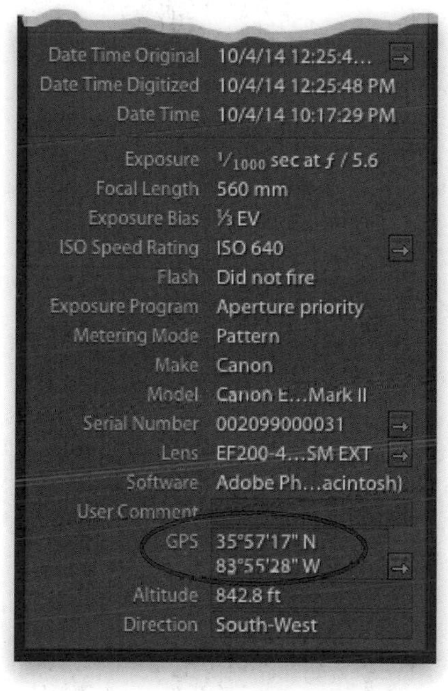

Step One:

There are two ways to organize your images using Lightroom's Map feature: (1) If you have photos that have embedded GPS coordinates in them, Lightroom will automatically add them to its world map. If you're thinking you don't have any of these, you actually probably do—in your cell phone. Most smartphones automatically embed the GPS info from where the photo was taken right into the image file itself, and if you have those in Lightroom, they're "on the map." If you don't have any GPS info in your images, you're not out of luck, because (2) you can search the map and place them on it yourself (it's simple). *Note:* To use the Map module, you'll need to be connected to the Internet, since it uses a version of Google Maps.

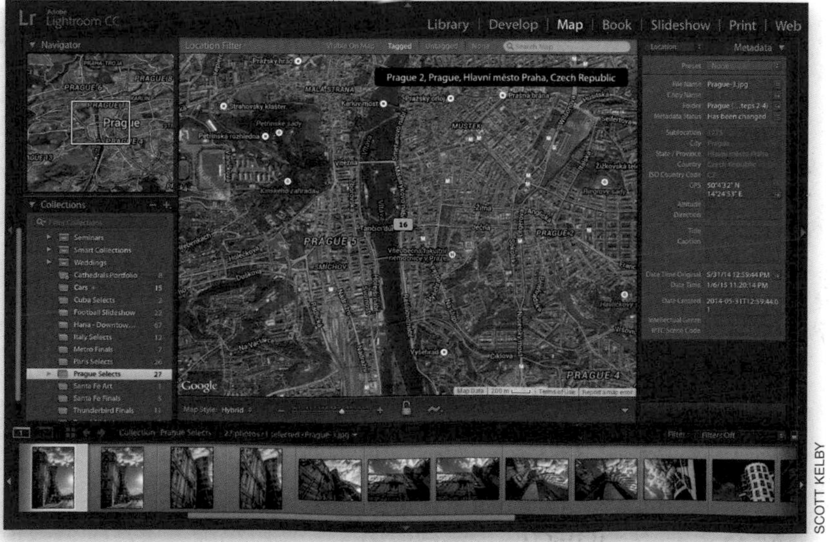

SCOTT KELBY

Step Two:

We'll look at the automated method first (which assumes that you have at least a few GPS-embedded images already in Lightroom. If you know you don't, import a few from your cell phone, so you can at least try this out). Now, click on the Map module up top, and then click on the collection of images you want to see plotted on the map. Click on your first image with GPS info (if you aren't sure which ones have it, click on Tagged in the Location Filter at the top of the preview area) and, on the map, you'll see a yellow pin marking where each photo was taken (it'll often look like one pin until you zoom in farther), and you'll see the number of photos taken right on the pin (as seen here).

Continued

Step Three:

To see the photos represented by that little pin, just hover your cursor over it and a little preview window pops up that shows you a thumbnail of the first image. (By the way, if you double-click on the pin, the preview window pops up and stays.) To see more photos, just click the left and right arrows on the sides of the preview window (or you can use the **Left/Right Arrow keys** on your keyboard). Double-click on any one of the image previews to open it in Loupe view in the Library module. If any of the photos represented by the pin is selected, the pin will be gold; if they are unselected, it will be orange. If you click on the orange map pin, it turns gold and selects all the photos. This is why this makes a pretty cool, very visual way to organize your photos.

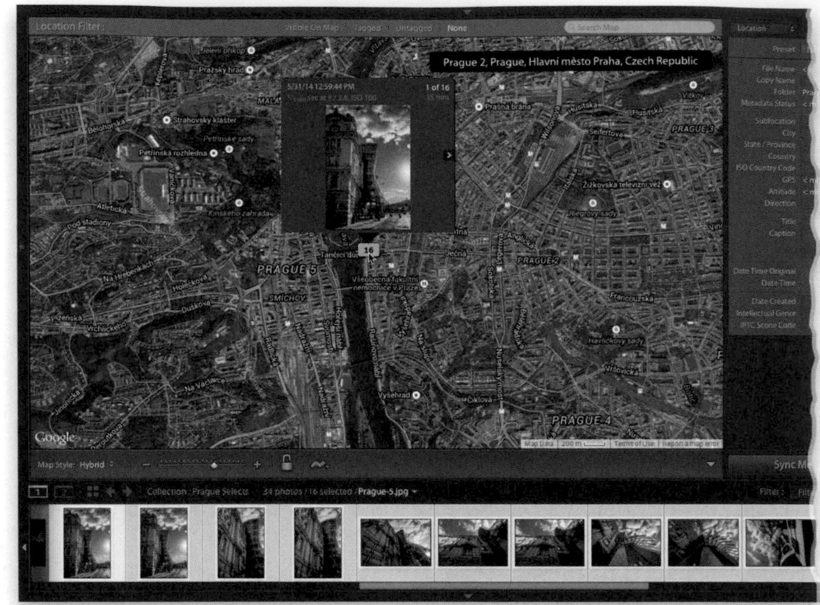

Step Four:

But, what if you don't have GPS data embedded into your photos? You can still add photos to the map—you just do it manually by searching for the location (this is easier than it sounds), and then dragging the images you want assigned to that location to the location on the map. For example, here are some more photos taken in Prague, but without any GPS data. All you do is go up to the Search field above the top-right corner of the map itself (if you don't see it, press **Command-F [PC: Ctrl-F]**), and type in "Prague, Czech Republic" and it locates Prague on the map for you. Now all you do is select all those photos from Prague in the Filmstrip, and drag-and-drop them right on the pin that represents Prague. Also, if you have images from a well-known monument, like the Charles Bridge, you can just type "Charles Bridge" (as I did here) and it will find it for you.

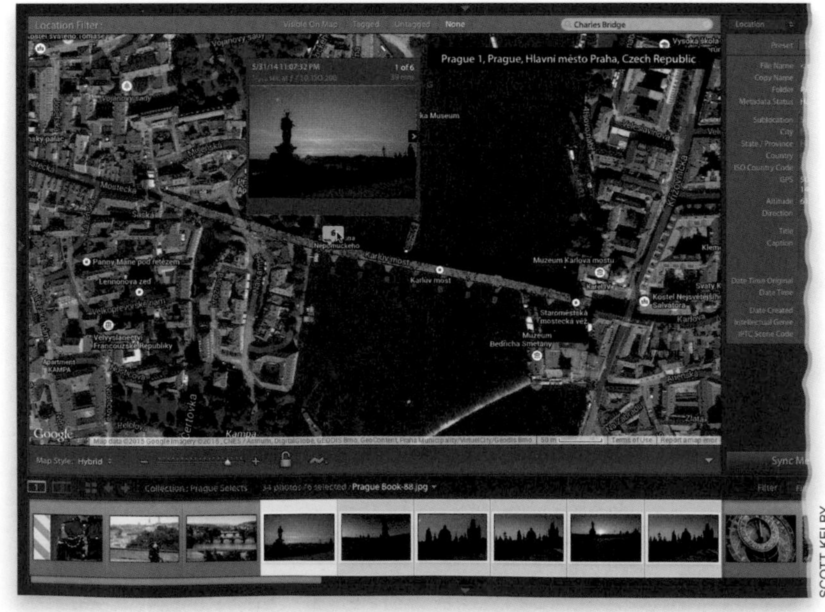

SCOTT KELBY

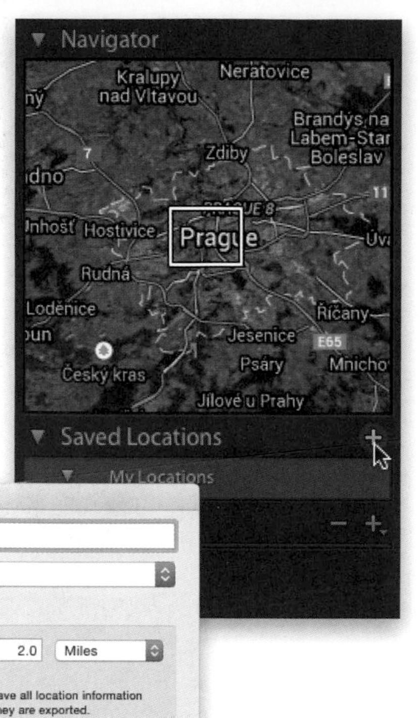

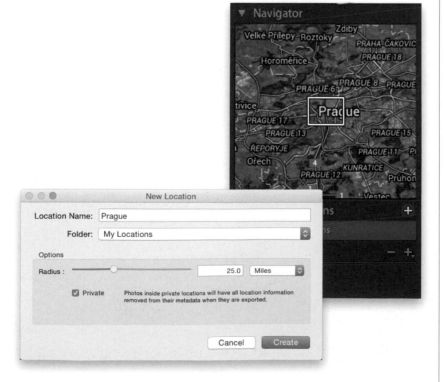

Step Five:

So, this is cool, but you might be thinking "Where's the organization part of all this?" Well, that comes once you've found a pin on the map that you might want to go back to. For example, let's say you added those photos from Prague, and you want to be able to see them anytime, without having to search the world (so to speak). Well, once you've found your Prague shots, save them as a Saved Location (kind of your "favorite shots on the map"). You do this over in the Saved Locations panel in the left side Panels area. First, click on the orange pin for Prague, then click the + (plus sign) button on the right side of the panel header to bring up the dialog you see here.

Step Six:

First, give your location a name, then use the Radius slider below it to determine how far out (in miles or kilometers) you want other nearby photos tagged to that same location. So, for example, if you shot around Prague for a week on vacation, but you took day trips to nearby areas, you could include photos taken in those other areas by setting a radius that includes them (so, if you know you stayed within 25 miles of Prague, set it at 25, and all your day trips would appear under the one pin). As you drag the slider, it visually shows the radius as a white circle on the map, kind of like a radar beacon, so you can see what's being covered (if you need to zoom in closer, use the Zoom slider in the toolbar below the map). Lastly, there's a Private checkbox, and turning this on tells Lightroom to automatically strip out your GPS data if you save these files outside of Lightroom (that way, nobody knows you were in Prague, except of course for people who see your images of Prague and say, "Hey, isn't that a shot from Prague?"). Click Create, and this location is added to your Saved Locations panel.

Continued

Step Seven:

There are a few other important Map module features you should know about. For example, if you have a GPS unit for your camera that, instead of embedding the GPS data directly into the images themselves, creates a tracklog (basically, it creates a text file with a list of everywhere you've been while your GPS was on) to be matched up to the images afterward, Lightroom lets you import that tracklog by clicking on the little chart (GPS Tracklog) icon in the toolbar below the map, which brings up a pop-up menu where you choose **Load Tracklog** (as shown here).

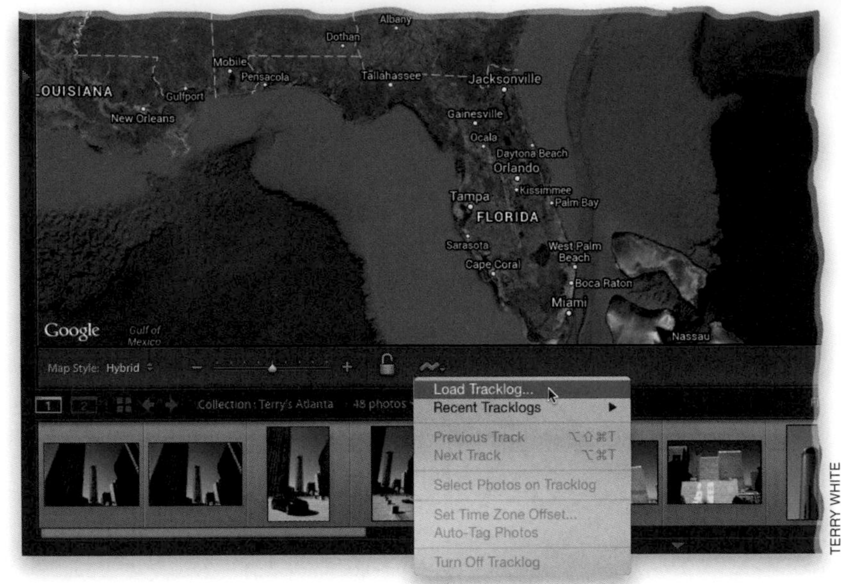

TERRY WHITE

Step Eight:

If you travel with a GPS unit that uses a tracklog, you'll need to remember to change the time to match the current time zone you're in when you're using the tracklog, because the tracklog matches up your images by comparing the time in the tracklog to the time embedded into each photo by your camera. If you don't remember to do that, when you import the tracklog into Lightroom, your time will be off by at least an hour (or more, depending on how far you strayed from home). Luckily, Lightroom figures you're like me, and that you forget to change your camera's time for the time zone that you're in, so what you do is select all the photos from your trip, then from that GPS Tracklog pop-up menu in the toolbar, choose **Set Time Zone Offset**, to bring up the dialog you see here, which lets you add (or subtract) hours to adjust for the time zone, so your time in your images and your tracklog are now in sync, and it can now match up the images and place them on the map. However, you're not done yet.

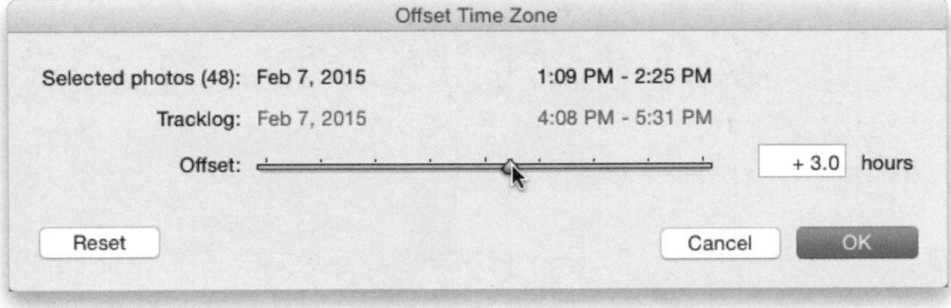

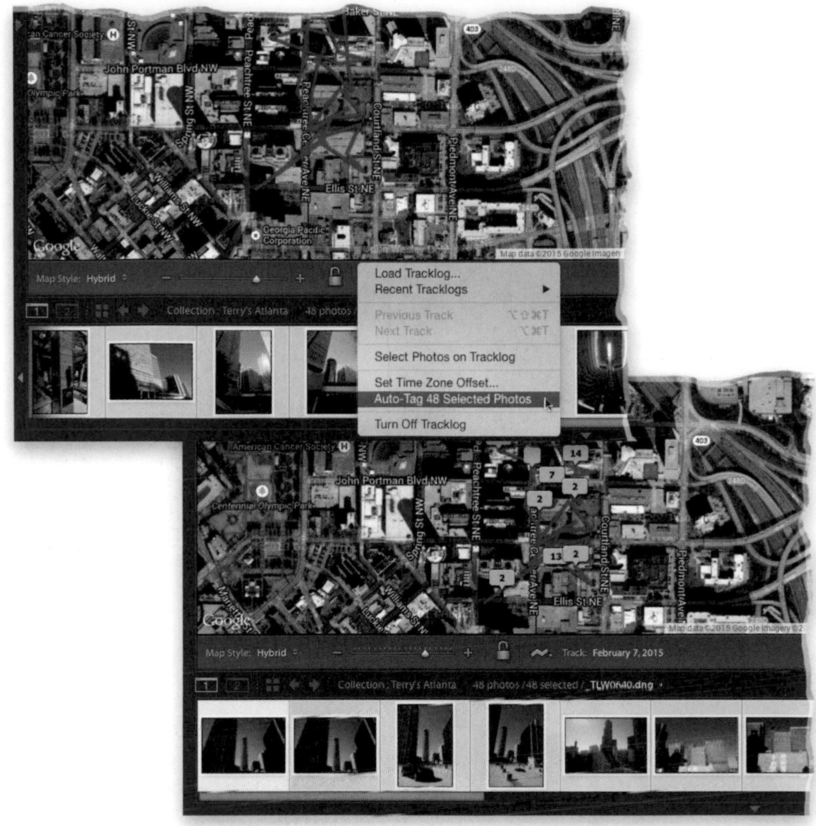

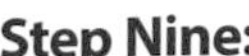

Step Nine:

So far, all you've done is change the time of the photos, but to actually have those photos move to the map, you need to select them, then go back to that same GPS Tracklog pop-up menu and choose **Auto-Tag Selected Photos**, as shown here, and now those images get added to the map.

TIP: Zooming In

To zoom in closer on a location on the map, you can just double-click on that area and it will zoom in one level tighter. You can use the Zoom slider in the toolbar, or the + (plus sign) and – (minus sign) keys on your keyboard. You can also press-and-hold the Option (PC: Alt) key, and click-and-drag out a selection around the area you want to zoom in tight on. Lastly, if your mouse has a scroll wheel, that works for zooming in/out, too.

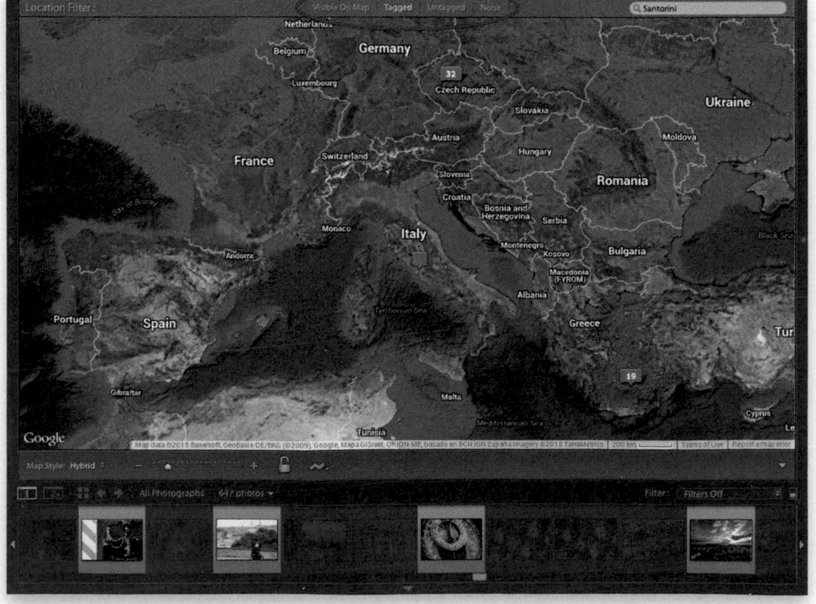

Step 10:

At the top of the map is a Location Filter, which is handy for helping you find which images in your library have been tagged on the map, or not. So, if you want to instantly see all the photos that do have embedded GPS info, go to the Library module, click on All Photographs in the Catalog panel, then go back to the Map module, and click the Tagged button (as I did here). All your tagged photos will be highlighted in the Filmstrip. To see the ones missing that data (so you can make sure they get added to the map), click the Untagged button and all the images that aren't tagged on the map appear highlighted down in the Filmstrip. To see all the images that are visible on your current map, just click the Visible On Map button. I won't insult you by explaining what None does. ;-)

Continued

Step 11:

We haven't really talked too much about the map itself, but you'll probably find it helpful to know a few options you have here. First, the default map view is Hybrid, which puts street names and other standard map data over a satellite view of the map, but you can switch to other views (like Road Map, or just the Satellite view, or Terrain) with the Map Style pop-up menu at the left end of the toolbar (as shown here, where I've chosen the Road Map view).

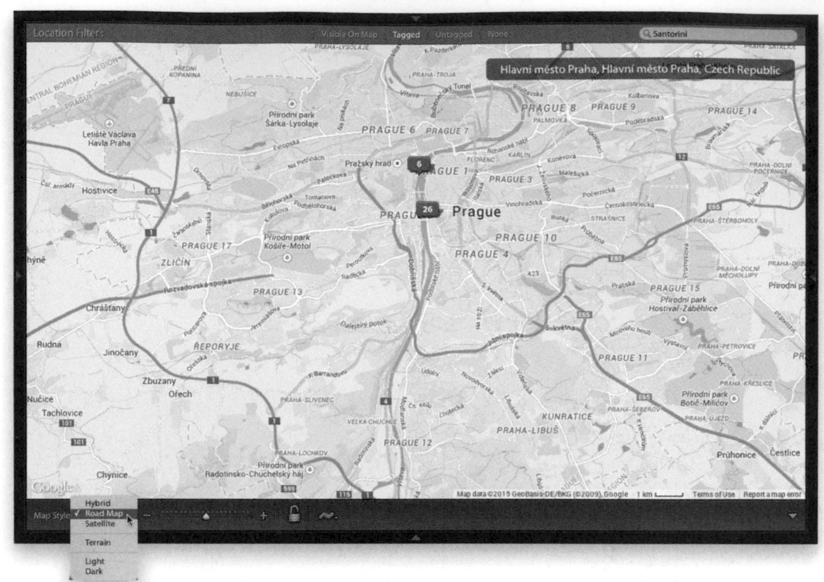

TIP: You Can Drag Pin Locations

If you're adding a pin, you can drag it anywhere you'd like. However, if you want to lock down your pins (so you don't accidentally drag one while you're moving around the map), just click the Lock Markers icon in the toolbar beneath the map.

Step 12:

I've been saving this for last, but there's actually another quick way to access your images on the map. You know those little badges that appear along the bottom of your thumbnail in the Library module's Grid view that show whether your photo has been cropped, or edited, and such? Well, there's a GPS badge, as well (it looks like a pin, as shown circled in red here), and if you click on the pin badge, it takes you to that photo's position on the map.

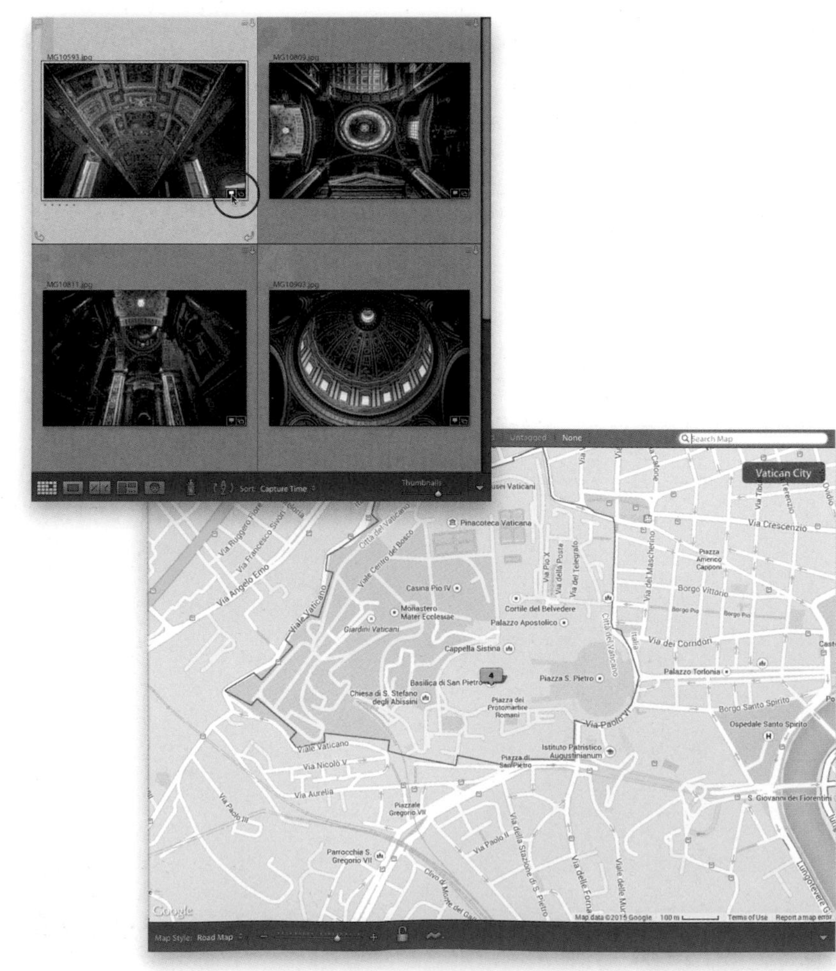

TIP: Seeing Your GPS Location

If you want to see the actual GPS data for your location (the longitude and latitude numbers), look over on the right side in the Metadata panel and it displays your GPS data there.

Okay, so to make finding our photos easier, we gave them names that make sense when we imported them, and we applied a few keywords to help make searching easier, and now we finally get the payoff: we can put our hands on exactly the photo (or photos) we need, in just seconds. This has been our goal from the very start—to set things up the right way from the beginning, so we have a fast, organized, streamlined catalog of our entire photo collection, and now we're ready to take 'er out for a spin.

Finding Photos Fast!

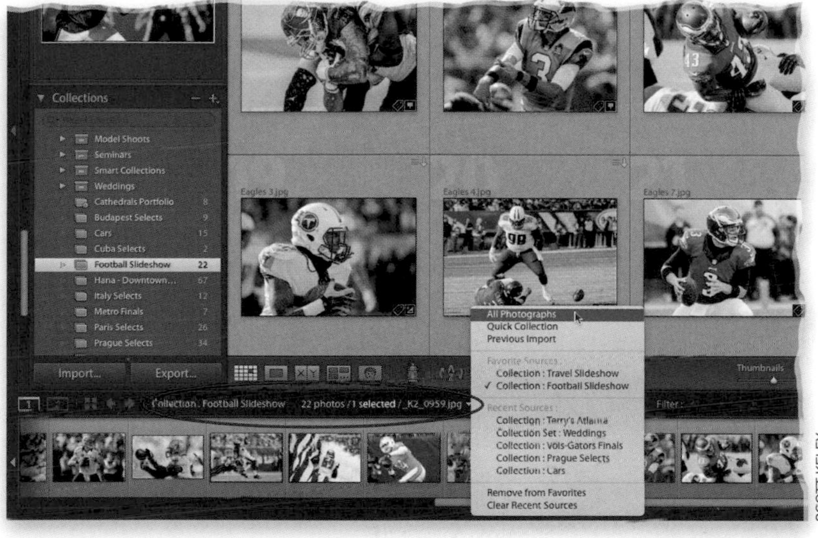

SCOTT KELEY

Step One:

Before you start searching, first you need to tell Lightroom where you want it to search. If you want to search just within a particular collection, go to the Collections panel and click on that collection. If you want to search your entire photo catalog, then look down on the top-left side of the Filmstrip and you'll see the path to the current location of photos you're viewing. Click-and-hold on that path and, from the pop-up menu that appears, choose **All Photographs** (other choices here are to search the photos in your Quick Collection, your last import of photos, or any of your recent folders or collections).

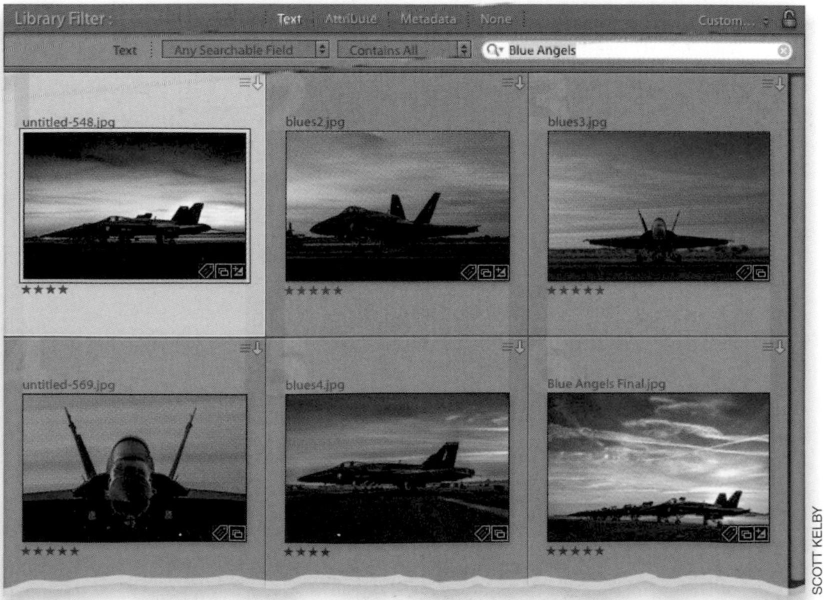

SCOTT KELBY

Step Two:

Now that you've chosen where to search, the easiest way to start a search is to use a familiar keyboard shortcut: **Command-F (PC: Ctrl-F)**. This brings up the Library Filter bar across the top of the Library module's Grid view. Chances are you're going to search by text, so just type in the word(s) you're searching for in the search field, and by default it searches for that word everywhere it can—in the photo's name, in any keywords, captions, embedded EXIF data, you name it. If it finds a match, those photos are displayed (here, I searched for "Blue Angels"). You can narrow your search using the two pop-up menus to the left of the search field. For example, to limit your search to just captions, or just keywords, choose those from the first pop-up menu.

Continued

Step Three:

Another way to search is by attribute, so click on the word Attribute in the Library Filter and those options appear. Earlier in this chapter, we used the Attribute options to narrow things down to where just our Picks were showing (you clicked on the white Pick flag), so you're already kind of familiar with this, but I do want to mention a few other things: As for the star ratings, if you click on the fourth star, it filters things so you just see any photos that are rated four stars or higher (so you'd see both your 4-star and 5-star images). If you want to see your 4-star rated images only, then click-and-hold on the ≥ (greater than or equal to) sign that appears to the immediate right of the word Rating, and from the pop-up menu that appears, choose **Rating Is Equal to**, as shown here.

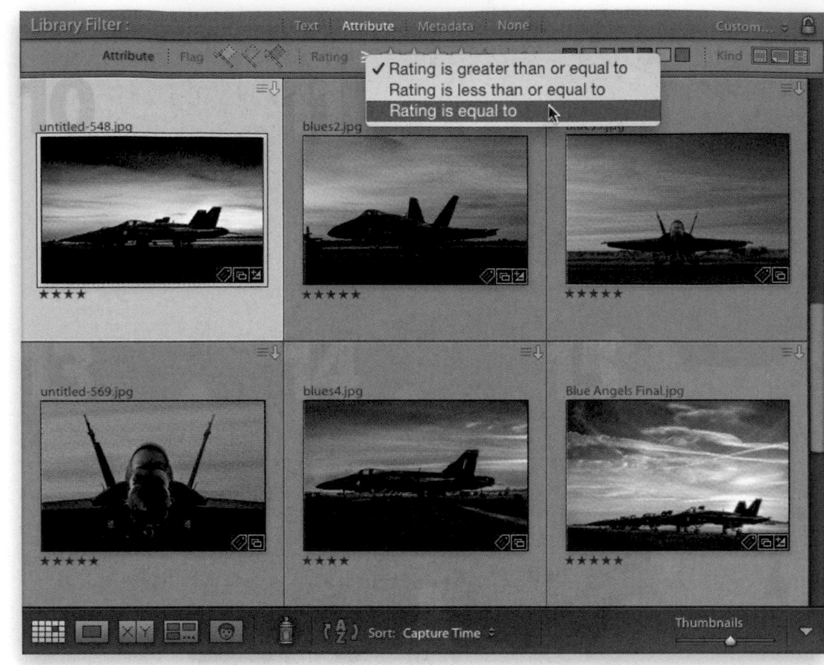

Step Four:

Besides searching by text and attributes, you can also find the photos you're looking for by their embedded metadata (so you could search for shots based on which kind of lens you used, or what your ISO was set to, or what your f-stop was, or a dozen other settings). Just click on Metadata in the Library Filter, and a series of columns will pop down where you can search by date, camera make and model, lenses, or labels (as shown here). However, I have to tell you, if the only hope you have of finding a photo is trying to remember which lens you used the day you took the shot, you've done a really lame job of naming and/or keywording your shots (that's all I'm sayin'). This should truly be your "search of last resort."

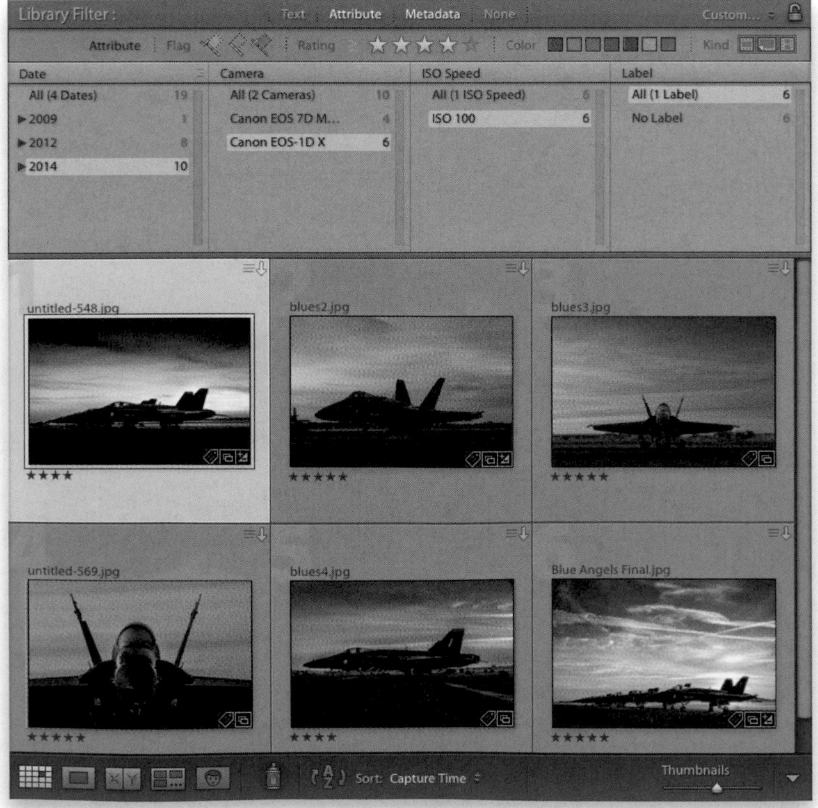

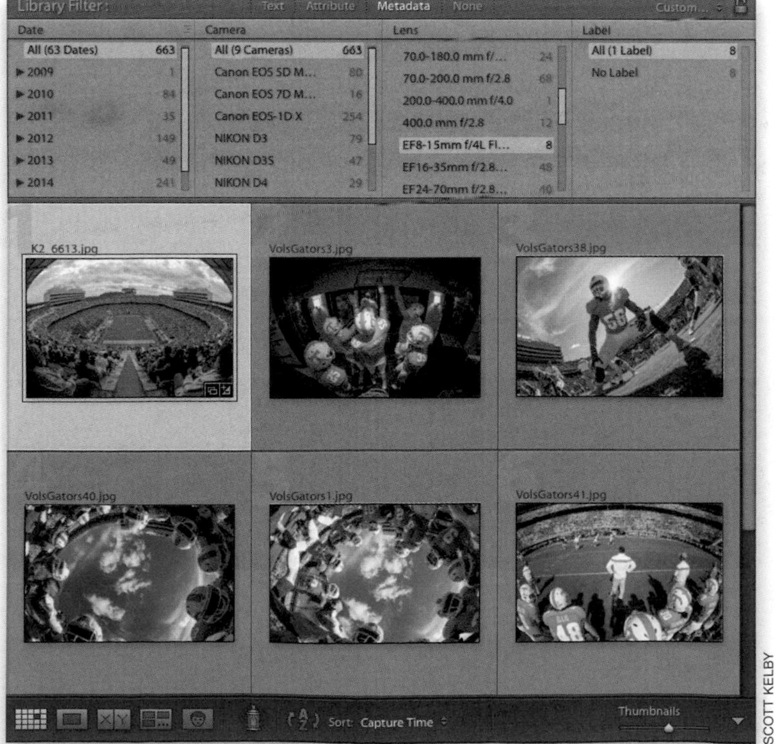

Step Five:

Again, there are four default ways to search using the Metadata options:

By Date: If you think you can remember which year the photo you're looking for was taken, in the Date column, click on that year, and you'll see just those photos appear. If you want to narrow it down further, click the right-facing arrow to the left of the year, and you'll find each month, and then you can drill down to the individual days (as shown here).

By Camera Body: If you don't remember the year you took the photo, but you know which camera body you took the shot with, then just go straight to the Camera column and click directly on the camera (you'll see how many photos you took with that camera listed to the right of the camera body). Click on the body, and those photos appear.

By Lens: If the shot you took was a wide angle, then go right to the Lens column, click on the lens you think it was taken with, and those images will appear. This helps if you know the photo was taken with a speciality lens, like a fisheye—you can just click right on that lens (as shown here), and you'll probably find the shot you're looking for pretty quickly. By the way, you don't have to start with the Date column, then Camera, then Lens. You can click on any column you'd like, in any order, as all of these columns are always "live."

By Label: The last column seems somewhat redundant to the Attribute search options, but it actually is helpful here if you've found 47 photos taken with a fisheye, and you know you have the best ones marked with a label. This will narrow things down even further.

Continued

Step Six:

Let's say you don't really ever need to search by date, but you do a lot of low-light shooting, so instead, searching by ISO might be more helpful. Luckily, you can customize each column, so it searches for the type of metadata you want, by clicking on the column header and choosing a new option from the pop-up menu (as shown here, where I've chosen ISO Speed for the first column). Now, all my ISOs will be listed in the first column, so I know to click on 800, 1600, or higher to find my low-light shots. Another helpful choice (for me anyway) is to set one column to Creator (the copyright info), so I can quickly find shots in my catalog taken by other people with just one click.

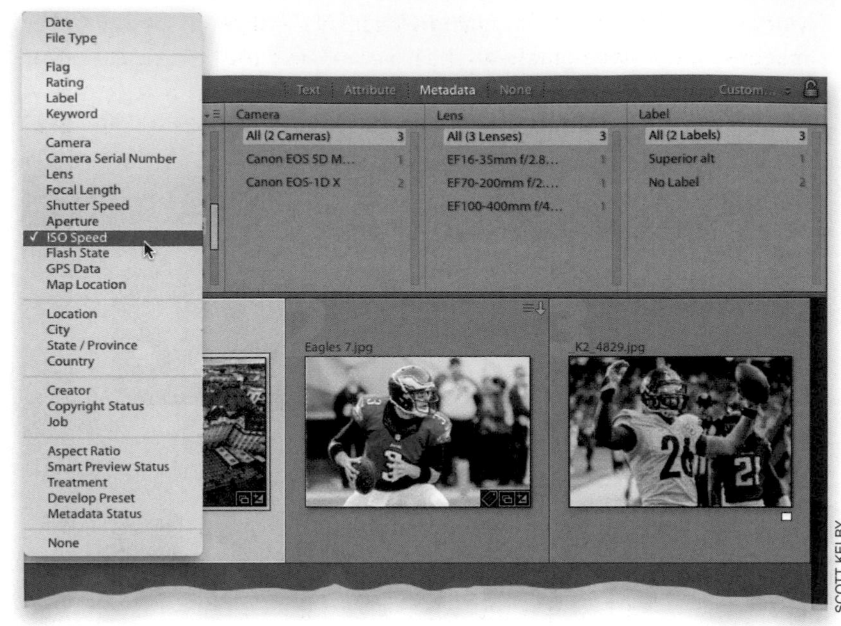

Step Seven:

Want to take things up one last notch? (Sure ya do!) If you Command-click (PC: Ctrl-click) on more than one of the three search options in the Library Filter, they're additive (go ahead, Command-click on Text, then Attribute, then Metadata, and they just pop down one after another). Now you can search for a photo with a specific keyword (in this case, "Vols") that's marked as a Pick, with a Red label, that was taken at ISO 400, with a Canon EOS 1-DX, using a 16–35mm lens, and is in Landscape (wide) orientation (the result of that search is shown here). Ya know what else is cool? You can even save these criteria as a preset. You have to admit, although you shouldn't have to resort to this type of metadata search in the first place, it's still really amazing.

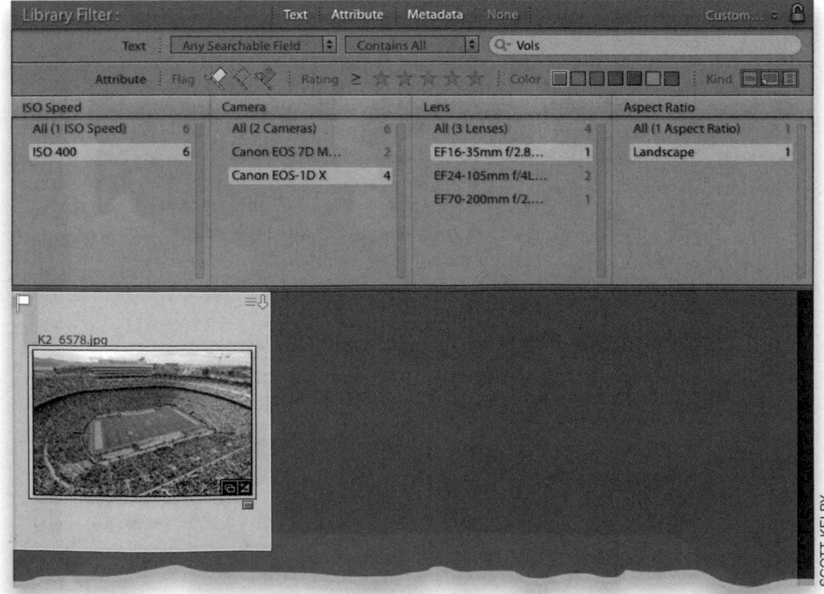

Creating and Using Multiple Catalogs

Lightroom is designed for managing a library of literally tens of thousands of images—I know photographers who have well over 100,000 images in their catalog, and Lightroom can handle it, no sweat. However, once your catalog gets that large, Lightroom can start to take a performance hit, so you might want to think about creating a second catalog (you can create more than one catalog and switch between them any time you like), so you can keep your catalog sizes manageable and Lightroom running at full speed.

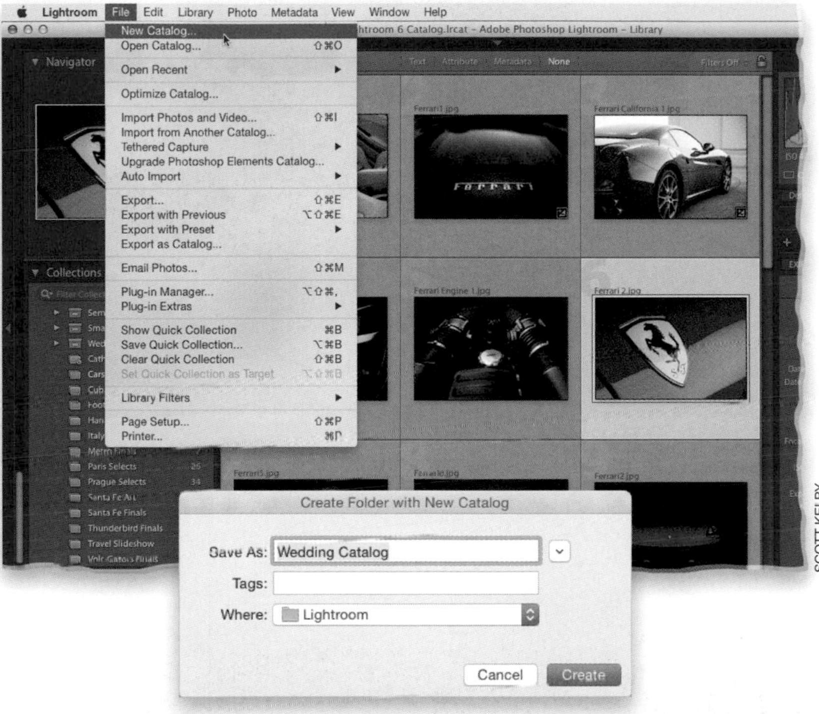

SCOTT KELBY

Step One:

So far, we've been working with a catalog of photos that was created for you when you launched Lightroom for the first time. However, if you wanted to, for example, create a separate catalog for managing all your travel photos, family photos, or sports photos, then you'd go under Lightroom's File menu and choose **New Catalog** (as shown here). This brings up the Create Folder with New Catalog dialog. Give your catalog a simple name (like "Wedding Catalog") and pick a place to save it to (just to keep things straight, I save all of my catalogs in my Lightroom folder, so I always know where they are).

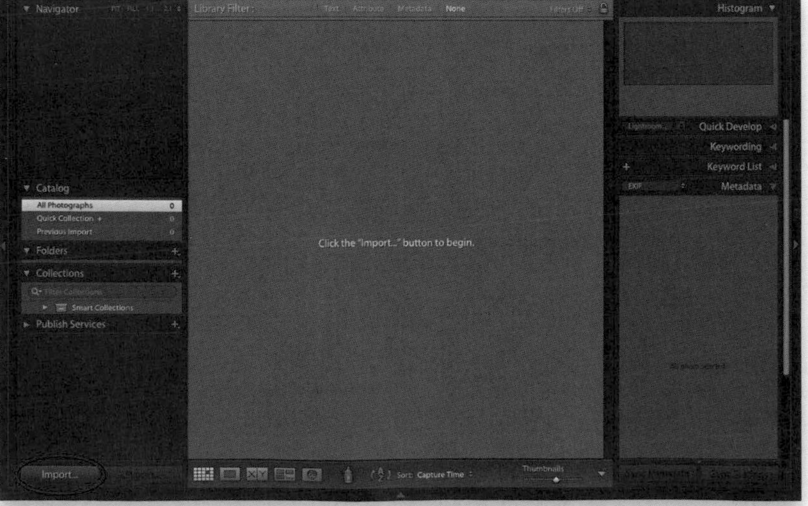

Step Two:

Once you click the Create button, Lightroom closes your database, then Lightroom itself quits and automatically relaunches with your brand new, totally empty catalog, with no photos in it whatsoever (as seen here). So, click on the Import button (near the bottom-left corner), and let's bring in some wedding photos to get the ball rolling.

Continued

Step Three:

You know what to do from here, as far as building a catalog of images (import more photos, add keywords, make your collections, etc., just like always). When you're done working with this new Wedding catalog, and you want to return to your original main catalog, just go under the File menu, under Open Recent, and choose your original catalog, as shown here. Click Relaunch in the Open Catalog dialog and Lightroom will save your wedding photos catalog, and once again, quit and relaunch with your main catalog. I know it's kinda weird that it has to quit and relaunch, but luckily it's pretty darn quick about it.

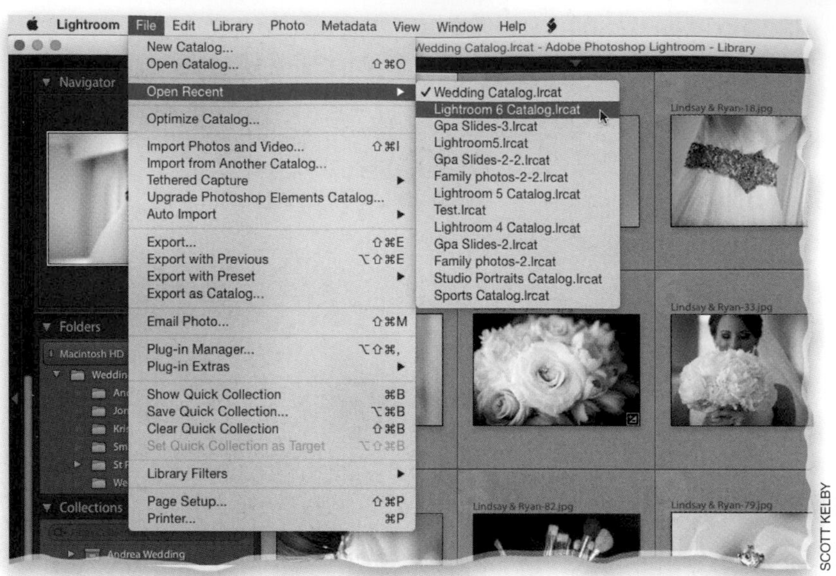

Step Four:

You can actually choose which catalog you want to work with when you launch Lightroom. Just press-and-hold the **Option (PC: Alt) key** while you launch Lightroom, and it will bring up the Select Catalog dialog you see here, where you can choose which catalog you want it to open. *Note:* If you want to open a Lightroom catalog you created, but it doesn't appear in the Select a Recent Catalog to Open section (maybe you didn't save it in your Lightroom folder when you created it or you haven't opened it recently), then you can click the Choose a Different Catalog button at the bottom left of the dialog and locate the catalog using a standard Open dialog. Also, I know I probably don't have to say this, but if you want to create a brand new empty catalog, just click the Create a New Catalog button.

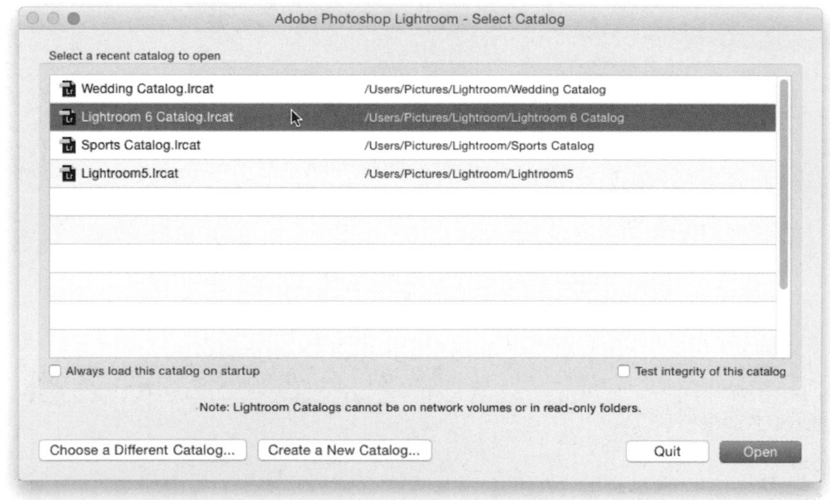

TIP: Always Launch the Same Catalog

If you always want to launch Lightroom with a particular catalog, click on the catalog in the Select Catalog dialog, then turn on the Always Load This Catalog on Startup checkbox (which appears beneath your catalog list).

From Laptop to Desktop: Syncing Catalogs on Two Computers

If you're running Lightroom on a laptop during your location shoots, you might want to take all the edits, keywords, metadata, and of course the photos themselves, and add them to the Lightroom catalog on your studio computer. It's easier than it sounds: basically, you choose which catalog to export from your laptop, then you take the folder it creates over to your studio computer and import it—Lightroom does all the hard work for you, you just have to make a few choices about how Lightroom handles the process.

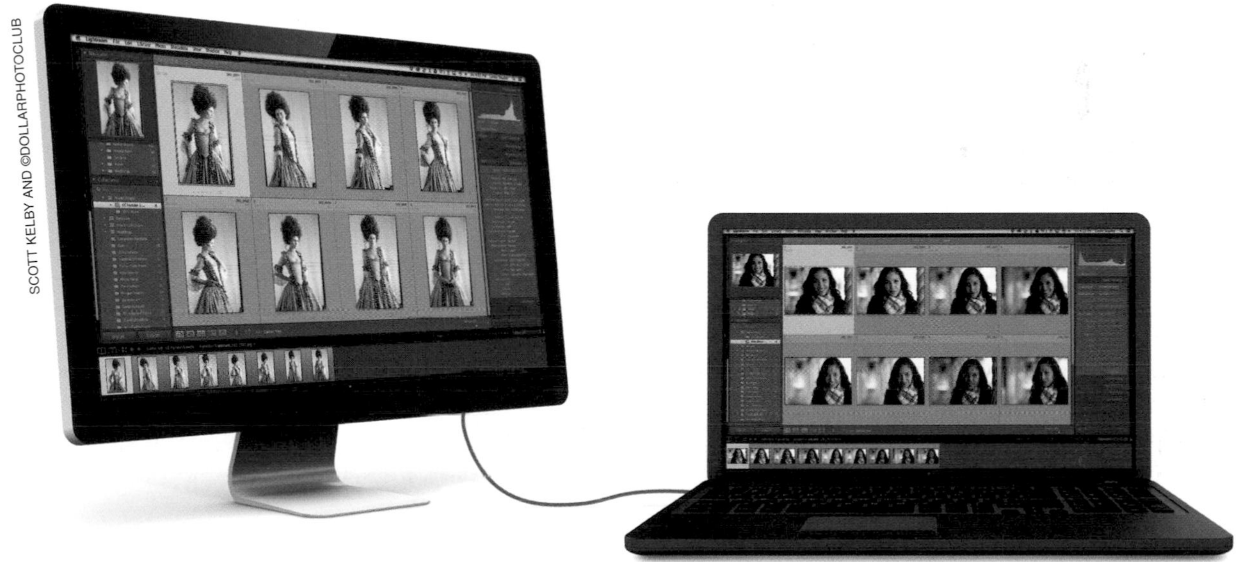
SCOTT KELBY AND ©DOLLARPHOTOCLUB

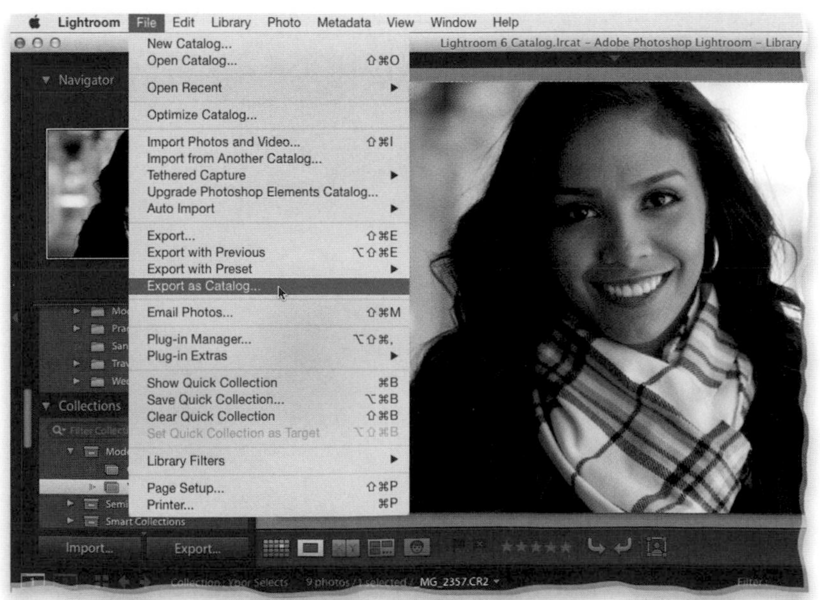

Step One:

Using the scenario described above, we'll start on the laptop. The first step is to decide whether you want to export a folder (all the imported photos from your shoot), or a collection (just your Picks from the shoot). In this case, we'll go with a collection, so go to the Collections panel and click on the collection you want to merge with your main catalog back in your studio. (If you had chosen a folder, the only difference would be you'd go to the Folders panel and click on the folder from that shoot instead. Either way, all the metadata you added, and any edits you made in Lightroom, will still be transferred over to the other machine.)

Step Two:

Now go under Lighroom's File menu and choose **Export as Catalog** (as shown here).

Continued

Step Three:

When you choose Export as Catalog, it brings up the Export as Catalog dialog (shown here), where you type in the name you want for your exported catalog at the top, but there are some very important choices you need to make at the bottom. By default, it assumes that you want to include the previews that Lightroom created when you imported the photos into Lightroom, and I always leave this option turned on (I don't want to wait for them to render all over again when I import them into my studio computer). You can also choose to have it build and include Smart Previews. If you turn on the top Export Selected Photos Only checkbox, then it will only export photos in that collection that you had selected before you chose Export as Catalog. But perhaps the most important choice is the second checkbox—Export Negative Files. With this off, it only exports previews and metadata, it doesn't really export the actual photos themselves, so if you do indeed want to export the actual photos (I always do), then turn the second checkbox on.

Step Four:

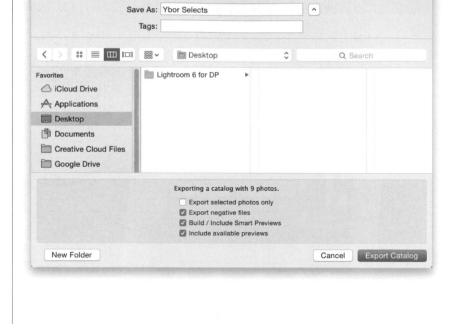

When you click the Export Catalog button, it exports your catalog (it usually doesn't take very long, but of course the more photos in your collection or folder, the longer it will take), and when it's done exporting, you'll see the folder on your computer that you exported (as seen here). I usually save this file to my desktop, because the next step is to copy it onto an external hard drive, so you can move this folder full of images over to your studio computer. So, go ahead and copy this folder onto an external hard drive now.

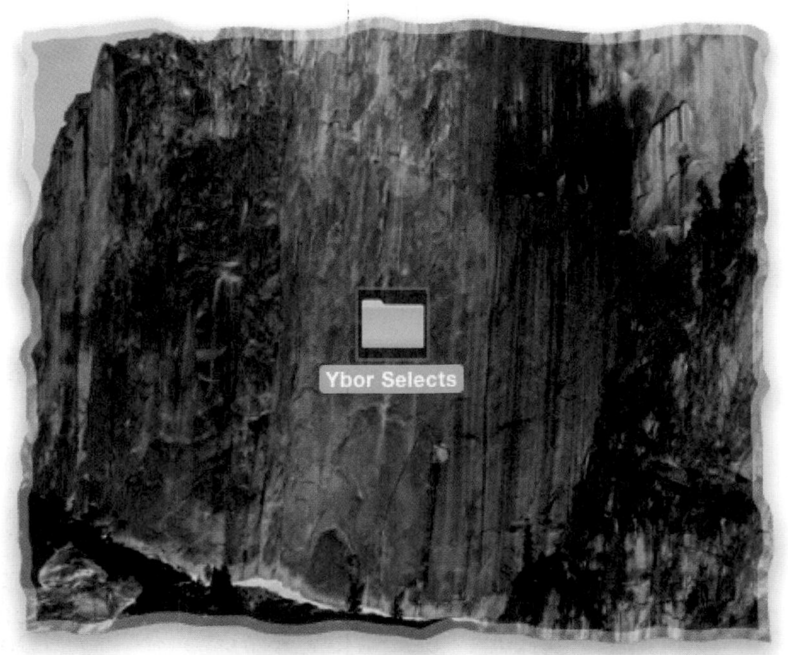

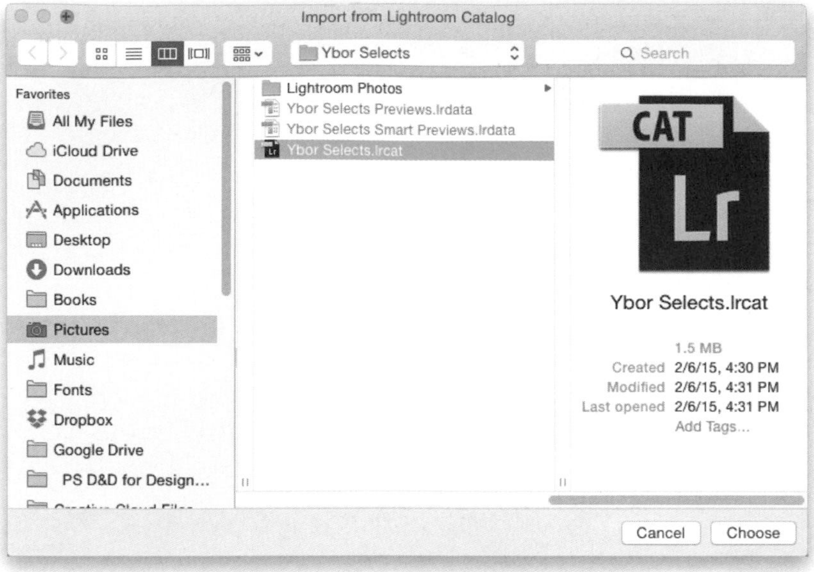

Step Five:

When you get to your studio, connect your hard drive to your studio computer, and copy that folder to the location where you store all your photos (which should be that Lightroom Photos folder we created in Chapter 1). Now, on your studio computer, go under Lightroom's File menu and choose **Import from Another Catalog** to bring up the dialog you see here. Navigate to that folder you copied onto your studio computer, and then inside that folder, click on the file that ends with the file extension LRCAT (as shown here), and click the Choose button. By the way, if you look at the capture shown here, you can see that Lightroom created four items inside this folder: (1) a file that includes the previews, (2) a file that includes the Smart Previews, (3) the catalog file itself, and (4) a folder with the actual photos.

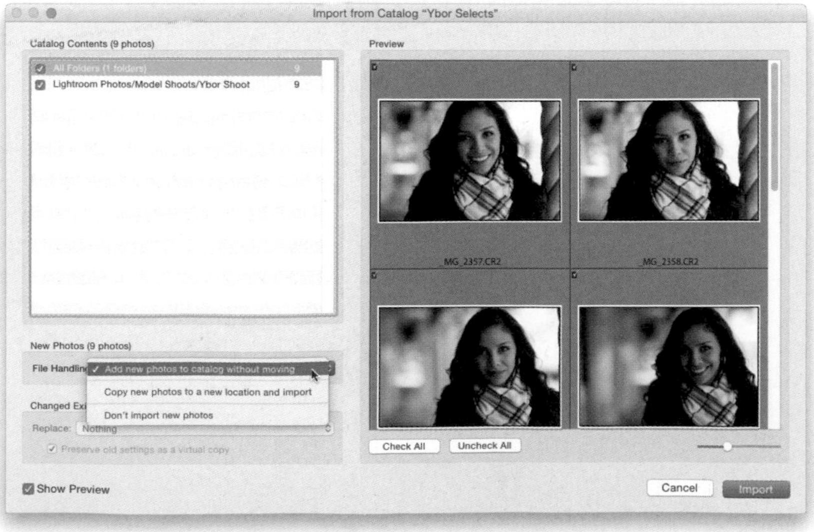

Step Six:

When you click the Choose button, it brings up the Import from Catalog dialog (seen here). Any photos in the Preview section on the right that have a checkbox turned on beside them will be imported (I always leave all of these turned on). In the New Photos section on the left is a File Handling pop-up menu. Since we already copied the photos into the proper folder on our studio computer, I'm using the default setting which is Add New Photos to Catalog Without Moving (as shown here), but if you want to copy them directly from your hard drive into a folder on your computer, you could choose the Copy option instead. There's a third option, but I have no idea why at this point you'd choose to not import the photos. Just click Import, and these photos will appear as a collection, with all the edits, keywords, etc., you applied on your laptop.

SCOTT KELBY

Continued

Backing Up Your Catalog (This Is VERY Important)

All the changes, edits, keywords, etc., you add to your photos in Lightroom are stored in your Lightroom catalog file, so as you might imagine, this is one incredibly important file. Which is also why you absolutely need to back up this catalog on a regular basis, because if for some reason or another your catalog database gets corrupted—you're completely hosed. (Of course, unless you backed up your catalog, in which case you're not hosed at all.) The good news is Lightroom will back up this catalog database for you, but you have to tell it to. Here's how:

Step One:

Start by going under the Lightroom (PC: Edit) menu and choosing **Catalog Settings**. When the Catalog Settings dialog appears, click on the General tab up top (shown highlighted here). At the bottom of this dialog is a Backup section, and a Back Up Catalog pop-up menu with a list of options (shown here) for having Lightroom automatically back up your current catalog. Choose how often you want that to be, but I recommend that you choose **Once a Day, When Exiting Lightroom**. That way, it backs up each time you're done using Lightroom, so if for some reason the catalog database becomes corrupt, you'd only lose a maximum of one day's editing.

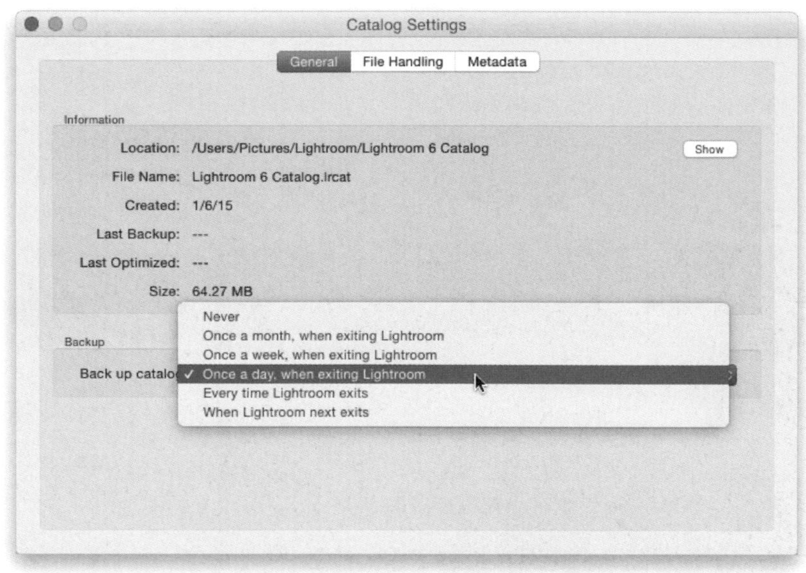

Step Two:

The next time you quit Lightroom, a dialog will appear reminding you to back up your catalog database. Click the Back Up button (as shown here), and it does its thing. It doesn't take long at all, so don't be tempted to click Skip Until Tomorrow or Skip This Time (those are sucker bets). By default, these catalog backups are stored in separate subfolders inside the Backup folder, which lives inside your Lightroom folder. To be safe, in case your computer crashes, you should really store your backups on an external hard drive, so click the Choose button, navigate to your external drive, then click Choose (PC: OK).

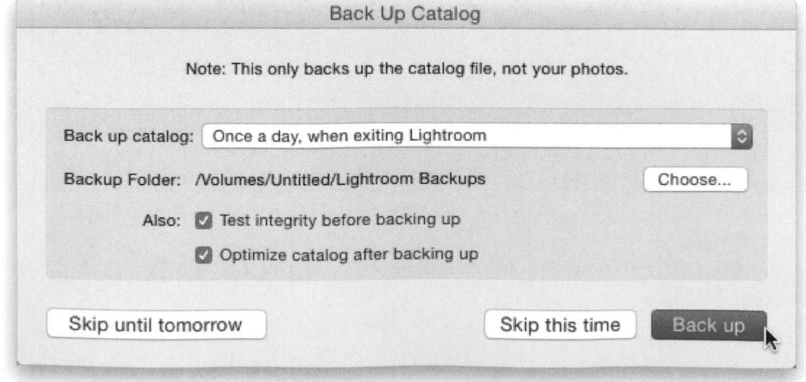

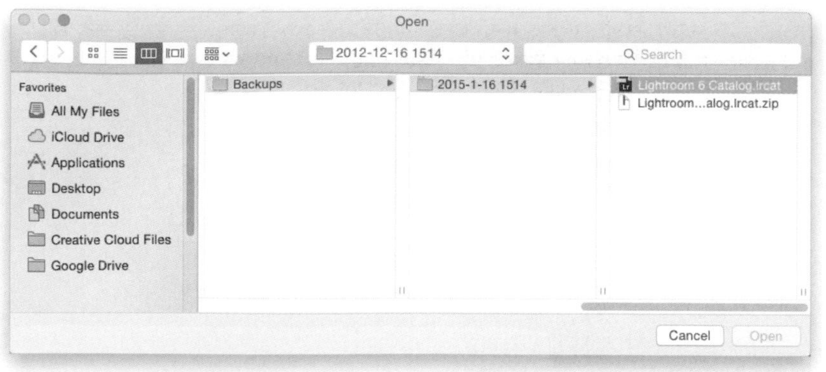

Step Three:

So now that you've got a backup of your catalog, what happens if your catalog gets corrupted or your computer crashes? How do you restore your catalog? First you launch Lightroom, then you go under the File menu and choose **Open Catalog**. In the Open dialog, navigate to your Backups folder (wherever you chose to save it in Step Two), and you'll see all your backups listed in folders by date and 24-hour time. Click on the folder for the date you want, then inside, click on the LRCAT file (that's your backup), click the Open button, and you're back in business.

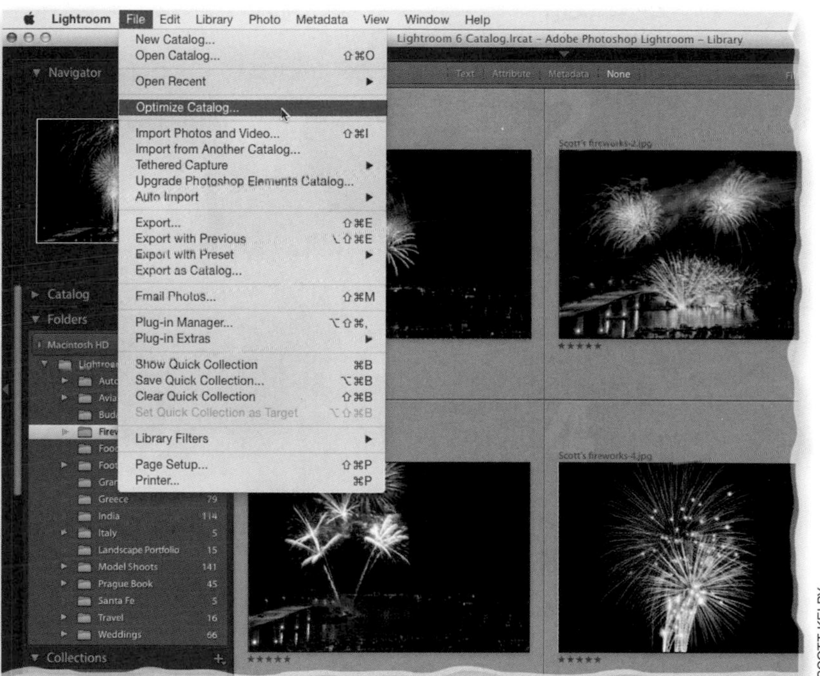

TIP: Optimizing Your Catalog If Things Start to Get Kinda Slow

Once you accumulate a lot of images in Lightroom (and I'm talking tens of thousands here), things can eventually start to get a little slow. If you notice this happening, go under the File menu and choose **Optimize Catalog**. This optimizes the performance of the currently open catalog, and while it might take a few minutes now, you'll get that time back really quickly with much faster performance. Even if you don't have tens of thousands of images in Lightroom, it's a good idea to optimize your catalog every couple of months or so to keep everything running at full speed. You can also do this when you back up your catalog by turning on the Optimize Catalog After Backing Up checkbox.

Relinking Missing Photos

If you work for any amount of time in Lightroom, at some point you're going to see a little exclamation point icon appear above the top right of a thumbnail, which means Lightroom can't find the original photo. You'll still be able to see the photo's thumbnail and even zoom in closer to see it in Loupe view, but you won't be able to do any serious editing (like color correction, changing the white balance, etc.), because Lightroom needs the original photo file to do those things, so you'll need to know how to relink the photo to the original.

Step One:

In the thumbnails shown here, you can see one of them has a little exclamation point icon, letting you know it has lost its link to the original photo. There are two main reasons why this probably happened: (1) The original photo is stored on an external hard drive and that hard drive isn't connected to your computer right now, so Lightroom can't find it. So, just reconnect the hard drive, and Lightroom will see that drive is connected, instantly relink everything, and all goes back to normal. But if you didn't store your photos on an external hard drive, then there's a different problem: (2) You moved or deleted the original photo, and now you've got to go and find it.

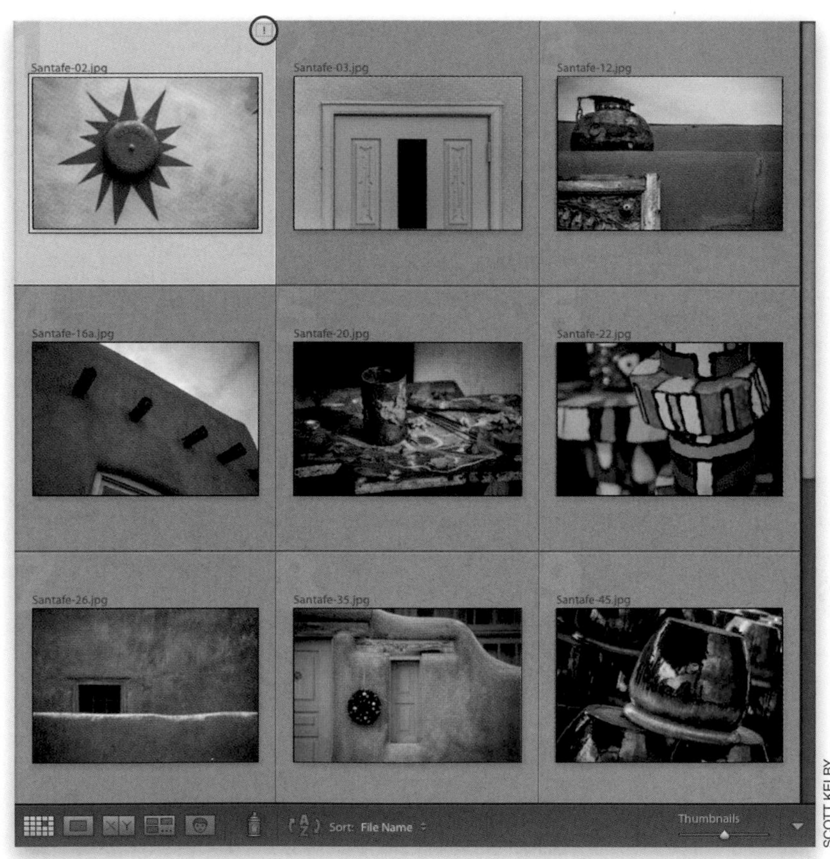

SCOTT KELBY

Step Two:

To find out where the missing photo was last seen, click on that little exclamation point icon and a dialog will pop up telling you it can't find the original file (which you already knew), but more importantly, under the scary warning it shows you its previous location (so you'll instantly be able to see if it was indeed on a removable hard drive, flash drive, etc.). So, if you moved the file (or the whole folder), you just have to tell Lightroom where you moved it to (which you'll do in the next step).

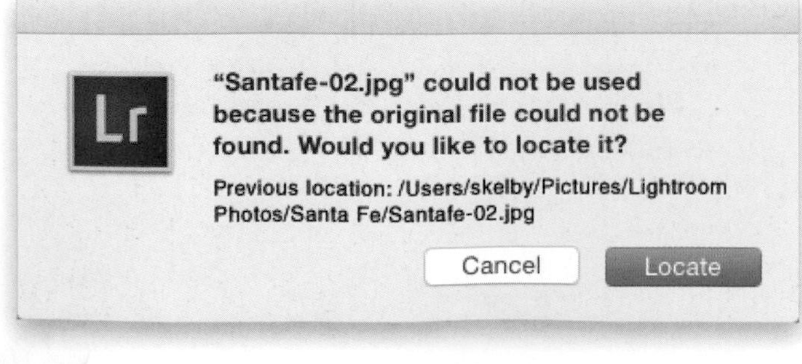

Lr
"Santafe-02.jpg" could not be used because the original file could not be found. Would you like to locate it?
Previous location: /Users/skelby/Pictures/Lightroom Photos/Santa Fe/Santafe-02.jpg
Cancel
Locate

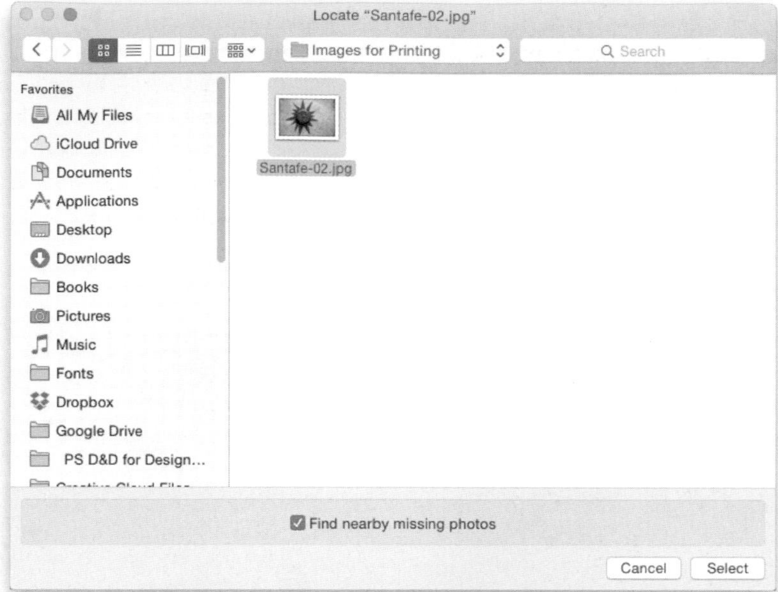

Step Three:

Click on the Locate button, and when the Locate dialog appears (shown here), navigate your way to where that photo is now located. (I know you're thinking to yourself, "Hey, I didn't move that file!" but come on—files just don't get up and walk around your hard drive. You moved it—you just probably forgot you moved it, which is what makes this process so tricky.) Once you find it, click on it, then click the Select button, and it relinks the photo. If you moved an entire folder, then make sure you leave the Find Nearby Missing Photos checkbox turned on, so that way when you find any one of your missing photos, it will automatically relink all the missing photos in that entire folder at once.

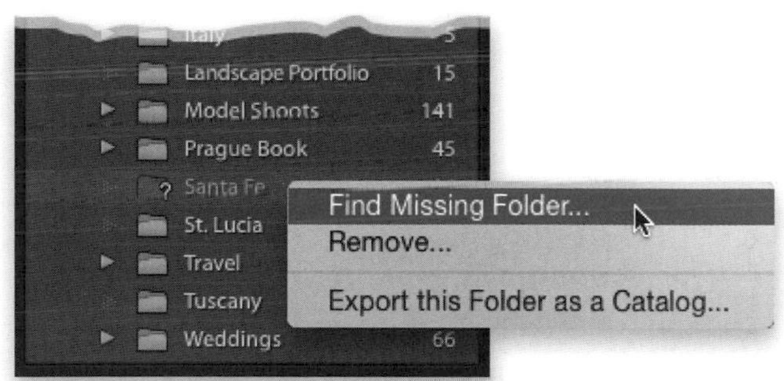

Step Four:

If an entire folder is missing (it will be grayed out and have a question mark on the folder), just Right-click on it in the Folders panel and choose **Find Missing Folder**. Then navigate to its new location, like you did with the single image in Step Three, and choose it.

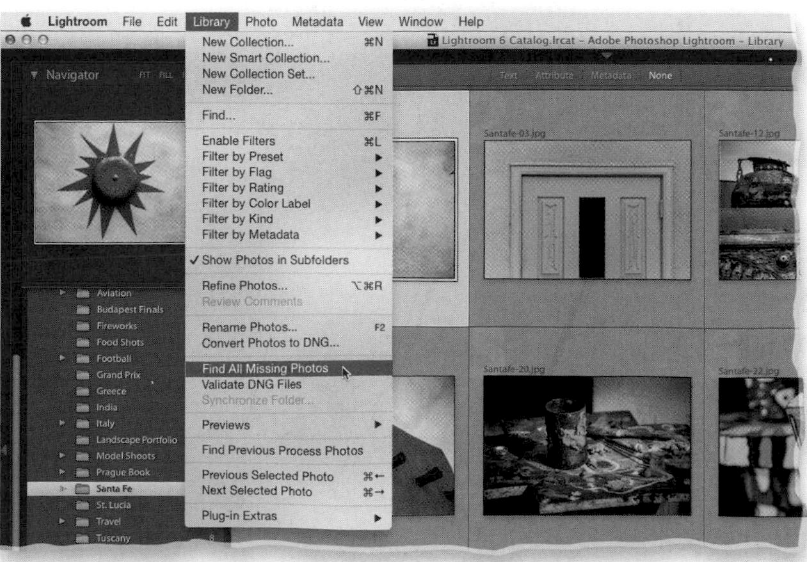

TIP: Keeping Everything Linked

If you want to make sure that all your photos are linked to the actual files (so you never see the dreaded exclamation point icon), go to the Library module, under the Library menu up top, and choose **Find All Missing Photos**. This will bring up any photos that have a broken link in Grid view, so you can relink them using the technique we just learned here.

Dealing with Disasters (Troubleshooting)

It's pretty unlikely that you'll have a major problem with your Lightroom catalog (after all these years of using Lightroom, it's only happened to me once), and if it does happen, chances are Lightroom can repair itself (which is pretty handy). However, the chances of your hard drive crashing, or your computer dying, or getting stolen (with the only copy of your catalog on it) are much higher. Here's how to deal with both of these potential disasters in advance, and what to do if the big potty hits the air circulation device:

Step One:

If you launch Lightroom and you get a warning dialog like you see here (at top), then go ahead and give Lightroom a chance to fix itself by clicking the Repair Catalog button. Chances are pretty likely it'll fix the catalog and then you're all set. However, if Lightroom can't fix the catalog, you'll see the bottom warning dialog instead, letting you know that your catalog is so corrupt it can't fix it. If that's the case, it's time to go get your backup copy of your catalog (ya know, the one we talked about a couple pages ago).

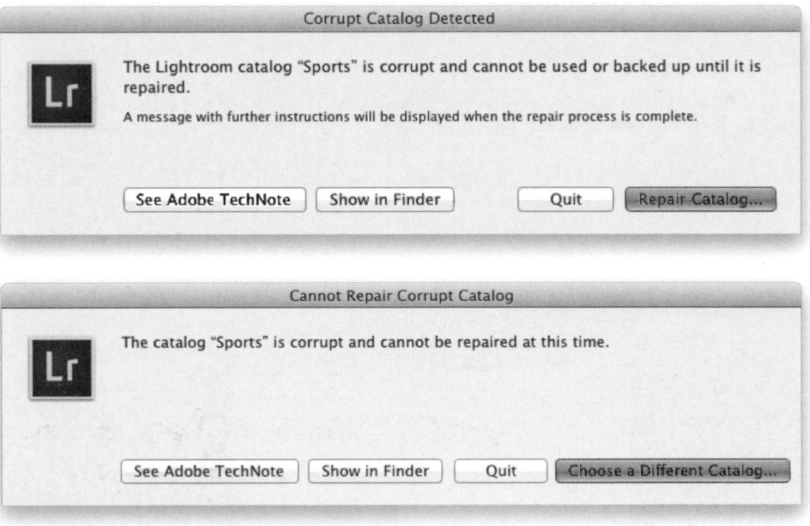

Step Two:

Now, as long as you've backed up your catalog, you can just go restore that backup catalog, and you're back in business (just understand that if the last time you backed up your catalog was three weeks ago, everything you've done in Lightroom since then will be gone. That's why it's so important to back up your catalog fairly often, and if you're doing client work, you should back up daily). Luckily, restoring from a backup catalog is easy. First, go to your backup hard drive (remember, your backup catalog should be saved to a separate hard drive. That way, if your computer crashes, your backup doesn't crash along with it), and locate the folder where you save your Lightroom catalog backups (they're saved in folders by date, so double-click on the folder with the most current date), and inside you'll see your backup catalog (as seen here).

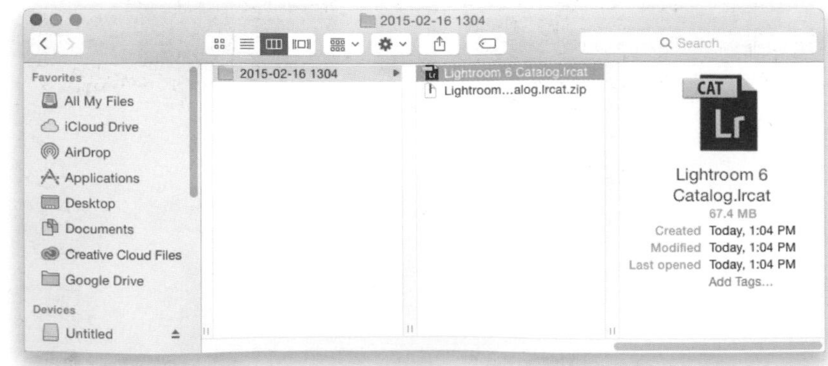

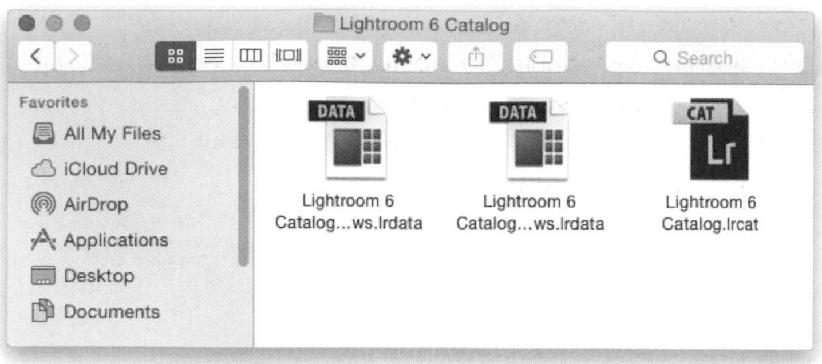

Step Three:

Next, go and find the corrupt Lightroom catalog on your computer (on my computer, it's in my Lightroom folder that's in my Pictures folder), and delete that file (drag it into the Trash on a Mac, or into the Recycle Bin on a PC). Now, drag-and-drop your backup catalog file into the folder on your computer where your corrupt file used to be (before you deleted it).

TIP: Finding Your Catalog

If you don't remember where you chose to store your Lightroom catalogs—don't worry—Lightroom can tell you. Go under the Lightroom (PC: Edit) menu and choose **Catalog Settings**. Click on the General tab, then under Location it will show the path to your catalog. Click on the Show button, and it will take you there.

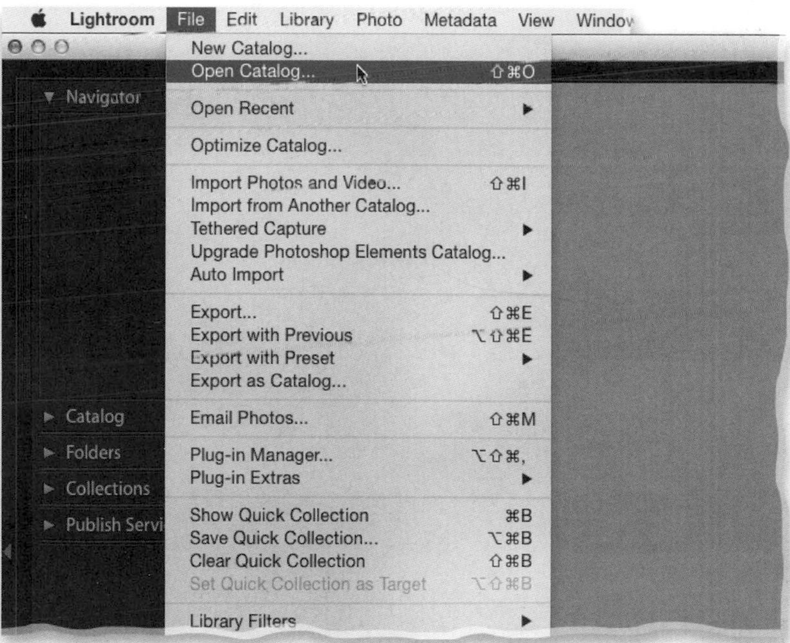

Step Four:

The final step is simply to open this new catalog in Lightroom by going under the File menu and choosing **Open Catalog**. Now, go to where you placed that backup copy of your catalog (on your computer), find that backup file, click on it, then click OK, and everything is back the way it was (again, provided you backed up your catalog recently. If not, it's back to what your catalog looked like the last time you backed it up). By the way, it even remembers where your photos are stored (but if for some strange reason it doesn't, go back to the last project to relink them).

TIP: If Your Computer Crashed...

If, instead of a corrupt catalog, your computer crashed (or your hard drive died, or your laptop got stolen, etc.), then it's pretty much the same process—you just don't have to find and delete the old catalog first, because it's already gone. So, you'll start by just dragging your backup copy of the catalog into your new, empty Lightroom folder (which is created the first time you launch Lightroom on your new computer, or new hard drive, etc.).

Continued

Step Five:

If you think your catalog's okay, but Lightroom has locked up or is just acting wonky, a lot of the time, simply quitting Lightroom and restarting will do the trick (I know, it sounds really simple, and kind of "Duh!" but this fixes more problems than you can imagine). If that didn't work, and Lightroom is still acting funky, it's possible your preferences have become corrupt and need to be replaced (hey, it happens). To do that, quit Lightroom, then press-and-hold **Option-Shift (PC: Alt-Shift)**, and then relaunch Lightroom. Keep holding those keys down until the dialog appears asking if you want to reset your preferences. If you click on Reset Preferences, it builds a new factory-fresh set of preferences, and chances are all your problems will be gone.

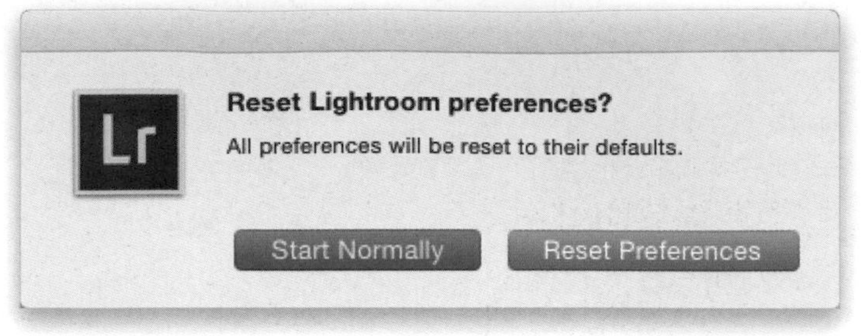

Step Six:

Next, if you have installed Lightroom plug-ins, it's possible one of them has gotten messed up or is outdated, so check the plug-in manufacturers' sites for updates. If your plug-ins are all up to date, then go under the File menu and choose **Plug-in Manager**. In the dialog, click on a plug-in, then to the right, click the Disable button, and see if the problem is still there. Turn each off, using the process of elimination, until you find the one that's messing things up. If you wind up disabling them all, and the problem is still there, then it's time to do a reinstall, either from the original install files (if you have Lightroom 6) or from the Adobe Creative Cloud (if you use Lightroom CC). Start by uninstalling Lightroom from your computer (it won't delete your catalogs), and then do your install. One of those will most surely fix your problem. If none of those worked, it may be time to call Adobe, 'cause something's crazy messed up (but at least you'll have already done the first round of things Adobe will tell you to try, and you'll be that much closer to a solution).

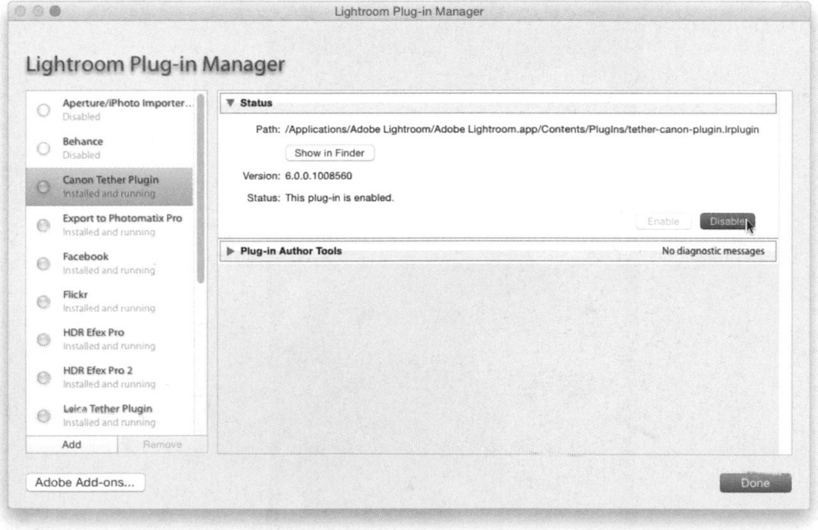

Lightroom Killer Tips > >

▼ Deleting a Collection

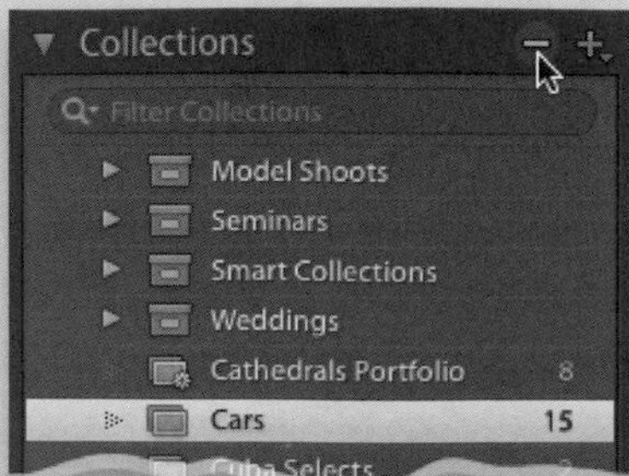

If you want to delete a collection, just click on it in the Collections panel and then click the – (minus sign) button on the right side of the panel header. This deletes just the collection, not the real photos themselves.

▼ Adding Photos to an Existing Collection

You can add photos to any existing collection by just dragging a photo from the grid (or Filmstrip) and dropping it onto your collection in the Collections panel.

▼ Filtering the Collections Panel

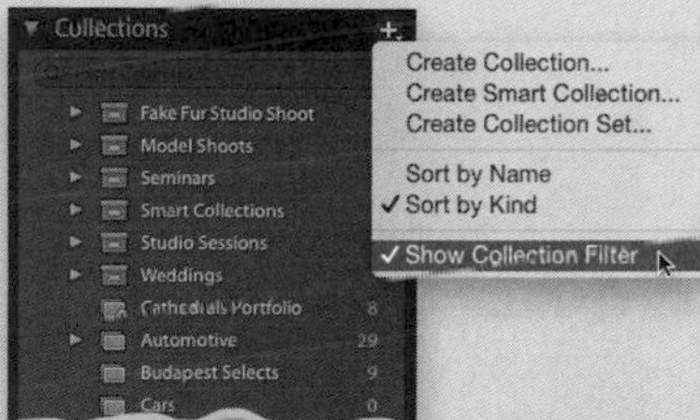

Got a bunch of collections? Want to cut through the clutter fast? Go to the top of the Collections panel, click on the + (plus sign) button in the panel header and choose **Show Collections Filter** to add a filter field to the top of the panel. Want to jump to a particular collection? Just start typing its name in this field and Lightroom filters everything else away and gets you to the one you want fast while hiding all the rest.

▼ Quickly Apply Keywords to Your Selected Photo

When you hover your cursor over a keyword in the Keyword List panel, a checkbox appears that lets you assign it to your selected photo.

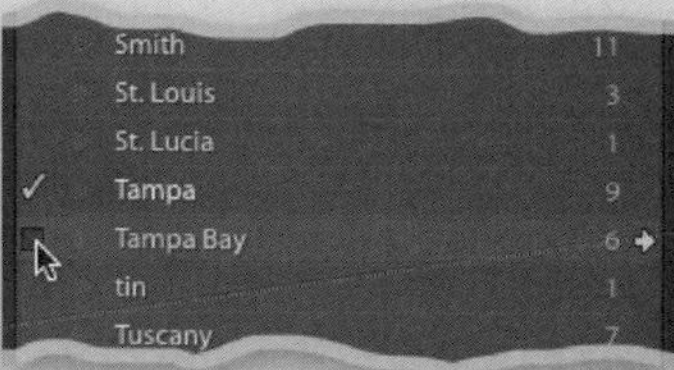

▼ How to Share Smart Collections Settings

If you Right-click on a smart collection, you can choose **Export Smart Collection Settings** from the pop-up menu to save the smart collection's criteria, so you can share it with a friend. After you send it to them, they can import it using the **Import Smart Collection Settings** command from the same pop-up menu.

▼ Using Keyword Sets with the Painter Tool

In Lightroom CC, instead of typing in the Painter tool's Keyword field, you can now load keywords from any Keyword set you've created. Start by getting the tool, then press-and-hold the Shift key, and a pop-up Keyword Set panel appears right where your cursor is so you can choose the set you want, and then the keywords you want. You can also load *all* the keywords at once by clicking the Select All button in that panel.

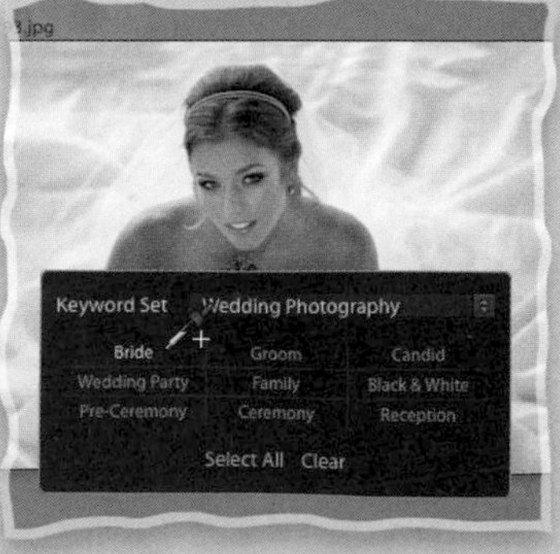

▼ Quickly Create Sub-Keywords

If you Right-click on a keyword in the Keyword List panel, there's a menu item called **Put New Keywords Inside This Keyword** and, until you turn it off (by choosing it again in the pop-up menu),

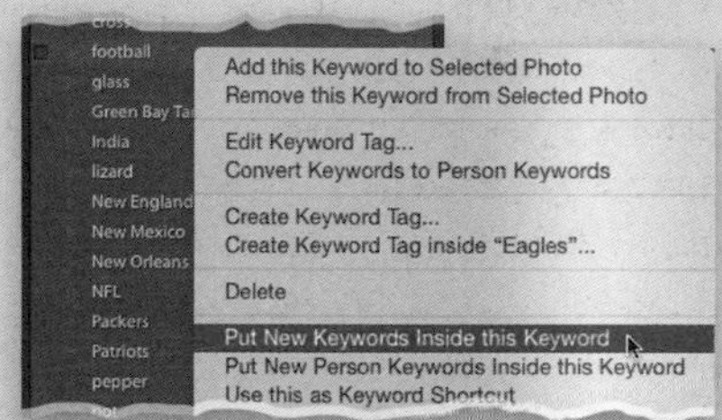

all keywords you create are created as sub-keywords of this keyword.

▼ Sharing Keywords

If you want to use your keywords in a copy of Lightroom on a different computer, or share them with friends or co-workers, go under the Metadata menu and choose **Export Keywords** to create a text file with all your keywords. To import these into another user's copy of Lightroom, go under the Metadata menu and choose **Import Keywords**, then locate that keyword file you exported earlier. Also, you can copy-and-paste keywords from text files directly into the Keywording panel.

▼ Removing Unused Keywords

Any grayed-out keywords in the Keyword List panel are not being used by any photos in Lightroom, so you can delete these orphaned keywords (which makes your keyword list cleaner and shorter) by going under the Metadata menu and choosing **Purge Unused Keywords**.

Lightroom Killer Tips > >

▼ Auto Hide the Top Taskbar

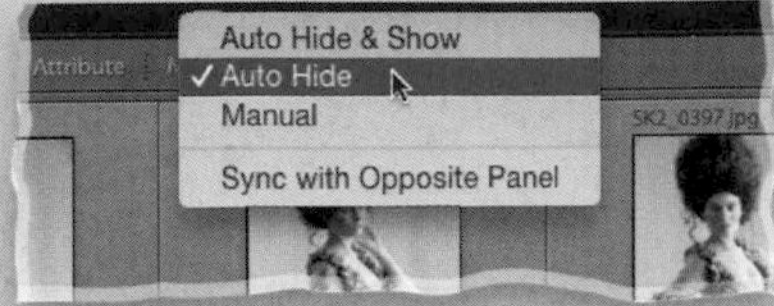

As I mentioned, the first thing I do is turn the Auto Hide feature off (so the panels stop popping in/out all day long), and instead I show/hide them manually as needed. But you might consider turning on Auto Hide just for the top taskbar. It's the most rarely used panel, but people do seem to like clicking to jump from module to module, rather than using the keyboard shortcuts. With Auto Hide turned on, it stays tucked out of sight until you click on the gray center triangle to reveal it. Then you can click on the module you want to jump to, and as soon as you move away from the top taskbar, it tucks away. Try it once, and I bet you'll totally dig it.

▼ More Options for the Toolbar

By default, Lightroom displays a number of different tools and options on the toolbar below the center Preview area, but you can choose which ones you want (including some you may not have realized were available) by clicking on the little triangle at the toolbar's far-right side. A menu will pop up with a list of toolbar items. The ones with checks beside them will be visible—to add one, just choose it.

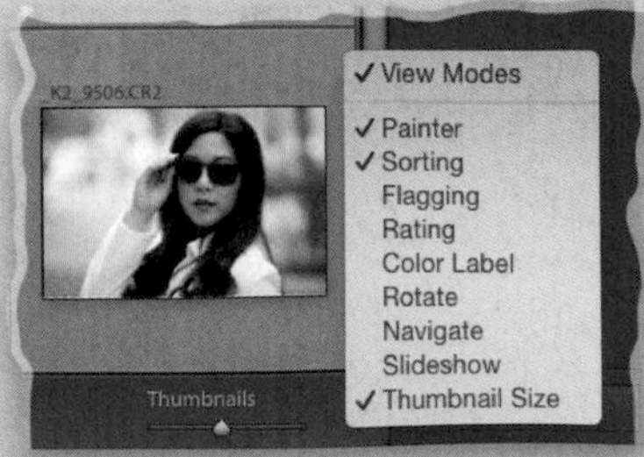

▼ Zooming In/Out

You can use the same keyboard shortcuts used by Photoshop to zoom in and out of your image when it's in Loupe view. Just press **Command-+ (PC: Ctrl-+)** to zoom in, and **Command-- (PC: Ctrl--)** to zoom back out.

▼ Finding Out Which Collection a Particular Photo Is In

If you're scrolling through your entire Lightroom catalog (you've clicked on All

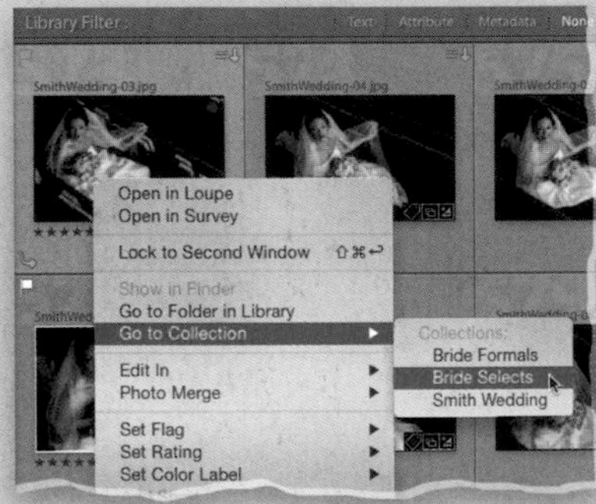

Photographs in the Catalog panel), and you see a photo and want to know which collection it lives in, just Right-click on the photo, and from the pop-up menu that appears, choose **Go to Collection**. If it's not in any collection, it will tell you so in the submenu.

▼ Making Your Panels Larger

If you want your panels to be wider (or thinner for that matter), just move your cursor right over the edge closest to the center Preview area and your cursor will change into a two-headed cursor. Now you can just click-and-drag your panels out wider (or drag them in to make them thinner). This also works for the Filmstrip at the bottom.

▼ Turning Your Filters On/Off

Just press **Command-L (PC: Ctrl-L)** to turn your filters (flags, ratings, metadata, etc., in the Library Filter bar) on/off.

▼ Filter Your Picks from the Filmstrip

Back in the original version of Lightroom, there wasn't a Library Filter bar at the top; instead, you showed your Picks and Rejects by clicking on little flag icons on the right side of the Filmstrip. Well, if you miss that way of doing things, Adobe left those filters there. So, you have your choice: do it from the top (which offers more features than just filtering by flags, stars, or colors), or the Filmstrip version. However, here's a tip within a tip: you're better off Right-clicking directly on the Filmstrip flags and making your choice from the pop-up menu, than you are

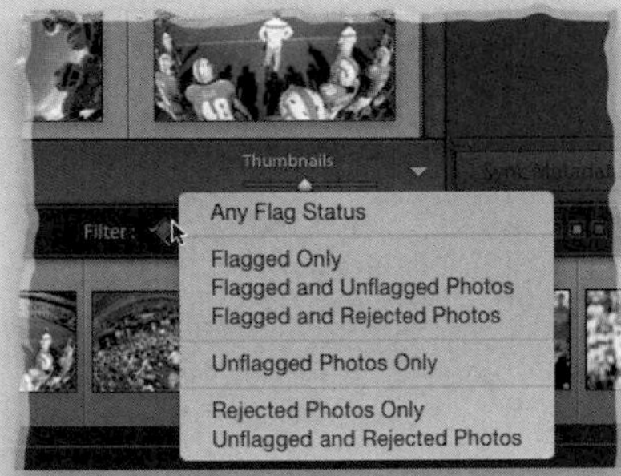

trying to click on them, because they toggle back and forth, and it can get really confusing as to what you're actually seeing, really fast.

▼ How Much Space Is Left on Your Hard Drive for More Photos

If you're using one or more external hard drives to store your Lightroom photos, you can quickly find out exactly how much storage space you have left on those drives without leaving Lightroom. Just go to the Folders panel (in the left side Panels area), and in the Volume Browser, you'll see a volume for each

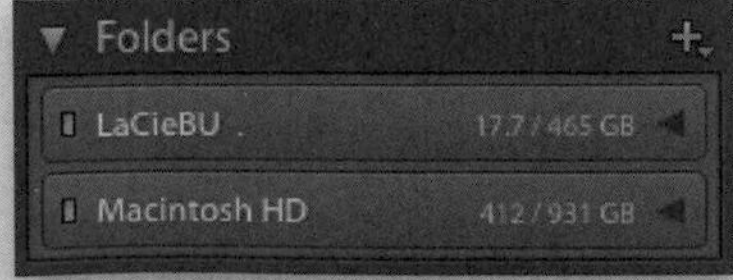

Lightroom Killer Tips > >

drive that you have Lightroom managing photos on (including your internal hard drive), and beside each name, it displays how much space is still available, followed by how much total space there is. If you hover your cursor over a volume, a message will pop up telling you exactly how many photos are stored on that drive that are managed by Lightroom.

▼ Add Metadata to Multiple Photos at Once

If you manually entered some IPTC metadata for a photo, and you want to apply that same metadata to other photos, you don't have to type it all in again—you can copy that metadata and paste it onto other photos. Click on the photo that has the metadata you want, then Command-click (PC: Ctrl-click) on the other photos you want to add the metadata to, to select them. Now, click the Sync Metadata button (at the bottom of the right side Panels area), which brings up the Synchronize Metadata

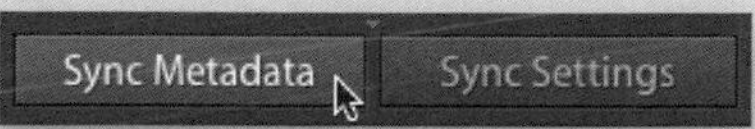

dialog. Click the Synchronize button to update those other photos with this metadata.

▼ Saving a Collection as a Favorite

If you find yourself using a particular collection fairly often (maybe your portfolio collection, or a client proofs collection), you can save it so it's always just one click away: Start by clicking on that collection in the Collections panel, then from the pop-up menu at the top

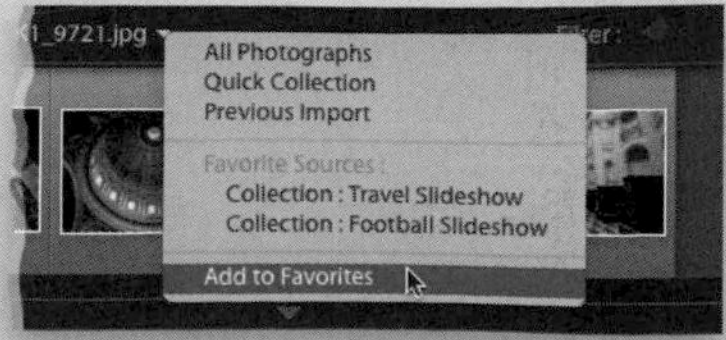

left of the Filmstrip, choose **Add to Favorites**. That collection will appear in this pop-up menu from now on. To remove a favorite, click on the collection, then chose **Remove From Favorites** from that same menu.

▼ Locking In a Filter

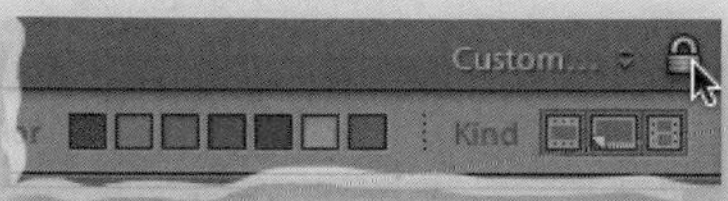

In previous versions of Lightroom, when you turned on a filter in the Library Filter bar (let's say you turned on the filter to show just your 5-star photos), that filter was only turned on for the current collection or folder you were in. When you changed collections or folders, it stopped filtering. Now, if you want to move from collection to collection and only see your 5-star images, click on the padlock icon at the right end of the Library Filter (at the top of the Grid view; if you don't see the Library Filter, press the / [backslash] key).

▼ Backing Up Your Presets

If you've created your own presets (anything from Import presets to Develop or Print module presets), you need to back these up at some point, too. If your hard drive crashes, or you lose your laptop, you'll have to create them all from scratch (if you can even remember what all the settings were). To find the folder where all the presets are on your computer, go to Lightroom's Preferences (under the Lightroom menu on a Mac or the Edit menu on a PC), click on the Presets tab, and then click the Show Lightroom Presets Folder button in the middle. Now copy that entire folder onto a separate hard drive (or a DVD) to back it up. That way, if things go horribly wrong, you can just drag-and-drop the contents of this backup folder into your new presets folder.

▼ The Auto Advance Advantage

You can have Lightroom automatically advance to the next image when you're adding a Pick flag or star rating to a photo—just go under the Photo menu and choose **Auto Advance**.

▼ Making Collections in a Set

The quickest way to create a collection inside an existing collection set is to Right-click on the set (in the Collections panel) and choose **Create Collection**. This auto-

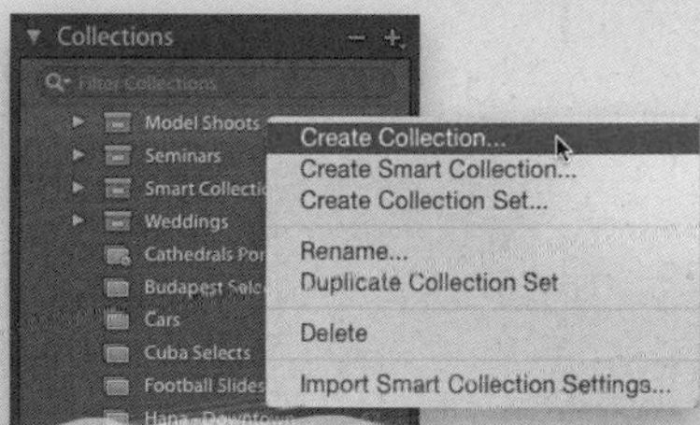

matically chooses that collection set when you turn on the Inside a Collection Set checkbox, so all you have to do is name your new collection and click Create.

▼ Use Keyword Suggestions

When you click on a photo and Lightroom sees you've tagged it with a keyword, it instantly looks to see if you've tagged any other photos with that keyword. If you did, it lists the other keywords you applied to those photos as Keyword Suggestions (in the middle of the Keywording panel) figuring you're likely to use some of these same keywords again for the current photo. To add these suggested keywords, just click on 'em (it even adds the comma for you).

▼ Create Search Presets

At the far-right end of the Library Filter is a pop-up menu with handy filtering presets. If you find yourself using a particular type of search often, you can save your own custom search presets here, too, by choosing **Save Current Settings as New Preset** from this same menu.

Photo by Scott Kelby | Exposure: 1/400 sec | Focal Length: 168mm | Aperture Value: ƒ/5.6

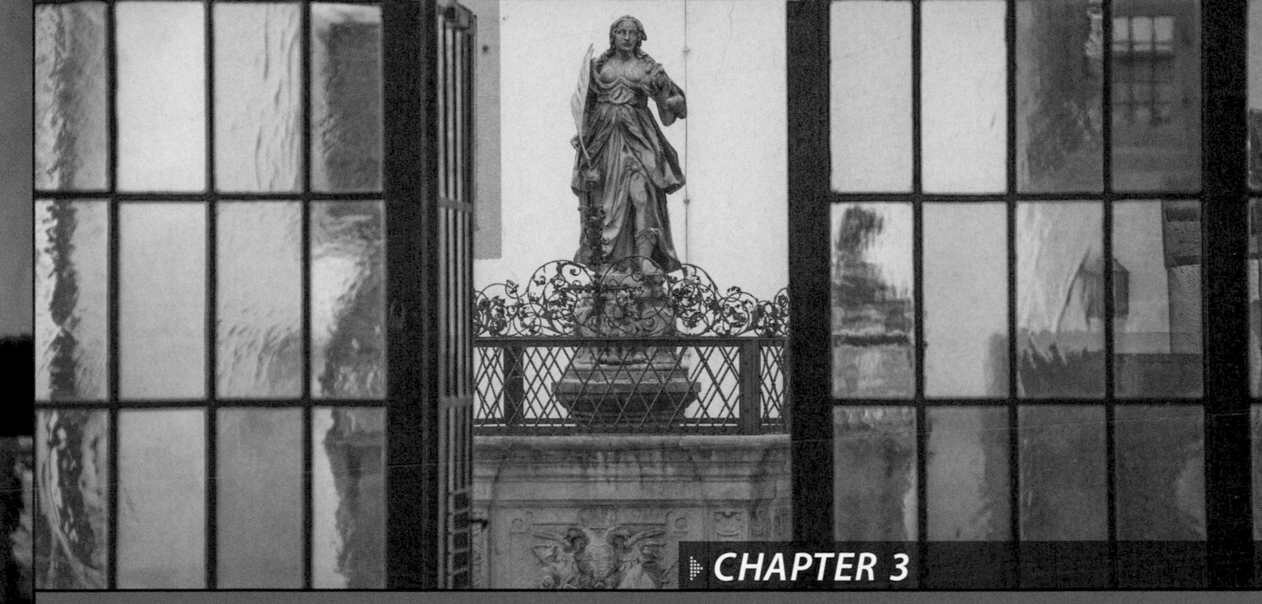

CHAPTER 3

CUSTOMIZING
how to set things up your way

A great name for this chapter would have been "Pimp My Ride" (after the popular MTV show of the same name), seeing as this chapter is all about customizing Lightroom to your own personal tastes. Kids these days call this "pimping" (by the way, I just checked with a nearby kid to confirm this and apparently that is correct. I said, "Hey, what does it mean if something is pimped?" and he said, "It means it has been customized." But then I called my older brother Jeff, who spent a number of years in the U.S. Navy, and asked him what it means if something is pimped and, surprisingly enough, he had an entirely different answer, but I'm not so sure our mom would be pleased with him for telling this to his impressionable younger brother). So, at this point, I wasn't sure if using the word "pimped" would be really appropriate, so I did a Google search for the word "pimped" and it returned (I'm not making this up) more than 2,500,000 pages that reference the word "pimped." I thought I would go ahead and randomly click on one of those search result links, and I was pleasantly surprised to see that it took me to a page of totally customized cars. So, at that point, I felt pretty safe, but I realized that using the term "pimped" was kind of "past tense," so I removed the "ed" and got a totally different result, which led me to a webpage with a "Pimp Name Generator" and, of course, I couldn't leave without finding out what my pimp name would be (just in case I ever wrote a book about customizing cars or my brother's life), and it turned out to be "Silver Tongue Scott Slither" (though personally I was hoping for something more like "Snoop Scotty Scott").

Choosing What You See in Loupe View

When you're in Loupe view (the zoomed-in view of your photo), besides just displaying your photo really big, you can display as little (or as much) information about your photo as you'd like as text overlays, which appear in the top-left corner of the Preview area. You'll be spending a lot of time working in Loupe view, so let's set up a custom Loupe view that works for you.

Step One:

In the Library module's Grid view, click on a thumbnail and press **E** on your keyboard to jump to the Loupe view (in the example shown here, I hid everything but the right side Panels area, so the photo would show up larger in Loupe view).

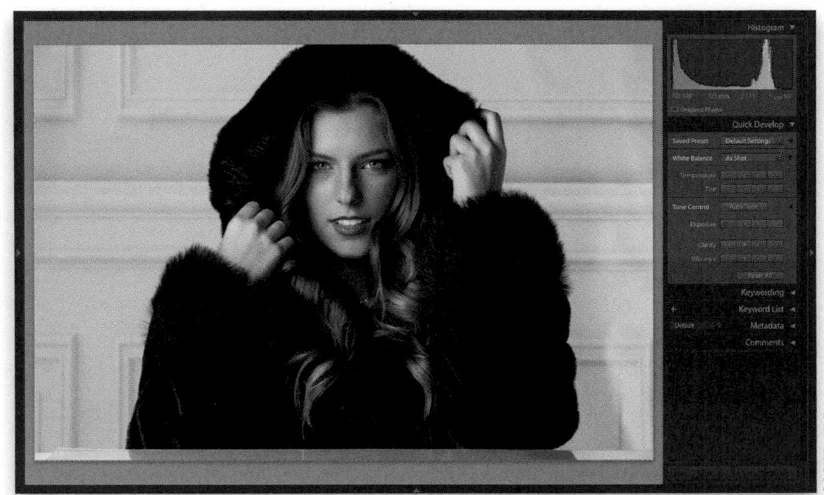

SCOTT KELBY

Step Two:

Press **Command-J (PC: Ctrl-J)** to bring up the Library View Options dialog and then click on the Loupe View tab. At the top of the dialog, turn on the Show Info Overlay checkbox. The pop-up menu to the right lets you choose from two different info overlays: Info 1 overlays the filename of your photo (in larger letters) in the upper-left corner of the Preview area (as seen here). Below the filename, in smaller type, is the photo's capture date and time, and its cropped dimensions. Info 2 also displays the filename, but underneath, it displays the exposure, ISO, and lens settings.

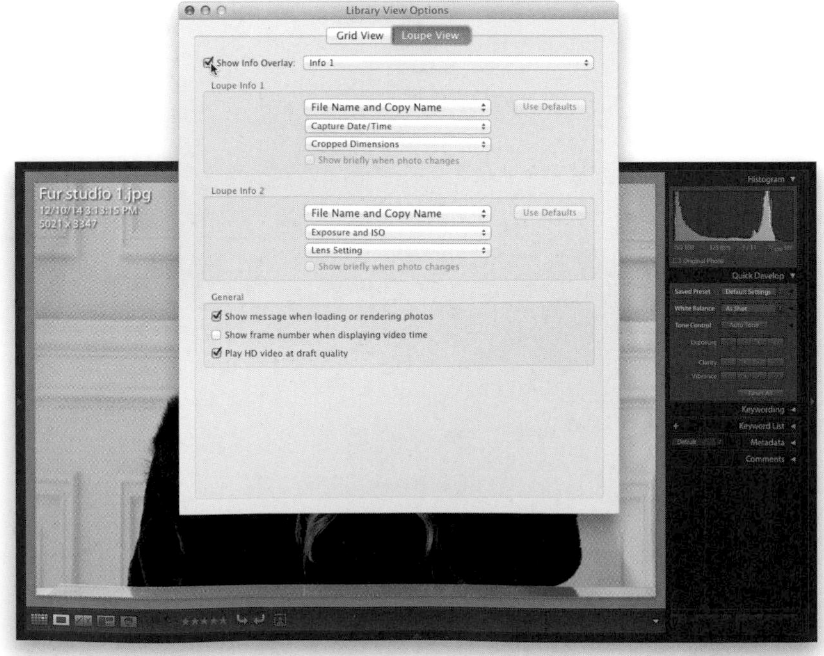

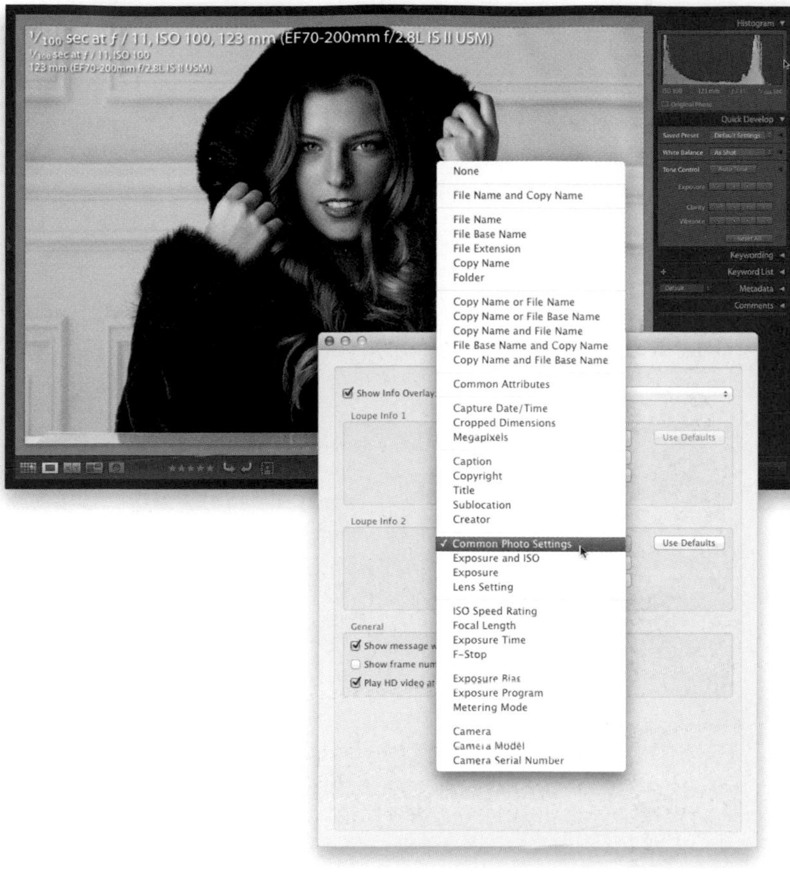

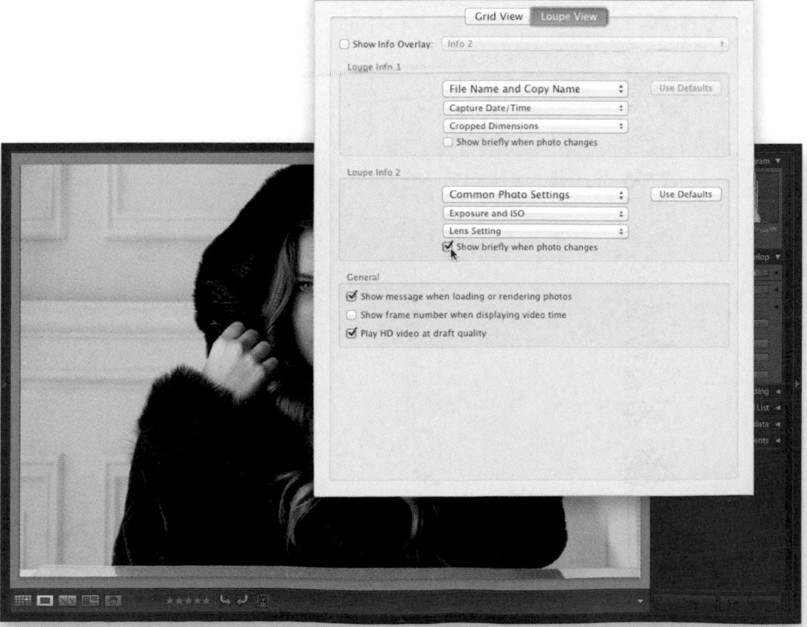

Step Three:

Luckily, you can choose which info is displayed for both info overlays using the pop-up menus in this dialog. So, for example, instead of having the filename show up in huge letters, for Loupe Info 2, you could choose something like **Common Photo Settings** from the pop-up menu (as shown here). By choosing this, instead of getting the filename in huge letters, you'd get the same info that's displayed under the histogram (like the shutter speed, f-stop, ISO, and lens setting) found in the top panel in the right side Panels area. You can customize both info overlays separately by simply making choices from these pop-up menus. (*Remember:* The top pop-up menu in each section is the one that will appear in really large letters.)

Step Four:

Any time you want to start over, just click the Use Defaults button to the right and the default Loupe Info settings will appear. Personally, I find this text appearing over my photos really, really distracting most of the time. The key part of that is "most of the time." The other times, it's handy. So, if you think this might be handy, too, here's what I recommend: (a) Turn off the Show Info Overlay checkbox and turn on the Show Briefly When Photo Changes checkbox below the Loupe Info pop-up menus, which makes the overlay temporary—when you first open a photo in Loupe view, it appears on the photo for around four seconds and then hides itself. Or, you can do what I do: (b) leave those off, and when you want to see that overlay info, press the letter **I** to toggle through Info 1, Info 2, and Show Info Overlay off. At the bottom of the dialog, there's also a checkbox that lets you turn off those little messages that appear onscreen, like "Loading" or "Assigned Keyword," etc., along with some video option checkboxes.

Choosing What You See in Grid View

Those little cells that surround your thumbnails in Grid view can either be a wealth of information or really distracting (depending on how you feel about text and symbols surrounding your photos), but luckily you get to totally customize not only how much info is visible, but in some cases, exactly which type of info is displayed (of course, you learned in Chapter 1 that you can toggle the cell info on/off by pressing the letter **J** on your keyboard). At least now when that info is visible, it'll be just the info you care about.

Step One:

Press **G** to jump to the Library module's Grid view, then press **Command-J (PC: Ctrl-J)** to bring up the Library View Options dialog (shown here), and click on the Grid View tab at the top (seen highlighted here). At the top of the dialog, there's a pop-up menu where you can choose the options for what's visible in either the Expanded Cells view or the Compact Cells view. The difference between the two is that you can view more info in the Expanded Cells view.

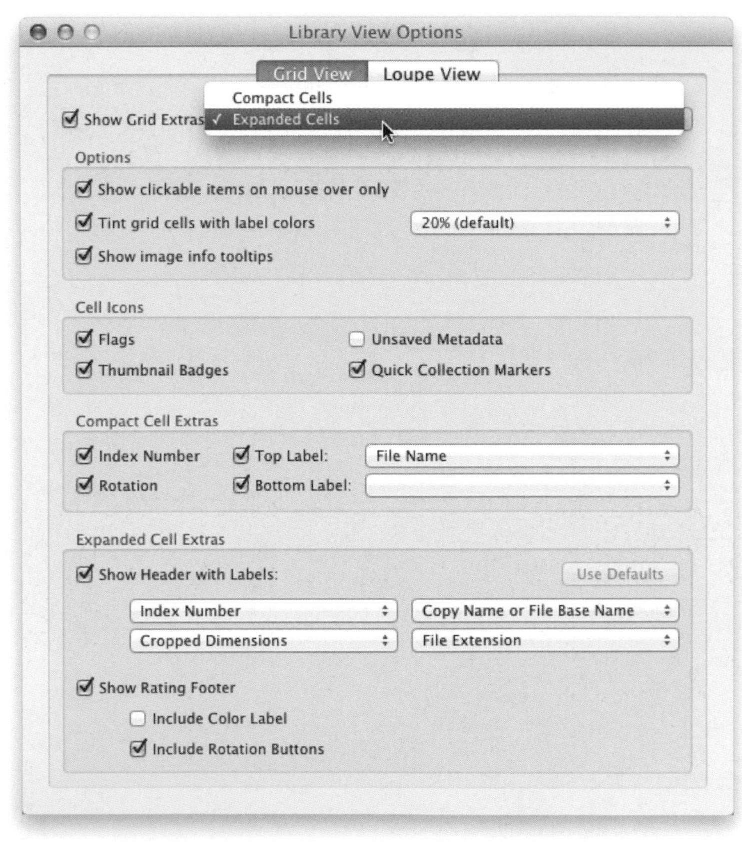

Step Two:

We'll start at the top, in the Options section. If you add a Pick flag and left/right rotation arrows to your cell, and turn on the Show Clickable Items on Mouse Over Only checkbox, it means they'll stay hidden until you move your mouse over a cell, then they appear so you can click on them. If you leave it unchecked, you'll see them all the time. The Tint Grid Cells with Label Colors checkbox only kicks in if you've applied a color label to a photo. If you have, turning this on tints the gray area around the photo's thumbnail the same color as the label, and you can set how dark the tint is with the pop-up menu. With the Show Image Info Tooltips checkbox turned on, when you hover your cursor over an icon within a cell (like a Pick flag or a badge), it'll show you a description of that item. Hover your cursor over an image thumbnail, and it'll give you a quick look at its EXIF data.

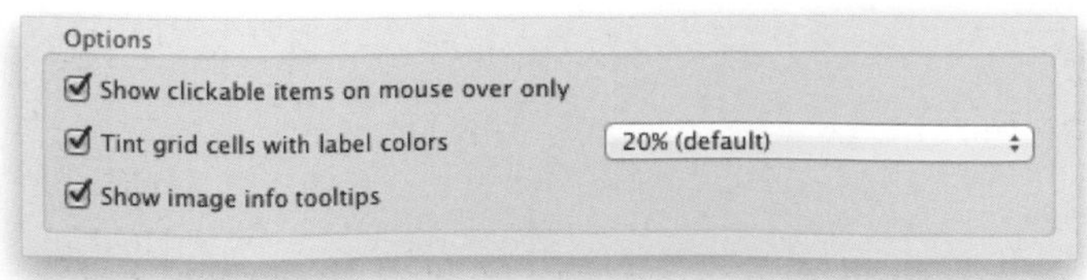

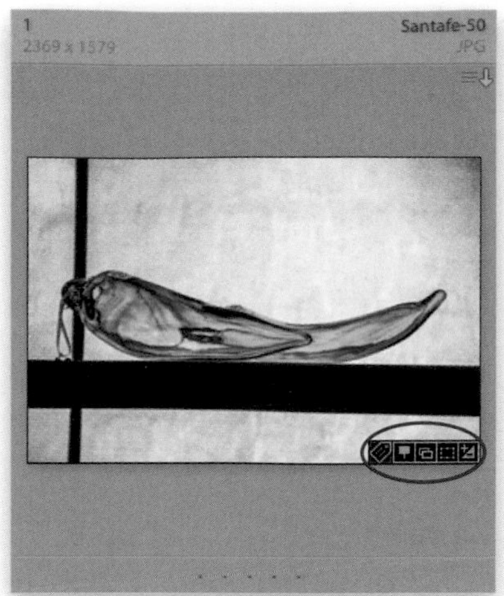

The thumbnail badges show you (from L to R) that a keyword has been applied, the photo has GPS info, it has been added to a collection, it has been cropped, and edited

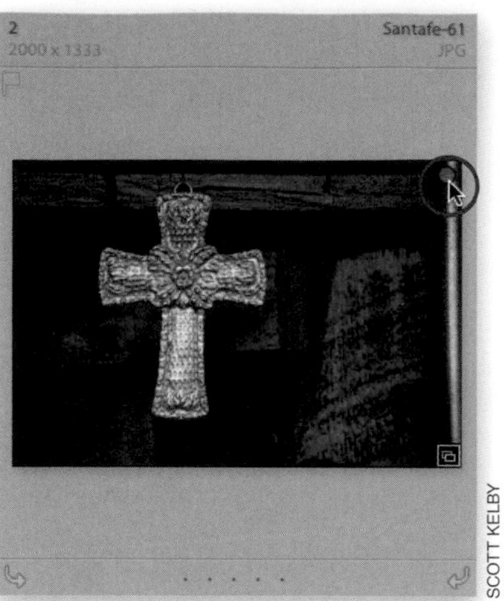

The black circle in the upper-right corner is actually a button—click on it to add this photo to your Quick Collection

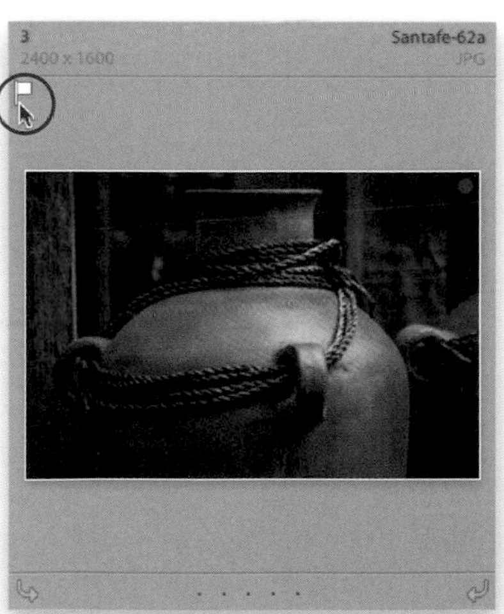

Click the flag icon to mark it as a Pick

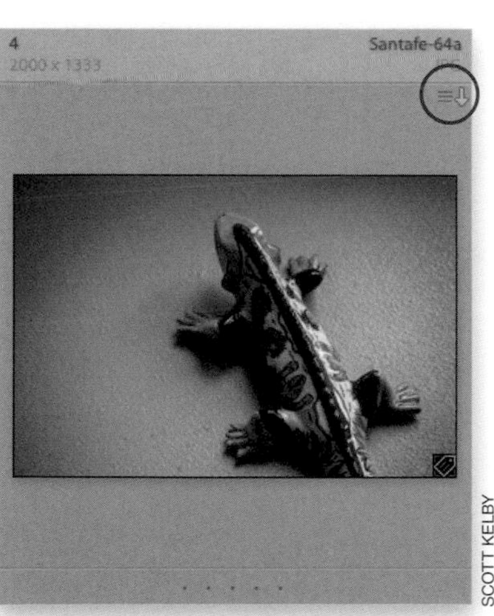

Click the Unsaved Metadata icon to save the changes

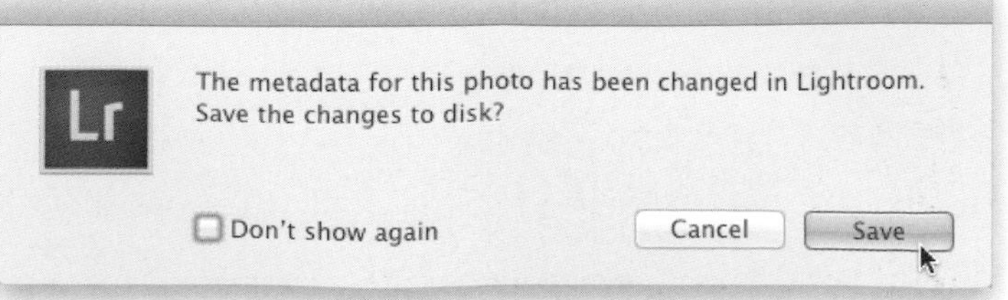

Step Three:

The next section down, Cell Icons, has two options for things that appear right over your photo's thumbnail image, and two that appear just in the cell. Thumbnail badges appear in the bottom-right corner of a thumbnail to let you see if: (a) the photo has GPS info, (b) the photo has had keywords added, (c) the photo has been cropped, (d) the photo has been added to a collection, or (e) the photo has been edited in Lightroom (color correction, sharpening, etc.). These tiny badges are actually clickable shortcuts, so for example, if you wanted to add a keyword, you could click the Keyword badge (whose icon looks like a tag), and it opens the Keywording panel and highlights the keyword field, so you can just type in a new keyword. The other option on the thumbnail, Quick Collection Markers, adds a black circle (that's actually a button) to the top-right corner of your photo when you mouse over the cell. Click on it to add the photo to (or remove it from) your Quick Collection (it becomes a gray dot).

Step Four:

The other two options don't put anything over the thumbnails—they add icons in the cell area itself. When you turn on the Flags checkbox, it adds a Pick flag to the top-left side of the cell, and you can then click on this flag to mark this photo as a Pick (shown here on the left). The last checkbox in this section, Unsaved Metadata, adds a little icon in the top-right corner of the cell (shown here on the right), but only if the photo's metadata has been updated in Lightroom (since the last time the photo was saved), and these changes haven't been saved to the file itself yet (this sometimes happens if you import a photo, like a JPEG, which already has keywords, ratings, etc., applied to it, and then in Lightroom you added keywords, or changed the rating). If you see this icon, you can click on it to bring up a dialog that asks if you want to save the changes to the file (as shown here).

Continued

Step Five:

We're going to jump down to the bottom of the dialog to the Expanded Cell Extras section, where you choose which info gets displayed in the area at the top of each cell in Expanded Cells view. By default, it displays four different bits of info (as shown here): It's going to show the index number (which is the number of the cell, so if you imported 63 photos, the first photo's index number is 1, followed by 2, 3, 4, and so on, until you reach 63) in the top left, then below that will be the pixel dimensions of your photo (if the photo's cropped, it shows the final cropped size). Then in the top right, it shows the file's name, and below that, it shows the file's type (JPEG, RAW, TIFF, etc.). To change any one of these info labels, just click on the label pop-up menu you want to change and a long list of info to choose from appears (as seen in the next step). By the way, you don't have to display all four labels of info, just choose None from the pop-up menu for any of the four you don't want visible.

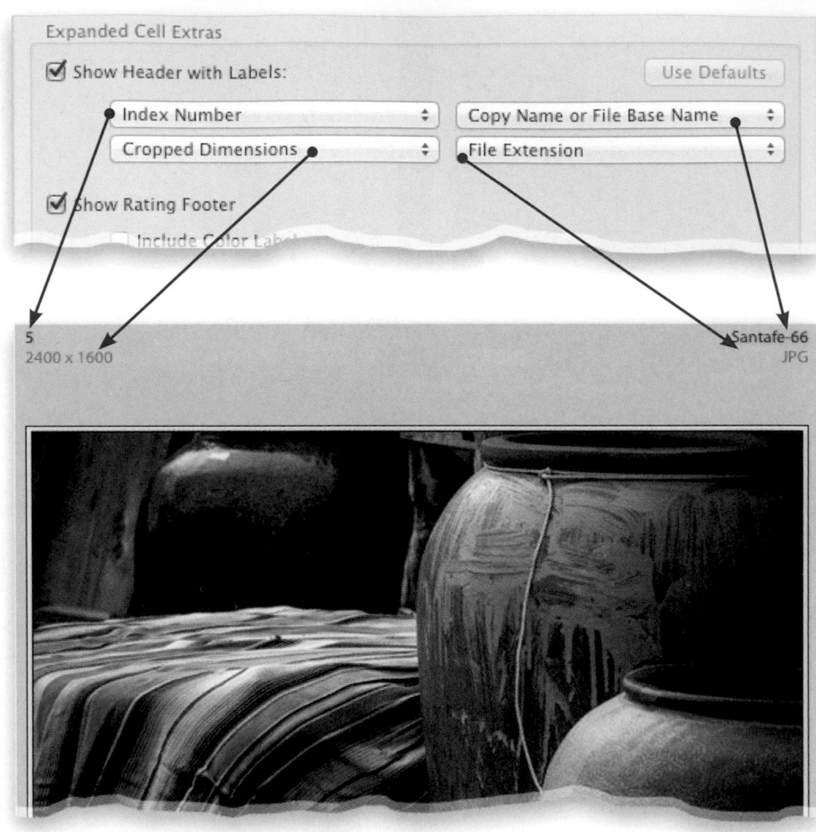

Step Six:

Although you can use the pop-up menus here in the Library View Options dialog to choose which type of information gets displayed, check this out: you can actually do the same thing from right within the cell itself. Just click on any one of those existing info labels, right in the cell itself, and the same exact pop-up menu that appears in the dialog appears here. Just choose the label you want from the list (I chose ISO Speed Rating here), and from then on it will be displayed in that spot (as shown here on the right, where you can see this shot was taken at an ISO of 400).

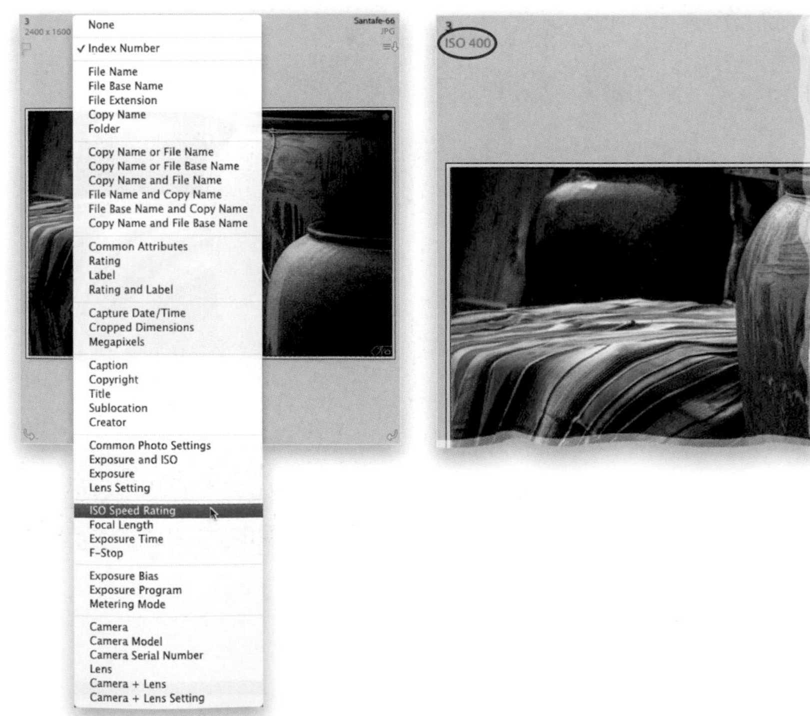

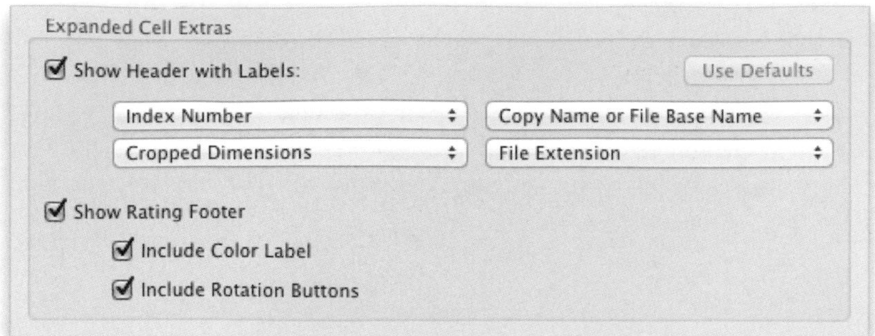

Step Seven:

At the bottom of the Expanded Cell Extras section is a checkbox, which is on by default. This option adds an area to the bottom of the cell called the Rating Footer, which shows the photo's star rating, and if you keep both checkboxes beneath Show Rating Footer turned on, it will also display the color label and the rotation buttons (which are clickable).

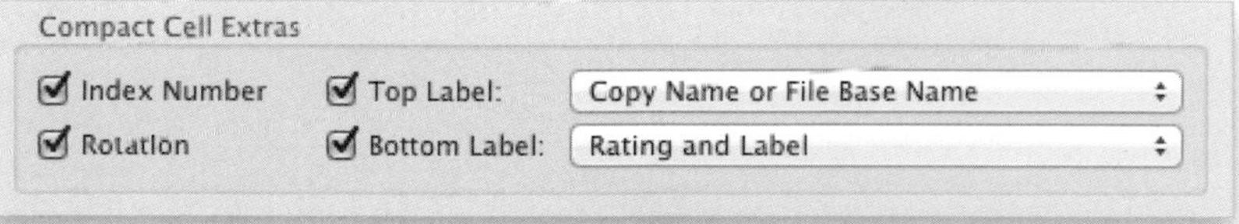

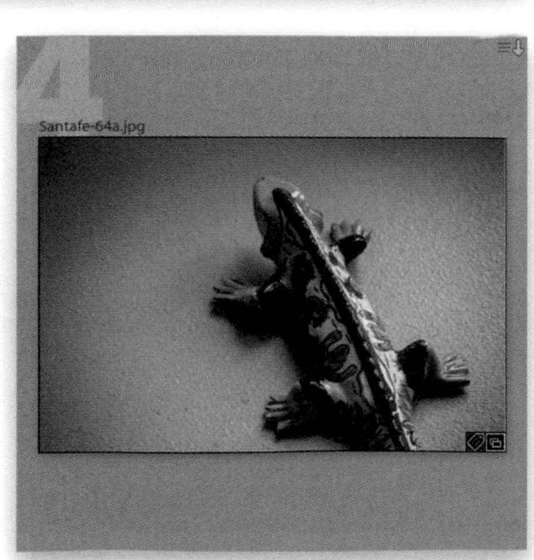

Step Eight:

The middle section we skipped over is the Compact Cell Extras section. The reason I skipped over these options is that they work pretty much like the Expanded Cell Extras, but with the Compact Cell Extras, you have only two fields you can customize (rather than four, like in the Expanded Cell Extras): the filename (which appears on the top left of the thumbnail), and the rating (which appears beneath the bottom left of the thumbnail). To change the info displayed there, click on the label pop-up menus and make your choices. The other two checkboxes on the left hide/show the index number (in this case, it's that huge gray number that appears along the top-left side of the cell) and the rotation arrows at the bottom of the cell (which you'll see when you move your cursor over the cell). One last thing: you can turn all these extras off permanently by turning off the Show Grid Extras checkbox at the top of the dialog.

Make Working with Panels Faster & Easier

Lightroom has an awful lot of panels, and you can waste a lot of time scrolling up and down in these panels just searching for what you want (especially if you have to scroll past panels you never use). This is why, in my live Lightroom seminars, I recommend: (a) hiding panels you find you don't use, and (b) turning on Solo mode, so when you click on a panel, it displays only that one panel and tucks the rest out of the way. Here's how to use these somewhat hidden features:

Step One:

Start by going to any side panel, then Right-click on the panel header and a pop-up menu will appear with a list of all the panels on that side. Each panel with a checkmark beside it is visible, so if you want to hide a panel from view, just choose it from this list and it unchecks. For example, here in the Develop module's right side Panels area, I've hidden the Camera Calibration panel. Next, as I mentioned in the intro above, I always recommend turning on Solo mode (you choose it from this same menu, as seen here).

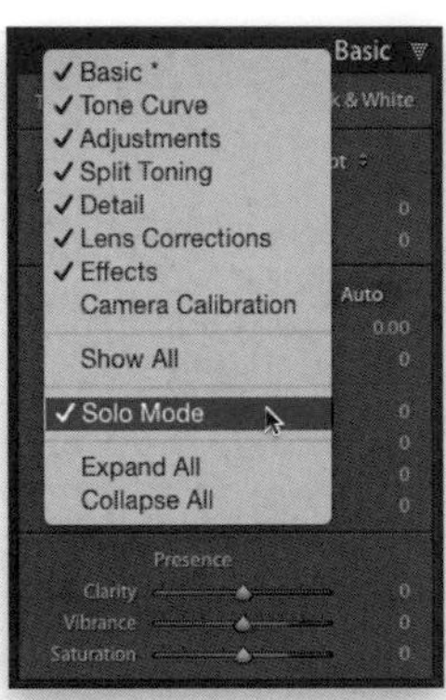

Step Two:

Take a look at the two sets of side panels shown here. The one on the left shows how the Develop module's panels look normally. I'm trying to make an adjustment in the Split Toning panel, but I have all those other panels open around it (which is distracting), and I have to scroll down past them just to get to the panel I want. However, look at the same set of panels on the right when Solo mode is turned on—all the other panels are collapsed out of the way, so I can just focus on the Split Toning panel. To work in a different panel, I just click on its name, and the Split Toning panel tucks itself away automatically.

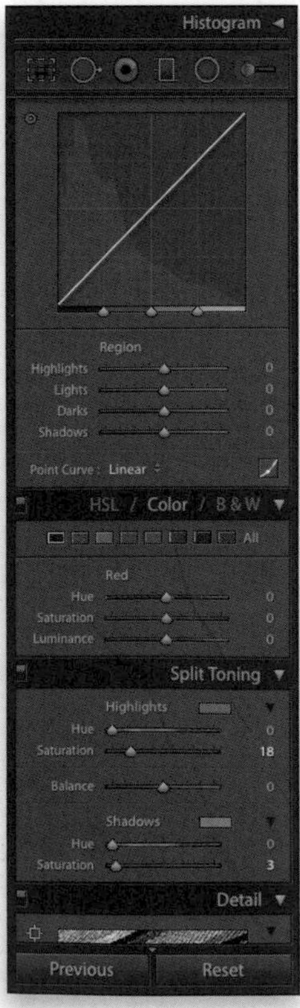

The Develop module's right side Panels area with Solo mode turned off

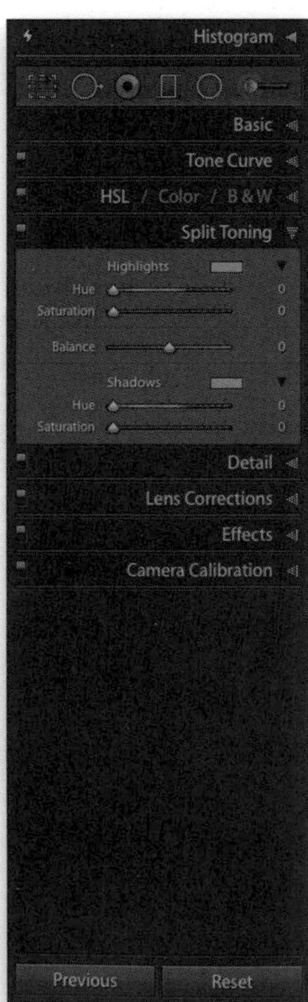

The Develop module's right side Panels area with Solo mode turned on

Using Two Monitors with Lightroom

Lightroom supports using two monitors, so you can work on your photo on one screen and also see a huge, full-screen version of your photo on another. But Adobe went beyond that in this Dual Display feature and there are some very cool things you can do with it, once it's set up (and here's how to set it up).

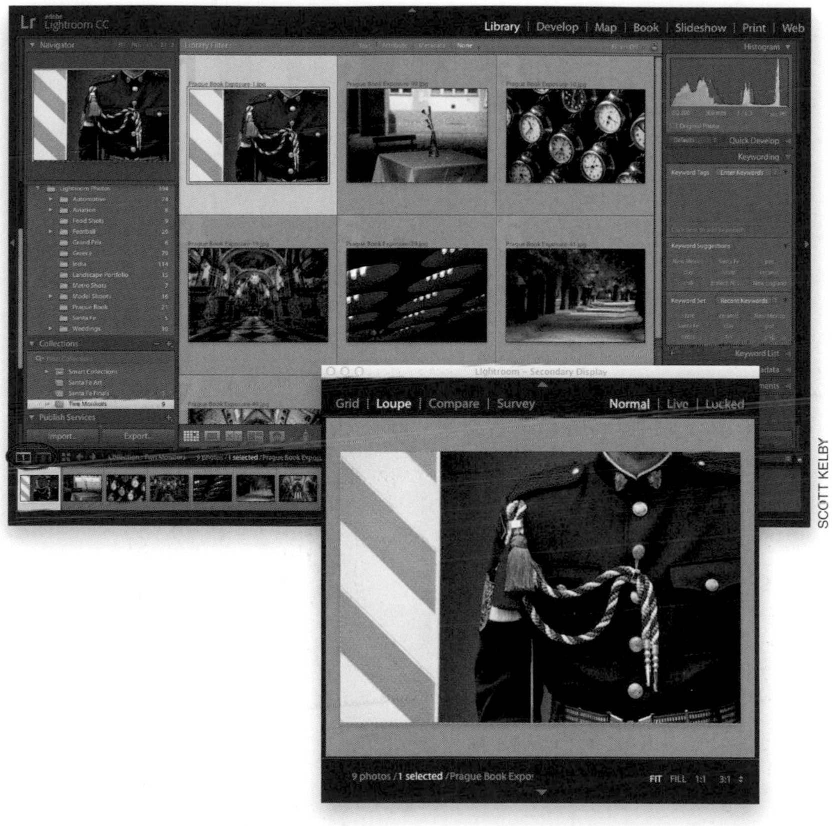

SCOTT KELBY

Step One:

The Dual Display controls are found in the top-left corner of the Filmstrip (shown circled in red here), where you can see two buttons: one marked "1" for your main display, and one marked "2" for the second display. If you don't have a second monitor connected and you click the Second Window button, it just brings up what would be seen in the second display as a separate floating window (as seen here).

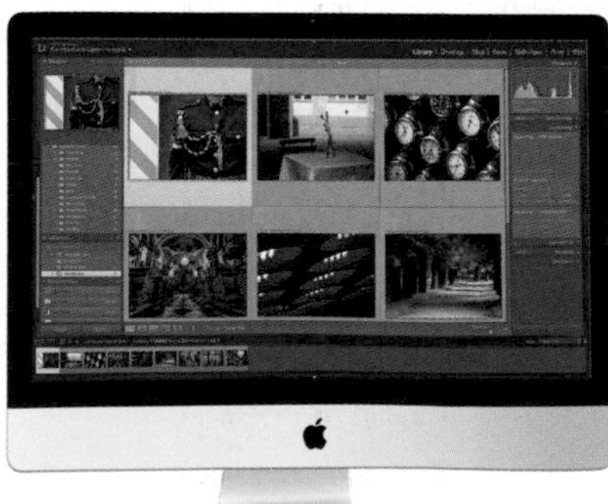

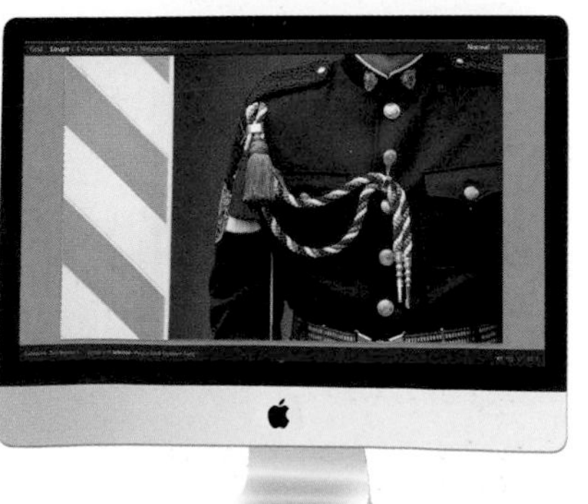

Step Two:

If you do have a second monitor connected to your computer, when you click on the Second Window button, the separate floating window appears in Full Screen mode, set to Loupe view, on the second display (as seen here). This is the default setup, which lets you see Lightroom's interface and controls on one display, and then the larger zoomed-in view on the second display.

Continued

Step Three:

You have complete control over what goes on the second display using the Secondary Window pop-up menu, shown here (just click-and-hold on the Second Window button and it appears). For example, you could have Survey view showing on the second display, and then you could be zoomed in tight, looking at one of those survey images in Loupe view on your main display (as shown at bottom). By the way, just add the **Shift key** and the Survey view, Compare view, Grid view, and Loupe view shortcuts are all the same (so, **Shift-N** puts your second display into Survey view, etc.).

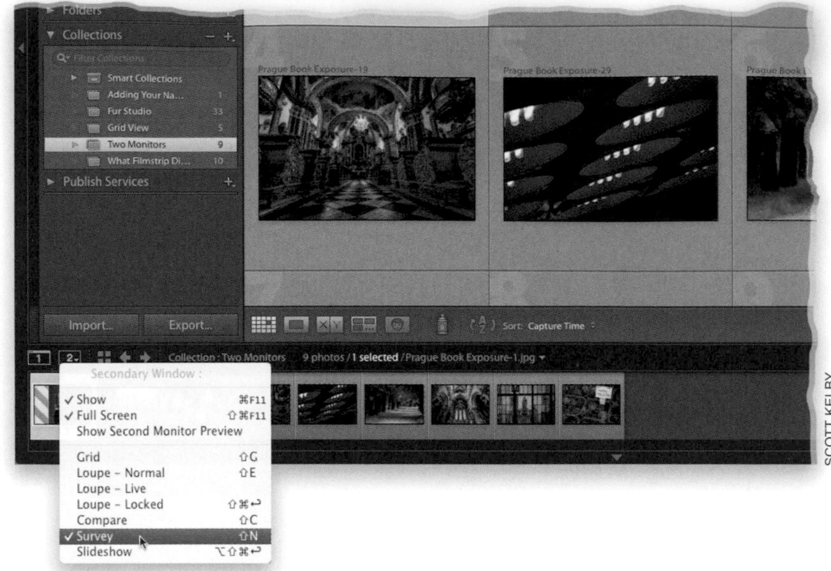

SCOTT KELBY

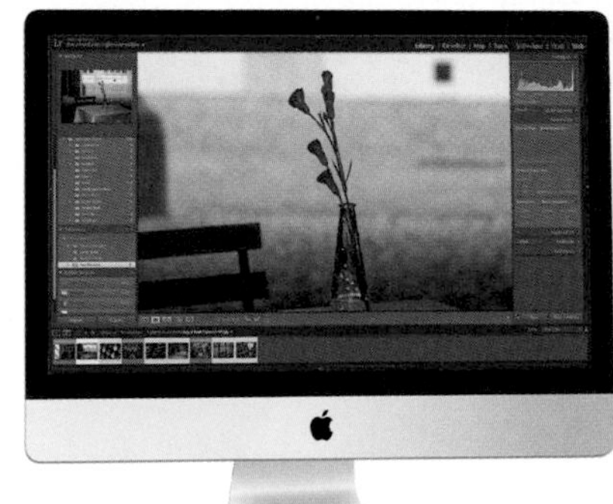

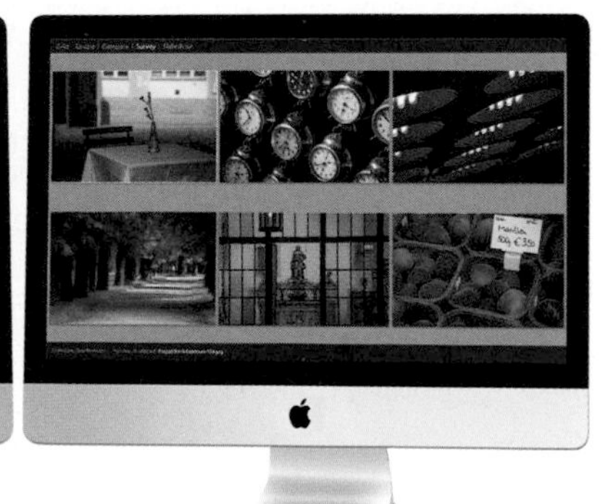

Step Four:

Besides just seeing things larger with the Loupe view, there are some other pretty cool Second Window options. For example, click on the Second Window button and choose **Loupe – Live** from the Secondary Window pop-up menu, then just hover your cursor over the thumbnails in the Grid view (or Filmstrip) on your main display, and watch how the second display shows an instant Loupe view of any photo you pass over (here, you can see on my main display the third photo is selected, but the image you see on my second display is the one my cursor is hovering over—the fifth image).

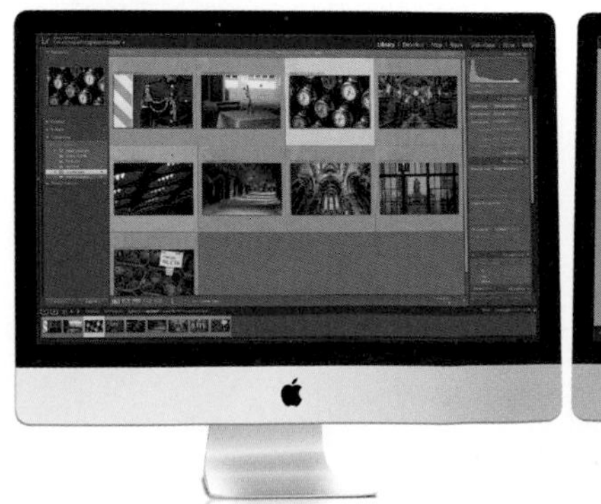

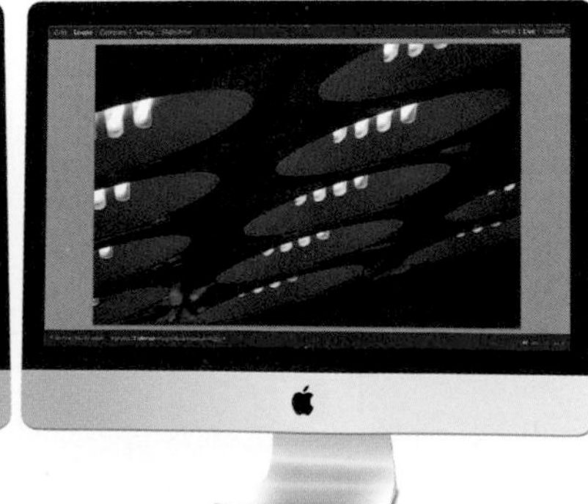

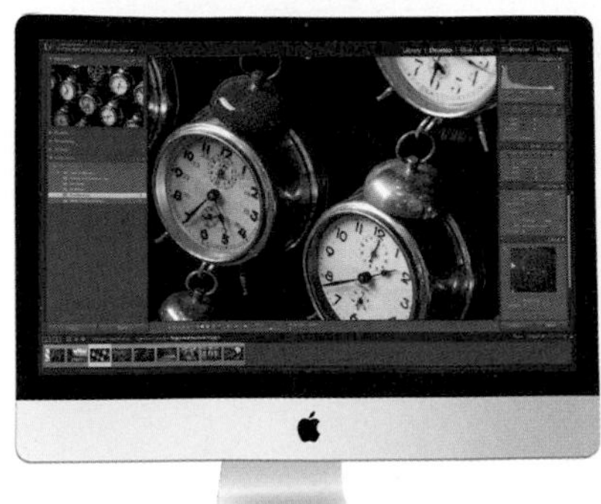
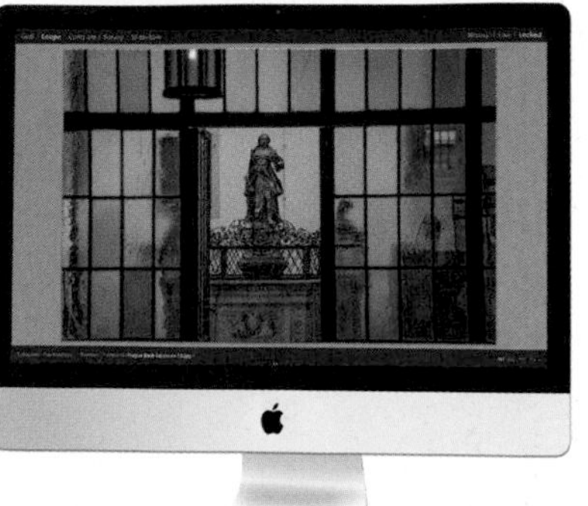

Step Five:

Another Second Window Loupe view option is called **Loupe – Locked** and when you choose this from the Secondary Window pop-up menu, it locks whatever image is currently shown in Loupe view on the second display, so you can look at and edit other images on the main display (to return to where you left off, just turn Loupe – Locked off).

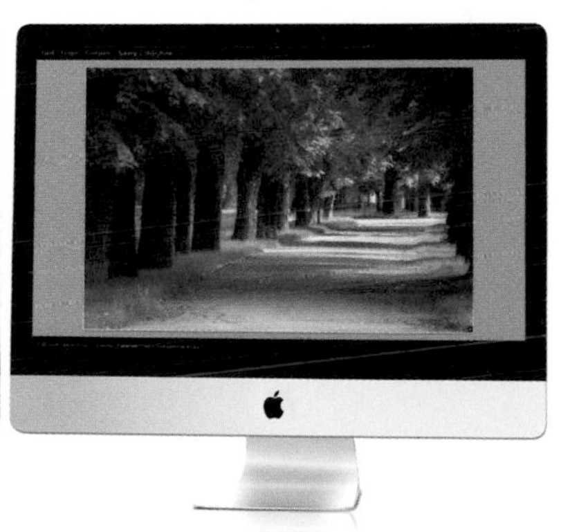

Here's the second display default view, with the navigation bars at the top and bottom visible

Step Six:

The navigation bars at the top and bottom of your image area will be visible on the second display. If you want those hidden, click on the little gray arrows at the top and bottom of the screen to tuck them out of sight, and give you just the image onscreen.

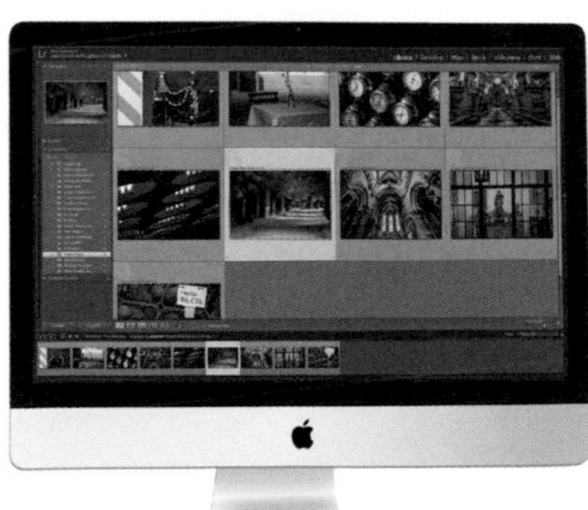
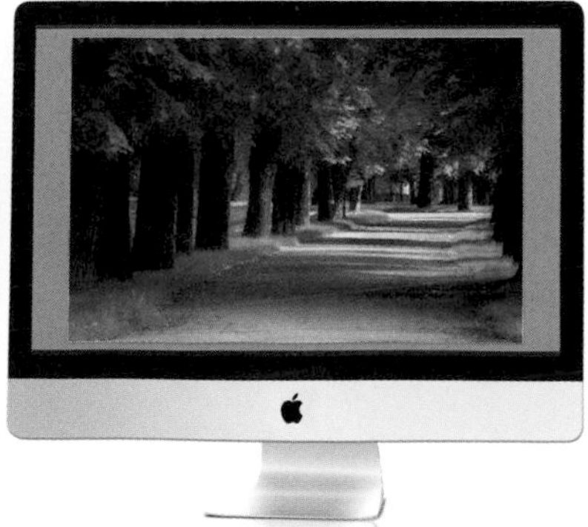

Here's the second display with the navigation bars hidden, which gives a larger view

Continued

TIP: Show Second Monitor Preview

There's a feature found under the Secondary Window pop-up menu called Show Second Monitor Preview, where a small floating Second Monitor window appears on your main display, showing you what's being seen on the second display. This is pretty handy for presentations, where the second display is actually a projector, and your work is being projected on a screen behind you (so you can face the audience), or in instances where you're showing a client some work on a second screen, and the screen is facing away from you (that way, they don't see all the controls, and panels, and other things that might distract them).

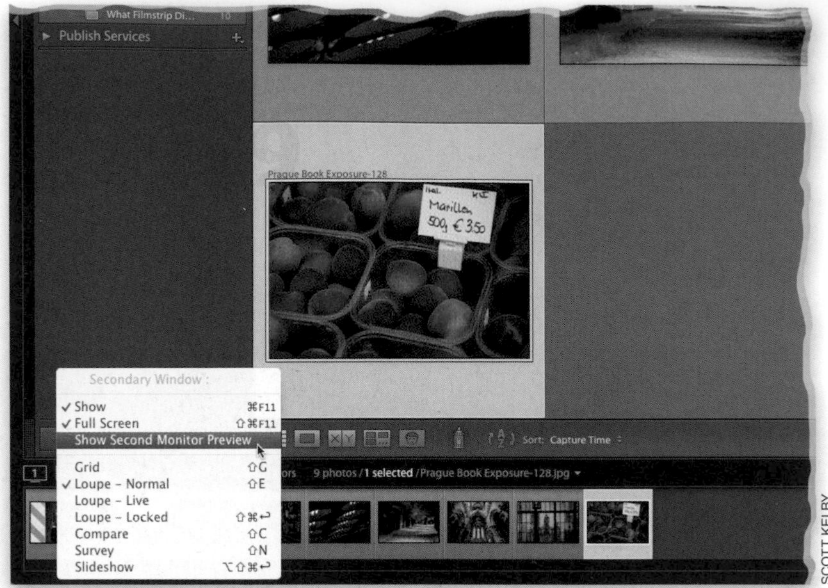

Choosing What the Filmstrip Displays

Just like you can choose what photo information is displayed in the Grid and Loupe views, you can also choose what info gets displayed in the Filmstrip, as well. Because the Filmstrip is pretty short in height, I think it's even more important to control what goes on here, or it starts to look like a cluttered mess. Although I'm going to show you how to turn on/off each line of info, my recommendation is to keep all the Filmstrip info turned off to help avoid "info overload" and visual clutter in an already busy interface. But, just in case, here's how to choose what's displayed down there:

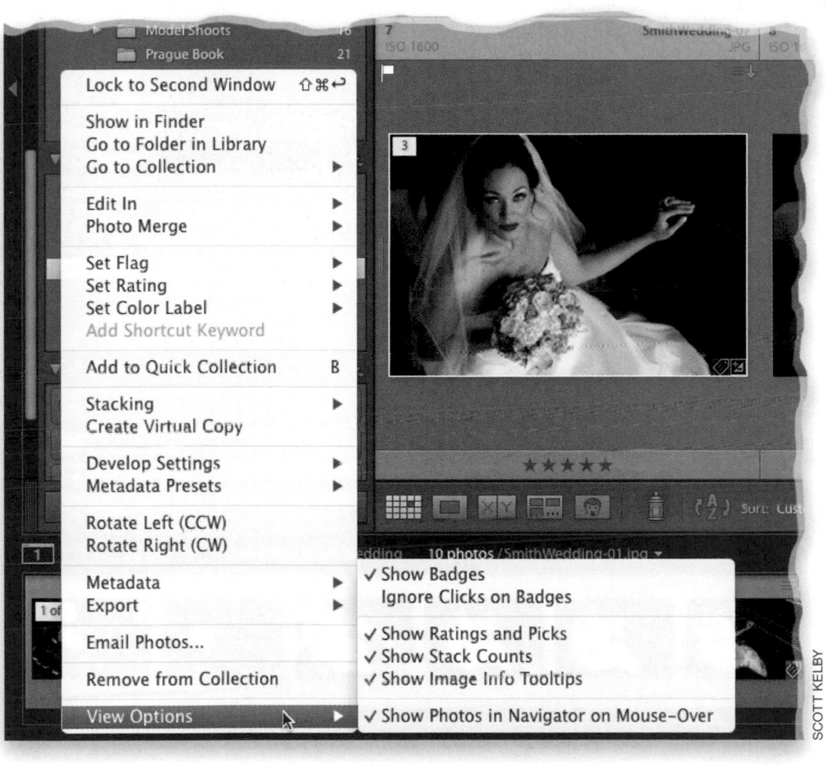

SCOTT KELBY

Step One:

Right-click on any thumbnail in the Filmstrip and a pop-up menu appears (seen here). At the bottom of it are the View Options for the Filmstrip. There are four options: Show Ratings and Picks adds tiny flags and star ratings to your Filmstrip cells. If you choose Show Badges, it adds mini-versions of the same thumbnail badges you see in the Grid view (which show if the photo is in a collection, whether keywords have been applied, whether it has been cropped, or if it has been adjusted in Lightroom). Show Stack Counts adds a stack icon with the number of images inside the stack. The last choice, Show Image Info Tooltips, kicks in when you hover your cursor over an image in the Filmstrip—a little window pops up showing you the info you have chosen in the View Options dialog for your Info Overlay 1. If you get tired of accidentally clicking on badges that launch stuff when you're navigating around the Filmstrip, you can leave the badges visible, but turn off their "clickability" (if that's even a word) by choosing **Ignore Clicks on Badges** here, too.

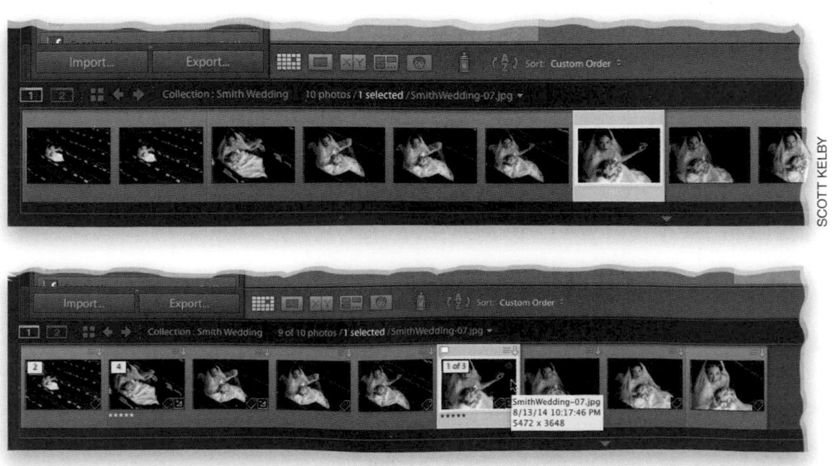

SCOTT KELBY

Step Two:

Here's what the Filmstrip looks like when these options are turned off (top) and with all of them turned on (bottom). You can see Pick flags, star ratings, and thumbnail badges (with unsaved metadata warnings), and I hovered my cursor over one of the thumbnails, so you can see the little pop-up window appear giving me info about the photo. The choice is yours—clean or cluttered.

Adding Your Studio's Name or Logo for a Custom Look

The first time I saw Lightroom, one of the features that really struck me as different was the ability to replace the Lightroom logo (that appears in the upper-left corner of the interface) with either the name of your studio or your studio's logo. I have to say, when you're doing client presentations, it does add a nice custom look to the program (as if Adobe designed Lightroom just for you), but beyond that, the ability to create an Identity Plate goes farther than just giving Lightroom a custom look (but we'll start here, with the custom look).

Step One:

First, just so we have a frame of reference, here's a zoomed-in view of the top-left corner of Lightroom's interface, so you can clearly see the logo we're going to replace starting in Step Two. Now, you can either replace Lightroom's logo using text (and you can even have the text of the modules in the taskbar on the top right match), or you can replace the logo with a graphic of your logo (we'll look at how to do both).

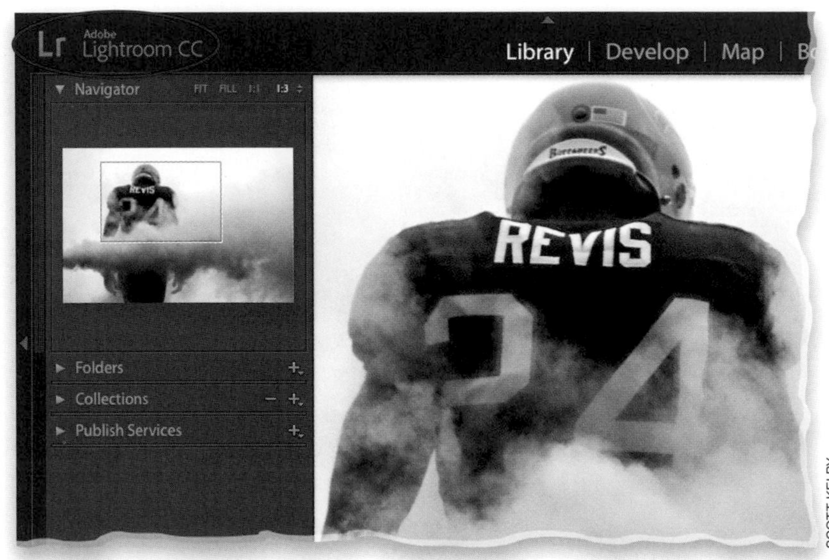

SCOTT KELBY

Step Two:

Go under the Lightroom menu (the Edit menu on a PC) and choose **Identity Plate Setup** to bring up the Identity Plate Editor (shown here). By default, the Identity Plate pop-up menu at the top is set to Lightroom Mobile, so you'll need to change it to **Personalized**. To have your name replace the Lightroom logo seen above, type it in the large black text field on the left side of the dialog. If you don't want your name as your Identity Plate, just type in whatever you'd like (the name of your company, studio, etc.), then while the type is still highlighted, choose a font, font style (bold, italic, condensed, etc.), and font size from the pop-up menus (directly below the text field).

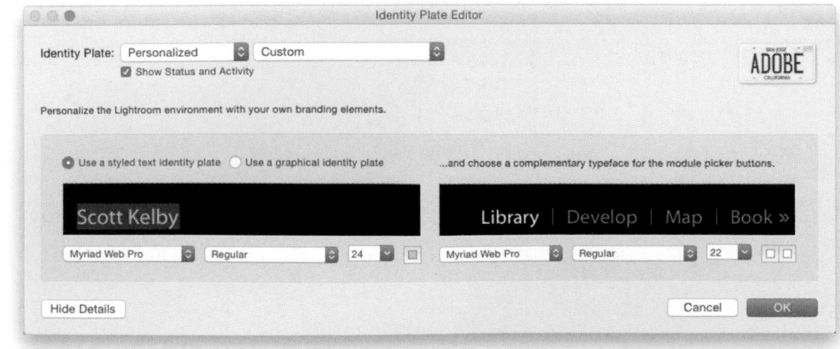

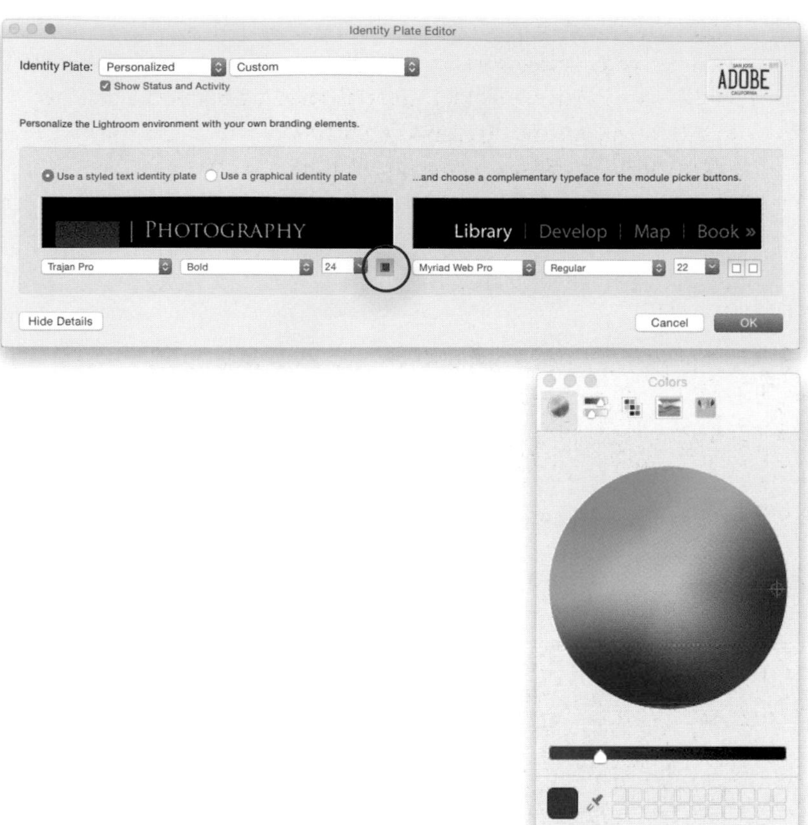

Step Three:

If you want to change only part of your text (for example, if you wanted to change the font of one of the words, or the font size or color of a word), just highlight the word you want to adjust before making the change. To change the color, click on the little square color swatch to the right of the Font Size pop-up menu (it's shown circled here). This brings up the Colors panel (you're seeing the Macintosh Colors panel here; the Windows Color panel will look somewhat different, but don't let that freak you out. Aw, what the heck—go ahead and freak out!). Just choose the color you want your selected text to be, then close the Colors panel.

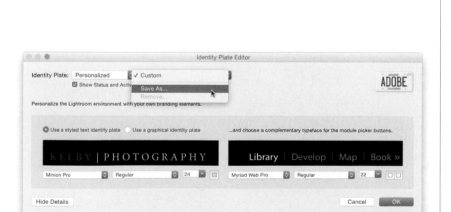

Step Four:

If you like the way your custom Identity Plate looks, you definitely should save it, because creating an Identity Plate does more than just replace the current Lightroom logo—you can add your new custom Identity Plate text (or logo) to any slide show, web gallery, or final print by choosing it from the Identity Plate pop-up menu in all three modules (see, you were dismissing it when you thought it was just a taskbar, feel good feature). To save your custom Identity Plate, from the Enable Identity Plate pop-up menu, choose **Save As** (as shown here). Give your Identity Plate a descriptive name, click OK, and now it's saved. From here on out, it will appear in the handy Identity Plate pop-up menu, where you can get that same custom text, font, and color with just one click.

Continued

Step Five:

Once you click the OK button, your new Identity Plate text replaces the Lightroom logo that was in the upper-left corner (as shown here).

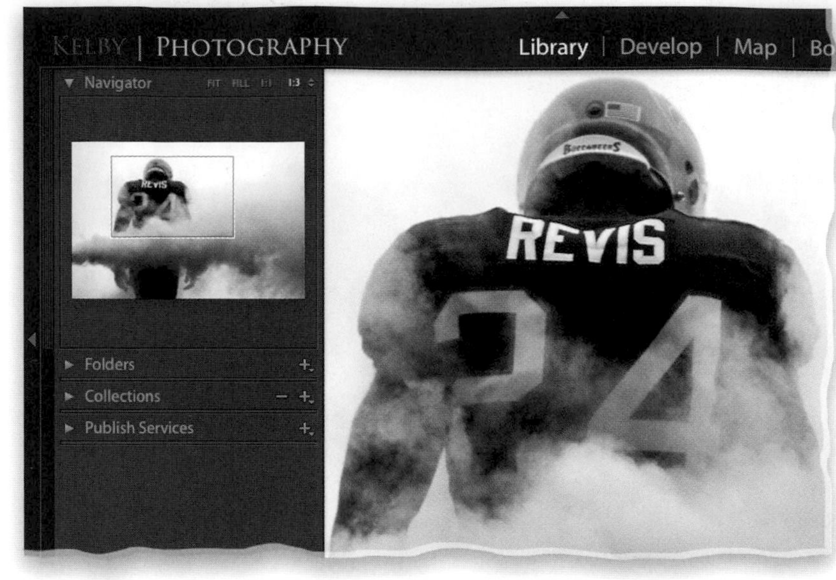

Step Six:

If you want to use a graphic (like your company's logo) instead, just go to the Identity Plate Editor again, but this time, click on the radio button for Use a Graphical Identity Plate (as shown here), instead of Use a Styled Text Identity Plate. Next, click on the Locate File button (found above the Hide/Show Details button near the lower-left corner) and find your logo file. You can put your logo on a black background so it blends in with the Lightroom background, or you can make your background transparent in Photoshop, and save the file in PNG format (which keeps the transparency intact). Now click the Choose button to make that graphic your Identity Plate.

Note: To keep the top and bottom of your graphic from clipping off, make sure your graphic isn't taller than 57 pixels.

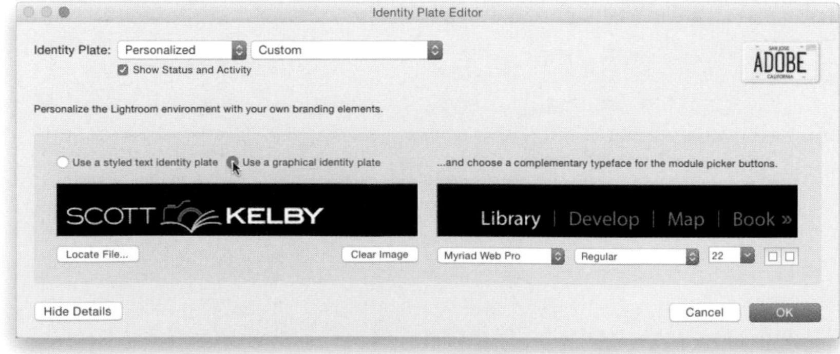

Step Seven:

When you click OK, the Lightroom logo (or your custom text—whichever was up there last) is replaced by the new graphic file of your logo (as shown here). If you like your new graphical logo file in Lightroom, don't forget to save this custom Identity Plate by choosing Save As from the Enable Identity Plate pop-up menu at the top of the dialog.

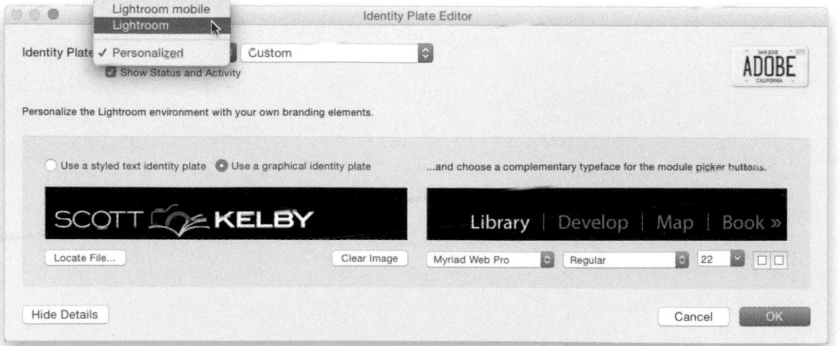

Step Eight:

If you decide, at some point, that you'd like the original Lightroom logo back instead, just go back to the Identity Plate Editor and change the first Identity Plate pop-up menu to **Lightroom** (as shown here). Remember, we'll do more with one of your new Identity Plates later in the book when we cover the modules that can use it.

Lightroom Killer Tips > >

▼ Spacebar Loupe Tricks

If you want to see your currently selected photo zoomed in to Loupe view, just press the **Spacebar**. Once it's zoomed in like that, press the Spacebar again, and it zooms in to whatever magnification (zoom factor) you chose last in the Navigator panel's header (by default, it zooms to 1:1, but if you click on a different zoom factor, it will toggle back and forth between the view you were in first and the zoom factor you clicked on). Once zoomed in, you can move around your image by just clicking-and-dragging on it.

▼ Hiding the Render Messages

If you chose Minimal or Embedded & Sidecar in the Render Previews pop-up menu in the Import window, Lightroom is only going to render higher-resolution previews when you look at a larger view, and while it's rendering these higher-res previews, it displays a little "Loading"

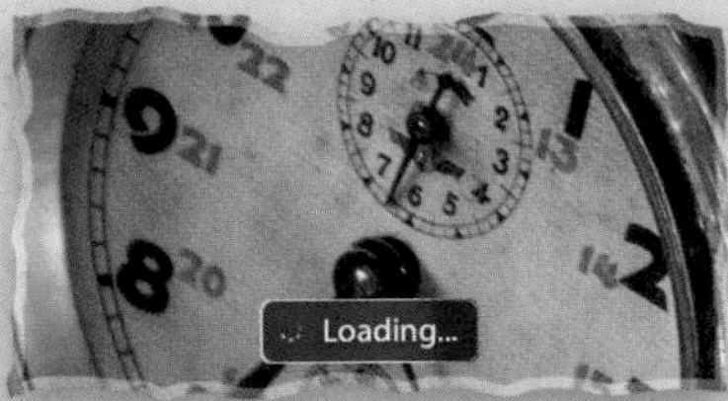

message. You'll see these messages a lot, and if they get on your nerves, you can turn them off by pressing **Command-J (PC: Ctrl-J)** and, in the View Options dialog that appears, click on the Loupe View tab (up top), then in that section, turn off the checkbox for Show Message When Loading or Rendering Photos.

▼ Give Your Labels Names

You can change the default names Lightroom uses for its Color Label feature from the standard names of Red, Blue, Green, etc. (for example, you might want to name

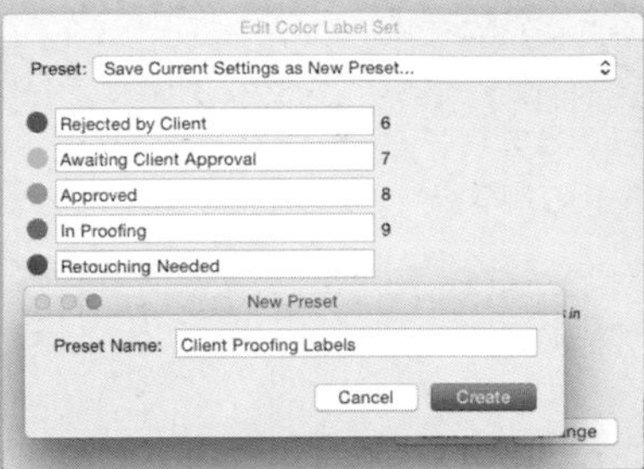

your Green label "Approved," and your Yellow label "Awaiting Client Approval," and so on). You do this by going under the Metadata menu, under Color Label Set, and choosing **Edit** to bring up the Edit Color Label Set dialog. Now, type in your new names (right over the old names). The numbers to the right of the first four color labels are the keyboard shortcuts for applying those labels (Purple doesn't have a shortcut). When you're done, choose **Save Current Settings as New Preset,** from the Preset pop-up menu at the top of the dialog, and give your preset a name. Now, when you apply a label, onscreen you'll see "Approved" or "In Proofing" or whatever you choose (plus, the Set Color Label submenu [found under the Photo menu] updates to show your new names).

▼ Opening All Panels at Once

If you want every panel expanded in a particular side panel, just Right-click on any panel's header, then choose **Expand All** from the pop-up menu.

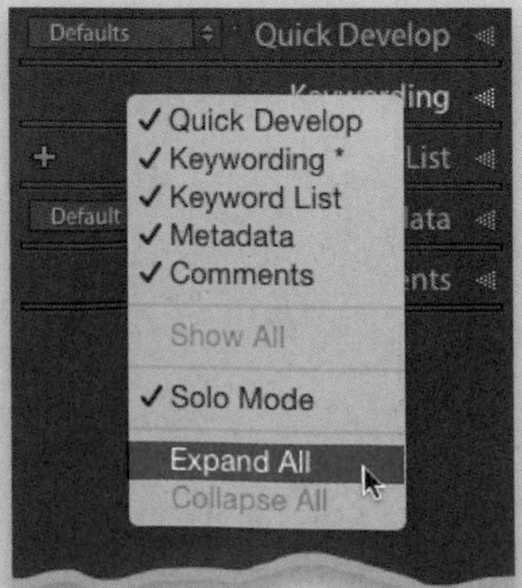

▼ How to Link Your Panels So They Close Simultaneously

If you set your side panels to Manual (you show and hide them by clicking on the little gray triangles), you can set them up to where if you close one side, the other side closes, too (or if you close

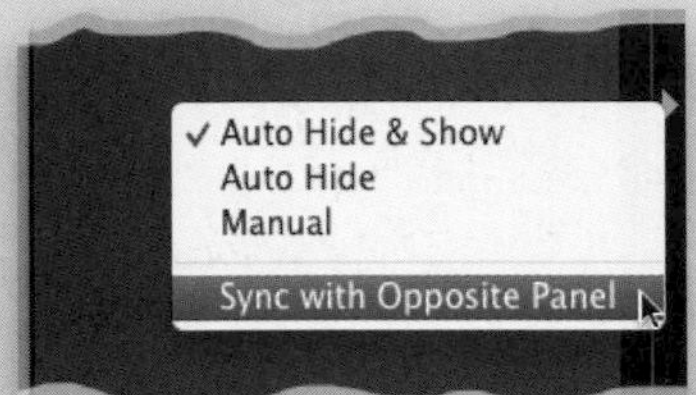

the top, the bottom closes, too). To do this, Right-click on one of those little gray triangles, and from the pop-up menu that appears, choose **Sync With Opposite Panel**.

▼ Jump to a 100% View

Any time you want to quickly see your image at a 100% full-size view, just press the letter **Z** on your keyboard.

▼ Changing Where Lightroom Zooms

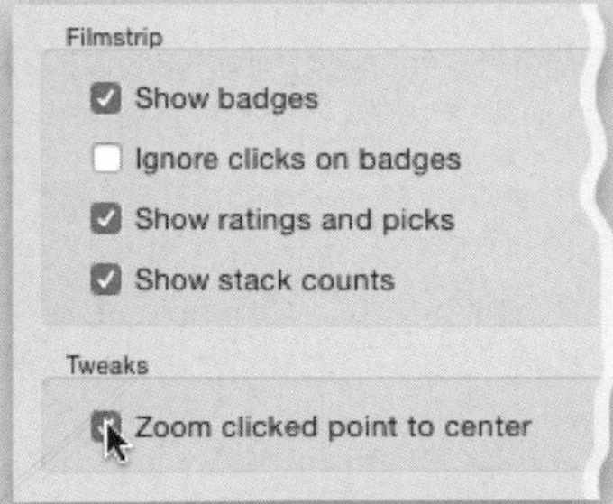

When you click to zoom in on a photo, Lightroom magnifies the photo, but if you want the area that you clicked on to appear centered on the screen, press **Command-,** (comma; **PC: Ctrl-,**) to bring up Lightroom's Preferences dialog, then click on the Interface tab, and at the bottom, turn on the checkbox for Zoom Clicked Point to Center.

Lightroom Killer Tips > >

▼ Hiding Modules You Don't Use

If there are some modules that you don't use at all (maybe you don't use the Web or Slideshow modules), you can actually hide those modules from view (after all, if you don't use 'em, why should you have to see them everyday, right?). Just Right-click directly on any of the module names (Develop, for example) and a pop-up menu will appear. By default, they've all got a checkmark beside them, because they're all visible. So, just chose whichever one you want hidden and it's out of sight. Want to hide another module? Do the same thing, again.

▼ See Common Attributes

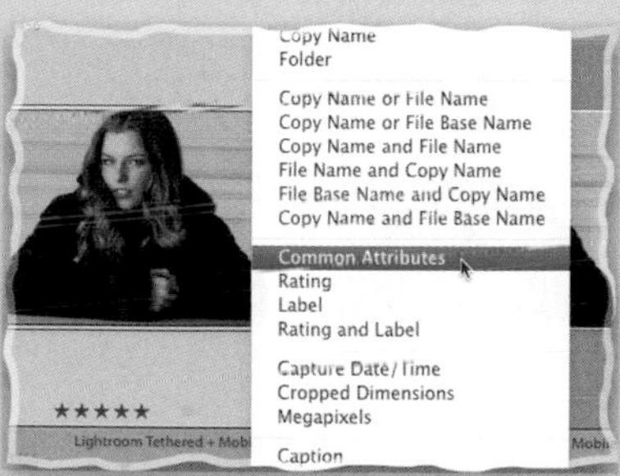

If you want to see if your image is flagged or has a star rating, there's a Common Attributes feature in the view pop-up menu (just Right-click at the top of a thumbnail cell), and if you choose it as one of your view criteria, it'll show those along the top of the image cell.

▼ Delete Old Backups to Save Big Space

I usually back up my Lightroom catalog once a day (when I'm done for the day and am closing Lightroom; see Chapter 2 for more on this). The problem is that after a while, you've got a lot of backup copies—and before long you've got months of old, outdated copies taking up space on your hard drive (I really only need one or two backup copies. After all, I'm not going to choose a backup from three months ago). So, go to your Lightroom folder from time to time and delete those outdated backups.

▼ Changing Lightroom's Background Color

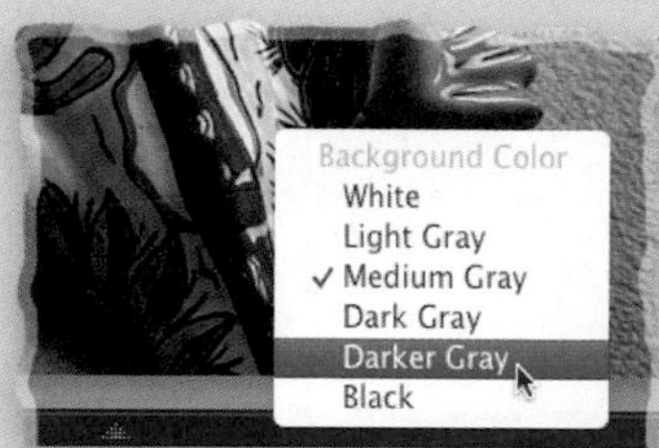

You can change that medium gray background color that appears behind your photos by Right-clicking anywhere on that gray area, and from the pop-up menu that appears, you can choose different background colors.

▼ Collection Badge

Lightroom has a Collection thumbnail badge (it looks like two overlapping rectangles), which, if you see it at the bottom-right corner of a thumbnail, lets you know the image is in a collection. Click on it, and a list of collections that photo appears within shows up, and you can click on any one to jump directly to that collection.

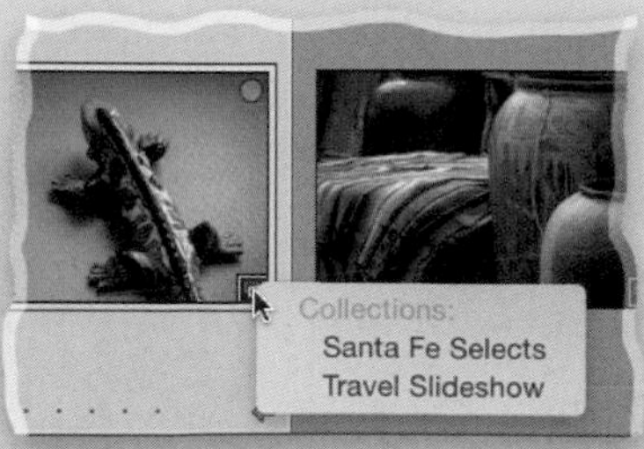

▼ The Secret Identity Plate Text Formatting Trick

It's surprisingly hard to format text inside the Identity Plate Editor window, especially if you want multiple lines of text (of course, the fact that you can have multiple lines of text—on a Mac only—is a tip unto itself). But, there's a better way: Create your text somewhere else that has nice typographic controls, then select and copy your text into memory. Then come back to the Identity Plate Editor and paste that already formatted text right into it, and it will maintain your font and layout attributes.

▼ You Can Add a Little Ornament Under the Last Panel

Lightroom used to have a little flourish thingy (called an end mark) at the bottom of the last panel in the side Panels areas that let you know you were at the last panel. It's gone, but you can add a built-in graphic or add your own. To add one, press **Command-,** (comma; **PC: Ctrl-,**) to open the Preferences dialog and click on the Interface tab. At the top, choose **Small Flourish** from the End Marks pop-up menu. You can also create your own

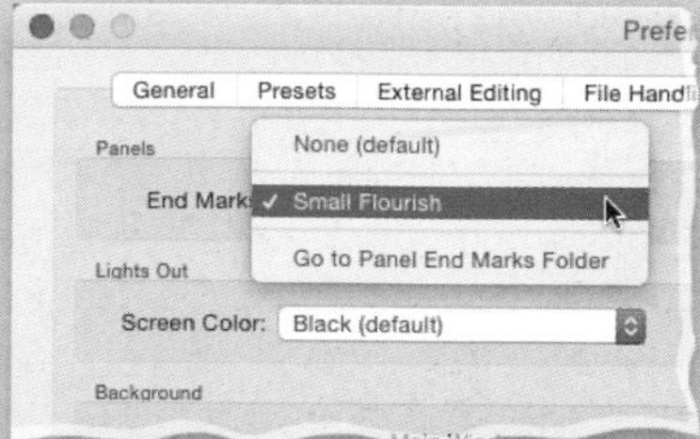

custom end marks (make sure they're on a transparent background, and saved in PNG format), then choose **Go to Panel End Marks Folder** instead. This is the folder you'll drop them into and choose them from.

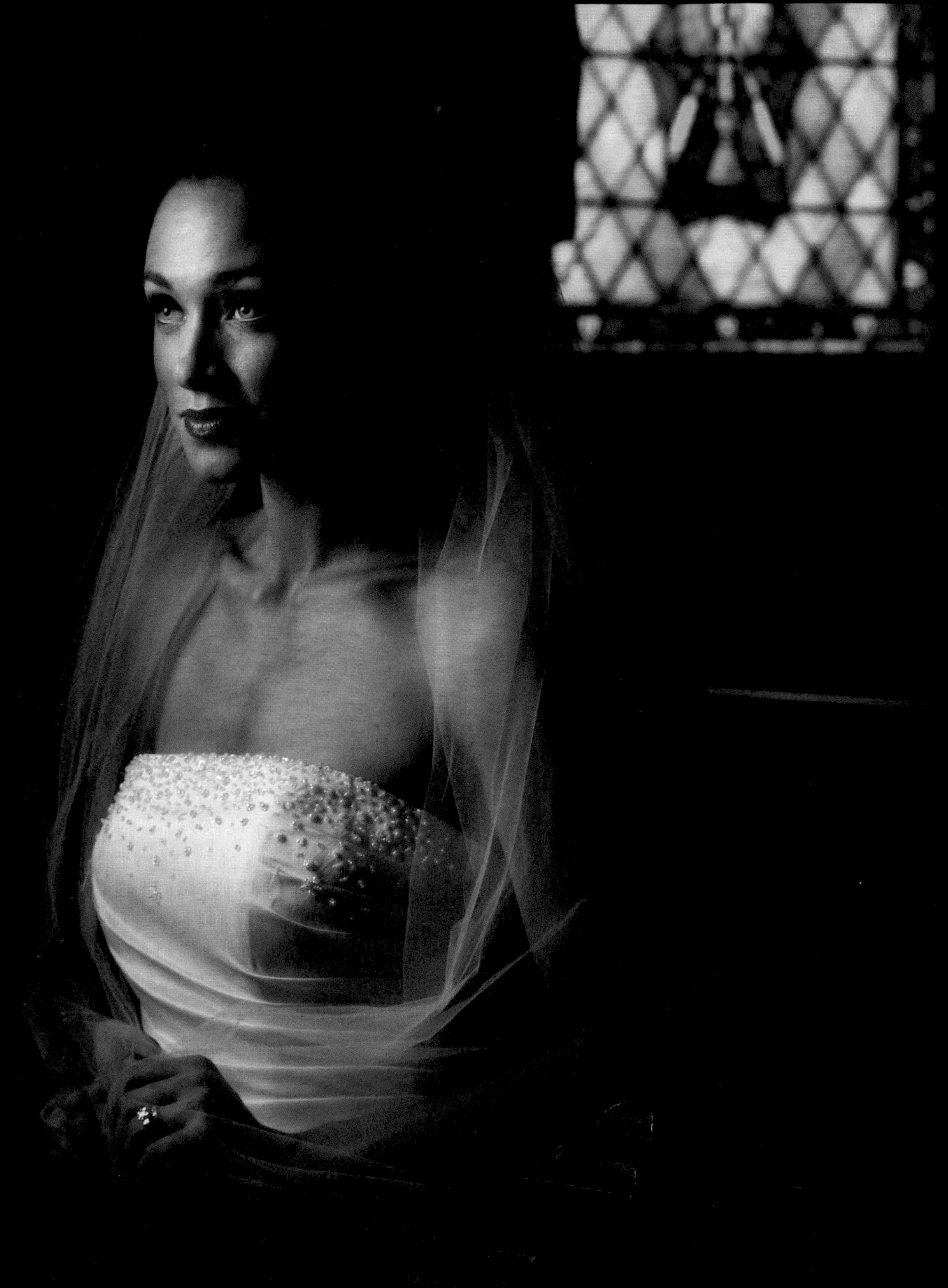

Photo by Scott Kelby | Exposure: 1/60 sec | Focal Length: 70mm | Aperture Value: ƒ/5.6

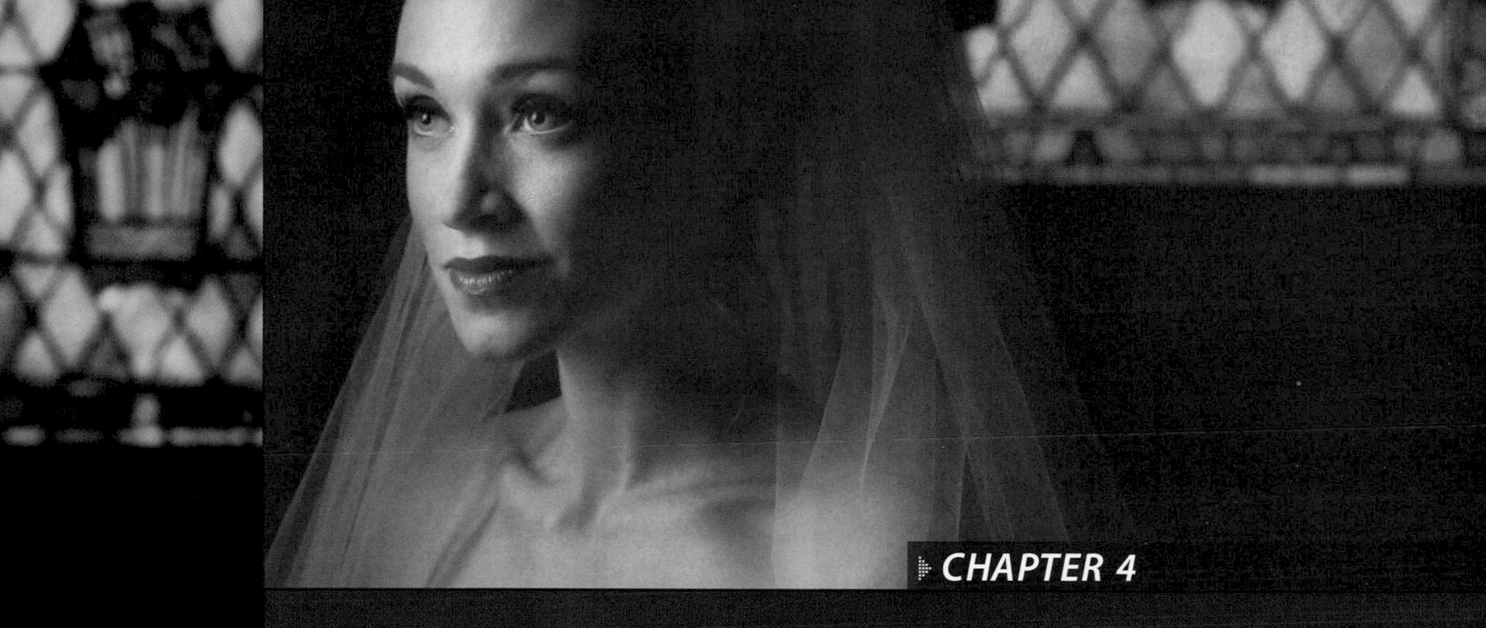

CHAPTER 4

EDITING ESSENTIALS

how to develop your photos

I kinda like that subhead above—How to Develop Your Photos—because even though it sounds like a direct reference to Lightroom's Develop module, the name of that module itself is a direct reference to what we used to do in the darkroom—develop our prints. Of course, this chapter isn't about prints, which pretty much throws that whole line of thought out the window, but we're not going to look that closely at things like that (or grammar, spelling, or ending sentences with a preposition), because instead we're going to bask in the fact that now we can develop our photos without having to mix dangerous chemicals. Now, of course, back in the old days (which was only about 10 years ago), we didn't realize these chemicals were dangerous, so we'd be in the darkroom, developing some T-MAX P3200, and somebody would get thirsty, so we'd just take a big swig of some Hypo Clearing Agent (which was a chemical we used to remove the fixing agent from fiber-based paper, but doggone it if that stuff didn't taste just like Welch's grape juice, so we'd usually finish off a bag or two before coming out and grabbing a Reuben and a bag of Doritos). Anyway, it seemed like a pretty good idea at the time, but then my darkroom buddy Frank got this huge goiter in the shape of the Transamerica building, so we backed off on the Hypo Clear, and just stuck to chugging the Indicator Stop Bath (we loved those little salmon-colored bottles. We'd keep 'em in the fridge and even take them on picnics). Anyway, that was a different time. Now we know better, and so we stick to chain smoking and strutting around in our asbestos photo vests.

Making Your RAW Photos Look More Like JPEGs

Why would we want our RAW photos to look more like JPEGs? It's because JPEGs look better straight out of the camera—they're sharpened, contrast is added, noise is reduced, etc., all in-camera. When you shoot in RAW, you're telling your camera to turn off all that stuff and just give you the raw, untouched photo. That's why RAW photos look so flat, and why the #1 complaint I hear is "When my photos first appear in Lightroom, they look great, but then they change and look terrible." That's because you see the JPEG preview first, then you see the actual RAW photo. Here's how to get a more JPEG-like starting place:

Step One:

First, let's take a look at how this will play out onscreen, so you'll know what to look for. When you first import photos into Lightroom, and you double-click on a thumbnail to look at one of them larger, you're likely to see "Loading..." appear either under or near the bottom of your image (as seen here, circled in red). That's letting you know that (a) you're now seeing the JPEG preview onscreen (the version that has been sharpened, had contrast added, and so on), and (b) it's loading the RAW image, which takes just a moment. While you're looking at this JPEG preview, you're probably thinking, "Hey, this looks pretty much like what I saw on the back of my camera when I took the shot."

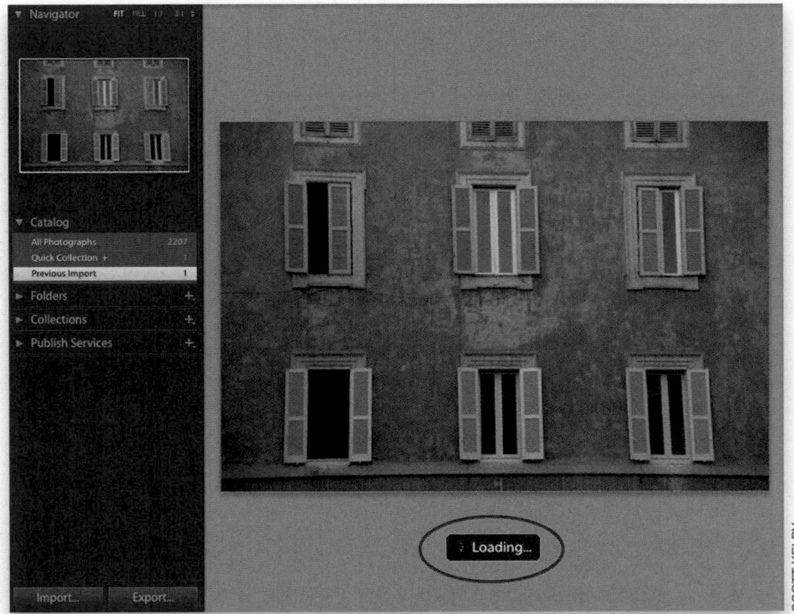

SCOTT KELBY

Step Two:

After your RAW image loads (it only takes a second or two), you now see the actual raw image (seen here), and you're probably thinking, "This looks nothing like the image I saw on the back of my camera! It's flatter and less contrasty and less sharp." That's because even when you shoot in RAW mode, the screen on the back of your camera still shows you the nice, sharp, contrasty JPEG image. This is why I hear so many users say, "It looked really good when it first imported, but now it looks really bad." That's because you saw the JPEG when it first imported and a few seconds later (after it loads the real RAW image), you see the rather flat-looking image you see here. So, if you'd like to start your editing process with an image that looks more like the JPEG did, go on to the next step.

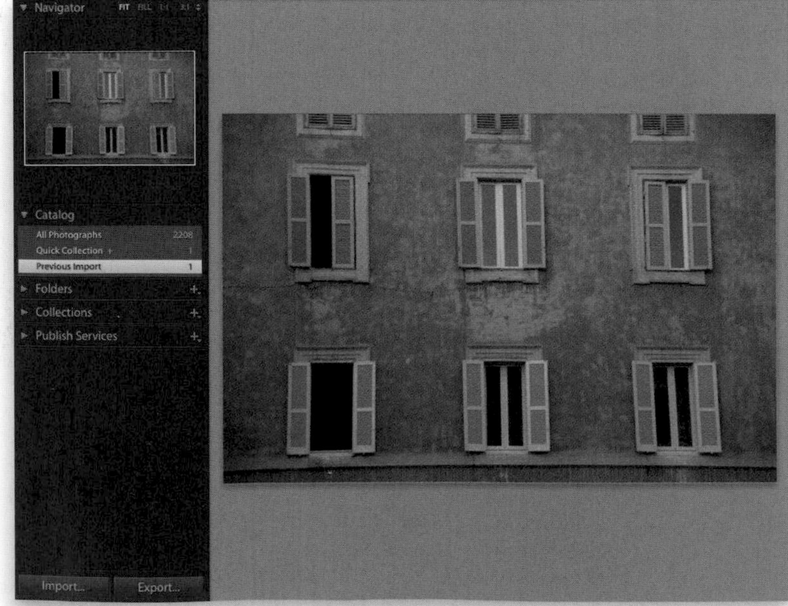

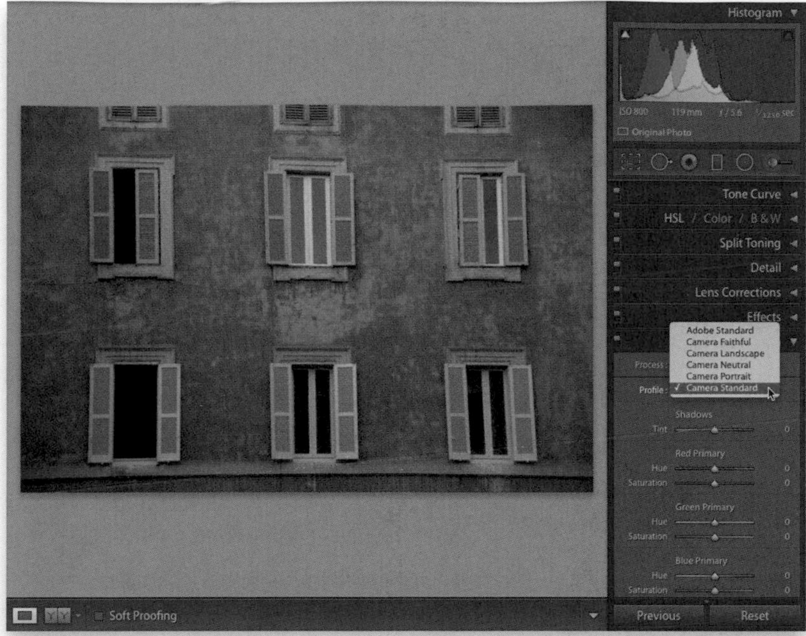

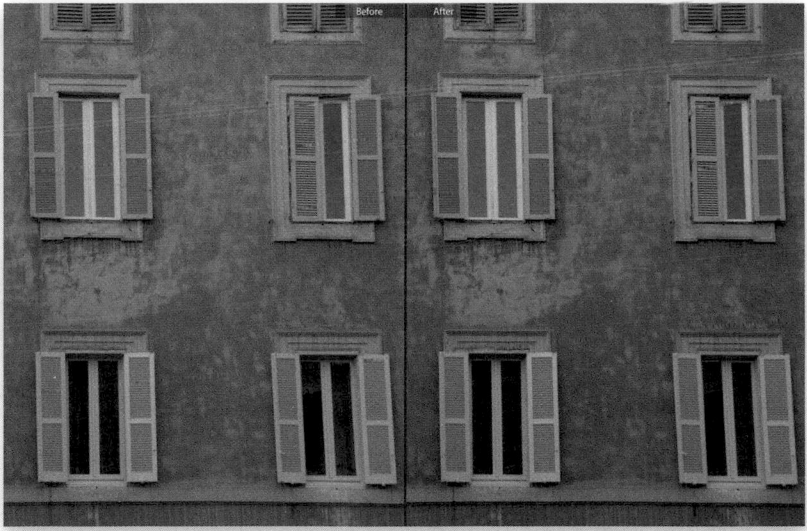

Step Three:

To get a more JPEG-like starting place for your RAW images, go to the Develop module and scroll down to the Camera Calibration panel. There's a Profile pop-up menu near the top of this panel, where you'll find a number of profiles based on your camera's make and model (it reads the image file's embedded EXIF data to find this. Not all camera brands or models are supported, but most recent Nikon and Canon DSLRs are, along with some Pentax, Sony, Olympus, Leica, and Kodak models). These profiles mimic camera presets you could have applied to your JPEG images in-camera (but are ignored when you shoot in RAW). The default profile is Adobe Standard, which looks pretty average (if you ask me). Here I chose Camera Standard and the image looks more vibrant and has more contrast.

Step Four:

Another one I think looks more JPEG-like is Camera Landscape (for Canon or Nikon images) or Camera Vivid for Nikons, both of which are more vivid and contrasty (choose the one that you like the best). I've learned that these profiles look different on different pictures. That's why I recommend trying a few different profiles to find the one that's right for the photo you're working with. Here's a before/after with the RAW image on the left and the same image with the Camera Standard profile applied on the right. *Note:* You only get these camera profiles if you shot in RAW. If you shot in JPEG mode, the profile is already embedded.

TIP: Apply Profiles Automatically

If you like a particular profile, Lightroom can automatically apply it to your RAW images as they're imported: Go to the Develop module, choose the profile (don't do anything else), and create a Develop preset with that name. Now, choose that preset from the Develop Settings pop-up menu in Lightroom's Import window. (For more on creating presets, see Chapter 6.)

Setting the White Balance

I always start editing my photos by setting the white balance first, because if you get the white balance right, the color is right, and your color correction problems pretty much go away. You adjust the white balance in the Basic panel, which is the most misnamed panel in Lightroom. It should be called the "Essentials" panel, because it contains the most important, and the most used, controls in the entire Develop module.

Step One:

In the Library module, click on the photo you want to edit, and then press the letter **D** on your keyboard to jump over to the Develop module. By the way, you're probably figuring that since you press D for the Develop module, it must be S for Slideshow, P for Print, W for Web, etc., right? Sadly, no—that would make things too easy. Nope, it's just Develop that uses the first letter. (Arrrrgggh!) Anyway, once you're in the Develop module, the White Balance controls appear at the top of the Basic panel, and the photo is displayed using whatever you had the white balance set on in your digital camera (that's why it says "As Shot" to the right of WB. You're seeing the white balance "as it was shot," which in this case is way too blue).

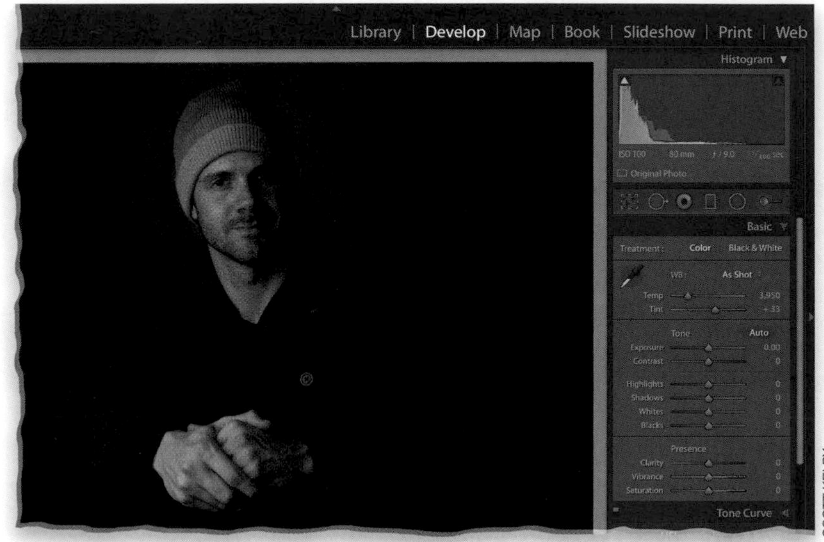

SCOTT KELBY

Step Two:

There are three main ways to set the white balance, and we'll start with trying out the different built-in White Balance presets (if you shot in RAW, Lightroom lets you choose the same white balance settings you could have chosen in the camera. If you shot in JPEG mode, all these presets won't be available—just Auto will be available because your white balance choice is already embedded in the file. We can still change the white balance for JPEG files, but aside from choosing Auto, not from this pop-up menu). Click-and-hold on As Shot and the pop-up menu of White Balance presets appears (as seen here).

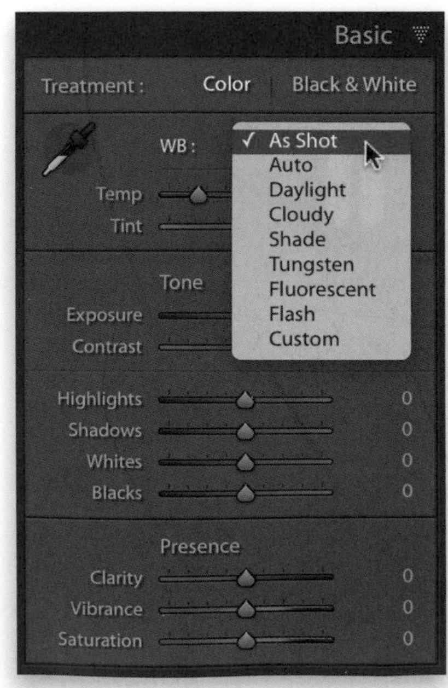

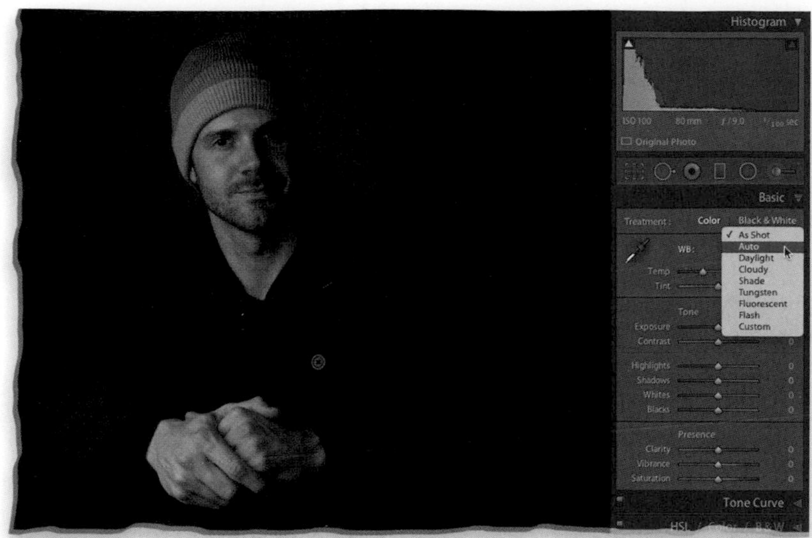

Step Three:

In our photo in Step One, the overall tone is really blue (not very flattering to most folks), so it definitely needs a white balance adjustment. (*Note:* If you want to follow along using this same image, you're welcome to download it from **http://kelbyone.com/books/lr6**.) We need to make it warmer, so choose Auto from the White Balance pop-up menu and see how that looks (as you can see here, it's much better all-around, but that doesn't mean it's the right one, so we have to try a few others to see which one gets us closest to how he looked in real life). The next three White Balance presets down will make things warmer (more yellow), with Daylight being a bit warmer, and Cloudy and Shade being a lot warmer. Go ahead and choose Cloudy (just so you can see it), and now the whole photo is much too warm.

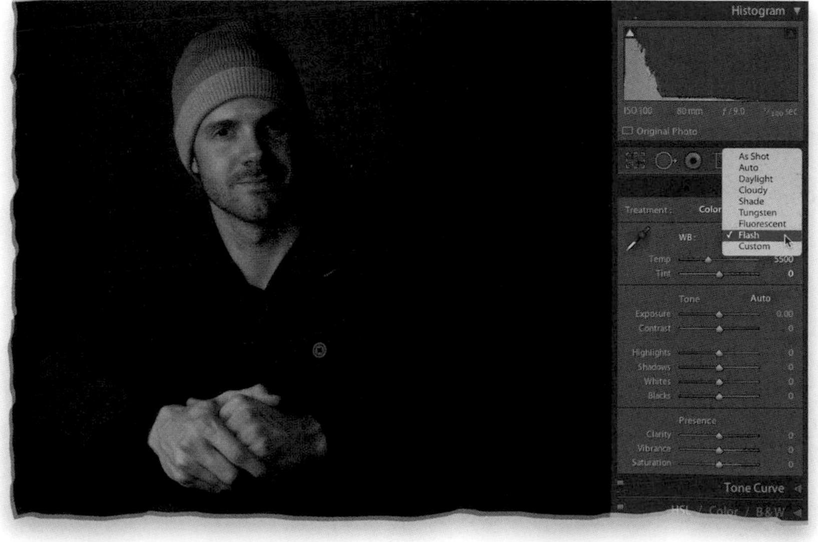

Step Four:

If you choose either of the next two down—Tungsten or Fluorescent—they're going to be way crazy blue, so you don't want either of those. In this case (since I lit the shot with flash), I tried the Flash preset (as shown here), and it looks pretty decent. It's warmer than Auto and people generally look better with a warmer skin tone, so I might stick with that one. By the way, the last preset isn't really a preset at all—Custom just means you're going to create the white balance manually using one of the two other methods we're going to look at. Now, here's what I do: First, quickly run through all the presets and see if one of them happens to be right on the money (it happens more than you might think). If one looks right on the money, that's it. I'm done. If not, then I just use the one that is closest as a starting point, and I go on to method #2 (on the next page).

Continued

Step Five:

Method #2 is, again, to start with a preset that is close to what you want, then tweak it using the Temp (short for Temperature) and Tint sliders found just below the WB preset menu. I zoomed in here on the Basic panel so you can get a nice close-up of these sliders, because Adobe did something really great to help you out here—they colorized the slider bars, so you can see what will happen if you drag in a particular direction. See how the left side of the Temp slider is blue, and the right side graduates over to yellow? That tells you exactly what the slider does. So, without any further explanation, which way would you drag the Temp slider to make the photo more blue? To the left, of course. Which way would you drag the Tint slider to make the image more magenta? See, it's a little thing, but it's a big help. *Note:* To reset both the Temp and Tint sliders to their original settings, double-click on the letters "WB."

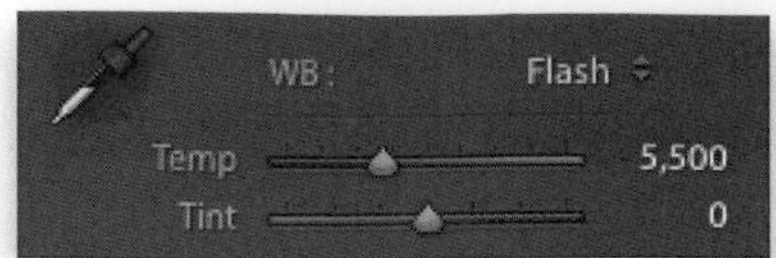

Here's the White Balance temperature settings when you choose the Flash preset

Step Six:

Let's put this to use. I wound up sticking with the Flash preset, but I felt it was a little too warm (yellowish). So, let's drag the Temp slider slowly toward the blue side (to the left), so the skin tone doesn't look quite so yellow. In this case, that had me dragging over to 5168 (when I chose the Flash preset, it set the Temperature to 5500—the higher the number, the warmer the color). That's all there is to it—use a White Balance preset as your starting place, then use the Temp and/or Tint sliders to tweak it until it looks right (here's a before/after from the original to the one we corrected). Okay, those are Methods #1 and #2, but Method #3 is my favorite and the way I think you'll usually get the best, most accurate results, and that is to use the White Balance Selector tool (it's that huge eyedropper on the top-left side of the white balance section, or press **W**).

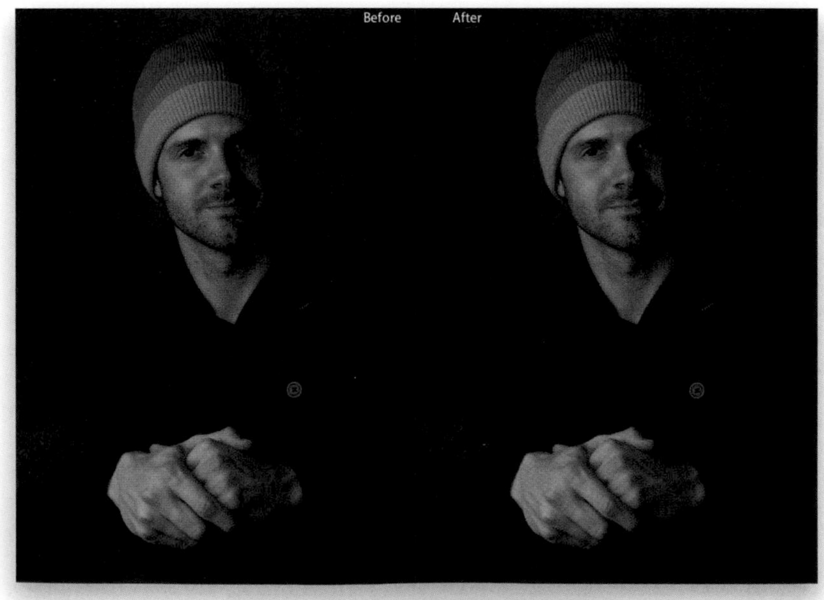

WB: Custom
Temp 5168
Tint 0

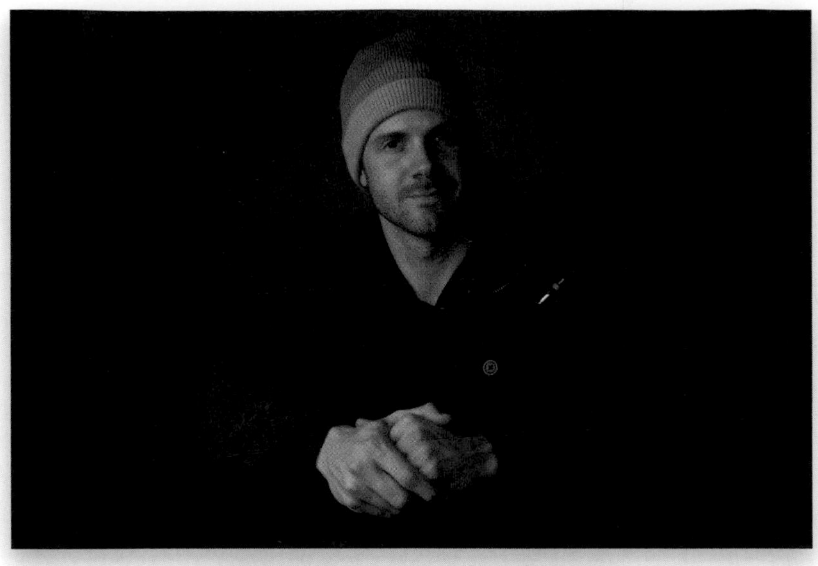

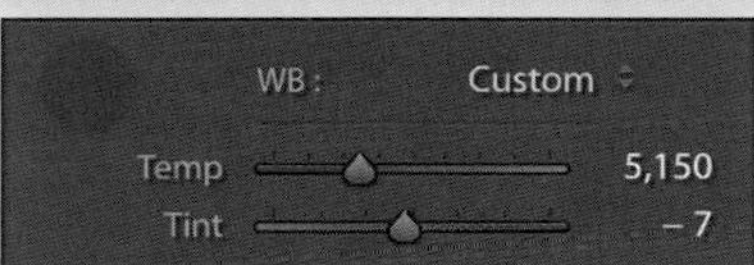

Step Seven:

First, choose **As Shot** from the White Balance pop-up menu, so we're starting from scratch with this. Now click on the tool to get it, then ideally, you'd click it on something in your photo that's supposed to be gray (that's right—don't click on something white, look for something gray. Video cameras white balance on solid white, but digital still cameras need to white balance on a gray instead). All you have to do for this image is click the White Balance Selector tool on his jacket (I clicked just to the right of his jacket collar) and the white balance is fixed (as seen here).

TIP: Dismiss the White Balance Selector Tool

In the toolbar, there's an Auto Dismiss checkbox. With this turned on, after you click the White Balance Selector tool once, it automatically returns to its home in the Basic panel.

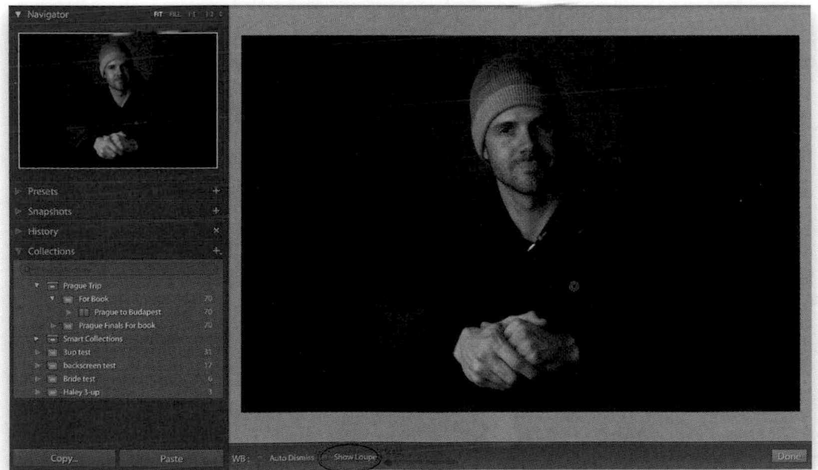

Step Eight:

This is more of a tip than a step, but it's super-helpful. When you're using the White Balance Selector tool, look over at the Navigator panel on the top of the left side Panels area. As you hover the White Balance Selector tool over different parts of your photo, it gives you a live preview (as shown here) of what the white balance would look like if you clicked there. This is huge, and saves you lots of clicks and lots of time when trying to find a white balance that looks good to you. Next, you'll probably notice a large pixelated grid that appears while you're using the White Balance Selector tool. It's supposed to magnify the area your cursor is over to help you find a neutral gray area but if it drives you crazy (like it does me), you can get rid of it by turning off the Show Loupe checkbox down in the toolbar (I've circled it here in red, because my guess is you'll be searching for that checkbox pretty quickly).

Setting Your White Balance Live While Shooting Tethered

The fact that you can shoot tethered directly from your camera, straight into Lightroom, is one of my favorite features in Lightroom, but when I learned the trick of having the correct white balance applied automatically, as the images first come into Lightroom, it just put me over the top. So much so that I was able to include a free, perforated tear-out 18% gray card in the back of this book, so you can do the exact same thing (without having to go out and buy a gray card. A big thanks to my publisher, Peachpit Press, for letting me include this). You are going to love this!

Step One:

Start by connecting your camera to your computer (or laptop) using a USB cable, then go under Lightroom's File menu, under Tethered Capture, and choose **Start Tethered Capture** (as shown here). This brings up the Tethered Capture Settings dialog, where you choose your preferences for how the images will be handled as they're imported into Lightroom (see page 29 in Chapter 1 for more details on this dialog and what to put in where).

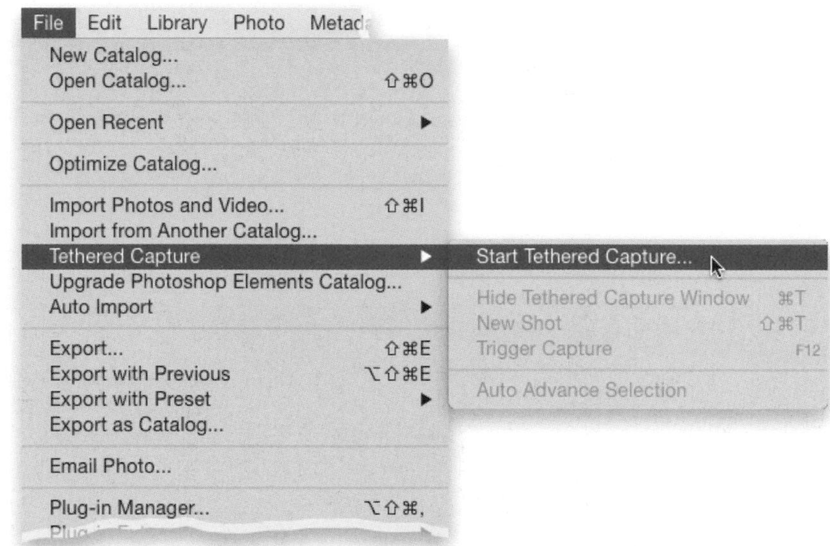

Step Two:

Once you get your lighting set up the way you want it (or if you're shooting in natural light), place your subject into position, then go to the back of this book, and tear out the perforated 18% gray card. Hand the gray card to your subject and ask them to hold it while you take a test shot (if you're shooting a product instead, just lean the gray card on the product, or somewhere right near it in the same light). Now take your test shot with the gray card clearly visible in the shot (as shown here).

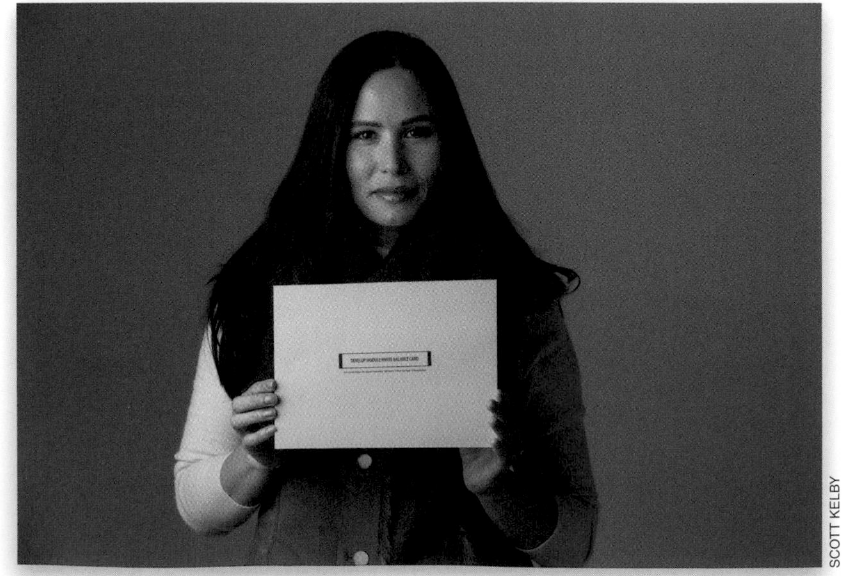

SCOTT KELBY

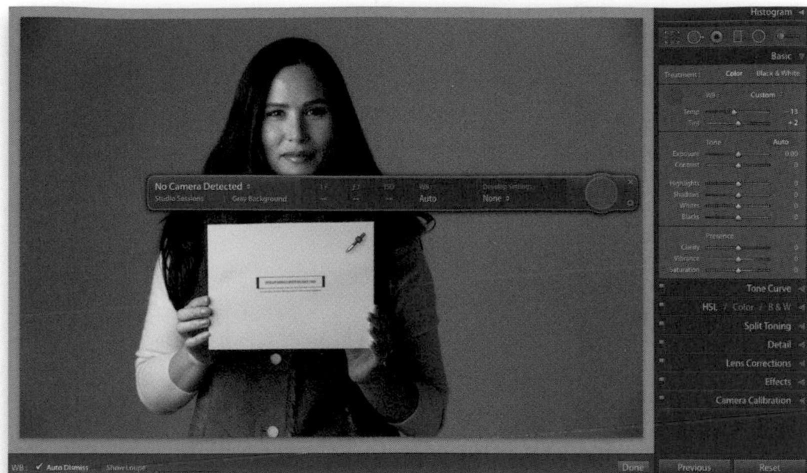

Step Three:

When the photo with the gray card appears in Lightroom, get the White Balance Selector tool **(W)** from the top of the Develop module's Basic panel, and click it once on the gray card in the photo (as shown here). That's it—your white balance is now properly set for this photo. Now, we're going to take that white balance setting and use it to automatically fix the rest of the photos as they're imported.

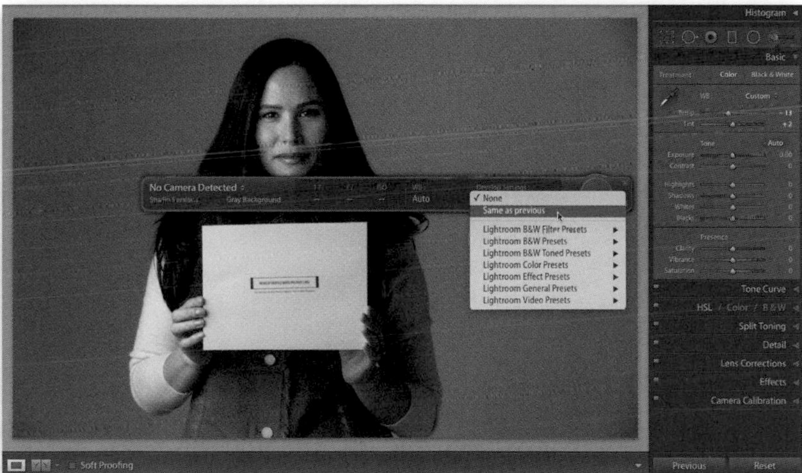

Step Four:

Go to the Tethered Capture window (press **Command-T [PC: Ctrl-T]** if it's no longer visible) and on the right side, from the Develop Settings pop-up menu, choose **Same as Previous**. That's it—now you can take the gray card out of the scene (or get it back from your subject, who's probably tired of holding it by now), and you can go back to shooting. As the next photos you shoot come into Lightroom, they will have that custom white balance you set in the first image applied to the rest of them automatically. So, now not only will you see the proper white balance for the rest of the shoot, that's just another thing you don't have to mess with in post-production afterwards. Again, a big thanks to my publisher, Peachpit Press, for allowing me to include this gray card in the book for you.

Seeing Befores and Afters

In the first white balance project at the beginning of this chapter, I ended with a before and after, but I didn't get a chance to show you how I did that. I love the way Lightroom handles the whole before and after process because it gives you a lot of flexibility to see these the way you want to see them. Here's how:

Step One:

Any time you're working in the Develop module and you want to see what your image looked like before you started tweaking it (the "before" image), just press the **\ (backslash) key** on your keyboard. You'll see the word "Before" appear in the upper-right corner of your image, as seen here. In this image, you're seeing the overly cool original image. This is probably the Before view I use the most in my own workflow. To return to your After image, press the \ key again (it doesn't say "After;" the Before just goes away).

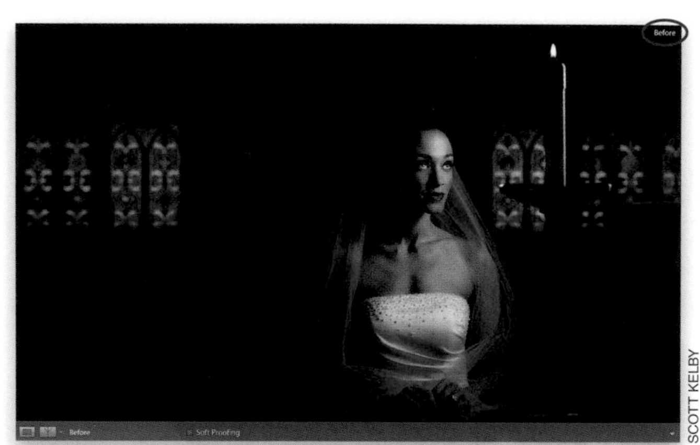

SCOTT KELBY

Step Two:

To see a side-by-side Before and After view (shown here on top), press the letter **Y** on your keyboard. If you prefer a split-screen view, then click the little Before and After Views button in the bottom-left corner of the toolbar under your preview (as shown here on the bottom. If you don't see the toolbar for some reason, press the letter **T** to make it visible). If you click the Y button again, instead of a side-by-side before and after, you get a top/bottom before and after. Click it again, and you get a top/bottom split screen before and after. The next set of buttons (to the right of Before & After) don't change your view, they change the settings. For example, the first one copies the Before image's settings to the After image, the second one copies the After's settings to the Before image, and the third one just swaps the Before/After settings. To return to Loupe view, just press the letter **D** on your keyboard.

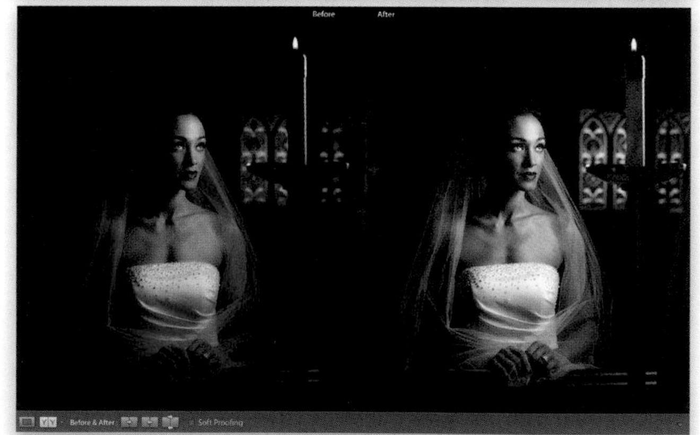

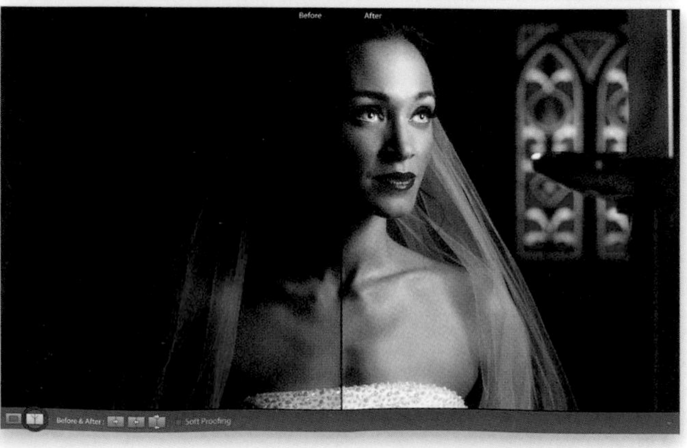

My Editing Your Images Cheat Sheet

Here's a quick look at the sliders in the Basic panel (this isn't "official"—it's just how I think of them). By the way, although Adobe named this the "Basic" panel, I think it may be the most misnamed feature in all of Lightroom. It should have been called the "Essentials" panel, since this is precisely where you'll spend most of your time editing images. Also, something handy to know: dragging any of the sliders to the right brightens or increases its effect; dragging to the left darkens or decreases its effect.

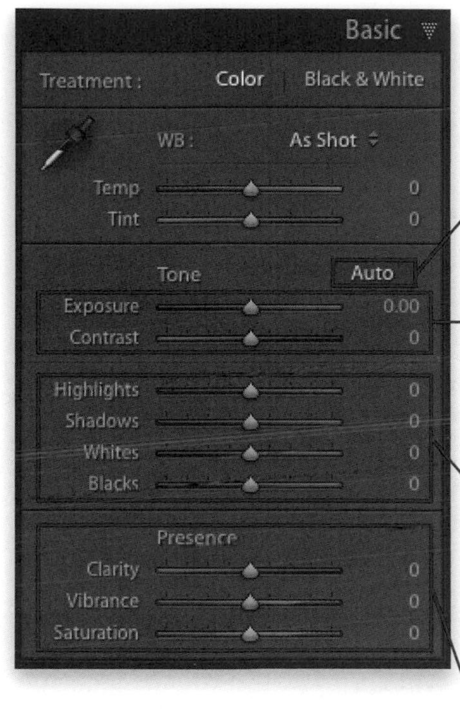

Automatic Toning

Click the Auto button and Lightroom automatically tries to balance the image for you. Sometimes it's great; other times… well, not so much. If you have no idea where to start, click this button and see how it looks. It might be a good starting place. If not, just click the Reset button (at the bottom of the right side Panels area).

Overall Exposure

These two sliders, Exposure and Contrast, do most of the heavy lifting when it comes to editing your images. Exposure controls the overall brightness of your photo, so you'll almost always wind up using it, at least a bit. Once it's set the way you want it, then add contrast (I rarely, if ever, lower the contrast).

Problems

I use these four sliders when I have a problem. I use the Highlights slider when the brightest areas of my photo are too bright (or the sky is way too bright). The Shadows slider can open up the darkest parts of my image and make things "hidden in the shadows" suddenly appear—great for fixing backlit subjects (see Chapter 8). The Whites and Blacks sliders are really for people used to setting white and black points in Photoshop's Levels feature. If that's not you, chances are you'll skip using these two.

Finishing Effects

These are effects sliders that add tonal contrast and make your colors more vibrant (or take the color away).

Controlling Overall Brightness Using the Exposure Slider

Lightroom has one main slider that controls the overall brightness of your image, making it either darker or brighter (depending on which way you drag the slider). Of course, there are other sliders that let you control specific parts of the image (like the highlights and shadows and such), but when I start to edit an image (after I have my white balance looking good), I usually want to make sure the overall exposure looks about right before I start tweaking anything else. So, this is a pretty important adjustment.

Step One:

All of the controls we're going to use at this point for editing our image are in the right side Panels area, so let's close the left side Panels area (press **F7** on your keyboard, or just click on the little gray left-facing triangle [shown circled here in red] on the far left to collapse it and tuck it out of sight). That way, our image appears much larger onscreen and that makes it much easier to see what's going on during the editing process. Okay, so here's our image opened in Lightroom's Develop module, and you can see that when I shot it, I totally trashed the exposure—it's way overexposed (I was shooting indoors at a high ISO, and then I walked outside and forgot to lower it back down).

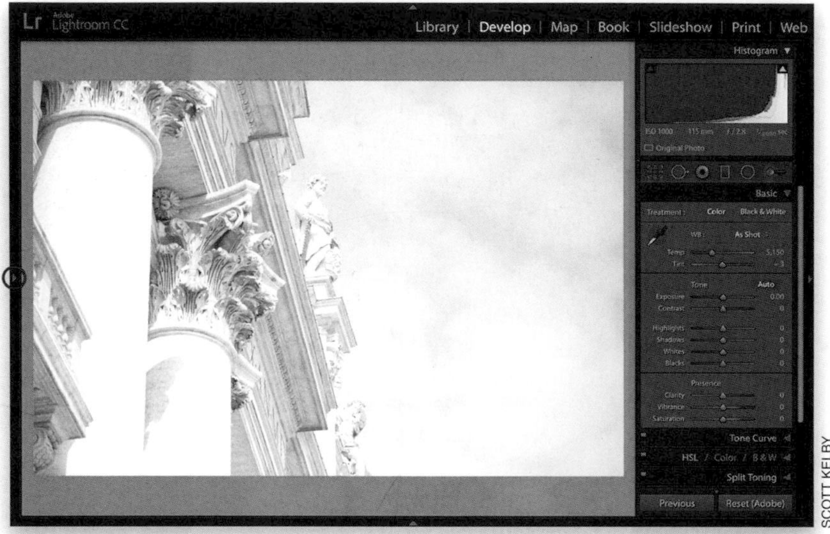

SCOTT KELBY

Step Two:

To darken the overall brightness of the image, all you have to do is drag the Exposure slider to the left until the exposure looks good to you. Here, I dragged it to the left quite a bit (down to –2.25, so I was more than two-stops overexposed. Each whole number is roughly equivalent to a stop). One way I knew I had an exposure problem back in Step One was to look at the histogram (at the top of the right side Panels area), where you'll see a highlight clipping warning (I call it the "White Triangle of Death"), which lets you know parts of the image have gotten so bright there's no detail. Sometimes just lowering the Exposure amount will fix the problem. But, when that doesn't work, see page 168 on correcting highlights—it works great in conjunction with the Exposure slider.

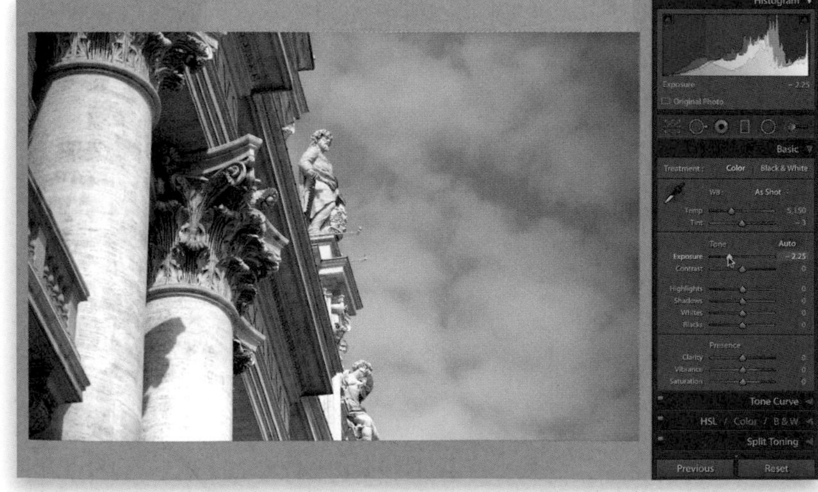

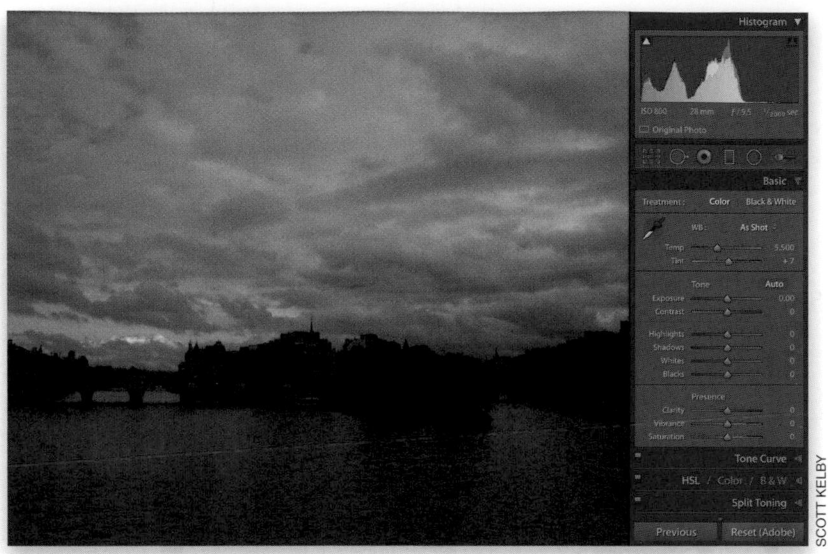

SCOTT KELBY

Step Three:

Of course, the Exposure slider doesn't just darken—it brightens, too, which is a good thing because this image is way too dark (underexposed). By the way, all the sliders here in the Basic panel start at zero and allow you to add more of a particular adjustment, or less depending on which way you drag. For example, if you were to drag the Saturation slider to the right, it makes the colors in your image more vivid; if you drag it to the left, it removes color (the farther you drag to the left, the more color it removes until you're left with a black-and-white image). Anyway, let's look at fixing this horribly underexposed image (I don't have a fancy reason why I underexposed it this time. I just messed up).

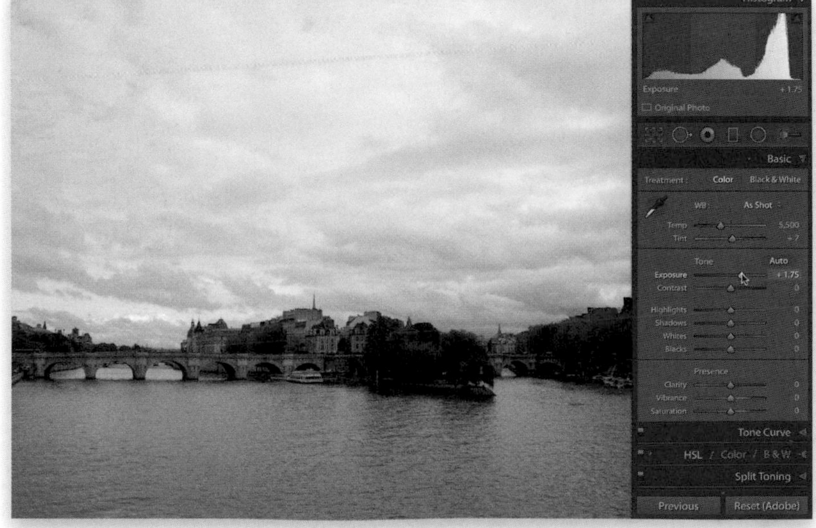

Step Four:

To make the image brighter, simply drag the Exposure to the right until the overall brightness looks good to you. In this case, I had to drag it over to +1.75 (so, I was about a stop and three-quarters underexposed. I think it was the wine. Yeah, that's it—the wine!). Of course, there's a lot more to do to this image to get it looking the way we want it to, but because we've started by setting the overall brightness first, we're now at a really good starting point for tweaking things like contrast, highlights, shadows, whites, and blacks (stuff you'll learn in the rest of this chapter).

Automatically Matching Exposures

If you've run into a situation where you have some images where the exposure or overall tone is off, Lightroom can usually fix it for you, pretty much automatically. This is great if you're shooting landscapes and the exposure changes on you as the light changes, or if you're shooting a portrait and your exposure changes as you're taking the shots, or about any time where you want a consistent tone and exposure across a set of images.

Step One:

Take a look at this set of images, taken with window light. The first one is too bright, the second one's too dark, the third looks about right (well, to me anyway), and the fourth and fifth look underexposed. So the exposure for these images is kind of all over the place. One brighter, three darker, and one looks okay.

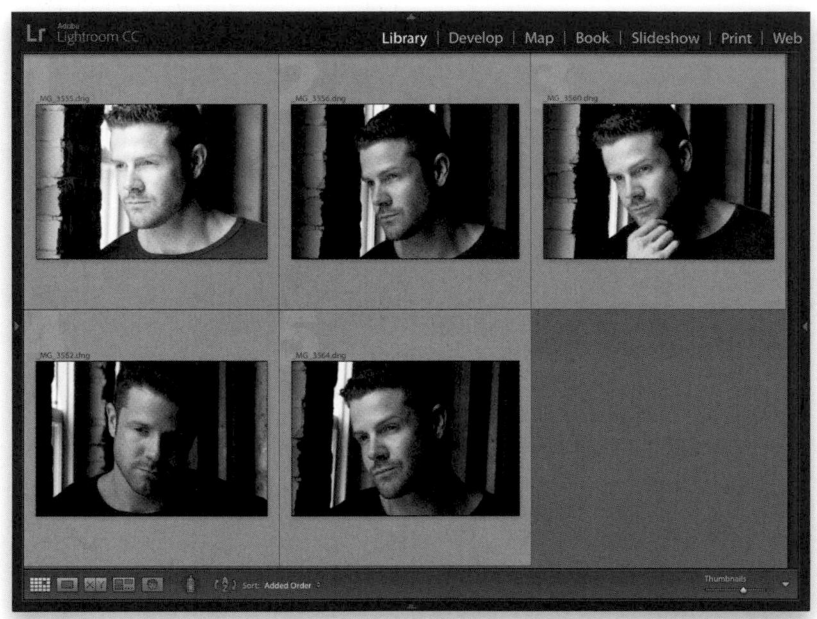

SCOTT KELBY

Step Two:

Click on the image that has overall exposure you want (to make it the "most selected" image), then press-and-hold the Command (PC: Ctrl) key and click on the other images to select them, as well. Now, press **D** to jump to the Develop module.

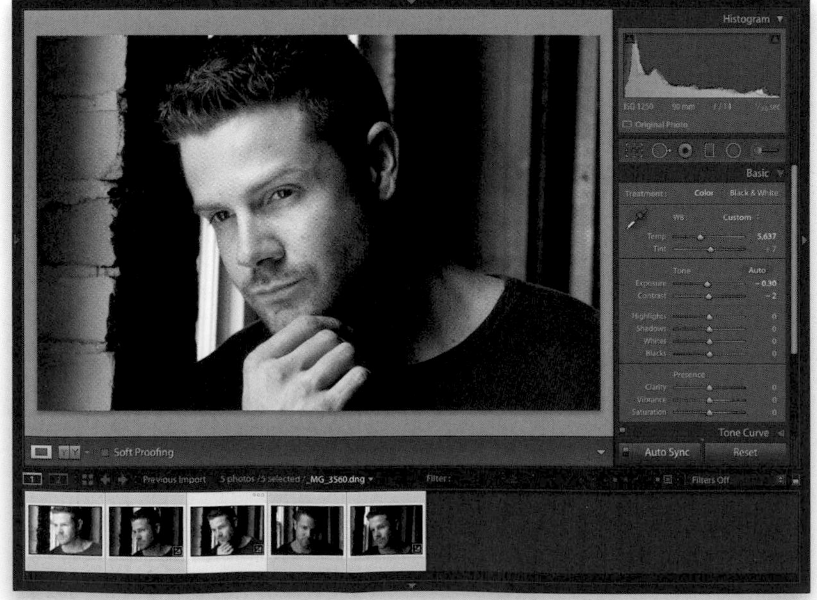

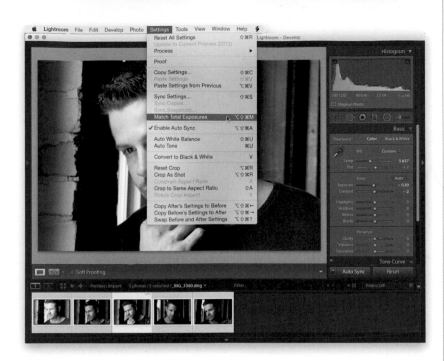

Step Three:

Go under the Settings menu and choose **Match Total Exposures** (as shown here). That's it. There are no settings. There's no dialog. No window. It just does its thing.

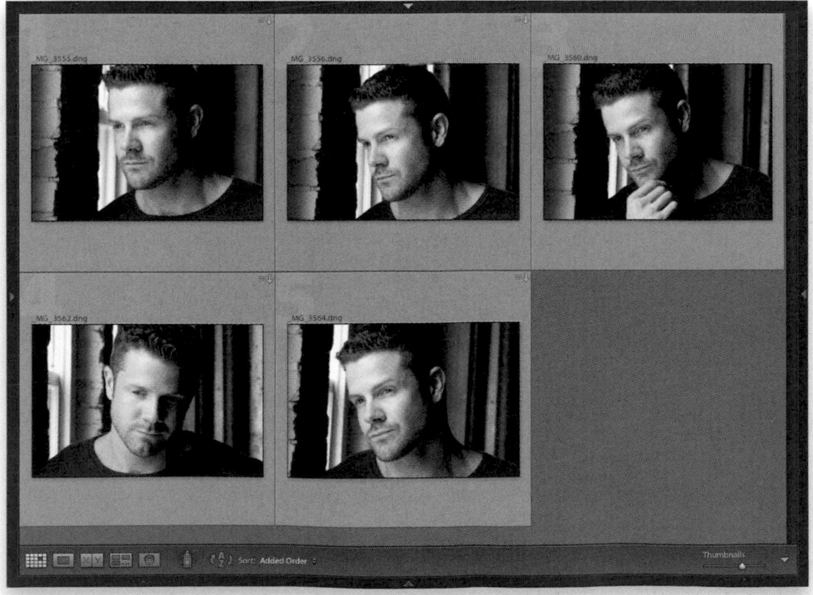

Step Four:

Press **G** to jump back to the Grid view, and now compare these images to the ones in Step One, and you can see that they all have a consistent exposure now. This works pretty darn well in most cases, which makes it pretty darn handy.

60 Seconds on the Histogram (& Which Slider Controls Which Part)

At the top of the right side Panels area is a histogram, which is basically what your image looks like if you charted the exposure on a graph. Reading a histogram is easier than it looks—the darkest parts (shadows) of your image appear on the left side of the graph, the midtones appear in the middle, and the brightest parts (highlights) are on the right side. If part of the graph is flat, there's nothing in your photo in that range (so if it's flat on the far right, that means your image doesn't have any highlights. Well, not yet anyway).

Exposure Slider: Midtones

Move your cursor over the Exposure slider and a light gray area appears over the part of the histogram that the Exposure slider affects. In this case, it's mostly the midtones (so the gray area is in the middle of the histogram), but it also affects some of the lower highlights, as well.

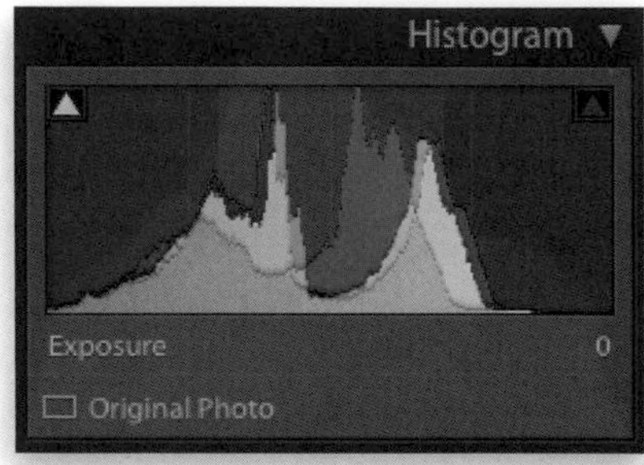

Highlights Slider: Highlights

The Highlights slider covers the next brightest areas above the midtones. If you look at the histogram shown here, it's flat right above that, which lets you know that this image doesn't have a full range of tones—it's missing the brightest parts. Moving the Highlights slider to the right can help fill in that gap, but there's actually a different slider that covers that range.

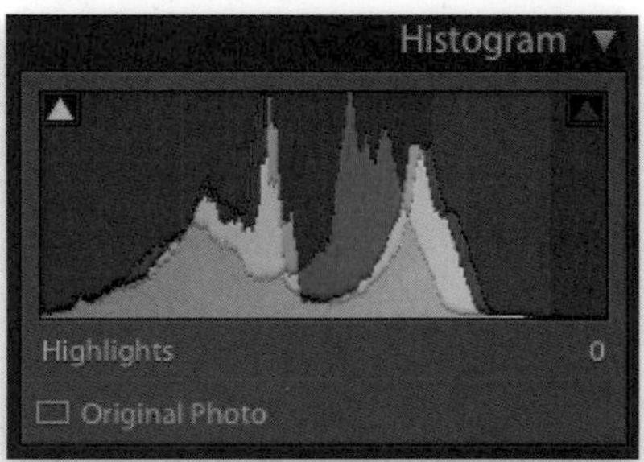

Shadows Slider: Shadows

This controls shadow areas. You can see it only controls a small area (but it's an important area because details can get lost in the shadows). Below that area is a flat area, and that means that this image is missing tone in the darkest part of the image.

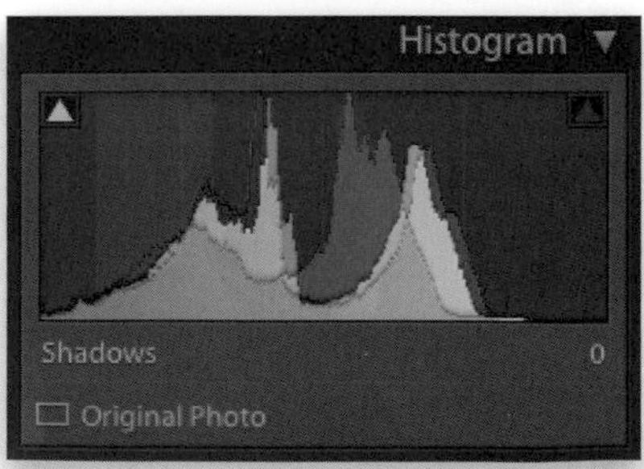

Blacks & Whites Sliders

These two sliders control the very brightest (Whites) and darkest (Blacks) parts of your image. If your image looks washed out, drag the Blacks slider to the left to add in more black (and you'll see the Blacks expand over to the left in the histogram). Need more really bright areas? Drag the Whites slider to the right (and you'll see that area in the histogram slide over to fill in that missing gap).

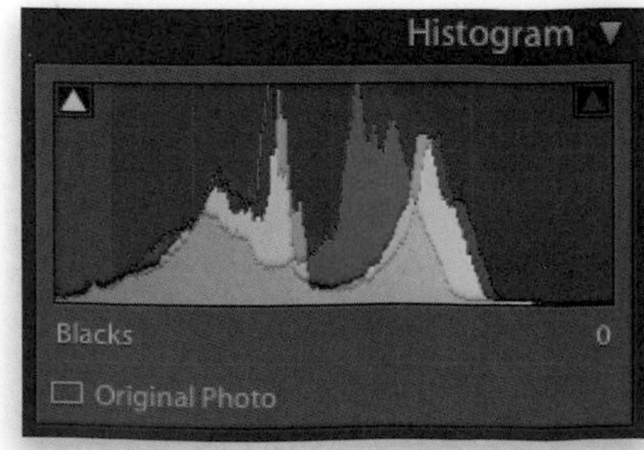

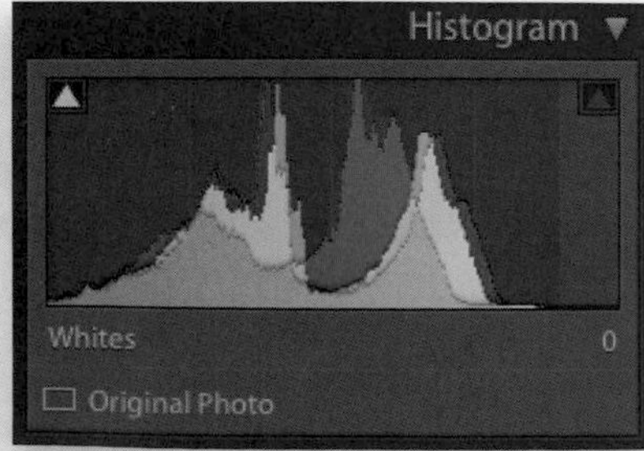

Auto Tone (Having Lightroom Do the Work for You)

Like I mentioned in my Editing Cheat Sheet earlier in this chapter, the Auto Tone feature lets Lightroom take a crack at editing your photo (basically, it evaluates the image based on what it sees in the histogram) and it tries to balance things out. Sometimes it does a pretty darn good job, but if it doesn't, no worries—just press Command-Z (PC: Ctrl-Z) to undo it.

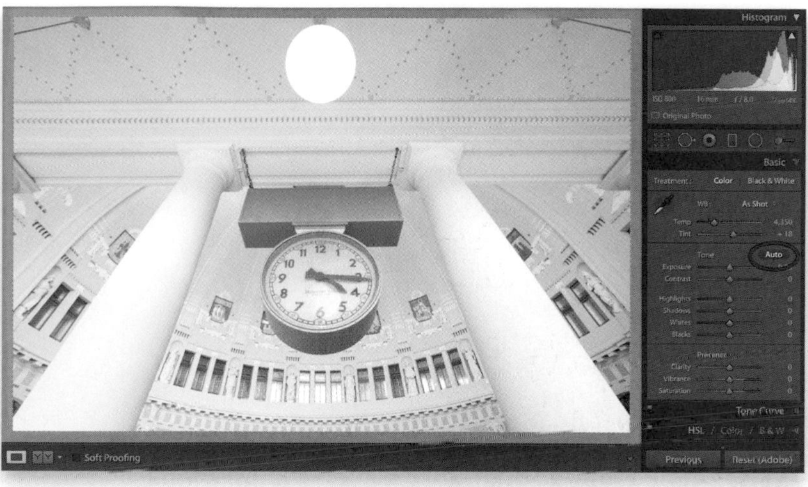

Step One:

Here's an image that's quite a bit overexposed, washed out, and flat-looking (this was taken inside the main train station in Prague). If you're not sure where to start in fixing an image, this is the perfect time to click on the Auto button (it's in the Basic panel, in the Tone section, just to the right of the word "Tone"). Just click on it and Lightroom analyzes the image and applies what it thinks is the proper correction for this photo. It will only move the sliders it thinks it needs, and they will only be the sliders in the Tone section of the Basic panel (so not things like Vibrance, Saturation, or Clarity, or stuff in other panels).

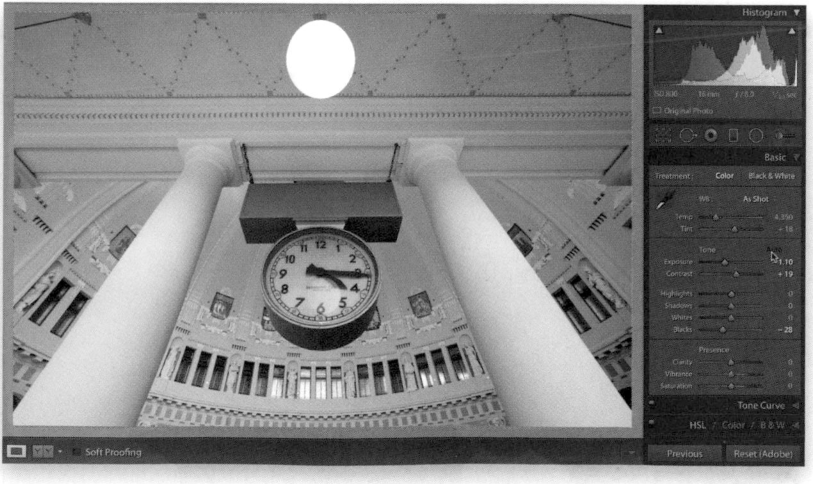

Step Two:

Just one click and look at how much better the image looks. Now, if the image doesn't look that great after clicking the Auto button, you can either: (a) just use it as a starting place and then tweak the sliders yourself, or (b) press **Command-Z (PC: Ctrl-Z)** to undo the Auto adjustment, so you can do your editing manually. It's worth at least trying Auto tone because it can actually do a pretty decent job sometimes—it just depends on the image. In my experience, it works really well on images that are too bright (like this one), but on images that are too dark, it often overexposes them, but you can usually fix that by simply lowering the Exposure amount.

Dealing With Highlight Problems (Clipping)

One potential problem we have to keep an eye out for is highlight clipping. That's when some of the highlights in an image got so bright (either when you took the shot, or here in Lightroom when you made it brighter) that there's actually no detail in those parts of the image at all. No pixels whatsoever. Just blank nothingness. This clipping happens in photos of nice cloudy skies, white jerseys on athletes, bright, cloudless skies, and a dozen other places. It happens, and it's our job to fix it so we keep detail throughout our image. Don't worry, the fix is easy.

Step One:

Here's a studio shot, and not only is our subject wearing a white coat, but I overexposed the image when I shot it. That doesn't necessarily mean we have clipping (see the intro above for what clipping means), but Lightroom will actually warn us if we do. It tells us with a white triangle-shaped highlight clipping warning, which appears in the upper-right corner of the Histogram panel (shown circled here in red). That triangle is normally black, which means everything's okay—no clipping. If it turns red, yellow, or blue, it means there's some clipping but only in a particular color channel, so I don't sound the alarm for that. But, if it's solid white (like you see here), we have a problem we need to fix.

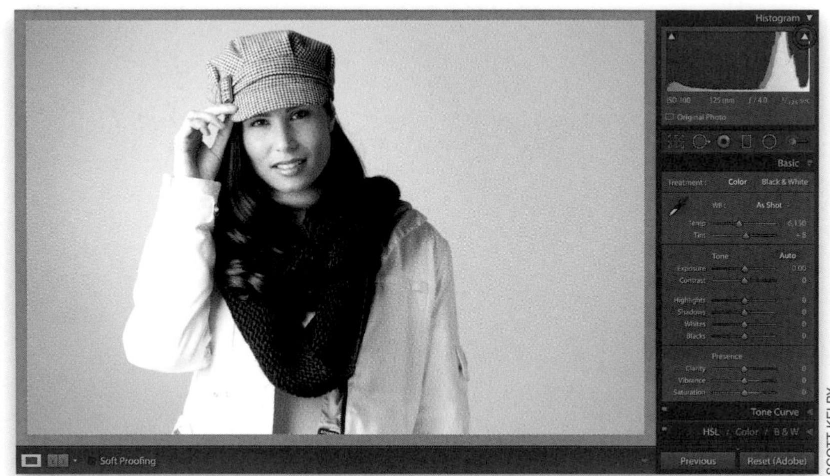

SCOTT KELBY

Step Two:

Okay, now we know we have a problem somewhere in our image, but exactly where? To find out exactly where the image is clipping, go up to that white triangle and click directly on it (or press the letter **J** on your keyboard). Now, any areas that are clipping in the highlights will appear in bright red (as seen here, where her arm, hand, and other parts of her jacket on the left side are clipping badly). Those areas will have *no* detail whatsoever (no pixels, no nuthin') if we don't do something about it.

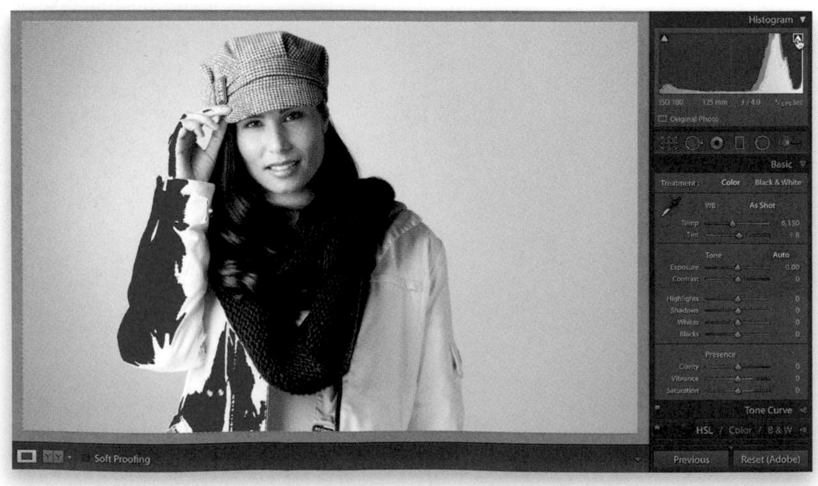

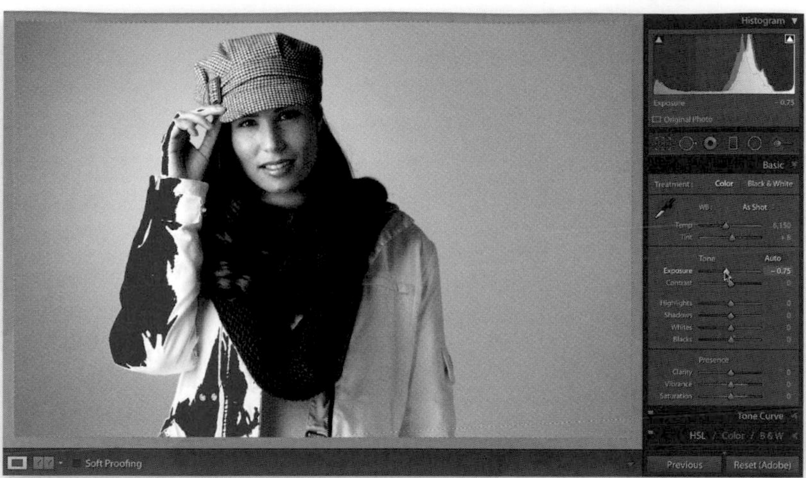

Step Three:
Sometimes just lowering the Exposure amount will do the trick and the clipping goes away and, in this case, the photo was overexposed a bit anyway, so let's start there. Here, I dragged the Exposure slider to the left to darken the overall exposure and while that looks decent now, the clipping problem is still there big time. Now, because the photo was already too bright, darkening the exposure actually helped the photo look better, but what if your exposure was okay? Then, dragging the Exposure slider to make the image darker would just make the image too dark (underexposed), so that's why we need something different—something that just affects the highlights and not the entire exposure. We want our clipping problem to go away; we generally don't want just a darker photo.

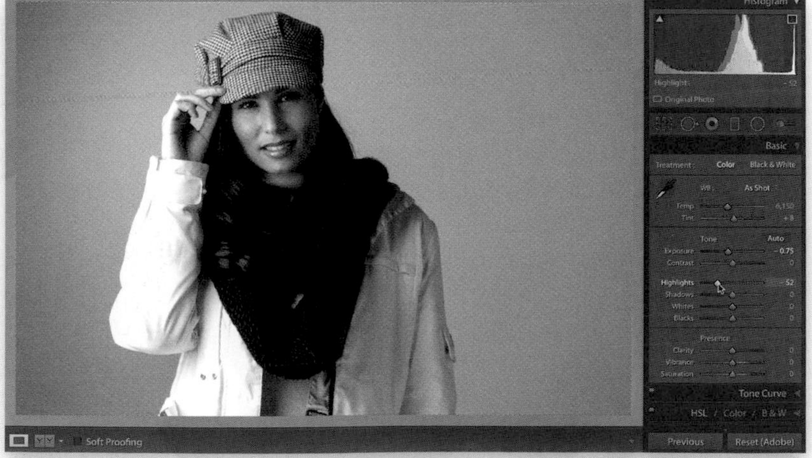

Step Four:
Let's put the Highlights slider to work. When you have a clipping problem like this, it's your first line of defense. Just drag it to the left a bit until you see the red onscreen clipping warning go away (as seen here). The warning is still turned on, but dragging the Highlights slider to the left fixed the clipping problem and brought back the missing detail, so now there are no areas that are clipping. I use this Highlight slider *a lot* on shots with bright skies and puffy clouds.

TIP: This Rocks for Landscapes
Next time you have a blah sky in a landscape or travel shot, drag the Highlights slider all the way to the left. It usually does wonders with skies and clouds, bringing back lots of detail and definition. Really an incredibly handy little tip.

Opening Up the Shadows (Like "Fill Light" on a Slider)

When you've got a subject that's backlit (so they look almost like a silhouette), or part of your image is so dark all the detail is getting lost in the shadows, help is just one slider away. The Shadows slider does an amazing job of opening up those dark shadow areas and putting some light on the subject (almost like you had a flash to add in a bit of fill light).

Step One:

Here's the original image and you can see the subject is backlit. While our eyes do an amazing job of adjusting for scenes like this with such a wide range of tones, as soon as we press the shutter button and take the shot, we wind up with a backlit image where our subject is in the shadows (like you see here). As good as today's cameras are (and they are the most amazing they've ever been), they still can't compete with the incredible tonal range of what our eyes can see. So, don't feel bad if you create some backlit shots like this, especially since you're about to learn how easy it is to fix them.

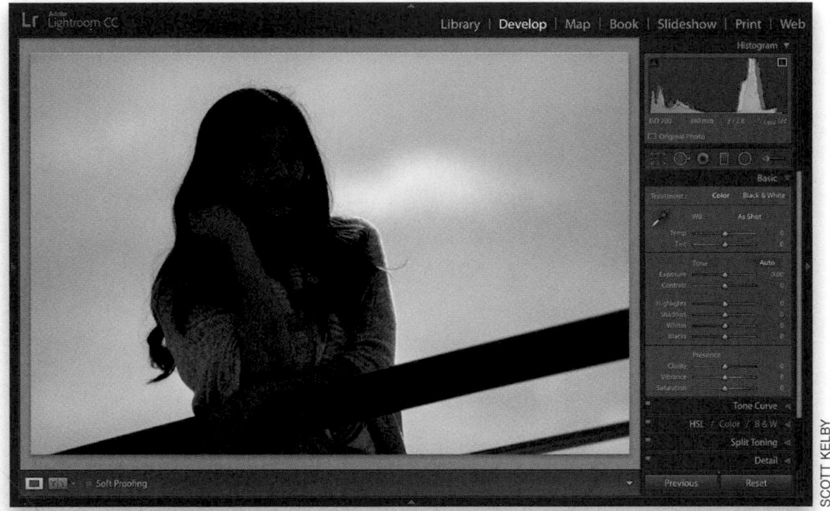

SCOTT KELBY

Step Two:

Just go to the Shadows slider, drag it to the right, and as you do, just the shadow areas of your photo are affected. As you can see here, the Shadows slider does an amazing job of opening up those shadows and bringing out detail in the image that was just hidden in the shadows. *Note:* Sometimes, if you really have to drag this slider way over to the right, the image can start to look a little flat. If that happens, just increase the Contrast amount (dragging to the right), until the contrast comes back into the photo. You won't have to do this very often, but at least when it happens you'll know to add that contrast right back in to balance things out.

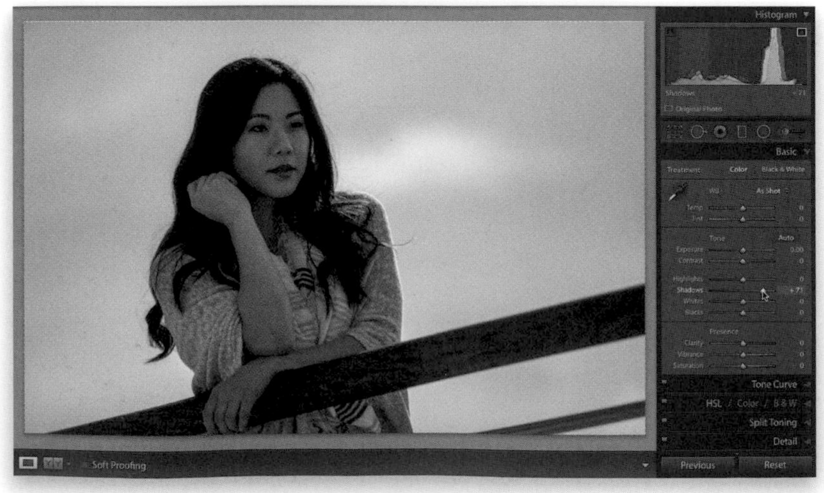

Setting Your White Point and Black Point

One way to get the most out of your image editing is to expand the tonal range of your photo by setting your white point and black point (this is something Photoshop users have done for many years using Photoshop's Levels control). We do this using the Whites and Blacks sliders. We increase the whites as far as we can without clipping the highlights, and increase the blacks as far as we can without clipping the deepest shadows too much (although, I personally don't mind a little shadow clipping), which expands the tonal range big time.

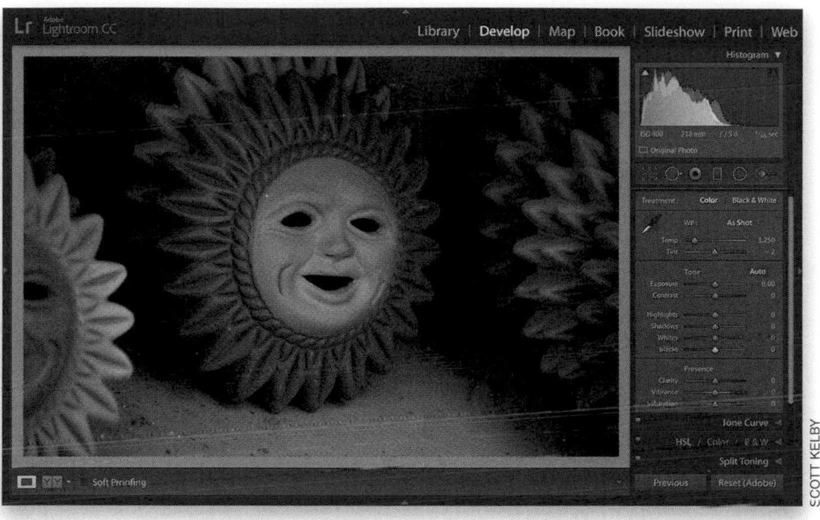

SCOTT KELBY

Step One:

Here's the original image and you can see it looks pretty flat. When you see a flat-looking shot like this, it's a perfect candidate for expanding its tonal range by setting the white and black points (right in the Basic panel, below Highlights and Shadows).

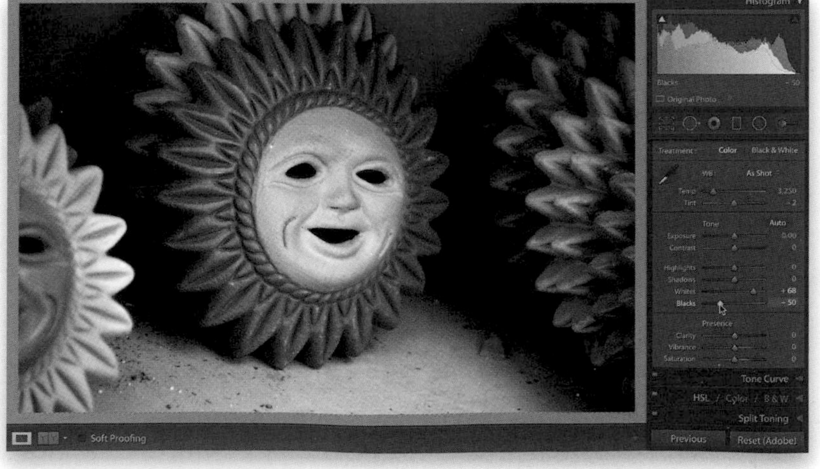

Step Two:

Start by dragging the Whites slider to the right until you see the "White Triangle of Death" (errrr, I mean the white triangle-shaped clipping warning) up in the top-right corner of the Histogram panel (at the top of the right side Panels area) and back it off a bit until the triangle turns solid black again. That's as far as you want to take it. Any farther and you can damage (clip) the highlights (see page 168 for more on clipping the highlights). You can do the same things with the Blacks slider, but to add more blacks (and expand the range), drag to the left until you see the shadow clipping warning (in the top-left corner of the Histogram panel) turn white. I think some things should actually be solid black in a photo, so if I clip the shadows a bit but the photo looks better to me, I go with it. Just sayin'. Anyway, I'm clipping the shadows a bit here and it still looks good to me.

Continued

Step Three:
You can get an onscreen preview of any clipping by pressing-and-holding the Option (PC: Alt) key before you drag either the Whites or Blacks sliders. When you do this with the Whites slider, the image turns black (as seen here). As you drag to the right, any areas that start to clip in individual channels (not as critical) start to appear in that color. So, if you're just clipping the Red channel, you'll see areas appear in red (as seen here) or if they're yellow or blue, you're just clipping those channels. I pretty much let that go for the most part, but if I see areas start to appear in white (all three channels are clipping. Ack!), I know I've gone too far and I back it off to the left a little. If you press-and-hold the Option key with the Blacks slider, it's the opposite. The image turns solid white and as you drag the Blacks slider to the left, any parts that become solid black start to appear in either the color of the channel that's clipping, or in black if all the channels are clipping.

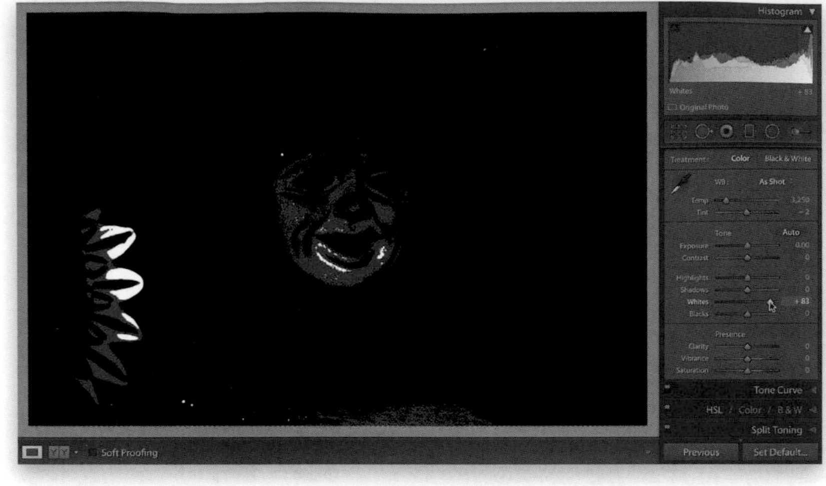

Step Four:
Okay, now that I've gone over the manual way to set your white and black points, and how to use the Option (PC: Alt) key to keep you from clipping either the highlights or shadows, here's what I actually do in my own workflow: I let Lightroom automatically set them for me. That's right, it can automatically set both for you, and it's pretty good at pushing the sliders as far out as they can go without clipping (it does, though, sometimes clip the shadows a bit, but, again, you know how I feel about that). Here's how you have it set them automatically (this is so simple): Just press-and-hold the Shift key, then double-click on the Whites slider knob and it sets your white point; double-click on the Blacks slider knob and it sets your black point. Yes, it's that easy, and that's what I use in my own workflow. By the way, if you Shift-double-click on either one and it doesn't move, then it's already set as far as it should go.

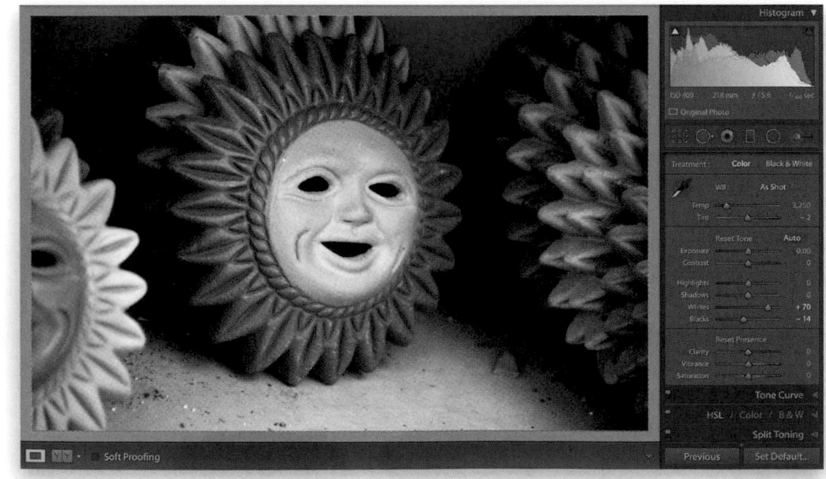

Adding "Punch" to Your Images Using Clarity

When Adobe was developing the Clarity control, they had actually considered calling the slider "Punch," because it adds midtone contrast to your photo, which makes it look, well…more punchy. It's great for bringing out detail and texture, and as of Lightroom 4, you can use a lot more Clarity than you could in the past. If you used a lot before, you'd often get little dark halos around edge areas, but now you can crank it up, bringing in detail galore, without the ugly halos. Plus, the Clarity effect just plain looks better now in Lightroom!

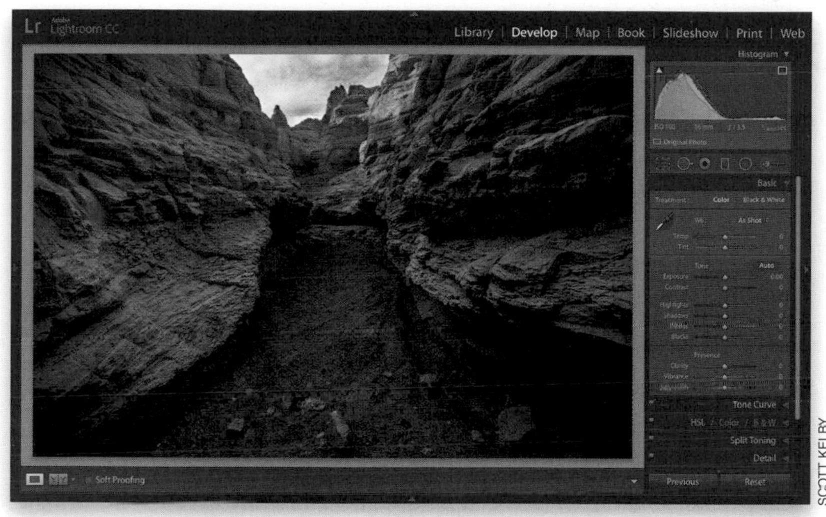

SCOTT KELBY

Step One:

Here's the original photo and it's a perfect candidate for adding Clarity because Clarity brings out detail in your image (what it actually does is increases midtone contrast, but that has the effect of enhancing detail). So, when I see an image with lots of texture and detail I want to enhance, I grab the Clarity slider. Which kinds of shots work best with Clarity? Usually anything with wood (from churches to old country barns), landscape shots (because they generally have so much detail), cityscapes (buildings love clarity, so does anything glass or metal), or basically anything with lots of intricate detail (even an old man's craggy face looks great with some Clarity). I don't add Clarity to photos where you wouldn't want to accentuate detail or texture (like a portrait of a mother and baby, or a close-up portrait of a woman).

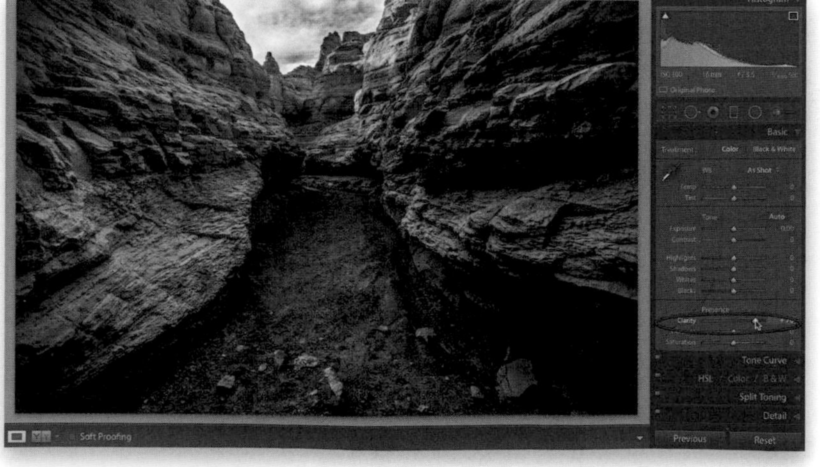

Step Two:

To add more punch and midtone contrast to our image here, drag the Clarity slider quite a bit to the right. Here, I dragged it to +76 and you can really see the effect. Look at the added detail in the rocks and the ground. If you drag too far in some photos, you might start to see a black glow appear around the edges. If that happens, back it off a bit until the glow goes away.

Note: The Clarity slider does have one side effect (which I happen to like) and that is that it tends to brighten the areas it affects a bit, as well as just enhancing the detail.

Making Your Colors More Vibrant

Photos that have rich, vibrant colors definitely have their appeal (that's why professional landscape photographers got so hooked on Velvia film and its trademark saturated color), and although Lightroom has a Saturation slider for increasing your photo's color saturation, the problem is it increases all the colors in your photo equally—the dull colors get more saturated, but the colors that are already saturated get even more so, and well…things get pretty horsey, pretty fast. That's why Lightroom's Vibrance control may become your Velvia.

Step One:

In the Presence section (at the bottom of the Basic panel) are two controls that affect the color saturation. I avoid the Saturation slider because everything gets saturated at the same intensity (it's a very coarse adjustment). In fact, I only use it to remove color—never to add it. If you click-and-drag the Saturation slider to the right, your photo gets more colorful, but in a clownish, unrealistic way. Here's our original image (a photo of my house) with no color boost (just seeing if you were paying attention). The sky is kind of "meh" and dull (colorwise), and the roof of the church is kind of washed-out looking, too, but at least the trees look okay.

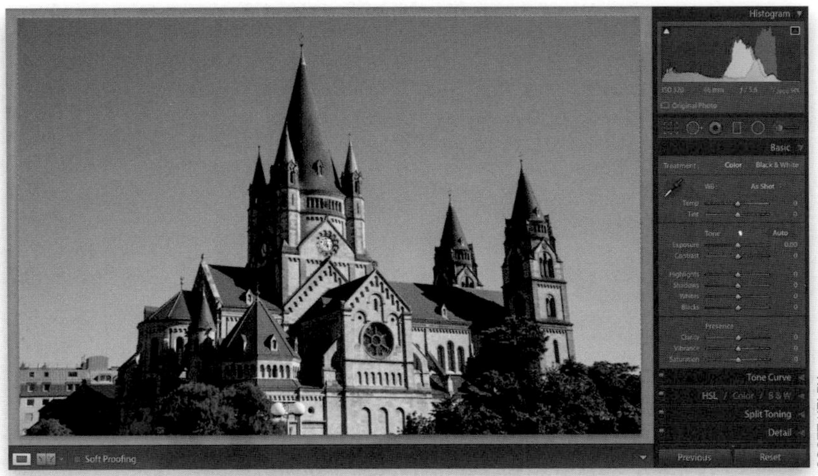

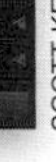

Step Two:

When you see a dull sky, a washed-out roof, a lifeless, monotone-looking color image, that's a job for the Vibrance slider! Here's basically what it does: It boosts the vibrance of any dull colors in the image quite a bit. If there are already saturated colors in the image, it tries not to boost them very much, so things don't get too vibrant. Lastly, if your photo has people in it, it uses a special mathematical algorithm to avoid affecting flesh tones, so the skin on your people doesn't start to look too colorful (of course, that doesn't come into play in this particular image). Anyway, using Vibrance gives a much more realistic-looking color boost than you'd ever get from Saturation. I pushed it pretty far here, but in my own workflow, I'm usually between 10 and 25 for my Vibrance amount, and only if I have an image that I think needs it.

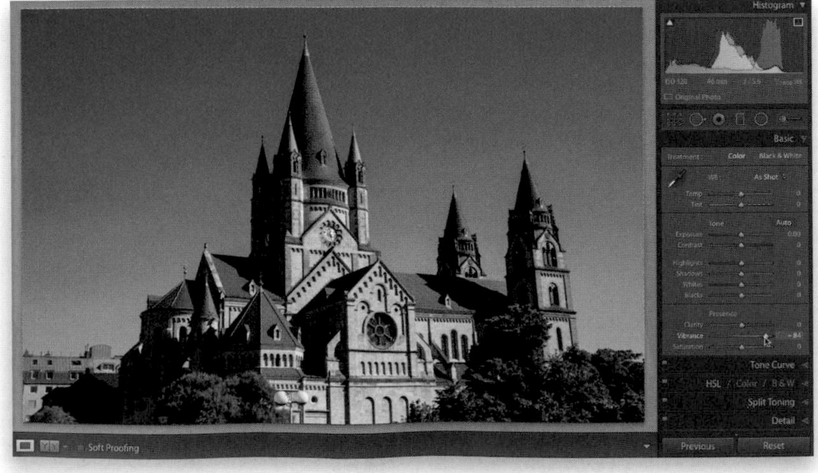

Adding Contrast (and How to Use the Tone Curve)—This Is Important Stuff!

If I had to point to the biggest problem I see in most people's images (we get hundreds sent to us each month for "Blind Photo Critiques" on our weekly photography talk show, *The Grid*), it's not white balance or exposure problems, it's that their images look flat (they lack contrast, big time). It's the single biggest problem, and yet it's about the easiest to fix (or it can be a bit complex, depending on how far you want to take this). I'll cover both methods here (the simple and the advanced):

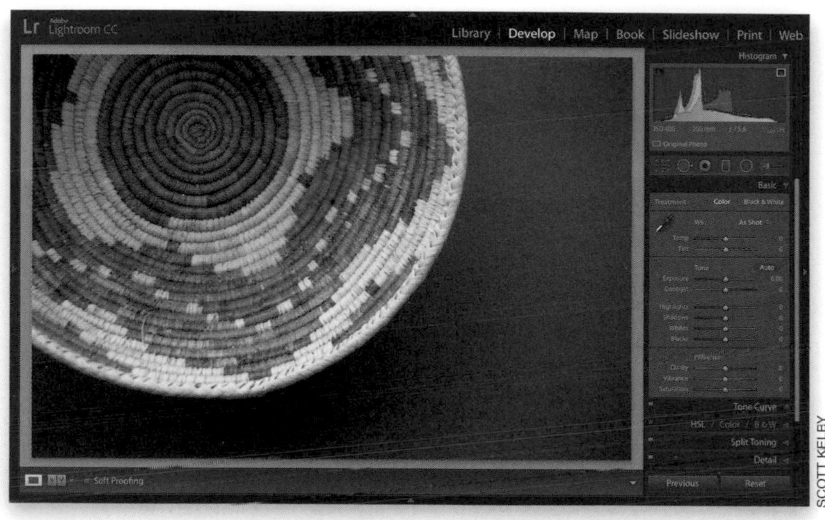

SCOTT KELBY

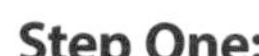

Step One:

Here's our flat, lifeless image. Before we actually apply any contrast (which makes the brightest parts of the image brighter and the darkest parts darker), here's why contrast is so important: when you add contrast, it (a) makes the colors more vibrant, (b) expands the tonal range, and (c) makes the image appear sharper and crisper. That's a lot for just one slider, but that's how powerful it is (in my opinion, perhaps the most underrated slider in Lightroom). Now, for those of you coming from a much earlier version of Lightroom, the Contrast slider used to have so little effect that we really didn't use it at all—we had to use the Tone Curve to create a decent amount of contrast. But, Adobe fixed the math behind it back in Lightroom 4, and now it's awesome.

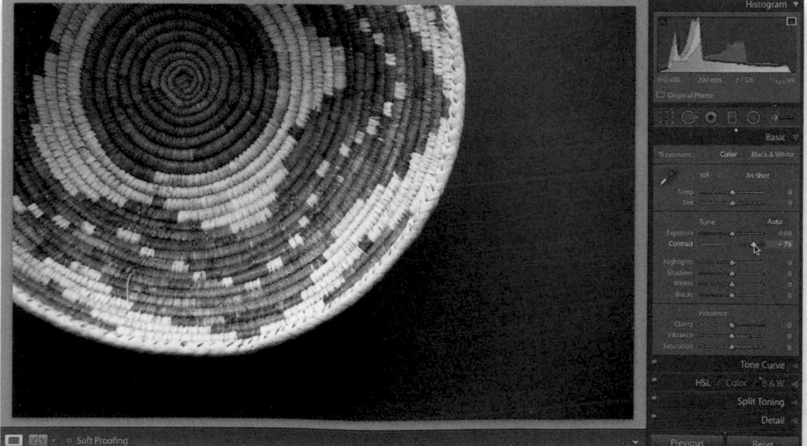

Step Two:

Here, all I did was drag the Contrast slider to the right, and look at the difference. It now has all the things I mentioned above: the colors are more vibrant, the tonal range is greater, and the whole image looks sharper and snappier. This is such an important tweak, especially if you shoot in RAW mode, which turns off any contrast settings in your camera (the ones that are applied when you shoot in JPEG mode), so RAW images look less contrasty right out of the camera. Adding that missing contrast back in is pretty important and, it's just one slider. By the way, I never drag it to the left to reduce contrast—I only drag it to the right to increase it.

Continued

Step Three:

Now, there's a more advanced method of adding contrast using the Tone Curve panel (this is what we used to do before Adobe fixed the Contrast slider. But, before we get into it, I just want to let you know up front that I no longer use this method myself—the effect of the new Contrast slider is all I need for my own image editing—but I wanted to include it here in the book for anyone who wants to learn it). If you scroll down past the Basic panel, you'll find the Tone Curve panel (shown here). Look in the bottom of the panel, and you'll see that Point Curve is set to Linear (shown circled here in red), which just means the curve is flat—there's no contrast applied to the image yet (unless, of course, you already used the Contrast slider, but in this case I didn't—the Contrast slider in the Basic panel is set to zero).

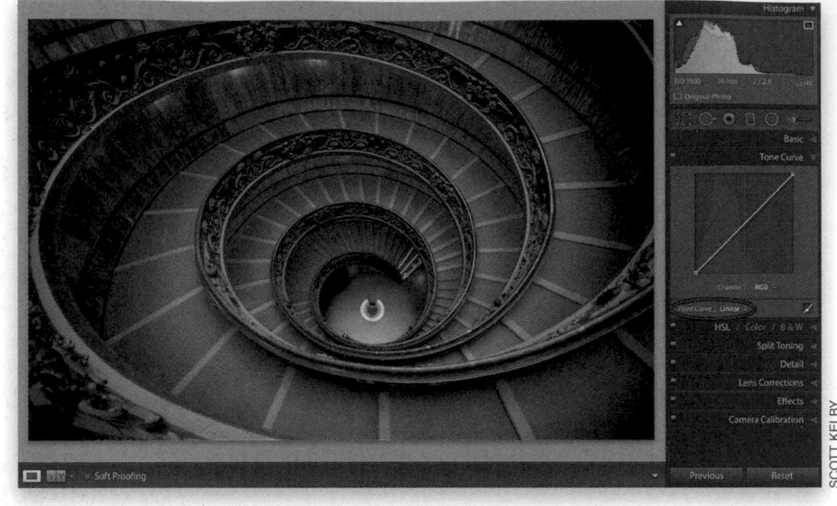

SCOTT KELBY

Step Four:

The fastest and easiest way to apply contrast here is just to choose one of the presets from the Point Curve pop-up menu. For example, choose **Strong Contrast** and look at the difference in your photo. Look how much more contrasty the photo now looks—the shadow areas are stronger and the highlights are brighter, and all you had to do was choose this from a pop-up menu. If you look at the curve, you can now see a slight bend in it, almost like it's forming a slight "S" shape. You'll also see adjustment points added to the curve. The bump upward at the top third of the line increases the highlights, and the slight dip downward at the bottom increases the shadows. (*Note:* If you see sliders beneath your curve graph, you're not quite in the right section of this panel, and you won't see these points on your curve. To get to the right section, click on the Point Curve button to the right of the Point Curve pop-up menu to hide the sliders and see the points.)

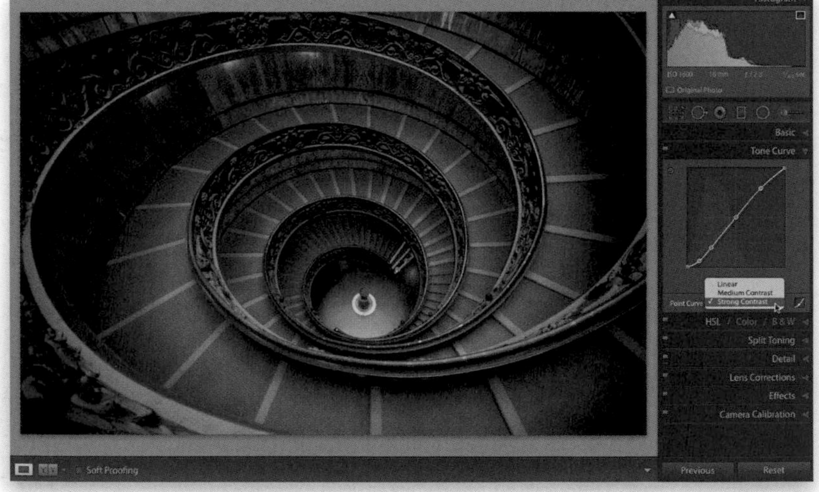

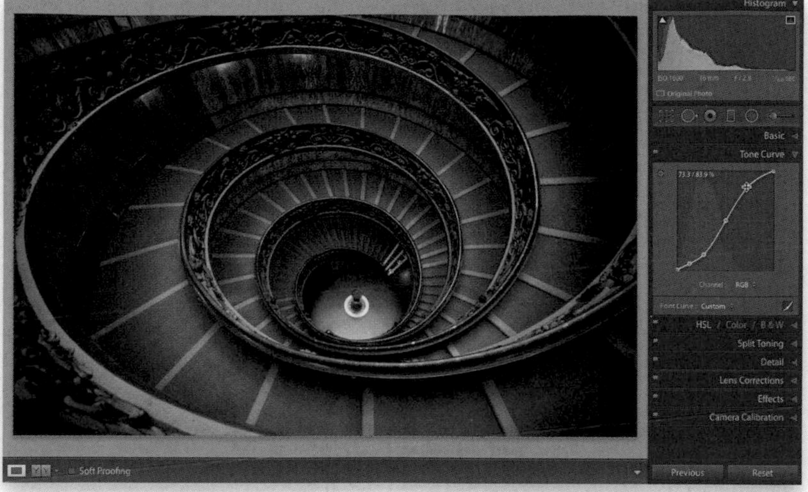

Step Five:

If you think the Strong Contrast preset isn't strong enough, you can edit this curve yourself, but it's helpful to know this rule: the steeper you make that S-curve, the stronger the contrast. So, to make it steeper (and the image more contrasty), you'd move the point near the top of the curve (the highlights) upward and the bottom of the curve (the darks and shadows) downward. To move your top point higher, move your cursor over the point, and a two-headed arrow appears. Click-and-drag it upward (shown here) and the image gets more contrast in the highlights. Do the same at the bottom to increase the contrast in the shadows. By the way, if you start with the Linear curve, you'll have to add your own points: Click about ¾ of the way up to add a highlights point, then drag it upward. Click about ¼ of the way up the curve to add a shadows point, and drag down until you have a steep S-curve and lots more contrast (as seen here).

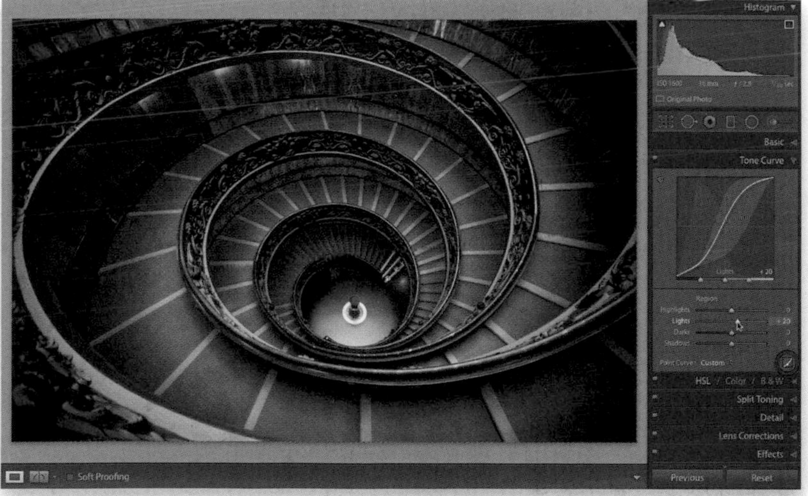

Step Six:

There's another way to add contrast, or stack more contrast on top of what you've already done, and that is by using the other section of the Tone Curve panel. To get to this, click on the little Point Curve button (shown circled here) to reveal the curve sliders. These sliders adjust the curve for you, and each represents part of the curve—dragging to the right increases the steepness of that tonal area and dragging to the left flattens out the tone curve in that area. The Highlights slider moves the top-right part of the curve and affects the very brightest parts of the image. The Lights slider affects the next brightest area (the ¼-tones). The Darks slider controls the midtone shadow areas (the ¾-tones). And, the Shadows slider controls the very darkest parts of the image. As you move a slider, you'll see the curve change. *Note:* If you created an S-curve for contrast earlier, moving these sliders adds more contrast on top of what you've already done.

Continued

Step Seven:

Besides using the sliders, you can also use the Targeted Adjustment tool (or TAT, for short). The TAT is that little round target-looking icon in the top-left corner of the Tone Curve panel (shown circled here in red). It lets you click-and-drag (up or down) directly on your image and adjusts the curve for the part you're clicking on. The crosshair part is actually where the tool is located (as shown on the right)—the target with the triangles is there just to remind you which way to drag the tool, which (as you can see from the triangles) is up and down.

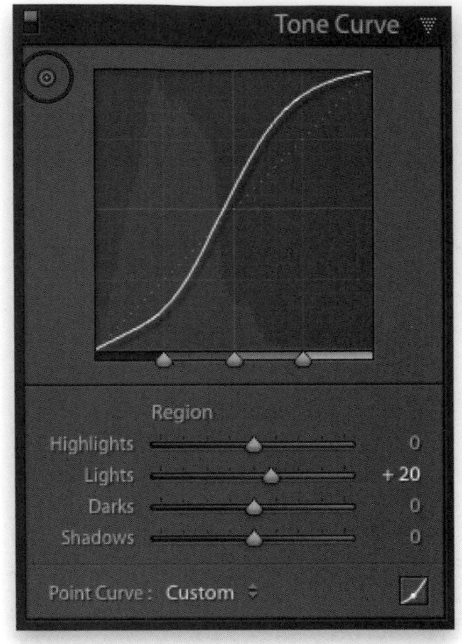

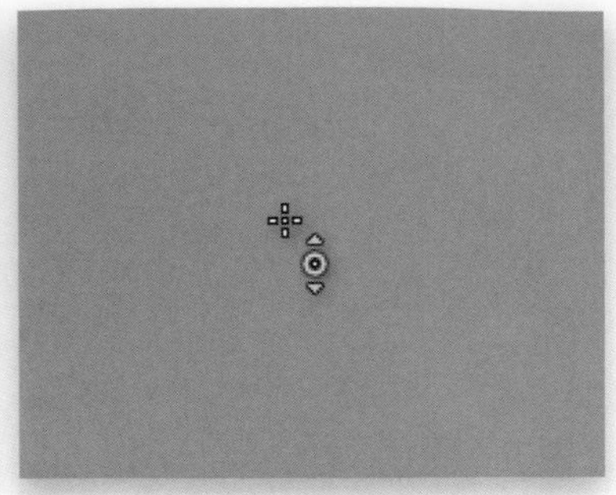

Step Eight:

You can have even more control over how the curve works by using the three Range slider knobs that appear at the bottom of the curve graph. They let you choose where the black, white, and midpoint ranges are that the tone curve adjusts (you determine what's a shadow, what's a midtone, and what's a highlight by where you place them). For example, the Range slider knob on the left (circled here in red) divides the shadows and darks—the area that appears to the left of it will be affected by the Shadows slider. If you want to expand the Shadows slider's range, click-and-drag that left Range slider knob to the right (as shown here). Now, your Shadows slider adjustments affect a larger range of your photo. The middle Range slider knob covers the midtones—clicking-and-dragging it to the right decreases the space between the midtone and highlight areas. So, your Lights slider now controls less of a range, and your Darks slider controls more of a range. To reset any of these sliders to their default position, just double-click directly on the one you want to reset.

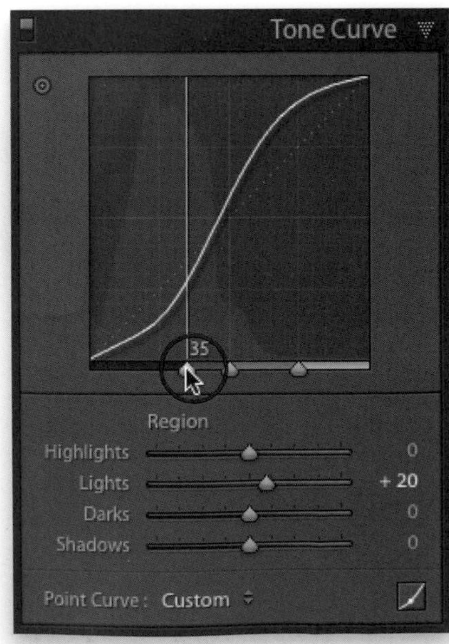

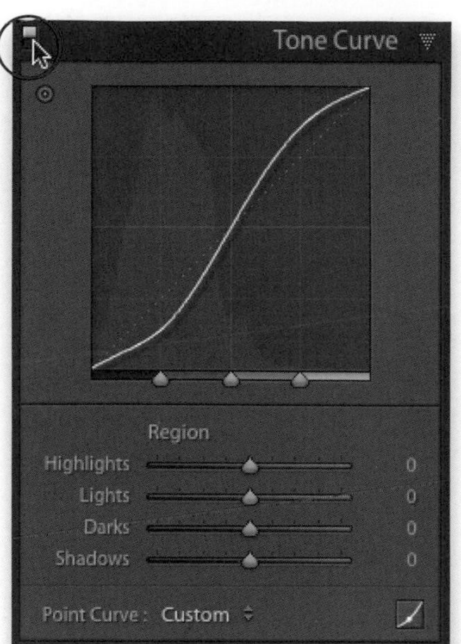

Step Nine:
Another thing you'll want to know is how to reset your tone curve and start over from scratch—just double-click directly on the word Region and it resets all four sliders to 0. Also, to see a before/after of just the contrast you've added with the Tone Curve panel, toggle the Tone Curve adjustments off/on using the little switch on the left side of the panel header (shown circled here). Just click it on or off.

TIP: Adding Mega-Contrast
If you did apply some Contrast in the Basic panel, using the Tone Curve actually adds more contrast on top of that contrast, so you get mega-contrast, when needed.

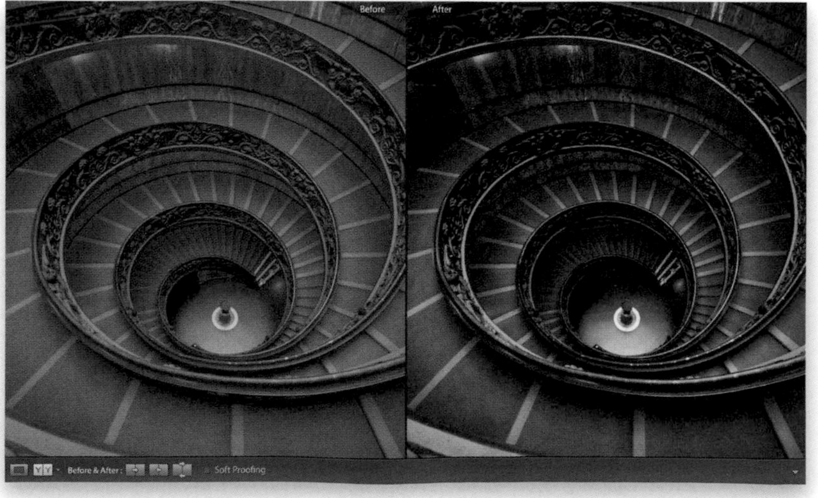

Step 10:
As we finish this off, here's a before/after with our original image and after adding a nice bit of contrast. Adding contrast is important and is a powerful way to give your images some life.

Applying Changes Made to One Photo to Other Photos

This is where your workflow starts to get some legs, because once you've edited one photo, you can apply those exact same edits to other photos. For example, at the beginning of this chapter, we fixed the white balance for one photo. But what if you shot 260 photos during one shoot? Well, now you can make your adjustments (edits) to one of those photos, then apply those same adjustments to as many of the other photos as you'd like. Once you've selected which photos need those adjustments, the rest is pretty much automated.

Step One:

Let's start by fixing the exposure and the white balance for this catalog shoot. In the Library module, click on a photo, then press **D** to jump over to the Develop module. In the Basic panel, go ahead and make your adjustments until the photo looks about right (you can see my adjustments in the overlay. I also pressed **Y**, so you could see a before/after side-by-side view here). So, those are the first steps—fix the exposure, white balance, and a few other things. Now press D to return to the regular view. (Just a reminder, you can download this photo and follow along at **http://kelbyone.com/books/lrcc**.)

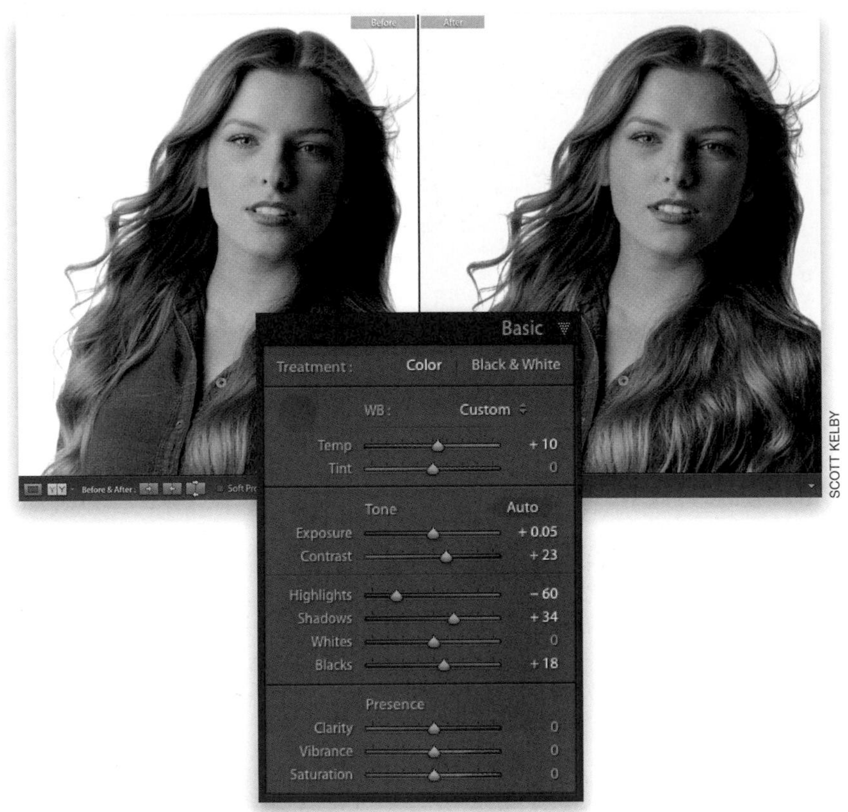

Step Two:

Now click the Copy button at the bottom of the left side Panels area. This brings up the Copy Settings dialog (shown here), which lets you choose which settings you want to copy from the photo you just edited. By default, it wants to copy a bunch of settings (several checkboxes are turned on), but since we only want to copy a few adjustments, click on the Check None button at the bottom of the dialog, then turn on just the checkboxes for White Balance and Basic Tone (which turns on all the checkboxes in that section), and then click the Copy button. (*Note:* Be sure to also turn on the Process Version checkbox if you're copying settings to images that are using an old process version.)

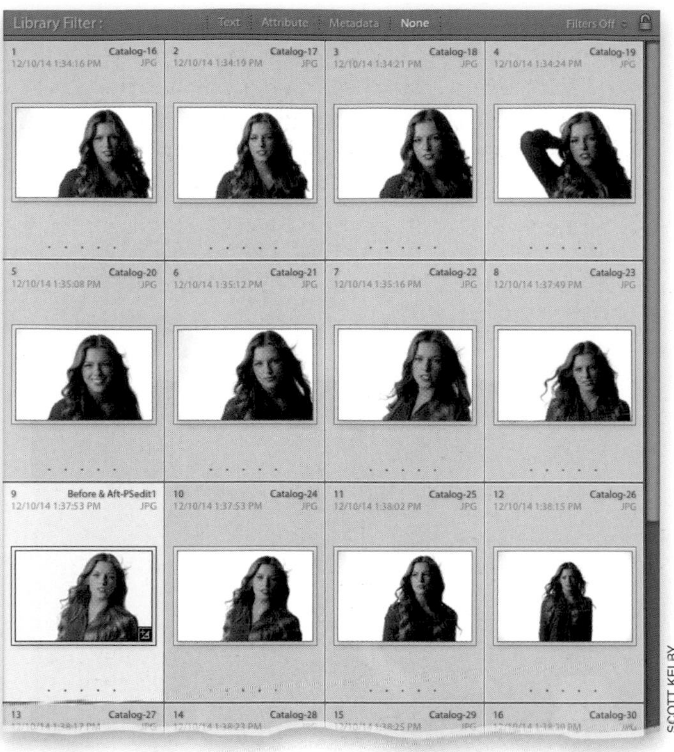

SCOTT KELBY

Step Three:

Next press **G** to return to the Grid view, and select all the photos you want to apply these changes to. If you want to apply the correction to all your photos from the shoot at once, you can just press **Command-A (PC: Ctrl-A)** to select them all (as shown here). It doesn't matter if your original gets selected again—it won't hurt a thing. If you look in the bottom row of the grid here, you can see that the first photo is the one I corrected.

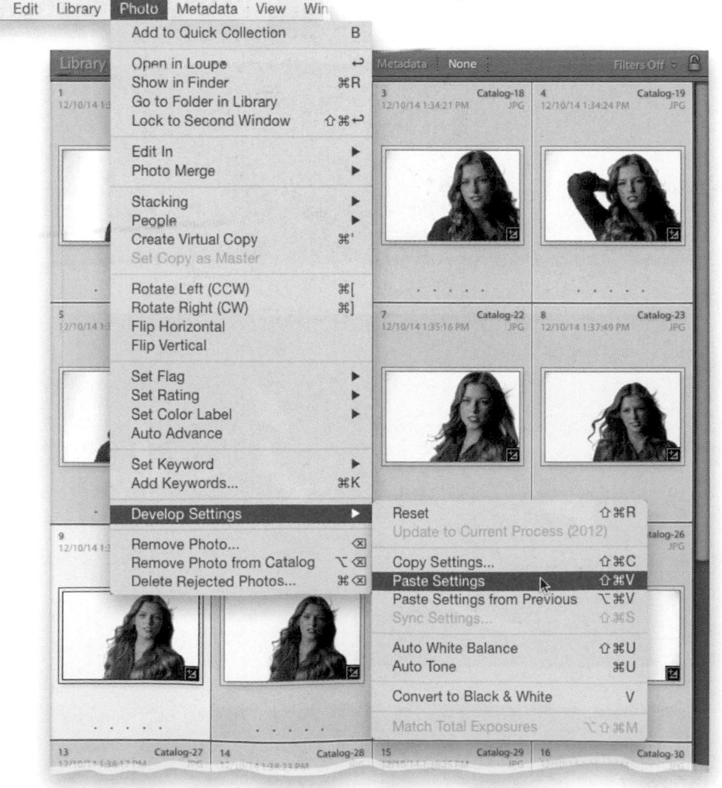

Step Four:

Now go under the Photo menu, under Develop Settings, and choose **Paste Settings**, or use the keyboard shortcut **Command-Shift-V (PC: Ctrl-Shift-V)**, and the settings you copied earlier will be applied to all your selected photos (as seen here, where the white balance, exposure, etc., have been corrected on all those selected photos).

TIP: Fixing Just One or Two Photos

If I'm in the Develop module, fixing just one or two photos, I fix the first photo, then in the Filmstrip, I move to the other photo I want to have the same edits and click the Previous button at the bottom of the right side Panels area, and all the changes I made to the previously selected photo are now applied to that photo.

Auto Sync: Perfect for Editing a Bunch of Photos at Once

So you learned earlier how to edit one photo, copy those edits, and then paste those edits onto other photos, but there's a "live-batch editing" feature called Auto Sync that you might like better (well, I like it better, anyway). Here's what it is: you select a bunch of similar photos, and then any edit you make to one photo is automatically applied to the other selected photos, live, while you're editing (no copying-and-pasting necessary). Each time you move a slider, or make an adjustment, all the other selected photos update right along with it.

Step One:

In the Develop module, down in the Filmstrip, click on the first photo you want to edit, then Command-click (PC: Ctrl-click) on all the other photos you want to apply the same adjustments to (here, I've selected a bunch of photos that need the shadows opened up a bit and sharpening). The first photo you clicked on appears large onscreen and, in the Filmstrip, you can see the selection is brighter than all the other selected images (Adobe calls this the "most selected" photo). Now, look at the two buttons at the bottom of the right side Panels area. The button on the left was Previous, but once you select multiple photos, it changes to Sync… (shown circled here).

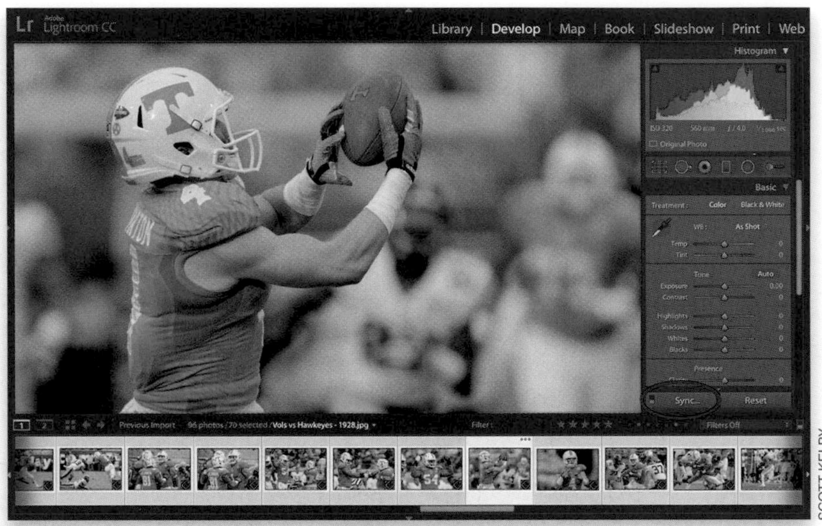

SCOTT KELBY

Step Two:

To turn on Auto Sync, click on that little switch on the left end of the Sync button Now that it's on, any change you make to your "most selected" photo is automatically applied to all your other selected photos simultaneously. For example, here I increased the Shadow amount to +22, and, in the Detail panel, increased the Sharpening Amount to 35 (as shown here). As you make these changes, you'll see your selected images' thumbnails update in the Filmstrip—they all get the exact same adjustments, but without any copying-and-pasting, or dialogs, or anything. By the way, Auto Sync stays on until you turn off that switch. To use this feature temporarily, press-and-hold the **Command (PC: Ctrl) key**, and Sync changes to Auto Sync. (*Note:* You won't see the Sync or Auto Sync buttons until you select multiple photos.)

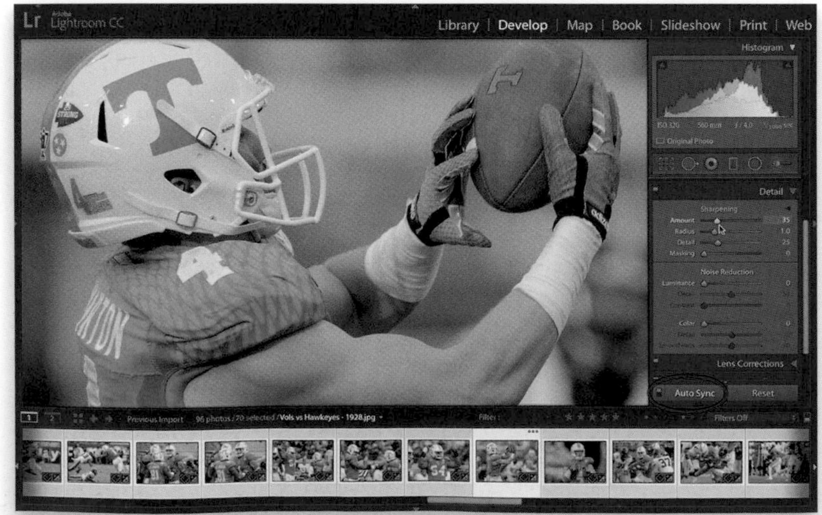

Using the Library Module's Quick Develop Panel

There's a version of the Develop module's Basic panel right within the Library module, called the Quick Develop panel. The idea is that you can make some quick, simple edits right there in the Library module, without having to jump over to the Develop module. The problem is, the Quick Develop panel stinks. Okay, it doesn't necessarily stink, it's just hard to use because there are no sliders—there are buttons you click instead that move in set increments (which makes it frustrating to get just the right amount)—but for a quick edit, it's okay (you can see I'm biting my tongue here, right?

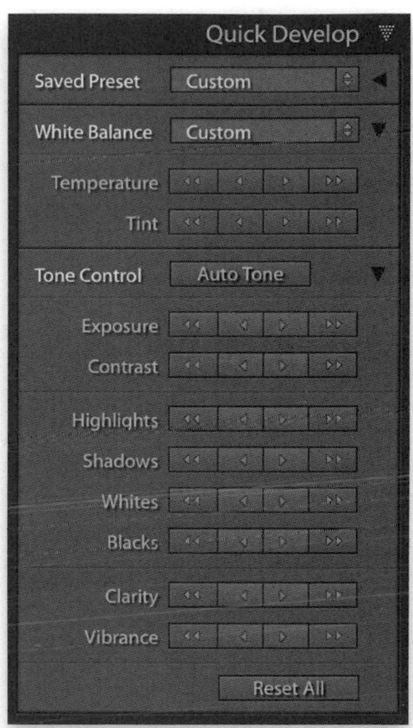

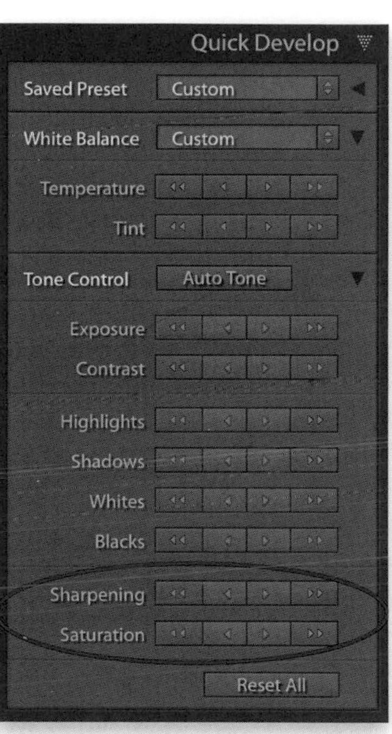

Step One:

The Quick Develop panel (shown here) is found in the Library module, under the Histogram panel at the top of the right side Panels area. Although it doesn't have the White Balance Selector tool, it has pretty much the same controls as the Develop module's Basic panel (like Highlights, Shadows, Clarity, etc.; if you don't see all the controls, click on the triangle to the right of the Auto Tone button). Also, if you press-and-hold the Option (PC: Alt) key, the Clarity and Vibrance controls change into the Sharpening and Saturation controls (as seen on the right). If you click a single-arrow button, it moves that control a little. If you click a double-arrow button, it moves it a lot. For example, if you click the single-right-arrow for Exposure, it increases the Exposure amount by 1/3 of a stop. Click the double-right-arrow and it increases it by a full stop.

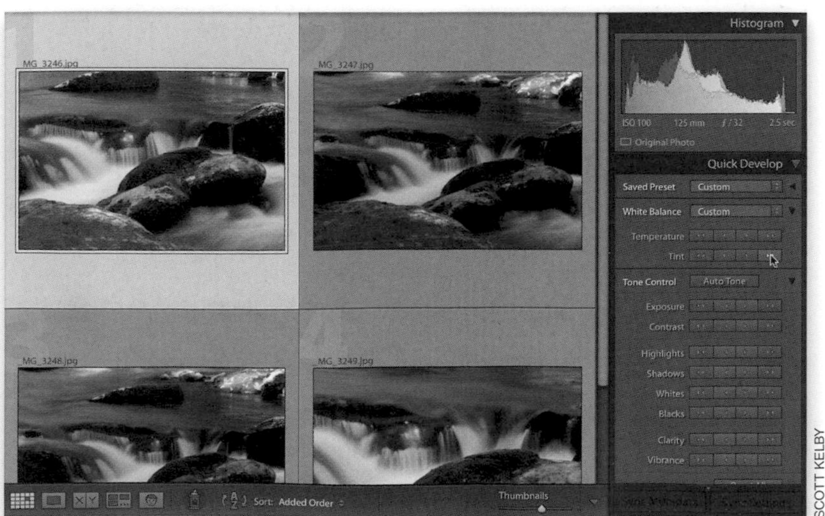

SCOTT KELBY

Step Two:

One way I use the Quick Develop panel is to quickly see if an image is worth working on, but without actually doing the full edit over in the Develop module. For example, these stream images have a white balance problem (too green), among other things, so to quickly see how it would look when edited, I'd click on the first image (or as many of the images as you'd like), then I'd go to Temperature and click once on the single-left-arrow to move it –5 toward blue to white balance the image, then for Tint, I'd click twice on the double-right-arrow to move the Tint to +40 (each click on the double-arrow moves it +20).

Continued

Step Three:

The other time I use Quick Develop is in Compare or Survey view (as shown here), because you can apply these edits while in a multi-photo view (just be sure to click on the photo you want to edit first, and make sure Auto Sync is turned off at the bottom of the right side Panels area). For example, I've selected four photos here and pressed **N** to enter Survey view. I clicked on the top-left photo to edit it while leaving the others alone, so I can compare the look between them. I clicked on the Exposure single-right-arrow, and the image got 1/3 of a stop brighter, then I clicked the Contrast double-right-arrow once, which increased it by +20. I clicked the double-right-arrow twice for Shadows and once for Clarity, and you can see how it compares to the rest.

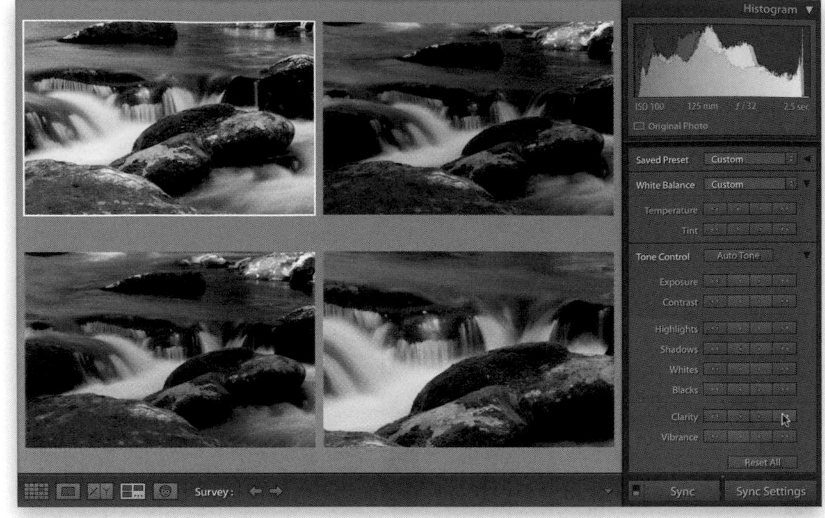

TIP: Finer Increments in Quick Develop

Now you can adjust in smaller increments when clicking the single-right-arrow: if you Shift-click on a single-right-arrow, it moves up/down 1/6 of a stop, instead of a 1/3 of a stop (so, instead of moving +33, it moves just +17 for each Shift-click).

Step Four:

Here's some other stuff you can do in Quick Develop: Apply any existing Develop module preset by choosing it from the Saved Preset pop-up menu at the top of the panel, and if you expand that black flippy triangle to the right of it, more features appear, like crop ratios and making the images black and white. There's the Auto Tone button (see page 167), and if you mess up, there's the Reset All button. You can also sync the individual changes you made to one photo to as many selected photos as you'd like using the Sync Settings button at the bottom of the right side panels. That brings up the dialog shown here, where you can choose which settings get applied to the rest of the selected photos. Just turn on the checkboxes beside those settings you want applied, and click the Synchronize button.

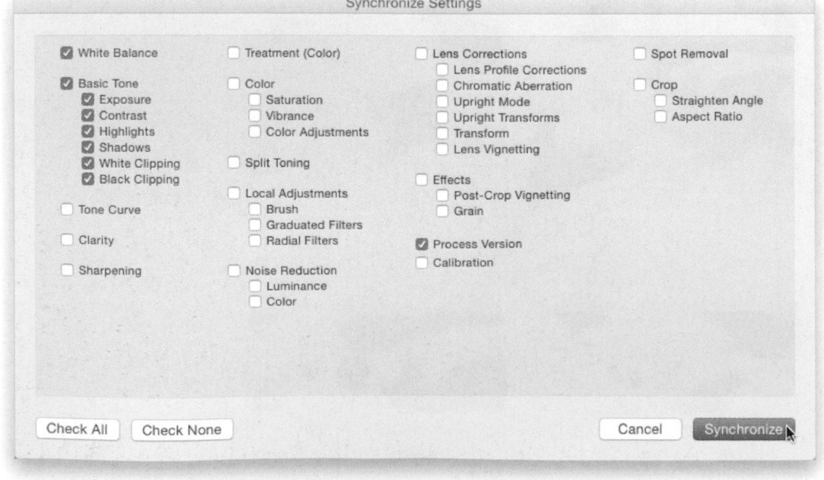

The "Previous" Button (and Why It Rocks!)

Let's say you spent a few minutes tweaking an image and you have it just the way you want it. Without using Copy and Paste, you can apply those exact same settings to any photo from that shoot. It can be the next photo in the Filmstrip, or one of 20 thumbnails down the line, but if you try this one out a few times, you will fall in love with how much this can speed your workflow. Basically, you click on an image, click on the Previous button, and whatever you did to the previously selected image is applied to the image you're on now.

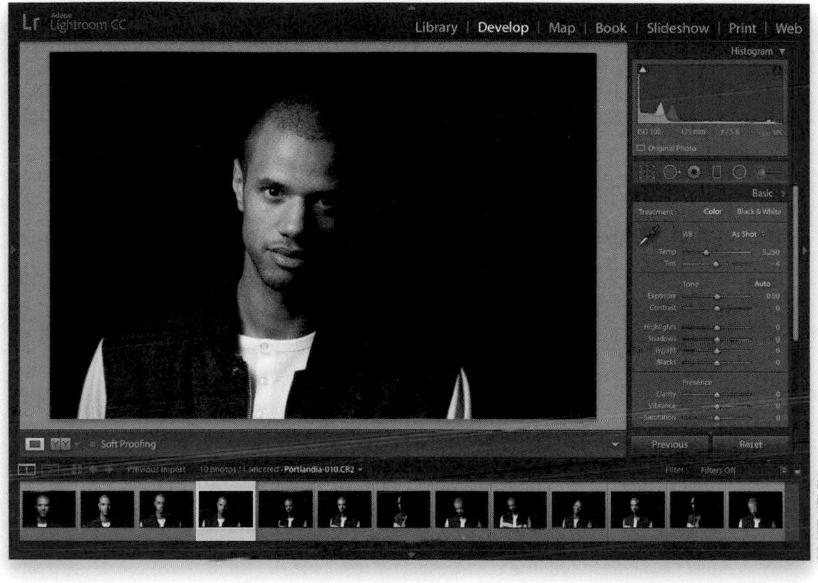

SCOTT KELBY

Step One:

Here's our original that needs some tweaking (in this case, I would just tweak the exposure a bit, add some clarity, and crop the photo in a bit tighter. Pretty standard stuff).

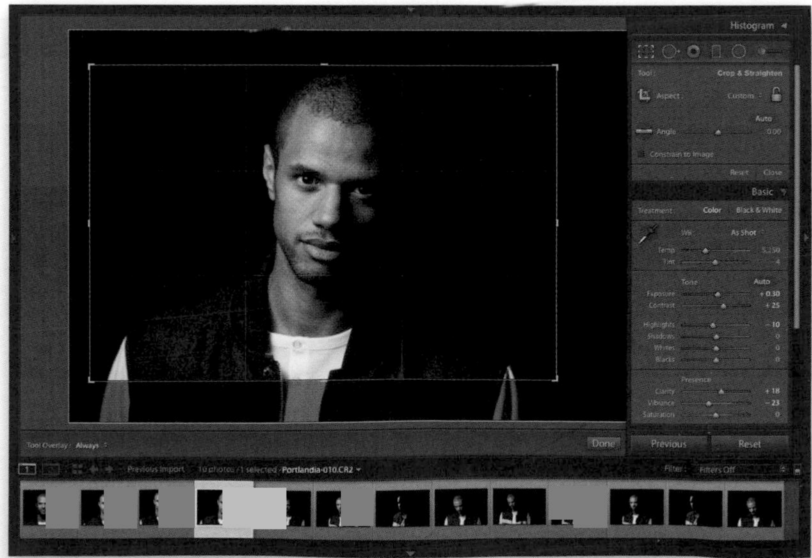

Step Two:

In the Develop module, grab the Crop Overlay tool **(R)** and crop the image, so it's a bit tighter in on our subject. Then, let's increase the exposure a little bit by dragging the Exposure slider to the right to +0.30, then increase the Contrast to +25. Next, let's lower the Highlights a bit (I dragged them down to –10), increase the Clarity to +18 (to bring out more detail in his skin), and lastly, desaturate his skin by dragging the Vibrance slider to the left to –23. Nothing earth shattering, just the typical little tweaks, but there are a few other images from this same shoot I'd like to have the same look.

Continued

Step Three:

Now, down in the Filmstrip, click on the next photo you want to have this same look (cropping and all). If the photo you want to have that same look is the next photo over in the Filmstrip, you can just press the **Right Arrow key** on your keyboard to move to that next image. If it's not, then click on any other image in the Filmstrip, like I did here where I clicked on the fourth image down from the one I was tweaking.

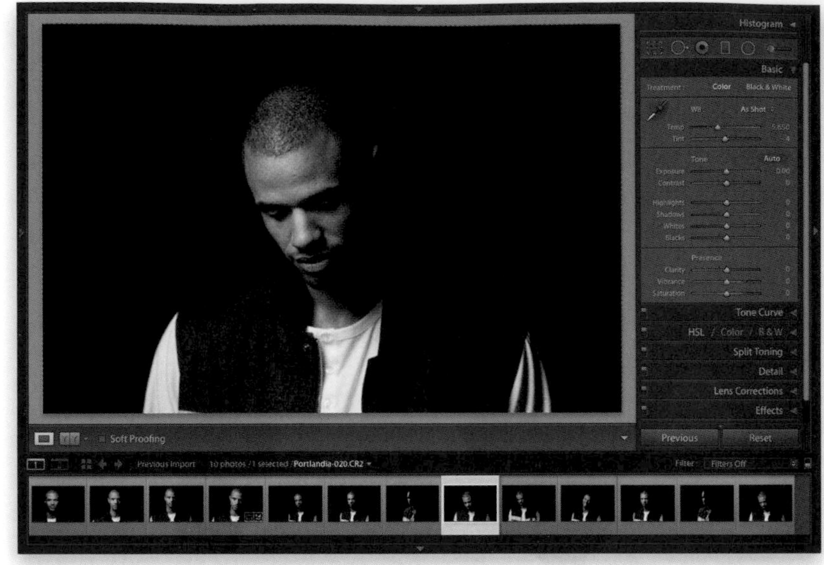

Step Four:

Next, just click the Previous button (at the bottom of the right side Panels area), and this image gets those exact same changes (cropping and all) that you applied to the previous image. Now, you can scroll to another photo in the Filmstrip and do the same thing to any single selected photo.

Note: Remember, this applies the settings of whichever photo you clicked on last. If you click on a photo and decide *not* to click the Previous button, that now becomes your "previous photo," because it's the last photo you clicked on. So, to be able to use the Previous button, you'll have to go back and click on any one of the photos you've already applied the changes to. That reloads the Previous button with your edits.

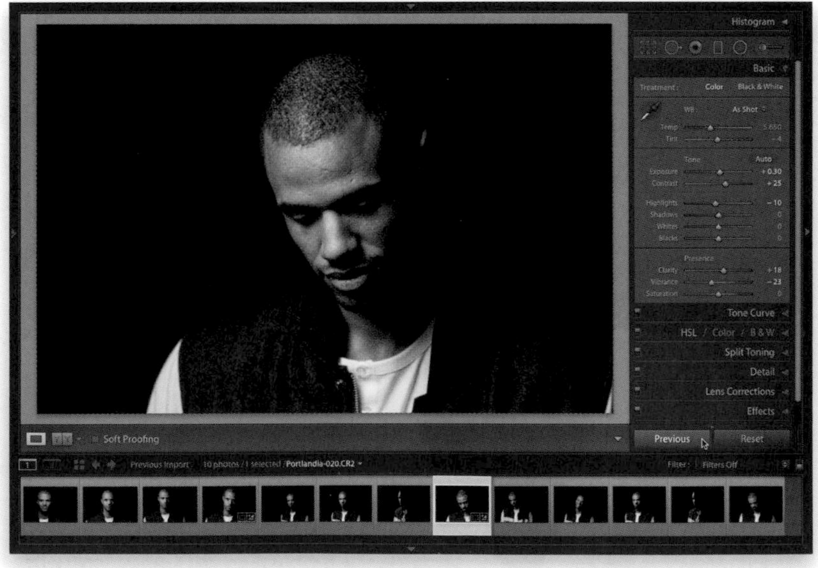

Putting It All Together (Doing a Start-to-Finish Tweak)

Okay, we're nearly done with what we do to edit our images here in Lightroom, but before we uncork the next chapter of adjustments, I thought it might be good for you to see how all these sliders in the Basic panel work together. So, go download this image and follow along (the download link is in the "Seven [or So] Things You'll Want to Know…" part up front that you skipped). I think this will really help you see how all these adjustments work together.

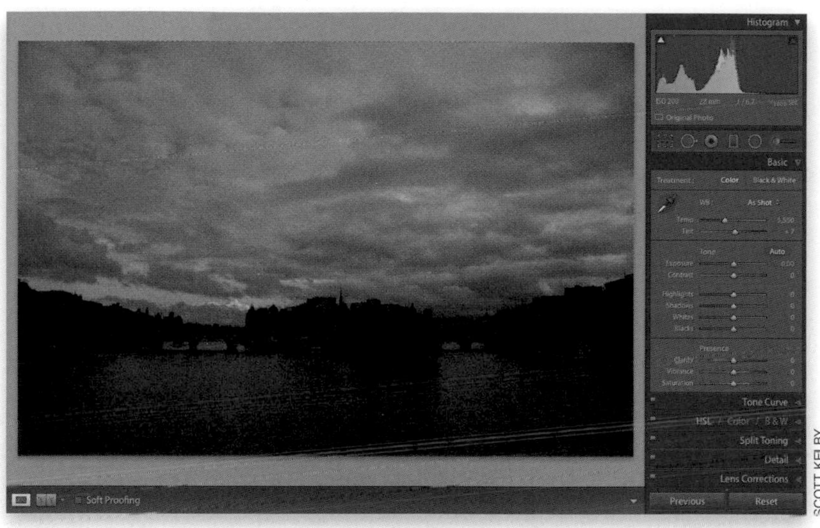

SCOTT KELBY

Step One:

Remember this image from earlier in the chapter (the one we used in the Exposure technique)? We'll it's back, but we're going to do more than just fix the overall brightness. Here's something that I do that I think might help you when you're sitting there in front of Lightroom looking at an image that needs help: each step of the way, just ask yourself, "What do I wish were different in this image?" Once you know what it is you want to do next, the controls are all right here in Lightroom, so that's the easy part. The hard part is really sitting back and analyzing the image and asking yourself that question after every step. I can tell you what I wish was different here. I wish it wasn't so dark, so we'll start there.

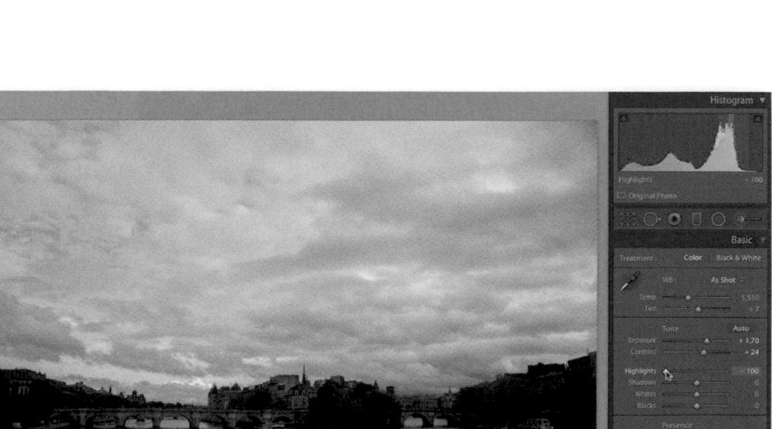

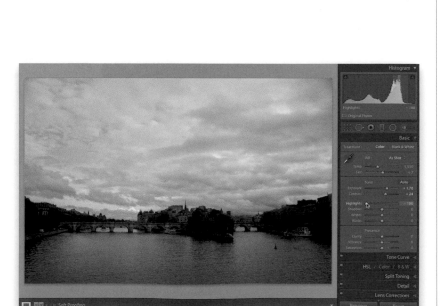

Step Two:

To make the overall image brighter, we drag the Exposure slider to the right until it looks good to us. I didn't drag it quite as far this time as I did earlier in the book (I dragged it to +1.70, here) because now I have more sliders I can use for particular areas. Next, the image looks kinda flat to me, so I want to add more contrast by dragging the Contrast slider a little to the right (here, I dragged it to +24). Then, I'm going to use that tip I mentioned in the Highlights technique back on page 168, and enhance the cloudy skies by dragging the Highlights slider all the way to the left to –100. Now the sky doesn't look as light and bright and the clouds have more detail.

Continued

Step Three:
Looking at the image back in Step Two, there's a lot of detail in the bridge and in the trees and buildings alongside the river, but it's kind of lost in the shadows. So, I'm going to bring out the detail in those areas by dragging the Shadows slider to the right quite a bit (here, I dragged it to +76). I knew when I first looked at the image that I'd be opening up these shadows (I use the Shadows slider a lot), and that's why I didn't drag the Exposure slider as far to start with. To set the white and black points using the Whites and Blacks sliders, I let Lightroom set them automatically, which you do by Shift-double-clicking directly on the Whites slider knob and then the Blacks slider knob. Okay, so far, so good, but there are some finishing moves that could help this image be more colorful and enhance the detail and texture overall.

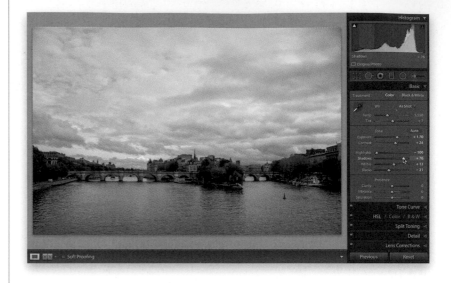

Step Four:
To bring out the texture in the buildings, trees, and river, I increased the Clarity a bit (cityscapes like this love Clarity and, honestly, I could have pushed it a lot farther than +13. It probably could have easily gone to +30 and not looked bad. Maybe higher. Photos with lots of fine detail like this love Clarity and Sharpening, but we haven't gotten to sharpening yet). Lastly, the color in the image is very muted and, under that cloudy sky, I don't want to make the colors "pop," but I would like to make the colors in the image a bit more vibrant. So, I dragged the Vibrance slider to +22. That whole process will take you just a minute or so. The thinking part takes a lot more than the dragging sliders part. There are still some things I'd definitely add to finish this photo off, but we don't cover them until the next chapter. Hey, it's something to look forward to. :)

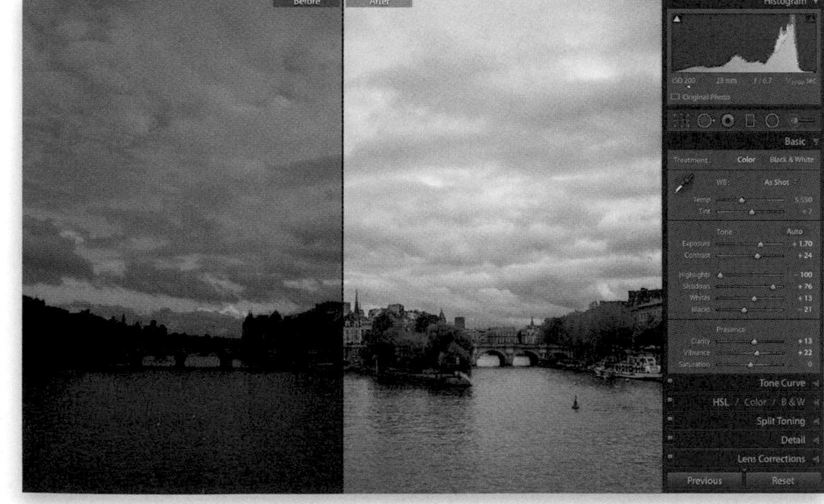

Lightroom Killer Tips > >

▼ Picking Zooms in the Detail Panel

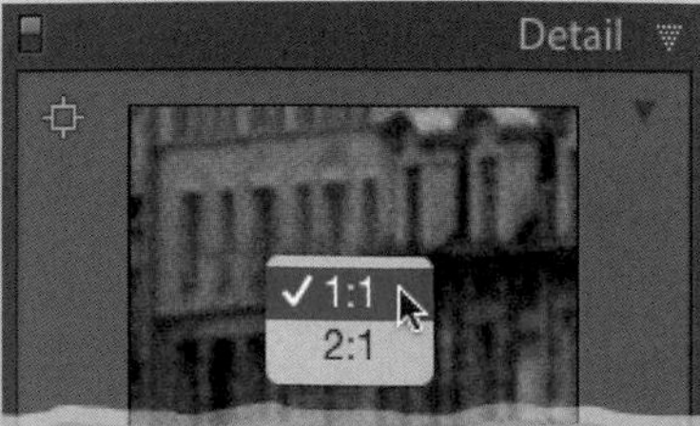

If you Right-click inside the little preview window in the Detail panel, a pop-up menu will appear where you can choose between two zoom ratios for the preview—1:1 or 2:1—which kick in when you click your cursor inside the Preview area.

▼ Hiding the Clipping Warning Triangles

If you don't use the two little clipping warning triangles in the top corners of the histogram (or you want them turned off when you're not using them), then just Right-click anywhere on the histogram itself and choose **Show Clipping Indicators** from the pop-up menu to turn it off,

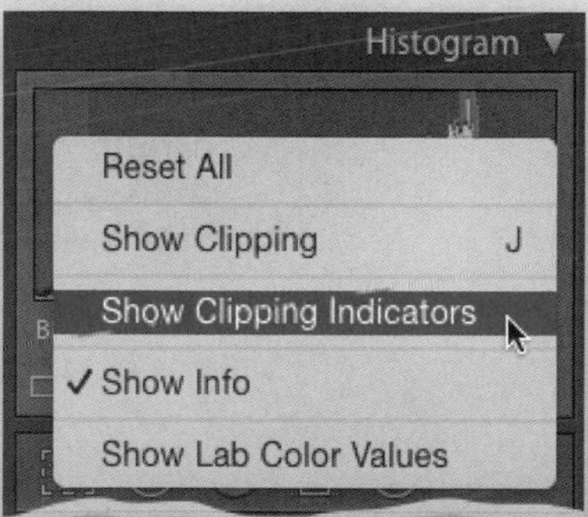

and they'll be tucked out of sight. If you want them back, go back to that same pop-up menu, and choose Show Clipping Indicators again.

▼ Separating Your Virtual Copies from the Real Images

To see just your virtual copies, go up to the Library Filter bar (if it's not visible, press the **\ [backslash] key**), and then

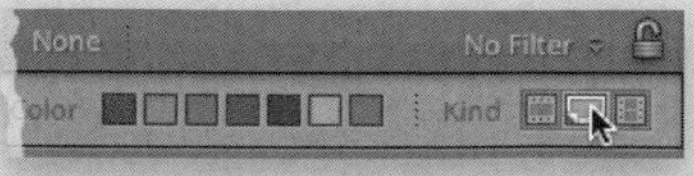

click on Attribute. When the Attribute options pop down, click on the little curled page icon at the far right of the bar to show just the virtual copies. To see the real original "master" files, click the filmstrip icon just to the left of it. To see everything again (both the virtual and original masters), click the None button.

▼ Quickly Flatten Your Curve

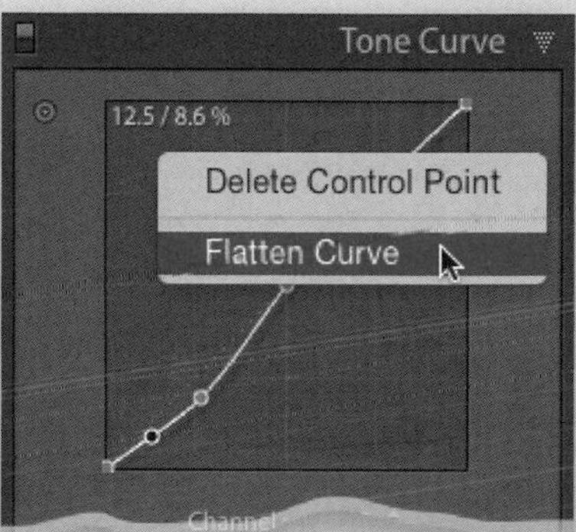

If you've created a Tone Curve adjustment (in the Develop module) and you want to quickly reset the curve to a flat (Linear) curve, just Right-click anywhere inside the curve grid and choose **Flatten Curve.**

▼ Tip for Using the Targeted Adjustment Tool (TAT)

If you're using the Develop module's TAT to tweak your image, you already know that you click-and-drag the TAT within your image and it moves the sliders that control the colors/tones underneath it. However, you might find it easier to move the TAT over the area you want to adjust, and instead of dragging the TAT up/down, use the **Up/Down Arrow keys** on your keyboard, and it will move the sliders for you. If you press-and-hold the Shift key while using the Up/Down Arrow keys, the sliders move in larger increments.

▼ Copy What You Last Copied

When you click the Copy button in the Develop module (at the bottom of the left side Panels area), it brings up a Copy Settings dialog asking which edits you want to copy. However, if you know you want to copy the same edits as you had previously (maybe you always copy everything), then you can skip having that Copy Settings dialog pop up completely by pressing-and-holding the Option (PC: Alt) key, then clicking the Copy button (it will change from Copy… to Copy).

▼ Making Lightroom Go Faster!

One of the most important new features of the current version of Lightroom is the speed increase in the Develop module, thanks to Adobe moving some of the heavy lifting off to your computer's GPU (Graphics Processing Unit). So, if your sliders or brush were lagging in previous versions, it should respond tremendously faster now. This acceleration is turned on by default, but to make sure it is, press

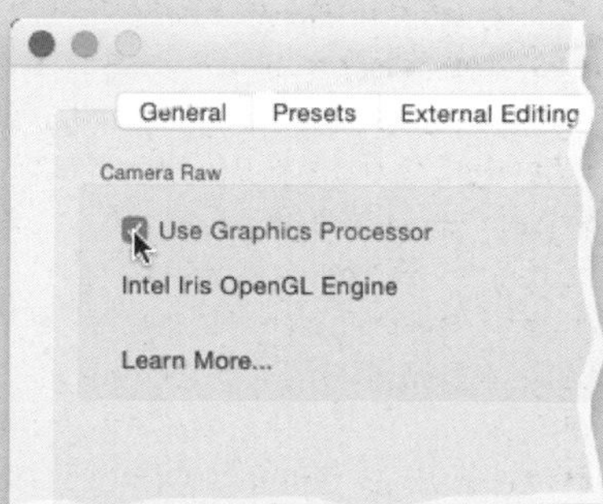

Command-, (comma; **PC: Ctrl-,**) to open the Preferences, click on the Performance tab, and then make sure Use Graphic Processor is turned on. If your computer supports this feature, you'll see the name of your graphic card appear right below this checkbox. If you see an error message instead, your computer can't take advantage of the GPU acceleration. Ack!

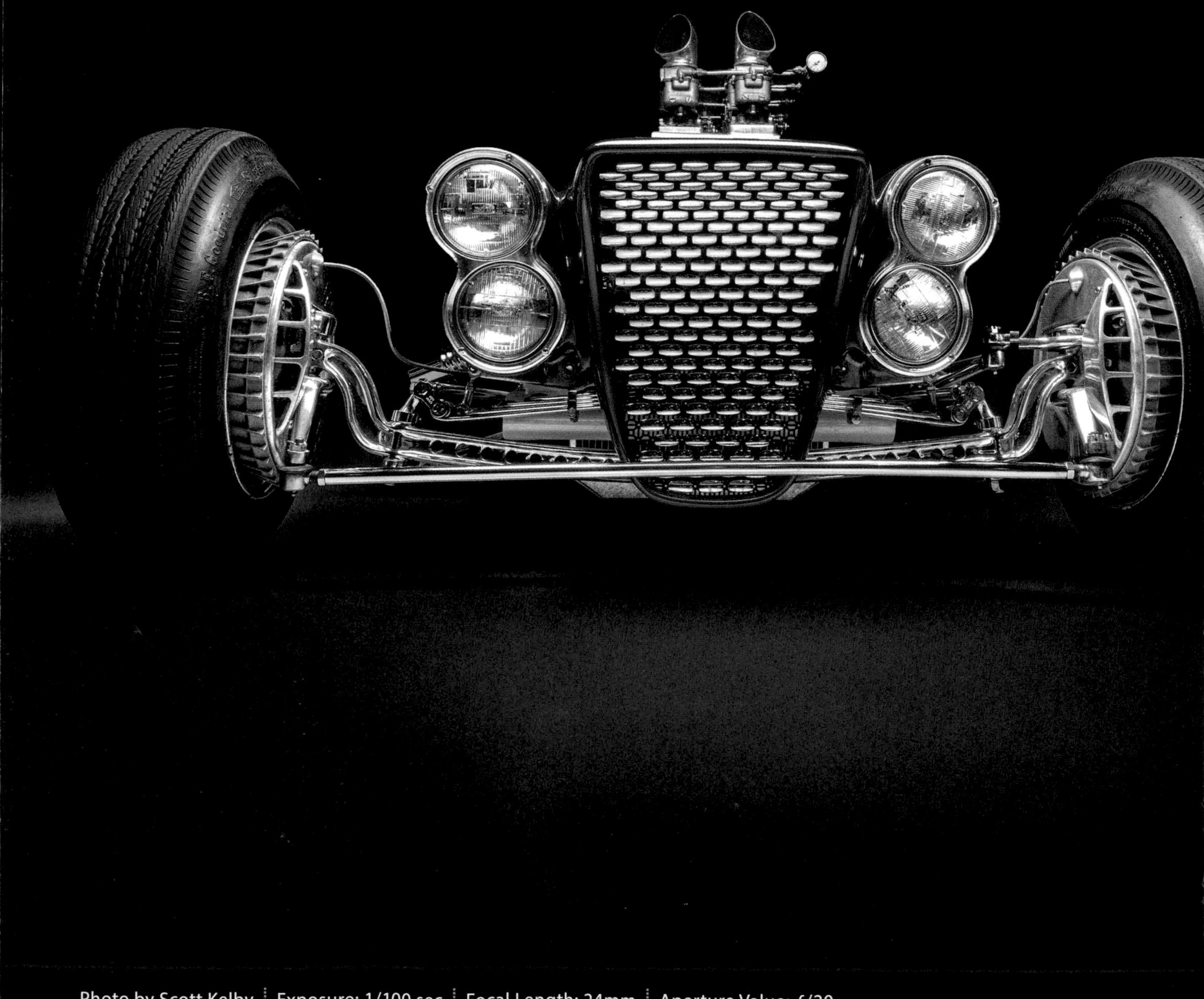

Photo by Scott Kelby | Exposure: 1/100 sec | Focal Length: 24mm | Aperture Value: ƒ/20

CHAPTER 5

LOCAL ADJUSTMENTS

how to edit just part of your images

I'll be the first to admit that "Local Adjustments" isn't a great name for a chapter on using the Adjustment Brush (and the other local adjustment tools), but it's an "Adobe-ism" for editing just one section of your image. Here's how they describe it: Everything you do in Lightroom is a global adjustment. It affects your entire image globally. So, if you're affecting just one part of your image, it's not global. It's local. So what you're making is a local adjustment. This would all make perfect sense if anyone in the world actually thought that way, but of course nobody does (not even the engineer who thought up this term). You see, we regular non-software-engineer people refer to adjustments that affect the entire photo as "adjustments that affect the entire photo" and we refer to adjustments that affect just one part as "adjustments that affect just one part." But, of course, Adobe can't actually name functions with those names, because then we'd clearly understand what they do. Nope, when it comes to stuff like this, it has to go before the official Adobe Council of Obscure Naming Conventions (known internally as ACONC, which is a powerful naming body whose members all wear flowing robes, carry torches, and sing solemn chants with their heads bowed). The ACONC types a simple, understandable phrase into the "Pimp Name Generator" (see page 131), and out comes an overly technical name that their sacred emissary (brother Jeff Schewe) will carry forward into the world (after which there is a great celebration where they sacrifice an intern from the marketing department, and a temp from accounting). And that's how I met your mother.

Dodging, Burning, and Adjusting Individual Areas of Your Photo

Everything we've done so far affected the entire image. If you drag the Temp slider, it changes the white balance for the entire image (it's a "global adjustment"). But what if you want to adjust one particular area of your image (a "local" adjustment)? Then you'd use the Adjustment Brush, which lets you paint changes just where you want them, so you can do things like dodging and burning (lightening and darkening different parts of your photo). There's a lot of important stuff in this chapter, but I think learning how to dodge-and-burn is the most important.

Step One:

Here's the original image—one of the amazing ceilings at St. Peter's Basilica in Vatican City, Italy. It needs a lot of work. The bright sunlight coming into the dome fooled the camera's metering system (and, apparently, the guy holding it, as well. Ahem…) and underexposed most of the image by quite a bit. That's the key—there are parts that are too bright, and areas I wish were brighter. This is where the Adjustment Brush, which lets you selectively dodge (make certain areas brighter) and burn (make certain areas darker), totally rocks. It was born for this stuff, but I don't use it until I at least get my basic exposure right, so let's do that first. In the Develop module's Basic panel, let's tweak the sliders to get us at least in the ballpark.

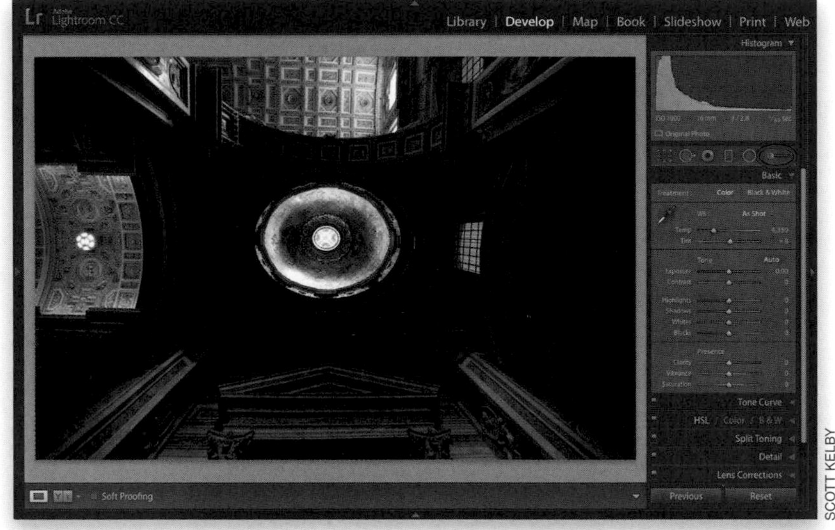

SCOTT KELBY

Step Two:

Since it's way underexposed, let's start by dragging the Exposure slider to the right to help the overall brightness. The light coming in from the top of the dome and the windows is pretty bright, so let's lower the highlights in those areas by dragging the Highlights slider to the left quite a bit. Finally, I'd like to see more detail in the shadow areas, so let's open up the Shadows a nice bit, too (as shown here). Okay, it already looks a lot better, but the areas right around the dome are still pretty dark, and the gold ceiling area on the left is too bright. The ceiling area at the top center is too bright, too, and so are the columns on either side of it. As is often the case, there are some areas that need to be brighter and some that need to be darker.

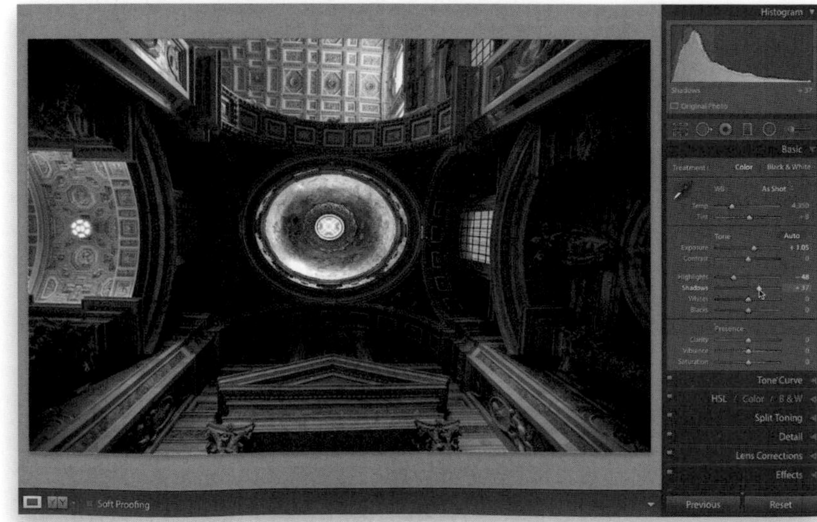

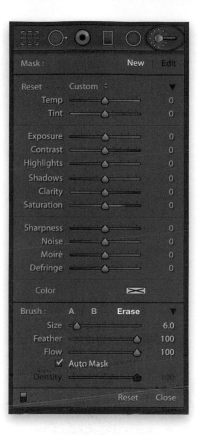

Step Three:

The Adjustment Brush is found in the toolbox right above the Basic panel (it's the tool on the far right, shown circled here), or just press the letter **K** on your keyboard. When you choose it, an options panel pops down (seen here) and you'll see that you can paint using nearly all the same controls you have in the Basic panel, except that Vibrance isn't there. (Rats!) But, at least we have other cool stuff, like noise reduction and moiré removal, so it kinda makes up for not having Vibrance. Kinda. With the Adjustment Brush, you choose which adjustment you want to paint with by dragging one or more of those sliders, and then you just start painting that adjustment right on your photo.

TIP: Changing Brush Sizes

To change your brush size, press the Left Bracket key to make it smaller or the Right Bracket key to make it bigger.

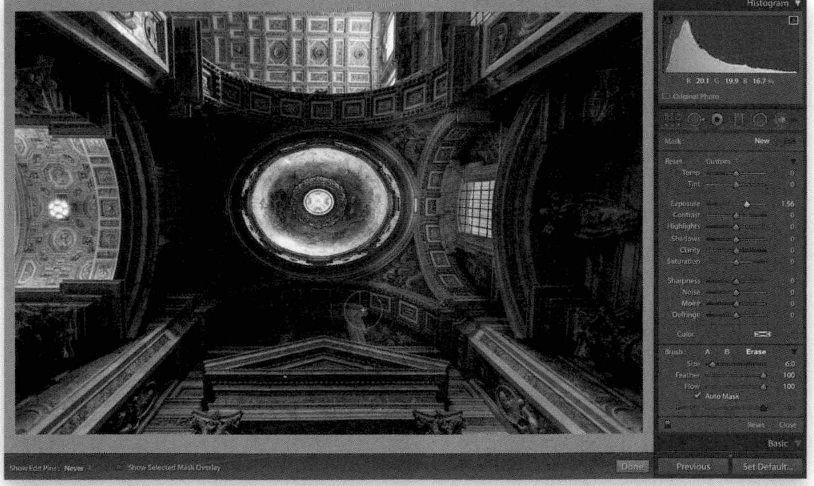

Step Four:

Since you don't actually see the effect until you start painting on your photo, how do you know how far to move the sliders? Well, this is going to sound weird, but you don't. You literally just make a blind guess at how much you think you might want of a particular adjustment, and then you paint over the area you want to adjust. Then, once you can see the adjustment, you go back to that slider and tweak the amount until it looks right. The good part is you get to make your final decision after you've painted over the area, so you can get it right on the money. For example, here I (1) got the brush, (2) dragged the Exposure slider to the right a bunch, (3) painted over the dark area on the right side of the dome to brighten it, and then (4) went back to the Exposure slider and lowered the amount until it looked right to me.

Continued

Step Five:

Once you stop painting, you'll see that a little white circle with a black dot in the center appears on your image right at the spot where you started painting. (If you don't see the black dot, look down in the toolbar under your image and make sure Auto, Always, or Selected appears after Show Edit Pins. If you don't see the toolbar, press **T**). That's called an Edit Pin (shown circled here in red), and it represents the change you just made to the right side of the dome. As long as you see a black dot in the center, it means that adjustment is "active," and if you start painting again right now it just adds to what you've already painted. So, let's continue painting around the rest of the dark areas surrounding the dome (as shown here, where that area is much brighter now). By the way, that little Edit Pin automatically hides as you paint

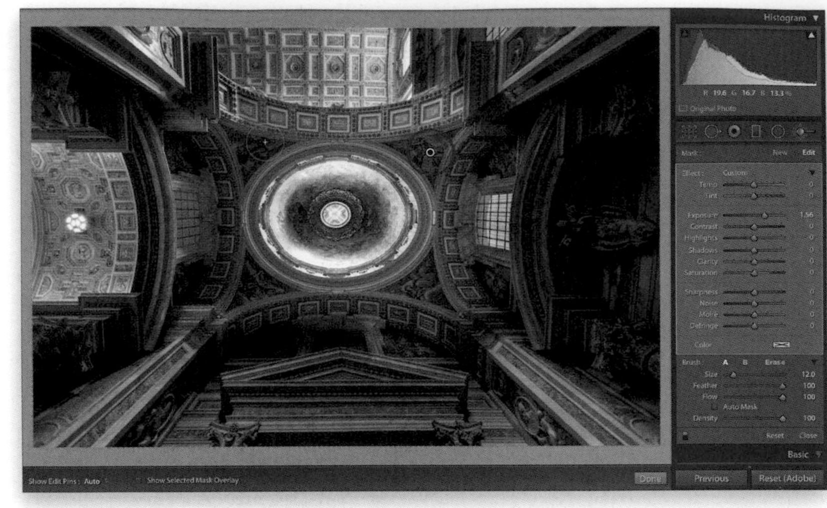

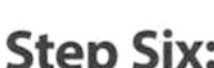

Step Six:

When you're done brightening around the dome, and you now want to adjust a different area (for example, let's say you want to darken [burn] the gold ceiling on the left center of the image, so it's not too bright), you can't just drag the Exposure slider over to the left and start painting. That's because your Edit Pin for the dome is still active. Moving the Exposure slider will make the area you painted around the dome darker. You have to tell Lightroom to "Leave what I did around the dome alone. Now, I want to paint a totally separate adjustment, somewhere else in the photo, with different settings." You do that by clicking the New button at the top of the Adjustment Brush panel. Now, you can lower the Exposure amount and start painting over that bright middle-left ceiling area without disturbing your original brightening of the area around the dome. Each time you want to paint with a different set of adjustments (so that area is controlled separately from the last area you painted), click the New button.

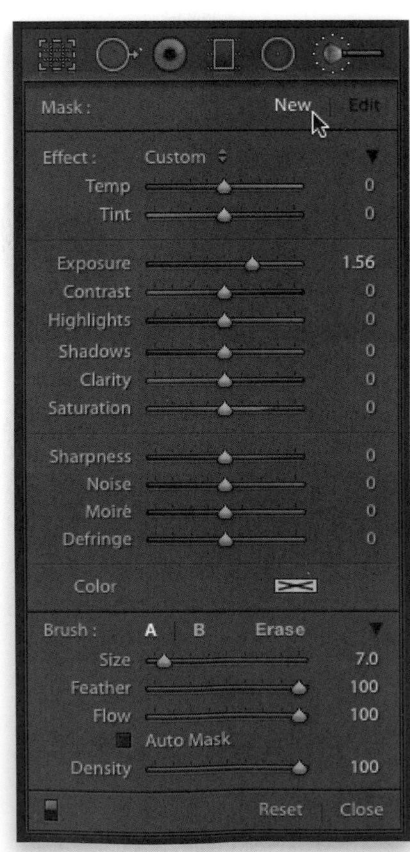

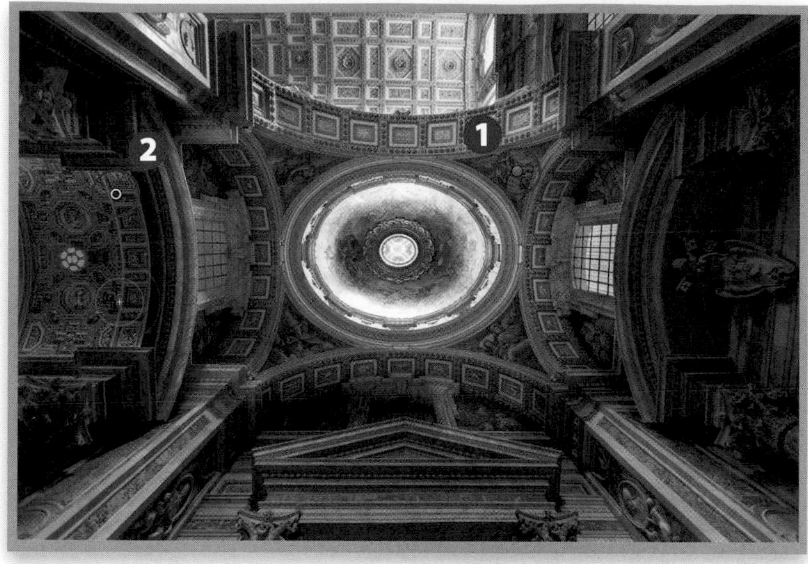

Step Seven:

Okay, after you click the New button, go ahead and lower the Exposure amount and the Highlights amount, and start painting over that middle-left gold ceiling area, so it's not so bright. I figured we'd take down the highlights at the same time since there's a bright light fixture right in the center of that ceiling area. When you're done painting, move your cursor out of the way (drag it over the panels on the right side), and now you'll see two Edit Pins: (1) which is now just solid gray—there's no black dot in the center because it's not the active pin—and represents the area brightened around the dome, and (2) which represents the area you just darkened (the gold ceiling on the middle left). It has a black dot in the center of the pin because it's still active, meaning if you move any sliders now, it will affect that gold ceiling area.

TIP: Deleting Edit Pins

To delete an Edit Pin, click on it then press the Delete (PC: Backspace) key.

Step Eight:

If you want to go back and work on the area around the dome, all you have to do is click on that gray pin. It becomes the active area, and all the sliders automatically update to the last settings you used on that pin, so you can continue right where you left off. It's not unusual for me to have five or six Edit Pins in a photo (occasionally more) because I needed to adjust five or six different areas. Now, what do you do if you make a mistake or paint over something that doesn't look good? For example, look at the light fixture in the center of the gold ceiling area on the left. It looks gray, which looks weird (light isn't usually gray). To remove the adjustment over just that light, press-and-hold the Option (PC: Alt) key, which switches you to the Erase brush. Now, just paint over the light fixture and it erases the adjustment in only that area, and the light looks normal again.

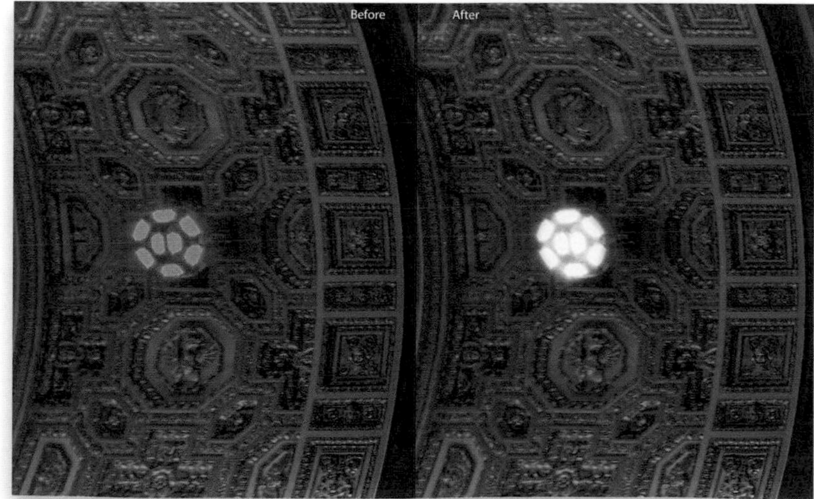

Above: Darkening the gold ceiling also darkened the light fixture, making it look gray

Above: Erasing the effect just over the light fixture brings back the original natural look

Continued

Step Nine:

Before we wrap up erasing, two quick things: (1) as with the brush, you have complete control over how your Erase brush works in the very bottom section of the Adjustment Brush panel. Click on the word Erase (as shown here) and it displays the settings for the Erase brush. You can choose the Size, Feather (how soft the edges are), Flow (whether it paints a solid stroke at 100% opacity or whether you want it to build up as you paint), and you can turn on/off Auto Mask (we'll talk about that next). (2) You have two regular brushes to choose from, as well, called "A" and "B," and you can choose their settings. I usually make my "A" brush have a soft edge and my "B" brush have a hard edge (I lower the Feather amount to 0), so if I run into a situation where I'm painting along a wall or other area where a soft edge looks weird, I can toggle over to my "B" brush using the **Backslash (/) key** on my keyboard.

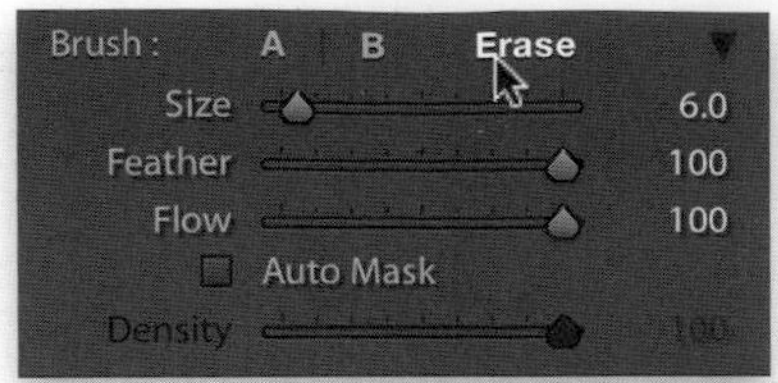

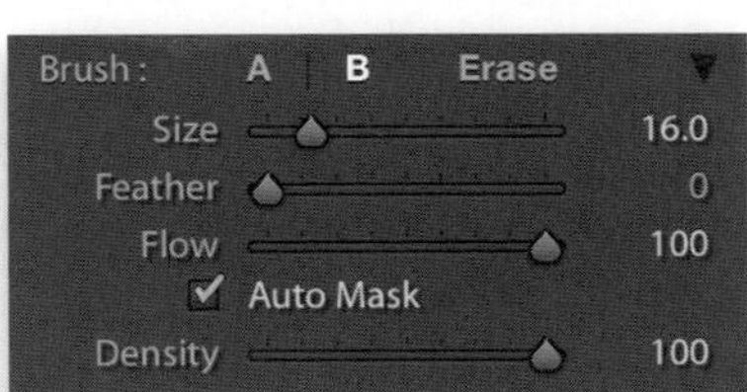

Step 10:

I'm going to switch to a new image for just a moment to talk about Auto Mask (you turn this on/off near the bottom of the panel). When it's on, it kind of senses where the edges of things are and keeps you from accidentally painting where you don't want to. Take a look at the image on top, here. I want to darken the background, but when I paint on it near the guard's arm, it also paints over his arm. However, look at the image at the bottom. When I turn Auto Mask on, it senses the edge and lets me paint over the background next to his arm without spilling over onto it (pretty amazing!). The trick is knowing how it works: You see that little + (plus sign) in the center of the brush? That determines what gets painted, and any area that + travels over gets painted. So, as long as that + doesn't go over his arm, it won't paint over it, even if the outer rim of the brush extends way over onto his arm (as shown here). As long as you keep that off the arm, it leaves that area alone.

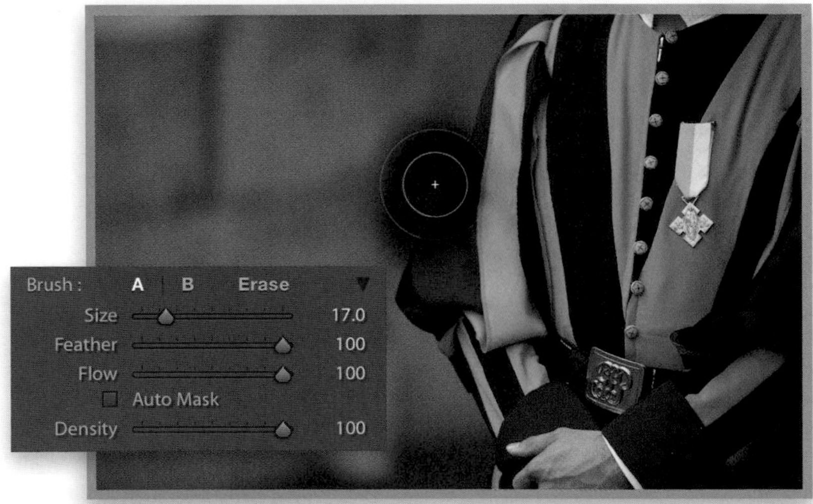

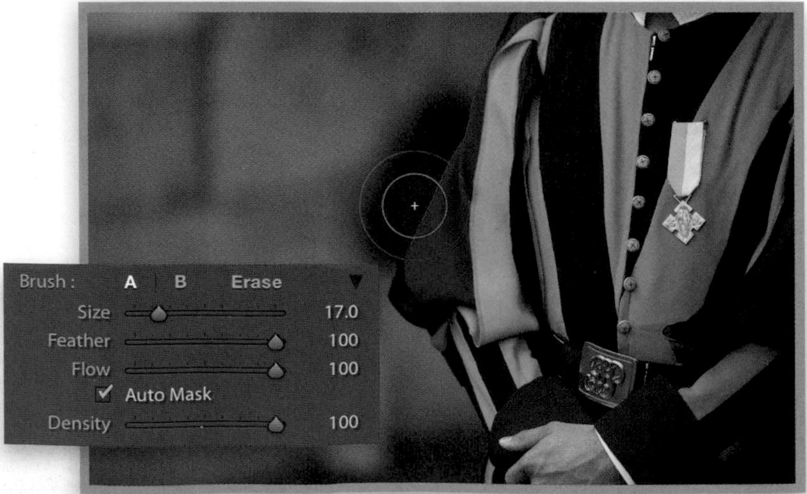

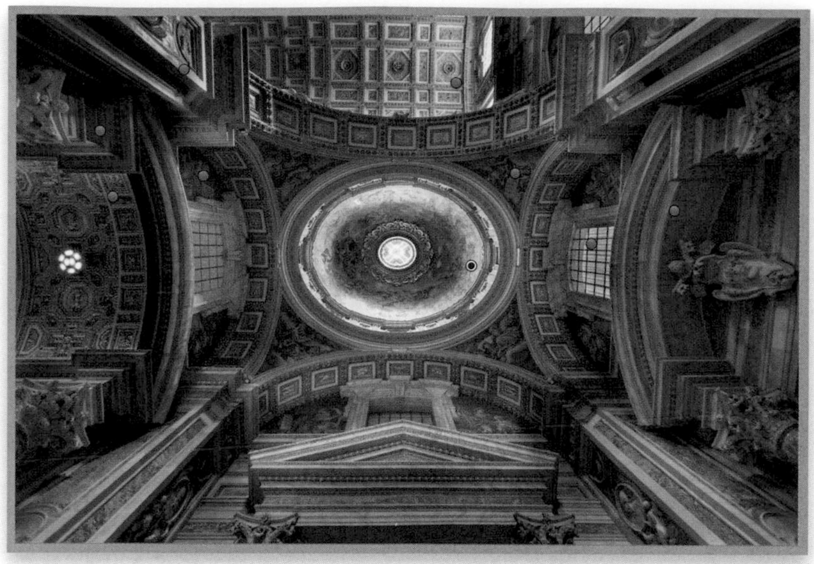

Step 11:

Before we get back to working on our church ceiling, I wanted to mention one more thing about Auto Mask. When it's turned on, the brush runs a bit slower, because it's doing "math" as you paint (determining where the edges are). So, if I'm painting over a big sky or wall or other area that doesn't need the brush doing fancy math, I turn it off so things go faster. Okay, back to our church. I think that, at this point, you've got the idea: In a lot of images, there are some areas you want brighter and some you want darker, and this brush not only lets you do that, but you can add any of the other sliders, as well. This is awesome because you can brighten an area and make it sharper, or darken an area and make the color more saturated, too (great for skies). Let's go ahead and darken and brighten a few more areas here (like darkening the dome at the top center. Then, I'd brighten the area along the bottom of the image, darken the two columns up top on the sides, and even lower the Highlights in the dome itself to bring back some detail there. You can see I've got nine Edit Pins now).

TIP: How Do You Know If You've Missed a Spot?

Press the letter **O** on your keyboard to show a red mask over the area you painted on the active pin (to see it temporarily, move your cursor over the pin). If you missed an area, paint over it; if you spilled over onto something you didn't want to, press-and-hold the Option (PC: Alt) key and paint it away.

Step 12:

Okay, now, how about a finishing move that I usually use in landscape photos to add an extra "kiss of light" to highlight areas in the image? Click the New button, make your brush pretty large, increase the Exposure to about 1.00, and then click once over highlight areas as though little beams of light are hitting them. (I created a video for you on this, which you can find on the book's companion webpage, mentioned in the book's introduction.) Here's a before/after.

Continued

Step 13:
By the way, dodging and burning isn't just for cathedrals and it isn't just for travel and landscape photos. I routinely use it for portrait work, and here's a typical example: when you're lighting an outdoor portrait and the flash not only lights your subject, but spills over onto the ground and lights that, as well (as seen here, which looks lame because our goal is to light the subject's face the brightest, and then have fall-off so the light gets darker and darker as it moves down your subject until it fades away. In short, it shouldn't make it to the ground).

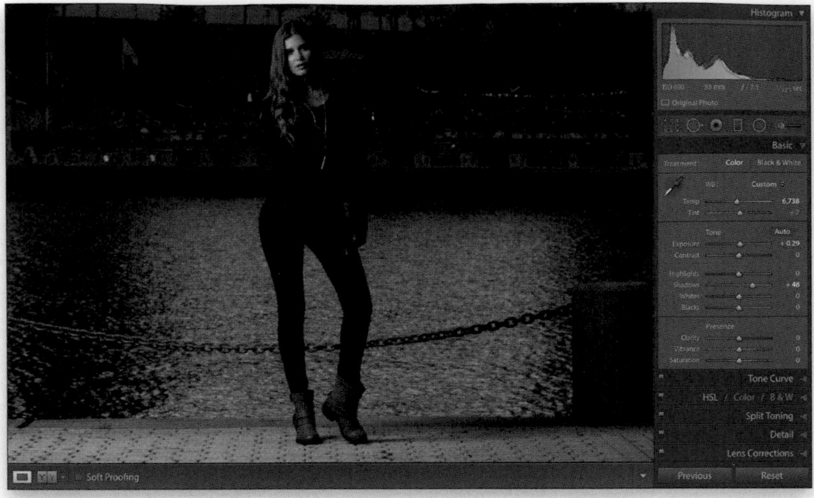

Above: You can see the light from the flash spilling onto the ground.

Step 14:
When this happens, here's a quick fix: get the Adjustment Brush, lower the Exposure amount, and paint over the ground until you don't see the flash spilling onto it, which gives you a much more professional look.

TIP: Moving Your Adjustment
In Lightroom CC, you can now drag a pin to move it to a new location once you've copied-and-pasted the Adjustment Brush edit onto other photos, like similar ones from the same shoot. If you didn't use a tripod, chances are either you or your subject moved a tiny bit from shot to shot. Now you can drag the adjustment a tiny bit, too! To return to the way clicking-and-dragging on a pin used to work (when you dragged over the pin, it moved all the adjustment sliders in tandem instead), just press-and-hold the Option (PC: Alt) key, then click directly on the pin and drag left or right.

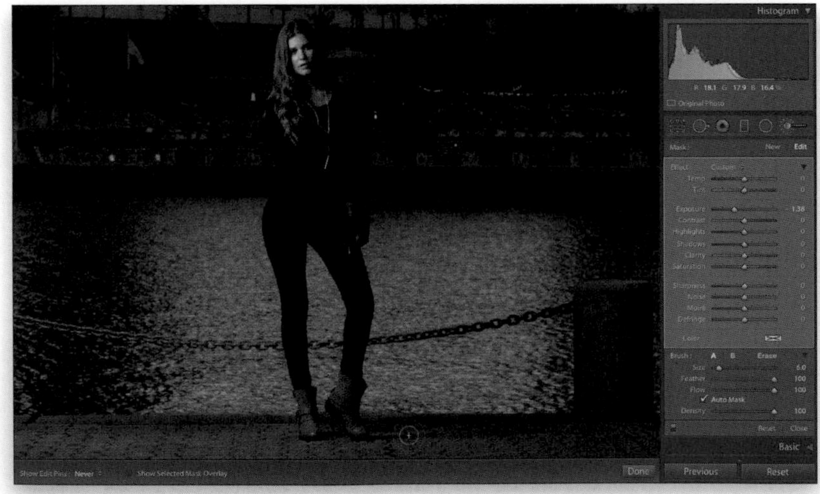

Above: Here's the photo after lowering the Exposure amount and painting over the ground. When it gets close to her boots, turn on Auto Mask, so it doesn't darken them (unless you want that). If you did darken them, I would hit the New button, then don't lower the Exposure quite as much, and then paint over just her boots separately.

Five More Things You Should Know About Lightroom's Adjustment Brush

There are a few other things you need to know that will help you get more comfortable with the Adjustment Brush, and once you learn these (along with the rest of the stuff in this chapter), you'll find yourself making fewer trips over to Photoshop, because you can do so much right here in Lightroom.

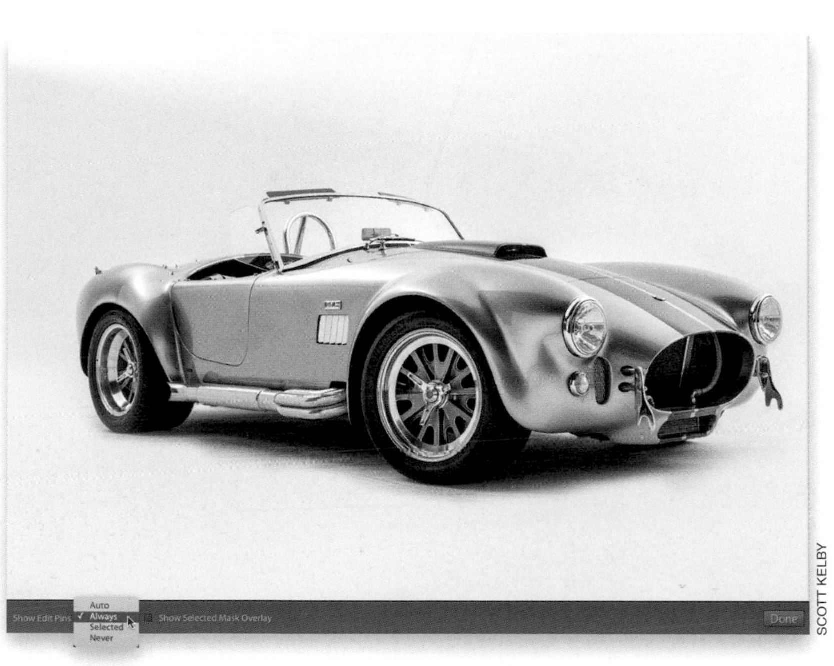

SCOTT KELBY

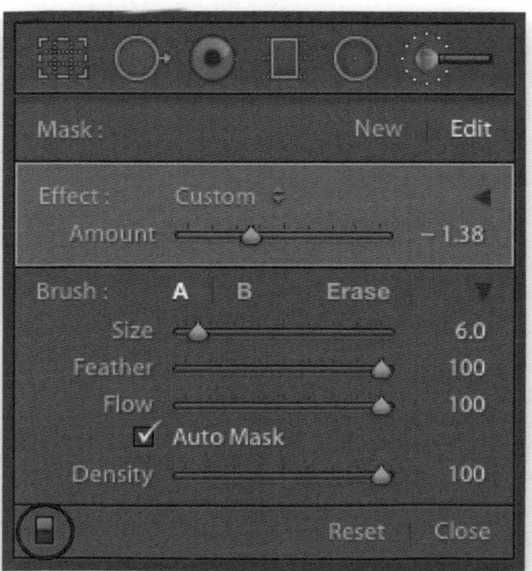

#1: You have a choice of how Lightroom displays the Edit Pins, and you make that choice from the Show Edit Pins pop-up menu down in the toolbar beneath the Preview area (as shown here). Choosing Auto means when you move your cursor outside the image area, the pins are hidden. Always means they're always visible and Never means you never see them. Selected means you only see the currently active pin.

#2: To see your image without the edits you've made with the Adjustment Brush, click the little switch on the bottom left of the panel (circled below in red).

#3: If you press the letter **O**, the red mask overlay stays onscreen, so you can easily see, and fix, areas you've missed.

#4: If you click on the little down-facing triangle to the far right of the Effect pop-up menu, it hides the Effect sliders, and instead gives you an Amount slider (as shown here) that provides a single, overall control over all the changes you make to the currently active Edit Pin.

#5: Below the Auto Mask checkbox is the Density slider, which kind of simulates the way Photoshop's Airbrush feature works, but honestly, the effect is so subtle when painting on a mask, that I don't ever change it from its default setting of 100.

Selectively Fixing White Balance, Dark Shadows, and Noise Issues

Fixing problems that only appear in certain parts of your image is where the Adjustment Brush comes up big, because you can paint away the problems in these areas. Things like white balance problems, when, for example, part of your image is in daylight and part is in the shade. Or painting away noise that just appears in the shadow areas, leaving the rest of the photo untouched (and saving it from the blurring that comes with noise reduction). Incredibly handy.

Step One:

Let's start with painting white balance. Take a look at the image here, where the bride is lit with late afternoon sun, but the part of her bridal gown that she's holding is in the shade. Because I shot this in Auto White balance on my camera, that part of her gown has a fairly strong blue tint to it (pretty typical when part of your image winds up in shade. I face this a lot shooting sports, when part of the field is in shade in the late afternoon games and part is in daylight) and most brides won't be happy to see part of their beautiful bridal gown in blue. This is where the ability to paint white balance in just certain areas is incredibly helpful, so press the letter **K** to get the Adjustment Brush.

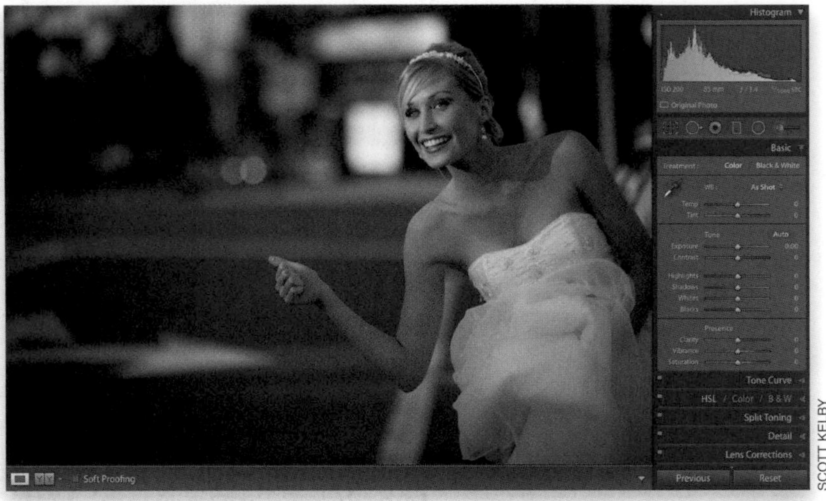

SCOTT KELBY

Step Two:

Double-click directly on the word "Effect" to reset all the sliders to zero. Then, drag the Temp slider over to the right a bit (toward yellow) and start painting over the part of the gown she's holding. As you do, the yellow white balance you're painting neutralizes the blue in her gown, and you wind up with a white gown (as seen here). Because you have to guess your starting point, the original amount of Temp I used (+31) made her dress look yellow, so I lowered the Temp amount to +18 and that looked better, but it did look a little reddish, so I dragged the Tint slider away from magenta and over toward green (to –28) until her dress looked white. Painting with white balance like this is a huge help. Next, let's paint away noise in the same way.

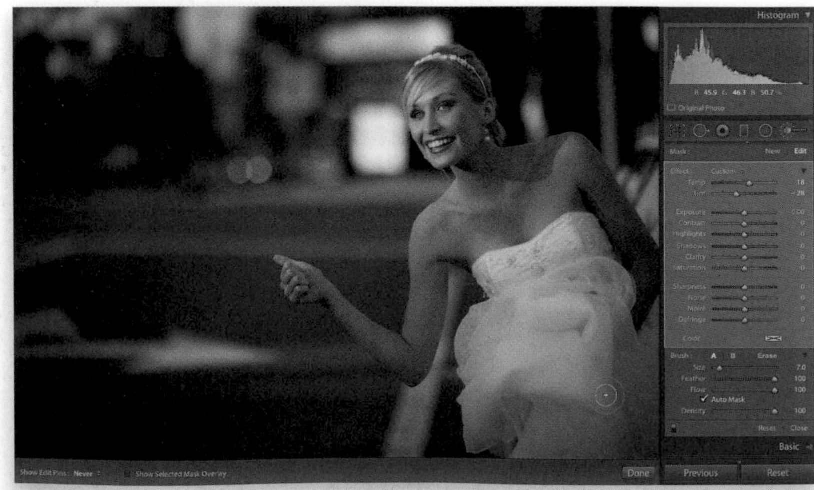

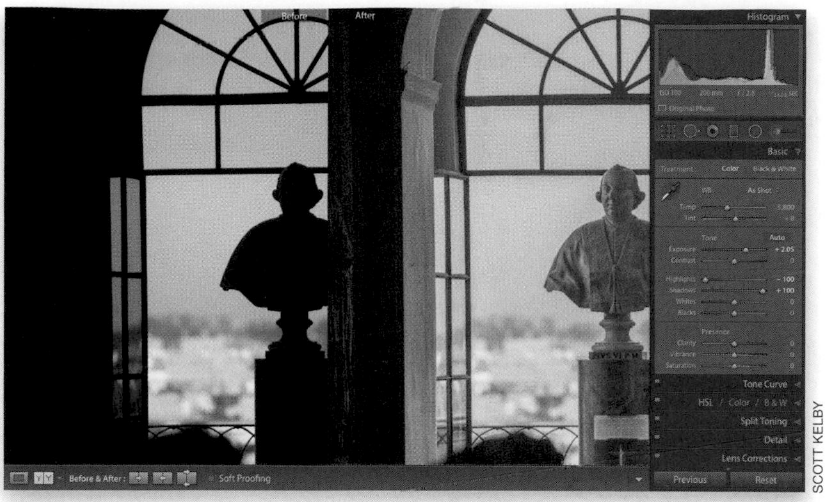

SCOTT KELBY

Step Three:

Here we have an image that is severely backlit from the window. If you look at the before image on the left, you can't even see any detail in the bust or in the room—it's all just a silhouette. However, when you crank up the Shadows slider and the Exposure slider enough to where the image is properly exposed (I also lowered the Highlights slider a lot to make the area outside the window not nearly as bright), you see all the noise big time. Noise usually hides in the shadows, and sometimes when you drastically open up those shadow areas (like we did here), any noise that was in the image is now magnified. So, the statue, windows, and the rest of the room look great, but the wall on the left is full of red, green, and blue noise dots that we need to deal with.

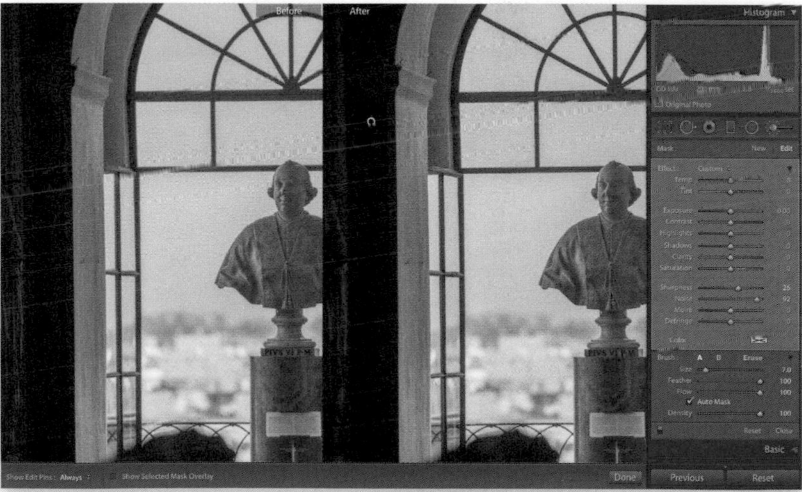

Step Four:

So, why don't we just use Lightroom's regular Noise Reduction controls in the Detail panel? It's because that affects the entire image equally—when it reduces noise, to do so, it also softens the entire image. Here, by using the Adjustment Brush, we can reduce the noise only on that wall on the left and leave the rest of the photo (the brighter areas that don't show much noise) sharp and untouched. By doing it this way, we only make that wall on the left a little soft and not the entire image. To do this, get the Adjustment Brush, and then double-click on the word "Effect" to reset all the sliders to zero. Now, drag the Noise slider nearly all the way to the right, and then paint over that wall on the left to reduce the noise there. How far are you supposed to drag that Noise slider? The idea is to find that sweet spot where it's not too noisy and it's not too blurry. Also, don't forget, all the other sliders here still work, so you could darken just that wall a little, while you're applying noise reduction, which would help to hide the noise, too. Here, I just increased the Sharpness slider to 26.

Retouching Portraits

When it comes to detailed retouching, I generally jump over to Adobe Photoshop, but if you just need to do a quick retouch, it's amazing how many things you can do right here in Lightroom using the Adjustment Brush and the Spot Removal tool, with its healing power. Here's a quick retouch using just those two tools:

Step One:

Here are the things we're going to retouch in this image: (1) remove any major blemishes and wrinkles, (2) soften her skin, (3) brighten the whites of her eyes, (4) add contrast to her eyes and sharpen them, and (5) add some highlights to her hair. Although we're seeing the full image here, for retouching, it's best to zoom in quite a bit. So, go ahead and zoom in nice and tight to start the next step. By the way, I thought her skin looked a little too warm in the original image, so here I reduced the Vibrance to –21 (just so you know).

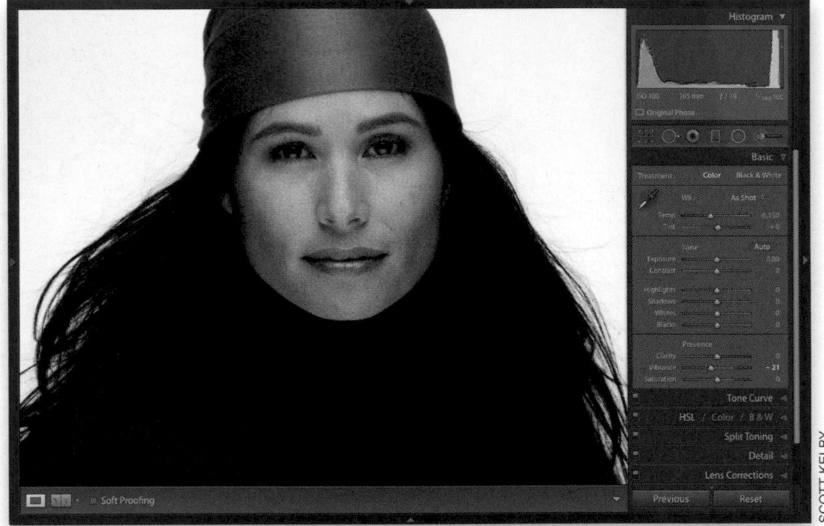

SCOTT KELBY

Step Two:

Here, I've zoomed in to a 1:2 view, so we can really see what we're doing (just select this zoom ratio from the pop-up menu at the top right of the Navigator panel, at the top of the left side Panels area). Click on the Spot Removal tool (in the toolbox near the top of the right side Panels area or just press the letter **Q**). This tool works with just a single click, but you don't want to retouch any more than is necessary, so make the brush Size of the tool just a little bit larger than the blemish you're going to remove. Move your brush cursor over the blemish and then just click once. A second circle will appear showing you from where it sampled a clean skin texture. Of course, it's not always 100% right, and if for some reason it chose a bad area of skin to sample from, just click on that second circle, drag it to a clean patch, and it will update your blemish removal. Go ahead and remove any blemishes now using this tool (as shown here).

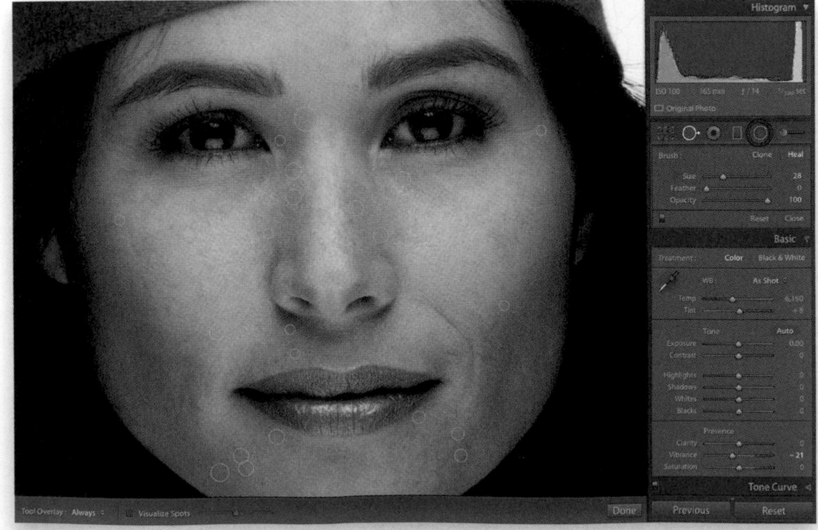

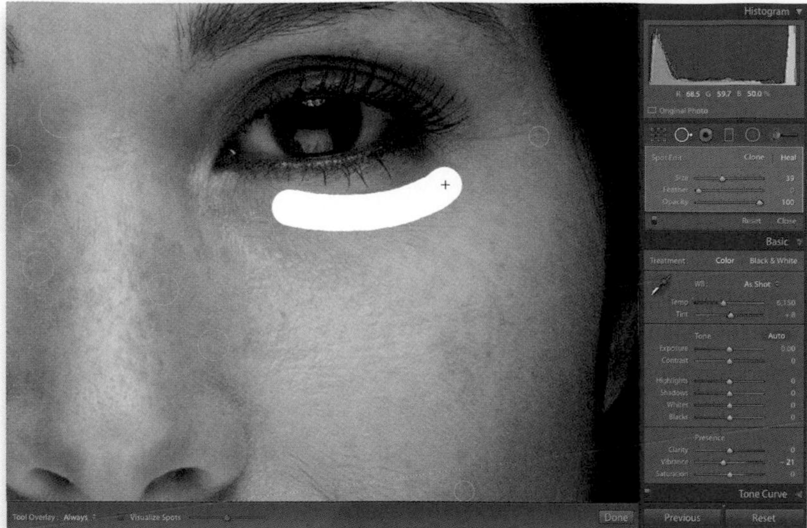

Step Three:

Now, let's remove some wrinkles under her eyes. Zoom in tighter (this is a 1:1 view), then take the same Spot Removal tool we've been using (make sure it's set to Heal) and paint a stroke over the wrinkles under her eye on the right (as shown here). The area you've painted over turns white (as seen here), so you can see the area you're affecting.

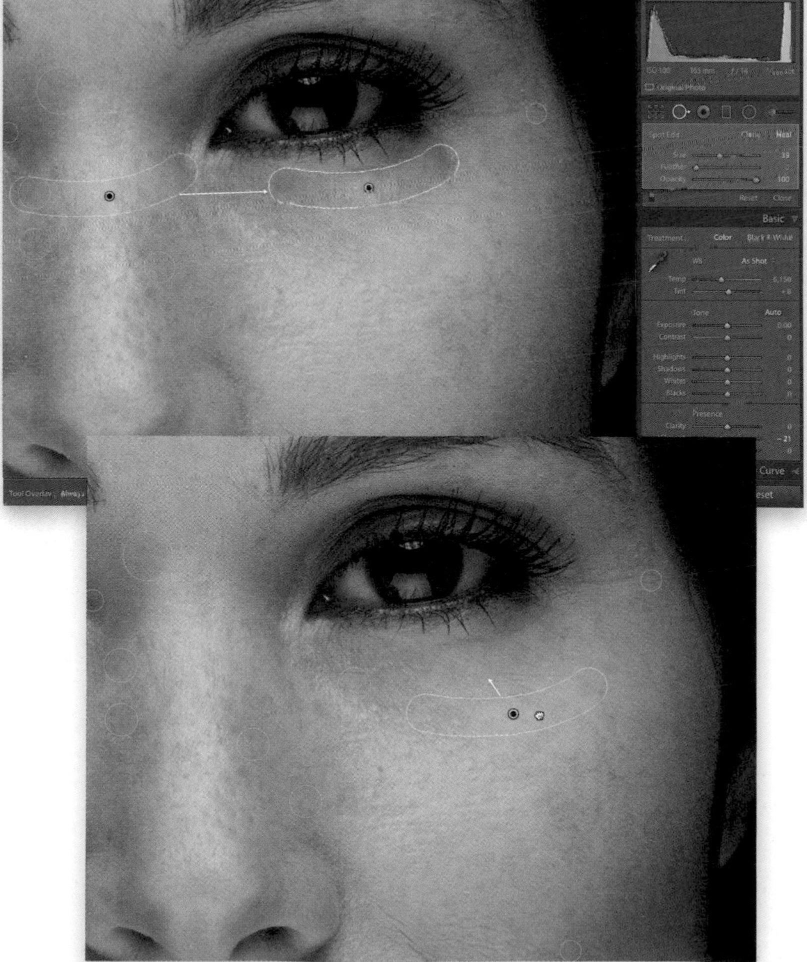

Step Four:

Lightroom analyzes the area and picks a spot somewhere else in the image to use to repair those wrinkles. It usually picks something nearby, but in this case it chose an area across the bridge of her nose, which, of course, created a bad retouch. Luckily, if you don't like where Lightroom chose to sample from, you can simply have it sample somewhere else by clicking on that second outline (the thinner one of the two) and dragging it somewhere on her face where you think the texture and tone will match better (here, I moved it right up under the original area where the wrinkles used to be, as shown in the overlay). Also, don't forget to remove the wrinkles from beneath the other eye (it's easier to forget than you'd think). *Note:* If your subject is at an age where fully removing the wrinkles would be unrealistic, we would instead need to "reduce" the wrinkles, so we would decrease the Opacity slider to lower the strength of the removal, bringing back some of the original wrinkles.

Continued

Step Five:

Now that the blemishes and wrinkles are removed, let's do some skin softening. Switch to the Adjustment Brush (also in the toolbox near the top of the right side Panels area, or just press the letter **K**), then choose **Soften Skin** from the Effect pop-up menu. Now paint over her face, but be careful to avoid any areas that you don't want softened, like her eyelashes, eyebrows, lips, nostrils, hair, the edges of her face, and so on. This softens the skin by giving you a negative Clarity setting (it's set at –100). Here, I've only painted over the right side of her face, so you can see the difference. This is quite a lot of softening, so once you're done, back off the Clarity amount so you can still see skin detail (I raised my amount to –55).

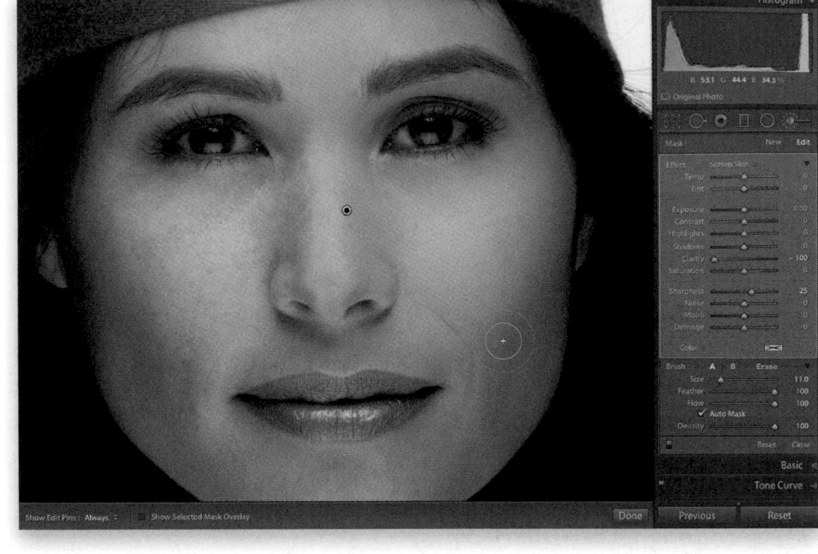

Step Six:

Next, let's work on her eyes, and we'll start by making the whites brighter. First, click the New button in the top right of the panel, then double-click on the word "Effect" to reset all the sliders to zero. Now, drag the Exposure slider to the right a little bit (here, I dragged it over to +1.04) and paint over the whites of her eyes. If you accidentally paint outside the whites, just press-and-hold the **Option (PC: Alt) key** to switch to the Erase tool and erase away any spillover. Do the same for the other eye and, when you're done, adjust the Exposure slider, as needed, to where the whitening looks natural. Next, let's brighten her irises. Click the New button, and increase the Exposure amount to +1.36 and paint over both irises. Then, to add some contrast, increase the Contrast slider to +33. Lastly, to make those eyes really nice and sharp, increase the Sharpness slider to +22, so the irises get brighter, more contrasty, and sharper all at the same time.

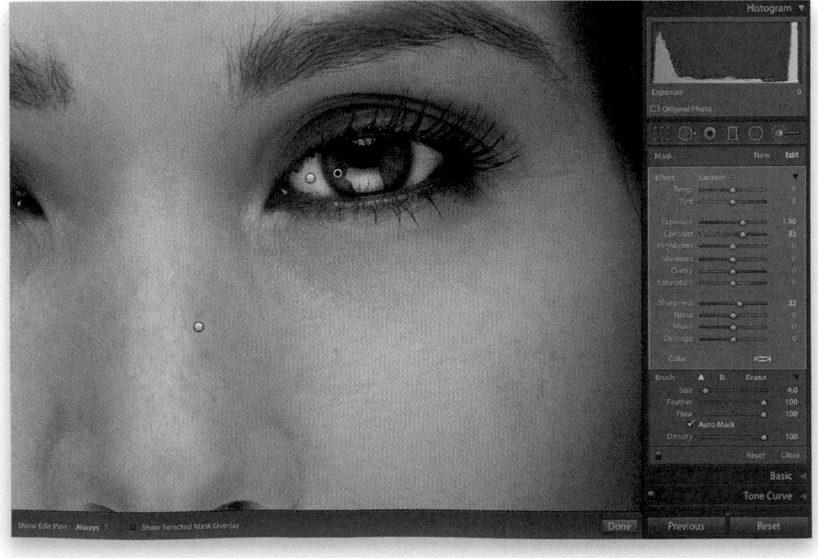

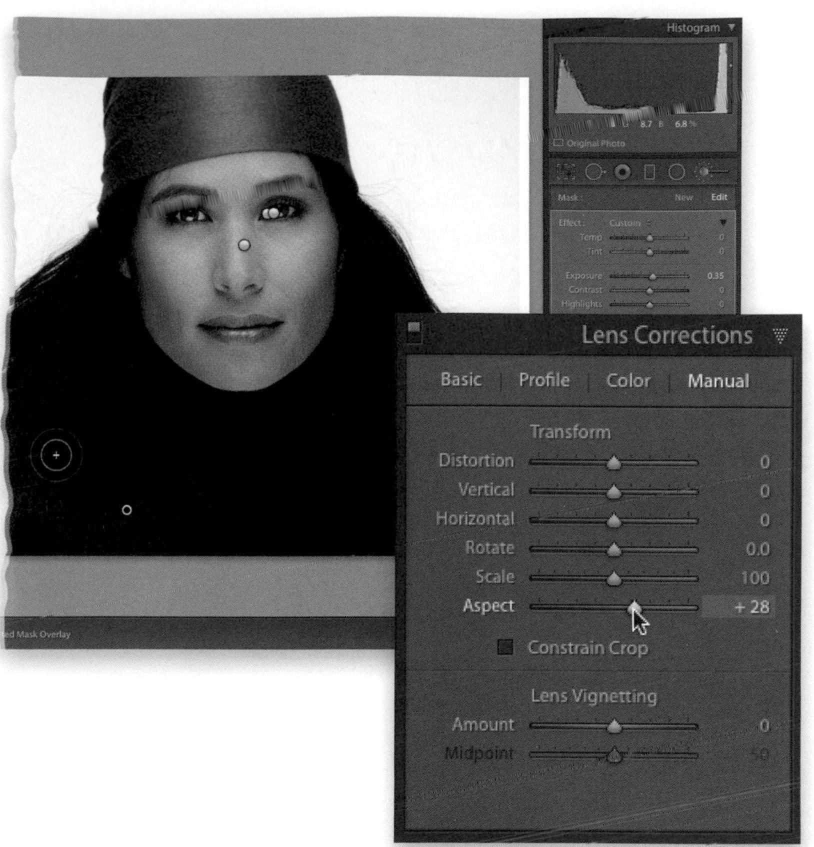

Step Seven:

Now, click the New button once again, and let's brighten the highlights in her hair. Start by resetting your sliders to zero, then drag the Exposure slider to the right a little bit (I dragged mine to +0.35), and then paint over the highlight areas to bring them out. Lastly, one of the retouches I get asked the most to do by subjects is to slim them up a bit. I don't think our subject here needs it at all, but if you're asked, here's how it's done: Go to the Lens Corrections panel; click on Manual (at the top right of the panel), then drag the Aspect slider to the right (as seen in the overlay here). As you do, it compresses (narrows) the photo, giving you an instant slimming effect. The farther to the right you drag, the more your subject gets slimmed (here, I dragged to +28). A before/after is shown below.

TIP: Keep from Seeing Too Many Pins

To see just the currently selected Edit Pin, choose **Selected** from the Show Edit Pins pop-up menu in the Preview area toolbar.

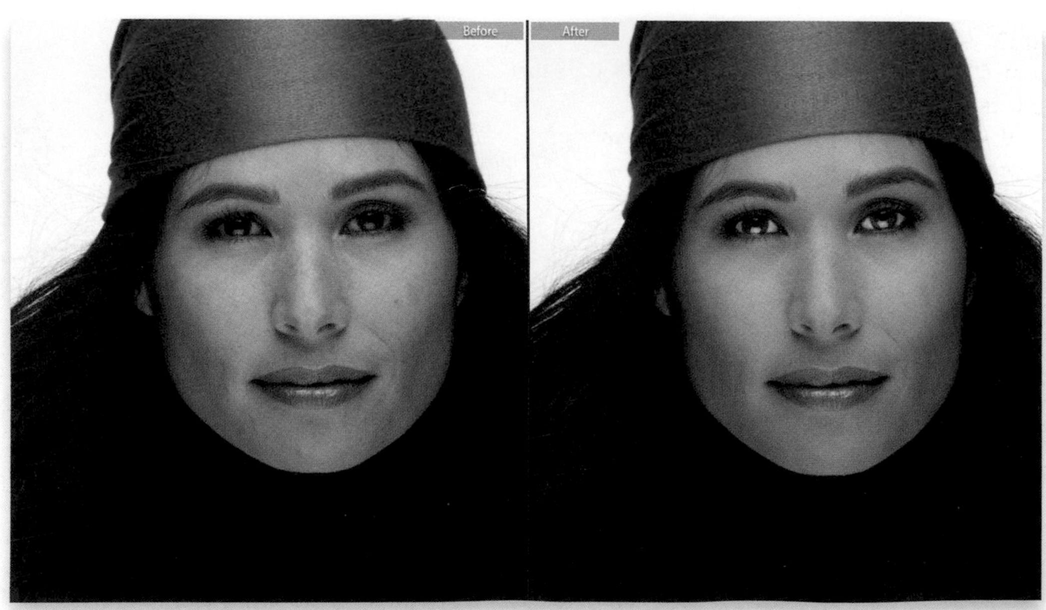

The After photo has clearer and smoother skin (plus it's desaturated a little bit), the eyes are brighter, have more contrast, and are sharper, we've enhanced the highlights in her hair, and we've slimmed her face a bit

Fixing Skies (and Other Stuff) with a Gradient Filter

The Graduated Filter (which is actually a tool) lets you recreate the look of a traditional neutral density gradient filter (these are glass or plastic filters that are dark on the top and then graduate down to fully transparent). They're popular with landscape photographers because you're either going to get a perfectly exposed foreground or a perfectly exposed sky, but not both. However, the way Adobe implemented this feature, you can use it for much more than just neutral density gradient filter effects (though that probably will still be its number one use).

Step One:

Start by clicking on the Graduated Filter tool in the toolbox (it's the second icon to the left of the Adjustment Brush, or press **M**), near the top of the right side Panels area. When you click on it, a set of options pops down that are similar to the effects options of the Adjustment Brush (shown here). Here, we're going to replicate the look of a traditional neutral density gradient filter and darken the sky. Start by choosing **Exposure** from the Effect pop-up menu and then drag the Exposure slider to the left to –1.22 (as shown here). Just like with the Adjustment Brush, at this point we're just kind of guessing how dark we're going to want our gradient, but we can darken or lighten it later.

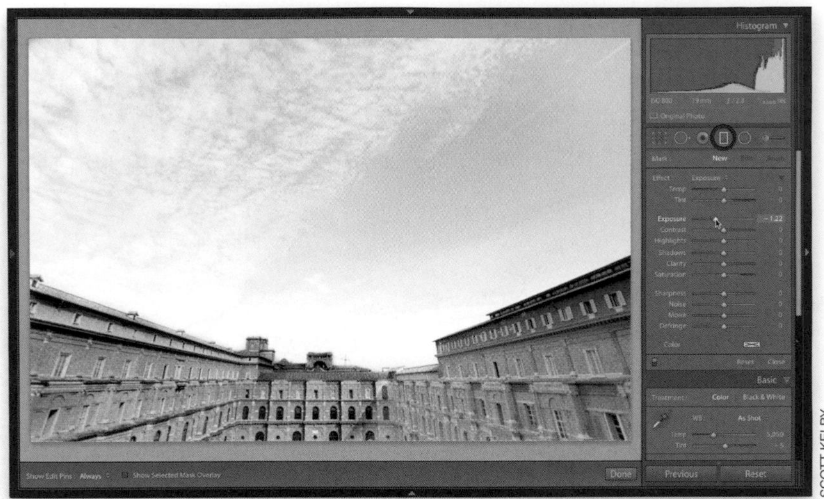

SCOTT KELBY

Step Two:

Press-and-hold the Shift key, click on the top center of your image, and drag straight down until you reach around the middle of the photo (the horizon line. You can see the darkening effect it has on the sky, and the photo already looks more balanced). You might need to stop dragging the gradient before it reaches the horizon line, if it starts to darken your properly exposed foreground (here, I dragged to the top of the building in the middle). By the way, the reason we held the Shift key down was to keep our gradient straight as we dragged. Not holding the Shift key down will let you drag the gradient in any direction.

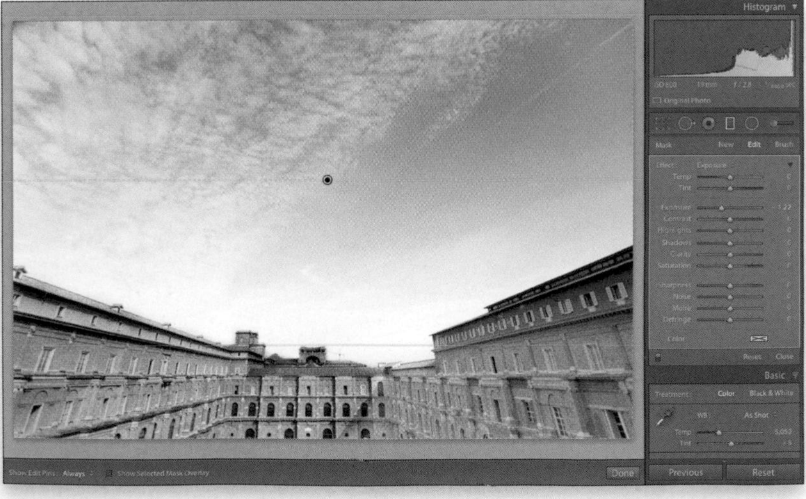

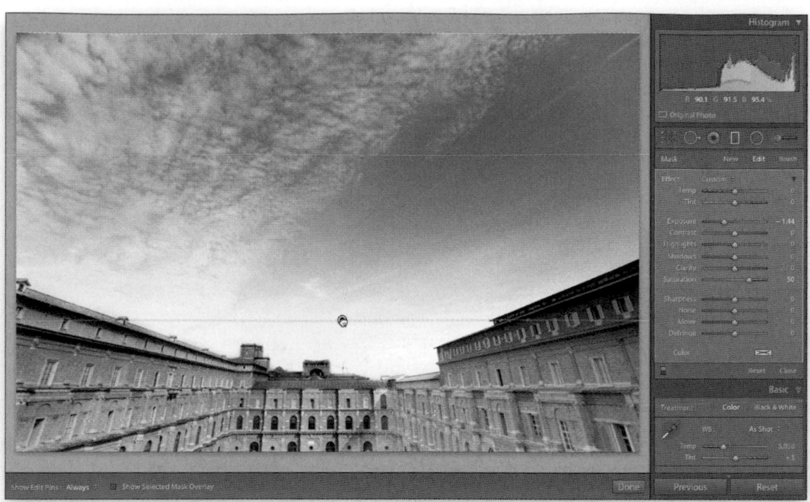

Step Three:

The Edit Pin shows where the center of your gradient is, and here, I think the darkening of the sky stopped a little short. Luckily, you can reposition your gradient after the fact—just click-and-drag that pin downward to move the whole gradient down (as shown here). Now, we can add other effects to that same area. For example, increase the Saturation to 50 (to make it more punchy), then decrease the Exposure to –1.44 (a before and after is shown below). Also, if you have a gray sky, you can add some blue by clicking on the Color swatch at the bottom of the panel and choosing a blue tint. *Note:* You can have more than one gradient (click the New button), and to delete a gradient, click on its pin and press the Delete (PC: Backspace) key. On the next page, we'll look at a handy new feature available with both the Graduated Filter and the Radial Filter.

Continued

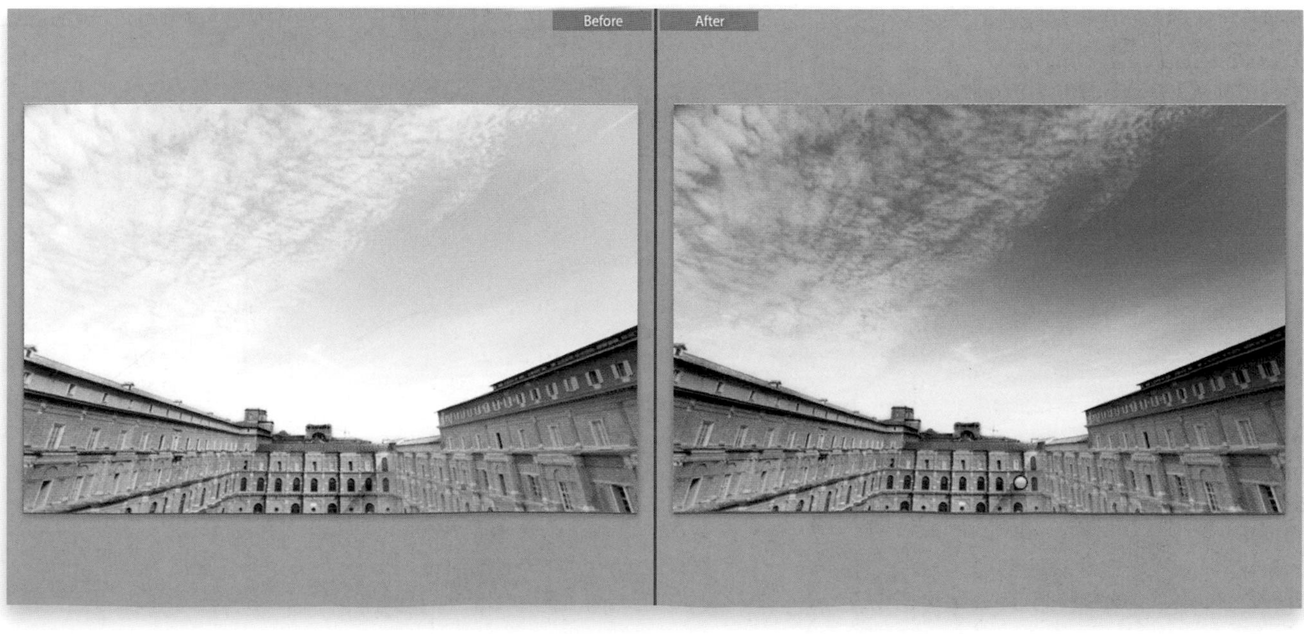

Step Four:

You're going to run into times where the Graduated Filter covers part of the image you don't want affected, like in this case, where we do want to darken and saturate the sky and graduate down to transparent, but it also darkens and saturates the lighthouse at the same time, which we don't want. Luckily, you can now edit that gradient and basically erase the filter just over that lighthouse area. While the Graduated Filter pin is selected, in the Mask section right below the toolbox, click on Brush, as shown here.

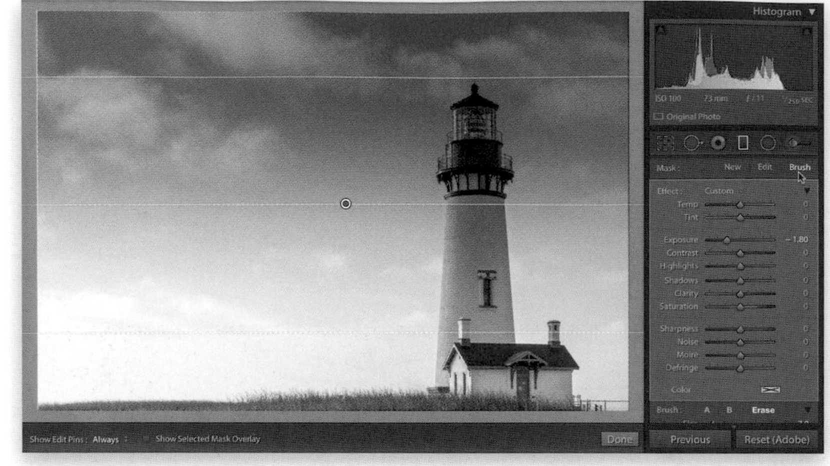

SCOTT KELBY

Step Five:

Now, scroll down to the bottom of the panel, just below the sliders, click on Erase, and start painting over the lighthouse, and as you do, it removes the darkening and saturation from the areas you're painting over (as seen here). All the same rules apply as you're painting with this that apply to the regular Adjustment Brush (you can press the letter **O** to see the mask as you paint, you can change the amount of feathering on the brush, etc.). Also, you can use this brush to add to a mask, instead of just removing like we did here. Just don't click on Erase, and then you're adding to the mask.

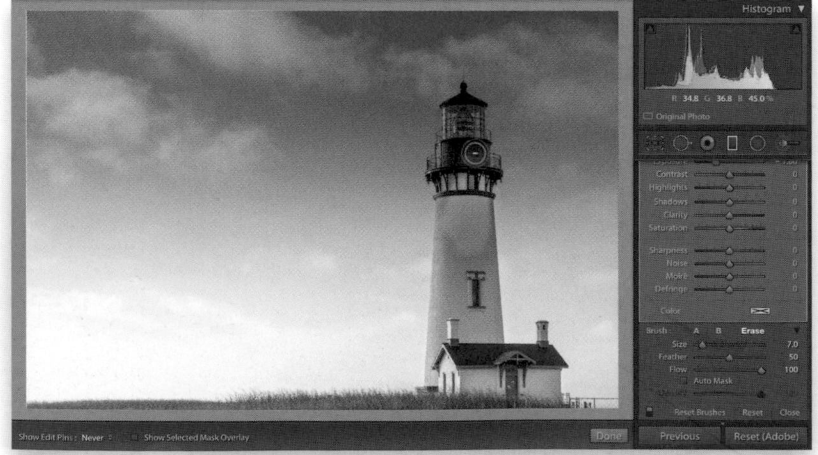

Vignettes (where you darken the outside edges all the way around your image) have become very popular in the past couple of years. Normally, we would apply them using the Effects panel, and it works great—as long as your subject is right in the middle of the frame (which, hopefully, isn't always the case). Now, not only can you create vignettes in any location within your image, but you can do more than just darken, and you can have more than one vignette, so you can also use it to re-light your image after the fact.

Custom Vignettes & Spotlight Effects Using the Radial Filter

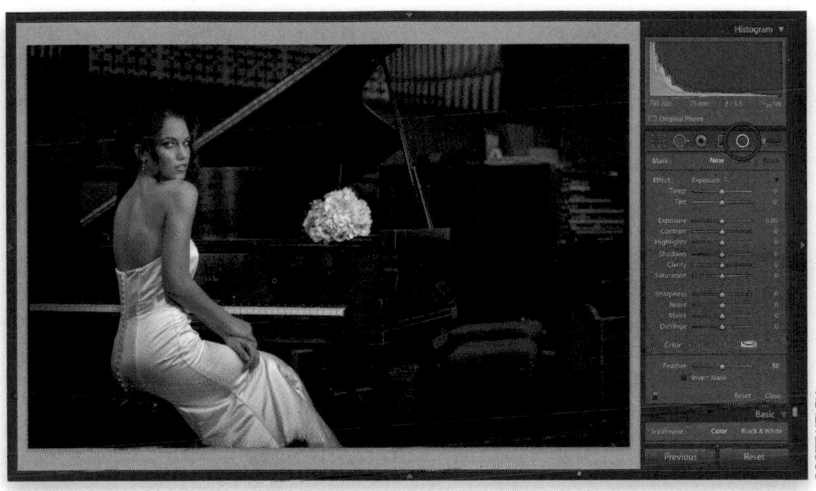

SCOTT KELBY

Step One:

The viewer's eye is drawn to the brightest part of the image first, but unfortunately, in this shot, the lighting is fairly even, so we're going to use the Radial Filter tool to "re-light the scene" and focus the viewer's attention on our bride. So, click on the Radial Filter tool in the toolbox near the top of the right side Panels area (it's shown circled here in red; or press **Shift-M**). This tool creates an oval or a circle and you get to decide what happens inside or outside this shape.

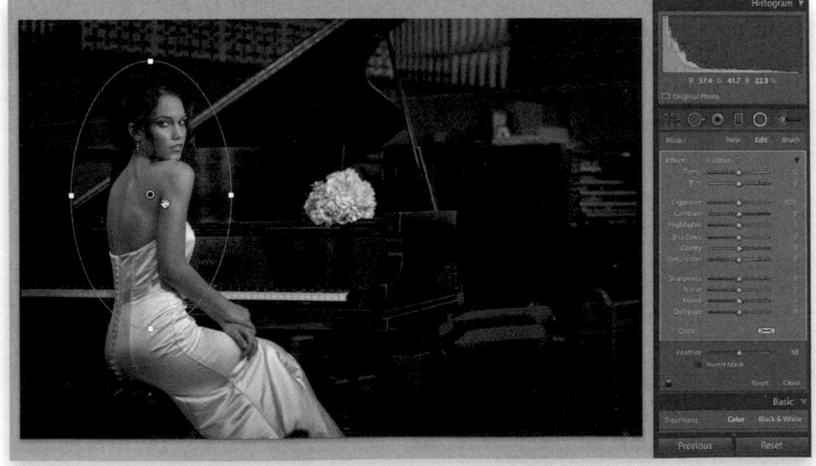

Step Two:

Click-and-drag out the tool in the direction you want your oval (or circular) pool of light to appear (here, I dragged it out over the bride). If it's not in the exact spot you want it, just click inside the oval and drag it wherever you want, just like I'm doing here (you can see my cursor has changed to the grabber hand cursor as soon as I started to drag the oval). *Note:* If you need to create a circle using the Radial Filter tool, press-and-hold the Shift key and it constrains the shape to a circle. Also, if you press-and-hold the Command (PC: Ctrl) key and double-click anywhere in your image, it creates an oval as large as it possibly can (you'd use this when you want to create one that affects nearly the entire image).

Continued

Step Three:

Here, we want to focus the attention on the bride, so we're going to make the area around her much darker. Drag the Exposure slider over to the left (as shown here, where I dragged it to –1.58), and you can see it darkens the entire area outside the oval (the area inside the oval stays the same as it was, and what's nice about this is that it kind of creates a spotlight effect on our bride). The transition between the brighter area and the darker area is nice and smooth because the edges of the oval have been feathered (softened), by default, to create that smooth transition (the Feather amount is set to 50. If you want a harder or more abrupt transition, just lower the amount using the Feather slider at the bottom of the panel).

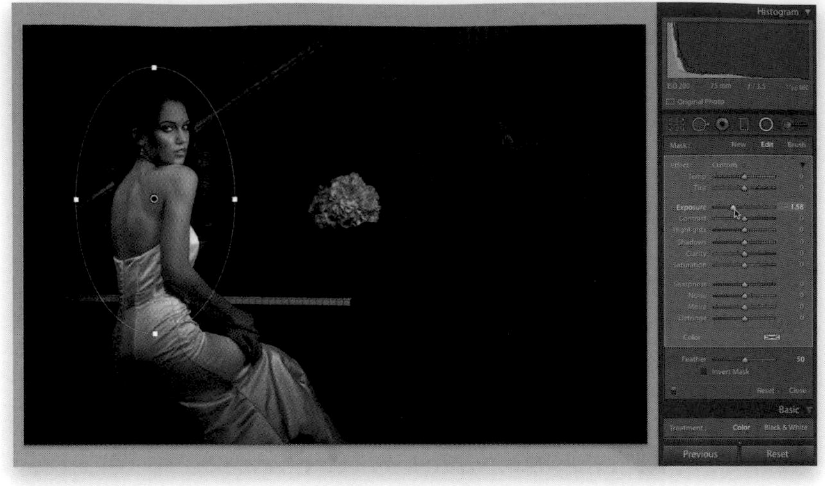

TIP: Removing Ovals

If you want to remove an oval you've created, click on it and then just hit the Delete (PC: Backspace) key.

Step Four:

Once your oval is in place, you can rotate it by moving your cursor just outside the oval (as seen here, where my cursor is just outside the right side of the oval, just above its center, and I'm rotating it a little to the right. The area where you can rotate is really small, so make sure you stay pretty darn close to the edges of the oval, and make sure you have the double-headed arrow cursor before you start dragging to rotate or it will create another oval. If that happens, just press **Command-Z [PC: Ctrl-Z]** to remove that extra oval). To resize the oval, just grab any one of the four little handles on the oval and drag out or in (here, I dragged it out to cover more of our bride). The nice thing about this filter is that you can do more than just adjust the exposure.

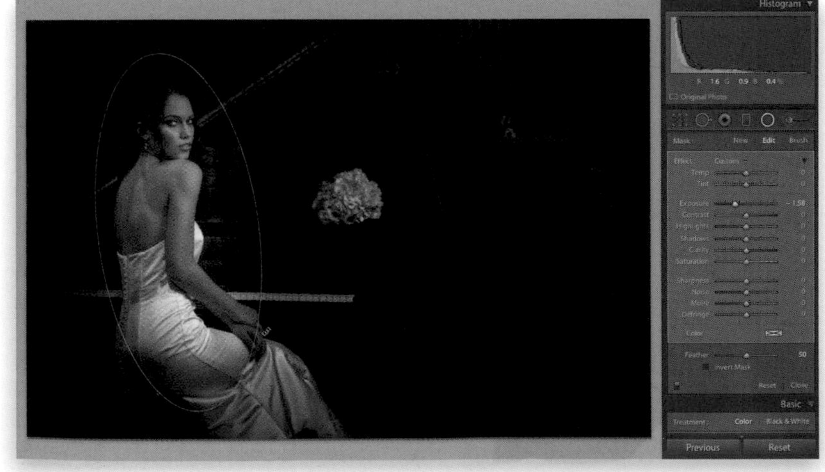

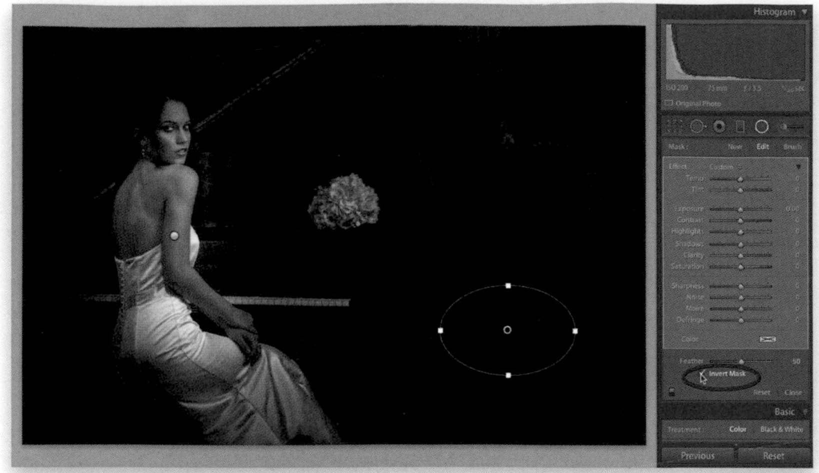

Step Five:

Now, let's create another oval—this time to help hide that bright area over on the right side. Just move your Radial Filter tool over there and click-and-drag out an oval about the size you see here. By default, it's going to affect what's outside the oval, but you can switch it to have the sliders control what happens inside the oval instead. You do that by turning on the Invert Mask checkbox at the bottom of the panel (shown circled here in red). Now, when you move the sliders, it affects what's inside the oval and the area outside it remains unchanged.

TIP: Swapping to the Inside/Outside

Pressing the **' (apostrophe) key** turns the Invert Mask checkbox on/off, swapping the effect to the inside/outside.

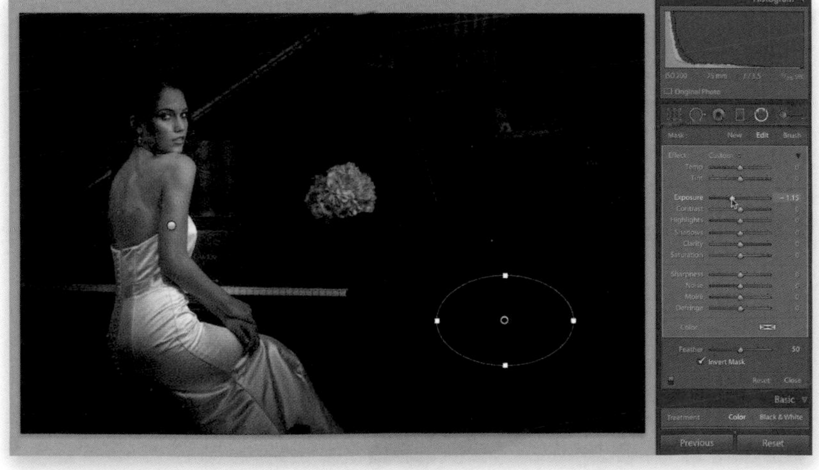

Step Six:

Drag the Exposure slider over to the left a bit (here, I dragged it to –1.15), until that area inside the oval gets dark enough to make it kind of blend in (instead of sticking out and drawing our eyes over there). Again, if you need to move the oval, just click inside it and drag, and if you need to rotate it, just click-and-drag in a circular motion right outside the oval. If you look at our bride now, you'll see a gray pin on her arm—that's an Edit Pin showing the first oval we placed there (the one that darkened the background). If you want to make any adjustments to that oval, just click on that gray pin and it becomes the active one.

Continued

Step Seven:

You can also add an oval inside another oval. Here, we want one that's inverted (so the center of the oval gets affected), so let's drag a copy of the one we just made. Press-and-hold **Command-Option (PC: Ctrl-Alt)**, and click-and-drag on the center of the second oval and a third oval appears (it's a duplicate of your second one). Place it over her face (as shown here), shrink the size way down, and rotate it. Now, to make her face just a little bit brighter, drag the Exposure slider a bit to the right (here, I dragged to 0.44) and it just affects her face. Next, press Command-Option once again, this time on this third oval, and then move this new one over onto the bouquet. For this one, drag the Highlights slider to the right to around 0.16 to brighten that area a bit. Instead, we also could have used the Radial Gradient's new Brush feature to erase the gradient over the bouquet (see the end of the Graduated Filter technique for more). A before/after is shown below.

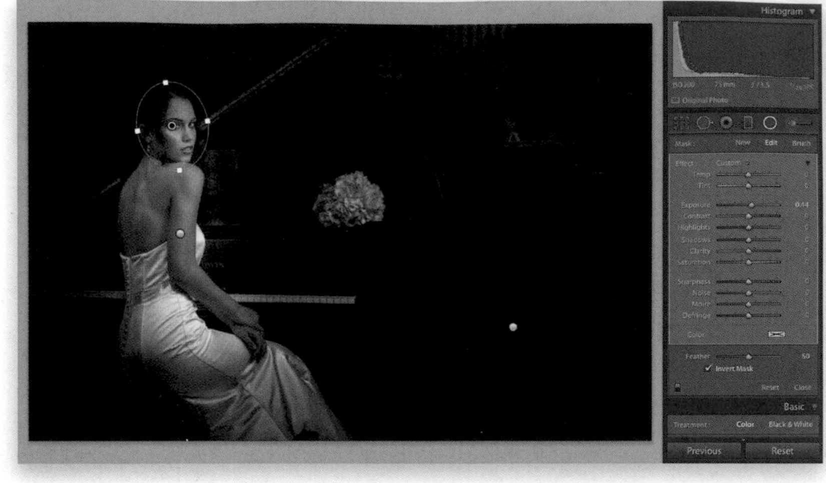

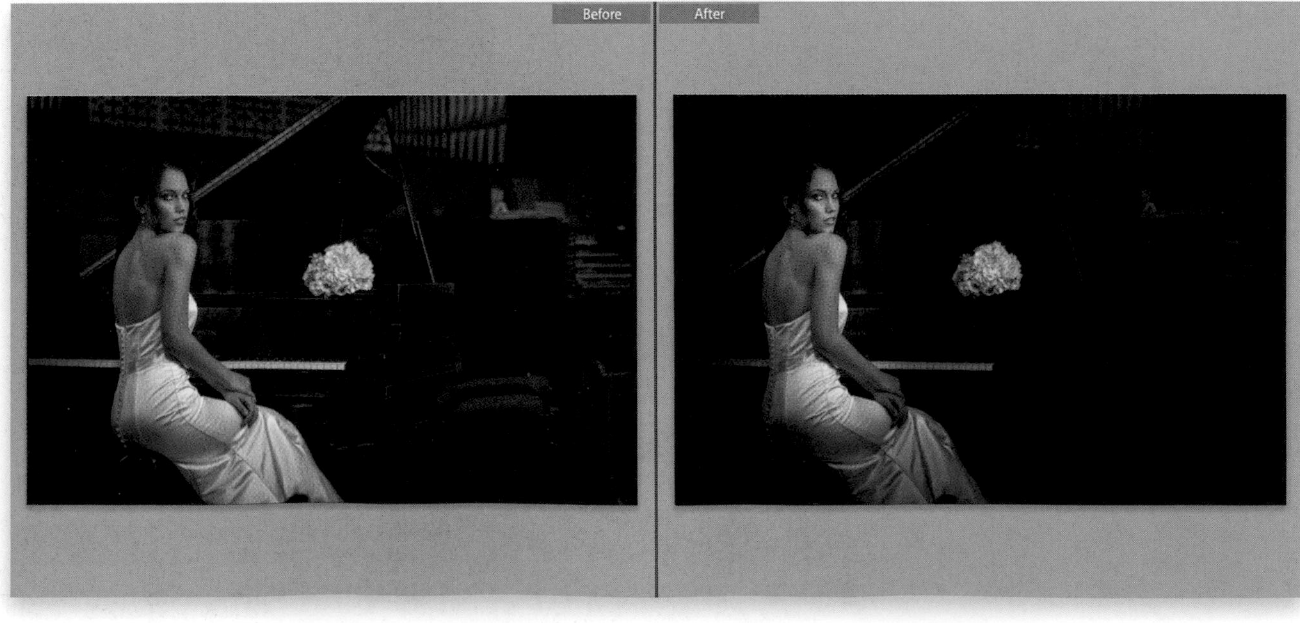

Lightroom Killer Tips > >

▼ Hiding Your Pins

You can hide the Adjustment Brush, Radial Filter, and Graduated Filter pins anytime by pressing the letter **H** on

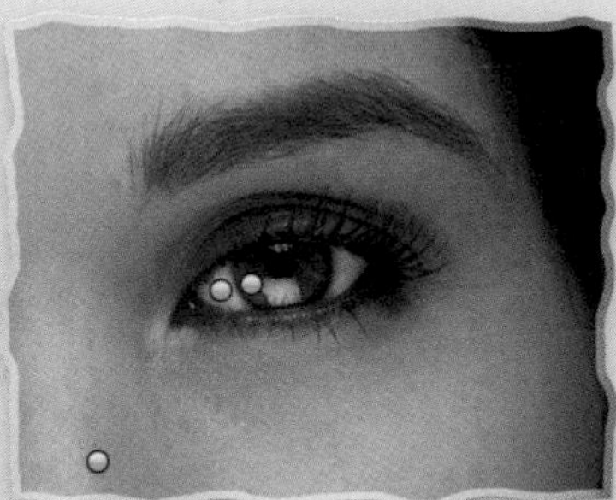

your keyboard. To bring them back, press H again.

▼ Shortcut for Adding New Edits

When you're making a local adjustment, if you want to quickly add a new pin (without going back to the panel to click on the New button), just press the **Return (PC: Enter) key** on your keyboard.

▼ Shrinking the Brush Options

Once you've set up your A/B brushes, you can hide the rest of the brush options by clicking on the little downward-facing triangle to the right of the Erase button.

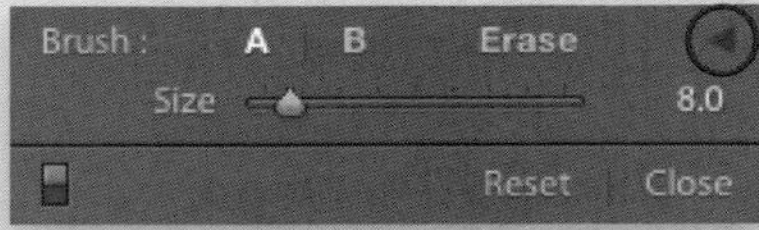

▼ Scroll Wheel Trick

If you have a mouse with a scroll wheel, you can use the scroll wheel to change the Size amount of your brush.

▼ Controlling Flow

The numbers **1** through **0** on your keyboard control the amount of brush Flow (**3** for 30%, **4** for 40%, and so on).

▼ The Erase Button

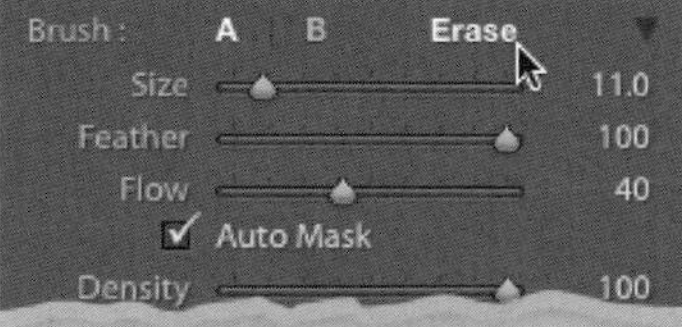

The Erase button (in the Brush section), doesn't erase your image, it just changes your brush, so if you paint with it selected, it erases your mask instead of painting one.

▼ Choosing Tint Colors

If you want to paint with a color that appears in your current photo, first

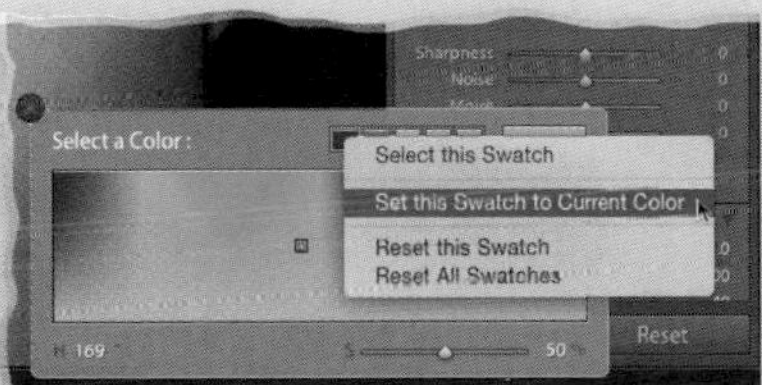

choose **Color** as your Effect, then click on the Color swatch, and when the color picker appears, click-and-hold the eyedropper cursor and move out over your photo. As you do, any color you move over in your photo is targeted in your color picker. When you find a color you like, just release the mouse button. To save this color as a color swatch, just Right-click on one of the existing swatches and choose **Set this Swatch to Current Color**.

▼ Seeing/Hiding the Adjustment Mask

By default, if you put your cursor over a pin, it shows the mask, but if you'd prefer to have it stay on while you're painting (especially handy when you're filling in spots you've missed), you can toggle the mask visibility on/off by pressing the letter **O** on your keyboard.

▼ Changing the Color of Your Mask

When your mask is visible (you've got your cursor over a pin), you can change

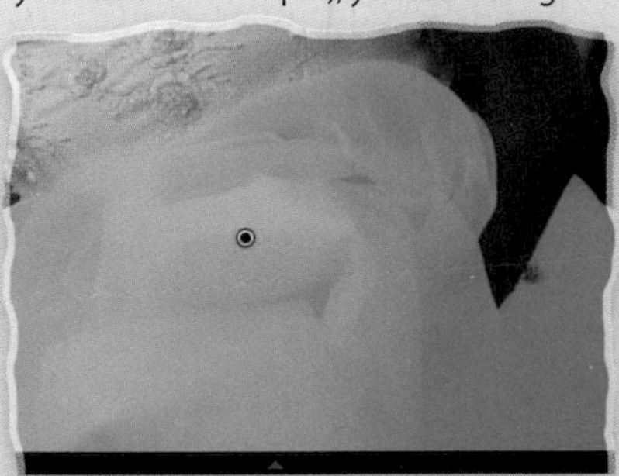

its color by pressing **Shift-O** on your keyboard (this toggles you through the four choices: red, green, white, and gray).

▼ Inverting Your Gradient

Once you've added a Graduated Filter to your image, you can invert that gradient by pressing the **' (apostrophe) key** on your keyboard.

▼ Scaling the Graduated Filter from the Center

By default, your gradient starts where you click (so it starts from the top or the bottom, etc.). However, if you press-and-hold the **Option (PC: Alt) key** as you drag the gradient, it draws from the center outward instead.

▼ Changing the Intensity of the Effects

Once you've applied a Graduated Filter, you can control the amount of the last-adjusted effect by using the **Left and Right Arrow keys** on your keyboard. With an Adjustment Brush effect, use the **Up and Down Arrow keys**.

Lightroom Killer Tips > >

▼ Switching Between the A and B Brushes

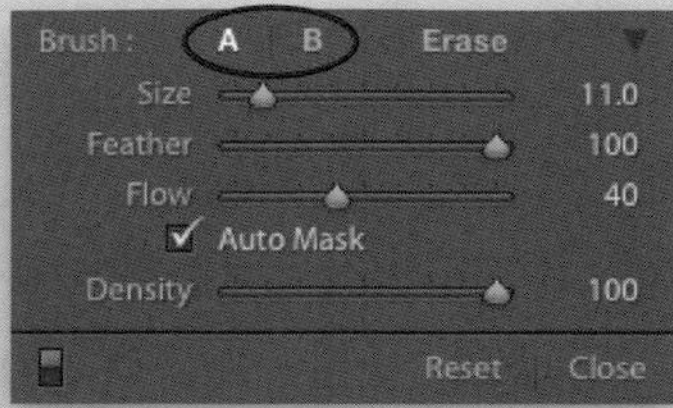

The A and B buttons are actually brush presets (so you can have a hard brush and a soft brush already set up, if you like, or any other combination of two brushes, like small and large). To switch between these two brush presets, press the **/ (Forward Slash) key** on your keyboard.

▼ Increasing/Decreasing Softness

To change the softness (Feather) of your brush, don't head over to the panel—just press **Shift-] (Right Bracket key)** to make the brush softer, or **Shift-[(Left Bracket key)** to make it harder.

▼ Auto Mask Tip

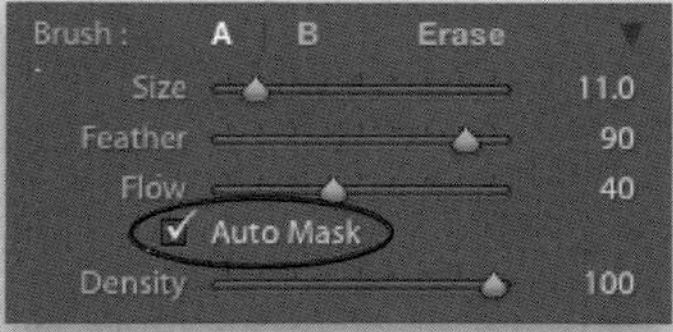

When you have the Auto Mask checkbox turned on, and you're painting along an edge to mask it (for example, you're painting over a sky in a mountain landscape to darken it), when you're done, you'll probably see a small glow right along the edges of the mountain. To get rid of that, just use a small brush and paint right over those areas. The Auto Mask feature will keep what you're painting from spilling over onto the mountains.

▼ Auto Mask Shortcut

Pressing the letter **A** toggles the Auto Mask feature on/off.

▼ Painting in a Straight Line

Just like in Photoshop, if you click once with the Adjustment Brush, then press-and-hold the **Shift key** and paint somewhere else, it will paint in a straight line between those two points.

▼ Resetting Sliders vs. Starting Over

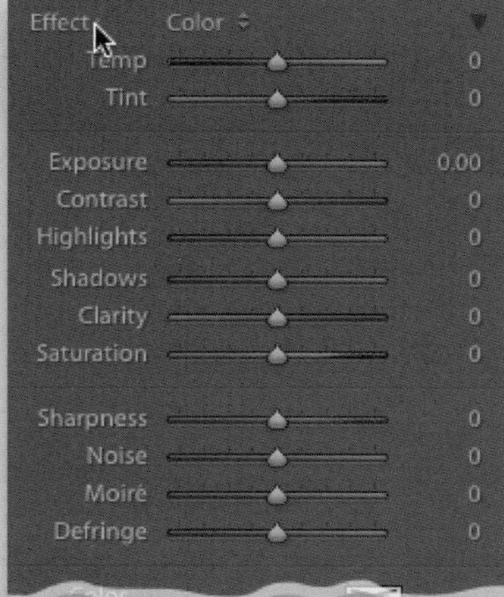

This one surprises a lot of folks because if you click the Reset button at the bottom of an adjustment panel, it doesn't reset your sliders, it deletes all the adjustments you've created like you're totally starting over from scratch. If you do just want to reset the sliders for your currently selected edit pin, just double-click directly on the word "Effect" at the top left of the panel, right above the sliders.

▼ A Gaussian Blur in Lightroom?

If you need a subtle blurring effect, kind of like a light amount of Gaussian Blur (well, probably more like a subtle version

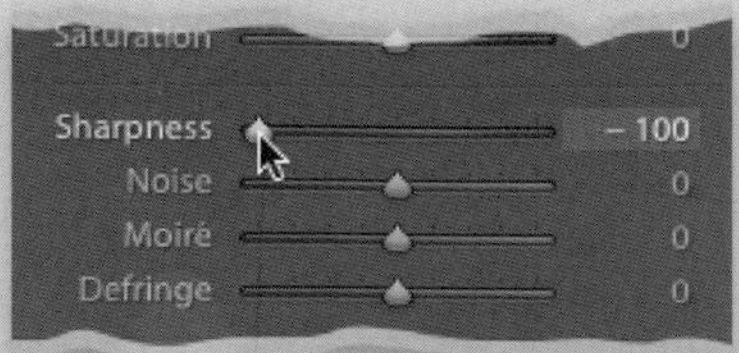

of the Lens Blur filter), just get the Adjustment Brush, choose **Sharpness** from the Effect pop-up menu (to reset the sliders), then drag the Sharpness slider all the way to the left (to –100), and now you're painting with a little blur. Great for creating a quick shallow-depth-of-field look.

▼ Doubling the Effect

To double the effect of an adjustment, **Command-Option-click (PC: Ctrl-Alt-click)** on an active Edit Pin and drag just a tiny bit away from the original to make a duplicate of your original, then drag it right back on top of the original. This duplicate "doubles" the effect (like stacking effects one on top of the other). If you need to adjust the bottom Edit Pin, just drag the top one a tiny bit to the side, and then click on the bottom one, make your changes, and then drag that other pin back on top.

▼ Deleting Adjustments

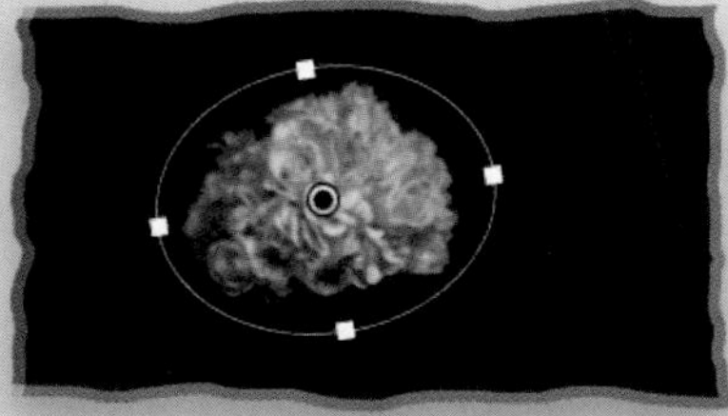

If you want to delete any adjustment you've made, click on the pin to select that adjustment (the center of the pin turns black), then press the Delete (PC: Backspace) key on your keyboard.

Lightroom Killer Tips > >

▼ Make It Easier to Choose Camera Profiles

To make things easier when choosing your Camera Calibration panel profiles, try this: Set your DSLR to shoot RAW+JPEG Fine, so when you press the shutter button it takes two photos— one in RAW and one in JPEG. When you import these into Lightroom, you'll have the RAW and JPEG photos side-by-side, making it easier to pick the profile for your RAW photo that matches the JPEG your camera produces.

▼ Choosing What Will Be Your Before and After

By default, if you press the **\ (backslash) key** in the Develop module, it toggles you back and forth between the original untouched image (the Before view) and the photo as it looks now with your edits. However, what if you don't want your Before photo to be the original? For example, let's say you did some Basic panel edits on a portrait, and then you used the Adjustment Brush to do some portrait retouching. Maybe you'd like to see the Before photo showing the Basic panel edits after they were applied, but before you started retouching. To do that, go to the History panel (in the left side Panels area), and scroll down until you find the step right before you started using the Adjustment Brush. Right-click on that history state and choose **Copy History Step Settings to Before**. That

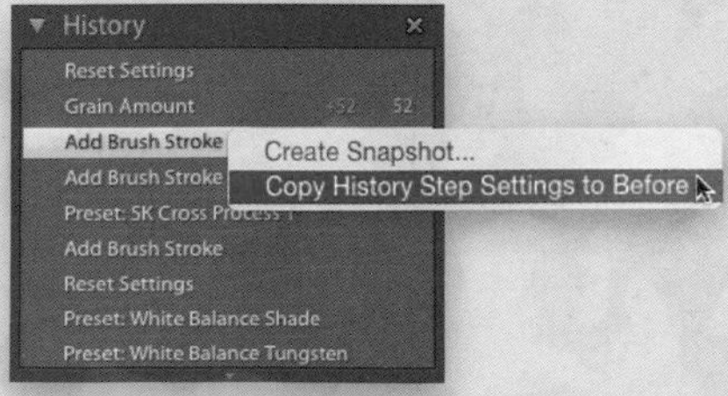

now becomes your new Before photo when you press the \ key. I know—that's totally cool.

▼ Making Your Current Settings the New Defaults for That Camera

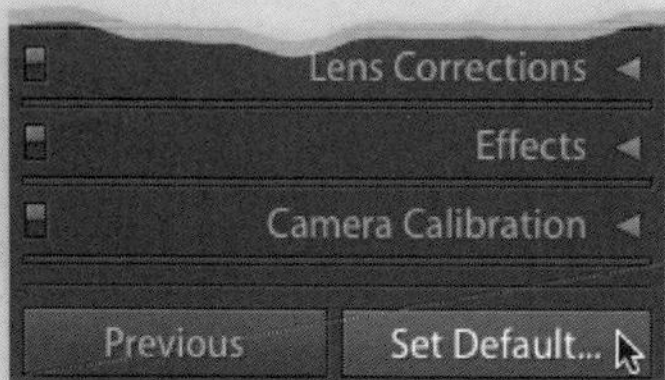

When you open a photo, Lightroom applies a default set of corrections based on the photo's file format and the make and model of the camera used to take the shot (it reads this from the built-in EXIF data). If you want to use your own custom settings (maybe you think it makes the shadows too black, or the highlights too bright), go ahead and get the settings the way you want them in Lightroom, then press-and-hold the Option (PC: Alt) key and the Reset button at the bottom of the right side Panels area changes into a Set Default button. Click on it and it brings up a dialog showing you the file format or the camera make and model of the current image. When you click Update to Current Settings, from now on, your current settings will be your new starting place for all images taken with that camera, or in that file format. To return to Adobe's default settings for that camera, go back to that same dialog, but this time click on the Restore Adobe Default Settings button.

▼ How the RGB Readouts Change When You Turn on Soft Proofing

In the Develop module, when you move your cursor out over your image, the red, green, and blue (RGB) values of what's under your cursor are displayed directly under the histogram, in the top of the right side Panels area, and they're displayed from 0% (black) to 100% (solid white). However, when you turn on Soft Proofing, these values change to a more traditional printing read scale, which measures 256 shades, ranging from 0 (solid black) to 255 (solid white) depending on which color profile you have selected. A lot of photographers who are into printing and have moved to Lightroom from Photoshop (which has always used the 0–255 readout scale) are cheering this subtle, but important change.

▼ B&W Conversion Tip

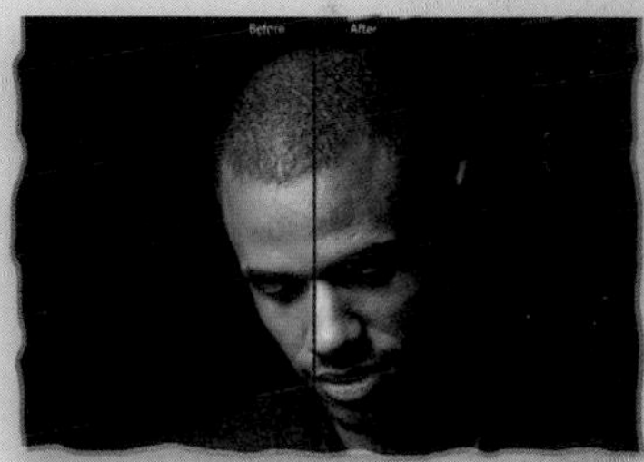

Clicking on B&W in the HSL/Color/B&W panel converts your photo to black and white—kind of a flat-looking conversion, but the idea is that you'll use those color sliders to adjust the conversion. However, it's hard to know which color sliders to move when the photo is in black and white. Try this: once you've done your conversion and it's time to tweak those color sliders, press **Shift-Y** to enter the Before & After split-screen view (if it shows a side-by-side view instead, just press Shift-Y again). Now you can see the color image on the left side of the screen, and black and white on the right, which makes it easier to see which color does what.

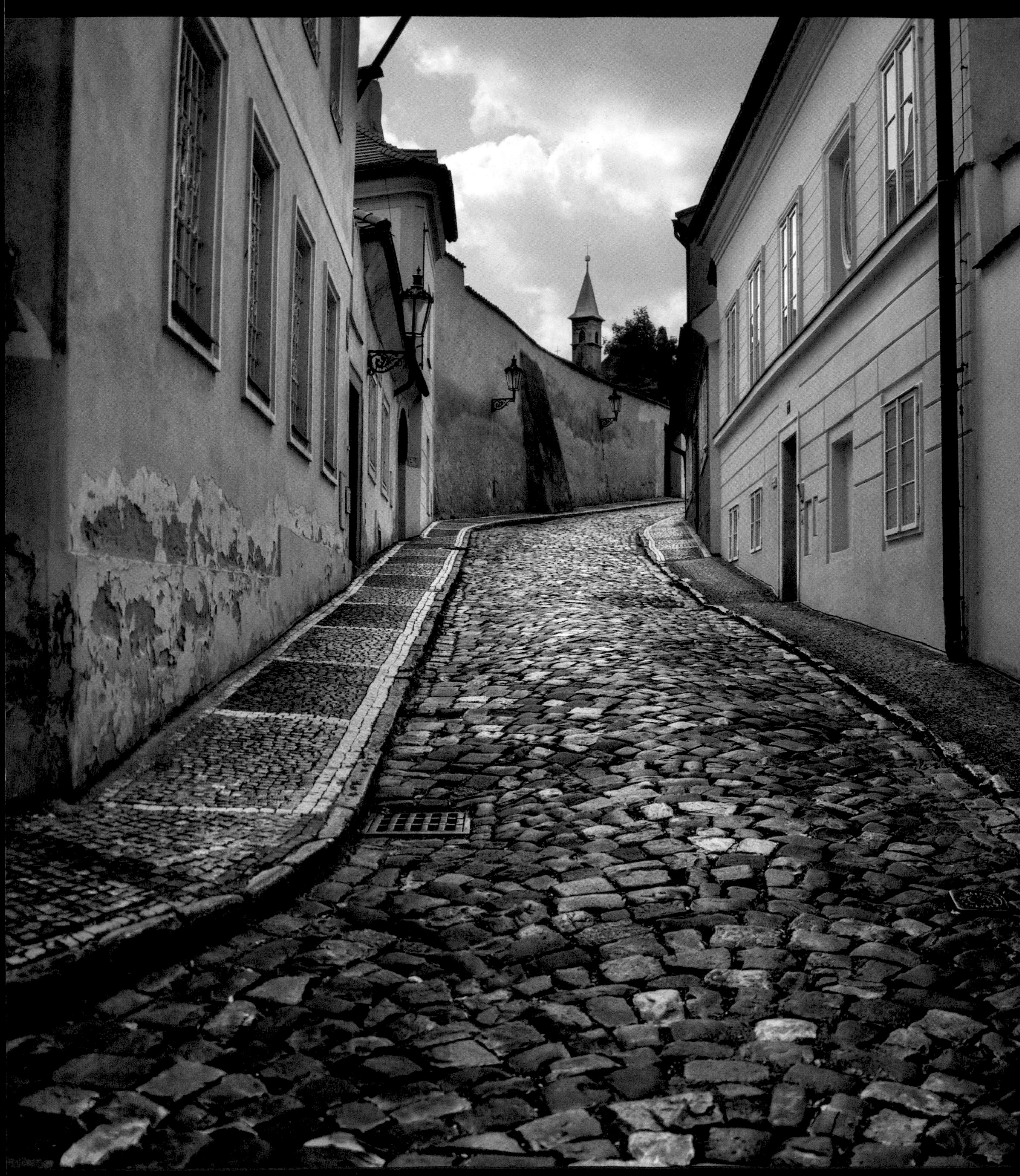

Photo by Scott Kelby | Exposure: 1/4000 | Focal Length: 28mm | Aperture Value: f/3.5

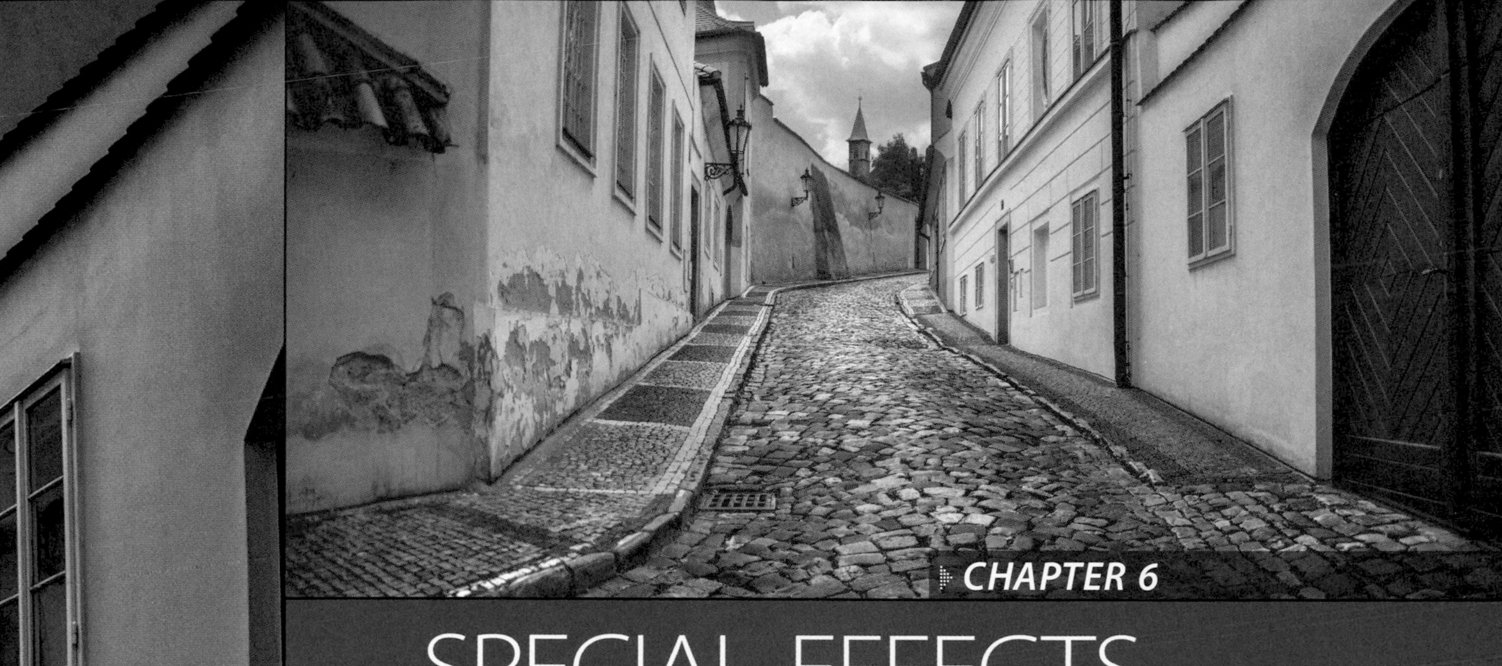

CHAPTER 6

SPECIAL EFFECTS

making stuff look...well...special!

When you hear the phrase "special effects," the first thing most people think of is "Hollywood special effects" and that might actually be something handy to learn if you lived in Hollywood, but have you seen what rents are in Hollywood? They're insane! I don't know how anybody can afford to live there if you're not a Hollywood mega-star like Fabio or Pauly Shore. Anyway, this chapter is not about Fabio or Pauly Shore, but I will tell you this (just between you and me), I cannot tell you the number of times I've been casually having lunch somewhere with my friends, and someone comes up and asks, "Mr. Fabio, could I get your autograph?" Now, quite frankly, this doesn't happen nearly as much when I don't have my hair down, but when my hair *is* down, and it's a windy day, and worse yet, I'm in slow motion, the number of people coming up asking for a signed promo photo (I carry a stack of black-and-white 8x10" headshots my agent at CAA had made for me) is really amazing. I'm totally cool with it unless they come up and start with the whole, "Come on, say 'I can't believe it's not butter'" and then honestly it gets a little old. But if I say the line (just to get rid of them), they're like, "Say it again! Say it again!" and I'm just like, "Ugh!" But that doesn't annoy me as much as when they come up and say "Hey Fabio! Or is it Mr. Fabio?" or "Is Fabio your first name or your last name?" (It's Lanzoni, thank you very much.) That's usually when I say, "How would you like a signed 8x10?" but then I sign it: Chillin' with The Weasel! Your pal, Pauly Shore. Luckily, they usually don't notice until they take the 405 to Sepulveda, take a right on Laurel Canyon Road, and make a left to get to Marina Del Rey.

Virtual Copies—The "No Risk" Way to Experiment

Let's say you added a vignette to a bridal shot. Well, what if you wanted to see a version in black and white, and a version with a color tint, and then a real contrasty version, and then maybe a version that was cropped differently? Well, what might keep you from doing that is having to duplicate a high-resolution file each time you wanted to try a different look, because it would eat up hard drive space and RAM like nobody's business. But luckily, you can create virtual copies, which don't take up space and allow you to try different looks without the overhead.

Step One:

You create a virtual copy by just Right-clicking on the original photo and then choosing **Create Virtual Copy** from the pop-up menu (as shown here), or using the keyboard shortcut **Command-'** (apostrophe; **PC: Ctrl-'**). These virtual copies look and act the same as your original photo, and you can edit them just as you would your original, but here's the difference: it's not a real file, it's just a set of instructions, so it doesn't add any real file size. That way, you can have as many of these virtual copies as you want, and experiment to your heart's content without filling up your hard disk.

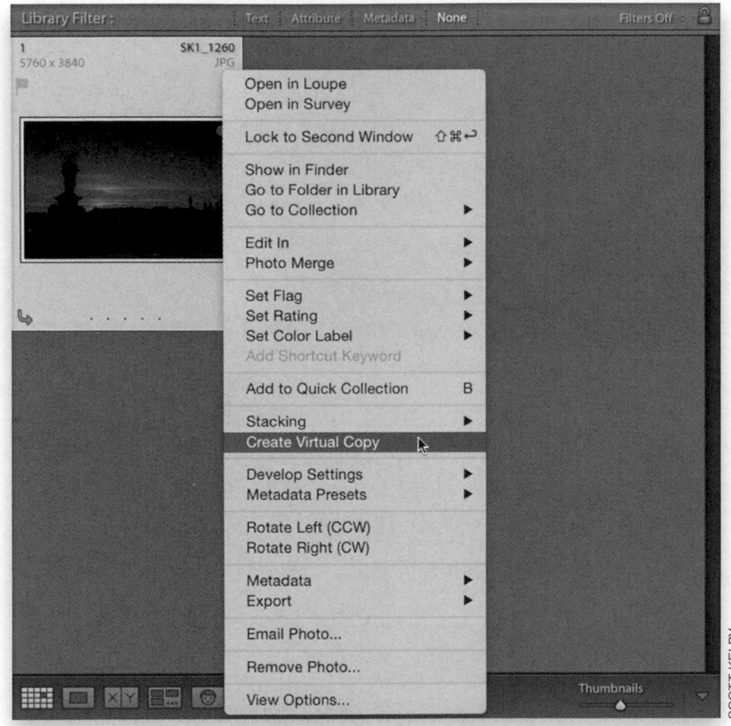

Step Two:

When you create a virtual copy, you'll know which version is the copy because the virtual copies have a curled page icon in the lower-left corner of the image thumbnail (circled in red here) in both the Grid view and in the Filmstrip. So now, go ahead and tweak this virtual copy in the Develop module any way you want (here, I increased the Exposure, Contrast, Shadows, Clarity, and Vibrance), and when you return to the Grid view, you'll see the original and the edited virtual copy (as seen here).

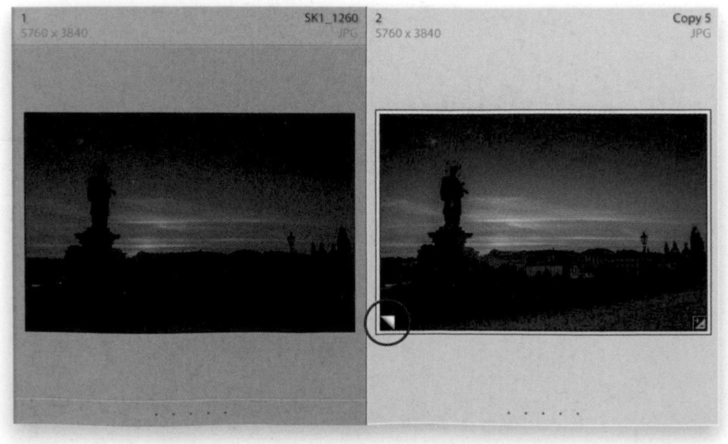

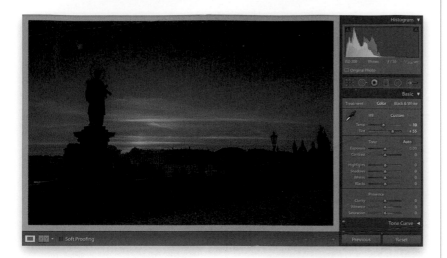

Step Three:

Now you can experiment away with multiple virtual copies of your original photo, at no risk to your original photo or your hard drive space. So, click on your first virtual copy, then press Command-' (PC: Ctrl-') to make another virtual copy (that's right—you can make virtual copies of your virtual copy), and then head over to the Develop module, and make some adjustments (here, I made changes to the White Balance, adding lots more blue and magenta [I took the Temp to –10 and set my Tint at +55] to give this a twilight look. I also decreased the Exposure a little). Now, make some more copies to experiment with (I made a few more copies and made some more White Balance, Exposure, and Vibrance setting changes). *Note:* When you make a copy, you can hit the Reset button at the bottom of the right side Panels area to return the virtual copy to its original unedited look. Also, you don't have to jump back to the Grid view each time to make a virtual copy—that keyboard shortcut works in the Develop module, too.

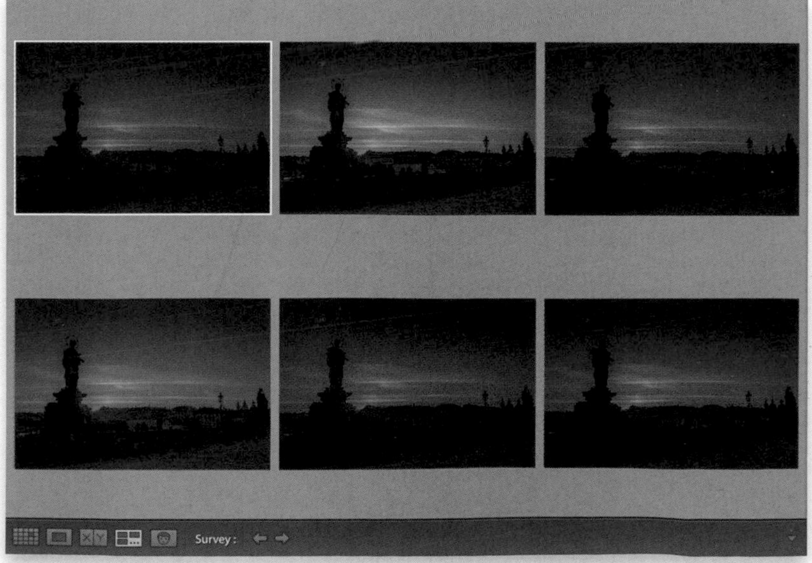

Step Four:

Now, if you want to compare all your experimental versions side by side, go back to the Grid view, select your original photo and all the virtual copies, then press the letter **N** on your keyboard to enter Survey view (as shown here). If there's a version you really like, of course you can just leave it alone, and then delete the other virtual copies you don't like. (*Note:* To delete a virtual copy, click on it and press the Delete [PC: Backspace] key, and then click Remove in the dialog that appears.) If you choose to take this virtual copy over to Photoshop or export it as a JPEG or TIFF, at that point, Lightroom creates a real copy using the settings you applied to the virtual copy.

Two Really Handy Uses for RGB Curves

Although Curves have been in Lightroom for a while now, Lightroom 4 was the first version to let you adjust the individual Red, Green, and Blue channels (just like Photoshop does), which can come in really handy for things like fixing sticky white balance problems by adjusting an individual color channel, or for creating cross processing effects (which are very popular in fashion and fine art photography). Here's how to do both:

Step One:

You choose which RGB color channel you want to adjust by going to the Tone Curve panel, and then choosing the individual color channel from the Channel pop-up menu (as shown here, where I'm choosing the Red channel to help me remove a color cast from her skin and hair—she looks a little red). So, now that you have just the Red channel selected, notice that the Curve readout is tinted red, as well, to give you a visual cue that you're adjusting just this one channel.

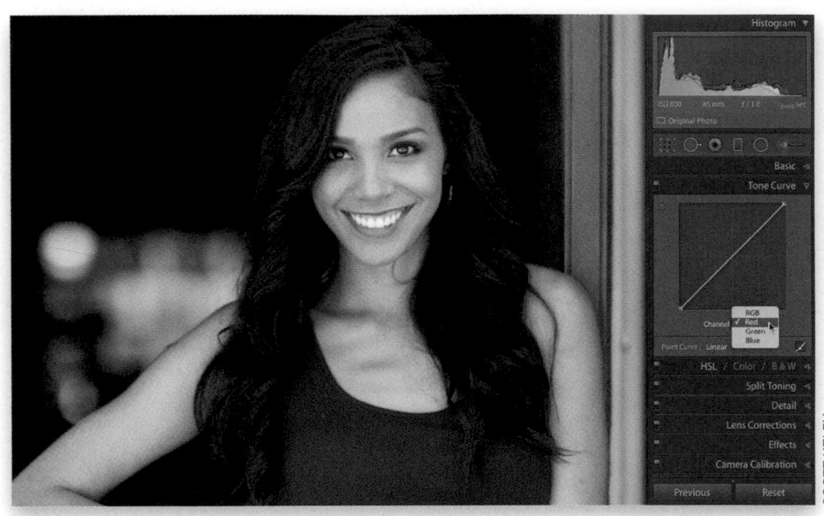

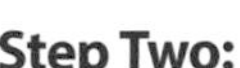

Step Two:

So, how do you know which part of the curve to adjust to remove this red tint problem? Well, Lightroom can actually tell you exactly which part to adjust. Get the TAT (Targeted Adjustment tool) from the top-left corner of the panel and then move it over the area you want to affect (in this case, her arm), and you'll see a point appear on the curve as you move your cursor. Just click once while you're over her arm and it adds a point to the curve that corresponds to the area you want to adjust. Take that new curve point and drag at a 45° angle down toward the bottom-right corner and it removes the red from her skin and hair (as seen here). Of course, since you have the TAT, you can use it, instead—click it directly on her arm and drag your cursor downward, and it edits that part of the curve for you.

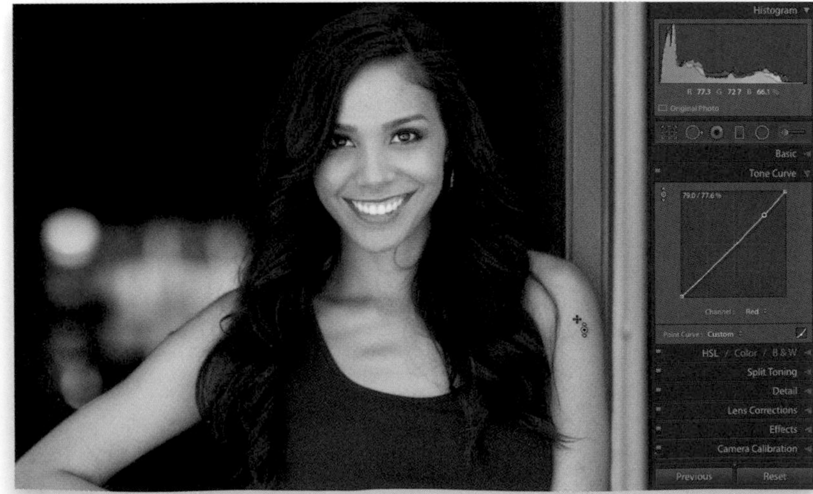

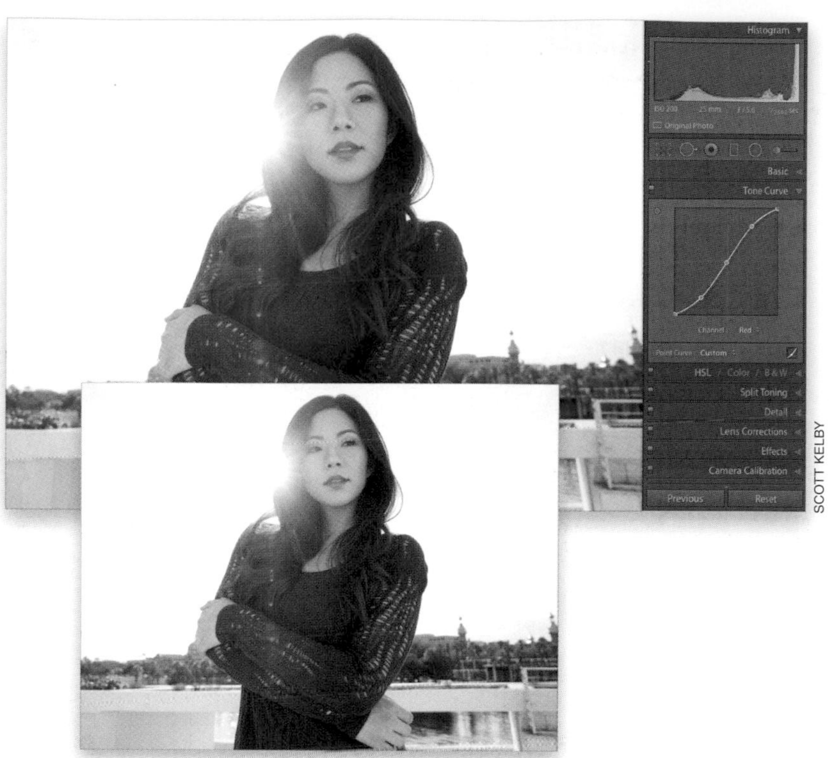

Step Three:

If you want to use these RGB curves to create a cross processing effect (a classic darkroom technique from the film days), it's actually fairly easy. There are dozens of different combinations, but here's one I use: Start by choosing **Red** from the Channel pop-up menu. Create an S-curve by clicking three times along the diagonal curve—once in the center, once at the next major grid line above, and once at the next major grid line below, so they're evenly spaced along the line. Leave the center point where it is, and click-and-drag the top point upward and the bottom point downward to create the curve you see here. By the way, I put the original image, without any RGB curves applied, at the bottom here, just so you can see our original starting point.

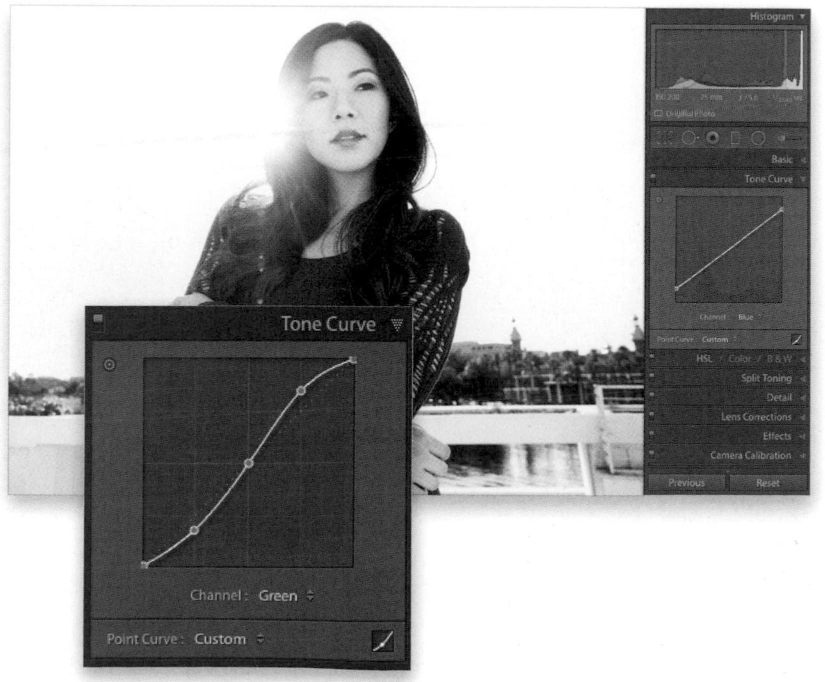

Step Four:

Then, switch to the Green channel and make another three-point S-curve (as seen here at the bottom). Lastly, go to the Blue channel. Don't add any points—just drag the bottom-left point straight upward along the left edge (as shown here). Then, drag the top-right point down along the right edge, as well. Of course, based on the particular image you use, you might have to tweak these settings (usually it's the amount you drag in the Blue channel, but again, it depends on the photo). By the way, if you come up with a setting you like, don't forget to save it as a Develop module preset (click the + [plus sign] button on the right side of the Presets panel header. When the New Develop Preset dialog appears, click Check None, then just turn on the checkbox for Tone Curve).

Changing Individual Colors

Anytime you have just one color you want to adjust in an image (for example, let's say you want all the reds to be redder, or the blue in the sky to be bluer, or you want to change a color altogether), one place to do that would be in the HSL panel (HSL stands for Hue, Saturation, Luminance). This panel is incredible handy (I use it fairly often) and luckily, because it has a TAT (Targeted Adjustment tool), using it is really easy. Here's how this works:

Step One:

When you want to adjust an area of color, scroll down to the HSL panel in the right side Panels area (by the way, those words in the panel header, HSL/Color/B&W, are not just names, they're buttons, and if you click on any one of them, the controls for that panel will appear). Go ahead and click on HSL (since this is where we'll be working for now), and four buttons appear in the panel: Hue, Saturation, Luminance, and All. The Hue panel lets you change an existing color to a different color by using the sliders. Just so you can see what it does, click-and-drag the Red slider all the way to the left and the Orange slider to –71, and you'll see it changes the red motorcycle to magenta.

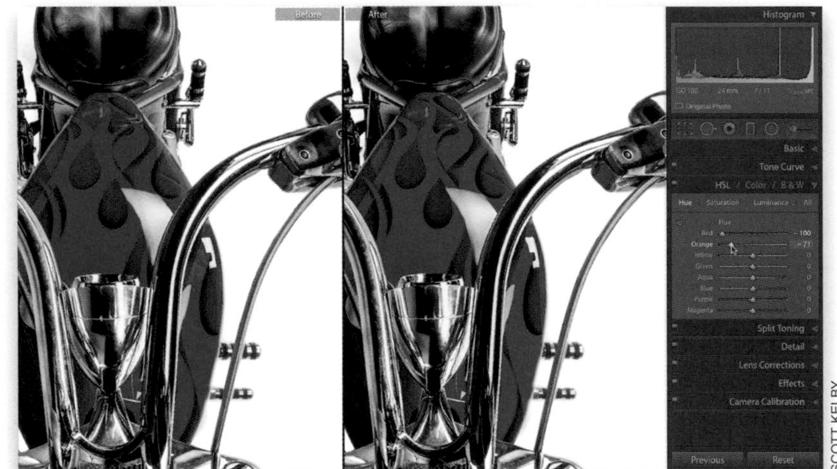

SCOTT KELBY

Step Two:

If you dragged the Red slider all the way to the right, and left the Orange slider at –71, it would change the color of the red motorcycle to more of an orangeish color. This is a perfect task for the Hue sliders of the HSL panel. Now, what if you wanted to make the orange color more orange, but you've pushed the sliders just about as far as they can go? Well, you'd start by clicking on the word "Saturation" at the top of the panel.

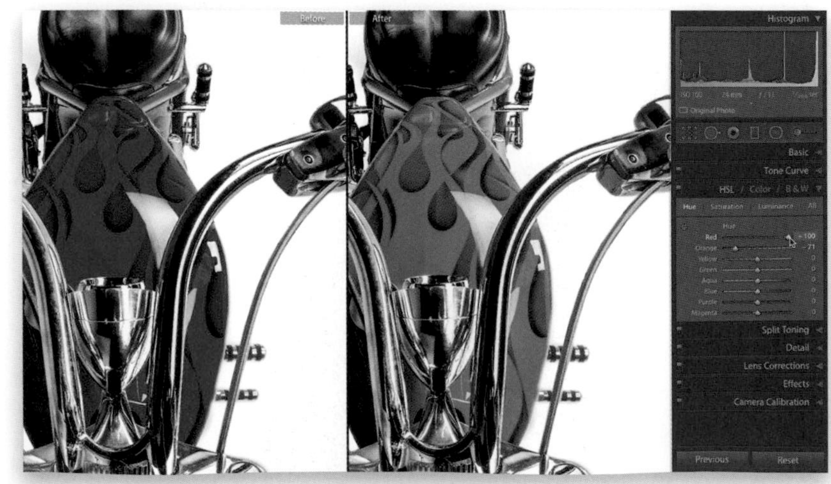

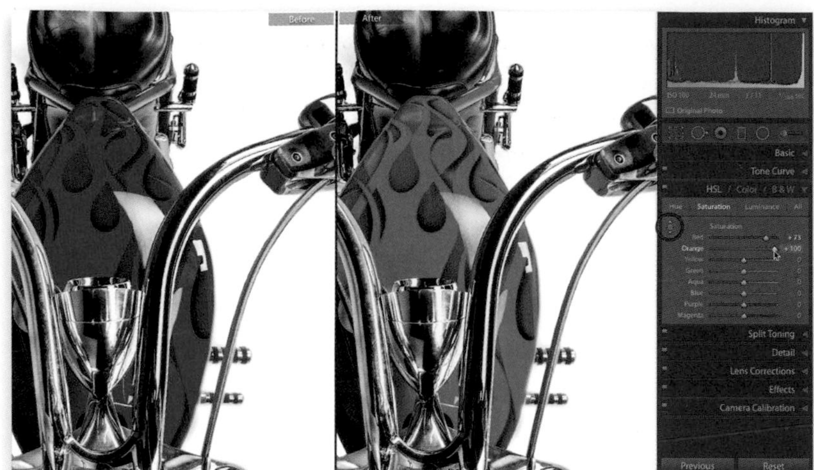

Step Three:

Now, these eight sliders control just the saturation of colors in your image. Drag the Orange slider way over to the right, and the Red not quite as far, and the orange in the motorcycle becomes much more vibrant (as seen here). If you know exactly which color you want to affect, you can just drag the sliders. But if you're not sure exactly which colors make up the area you want to adjust, then you can use the TAT (the same Targeted Adjustment tool you used in the Tone Curve panel). So, if you had a blue sky and wanted to make it more vibrant, you'd click on the TAT, then click it on the sky, and drag it upward to make it bluer (downward to make it less blue). And it wouldn't just move the Blue slider, but would increase the Aqua Saturation slider, as well. You probably wouldn't have realized that there was any aqua in that blue sky, and this is exactly why this tool is so handy here. In fact, I rarely use the HSL panel without using the TAT!

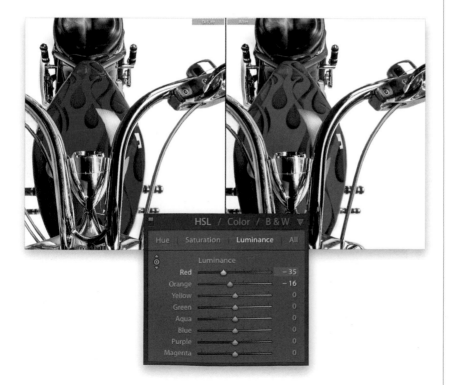

Step Four:

To change the brightness of the colors, click on Luminance at the top of the panel. To darken the orange color on the motorcycle, take the TAT and click-and-drag straight downward on it, and its color gets deeper and richer (the Luminance for both Red and Orange decreased). Two last things: Clicking the All button (at the top of the panel) puts all three panels in one scrolling list and the Color panel breaks them all into sets of three for each color—a layout more like Photoshop's Hue/Saturation. But, regardless of which layout you choose, they all work the same way. A before/after is shown here, after we changed and darkened the motorcycle.

How to Add Vignette Effects

An edge vignette effect (where you darken all the edges around your image to focus the attention on the center of the photo) is one of those effects you either love or that drives you crazy (I, for one, love 'em). Here we're going to look at how to apply a simple vignette; one where you crop the photo and the vignette still appears (called a "post-crop" vignette); and how to use the other vignetting options.

Step One:

To add an edge vignette effect, go to the right side Panels area and scroll down to the Lens Corrections panel (the reason it's in the Lens Corrections panel is this: some particular lenses darken the corners of your photo, even when you don't want them to. In that case, it's a problem, and you'd go to the Lens Corrections panel to fix a lens problem, right? There you would brighten the corners using the controls in this panel. So, basically, a little edge darkening is bad, but if you add a lot intentionally, then it's cool. Hey, I don't make the rules—I just pass them on). Here's the original image without any vignetting (by the way, we'll talk about how to get rid of "bad vignetting" in Chapter 8—the chapter on how to fix problems).

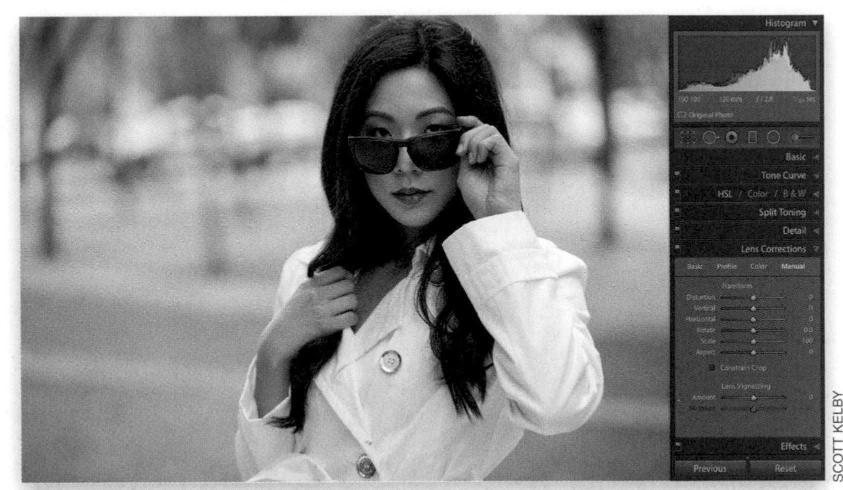

SCOTT KELBY

Step Two:

We'll start with regular full-image vignetting, so click on Manual at the top of the panel, then drag the Lens Vignetting Amount slider all the way to the left. This slider controls how dark the edges of your photo are going to get (the further to the left you drag, the darker they get). The Midpoint slider controls how far in the dark edges get to the center of your photo. So, try dragging it over quite a bit, too (as I have here), and it kind of creates a nice, soft spotlight effect, where the edges are dark, your subject looks nicely lit, and your eye is drawn right where you want it to look.

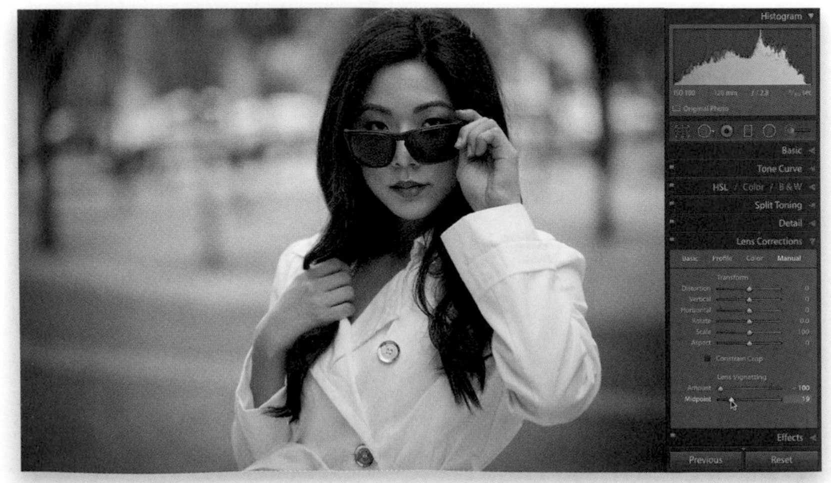

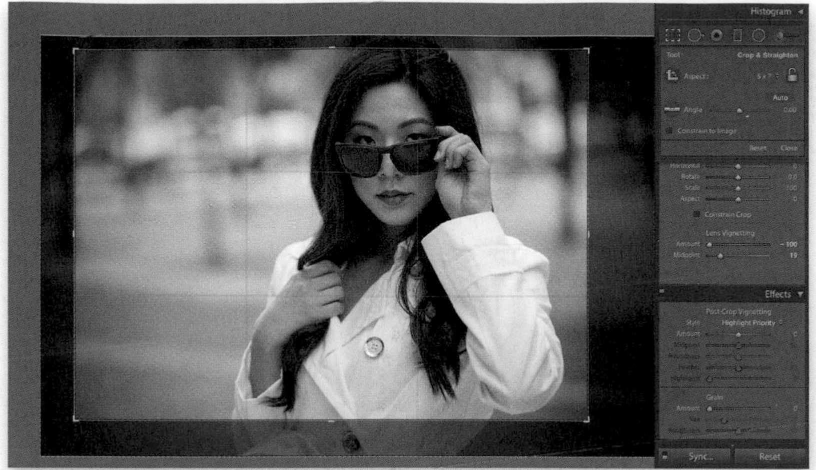

Step Three:

Now, this works just fine, until you wind up having to crop the photo, because cropping will crop away the edge vignette. To get around that problem, Adobe added a control called "Post-Crop Vignetting," which lets you add vignetting effects after you've cropped. I'm cropping that same photo in tight here, and now most of the edge vignetting I added earlier will be cropped away. So, scroll down to the Effects panel and at the top you'll see Post-Crop Vignetting. Before we try that, reset your Lens Vignetting Amount slider to 0 (zero), so we don't add the post-crop vignetting on top of the little bit of original vignetting still in our photo.

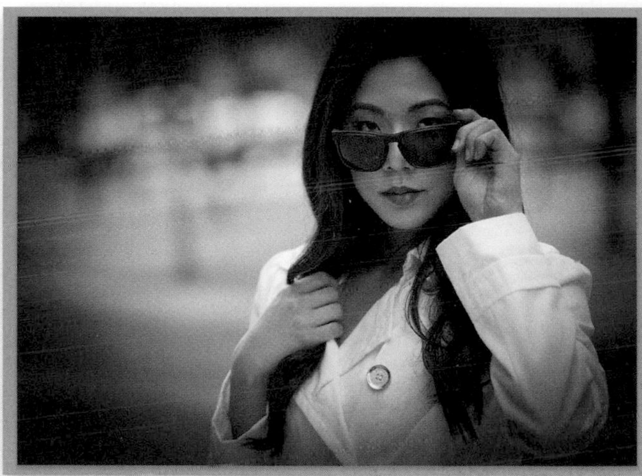

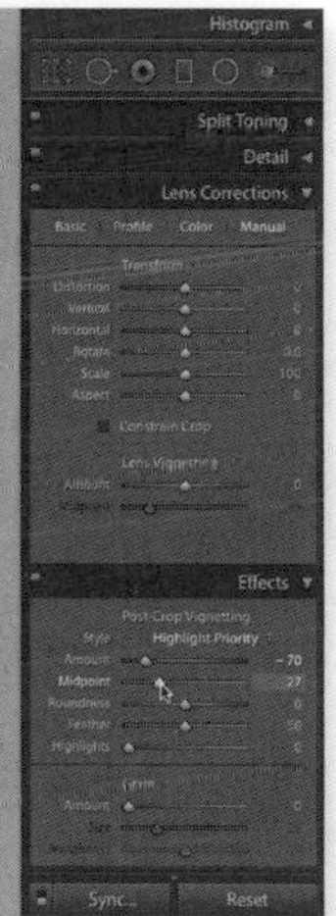

Step Four:

Before we get to the sliders, let's talk about the Style pop-up menu. You have three choices: (1) Highlight Priority, (2) Color Priority, and (3) Paint Overlay (though the only one that really looks good is Highlight Priority, so it's the only one I ever use. The results are more like what you get with the regular vignette. The edges get darker, but the color may shift a bit, and I'm totally okay with the edges looking more saturated. This choice gets its name from the fact that it tries to keep as much of the highlights intact, so if you have some bright areas around the edges, it'll try to make sure they stay bright). I made the edges pretty darn dark here—darker than I would make mine, but I wanted you to really see the effect on the cropped image (just for example purposes). The Color Priority style is more concerned with keeping your color accurate around the edges, so the edges do get a bit darker, but the colors don't get more saturated, and it's not as dark (or nice) as the Highlight Priority style. Finally, Paint Overlay gives you the look we had back in Lightroom 2 for post-crop vignetting, which just painted the edges dark gray (yeech!).

Continued

Step Five:

The next two sliders were added to give you more control to make your vignettes look more realistic. For example, the Roundness setting controls how round the vignette is. Just so you know exactly what this does, try this: leave the Roundness set at 0, but then drag the Feather amount (which we'll talk about in a moment) all the way to the left. You see how it creates a very defined oval shape? Of course, you wouldn't really use this look (well, I hope not), but it does help in understanding exactly what this slider does. Well, the Roundness setting controls how round that oval gets (drag the slider back and forth a couple of times and you'll instantly get it). Okay, reset it to zero (and stop playing with that slider). ;-)

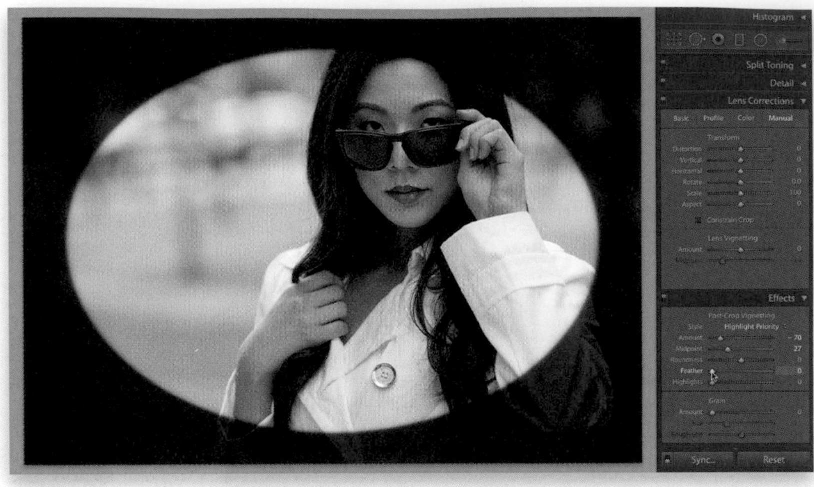

Step Six:

The Feather slider controls the amount of softness of the oval's edge, so dragging this slider to the right makes the vignette softer and more natural looking. Here I clicked-and-dragged the Feather amount to 57, and you can see how it softened the edges of the hard oval you saw in the previous step. So, in short, the farther you drag, the softer the edges of the oval get. The bottom slider, Highlights, helps you to maintain highlights in the edge areas you're darkening with your vignette. The farther to the right you drag it, the more the highlights are protected. The Highlights slider is only available if your Style is set to either Highlight Priority or Color Priority (but you're not going to set it to Color Priority, because it looks kind of yucky, right?). So there ya have it—how to add an edge vignette to focus the viewer's attention on the center of your image by darkening the edges all the way around.

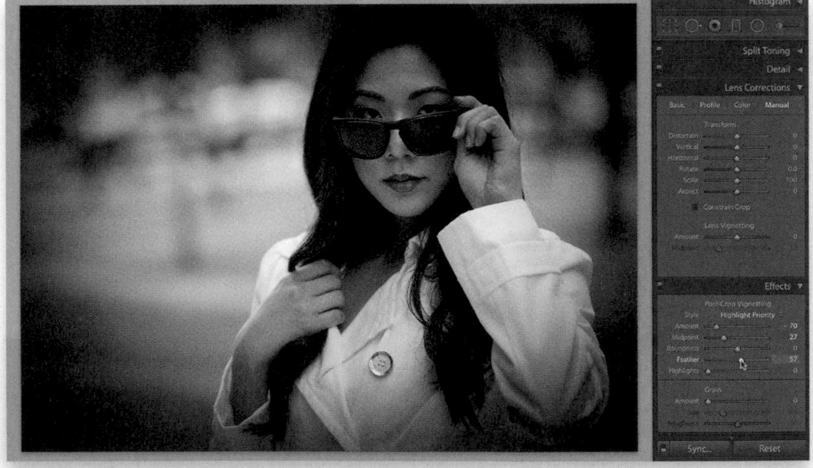

Getting That Trendy High-Contrast Look

There's a Photoshop effect that started making the rounds a couple years ago, and now it's one of the hottest and most requested looks out there—you see it everywhere from big magazine covers to websites to celebrity portraits to album covers. Anyway, you can get pretty darn close to that look right within Lightroom itself. Now, before I show you the effect, I have to tell you, this is one of those effects that you'll either absolutely love (and you'll wind up over-using it), or you'll hate it with a passion that knows no bounds. There's no in-between.

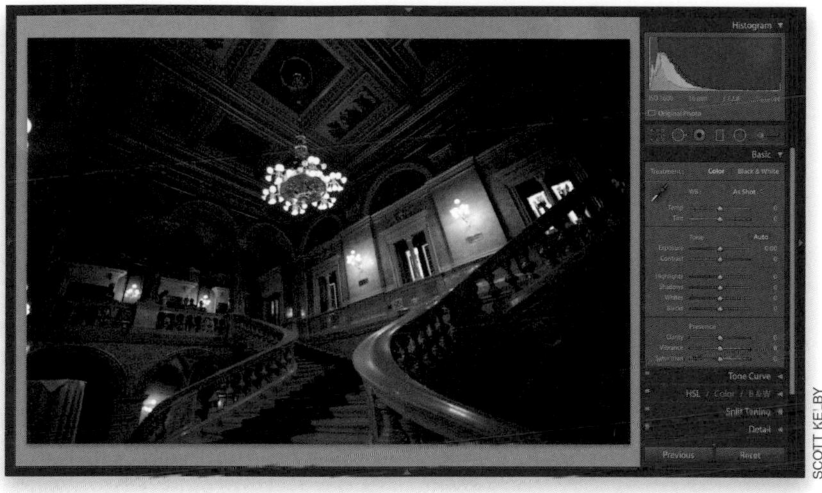

SCOTT KELBY

Step One:

Before we apply this effect, I have a disclaimer: this effect doesn't look good on every photo. It looks best on photos that have lots of detail and texture, so it looks great on city shots, landscapes, industrial shots, and even people (especially guys)—anything you want to be gritty and texture-y (if that's even a word). So, you're usually not going to apply this effect to anything you want to look soft and/or glamorous. Here's a shot with lots of detail and that has lots of textures. It's just screaming for this type of treatment.

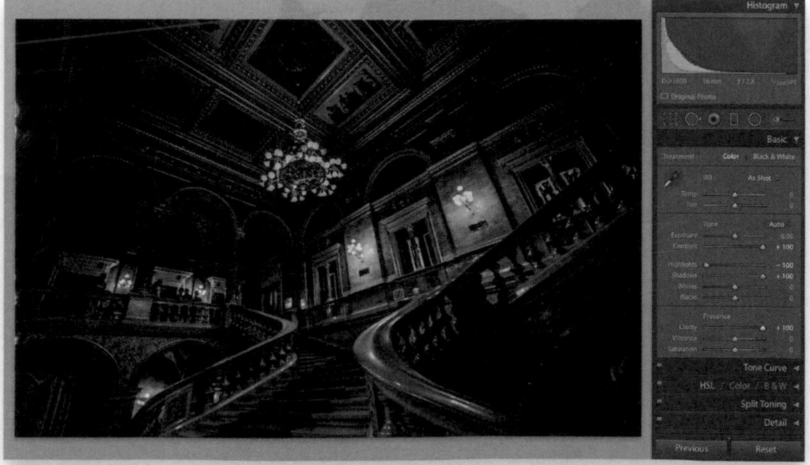

Step Two:

You're going to really crank up four sliders in the Develop module's Basic panel: (1) drag the Contrast slider all the way over to +100, (2) drag the Highlights slider all the way to –100, (3) drag the Shadows slider all the way to +100 (that opens up the shadows), and (4) drag the Clarity slider all the way to the right to +100. Now, the whole image has that high-contrast look already, but we're not done yet.

Continued

Step Three:

Now, at this point, depending on the photo you applied this effect to, you might have to drag the Exposure slider to the right a bit if the entire image is too dark (that can happen when you set the Contrast at +100), or if the photo looks washed out a bit (from cranking the Shadows slider to +100), then you might need to drag the Blacks slider to the left to bring back the color saturation and overall balance (I increased the Exposure to +0.30 and decreased the Blacks to –11). Outside of those potential tweaks, the next step is to desaturate the photo a little bit by dragging the Vibrance slider to the left (here, I dragged it over to –45). This desaturation is a trademark of this "look," which kind of gives the feel of an HDR image without combining multiple exposures.

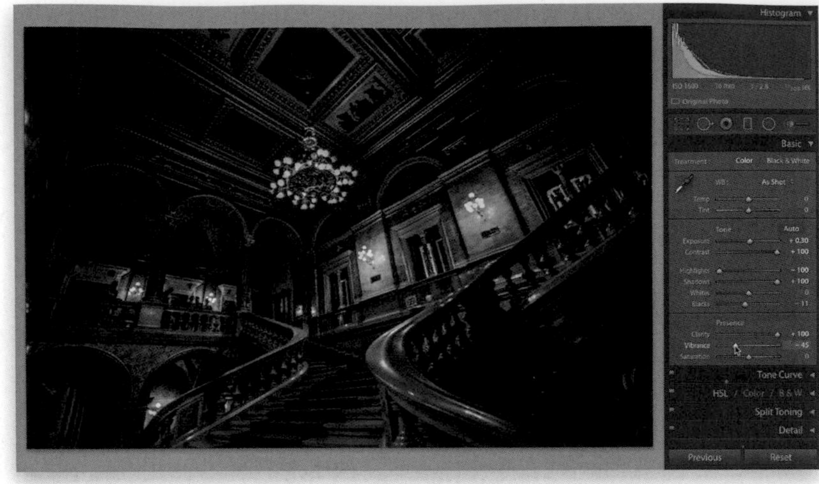

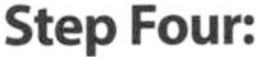

Step Four:

The final step is to add an edge vignette to darken the edges of your photo, and put the focus on your subject. So, go to the Lens Corrections panel (in the right side Panels area), click on Manual at the top, and drag the Lens Vignetting Amount slider to the left (making the edges really dark). Then drag the Midpoint slider pretty far to the left, as well (the Midpoint slider controls how far the darkened edges extend in toward the middle of your photo. The farther you drag this slider to the left, the farther in they go). This made the whole photo look a little too dark, so I had to go back to the Basic panel and increase the Exposure amount a little bit more (to +0.55) to bring back the original brightness before the vignette. I included a few befores and afters on the next page just to give you an idea of how it affects different images. Hey, don't forget to save this as a preset (see page 234), so you don't have to do this manually every time you want to apply this look.

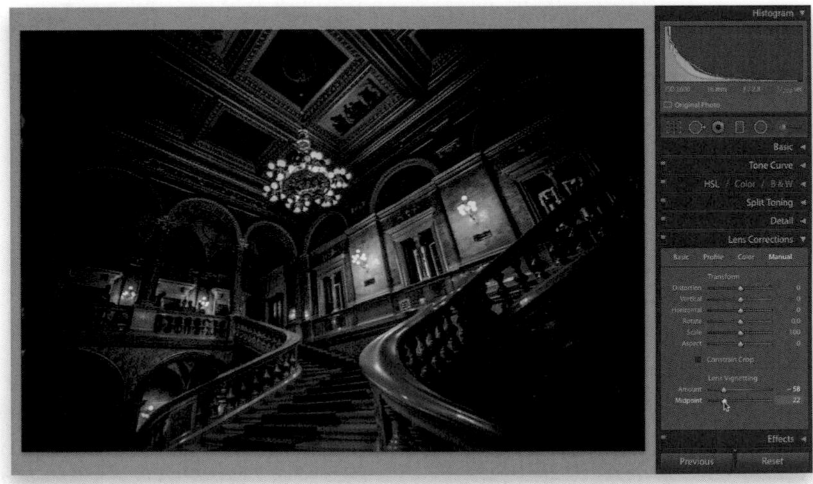

Before After

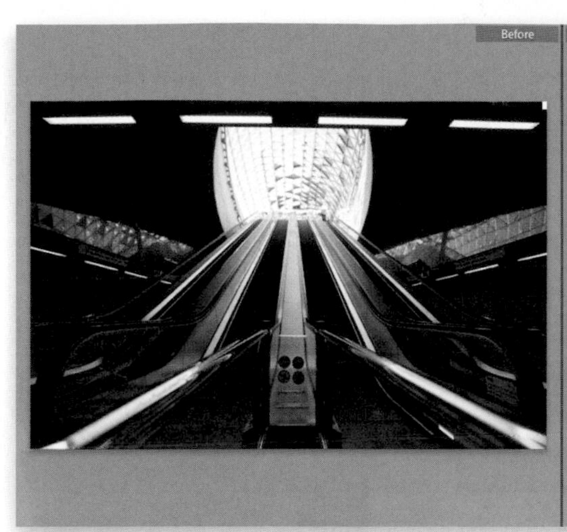

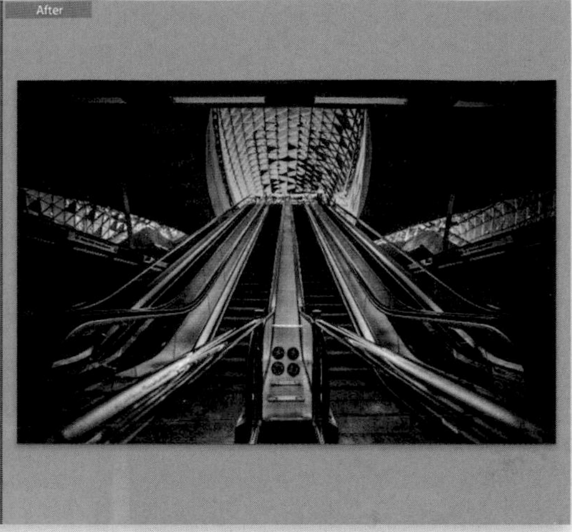

SCOTT KELBY

Before After

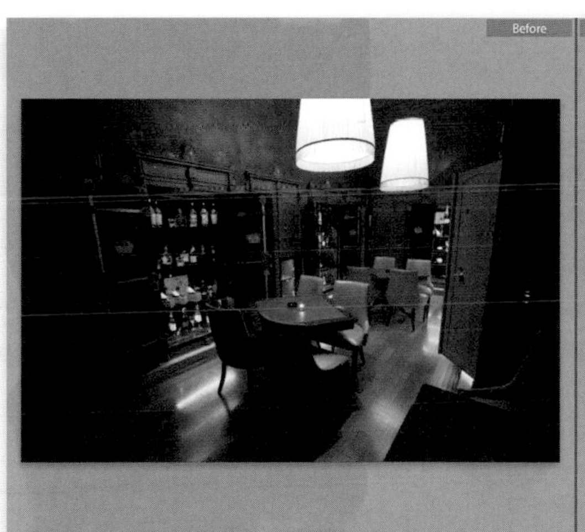

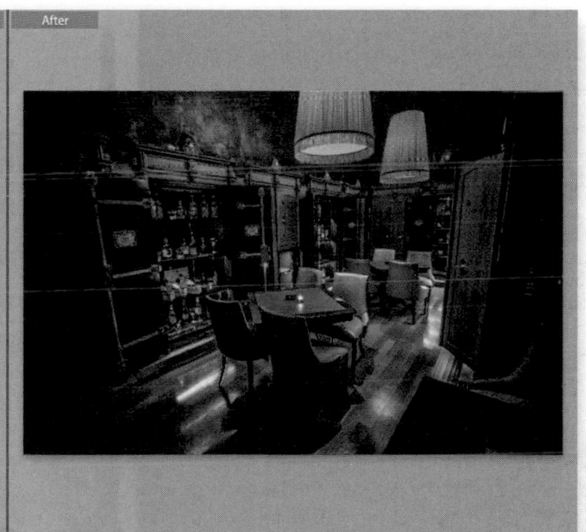

SCOTT KELBY

Before After

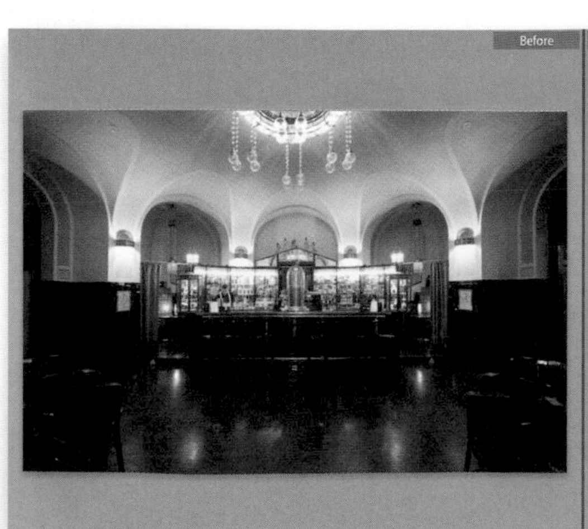

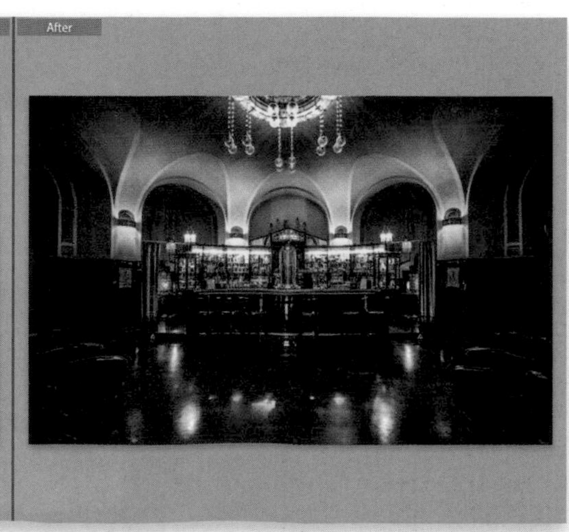

SCOTT KELBY

Creating Black-and-White Images

There are two auto conversion methods for converting your images from color to black and white (one in the Basic panel and another in the HSL/Color/B&W panel), and no matter where you choose to do it from, the results are the same. Now, to me they just look really flat, and I honestly think you can do much better by doing it yourself. We'll start with my preferred method for most color-to-black-and-white conversions, which lets you build on what you've already learned in this chapter.

Step One:

In the Library module, find the photo you want to convert to black and white, and first make a virtual copy of it by going under the Photo menu and choosing **Create Virtual Copy**, as shown here (the only reason you do this is so when you're done, you can compare your do-it-yourself method with Lightroom's auto-conversion method side by side. By the way, once you learn to do the conversion yourself, I doubt you'll ever want to use the auto method again). Press **Command-D (PC: Ctrl-D)** to deselect the virtual copy, and then go down to the Filmstrip and click on the original photo.

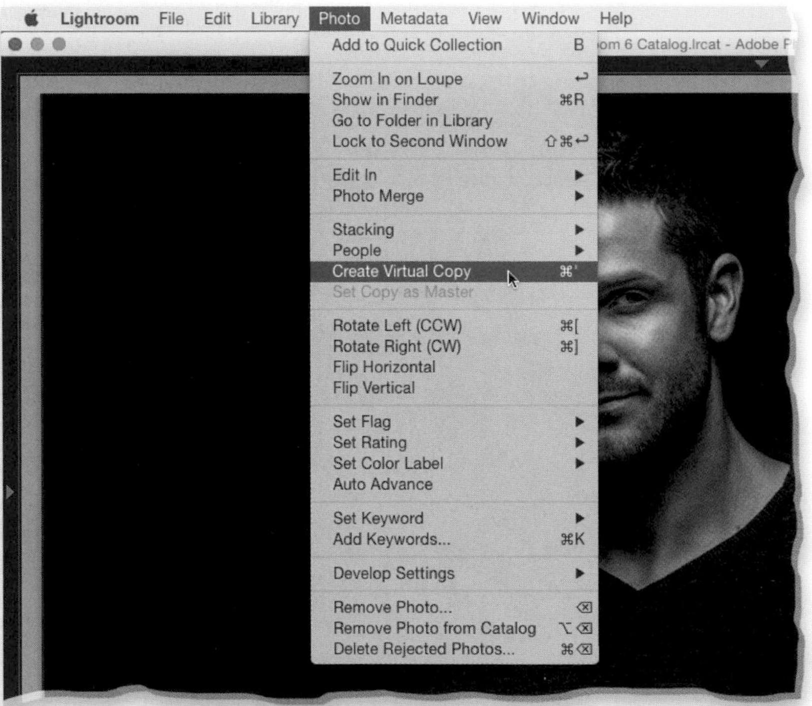

SCOTT KELBY

Step Two:

Now press **D** to jump to the Develop module and, in the right side Panels area, scroll down to the HSL/Color/B&W panel, then click directly on B&W on the far right of the panel header (as shown here). This applies an automatic conversion from color to black and white, but sadly it usually gives you the flat-looking B&W conversion you see here (consider this your "before" photo). The idea here is that you adjust the B&W auto conversion by moving the color sliders. The thing that makes this so tricky, though, is that your photo isn't color anymore. Go ahead and move the sliders all you want, and you'll see how little they do by themselves. By the way, if you toggle the panel on/off button (circled here in red), you can see how bad this black-and-white would have looked if Lightroom had done the auto conversion for you without using the default conversion settings.

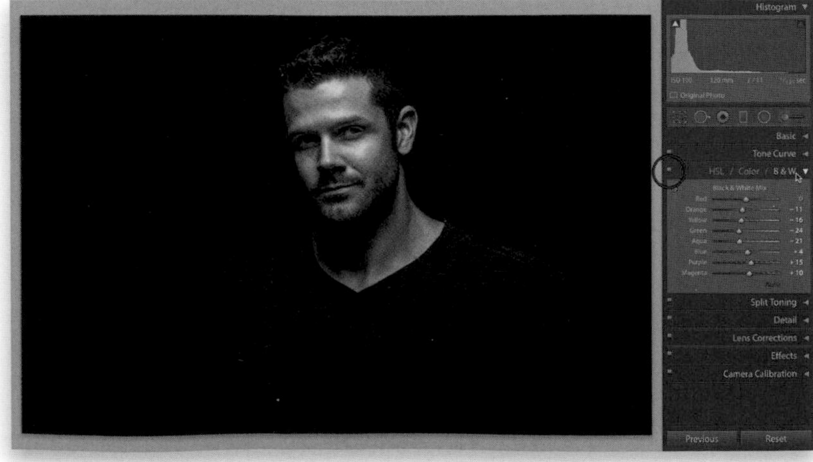

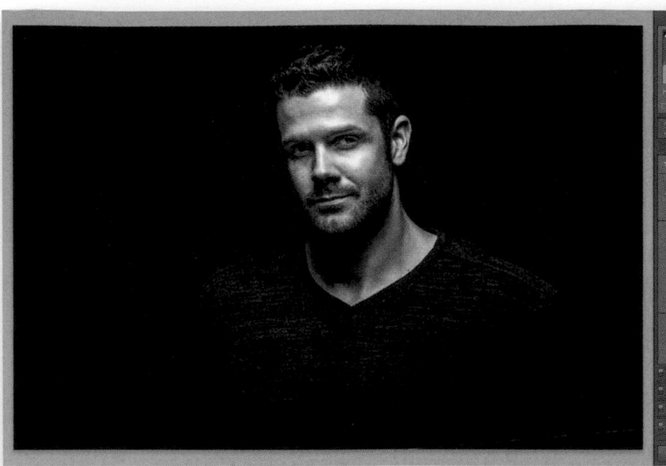
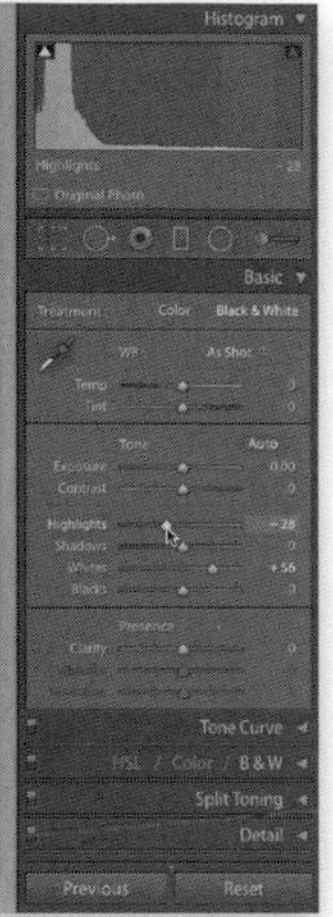

Step Three:

Now, press the **Right Arrow key** on your keyboard to switch to that virtual copy you made, and I'll show you my preferred do-it-yourself method. Go to the Basic panel (at the top of the right side Panels area), and in the Treatment section at the top, click on Black & White, and you get another flat-looking image (but that's about to change). Most photographers want to create a really rich, high-contrast B&W image, so the first thing to do is make sure we've gotten all we can out of the highlights in the photo, so drag the Whites slider over to the right until the moment the "white triangle of death" (in the upper-right corner of the histogram) appears, then stop. Next, drag the Highlights slider just a tiny bit to the left until that white triangle turns dark gray again. Now you know you've gotten the maximum amount of highlights without clipping any of them away.

Step Four:

Next, drag the Blacks slider over to the left a little until the photo doesn't look so flat and washed out, and then increase the Contrast quite a bit. Now, there are those who believe that you should never let any part of your photo turn solid black, even if it's a non-essential, low-detail area like a shadow under a rock. I'm not one of those people. I want the entire photo to have "pop" to it, and in my years of creating B&W prints, I've found that your average person reacts much more positively to photos with high-contrast conversions than to the flatter conversions that retain 100% detail in the shadows. If you get a chance, try both versions, show your friends, and see which one they choose. His face seemed a little too bright, so I also decreased the Exposure a little.

Continued

Step Five:

We're going for a high-contrast black and white, so we can add even more contrast by clicking-and-dragging the Clarity slider quite a bit to the right (here I dragged to +46), which gives the midtones much more contrast and makes the overall photo have more punch and crispness.

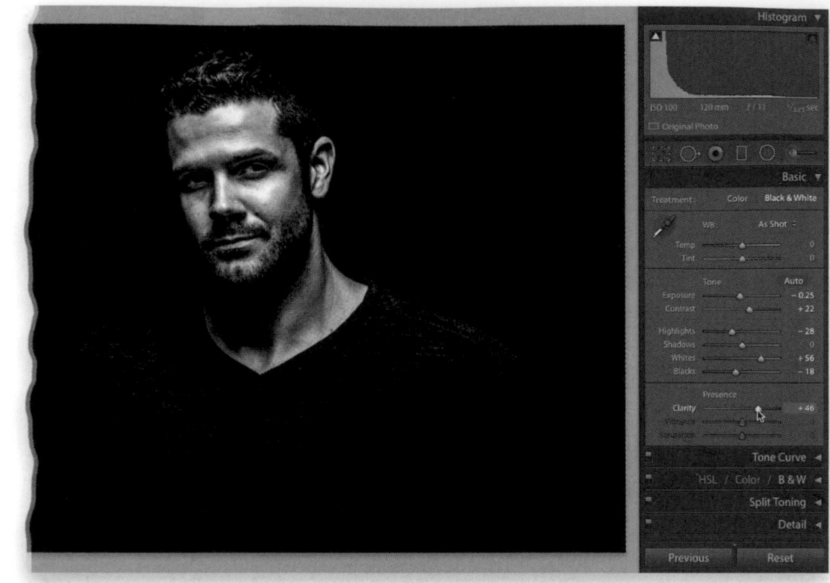

TIP: Finding Out Which Shots Make Great B&W Images

Go to a collection, press **Command-A (PC: Ctrl-A)** to select all of the photos, then press the letter **V** to temporarily convert them all to black and white, and now you can see which ones (if any) would make great B&W images. Press **Command-D (PC: Ctrl-D)** to Deselect all the photos. When you see a great B&W candidate, click on it, then press **P** to flag it as a Pick. When you're done, select all of the photos again and press V to return them to full color. Now all the photos that you think would make great B&W images are tagged with a Picks flag. Pretty handy.

Step Six:

The final step is to add some sharpening. Since this is a portrait, the easiest thing to do is to go over to the left side Panels area, and in the Presets panel, under the Lightroom General Presets, choose Sharpen–Faces (as shown here) to apply a nice amount of sharpening for portraits. By the way, if that's not enough sharpening, try the next preset down (which is really for landscape shots, and is called Sharpen–Scenic, but it's worth trying). So that's it. It's not that much different from adjusting a color photo, is it? Now, I didn't want to tell you this earlier, because I wanted you to learn this technique, but there's a built-in preset that pretty much does all this for you. Click on the Reset button at the bottom right to reset your photo to the original color image, then go to the Presets panel, and under Lightroom B&W Presets, click on B&W Look 5. Don't hate the playa. Hate the game.

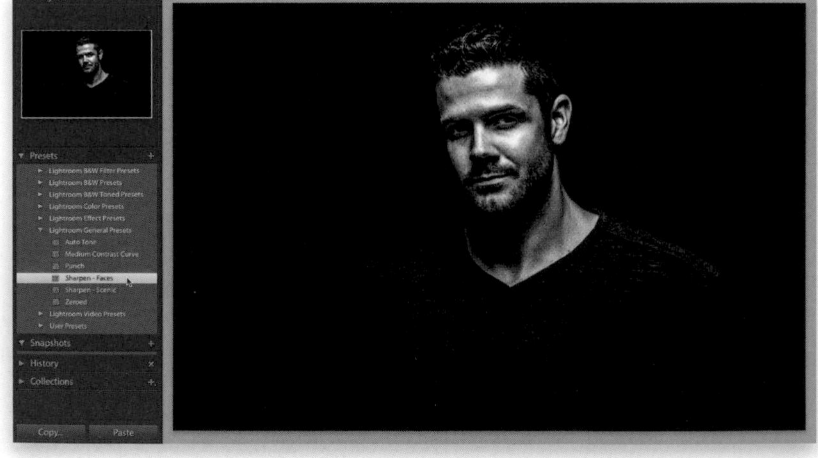

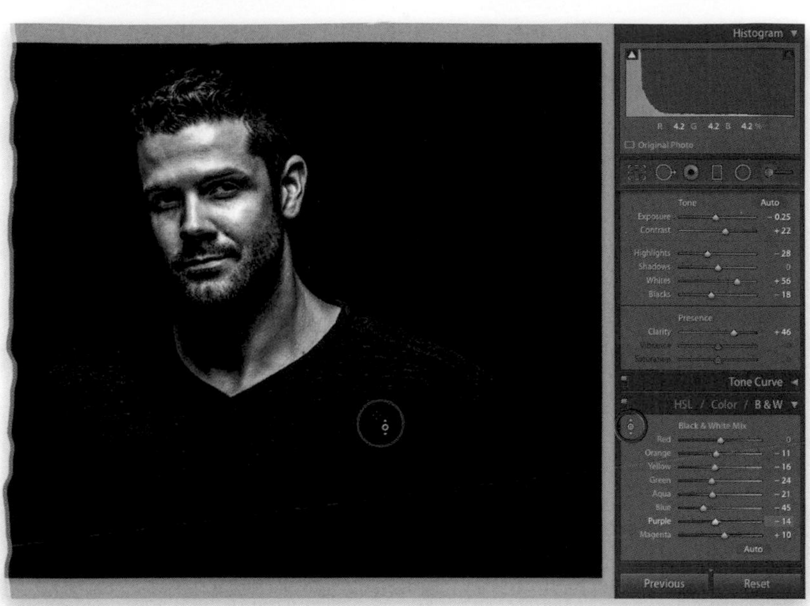

Step Seven:

Okay, we're done with our conversion, but there's one other thing you'll want to know about, and that's how to tweak an individual area of your B&W photo. For example, let's say you wanted his sweater to be a little darker. You'd just go to the B&W panel again, click on the TAT (Targeted Adjustment tool—shown circled here), then click it on his sweater, and drag straight downward. Even though the photo is now a black and white, it knows which underlying colors make up that area, and it moves the sliders for you to darken that area (as shown here). The next time you need to darken or brighten (you'd drag up instead) a particular area, try using the TAT and let it do the work for you.

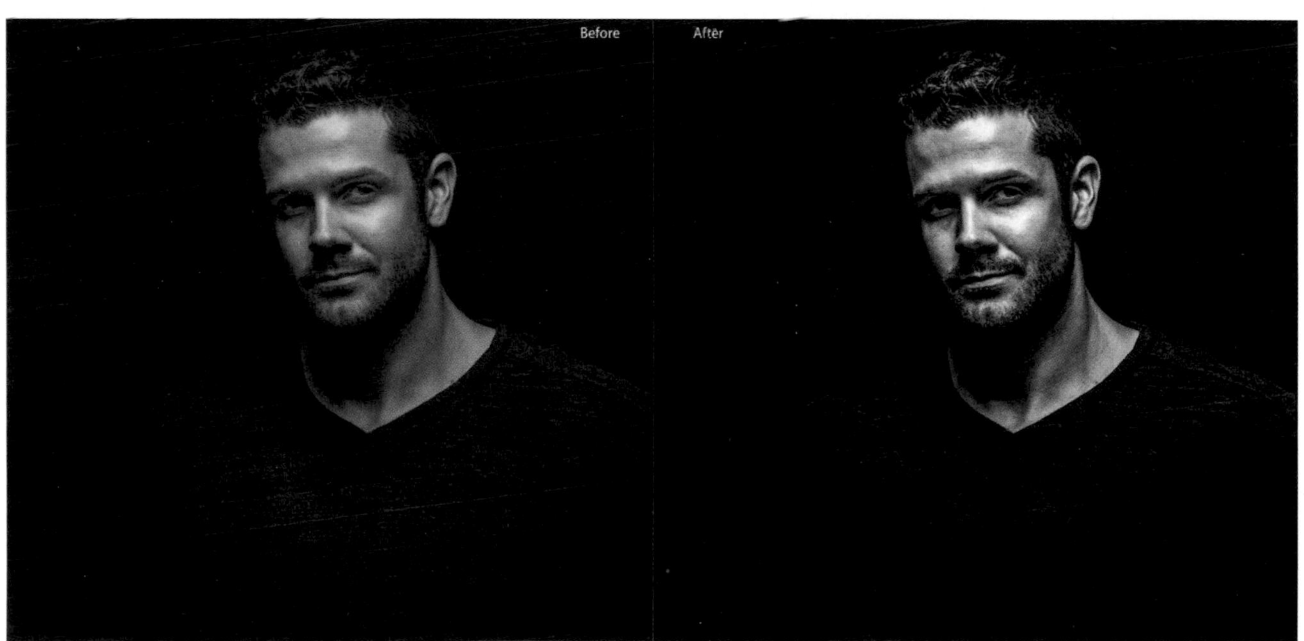

The auto conversion to black and white

Doing the black-and-white conversion yourself

Getting Great Duotones (and Split Tones)

Okay, I need to clarify here a bit: This trick is for getting great duotones, but I also cover how to do a split-tone effect, since it kind of uses the same controls. A duotone generally starts with a B&W photo, then you expand the visual depth of the image with a deep color tint. Split toning is where you apply one color tint to the highlights and another to the shadow areas. We'll cover duotones first, because not only are you more likely to do a duotone, they just look better (I'm not a big split-toning fan myself, but hey, I'm still happy to show ya how to do one, just in case).

Step One:

Although the actual duotone or split tone is created in the Split Toning panel (in the right side Panels area), you should convert the photo to black and white first. (I say "should" because you can apply a split-toning effect on top of your color photo, but…well…yeech!) In the Develop module's Presets panel, under Lightroom B&W Presets, click on B&W Look 5 to convert the photo. Then, in the Basic panel, increase the Clarity a bit more, and decrease the Exposure a little.

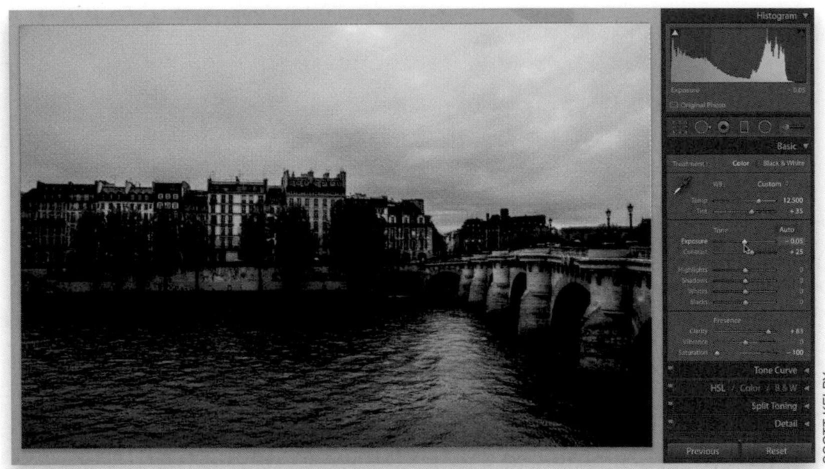

Step Two:

The trick to creating duotones is actually incredibly simple: you only add the color tint in the shadows, and you leave the highlights untouched. So, go to the Split Toning panel, in the right side Panels area, and start by dragging the Shadows Saturation slider to around 25, so you can see some of the tint color (as soon as you start dragging the Saturation slider, the tint appears, but, by default, the hue is a reddish color). Now, drag the Shadows Hue slider over to 41 to get more of a traditional duotone look (while you're there, increase the Saturation amount to 35, as shown here). That's it. Couldn't be simpler. Of course, you can choose any hue you want (this one just happens to be my favorite for duotones).

TIP: Reset Your Settings

If you want to start over, press-and-hold the Option (PC: Alt) key, and the word "Shadows" in the Split Toning panel changes to "Reset Shadows." Click on it to reset the settings to their defaults.

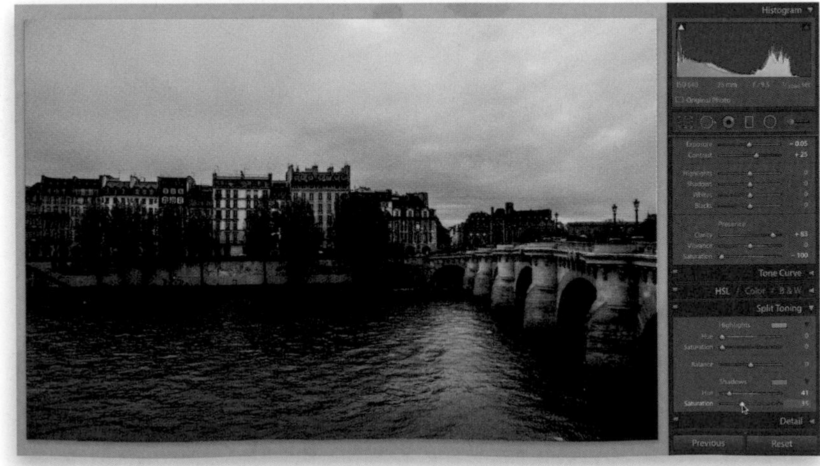

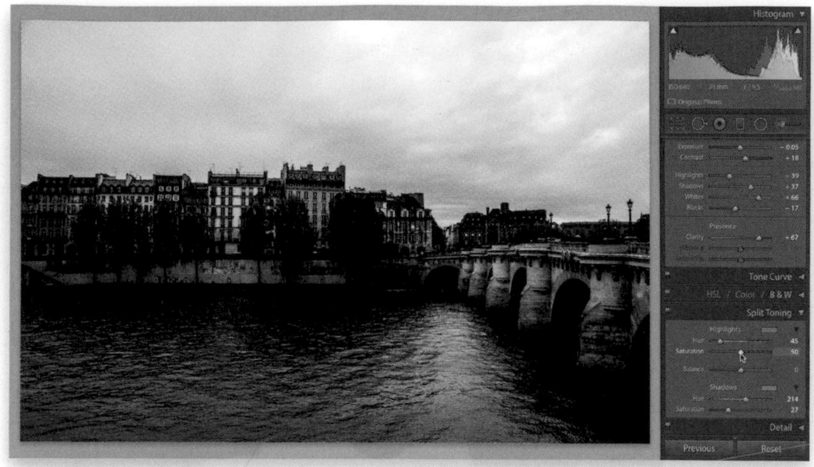

Step Three:

Now, on to split tones. To create a split-tone effect, start with a good-looking B&W photo (you know how to convert from color to black and white now), then you're going to do the same thing you did to create a duotone, but you're going to choose one hue for the highlights and a different hue for the shadows. That's all there is to it (I told you this was easy). Here, I set the Highlights Hue to 45 and the Shadows Hue to 214. I then set the Shadows Saturation slider to 27 and the Highlights Saturation slider to 50 (a little bit higher than usual, just to add more color).

TIP: See a Tint Color Preview

To make it easier to see which color tint you're choosing, press-and-hold the Option (PC: Alt) key and drag the Hue slider, and it will give you a temporary preview of your color tint as if you bumped up the Saturation amount to 100%.

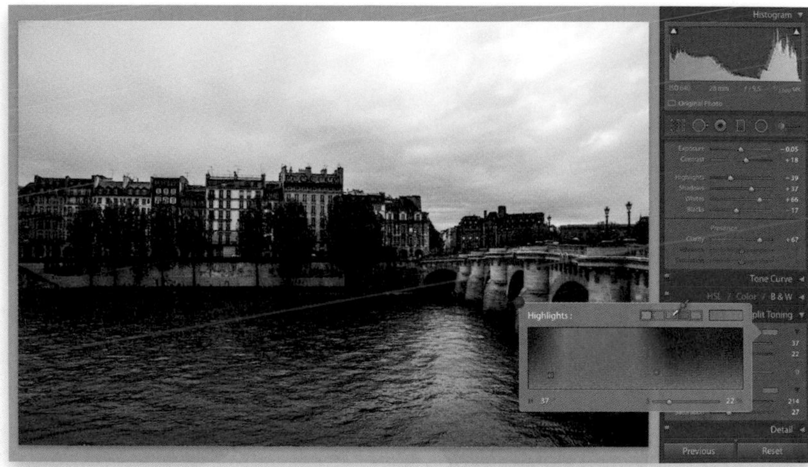

Step Four:

You can also choose your colors from a color picker: click on the color swatch next to Highlights to bring up the Highlights color picker. Along the top are some common split-tone highlight colors. For example, click on the beige swatch (the third from the left) to apply a beige tint to the highlights (you can see the result in the Preview area). To close the color picker, click on the X in the upper-left corner. The Balance slider (found between the Highlights and Shadows sections) does just what you'd think it would—it lets you balance the color mix between the highlights and shadows. For example, if you want the balance in your image more toward the beige highlights, you'd just click-and-drag the Balance slider to the right. Now, if you've created a particular duotone or split-tone combination that you like, save it as a preset by going to the Presets panel and clicking the little + (plus sign) button on the right side of the panel header.

Using One-Click Presets (and Making Your Own!)

Lightroom comes with a number of built-in Develop module presets that you can apply to any photo with just one click. These are found in the Presets panel over in the left side Panels area, where you'll find eight different collections of presets: seven built-in collections put there by Adobe and a User Presets collection (that one's empty for now, because this is where you store the ones you create on your own). These are huge time savers, so take just minute or two and learn how to put them to use (and how to create your own).

Step One:

We'll start by looking at how to use the built-in presets, then we'll create one of our own, and apply it in two different places. First, let's look at the built-in presets by going to the Presets panel (found in the left side Panels area). There are seven built-in Lightroom collections (and a User Presets collection, where you can save and store your own presets). When you look inside each collection, you'll see that Adobe named these built-in presets by starting each name with the type of preset it is (for example, within the Lightroom Effect presets, you'll find Grain. That's the type of preset, then it says, "Heavy," "Light," or "Medium").

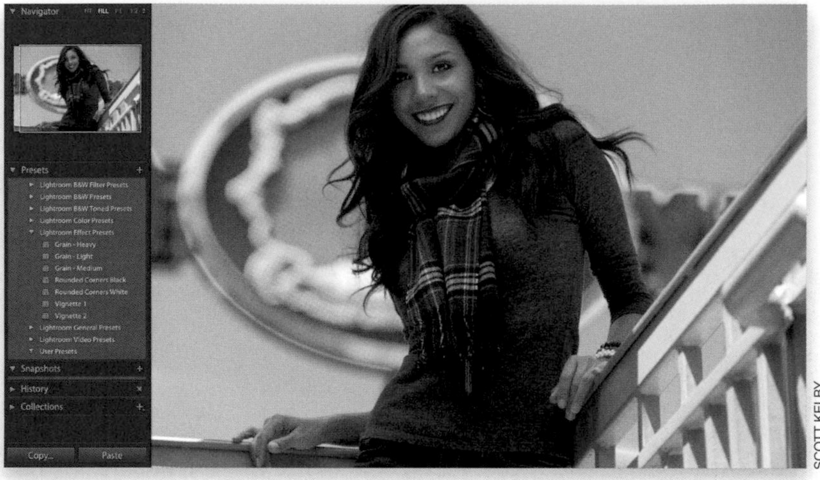

SCOTT KELBY

TIP: Renaming Presets

To rename any preset you created (a user preset), just Right-click on the preset and choose **Rename** from the pop-up menu.

Step Two:

You can see a preview of how any of these presets will look, even before you apply them, by simply hovering your cursor over the presets in the Presets panel. A preview will appear above the Presets panel in the Navigator panel (as shown here, where I'm hovering over a Color preset called Cross Process 3, and you can see a preview of how that color effect would look applied to my photo, up in the Navigator panel, at the top of the left side Panels area).

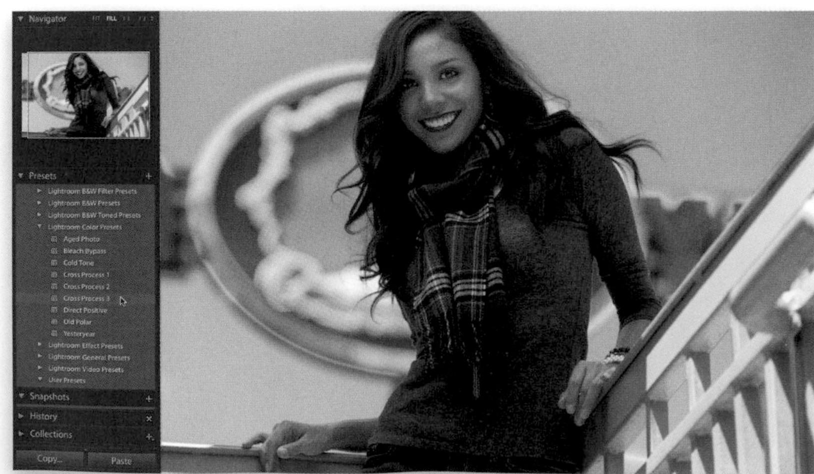

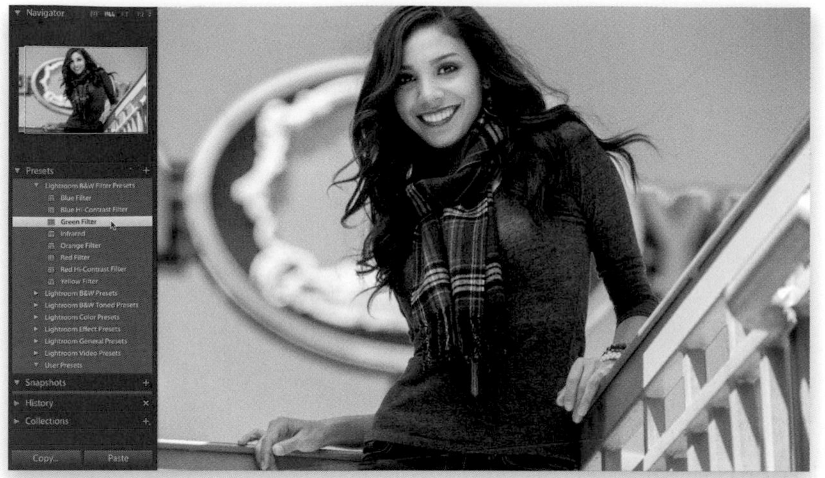

Step Three:

To actually apply one of these presets, all you have to do is click on it. In the example shown here, I went to the Lightroom B&W Filter presets and clicked on the Green Filter preset to create this black-and-white conversion. I could be done right there with one click, but the nice thing is if you want to tweak things after the preset has been applied, you can just grab the sliders in the Basic panel and go to town!

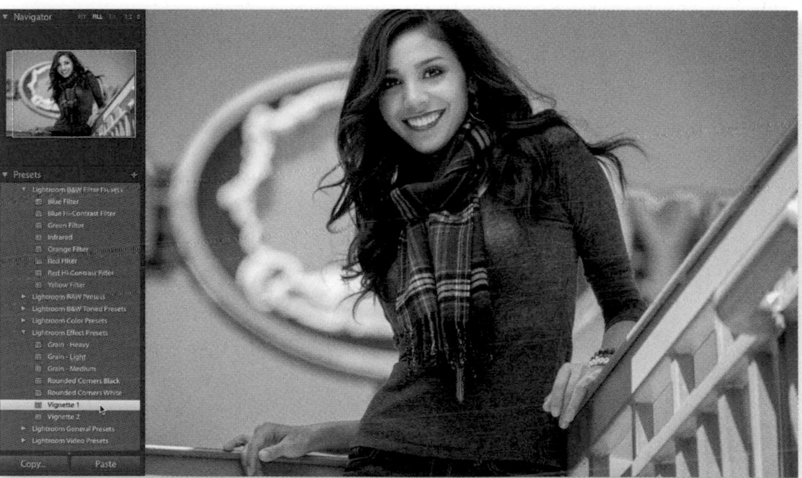

Step Four:

For example, here I lowered the Contrast to –17 (lowering contrast is something I rarely do, but it looked way too contrasty), and I lowered the Highlights a bit more than the preset had (to –95), so I could darken the sky a bit. I opened up the Shadows a bit to +10, so you could see more detail in the dark parts of her hair, and I backed off the Clarity amount to +16 to keep the image from looking so "crunchy." Also, once you've applied a preset, you can apply more presets and those changes are added right on top of your current settings, as long as the new preset you chose doesn't use the same settings as the one you just applied. So, if you applied a preset that set the Exposure, White Balance, and Highlights, but didn't use vignetting, if you then chose a preset that just uses vignetting, it adds this on top of your current preset. Otherwise, if the new preset uses Exposure, White Balance, or Highlights, it just moves those sliders to new settings, so it might cancel the look of the original preset. For example, after I applied the Green Filter preset, and tweaked the settings I mentioned above, I went to the Effect Presets collection and applied the preset called "Vignette 1" (as shown here) to add a dark edge effect. The Green Filter didn't have a vignette, so it added it on top.

Continued

Step Five:

Now, of course you can use any built-in preset as a starting place to build your own preset, but let's just start from scratch here. Click the Reset button at the bottom of the right side Panels area (shown circled here in red) to reset our photo to how it looked when we started. Now we'll create our own cross-process fashion look: Increase the Exposure amount to +1.15 to brighten things up, and the Contrast to +64, set the Highlights to +64 to make it even brighter, the Whites to –58 (a more high-key look), Blacks to –15, Clarity to +4, and Vibrance to –32 to desaturate the image a bit. That's it for the Basic panel.

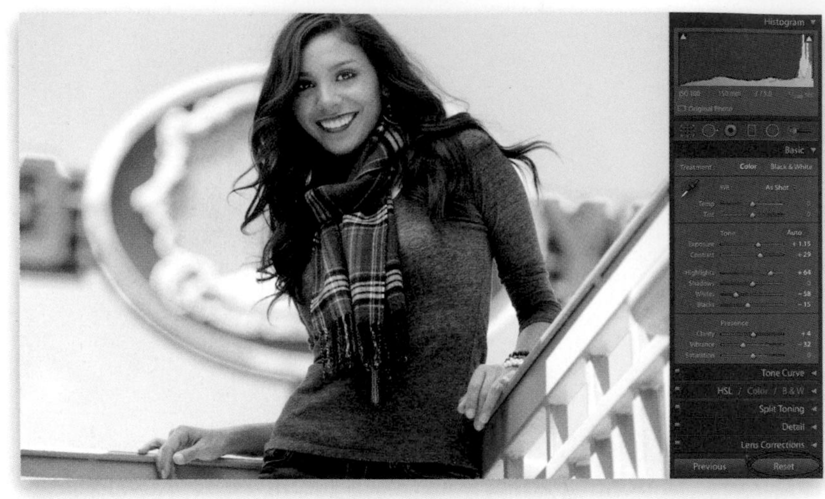

Step Six:

Now, go the Split Toning panel. In the Highlights section, set the Hue to 54 (for an amber tone) and Saturation to 80, so there's a lot of it. In the Shadows section, set the Hue to 218 (kind of a powder blue) and the Saturation to 45. The Balance slider in the middle lets you choose the balance between the Highlights Hue and the Shadows Hue. Drag the Balance to –36, so the image is learning toward the blues in the shadows. Now, let's save it as a preset. In the Presets panel, click on the + (plus sign) button on the right side of the panel header to bring up the New Develop Preset dialog (shown here). Give your new preset a name (I named mine "SK Cross Process 1"), click the Check None button at the bottom of the dialog (to turn off all the checkboxes), then turn on the checkboxes beside all the settings you edited (as seen here). Now, click the Create button to save all the edits you just made as your own custom preset, which will appear under the User Presets collection in the Presets panel.

Note: To delete a user preset, just click on the preset, then click on the – (minus sign) button, which will appear to the left of the + button on the right side of the Presets panel header.

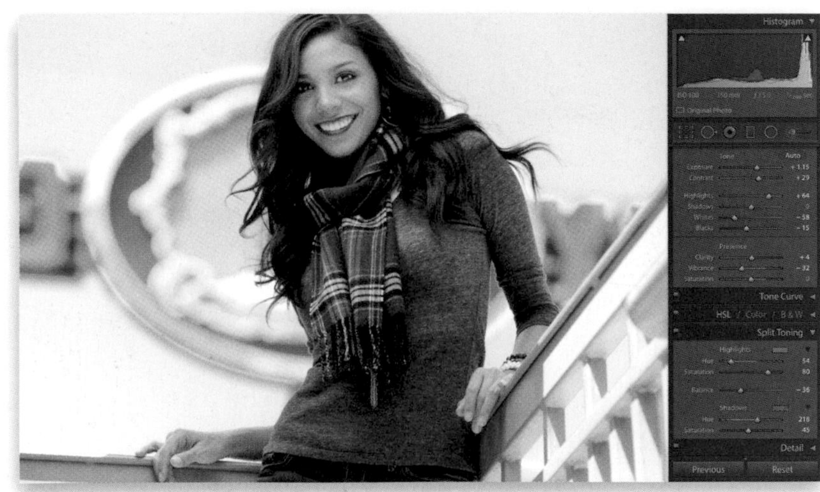

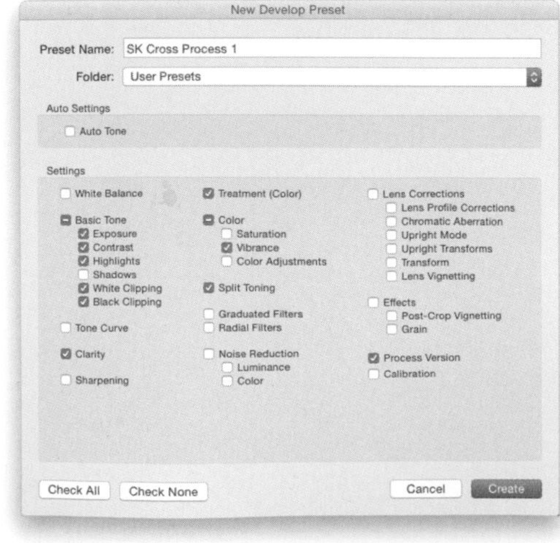

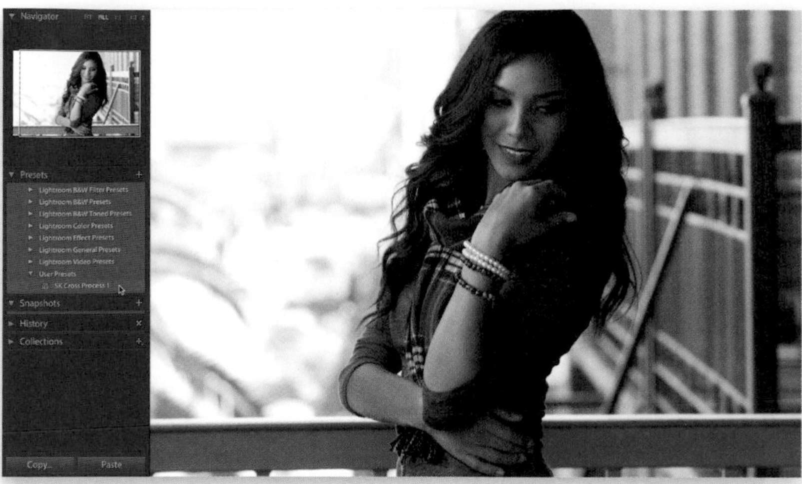

Step Seven:

Now click on a different photo in the Filmstrip, then hover your cursor over your new preset. Look up at the Navigator panel, and you'll see a preview of the preset (as seen here). Seeing these instant live previews is a huge time saver, because you'll know in a split second whether your photo will look good with the preset applied or not, before you actually apply it.

TIP: Updating a User Preset

If you tweak a User Preset and want to update it with the new settings, Right-click on your preset and choose **Update with Current Settings** from the pop-up menu.

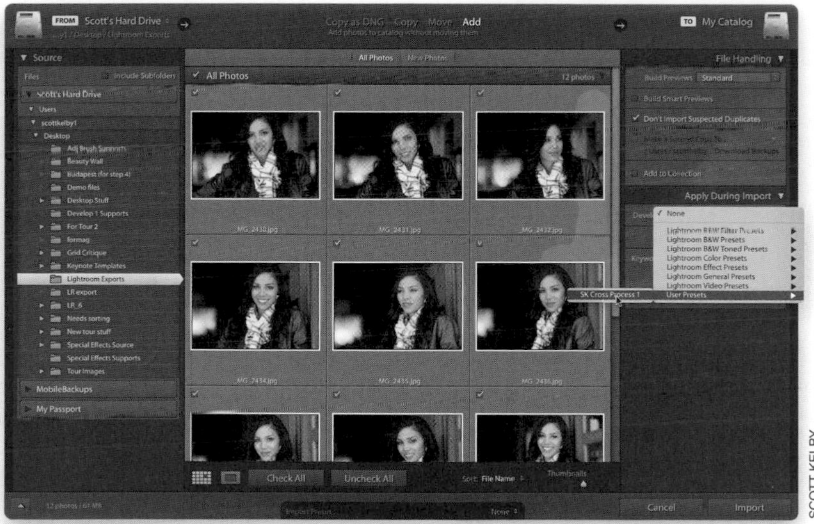

SCOTT KELBY

Step Eight:

If you're going to apply a particular preset (either a built-in one or one you created) to a bunch of images you're importing, you can actually have that preset applied to your images as they're imported, so when they appear, they already have your preset applied. You do this right within the Import window. Just go to the Apply During Import panel (seen here), where you'd choose which preset you want from the Develop Settings pop-up menu (as shown here, where I chose that SK Cross Process 1 preset I just created), and now that preset is automatically applied to each photo as it's imported. There's one more place you can apply these Develop presets, and that's in the Saved Preset pop-up menu, at the top of the Quick Develop panel, in the Library module (more about the Quick Develop panel in Chapter 4).

TIP: Importing Presets

There are lots of places online where you can download free Develop module presets (like from this book's companion website [see Chapter 14] and my LightroomKillerTips.com site). Once they're downloaded, go to the Presets panel, Right-click on User Presets, and choose **Import** from the pop-up menu. Locate the preset you downloaded and click the Import button, and it will now appear in your User Presets.

Stitching Panoramas Right in Lightroom

We can now create panoramic images (stitching multiple frames into one very wide, or very tall shot) right in Lightroom—no more trips over to Photoshop necessary. And, I gotta tell ya, I like the way Lightroom does it better than Photoshop anyway. It's quick and easy and it does a great job. Here's how to start stitching your own panos:

Step One:

Start by selecting the images you want combined into a panorama (or pano, for short) in the Library module. Then, go under the Photo menu, under Photo Merge, and choose **Panorama** (as seen here) or just press **Control-M (PC: Alt-M)**.

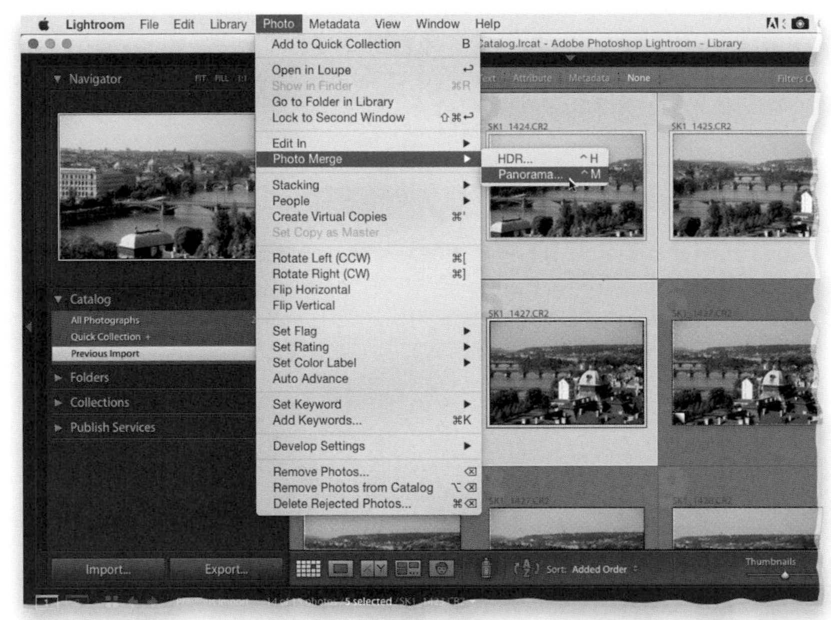

SCOTT KELBY

Step Two:

This brings up the Panorama Merge Preview dialog, and you'll see that it's creating your pano preview. Also, the dialog itself won't look wide like this—it'll have a more standard Photoshop dialog dimensions—but since it's resizable, I figured I'd just drag it way out to the right to make it more like the shape of a horizontal pano. But, you can resize it to whatever size and dimensions you like by just dragging its edges.

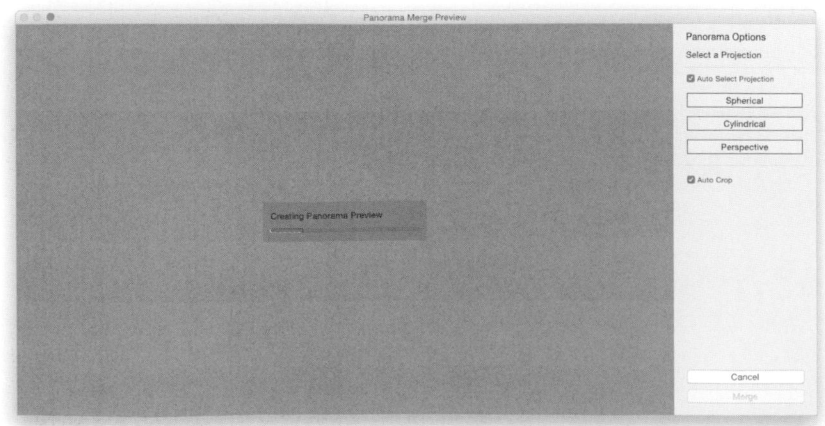

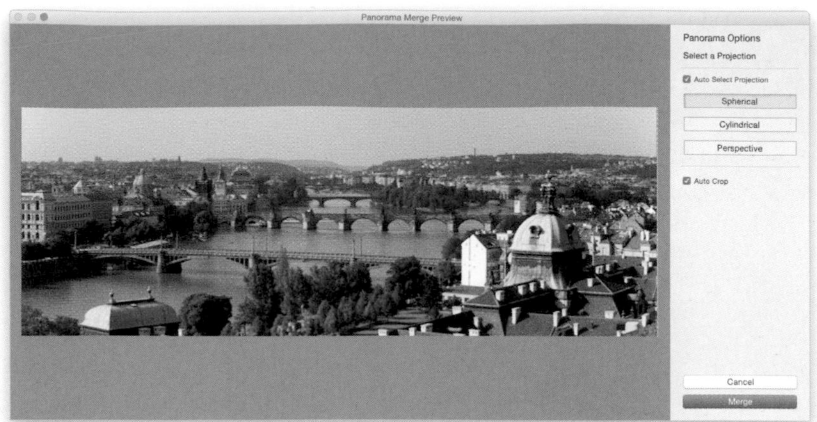

Step Three:

After a few seconds, a preview of your stitched pano will appear (as seen here). In the Panorama Options on the right, there's an option to crop away any of the white gaps that normally appear around the edges of your image from the process of putting this all together into one image (you folks that use Photoshop know those gaps all too well); if you prefer to do the cropping yourself manually, keep the Auto Crop checkbox turned off (or turn it on, then after your pano is stitched, just click on the Crop Overlay tool in the Develop module and it reveals the cropped away areas, so you can re-crop).

Panorama Options
Select a Projection
Auto Select Projection
Spherical
Cylindrical
Perspective
Auto Crop

Step Four:

At the top of the Panorama Options are your options for choosing your projection (the method Lightroom uses for creating your pano) but, honestly, just leaving the Auto Select Projection checkbox on (the default) does an awesome job of picking the right projection, and personally it's the only choice I ever use. However, here's what these three do: Perspective assumes the center image that makes up the pano is the focal point, and it does whatever it needs to do (including tweaking, warping, bending, etc.) to the other images so they fit nicely with that center one. Cylindrical seems to work best with really wide panos, and it tries to keep the height of all the images consistent so your pano doesn't wind up with the "bowtie" effect—where the ends of the pano are tall and then they angle inward toward the center image like a real bowtie. Spherical is for stitching 360° panos (of course, you'd have to have shot a 360° pano for this to work).

Continued

Step Five:

Okay, now you can click the Complete Merge button and your final pano is rendered (it takes a minute. Or two. Or more). Of course, this all holds true unless there's a problem. Luckily, the most common problem is a pretty minor one, and it's one where there's a quick fix. You'll know if you have this problem because right under the Auto Crop checkbox, you'll see a warning icon (an exclamation point in a gray circle) and it warns you that Lightroom is "Unable to match a lens profile automatically. For best results, apply the appropriate lens profile to the photos before merging." Here's basically what that means: When making a pano, Lightroom first looks at the camera data embedded into your photos. When it finds out which lens you used, it applies one of Lightroom's built-in lens profiles to help make the best quality pano it can. If it can't find a profile for your lens, or it doesn't find the lens info it needs, it still puts the pano together, but it's not quite as good as it could be. It's not awful. Just not ideal.

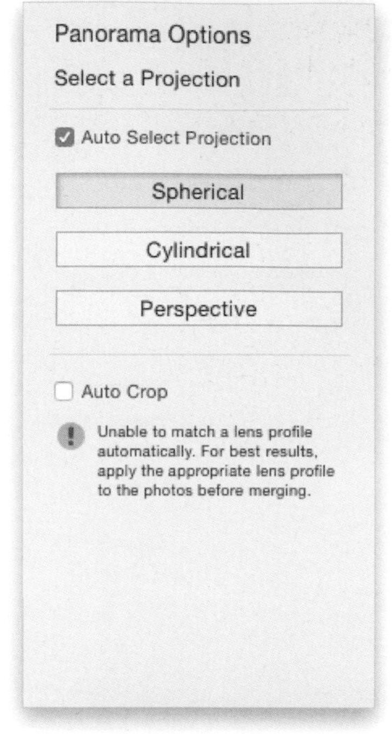

Step Six:

Here's how to fix this: All you have to do is tell Lightroom which lens you used. Here, it couldn't find a profile for the Tamron 28–300mm lens I used to make this pano. So, first, hit the Cancel button to close the dialog. Then, while your images are all still selected, go to the Develop module. With Auto Sync turned on (see Chapter 4), go to the Lens Corrections panel, click on the Profile tab (along the top of the panel), and then turn on the Enable Profile Corrections checkbox. Next, choose your lens make and model from the pop-up menus. If they don't have your exact lens profile, choose the closest one you can find. That's it. Go ahead and create your pano again and this time your results will be better.

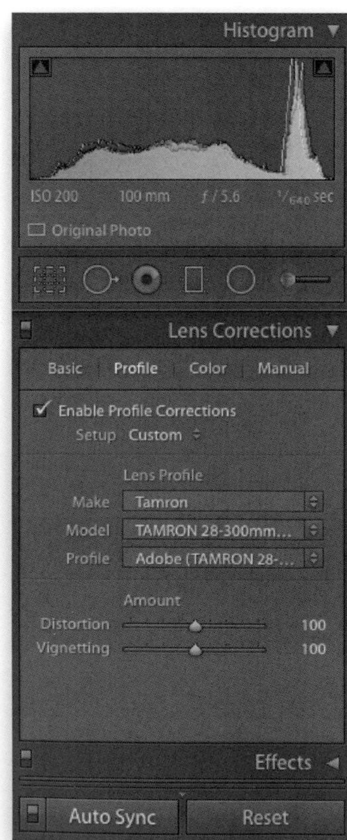

Here's where you choose the make and model of your lens

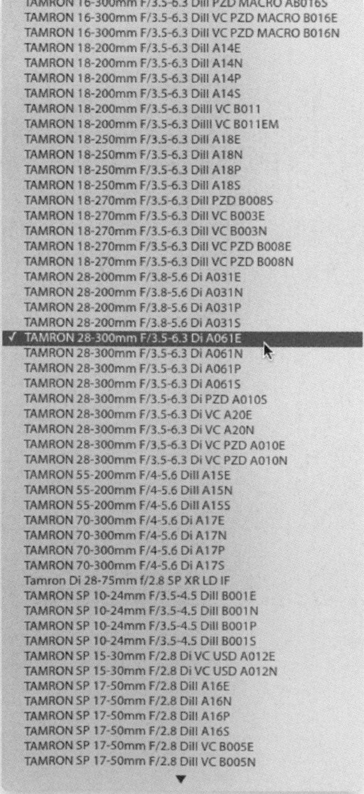

For some makes, there are a lot of built-in lens profiles

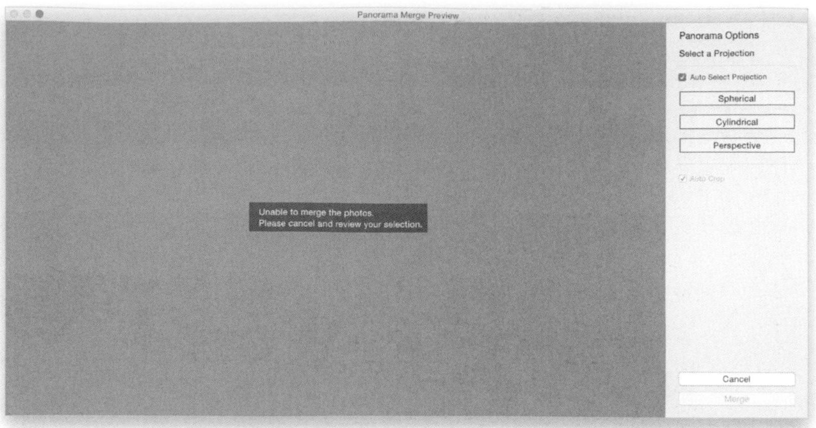

Step Seven:

Now that you know how to stitch a pano, and how to fix the most likely problem (another problem would be when it just can't stitch it together—maybe you didn't overlap each frame enough when you shot, or you tilted the camera too much so it just won't work. If that happens, it'll tell you, "I can't stitch this" [but in a much more formal way], and there's not much you can do at that point except go reshoot the pano), it's time to learn how to do it faster. To skip the Panorama Merge Preview dialog altogether, just press-and-hold the Shift key when you choose Panorama from the Photo Merge menu (or just press **Control-Shift-M [PC: Alt-Shift-M]**. It'll put the final stitched image together in the background, so you can continue doing whatever else you want to do in Lightroom, including creating another pano (yes, it can be rendering one when you work on another. Sweet!). Adobe calls this hidden dialog rendering "Headless" mode.

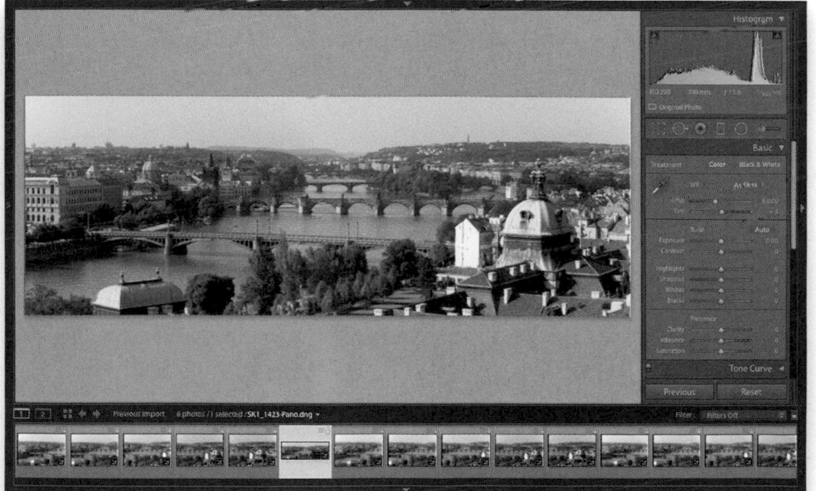

Step Eight:

When it's finished rendering in the background, your final stitched pano appears as a (RAW) DNG file in the same collection as the images you used to create the pano (provided, of course, that the images were in a collection when you started. If not, it'll appear in the same folder) and you can continue tweaking the pano like you would any regular single image. *Note:* When your pano is created, Lightroom adds the word "Pano" to the end of its filename.

TIP: Making HDR Panos

If you shot bracketed images when you were making your pano, first use the Photo Merge HDR feature to combine each set of bracketed photos into individual HDR images, then select all the compiled HDR images and choose Panorama from the Photo Merge menu to turn those into an HDR pano.

Creating 32-bit HDR Images in Lightroom

Lightroom lets you take a series of shots that were bracketed in-camera and combine them into a single 32-bit HDR image (something we used to have to jump to Photoshop for in the past). But, I want to tell you up front—it doesn't create the traditional tone-mapped HDR "look" (like Photoshop's HDR Pro does). In fact, the 32-bit HDR will look a lot like the normal exposure. But, when you edit it, this 32-bit image has increased highlight range and better low noise results when you really have to open up the shadows, so the image has a greater tonal range overall to work with from the start. Plus, the final HDR image is a RAW image.

Step One:

Select your bracketed shots in the Library module. Here, I selected three shots: the regular exposure, one shot that is two stops *underexposed*, and one shot that is two stops *overexposed*. Then, go under the Photo menu, under Photo Merge, and choose **HDR** (as shown here; or just press **Control-H [PC: Alt-H]**). *Note:* If you have Adobe Photoshop, you still have the option to jump over to it from Lightroom and use its HDR Pro feature instead. To do that, just select your images, then go under the Photo menu, under Edit In, and choose **Merge to HDR Pro in Photoshop**.

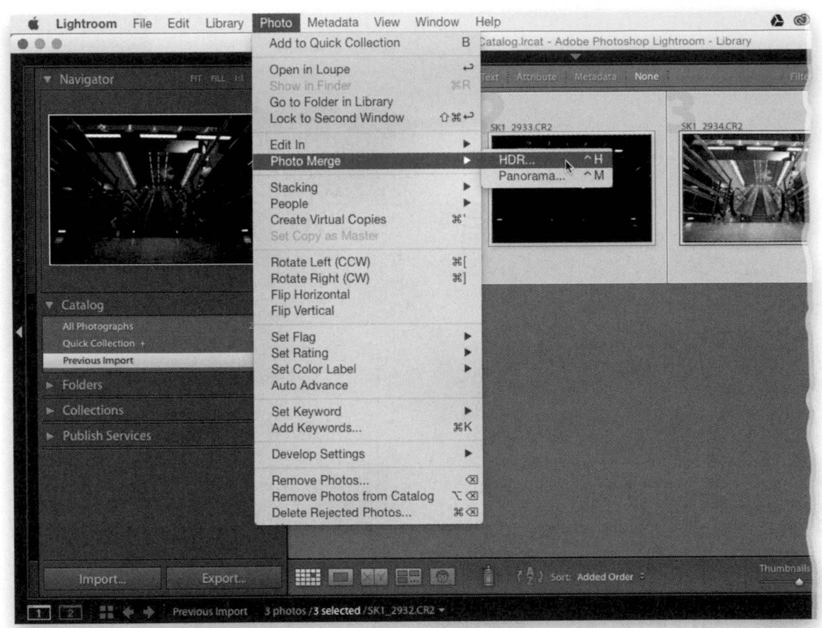

SCOTT KELBY

Step Two:

This brings up the HDR Merge Preview dialog you see here, and it looks gray like this while it's building a preview of how your combined single HDR image will look. *Note:* This dialog is resizable—just click-and-drag the edges of the dialog to resize it.

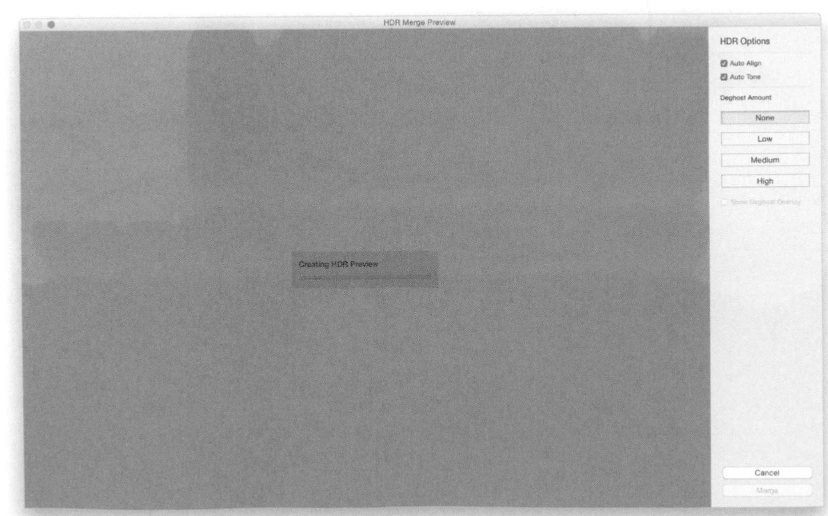

TIP: Faster HDR Processing

If you want to skip this dialog altogether and just have Lightroom combine your bracketed images into a 32-bit HDR in the background, using the settings you last used, just select the images, then press **Command-Shift-H (PC: Ctrl-Shift-H)** and it'll do the rest. Adobe calls this skipping-the-dialog feature "Headless" mode. I am not making this up.

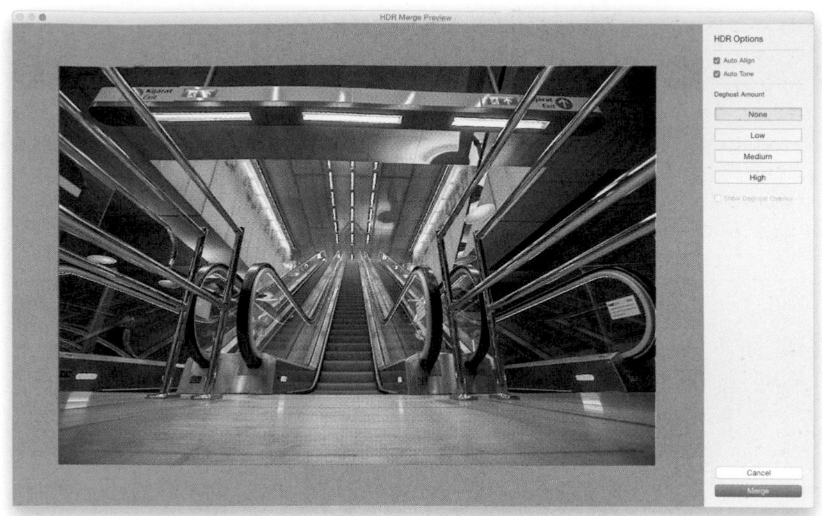

Step Three:

After 20 or 30 seconds (or so), a preview of the combined HDR image will appear. Like I said up top in the intro, it'll probably look very much like the normal exposure. But, depending on the image, I can have more detail or it can look brighter in the shadow areas, but it won't look a whole lot different (with Lightroom's brand of 32-bit HDR, you don't really see the benefits until you "tone" the image in the Develop module using the Basic panel).

TIP: Less Bracketed Image Is More

For the type of math Lightroom's HDR Photo Merge does, you don't need a lot of bracketed images. In fact, according to Adobe, not only are three bracketed images enough (one normal, one two stops under, one two stops over), you can even skip the normal exposure and just use two images and have lots of detail (versus using more bracketed images). Pretty wild, I know.

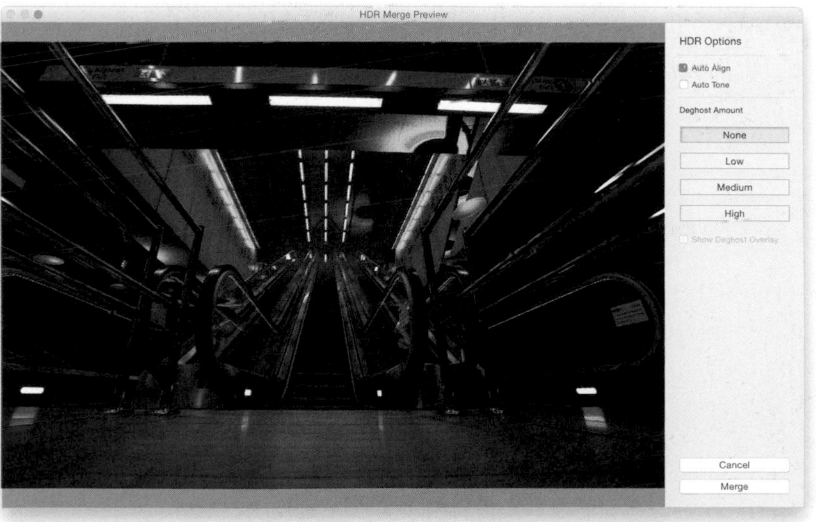

Step Four:

Before you click Merge, I would recommend turning the Auto Tone checkbox on/off to see how it looks (this is the same Auto Tone checkbox found in the Basic panel, and covered in Chapter 4). In nearly all the HDR images I've tested (and it's a bunch), Auto Tone has looked at least a little, if not a lot, better, so it's worth toggling it on/off to see what you think. You can see the difference here between this one with Auto Tone turned off and the auto-toned image in Step Three. If you ask me, that one looks quite a bit better (and I usually leave Auto Tone turned on when I'm processing my own HDR images). While we're talking checkboxes, the Auto Align checkbox is on by default, but what it helps with (mostly) are shots you hand-held while bracketing. If the alignment is off a little (or a lot), it'll fix that automatically. If you shot your HDR on tripod, it doesn't need to align anything, so you can skip it and it'll process faster.

Continued

Step Five:

The Deghosting feature helps if something was moving in your photo (like someone walking in your frame, who now appears like a fully or semi-transparent ghost, but it doesn't look cool, it looks like a mistake). By default, Deghosting is turned off (only turn it on if you have visible ghosting). To turn it on, click either Low (for mild deghosting), Medium (for more), or High (if there's a lot of ghosting in the image), and it does a pretty amazing job of basically pulling a non-moving area from one of the three bracketed exposures and seamlessly displaying it, rather than the ghosted movement. I always start with the Low setting and only move up to Medium or High if the ghosting is still visible. By the way, when you turn this on, it has to rebuild the preview again, so it'll take a few seconds (and you'll see a "Building Preview" message appear).

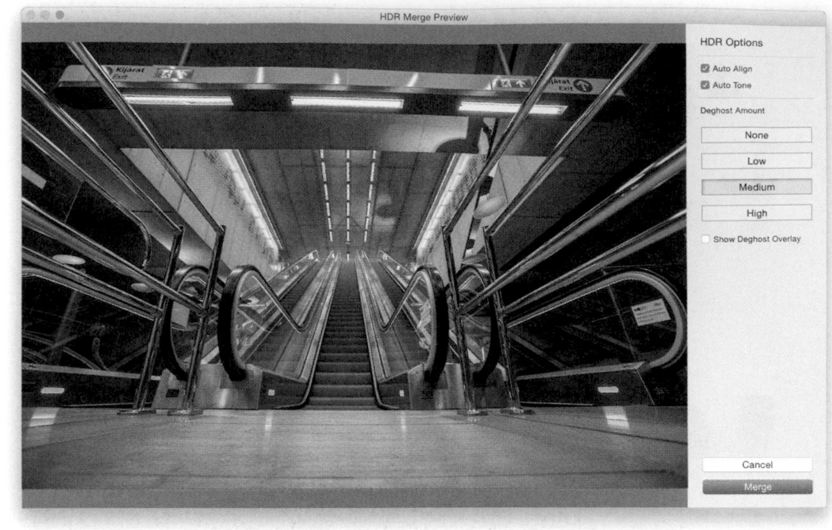

Step Six:

If you want to see the areas that are being deghosted in your image, you can turn on the Show Deghost Overlay checkbox and after a few seconds (it has to rebuild a new preview), the areas that are being deghosted will appear in red, as seen here, where I turned on Medium deghosting. There's not a lot moving in this image, which was shot on a tripod, but you can see a guy on the far left who was moving and the deghosting helped a bit here. Since it didn't do much, I turned it off again.

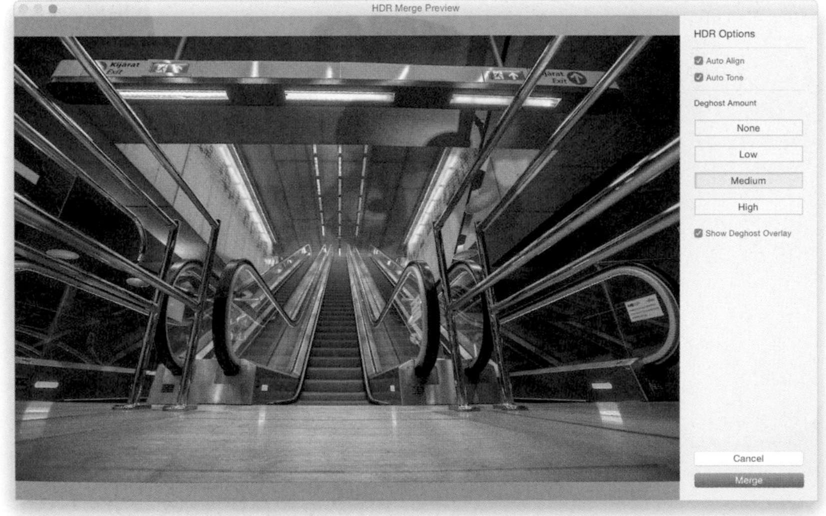

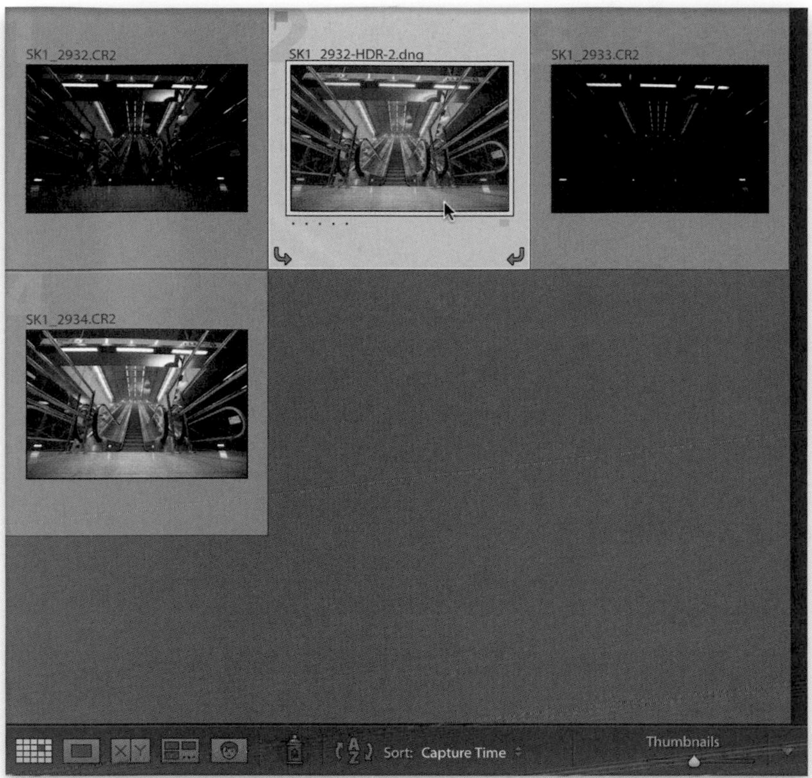

Step Seven:

So far, you're looking at a preview of how your merged HDR will look, but it's just a preview. When you're finished making your checkbox choices, click the Merge button and it starts processing the actual HDR image in the background. It takes a minute or so (depending on how many bracketed images you used, the size of your images, the speed of your computer, etc.). When its done merging, this new 32-bit HDR appears as a RAW DNG file in the same collection you started in, as seen here (you read that right—your combined HDR image is a RAW file, which is pretty amazing unto itself). By the way, if you didn't start this process from a collection, then it saves the single 32-bit HDR image in the same folder as the bracketed images. Let's go ahead and take a look at our HDR image. Click on its thumbnail and go to the Develop module.

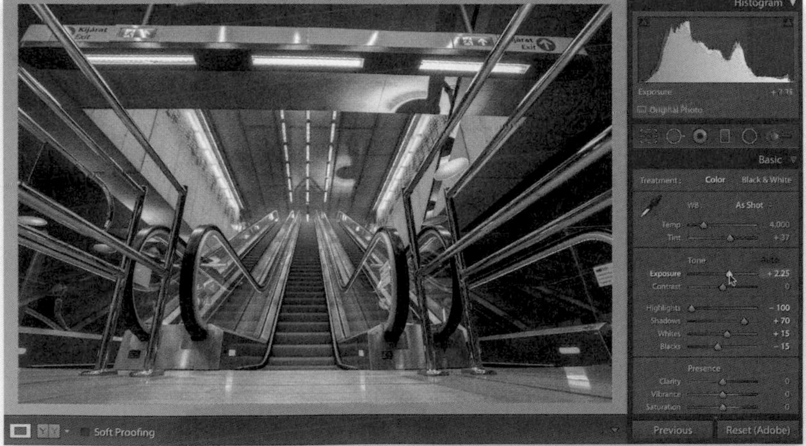

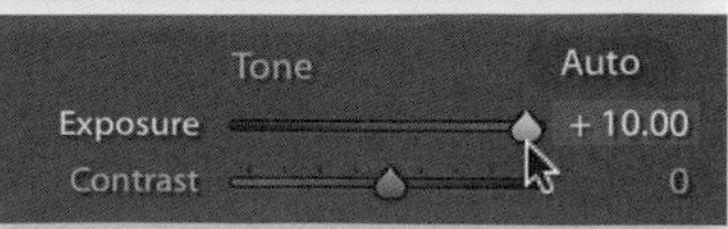

Step Eight:

Normally, you can drag the Exposure slider to +5.00 or –5.00. Well, because of the hugely expanded tonal range in 32-bit images, that range is now +10.00 (as seen in the inset) or –10.00. Hopefully, you'll never take an image whose exposure is off by 10 stops, so I'm just letting you know the 32-bit HDR image has a greatly expanded range, and that helps us by giving us some highlight headroom and better results when it comes to noise when you open up the shadow areas a lot. Aside from that stuff, if you look at the image, you can see some lens problems (take a look at the long horizontal sign up top—the whole thing is arcing down on the right). It's not fully level, either.

Continued

Step Nine:

Luckily, these lens problems are an easy fix using the Lens Corrections panel (so scroll down to it in the right-side panels). On the Basic tab, turn on the Enable Profile Corrections checkbox (Lightroom reads the camera data embedded in the file and chooses the proper lens profile for you), and just doing that helps a lot. If, for whatever reason, it can't find a matching lens profile, then click on the Profile tab and choose your lens make and model from the pop-up menus. Once that's done, back on the Basic tab, turn on the Constrain Crop checkbox and click the Auto button to apply an automatic lens correction. As you can see, it's dramatically better (compare it with the original in the previous step).

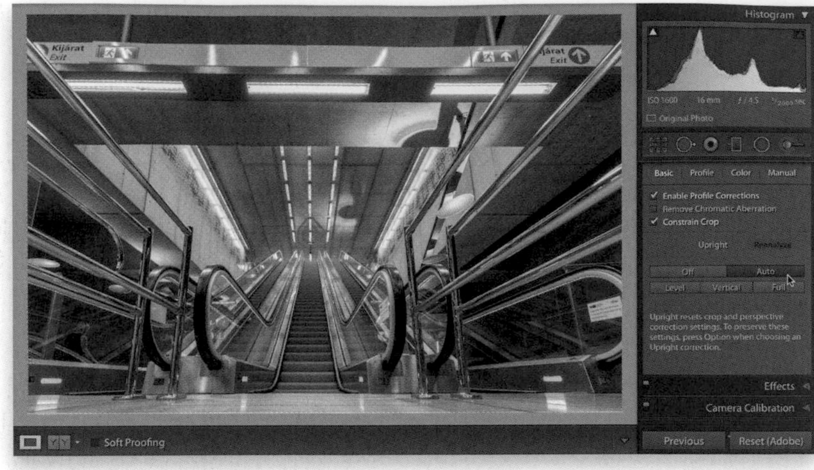

Step 10:

Okay, now we can start toning the image in the Develop module's Basic panel, and in this particular image, there's just not that much to do (especially since we already applied an Auto Tone when we created the HDR image in the first place). In fact, all I did here was to crank up the Clarity amount to +42 (chrome and metal love clarity—it really makes them "pop"), then I went to the Detail panel, and in the Sharpening section, I increased the Amount to +50. That's it, your first 32-bit HDR image in Lightroom.

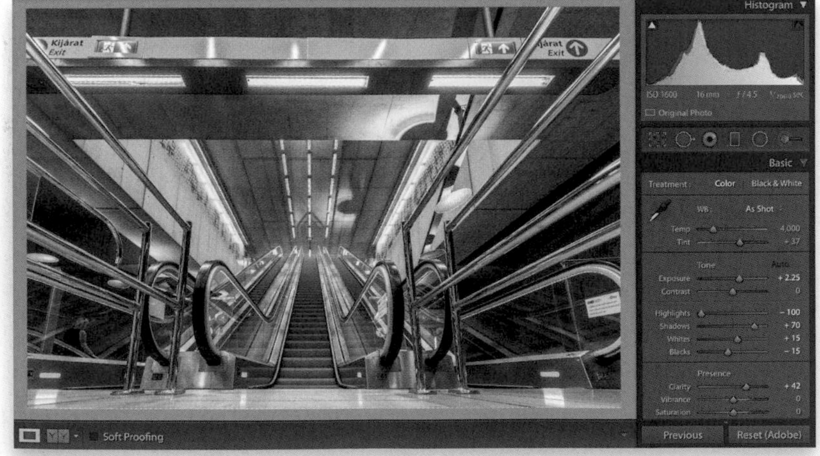

Making Streets & Cobblestones Look Wet

This is a trick I've been using for a while to make streets look wet in my travel photos, and what I love about it is that it's so simple (you just use two sliders) and yet it's amazingly effective (especially on cobblestone streets, where it look especially good, but also on just regular ol' asphalt streets, too).

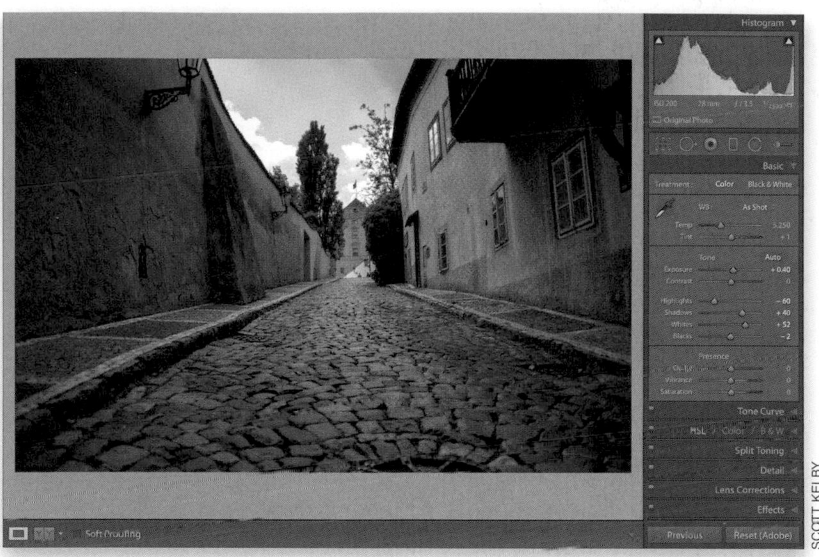

SCOTT KELBY

Step One:

In the Develop module, go ahead and make any regular tweaks to the image in the Basic panel (I Shift-double-clicked on the Whites slider and the Blacks slider to have Lightroom automatically set the white and black points. I also increased the Shadows a bit to bring out detail in the buildings, and I lowered the Highlights slider quite a bit because the sky looked really washed out). None of these adjustments have anything to do with the effect you're about to learn, but I thought you might at least want to know what the basic edits I applied to prep the photo were.

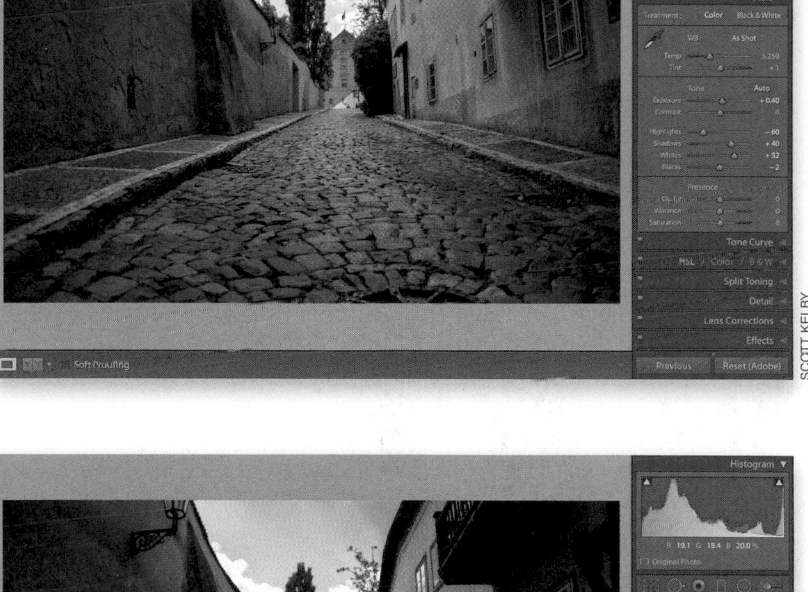

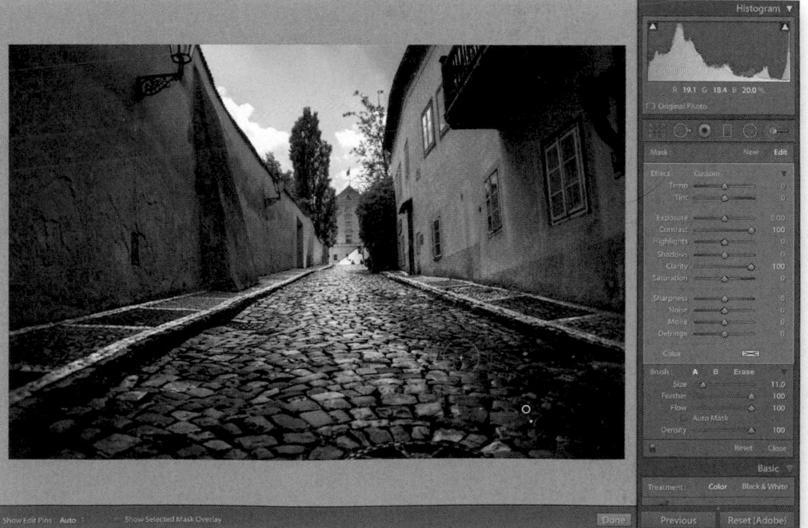

Step Two:

Click on the Adjustment Brush tool **(K)** up in the toolbar and then double-click on the word "Effects" to zero out all the sliders. You've got just two sliders to adjust here: (1) Drag the Contrast slider to 100, then drag the Clarity slider to 100, as well. That's it—that's the recipe. Now, paint over the surface you want to appear wet (here, I'm painting over the street in the foreground). As you paint, the area looks wet and appears to add reflections like an actual wet street.

Continued

Step Three:

Don't forget to paint over the sidewalk and curb, as well. Also, if you paint over the street and it doesn't look "wet" enough, click the New button at the top-left corner of the Adjustment Brush panel and start painting over the same area, but start in a different part of the street (that way, you're stacking this second pass of the look over the first coat of "wet"). By the way, if for any reason the street looks too bright from applying that much Clarity, just lower either the Exposure slider or Highlights slider a little bit for each pin, so it looks to have about the same brightness overall (here, I lowered the Highlights slider to –16. I tried lowering Exposure, as well, but lowering just the Highlights looked better to me).

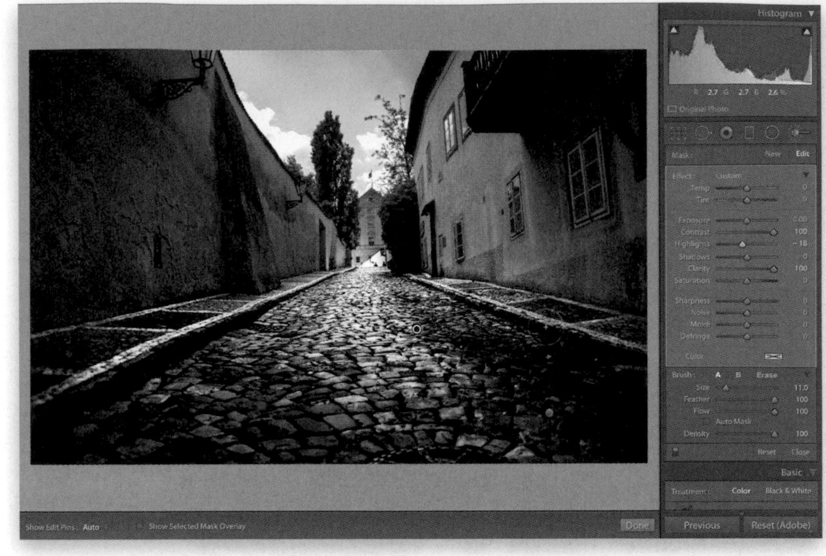

Step Four:

This technique looks particularly great on cobblestone streets, but it also works for most regular paved streets. I did a before/after here, so you can see an example. Okay, that's it. Instant wet streets.

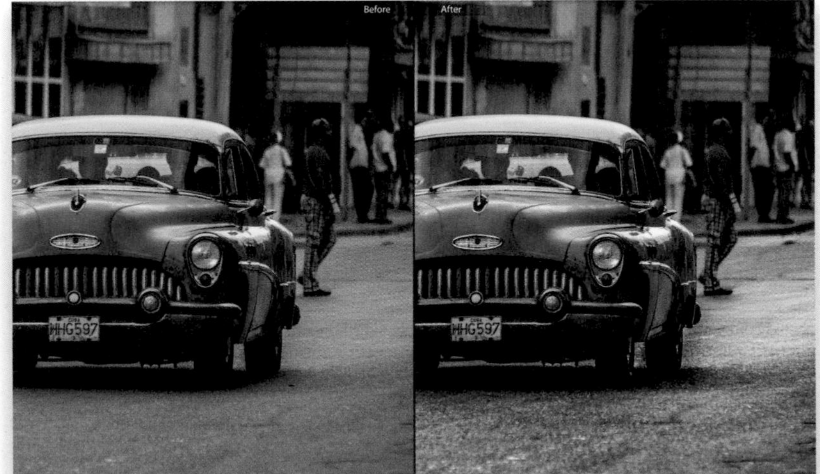

SCOTT KELBY

Lightroom Killer Tips > >

▼ Get Different Versions of Photos Without Making Virtual Copies

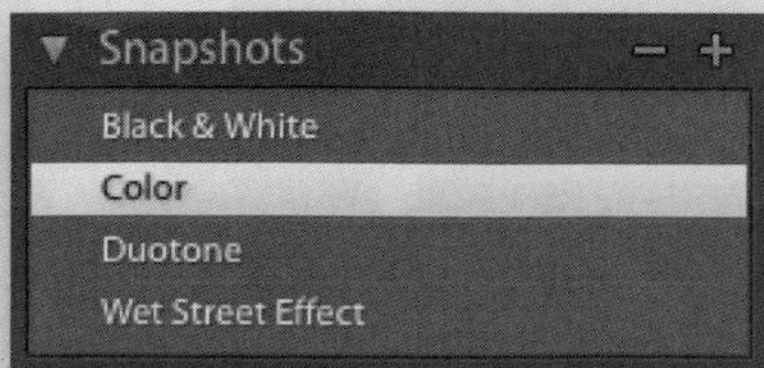

Think of snapshots as another way to have one-click access to multiple versions of your photo. When you're working in the Develop module and see a version of your photo you like, just press **Command-N (PC: Ctrl-N)** and how your photo looks at that moment is saved to your Snapshots panel (you just have to give it a name). So, that way, you could have a B&W version as a snapshot, one version as a duotone, one version in color, one with an effect, and see any of those in one click, without having to scroll through the History panel to try to figure out where each look is.

▼ Create White Balance Presets for JPEG and TIFF Images

I mentioned in Chapter 4 that with JPEG or TIFF images the only White Balance preset available to you is Auto. However, here's a cool workaround to get you more choices: Open a RAW image and only make one edit—choose the White Balance preset Daylight. Now, save just that change as a preset and name it White Balance Daylight. Then do that for each of the White Balance presets, and save them as presets. When you now open

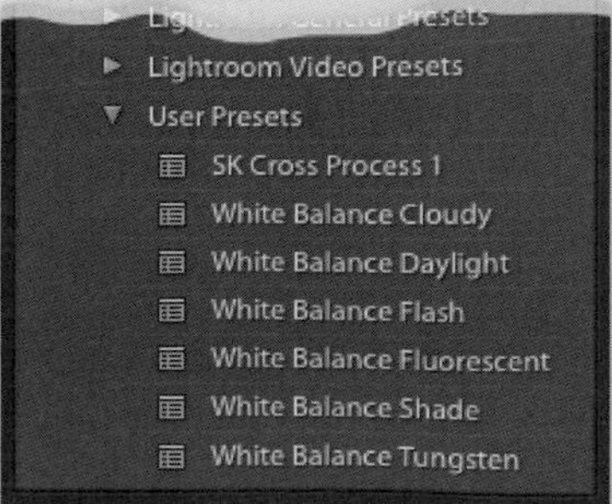

a JPEG or TIFF image, you'll have these one-click White Balance presets you can use to get a similar look.

▼ Using the HSL/Color/B&W Panel? Color Correct Your Photo First

If you're going to be using the B&W panel to make your B&W conversion, before you go there, start by making the color image look right first (balance the exposure, blacks, contrast, etc., first,

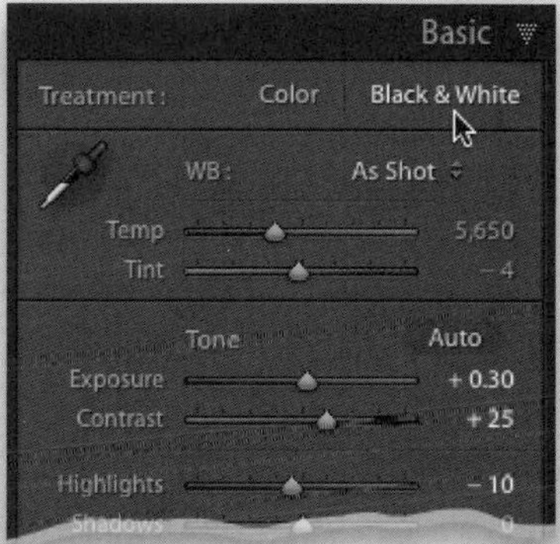

then you'll get better results from the B&W panel).

▼ Getting a Film Grain Look

If you want to simulate the look of film grain, there's a feature that does just that in the Effects panel (to really see the grain, you'll first want to zoom in to a 100% [1:1] view). The higher you drag the Grain Amount, the more grain is added to your photo (I don't generally go over 40 as a maximum, and I usually try to stay between 15 and 30). The Size slider lets you choose how large the grain appears (I think it looks more realistic at a fairly small size) and the Roughness slider lets you vary the consistency of the grain (the farther to the right you drag the Roughness slider, the more it's varied). Lastly, Grain tends to disappear a bit when you make a print, so while the amount may look right onscreen, don't be surprised if it's barely visible in print. So, if your final output is print, you might have to use a little more grain than you think you should.

▼ Painting Duotones

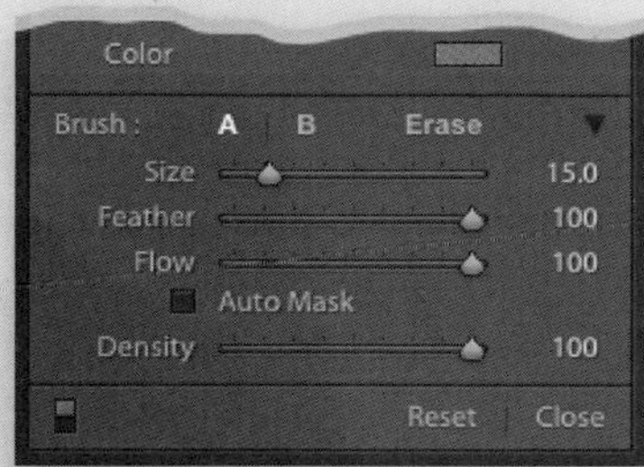

Another way to create a duotone effect from your B&W photo is to click on the Adjustment Brush, and then in the options that pop down, choose **Color** from the Effect pop-up menu. Now, click on the Color swatch to bring up the color picker, choose the color you want, and close the picker. Then, turn off the Auto Mask checkbox and paint over the photo, and as you do, it will retain all the detail and just apply the duotone color.

▼ Getting a Before/After of Your B&W Tweaking

You can't just press the **\ (backslash) key** to see your before image after you've done the edits to your B&W image, because you're starting with a color photo (so pressing \ just gives you the color original again). There are two ways to get around this: (1) As soon as you convert to black and white, press **Command-N (PC: Ctrl-N)** to save the conversion as a snapshot. Now you can get back to your B&W original anytime by clicking on that snapshot in the Snapshots panel. Or, (2) after you convert to black and white, press **Command-' (PC: Ctrl-')** to make a virtual copy, and then do your editing to the copy. That way you can use \ to compare the original conversion with any tweaks you've been making.

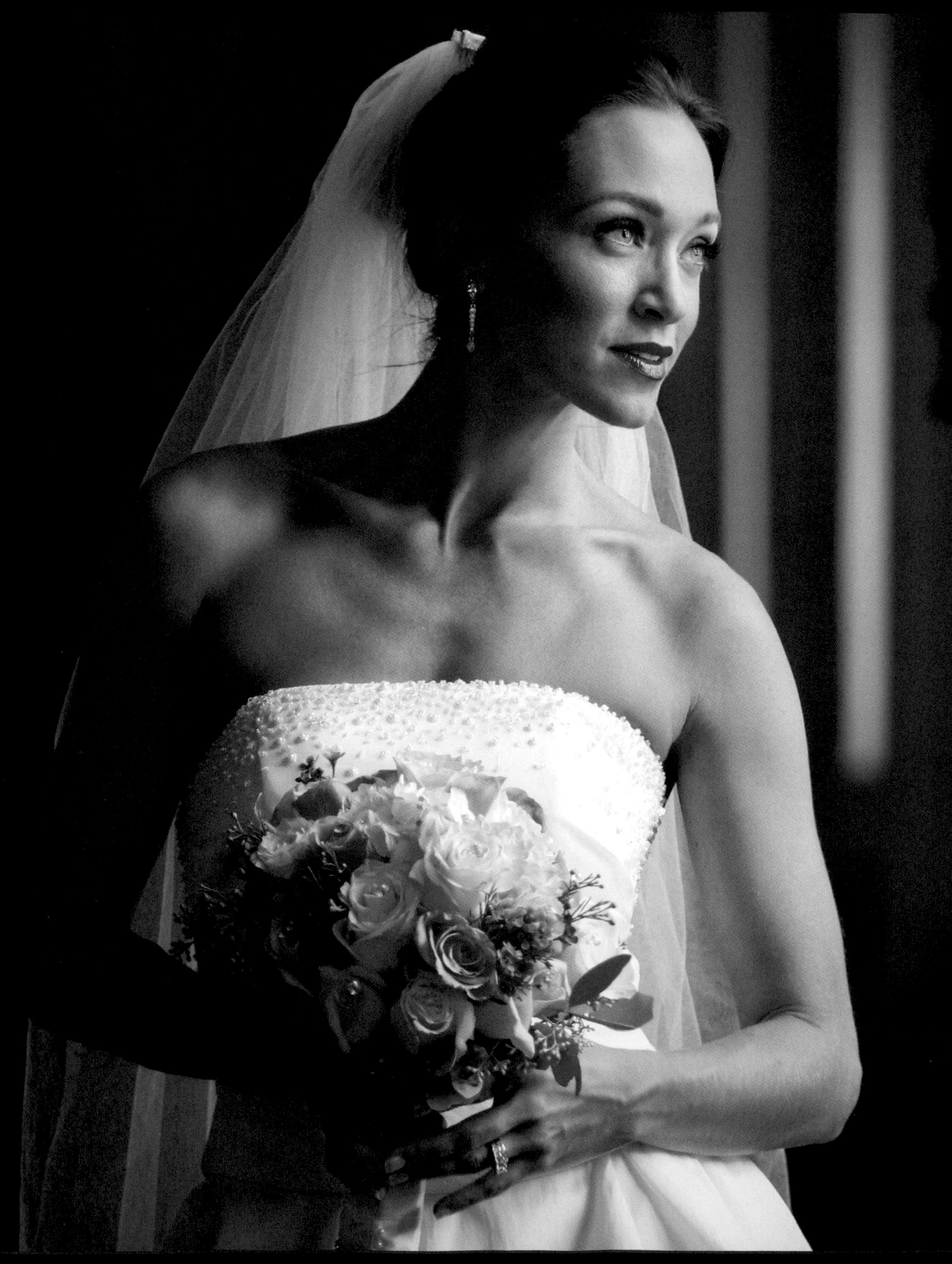

Photo by Scott Kelby | Exposure: 1/50 sec | Focal Length: 145 mm | Aperture Value: ƒ/2.8

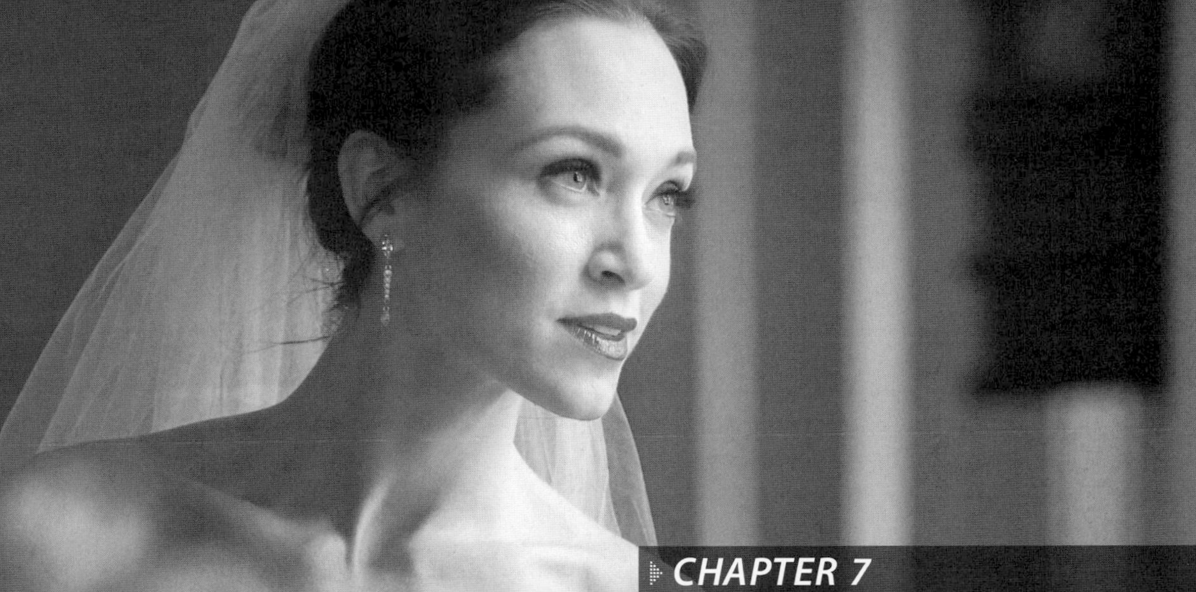

CHAPTER 7

LIGHTROOM FOR MOBILE
using the mobile app

This is the first version of this book that has a chapter in it on using the Lightroom app for mobile devices, and I think the reason I waited so long to include one is that there actually was no Lightroom mobile app before now, but honestly, that's never stopped me from filling pages of a chapter with totally made up stuff. Now, I kind of hate to admit this, especially in print, but back when I wrote the Lightroom 2 version of this book (I think it was back in 2008), I had a chapter named "Adjustments, Shadows, Saturation, Filters, Autosync, Reset, and Temperature" and I was pretty psyched about it, but my editors said the name was way too long, and so we'd have to use an acronym instead because it would be too clumsy for the reader, but then when my editors actually created the acronym, they came to my office all upset, and I knew something smelled as soon as they walked in and said the acronym made for an uncomfortable phrase. So I said, "Well, that really stinks," and they all started giggling and I got really cheesed about it. Anyway, the book was due to go to press, so I made a deal with them to shorten the name to just "Grid, Adjustments, Saturation, Shadows, and Yellow" and they were okay with that, but honestly, I didn't have any real content that matches those topics (Yellow? Really?), so I just kind of typed a bunch of gibberish in that chapter (I made up words, and even copied-and-pasted entire paragraphs of Latin in there). I made up names for features that are not even in Lightroom (like the Air Biscuit), but the program was so new nobody really caught on. I fixed it in the Lightroom 3 book, and since there was no harm done, can we just keep this between us? I don't want anyone to get wind of it. ;-)

Four Really Cool Things About Lightroom on Your Mobile Device

It's something Lightroom users have been begging for, for years and it's finally here—a version of Lightroom for your iPad, iPhone, and Android device. Well, I kind of feel like it's more of an extension of the regular desktop (computer) version, but it's a really handy one that lets you do a lot of the main things we use the desktop version for. Plus, it's "free," and that's a hard price to beat. (*Note:* As of the writing of this book, Lightroom is only available on Android phones, not Android tablets. But, of course, that could change at any time if/when Adobe releases an Android tablet version.)

(#1) You Can Sync Collections: While you're working in Lightroom on your computer, you get to choose which collections you want synced to Lightroom on your mobile device. If you make changes in Lightroom on your computer, it automatically sends those changes to those synced images in your collections in Lightroom on your mobile device (and vice versa—make a change in Lightroom on your mobile device, and it sends those changes back to your computer). But, it's not just syncing—you can create new collections, organize collections, put images on your phone or tablet into collections, you can add Pick flags, star ratings, and more from your mobile device.

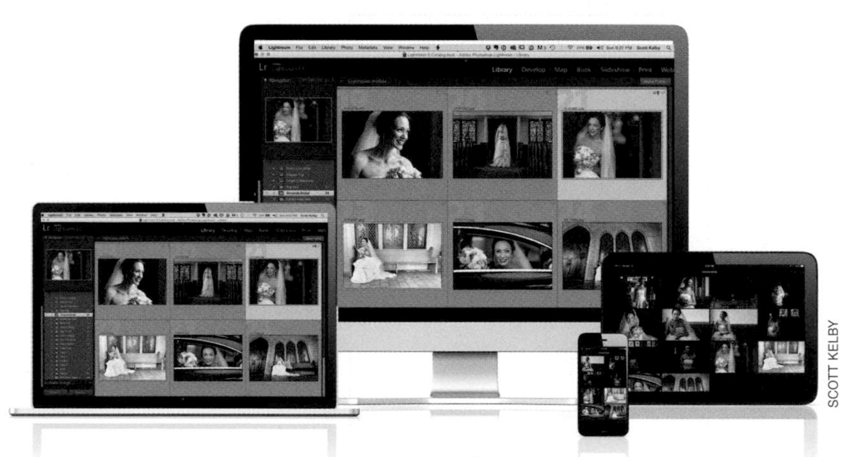

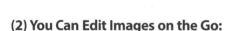

SCOTT KELBY

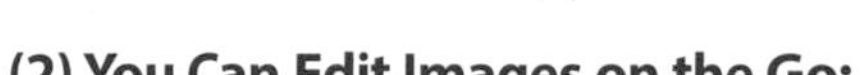

(2) You Can Edit Images on the Go: Lightroom on your mobile device has the same Basic panel as Lightroom on your computer built right in, so you can edit your images right on your mobile device (even RAW images), and any changes you make there can be sent back to Lightroom on your computer. It has the same sliders, with the same names and the same math underlying it all. There is no Adjustment Brush, but this is supposed to be "Four Really Cool Things About Lightroom on Your Mobile Device," so forget I brought that up. Next!

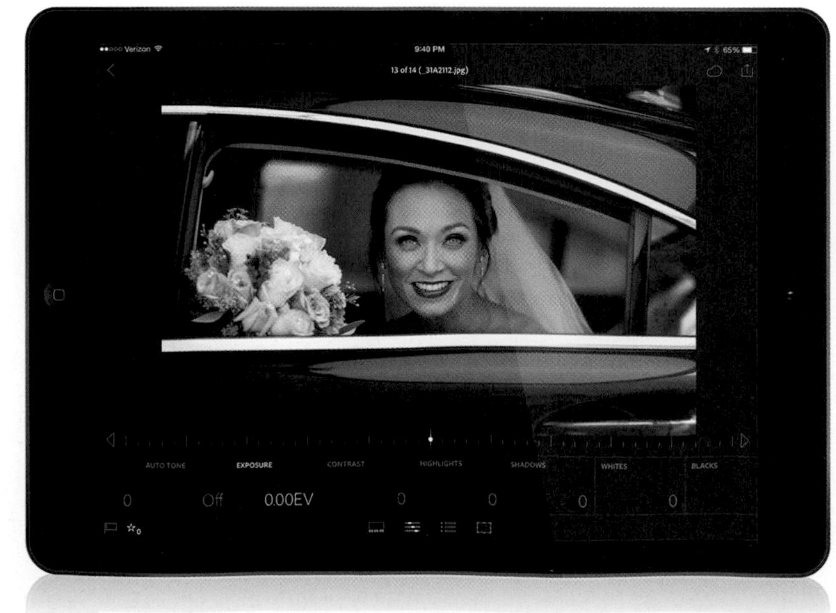

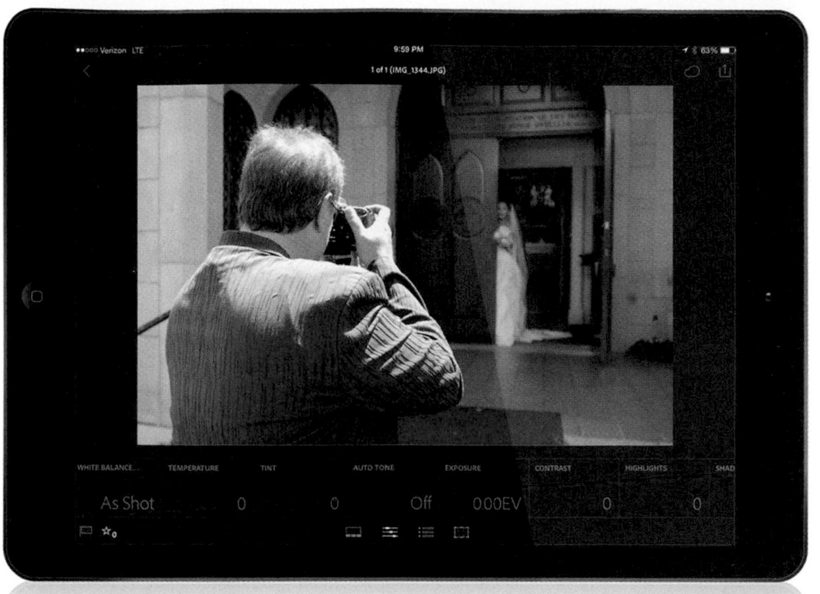

(#3) You Can Use It Without Using Lightroom on Your Computer

You don't have to sync your images and all that stuff. You can just use Lightroom on your mobile device to import and edit the images you took with your cell phone camera or your tablet camera—no matter how ridiculous it looks holding up a huge tablet to take photos (wait…who said that?!). So, basically, you can apply the editing power of Lightroom to images already on your mobile device (or what the rest of the world just calls their phone).

(#4) You Can Share What You're Working On, While You're Working On It

One of my favorite features lets anyone you choose not only see a particular collection (you send them a web link to it and, as long as they have a web browser, they can see it), but they can also add Pick flags, assign star ratings, or even leave a written comment on a photo, and all of this feedback comes straight back to you in Lightroom on your computer. You can be in Cincinnati, they can be in Venice, and the two of you are collaborating over a shoot. Seriously, how amazing is that? They don't need an Adobe account; they don't need anything special—just a web browser and an Internet connection. Of course, there's more to Lightroom on your mobile device than just these four things, but these four things make a great case for why you'd want to extend Lightroom on your computer's power and reach by adding this mobile version to your workflow when you want it. The rest of this chapter is about how to put Lightroom on your mobile device to use (luckily, it's pretty easy because you've already learned about collections, and Pick flags, and the Basic panel, and all that stuff. Now, all you're doing is learning how to do the stuff you already know, but on a touchscreen mobile device). Okay, let's get to it!

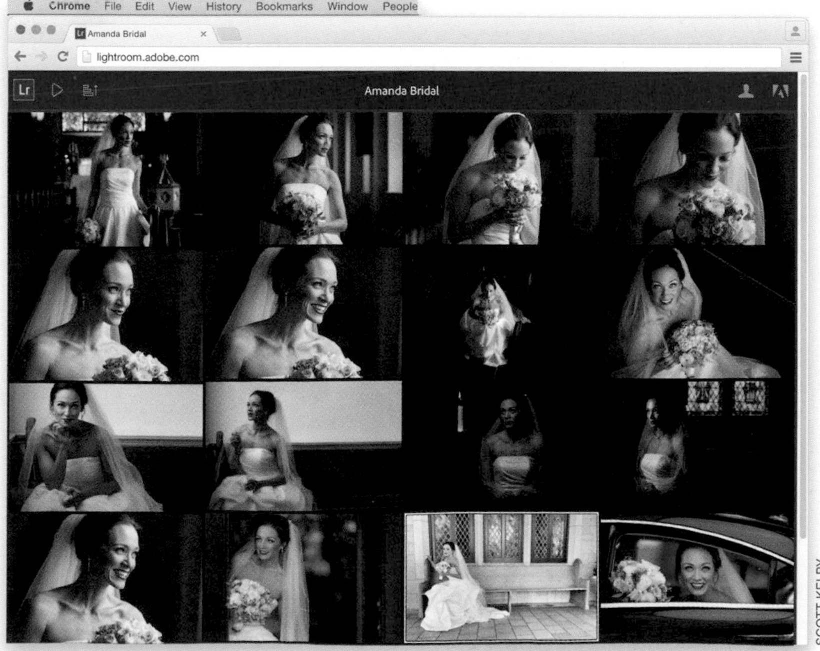

SCOTT KELBY

Setting Up Lightroom on Your Mobile Device

This is really easy, but kind of "pain-in-the-butt," stuff because you have to log into your Adobe account in a couple of different places. But, what's nice is, once you've done it, you're done, and it really doesn't get in the way again. Here's how to get up and running quickly:

Step One:

You start in regular ol' Lightroom on your computer by going to Lightroom's Preferences (**Command-,** [comma; **PC: Ctrl-,**]) and clicking on the Lightroom Mobile tab (it's the last tab on the far right, as seen here). Now, just click on the Sign In button and then, in the Lightroom Mobile window, enter your Adobe ID and password. If you don't have an Adobe ID yet (it's just a simple user account), you can sign up for one (it's free) by clicking on the Get an Adobe ID link below the Sign In button. It takes you to another window where you can create your account (no credit card info; just your name, address, and stuff like that).

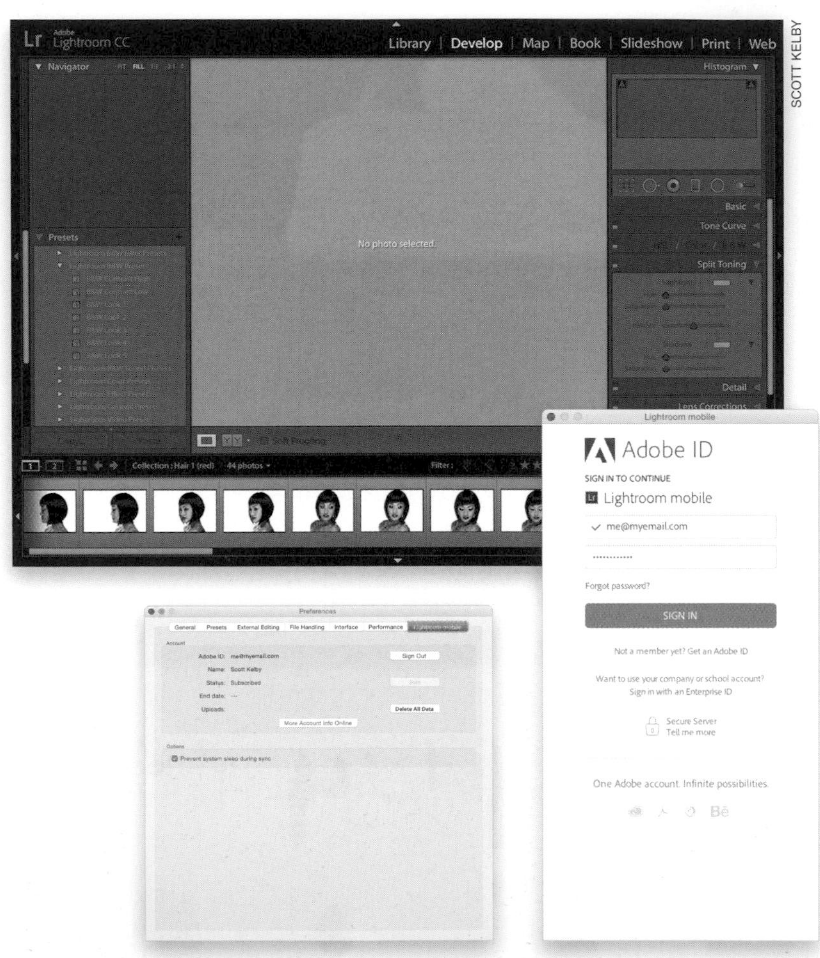

Step Two:

Okay, this next part may win the international "I hide commands in the most unlikely places" award for Adobe, but if you move your cursor over the Lightroom logo (up in the left-hand corner of the window), a little white down-facing triangle appears, indicating that there's something that happens if you click there. So, go ahead and click there and the Activity panel will appear. At the top, there's a control for turning the Sync with Lightroom Mobile feature on/off. Make sure that's turned on (if it's not, just click on it to turn it on), and now you're good to go.

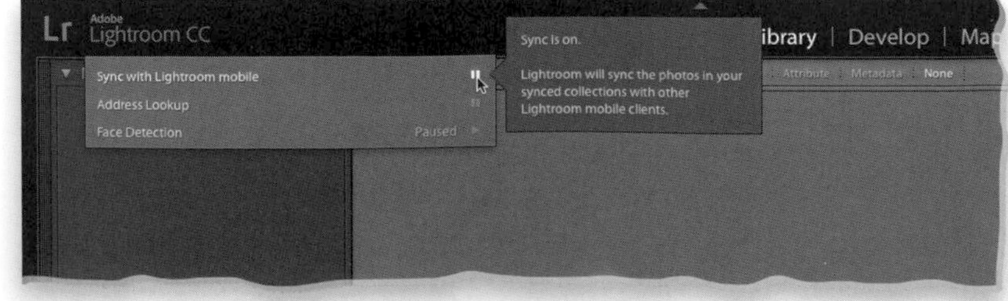

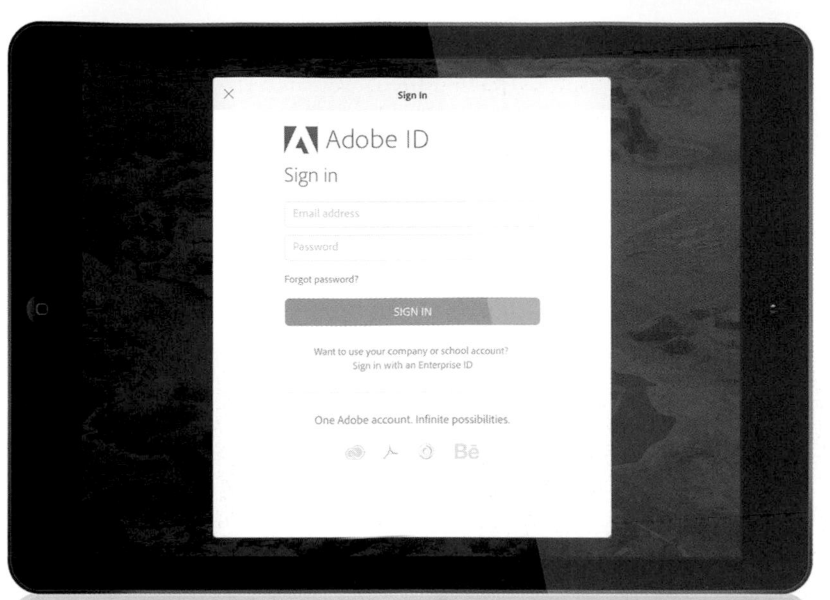

Step Three:

Now, go to your iPad, iPhone, or Android device and download the Lightroom app (it's free). When you launch it, it's going to ask you to sign in with your Adobe ID (this is how it knows Lightroom on your computer and Lightroom on your mobile device are linked to each other). At this point, you haven't imported any photos and we haven't chosen which collections to sync with Lightroom on your mobile device, so there's nothing there yet (but there will be in a page or two). For now, I just wanted you to know where your options and preferences are located.

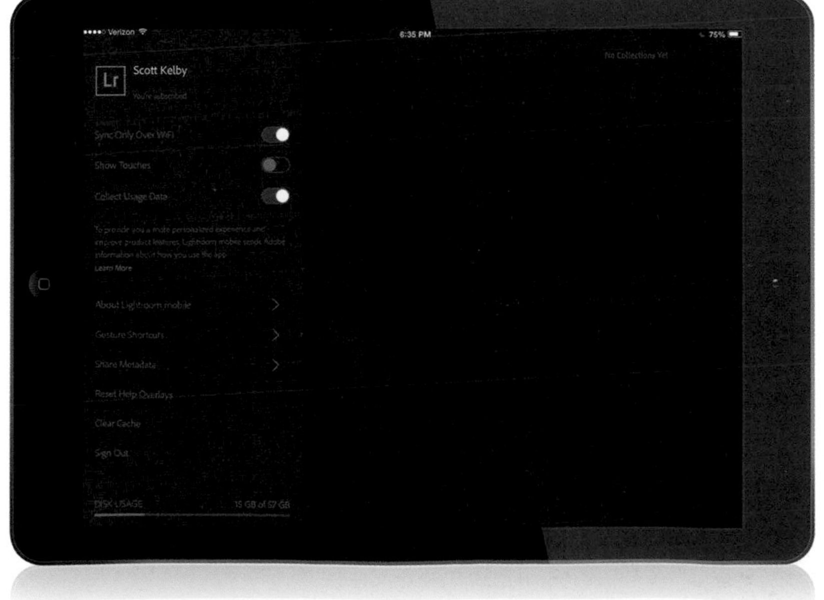

Step Four:

When you launch Lightroom on your mobile device, you'll be in the Collections view and you'll see the little LR logo in the top-left corner of the screen. Tap on it and the Sidebar slides out from the left side with your options, including whether you choose to sync photos just over wireless or whether you're okay with them syncing over cellular, too (which might affect your data plan charges). Turning on Show Touches shows a red "dot" when you tap the screen (helpful when doing a Lightroom demo from your mobile device or teaching someone how to use Lightroom on their mobile device for the first time). Also, as Adobe continues to develop this app, they collect anonymous data to help them see how people are using it. If you'd prefer they didn't collect that data from you, you can turn off Collect Usage Data. The rest are options for help, signing out of your account, and so on. To hide that Sidebar panel again, just tap on it. Okay, let's get some photos in here!

Getting Images Into Lightroom on Your Device (and Working with Collections)

Believe it or not, all the hard parts are done—now comes the fun stuff, which is telling Lightroom on your computer which collections you want access to over in Lightroom on your mobile device. Once you tell it which ones, it does the rest behind-the-scenes. Plus, we'll look at how to manage your collections, move images, play slide shows, and a bunch of other important stuff you'll want to know right up front, and it all works the same on your iPhone, iPad, or Android device.

Step One:

We start in Lightroom on your computer (once you're signed in with your Adobe ID). Go to the Collections panel and you'll see a gray box to the left of each collection. We use these boxes to choose which collections get synced over to Lightroom on our mobile device—just click in a box and a little sync icon appears in that box (kind of like a checkmark; shown circled here in red), and that collection is now automatically copied over to Lightroom on your mobile device. If you look in the top left of the thumbnail grid, you'll see the sync icon and "Lightroom mobile" appear, and a little sync icon appears in the top-right corner of each thumbnail of a synced image, once again, just letting you know that the images in this collection are synced.

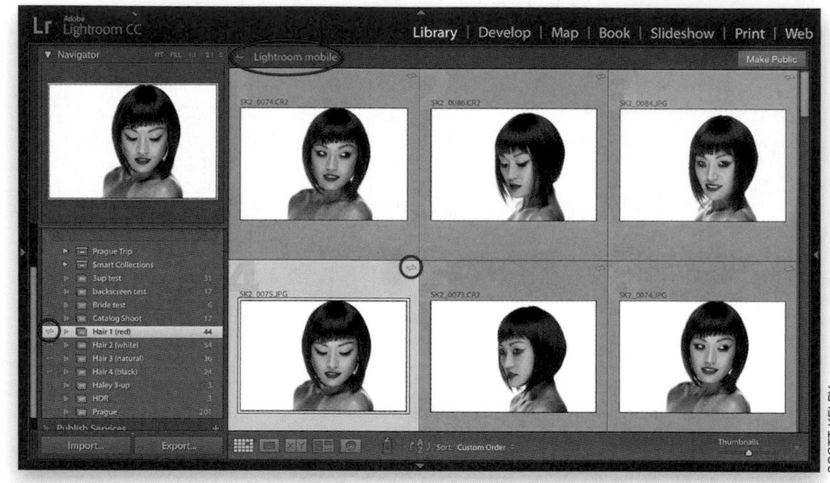

Step Two:

Luckily for us, when it syncs these images, it doesn't send the full high-resolution RAW or JPEG photo over to our mobile devices, or we'd run out of storage space pretty quickly. Instead, it sends a smart preview (stored in the cloud), which still looks great, and which we can still edit, but at a fraction of the size of the full-resolution image (see Chapter 1 for more on smart previews). Okay, let's head over to Lightroom on your mobile device to see if our four collections made it over there (I turned on the checkboxes beside four collections, as seen above). On my mobile device, in the Collections view (kind of like the homepage), if you look at the top of the screen, it says "4 Collections with 158 Photos" (or just "4 Collections," depending on the device).

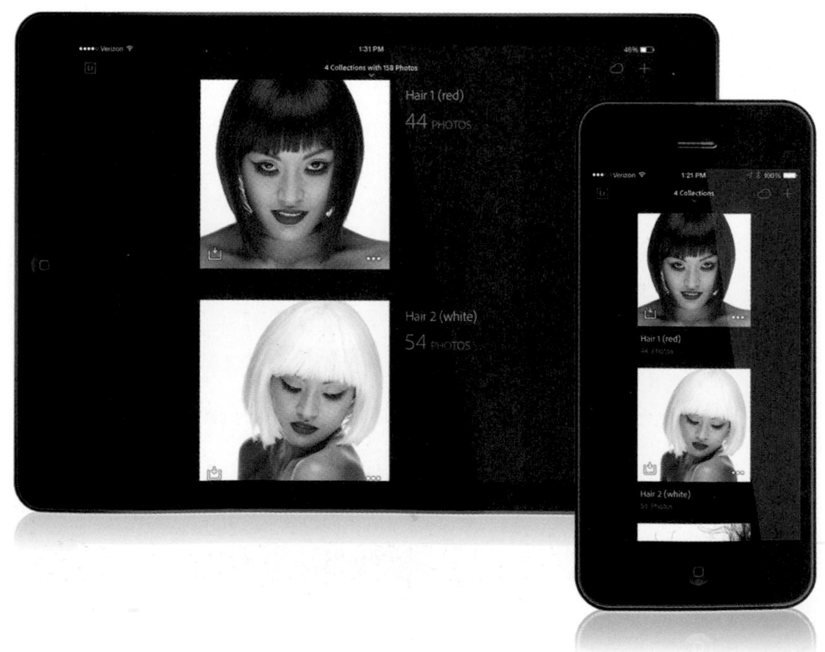

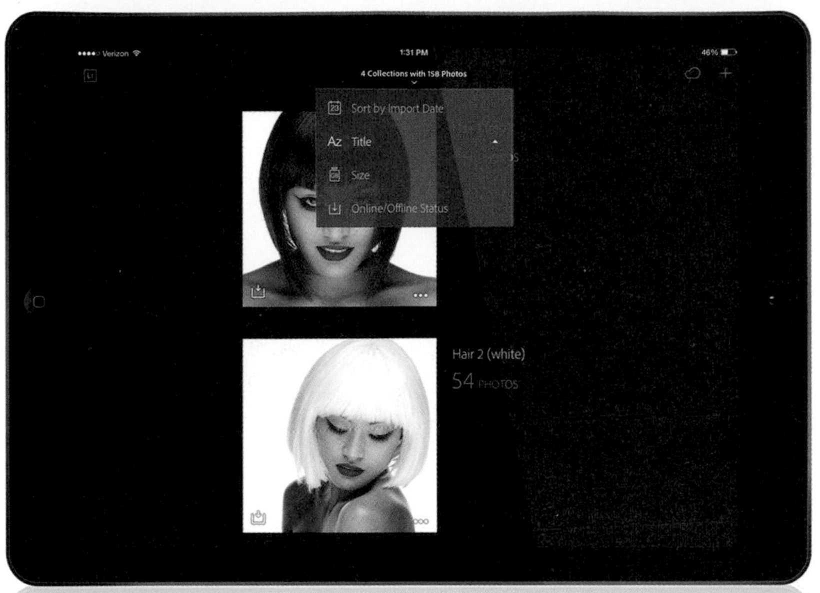

Step Three:

If you tap directly on that "4 Collections," a pop-up menu appears with sorting options (you can sort the collections by the date you imported them, by their name, or by the file size of the images in each collection). If you tap on any of those sort options, a little white up-facing triangle appears to the right of that option, which lets you choose ascending or descending for your sort order (in other words, if you chose Sort by Import Date, do you want the collection at the top to be the most recently taken photos, or do you want the oldest photos at the top?). Just tap on that arrow to toggle back and forth between the two options.

Note: Lightroom on your mobile device only works with collections, not folders. So, if you have a folder you want synced, you have to make it a collection first by clicking on it in the Folders panel and dragging it to the Collections panel. Now, you can sync that collection.

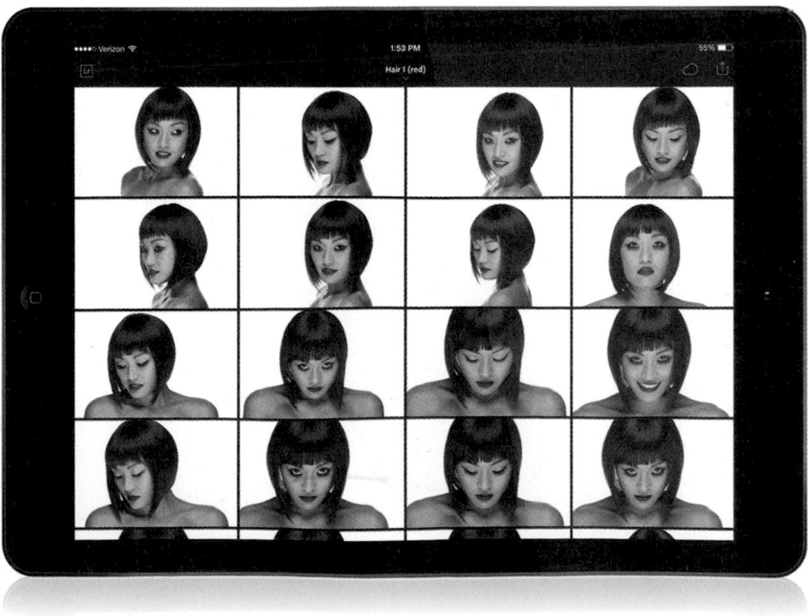

Step Four:

To see the images inside any collection, just tap on a collection and it displays those images in Grid view (as seen here). To scroll through all the images in the collection, just swipe up or down.

Continued

Step Five:
To see one of the images in the grid larger, just tap on it and it zooms up to the size you see here (this is called Loupe view), and it displays the filename at the top of the screen (along with how many images are in this current collection). It also displays the EXIF camera data up near the top-left corner of the screen, much like you'd see in Lightroom on your computer, a histogram of the image up near the top-right corner, and down below the image are the editing controls (more on these in a few moments). Sharing options (along with some other options) are found up in the top-right corner. To see the next image in the grid at this full-size view, just swipe to the left (or to the right to see the previous image).

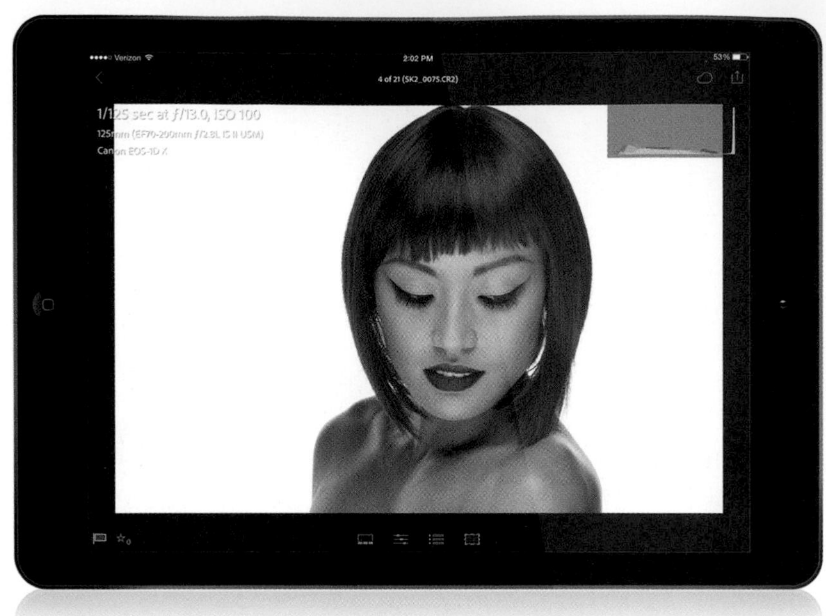

TIP: Zooming In with Lightroom Mobile
To zoom in to a tighter view, just double-tap the screen; same thing to zoom back out. You can also "pinch" the screen to zoom in/out.

Step Six:
If you want hide all that extra Loupe view info and just see your image presented full screen, tap once on your image and it all quickly hides away (as seen here). Of course, you can still swipe left/right to see more images in this collection. To return to the regular Loupe view, just tap the screen once. To return to Grid view, once you're back in regular Loupe view, just tap the Back arrow at the top left of the screen (you can see that arrow in the previous step). So, to get from this full-screen view back to Grid view, it's two taps: (1) tap on the image once to return to Loupe view, (2) then tap the Back arrow.

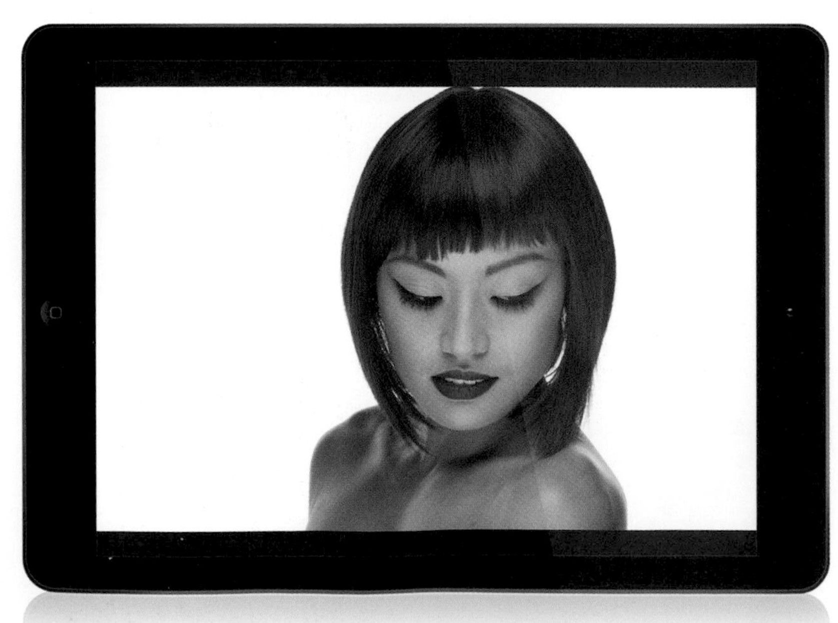

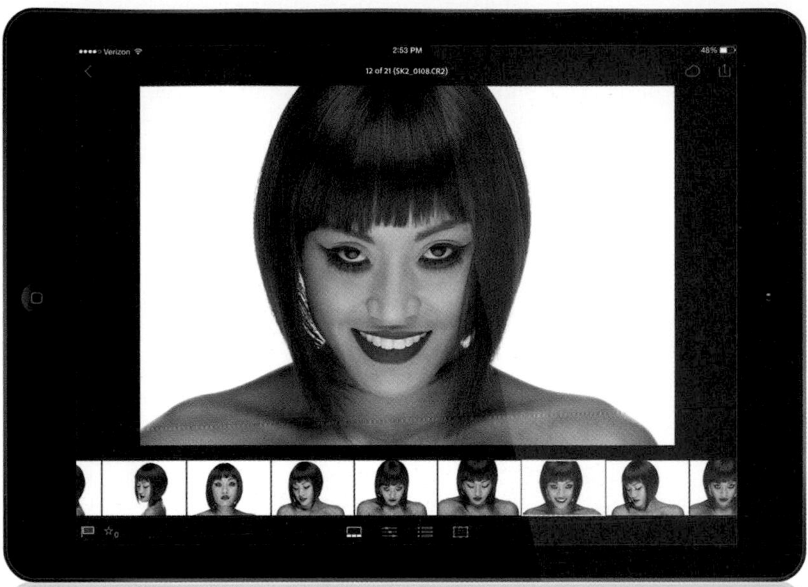

Step Seven:

When you're in regular Loupe view, there are four icons beneath your image. Tap on the Filmstrip icon (the first one on the left) to bring up the Filmstrip below your image with all the thumbnails for the images in that collection. To hide the Loupe view extras here, just tap with two fingers to cycle through the EXIF data and histogram (as seen here, where I've hidden them both). You can scroll through the images in this Filmstrip by swiping left or right directly on it. To hide it, either tap the Filmstrip icon again or tap on the image to enter full-screen view (which, again, hides all the interface controls).

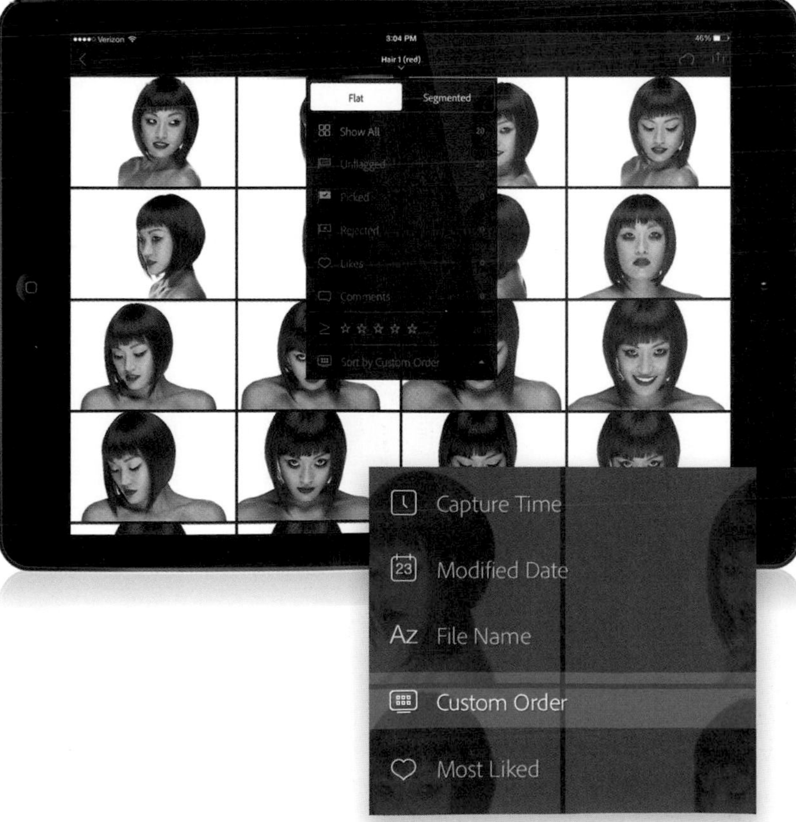

Step Eight:

When you're back in the Grid view, if you tap on the name of the collection at the top of the screen, you'll get a pop-up menu with a bunch of filtering choices (which we're going talk more about in just a minute, in the next project). For now, look at the last option at the bottom of that menu (mine says, "Sort by Custom Order" here, but yours will show whatever you have selected in Lightroom on your computer). If you tap on that sort option, it brings up another pop-up menu (seen here in the overlay), where you can choose the sort order of these images. If this menu looks familiar, it's because it's kind of like the one for sorting collections in Collections view, but there's another choice here, called "Custom Order." Now, I have good news and bad news, and I'll start with the bad news: Custom Order makes it sound like you can drag the thumbnails into the order you want them. Currently, you can't. (Ugh. Don't get me started.) So what could possibly be the good news? The good news is choosing this option at least puts them in the same order as they are in Lightroom on your computer. "So, Scott, are you telling me that I have to go back to Lightroom on my computer if I want one or two thumbnails moved to a different location in the collection?" Yes I am. Don't shoot the messenger.

Continued

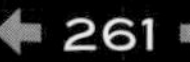

Step Nine:

Just a few more things about working with collections: When you're in Grid view, if you tap on one of the thumbnails with *two* fingers, it'll show you badges to let you know if there are any flags, stars, or edits applied to your images (kind of like the way Lightroom on your computer does in its Grid view). The second time you two-finger tap, it will show you if the images have any comments or likes (if you made them Public). The third time you two-finger tap, it shows you some EXIF camera data (the f-stop, ISO, and shutter speed, as seen in the overlay here). And, a fourth two-finger tap will display the time and date the image was taken, the pixel dimensions, and the filename (as seen here).

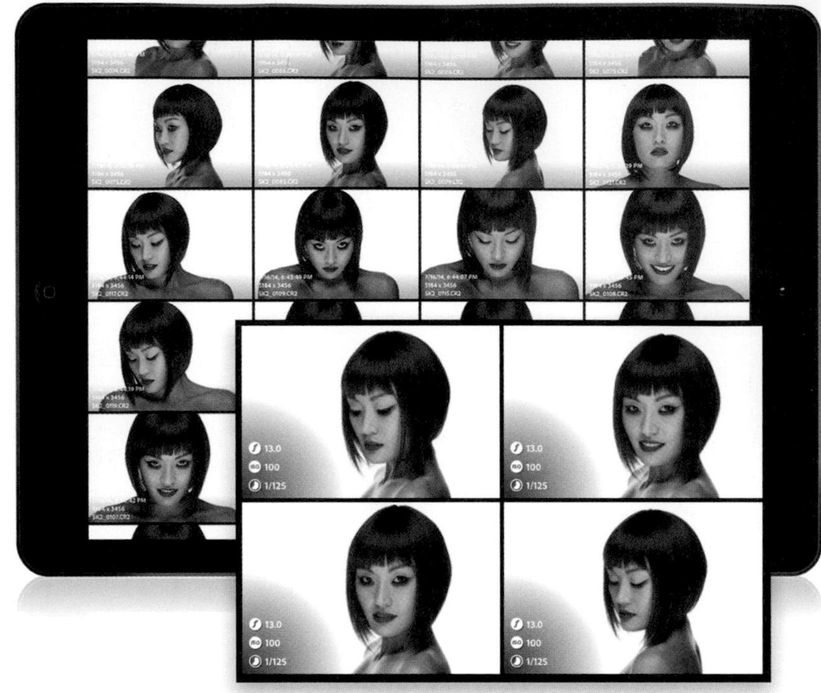

Step 10:

If you tap on the Collection Options icon up in the top-right corner of the screen (the one with the arrow pointing up), it brings up another pop-up menu. At the top, if you tap on Share, you can then tap on any photos you want to share to select them (as seen in the overlay, here). Once they're selected, tap on the checkmark icon in the top-right corner to bring up a pop-up menu with a bunch of sharing options (depending on which device you're on), which range from emailing them, to texting, to sharing to Facebook, or saving them to your device.

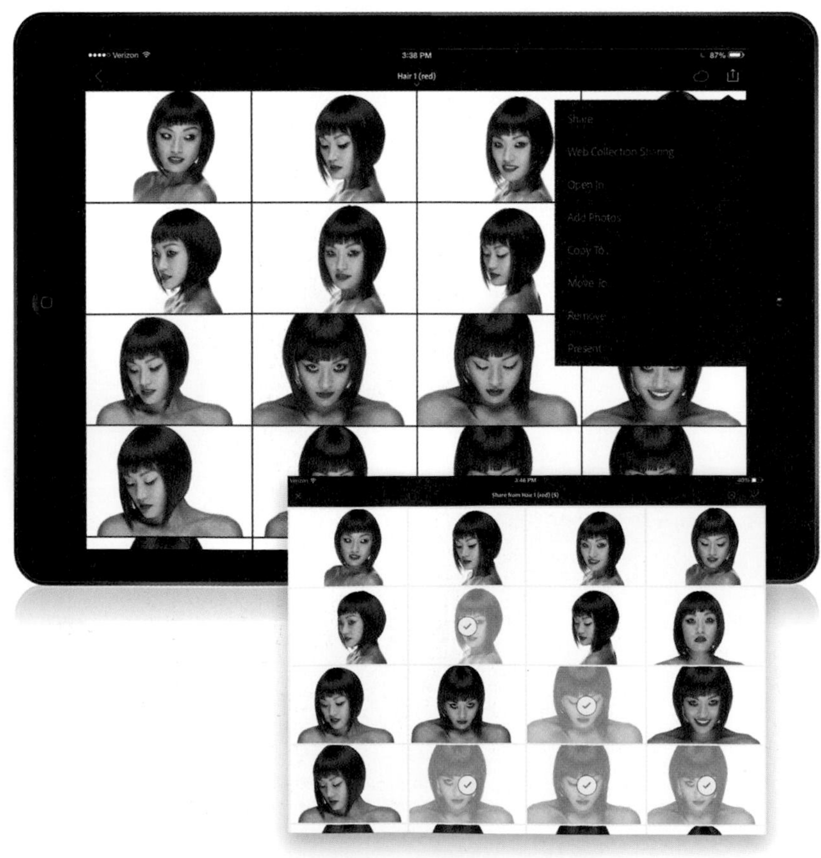

TIP: Selecting Multiple Images

If the images you want to select are nearby each other, you can tap, hold, and drag over the thumbnails to select multiple images at once. To select them all, tap-and-hold to bring up a pop-up menu, then tap **Select All**. You can deselect images the same way. You can also select a range of images from here, too—the image you first tapped on starts blinking, then tap the last image you want to select, and it selects everything in between them.

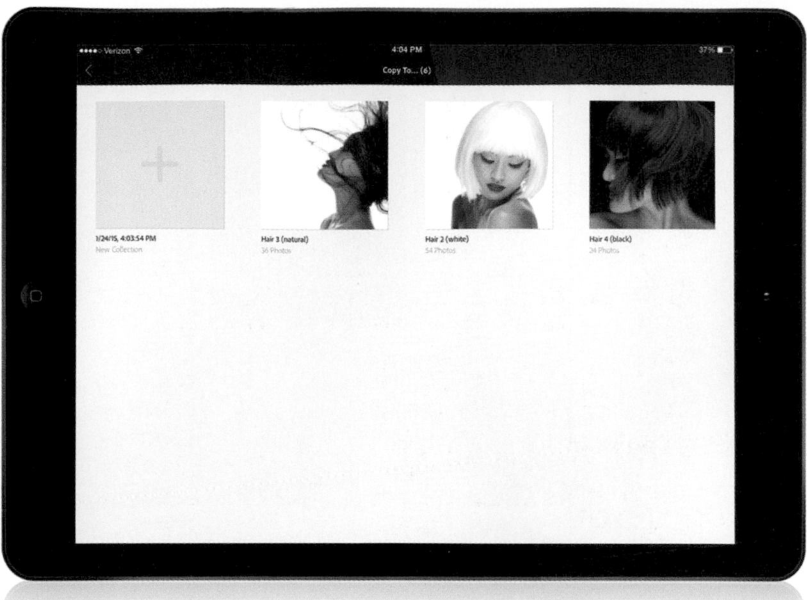

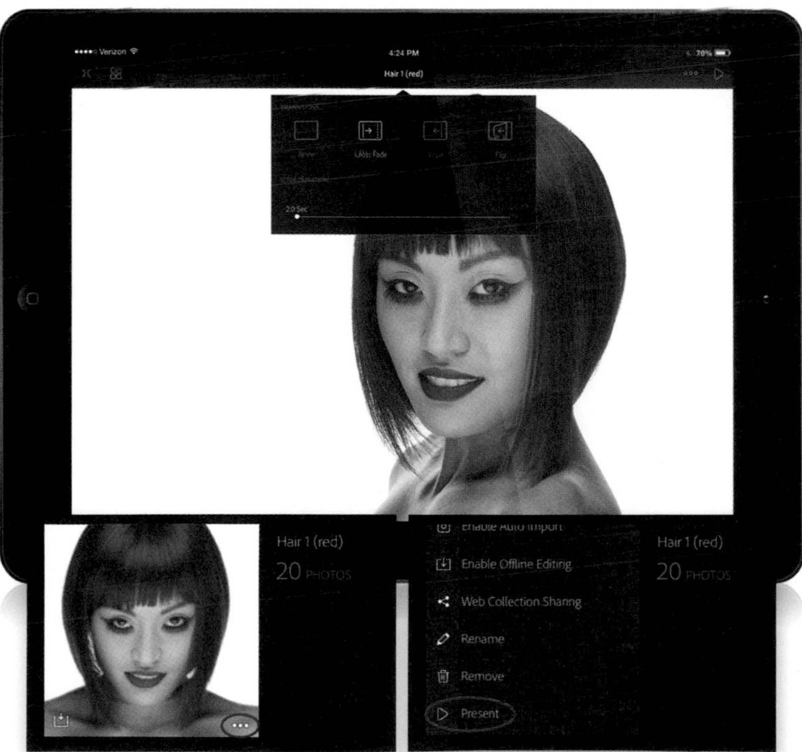

When you tap the three dots on the Collections view tile (on the left), it flips over to reveal a list of options (seen on the right) where you'll find Present

Step 11:

The other options in the Collection Options pop-up menu let you copy or move images from one collection to another without having to go back to Lightroom on your computer. They work very much like the Share option. For example, if you tap on Copy To, and then tap on the image(s) you want to copy, then tap on the right-facing arrow in the top-right corner, it displays all your collections in Lightroom on your mobile device (as seen here). Tap on the one you want to copy it to (there's also an option to add it to a New Collection), and you're done. Same process with choosing Move To. If you choose Remove, you choose which image(s) you want removed from this collection, and then tap on the trash icon in the top-right corner. *Note:* It removes those images from your collection here, and back in Lightroom on your computer, but it does not delete the original file—that's still in the original folder on your computer. After you select some images for any of these options, if you change your mind, just tap the "X" icon in the upper-left corner to cancel.

Step 12:

Choosing Present from that pop-up menu, and then tapping on the right-facing arrow in the top-right corner, starts a self-running slide show of the images in this collection with a soft dissolve between each image. Another way to start this slide show is from the Collections view screen—just tap on the three dots in the bottom-right corner of a collection's cover image and it flips over to reveal a set of options. If you scroll to the bottom of the options list, you'll see Present (as seen in the overlay, here). Also, once the slide show is running, if you tap on the screen, then tap on the three dots in the top-right corner, a pop-up menu of options appears (seen here), where you can choose the length of time between images (using the slider), and your preferred style of transition between images (to turn off the transitions altogether, just choose None).

Continued

Step 13:

Lastly, if you choose Open In from this pop-up menu, you can open the selected image in another app on your mobile device. If that app supports metadata from Lightroom, you can choose to include that, as well. You'll also want to know how to choose which image appears as the thumbnail for a collection (when you're in the Collections view, like you saw back in Step Two, or in the next step). By default, it chooses the first image in the collection, but if you'd like a different image as the cover, just go to Grid view, tap-and-hold on the image you'd like for your collection cover, and choose **Set as Cover** (as shown here. By the way, it doesn't highlight in yellow like you see here or in blue like in Step Eight. I added that so you could see it more easily).

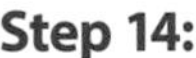

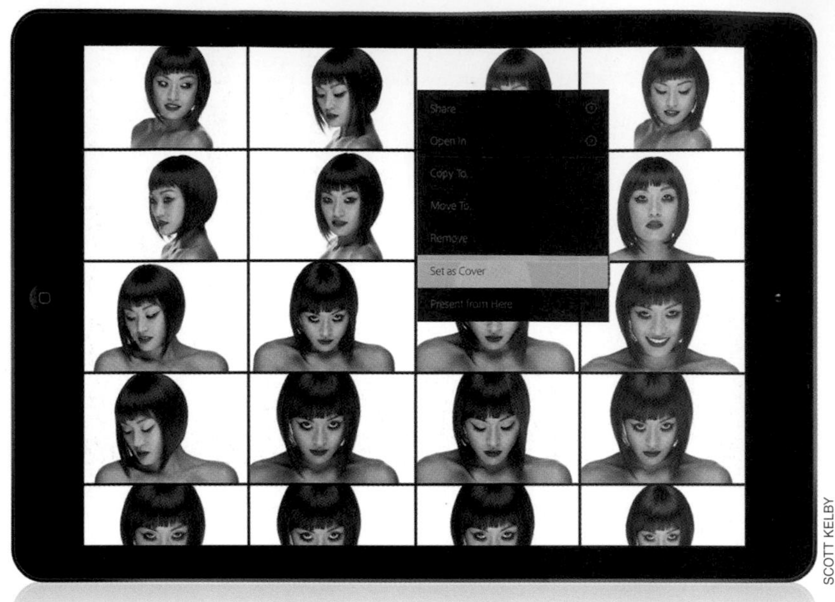

SCOTT KELBY

Step 14:

If you want to create a totally new collection from scratch, go back to Collections view and tap on the plus sign icon in the top-right corner of the screen. This brings up a dialog where you can name your new collection, as seen here (by default, it names your collection with today's time and date, but you'll probably want to make it something more useful, so tap the little "X" on the far right of the text field to erase that, and then type a new name), then tap OK. It adds a new gray thumbnail at the top of your Collections view screen. Tap on it, and it goes to your Camera Roll, where you can choose images already on your mobile device to import. To add photos from other existing collections , tap on a collection, tap on the Collection Options icon in the top-right corner, choose Copy To or Move To, select the photos, tap the arrow icon in the top-right corner, and tap on that new collection and as their destination (it gets marked with a checkmark). To complete the move (or copy), tap the checkmark in the top-right corner.

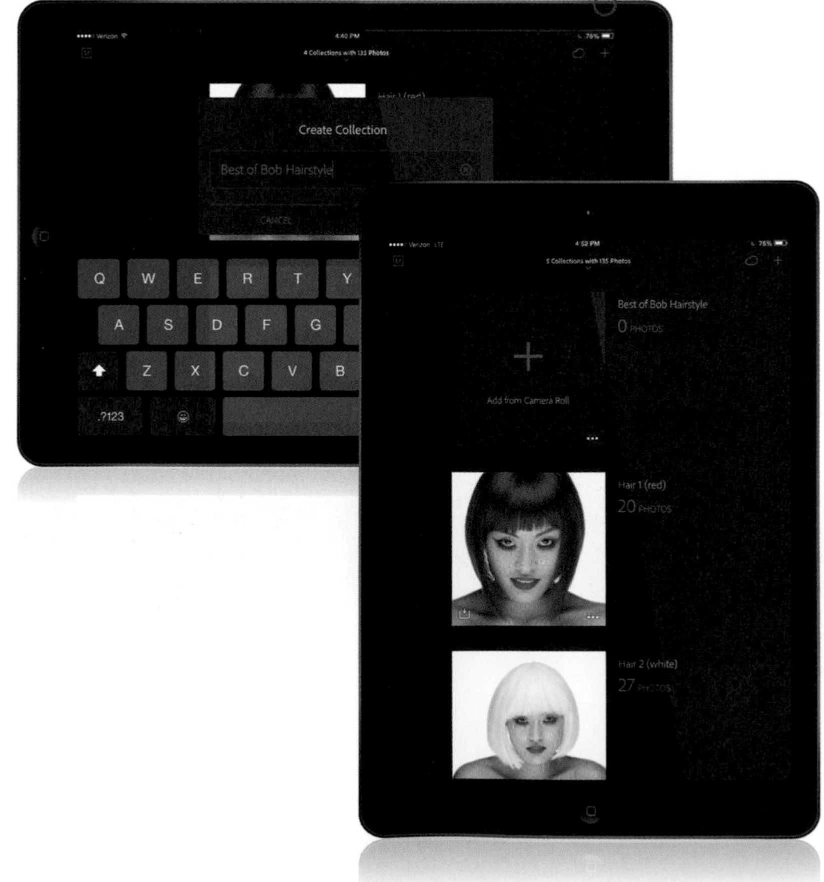

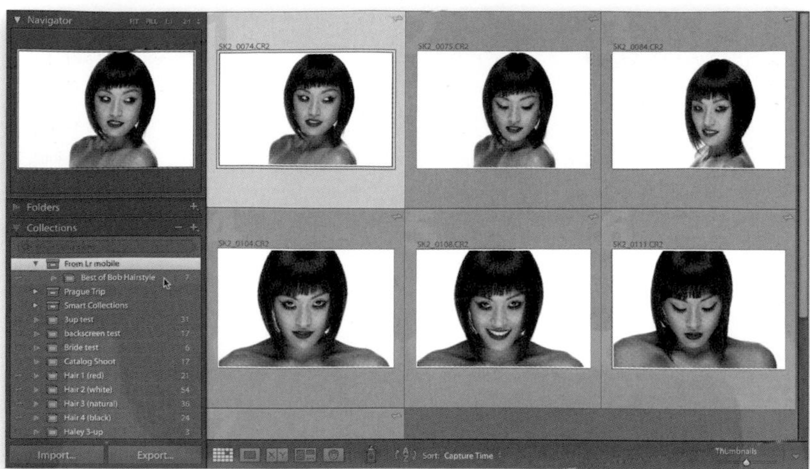

Step 15:

When you create a new collection in Lightroom on your mobile device like we just did, that new collection is synced over to Lightroom on your computer. To help you keep things straight, when this collection appears in your Collections panel, it adds a Collection Set called, "From Lr mobile," and if you look inside that set, you'll see any collections you've created in Lightroom on your mobile device (as seen here, where our "Best of Bob Hairstyle" collection was synced). So, if you've created a bunch of different collections in Lightroom on your mobile device, they all would be listed here. To see only what's in any individual collection, just click on it.

BRAD MOORE

Step 16:

Here's another thing you'll want to know: If you add images that were on your mobile device (like these behind-the-scenes images that were in the Camera Roll of my iPad) to one of your collections, not only does that collection get synced to Lightroom on your computer, but those full-resolution images get copied over, as well. So, you'll be able to see them in the synced collection of course, but if you want to get to the originals for some reason, you'll find them in the Folders panel. In there, you'll see a source with the name of your mobile device (as seen here, where mine's listed as "Scott's iPad Air"). When I click on that, I see a folder containing the original nine images copied over from my iPad to my computer. This works the same way with your phone—if you add images taken with your phone's camera to a Lightroom collection, those full-resolution files will be copied back over to Lightroom on your computer. See, you did want to know that now, didn't you? :-)

Flagging, Rating, and Sorting Your Images

Adding Pick flags and star ratings is definitely more fun here in Lightroom on your mobile device than it is in Lightroom on your computer. Plus, it's nice to just sit back after a shoot, get comfy on the couch, pour a glass of Silver Oak (er, I mean vitamin water or tea…yeah…tea), and just swipe through your images tagging your favorites. There's only one thing missing: color labels. Believe me, I've whined about it to Adobe until the cows come home. Well, maybe one day, but until then, let's flag and rate.

Step One:

When I'm going through my images from a shoot and flagging my Picks (the "keepers" from a shoot), I don't like any distractions onscreen—I want my focus to be on the images—so I do my reviewing in full-screen mode. But, the technique I'm going to show you not only works in full-screen, but also in the Loupe view, or with the Filmstrip visible, too. As you swipe left/right through the images in your collection, when you see one you want to flag as a Pick, just swipe up. A circle with a Pick flag it in will appear onscreen (as seen here) letting you know you tagged it as a Pick. If you tag an image as a Pick and then change your mind, just swipe down to "unflag" it, and you'll see a circle with an Unflag symbol onscreen (as seen in the phone at the bottom right). Swipe down again, and it'll flag the image as a Reject.

Step Two:

If you'd prefer to use star ratings instead (from 1 to 5 stars), you can do that by going to the Loupe view (seen here) and, in the bottom left corner of the screen, tap on the small star icon to turn on star ratings. Now, when you're swiping through you're images and you see one you want to rate with a star rating, just slowly swipe up and a ratings bar appears. The higher you swipe, the more stars it adds. If you add too many by mistake, just slowly swipe down to remove them one by one. To switch back to Pick flags for tagging, just tap on the tiny Flag Status icon in the bottom-left corner.

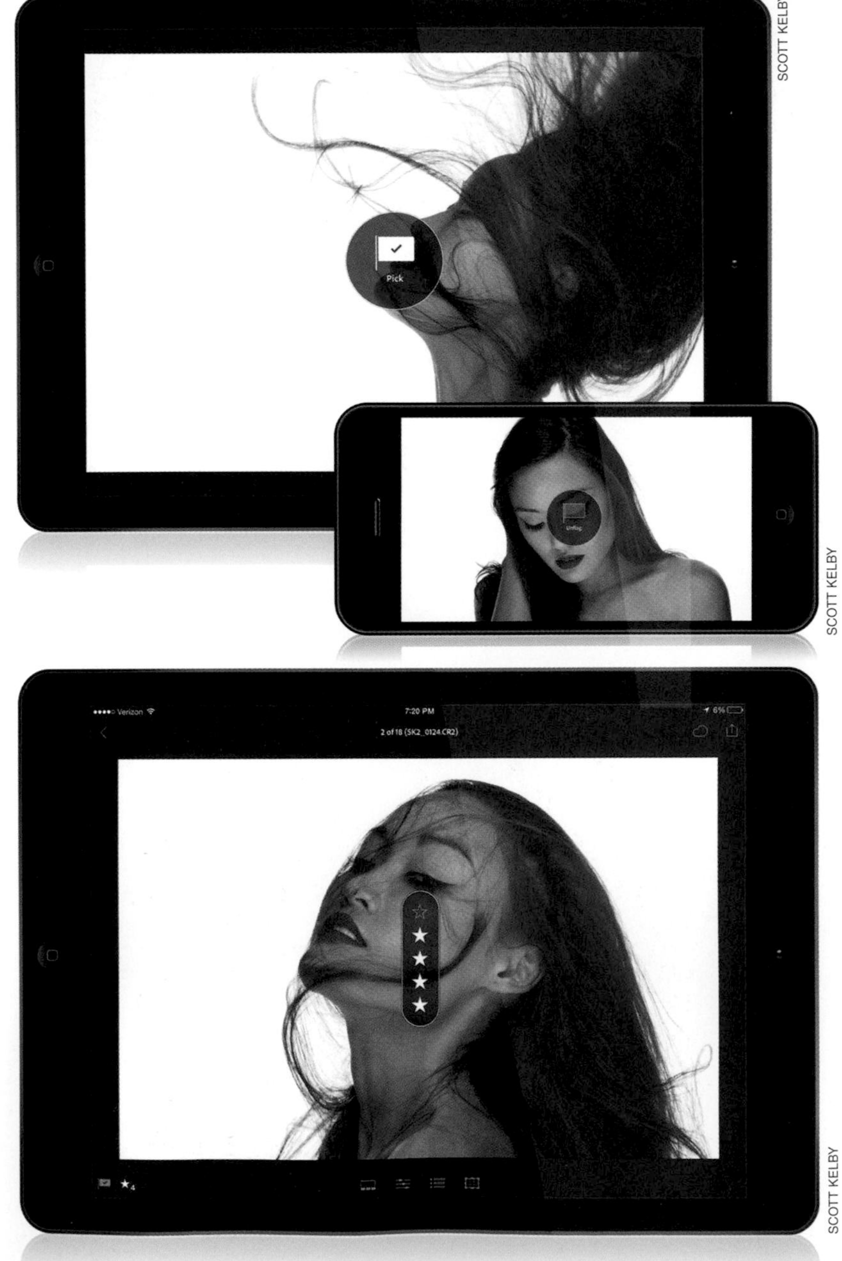

SCOTT KELBY

SCOTT KELBY

SCOTT KELBY

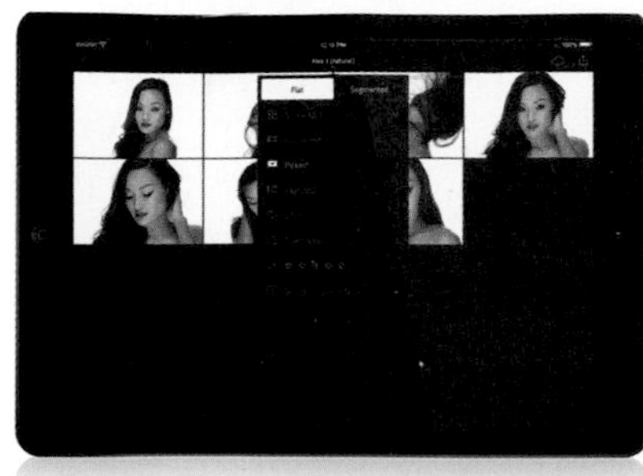

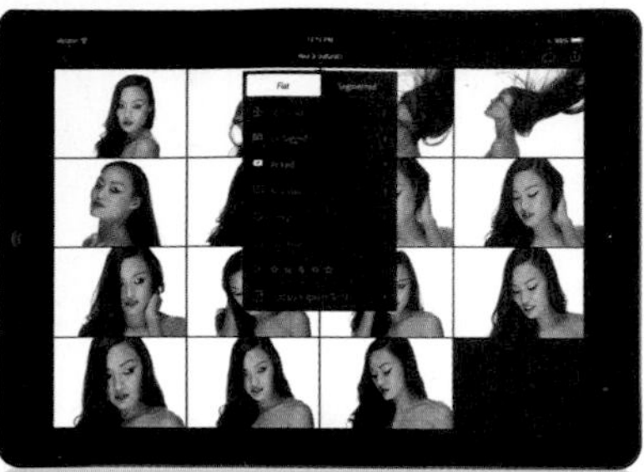

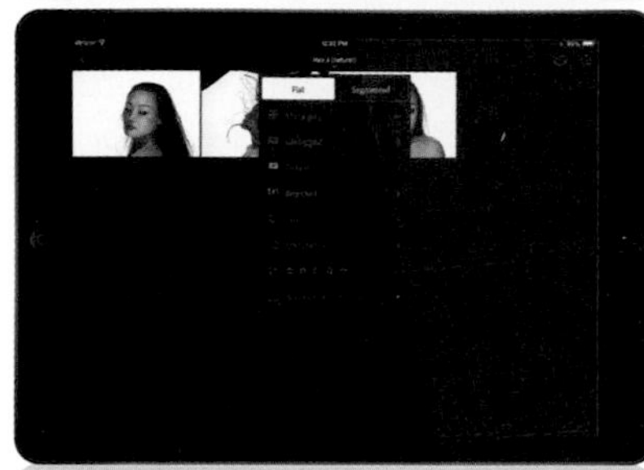

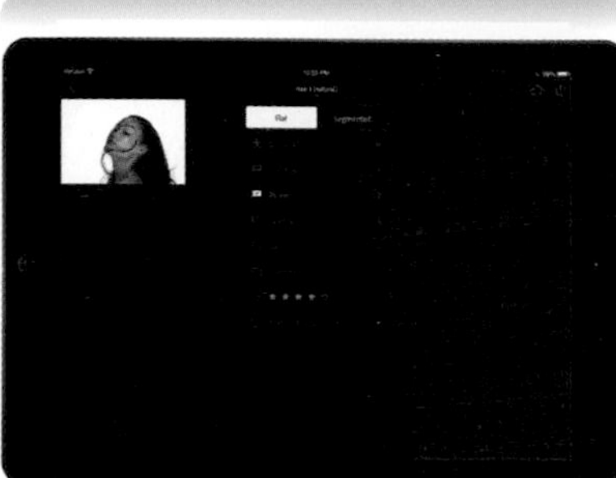

Step Three:

Once you've applied your Pick flags and/or star ratings, you can apply filters so you only see what you want to see. To get to these filters, tap on the name of the collection up at the top center of Grid view to bring up the Grid View options. Then, just tap on the filter you want to turn on. In the examples I'm showing here, in the view you see at the top left, I tapped on Picked and now it just displays the images I marked as Picks in that collection. Here's the cool thing: you can assign more than one filter. In the next one over (top right), I also tapped on Unflagged, so now you're seeing both my Picks and images I haven't tagged with anything. At the bottom left, I tapped on just Rejected and then, lastly, at the bottom right, I tapped on Picked (which narrowed it down just seven images), but then I also set it to four stars and it narrowed things down to just that one image, which has both a Picks flag and a 4-star rating. These filters are incredibly handy.

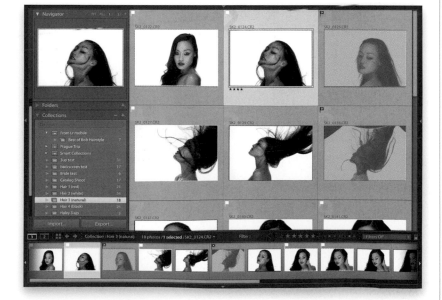

Step Four:

When you go back to Lightroom on your computer, you'll notice that all the flags (Picks and Rejects), plus any star ratings have been synced back to your collection there.

Editing Your Images in Lightroom on Your Device (Its Version of the Basic Panel)

If you were in Lightroom on your computer, and there was a switch that would put your Basic panel along the bottom instead of on the right side of the window, you'd pretty much have this. It's the same sliders that do the same thing, and it's even in the same order. But, it's just the Basic panel—no Tone Curve, no HSL, no Lens Corrections, or any of that other stuff. And, like I said earlier in the book, the Basic panel is horribly misnamed. It should be called the "Absolute Essentials" panel.

Step One:

To edit an image using the same controls as you would in Lightroom on your computer, just tap on an image in Grid view to enter Loupe view (seen here), and then tap on the Adjustments icon (it's the second one from the left in the Actions options across the bottom). This brings up the same controls you have for editing in Lightroom's Basic panel on your computer (it's all there—everything from White Balance to Exposure; Shadows to Whites and Blacks; Clarity to Vibrance; it's all there), in the same order, it just runs across the bottom of the screen instead of along the right side like it does on your computer. Adobe calls each of these controls "adjustment tiles," so you tap on a tile to access its features (or slider).

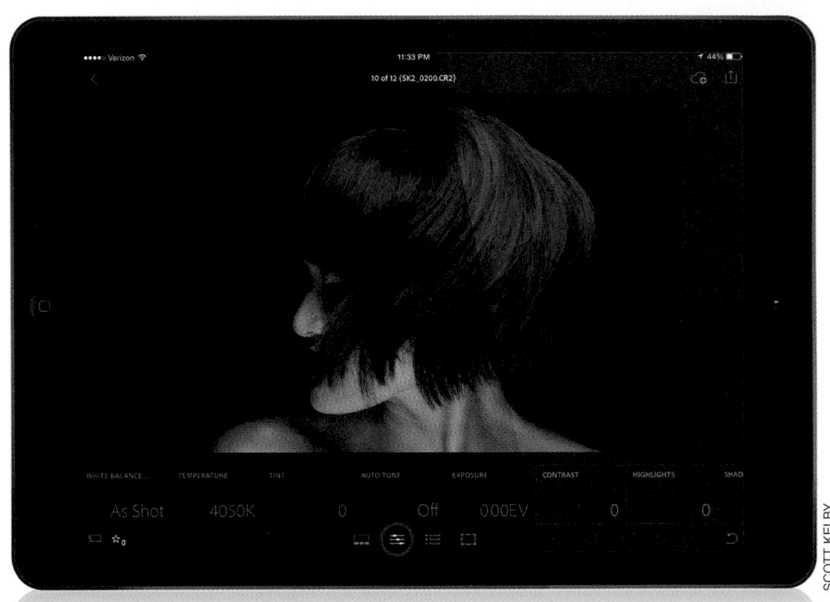

SCOTT KELBY

Step Two:

If you look at her hair in Step One, you'll notice it has a pretty strong blue tint to it, but her hair is supposed to black. So, we have to fix the white balance. In the row of adjustment tiles across the bottom, tap on the White Balance tile and a menu pops up with a list of White Balance presets and a thumbnail preview of how each would look if applied to your image. Just taking a quick glance at these, it looks like the Flash preset would look best (well, at least the blue tint is gone from her hair with it), so tap once on the Flash preset to apply it (as seen here).

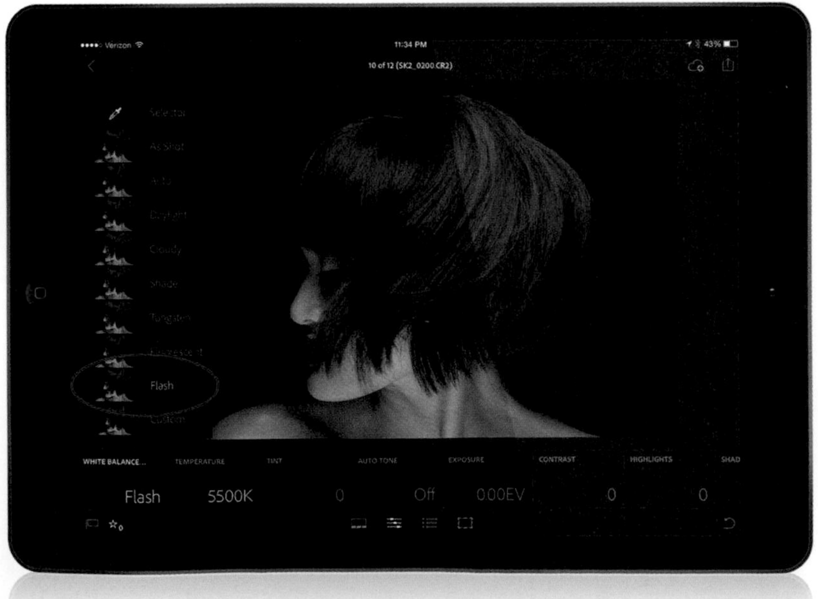

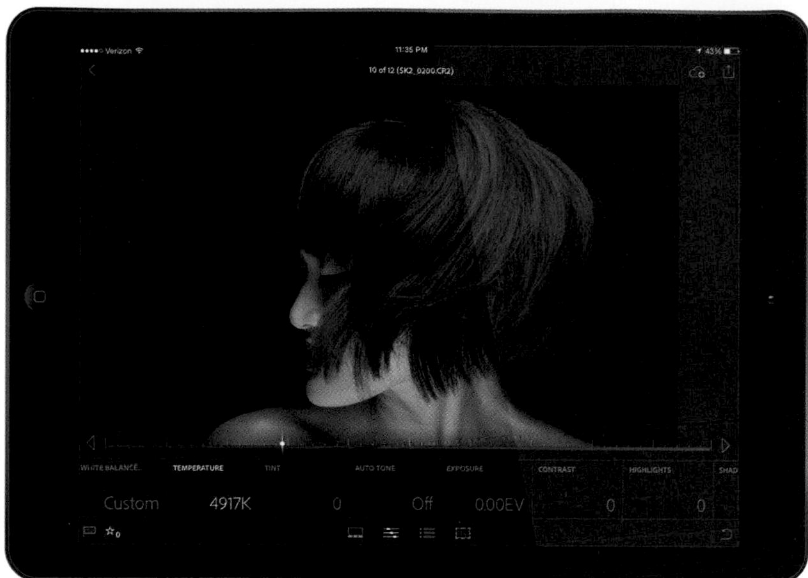

Step Three:

The nice thing about applying a preset like this is if it's not right on the money, you can still tweak it. In this case, it might be a little too warm, but you can just tap on the Temperature tile and a slider appears right above the row of tiles. Just tap-and-hold on the little knob on the slider and it works just like the sliders in regular ol' Lightroom on your computer—drag to the left to make the white balance cooler; to the right to make it warmer. In this case, I'd drag a little to the left, so it's not so warm (the Temperature reading was 5500K, but now it's down to a little cooler 4917K).

TIP: Resetting a Slider

If you make a mistake, or don't like the change you applied, just double-tap anywhere along that slider to reset the it to where you started, or you can just double-tap on the name of the adjustment tile.

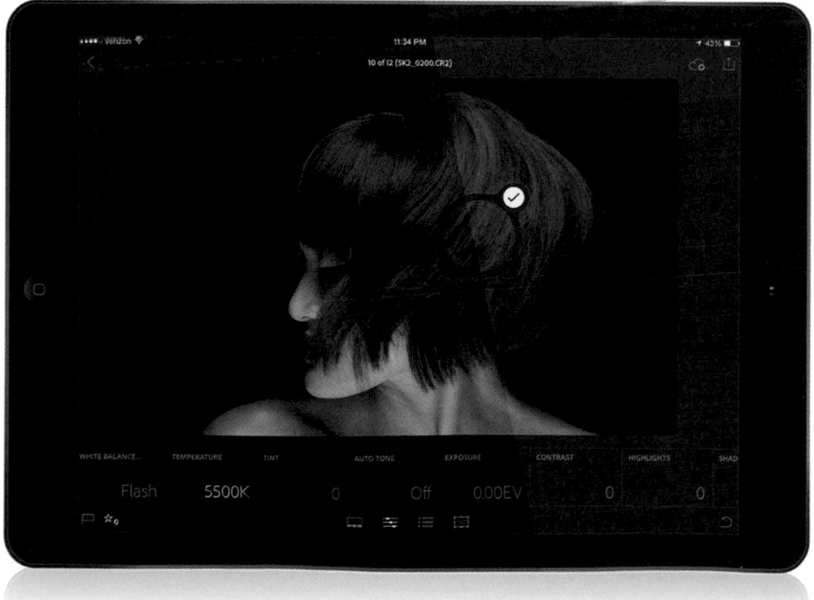

Step Four:

One last thing about White Balance: the White Balance Selector tool is here in Lightroom on your mobile device, too. Look back in Step Two—it's at the top of the White Balance preset pop-up menu. Just tap on it, and it appears over your image. It has a loupe to help you isolate where you're picking your neutral gray color from. Here, I tapped-and-dragged it over her hair—as you drag-and-release, it gives you a live preview of what it would look like if you tapped on the white checkmark at the top right of the loupe (which confirms you're choosing that spot to base your white balance upon). So, I guess you know now that when it looks good to you, tap on that checkmark to lock in your choice. When you do, the White Balance Selector tool disappears.

Continued

Step Five:

To scroll through the rest of the Basic panel controls you already know and love, just swipe to the left to reveal the rest of them. Here, I swiped over near the end to Vibrance where I tapped once on that tile to bring up its slider, then I tapped-and-held the knob on the slider and dragged it to the left to –41 to desaturate the photo a bit (as seen here). All the sliders here pretty much work the same way—you tap once on a tile to reveal its slider, then you tap, hold, and drag it to the left or right to decrease or increase the amount (respectively).

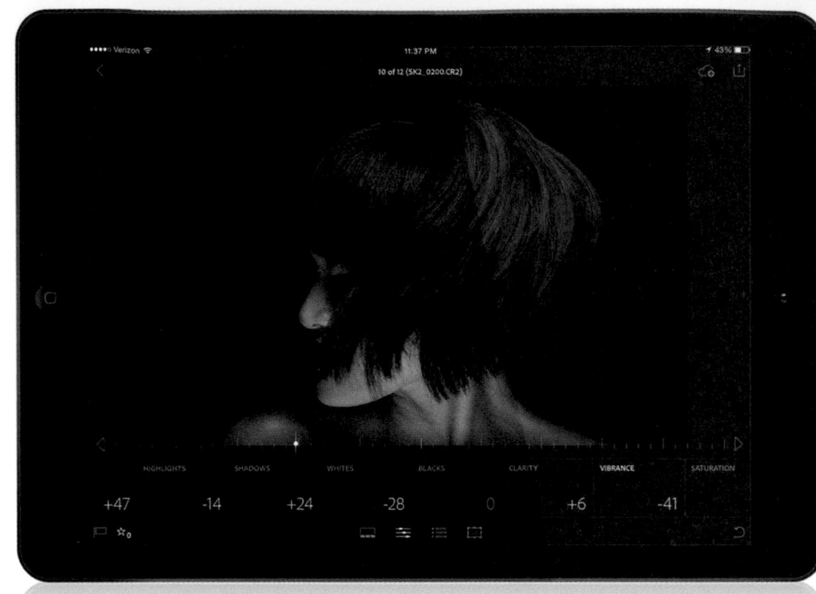

TIP: You Can Add Pick Flags & Star Ratings While You're Here

While you're editing in Loupe view, you can also apply a Pick flag or a star rating by tapping on them in the bottom-left corner. To increase the number of stars, keep tapping on that tiny star icon.

Step Six:

One of my favorite features in Lightroom on your computer is here in Lightroom on your mobile device—it's just kind of hidden—and that's the ability to get a clipping warning if you're blowing out your pixels. You can see this warning onscreen when adjusting Exposure, Shadows, Highlights, Whites, and Blacks. Just press two fingers anywhere on the slider for that control, and it will black out the screen and display only areas that are clipping, like you see here where cranking up the Whites too much clipped her skin in just the Red channel, but clipped all three channels on her cheek, which is some pretty serious damage, and now I know to back down the Whites to avoid this clipping.

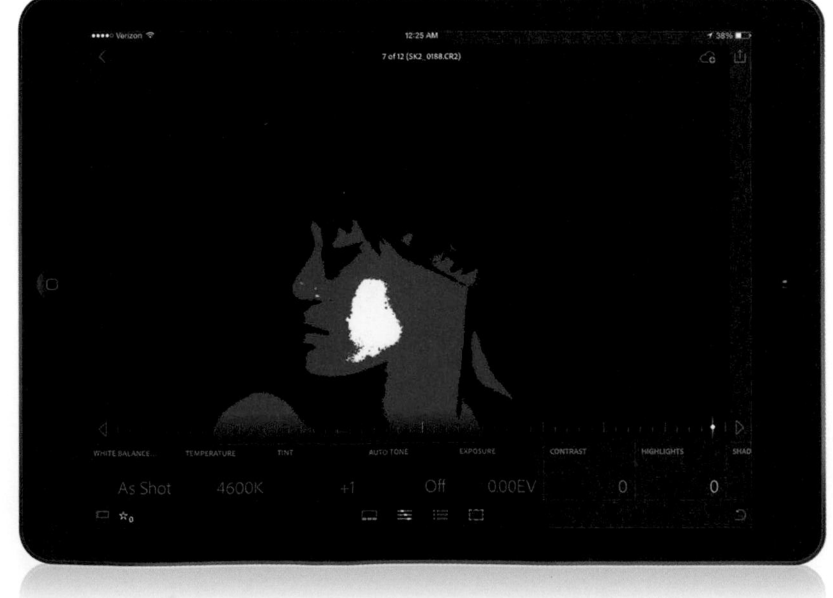

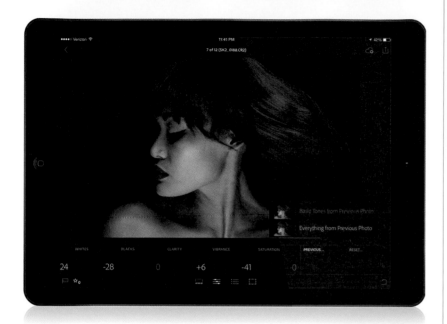

Step Seven:

One of the most powerful time savers from Lightroom on your computer is here, too: the Apply Previous button. It takes the adjustments you made to the previous image, and applies them to the current image with one tap (super handy and fast!). To use it, tweak a photo the way you like it, tap on the Filmstrip icon to bring it up along the bottom, then swipe to the image you want to apply this look to, and tap on it. Now, tap back on the Adjustments icon and in the adjustment tiles across the bottom, scroll to the right (er, I mean swipe to the right) down near the very end, where you'll see a tile named simply, "Previous…." Tap on it, and a pop-up menu appears (seen here) asking if you want just basic tonal edits from the tiles below, or everything you did to the previous photo, including cropping, rotating, etc. Make your choice and the edits are applied immediately.

TIP: Seeing a Before/After

To see a before image (what the image looked like before you started adjusting it), just tap-and-hold three fingers right on your image (you'll see "Before" appear above the image).

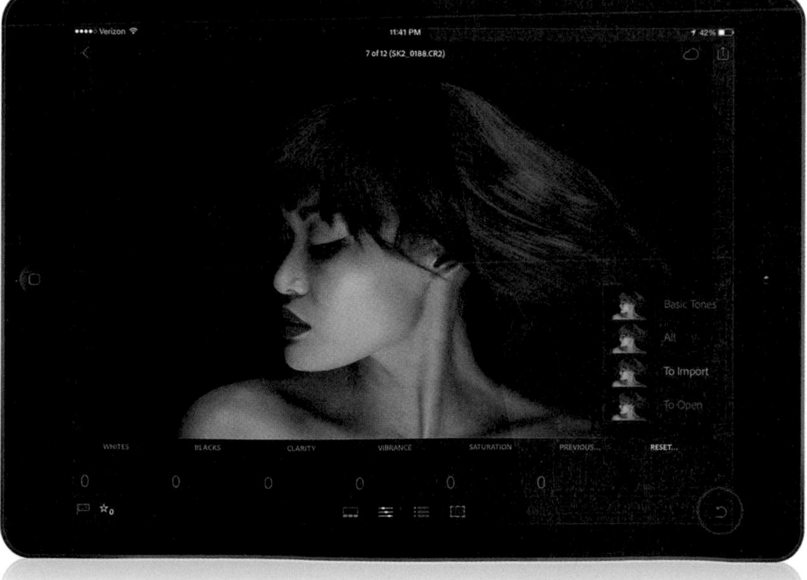

Step Eight:

If you swipe over to the very end of the adjustment tiles, there's a Reset tile, which lets you start over. Just tap once on it and a pop-up menu appears (seen here) asking if you just want to reset the Basic Tones, or reset everything (cropping including), or if you want to reset the image to how it looked when you first imported it in Lightroom or when you last opened it. It's great to know how to reset your image, but something that's probably at least as, if not more, important is just below that tile in the bottom-right corner. That's the Undo icon. Each time you tap on it, it undoes another step, so you can go back in time, step by step, and undo anything you didn't like in the order it was applied.

Continued

Step Nine:

This next thing is either really cool, or really frustrating, or a little of both (I lean toward "it's really cool"), but here goes: In Loupe view, the Presets icon (the third one from the left in the Actions options across the bottom) gives you access to a ton of Develop module presets (each tile has a pop-up menu, as seen here where I tapped on the Creative tile). These are one-tap effects that we just tap and—boom—done! Of course, once we apply a preset, we can still adjust our Basic panel adjustments (Exposure, Highlights, etc.). But, we can't adjust some of the things included in the presets, which were created in Lightroom on your computer, because they contain effects (like vignetting, and black and white, and noise, and split toning) that aren't available here in Lightroom on your mobile device. I'm taking the "Hey, this is cool because these things aren't in Lightroom on your mobile device, but I can still get these effects" line of thinking, here.

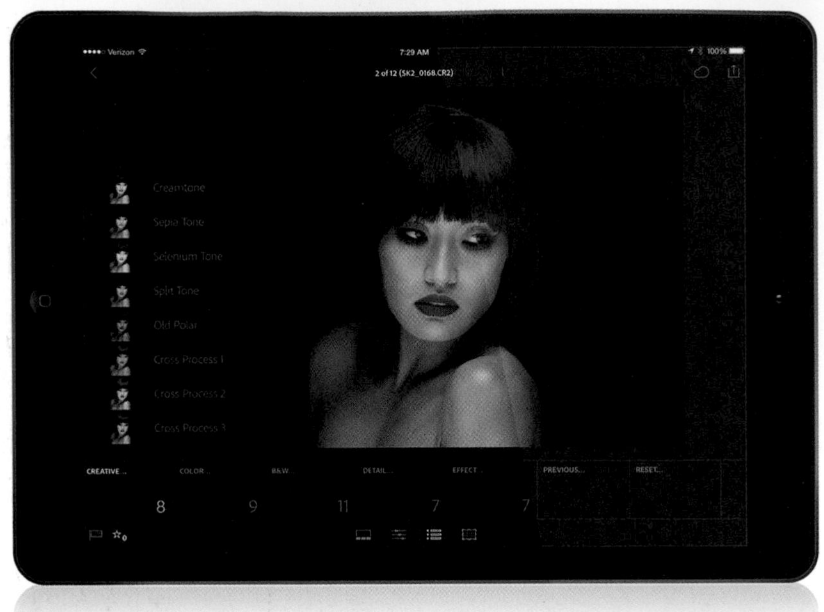

Step 10:

I tapped on Creamtone to apply the look you see here. One thing I really like about how Adobe designed these preset pop-up menus is that you can see a mini-thumbnail preview right there for each preset. That way, you can see which ones look good without even tapping anything—you don't have to waste a lot of time trying out ones that just don't look good for a particular image. *Note:* The number you see displayed on each preset tile is the number of presets available under that category (for example, the Creative tile has an "8," and there are eight presets to choose from in its pop-up menu). *Note:* If you're wondering if you can create a preset in Lightroom on your computer and bring it over here into Lightroom on your mobile device, sadly... no. That would be awesome, though. Maybe one day.

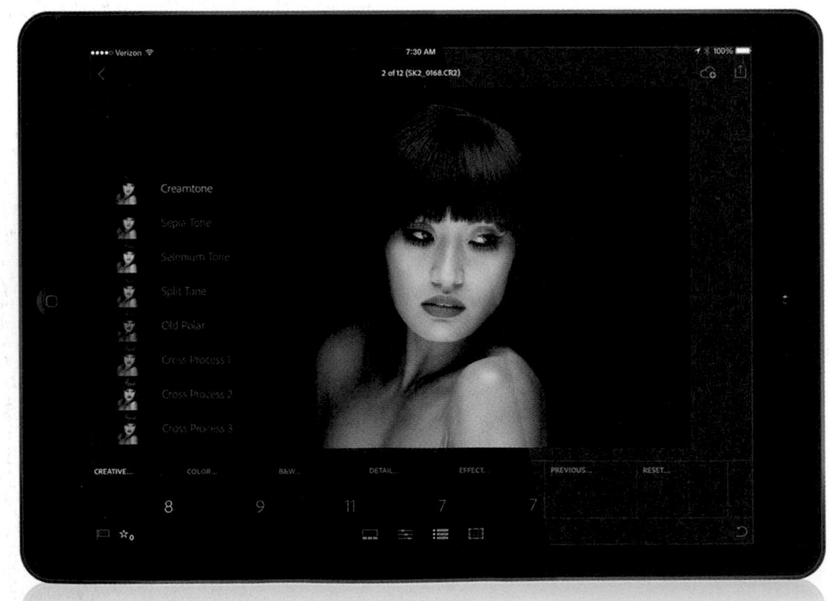

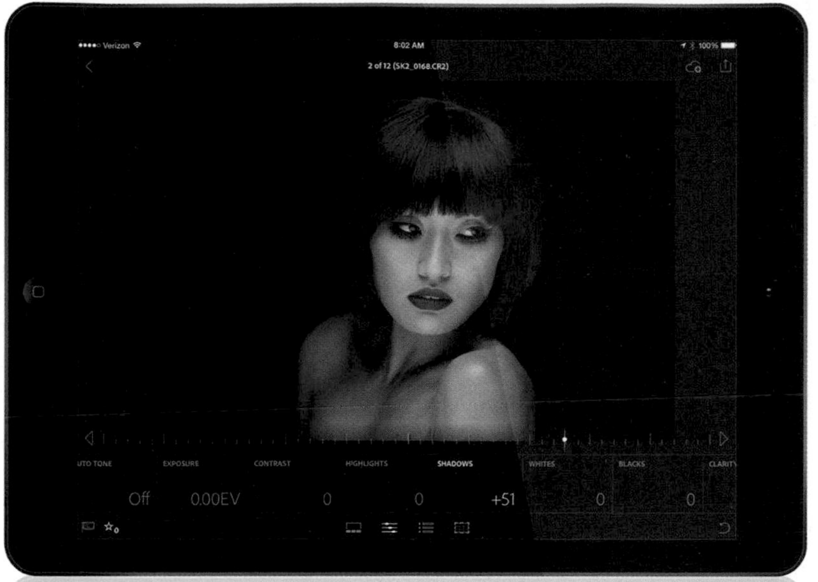

Step 11:

Here, I tapped on the Color tile and chose Cool as my preset, but when I looked at the result, I wanted her hair a little brighter (it was getting lost in the black background with this particular preset applied). Luckily, again, you can edit things like exposure and shadows after applying a preset, so tap on the Adjustments icon to return to the adjustment tiles. Here, I tapped on Shadows to bring up the slider, and I tapped-and-dragged over to +51 to really open up those shadow areas in her hair. So, while I can't change the balance or intensity or hue of the colors in the split-tone color effect from that preset, I can still adjust things like exposure, shadows, clarity, and such.

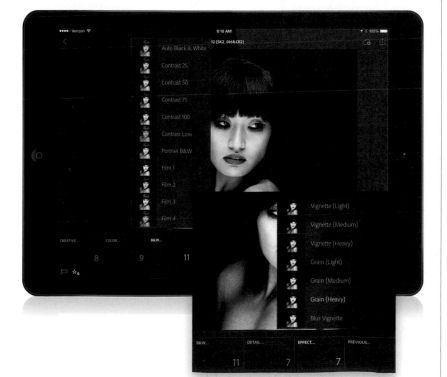

Step 12:

In some cases, you can "stack" presets—having one add its effect on top of another—and a great place to see this in action is when you use the Effect presets, which add things like vignette looks (darkening the outside edges of your image) or adding noise (grain) or a blur vignette. The reason these add on is that they don't use the Split Toning panel or the HSL panel or any other options that might get changed by applying another preset. For example, if you apply a B&W preset, then apply a Color preset, the color overrides the black and white and changes the image back to color. But, adding noise (grain) or a vignette adds on to the look you applied with the first preset. Here, I started by applying the B&W preset, Film 2. In the overlay shown, I tapped on the Effect presets and added Grain (Heavy) to enhance the grainy film look.

Continued

Cropping & Rotating

The last of the four Actions options in Loupe view is the Crop Tool icon, and I gotta tell you, I'm not sure if I don't like this one better than the one in Lightroom on your computer. It really feels quick and intuitive and you can pretty much do all of the stuff you do on your computer, but somehow it seems smoother and easier here. In short: you'll dig it.

Step One:

If you need to crop your images, just tap on the Cropping Tool icon (the fourth icon in the Actions options across the bottom; its icon looks like a cropping border), which actives the Cropping tool. You'll know it's active because it puts a cropping border around your entire image (as seen here), and the tiles along the bottom are now one-click cropping aspect ratios (1x1, 5x4, and so on).

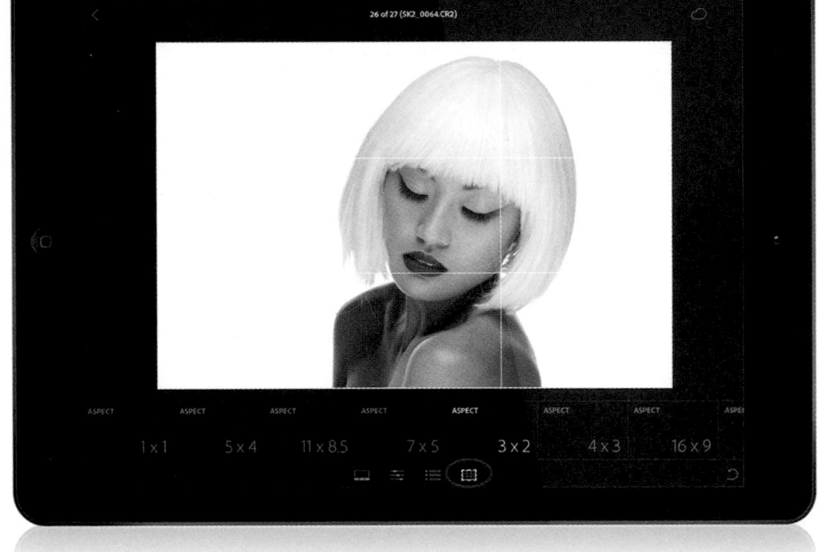

Step Two:

To apply any of those preset cropping ratios, just tap once on the ratio you want applied (here, I tapped on 16x9 and the cropping border updates to the new ratio). The areas that will be cropped away are still visible, but they're shown in dark gray (you can see here a horizontal strip would be cropped off along the top and bottom if I were to go with this cropping ratio). Now that you've applied a crop, you can reposition your image within that cropping border by just tapping-and-dragging the image right where you want it.

TIP: Resetting the Crop

To return to the original uncropped image, just double-tap anywhere within the cropping border.

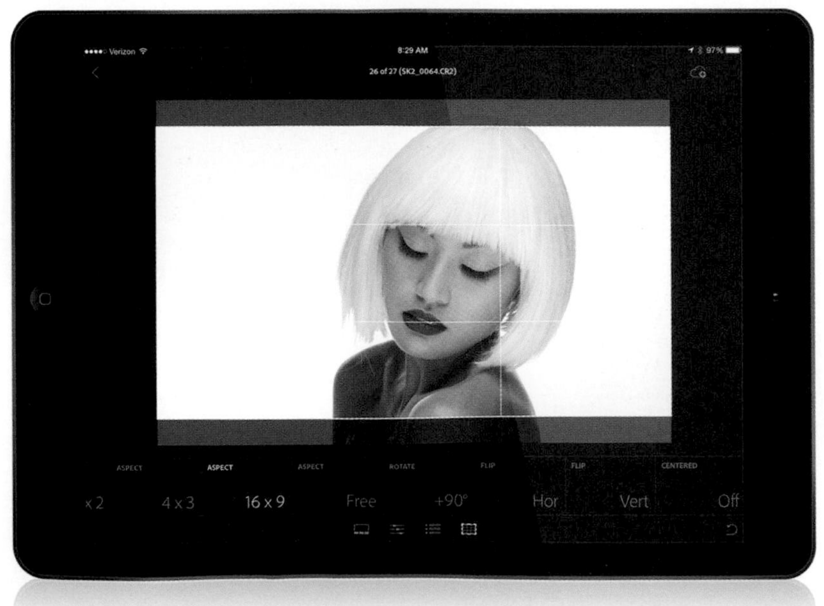

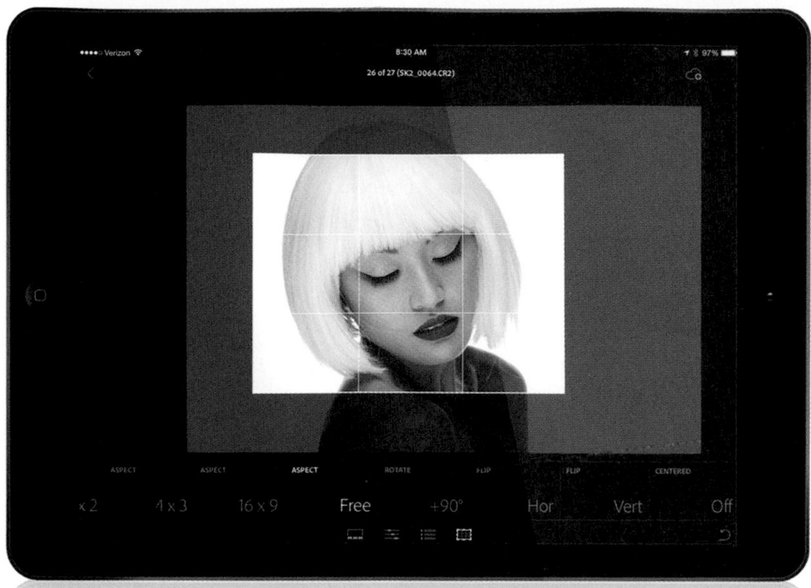

Step Three:

If you swipe through the cropping ratio tiles, towards the right end, you'll see some other options besides just cropping ratios. For example, there's the Free aspect ratio, which means you're not constrained to any preset ratio. So, once you tap on it, you can tap on any corner or side of the cropping border and move just that part right where you want, without affecting the other three sides (it's like clicking on the Unlock icon for the Crop Overlay tool in Lightroom on your computer). Here, I tapped on Free and then just tapped-and-dragged each side of the cropping border right where I wanted it. If you tap on Hor, it flips your image horizontally (like I did here—she's now looking to the right), and, of course, tapping Vert flips your image upside down.

TIP: Changing the Crop Overlay

By default, when you choose the Cropping Tool it displays a Rule of Thirds overlay grid. Just do a two-finger tap within the cropping border to cycle through different crop overlays or to turn the overlay off altogether.

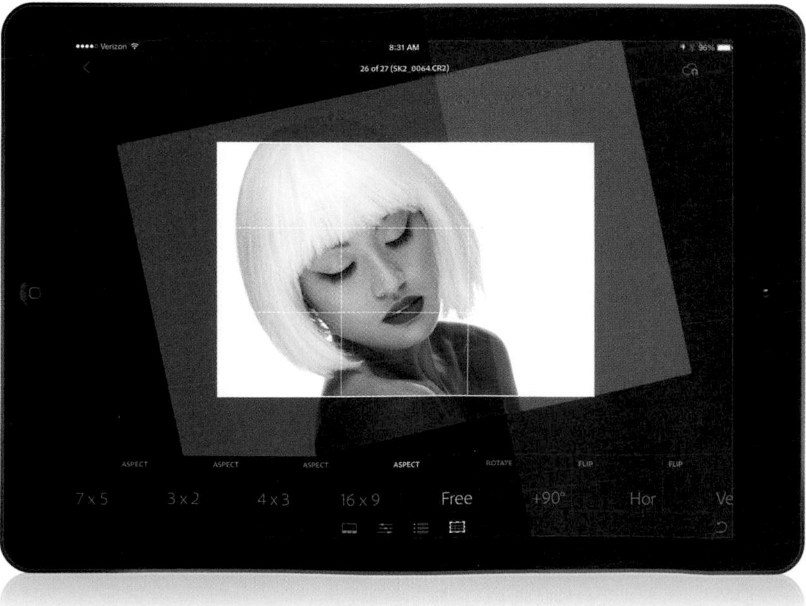

Step Four:

If you want to rotate your image within the cropping border, just tap-and-hold outside the cropping border and drag up/down and the image will rotate within the cropping border (so you're rotating the image—not the border). Here, I tapped on Free (so I could move any side of the border), and then I tapped-and-dragged outside the border to rotate it.

TIP: Flipping the Crop to Tall

By default, a crop is applied wide (landscape), but if you want to flip it to the same ratio, but tall (portrait), just tap again on the Aspect ratio tile.

Client Proofing Using Lightroom on Your Mobile Device

I think this is one of the coolest features of Lightroom on your mobile device, and it really impresses clients because the technology here is really pretty cool. We're going to set up Lightroom on your computer and Lightroom on your mobile device, so that during our shoot, we can hand our client our tablet and not only can they see the images coming in live as we shoot, they can make their own Picks, comments, and even share the link with someone at a different location, so they can be part of the shoot, and the approval process, too!

Step One:

When I'm shooting in the studio (or even on location, if possible), I shoot tethered directly into Lightroom on my laptop (see Chapter 1 for how to set up to shoot tethered, so your images go directly from your camera straight into Lightroom). Here's a behind-the-scenes shot from a fashion shoot (yes, it took four assistants and a high-powered fan underneath to get the 10-foot train on her dress into the air). As I shoot the images, they come straight into Lightroom on my laptop, as seen here. Now, let's set up Lightroom on our mobile device to make it a part of this shoot.

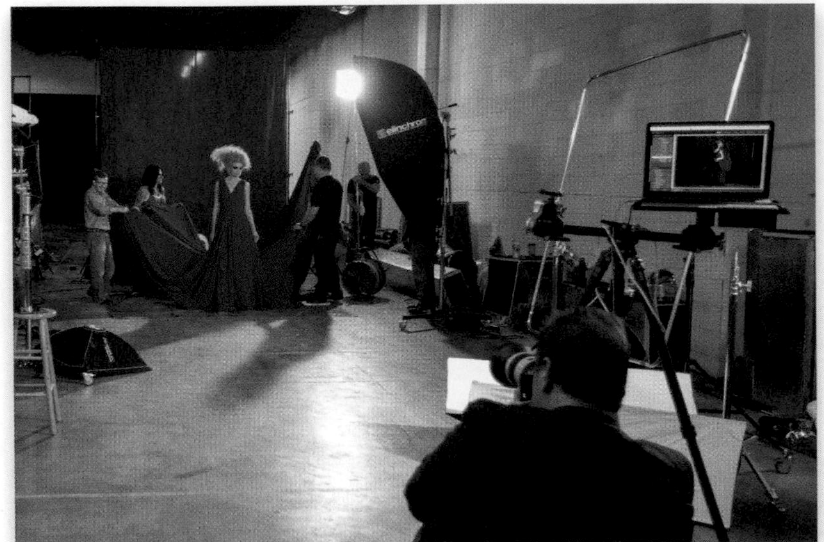

BRAD MOORE

Step Two:

When you shoot tethered into Lightroom, the images come into a folder in Lightroom, but of course Lightroom on your mobile device only syncs collections, right? Of course, you could drag that entire folder into the Collections panel and sync that, but then my client would see every shot—ones where the model's eyes are closed, ones where the light didn't fire, ones where my composition was off, and well…they'd just see lots of lame shots. I only want my client seeing good solid shots, not those that should be deleted. So, here's what I do: First, create a new collection in Lightroom on your computer. When the Create Collection dialog appears, give it a name (I named mine "Red Dress Shoot"), then turn on the Set as Target Collection checkbox (a very important checkbox for this workflow to work).

Create Collection
Name: Red Dress Shoot
Location
Inside a Collection Set
Options
Set as target collection
Sync with Lightroom mobile
Cancel
Create

Step Three:

Go the little gray Sync checkbox to the left of this new collection and click on it to turn on syncing for this collection (you'll see a message appear onscreen for a second or two letting you know that this collection will be synced with Lightroom on your mobile device, as seen here). Now that everything's set up and ready to go, I launch Lightroom on my iPad and hand it to my client, or Art Director (a friend, an assistant, a guest on the set, etc.), who is there on the set well behind where I'm shooting from (most photographers don't like someone looking over their shoulder when they're trying to shoot).

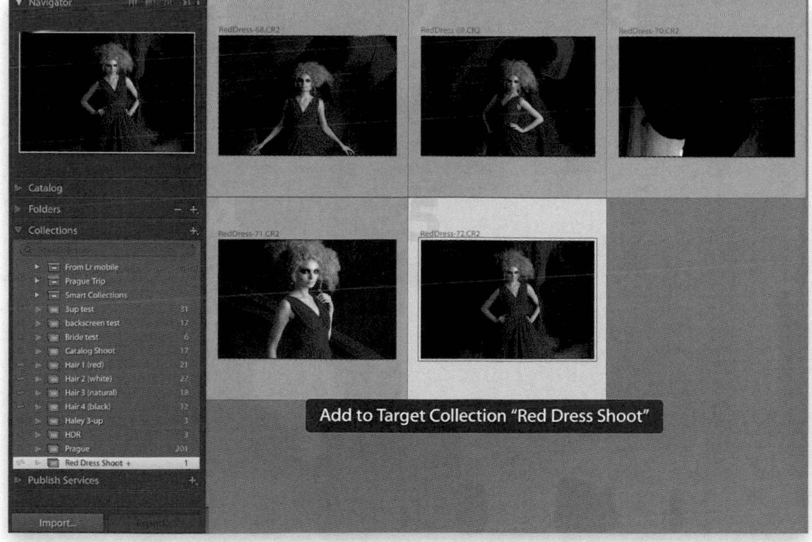

Step Four:

So, here are the shots coming in to Lightroom on my laptop from the shoot. Check out that third shot where only the background light fired and the main light didn't fire—why would I want my client to see that? Or the first frame where the model looks startled. But, when I see an image come in that I like, I just press the letter **B** on my keyboard and that image is sent to my iPad, and the client sees that image a few seconds later. The reason this works is because when I press B, that image is sent to the Red Dress Shoot collection (remember I made that my target collection when I created it? Making it a target collection means that anytime I hit the letter B for a selected image, that image goes to that collection I've targeted), and that collection is synced to Lightroom on my iPad, so my client sees only the images I hit the letter B on. How cool is that? So, that's my process: hit B on good shots, and the client sees just those keepers. But, we're just getting started (this gets even better).

Continued

Step Five:

Here's a look at the iPad my client is holding, and instead of there being 100 or 200 images flowing in there, it's just the images I hit the letter B on.

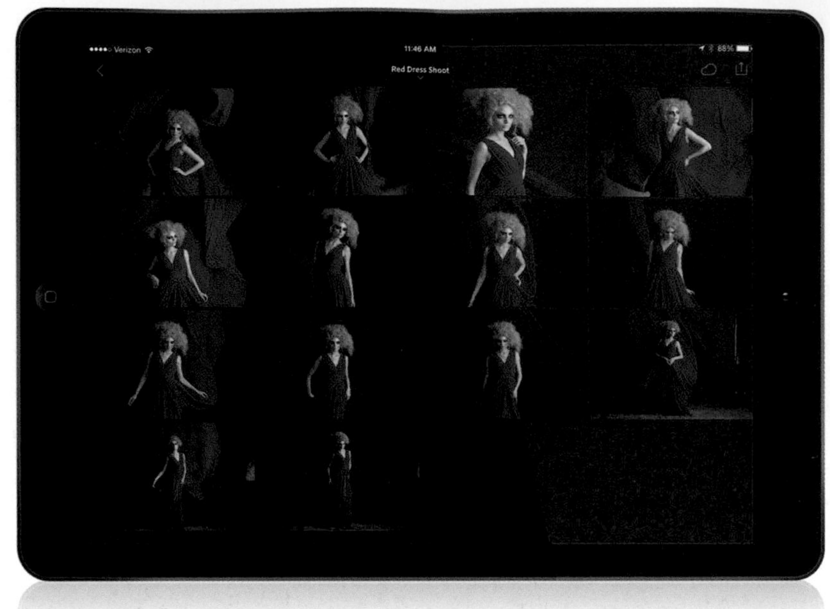

Step Six:

Now, when I hand the client the iPad, I show them how to swipe up to flag an image as a Pick and how to swipe down if they change their mind. I also let them know that can just tap the Pick flag in the bottom-right corner, or they can tap on the Star icon—once for each star they want the image to have (I tell them to only add a star rating to one that really stands out to them—one of their very favorites—and the rest that they like just mark them as a Pick). Since we're synced, when they choose a photo to get a Pick flag or star rating, those get sent back to my collection (as seen in the overlay below), so I can instantly see which ones they like (and which to try and do more of). So, your client is seeing your images appear on the iPad she's holding. What if you could also share this same collection with someone else who's not even there? Maybe they're back at the office, or out of town, or even out of the country? Well, they can not only follow along with your shoot, they can be a part of it.

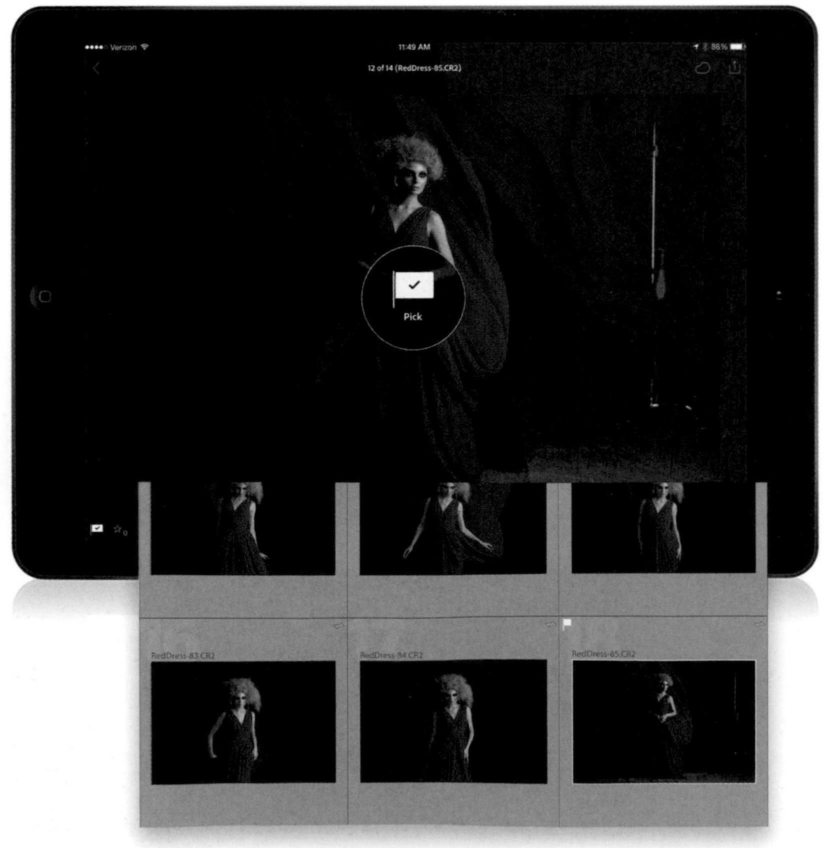

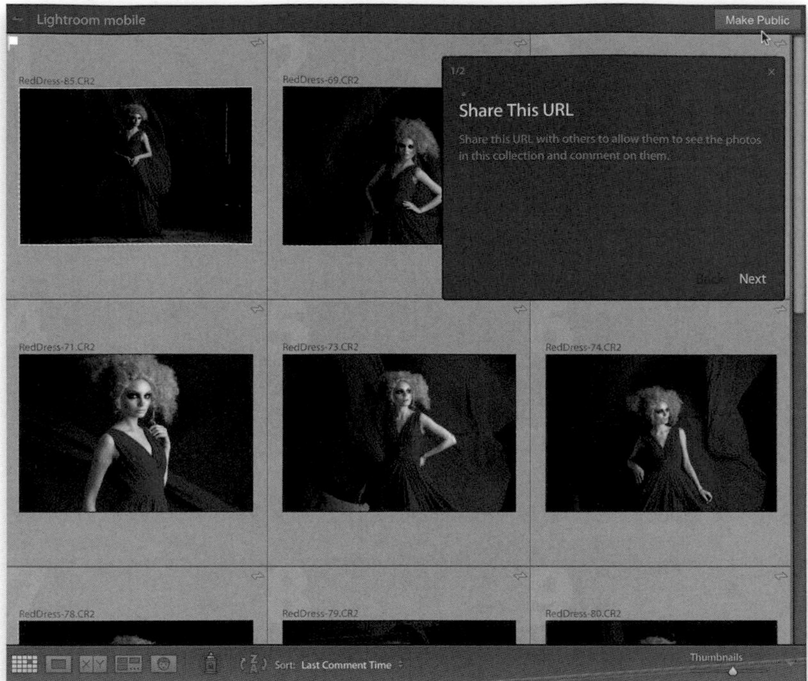

Step Seven:

In Lightroom on your computer, at the top of the Preview area in Grid view, on the right, you'll see the Make Public button. If you click on that button, it generates a URL (web address) that, at this point, only you have access to (even though the button says, "Make Public"), that you can now email or text to someone anywhere in the world, so they can follow along—see the same images your client is seeing on your iPad—and they can do this all right from any web browser. They don't need an Adobe ID. They don't need special software—just Internet access and a web browser. By the way, that "Share This URL" pop-up (as seen here) gives you the URL to copy-and-paste to your client, but it'll also list the URL just to the left of the Make Public button (which, after you click, changes to Make Private, if you want to turn off access to the person you sent it to, as seen at the bottom). By the way, you can send that URL to more than just one person, so multiple people in different locations can see.

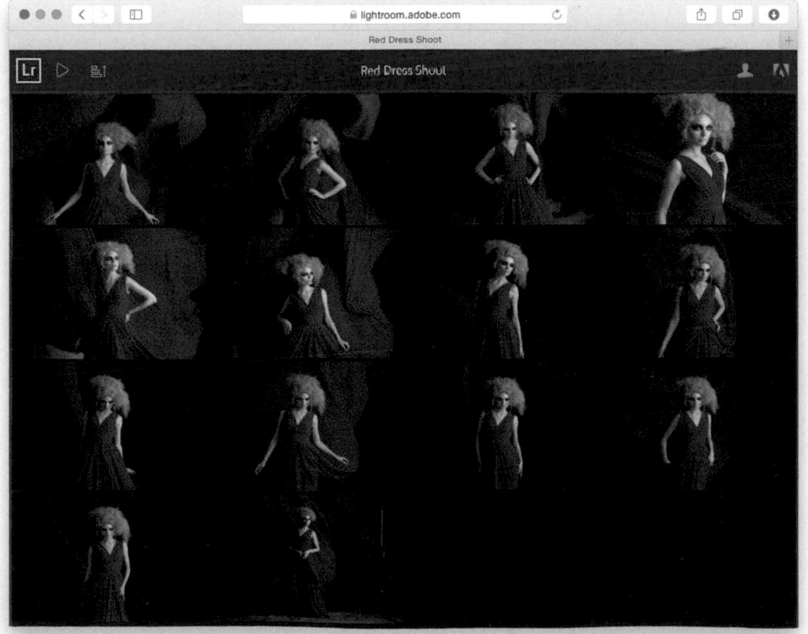

Step Eight:

When the offsite person goes to that URL you sent them, they see what you see here: the same images the client right beside you there in the studio is seeing. If they hit the Play icon in the upper-left corner, they'll get a slide show of the images in your Red Dress Shoot collection. If they want to change the sort order, they can click on the Sort Order icon to the right of the Play icon (if they hover their mouse over any of the icons, a little pop-up explains what they do, so you don't have to give them a demo). So, at this point, yes they can see the images, but they're not really "part of the shoot," right? Well, it's about to get ever better (though, they will need to sign in with an Adobe ID in order to use some of the features we'll look at next).

Continued

Step Nine:

If the offsite person viewing through their web browser clicks on one of those full thumbnails, it zooms in to the larger size you see here. Here, they can tag a photo they like as a Favorite by clicking on the little heart icon in the lower-left corner of the window (they need to use something different than a Pick flag, because your client there with you on the iPad is using Pick flags). Any image they tag in their web browser as a favorite is sent back to you, as well, to Lightroom on your laptop. But, they actually have a feature here in the web browser that your client doesn't even have in the iPad in their hands: the ability to send written comments directly to you.

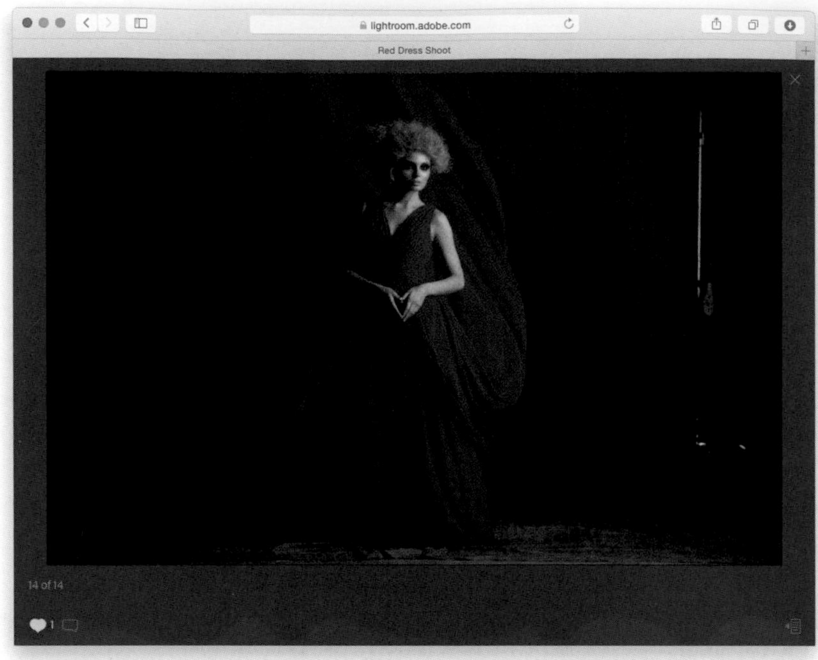

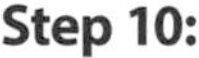

Step 10:

To send a comment on a photo, they just click on the Comment icon in the bottom-left corner of the window (or the Show Activity & Info icon in the bottom right) and an Activity sidebar slides out from the right side. They type in their comment (as seen here, where I wrote "I really like this one, but can we remove the light stand or hide it somehow?"). Once they hit the Post Comment button, that comment is sent directly to Lightroom on your computer (on my laptop, in this case) where you can not only see their comment, but you can even respond back.

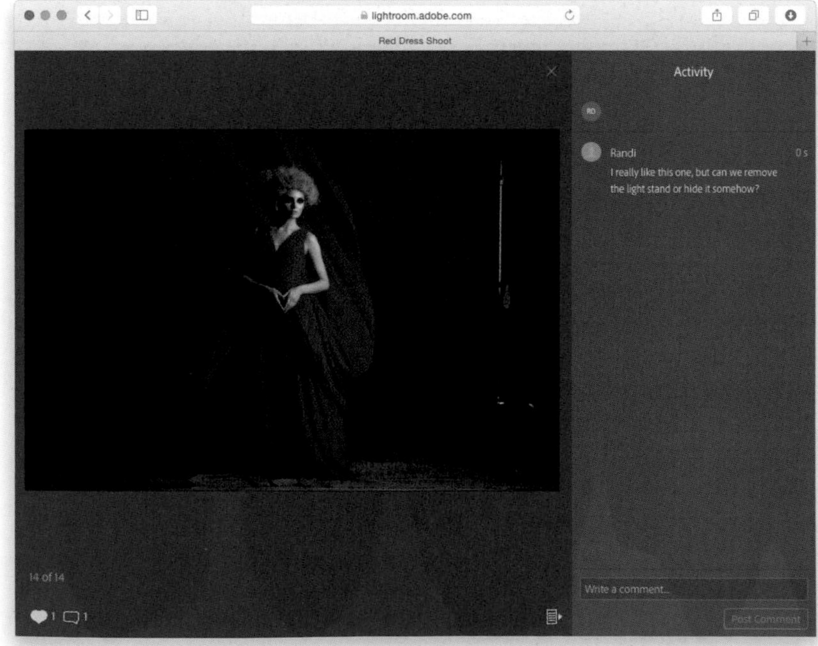

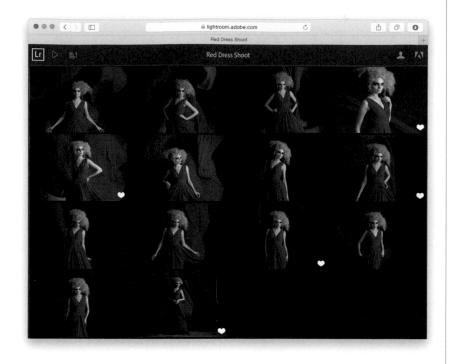

Step 11:

When your offsite viewer returns to the Grid view (they just click the X in the top right), they will see which ones they "Liked" (a white heart will appear in the bottom-right corner of the thumbnail) and which ones they commented on (a comment bubble icon will appear in the top right corner of the thumbnail). Now, back to you, in the studio as the shoot is still in progress.

Note: Only people you send the web link to will be able to see your shoot images in their web browser, even though the button says, "Make Public." A better name for that button might be "Invite." Just sayin'.

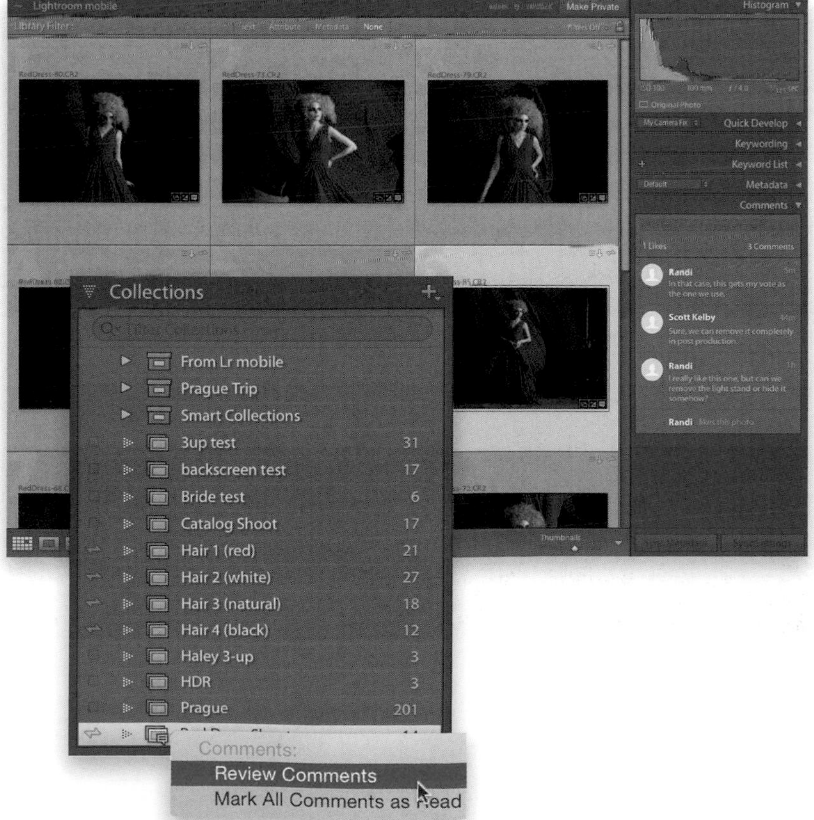

Step 12:

When you look in Lightroom on your computer, you'll know if the offsite person commented or "Liked" a photo because you'll see a little yellow comment icon on your synced collection in the Collections panel (as seen here in the overlay). If you click directly on that yellow icon you can choose to Review Comments now, or to ignore them by choosing Mark All Comments as Read. To read them, look in the Comments panel at the bottom of the right side Panels area in the Library module (this is a new panel in Lightroom). Now, those images that have comments and Favorite tags appear at the top of your collection in Grid view, and once you've looked at them once, the yellow comment icon goes away. You'll still know they have a comment because you'll see a little comment badge appear at the bottom right of those image thumbnails. But, what I do is select all of those images with comments and create a new collection, and either put it in the same collection set (if I made a Collection Set for it), or I just give this new collection a very similar name (like "Red Dress Comments"), so it appears right next to it alphabetically in the Collections panel. That's it!

Four Last Things You'll Want to Know (and They're All Pretty Cool)

There are some other handy features you'll want to know about, but they're so simple they don't each require a full technique, so I put them right here in one. One gives you peace of mind when you hand someone your mobile device to look at your images that they won't mess anything up. One is a new view that groups your images by the time they were taken. Then, there's how to copy-and-paste not only adjustments from one image to another, but also desktop-only features. All cool stuff.

Presentation Mode:

If you want to hand someone your mobile device and let them swipe through your images in Lightroom, there's always the chance that they might swipe up/down and change a star rating or a Pick flag for an image, or maybe they'll accidentally click on the icon that takes them to the adjustment tiles (ack!). That's why Presentation mode was invented—it disables all that stuff, so you don't have to worry about them accidentally changing anything. You enter Presentation mode by tapping on the collection you want, then tapping on the Collection Options icon at the top-right corner, and choosing **Present** from the pop-up menu. When they hand your mobile device back to you, just tap the X in the upper-left corner to exit Presentation mode.

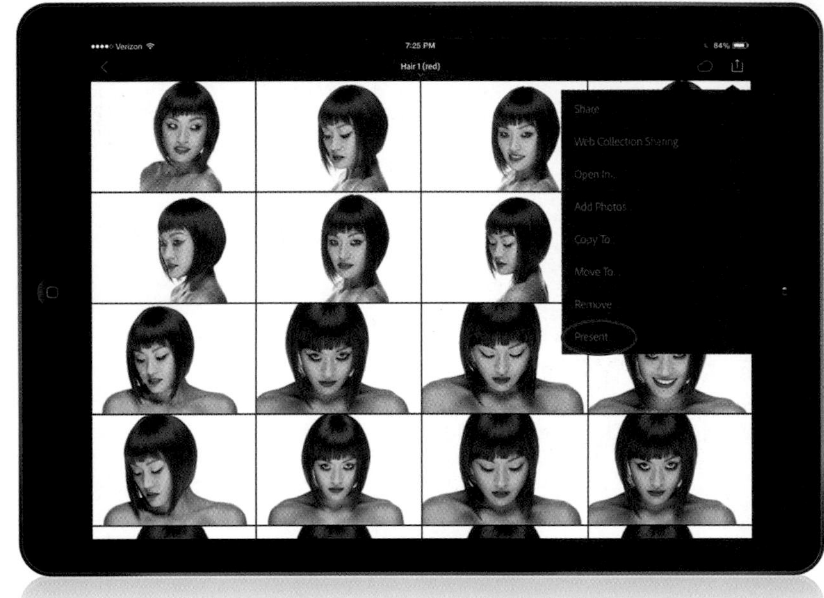

Segmented View:

This view allows you to see your images grouped together automatically by when they were taken. To enter this view, tap on a collection's name at the top of the screen and then tap on **Segmented** (the regular view is called "Flat"). The date the first image was taken will appear at the top left. Tap-and-hold on it to choose which time frame you want them segmented by (year, month, day, or hour) from the pop-up menu (as seen here in the overlay) and it takes it from there (you can still filter to just see your Picks, 5-star images, etc., from the Grid View Options pop-up menu in the top center of the screen). To return to Flat view, choose No Segmentation from that same pop-up menu (or tap on it in the Grid View Options pop-up menu).

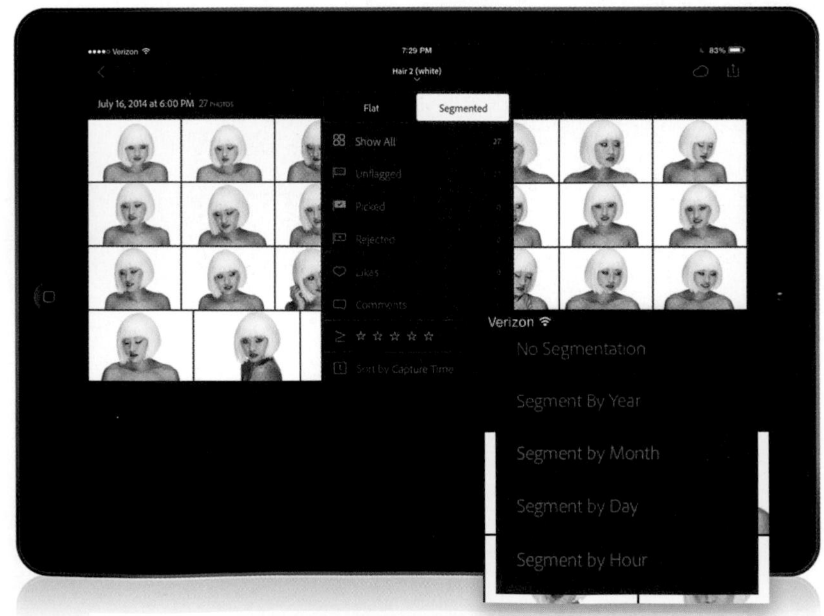

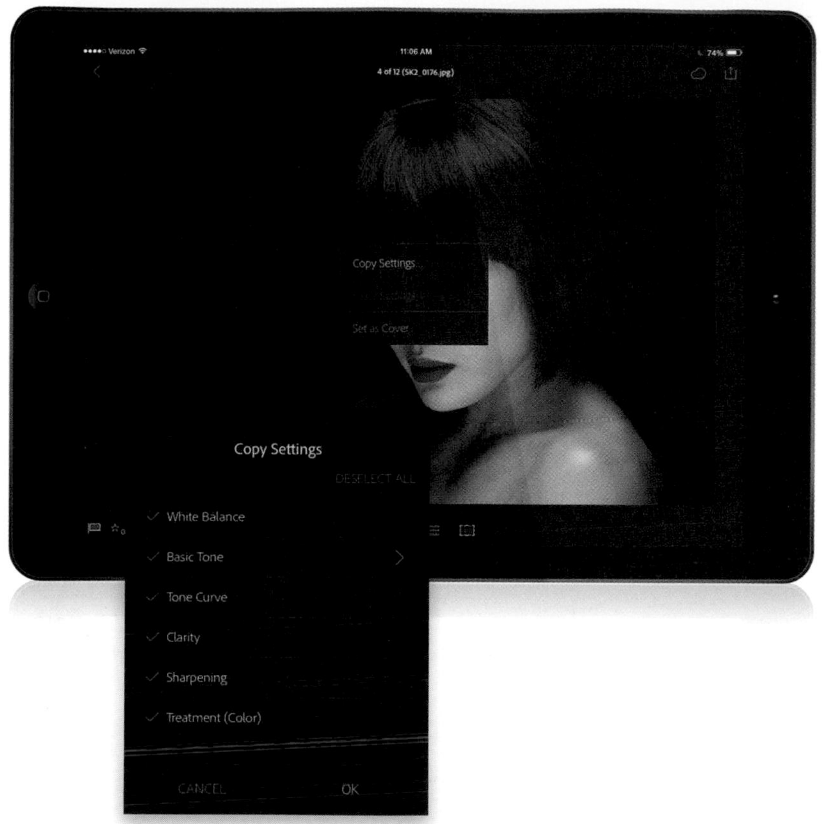

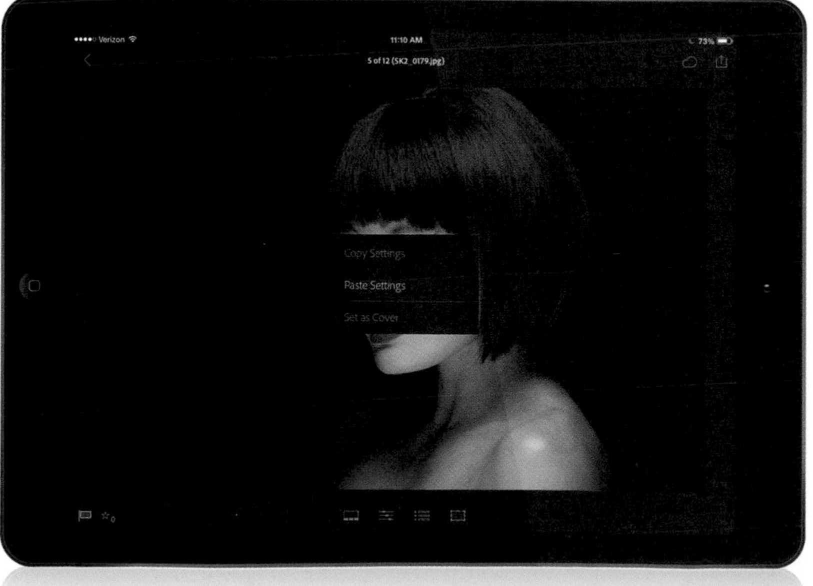

Copying-and-Pasting Settings from One Image to Another:

We do this all the time in Lightroom on our computers (well, even if you don't, you at least you know you can), and now that same feature is in Lightroom on your mobile device. Here's how it works: In Loupe view, tap-and-hold on the photo that has the settings you want to copy. When the pop-up menu appears, tap on **Copy Settings**. This brings up the menu you see here in the overlay and, by default, it's going to copy all the settings from this image. But, if there are certain settings you don't want copied, tap on them to deselect them, so it only copies the ones you want. Tap OK, then swipe over to any image you want to have these copied settings applied to, tap-and-hold on the that image, and when the pop-up menu appears, choose Paste Settings (as shown below), and you're done.

Copying-and-Pasting Features That Aren't Even in Lightroom on Your Mobile Device:

This is pretty slick, because it allows you to do something you shouldn't be able to do in Lightroom on your mobile device, and that's because Lightroom on your mobile device pretty much just has the editing features of Lightroom on your computer's Basic panel, right? There's no Graduated Filter, or Adjustment Brush, or the HSL panel, or stuff like that. However, if you bring an image over to Lightroom on your mobile device that already has stuff like that applied, you can copy-and-paste those settings over to another image inside of Lightroom on your mobile device. Here's how: When you choose Copy Settings on an image that has had some of those features from Lightroom on your computer added (that Lightroom on your mobile device doesn't have), when the Copy Settings pop-up menu appears, keep scrolling down. You can now copy those edits from that photo into memory, and then you can paste them into another image right in Lightroom on your mobile device. I know. Pretty sweet, right?

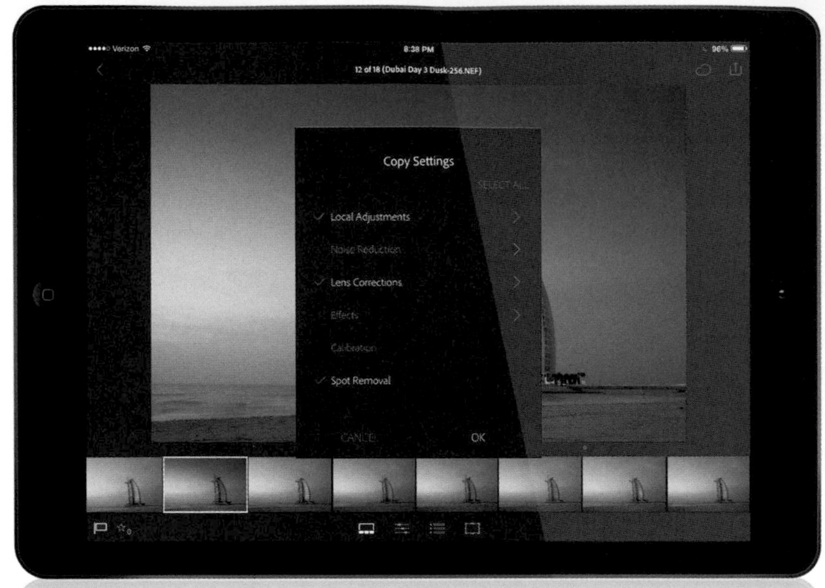

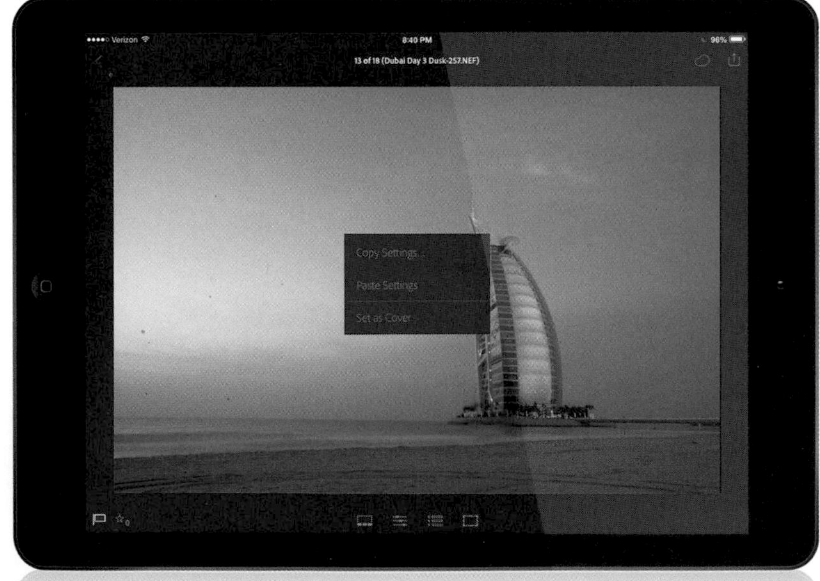

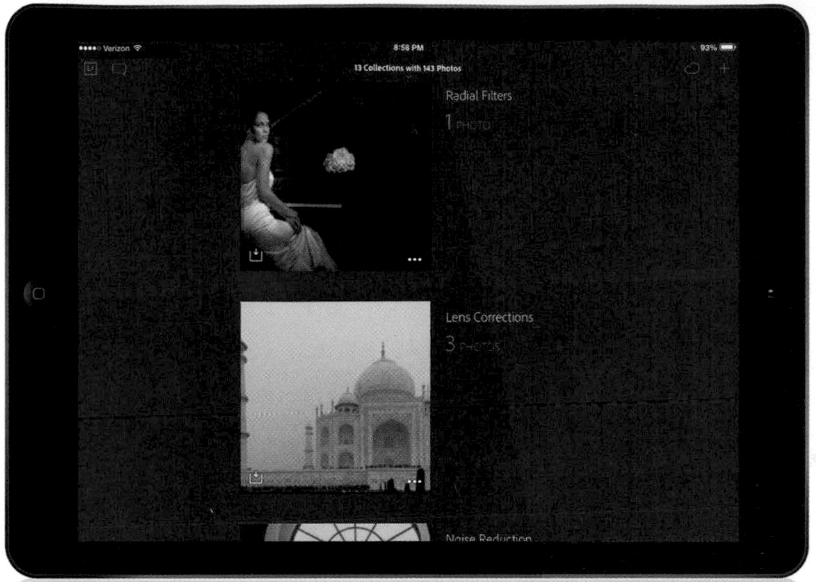

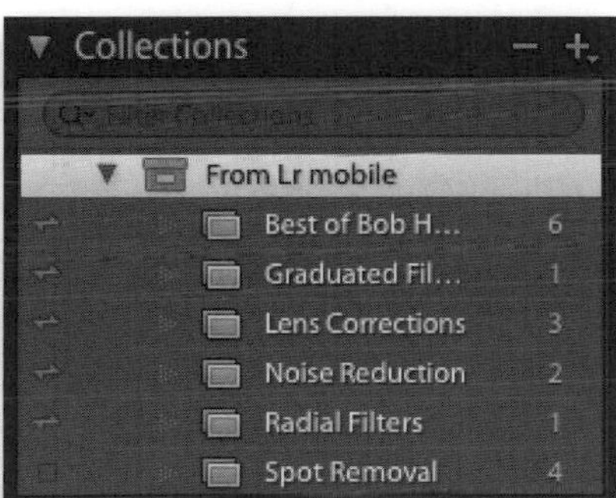

TIP: Make Collections of Adjustments Not in Lightroom on Your Mobile Device:

Now that you can know you can copy-and-paste settings that were applied to an image in Lightroom on your computer (but that aren't yet in Lightroom on your mobile device), why not create a collection of images with edits applied in Lightroom on your computer to sync with Lightroom on your mobile device? Stuff like separate images, each with a different lens correction profile applied for the lenses you use most. Name them with the name of the profile (like 14mm wide-angle), then you can copy-and-paste just that profile to images on your mobile device that need it, even though Lightroom on your mobile device doesn't have a Lens Corrections feature. Or, create a series of graduated filters (one that extends down 25%; one 50%, and one 75%), so you can apply them to landscape photos. Or how about different radial filters with different size clear areas, where the outside is either dark or blurry? Remember to give them descriptive names so you'll know what you're pasting. The mind reels over this one, doesn't it?

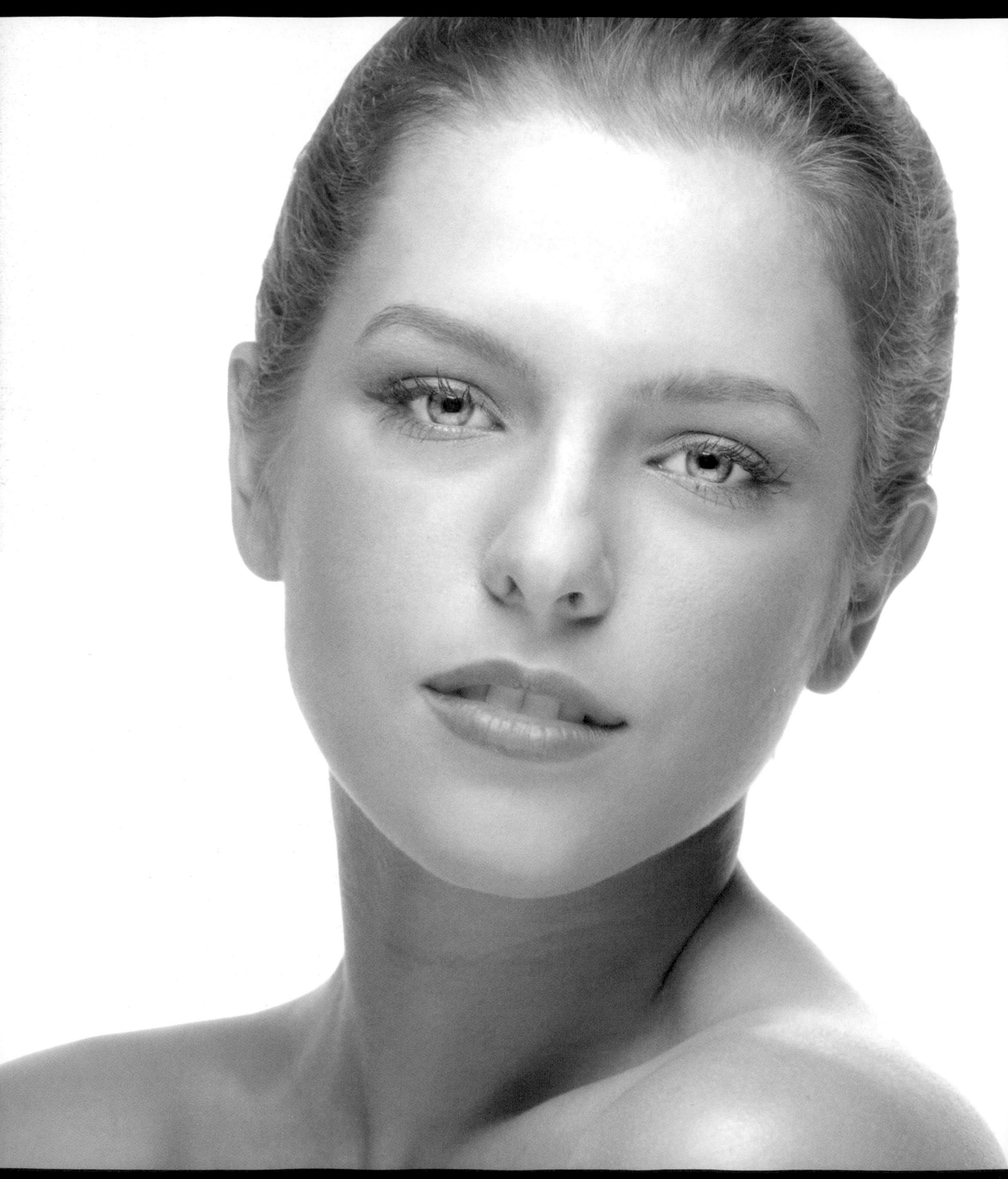

Photo by Scott Kelby | Exposure: 1/125 sec | Focal Length: 150mm | Aperture Value: ƒ/11

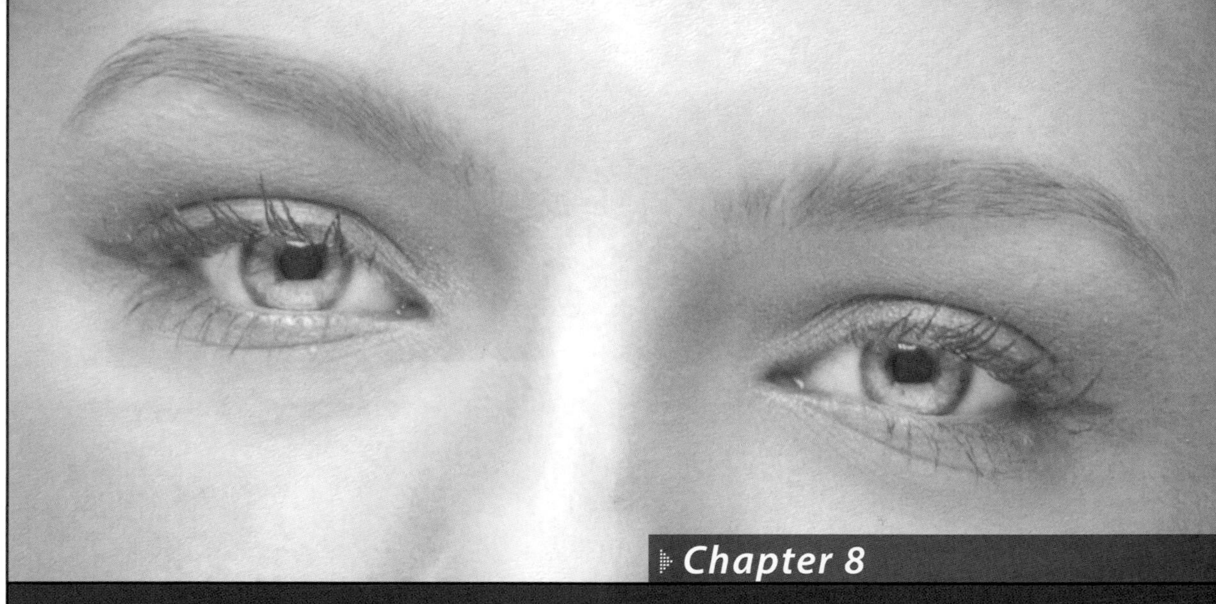

Chapter 8

PROBLEM PHOTOS
fixing common problems

Of all the chapter names, this one is probably the most obvious, because what else could this chapter be about, right? I mean, you wouldn't name it "Problem Photos" and then have it be about creating problems with your photos, or the book would never sell. Well, the book might sell, but this chapter certainly wouldn't help sales. You know what does help sales? Using the word "pimp" not just once, but three times (in three chapter intros). Here's why: Google started this thing a few years back where they index all the pages to printed books, and then add that information to their search database (deep inside Cheyenne Mountain), so if what you're searching for only appears within the pages of a printed book (rather than a webpage), it would still appear as a Google search result, and it would lead you directly to that book. Of course, you'd have to buy the book, but as an author, I can tell you that's not the worst outcome of a search. Anyway, now when people search for the word "pimp," this book will appear as one of Google's search results. Of course, people looking for a pimp will see that this is, in fact, a Lightroom CC book, which will probably initially dissuade them from buying it, but what I'm hoping is that they'll start to wonder why a book about Lightroom contains the word "pimp" at all, and that curiosity will start to eat at them. They'll be dying to know the mystery that lies deep within its crumpled pages, so they'll wind up buying the book anyway to unearth it's hidden pimpy agenda, but then of course, they'll realize that's not the way I was using the word "pimp," and while they'll still be somewhat disappointed, we know from more than a fiftieth of a century's research that approximately 6.7% of those people will start learning Lightroom. Hey, serves the rest right for trying to find a pimp using Google. They should have tried Craigslist.

Fixing Backlit Photos

One of the most common digital photography problems is photos where the subject is backlit, so it is almost a black silhouette. I think it's so common because the human eye adjusts for backlit situations so well that, to our naked eye, everything looks great, but the camera exposes much differently and that shot that looked very balanced when you took it, really looks like what you see below. The Shadows slider (which replaced the Fill Light slider in the Basic panel), does the best job of fixing this problem of anything I've ever seen, but there is one little thing you need to add.

Step One:

In this image, the sky looks properly exposed, but the building is totally in the shadows. While I was looking at the scene, everything looked fine because our eyes instantly balance the exposure of the scene, but unfortunately, our camera doesn't—it exposed for just the sky, leaving the building in shadows. Before we fix the backlit problem, increase the Exposure a little to see if that helps (I dragged it over to +0.65 without blowing out the highlights), then drag the Highlights slider to the left to –50 to lower the brightest highlights in the overly bright sky (hey, it helps).

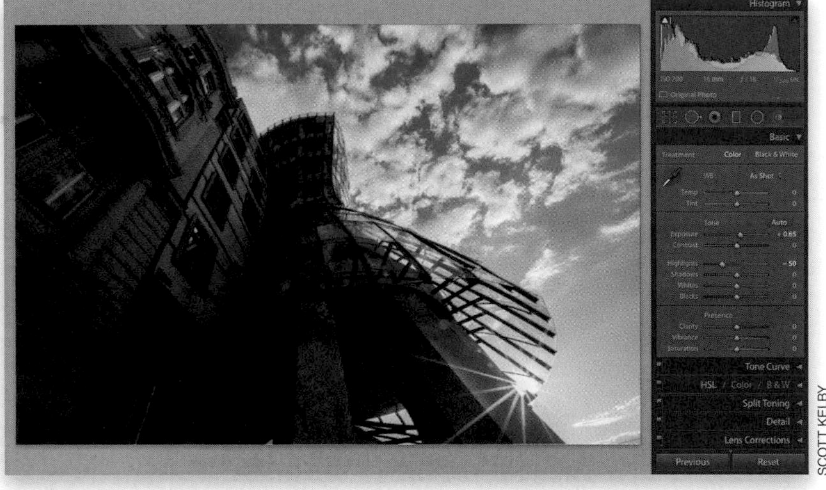

SCOTT KELBY

Step Two:

To open up the foreground, click-and-drag the Shadows slider to the right (here, I dragged to around +80). Back in Lightroom 3, you didn't want to drag the Fill Light slider (the Shadows slider's lesser-quality LR3 counterpart) that far, because it made the image look funky. Luckily, you don't get that same heavy-handed look in Lightroom CC. If you do crank up the Shadows slider pretty high (like I did here), then the photo may start to look washed out (as seen here), but in the next step, we'll fix that with just one simple move.

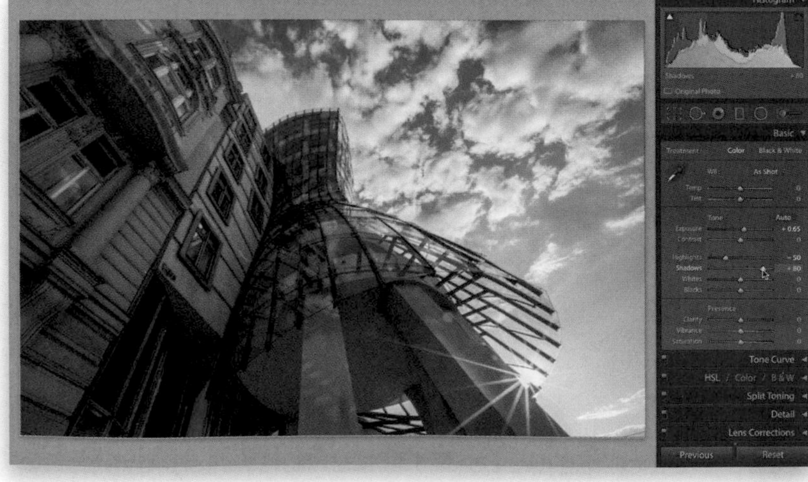

TIP: Watch Out for Noise

If an image has noise in it, it's usually in the shadow areas, so if you do open the shadows a lot, any noise gets amplified. Keep an eye out for it as you drag, and if you do see a lot, go to the Detail panel to reduce the luminance and color noise (see the next project for more on this).

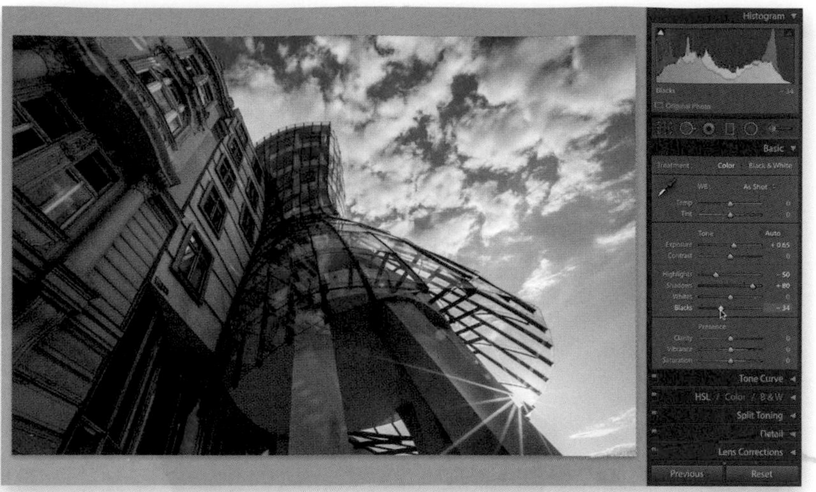

Step Three:

The way to get rid of that washed-out look is simply to push a little bit of blacks into the image by clicking-and-dragging the Blacks slider to the left just a little bit (here, I dragged it to –34). Luckily, this washed-out look doesn't happen nearly as often now as it did back in Lightroom 3, thanks to the new process version. In most cases, you'll be able to move it just a little bit to bring back the blacks.

Step Four:

Here, I used Lightroom's Before/After view (press **Y**) to show what a big difference this technique (using Shadows, then bringing back the deep shadows by increasing the Blacks slider) can do for our backlit photos.

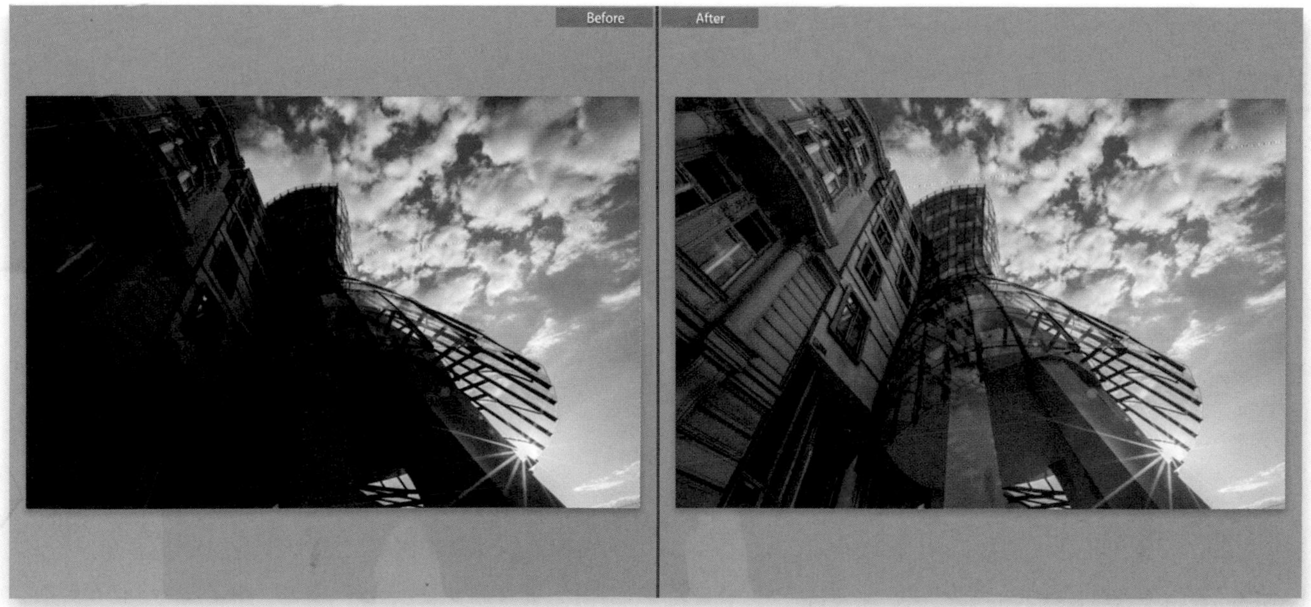

Reducing Noise

If you wind up shooting at a high ISO or in very low light, chances are your image is going to have some noise—either luminance noise (a visible graininess throughout the photo, particularly in shadow areas) or color noise (those annoying red, green, and blue spots). Although the noise reduction in previous versions of Lightroom was kind of weak, in Lightroom 3 Adobe completely reworked the Noise Reduction feature, so now it's not just good, it absolutely rocks. Not only is it more powerful, but it maintains more sharpness and detail than ever before.

Step One:

To reduce the noise in a "noisy" image like this, go to the Develop module's Detail panel, to the Noise Reduction section. To really see the noise, zoom in to at least a 1:1 (as seen below, where I zoomed in on the windows).

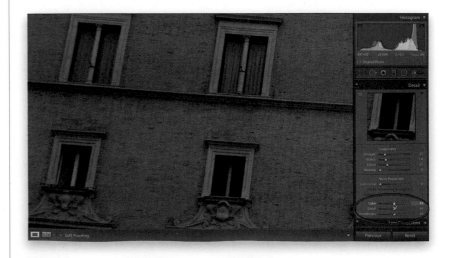

SCOTT KELBY

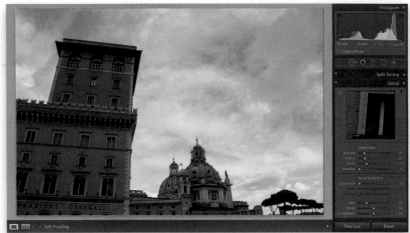

Step Two:

I usually reduce the color noise first, because it's so distracting (if you shoot in RAW, it automatically applies some noise reduction, but I dragged the Color slider back to 0 [zero] so you could see how this works). So, start with the Color slider at 0, and slowly drag it to the right. As soon as the color goes away, stop, because once it's gone, it doesn't get "more gone." Here, there's no visible improvement between a Color setting of 49 (where the color first went away) and 100. The Detail slider controls how the edges in your image are affected. If you drag it way over to the right, it does a good job of protecting color details in edge areas, but you run the risk of having color speckles. If you keep this setting really low, you avoid the speckles, but you might get some colors bleeding (expanding, like they're glowing a bit). So, where do you set it? Look at a colorful area of your image, and try both extremes. I tend to stay at 50 or below for most of my images, but you may find an image where 70 or 80 works best, so don't be afraid to try both ends. Luckily, the Color slider itself makes the most visible difference.

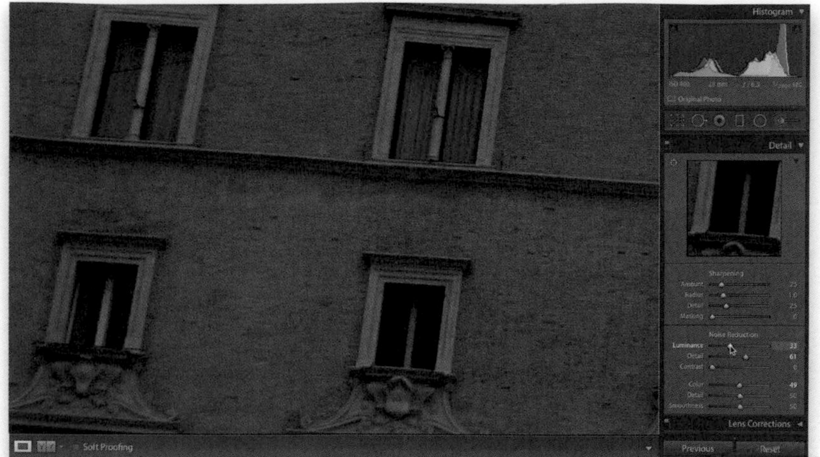

Step Three:

Now that the color noise has been dealt with, chances are your image looks grainy. So to reduce this type of noise (called luminance noise), drag the Luminance slider to the right until the noise is greatly reduced (as shown here). I gotta tell you, this baby works wonders all by itself, but you have additional control with the other two sliders beneath it. The "catch" is this: your image can look clean, or it can have lots of sharp detail, but it's kinda tricky to have both. The Detail slider (in Adobe speak, the "luminance noise threshold") really helps with seriously blurry images. So, if you think your image looks a little blurry now, drag the Detail slider to the right—just know this may make your image a little more noisy. If, instead, you want a cleaner looking image, drag the Detail slider to the left—just know that you'll now be sacrificing a little detail to get that smooth, clean look (there's always a trade-off, right?).

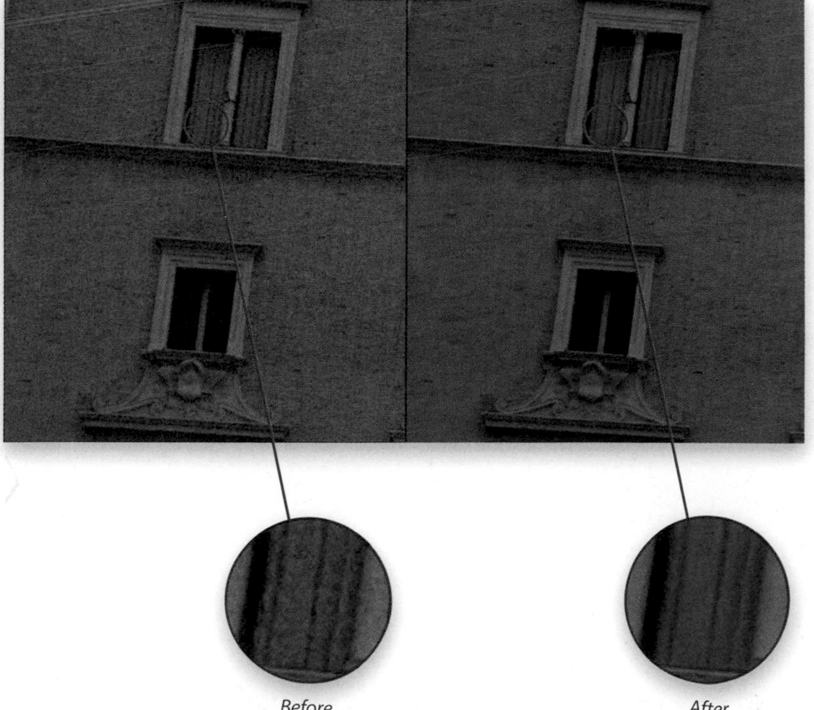

Before *After*

Step Four:

The other slider under Luminance is the Contrast slider. Again, this one really makes a difference on seriously noisy images. Of course, it has its own set of trade-offs. Dragging the Contrast slider to the right protects the photo's contrast, but it might give you some blotchy-looking areas (the key word here is "might"). You get smoother results dragging the slider to the left, but you'll be giving up some contrast. I know, I know, why can't you have detail and smooth results? That's coming in Lightroom 9. The real key here is to try to find that balance, and the only way to do that is experiment on the image you have onscreen. For this particular image, most of the luminance noise was gone after dragging the Luminance slider to around 33 (dragging much higher didn't yield better results). I wanted to keep more detail, so I increased the Detail amount to around 61. I left the Contrast slider as is. The before/after is shown here.

Undoing Changes Made in Lightroom

Lightroom keeps track of every edit you make to your photo and it displays them as a running list, in the order they were applied, in the Develop module's History panel. So if you want to go back and undo any step, and return your photo to how it looked at any stage during your editing session, you can do that with just one click. Now, unfortunately, you can't just pull out one single step and leave the rest, but you can jump back in time to undo any mistake, and then pick up from that point with new changes. Here's how it's done:

Step One:

Before we look at the History panel, I just wanted to mention that you can undo anything by pressing **Command-Z (PC: Ctrl-Z)**. Each time you press it, it undoes another step, so you can keep pressing it and pressing it until you get back to the very first edit you ever made to the photo in Lightroom, so it's possible you won't need the History panel at all (just so you know). If you want to see a list of all your edits to a particular photo, click on the photo, then go to the History panel in the left side Panels area (shown here). The most recent changes appear at the top. (*Note:* A separate history list is kept for each individual photo.)

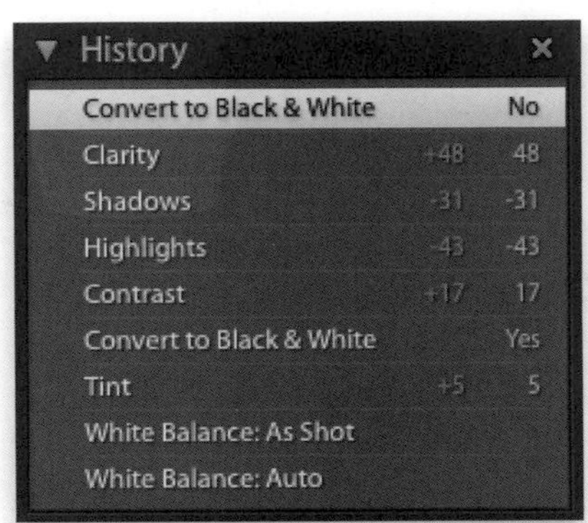

Step Two:

If you hover your cursor over one of the history states, the small Navigator panel preview (which appears at the top of the left side Panels area) shows what your photo looked like at that point in history. Here, I'm hovering my cursor over the point a few steps back where I had converted this photo to black and white, but since then I changed my mind and switched back to color.

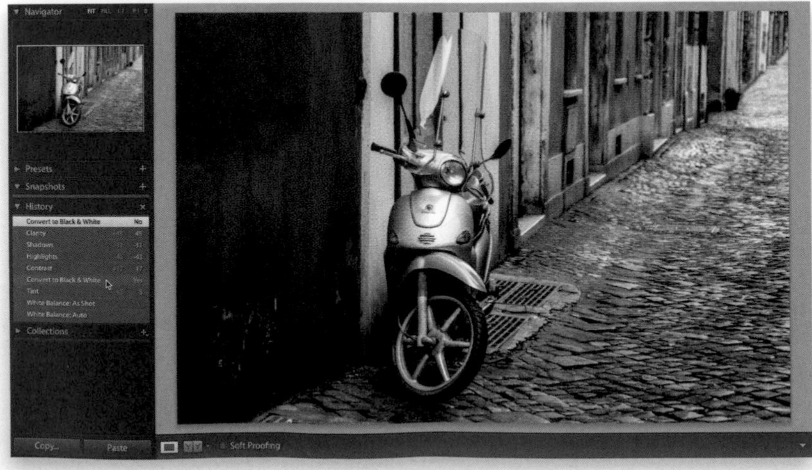

SCOTT KELBY

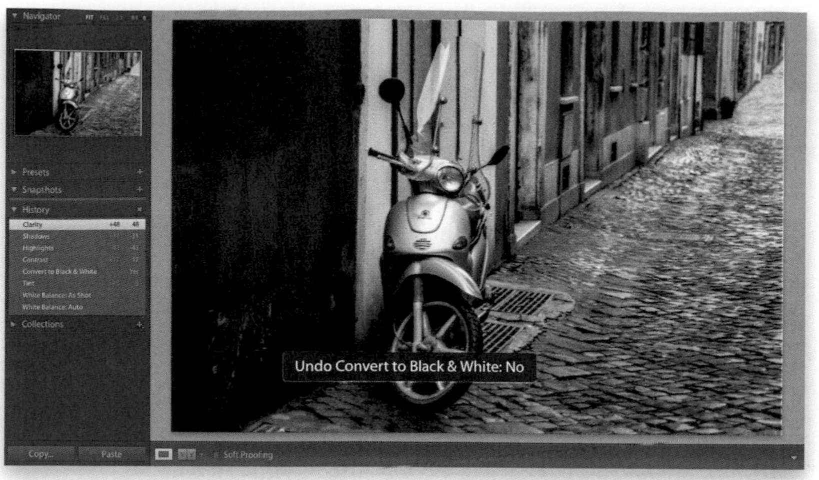

Step Three:

If you actually want to jump back to what your photo looked like at a particular stage, then instead of hovering over the state, you'd click once on it and your photo reverts to that state. By the way, if you use the keyboard shortcut for your undos (instead of using the History panel), the edit you're undoing is displayed in very large letters over your photo (as seen here). This is handy because you can see what you're undoing, without having to keep the History panel open all the time.

TIP: Undos Last Forever

Photoshop's History panel only lets you have 20 undos, and if you close the file, they go away. However, in Lightroom, every single change you make to your photo inside Lightroom is tracked and when you change images, or close Lightroom, your unlimited undos are saved. So even if you come back to that photo a year later, you'll always be able to undo what you did.

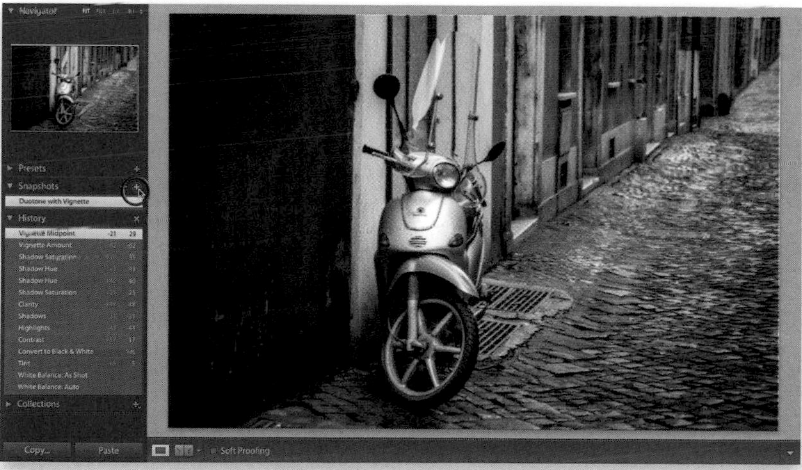

Step Four:

If you come to a point where you really like what you see and you want the option of quickly jumping back to that point, go to the Snapshots panel (right above the History panel), and click on the + (plus sign) button on the right side of the panel header (as shown here). That moment in time is saved to the Snapshots panel, and it appears with its name field highlighted, so you can give it a name that makes sense to you (I named mine "Duotone with Vignette," so I'd know that if I clicked on that snapshot, that's what I'd get—a duotone with a vignette. You can see my snapshot highlighted in the Snapshots panel shown here). By the way, you don't have to actually click on a previous step in the History panel to save it as a snapshot. Instead, you can just Right-click on any step and choose **Create Snapshot** from the pop-up menu. Pretty handy.

Cropping Photos

When I first used the cropping feature in Lightroom, I thought it was weird and awkward—probably because I was so used to the Crop tool in older versions of Photoshop—but once I got used to it, I realized that it's probably the best cropping feature I've ever seen. This might throw you for a loop at first, but if you try it with an open mind, I think you'll wind up falling in love with it. If you try it and don't like it, make sure you read Step Six for how to crop more like you used to in Photoshop (but don't forget that whole "open mind" thing).

Step One:

Here's the original photo. The shot is so wide and your eye kinda wanders around the image, so we're going to crop in tight to isolate the fireworks. Go to the Develop module and click on the Crop Overlay tool (circled here in red) in the toolbox above the Basic panel, and the Crop & Straighten options will pop down below it. This puts a "rule of thirds" grid overlay on your image (to help with cropping composition), and you'll see four cropping corner handles. To lock your aspect ratio (so your crop is constrained to your photo's original proportion), or unlock it if you want a non-constrained freeform crop, click on the lock icon near the top right of the panel (as shown here).

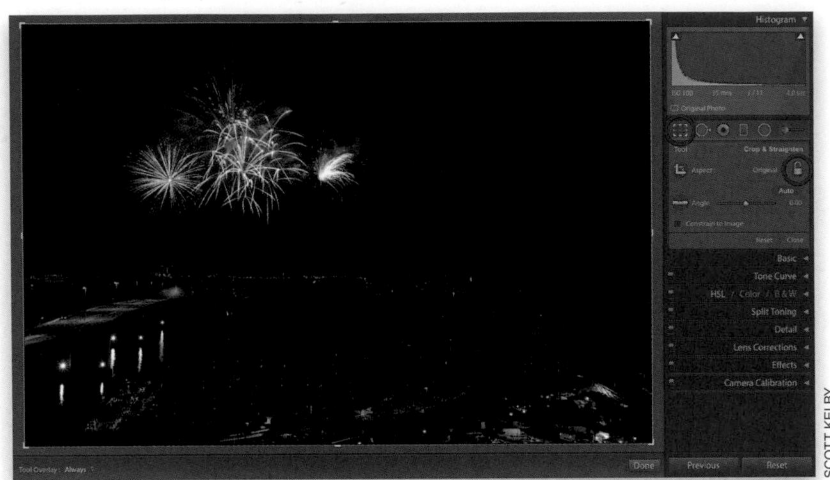

SCOTT KELBY

Step Two:

To crop the photo, grab a corner handle and drag inward to resize your Crop Overlay border. Here, I grabbed the bottom-right corner handle and dragged diagonally inward.

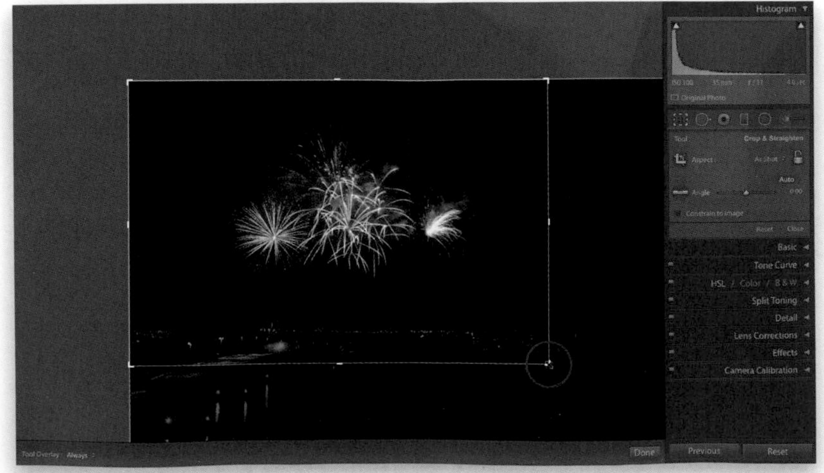

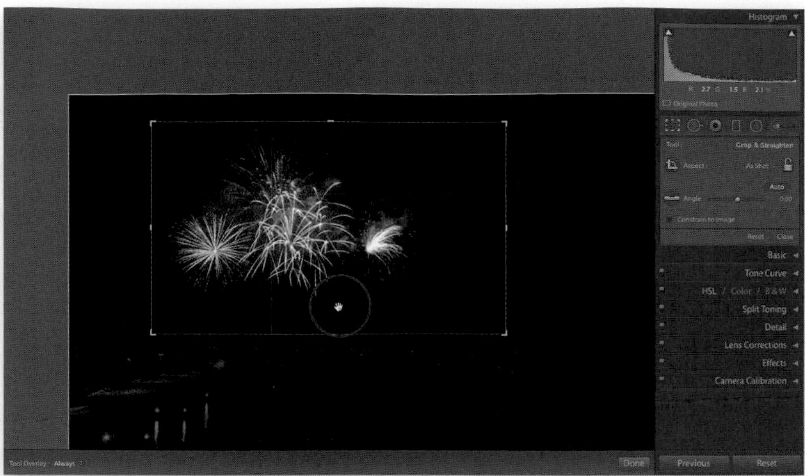

Step Three:

Now let's crop in tight on the fireworks (you did download this photo, right? The URL for the downloads is in the book's introduction). Just grab the bottom-right corner and drag it diagonally outward for a nice, tight crop (as seen here). If you need to reposition the photo inside the cropping border, just click-and-hold inside the Crop Overlay border. Your cursor will change into the "grabber hand" (shown here), and now you can drag it where you want it.

TIP: Hiding the Grid

If you want to hide the rule-of-thirds grid that appears over your Crop Overlay border, press **Command-Shift-H (PC: Ctrl-Shift-H)**. Or, you can have it only appear when you're actually moving the crop border itself, by choosing **Auto** from the Tool Overlay pop-up menu in the toolbar beneath the Preview area. Also, there's not just a rule of thirds grid, there are other grids—just press the letter **O** to toggle through the different ones.

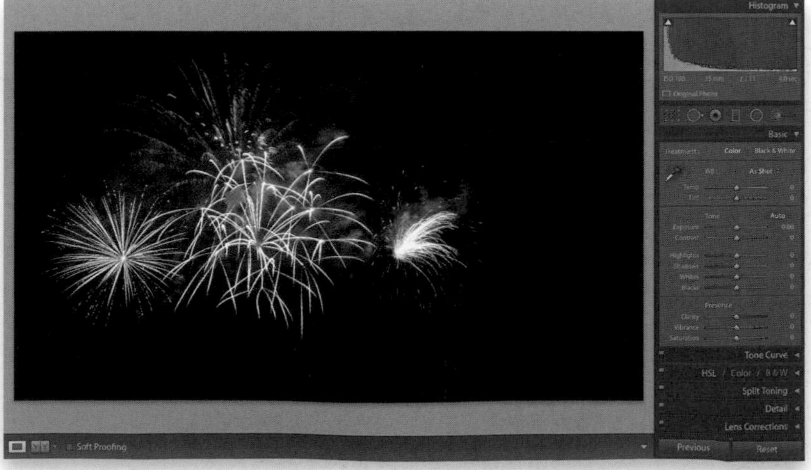

Step Four:

When the crop looks good to you, press the letter **R** on your keyboard to lock it in, remove the Crop Overlay border, and show the final cropped version of the photo (as seen here). But there are two other choices for cropping we haven't looked at yet.

Continued

Step Five:

If you know you want a particular size ratio for your image, you can do that from the Aspect pop-up menu in the Crop & Straighten options. Go ahead and click the Reset button, below the right side Panels area, so we return to our original image, and then click on the Crop Overlay tool, again. Click on the Aspect pop-up menu at the top-right side of the Crop & Straighten options, and a list of preset sizes appears (seen here). Choose **4x5/8x10** from the pop-up menu, and you'll see the left and right sides of the Crop Overlay border move in to show the ratio of what a 4x5" or 8x10" crop would be. Now you can resize the cropping rectangle and be sure that it will maintain that 4x5/8x10 aspect ratio.

Step Six:

The other, more "Photoshop-like," way to crop is to click on the Crop Overlay tool, then click on the Crop Frame tool (shown circled here in red) to release it from its home near the top left of the Crop & Straighten options. Now you can just click-and-drag out a cropping border in the size and position you'd like it. Don't let it freak you out that the original cropping border stays in place while you're dragging out your new crop, as seen here—that's just the way it works. Once you've dragged out your cropping border, it works just like before (grab the corner handles to resize, and reposition it by clicking inside the cropping border and dragging. When you're done, press **R** to lock in your changes). So, which way is the right way to crop? The one you're most comfortable with.

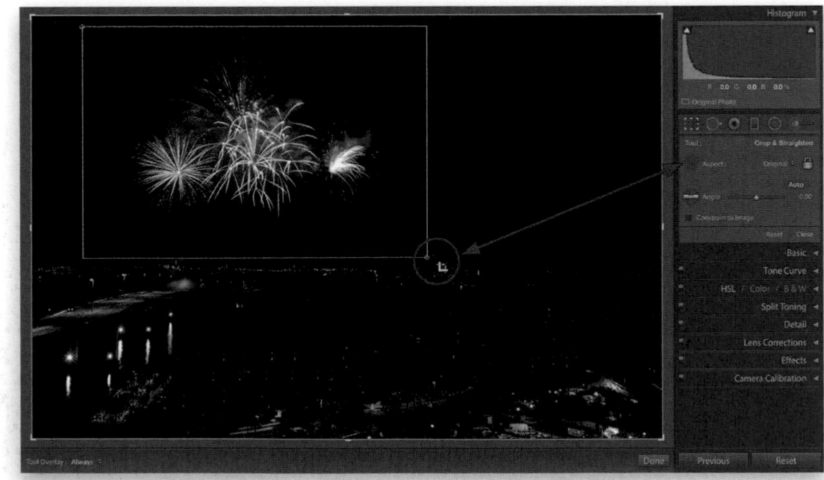

TIP: Canceling Your Crop

If, at any time, you want to cancel your cropping, just click on the Reset button at the bottom-right side of the Crop & Straighten options panel.

When you crop a photo using the Crop Overlay tool in the Develop module, the area that will get cropped away is automatically dimmed to give you a better idea of how your photo is going to look when you apply the final crop. That's not bad, but if you want the ultimate cropping experience, where you really see what your cropped photo is going to look like, then do your cropping in Lights Out mode. You'll never want to crop any other way.

Lights Out Cropping Rocks!

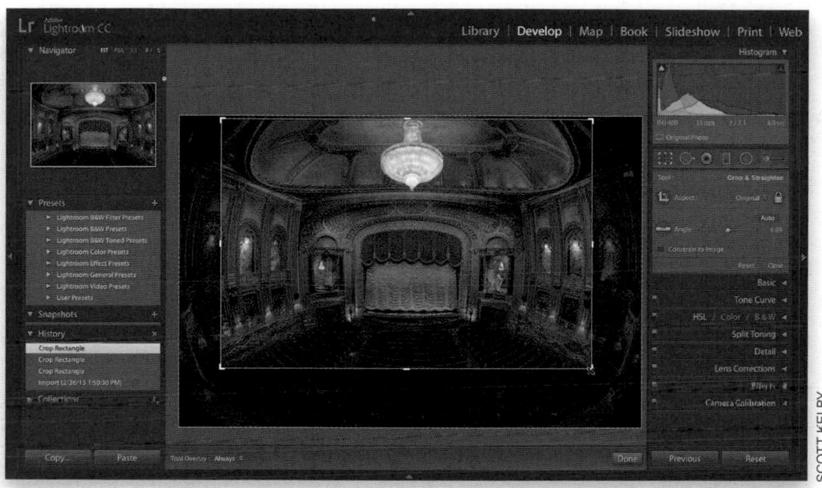

SCOTT KELBY

Step One:

To really appreciate this technique, first take a look at what things look like when we normally crop an image—lots of panels and distractions, and the area we're actually cropping away appears dimmed (but it still appears). Now let's try Lights Out cropping: First, click on the Crop Overlay tool to enter cropping mode. Now press **Shift-Tab** to hide all your panels.

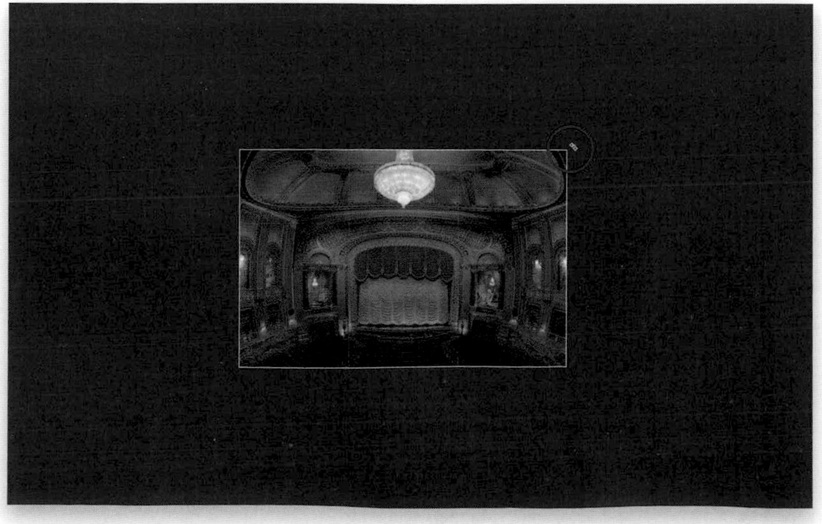

Step Two:

Press the letter **L** twice to enter Lights Out mode, where every distraction is hidden, and your photo is centered on a black background, but your cropping border is still in place. Now, try grabbing a corner handle and dragging inward, then clicking-and-dragging outside your cropping border to rotate it, and watch the difference—you see what your cropped image looks like live as you're dragging the cropping border. It's the ultimate way to crop (it's hard to tell from the static graphic here, so you'll have to try this one for yourself—you'll never go "dim" again!).

Straightening Crooked Photos

If you've got a crooked photo, Lightroom's got four great ways to straighten it. One of them is pretty precise, one's automatic, and with the other two you're pretty much just "eyeing it," but with some photos that's the best you can do.

Step One:

The photo shown here has a crooked horizon line, which is pretty much instant death for a landscape shot. To straighten the photo, start by getting the Crop Overlay tool **(R)**, found in the toolbox, right under the histogram in the Develop module's right side Panels area (shown here). This brings up the Crop Overlay grid around your photo, and while this grid might be helpful when you're cropping to recompose your image, it's really distracting when you're trying to straighten one, so I press **Command-Shift-H (PC: Ctrl-Shift-H)** to hide that grid.

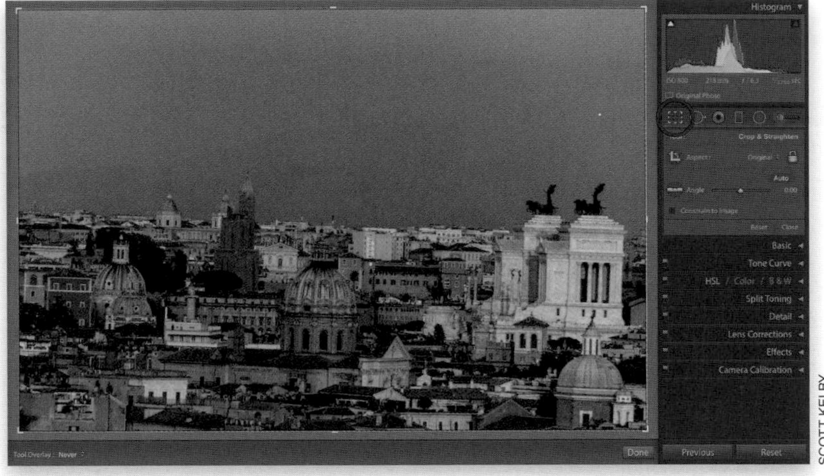

SCOTT KELBY

Step Two:

As I mentioned above, there are four different ways to straighten your photo and we'll start with my favorite, which uses the Angle tool. I think it's the fastest and most accurate way to straighten photos. Click on the Angle tool, found in the Crop & Straighten options (it looks like a level), then click-and-drag it left to right along something that's supposed to be level in the image (as shown here, where I've dragged it along the tops of the buildings). See why I like straightening like this? However, there is one catch: you have to have something in the photo that's supposed to be level—like a horizon, or a wall, or a window frame, etc.

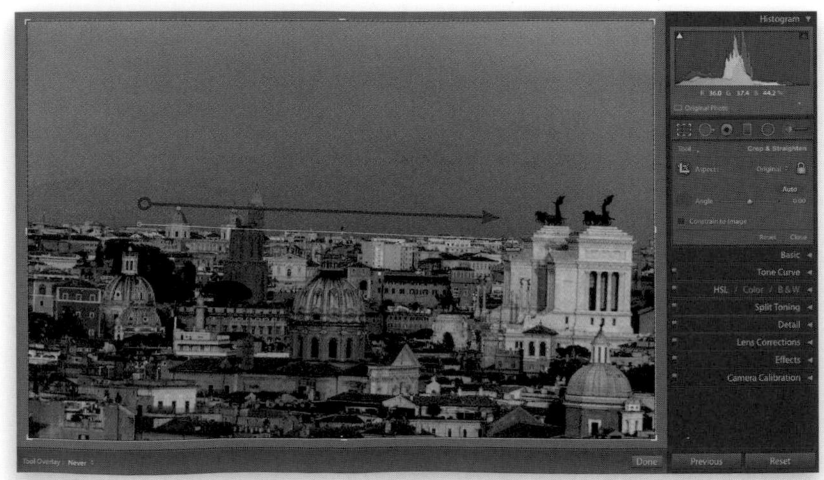

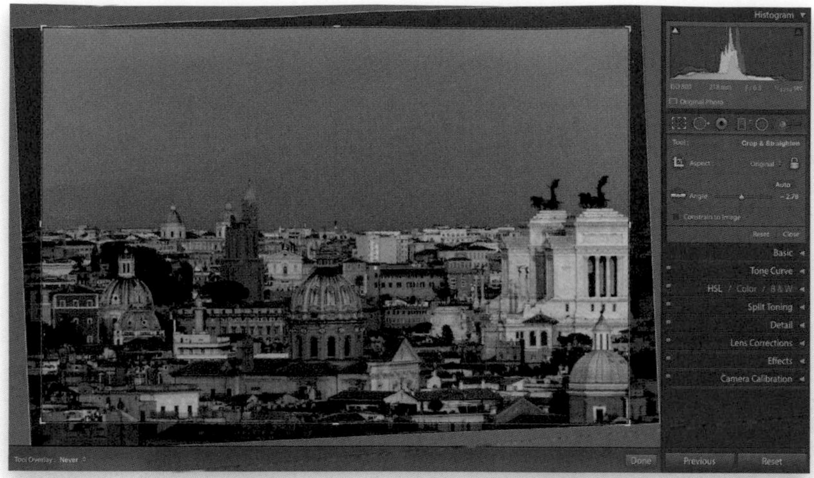

Step Three:

When you drag that tool, it shrinks and rotates the cropping border to the exact angle you'd need to straighten the photo (without leaving any white gaps in the corners). The exact angle of your correction is displayed in the Crop & Straighten options next to the Angle slider. Now all you have to do is press **R** to lock in your straightening. If you decide you don't like your first attempt at straightening, just click the Reset button at the bottom of the options, and it resets the photo to its unstraightened and uncropped state. So, to try again, grab the Angle tool and start dragging.

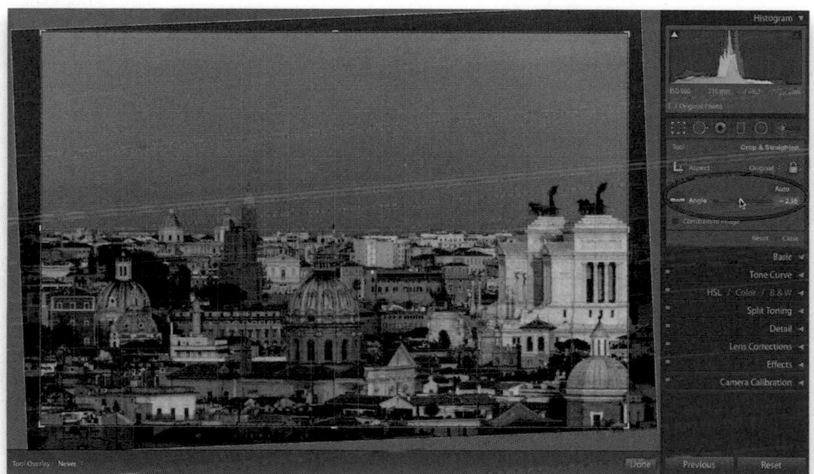

Step Four:

To try the three other methods, we need to undo what we just did, so click the Reset button at the bottom of the right side Panels area, then click on the Crop Overlay tool again (if you locked in your crop after the last step). The first of the three methods is to just drag the Angle slider (shown circled here in red)—dragging it to the right rotates the image clockwise; dragging left, counterclockwise. As soon as you start to drag, a rotation grid appears to help you line things up (seen here). Unfortunately, the slider moves in pretty large increments, making it hard to get just the right amount of rotation, but you can make smaller, more precise rotations by clicking-and-dragging left or right directly over the Angle amount field (on the far right of the slider). The second method is to just move your cursor outside the Crop Overlay border (onto the gray background), and your cursor changes into a two-headed arrow. Now, just click-and-drag up/down to rotate your image until it looks straight. And, the third method is to try to have Lightroom straighten the image for you by just clicking on the Auto button above the Angle slider (or just press-and-hold the Shift key and double-click directly on the word "Angle").

Finding Spots and Specks the Easy Way

There is nothing worse than printing a nice big image, and then seeing all sorts of sensor dust, spots, and specks in your image. If you shoot landscapes or travel shots, it is so hard to see these spots in a blue or grayish sky, and if you shoot in a studio on seamless paper, it's just as bad (maybe worse). I guess I should say, it used to be bad—now it's absolutely a breeze thanks to a feature added back in Lightroom 5 that makes every little spot and speck really stand out so you can remove them fast!

Step One:

Here's an image of the Burj Khalifa, and you can see a few spots and specks in the sky pretty clearly (but it's the spots that you can't see clearly at this size, or against this flat sky, that "Getcha!"). Of course, you eventually do see them—like after you've printed the image on expensive paper, or when a client asks, "Are these spots supposed to be there?"

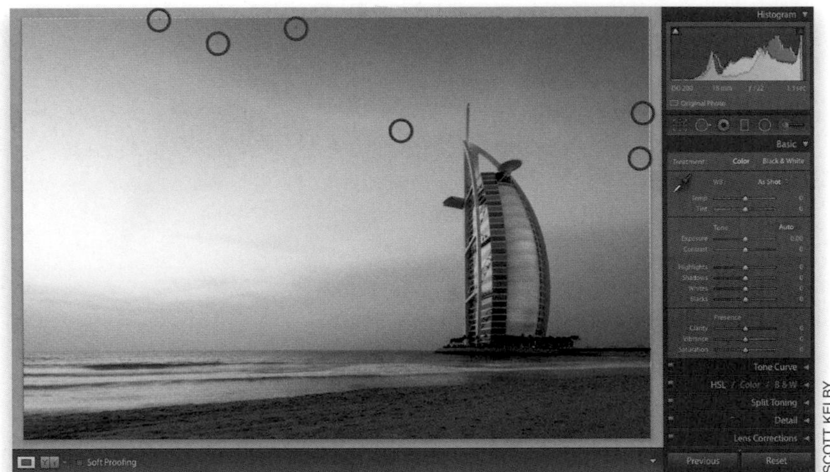

Step Two:

To find any spots, specks, dust, or junk in your image, click on the Spot Removal tool (**Q**; it's shown here circled in red) in the toolbox near the top of the right side Panels area. Down in the toolbar, directly below the main Preview area, is a Visualize Spots checkbox (also circled here). Turn this checkbox on and you get an inverted view of your image, where you can instantly see some more spots now.

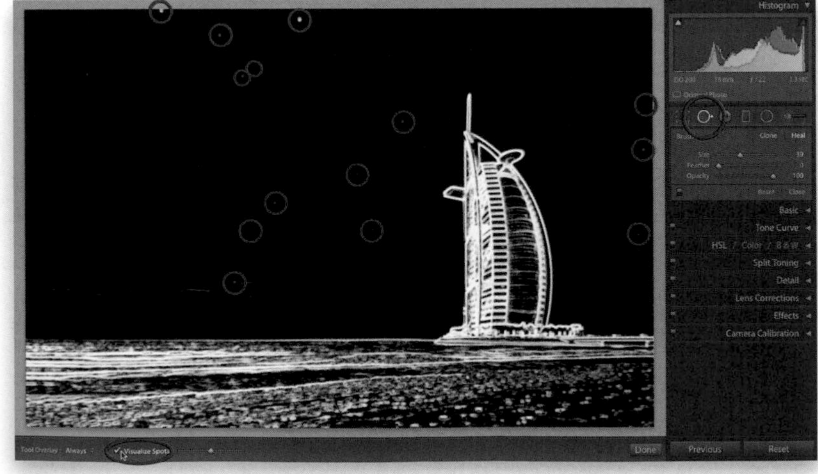

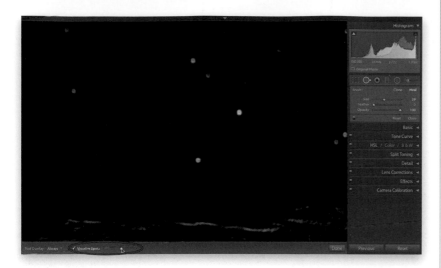

Step Three:
I zoomed in a bit here, so you can see the spots better, but another reason why they stand out so amazingly is because I increased the Visualize Spots threshold level (drag the Visualize Spots slider to the right, and now if there are any spots, specks, dust, etc., still hiding, you'll see them in an instant). I drag this slider to the right until I find that point where the spots stand out, but without the threshold overwhelming everything by bringing out what, if you drag too far, looks like snow or noise.

TIP: Choosing Brush Size
When using the Spot Removal tool, you can press-and-hold Command-Option (PC: Ctrl-Alt) and click-and-drag out a selection around your spot (start by clicking just to the upper left of the spot, then drag across the spot at a 45° angle). As you do, it lays down a starting point and then your circle drags right over the spot.

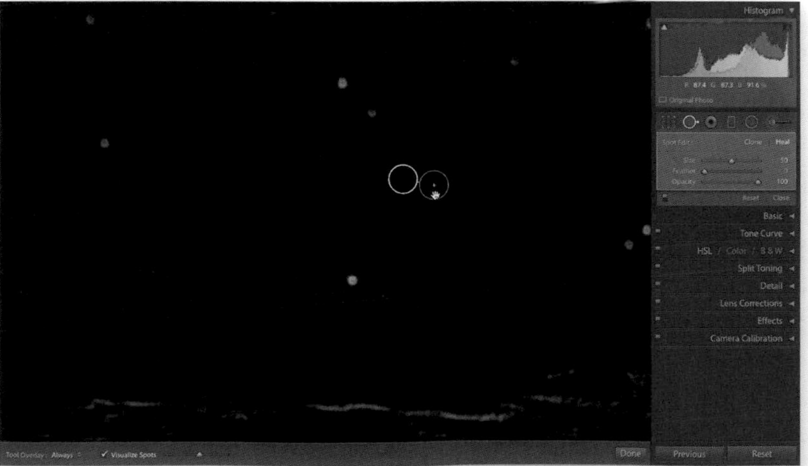

Step Four:
Now that the spots are so easily visible, you can take the Spot Removal tool and just click it once, right over each spot, to remove them (as shown here, where I've removed most of the visible spots). Use the Size slider or the **Left and Right Bracket keys** to make the tool a little larger than the spot you want to remove. When you're done, turn the Visualize Spots checkbox off and make sure the Spot Removal tool sampled from matching areas. If you see a spot where it didn't, just click on that circle to make it active, then click inside the sampling circle and drag it to a matching area (as shown here, where I still have Visualize Spots on and am moving the sampling circle).

Continued

Step Five:

Often, it's dust on your camera's sensor that creates these annoying spots and they'll be in the exact same position in every shot from that shoot. If that's the case, then once you've removed all the spots, make sure the photo you fixed is still selected in the Filmstrip, and select all the similar photos from that shoot, then click the Sync button at the bottom of the right side Panels area. This brings up the Synchronize Settings dialog, shown here. First, click the Check None button, so everything it would sync from your photo is unchecked. Then, turn on the checkboxes for Process Version and Spot Removal (shown here), and click the Synchronize button.

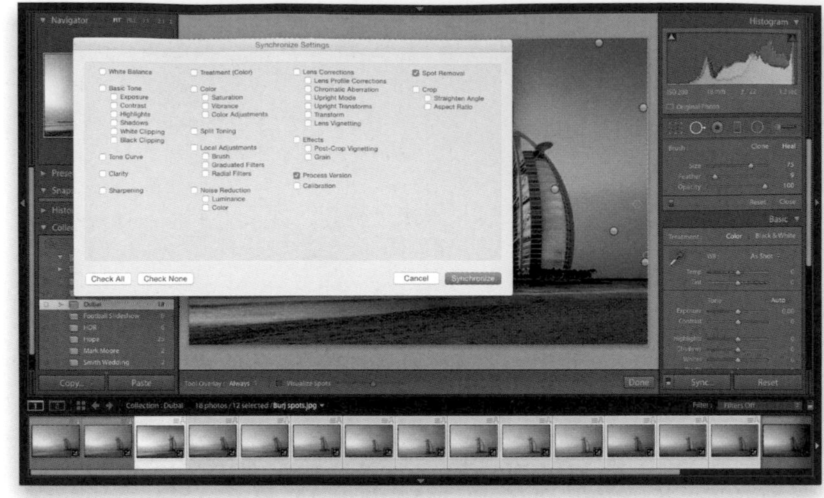

Step Six:

Now, it applies that same spot removal you did to the first photo, to all these other selected photos—all at once (as you can see it did here). To see these fixes applied, click on the Spot Removal tool again. I also recommend you take a quick look at the fixed photos, because depending on the subject of your other shots, the fixes could look more obvious than on the photo you just fixed. If you see a photo with a spot repair problem, just click on that particular circle, hit the **Delete (PC: Backspace) key** on your keyboard to remove it, then use the Spot Removal tool to redo that one spot repair manually.

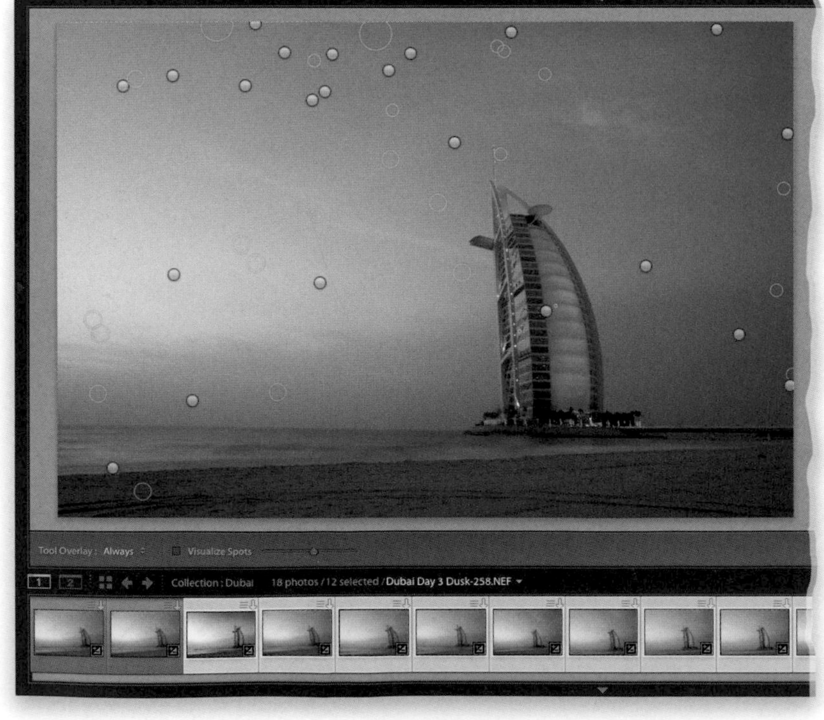

TIP: When to Use Clone

There are two choices for how this tool fixes your spots—Clone or Heal. The only reason ever to switch it to Clone is if the spot you're trying to remove is on or near the edge of an object in your image, or near the edge of the image itself. In these cases, Heal often smudges the image.

Removing Stuff With the Spot Removal Tool

One thing we had to always go to Photoshop for was to use the Healing Brush. Sure, if you wanted to remove a spot or a blemish, you could use Lightroom's Spot Removal tool, but since it did "circular healing" (it would only heal inside a circular shape), you couldn't paint a stroke to remove a wrinkle, or a power line, or well… much of anything other than a spot—all you could do was create more circles. Well, back in Lighroom 5, Adobe turned the tool into a brush, and now we can paint those problems away right in Lightroom—no Photoshop necessary.

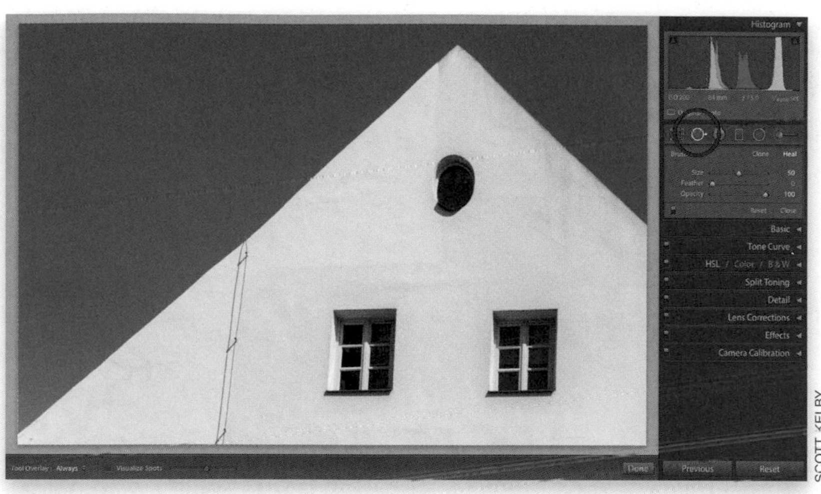

SCOTT KELBY

Step One:

Here's the image we want to retouch. In this case, we want to remove the cable running along the left side of the building, and later we'll remove the window on the right (just because we can). So, click on the Spot Removal tool (shown circled here in red) in the toolbox near the top of the right side Panels area, or just press **Q**. By the way, I think they totally should rename this tool now that it works more like Photoshop's Healing Brush and it does more than just remove spots. Just sayin.'

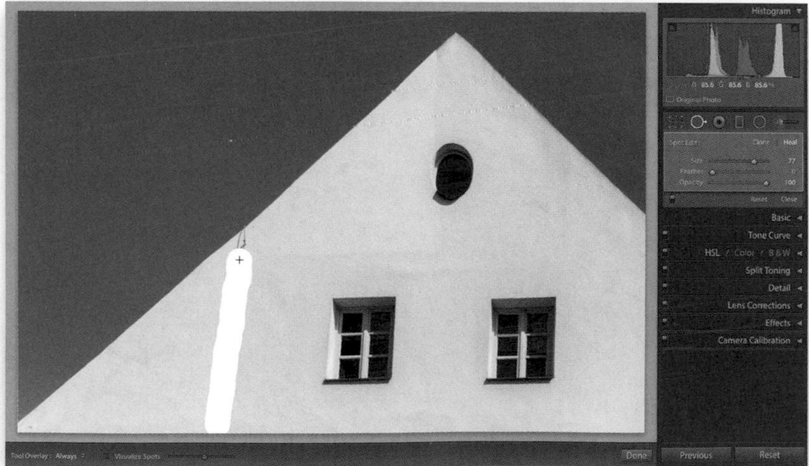

Step Two:

Take the Spot Removal tool and just paint a stroke over the cable (as seen here, where I started at the bottom and dragged it upward). As you do, you'll see a white area appear showing the area you're "healing" as you paint.

TIP: Drawing Straight Lines with the Healing Brush

If you want to remove something distracting from your image that's in a straight line, like a telephone wire, start by clicking once on one end of the wire. Then, press-and-hold the Shift key, go to the other end of the wire, and just click once to have it paint a straight brush stroke between those two points, and remove the wire completely.

Continued

Step Three:

When you finish your stroke, you'll see two outlined areas: (1) the one with the slightly thicker outline is the one showing the area you're healing, and (2) the other one (the thinner one) is showing you the area that the Spot Removal tool chose to sample to use to cover the wires. Usually, this sample area is pretty close to the area you're trying to fix, but sometimes (for reasons I can't begin to understand) it decides to sample somewhere totally weird (like the middle of the window). Luckily, it didn't happen in this case, but when it does happen (notice I didn't say "if"), you can choose a different area to sample from by just clicking inside the thinner outline and dragging it to a different area (as seen here). Once you drag it over a new area, let go of the mouse button and it draws a preview of how this new sample area looks (that way, you can see if moving it actually helped or not). *Note:* If parts of the repair look see-through, just adjust the Feather amount.

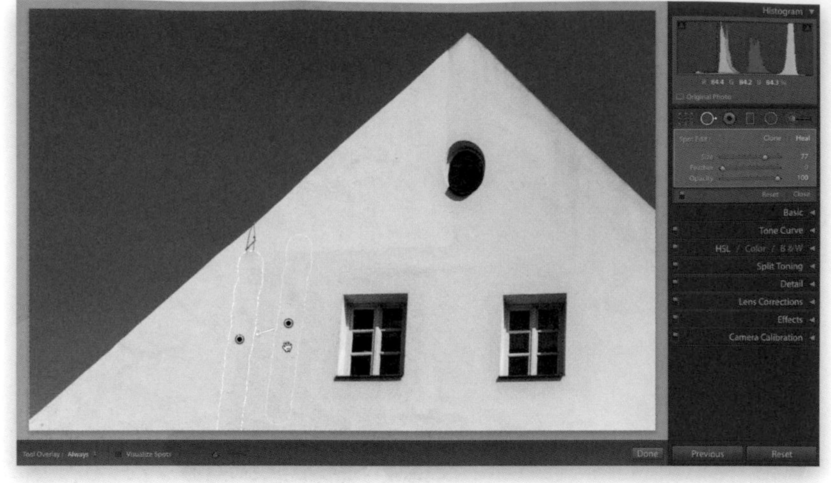

Step Four:

If it still doesn't look good, just drag the sample outline somewhere else and release the mouse for a quick preview of how it looks now. Another method is to just press the **/ (Forward slash) key** (named after the lead guitarist for Guns N' Roses) and Lightroom will choose a new area to sample from. If it's first try just doesn't look good, just press the / key again and it tries a different area. Okay, back to our retouch. We'll need to add a second stroke to remove the wires along the edge, so paint over that area, too. In this case, when it picked the edge area to sample from, it was off by about 1/16 of an inch. You can try to move the area it sampled from, but clicking-and-dragging the brush stroke outline actually worked better here. There was one little area left over that the two strokes missed, so I added a third smaller one (see the overlay).

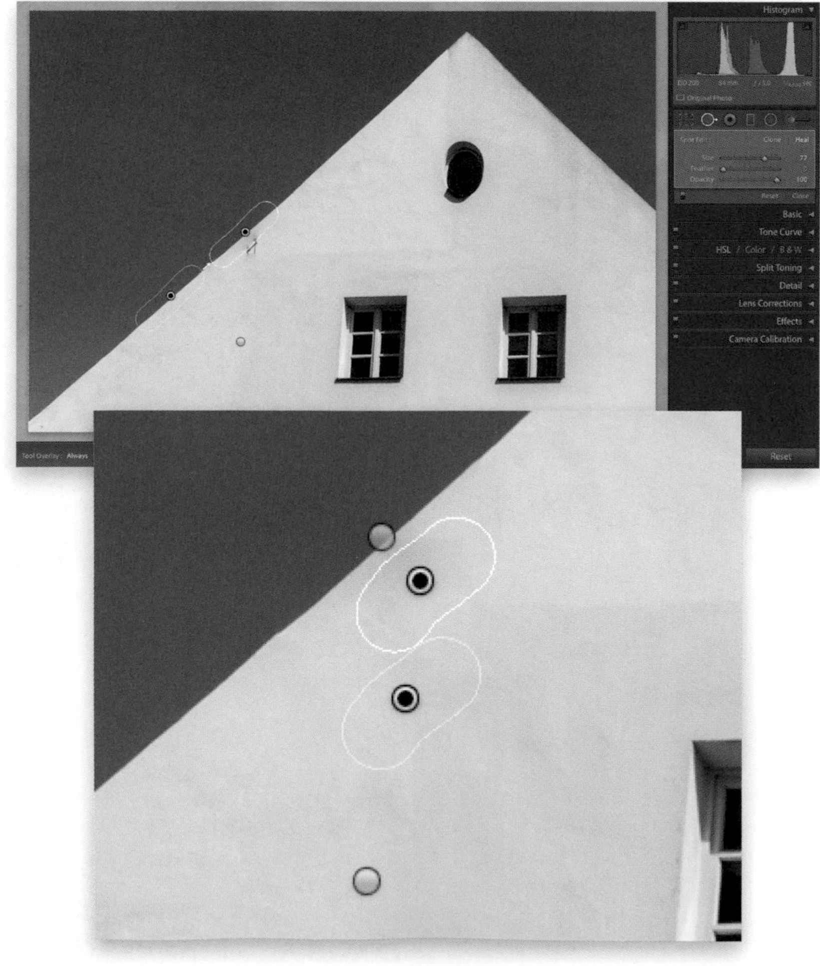

Step Five:

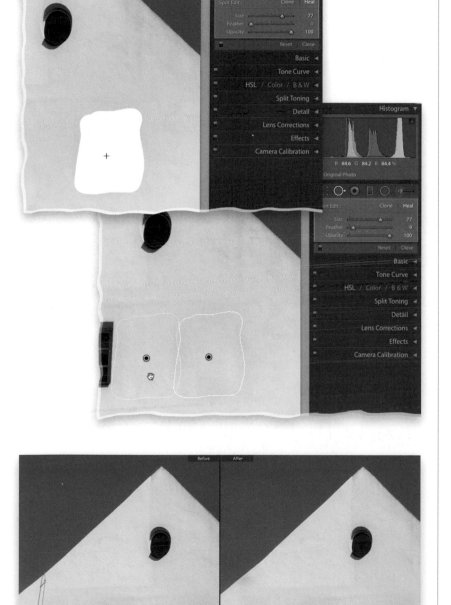

Now, let's remove something larger, like that window on the right (again, not that it needs it, but just because we can). Take the Spot Removal tool, paint over the entire window, including a little bit just outside it (as seen here). When you release the mouse button, it picks a spot to sample from and tries to remove the window. The first spot it chose when I did it wasn't that great—it left some little areas around the edge and the middle. If this happens, try raising the Feather amount (this softens the edges of the patched area, and it usually works well with small areas, but with a large area it sometimes leaves junk behind. In this case, though, raising the Feather amount helped a lot). When you're removing something large like a window, there's often not a lot of good, clean open areas for it to choose from nearby, so you'll probably have to wind up dragging the thinner outline to different spots around the image until you come up with an area that looks good (well, at least that's what I had to do).

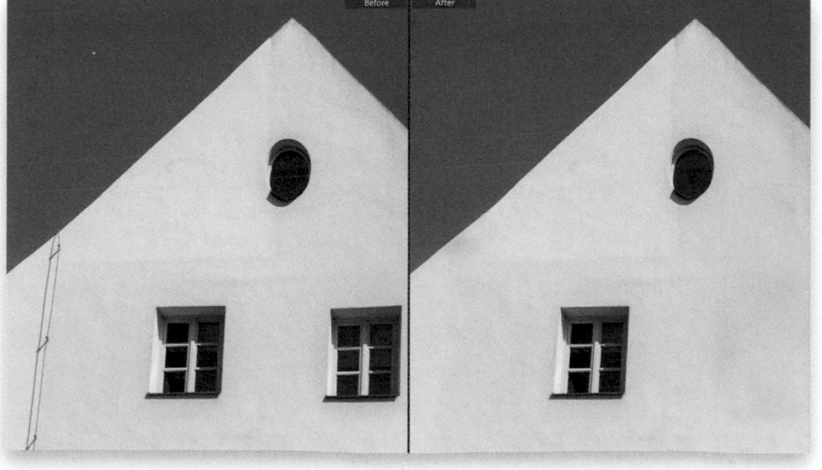

Step Six:

Here's a before/after, with the cables gone and after removing the window. Again, this is something we almost surely would have had to jump to Photoshop to do, but now we can do it all here in Lightroom, which is pretty darn sweet.

Removing Red Eye

If you wind up with red eye in your photos (point-and-shoots are notorious red-eye generators thanks to the flash being mounted so close to the lens), Lightroom can easily get rid of it. This is really handy because it saves you from having to jump over to Photoshop just to remove red eye from a photo of your neighbor's six-year-old crawling through a giant hamster tube at Chuck E. Cheese. Here's how it works:

Step One:

Go to the Develop module and click on the Red Eye Correction tool, found in the toolbox right under the Histogram panel (its icon looks like an eye, and it's circled here in red). Click the tool in the center of one of the red eyes and drag down and when you release the mouse button, it removes the red eye. If it doesn't fully remove all the red, you can expand how far out it removes it by going to the Red Eye Correction tool's options (they appear in the panel once you've released the mouse button), and dragging the Pupil Size slider to the right (as shown here) or clicking-and-dragging the edge of the circle itself (it allows you to reshape it, as well). If you need to move the correction, click-and-drag inside the circle.

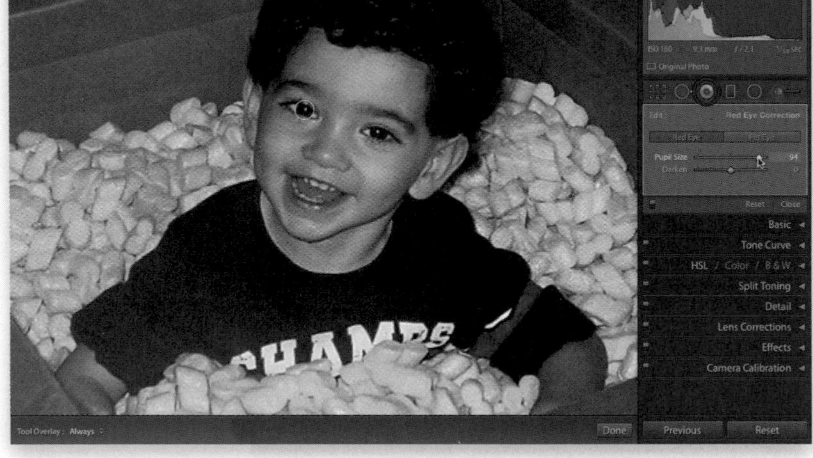

KIM DOTY

Step Two:

Now do the same thing to the other eye (the first eye you did stays selected, but it's "less selected" than your new eye selection—if that makes any sense). As soon as you click, this eye is fixed, too. If the repair makes it look too gray, you can make the eye look darker by dragging the Darken slider to the left (as shown here). The nice thing is that these sliders (Pupil Size and Darken) are live, so as you drag, you see the results right there onscreen—you don't have to drag a slider and then reapply the tool to see how it looks. If you make a mistake and want to start over, just click the Reset button at the bottom right of the tool's options.

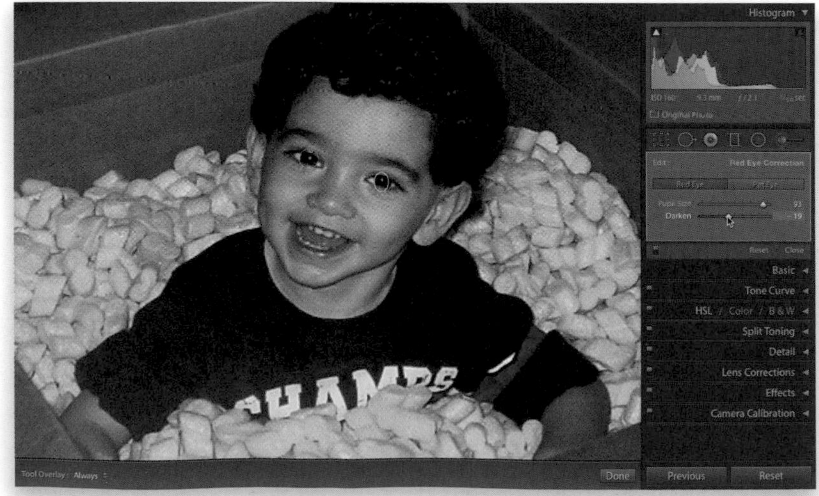

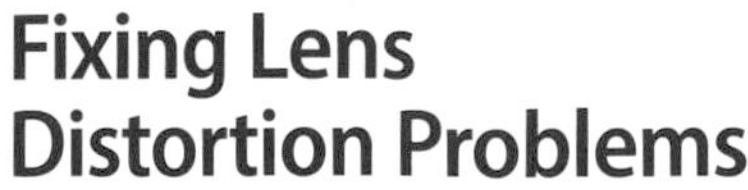

Fixing Lens Distortion Problems

Ever shoot some buildings downtown and they look like they're leaning back? Or maybe the top of a building looks wider than the bottom, or a doorway or just a whole image seems like it's "bulging" out. All these types of lens distortion problems are really pretty common (especially if you use wide-angle lenses), but luckily for us, fixing them is usually just a one- or two- (maybe three-, seldom four-, rarely five-, but I once did six-) click fix.

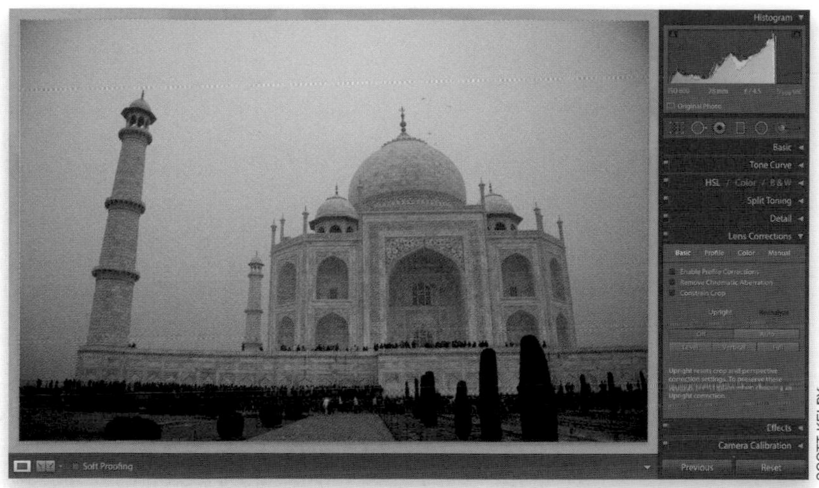

SCOTT KELBY

Step One:

Open an image that has a lens distortion problem. This one has a bunch—from lens vignetting in all four corners to the bulging of the Taj Mahal (just look at how the wall is bowing down from left to right and the tower on the left looks like it's going to fall over on the Taj). We can probably fix most of these problems with one click just by turning the lens profile correction on (and this is *always* the first thing I try, because even if the automated profile doesn't do the full job, if I have to go to the next phase of correction, it works better once a profile has been applied). So, applying a lens profile correction is always my first step. Let's go to the Lens Corrections panel (seen here), and click on the Basic tab at the top to see those options.

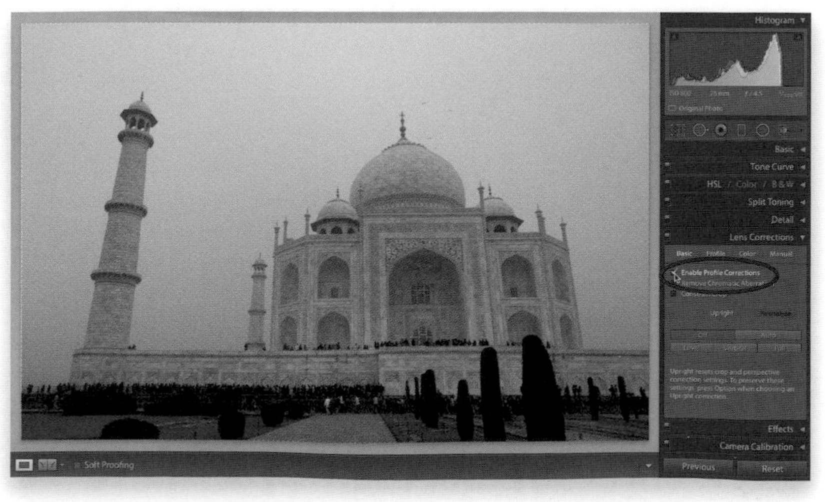

Step Two:

Lightroom has a bunch of profiles built-in for the most commonly used lenses from most lens manufacturers. When you turn on the Enable Profile Corrections checkbox (as shown here), most of the time it will find the proper lens profile for you and apply it (it knows which lens you used by looking at the EXIF camera data embedded in the file by your camera when you took the shot). If it can't find one, you just have to help it out a bit by telling it your camera make and model (in the Profile tab) and it does the rest. In this case, it found the profile and we know it did, because it actually did something—the vignetting in the corners is almost gone as is most of the bulging (look at the wall now). There are still other problems, but we're on our way.

Continued

Step Three:

If you want to see the profile it applied (or if it didn't apply a lens correction profile at all), click on the Profile tab at the top to see its options. If you don't see your lens's make and model in these pop-up menus, then just start by choosing your make. That alone will often nudge Lightroom enough to pick the model automatically for you, but if it doesn't, just choose yours from the pop-up menu. What if you don't see your exact lens there? Just pick the closest match you can find. Even if you find the exact make and model match, I often have to tweak the automatic settings a bit using the Amount sliders at the bottom of the panel. For example, if you thought it didn't remove enough distortion, you can drag the Distortion slider to the right a little, and it lessens the amount of rectilinear correction it applied to the photo (notice how the wall is a little flatter now?). Do the same with the Vignetting slider (as shown here). Having these sliders to tweak the results is pretty handy (and you'll probably use them more than you think).

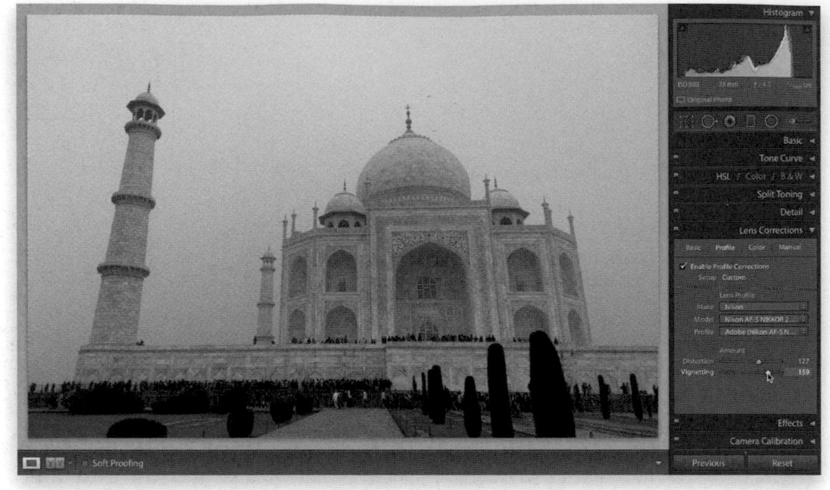

Step Four:

One of the most useful features here is Upright. These are automated, one-click corrections. You choose which kind you want, from just straightening the horizontal or vertical lines to a full one-perspective correction, and it usually does a really great job of it. However, to get the best results from Upright, you need to turn on the lens profile corrections first (by turning on the Enable Profile Corrections checkbox). To use Upright, click on the Basic tab again, and you'll see five buttons: Off, Auto, Level, Vertical, and Full. The one that seems, to me, to work the best consistently is the Auto button. It doesn't "overcorrect" (which Vertical and Full seem to sometimes do), and it's usually the one I wind up going with. I clicked Auto here, and it pretty much stopped the building from leaning back, and the tower on the left isn't leaning nearly as far.

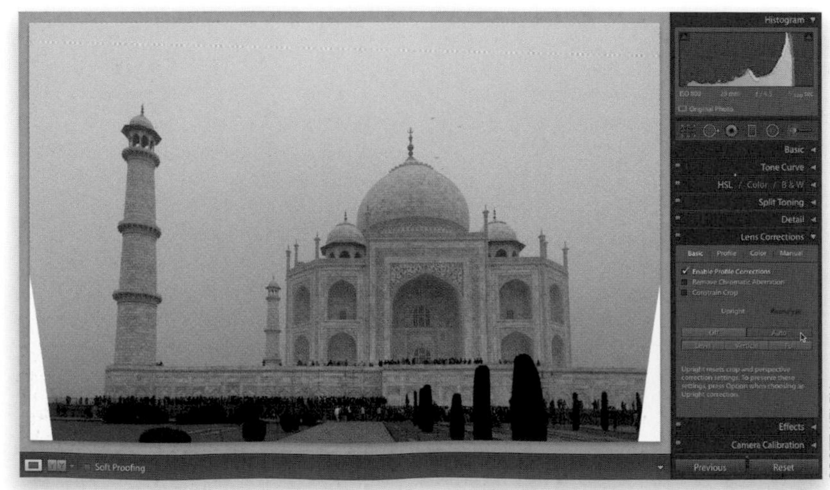

SCOTT KELBY

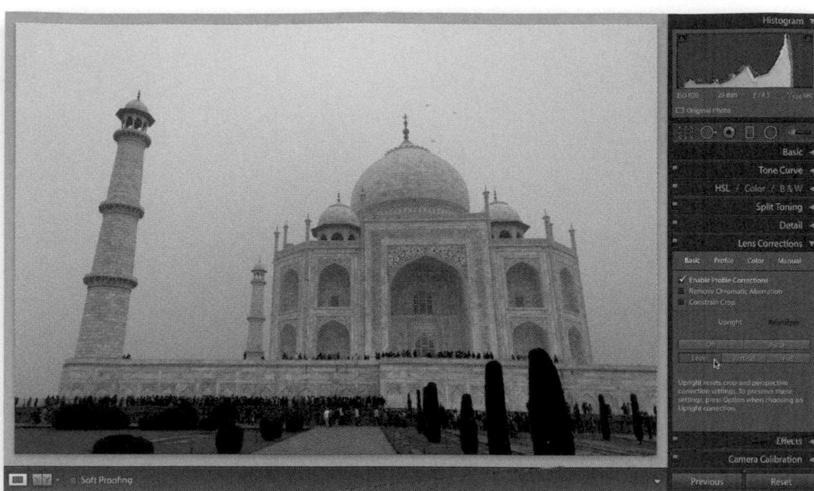

Step Five:

Before we move on to the next Upright button, did you notice in the previous step that to make its correction it wound up leaving white triangular-shaped gaps in the bottom corners of the image? There are three ways to fix this: (1) Crop those areas away with the Crop Overlay tool. (2) Click on the Manual tab and drag the Scale slider to the right to scale the photo up in size until those white triangles go away (though you lose a little quality scaling up, but none from cropping down, so I'd prefer to crop it). (3) Take the image over to Photoshop, select those white areas and use Content-Aware Fill. Okay, back to Upright. If you click on the Level button, it does just one thing—it tries to straighten your image. Even though it didn't do much here (in fact, it actually looks worse than the Auto correction because all it's doing is just straightening—nothing else), it usually does a great job of the simple act of straightening, so if that's all your image needs, then click on Level.

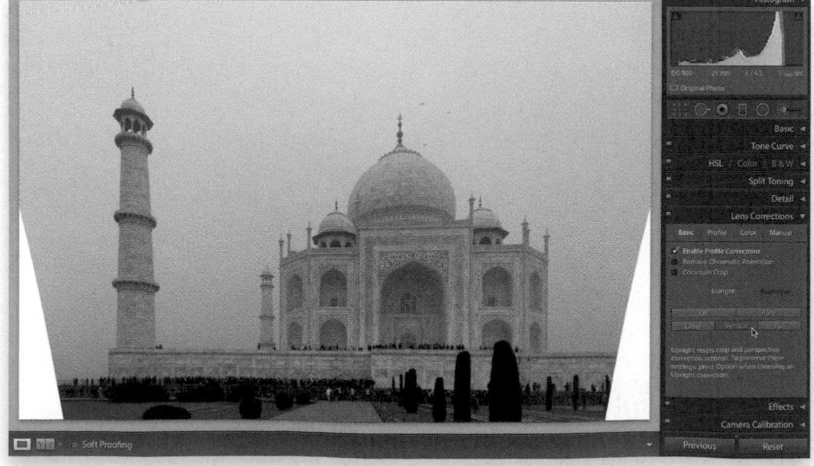

Step Six:

When you click on the Vertical button, it tries to make the vertical lines perfectly straight. Take a look at the sides of the Taj now, and it looks pretty darn straight, but it also looks a little like it has been stretched upward (making it look a little taller and skinnier). You can fix this by going to the Manual tab and dragging the Aspect slider to the left a little bit, which stretches the image out wider, so you can make it look normal again. Of course, either way, you'll have to deal with those white triangle-shaped gaps like I mentioned in the previous step, but at least the building looks right.

Continued

Step Seven:

If you click on the Full button, it applies of full dose of all three—horizontal, vertical, and a perspective correction. It's a little more extreme than choosing the Auto button, which is a bit more balanced. So, don't be surprised if, on a particular photo, you click on Full and it looks totally whacked, but Auto looked fine. I rarely wind up using the Full correction because it usually is too extreme, too wild, or it just doesn't look good.

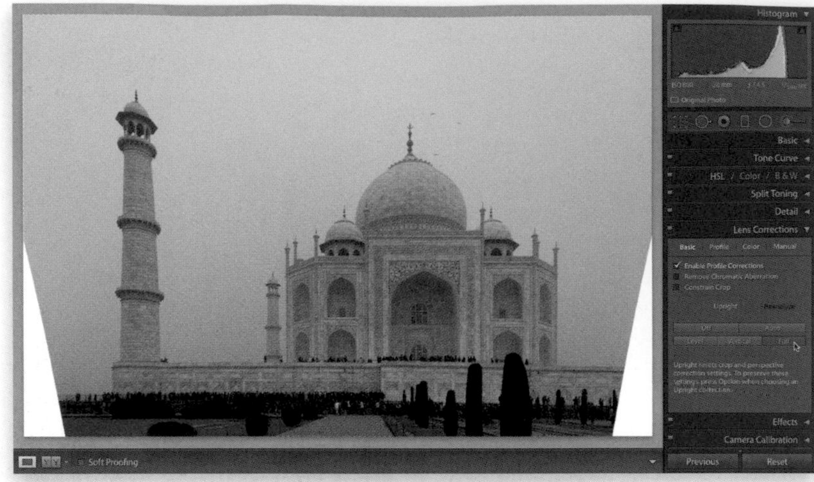

Step Eight:

For this particular image, I felt the Auto correction looked best (but, of course, I usually think the Auto Upright correction choice looks best). We do, though, have that white triangle issue to deal with and, as I mentioned earlier, I prefer cropping the image rather than scaling it up to fill the space. But, what's nice is Lightroom can auto crop away those areas for you. In the Basic tab, just turn on the Constrain Crop checkbox, and it auto-crops the image so those white areas are trimmed away (as you see here). Below, is a before/after up to this point.

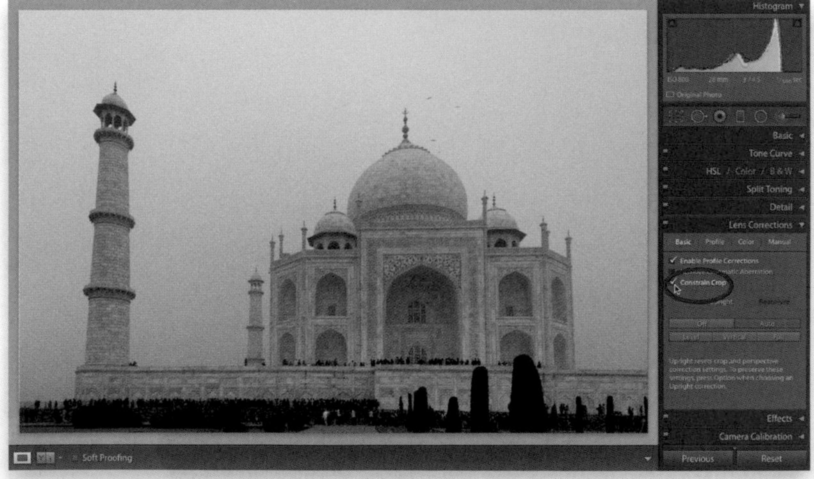

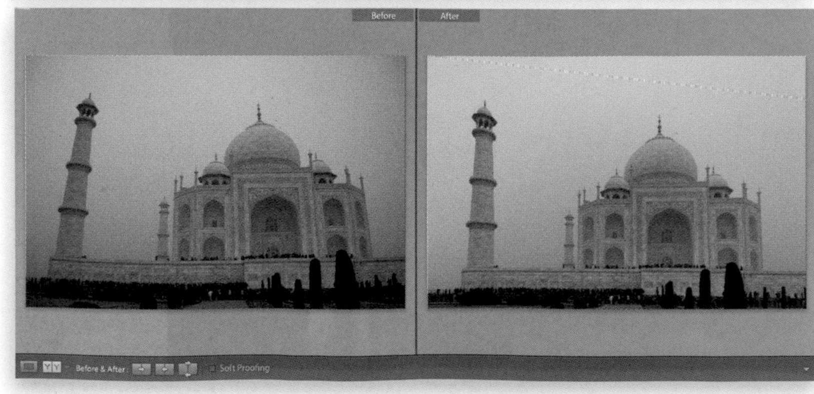

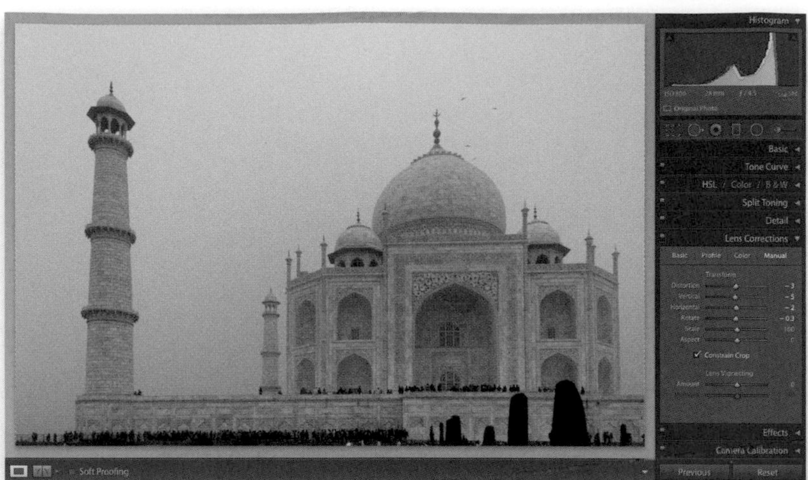

Step Nine:

If you don't like the results you get from the automated Upright fixes (or if you just want to tweak the results), click on the Manual tab and you'll see some sliders that you can adjust: Distortion (the bowing in/out), Vertical (if the building is tipping back or forward), Horizontal (if the scene needs to be tilted horizontally—as if you were holding a print in front of you and you moved one hand on one side toward you or away from you), Rotate (just lets you rotate the image to make it straight), Scale (zooms in the image toward you if you have white areas that appear after you apply a correction), and Aspect (if any of the corrections made the image look squashed/squatty or thin and stretched upward, this lets you counteract both). I tweaked this a little here to make the wall and the tower straighter.

TIP: Using the Adjustable Grid

When you're trying to straighten things out like this, you might find it helpful to have a grid appear as you're rotating. To do that, go under the View menu, under Loupe Overlay, and choose **Grid**. Once it appears, you can change its Size and Opacity by pressing-and-holding the Command (PC: Ctrl) key and clicking-and-dragging left/right on the two controls that appear at the top of the Preview area.

SCOTT KELBY

Step 10:

Let's look at just working on a very common lens problem using just the Manual sliders. In this case, the building looks like it's leaning back (you see this a lot, especially when shooting up close with a wide-angle lens, like a 24mm, an 18mm, 16mm, and so on). Click on the Manual tab at the top of the Lens Corrections panel, so we can drag these sliders to fix the problem.

Continued

Step 11:

The quickest way to really understand what the Vertical slider does, is literally to just drag it way over to the right, then back way over to the left, and in a split second, you'll totally "get it." Try it (go ahead, I'll wait). See, told ya! Now that you get it, just drag it to the left until the building looks straight (I generally look for a column or a straight edge of a building and try to get it straight).

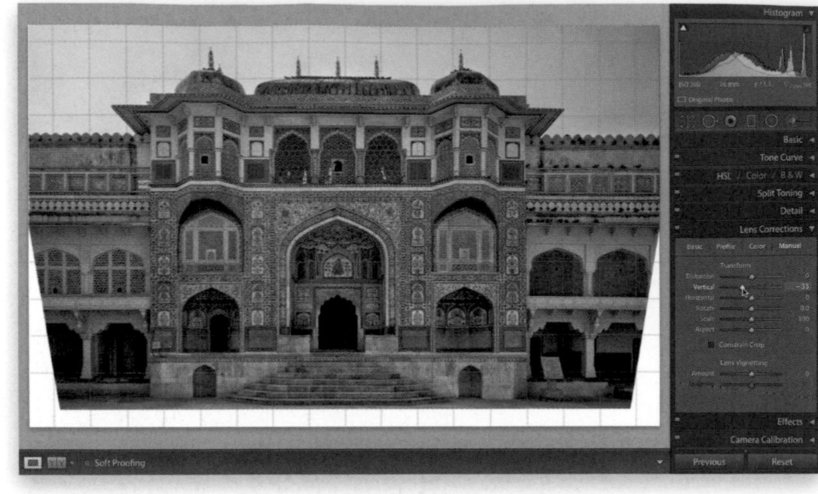

Step 12:

Here, I dragged the Vertical slider over to –32 to get that main column (one of four columns in the center) fairly straight. Of course, this left the white triangle gaps (from making such an extreme correction), so I turned on the Constrain Crop checkbox to crop away those areas. A final before/after is seen below. Now, let's look at a more subtle problem (they won't always be as obvious as this).

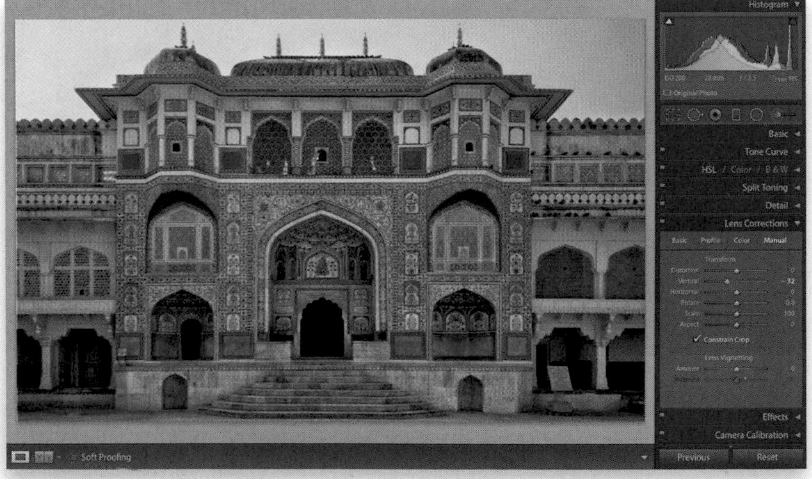

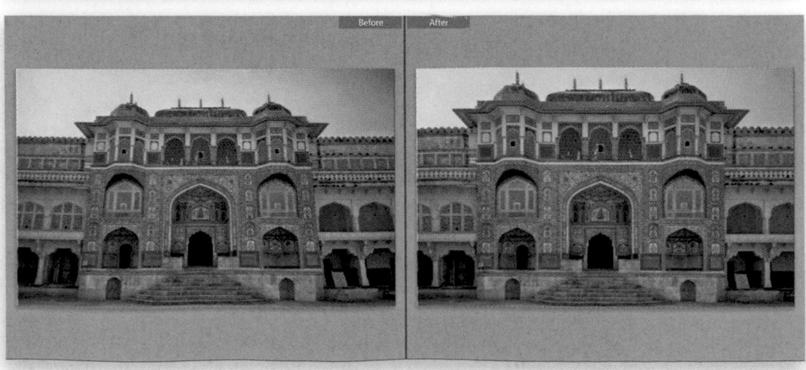

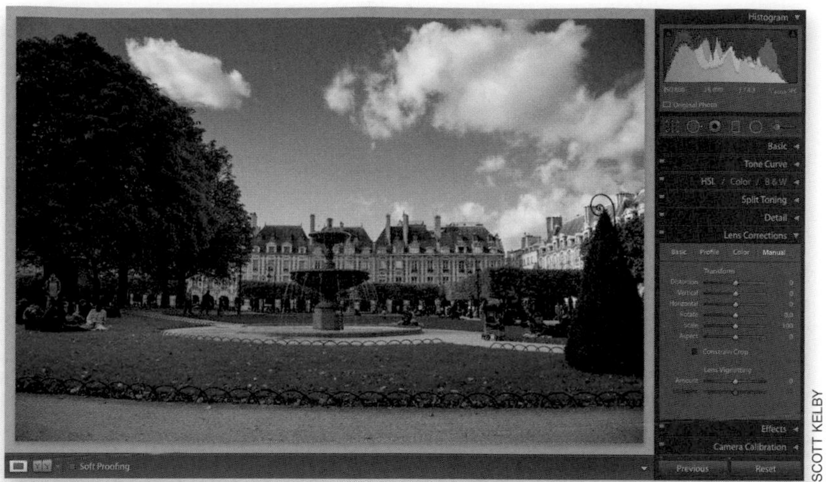

Step 13:

At first glance, this one looks okay, until you look at the sidewalk and realize it's bowing downward from left to right (look how much higher it is in the left corner than it is on the right). That bowing is a dead giveaway that there's a lens distortion problem. There's lens vignetting in the corners, too.

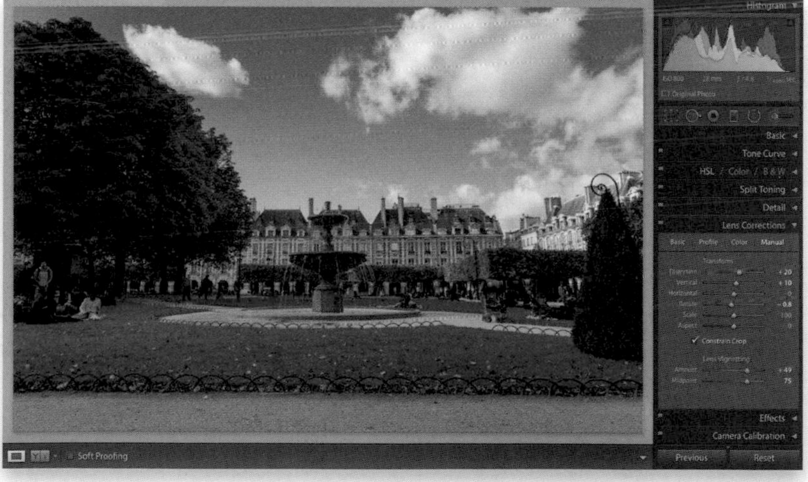

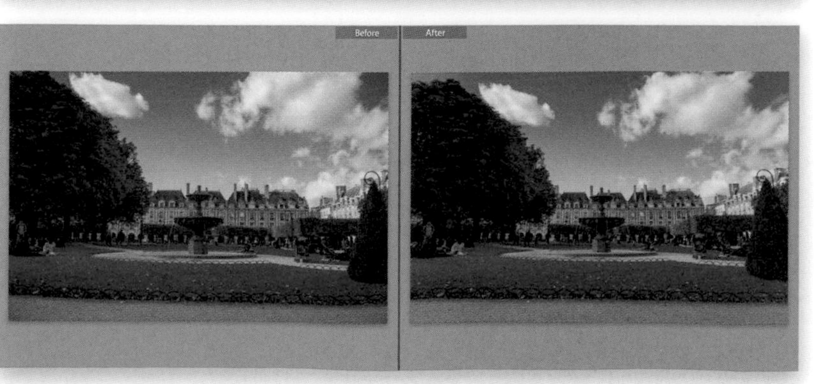

Step 14:

Let's drag the Distortion slider over to the right until the sidewalk flattens out and looks even on both sides (if you drag too far, the ends will start to bow upward). Here, I dragged to +20. Now, drag the Vertical slider until the building looks right in the background (to +10), and then rotate the entire image, so the sidewalk is flat (by dragging the Rotate slider to the left to –0.8). Turn on the Constrain Crop checkbox to remove all white caps caused by the correction and, lastly, drag the Lens Vignetting Amount slider to the right (to +49) to brighten the corners, and drag the Midpoint slider to the right (to 75), as well, since the vignetting problem is just up tight in the corners (that slider controls how wide the brightening extends into the image, and here we didn't need much—it's all pretty much right up in the corners). Okay, that's it—it's much more subtle than our other edits, but totally worth the 30 seconds it takes to fix it.

Continued

Step 15:

Now, let's look at correcting a super-wide-angle fisheye lens (in this case, a 15mm fisheye). Before we correct this, though, let me just say that when I put a fisheye lens on my camera, it's because I want that rounded fisheye look. Because of that, I like the original image, here, more than the "fixed" image we're going to create, but you should at least know how to do this just in case (and I do have a case or two where I went with the corrected version, so ya never know). Here's the original, where I turned on the Enable Profile Corrections checkbox in the Basic tab, but since it didn't recognize the lens profile, it did just about nuthin'.

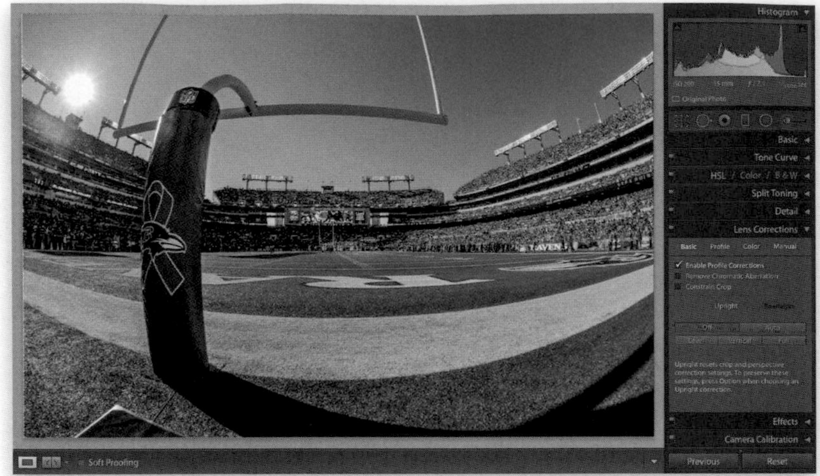

SCOTT KELBY

Step 16:

If it doesn't recognize your lens, then remember, you have to help it out. So, click on the Profile tab and choose your lens manufacturer from the Make pop-up menu, as seen here (in my case, it was a Canon lens—an 8–15mm fisheye zoom).

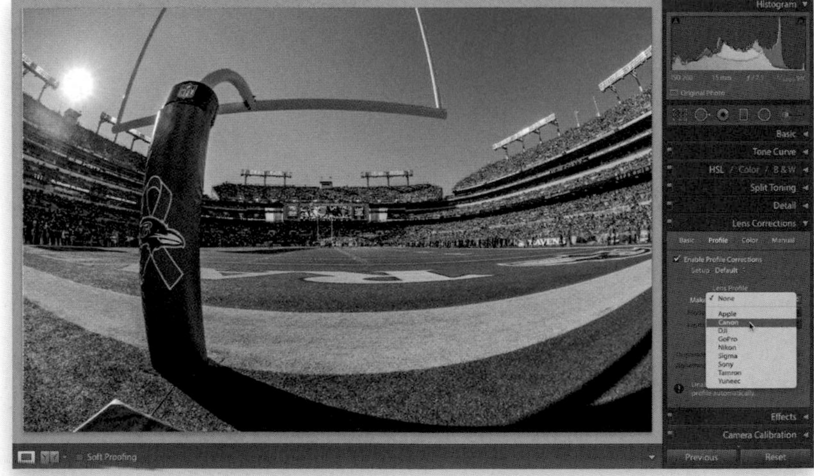

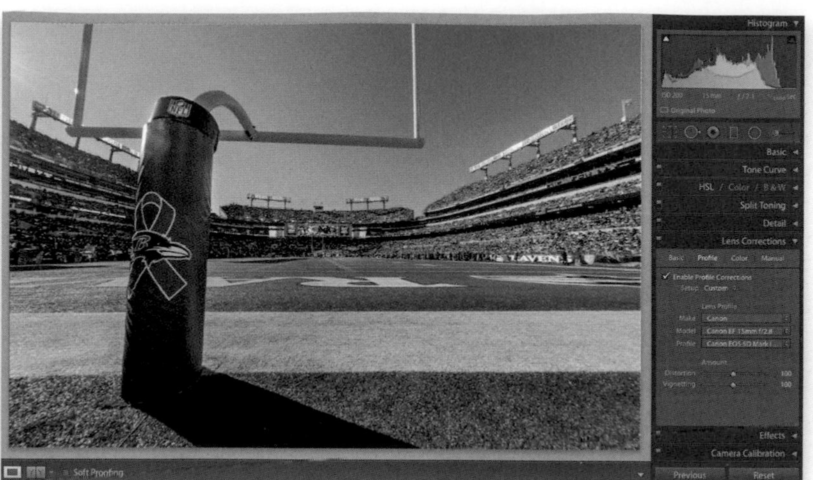

Step 17:

As soon as I choose Canon, it immediately found a matching profile for the 15mm fisheye, applied the profile correction (as seen here), and turned the rounded fisheye lens into a super-wide-angle regular look. Now, if you look at the white end zone border, you can see it's a little crooked, and so are the goal posts (they're leaning to the right). So, while it's really close, it's not 100%.

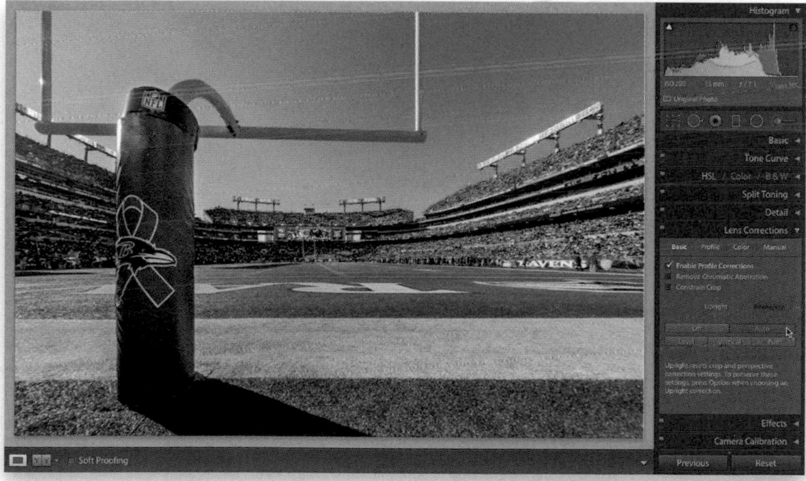

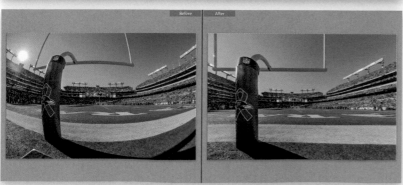

Step 18:

Let's give Upright a shot at this. Click on the Basic tab and then click on the Auto button. This helped a lot (look at the goal posts now). Lastly, you can try the other buttons to see how they affect the look (hey, it's worth a try). Actually, in this case, I think the Full button actually added a nice final tweak of changing the horizontal perspective a little (like holding a printed image out in front of you and moving your right hand a little toward you). I show that tweak in the before/after here. So, that's it for lens correction (except for chromatic aberrations which we cover later in this chapter and a little more on lens vignetting, which we cover next).

Fixing Edge Vignetting

Vignetting is a lens problem that causes the corners of your photo to appear darker than the rest of the photo. This problem is usually more pronounced when you're using a wide-angle lens, but can also be caused by a whole host of other lens issues. Now, a little darkness in the edges is considered a problem, but many photographers (myself included) like to exaggerate this edge darkening and employ it as a lighting effect in portraits, which we covered in Chapter 6. Here's how to fix it if it happens to you:

Step One:

In the photo shown here, you can see how the corner areas look darkened and shadowed. This is the bad vignetting that I mentioned above.

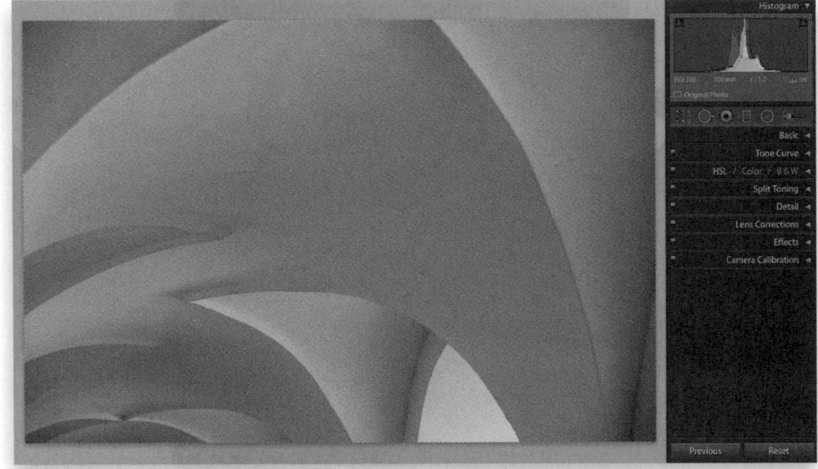

SCOTT KELBY

Step Two:

Scroll down to the Lens Corrections panel in the Develop module's right side Panels area, click on Profile at the top, then turn on the Enable Profile Corrections checkbox, and Lightroom will try to automatically remove the edge vignetting, based on the make and model of the lens you used (it learns all this from the EXIF data embedded in your image. See page 307 for more on how it reads this data). Since this image has no lens information, we have to tell it what make of lens it was (in this case, Canon) in the Make pop-up menu. Then, choose the lens model, or one close to it. In this case, the profile for the 70–200mm lens (in the Model pop-up menu) works the best. If the image still needs a little correction (as this one does), you can try the Vignetting slider under Amount.

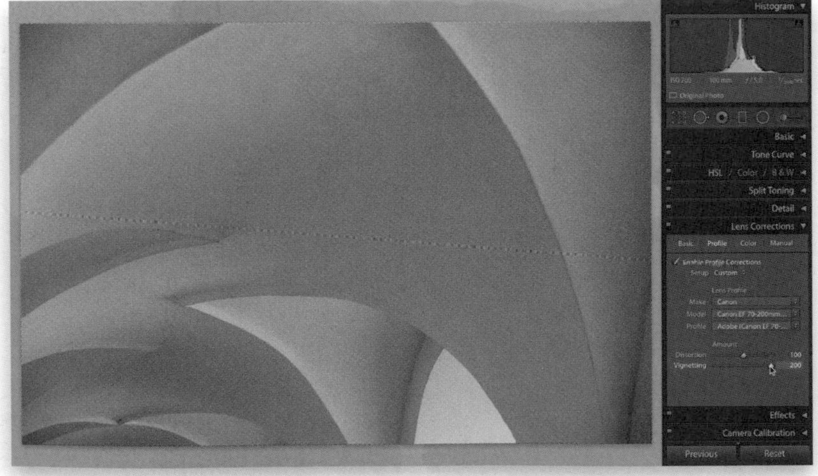

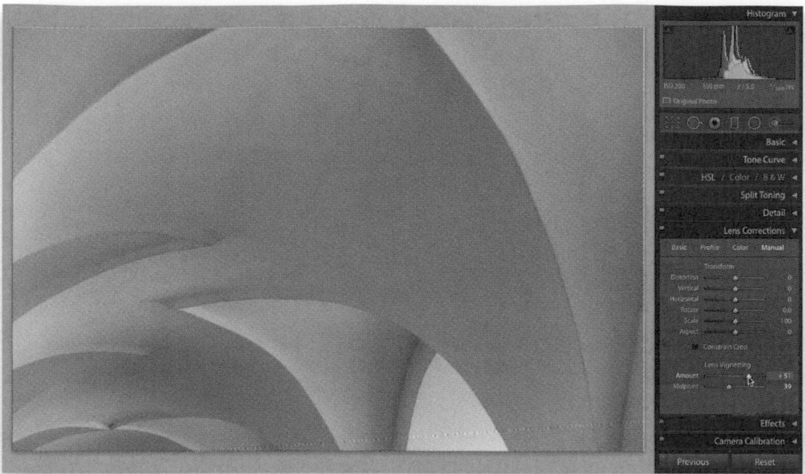

Step Three:

If you still think the automatic way isn't working well enough, you can do it manually by clicking on the Manual tab, and you'll see a section for Lens Vignetting at the bottom. There are two vignetting sliders here: the first controls the amount of brightening in the edge areas, and the second slider lets you adjust how far in toward the center of your photo the corners will be brightened. In this photo, the edge vignetting is pretty much contained in the corners, and doesn't spread too far into the center of the photo. So, start to slowly click-and-drag the Amount slider to the right, and as you do, keep an eye on the corners of your image. As you drag, the corners get brighter, and your job is to stop when the brightness of the corners matches the rest of the photo (as shown here). If the vignetting extends toward the center of the photo, drag the Midpoint slider to the left to make your brightening cover a larger area (as I did here). That's how easy removing this problem is.

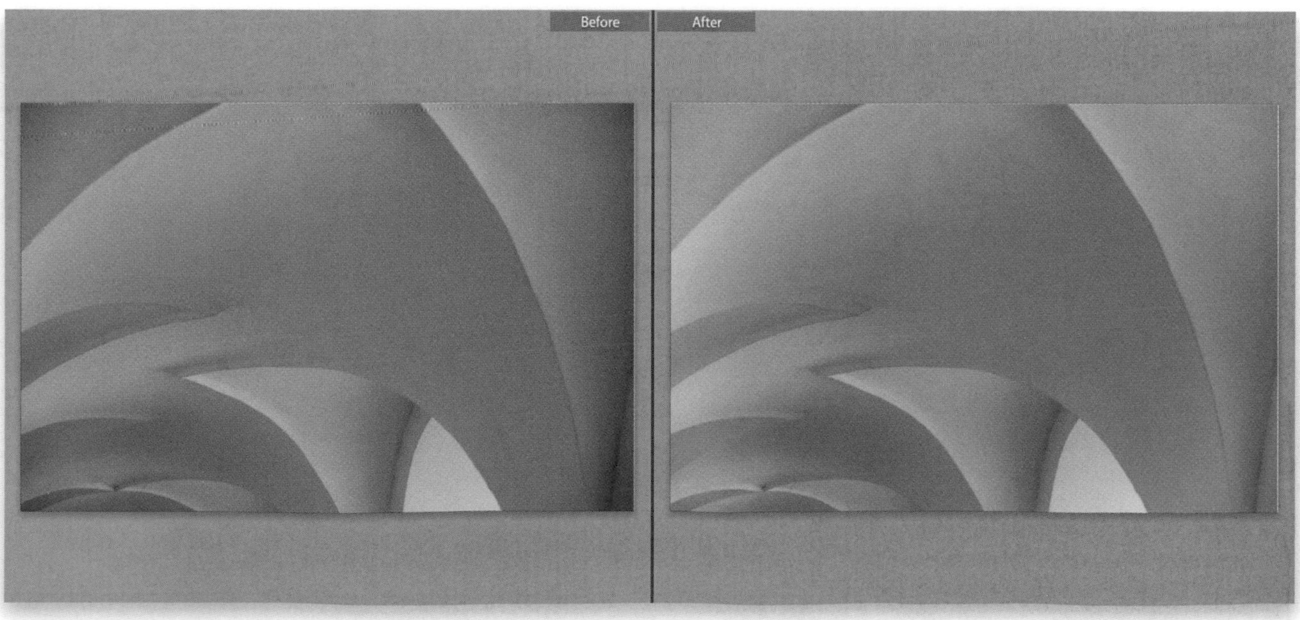

Sharpening Your Photos

There are two types of sharpening you can do in Lightroom: The first is called capture sharpening (covered here), which is sharpening that would normally happen in your camera if you're shooting JPEG. If you shoot RAW, the sharpening in your camera is turned off, so we apply it in Lightroom instead (by default, all RAW photos have sharpening applied in Lightroom, but if you want more sharpening, or if you want to control which type of sharpening is applied, and how, then you definitely want to read this).

Step One:

In early versions of Lightroom, you had to view your image at a 1:1 (100%) view to be able to see the effects of sharpening, but now, not only can you view it at other magnifications, they've also improved the sharpening technology itself, so you can apply more sharpening without damaging your image. To sharpen your image, go to the Detail panel in the Develop module. There's a preview window in this panel that lets you zoom in tight on one area of the image, while you see the normal-size image in the main Preview area (if you don't see the preview window, click on the left-facing triangle to the right of Sharpening at the top of the panel).

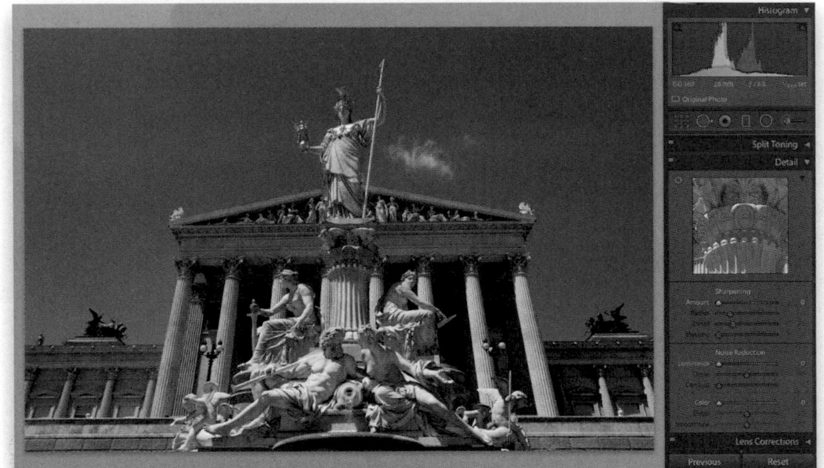

SCOTT KELBY

Step Two:

To zoom in on an area in the preview window, just click your cursor on the spot you want to zoom in on. Once you've zoomed in, you can navigate around by clicking-and-dragging inside the preview window. Although I use just the default 1:1 zoom, if you want to zoom in even tighter, you can Right-click inside the preview window, and choose a 2:1 view from the pop-up menu (shown here). Also, if you click the little icon in the upper-left corner of the panel (shown circled here in red), you can move your cursor over your main image in the center Preview area, and that area will appear zoomed in the preview window (to keep the preview on that area, just click on the area in the main image). To turn this off, click that icon again.

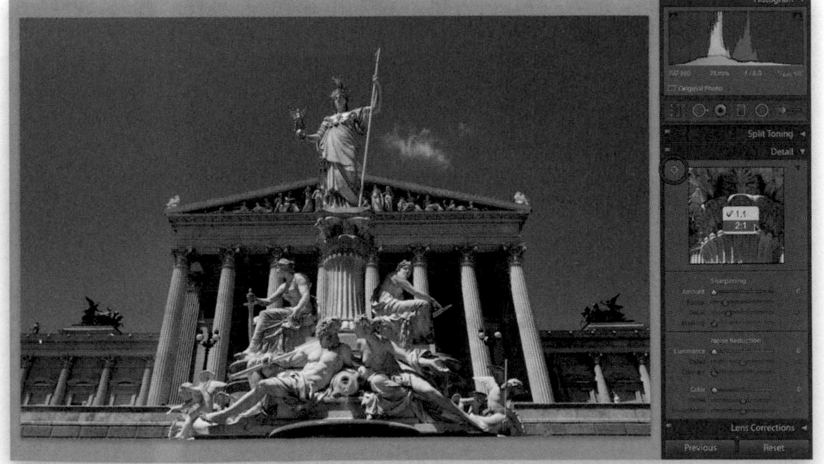

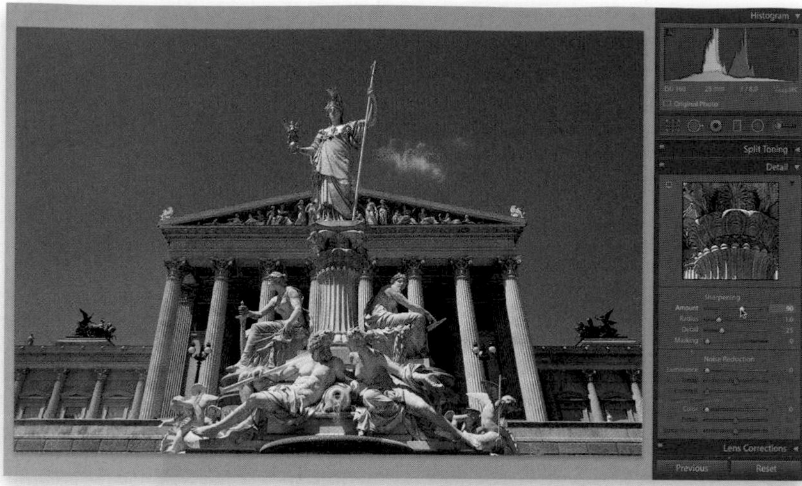

Step Three:

The Amount slider does just what you think it would—it controls the amount of sharpening applied to your photo. Here I increased the Amount to 90, and while the photo in the main Preview area doesn't look that much different, the Detail panel's preview looks much sharper (which is why it's so important to use this zoomed in preview). The Radius slider determines how many pixels out from the edge the sharpening will affect, and personally I leave this set at 1 (as seen here), but if I really need some mega sharpening I'll bump it up to 2.

TIP: Toggling Off the Sharpening

If you want to temporarily toggle off the changes you've made in the Detail panel, just click on the little switch on the far left of the Detail panel's header.

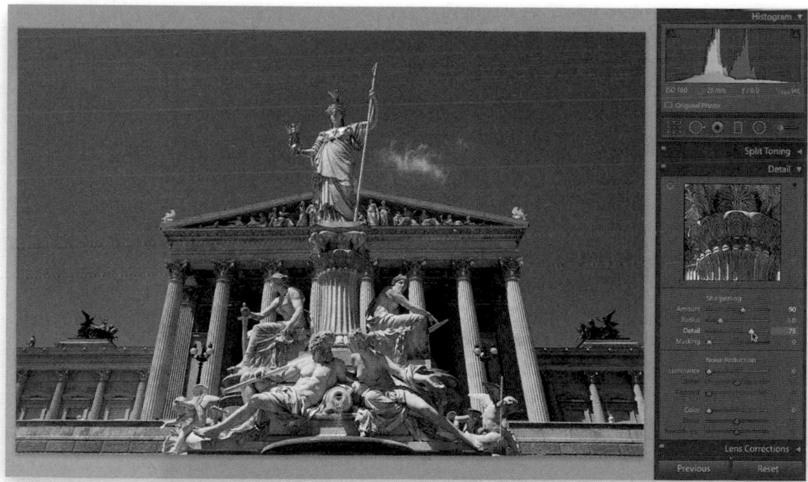

Step Four:

One of the downsides of traditional sharpening in Photoshop is that if you apply a lot of sharpening, you'll start to get little halos around the edge areas within your photos (it looks like somebody traced around the edges with a small marker), but luckily, here in Lightroom, the Detail slider acts as kind of a halo prevention control. At its default setting of 25, it's doing quite a bit of halo prevention, which works well for most photos (and is why it's the default setting), but for images that can take a lot of sharpening (like sweeping landscape shots, architectural images, and images with lots of sharply defined edges, like the one you see here), you would raise the Detail slider up to around 75, as shown here (which kind of takes the protection off quite a bit and gives you a more punchy sharpening). If you raise the Detail slider to 100, it makes your sharpening appear very much like the Unsharp Mask filter in Photoshop (that's not a bad thing, but it has no halo avoidance, so you can't apply as much sharpening).

Continued

Step Five

The last sharpening slider, Masking, is to me the most amazing one of all, because what it lets you do is control exactly where the sharpening is applied. For example, some of the toughest things to sharpen are things that are supposed to be soft, like a child's skin, or a woman's skin in a portrait, because sharpening accentuates texture, which is exactly what you don't want. But, at the same time, you need detail areas to be sharp—like their eyes, hair, eyebrows, lips, clothes, etc. Well, this Masking slider lets you do just that—it kind of masks away the skin areas, so it's mostly the detail areas that get sharpened. To show how this works, we're going to switch to a portrait.

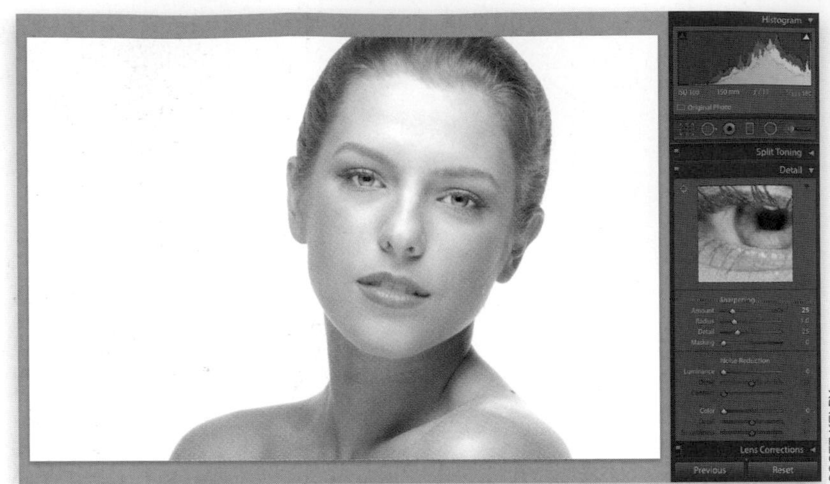

SCOTT KELBY

Step Six:

First, press-and-hold the Option (PC: Alt) key and then click-and-hold on the Masking slider, and your image area will turn solid white (as shown here). What this solid white screen is telling you is that the sharpening is being applied evenly to every part of the image, so basically, everything's getting sharpened.

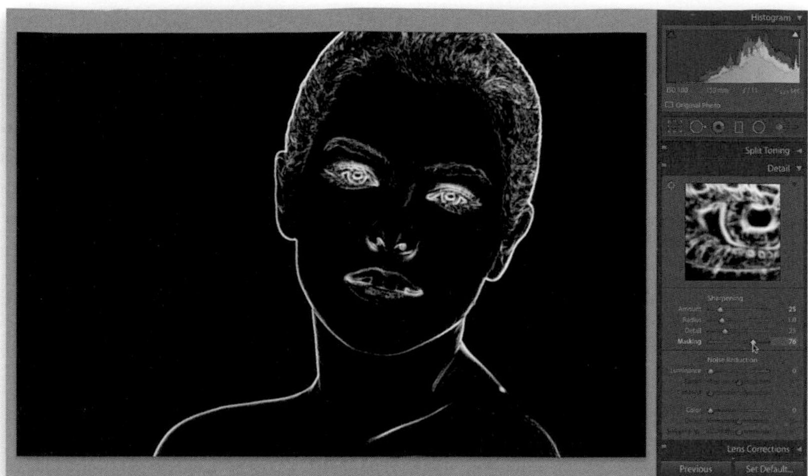

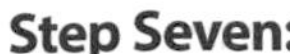

Step Seven:
As you click-and-drag the Masking slider to the right, parts of your photo will start to turn black, and those black areas are now not getting sharpened, which is our goal. At first, you'll see little speckles of black area, but the farther you drag that slider, the more non-edge areas will become black—as seen here, where I've dragged the Masking slider over to 76, which pretty much has the skin areas in all black (so they're not being sharpened), but the detail edge areas, like the eyes, lips, hair, nostrils, and outline, are being fully sharpened (which are the areas still appearing in white). So, in reality, those soft skin areas are being automatically masked away for you, which is really pretty darn slick if you ask me.

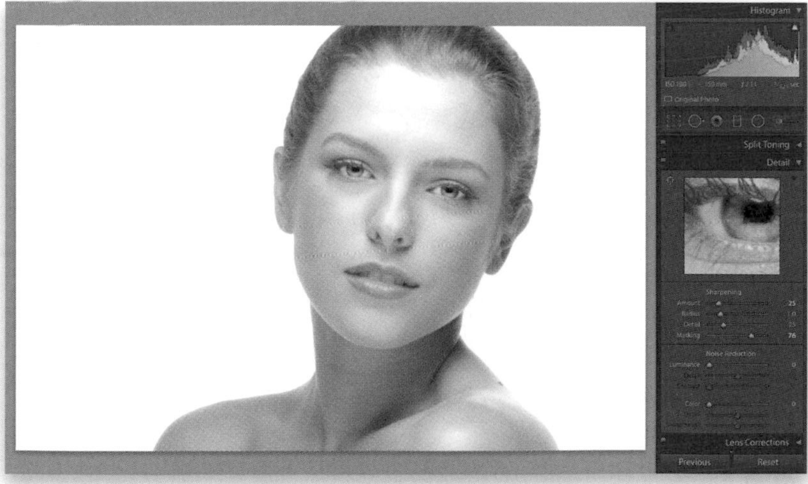

Step Eight:
When you release the Option (PC: Alt) key, you see the effects of the sharpening, and here you can see the detail areas are nice and crisp, but it's as if her skin was never sharpened. Now, just a reminder: I only use this Masking slider when the subject is supposed to be of a softer nature, where we don't want to exaggerate texture. Okay, on the next page, we're going to switch back to the first photo and finish up our sharpening there.

TIP: Sharpening a Smart Preview
If you apply sharpening (or noise reduction) to a low-res smart preview of an image, the amount you apply might look just right. But, when you reconnect your hard drive, and it links to the original high-res file, that amount of sharpening (or noise reduction) will actually have much less of an effect. So, you might want to leave the sharpening (and noise reduction) for when you're working on the original file.

Continued

Step Nine:

Here, I reopened the first photo and, at this point, you know what all four sliders do, so now it's down to you coming up with the settings you like. But if you're not comfortable with that quite yet, then take advantage of the excellent sharpening presets that are found in the Presets panel in the left side Panels area. If you look under the Lightroom General presets (the built-in ones), you'll find two sharpening presets: one called Sharpen - Scenic and one called Sharpen - Faces. Clicking the Scenic preset sets your Amount at 40, Radius at 0.8, Detail at 35, and Masking at 0 (see how it raised the detail level because the subject matter can take punchier sharpening?). The Faces one is much more subtle—it sets your Amount at 35, Radius at 1.4, Detail at 15, and Masking at 60.

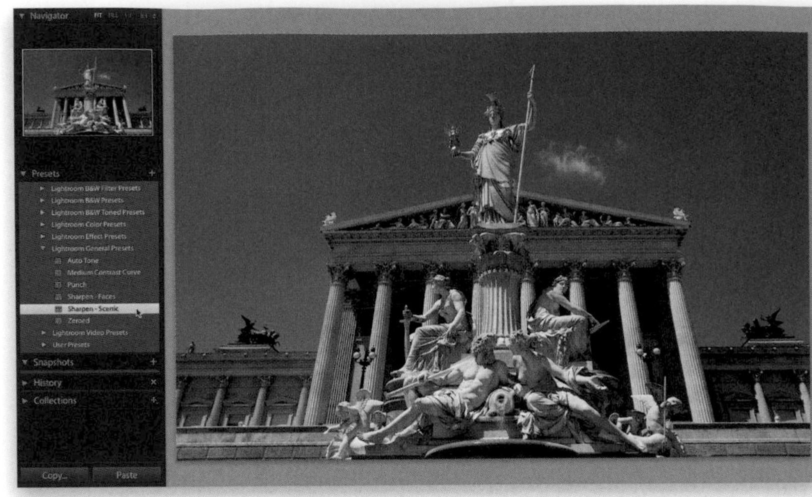

Step 10:

Here's the final before/after image. I started by clicking on the Sharpen - Scenic preset, then I increased the Amount to 125 (which is more than I usually use, but I pumped it up so you could see the results more easily here in the book). I set the Radius at 1.0 (which is pretty standard for me), the Detail at 75 (because a detailed photo like this can really take that punchy sharpening), and I left the Masking at 0 (because I want all the areas of the photo sharpened evenly—there are no areas that I want to remain soft and unsharpened). Now, at this point I'd save this setting as my own personal "Sharpening - High" preset, so it's always just one click away. (You learned how to do that back in Chapter 4.)

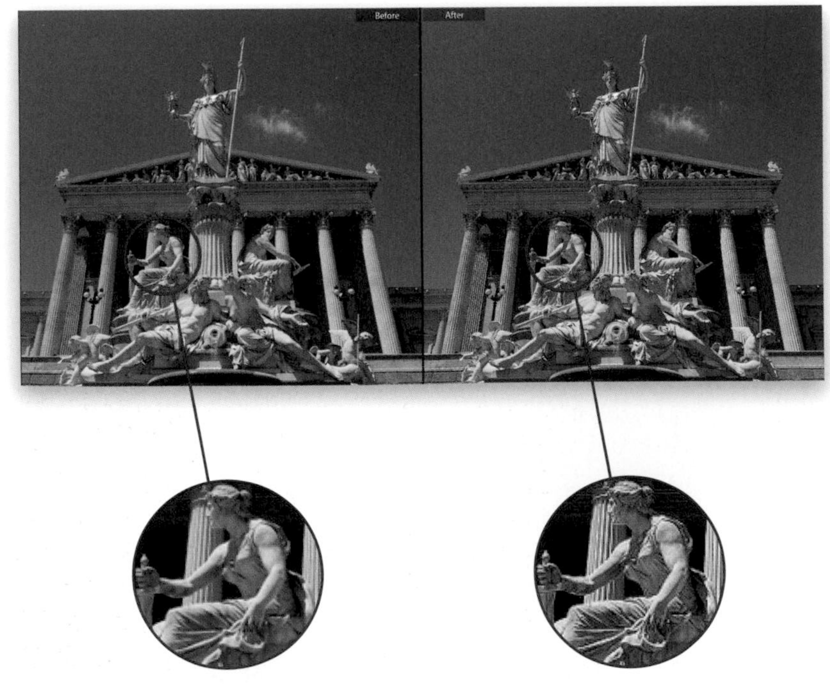

Fixing Chromatic Aberrations (a.k.a. That Annoying Color Fringe)

Sooner or later, you're going to run into a situation where some of the more contrasty edges around your subject have either a red, green, or more likely, a purple color halo or fringe around them (these are known as "chromatic aberrations"). You'll find these sooner (probably later today, in fact) if you have a really cheap digital camera (or a nice camera with a really cheap wide-angle lens), but even good cameras (and good lenses) can fall prey to this problem now and again. Luckily, it's easy enough to fix in Lightroom.

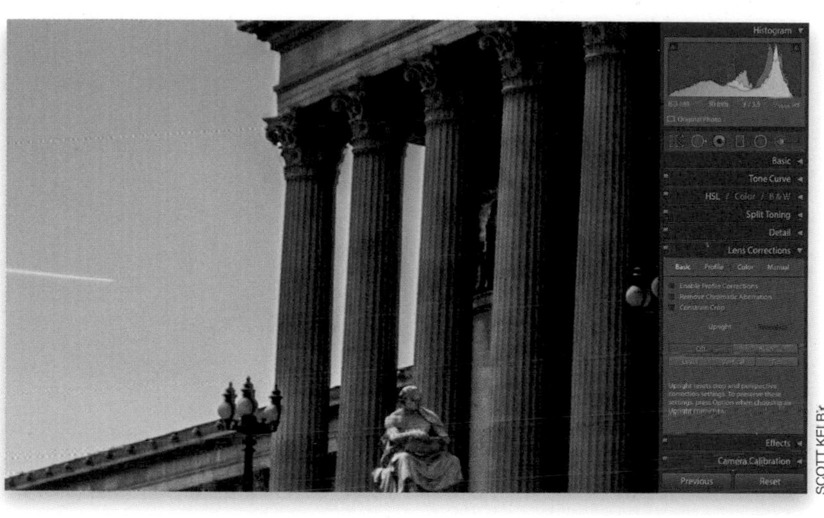

SCOTT KELBY

Step One:

Here I've zoomed in tight on these columns, and you'll see that it looks like someone traced the left sides with a thin green marker and the right sides with a pale purple marker. If this is happening to one of your images, first go to the Lens Corrections panel and click on Basic at the top, then zoom in on an edge area with the color fringe (I zoomed in to 1:1), so you can see how your adjustments affect the edge.

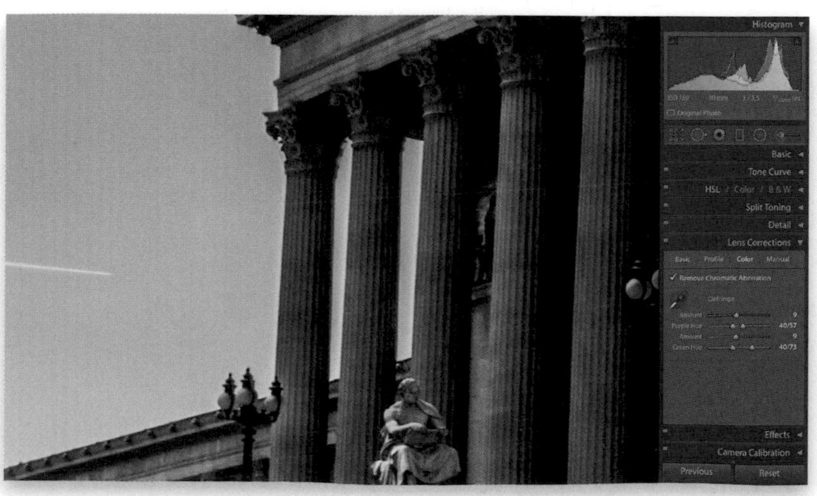

Step Two:

At the top of the panel, turn on the Remove Chromatic Aberrations checkbox. If this doesn't fully do the trick, then try clicking on Color at the top of the panel. Under Defringe, drag the top Amount slider to the right a little to remove the purple fringe. Then, move the Purple Hue sliders, so any color left is between the two slider knobs. Do the same thing with the Green Hue and Amount sliders to get the results shown here. Now, if you're not sure which slider to move (or moving the sliders doesn't seem to do much), then let Lightroom set them for you. Just click on the Fringe Color Selector tool (the eyedropper right above the sliders) and click it once directly on the color that is fringing. Now, the sliders will move automatically right where they need to remove that color fringe.

Basic Camera Calibration in Lightroom

Some cameras seem to put their own color signature on your photos, and if yours is one of those, you might notice that all your photos seem a little red, or have a slight green tint in the shadows, etc. Even if your camera produces accurate color, you still might want to tweak how Lightroom interprets the color of your RAW images. The process for doing a full, accurate camera calibration is kinda complex and well beyond the scope of this book, but I did want to show you what the Camera Calibration panel is used for, and give you a resource to take things to the next level.

Step One:

Before we start, I don't want you to think that camera calibration is something everybody must do. In fact, I imagine most people will never even try a basic calibration, because they don't notice a big enough consistent color problem to worry about it (and that's a good thing. However, in every crowd there's always one, right?). So, here's a quick project on the very basics of how the Camera Calibration panel works: Open a photo, then go to the Develop module's Camera Calibration panel, found at the very bottom of the right side Panels area, as shown here (see, if Adobe thought you'd use this a lot, it would be near the top, right?).

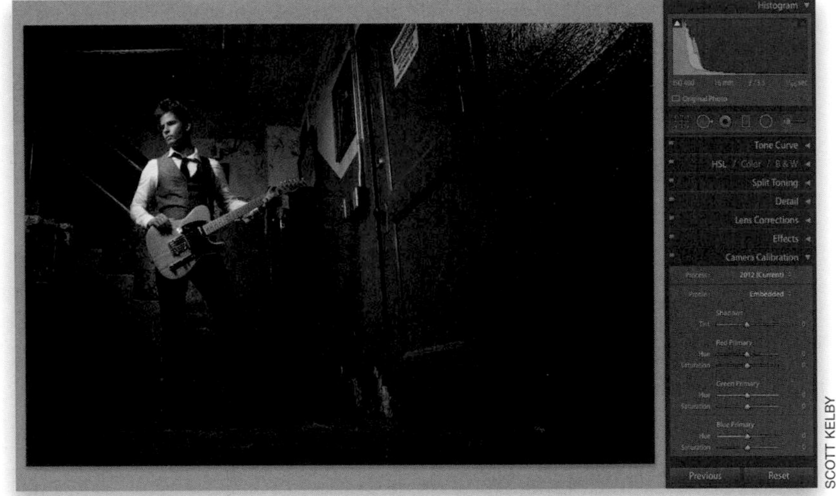

SCOTT KELBY

Step Two:

The topmost slider is for adjusting any tint that your camera might be adding to the shadow areas of your photos. If it did add a tint, it's normally green or magenta—look at the color bar that appears inside the Tint slider itself. By looking at the color bar, you'll know which way to drag (for example, here I'm dragging the Tint slider away from green, toward magenta, to reduce any greenish color cast in the shadow areas, but the change in this particular photo is very subtle).

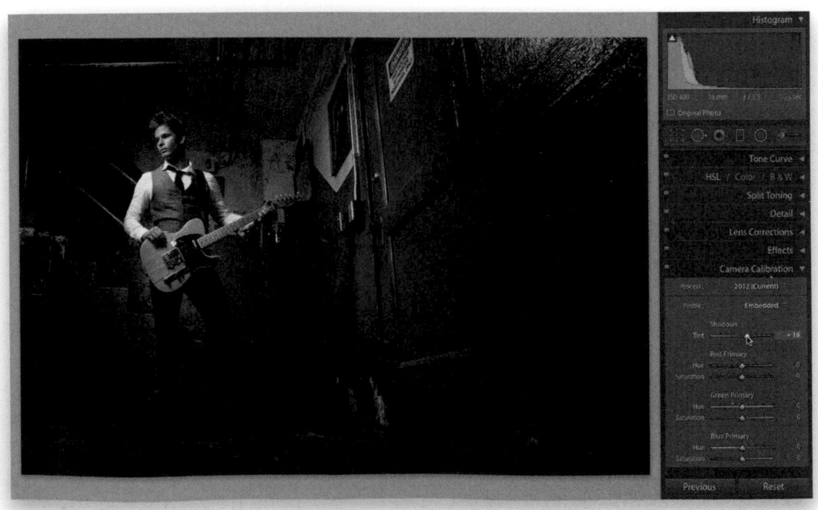

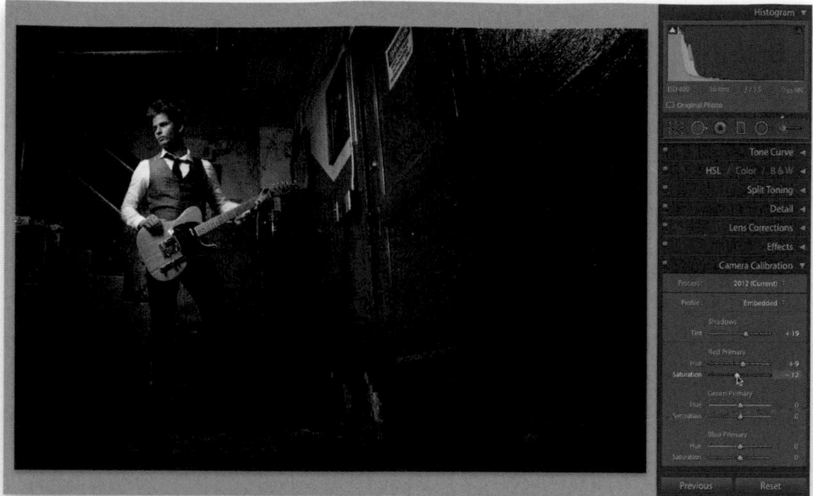

Step Three:

If your color problems don't seem to be in the shadows, then you'll use the Red, Green, and Blue Primary sliders to adjust the Hue and Saturation (the sliders that appear below each color). Let's say your camera produces photos that have a bit of a red cast to them. You'd drag the Red Primary Hue slider away from red, and if you needed to reduce the overall saturation of red in your photo, you'd drag the Red Primary Saturation slider to the left until the color looked neutral (by neutral, I mean the grays should look really gray, not reddish gray).

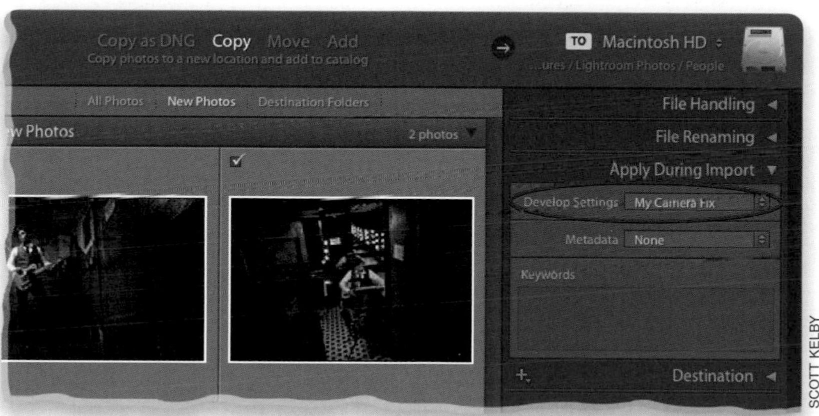

SCOTT KELBY

New Develop Preset

Preset Name: My Camera Fix

Folder: User Presets

Auto Settings

Auto Tone

Settings

White Balance, Basic Tone (Exposure, Contrast, Highlights, Shadows, White Clipping, Black Clipping), Tone Curve, Clarity, Sharpening

Treatment (Color), Color (Saturation, Vibrance, Color Adjustments), Split Toning, Graduated Filters, Radial Filters, Noise Reduction (Luminance, Color)

Lens Corrections (Lens Profile Corrections, Chromatic Aberration, Upright Mode, Upright Transforms, Transform, Lens Vignetting), Effects (Post-Crop Vignetting, Grain), Process Version, Calibration

Check All | Check None | Cancel | Create

Step Four:

When you're happy with your changes, press **Command-Shift-N (PC: Ctrl-Shift-N)** to bring up the New Develop Preset dialog. Name your preset, click the Check None button, then turn on the Calibration and Process Version checkboxes, and click Create. Now, not only can you apply this preset in the Develop module and Quick Develop panel, you can have it applied to all the photos you import from that camera by choosing it from the Develop Settings pop-up menu in the Import window (also shown here).

Lightroom Killer Tips > >

▼ Using the Detail Panel's Preview for Cleaning Up Spots

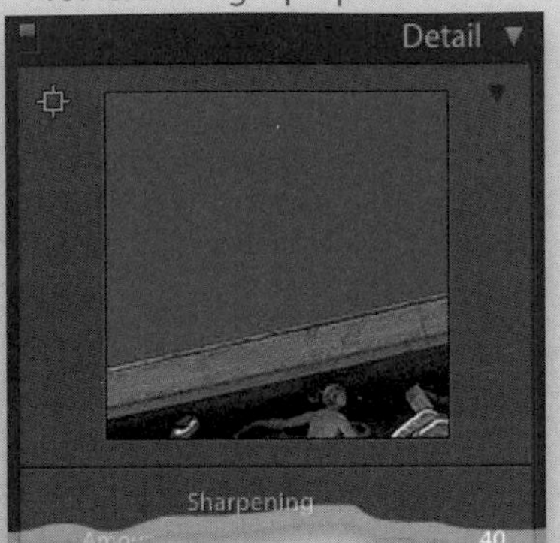

The Detail panel's preview window was designed to give you a 100% (1:1) view of your image, so you can really see the effects of your sharpening and noise adjustments. But it's also great to keep it open when you're removing spots, because you leave the main image at Fit in Window size, and still see the area you're fixing up close in the Detail panel's preview window.

▼ You Can Always Start Over—Even with Virtual Copies

Since none of your edits in Lightroom are applied to the real photo, until you actually leave Lightroom (by jumping over to Photoshop, or exporting as a JPEG or TIFF), you can always start over by pressing the Reset button at the bottom

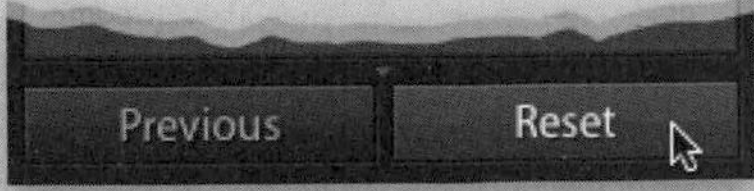

of the right side Panels area. Better yet, if you've been working on a photo and make a virtual copy, you can even reset the virtual copy to how the image looked when you first brought it into Lightroom.

▼ Another Noise Reduction Strategy

The Noise Reduction section, in the Detail panel, does a pretty good job, but if you're not happy with it or it's not working for you, try what I've done in previous versions of Lightroom: jump over to Photoshop and use a plug-in called Noiseware, which does just an amazing job. You can download a trial copy from their website at www.imagenomic.com and install it in Photoshop (so, you'd jump from Lightroom to Photoshop, run the Noiseware plug-in using their excellent built-in presets, and then save the file to come back into Lightroom).

▼ What to Do If You Can't See Your Adjustment Brush

If you start painting and can't see the brush or the pins it creates, go under the Tools menu, under Tool Overlay, and choose **Auto Show**. That way, the pins

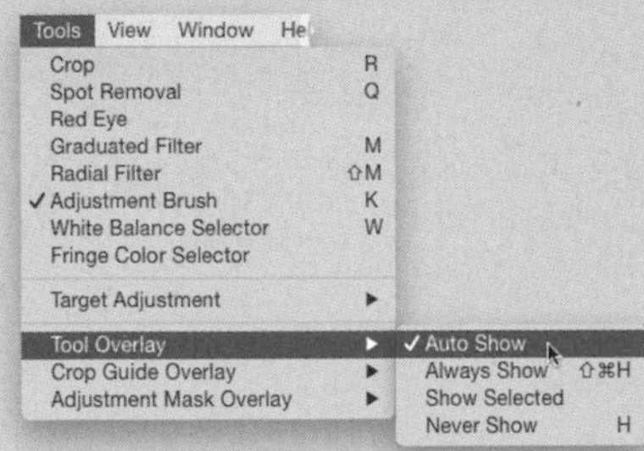

disappear when you move the cursor outside your photo, but then if you move your cursor back over it again to start painting, they reappear.

▼ Fixing "Pet Eye"

If you photograph pets, you've probably already realized that the Red Eye Correction tool doesn't help much when it comes to fixing eye reflection problems on pets, but now the tool has a new Pet Eye button, which corrects for the most common pet eye discoloration problems. It works just like the Red Eye Correction tool, but there's also a checkbox you can

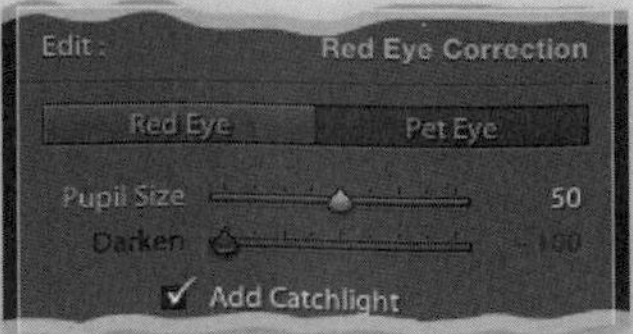

turn on/off to add a small white catchlight to the pupils, and you can click-and-drag directly on the catchlight to move it.

▼ The Constrain Crop Gotcha in Upright

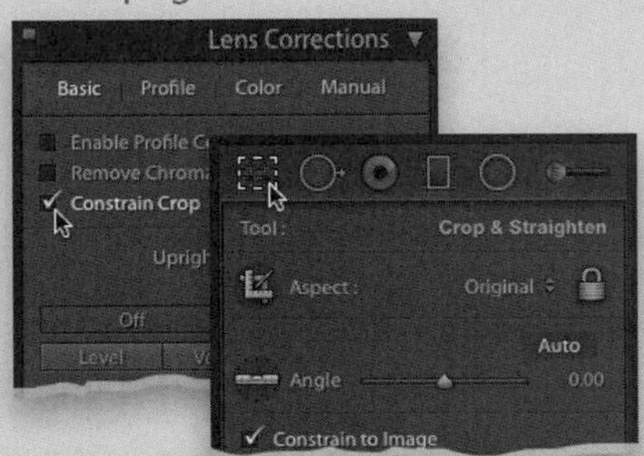

I love the Constrain Crop feature because when I turn it on, it automatically crops away any white border areas left over from Upright's automated correction. However, there's a little gotcha: If I decide I don't like the way it cropped the image (or I want to see more of the top or sides of my image), just turning off the Constrain Crop checkbox won't let me do that. In fact, turning it off (once it was on) doesn't do anything at all. You have to turn it off, then click on the Crop Overlay tool up in the toolbox, and only then does it show you the entire pre-cropped image with the cropping border, so you can crop it yourself. Thought you'd want to know that one.

▼ Auto Upright Auto Crops for You

When you click the Upright Auto button for correcting a perspective problem, you're basically saying, "Do it all for me," so it usually will automatically crop the image down to size, as though you had Constrain Crop turned on (even if you don't). By the way, you noticed I said it "usually" will automatically crop. Sometimes, depending the image, it doesn't. One more thing: if it does auto crop, you can no longer adjust the cropping at all—even if you click on the Crop Overlay tool,

Lightroom Killer Tips > >

it won't show you the original uncropped image. You can only crop what's left tighter, unless you go back to Upright and either turn it off or choose a different Upright Auto correction, like Vertical or Full. It's weird. I know.

▼ Keeping Your Own Cropping in Place and Still Using Upright

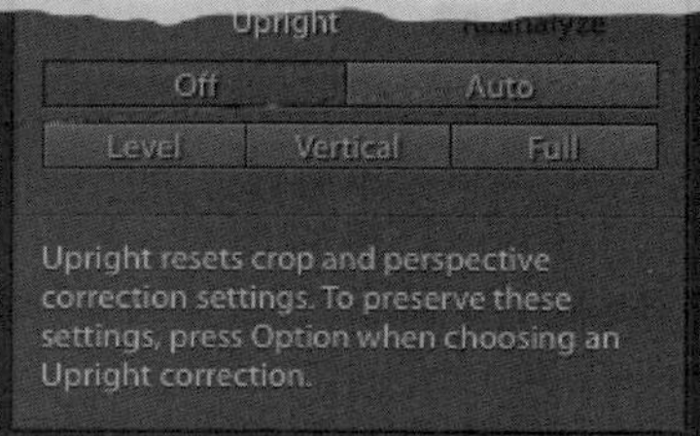

This tip actually appears in the Upright panel itself, but I talk to so many people who have missed it there that I thought it was worth mentioning. If you've cropped an image already, and then you use Upright, it automatically removes your cropping. If you want to keep your cropping in place and still use Upright, press-and-hold the Option (PC: Alt) key, and then click on one of the Upright buttons.

▼ New Common Print Sizes Cropping Overlay

Lightroom has different cropping overlays, like a grid, the rule of thirds, the golden spiral, and so on, but it also has one that shows you print aspect overlays (like a 5x7 crop, a 2x3, etc.). To get to this Aspect Ratios overlay, get the Crop Overlay tool, then press the letter **O** until you see the overlay with the ratios appearing.

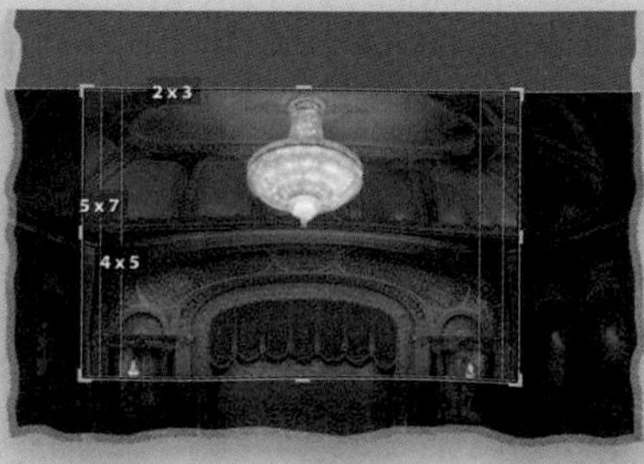

▼ Customizing the Crop Overlay Tool's Aspect Ratio

You're not stuck with the print size ratios Adobe chose for the Crop Overlay tool's new Aspect Ratios overlay. Choose the ratios you want to see by going under the Tools menu (in the Develop module), under Crop Guide Overlay, and selecting **Choose Aspect Ratios** to bring up a dialog where you can choose which of the preset sizes you'd like displayed.

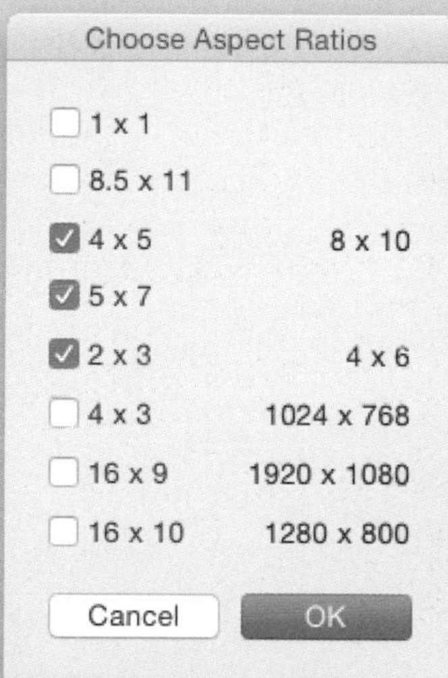

▼ Hiding Crop Overlays You Don't Use

If you have the Crop Overlay tool active, each time you press the letter O, it toggles you through another one of the crop overlays (Thirds, Golden Spiral, the new Aspect Ratios overlay, and so on), but if you find there are some of them you don't ever use, you can hide them (that way, it takes less time to toggle through them to get to the one you actually want, right?). Just go under the Tools menu, under Crop Guide Overlay, and select **Choose Overlays to Cycle** to bring up a dialog where you can choose which of the Overlays you want to hide.

▼ Deleting Multiple Spot Repairs at the Same Time

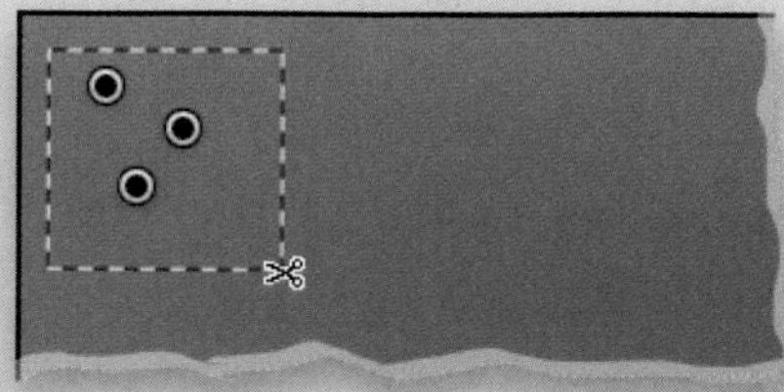

If you've repaired multiple areas of your photo using the Spot Removal tool (maybe you used it to remove sensor dust on your image, or a spot or speck on your lens that now shows up on your image), you can remove any individual spot repair by pressing-and-holding the Option (PC: Alt) key and clicking on that individual spot. To remove multiple edits at once, press-and-hold the Option key, but then click-and-drag out a selection around the repairs you want to remove, and it instantly removes all those edits inside that selected area. If you want to remove all your repairs at once, just hit the Reset button at the bottom of the Spot Removal tool panel.

▼ Have Lightroom Remember Your Zoom Position

If you want Lightroom to remember the amount of zoom and the zoom location between images, go under the View menu and choose **Lock Zoom Position**. Now, as you swap between images and click to zoom, it will zoom to the same amount and position automatically. Helpful when you're comparing the same area between multiple images.

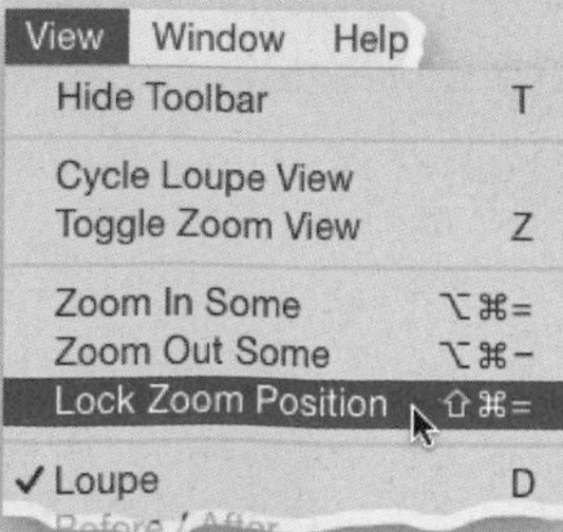

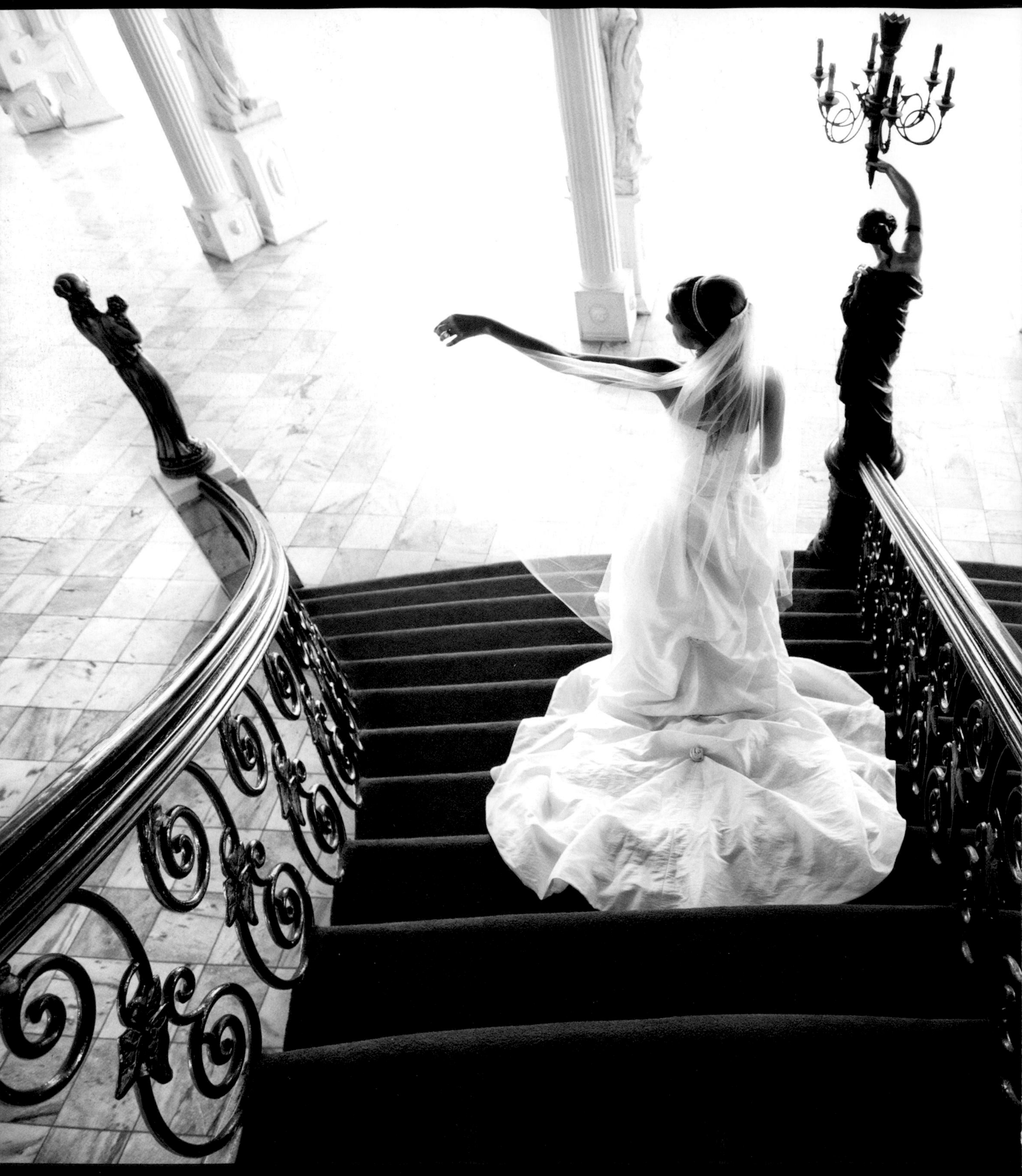

Photo by Scott Kelby | Exposure: 1/10 sec | Focal Length: 16mm | Aperture Value: ƒ/3.2

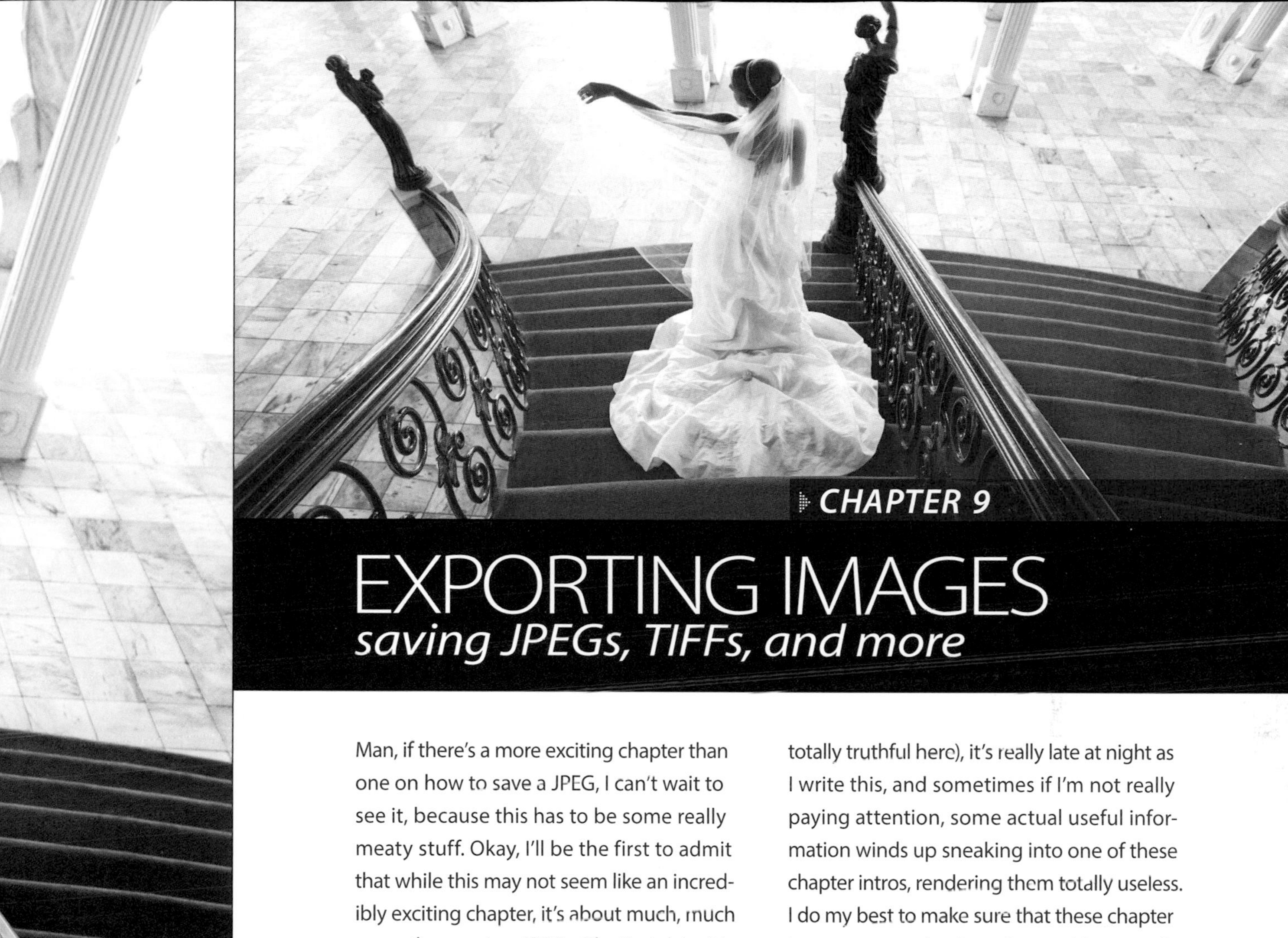

CHAPTER 9

EXPORTING IMAGES

saving JPEGs, TIFFs, and more

Man, if there's a more exciting chapter than one on how to save a JPEG, I can't wait to see it, because this has to be some really meaty stuff. Okay, I'll be the first to admit that while this may not seem like an incredibly exciting chapter, it's about much, much more than saving JPEGs. That's right—it's also about saving TIFFs. Okay, I gotcha on that one (come on—you know I did), but in reality there is more to this process than you might think, so if you spend just a few minutes now reading this short chapter, I promise you it will pay off in saved time and increased productivity in the future. Now, at this point you might be thinking, "Hey Scott, that last part was actually somewhat helpful. What's that doing in a chapter intro?" I honestly don't know how that snuck in here, but I can tell you this (and I'm being totally truthful here), it's really late at night as I write this, and sometimes if I'm not really paying attention, some actual useful information winds up sneaking into one of these chapter intros, rendering them totally useless. I do my best to make sure that these chapter intros are completely unfettered (I can't tell you how few times I've been able to use the word "unfettered" in a sentence, so I'm pretty psyched right now), but sometimes, against my better judgment, everything just starts to make sense, and before you know it—something useful happens. I try to catch these in the editing process by copying-and-pasting the entire chapter intro into the Pimp Name Generator (that's four times in one book. Cha-ching!), and then those results get copied-and-pasted back here as the final edited version for print. See, I do care. Pimp!

Saving Your Photos as JPEGs

Since there is no Save command for Lightroom (like there is in Photoshop), one of the questions I get asked most is, "How do you save a photo as a JPEG?" Well, in Lightroom, you don't save it as a JPEG, you export it as a JPEG (or a TIFF, or a DNG, or a Photoshop PSD). It's a simple process, and Lightroom has added some automation features that can kick in once your photo is exported.

Step One:

You start by selecting which photo(s) you want to export as a JPEG (or a TIFF, PSD, or DNG). You can do this in either the Library module's Grid view or down in the Filmstrip in any other module by Command-clicking (PC: Ctrl-clicking) on all the photos you want to export (as shown here).

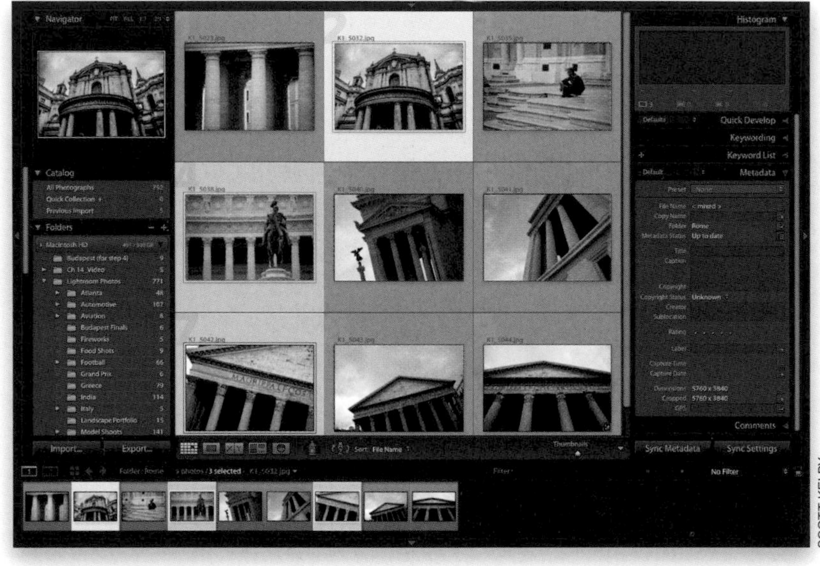

SCOTT KELBY

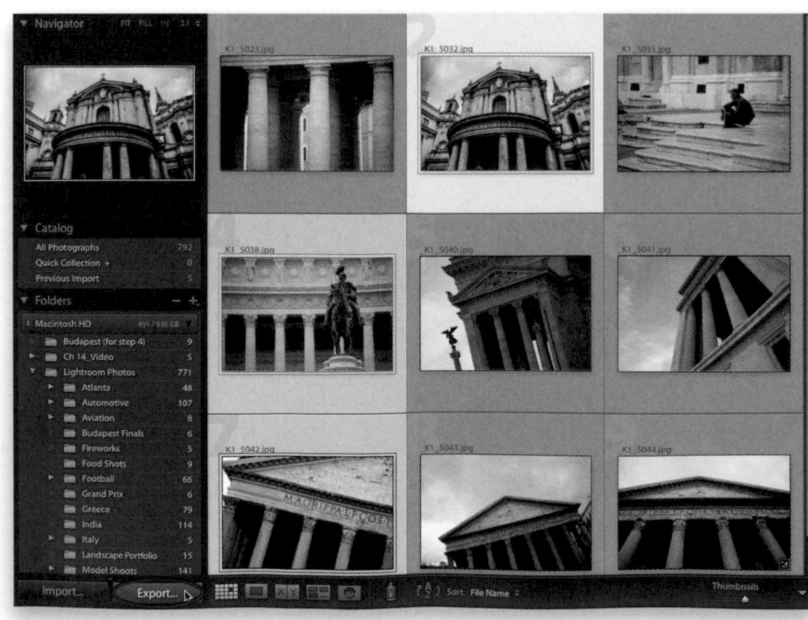

Step Two:

If you're in the Library module, click on the Export button at the bottom of the left side Panels area (circled here in red). If you're in a different module and using the Filmstrip to select your photos for export, then use the keyboard shortcut **Command-Shift-E (PC: Ctrl-Shift-E)**. Whichever method you choose, it brings up the Export dialog (shown in the next step).

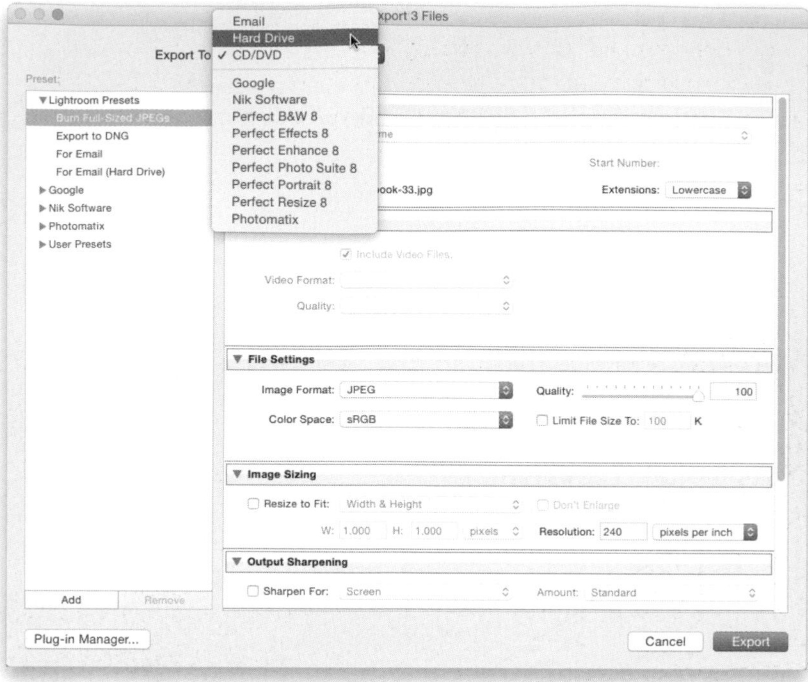

Step Three:

Along the left side of the Export dialog, Adobe put some Export presets, which are basically designed to keep you from having to fill out this entire dialog every time from scratch. It ships with a few presets from Adobe, but the real power of this is when you create your own (those will appear under the User Presets header). The built-in Lightroom Presets are at least a good starting place to build your own, so for now click on Burn Full-Sized JPEGs, and it fills in some typical settings someone might use to export their photos as JPEGs and burn them to a disc. However, we'll customize these settings so our files are exported where and how we want them, then we'll save our custom settings as a preset, so we don't have to go through all this every time. If, instead of burning these images to disc, you just want to save these JPEGs in a folder on your computer, go to the top of the dialog, and from the Export To pop-up menu, choose **Hard Drive**, as shown here.

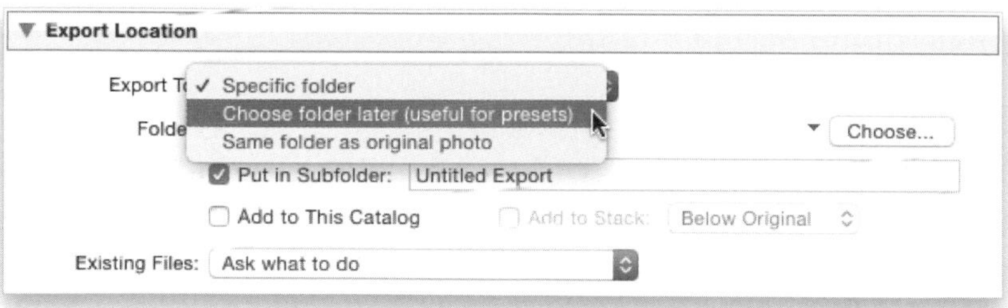

Choose where to save your exported images from the Export To pop-up menu

Step Four:

Let's start at the top of the dialog: First, you need to tell Lightroom where to save these files in the Export Location section. If you click on the Export To pop-up menu (as shown here, at top), it brings up a list of likely places you might choose to save your files. The second choice (Choose Folder Later) is great if you're making presets, because it lets you choose the folder as you go. If you want to choose a folder that's not in this list, choose Specific Folder, then click the Choose button to navigate to the folder you want. You also have the option of saving them into a separate subfolder, like I did here, at the bottom. So, now my images will appear in a folder named "Rome" on my desktop. If these are RAW files and you want the exported JPEGs added into Lightroom, turn on the Add to This Catalog checkbox.

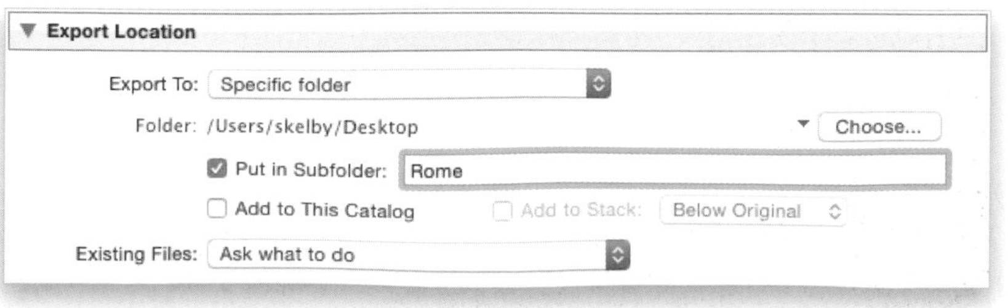

Turn on the Put in Subfolder checkbox to save your images in a separate subfolder

Continued

Step Five:

The next section down, File Naming, is like the file naming feature you learned about back in the Importing chapter. If you don't want to rename the files you're exporting, but want to keep their current names, leave the Rename To checkbox turned off, or turn it on and choose Filename from the pop-up menu. If you do want to rename the files, choose one of the built-in templates, or if you created a custom file naming template (we learned this back in Chapter 1), it will appear in this list, too. In our example, I chose Custom Name – Sequence (which automatically adds a sequential number, starting at 1, to the end of my custom name). Then, I simply named these shots "Rome," so the photos will wind up being named Rome-1, Rome-2, and so on. There's also a pop-up menu for choosing whether the file extension appears in all uppercase (.JPG) or lowercase (.jpg).

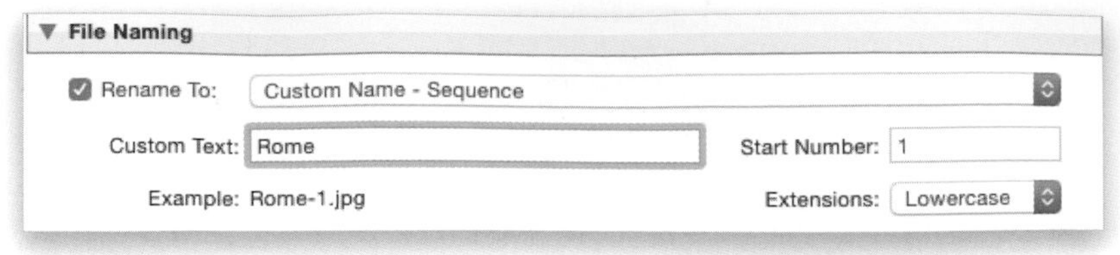

Step Six:

Let's say you're exporting an entire collection of images, and inside that collection are some video clips that were shot with your DSLR. If you want them included in your export, in the Video section, turn on the Include Video Files checkbox (shown here). Below that checkbox, you'll choose the video format (H.264 is really compressed, and is for playing on a mobile device; DPX is usually for visual effects). Next, choose your video Quality: Max will keep the quality as close to your original video as possible, and High is still good, but may be slower. Choose Medium if you're going to post it to the web, or if you're planning to view it on a high-end tablet. Choose Low for viewing on all other mobile devices. You can see the differences between your format and quality choices by watching the Target size and speed listed to the right of the Quality pop-up menu. Of course, if you don't have any videos chosen when you export, this section will be grayed out.

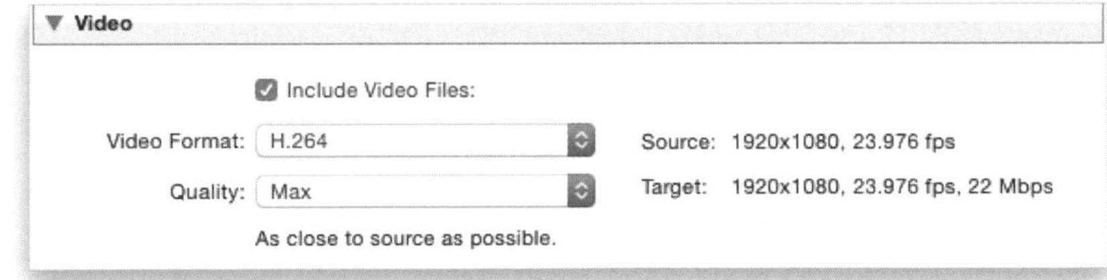

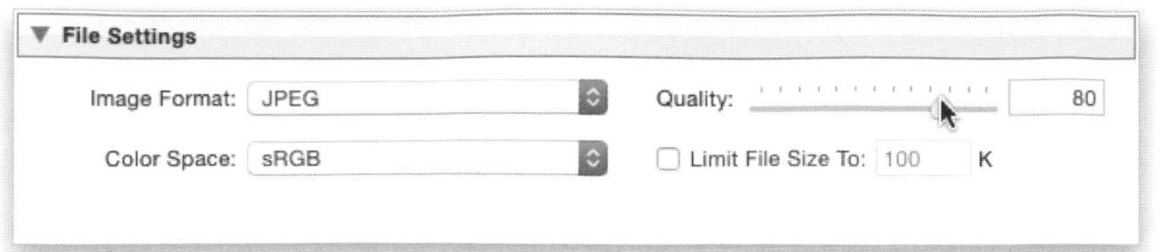

Step Seven:

Under File Settings, you choose which file format to save your photos in from the Image Format pop-up menu (since we chose the Burn Full-Sized JPEGs preset, JPEG is already chosen here, but you could choose TIFF, PSD, DNG, or if you have RAW files, you could choose Original to export the original RAW photo). Since we're saving as a JPEG, there's a Quality slider (the higher the quality, the larger the file size), and I generally choose a Quality setting of 80, which I think gives a good balance between quality and file size. If I'm sending these files to someone without Photoshop, I choose sRGB as my color space. If you chose a PSD, TIFF, or DNG format, their options will appear (you get to choose things like the color space, bit depth, and compression settings).

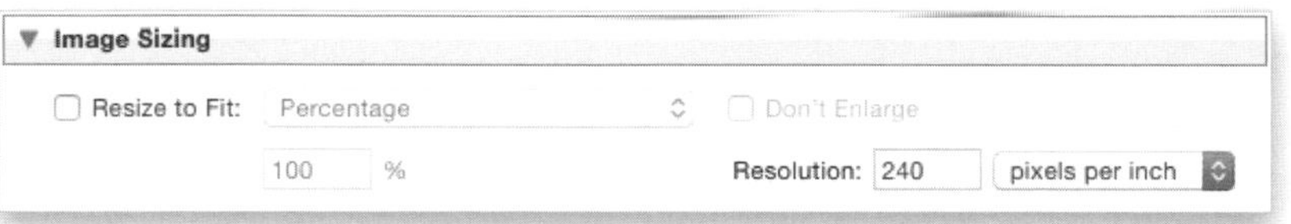

You can skip the Image Sizing section altogether, unless you need to make the image you're saving smaller than its original size

Step Eight:

By default, Lightroom assumes that you want to export your photos at their full size. If you want to make them smaller, in the Image Sizing section, turn on the Resize to Fit checkbox, then type in the Width, Height, and Resolution you want. Or you can choose to resize by pixel dimensions, the long edge of your image, the short edge of your image, the number of megapixels in your image, or a percentage from the top pop-up menu.

Continued

Step Nine:

Also, if these images are for printing in another application, or will be posted on the web, you can add sharpening by turning on the Sharpen For checkbox in the Output Sharpening section. This applies the right amount of sharpening based on whether they're going to be seen only onscreen (in which case, you'll choose Screen) or printed (in which case, you'll choose the type of paper they'll be printed on—glossy or matte). For inkjet printing, I usually choose High for the Amount, which onscreen looks like it's too much sharpening, but on paper looks just right (for the web, I choose Standard).

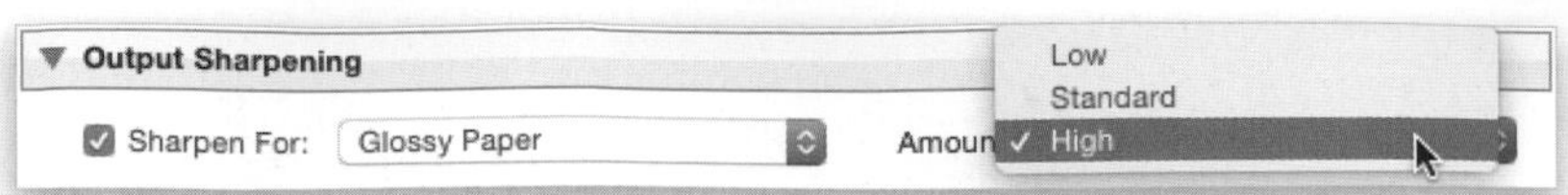

You can add Output Sharpening for wherever these images will be viewed, either onscreen (on the web or in a slide show), or on a print

Step 10:

In the Metadata section, you start by choosing what metadata you want to be exported with your images: everything, everything but your camera and Camera Raw data (this hides all your exposure settings, your camera's serial numbers, and other stuff your clients probably don't need to know), just your copyright and contact info (if you're including your copyright, you probably want to include a way for people to contact you if they want to use your photo), or just your copyright. If you choose All Metadata or All Except Camera & Camera Raw Info, you can still have Lightroom remove any Person keywords by turning on the Remove Person Info checkbox or any GPS data by turning on the Remove Location Info checkbox.

The next section down lets you add a visible watermark to the images you're exporting (watermarking is covered in detail in the next project), and to add your watermark to each image you're exporting, turn on the Watermark checkbox, then choose a simple copyright or your saved watermark from the pop-up menu.

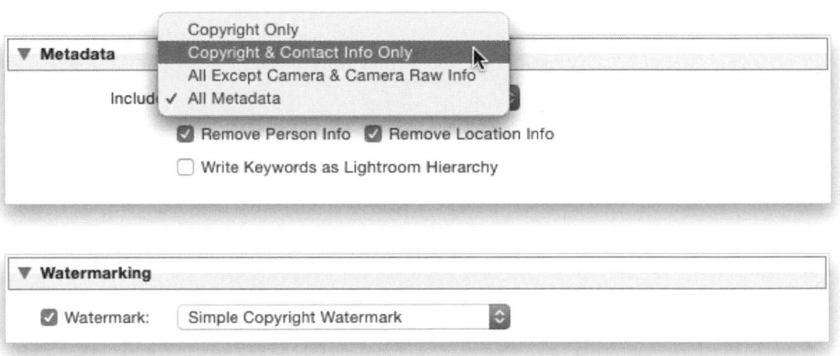

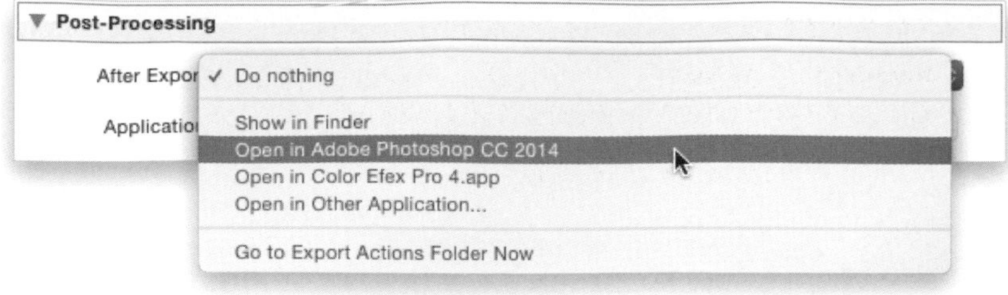

Step 11:

The final section, Post-Processing, is where you decide what happens after the files are exported from Lightroom. If you choose Do Nothing (from the After Export pop-up menu), they just get saved into that folder you chose back in the beginning. If you choose Open in Adobe Photoshop, they'll automatically be opened in Photoshop after they're exported. You can also choose to open them in another application or in a Lightroom plug-in. Go to Export Actions Folder Now opens the folder where Lightroom stores your export actions. So, if you want to run a batch action from Photoshop, you could create a droplet and place it in this folder. That droplet would then show up in the After Export pop-up menu, and choosing it would open Photoshop and run your batch action on all the photos you were exporting from Lightroom. (*Note:* I show you how to create a batch action in Chapter 10.)

Step 12:

Now that you've customized things the way you want, let's save these settings as your own custom preset. That way, the next time you want to export a JPEG, you don't have to go through these steps again. Now, there are some changes I would suggest that would make your preset more effective. For example, if you saved this as a preset right now, when you use it to export other photos as JPEGs, they'll be saved in that same Rome folder. Instead, this is where it's a good idea to select **Choose Folder Later** (in the Export Location section, as shown here), like we discussed back in Step Four.

Continued

Step 13:

If you know you always want your exported JPEGs saved in a specific folder, then in the Export Location section, click the Choose button, and choose that folder. Now, what happens if you go to export a photo as a JPEG into that folder, and there's already a photo with the same name in it (maybe from a previous export)? Should Lightroom just automatically overwrite this existing file with the new one you're exporting now, or do you want to give this new file a different name, so it doesn't delete the file already in that folder? You get to choose how Lightroom handles this problem using the Existing Files pop-up menu (shown here). I pick **Choose a New Name for the Exported File** (as seen here). That way, I don't accidentally overwrite a file I meant to keep. By the way, when you choose Skip, if it sees a file already in that folder with the same name, it doesn't export the JPEG image—instead, it just skips it.

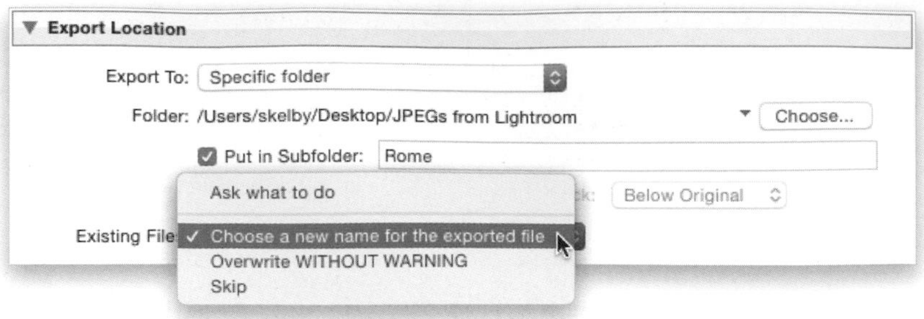

TIP: Rename Files When Using a Preset

Before you export your photos, make sure you give your files a new custom name, or the shots from your football game will be named Rome-1.jpg, Rome-2.jpg, and so on.

Step 14:

Now you can save your custom settings as a preset: click the Add button at the bottom-left corner of the dialog (shown circled here in red), and then give your new preset a name (in this case, I used Hi-Res JPEGs/Save to Hard Drive. That name lets me know exactly what I'm exporting, and where they're going).

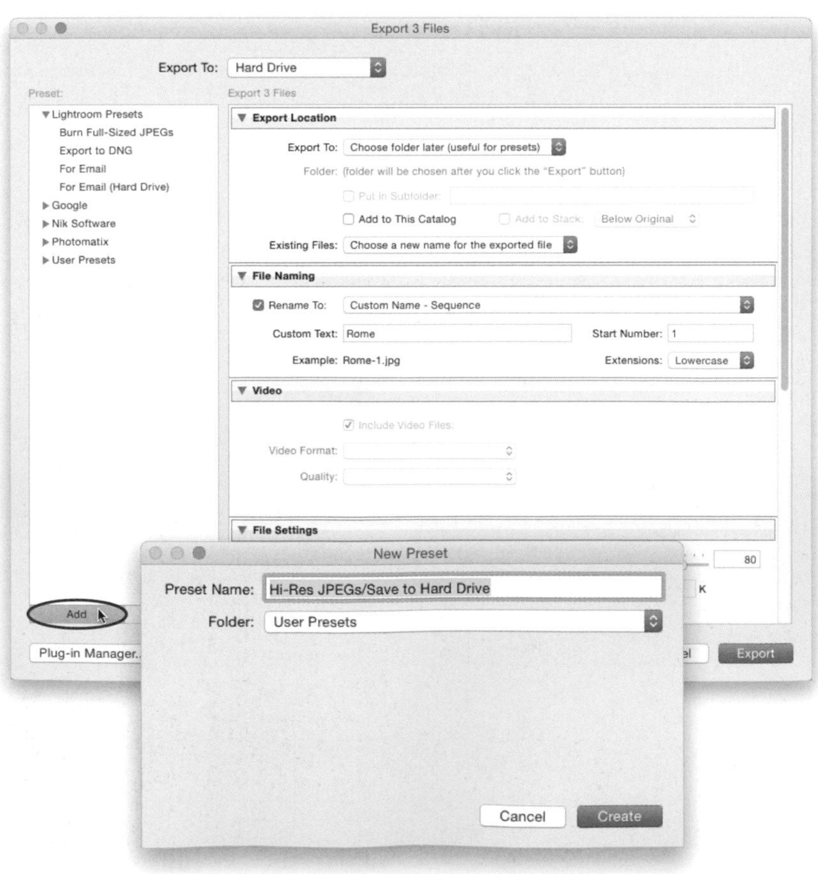

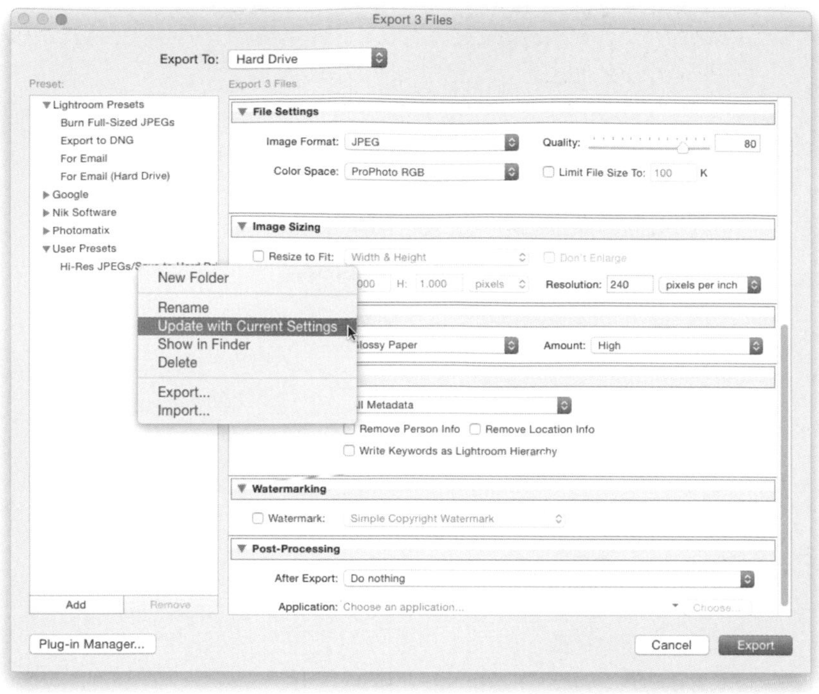

Step 15:

Once you click the Create button, your preset is added to the Preset section (on the left side of the dialog, under User Presets), and from now on you're just one click away from exporting JPEGs your way. If you decide you want to make a change to your preset (as I did in this case, where I changed the Color Space to ProPhoto RGB, and I turned the Watermark checkbox off), you can update it with your current settings by Right-clicking on your preset, and from the pop-up menu that appears, choosing **Update with Current Settings** (as shown here).

While you're here, you might want to create a second custom preset—one for exporting JPEGs for use in online web galleries. To do that, you might lower the Image Sizing Resolution setting to 72 ppi, change your sharpening to Screen, set Amount to Standard, set the Metadata to Copyright & Contact Info Only, and you might want to turn the Watermark checkbox back on to help prevent misuse of your images. Then you'd click the Add button to create a new preset named something like Export JPEG for Web.

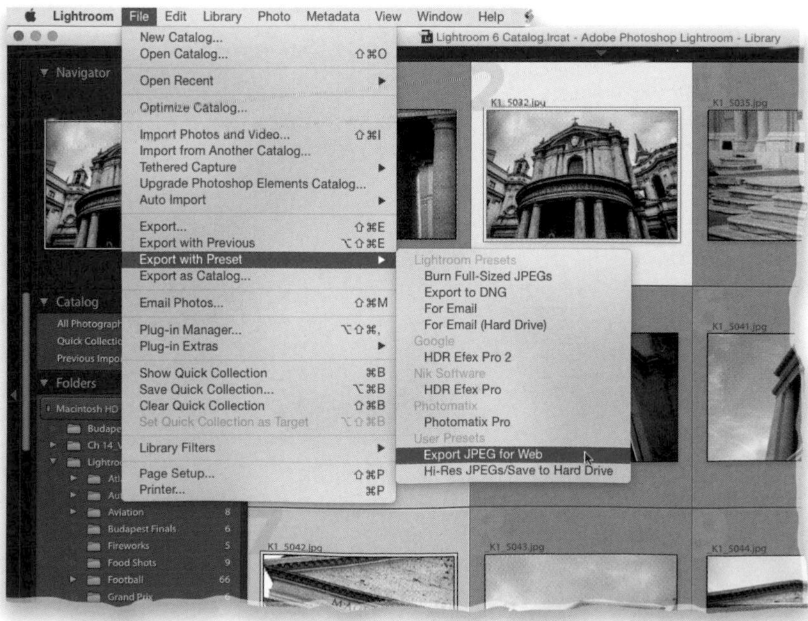

Step 16:

Now that you've created your own presets, you can save time and skip the whole Export dialog thing altogether by just selecting the photos you want to export, then going under Lightroom's File menu, under **Export with Preset**, and choosing the export preset you want (in this example, I'm choosing the Export JPEG for Web preset). When you choose it this way, it just goes and exports the photos with no further input from you. Sweet!

Adding a Watermark to Your Images

If your images are going on the web, there's not much to keep folks from taking your images and using them in their own projects (sadly, it happens every day). One way to help limit unauthorized use of your images is to put a visible watermark on them. That way, if someone rips them off, it'll be pretty obvious to everyone that they've stolen someone else's work. Also, beyond protecting your images, many photographers are using a visible watermark as branding and marketing for their studio. Here's how to set yours up:

Step One:

To create your watermark, press **Command-Shift-E (PC: Ctrl-Shift-E)** to bring up the Export dialog, then scroll down to the Watermarking section, turn on the Watermark checkbox, and choose **Edit Watermarks** from the pop-up menu (as shown here). *Note:* I'm covering watermarking here in the Export chapter, because you can add your watermark when you're exporting your images as JPEGs, TIFFs, etc., but you can also add these watermarks when you print an image (in the Print module), or put it in a web gallery (in the Web module).

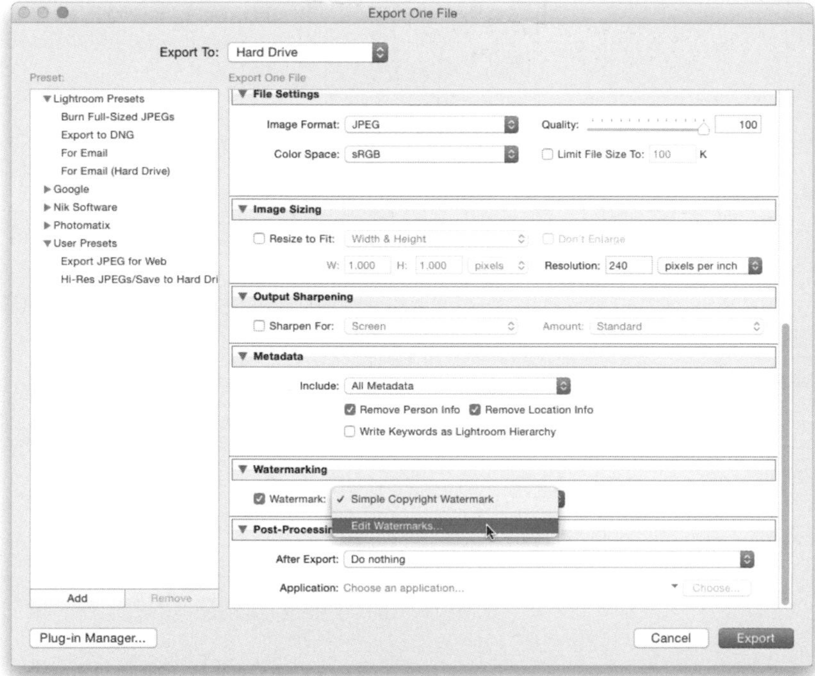

Step Two:

This brings up the Watermark Editor (seen here), and this is where you either (a) create a simple text watermark, or (b) import a graphic to use as your watermark (maybe your studio's logo, or some custom watermark layout you've created in Photoshop). You choose either Text or Graphic up in the top-right corner (shown circled here in red). By default, it displays the name from your user profile on your computer, so that's why it shows my copyright down in the text field at the bottom of the dialog. The text is also positioned right up against the bottom and left borders of your image, but luckily you can have it offset from the corners (I'll show you how in Step Four). We'll start by customizing our text.

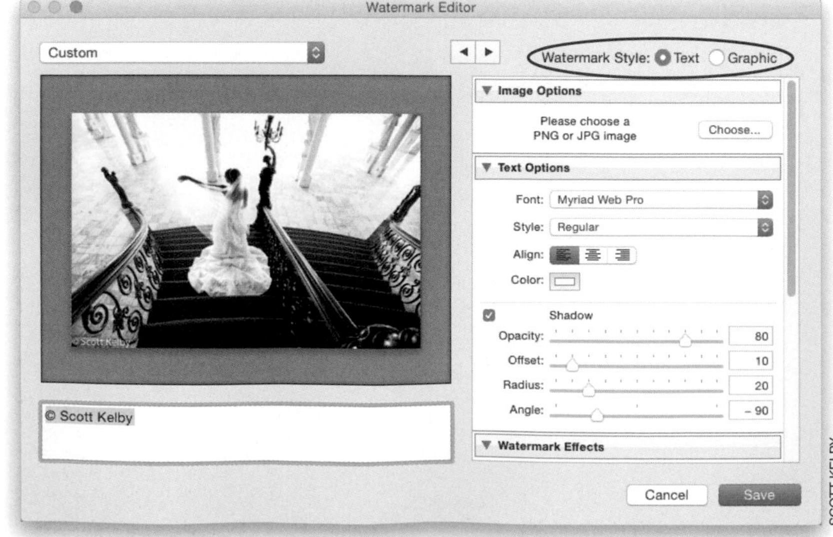

SCOTT KELBY

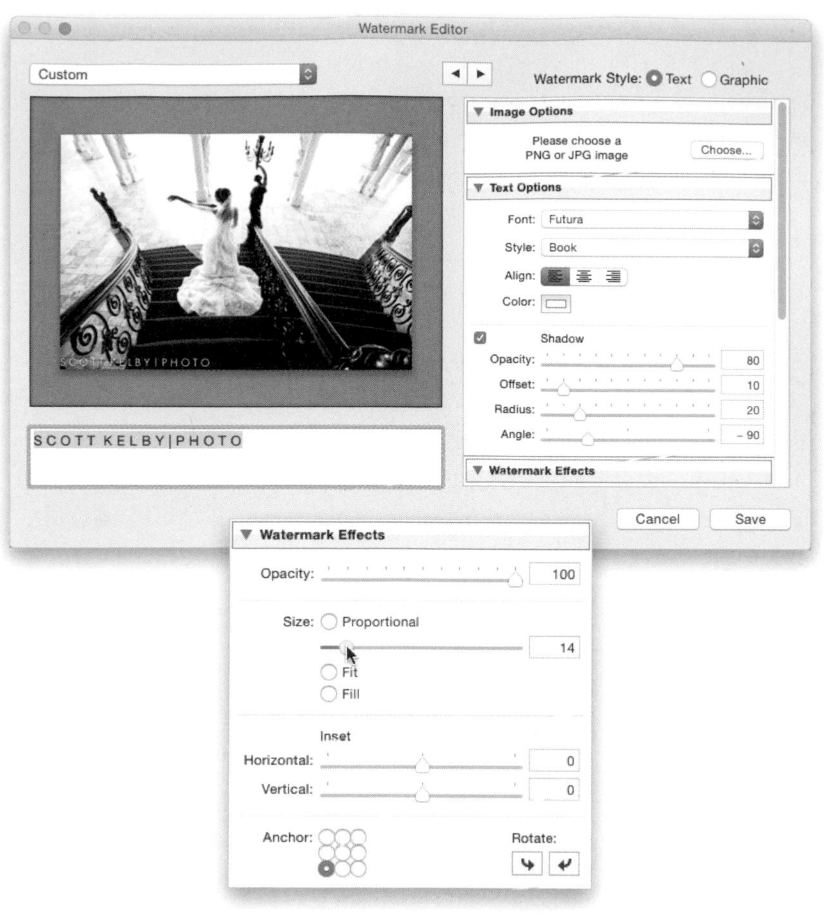

Step Three:

Type in the name of your studio in the text field at the bottom left, then choose your font in the Text Options section on the right side of the dialog. In this case, I chose Futura Book. (By the way, the little line that separates SCOTT KELBY from PHOTO is called a "pipe," and you create one by pressing Shift-Backslash.) Also, to put some space between the letters, I pressed the Spacebar after each one. You also can choose the text alignment (left justified, centered, or right justified) here, and you can click on the Color swatch to choose a font color. To change the size of your type, scroll down to the Watermark Effects section, where you'll find a Size slider (seen here) and radio buttons to Fit your watermark to the full width of your image, or Fill it at full size. You can also move your cursor over the type on the image preview and corner handles appear—click-and-drag outward to scale the text up, and inward to shrink it down.

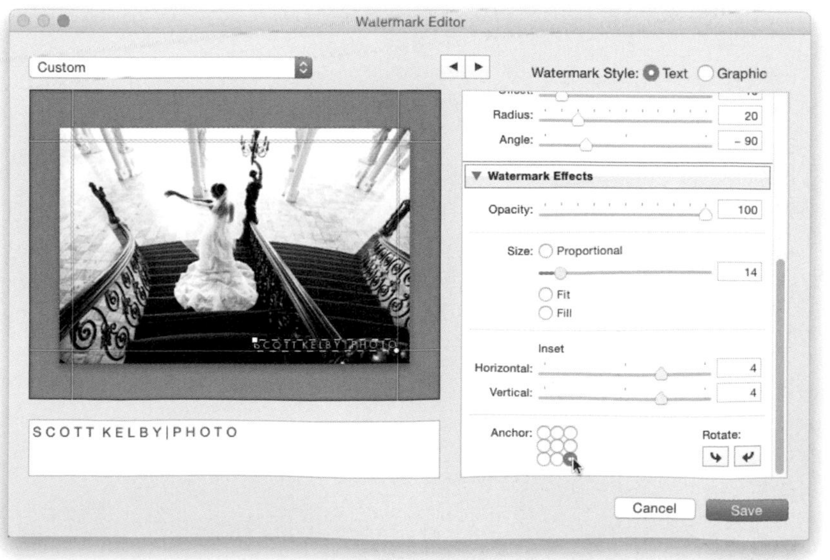

Step Four:

You get to choose the position of your watermark in the Watermark Effects section. At the bottom of the section, you'll see an Anchor grid, which shows where you can position your watermark. To move it to the bottom-right corner, click the bottom-right anchor point (as shown here). To move it to the center of your image, click the center anchor point, and so on. To the right of that are two Rotate buttons if you want to switch to a vertical watermark. Also, back in Step Two, I mentioned there's a way to offset your text from the sides of your image—just drag the Horizontal and Vertical Inset sliders (right above the Anchor grid). When you move them, little positioning guides will appear in the preview window, so you can easily see where your text will be positioned. Lastly, the Opacity slider at the top of the section controls how see-through your watermark will be.

Continued

Step Five:

If your watermark is going over a lighter background, you can add a drop shadow using the Shadow controls in the Text Options section. The Opacity slider controls how dark the shadow will be. The Offset is how far from the text your shadow will appear (the farther you drag to the right, the farther away the shadow will be). The Radius is Adobe's secret code name for softness, so the higher you set the Radius, the softer your shadow will become. The Angle slider is for choosing where the shadow appears, so the default setting of –90 puts the shadow down and to the right. A setting of 145 puts it up and to the left, and so on. Just drag it, and you'll instantly see how it affects the position of your shadow. The best way to see if the shadow really looks better or not is to toggle the Shadow checkbox on/off a couple of times.

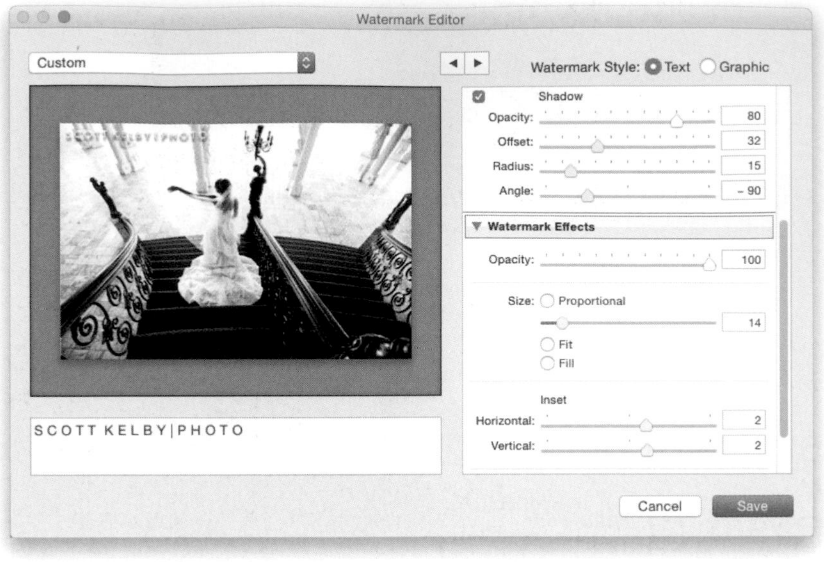

Step Six:

Now let's work with a graphic watermark, like your studio's logo. The Watermark Editor supports graphic images in either JPEG or PNG format, so make sure your logo is in one of those two formats. Scroll back up to the Image Options section, and where it says Please Choose a PNG or JPEG Image, click the Choose button, find your logo graphic, then click Choose, and your graphic appears (unfortunately, the white background behind the logo is visible, but we'll deal with that in the next step). It pretty much uses the same controls as when using text—go to the Watermark Effects section and drag the Opacity slider to the left to make your graphic see-through, and use the Size slider to change the size of your logo. The Inset sliders let you move your logo off the edges, and the Anchor grid lets you position the graphic in different locations on your image. The Text Options and Shadow controls are grayed out, since you're working with a graphic.

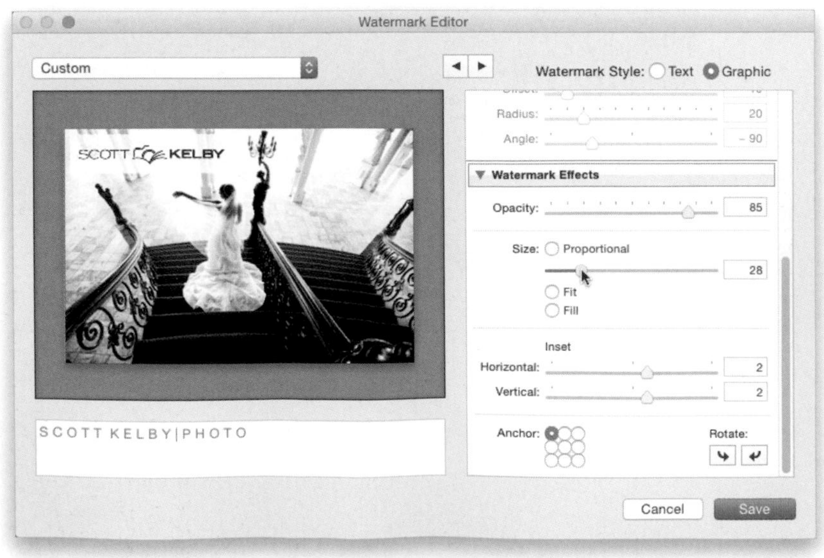

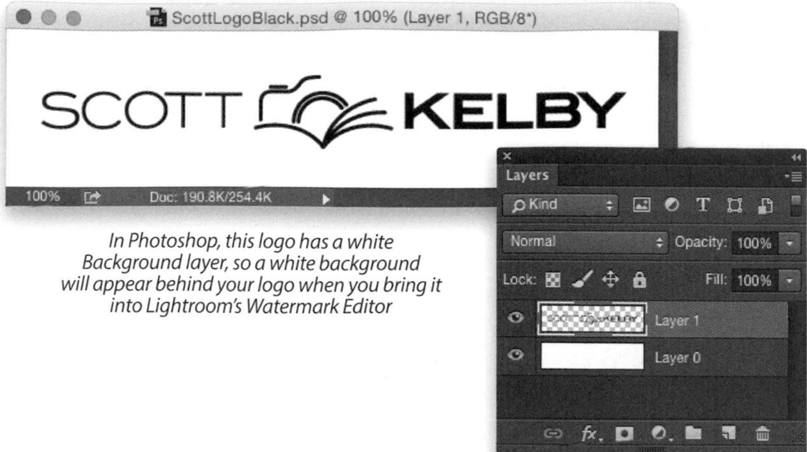

In Photoshop, this logo has a white Background layer, so a white background will appear behind your logo when you bring it into Lightroom's Watermark Editor

Step Seven:

To make that white background transparent, you have to open the layered file of your logo in Adobe Photoshop and do two things: (1) Delete the Background layer by dragging it onto the Trash icon at the bottom of the Layers panel, leaving just your graphics (and text) on their own transparent layers. Then, (2) save the Photoshop document in PNG format. This saves a separate file, and the file appears flattened, but the background behind your logo will be transparent (as shown here at the bottom).

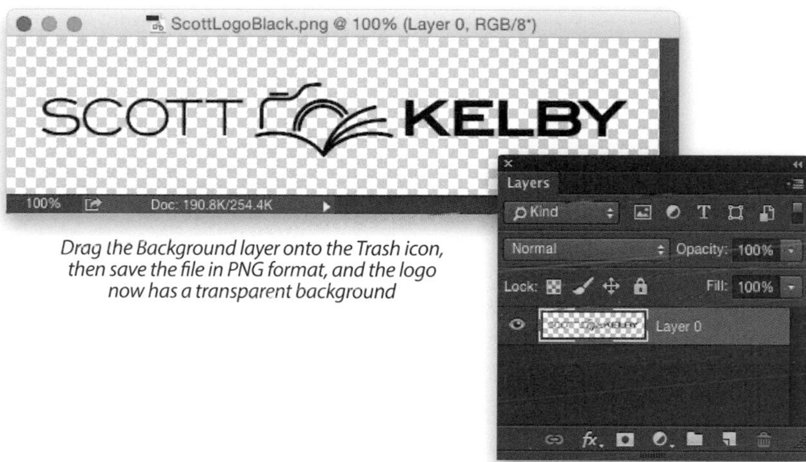

Drag the Background layer onto the Trash icon, then save the file in PNG format, and the logo now has a transparent background

Step Eight:

Now choose this new PNG logo file (in the Image Options section of the Watermark Editor), and when you import it, it appears over your image without the white background (as seen here). You can now resize, reposition, and change the opacity of your logo graphic in the Watermark Effects section. Once you get it set up the way you want it, you should save it as a watermark preset (so you can use it again, and you can apply it from the Print and Web modules). You do that by clicking the Save button in the bottom right or choosing **Save Current Settings as New Preset** from the pop-up menu in the top-left corner of the dialog. Now your watermark is always just one click away.

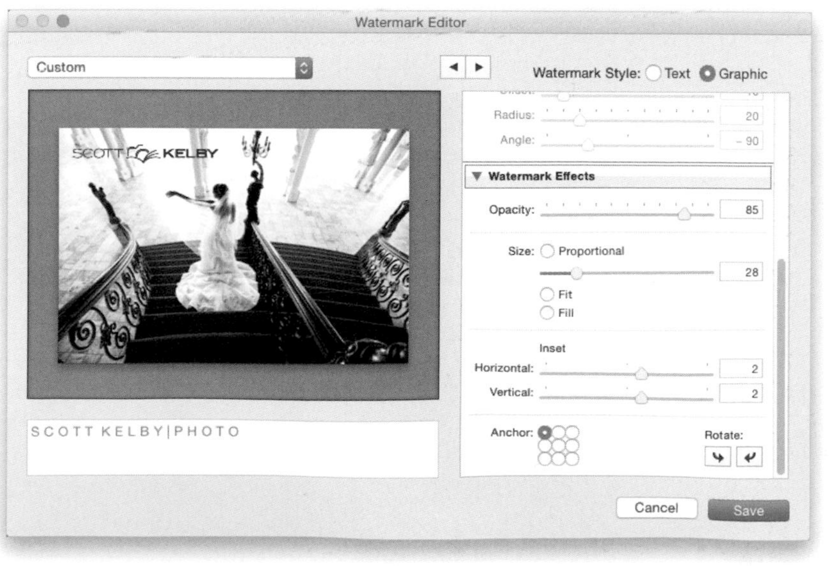

Emailing Photos from Lightroom

Back in Lightroom 3 (and earlier versions), if you wanted to email images from Lightroom, it was...well...it was a workaround. You had to jump through a lot of hoops (creating aliases/shortcuts to your email program, and placing those inside one of Lightroom's folders, and on and on). It kinda worked, but it was kinda clunky. Luckily, now, it's built right in, and it couldn't be easier.

Step One:

In the Grid view, Command-click (PC: Ctrl-click) on the images you want to email. Now, go under the File menu and choose **Email Photos** (as shown here) to bring up Lightroom's email dialog (shown in the next step).

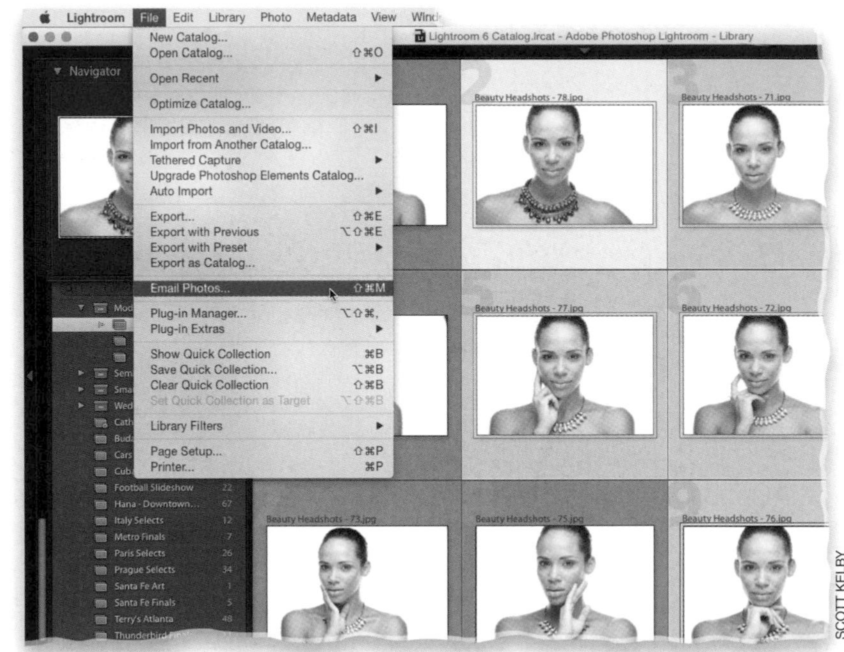

SCOTT KELBY

Step Two:

Here's where you enter the email address of the person you want to email the images to and type in the subject line of your email, and it chooses your default email application (but you can choose a different email application if you like from the From pop-up menu). You'll also see the thumbnails of the images you just selected in Lightroom's Grid view.

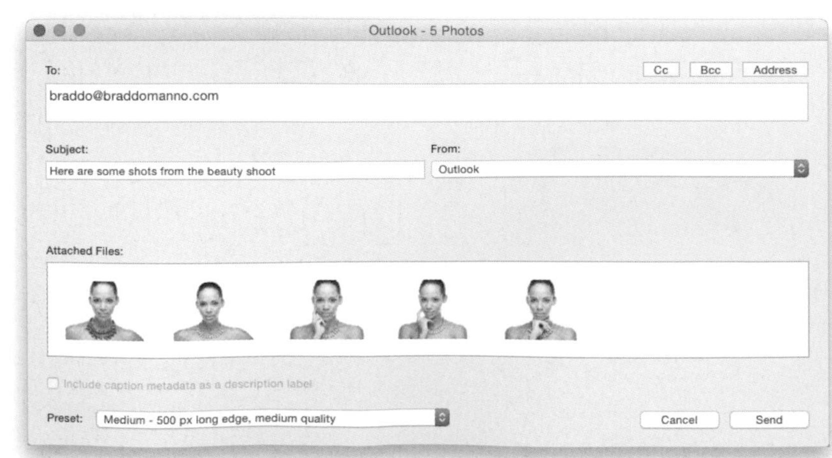

TIP: What If Your Email App Isn't Listed?

Then, from the From pop-up menu, choose **Go to Email Account Manager**. There, click the Add button (in the bottom left) and when the New Account dialog appears, choose your email provider from the Service Provider pop-up menu (you'll see AOL, Gmail, Hotmail, etc.). If yours isn't listed there, then choose Other, and you'll have to add the server settings yourself. Now, add your email address and password in the Credential Settings section (it will verify that it's correct), and your email server will be added to your From pop-up menu.

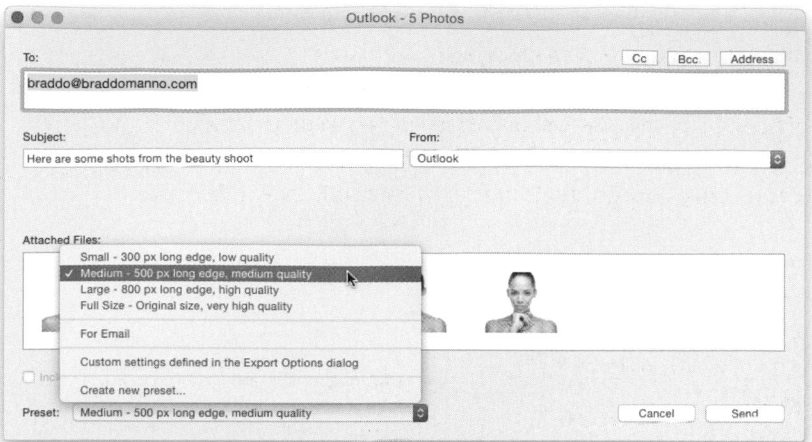

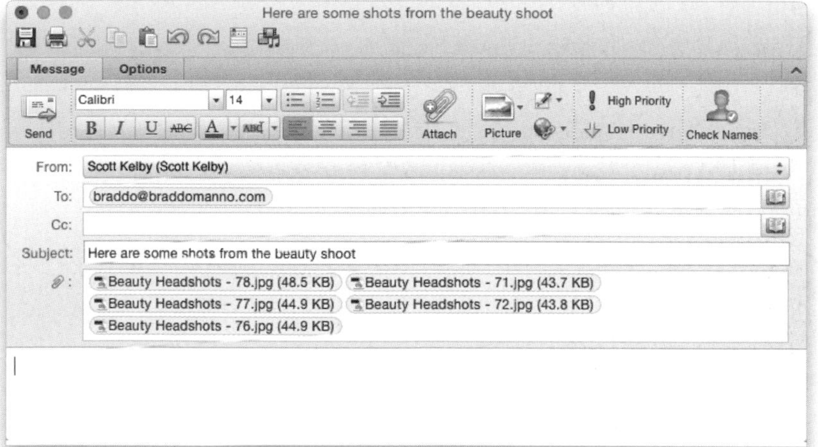

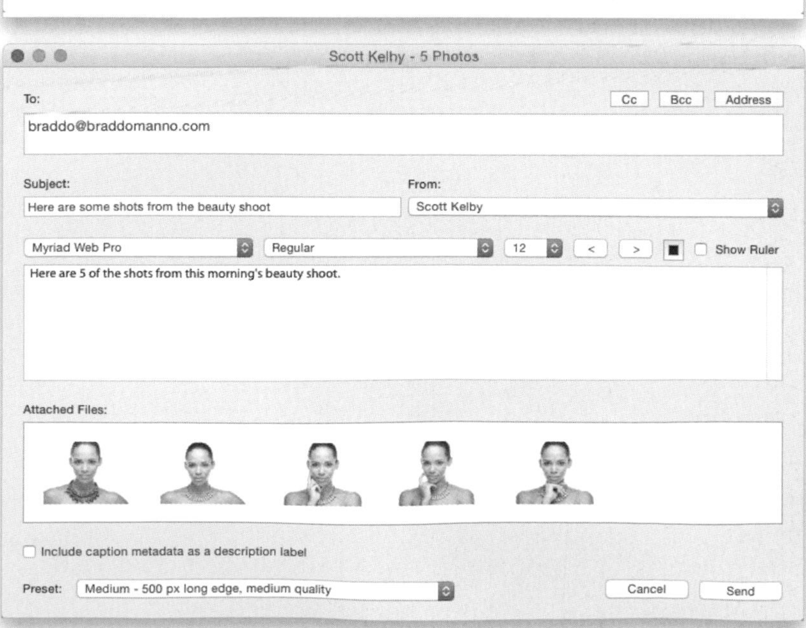

Step Three:

You also get to choose the physical size of the images you're emailing (after all, if you attach enough of them at their full size, chances are your email will bounce back for being too large). There are four built-in size presets you can choose from the pop-up menu in the bottom-left corner of the dialog (as shown here), where you choose both the size and quality. If you've created any presets for emailing, those will appear here, too, or to create one now, choose Create New Preset at the bottom of the menu, and it brings up the Standard Export dialog. Enter the settings you want, save it as a preset (click the + [plus sign] button in the bottom-left corner of the Export dialog), and now that preset will appear in your email Preset pop-up menu.

Step Four:

If you're using an email app, when you click the Send button, it launches your email program, fills in all the info you entered in the Lightroom email dialog (address, subject, and so on), and then it attaches your images at the size and quality you selected, so type your message and hit the Send button in your email program, and off it goes. If you're using webmail, once you choose it in the From pop-up menu, the dialog changes to include a message area. Type your message and click the Send button.

TIP: Using the Two Email Presets

Adobe included two email presets in Lightroom's Export dialog: one that brings up the regular email dialog you just learned about (called "For Email"), and the other simply saves your images to your hard drive for you to email later (manually). To save the images for emailing later, go under the File menu, under Export with Preset, and choose For Email (Hard Drive). You'll choose which folder you want to save your images into, and then it just saves them as JPEGs at a small size (640x640 pixels at a quality setting of 50).

Exporting Your Original RAW Photo

So far, everything we've done in this chapter is based on us tweaking our photo in Lightroom and then exporting it as a JPEG, TIFF, etc. But what if you want to export the original RAW photo? Here's how it's done, and you'll have the option to include the keywords and metadata you added in Lightroom—or not.

Step One:

First, click on the RAW photo you want to export from Lightroom. When you export an original RAW photo, the changes you applied to it in Lightroom (including keywords, metadata, and even changes you made in the Develop module) are saved to a separate file called an XMP sidecar file, since you can't embed metadata directly into the RAW file itself (we talked about this in Chapter 2), so you need to treat the RAW file and its XMP sidecar file as a team. Now press **Command-Shift-E (PC: Ctrl-Shift-E)** to bring up the Export dialog (shown here). Click on Burn Full-Sized JPEGs just to get some basic settings. From the Export To pop-up menu up top, choose **Hard Drive**, then, in the Export Location section, choose where you want this original RAW file saved to (I chose my desktop). In the File Settings section, from the Image Format pop-up menu, choose **Original (unedited)**, shown circled here in red. When you choose to export the original RAW file, most of your other choices are grayed out.

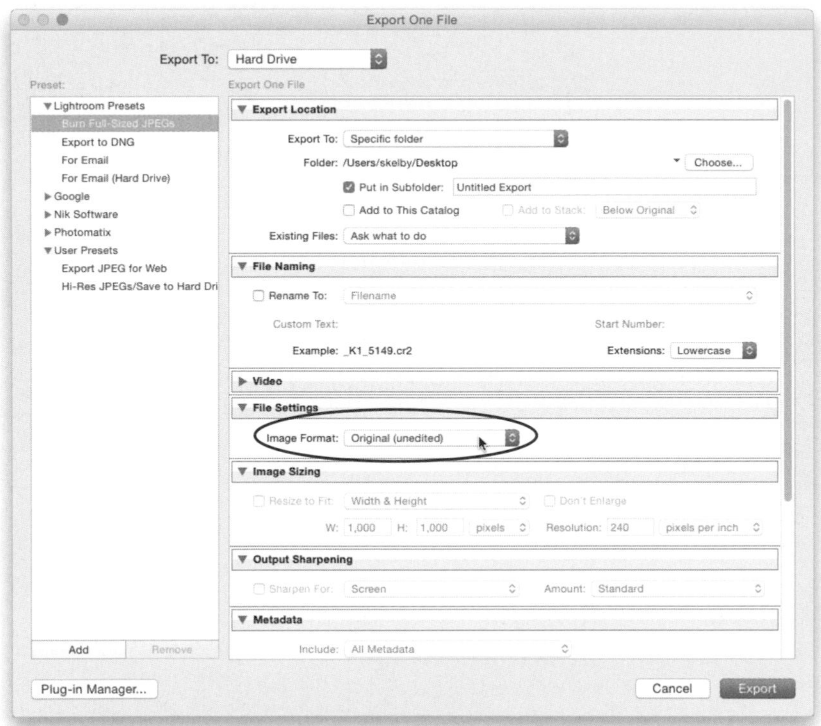

TIP: Saving Your RAW Photo as a DNG

From the Image Format pop-up menu, choose **DNG** to bring up the DNG options. Embed Fast Load Data affects how fast the preview appears in the Develop module (it adds a little size to your file). Use Lossy Compression does to RAW images what JPEG compression does to other images—it tosses some info to give you files that are around 75% smaller in size (good for archiving the images the client didn't pick, but you don't want to delete).

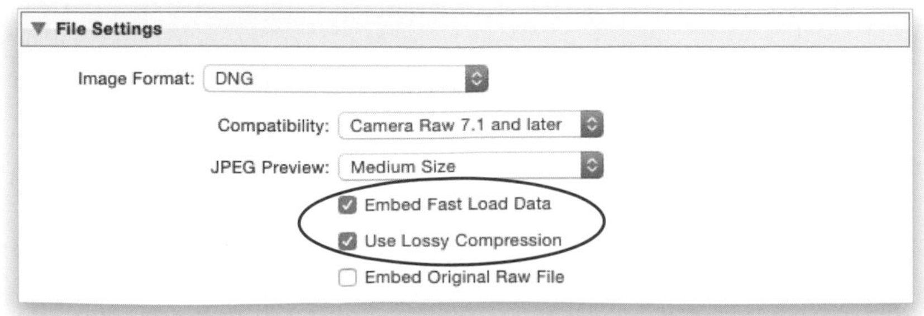

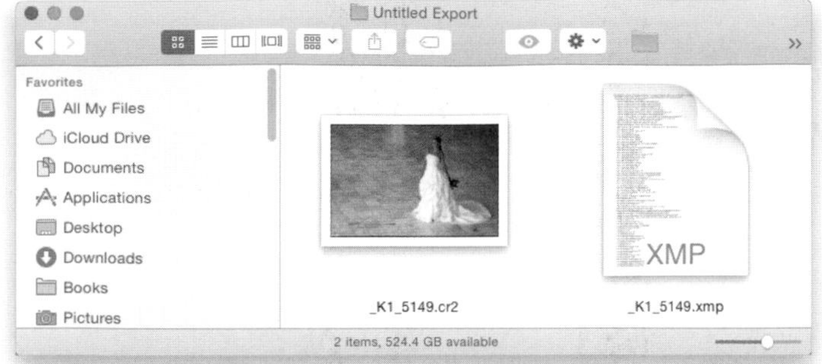

Step Two:

Now click Export, and since there's no processing to be done, in just a few seconds your file appears on your desktop (or wherever you chose to save it)—you'll see your file and its XMP sidecar (with the same exact name, but XMP as its file extension) in a folder (as seen here, on my desktop). As long as these two stay together, other programs that support XMP sidecar files (like Adobe Bridge and Adobe Camera Raw, for example) will use that metadata, so your photo will have all the changes you applied to it. If you send this file to someone (or burn it to disc), make sure you include both files. If you decide you want the file to not include your edits, just don't include the XMP file with it.

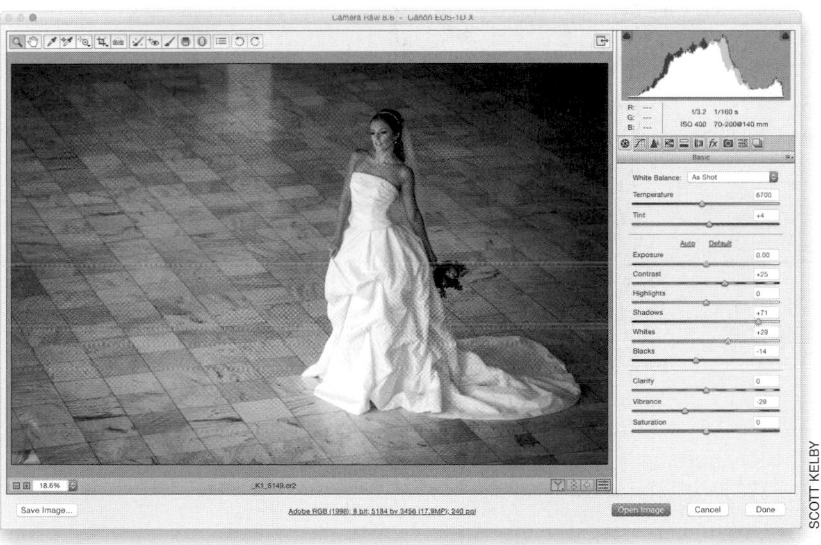

Here's the image with contrast, shadows, whites, blacks, and vibrance adjustments, and post-crop vignetting added, when you include the XMP sidecar file

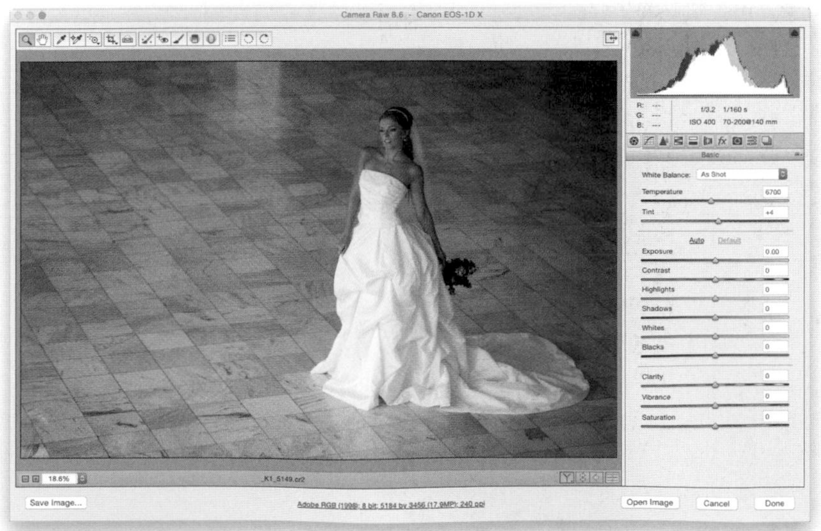

Here's the original image, without contrast, shadows, whites, blacks, and vibrance adjustments, and no post-crop vignetting, when you don't include the XMP sidecar file

Step Three:

If you export the original RAW file and send it to someone with Photoshop, when they double-click on it, it will open in Camera Raw, and if you provided the XMP file, they'll see all the edits you made in Lightroom, as seen in the top image shown here, where the contrast, shadows, whites, blacks, and vibrance were adjusted, and post-crop vignetting was added. The bottom image shown here is what they'll see in Camera Raw when you don't include the XMP file—it's the untouched original file with none of the changes I made in Lightroom.

Publish Your Images with Just Two Clicks

If you upload your images pretty regularly to sites like Flickr or Facebook, or maybe you just save them to other hard drives, or even to your iPhone, there's a drag-and-drop way to automate the process. Beyond that, it also helps you keep track of your published images, so the most recent versions of them are the ones that are published. This feature is called Publish Services, and if you take just a few minutes to set this up now, it'll save you a load of time whenever you want to post images online, or save images to your hard drive or external hard drive.

Step One:

The Publish Services panel is in the Library module's left side Panels area. By default, it has four templates you can set up: (1) your hard drive, (2) Behance, (3) Facebook, and (4) Flickr. Set these up by clicking on the Set Up button on the right side of each. Here, we'll start with the Flickr process, which is the most complicated, and at the end, we'll take a quick look at setting up your hard drive. The Behance and Facebook processes are pretty similar to Flickr's—click the Set Up button, authorize your account, and you're pretty much good to go. So, click on Set Up next to Flickr.

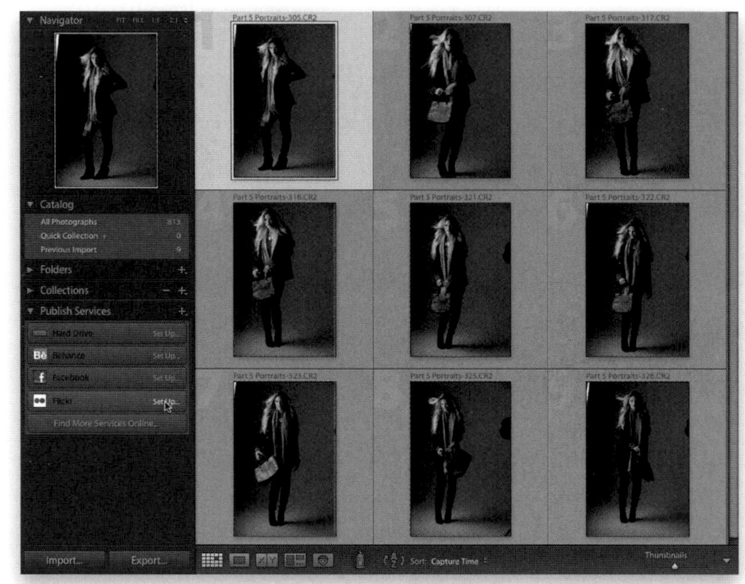

Step Two:

The main section of the Lightroom Publishing Manager dialog looks like the Export dialog, with two exceptions: (1) near the top, there are Publish Service, and Flickr Account and Title sections, and (2) at the bottom are Flickr's Privacy and Safety options. Start up top by clicking the Authorize button, and a dialog appears (shown on the bottom left) asking you to click another Authorize button to jump over to the Flickr website, so you can log in and give Flickr permission to work with Lightroom, so go ahead and click Authorize. Now the dialog changes to tell you that once you're done at Flickr.com, you need to come back to Lightroom to finish setting everything up (shown on the bottom right).

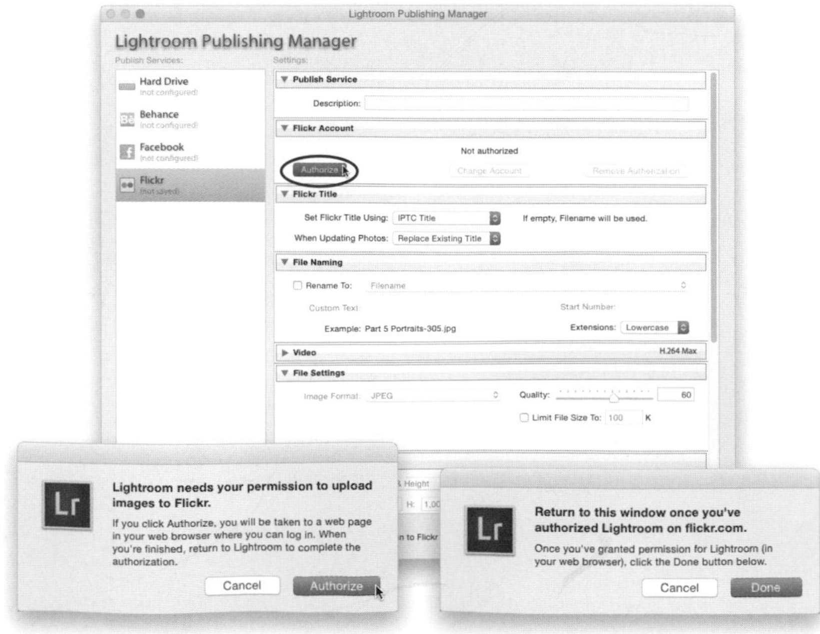

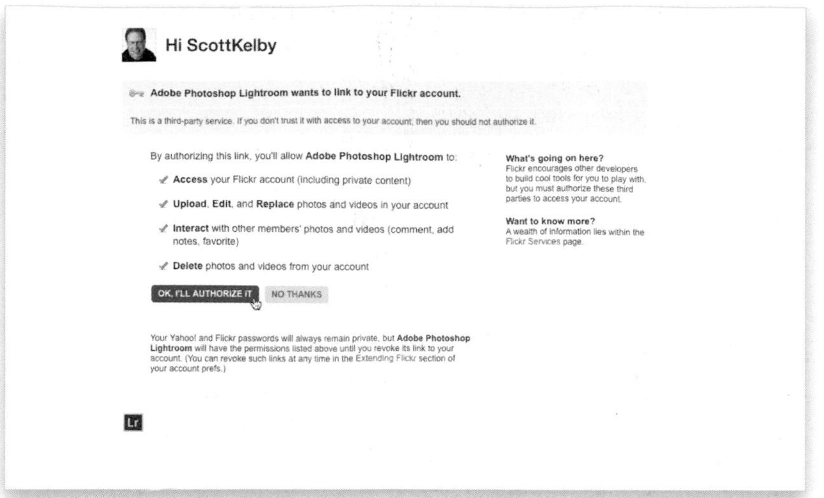

Step Three:

Once you log into your Yahoo account and get to Flickr (if you don't already have a Flickr account, and want to use this feature, go ahead and at least sign up for their free account through Yahoo), you'll find a page with something similar to what you see here, asking you to authorize Flickr to talk back and forth to Lightroom. Once you do, you'll get a confirmation page. Now, back to the Lightroom part.

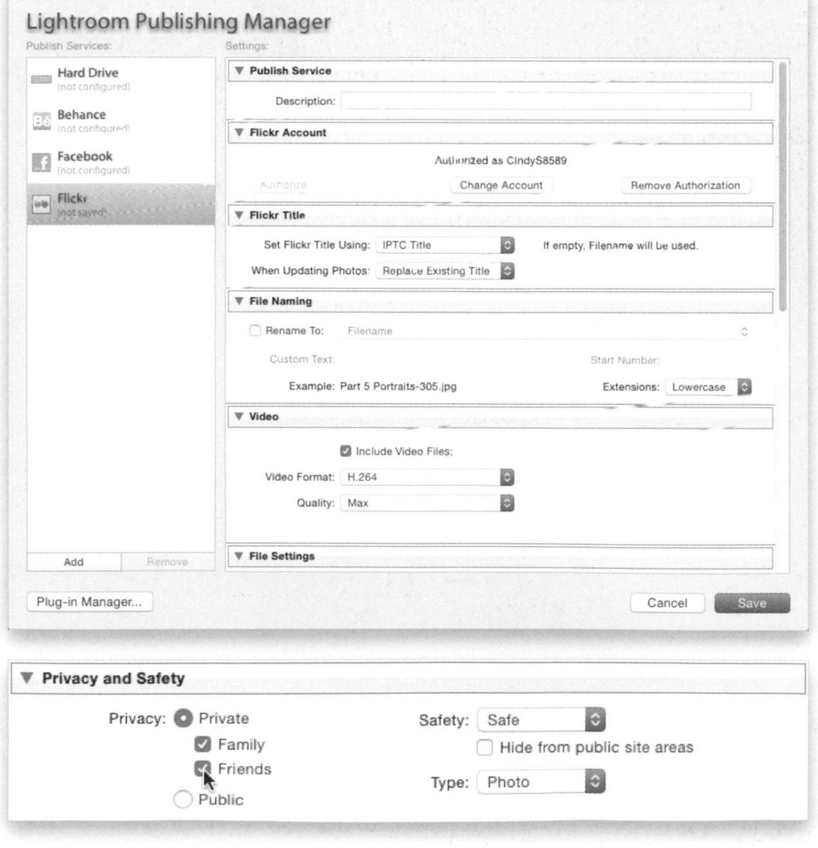

Step Four:

Once you're done on the Flickr approval page, go back to Lightroom, and click Done in that dialog we saw in Step Two. Now all you have to do is set up the export options like usual (choosing your file format, whether you want sharpening added, watermarking added, etc.), but when you get to the bottom, you'll see options for Flickr's Privacy and Safety control (shown here at the bottom) for the images you're going to upload, so make your choices there now, then click the Save button to save this setup as your Flickr Publish Service.

TIP: Download More Plug-Ins from Adobe

You can add more Publish Services and Export plug-ins by clicking on the Find More Services Online button at the bottom of the Publish Services panel to take you to the Adobe Add-Ons website. Once downloaded and installed, a new Publish Service will show up below your others. To install an Export plug-in, in the Lightroom Plug-In Manager, click Add below the list on the left, locate your downloaded plug-in, and click the Add Plug-In button. You can access it in the Export To pop-up menu at the top of the Export dialog.

Continued

Step Five:

Now select the photos that you'd like to publish to Flickr, and drag-and-drop them onto the Flickr Photostream in the Publish Services panel (you'll see Photostream appear right underneath Flickr, shown here). Once you've dragged them into this collection (yup, it's a collection), click directly on Photostream (as shown here) and you'll see that the images you just dragged there are waiting to be published (they're not actually published to Flickr until you click the Publish button at the bottom of the left side Panels area or the top right of the center Preview area). What's nice about this is it lets you gather up as many photos, from as many different collections as you'd like, and then publish them all at once with just one click. But for our example here, we'll assume that you just want to publish these five images.

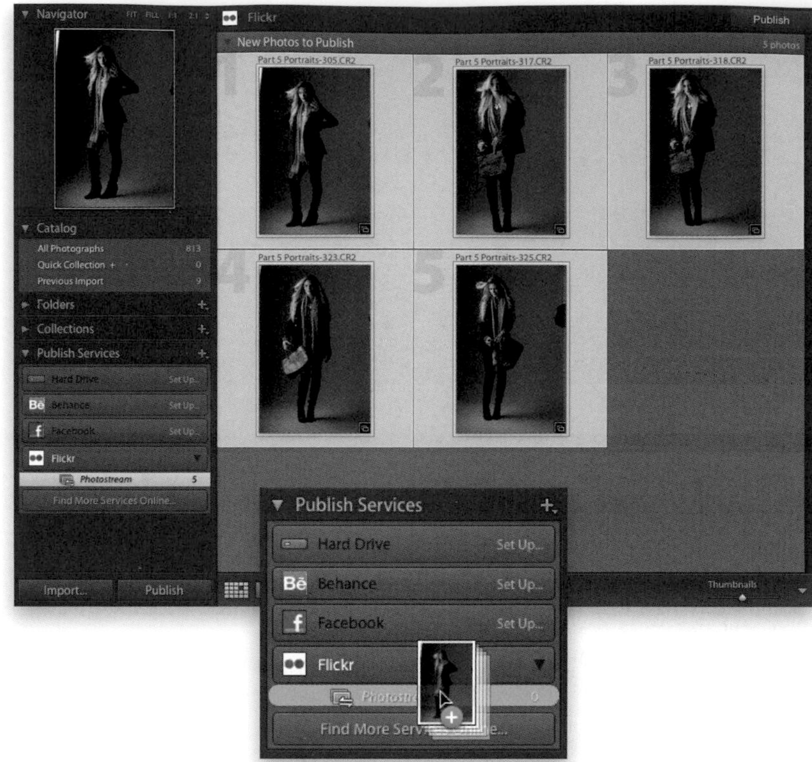

Step Six:

Click the Publish button now, and a split-screen appears in the Preview area, with the five New Photos to Publish appearing in the section on top first. One by one, they'll move down to the Published Photos section below (here, three of the five images have been published). Once all your photos have been published, the New Photos to Publish section disappears, because there are no photos waiting to be published. (By the way, while your photos are being published, a small status bar will appear at the top-left corner to let you know how things are moving along.)

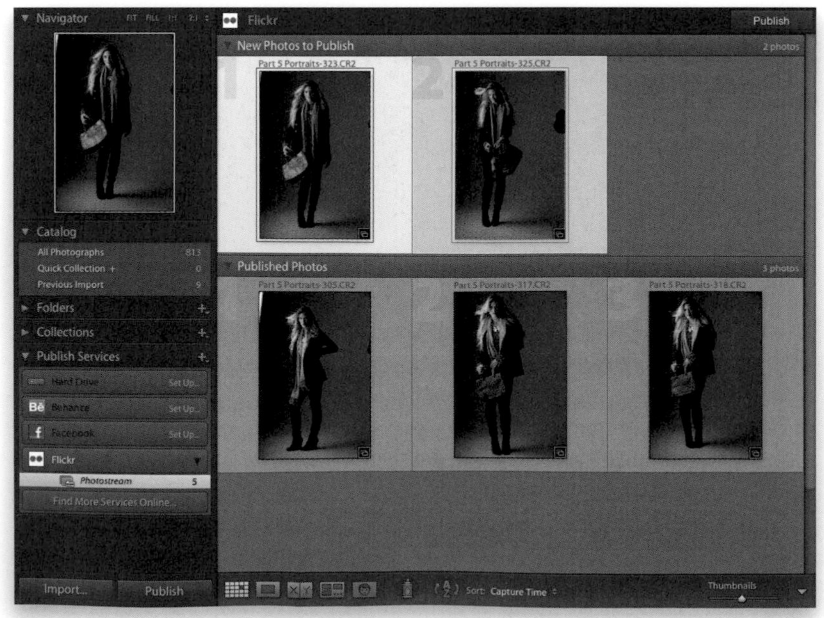

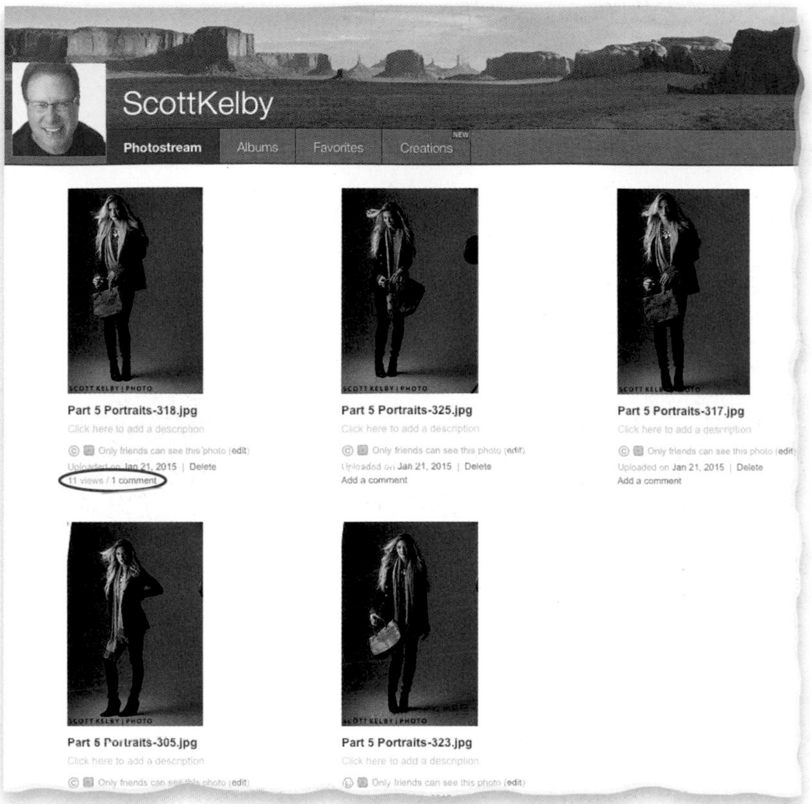

Step Seven:

Switch to your web browser, go to your Flickr photostream page, and you'll see your images have now been published there (as seen here). Now, you can take things a step further, because the comments that people post online about your published photos can be synced back to Lightroom, so you can read them right there in the Comments panel (in the right side Panels area). For example, on the Flickr website itself, I clicked on the first image and added a comment in the field below it. I wrote: "That watermark is really dark. It should be changed to white with the opacity lowered." (It's true, by the way.)

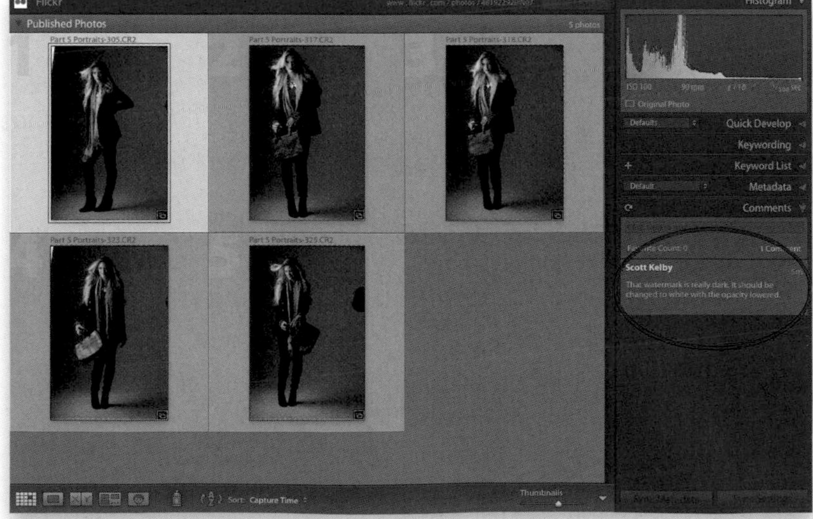

Step Eight:

To see the comments in Lightroom, go to the Publish Services panel, click on your Flickr Photostream, and it displays your published photos. Then, Right-click on your Photostream and choose **Publish Now** from the pop-up menu, and it goes and checks your Flickr account to see if any comments have been added, and downloads them into Lightroom. Now, click on a photo, and then look in the Comments panel (at the bottom of the right side Panels area), and any comments that were added to that image in Flickr will appear there. Also, it displays how many people have tagged that published photo as one of their favorites on Flickr.

Continued

Step Nine:

Okay, so far so good, but what if you make a change to one of those published photos in Lightroom? Here's what to do (and here's where this Publish Services thing works so well): First, click on the Flickr Photostream to display the photos you've already published to Flickr, then click on the photo you want to edit, and press **D** to jump over to the Develop module. In our case, we'll adjust two things here: (1) we'll click the White Balance Selector tool on the background just to the right of her head, so the photo is a little warmer, then (2) we'll bring up the Shadows a bit to brighten her face and bring back some detail in her clothing, as seen here. Now that our edits are done, it's time to get this edited version of the photo back up to our Flickr photostream.

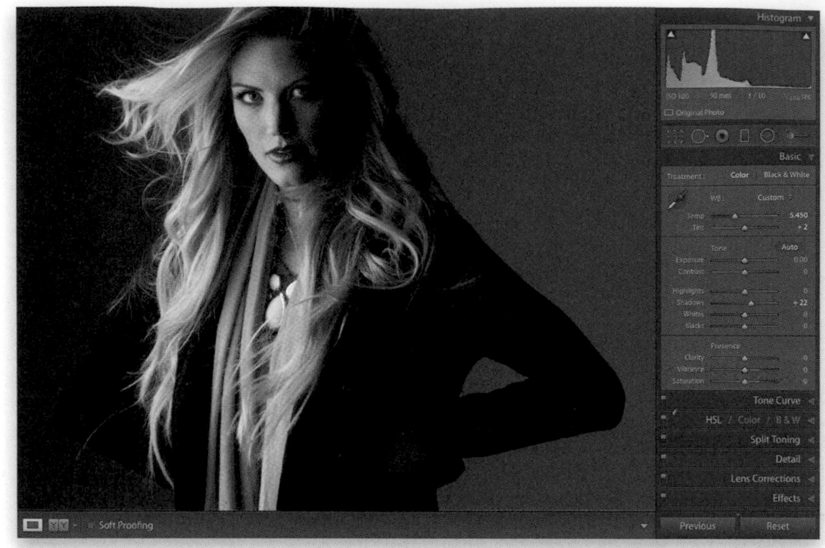

Step 10:

Go back to the Library module, to the Publish Services panel, and click on your Photostream, and you'll see a split screen again, but this time it's showing your edited photo up top waiting to be re-published. Click the Publish button and it updates the image on Flickr, so your most recent changes are reflected there. Of course, once you do this, the Modified Photos to Re-Publish section goes away, because now all your photos are published. Okay, so that's the Flickr Publish Services, and now that you've learned how that works, setting up your hard drive for drag-and-drop publishing is a cinch, so we'll do that next.

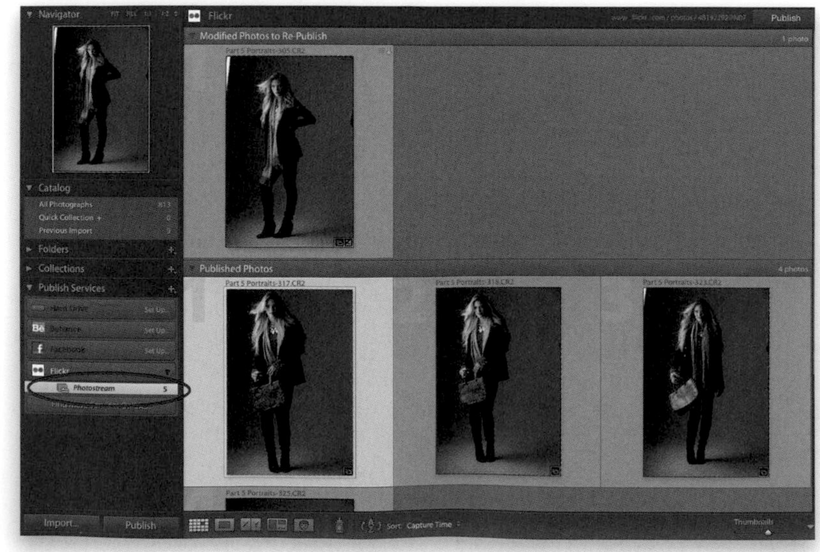

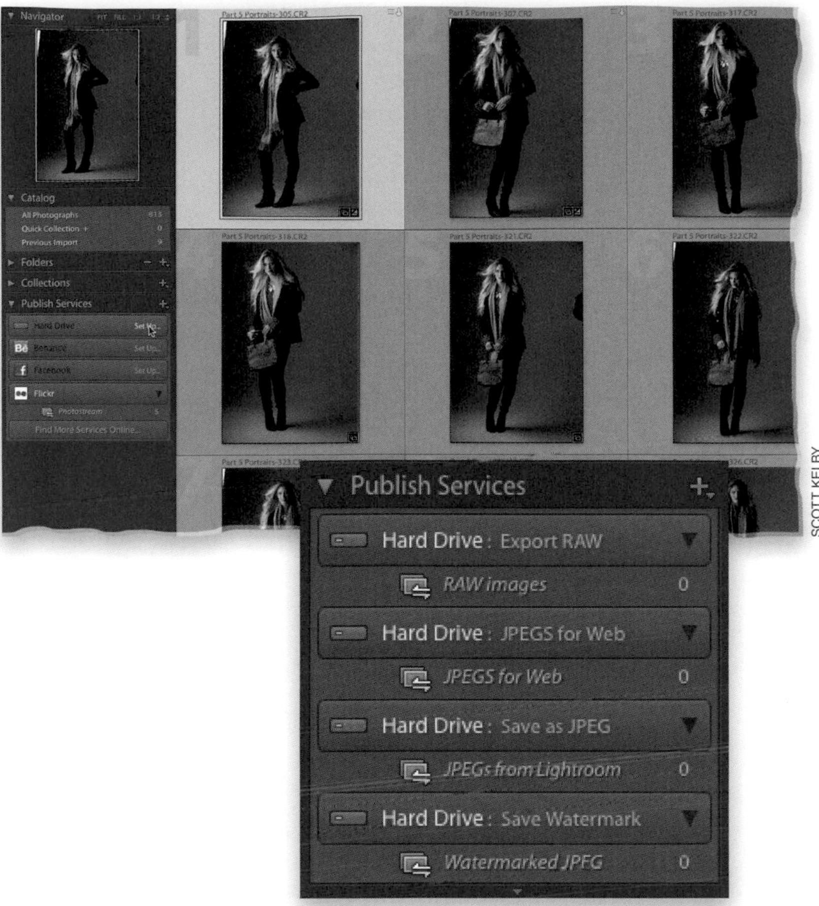

Step 11:

Start by clicking on the Set Up button next to Hard Drive in the Publish Services panel. We'll configure this one so it saves any files we drag onto it as high-resolution JPEGs to your hard drive (so think of this as a drag-and-drop shortcut to make JPEGs, rather than having to go through the whole Export dialog). Give this publish service a name now—call this one "Save as JPEG"—then fill out the rest just like you would for exporting a high-res JPEG to your hard disk (like we did back on page 330). When you click Save, it replaces Set Up with the name of your service (in this case, now it reads: "Hard Drive: Save as JPEG," so you know at a glance that it's going to save images you drag-and-drop on it to your hard drive as JPEGs). You can add as many of these as you'd like by Right-clicking next to Hard Drive and choosing **Create Another Publish Service via "Hard Drive."** That way, you can have some that export your images as originals, or some for emailing, or…well…you get the idea (look at the Publish Services panel here where I published a few extra setups, just so you can see what they'd look like).

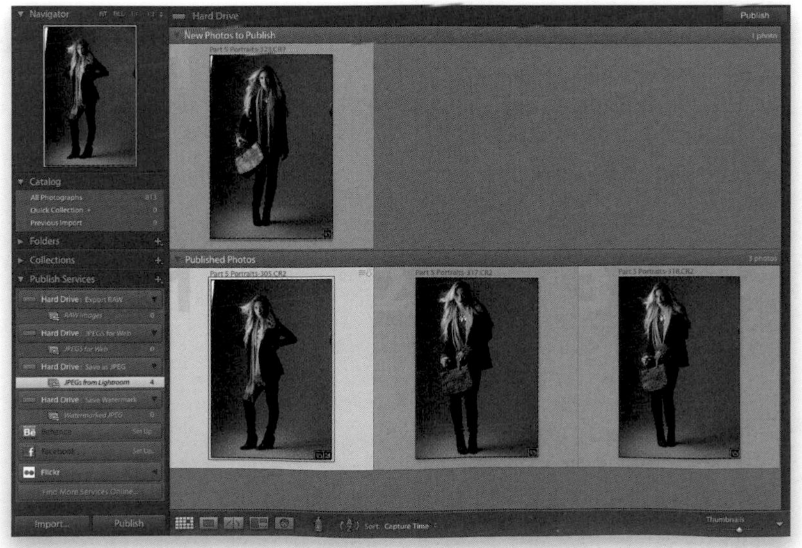

Step 12:

Now that you've got at least one configured, let's put it to work. In the Library module, go ahead and select four RAW files you want saved as JPEGs (they don't have to be RAW files—they can already be JPEGs that you just want exported from Lightroom), and drag-and-drop those selected photos onto your Hard Drive: Save as JPEG publish service. From here, it's pretty much the same as you just learned with Flickr—the images appear in a New Photos to Publish section until you click the Publish button, then it writes them as JPEGs into whichever folder you chose when you set this publish service up (here, one of the four images being saved as JPEGs is in progress).

Lightroom Killer Tips > >

▼ Exporting Your Catalog Shortcut

If, instead of just exporting a photo, you want to export an entire catalog of photos, press-and-hold the Option (PC: Alt) key, and the Export button in the

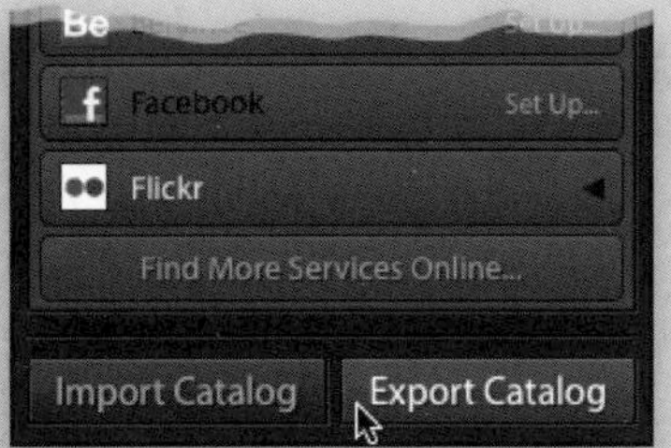

Library module changes into the Export Catalog button.

▼ Using Your Last Export Settings

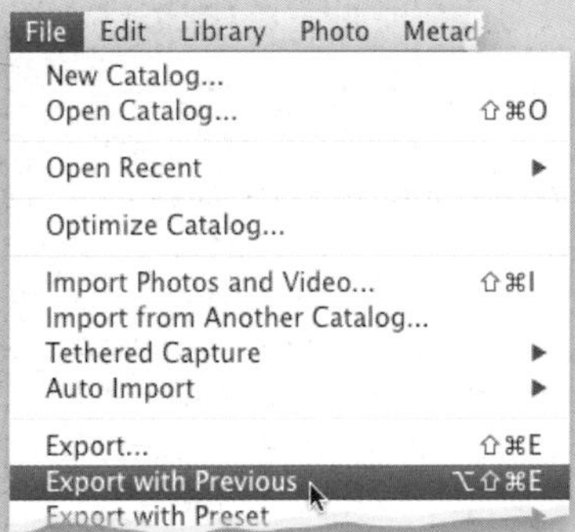

If you want to export some photos and use the same export settings you used the last time, you can skip the whole Export dialog and, instead, just go under the File menu and choose **Export with Previous**, or use the keyboard shortcut **Command-Option-Shift-E (PC: Ctrl-Alt-Shift-E)**, and it will immediately export the photos with your last used settings.

▼ Using Export Presets Without Going to the Export Dialog

If you've created your own custom Export presets (or you want to use the built-in ones, as is), you can skip the Export dialog by Right-clicking on the photo, and from the pop-up menu, going under **Export**, and you'll see both the built-in and cus-

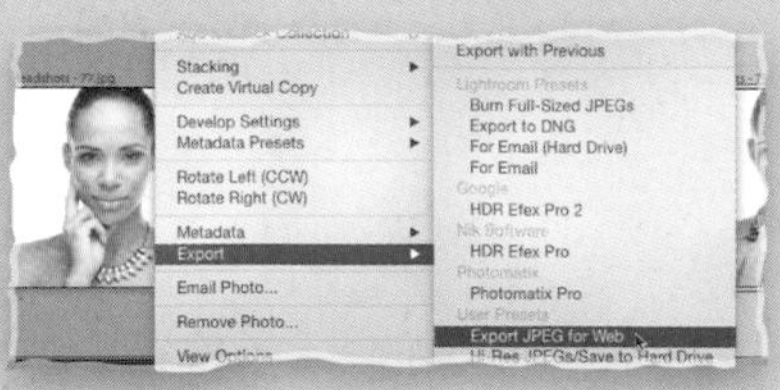

tom Export presets listed. Choose one from there, and off it goes.

▼ Lightroom's Built-In Address Book for Emailing

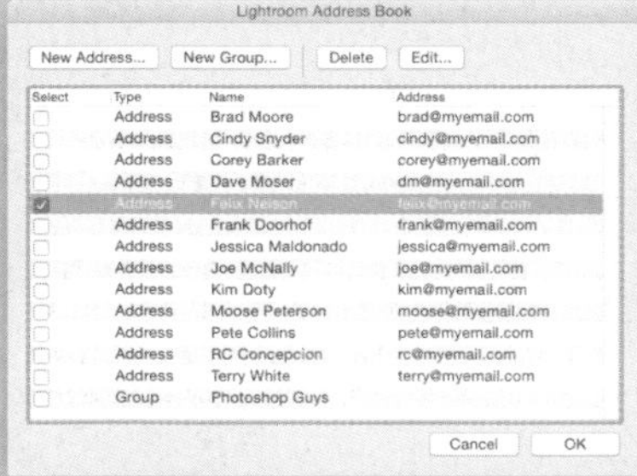

If you find yourself emailing from Lightroom a lot, you might want to create your own Lightroom email Address Book. You get to this from the main email dialog—just click on the Address button in the top right, and the Address Book appears. Here, you can enter names and email addresses, and even create groups to organize your emails. To use an address from your Address Book, just click on the checkbox beside the name you want to use.

▼ Sharing Your Export Presets

If you've come up with a really useful Export preset that you'd like to share with co-workers or friends (by the way, if you're sharing Export presets with friends, maybe you need some new friends), you can do that by pressing **Command-Shift-E (PC: Ctrl-Shift-E)** to bring up the Export dialog. Then, in the list of presets on the left side, Right-click on the preset you want to save as a file, then choose **Export** from the pop-up menu. When you give this Export preset

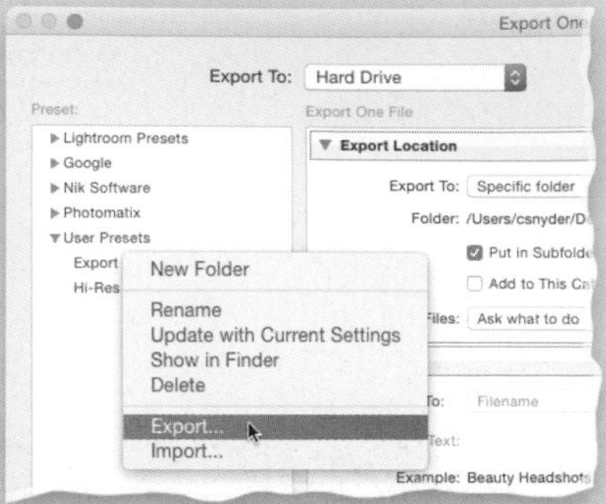

to a co-worker, have them choose **Import** from this same pop-up menu.

▼ My "Testing Panos" Trick

If you shoot multi-photo panoramas, you know that once they get to Photomerge Panorama for stitching, it can take… well…forever (it feels like forever, anyway). And sometimes you wait all this time, see your finished pano, and think, "Ah, that's nothing special." So, if I shot a pano I'm not 100% sure is going to be a keeper, I don't use the direct Photomerge Panorama command in Lightroom. Instead, I go to the Export dialog and use the For E-mail (Hard Drive) preset to export the files as small, low-resolution JPEGs, with a low Quality setting and the Add to This Catalog checkbox turned on. Then, I run the Photomerge Panorama feature, and because they're small, low-res files, they stitch together in just a couple of minutes. That way, I can see if it's going to be a good-looking pano (one worth waiting 20 or 30 minutes to stitch at high resolution). If it does look good, that's when I use the **Photomerge Panorama** feature in the Photo menu in the Library, Develop, and Map modules with the full-size, full-resolution, full-quality images. Then I go get a cup of coffee. And maybe a sandwich.

▼ Emailing or Posting Smart Previews Online

Smart previews of images actually have enough quality and resolution in them

Lightroom Killer Tips > >

that you can export these as JPEGs. That way, you have a decent-sized JPEG you can email to someone as a proof, or post them online to Facebook, Twitter, and so on, all without having to access the original high-resolution file.

▼ Exporting Directly to a Photo-Sharing Website

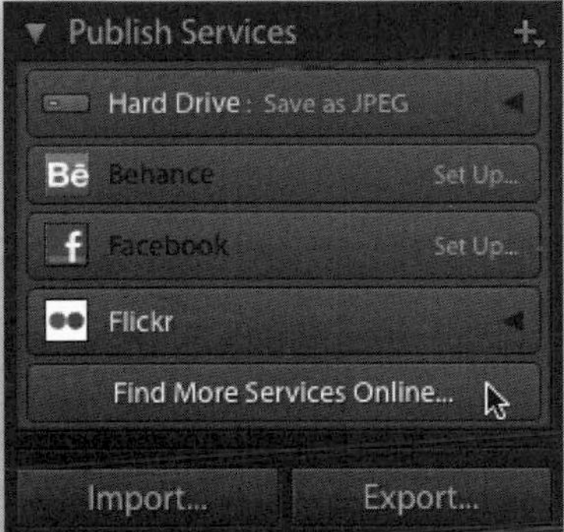

In this chapter, we talked about how you can publish images directly from Lightroom to Flickr.com, but there are now Export plug-ins available for most of the major photo-sharing sites (including Smugmug, Picasa Web Albums, and a dozen others) on the Adobe Add-Ons site. Click on the Find More Services Online button at the bottom of the Publish Services panel.

▼ Yes, You Sharpen Twice

I get asked this question all the time, because, by default, Lightroom adds sharpening to your RAW photos. So, do you sharpen again when you export the photos? Absolutely!

▼ Installing Export Plug-Ins

Although Adobe introduced Export plug-ins back in Lightroom 1.3, they've made the process of installing them much easier since then. Just go under the the File menu and choose **Plug-in Manager**. When the dialog appears, click the Add button below the left

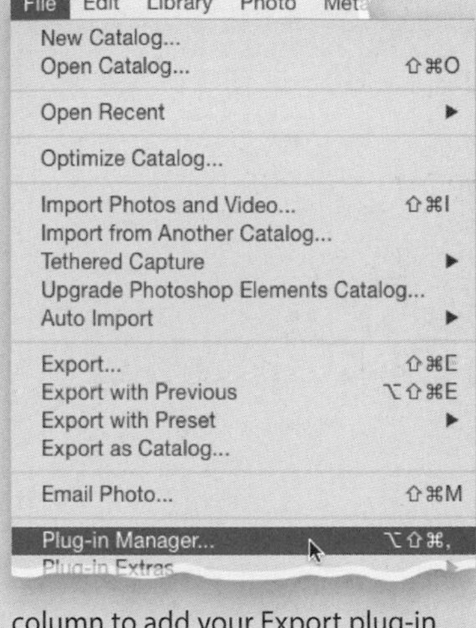

column to add your Export plug-in (I told you it was easier).

▼ Making Your Files Look Right on Somebody Else's Computer

I get emails from people all the time who have exported their photos as JPEGs, emailed them to somebody, and when they see them on the other person's machine, they're shocked to find out the photos don't look anything like they did on their computer (they're washed

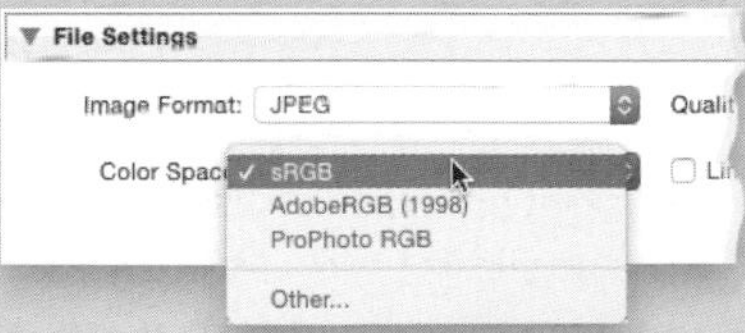

out, dull looking, etc.). It's a color space problem, and that's why I recommend that if you're emailing photos to someone, or that photo is going to be posted on a webpage, make sure you set your color space to **sRGB** in the File Settings section of the Export dialog.

▼ No XMP with DNG Files

If you convert your RAW image to DNG format before you export your original (go under the Library menu and choose **Convert Photo to DNG**), your changes are embedded in the file, so you don't

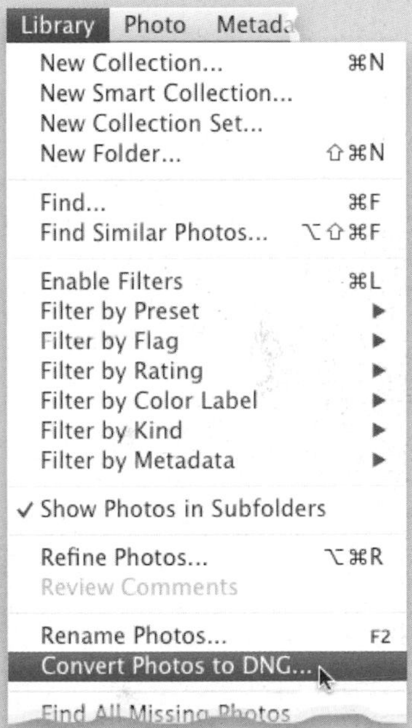

need an XMP file at all. There's more about DNG format in Chapter 1.

▼ Creating Flickr Photosets

If you want your published images to appear in their own Flickr Photoset or Smart Photoset, click on the + (plus sign) button on the right side of the Publish Services panel header and, in the pop-up menu, you'll see a Flickr section where

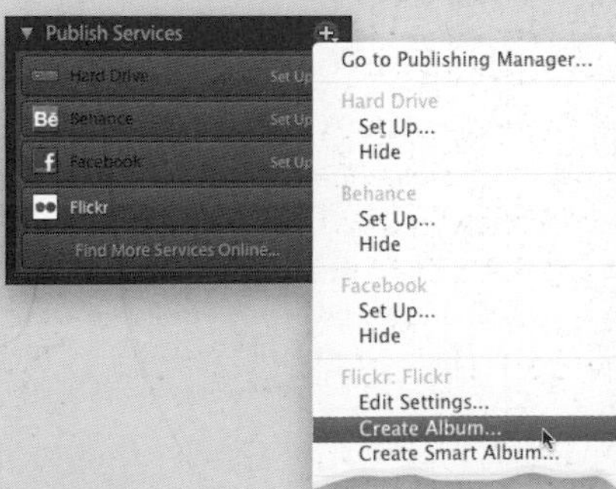

you can choose **Create Album** or **Create Smart Album**. Choose one and it adds it underneath your Flickr collection, so you can drag-and-drop to publish to those sets directly.

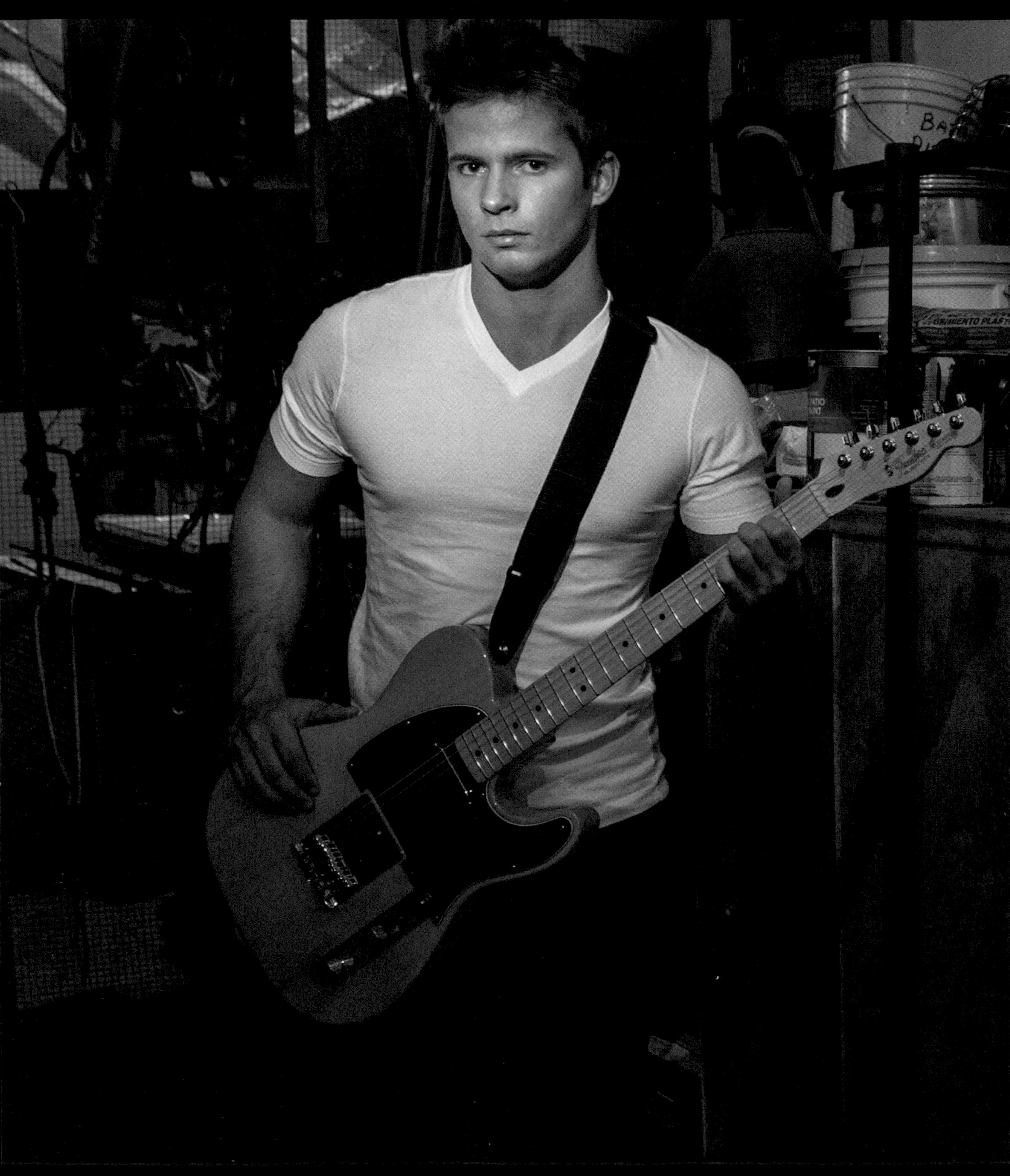

Photo by Scott Kelby | Exposure: 1/40 sec | Focal Length: 16mm | Aperture Value: ƒ/4

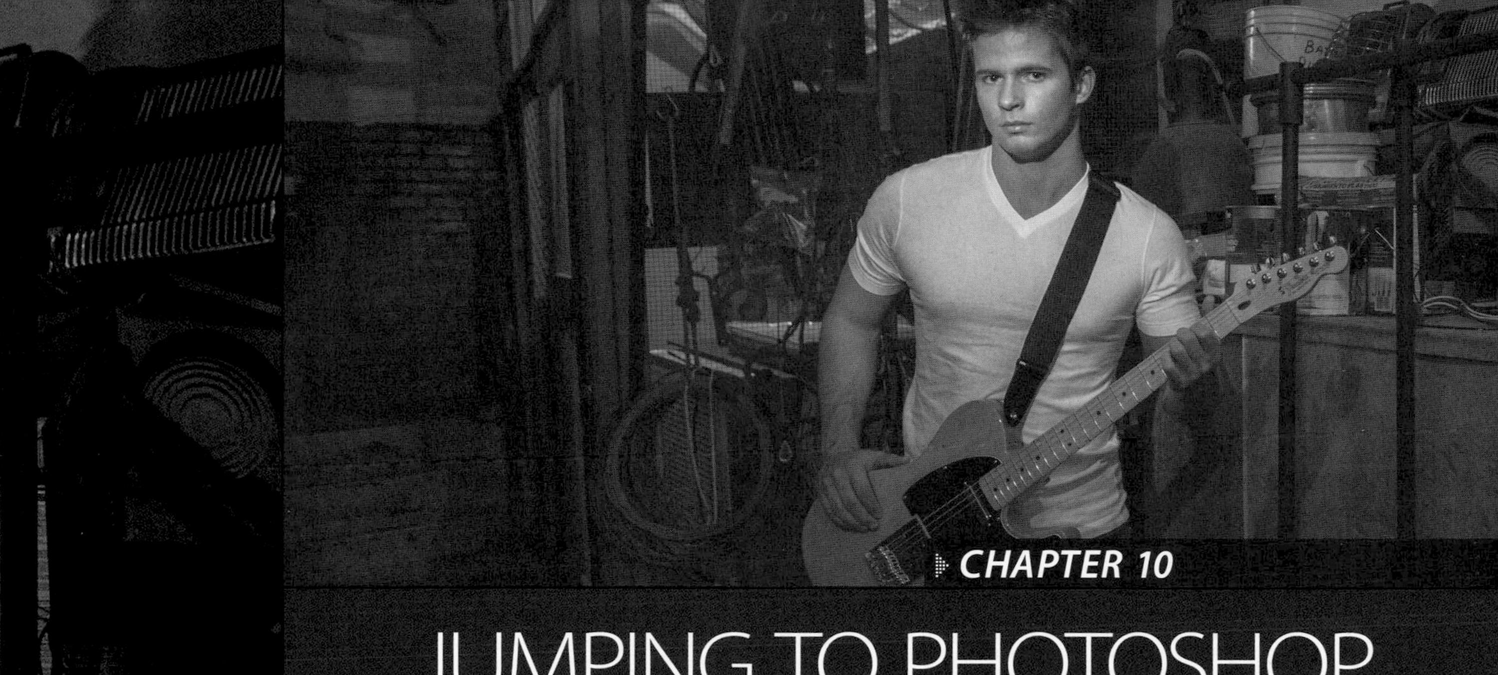

CHAPTER 10

JUMPING TO PHOTOSHOP
how and when to do it

Even though this book was written so you can jump in anywhere, I can tell you right now that if this is the first chapter intro you're reading, you probably should turn back to the Chapter 1 intro and start by reading that first, then work your way back to here, just reading chapter intros (not the whole chapters). Actually, go back a page or two further (to the part where I tell you not to read these chapter intros if you're a Mr. Fussypants), and then you can determine if you should take the mental break imposed by these chapter intros or not. Now, the chapter you're about to embark upon is about using Adobe Photoshop with Lightroom, and there are still a bunch of reasons why we still need to use Photoshop (or Photoshop Elements) to get the job done. For example, Lightroom doesn't have things like layers, or filters, or blend modes, or pro-level type control, or the Quick Selection tool, or HDR Pro, or serious portrait retouching (I could go on and on), so we still need it. We don't need Photoshop for every image, but you'll know when you need it, because you'll hit that moment when you realize what you want to do can't be done in Lightroom. Let's take creating counterfeit currency, for example. Lightroom kind of stinks for that, but if you're going to buy the full version of Photoshop (which runs around $700 U.S.), you're just about going to need to be printing your own money. The Catch-22 is that you need counterfeit money to buy Photoshop, but you need Photoshop first to create realistic counterfeit money. It's this conundrum that has kept so many of us out of the Federal prison system.

Choosing How Your Files Are Sent to Photoshop

When you take a photo from Lightroom over to Photoshop for editing, by default, Lightroom makes a copy of the file (in TIFF format), embeds it with the ProPhoto RGB color profile, sets the bit depth to 16 bits, and sets the resolution to 240 ppi. But if you want something different, you can choose how you'd like your files sent over to Photoshop—you can choose to send them as PSDs (that's how I send mine) or TIFFs, and you can choose their bit depth (8 or 16 bits) and which color profile you want embedded when your image leaves Lightroom.

Step One:

Press **Command-, (comma; PC: Ctrl-,)** to bring up Lightroom's preferences, and click on the External Editing tab up top (seen here). If you have Photoshop on your computer, it chooses it as your External Editor, so in the top section, choose the file format you want for photos that get sent to Photoshop (I set mine to PSD, because the files are much smaller than TIFFs), then from the Color Space pop-up menu, choose your file's color space (Adobe recommends ProPhoto RGB. If you keep it at that, I'd change Photoshop's color space to ProPhoto RGB, as well—whatever you choose, just use the same color space in Photoshop). Adobe also recommends choosing a 16-bit depth for the best results (although, I personally use an 8-bit depth most of the time). You also get to choose the resolution (I leave mine set at the default of 240 ppi). If you want to use a second program to edit your photos, you can choose that in the Additional External Editor section.

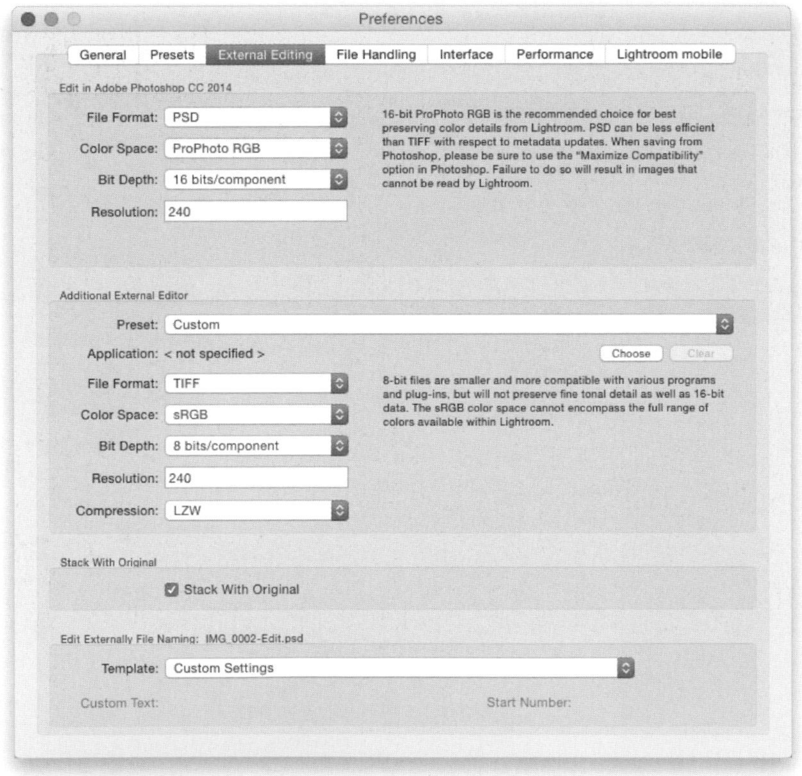

Step Two:

Next, there's a Stack With Original checkbox. I recommend leaving this on, because it puts the edited copy of your image right beside your original file (more on this in the next project), so it's easy to find when you return to Lightroom. Lastly, you can choose the name applied to photos sent over to Photoshop. You choose this from the Edit Externally File Naming section at the bottom of the dialog, and you have pretty much the same naming choices as you do in the regular Import window.

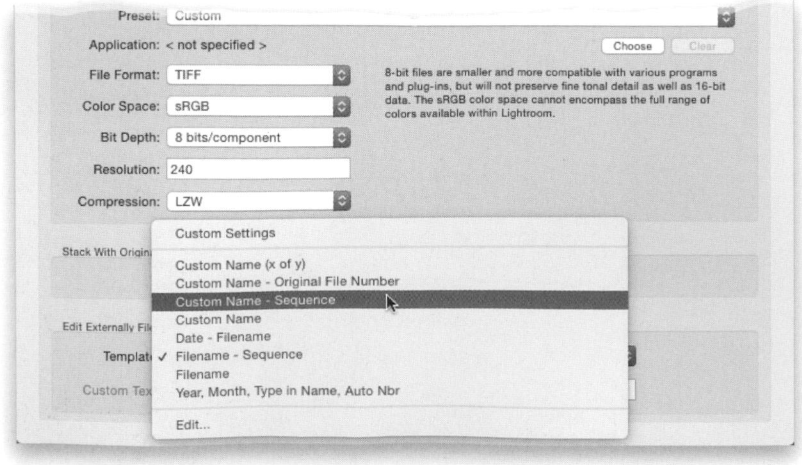

How to Jump Over to Photoshop, and How to Jump Back

While Lightroom is great for so many everyday editing things, it doesn't do heavy special effects or major photo retouching; there are no layers, no filters, and it's type controls are very limited, and it doesn't do many of the bazillion (yes, bazillion) things that Photoshop does. So, there will be times during your workflow where you'll need to jump over to Photoshop to do some "Photoshop stuff" and then jump back to Lightroom for printing or presenting. Luckily, these two applications were designed to work together from the start.

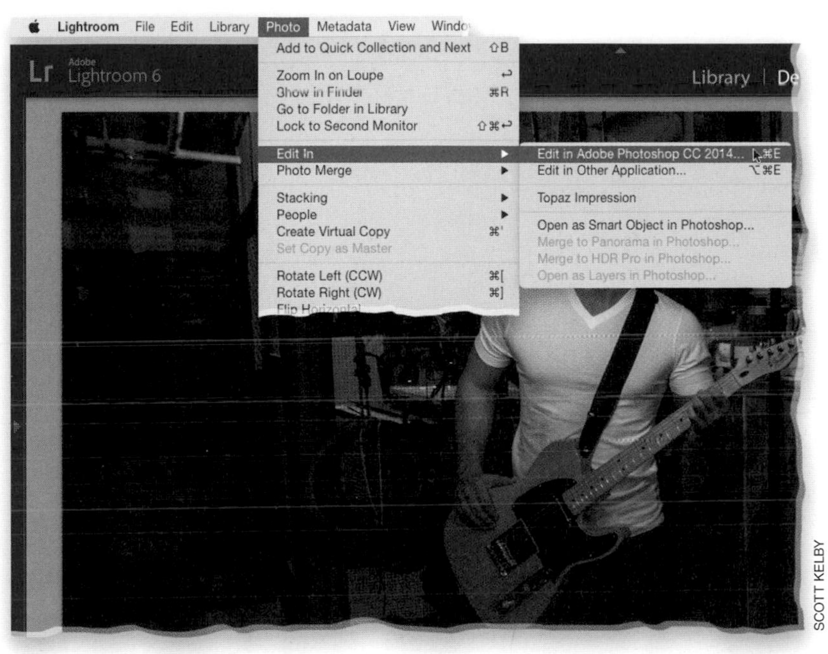

SCOTT KELBY

20-Second Tutorial:

To take the image you're working on over to Photoshop, go under the Photo menu, under Edit In, and choose **Edit in Adobe Photoshop** (as shown here), or just press **Command-E (PC: Ctrl-E)**, and Lightroom sends a copy of your image over to Photoshop. Do anything you want to it in Photoshop and then simply save the image, close the window, and it comes right back to Lightroom. However, if you want to follow along with project here, I'll take you through the process (plus, you'll get to learn a few Photoshop things along the way). Here's our original image in Lightroom.

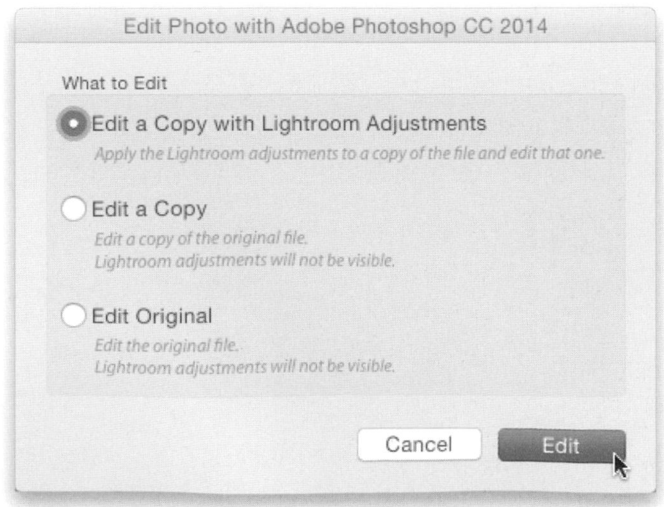

Step One:

Now, press Command-E (PC: Ctrl-E) to open the image in Photoshop. If you took the shot in RAW, it just "loans" Photoshop a copy of the image and opens it. However, if you shot in JPEG or TIFF mode, this brings up the Edit Photo with Adobe Photoshop dialog, where you choose (1) to have a copy of your original photo sent to Photoshop, with all the changes and edits you made in Lightroom applied to it, (2) to have Lightroom make a copy of your original untouched photo and send that to Photoshop, or (3) to edit your original JPEG or TIFF in Photoshop without any of the changes you've made thus far in Lightroom. Since we're working with a JPEG here, we'll choose the first option, and work on a copy that has our Lightroom adjustments.

Continued

Step Two:

Here's a copy of our image open in Photoshop CC. We're going to make a splash screen for a slide show (or it could also be used for a book cover in Lightroom's Book module) from a backstage photo shoot at an old theater.

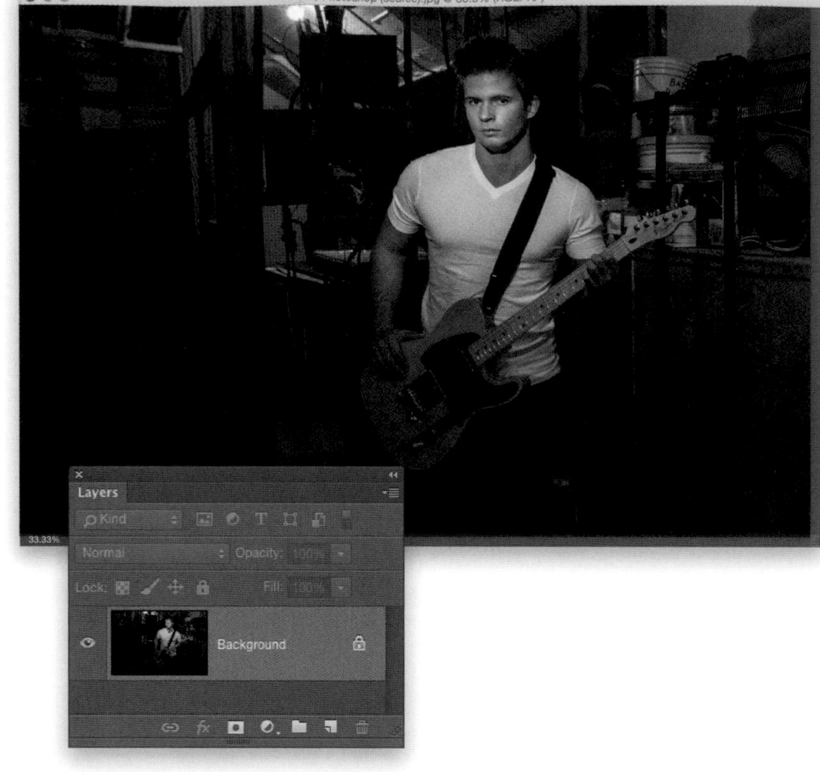

Step Three:

We'll start by converting the image to black and white (of course, we could've done this black and white conversion in Lightroom, but since we didn't, we'll do it here in Photoshop). Press **Command-Shift-U (PC: Ctrl-Shift-U)** to remove the color and create a black-and-white image (like you see here).

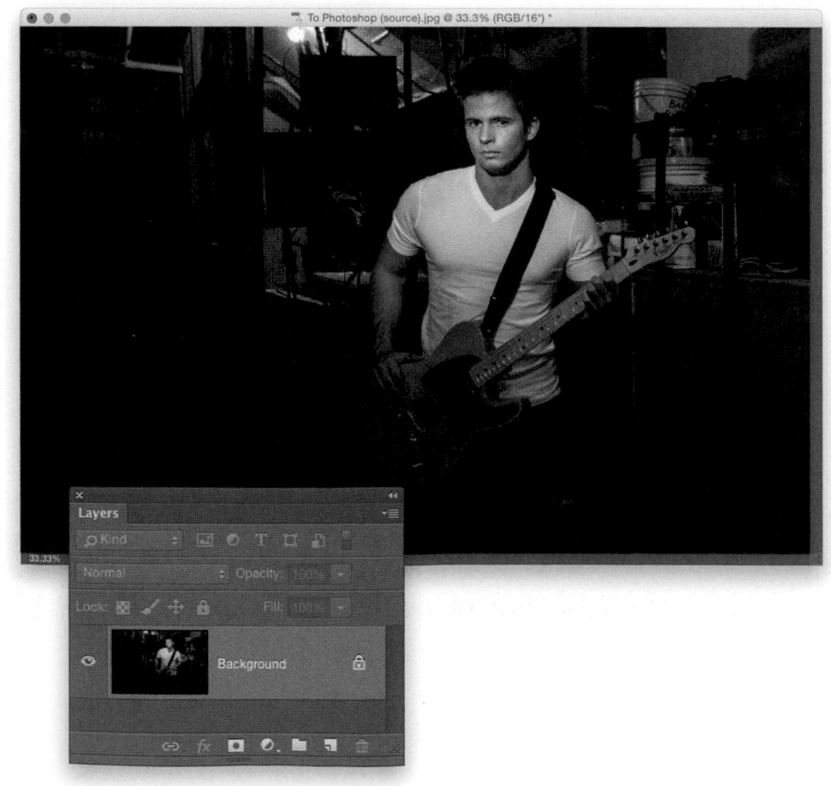

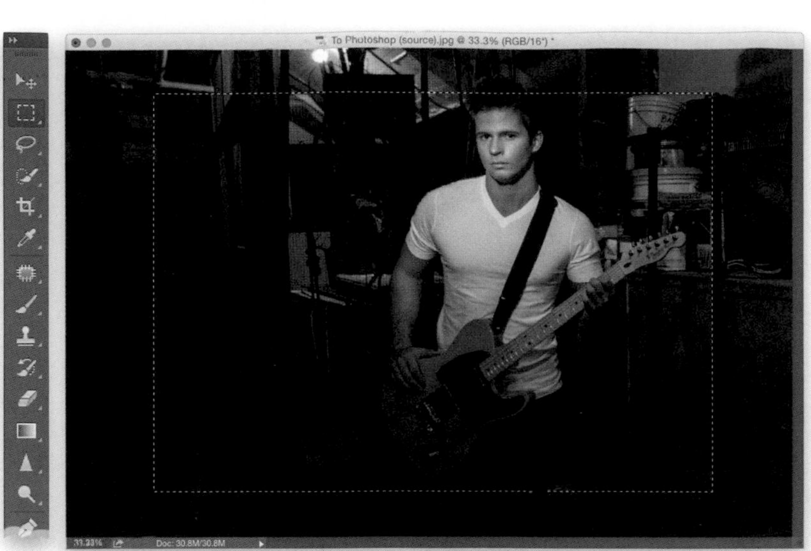

Step Four:
We're going to darken part of the image, so we can put text over it, blur the outside edges, backscreen the image, and then add some custom type (all things Lightroom either doesn't do at all or it takes a workaround to kinda do it). We'll start by getting the Retangular Marquee tool **(M)** from the Toolbox (along the left side of Photoshop) and dragging out a large rectangular selection like the one you see here.

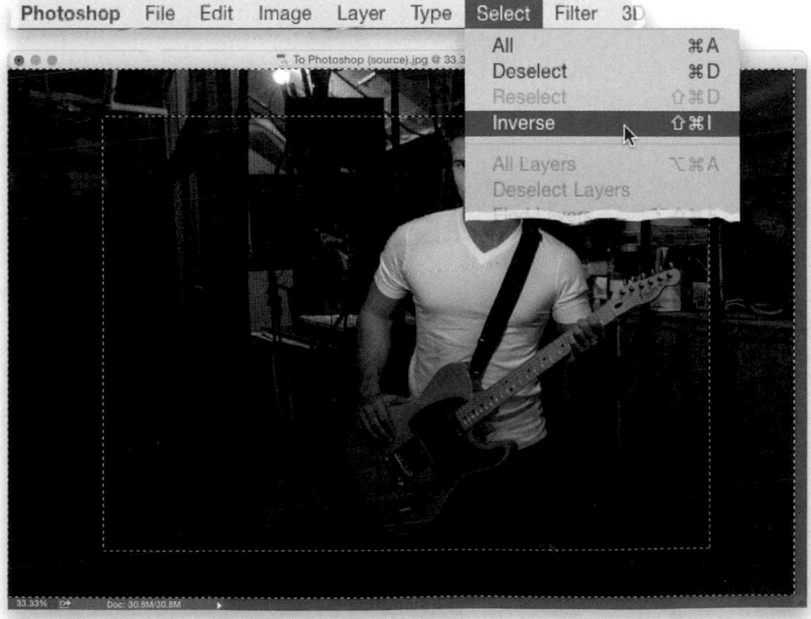

Step Five:
Now, anything we do in Photoshop will just affect the area inside that selection. However, at this moment, we need to just affect the stuff outside the rectangle. So, go up to the Select menu and choose **Inverse** (as seen here) to select everything outside that rectangular area.

Continued

Step Six:

With your inversed selection in place, go under the Filter menu, under Blur, and choose **Gaussian Blur**. When the filter dialog appears, enter around 26 pixels (as seen here) and click OK to blur the entire area outside the rectangle.

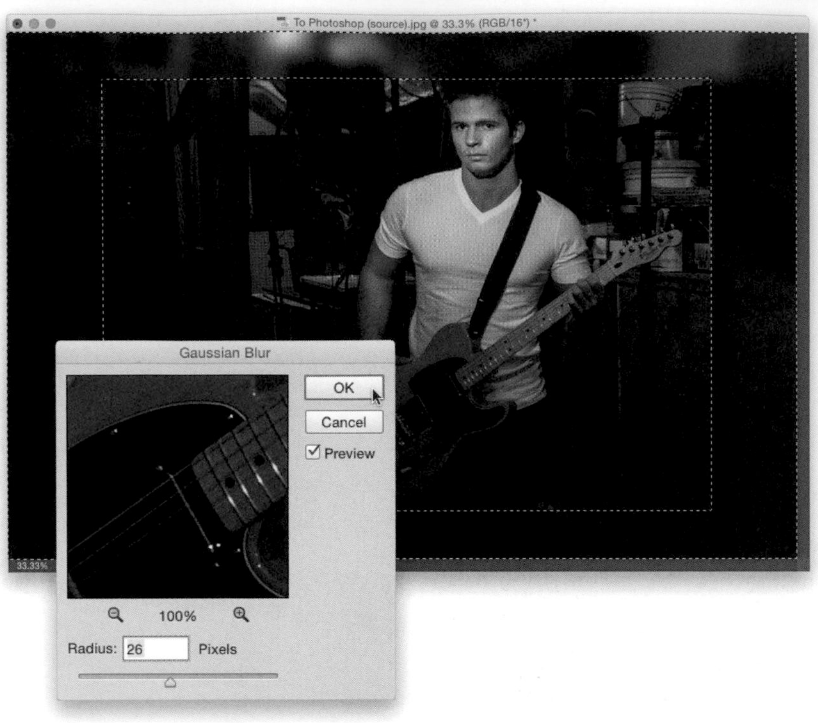

Step Seven:

Let's now switch our selection back to where we started, so go back up under the Select menu up top and choose Inverse (or just press **Command-Shift-I [PC: Ctrl-Shift-I]**). Now, we're back to where we started with just affecting what's inside our rectangular selection. Next, go to the Layers panel and click on the Create a New Layer icon at the bottom of the panel (it's the sixth icon from the left) to create a new blank layer (as seen here). We're going to add a white stroke around this selection, so go under the Edit menu and choose **Stroke**. When the dialog appears, enter 5 pixels, click on the Color swatch and change the color to white, choose Center for the Location (so the stroke is split half on one side of the selection, half on the other side), then click OK. Now, you can remove your selection by pressing **Command-D (PC: Ctrl-D)**, which is the shortcut for Deselect.

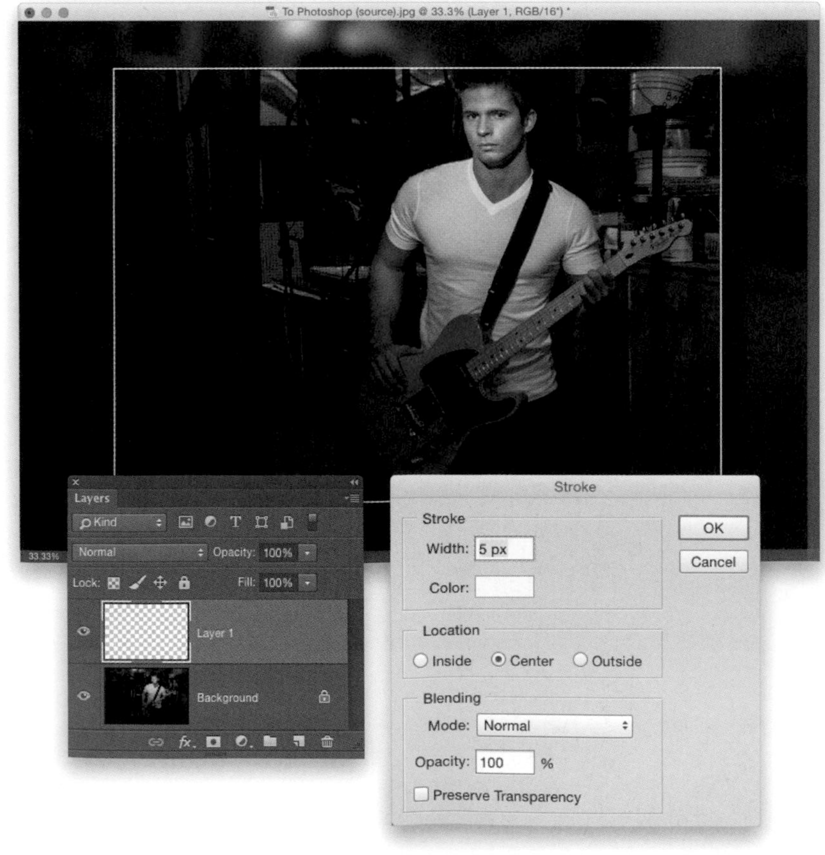

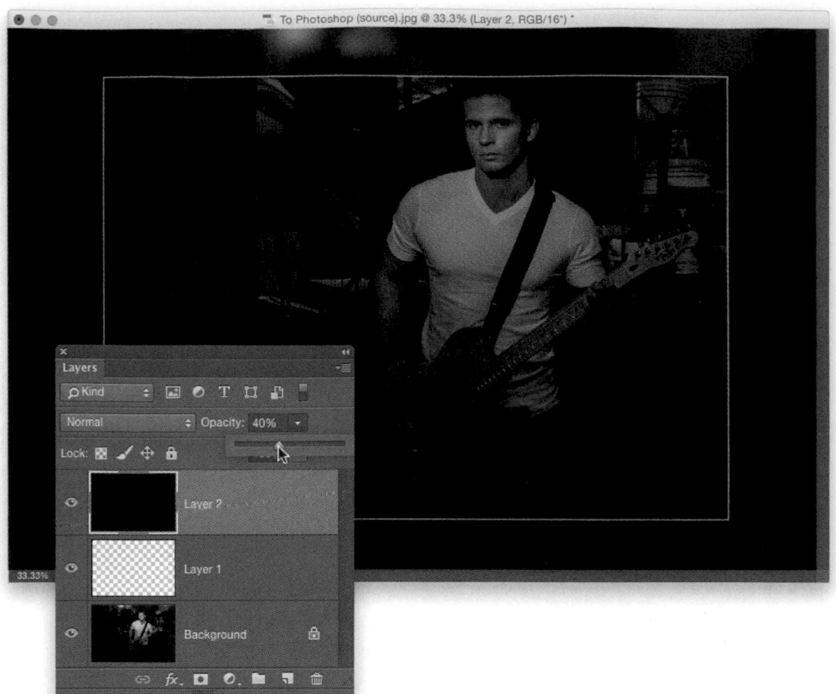

Step Eight:

Add another new blank layer (click on that Create a New Layer icon again), and then fill this new layer with black by first pressing the letter **D** on your keyboard to set your Foreground color to black, and then pressing **Option-Delete (PC: Alt-Backspace)**. To create our back-screen effect, lower the Opacity of this black-filled layer by clicking the little down-facing arrow to the right of the Opacity field at the top-right corner of the Layers panel, and dragging the little Opacity slider to the left to 40% (as seen here). You've now put a dark backscreen effect over the image.

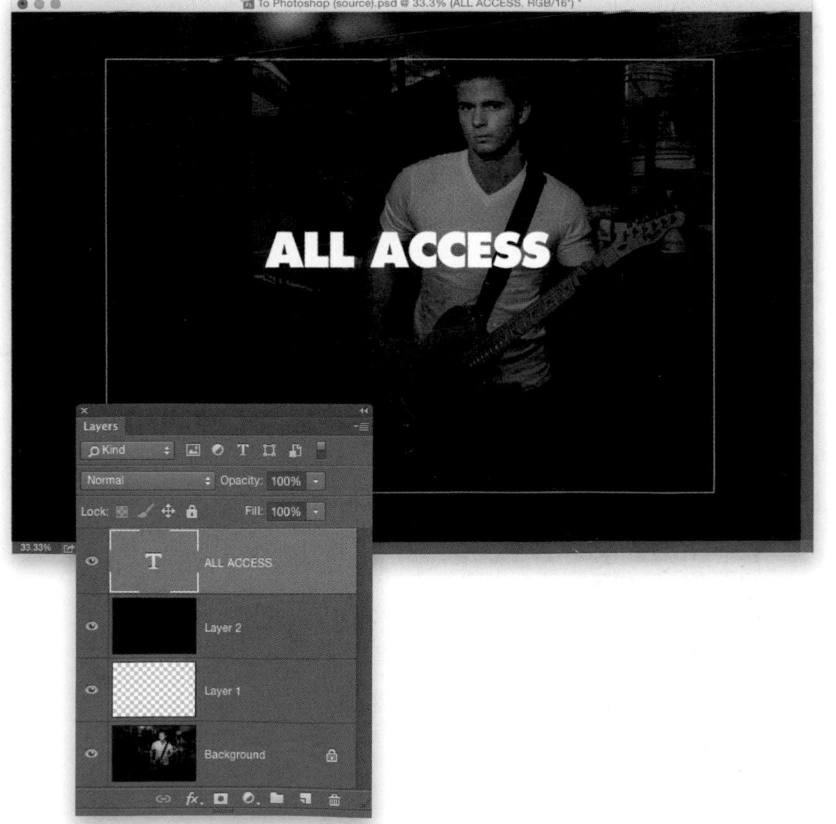

Step Nine:

Now, let's add some type. Get the Horizontal Type tool from the Toolbox (**T**; its icon looks like a capital "T") and type "ALL ACCESS" in all caps using a very bold typeface (I used Futura Bold, 50 pt., here). Once you've created your type, we're going to tighten up the space between the letters to give it a more professional look at that size. You do this by highlighting the words "ALL ACCESS," and then pressing **Option-Left Arrow key (PC: Alt-Left Arrow key)** on your keyboard. Each time you press that, it tightens the space between the letters. Get it nice and snug like you see here.

Continued

Step 10:

Next, we'll create a second line of type. Click the Horizontal Type tool somewhere away from your original type to create a new Type layer. This time, type (in all caps) "Behind the scenes photos from Mark Moore in concert" (as seen here). For the sake of contrast, choose a thinner, lighter typeface for this second line (here, I chose a lighter weight of the same font—Futura Medium, 16 pt.), and this time we're going to add space between the letters (instead of tightening them). So, highlight the letters, but this time press **Option-Right Arrow key (PC: Alt-Right Arrow key)**. Each time you press that, it puts more space between the letters. Make it nice and airy like you see here. If you need to reposition your type, just switch to the Move tool (click on it in the Toolbox), then drag it where you want it.

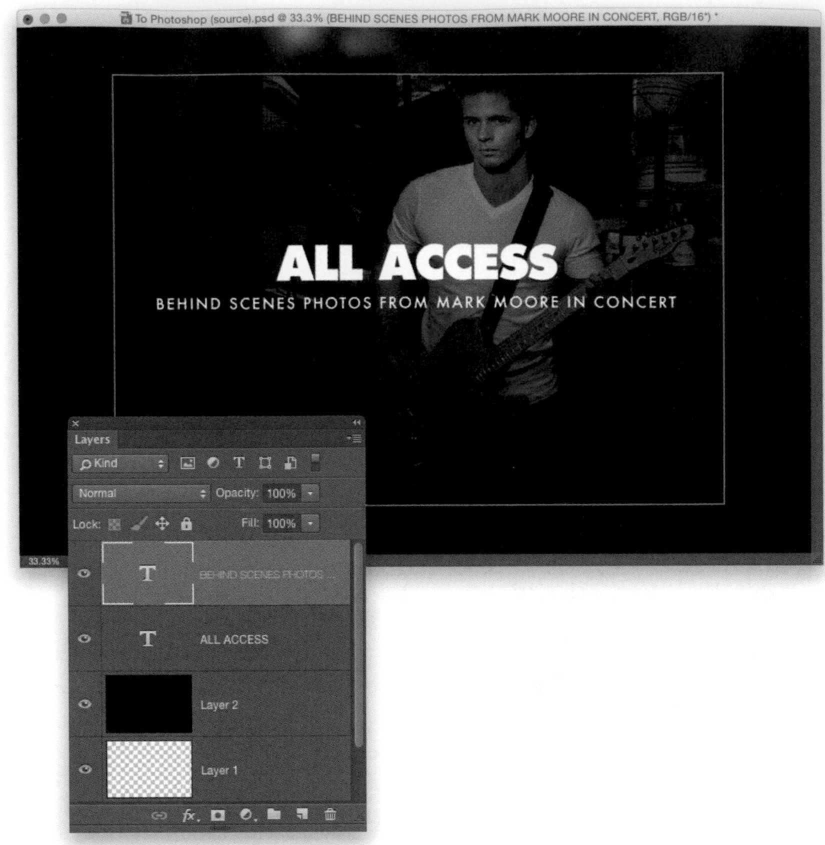

Step 11:

Okay, now that I look at where we are with our image, I think it needs a little something more to offset the area in the middle visually, like brightening that blurry area around the outside. So, let's start by doing what we did in Step Four all over again. Click on the Background layer in the Layers panel, take the Rectangular Marquee tool and put a selection around that center area, then Inverse the selection just like we did in Step Five. But, now, instead of blurring that outside area, we're going to brighten it. So, go under the Image menu, under Adjustments, and choose **Levels**. When the Levels dialog appears (seen here), drag the highlights (white) slider (the one on the right, under the histogram) to the left, as seen here (it's kind of like dragging the Whites slider in Lightroom to the right) to brighten the selected area. Click OK, then press Command-D (PC: Ctrl-D) to Deselect.

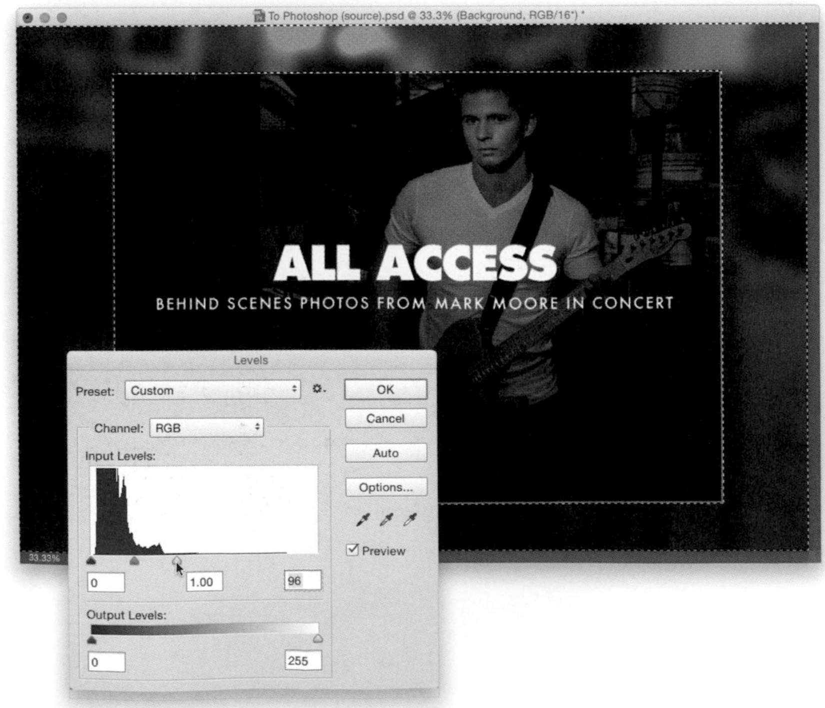

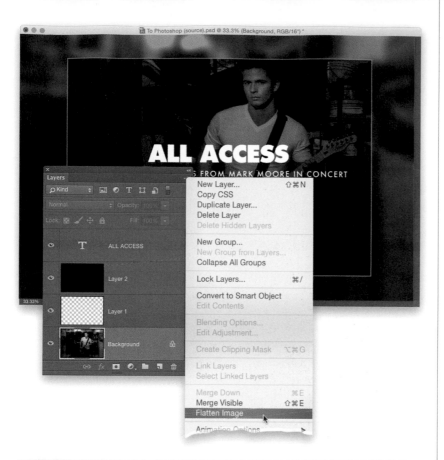

Step 12:
We're done tweaking the image here in Photoshop, so at this point, you can choose to flatten the image (by choosing **Flatten Image** from the Layers panel's flyout menu, as shown here), which removes all the layers and leaves you with a single-layer regular image like we normally have in Lightroom. Or, you can keep all the layers intact and send them over to Lightroom (more on this choice in a moment). But, no matter which you choose to do (flattening the image, or skipping that step), what you do next is the same. Just press **Command-S (PC: Ctrl-S)** to Save the changes, then press **Command-W (PC: Ctrl-W)** to Close the image window. Save and Close. That's it. That's the magic combination that sends your image back to Lightroom and closes your image here in Photoshop.

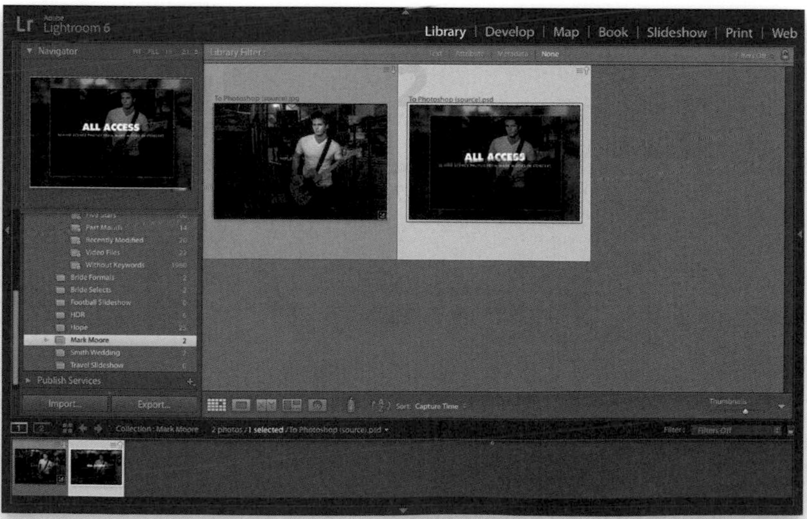

Step 13:
Now, lets switch back to Lightroom. If you look in the collection where your original Image is, you'll see the image you just edited in Photoshop right beside it (as seen here, where you can see the black-and-white image with text added next to the original color image we started with). It works this way whether you started with a RAW image, TIFF, JPEG, whatever. Okay, that's it. So, to recap: you press **Command-E (PC: Ctrl-E)** to take the selected image over to Photoshop, do all the tweaking and adjusting you want there, and when you're done, simply save and close, and your edited image now appears in Lightroom. Be sure to read the next step, though, because it's something you'll want to know about saving a layered file back to Lightroom.

Continued

Step 14: Working with Layered Files

If you have multiple layers (like we did with this image), and you save and close the document without flattening it first, Lightroom keeps all those layers intact in the background. So, in Lightroom, what you'll see appears to be a flattened image, but the layers are still there (you can't see them because Lightroom doesn't have a layers feature). If you want to see the layers, or work with them, you have to go back to Photoshop. *However*, to do that, when you click on the layered image in Lightroom and press Command-E (PC: Ctrl-E) to open it in Photoshop, when the dialog appears asking you if you want to edit a copy with your Lightroom changes, you must choose Edit Original (as seen here). When you do that, all the layers appear. Otherwise, it sends Photoshop a flattened version of the image. By the way, this is the only time I ever choose to open the original file—when I want to see a layered file.

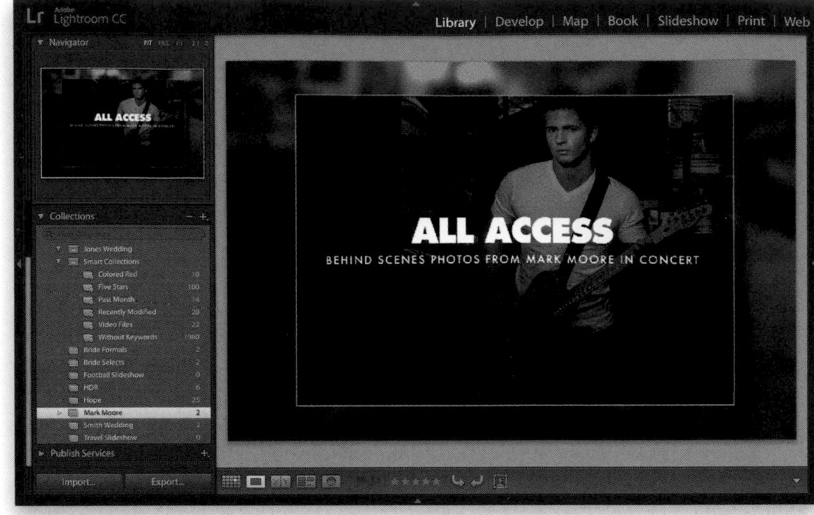

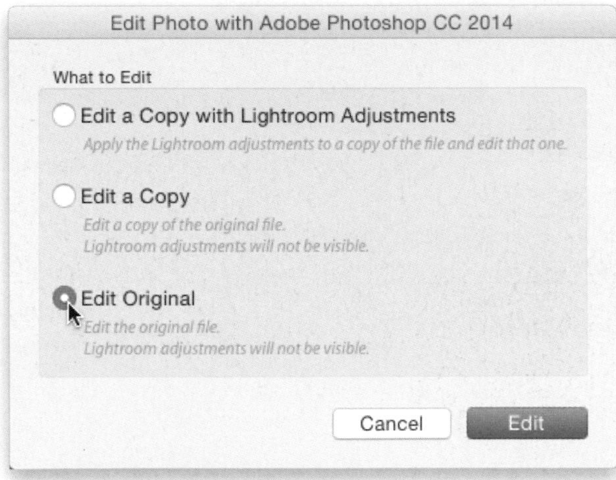

Adding Photoshop Automation to Your Lightroom Workflow

If there's a "finishing move" you like to do in Photoshop (after you're done tweaking the image in Lightroom), you can add some automation to the process, so once your photos are exported, Photoshop launches, applies your move, and then resaves the file. It's based on you creating an action in Photoshop (an action is a recording of something you've done in Photoshop, and once you've recorded it, Photoshop can repeat that process as many times as you'd like, really, really, fast). Here's how to create an action, and then hook that directly into Lightroom:

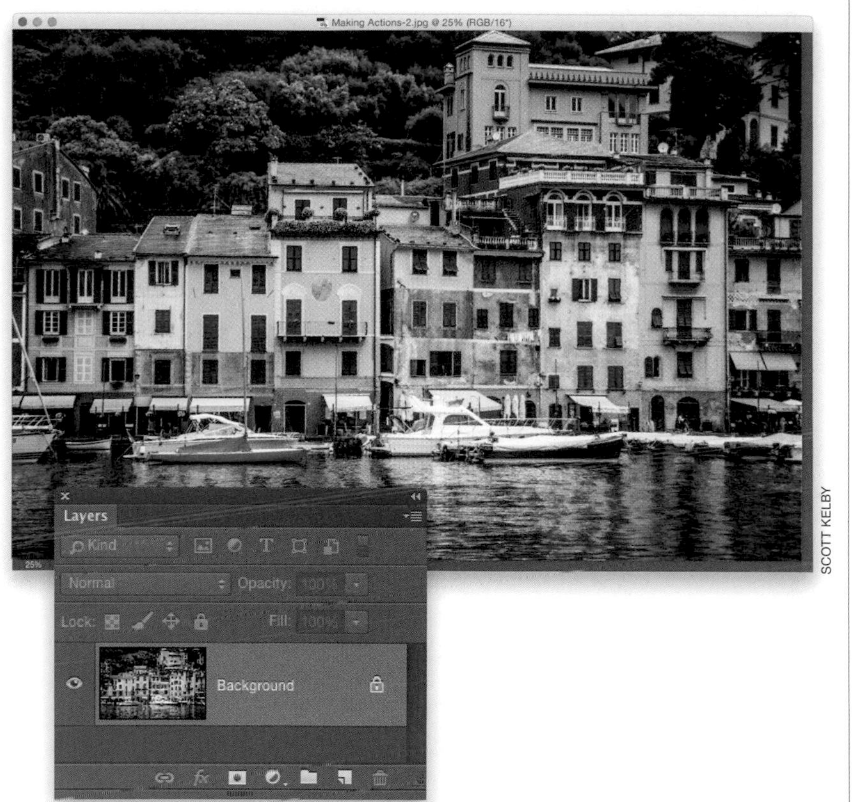

SCOTT KELBY

Step One:

We start this process in Photoshop, so go ahead and press **Command-E (PC: Ctrl-E)** to open an image in Photoshop (don't forget, you can follow along with the same photo I'm using here, if you like, by downloading it from the site I gave you back in the book's introduction). What we're going to do here is create a Photoshop action that adds a nice, simple softening effect to the image, and you can use it on everything from landscapes to portraits. (When I post a photo using this technique on my blog, I always get emails asking: "How is it that the image looks soft, but it still looks sharp?") Because this technique is repetitive (it uses the same steps in the same order every time), it makes it an ideal candidate for turning into an action, which you can apply to a different photo (or group of photos) much faster.

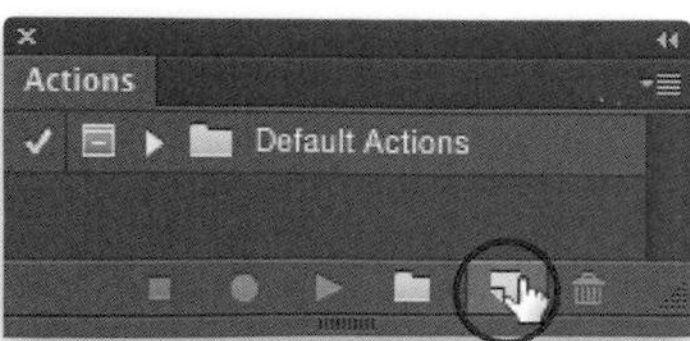

Step Two:

To create an action, go to the Window menu and choose **Actions** to make the Actions panel visible. Click on the Create New Action icon at the bottom of the panel (it looks just like the Create a New Layer icon in the Layers panel and is circled here). This brings up the New Action dialog (shown here). Go ahead and give your action a name (I named mine "Soften Finishing Effect") and click the Record button (notice the button doesn't say OK or Save, it says Record, because it's now recording your steps).

Continued

Step Three:

Make two duplicates of the Background layer by pressing **Command-J (PC: Ctrl-J)** twice. Then go to the Layers panel and click on the center layer (shown highlighted here). Now go under the Filter menu, under Sharpen, and choose **Unsharp Mask**. This is a low-resolution image we're working on, so apply an Unsharp Mask with the Amount set to 85%, the Radius set to 1 pixel, and the Threshold set to 4 levels, and click OK to apply the sharpening. (*Note:* If this had been a full-resolution image from a digital camera, I would have used Unsharp Mask settings of Amount: 120, Radius: 1, and Threshold: 3.)

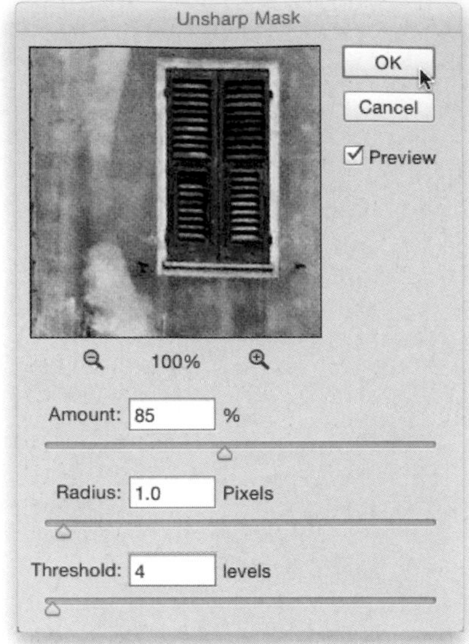

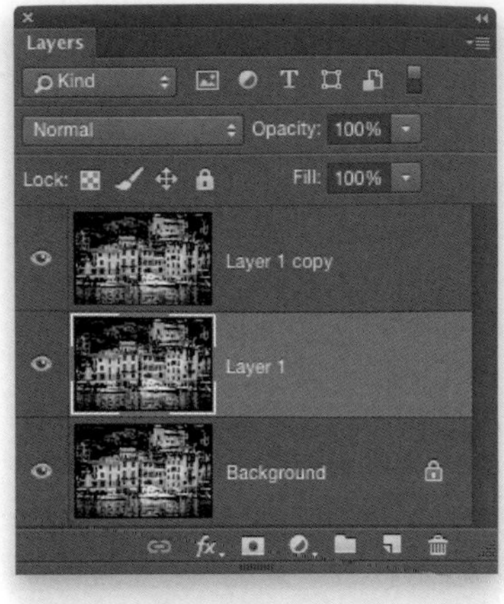

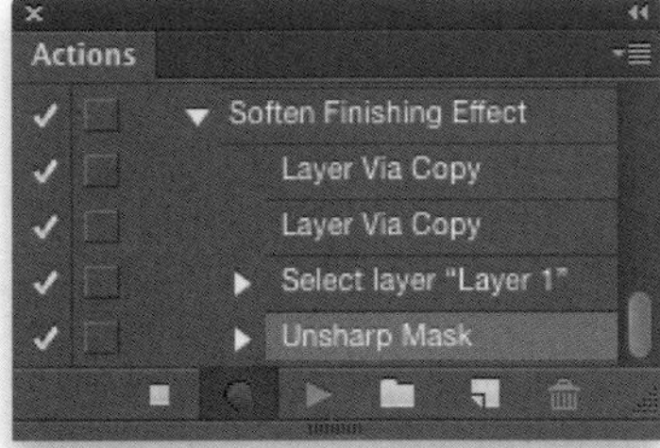

Step Four:

Now, after the sharpening, you're going to apply a huge blur to this image. So, click on the top layer in the Layers panel (Layer 1 copy). Go under the Filter menu, under Blur, choose **Gaussian Blur**, and enter 25 pixels as the Radius, so it's really blurry (like you see here).

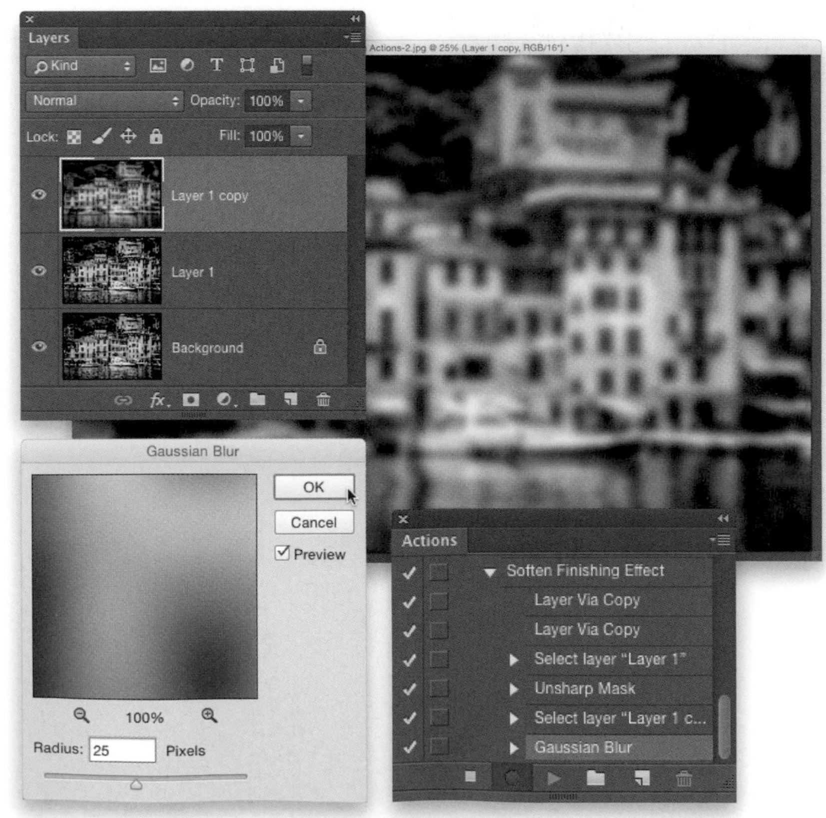

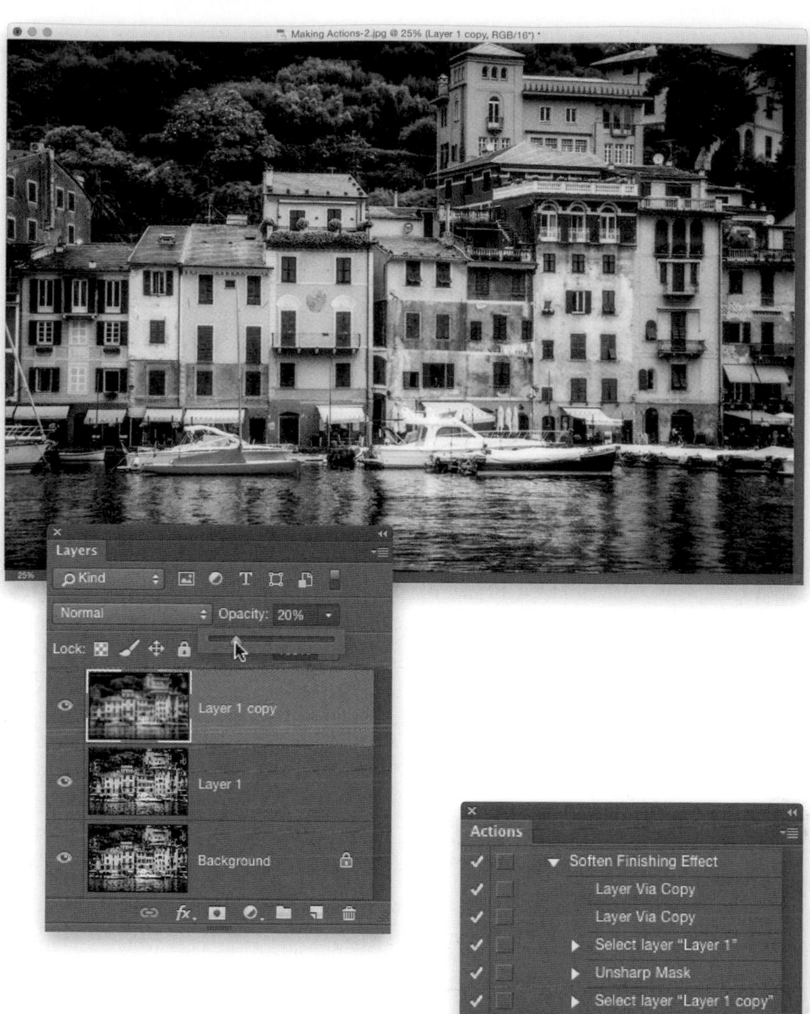

Step Five:

In the Layers panel, lower the Opacity of this blurry layer to 20%, which gives us our final look (as seen here). Now, go to the Layers panel's flyout menu (near the top-right corner of the panel) and choose **Flatten Image** to flatten the layers down to just the Background layer. Next, save the file by pressing **Command-S (PC: Ctrl-S)** and close it by pressing **Command-W (PC: Ctrl-W)**.

Step Six:

You may have forgotten by now, but we've been recording this process the whole time (remember that action we created a while back? Well, it's been recording our steps all along). So, go back to the Actions panel and click the Stop icon at the bottom left of the panel (as shown here). What you've recorded is an action that will apply the effect, then save the file, and then close that file. Now, I generally like to test my action at this point to make sure I wrote it correctly, so open a different photo, click on the Soften Finishing Effect action in the Actions panel, then click the Play Selection icon at the bottom of the panel. It should apply the effect, then save and close the document.

Continued

Step Seven:

Now we're going to turn that action into what's called a droplet. Here's what a droplet does: If you leave Photoshop and find a photo on your computer, and you drag-and-drop the photo right onto this droplet, the droplet automatically launches Photoshop, opens that photo, and applies that Soften Finishing Effect action to the photo you dropped on there. Then it saves and closes the photo automatically, because you recorded those two steps as part of the action. Pretty sweet. So, to make a droplet, go under Photoshop's File menu, under Automate, and choose **Create Droplet** (as shown here).

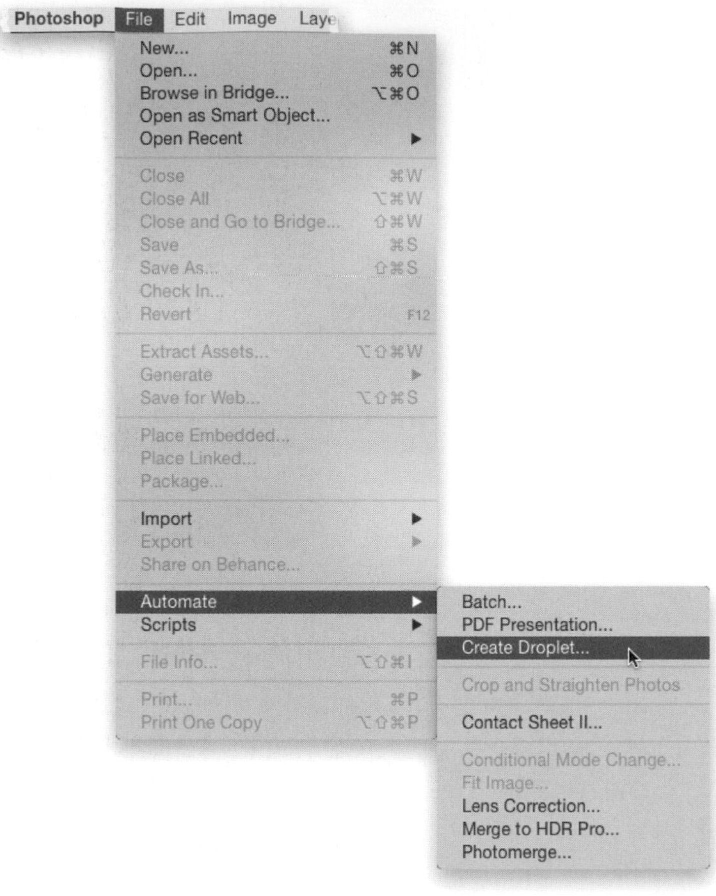

Step Eight:

This brings up the Create Droplet dialog (shown here). At the top left of the dialog, click the Choose button, choose your desktop as the destination for saving your droplet, and then name your droplet "Soften." Now, in the Play section of this dialog, make sure to choose **Soften Finishing Effect** (that's what we named our action earlier) from the Action pop-up menu (as shown here). That's it—you can ignore the rest of the dialog, and just click OK.

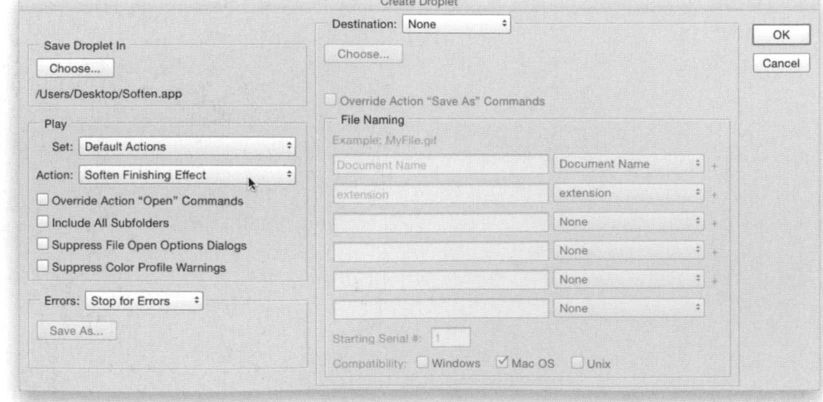

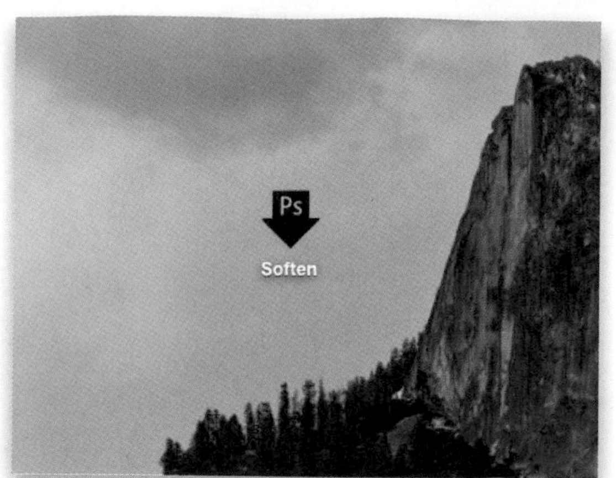

Step Nine:

If you look on your computer's desktop, you'll see an icon that is a large arrow, and the arrow is aiming at the name of the droplet (as shown here).

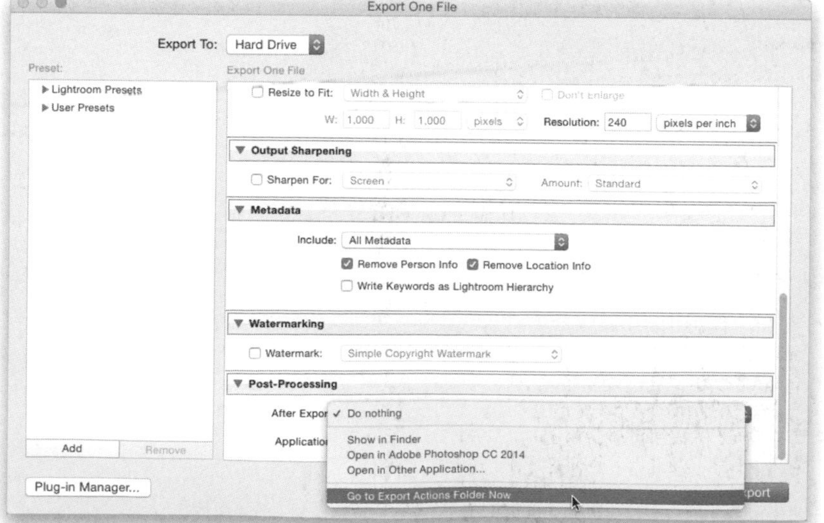

Step 10:

Now that we've built our Soften droplet in Photoshop, we're going to add that to our Lightroom workflow. Back in Lightroom, go under the File menu and choose **Export**. When the Export dialog appears, go down to the Post-Processing section, and from the After Export pop-up menu, choose **Go to Export Actions Folder Now** (as shown here).

Continued

Step 11:

This takes you to the folder on your computer where Lightroom stores Export Actions (and more importantly, where you can store any you create). All you have to do is click-and-drag that Soften droplet right into that Export Actions folder to add it into Lightroom. Now you can close this folder, head back to Lightroom, and click Cancel to close the Export dialog (you only needed it open at this point to get you to that Export Actions folder, so you could drag that droplet in there).

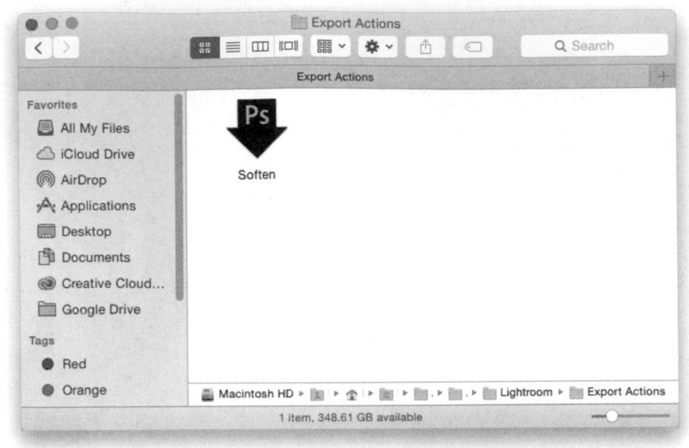

Step 12:

Okay, now let's put it to work: In Lightroom's Grid view, select the photo (or photos) you want to have that effect applied to, then press **Command-Shift-E (PC: Ctrl-Shift-E)** to bring back the Export dialog. From the Preset section on the left, click on the right-facing triangle to the left of User Presets, and then click on the Export JPEGs for Web preset we talked about creating at the beginning of Chapter 9 (if you didn't create that one, go ahead and do it now). In the Export Location section, click on the Choose button and select the destination folder for your saved JPEG(s) (if you want to change it). Then, in the File Naming section, you can give your photo(s) a new name, if you like. Now, in the Post-Processing section at the bottom, from the After Export pop-up menu, you'll see Soften (your droplet) has been added, so choose it (as shown here). When you click Export, your photo(s) will be saved as a JPEG, then Photoshop will automatically launch, open your photo(s), apply your Soften Finishing Effect, then save and close the photo(s). Pretty slick stuff!

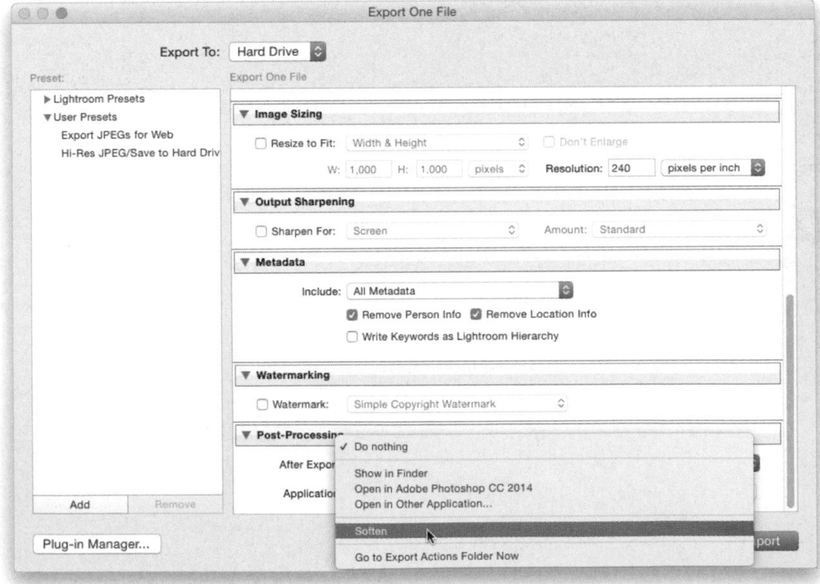

Lightroom Killer Tips > >

▼ Choosing the Name of Your Photoshop Edited Files

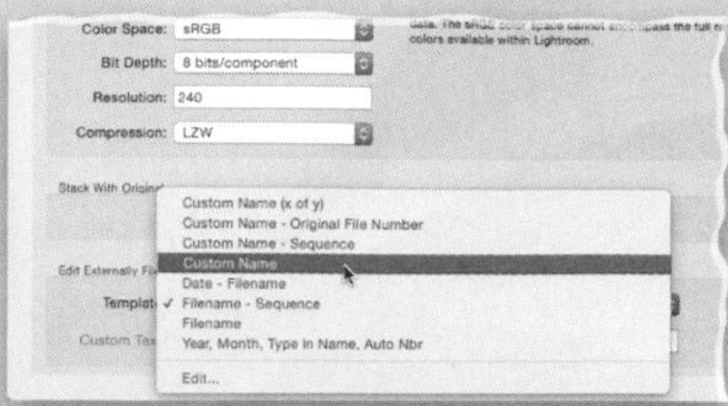

Back in Lightroom 1, it automatically added "Edit in CS3" to end of any photo you edited over there, but now you get to choose exactly what these edited files are named. Just go to Lightroom's preferences (press **Command-, [comma; PC: Ctrl-,]**), and then click on the External Editing tab, and at the bottom of the dialog, you'll see the Edit Externally File Naming section, where you can choose your own custom name or one of the preset file naming templates.

▼ Cutting Files' Ties to Lightroom

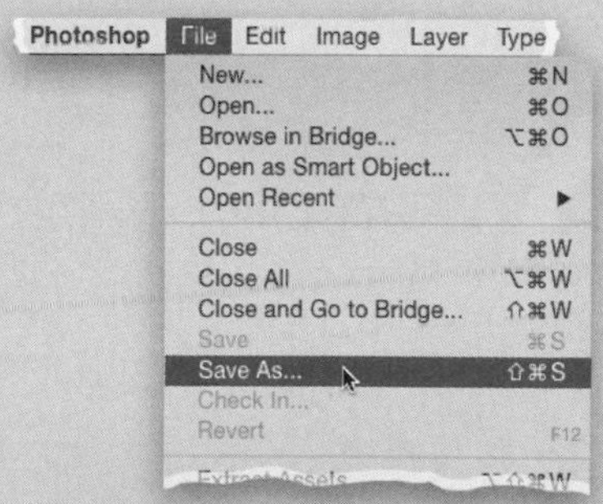

When you move a file over to Photoshop for editing, and you save that file, the saved file comes right back to Lightroom. So, how do you break this chain? When you're done editing in Photoshop, just go under Photoshop's File menu and choose **Save As**, then give the file a new name. That's it, the chain is broken and the file won't go back to Lightroom.

▼ Get Rid of Those Old PSD Files

If you upgraded from Lightroom 1, each time you jumped over to Photoshop, it created a copy of your photo and saved it alongside the original in PSD format, even if you never made a change to it in Photoshop. If you're like me, you probably had a hundred or more PSDs with no visible changes, just taking up space on your drive and in Lightroom. If you still haven't gotten rid of them, go to the Library module, and in the Catalog panel, click on All Photographs. Then, up in the Library Filter, click on Metadata. In the first field on the left, click on the header and choose **File Type** from the pop-up

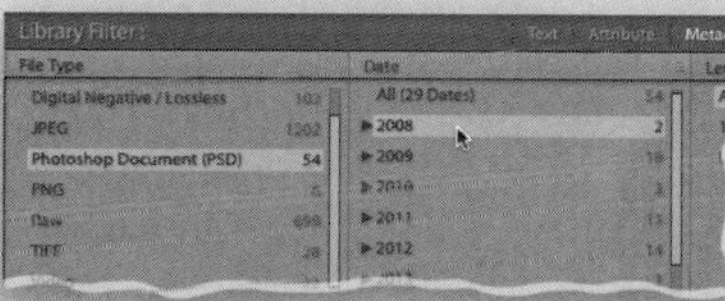

menu, then click on Photoshop Document (PSD). Choose **Date** for the second field and click on the oldest dates, so you can see which ones you never used or don't need, and you can delete them so you get that space back.

▼ How to Get Photos Back Into Lightroom After Running an Export Action

If you created an action in Photoshop and saved it as an export action in Lightroom (earlier this chapter), when your photos leave Lightroom and go to Photoshop to run the action, that's the "end of the line" (the photos don't come back to Lightroom). If you want those processed photos to be automatically imported back into Lightroom, you can use Lightroom's Auto Import feature (under the File menu) to watch a folder, and when you write your Photoshop action, have it save your processed files to that folder. That way, as soon as the action is run, and the file is saved out of Photoshop, it will automatically be re-imported into Lightroom.

▼ Getting Consistent Color Between Lightroom and Photoshop

If you're going to be going back and forth between Lightroom and Photoshop, I'm sure you want consistency in your color between the two programs, which is why you might want to change your color space in Photoshop to match Lightroom's default color space of ProPhoto RGB. You do this under Photoshop's Edit menu: choose **Color Settings**, then under Working Spaces, for RGB, choose **ProPhoto RGB**. If you prefer to work in

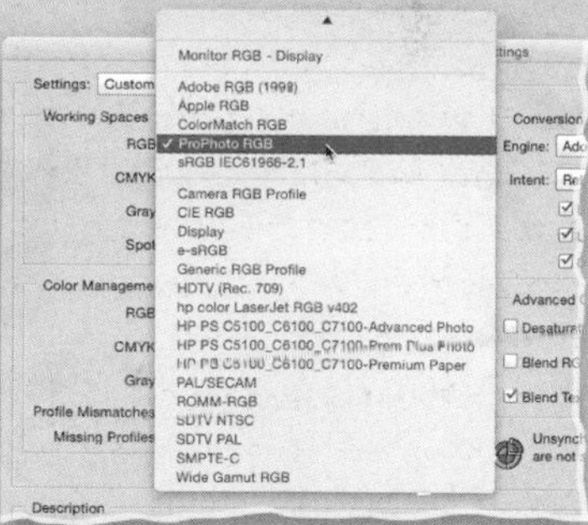

the Adobe RGB (1998) color space in Photoshop, then just make sure you send your photo over to Photoshop in that color space: go to Lightroom's Preferences dialog, click on the External Editing tab up top, then under Edit in Photoshop, for Color Space, choose **AdobeRGB (1998)**.

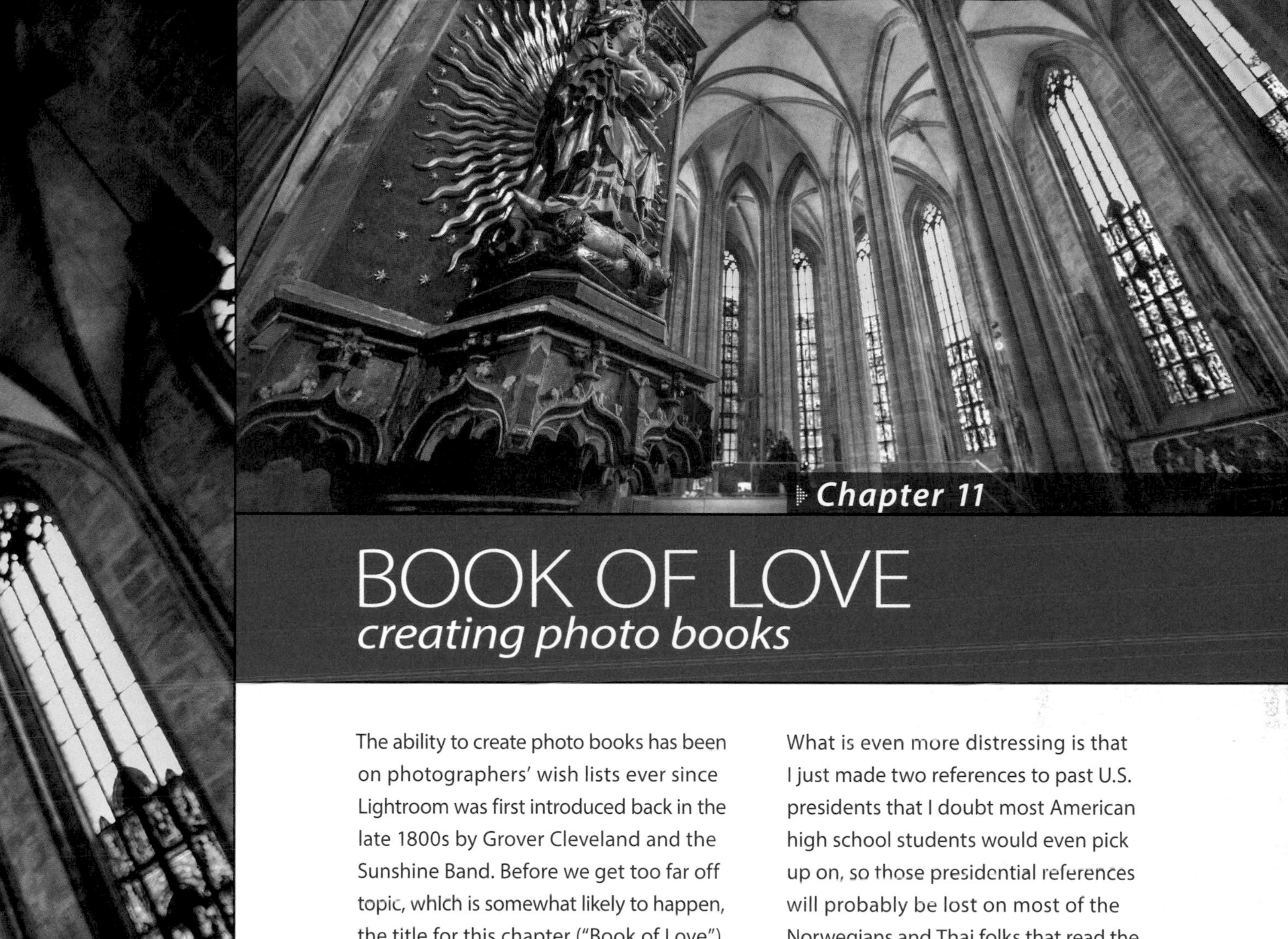

Chapter 11

BOOK OF LOVE
creating photo books

The ability to create photo books has been on photographers' wish lists ever since Lightroom was first introduced back in the late 1800s by Grover Cleveland and the Sunshine Band. Before we get too far off topic, which is somewhat likely to happen, the title for this chapter ("Book of Love") is from the band called (in fact) Book of Love. I'm willing to set aside the fact that they really should be called something like The Book of Love, or perhaps James Buchanan and the Book of Love, but I find it really hard to separate their name (and their song of the same name—a bouncy synth-pop song recorded back in 1986 when people wore skinny ties and sport coats with the sleeves rolled up) from the original (and actually kind of good) song, "Who Wrote the Book of Love," which was recorded by The Monotones. What is even more distressing is that I just made two references to past U.S. presidents that I doubt most American high school students would even pick up on, so those presidential references will probably be lost on most of the Norwegians and Thai folks that read the translations of this book. It won't be the first time I've actually heard from readers around the world that read the English-language version of the book first, and then the foreign translation, and who have told me my chapter intros don't make sense in translation. I always write back and remind them that they don't really make sense in English either, to which they usually reply, "Den hund er på kjøkkenet drive en båt gjort av bønner." See? When you read something like that, that's what makes it all worthwhile.

Before You Make Your First Book

Here are just a couple of quick things you'll want to know before you actually build your first book, including what kind of books, sizes, and covers are available through Adobe's partner in book building, Blurb (www.blurb.com).

Step One:

When you jump over to the Book module (up in the Module Picker, or just press **Command-Option-4 [PC: Ctrl-Alt-4]**), a Book menu appears up top, and if you go under that menu, at the bottom of it, you'll find **Book Preferences**. Go ahead and choose that before we get rollin' here. Okay, let's start at the top: Just like in the Print, Slideshow, or Web modules, in the Book module, you get to choose whether the default setting for your frames is Zoom to Fill or Zoom to Fit (I leave it set at Zoom to Fill, simply because it usually looks better, but you can choose whichever you like best).

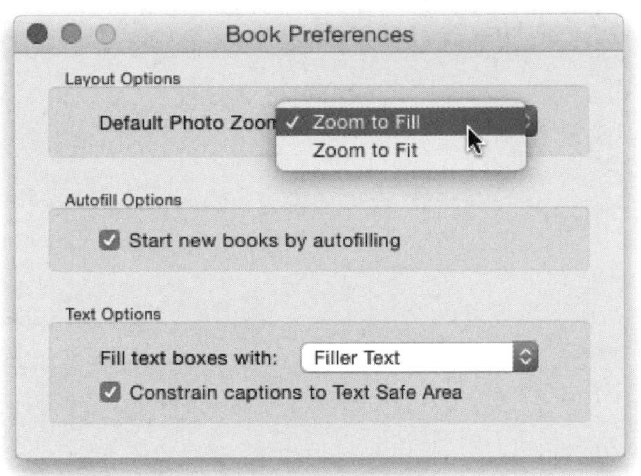

Step Two:

When we build our book project together (after these two pages), you'll have the option of having Lightroom automatically fill all the pages of your book with the photos you've chosen to be in the book (so you don't have to drag-and-drop them into the book one by one). So, with this preference turned on, as soon as you go to the Book module, it flows your Filmstrip photos into the photo frames on each page and—boom—you've got a book (of course, you can rearrange any pages or swap out photos after the fact, but it's a good starting place).

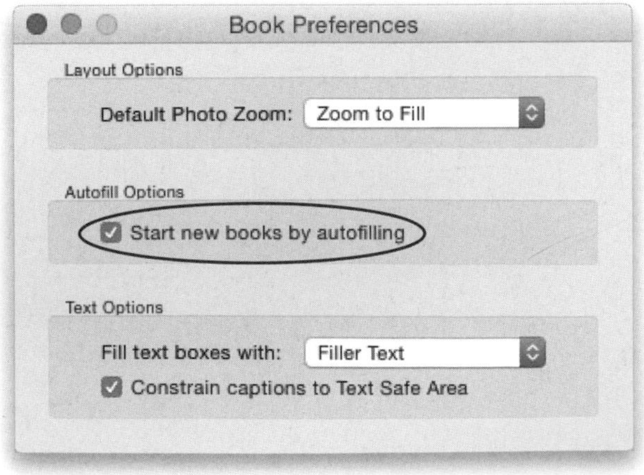

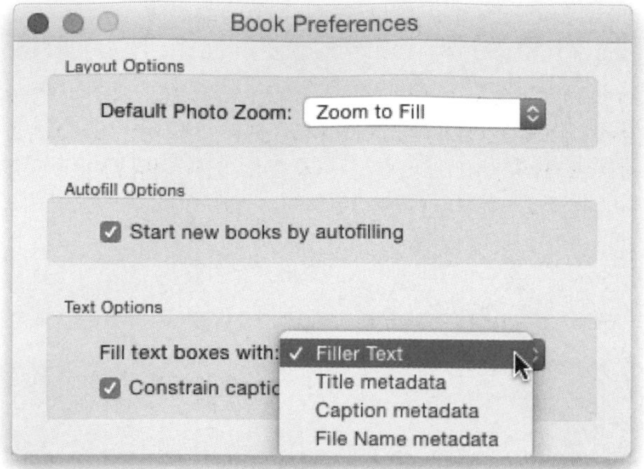

Step Three:

In the final section, there's a preference to help you visually see where you can add text. Some of the layouts have areas where you can put text, and it's easy to see in the thumbnail, but once you apply it to your actual page, unless there's some text already in place (Filler Text), then you wouldn't know there was a text box there at all. So, choosing Filler Text acts as a reminder (but don't worry—it's just for looks. It doesn't actually print until you erase it and start typing your own text, so you don't have to worry about it showing up in your final book—just like you don't have to worry about guides printing in your final book). Besides Filler Text, if you actually added captions or titles (in the Metadata panel fields in the Library module), you can choose to have Lightroom pull that text instead (which will definitely save you some time). Lastly, Constrain Captions to Text Safe Area just means it will keep your captions from extending into areas where it might get cut off, or extend into the page gutter between pages.

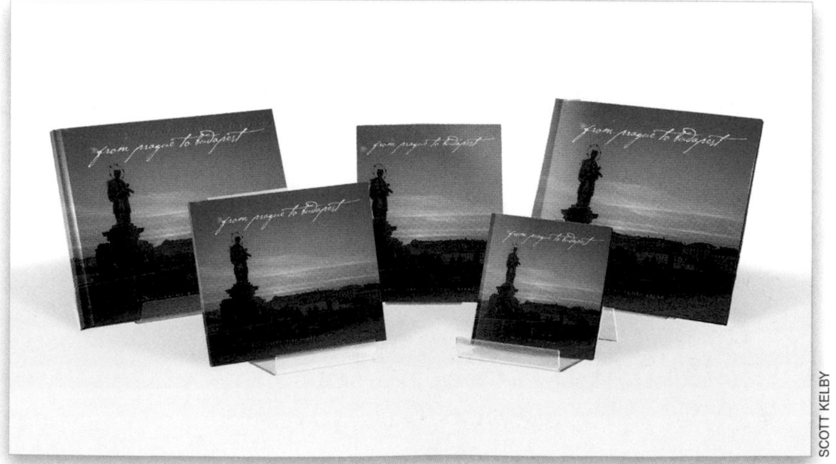

SCOTT KELBY

Step Four:

Before you turn the page and we start building a book together, I thought I'd show you the different sizes and types of books you can order directly from Lightroom through Blurb (an online photo book lab that's very popular with photographers, and Adobe's printing partner for Lightroom):

There are five different sizes: Small Square 7x7", Standard Portrait (tall) 8x10", Standard Landscape (wide) 10x8", Large Landscape 13x11", and Large Square 12x12". There are three different cover choices for each: a Softcover, a Hardcover Image Wrap (shown here, on the left and right), and a Hardcover Dust Jacket (you get to choose the inside flap covers and text if you want it, too!). Okay, let's build our book.

Building Your First Book from Scratch

Lightroom 4 was the first version of Lightroom to have a built-in book feature, and I have to say Adobe really did this one right! I thought the best way to learn this would be just to go ahead and build a book from scratch (it doesn't take long at all), and then when you're done with this one book, you'll totally have it down (yes, it's that easy). The hard part will be picking the images you want in the book—the actual building of the book is surprisingly easy, especially since Adobe included about 180 pre-designed page layout templates.

Step One:

In the Library module, create a new collection with just the photos you want in your book (as I did here). If you know the order in which you want your photos to appear in your book, go ahead and drag-and-drop them into that order. You can decide the order later, but if you have some idea now, it's handy to have them in order before the next step. Go to the Book module and, in the Book Settings panel (at the top of the right side Panels area), choose your book's size, paper type, and cover, and you'll get an estimated price (based on how many pages your book will be and in the currency you choose).

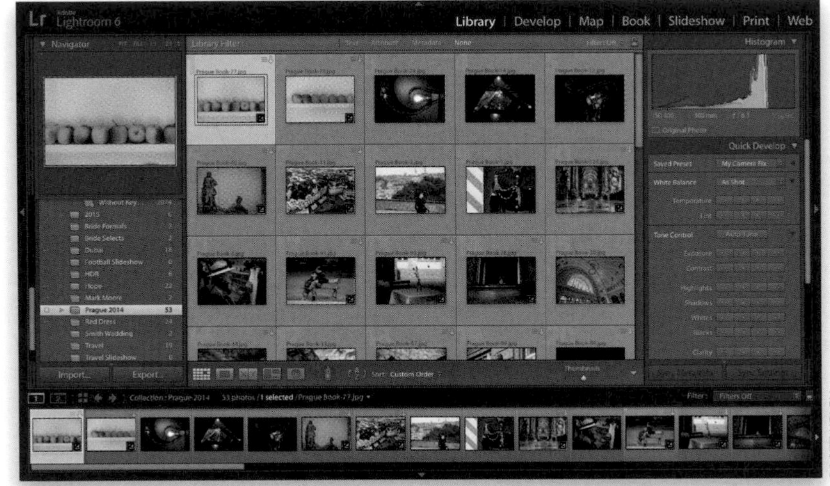

SCOTT KELBY

Step Two:

At this point, if you turned Autofill off in the Book preferences, all the pages are blank, but you can have Lightroom automatically fill them for you by clicking the Auto Layout button in the Auto Layout panel in the right side Panels area—it puts your photos in the book in the order they appear in your collection (ahhh, you see why it pays to put them into the order you want before you get here?). But, before you click the Auto Layout button, you can customize how it does the auto layout, from only putting one photo on each right page, with room for a caption, and leaving all the left pages blank, to the same layout without captions, to having one photo per page (that's what I generally do to start, and what we'll choose here). You choose which preset you want at the top of the Auto Layout panel.

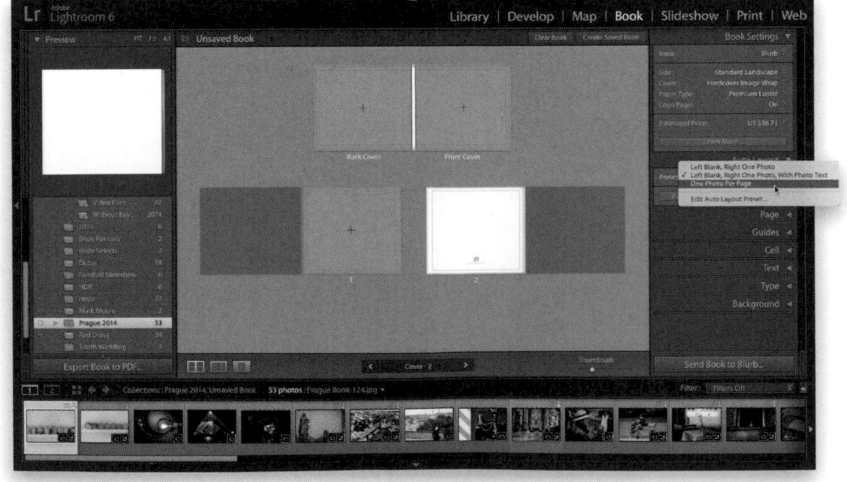

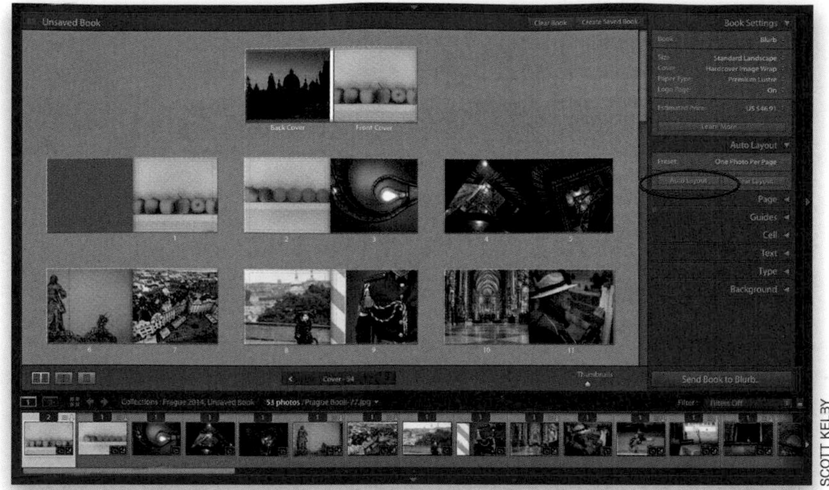

SCOTT KELBY

Step Three:

Now, so you have more room to see how your book is looking as you build it, I recommend hiding the left side and top panels (press **F5** on your keyboard to hide the top and **F7** to hide the left side) to make your Preview area much larger (as seen here). Click the Auto Layout button (shown circled here in red) and it automatically puts one photo on each page (as seen here). To see the rest of your pages, just scroll down. If you arranged them in the order you wanted them, then it's just a matter of choosing the right size for each image (if you don't want them all full-page). If they're not in the order you'd like, then drag-and-drop them on the book pages in the order you want.

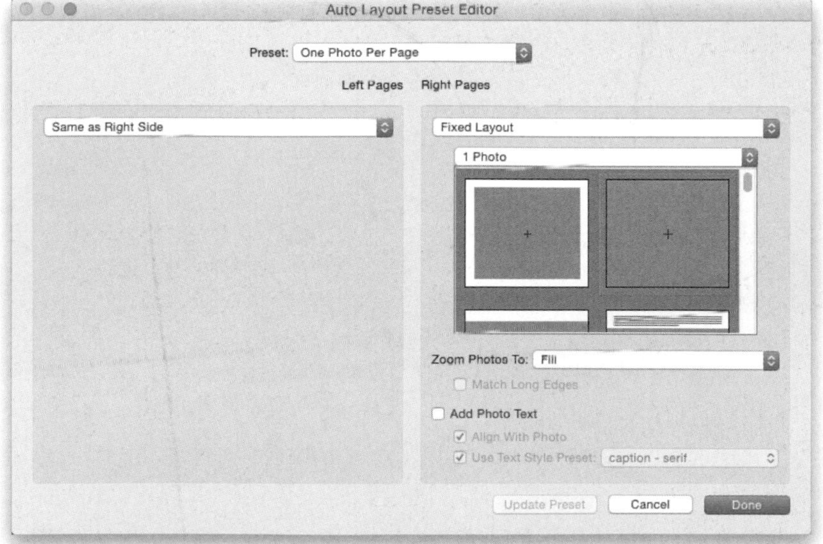

Step Four:

Before we get to sorting, there is a very cool feature that can help you with your next book. Remember when you chose one of the built-in Auto Layout presets (back in Step Two)? Well, you can create your own custom presets and save them to that same pop-up menu. That way, you can have it auto fill exactly the way you want it (for example, let's say you want the entire book to have square-shaped images—you can set that up as a preset). To create a custom preset, from the Auto Layout panel's Preset pop-up menu, choose **Edit Auto Layout Preset** and the Auto Layout Preset Editor dialog appears. It's split into two parts: the left pages and the right pages. Right now it's set so whatever you choose on the right page, the left page will do the same (Same as Right Side), but let's create our own from scratch.

TIP: Adding More Pages

If you didn't do the Auto Layout thing, you can add more pages to your book by going to the Page panel (in the right side Panels area) and clicking the Add Page button.

Continued

Step Five:

Let's set up a preset to make the left-page images square and the right-page images full page (like you see here). Here's what you do: In the Left Pages section, first choose Fixed Layout from the pop-up menu at the top, then choose **1 Photo** from the pop-up menu below that. Now, scroll down to the square image page layout and click on it (as shown here), then just leave the right side at Fixed Layout, 1 Photo, and full page. Click the Save button, give your preset a name, and this layout will now be a preset choice for you. Sweet!

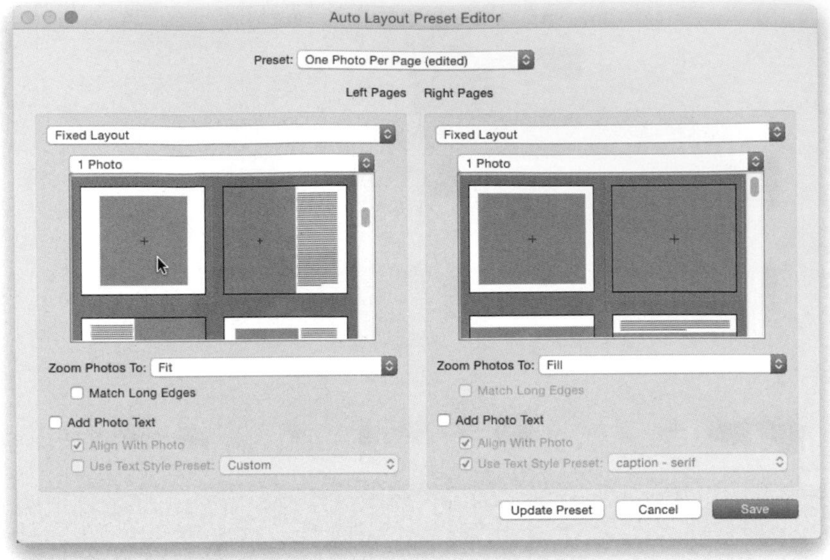

TIP: Hide Info Overlay

By default, info about your book appears in the top left of the preview window (size, page count, and price). If you'd rather not see this information (it's pretty distracting), then just go under the View menu and choose **Show Info Overlay** (or press the **I** key) to turn it off.

Step Six:

There's another option you need to know about with these custom layout presets: you get to choose how your image appears, once you drag it into place, using the Zoom Photos To pop-up menu in the Auto Layout Preset Editor dialog. If you choose Fit, it scales your image down to fit inside the frame. So, if you choose Fit with a square layout like we chose, the image will fit fully inside the square (like the image shown here on the top), but because it fits fully inside that square, your photo won't actually appear square. For that to happen, you'd have to choose Fill (like you see on the bottom). Luckily, you can always change this after the fact, on a per-page basis, by Right-clicking on a photo, and choosing **Zoom Photo to Fill Cell** from the pop-up menu to turn it on or off.

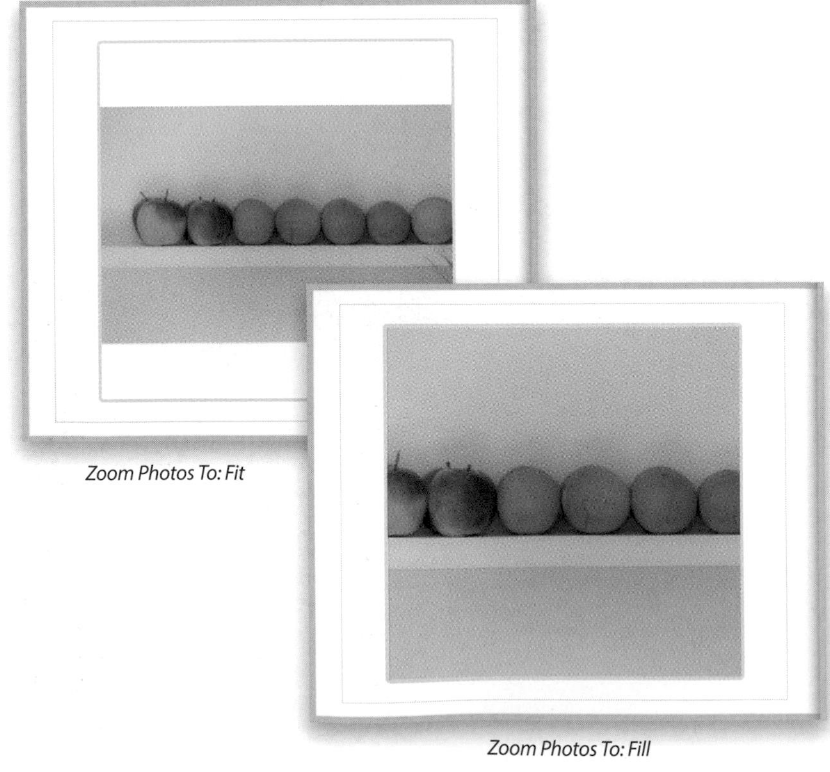

Zoom Photos To: Fit

Zoom Photos To: Fill

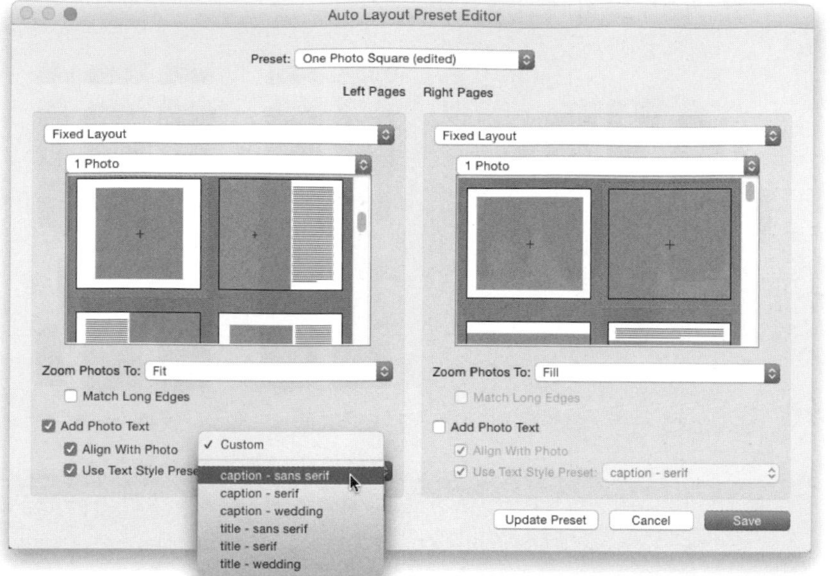

Step Seven:

If you know you're going to want to add a caption along with your photo, there's a checkbox for adding that, as well, and you can choose built-in text presets that work well for captioning.

TIP: If You Choose Fill, You Can Reposition Your Image in the Cell

Just click right on the image and drag it left or right, so the part you want to be visible appears within the frame.

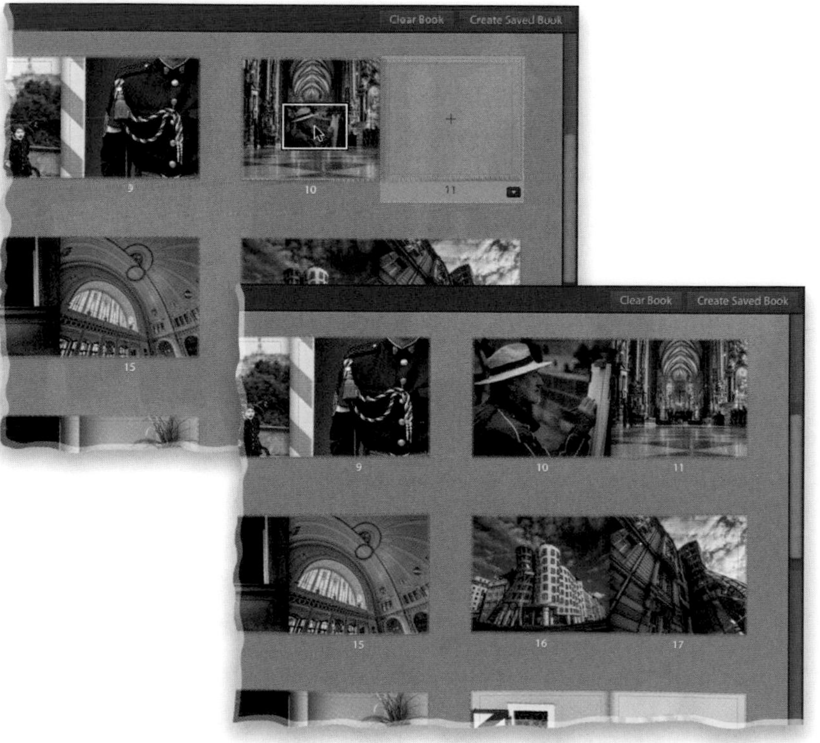

Step Eight:

Okay, now back to our layout. If you look back to Step Three, you'll see that the images on pages 10 and 11 probably need to be swapped (for design purposes, you generally don't want people looking off the page. It's more pleasing, and has less tension for the viewer, if they're looking in toward the spine, so let's swap those two pictures with each other). Click on the photo on page 11 and drag it over on top of page 10 (as shown here, top). When you release your mouse button, the two photos swap places (as shown here, bottom). Now he's kind of facing in toward the center of the book.

Continued

Step Nine:

Thus far, we've been building our book in Multi-Page View mode, but I usually prefer to work in the two-page Spread View while I'm putting pages together. I only use the Multi-Page View near the end of the process, when I want to re-order the pages themselves (more on this in Step 20). To get to this two-page view, just click the Spread View button (second from the left) on the left side of the toolbar that appears right below the Preview area (as seen here). The button to its right is the Single Page View, and the button to its left is the Multi-Page View. So, to recap: I use this two-page Spread View most of the time while building my books, so you'll see a lot of this view from here on out. Once you're in this Spread View, you can move through the book using the left/right arrows in the center of the toolbar, but I just use the **Left/Right Arrow keys** on my keyboard to move through the book.

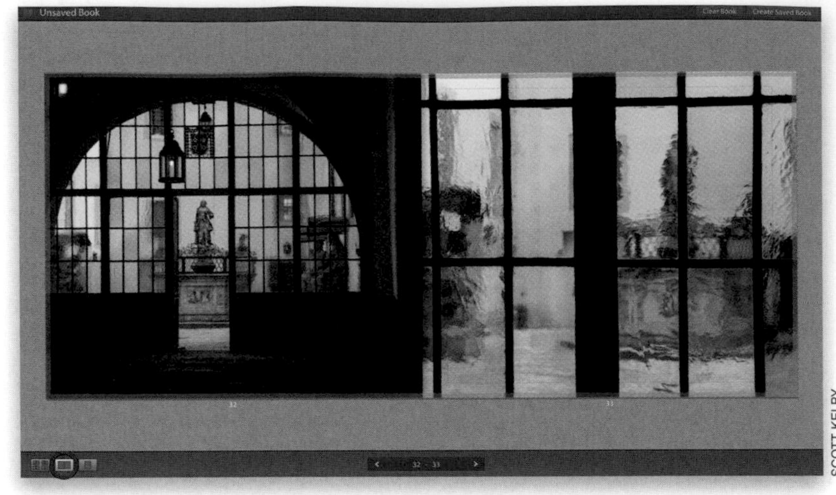

Step 10:

You can choose how many photos you want on a particular page, and then the layout of that page, by clicking on the little black button in the bottom-right corner of the currently selected page (if you don't see this button, click on the page first to select it—your page will appear highlighted in yellow—then you'll see the button). Once you click the Change Page Layout button, the Modify Page menu appears (shown here). First, choose how many photos you want on your page (in this case, we'll stick with one for now), and then a list of page layout thumbnails will appear at the bottom of the menu (notice that scroll bar to their right? That's right—there are a whole bunch of them!). The currently selected layout appears highlighted in gold. Layouts with lines of text show where you can add stories, captions, and headlines. They also show where that text will be positioned (to the left, right, top, bottom, etc.).

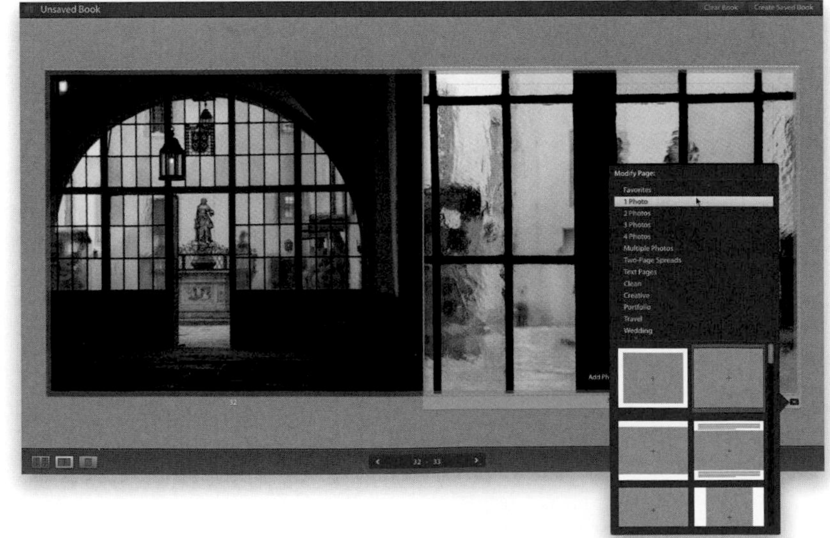

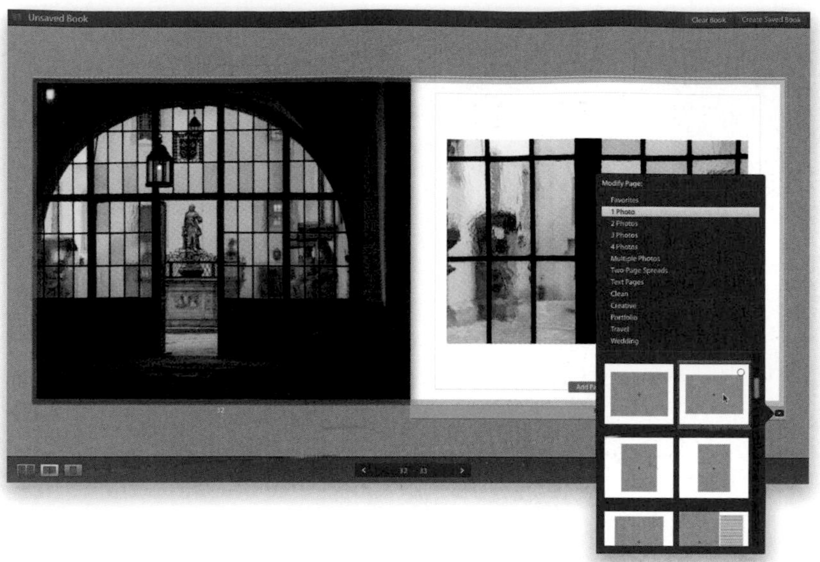

Step 11:

Let's go ahead and change the right page to have a smaller photo size, so scroll down the list until you come to a horizontal gray photo box and click on it (as seen here) to make that your new page layout. One of the things I love about Lightroom's Book module is that you can have a custom layout for every single page, rather than just applying a theme for the entire book. That way, you can mix and match pages from any themed layout you like (for example, you could pick the left page from the Travel theme, and the right page from the Portfolio theme).

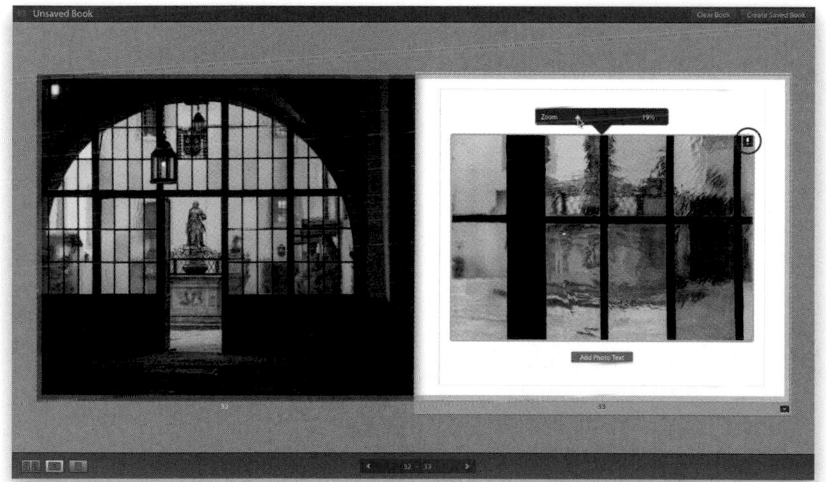

Step 12:

Now that you've created a new page layout, you still have lots of control. Click on the image and a Zoom slider appears above it, so you can zoom in/out on your image (this is kind of like cropping the image, because as you zoom in, the image stays within the "cell"). Here, I've zoomed the image in a bit. However, if you zoom in too tight, you won't have enough resolution to print the image, and if that happens, Lightroom gives you a warning (see that "!" in the upper-right corner of the photo?), letting you know you've zoomed in too close and now your image won't print as crisply or will look pixelated (or both).

DESIGN TIP: Make One Photo Larger

When putting together a photo book in two-page layouts, try to make one photo larger, so it becomes the focal point—the main attraction on that spread, which draws the viewer's eye. Not only does it create a more pleasing layout, it also lets the viewer know which photo to look at first, since people generally feel like the most important object on a page is the largest, like a newspaper headline.

Continued

Step 13:

If you want more white space around your photo, you can shrink the size of its cell by clicking on the photo, and then grabbing the top, bottom, or side of it (as your cursor gets near the edges, it will change to a double-headed arrow) and dragging inward (as shown here). Another way to do this is to go to the Cell panel (in the right side Panels area) and drag the Padding Amount slider. As you drag it to the right, it shrinks the size of the photo in the cell. If you click on the black, left-facing triangle, it'll reveal four sliders, so you can individually adjust the top, bottom, left, and right margins. They are linked together by default, so to move an individual slider, click on Link All to turn that feature off. *Note:* If you chose a layout with multiple photos right up against each other, you can also add space between them this way.

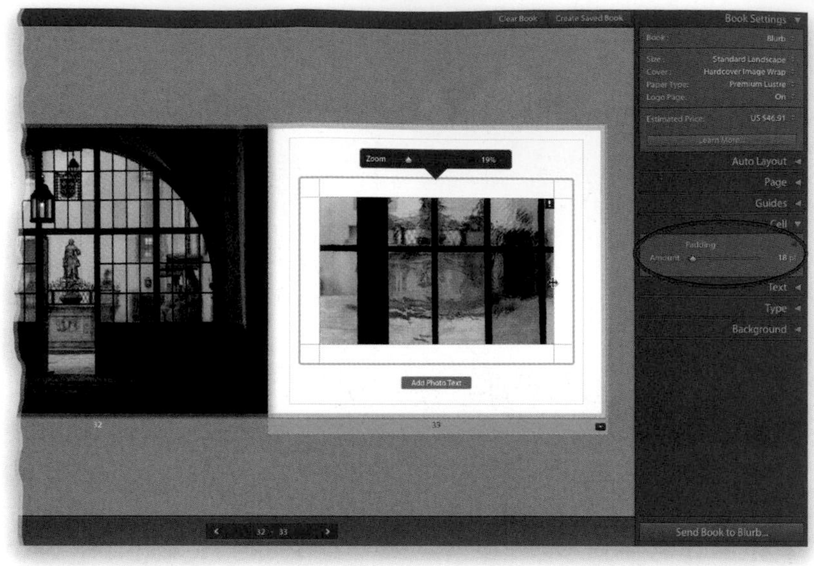

TIP: Removing a Photo

To remove a photo from a cell, click on it and hit the **Delete (PC: Backspace) key**. It doesn't delete it from your collection, so you can still find it down in your Filmstrip and drop it onto another a page.

Step 14:

Before we move on, I zoomed back out a bit until the resolution warning went away. Now, if you want to change the background color of your page, go to the Background panel (in the right side Panels area) and turn on the Background Color checkbox. Choose a new color by clicking on the color swatch to the right to bring up the Background Color picker, and click on any of the preset color swatches at the top, or choose any shade from the gradient bar below. To access full colors, click-and-drag the little horizontal bar on the gradient bar on the right upward to at least the middle of the bar to reveal the colors. Now, you can choose any color you'd like for your background.

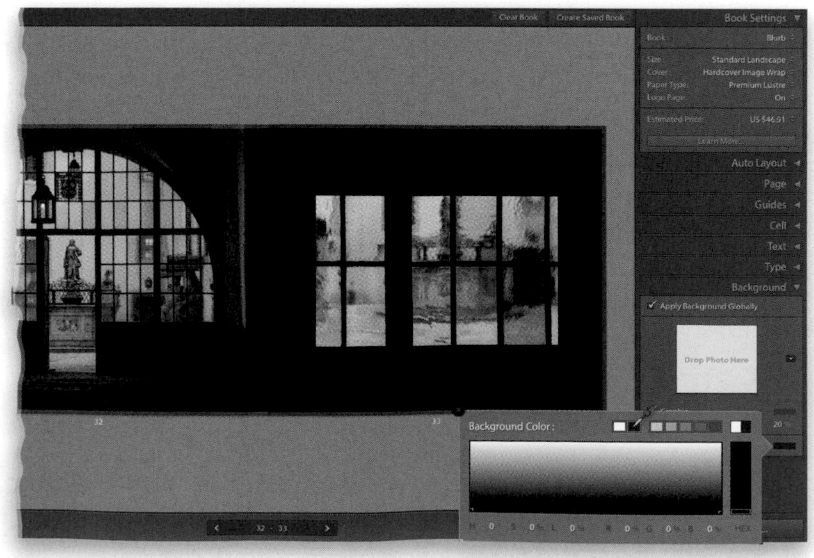

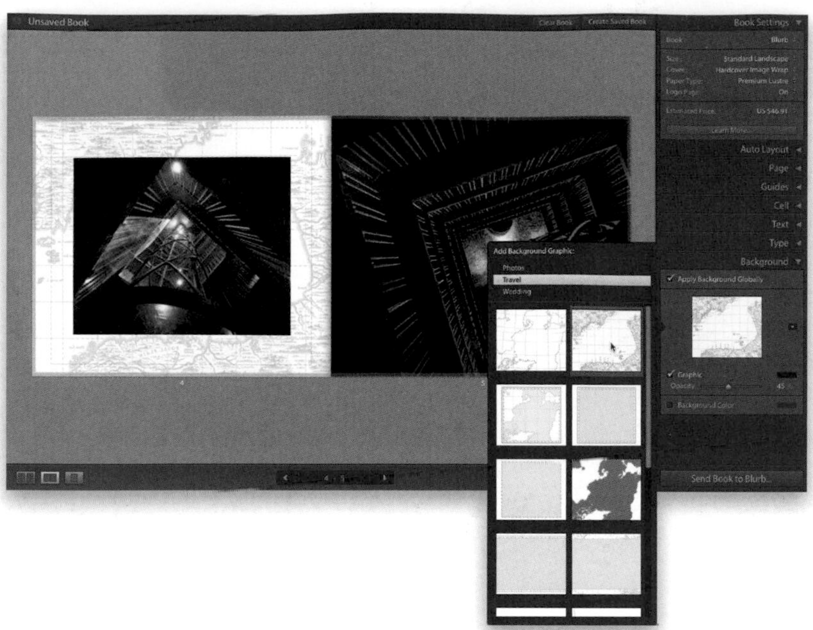

Step 15:

Okay, I am seriously sick of seeing this same two-page spread (I'm sure you are, too), so for the sake of variety (and our mutual sanity), I'm changing pages for the rest of this Background panel stuff (and resizing the photo on the left page). Besides just a solid color for your background, you can also choose from a collection of built-in background graphics, including one for travel with things like maps and page borders, and one for weddings with elegant little page ornaments. To get to these, turn on the Graphic checkbox in the Background panel, then to the right of the square background graphic well in the center of the Background panel, click the little black button to bring up the Add Background Graphic menu, with a thumbnail list of built-in backgrounds (as seen here). Just click on the category at the top, then scroll down to the graphic you want to use, click on it, and it appears behind your photo (as seen here). You can control how light/dark the graphic appears using the Opacity slider near the bottom of the panel.

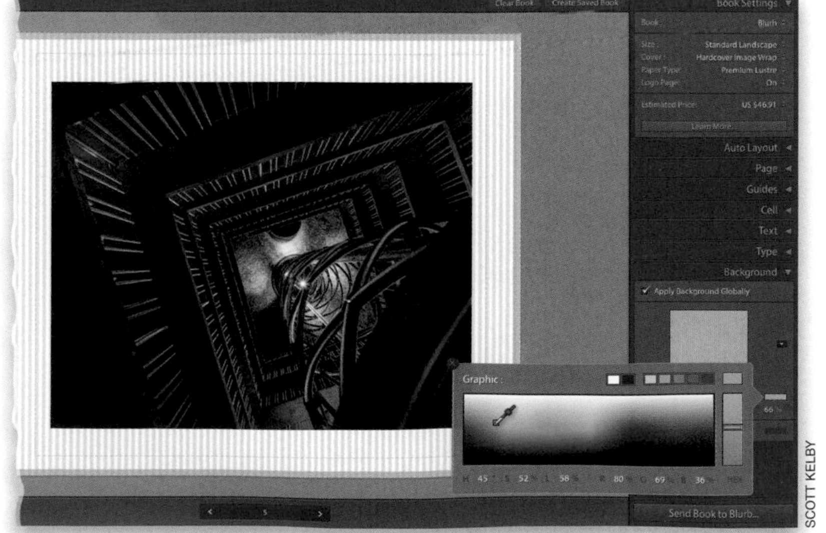
SCOTT KELBY

Step 16:

If you want a pattern, rather than ornaments, you can add vertical lines, and better yet, you get to choose their color. (By the way, I switched to the Single-Page View here, so you can see what's going on a little better.) First, go to the Travel category and choose the lines background from the pop-up menu, set its Opacity (lightness or darkness), then click on the color swatch to the right of the Graphic checkbox to bring up the Graphic color picker (seen here). Choose any color you'd like for your graphic (I chose a yellow color here, and I increased the Opacity to 66% to make it more visible).

Continued

Step 17:

There is one more Background option, but before we get to that, look up at the top of the Background panel and you'll find a checkbox that repeats your current background throughout the entire book (if that's what you want. It saves you the time of adding a background manually to every single page). Okay, now on to the last option: using a photo as a background (very popular in wedding albums). Start by turning off the Graphic checkbox, then in the Filmstrip, find the photo you want to use as a background, and drag-and-drop it onto the square background graphic well in the center of the Background panel (as shown here) and that photo becomes your page background. I usually like this background photo to be very light behind my main photo (so it doesn't compete with it), so I lower the Opacity quite a bit—usually to between 10% and 20%. By the way, to remove your background image altogether, Right-click on the background graphic well and choose **Remove Photo**.

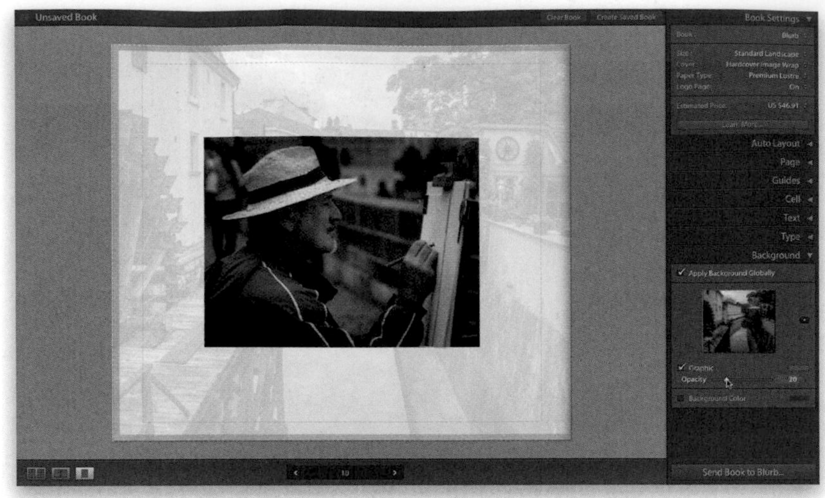

SCOTT KELBY

Step 18:

Okay, now I want to show you another of my favorite book features—having one photo appear all the way across a two-page spread. This really adds a lot of impact to a book, and I usually include at least two or three two-page spreads like this per photo book. To create one, click on the photo page that you want to make a two-page spread, then click the Change Page Layout button in the bottom-right corner of the page to get the Modify Page menu, and choose **Two-Page Spreads**. This brings up a scrolling list of different layouts (the top one is a full-bleed—all the way to the edges—the next puts a small border around it, and the rest are really cool, as well. Some cover 2/3 of the two pages, leaving room for text). For this project, we'll choose the full-bleed template.

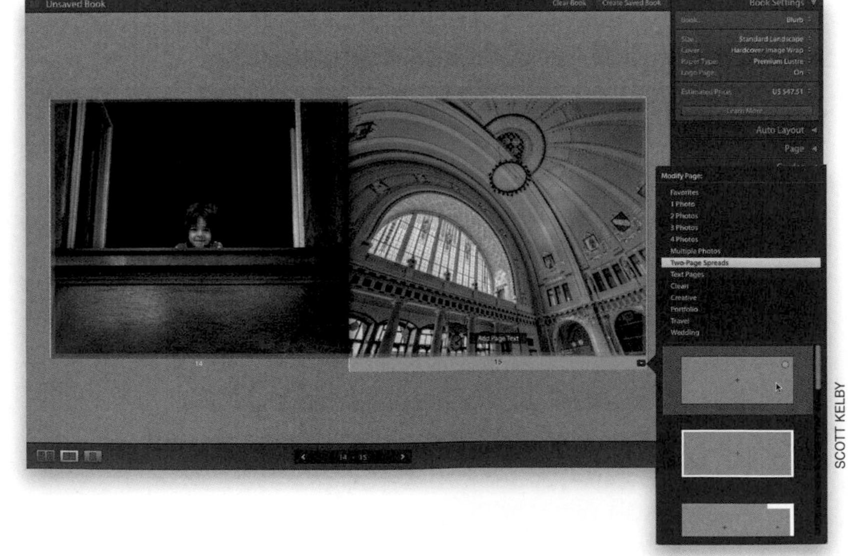

SCOTT KELBY

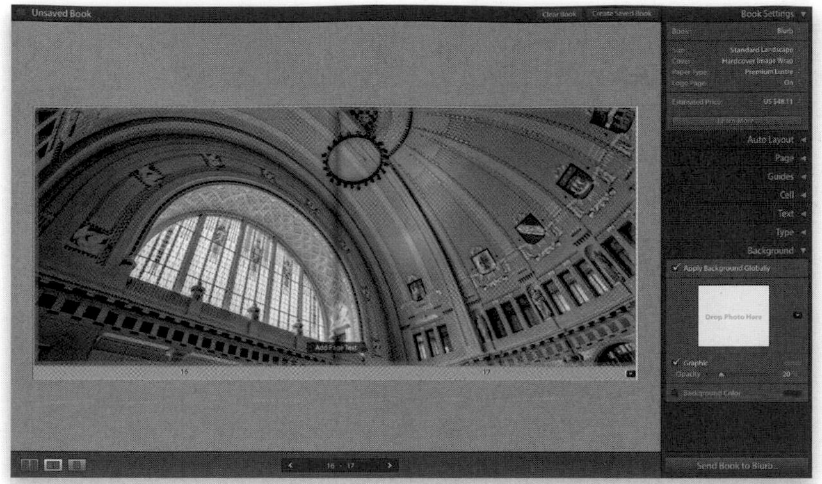

Step 19:

Once you make your two-page spread template choice, the photo on the second page moves to the next page and your photo now extends across two pages, and Lightroom simulates where the page break will appear in the center of the two-page spread. If you want to be able to reposition your photo on the two pages, you may have to zoom in a bit, so click on the photo to bring up the Zoom slider. Drag the slider to zoom it until the photo size looks good to you (don't forget to keep an eye out for the resolution warning in the upper-right corner of the photo, which you get if you zoom in too far). Once you zoom in, you can position your photo by just clicking-and-dragging directly on the photo (as I did here, where I clicked-and-dragged downward a bit. *Note:* I know we haven't covered text yet. I thought it needed its own separate pages, so that's coming shortly in the next technique.

SCOTT KELBY

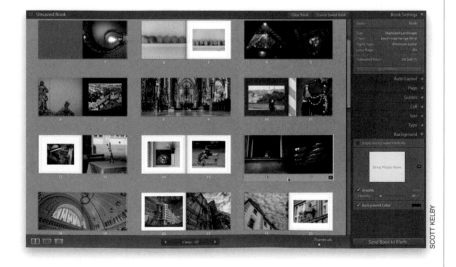

Step 20:

At this point, I work on getting everything into the final order I want, moving spreads around in the Multi-Page View, so the book flows in the order I want (by the way, the shortcut to get to this Multi-Page View is **Command-E [PC: Ctrl-E]**). To move a two-page layout, click on the first page (the left page), press-and-hold the Shift key, and then click on the right page to select it, as well. Now (this is important), click on the bottom of the two selected pages—where the page numbers are—then drag-and-drop the two-page spread anywhere you want in the book. If you don't click in that lower page-number area, it will think you want to move an individual photo. So, at this point, it's time to put the spreads in the final order you want them by dragging-and-dropping them into place.

Continued

Step 21:

Before we actually buy our book, I wanted to let you know about one more layout feature, even though I don't use it (it makes things look too cluttered to me, but you might find it useful): turning on/off visual guides. You turn on/off these non-printing guides in the Guides panel in the right side Panels area. There are four types of guides: (1) Page Bleed, so you see the small area on the very outside edge of your page that will be cropped off if you choose to have a photo fill the page. It's perfectly fine, and they only crop off around 1/8", so you won't even notice it. (2) The Text Safe Area guide shows the area where you can add text without it getting lost in the gutter between spreads or being too close to the outside edges. (3) The Photo Cells guide is the one that appears when you click on a photo anyway, so I leave that off for sure, and lastly, (4) the Filler Text guide only appears if you choose a layout with text, and it puts a word(s) in place so you know where to type.

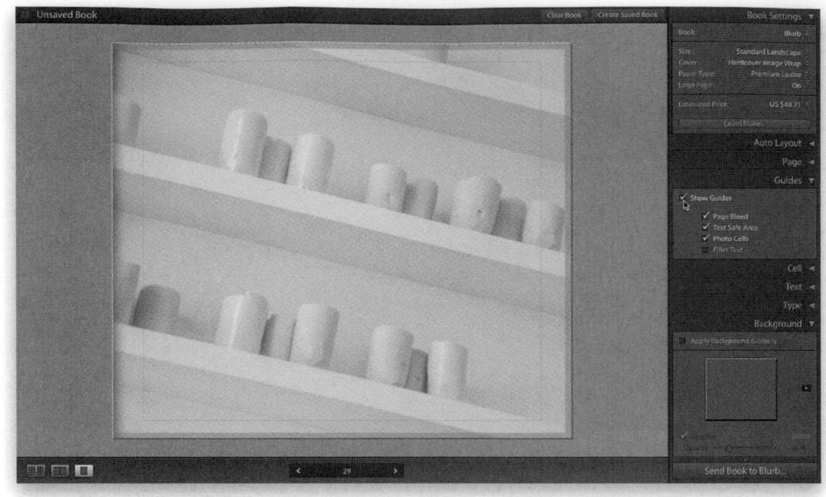

SCOTT KELBY

Step 22:

When everything looks just the way you want it (make sure to check for typos), it's time to: (a) send the book to Blurb, or (b) save the book as a PDF or JPEG and have it printed wherever you'd like. You do all of this in the topmost panel—Book Settings. At the top, you choose either to print to Blurb, or make a PDF or JPEG (it creates an individual JPEG of each page). If you choose Blurb, you then choose your Paper Type and whether you'll let them add a Blurb logo page to the end of the book (if you do, they give you a discount). Below that, it gives you the estimated price for your book. If you choose PDF or JPEG, instead you choose the quality of the photos (I use 80), the color profile (many photo labs recommend sRGB), the resolution (I set mine to 240 ppi), the sharpening strength, and the type of paper (I use High and Glossy).

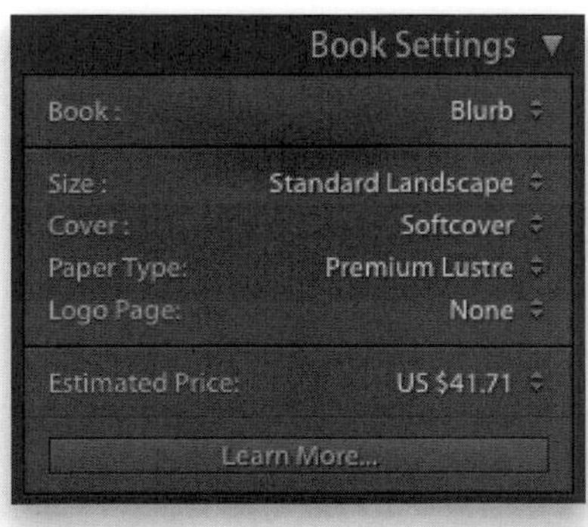

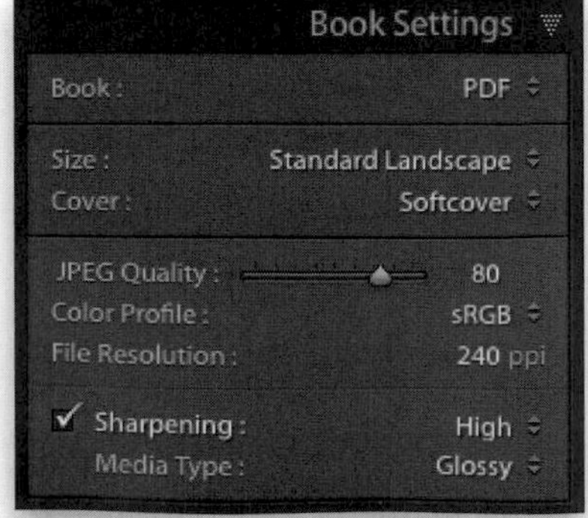

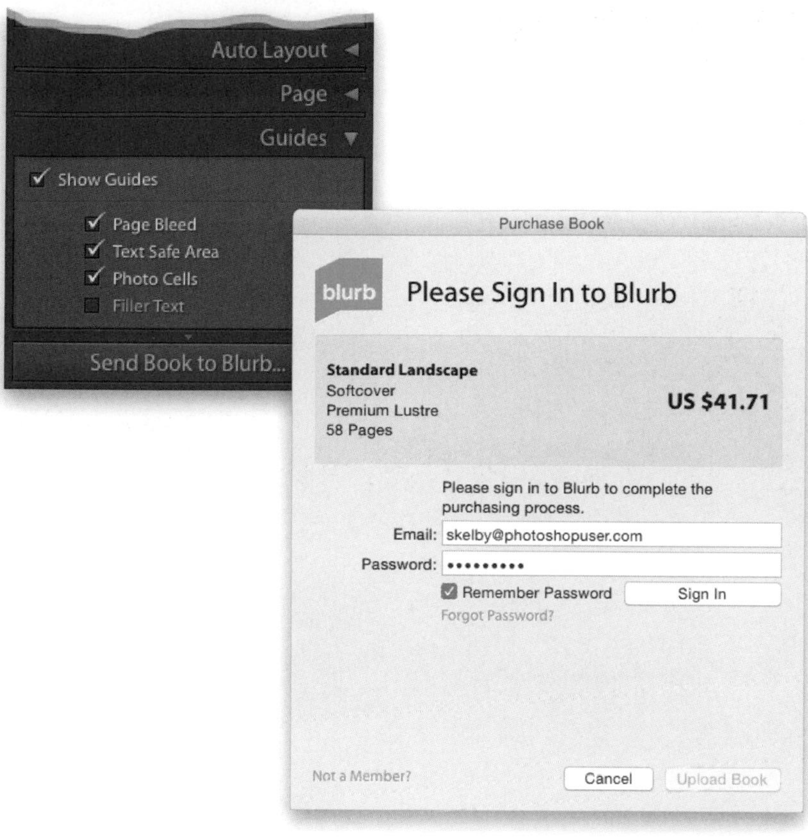

Step 23:

If you choose to have your book printed directly from Lightroom to Blurb, then you've got one more step: go to the bottom of the right side Panels area and click the Send Book to Blurb button (shown at left). This brings up the Purchase Book dialog, where you sign into your Blurb account (if you don't have one, you can set one up for free—click the Not a Member button in the bottom left). Once you log in, choose a Book Title, Book Subtitle (if any), and add the author's name (you, presumably), then click the Upload Book button. In a few days, your book will arrive (as shown below—my Blurb-printed version of the book).

TIP: The Numbers Above the Filmstrip Thumbnails

If you see a number (like 1 or 2) above an image in the Filmstrip, that's letting you know that photo has been placed into the book and how many times it has been used.

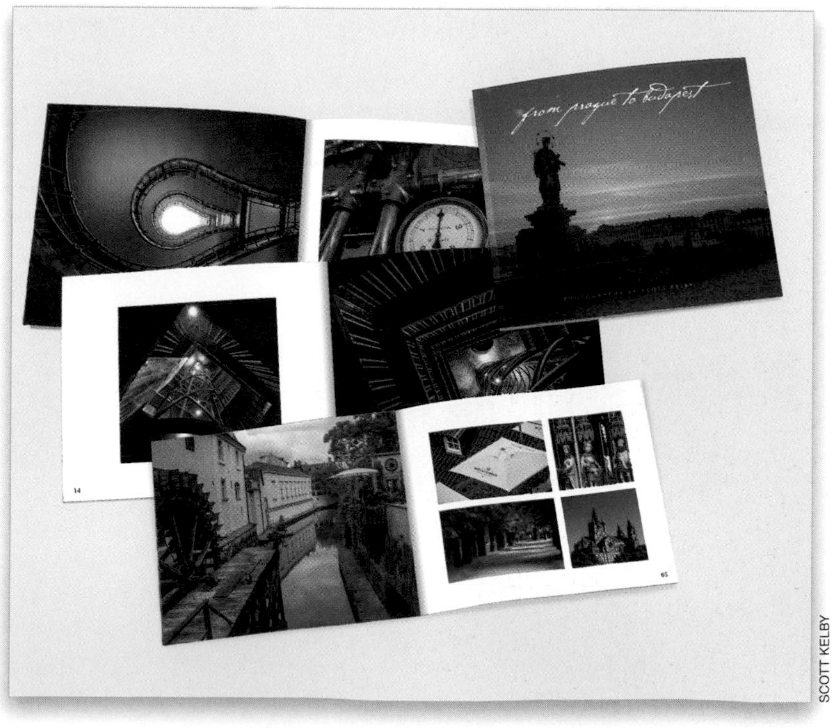

SCOTT KELBY

Step 24:

Now, before you do anything else, let's save your book (in case you want to make more of these later) by clicking on the Create Saved Book button at the top right of the Preview area. This saves your book layout to the Collections panel, so it's saved and just one click away. Okay, that's it—you've created your first book. If you noticed that we didn't go into adding text to your photo book, that's because there are a number of type features, so I thought we should go in-depth into them, and we do—starting on the next page.

Adding Text and Captions to Your Photo Book

If you've been using Lightroom for a while, you know the text capabilities have been really limited. But, when it came to books, Adobe added their full-featured type engine right into the Book module, so you have a surprising amount of control over how your type looks and where you can put it. Now, if we can only get them to put a copy of the Book module's type feature over into the Slideshow and Print modules (don't get me started).

Step One:

There are two ways to add text to your photo book: (1) Choose a page layout that has a text area already in place, so all you have to do is click in the text box and start typing. Or, (2) you can add a text caption to any page by going to the Text panel (in the right side Panels area) and turning on the Photo Text checkbox, as shown here. Now you'll see a yellow horizontal text box appear across the bottom of your image. To add your caption, just click and start typing.

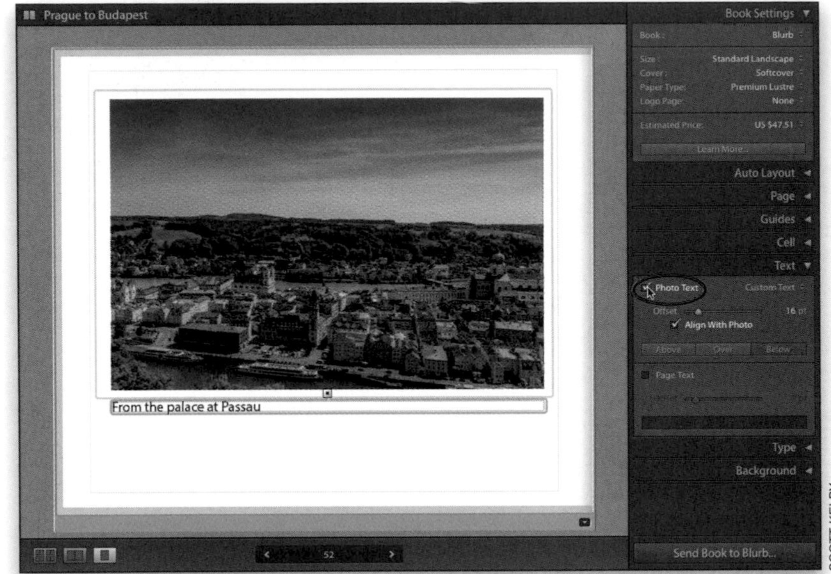

SCOTT KELBY

Step Two:

The Align with Photo checkbox keeps your caption aligned with your photo when you add padding to the photo's cell. So, as you shrink your photo within the cell, your caption will shrink within its cell, too. You can tweak exactly how far away your caption is from your photo using the Offset slider—the farther you drag it to the right, the farther away the text moves from your image (as seen here). *Note:* If you want to have Lightroom select a text box for you, go under the Edit menu and choose Select All Text Cells (this is handy if you have a page with three photos and three captions, and you want to turn all the captions off—just choose Select All Text Cells and then turn the Photo Text checkbox off to hide them from view).

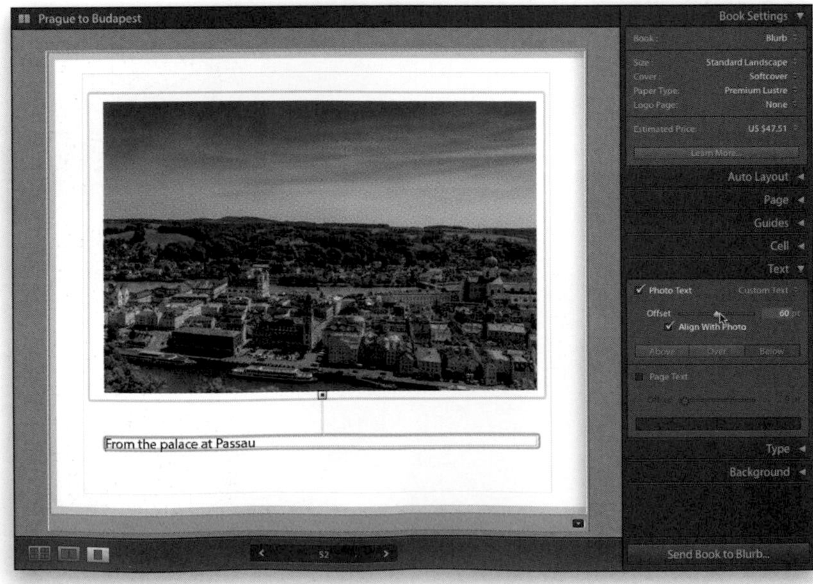

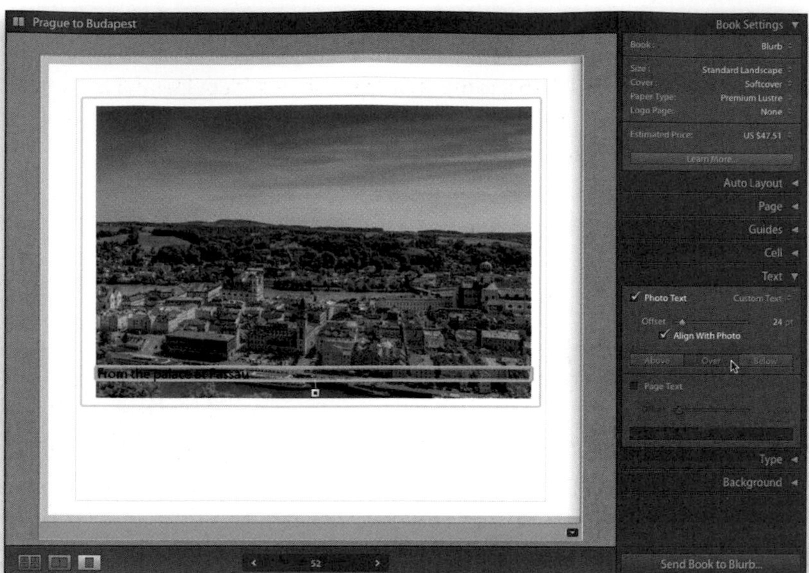

Step Three:

You also have the choice to move your caption above your photo, or to put your caption right over the photo itself (as seen here) using the three buttons below the Offset slider: Above, Over, and Below. Click the Over button and your text box now appears right over the photo, and the Offset slider controls how high your caption appears over it (as you slide it back and forth, you'll see your caption move up and down the photo). *Note:* If you choose to add a caption to a full-page photo layout, the only option you'll have for placement is Over, since there's no white space above or below the photo to fit a caption.

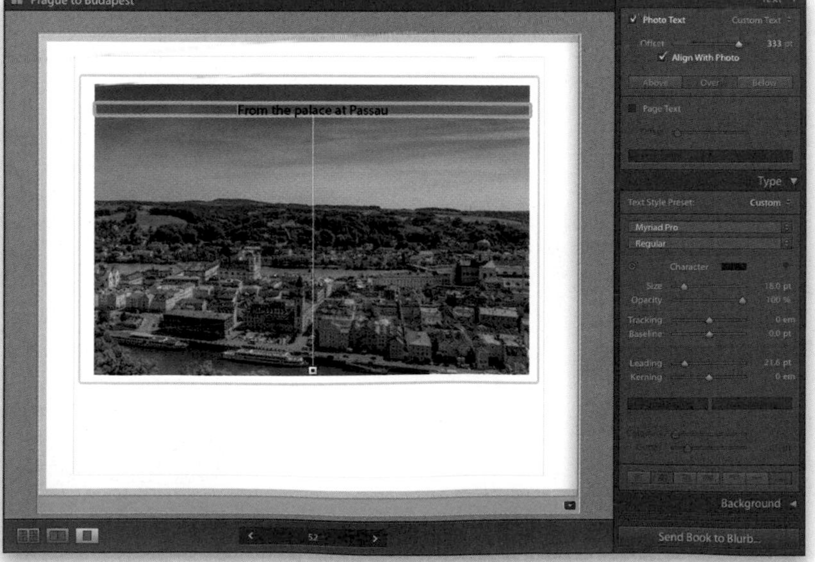

Step Four:

By default, your text is aligned with the left side of your photo, but if you go to the bottom of the next panel down, the Type panel, you'll see alignment buttons—you can choose Align Left, Align Center (as shown here), or Align Right (the fourth choice is Justification, which only comes into play if you're using columns of text). *Note:* If your Type panel doesn't look like this one (you see a lot fewer sliders), then you just need to click on the little black left-facing triangle to the far right of the word "Character" and this expands the panel down to show more options.

Continued

Step Five:

While we're in the Type panel, let's go ahead and highlight our text so we can change the color to white (easier to read over this particular photo) by clicking on the black Character color swatch, and when the Character color picker appears, clicking on the white swatch. Now, click on the Align Left button at the bottom of the Type panel. Look how close the text is to the left edge (it's right on it). If you want to offset that text (scoot it out a little from the edge), there isn't a slider for that. Instead, click off the photo (in that white area around it), then hover your cursor over the left end of the text box and it will change to a two-headed arrow. Now you can click-and-drag your text over to the right a bit (as shown here). *Note:* I have to warn you: getting this two-headed arrow cursor to actually appear may take a few tries. It's, shall we say, "finicky." You can also use it to drag the text box up/down by moving it over the top/bottom of the text box. Again, finicky though.

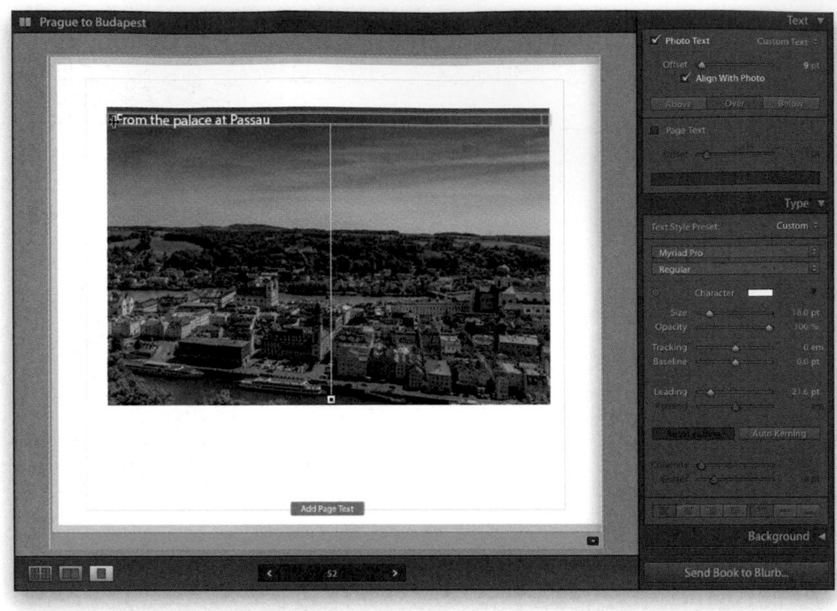

Step Six:

All the other standard controls that you'd expect for working with type are here (like Size, Opacity, and Leading [the space between two lines of text]), but there are also some more advanced type controls that I didn't expect (like Tracking [the space between all the letters in a word], Kerning [the space between two individual letters], and Baseline [shifting a letter or number above or below the line the text sits on—helpful for writing things like H_2O]). And, of course, you can choose your Font and Style (bold, italic, and so on) from the menus near the top. But, at the top is a very handy thing—Text Style presets, which are already set up using popular fonts and styles. So, if you're working on a travel book and choose Caption - Serif, you get a font style that's appropriate for travel photo books. A nice time saver.

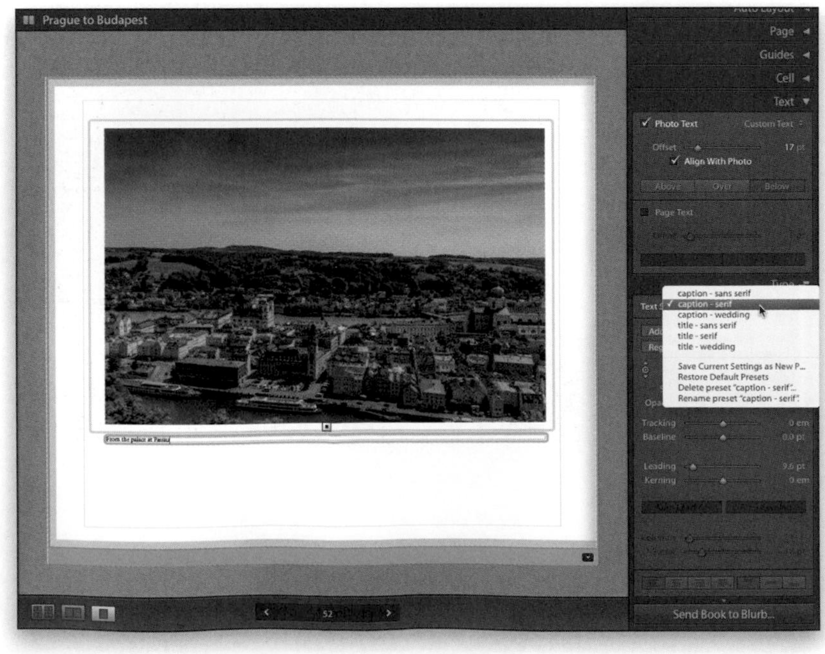

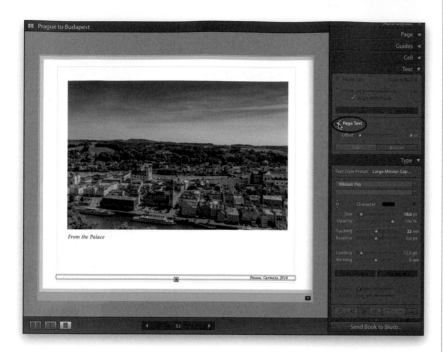

Step Seven:

While we're talking presets: if you tweak your text and like it, you can save the settings as a preset (choose **Save Current Settings as New Preset** from the Text Style Preset pop-up menu). That way, next time you don't have to start from scratch. If you'd like to add another line of text (besides your caption), go back to the Text panel and turn on Page Text (as shown here). This adds another line of text, lower down the page (you can control how far below the photo it appears using the Offset slider, just like the Photo Text). Of course, you can use the Type panel to choose your font, alignment, and all that stuff just like usual, but remember to highlight your text first.

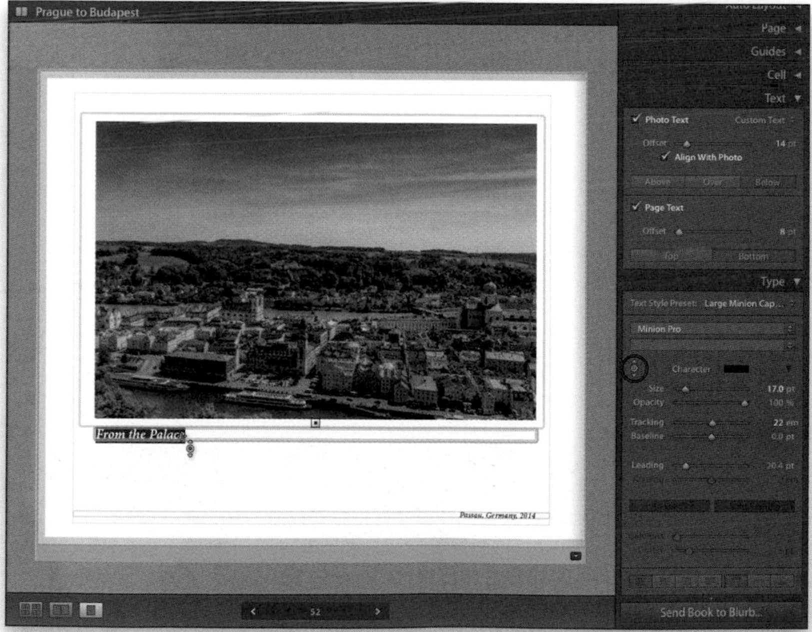

Step Eight:

If you'd like a more visual approach to your type tweaks (rather than dragging sliders or choosing numbers), then click on the Targeted Adjustment tool (TAT, for short—it's circled in red here). Now you can click-and-drag on your highlighted text to change the Size or Leading. Just move your cursor directly over your text, and click-and-drag up/down to control the space between two lines of text (Leading) or drag left/right to control the Size of your type (that's what I'm doing here). Honestly, I don't find myself using the TAT for Type tasks—it seems easier and faster to just move the sliders, but hey, that's just me. So, that's the scoop on adding captions and text to your photo book. *Note:* If you chose a layout where you can add a lot of text, you can split that text into multiple columns using the Columns slider at the bottom of the Type panel. The Gutter slider controls the amount of space between your columns—dragging to the right increases the amount of space between them.

Adding and Customizing Page Numbers

Another nice Book module feature in Lightroom is automatic page numbering. You have the ability to control the position, the formatting (font, size, etc.), and even which page the numbering starts on (along with how to hide the page numbers on blank pages if you want).

Step One:

To turn on page numbering, go to the Page panel and turn on the Page Numbers checkbox (shown circled here in red). By default, it places page numbers in the bottom-left corner of left pages and bottom-right of right pages.

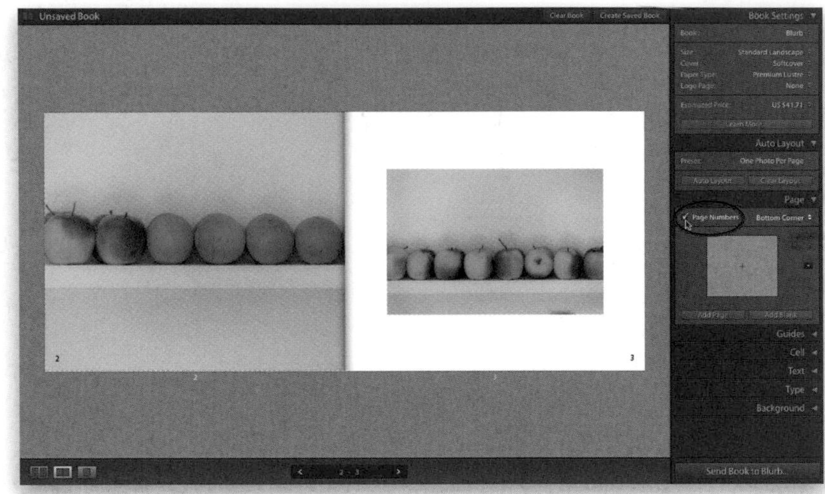

Step Two:

You can choose where you'd like them to appear using the pop-up menu to the right of the Page Numbers checkbox. The Top and Bottom options center the page number at the top or bottom of the page (respectively; as shown here, where I moved them to the bottom center). Choosing Side places the page number at the outside center of the page and, obviously, choosing Top Corner will move it to the top corner of the page.

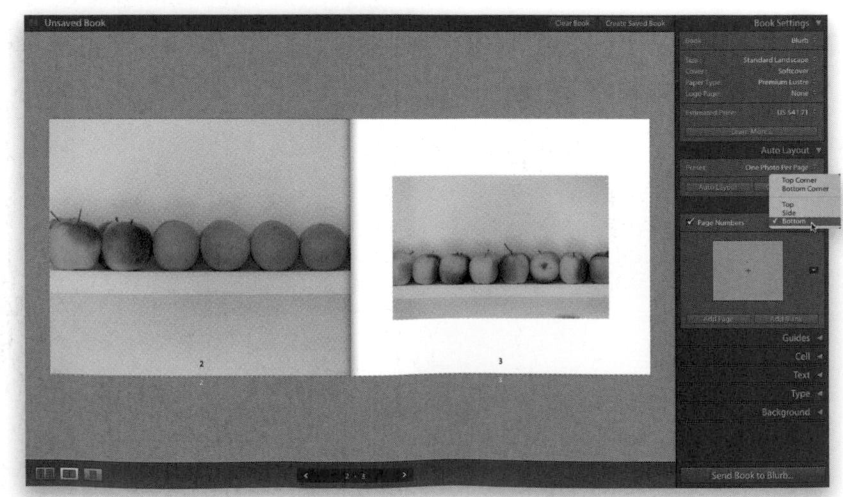

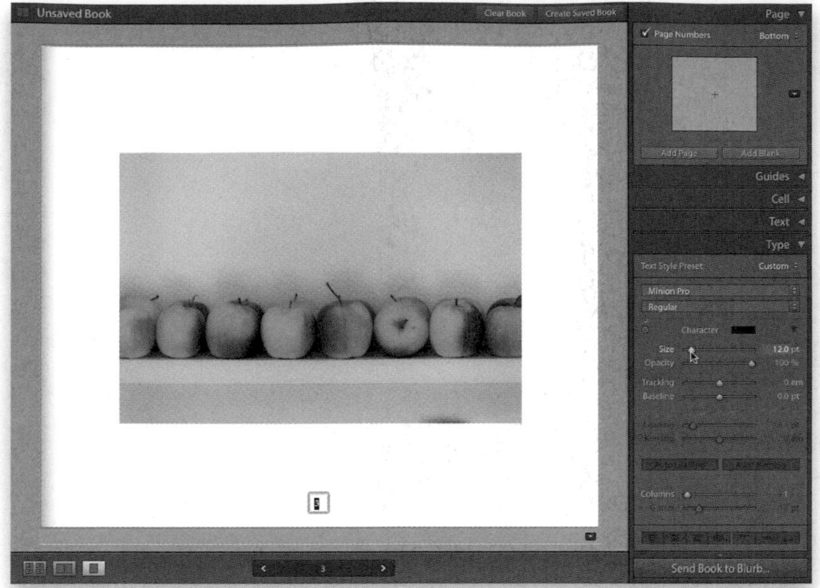

Step Three:

Once your numbers are visible, you can format them (choosing a custom font, size, etc.) by clicking on any page number, then going to the Type panel and choosing how you want them to appear (here, I changed the font to Minion Pro and I lowered the Size to 12 pt).

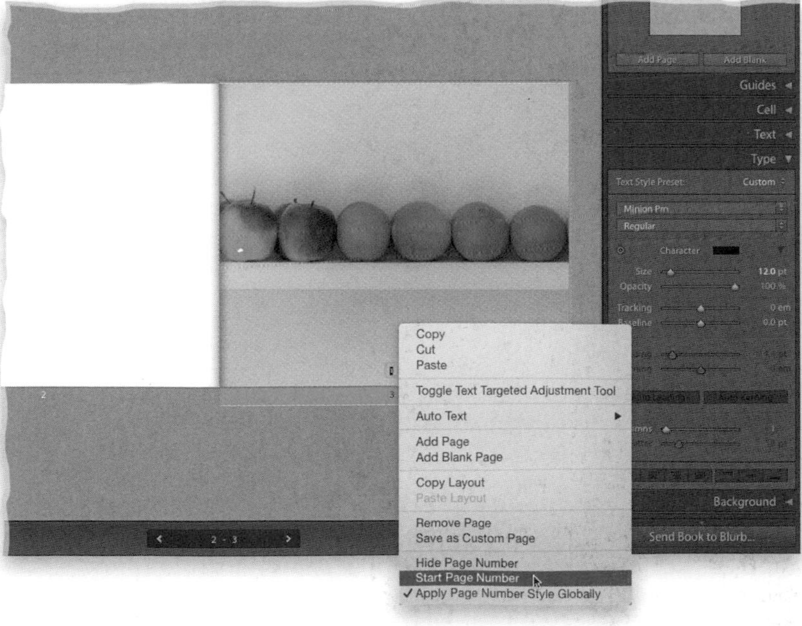

Step Four:

Besides just customizing their look, you can also choose which page the numbering starts on. For example, if the first page of your photo book is blank (so the images or opening story start on a right page), you can have that right page become page 1 by Right-clicking directly on the page number itself on the right page and, from the pop-up menu that appears, choosing **Start Page Number** (as shown here). Lastly, if you have a blank page(s) in your book (maybe all the left pages), and you don't want it to have a printed page number, just Right-click on the number on the blank page, and from the pop-up menu that appears choose **Hide Page Number**.

Four Things You'll Want to Know About Layout Templates

There are a few things about making books in Lightroom that aren't really obvious, so I thought I'd put them all together here so you don't have to go digging for them. It's all easy stuff, but since Adobe likes to sneak some features in "under the radar," or give them names that only Stephen Hawking can figure out, I thought this might keep you from reaching for a pistol. Ya know, metaphorically speaking. ;-)

One: The Advantage of Match Long Edges (and How to Do It Manually)

If you create an Auto Layout preset (see page 377) and choose Zoom Photos to Fit, there's a checkbox for Match Long Edges. With that turned off, if you put a wide photo and a tall photo on the same page, the tall photo will be much larger than the wide photo (as shown here, left). If you turn on Match Long Edges, then it balances the size, even though the two photos have different orientations (as shown here, right). If you didn't use Auto Layout, and you still want that balanced look, just hover your cursor over the corner of the tall image and it changes into a two-headed arrow. Click-and-drag inward to visually shrink the photo until it balances the size.

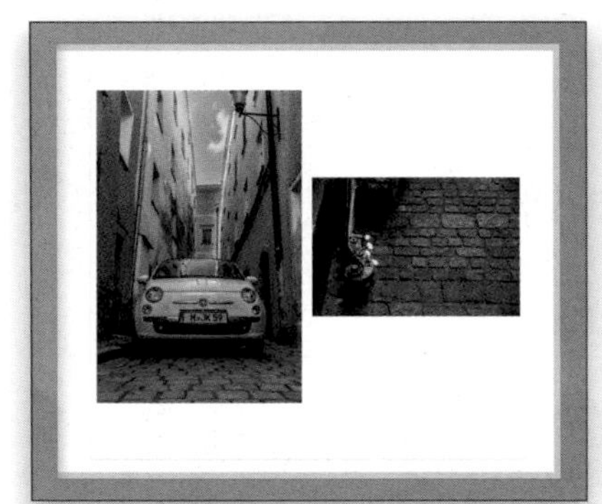

Match Long Edges off looks way out of balance

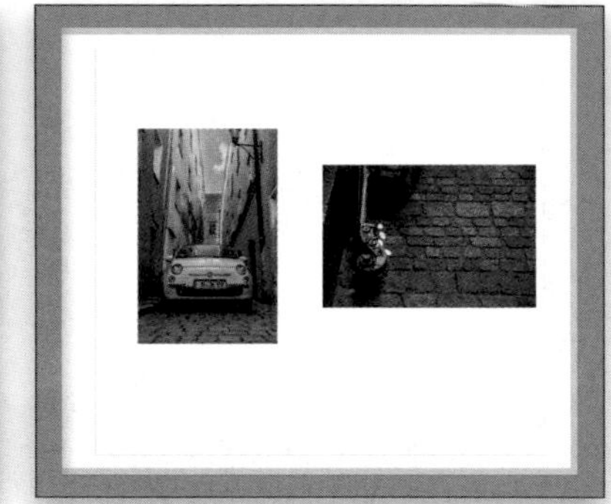

Match Long Edges on sizes it down to look more balanced

Two: Saving Your Favorite Layouts

If you see a layout you like and want to use again (without having to remember where to find it), you can save it to your Favorites at the top of the Modify Page pop-up menu by hovering your cursor over it, then clicking on the little circle that looks like a Quick Collection marker (as shown here). If you change your mind, go to your Favorites, and click on the now-gray circle to turn it off. Also, once you've set up some favorites, if you create an Auto Layout preset, one of the page choices in the Editor will be Random from Favorites—it pulls the layout from ones you like. You even get to choose how many photos per page it includes (that way, if you only want 1- or 2-photo favorites, it'll only use those). Cool!

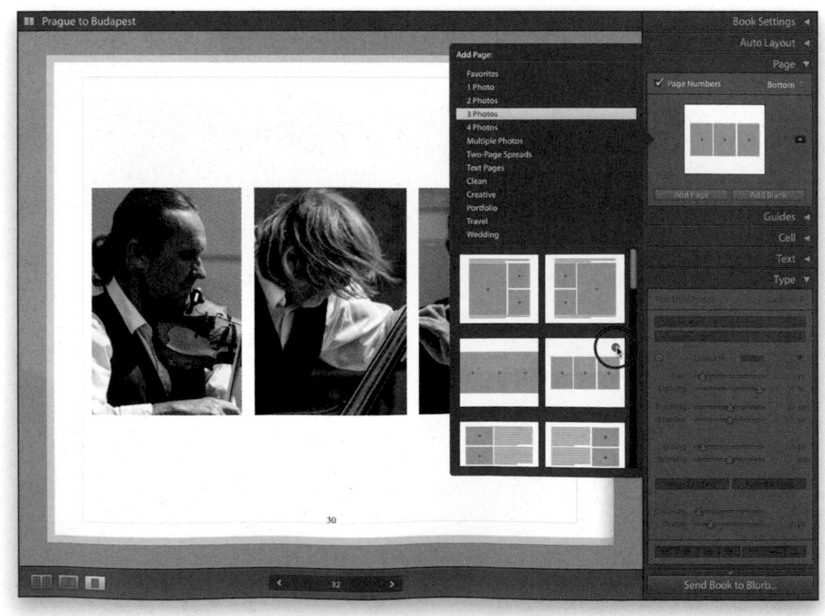

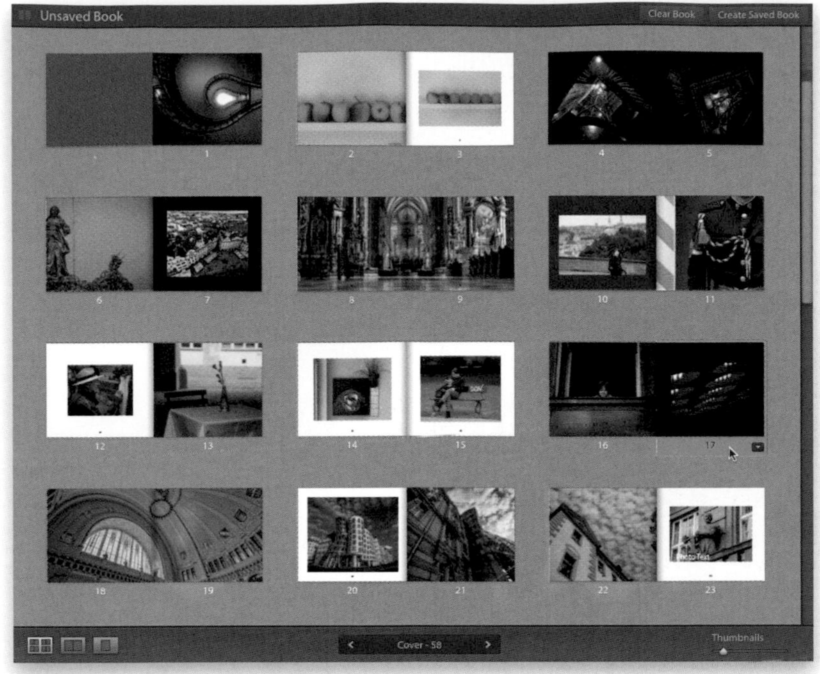

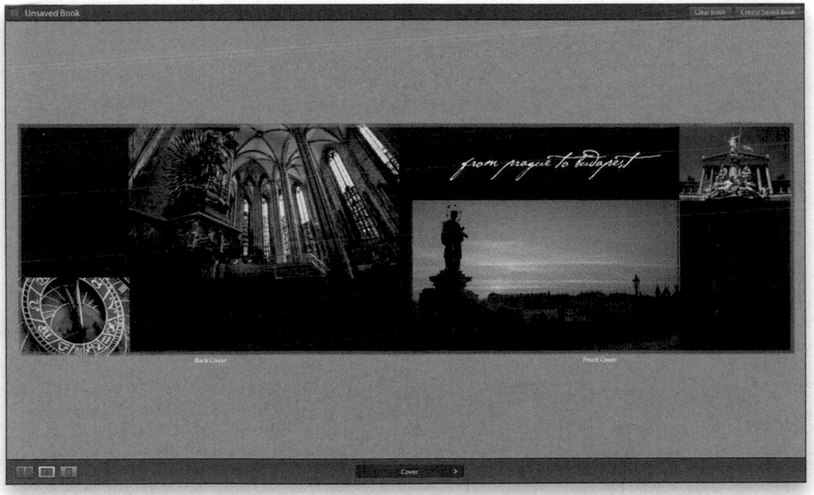

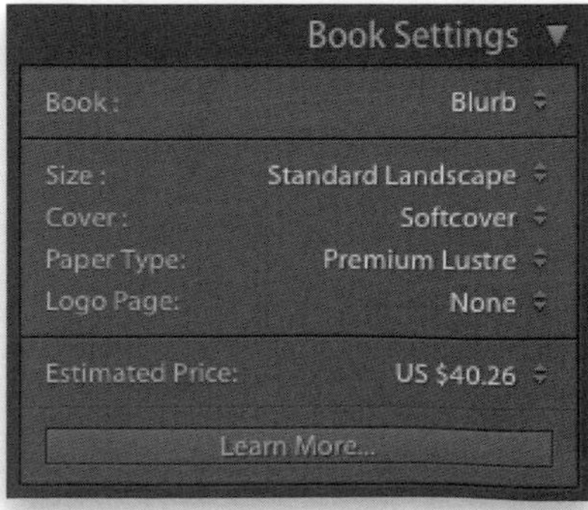

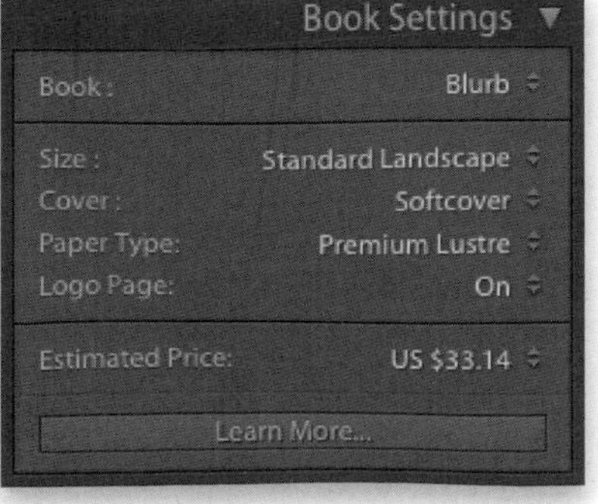

Three: Sorting Pages

You sort pages in Multi-Page View by clicking on the page you want to move to select it, then you click directly on the yellow bar at the bottom where the page number is (as shown here, where I've clicked on page 17), and then you just drag-and-drop that page where you want it in your book. If you want to move a two-page spread, click on the first page to select it, Shift-click on the second page to select it, and then click on either page number area to drag-and-drop the spread to a new location. You can even move groups of pages at once (like pages 10 through 15) by Shift-clicking on those pages to select them, then clicking on any one of the selected pages' yellow bar at the bottom, and dragging them where you want them. By the way, you can swap photos from page to page when you're in the Multi-Page View by just clicking-and-dragging them.

Four: The Front & Back Covers Change If You Choose Dust Jacket

If you choose the Hardcover Dust Jacket cover option for your book, you get to add two extra images on the flaps that fold inside the covers to keep your dust jacket in place (as seen here). You'll only see these side flaps appear if you choose the dust jacket option.

Five: I Know, I Said There Were Only Four, But…

There's one more page you might want to consider in your book: Blurb's logo page, which is the last page in the book. If you let them put their logo at the bottom of the last page, they give you a discount on the price of your book. How much? Well, on this book, the regular price was $40.26 without the logo page. If you turn on the option to allow a logo page (in the Book Settings panel), then the price comes down to $33.14 (that's around a 20% discount for giving them a logo on a page that was going to be blank anyway. Definitely worth considering).

Creating & Saving Your Own Custom Layouts

Back in Lightroom 4, the one Book module feature I really felt was missing was the ability to save your own custom layouts. I mean, technically you could *create* a custom layout, like we did earlier in this chapter (it wasn't really obvious—still isn't), but there was no way to save it to use it again. Sure you could mark some of the ones Adobe created as your favorites, but not ones you created from scratch. Well, until now anyway (whoo hooo!).

Step One:

Start by clicking on an image in your book layout, then click on the Change Page Layout button at the bottom-right corner of the page, and choose 1 Photo, then the full bleed (edge-to-edge) layout preset. The reason we choose this one is because it's the preset that gives us the most flexibility in customizing. Now, click on the outside edge of the page and drag inward a bit, so you can see all the sides of the cell (as shown here).

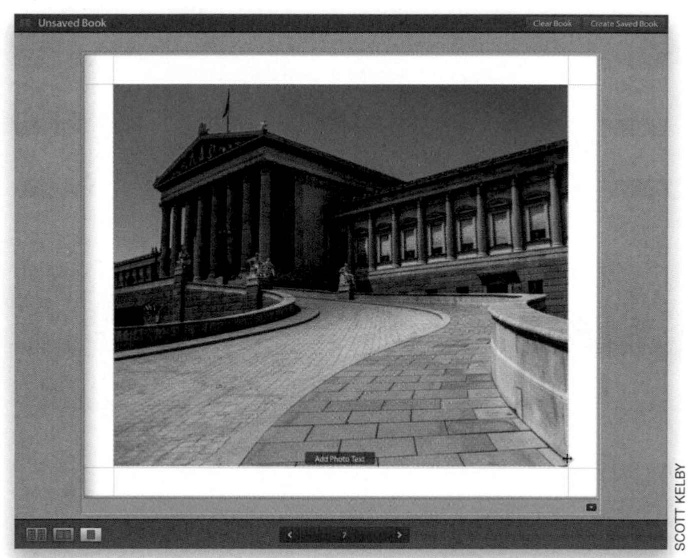

SCOTT KELBY

Step Two:

Go to the Cell panel (in the right side Panels area) and make sure the Link All checkbox is turned off (as seen in the overlay below), so that you can move the cell borders anywhere you'd like, independently of each other. For this page, we want to create more of a panoramic crop for our images, so start by grabbing the bottom cell border and dragging upward (as shown here).

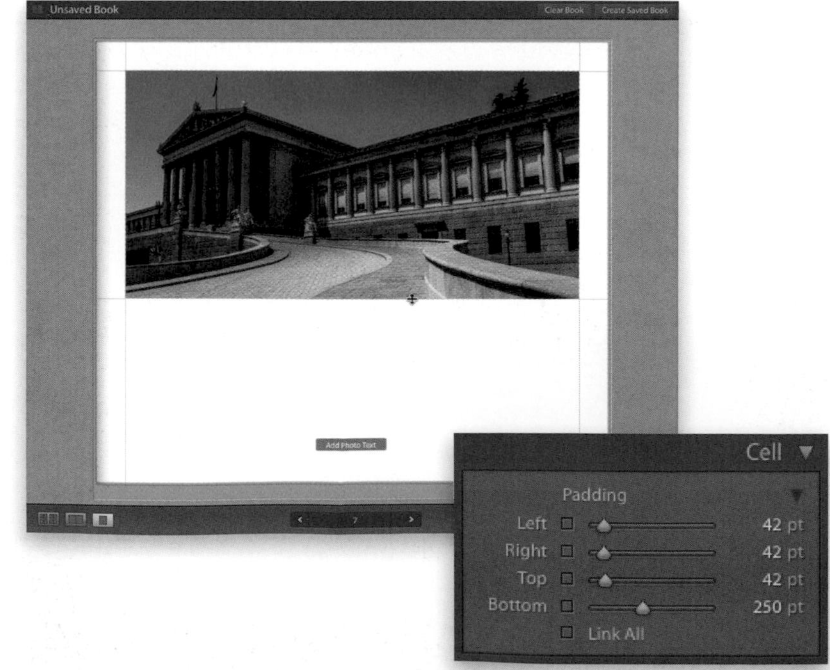

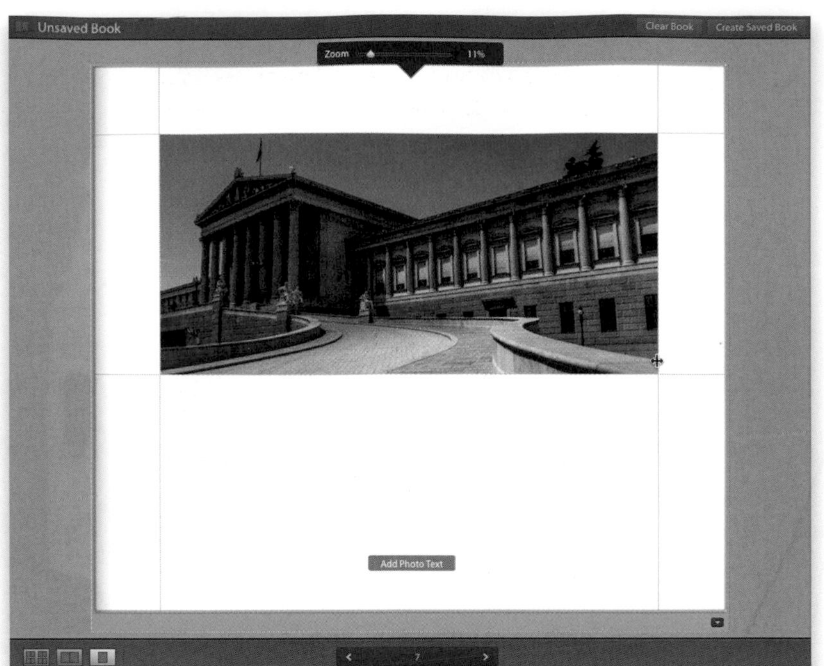

Step Three:

Now tuck in the sides of the cell, and adjust the top and bottom, until the photo layout looks like the pano-like crop you see here.

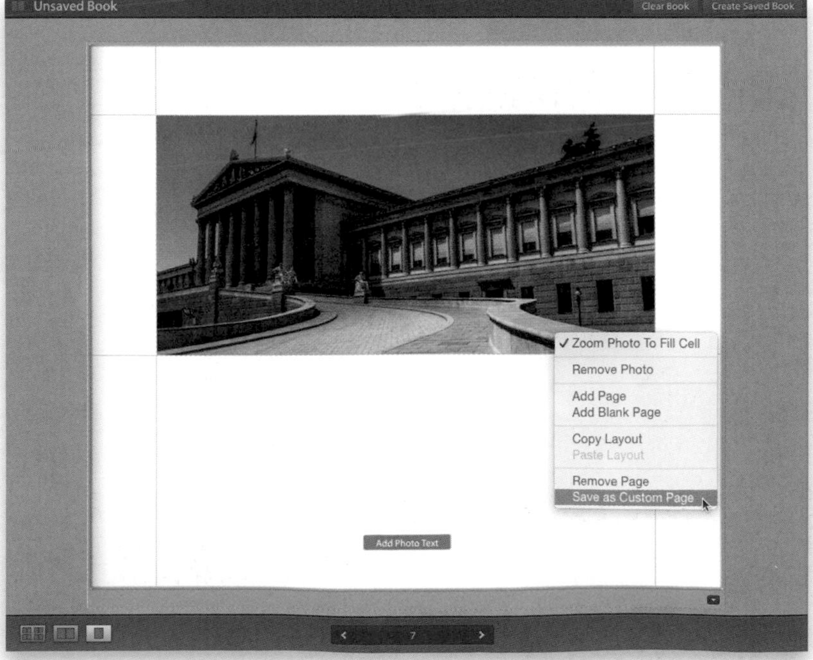

Step Four:

Once you have the page laid out the way you'd like it, Right-click anywhere on the page and from the pop-up menu that appears, choose **Save as Custom Page**. That's all there is to it! Now, on the next page, we'll look at where these custom pages are (and how to use them).

Continued

Step Five:

Click on the Change Page Layout button at the bottom-right corner of your page, and in the Modify Page pop-up menu, near the top, right under Favorites, will be your Custom Pages preset option. Click on it and it shows thumbnails of the custom layouts you've saved (in this case, I've saved three different layouts, the last one being the one we just created).

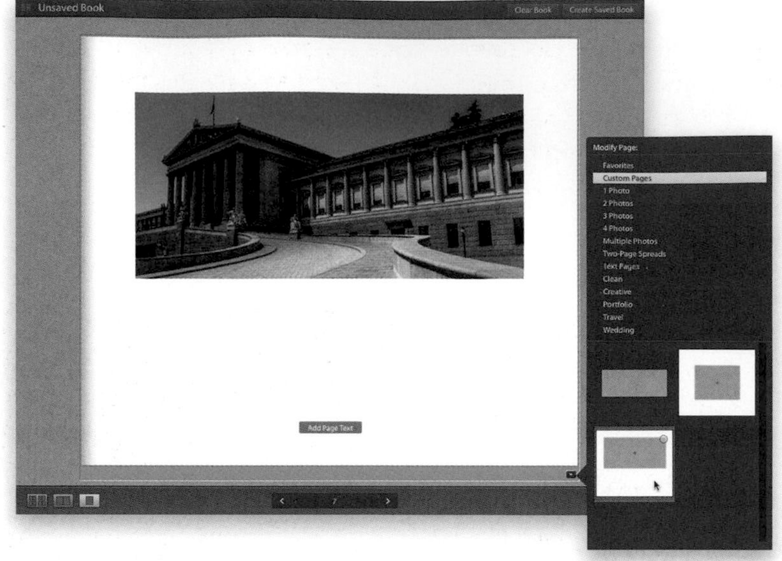

Step Six:

Now, to apply your custom layout to an existing book page, first go to that page (here, I'm going to change the layout of the photo of the man on page 46). Click on the page and then, from the Modify Page pop-menu, click on Custom Pages to see your layout thumbnails at the bottom of the menu, then click on the layout you want to use (as seen here), and that layout is applied to that page (as shown at the bottom here).

Note: Depending on how the original page was laid out (i.e., whether it was set to Fit or Fill), you might have to increase the zoom amount (using the Zoom slider that appears above the image when you click on it), so the image now fills the cell.

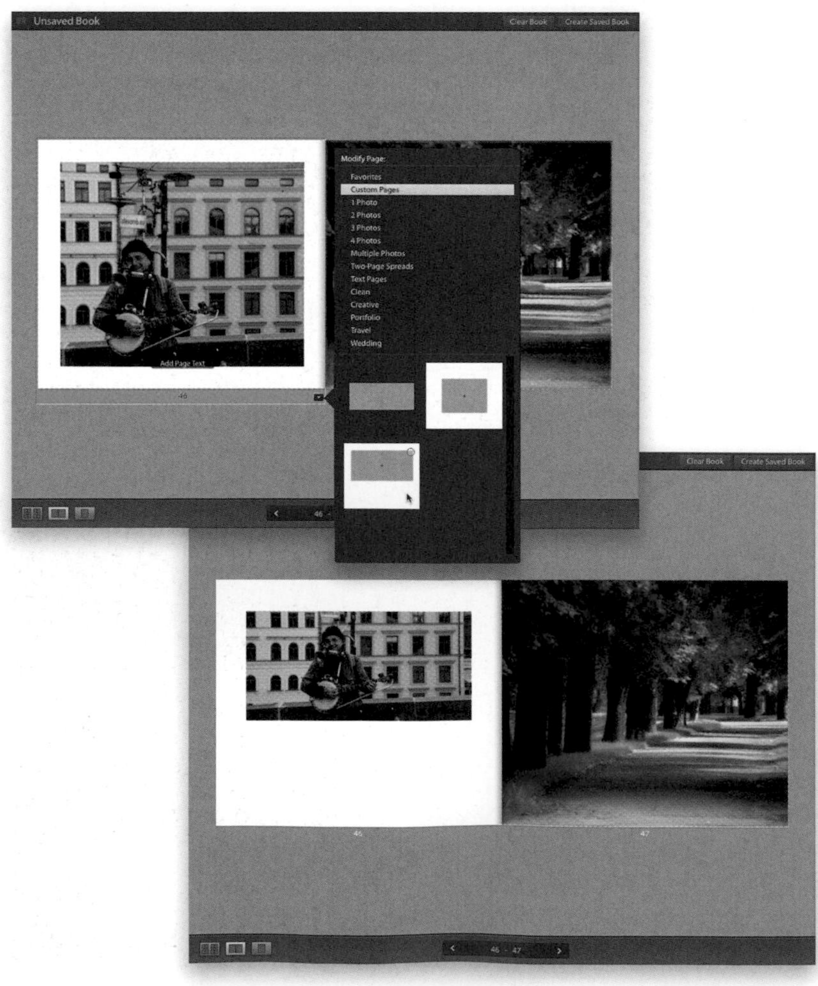

Creating Cover Text

If you want to create your cover text here in Lightroom's Book module, you're in luck, because it's more powerful and flexible than you might think. You can create multiple lines on the cover, different text blocks with different typefaces, and you can even add text to the spine for hardcover wrap layouts.

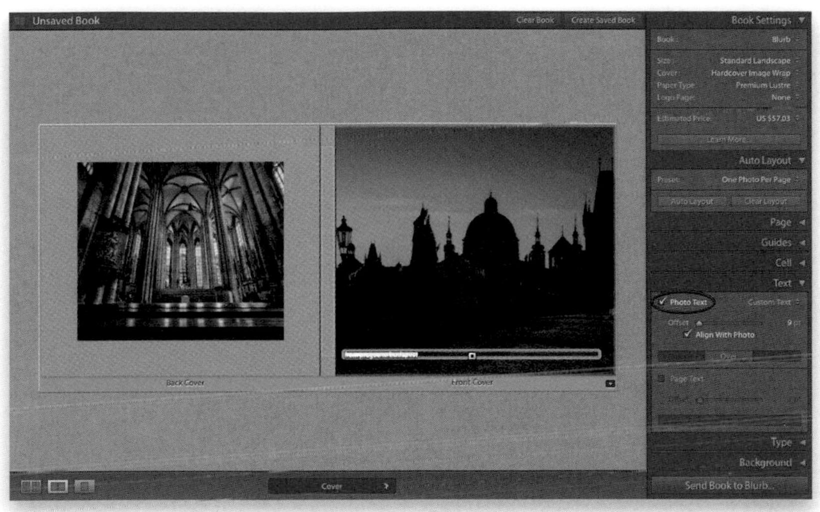

Step One:

Click on the Front Cover page to make it active, and you'll see "Add Photo Text" appear over the bottom center of the image. Click on that and a text block appears at the bottom of your image. Any text you enter in this text block will appear over your image. By the way, if for any reason you don't see the Add Photo Text button, go to the Text panel (in the right side Panels area) and turn on the Photo Text checkbox (as seen circled here) and it will appear. In our case, I typed in "From Prague to Budapest," but it's hard to see because the default type is small and black (don't worry, we'll change that type color in a few moments).

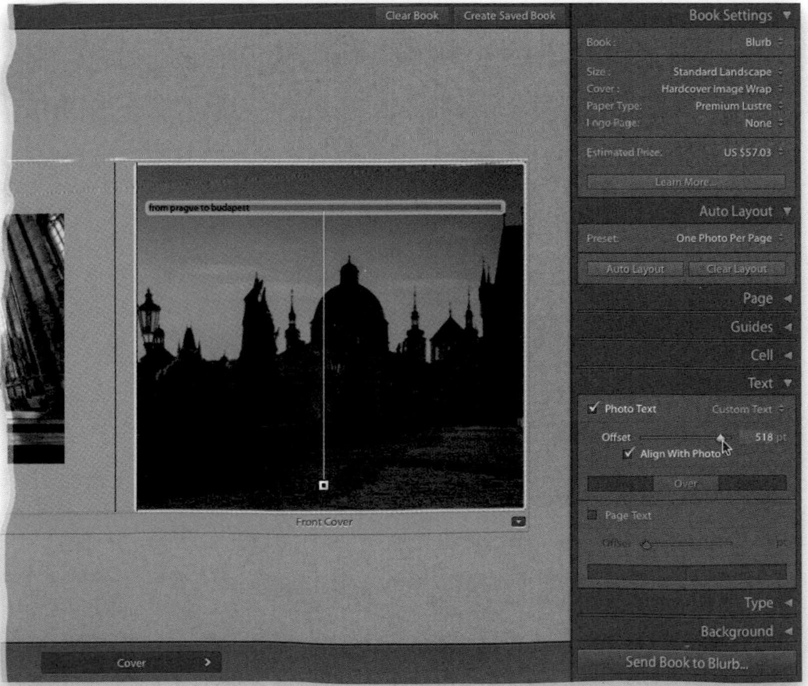

Step Two:

Like I mentioned, by default your text block appears near the bottom of the image, but you can choose how high on the page this text block appears using the Offset slider in the Photo Text section of the Text panel (as shown here). The farther you drag the Offset slider, the farther up that text block moves (as seen here, where I moved it to the top).

Continued

Step Three:

Once you have your text block positioned where you want it, you can control everything from the color of the text to the size, leading (space between two or more lines of type), tracking (the space between all the letters in your text), and even the justification (left, center, right, justified) in the Type panel. This is a pretty darn surprisingly powerful panel, with lots of nice options to make your type look great. We'll start by changing our font and font size. So, click-and-drag over your text to select it, then in the Type panel, choose a font from the first pop-up menu and then adjust the Size (I choose Cezanne at 54 points). If you need to change the color of the type, just click on the Character color swatch to bring up the Character color picker and choose a new color there (we're just going to leave it black here, though).

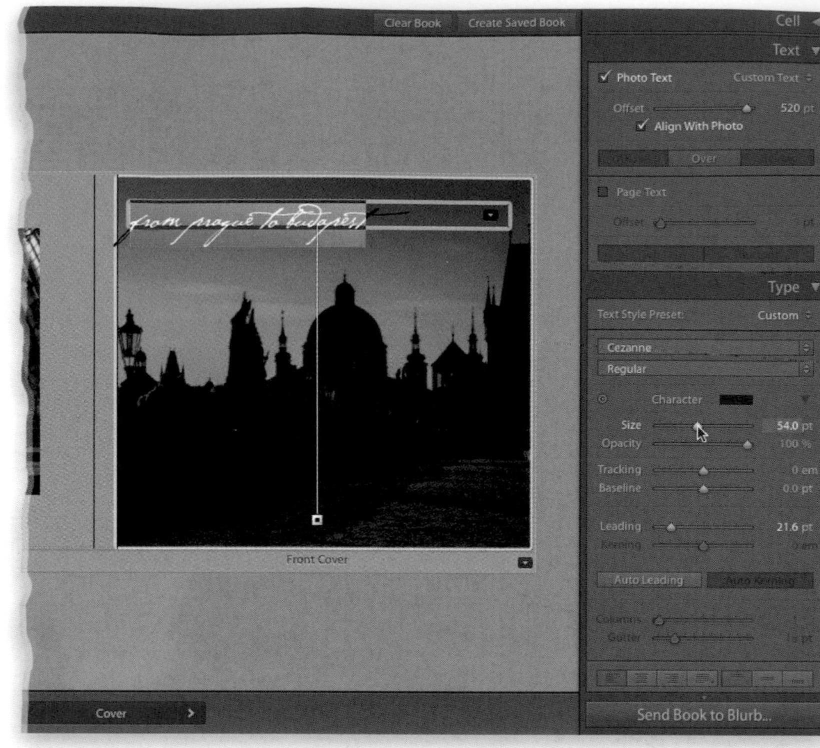

Step Four:

Now, all we have to do is adjust the placement, as needed. Here, I clicked on the Align Center button at the bottom of the panel to move the type in the middle.

TIP: Getting a Second Text Block

If you go back to the Text panel and turn on the Page Text checkbox, you can add a second block of text that you can position and style just like we've done here.

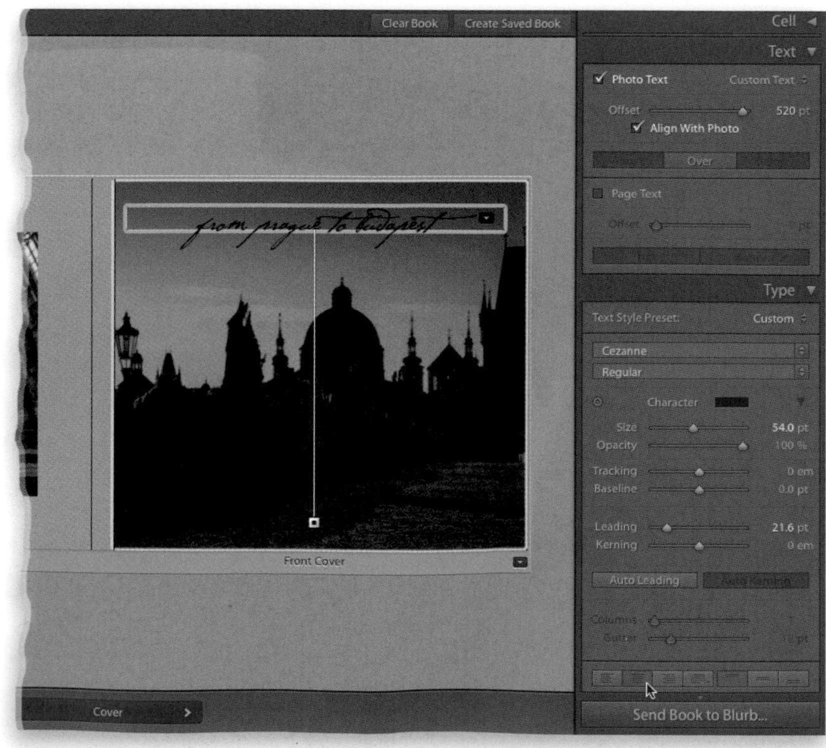

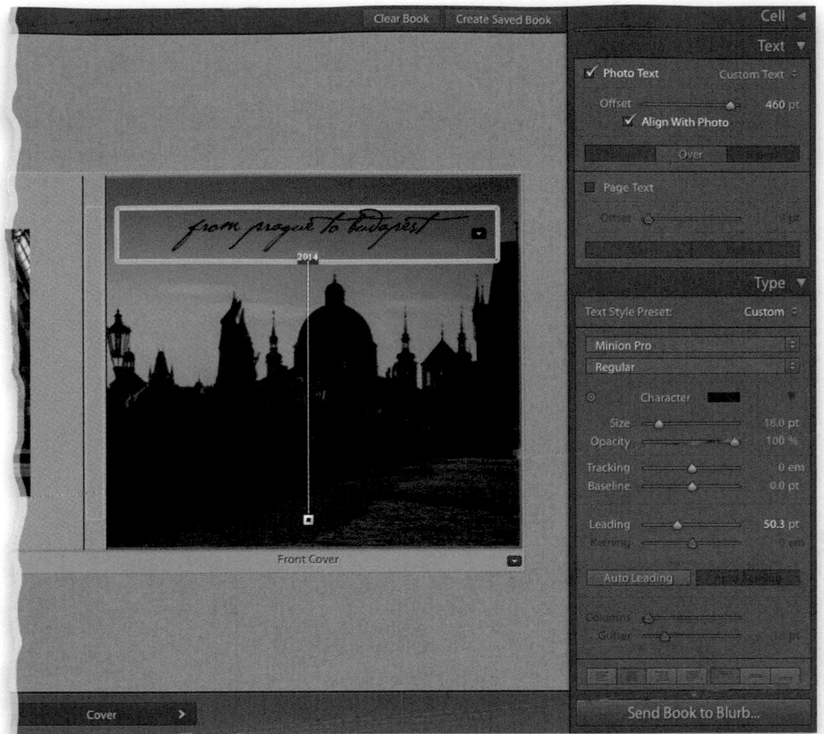

Step Five:

If you want a second line of type in the same text block, just put your cursor after the last letter and hit the Return (PC: Enter) key on your keyboard. The nice thing is this second line can be edited completely separately from the first line, so you can type in your text, select it, then choose a different font (I chose Minion Pro), change the size (I made it 18 points), and you can control the space between the letters using the Tracking slider. I also used the Leading slider (it controls the distance between two lines of text) to add more space between them (here, I increased it to 50.3). Finally, I clicked on the top of the text box and dragged it down a bit.

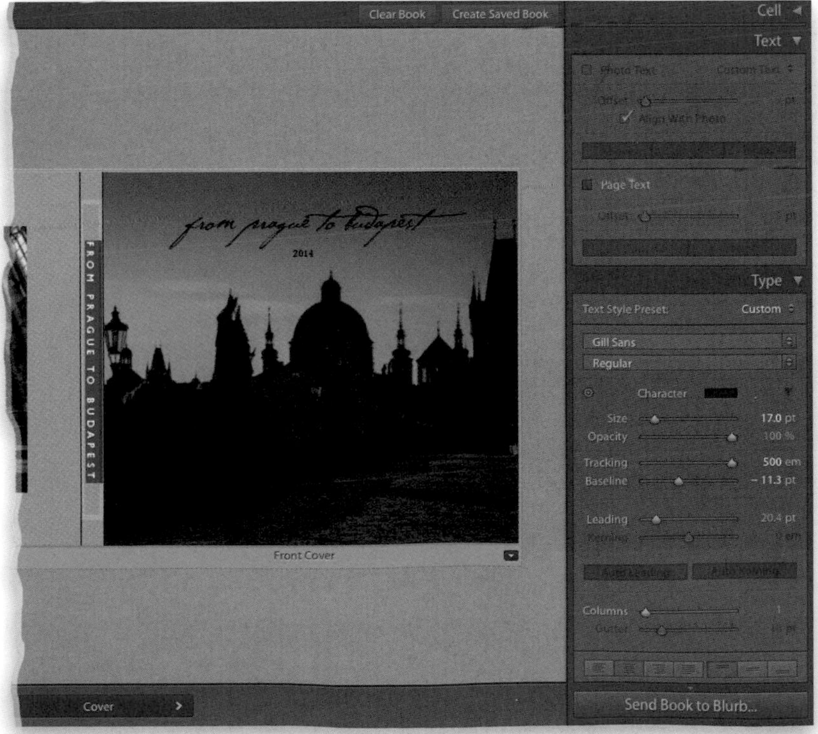

Step Six:

If you're printing a hardcover image wrap book, you also have the option of adding type to the spine. Just move your cursor over the spine (between the front and back cover) and a vertical text block will appear. Click inside it and start typing to add your text sideways down the spine (as seen here). You can edit the font, color, position, etc., just like you would any other text block.

TIP: Choosing a Color for the Spine

Go to the Background panel, turn on the Background Color checkbox, then click on its color swatch and choose a new color. Even better tip: when the Background Color picker appears, click-and-hold your mouse button down anywhere in the picker and, while still holding down the mouse, move the Eyedropper tool out over your cover photo and steal a color.

Custom Template Workaround

If you want a layout for your photo book that is more ambitious than the simple Custom Page layouts you just learned about, then you can do a pretty slick little workaround (which I learned from Adobe's own Lightroom Evangelist, Julieanne Kost), which is to go to the Print module, design any custom page layout you want (at the same size as your book) with the photos you want, save it as a JPEG file, and import that finished layout into Lightroom as if it was just one photo. It's not actually a template, but it looks like you used one.

Step One:

First, jump over to Lightroom's Print module, and click on the Page Setup button in the lower-left corner. When the Page Setup (PC: Print Setup) dialog appears, from the Paper Size pop-up menu, choose **Manage Custom Sizes** to bring up the dialog you see here (on a PC, click the Properties button, then in the Paper Options section, click the Custom button). You're going to create a new preset size (so you don't have to go through this again). Click the + (plus sign) button (shown circled here in red), and enter 7 in for both Width and Height (PC: Length), for Blurb's Small Square 7x7" book. On a Mac, you'll need to set all your margins (left, top, right, bottom) to 0 in, then click OK twice. Now this template is one click away in the future. While you're here, though, you might want to create presets for all the Blurb sizes (like 10x8", 8x10", 13x10", and 13x13").

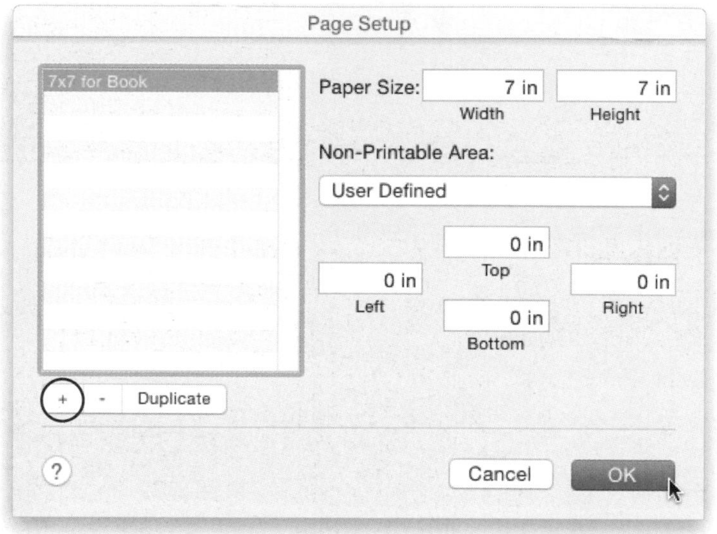

Step Two:

Now design any layout you'd like in the Print module. For this layout, I used one of the built-in presets that comes with Lightroom called 4 Wide (found in the Template Browser panel in the left side Panels area). Once the template appeared, I selected the four photos I wanted in this layout, then I turned the Identity Plate checkbox off in the Page panel in the right side Panels area. I only changed two small settings in the Layout panel, so it all fits nicely in the 7x7 square we're using. I set the bottom and top margins to 0.44 in and left the sides at 0.50 in, which gives you the layout you see here (there isn't a layout exactly like this in the Book module's templates).

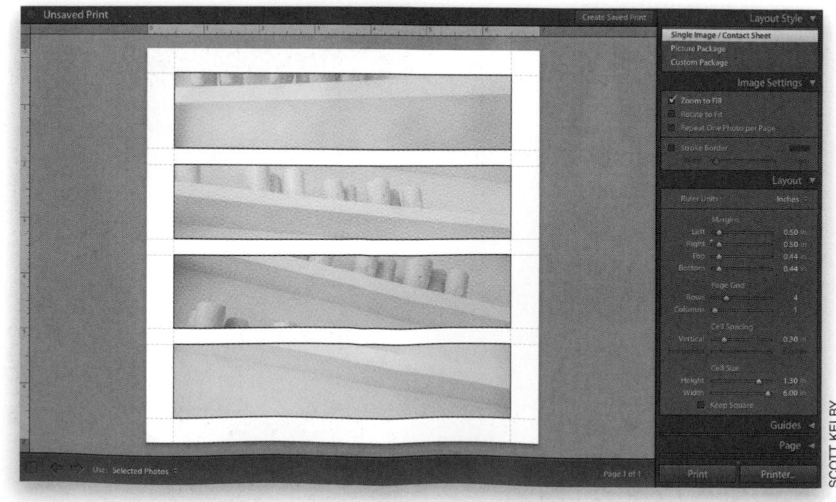

SCOTT KELBY

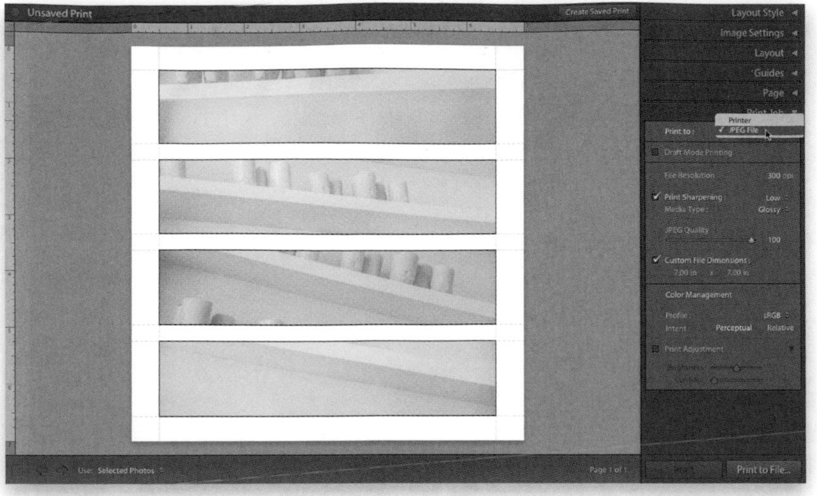

Step Three:

Although I used a built-in print template here, you can use the Print module's Custom Package feature (found up in the Layout Style panel at the top of the right side Panels area) to start with a blank page and create any type of layout you want (see page 450). Okay, once you've got your page set up the way you want it to look here in the Print module, scroll down to the Print Job panel and, where it says Print To, go ahead and choose **JPEG File** (as shown here). Set your Print Sharpening and Media Type to whichever settings you use (see Chapter 13 for more on this), then turn on the checkbox for Custom File Dimensions (so it uses the 7x7" custom size you created). Click the Print to File button to save this single 7x7" page as a JPEG file.

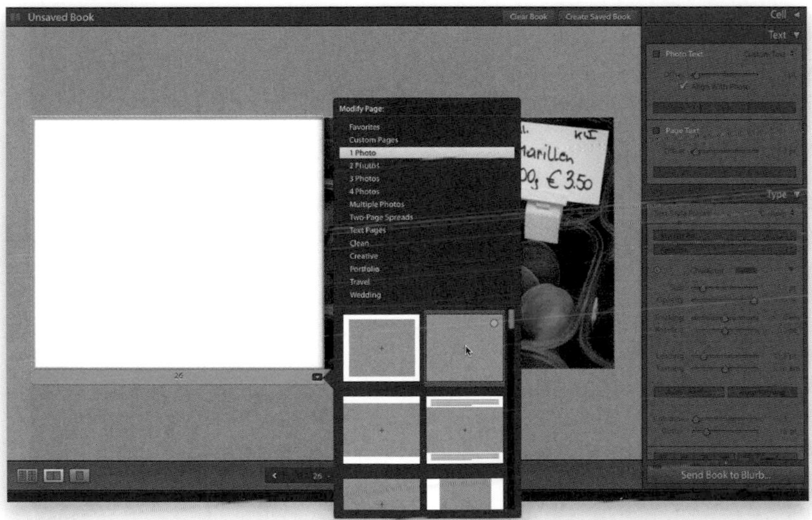

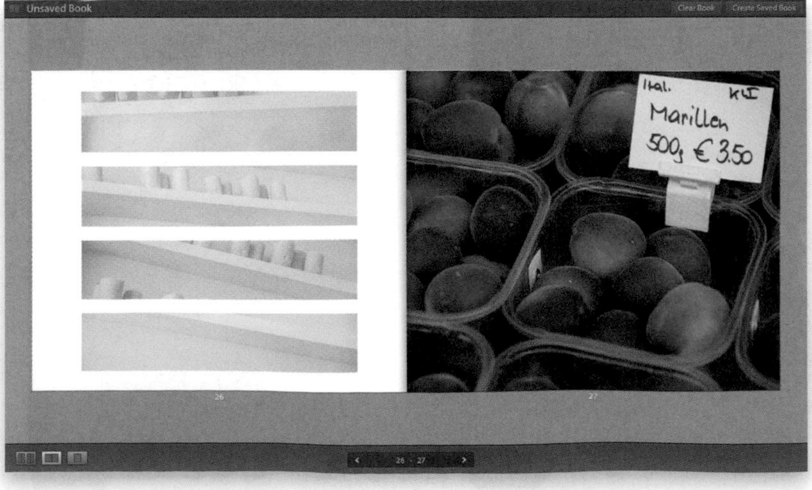

Step Four:

Now go to the Library module, and press **Command-Shift-I (PC: Ctrl-Shift-I)** to bring up the Import window. Find that JPEG file you just created and import it into Lightroom. Once it comes in, drag it into the collection you created for your photo book, then jump back to the Book module. Go to the page in your book where you want this 4 Wide image to appear. Right-click on the image on that page and choose **Remove Photo**, so it's just an empty page. From the Modify Page pop-up menu, choose a layout where the photo will fill the entire page (as shown at the top here). Then, simply find your 4 Wide image in the Filmstrip and drag it onto this empty page to get the layout you see here. The downside is that it's not a template—it's a fixed page (a flattened JPEG like any other photo). The upside is that you've got a page in your book where you created the layout from scratch exactly the way you wanted it.

Lightroom Killer Tips > >

▼ Zooming In/Out on Pages

You can use Photoshop's keyboard shortcuts for zooming in/out on your pages: press **Command-+ (PC: Ctrl-+)** to zoom in tighter on your page, or **Command-- (PC: Ctrl--)** to zoom back out.

▼ Zoom Multiple Photos

If you're working with more than one photo on a page, and you want to zoom all those photos in tighter, just select the first photo, press-and-hold the Shift

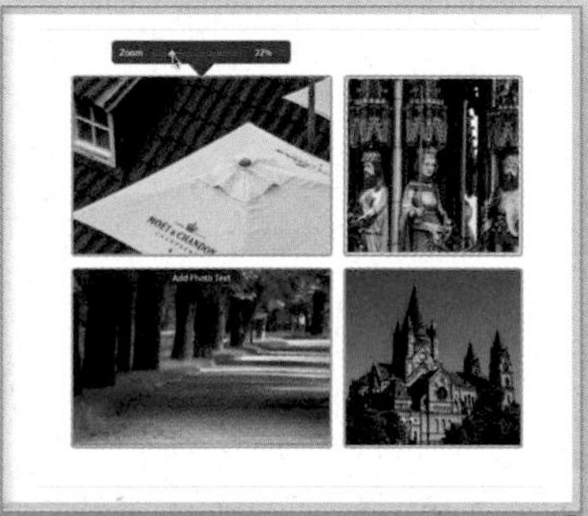

key, select any other photos you want zoomed on the page, and then drag the Zoom slider, and all the selected photos will zoom at the same time.

▼ Lightroom Converts Your Book to sRGB for Printing

Most photo labs ask that images sent to their lab for printing be converted to the sRGB format, but when printing your book, you won't have to worry about this because the images in your book are automatically converted to sRGB when the book is sent to Blurb.

▼ Tweaking an Image on a Page

If you're looking at an image in your book and you feel like it needs to be lighter, darker, more contrasty, etc., just click on the image, then press the letter **D** to take that image over to the Develop module. Make your tweaks there, and then press **Command-Option-4 (PC: Ctrl-Alt-4)** to jump back to the Book module and pick up right where you left off.

▼ Getting Larger Multi-Page Views

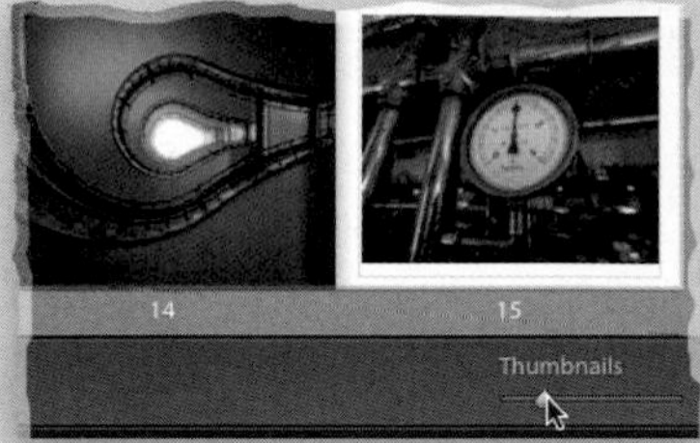

One thing a lot of folks miss when they're in Multi-Page View mode (the mode where you can see the two-page spreads in your book) is that you can change the size of your thumbnails, so you can either see more pages in the same space, or have a larger view of your spreads. You do this on the far-right side of the toolbar (right under the Preview area)—you'll see a Thumbnails slider. This works particularly well when you use the next tip (pressing Shift-Tab before you enter Multi-Page View mode).

▼ A Bigger View for Sorting Your Pages in Multi-Page View

When you start to do your page sorting (sorting the order of two-page spreads in your book), try this: press **Shift-Tab** to hide all your panels, which gives you a much larger view of your book, and it's easier to move spreads around when you have more space like this.

▼ Four Keyboard Shortcuts That Save a Lot of Time

You don't have to learn a bunch of shortcuts for making books, but these four will make the process that much faster

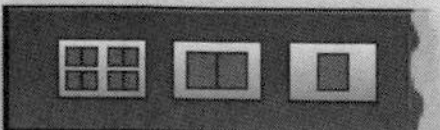

for you: (1) **Command-E (PC: Ctrl-E)** switches you to the Multi-Page View; (2) **Command-R (PC: Ctrl-R)** switches you to the Spread View; (3) **Command-T (PC: Ctrl-T)** switches you to Single Page View; and (4) **Command-U (PC: Ctrl-U)** switches you to Zoomed Page View (zoomed in really tight), which is particularly handy when you need to quickly check some caption text for a typo.

▼ Adding Pages

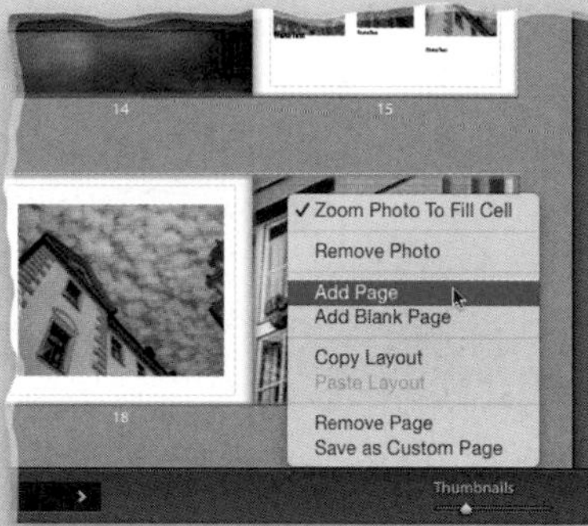

If you click the Add Page button in the Pages panel, it adds a new blank page to the end of your book, but more likely you're going to want to add a page at the spot you're currently working on in your book. To do that (add a page in front of the page you're on, rather than at the end), just Right-click on the page and choose **Add Page**, and it adds it right there.

▼ Why You Should Try Auto Layout Before You Put Your Photos in Order

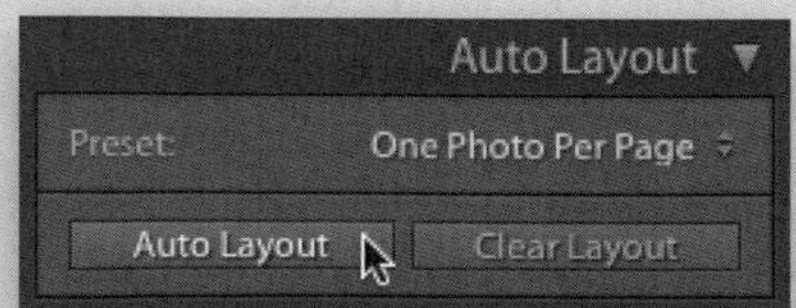

One big benefit of letting Lightroom do an Auto Layout of your book pages with your photos in a random order is that you'll generally find a couple of two-page layouts that look fantastic together, but they're photos that you might never have put together yourself. I find this happens every time I try this—I come up with at least three or four two-page layouts that look fantastic, just out of sheer luck of the pairing. Try it once and you'll see what I mean.

▼ Custom Page Save "Gotcha!"

When you create a custom page design and save it as one of your own custom pages, it remembers how many cells

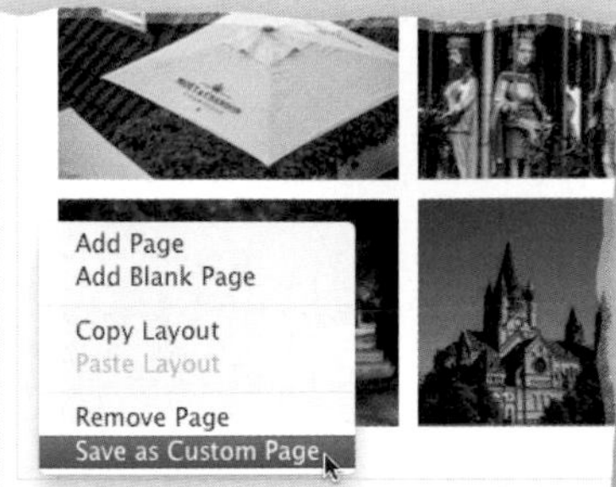

you had and what their positions were, and it even remembers if you had a text field, along with its position. The "gotcha" is what it doesn't remember. It doesn't remember whether you had these cells set to Zoom Photo to Fill and it doesn't remember your text formatting (font, size, etc.), or whether your text had multiple columns. Hey, they have to have something to fix in the future, right?

▼ Changing the Format of a Page Number for Just One Page

By default, page numbers automatically added to your book using the Page Numbers feature in the Page panel all share the same formatting (they all use whichever font, size, and other formatting choice you make). But, what if you have a full-page image that's dark, and you need to have that one page have its page number appear in white? Or what if there are a handful of pages where the font is either too dark, too light, or the wrong size? In that case, you can Right-click directly on the page number itself on the page where you need to change the color (size, etc.), and from the pop-up menu that appears, choose **Apply Page Number**

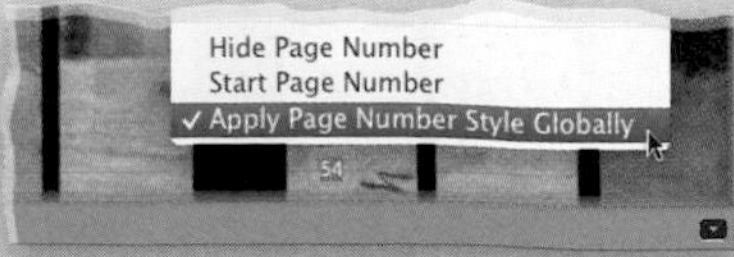

Style Globally to turn it off. Now, you can highlight the page number on that page, go to the Type panel, and choose white for its color (and now all the other page numbers can be edited individually, as well).

▼ Adding Captions Under Multiple Photos

If you have a page with multiple images (let's say a page with three cells), and you want a caption to appear under each individual image (rather than just one caption for the entire page), start by clicking on the first photo, then press-and-hold the Command (PC: Ctrl) key and click on the other two images to select all three.

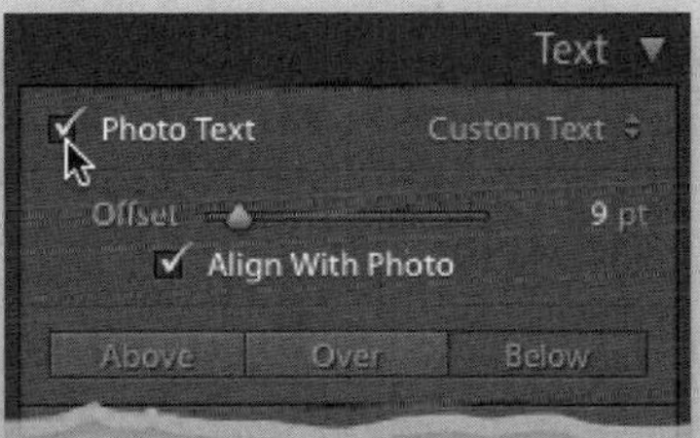

Now, go to the Text panel and turn on the Photo Text checkbox and now each of the selected images will have their own separate caption field right under them.

▼ Automatic Captions from Your Image's Metadata

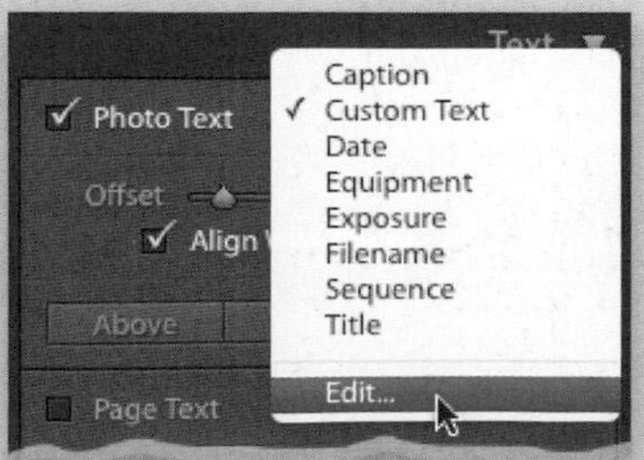

If you turn on the Photo Text checkbox (in the Text panel), just to the right of that checkbox is a pop-up menu of automated captions, including choices like the ability to pull info from the image metadata—stuff like Exposure or Equipment (camera make and model). Or, you can totally customize your caption by choosing **Edit**, which brings up the Text Template Editor, where you can pretty much have it generate whatever you want. By the way, you can format the font, size, and specs for this caption text in the Type panel.

▼ Locking a Text Caption's Position

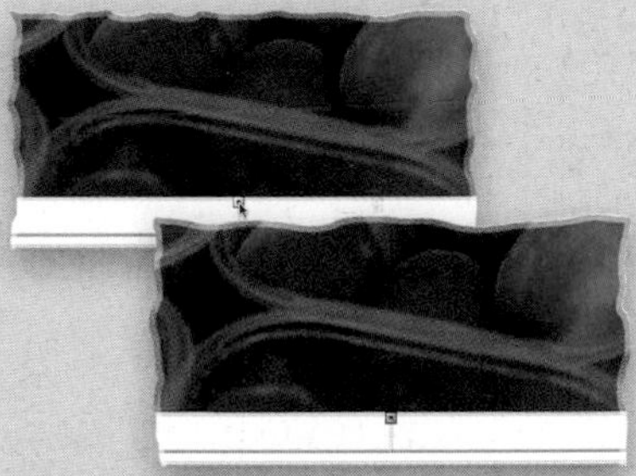

If you've positioned a text caption somewhere on your page and you want to make sure it doesn't get moved accidentally (when you're swapping out images or moving cells), just click on the square with a small black square inside that appears on the edge of the caption field. It will fill with yellow, showing that its position is now locked. To unlock it, click on that same little square again.

▼ Money-Saving Paper Option

If you want to save a few bucks on your photo book, back in Lightroom 5, Blurb added a new paper option called "Standard," which uses a lesser-quality paper (perfect if you're just creating a small proof book before you print the larger, more expensive final book). For example, for a Standard Landscape size book, with a Hardcover Image Wrap, switching from Premium Luster to this new Standard paper equaled around a 13% savings for me. Definitely worth considering (even though the pages won't be as thick, so you might see some bleed-through if you print images on both sides of the page).

▼ Jump to a Single-Page View

Double-click on any page to jump to a large Single Page View of that page.

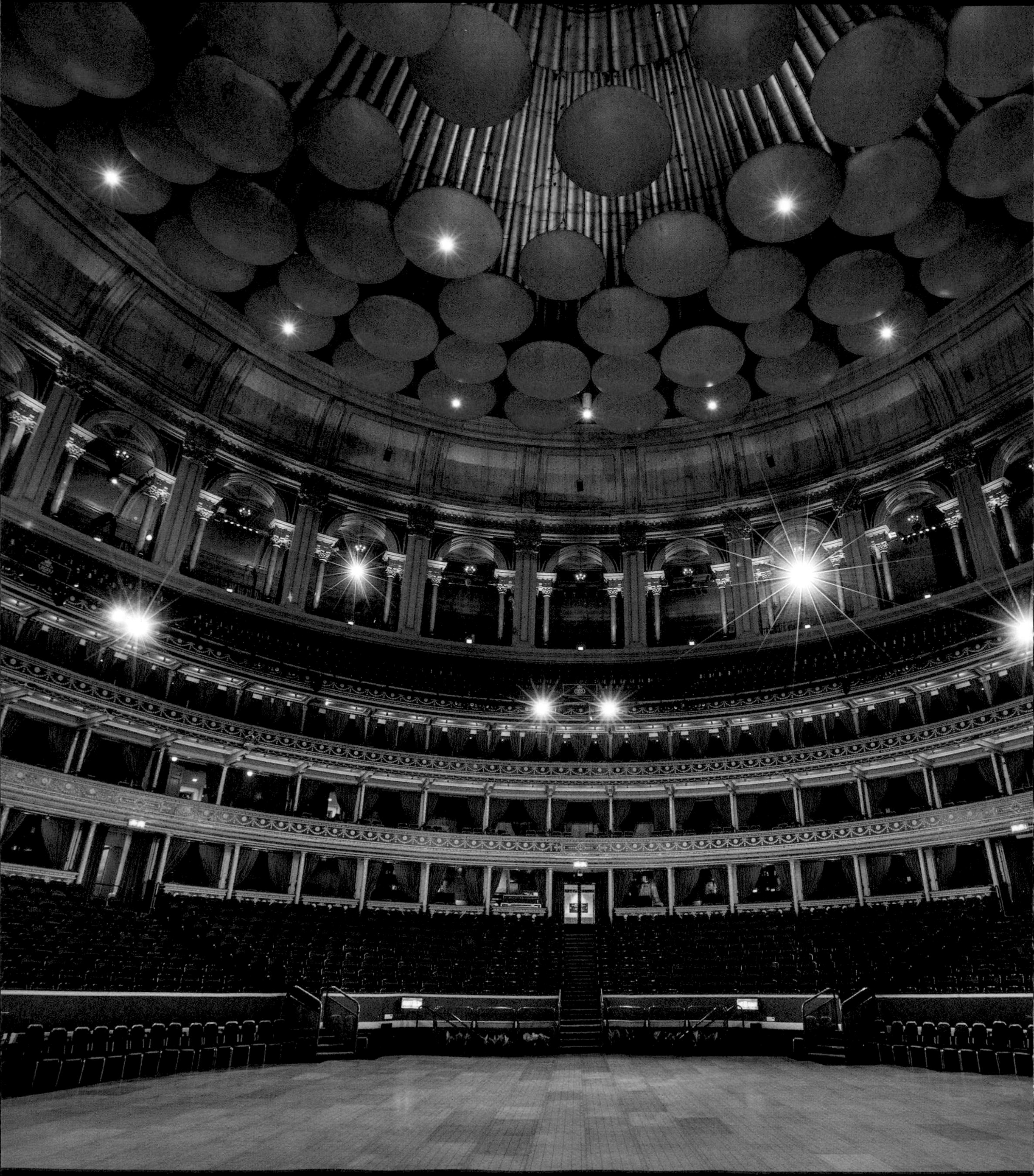

Photo by Scott Kelby | Exposure: 1 sec | Focal Length: 16mm | Aperture Value: ƒ/6.3

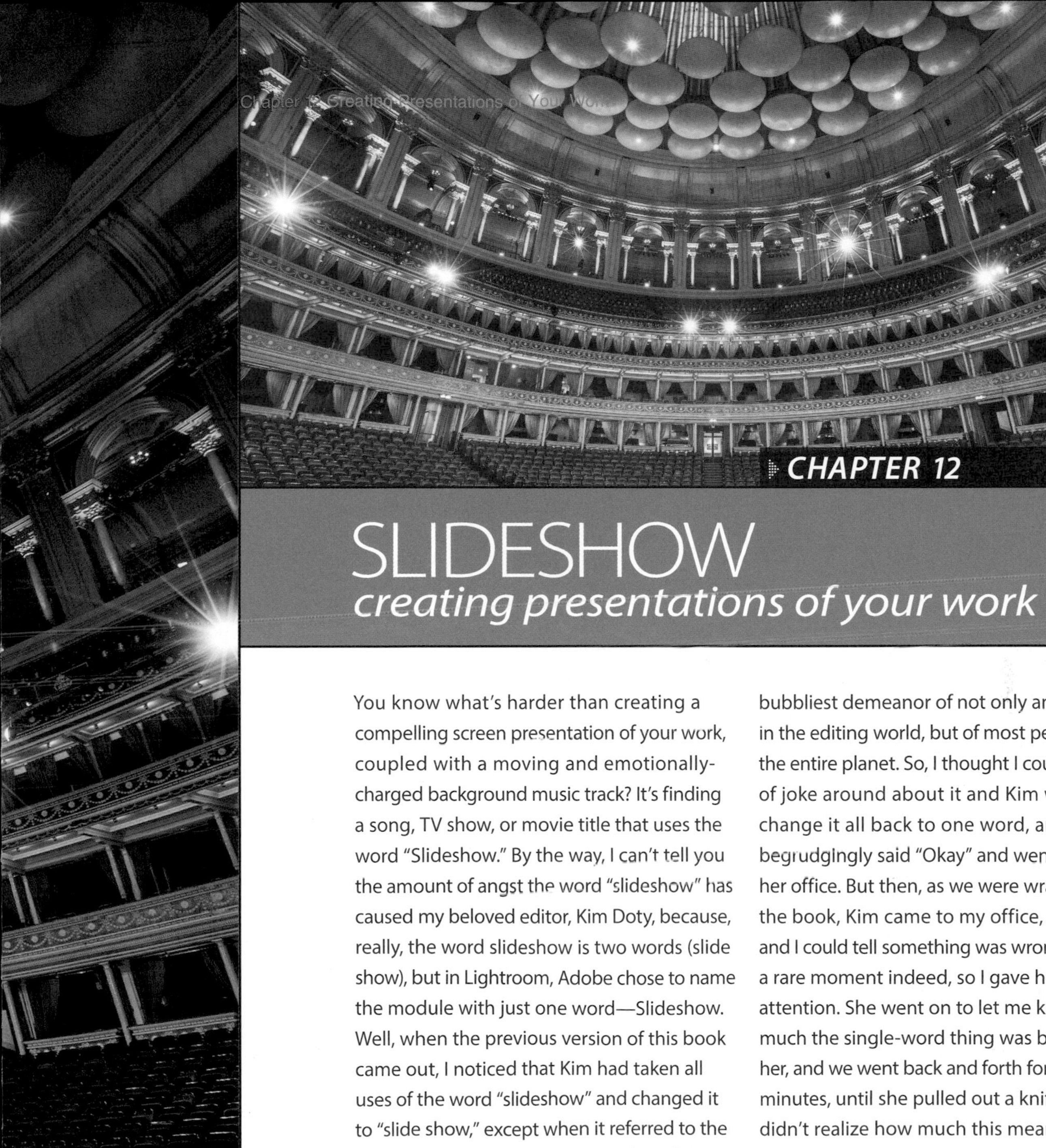

CHAPTER 12

SLIDESHOW
creating presentations of your work

You know what's harder than creating a compelling screen presentation of your work, coupled with a moving and emotionally-charged background music track? It's finding a song, TV show, or movie title that uses the word "Slideshow." By the way, I can't tell you the amount of angst the word "slideshow" has caused my beloved editor, Kim Doty, because, really, the word slideshow is two words (slide show), but in Lightroom, Adobe chose to name the module with just one word—Slideshow. Well, when the previous version of this book came out, I noticed that Kim had taken all uses of the word "slideshow" and changed it to "slide show," except when it referred to the actual module name itself. So, in this edition, I asked Kim to make it consistent and always refer to it as one word—slideshow. This didn't go over very well with Kim, which troubled me because Kim, by nature, has the happiest, bubbliest demeanor of not only any editor in the editing world, but of most people on the entire planet. So, I thought I could kind of joke around about it and Kim would change it all back to one word, and she begrudgingly said "Okay" and went back to her office. But then, as we were wrapping up the book, Kim came to my office, sat down, and I could tell something was wrong. This is a rare moment indeed, so I gave her my full attention. She went on to let me know how much the single-word thing was bothering her, and we went back and forth for about 10 minutes, until she pulled out a knife. I clearly didn't realize how much this meant to Kim, so of course, I relented and the chapter has been adjusted so the two-word "slide show" appears where appropriate. Also, the other good news is: the doctor says my stitches should be out within two weeks.

Creating a Quick, Basic Slide Show

Here's how to create a quick slide show using the built-in slide show templates that come with Lightroom. You'll probably be surprised at how easy this process is, but the real power of the Slideshow module doesn't really kick in until you start customizing and creating your own slide show templates (which we cover after this, but you have to learn this first, so start here and you'll have no problems when we get to customizing).

Step One:

Start by jumping over to the Slideshow module by pressing **Command-Option-5 (PC: Ctrl-Alt-5)**. There's a Collections panel in the left side Panels area, just like there is in the Library module, so you have direct access to the photos in any collection. First, click on the collection that has the photos you want to appear in your slide show, as shown here. (*Note:* If the photos you want in your slide show aren't in a collection, it will make your life a lot easier if they are, so head back to the Library module [press the letter **G**], and make a new collection with the photos you want in your slide show, then jump back over to the Slideshow module, and click on that collection in the Collections panel.)

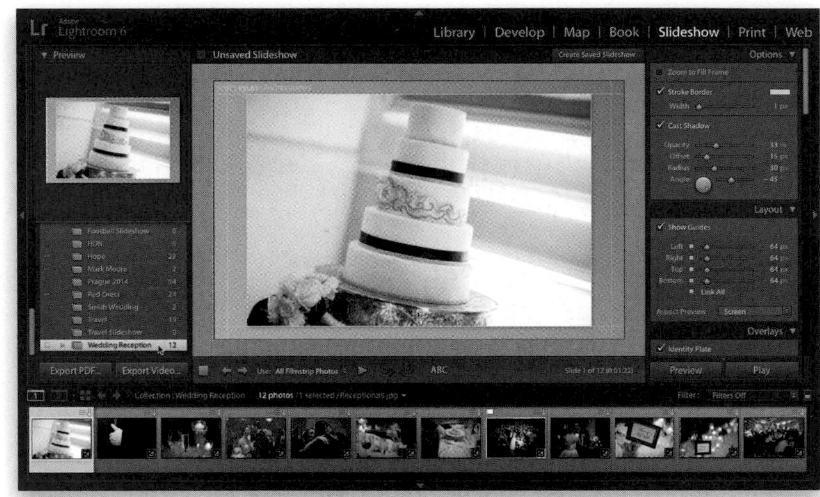

SCOTT KELBY

Step Two:

By default, it's going to play the slides in the order they appear down in the Filmstrip (the first photo from the left appears first, the second photo appears next, and so on), with a brief dissolve transition between slides. If you only want certain photos in your collection to appear in your slide show, then go to the Filmstrip, select just those photos, and choose **Selected Photos** from the Use pop-up menu in the toolbar below the center Preview area (as shown here). As you can see, you can also choose to have just flagged photos in your slide show.

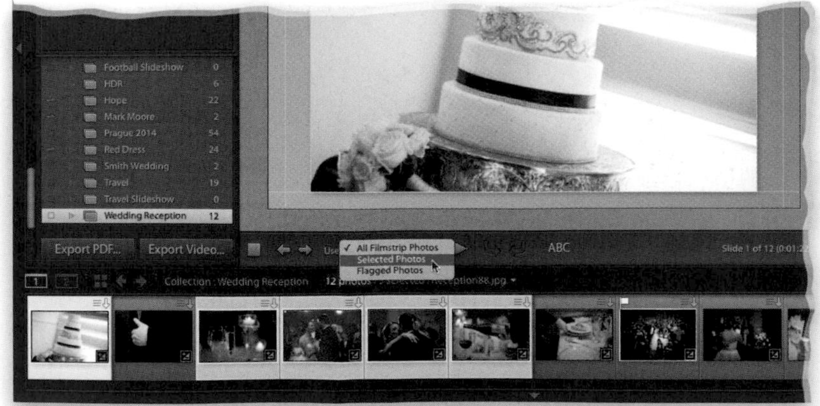

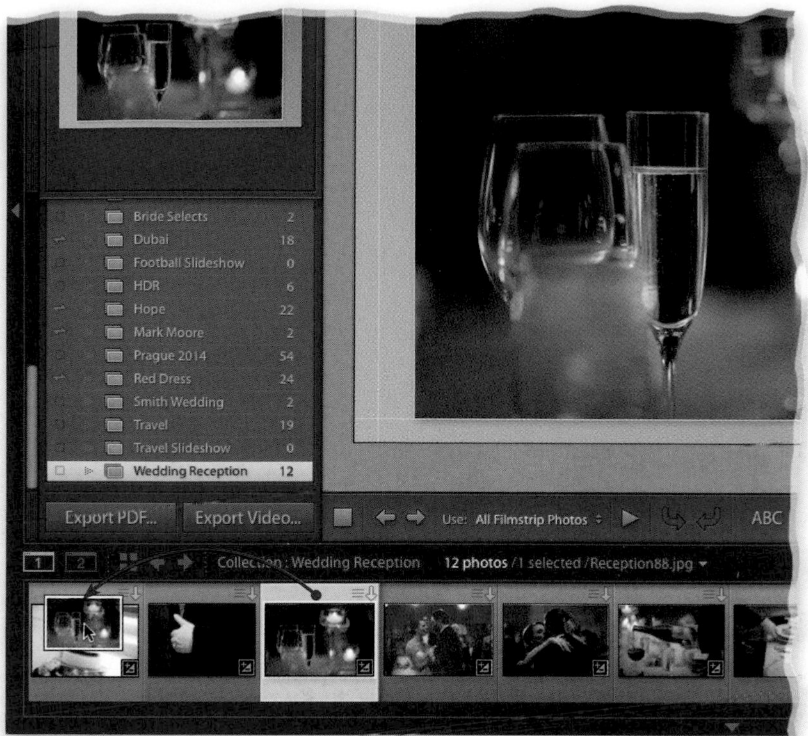

Step Three:

If you want to change the order of your slides, just click-and-drag them into the order you want them. (In the example shown here, I clicked on the third photo and dragged it over so it was the first photo in the Filmstrip.) So, go ahead and do that now—click-and-drag the photos into the order you'd like them to appear in your slide show. (*Note:* You can always change your mind on the order any time by clicking-and-dragging right within the Filmstrip.)

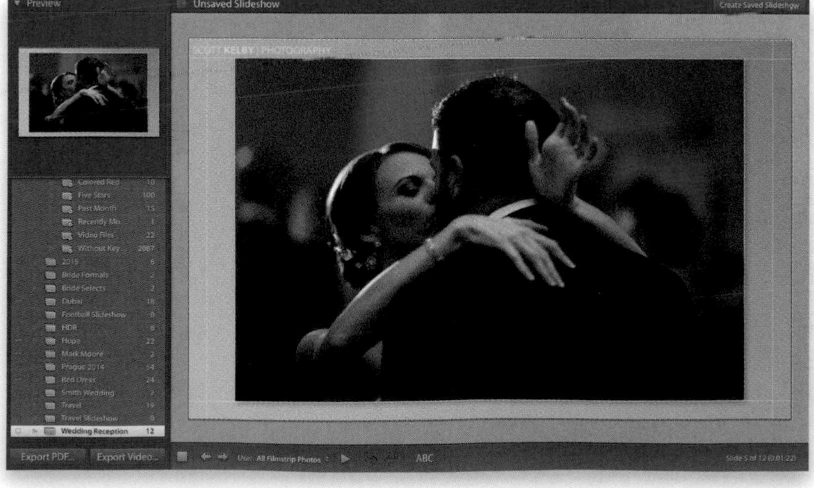

Step Four:

When you first switch to the Slideshow module, it displays your photos in the default slide show template, which has a light gray gradient background and your Main Identity Plate in the upper-left corner in white letters (now this is not to be confused with the Default template in the Template Browser, and yes, it usually looks pretty bad, as seen here, but we'll deal with that later on). Click on any other photo in the Filmstrip to see how that slide will look in the current slide show layout.

Continued

Step Five:

If you want to try a different look for your slide show, you can use any of the built-in slide show templates that come with Lightroom (they're in the Template Browser in the left side Panels area). Before you start clicking on them, however, you can get a preview of how they'll look by just hovering your cursor over their names in the Template Browser. Here, I'm hovering over the Caption and Rating template, and the Preview panel shows that template has a light gray gradient background, and the images have a thin white stroke and a drop shadow. While this is similar to the default template, with this template, if you've added a star rating to your photo, the stars appear over the top-left corner of your image, and if you added a caption in the Library module's Metadata panel, it appears at the bottom of the slide. Let's go ahead and try this one.

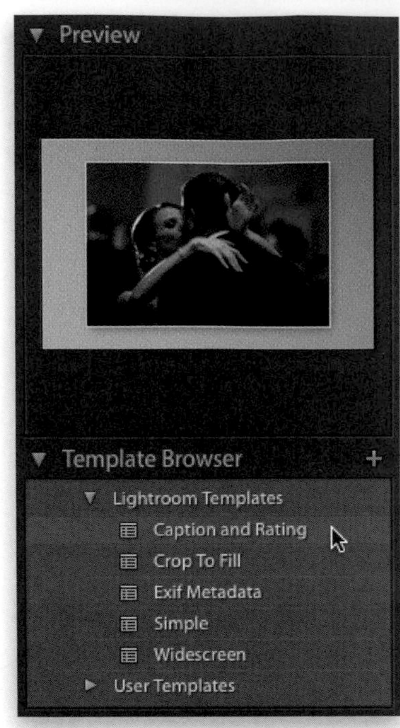

Step Six:

To see a quick preview of how your slide show will look, go to the toolbar below the center Preview area, and click the Preview button (it's a right-facing triangle—just like the Play button on a DVD player). This plays a preview of your slide show within that center Preview area, and although the slide show is the exact same size in that window, you're now seeing it without guides, with transitions, and with music (if you chose to add music, which we haven't covered yet, so you probably haven't, but hey, ya never know). To stop your preview, press the square Stop button on the left side of the toolbar; to pause it, press the two vertical lines where the Play button used to be (as shown here).

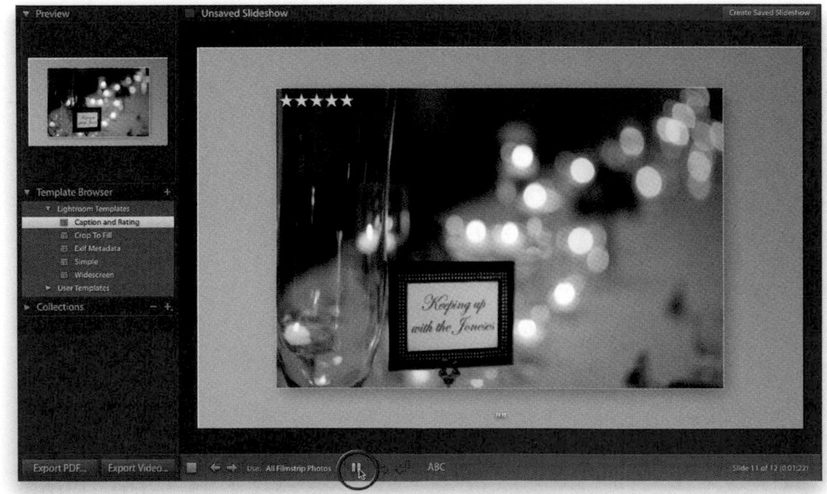

TIP: Life Is Random

Your slides play in the order that they appear in the Filmstrip, but if you want your slides to appear in a completely random order, go to the Playback panel in the right side Panels area and turn on the Random Order checkbox.

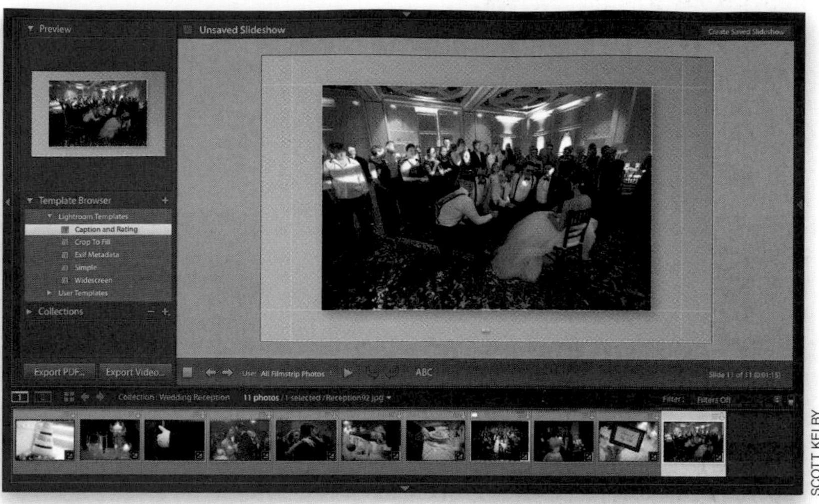

SCOTT KELBY

Step Seven:

If you want to remove a photo from your slide show, just remove the photo from your collection by clicking on it in the Filmstrip and pressing the Delete (PC: Backspace) key on your keyboard (or choose Selected Photos from the Use pop-up menu in the toolbar and just make sure you don't select that photo). Here, I removed that photo shown in Step Six from the slide show by hitting the Delete key, so the next photo in the Filmstrip is now displayed. By the way, this is another advantage of collections vs. folders. If you were working with a folder here, instead of a collection, and you deleted a photo, it would actually remove it from Lightroom and from your computer. Yikes!

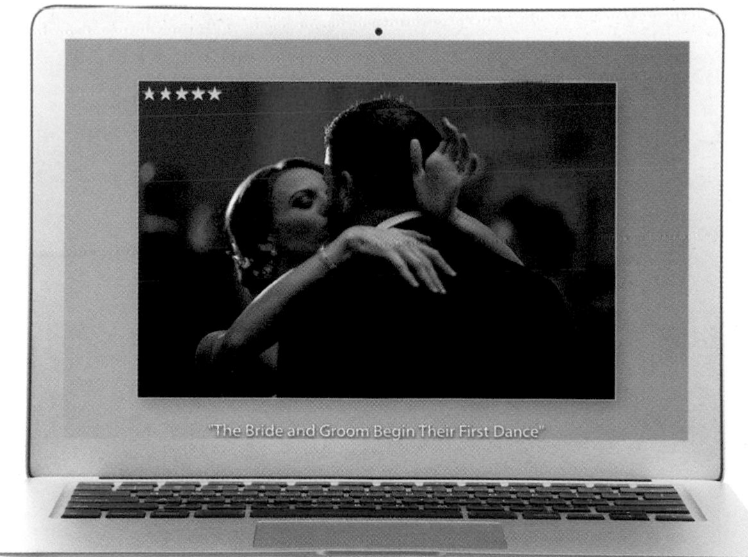

Step Eight:

When you're done tweaking things, it's time to see the full-screen final version. Click the Play button at the bottom of the right side Panels area, and your slide show plays at full-screen size (as shown here). To exit full-screen mode and return to the Slideshow module, press the Esc key on your keyboard. Okay, you've created a basic slide show. Next, you'll learn how to customize and create your own custom slide shows.

TIP: Creating an Instant Slide Show

I mentioned this in an earlier chapter, but you can create an impromptu slide show anytime without even going to the Slideshow module. Whichever module you're in, just go to the Filmstrip, select the photos you want in your slide show, then press **Command-Return (PC: Ctrl-Enter)**, and it starts—full screen.

Customizing the Look of Your Slide Show

The built-in templates are okay, but after you create a slide show or two with them, you're going to be saying stuff like, "I wish I could change the background color" or "I wish I could add some text at the bottom" or "I wish my slide show looked better." Well, this is where you start to create your own custom look for your slides, so not only does it look just the way you want it, your custom look is just one click away from now on.

Step One:

Although you might not be wild about Lightroom's predesigned slide show templates, they make great starting points for creating your own custom look. Here, we're going to create a vacation slide show, so start by going to the Slideshow module's Collections panel (in the left side Panels area) and click on the vacation collection you want to use. Then, go up to the Template Browser and click on Exif Metadata to load that template (seen here, which puts your photos over a black background with a thin white border, info about your photo in the top right, bottom right, and below your photo, and your Identity Plate in the upper-left corner).

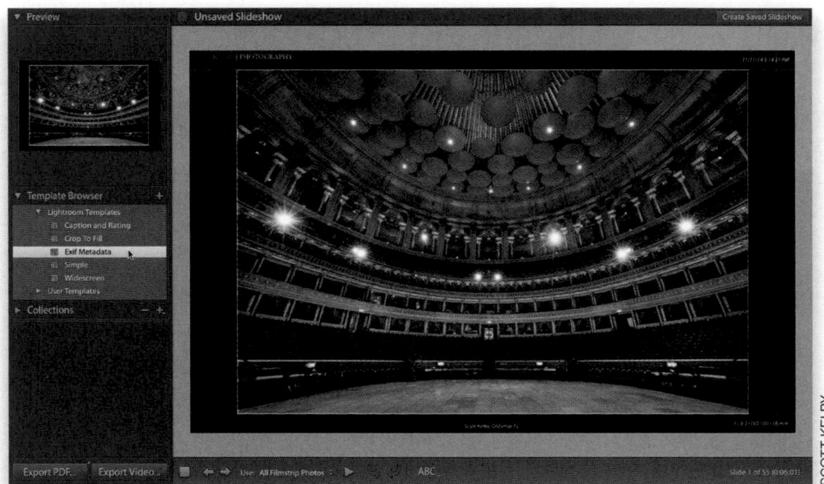

SCOTT KELBY

Step Two:

Now that we've got our template loaded, we don't need the left-side panels anymore, so press **F7** (or **Fn F7**) on your keyboard to hide them. The first thing I do is get rid of all the EXIF info (after all, people viewing your vacation slide show probably won't care what your ISO or exposure settings were), so go to the right side Panels area, to the Overlays panel, and turn off the Text Overlays checkbox (as shown here). Your Identity Plate is still visible, but the info in the upper- and lower-right corners and below the photo is now hidden.

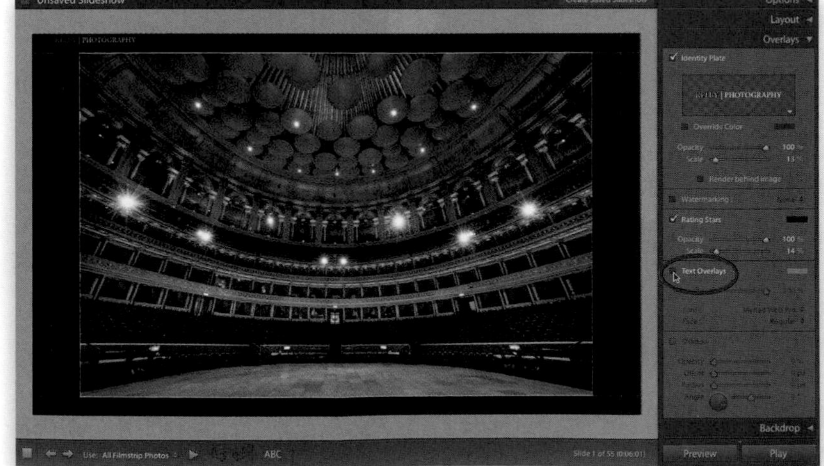

TIP: Resizing Custom Text

Once you create custom text, you can change the size by clicking-and-dragging the corner points outward (to make it larger), and inward (to make it smaller).

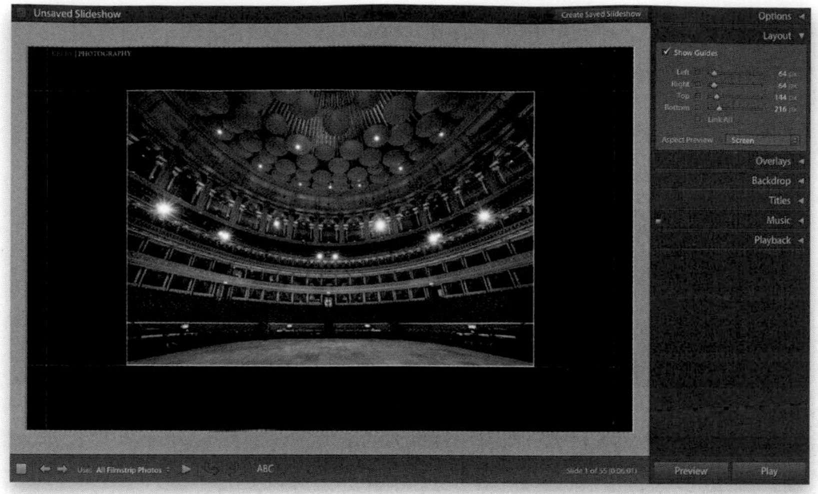

Step Three:

Now let's choose how big your photos are going to appear on the slide. For this design, we're going to shrink the size of the photos a bit, and then move them up toward the top of the slide, so we can add our studio's name below them. Your photo is positioned inside four page margins (left, right, top, and bottom), and you can control how big/small these margins are in the Layout panel found in the right side Panels area. To see the margins, turn on the Show Guides checkbox. By default, all four margin guides are linked together, so if you increase the left margin to 81 pixels, all of the other margins adjust so they're 81 pixels, as well. In our case, we want to adjust the top and bottom separately, so first click on Link All to unlink the margins (the little "lights" beside each margin go out). Now, click-and-drag the Bottom margin slider to the right to 216 px and the Top margin slider to 144 px, and you'll see the photo scale down in size inward, leaving a larger margin below the photo (as shown here).

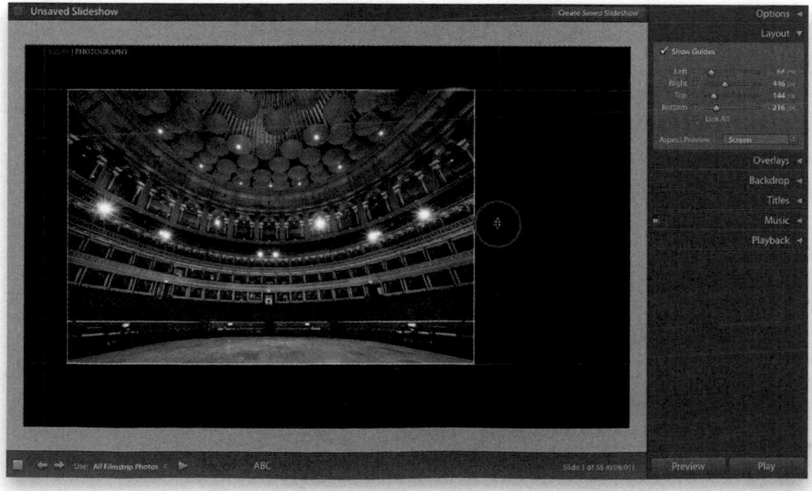

TIP: Moving Guides

You don't actually resize the photos on your slide—you move the margin guides and your photo resizes within the margins you create. You can do this visually (rather than in the Layout panel) by moving your cursor over a guide, and you'll see it change into a "moving bar" cursor (by the way, I have no idea if "moving bar" is its official name, but it is a double-headed arrow), and now you can click-and-drag the margins to resize the photo. If you move your cursor over a corner (where two guides intersect), you can drag diagonally to resize those two guides at the same time.

Continued

Step Four:

Now that our photo is in position, let's move our studio name Identity Plate below the photo. Click on it (up in the top-left corner of your slide) and drag it so it appears under your photo (when you drag it, it does this weird Spiderman thing of clinging to the edges. This is supposed to help you center your text by having it snap to the edges. At least, that's the theory).

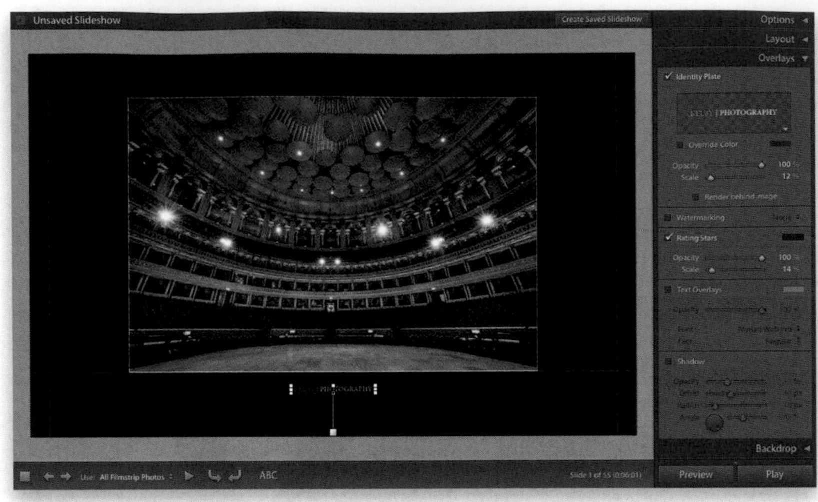

TIP: Zoom to Fill Frame

If you see a gap between the edges of your photo and the margin guides, you can fill that gap instantly with a very cool feature called Zoom to Fill Frame. Turning on this checkbox (found in the Options panel at the very top of the right side Panels area) increases the size of your photos proportionally until they completely fill the area inside the margins. Give this a try—you'll probably use it more than you'd think.

Step Five:

To customize your Identity Plate text, go to the Overlays panel, click on the little triangle in the bottom-right corner of the Identity Plate preview, and choose **Edit** to bring up the Identity Plate Editor (seen here). Type in the name you want to appear below each photo (in my case, I'm using one of my studio Identity Plates, where I typed in Scott Kelby | Photography in the font Myriad Web Pro at 24 points—you get that little bar by typing Shift-\ [backslash] on your keyboard. I clicked on the color swatch here and changed the font color temporarily to black, to make it easier to see), and click OK. Choosing the right point size isn't so critical, because you can change the size of your Identity Plate by either using the Scale slider (in the Overlays panel), or by clicking on your Identity Plate text on the slide and then clicking-and-dragging any corner point outward (which scales the text up).

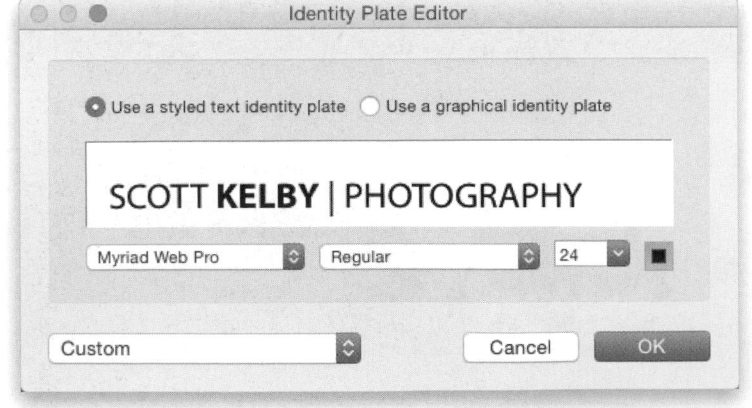

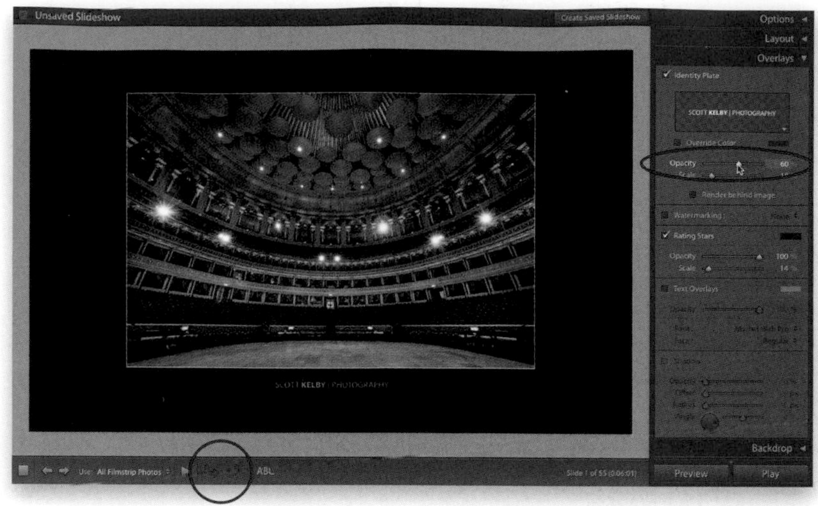

Step Six:

Let's take a look at how our custom slide layout is coming together by hiding the margin guides—press **Command-Shift-H (PC: Ctrl-Shift-H)**, or you could go to the Layout panel and turn off the checkbox for Show Guides. If you look at the text below the photo, you can see it's not bright white—it's actually a very light gray (I like that better, because it doesn't draw the eye as much if it's not solid white), and to get this more subtle light gray look, you just lower the Opacity amount up in the Identity Plate section of the Overlays panel (here you can see I've got the Identity Plate Opacity lowered to just 60%). Also, if you want to rotate your Identity Plate text, click on it first, then use the two Rotate arrows found down in the toolbar (I've circled them here in red for you).

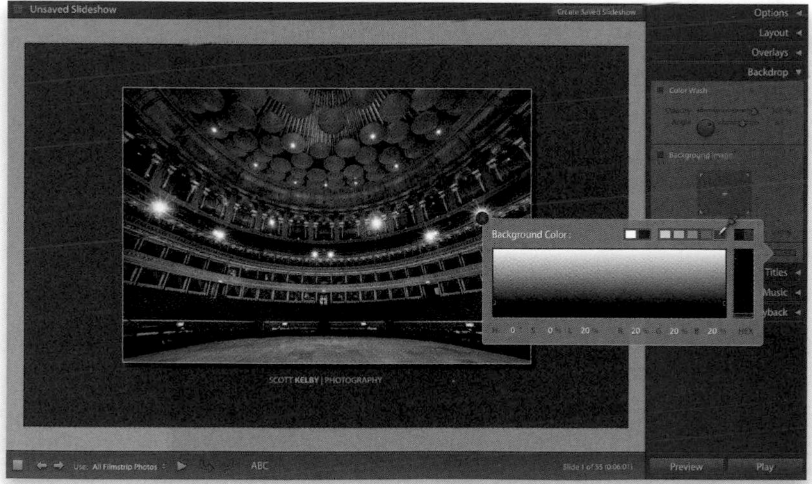

Step Seven:

You can change the background color of your slide to any color you'd like, so let's change it to a dark gray. Go down to the Backdrop panel, and to the right of the Background Color checkbox, you'll see a color swatch. Click on that swatch and the color picker appears, where you can choose any color you'd like (I chose a dark gray from the swatches at the top of the picker, as seen here). For more on customizing your background, go to the next project.

TIP: Add a Shadow to Your Identity Plate Text

If your slide has a lighter background color, you can add a drop shadow to your Identity Plate text. Just go to the bottom of the Overlays panel and turn the Shadow checkbox on. You can now control the opacity, how far offset your shadow is from your text, the radius (softness) of your shadow, and the angle (direction) of the shadow. *Note:* As of the writing of this book, this feature is not available in the PC version of Lightroom.

Continued

Step Eight:

Now that we're on a gray background, rather than black, you can see that this Exif Metadata template actually has a drop shadow on the image included in the design, but of course you can't see it when you're on a solid black background (which makes you wonder why Adobe had that feature turned on in the first place, eh?). Anyway, you can control the size, opacity, and direction of the drop shadow (see page 426 for more on drop shadows) in the Options panel, but for now we'll just increase the Radius to soften the shadow and increase the Opacity a bit to give us the look you see here.

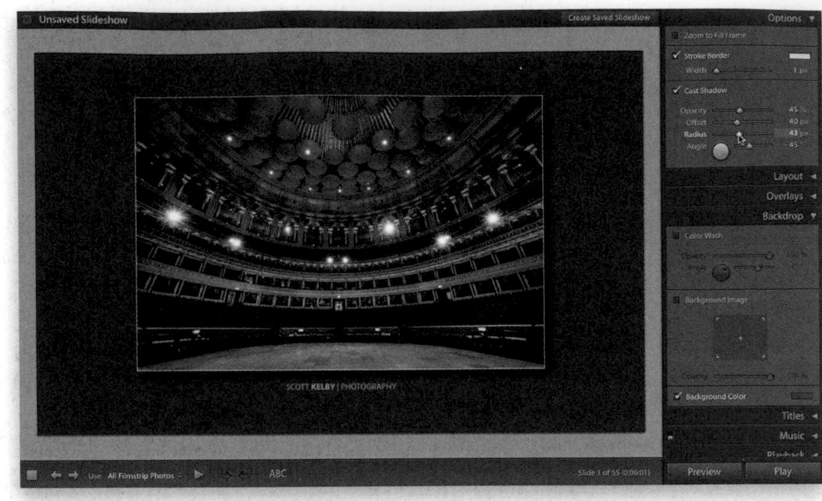

Step Nine:

Let's give this layout a little more of a fine art slide show feel by making the image area square. It's not real obvious how to do this, but luckily it's fairly easy. You start by moving the guides (press Command-Shift-H [PC: Ctrl-Shift-H] to turn them back on), so they make a square. This makes perfect sense at first, but once you see that it just resizes your photo, at the same aspect ratio, inside that square cell (rather than cropping it to square), you start scratching your head (well, I did anyway, but it was only because my head was itchy. That was pretty bad. I know). The trick is to go up to the Options panel and turn on the checkbox for Zoom to Fill Frame. That fills the square cell with your image, and now you get the square look you see here. While we're here, let's go and add a thicker stroke around the image using the Stroke Border Width slider in that same panel (more on adding a stroke on page 426).

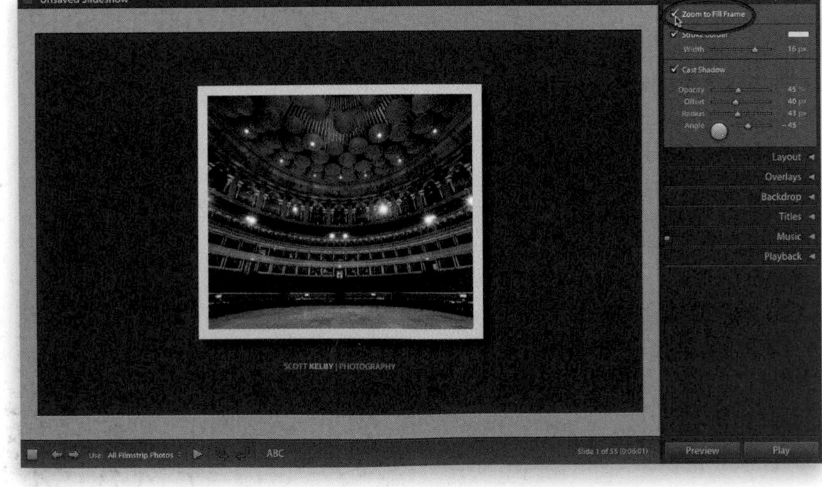

Step 10:

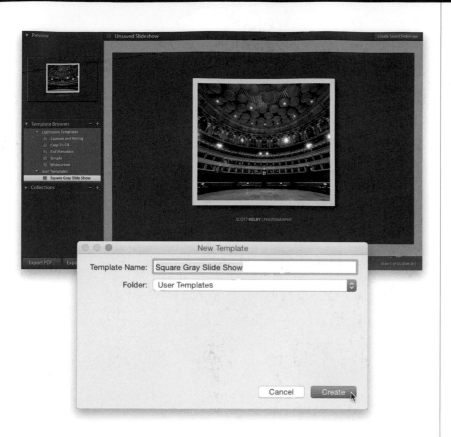

Now we're going to save our template, so in the future we can apply it with just one click in the Template Browser (it remembers everything: the text, the background color, the opening and closing title slides [more on those on page 428]—you name it). To do this, press **F7** to make the left side Panels area visible again, then go to the Template Browser and click on the + (plus sign) button on the far right of the panel header. This brings up the New Template dialog (shown here), where you can name your template and choose where you want to save it (I save mine in the User Templates folder, as shown here, but you can create your own folders and choose to save into one of them by choosing it from the Folder pop-up menu).

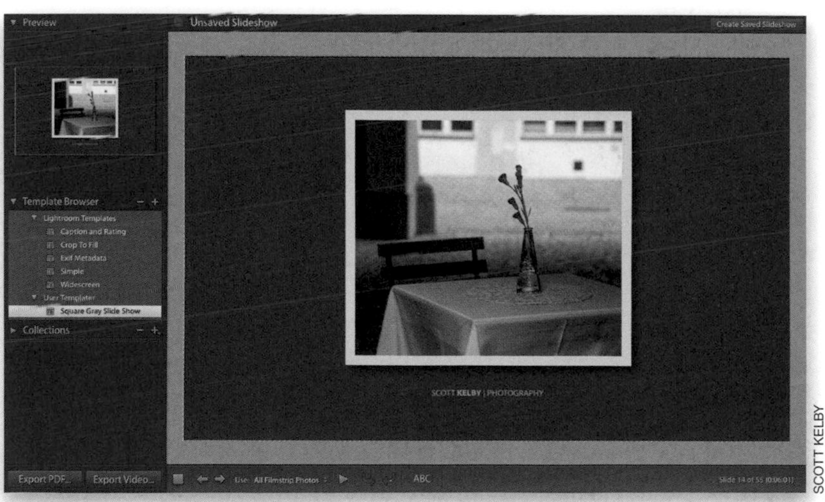

SCOTT KELBY

Step 11:

Now that you've saved your custom slide design as a template, you can apply this same exact look to a totally different set of images by going to the Slideshow module, and in the Collections panel, clicking on a different collection. Then, in the Template Browser, under User Templates, click on Square Gray Slide Show, and this look will be instantly applied to your collection of photos (as shown here).

Adding Video to Your Slide Show

Adobe didn't add a bunch of new features to the Slideshow module back in Lightroom 5, but the one they did add was a biggie: the ability to have video clips and stills together in the same slide show. This expands what we can do in a big way. If you're a wedding photographer, or if you want to make a promo video for your business, or for behind-the-scenes videos, or even your family vacation, you no longer need to learn a dedicated video program to make a simple movie.

Step One:

Start in the Library module by creating a collection with the videos and stills you want in your slide show (in our example, we've got video clips of a bride and some still images). Now, press **Command-Option-5 (PC: Ctrl-Alt-5)** to switch to the Slideshow module.

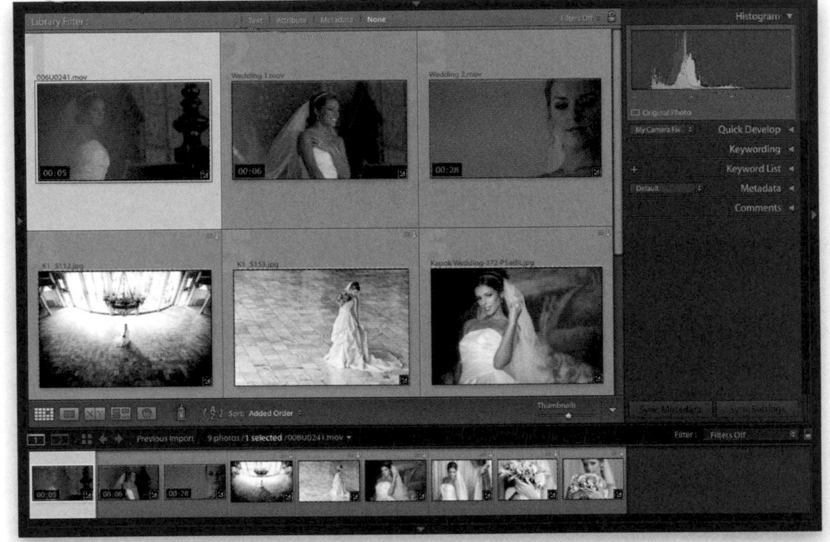

SCOTT KELBY

Step Two:

The order that you see the images down in the Filmstrip is the order your videos and still photos will appear, so go ahead and arrange them in the order you want them. (*Note:* I generally find it looks better if you start with a video clip and then put a similar-looking still right after it.) Choose the Crop To Fill or Widescreen preset in the Template Browser on the left. Now, there are a few things I would definitely add to make this slide show more like a short movie, and we'll cover that next.

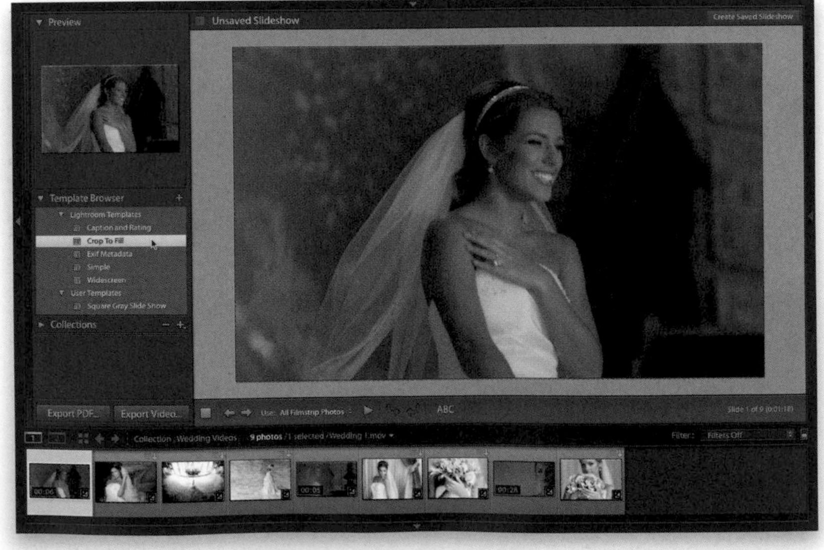

TIP: Editing Video Clips

If you want to learn how to trim clips and choose the opening frame for your video and stuff like that, turn to Chapter 15 here in the book for my chapter on using DSLR video in Lightroom.

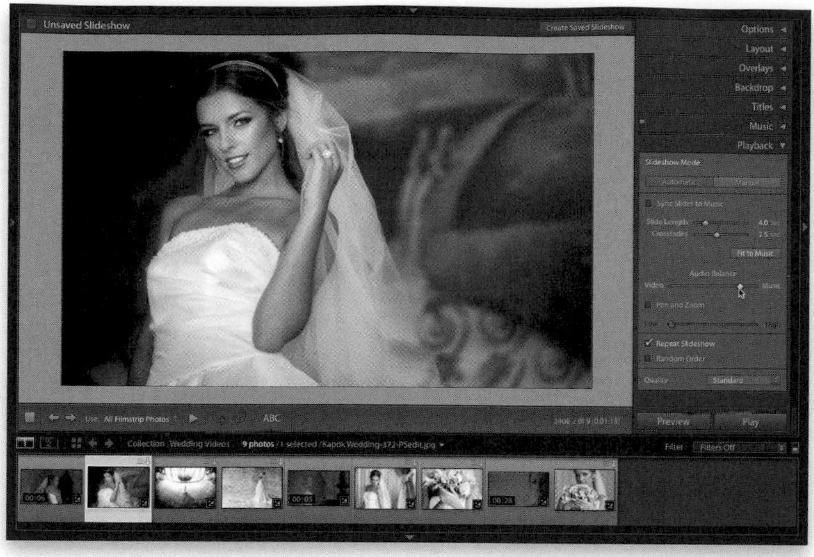

Step Three:

First, I'd start with an intro screen (see page 428 in this chapter) with the name of the bride and groom (in our case, Elizabeth & Alexander), and an ending screen (but I'd avoid writing "The End," unless you want a really awkward moment for everyone watching). Of course, for a wedding video like this, you need a background music track (see page 430). However, in Lightroom CC, since you're mixing video and stills, there's an important slider in the Playback panel. It's the Audio Balance slider and it lets you control the balance between the background music and any audio that was recorded by your camera when you shot the video. If you drag this slider all the way to the right, you'll only hear the background music. Drag it all the way to the left and you'll hear nothing but the audio in the video file. Put it in the middle, and you hear equal amounts of both, and you can drag it left or right to balance the two any way you want.

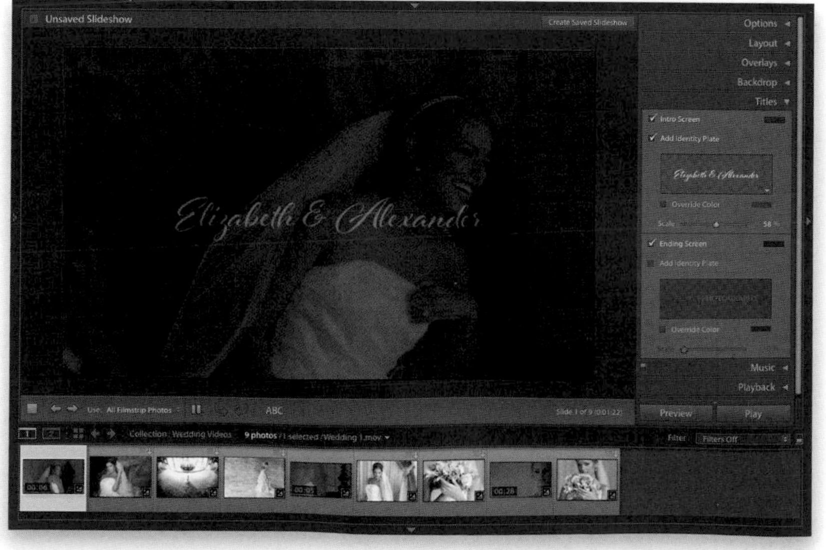

Step Four:

To see a preview of your slideshow, click the Preview button at the bottom of the right side Panels area. When you click that button, the slide show starts (with the intro screen, as seen here), and then moves through the videos and stills in order, with a dissolve between each one (controlled by the Crossfades slider in the Playback panel). That's all there is to it!

Getting Creative with Photo Backgrounds

Besides a solid color and a gradient fill, you can choose a photo as your slide background, and you can control the opacity of this background photo, so you can create a backscreened effect. The only downside is that the same background appears on every slide (except the title slides, of course), so you can't vary the background effect from slide to slide. Here, we're going to look at a simple photo background, then take it up a notch, and then finally pull a few tricks that will let you create some very creative slide show layouts.

Step One:

First a little setup: go to the Template Browser and click on the template named Caption and Rating. Now, let's simplify the layout: In the Options panel (at the top of the right side Panels area), turn off the checkboxes for Stroke Border and Cast Shadow, then click on the top-left corner of the guides and drag inward until your photo is smaller and closer to the bottom-right corner (like the one shown here. After I did this, I turned off the Show Guides checkbox in the Layout panel). Now go down to the Overlays panel and turn off both the Text Overlays checkbox and the Rating Stars checkbox (so we don't see stars over our photo).

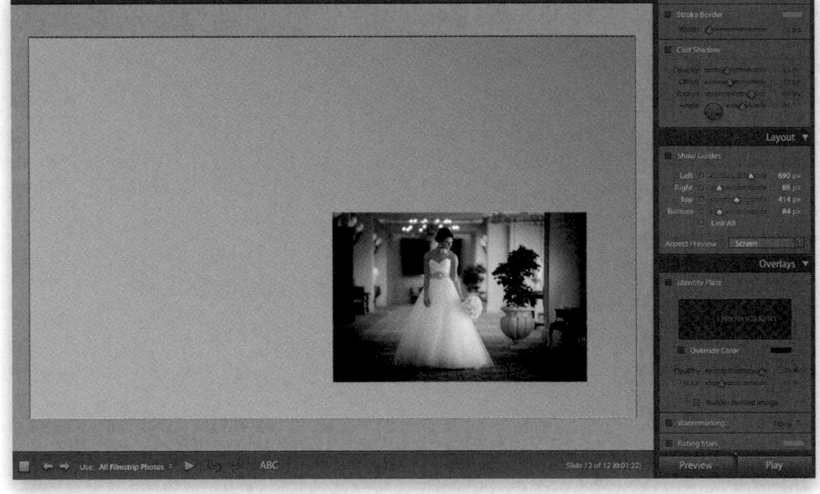

SCOTT KELBY

Step Two:

Go to the Backdrop panel, and turn the Color Wash checkbox off, so you no longer have a gradient over the background. Now, go to the Filmstrip and drag-and-drop the photo you want to use as a background image onto the Background Image well in the Backdrop panel (as shown here; you may have to turn the Background Image checkbox on first), and that image now appears as the background behind your currently selected photo. The background photo appears at 100% opacity, which usually means it's going to compete with your foreground photo, and for that reason we usually create a "backscreened" effect for the background photo, so it appears washed out and more subtle, and your main image stands out again.

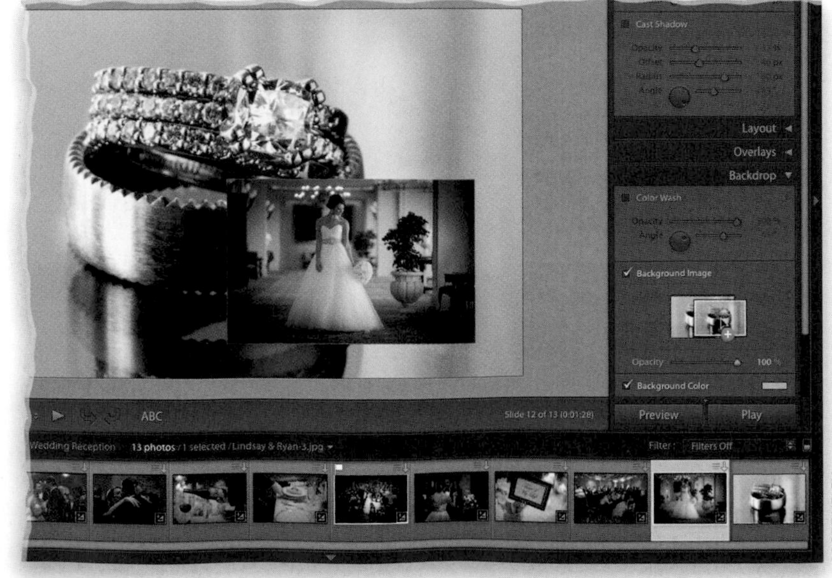

SCOTT KELBY

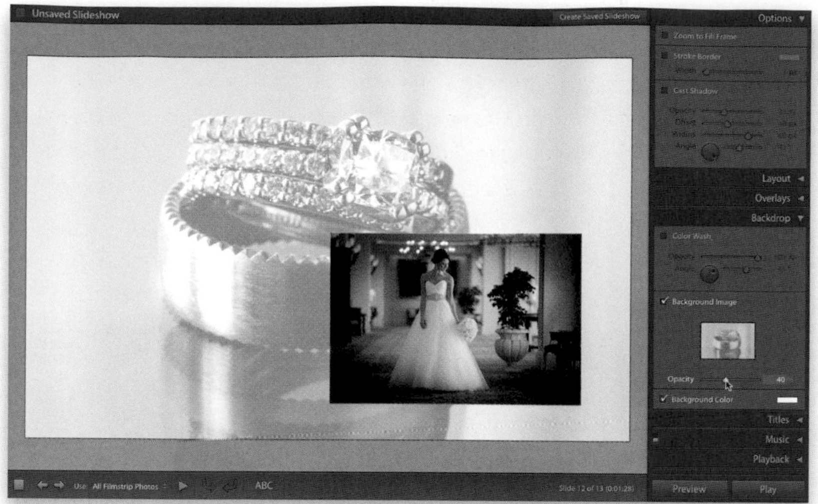

Step Three:

To create that backscreened effect, lower the Background Image Opacity to 40% (this will vary, depending on your image), and the photo fades to gray. If you prefer to have a white backscreened look, set your Background Color to white (click on the color swatch, then choose white in the color picker, as I did here), or if you want a black backscreened look (rather than gray or white), set the Background Color to black (which color looks best kind of depends on the photo you choose).

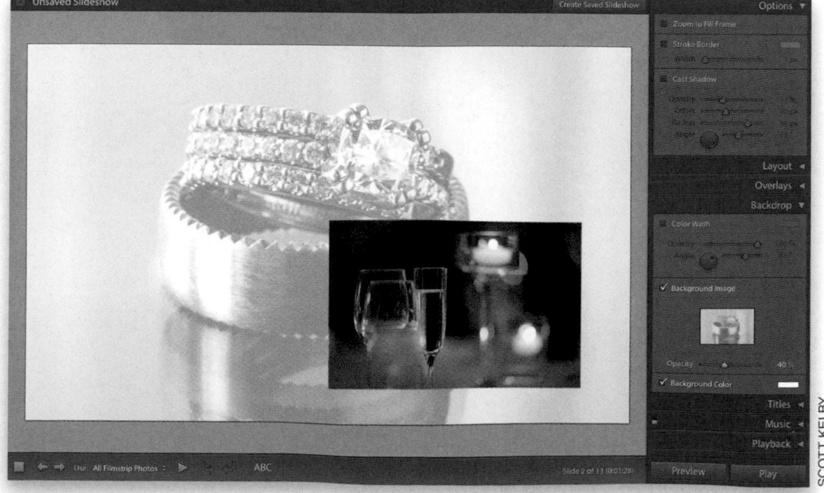

SCOTT KELBY

Step Four:

When you click the Preview button, or the Play button, you'll see the slides play with the photo you chose as the background image (as I mentioned in the intro, this same background will appear behind each photo).

Continued

Step Five:

Now, thus far, we've just used one of our regular photos from the shoot as our background image, but if you use images that were designed to be backgrounds, you get an entirely different look. For example, the image shown here is a background image I bought from Fotolia. I just went to their site (www.fotolia.com), did a search for "photo frames," and this came up as one of the results. So I bought it, then imported it into Lightroom. Once it appeared in Lightroom, I dragged it into the collection where I wanted to use it, then I dragged it onto the Background Image well in the Backdrop panel for the effect you see here. (*Note:* I buy royalty-free stuff like this from either iStockphoto [www.istockphoto.com], Fotolia, or Dollar Photo Club [www.dollarphotoclub.com], but almost every microstock site has lots of frames and borders you can buy for just a few bucks.)

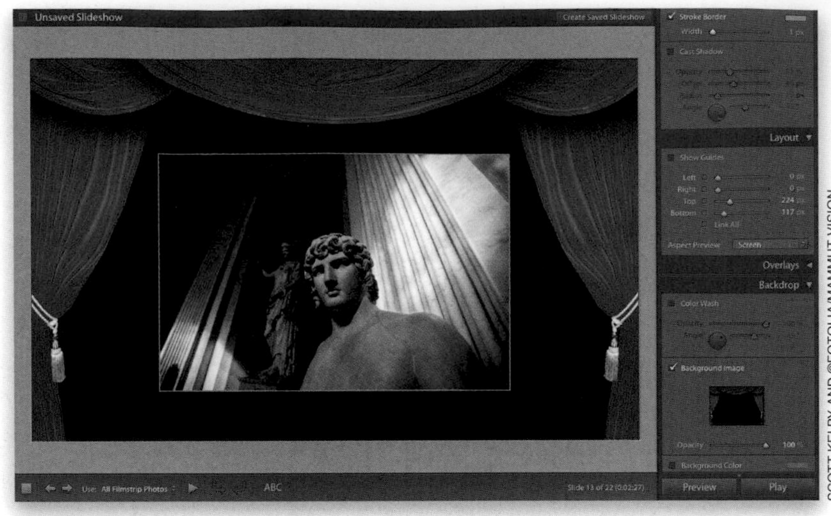

SCOTT KELBY AND ©FOTOLIA/MAMMUT VISION

Step Six:

Here's another example of the kind of simple backgrounds you can download for your slide shows. Once you've imported the background image into Lightroom, remember to drag that image into the collection where you want to use it, then drag it onto the Background Image well in the Backdrop panel. Now, as your slide show plays, the images will appear inside the iPad. The only tricky part of this is getting the image to fit right inside the iPad. The trick is to (1) go to the Options panel and turn on the Zoom to Fill Frame checkbox. Then, (2) go to the Layout panel, click on Link All to turn this off, make your guides visible, and move them so they're just about the same size (on all sides) as the iPad's screen. It's easier than it sounds, since you can just drag the guides around right in the Preview area.

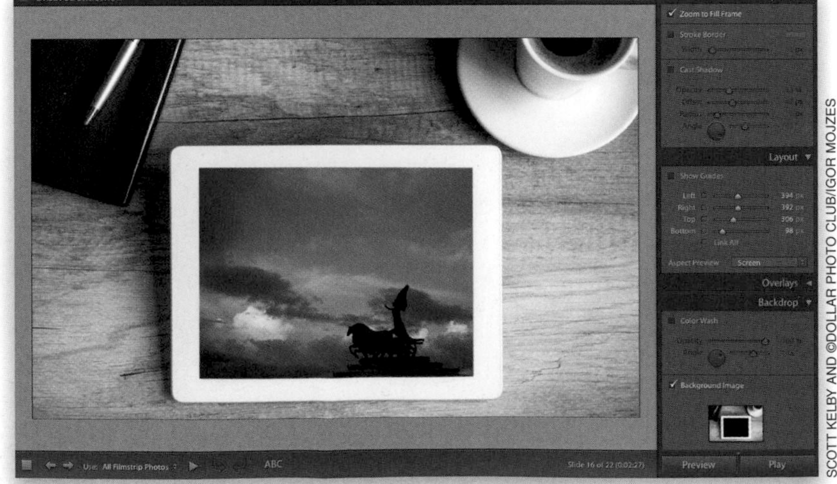

SCOTT KELBY AND ©DOLLAR PHOTO CLUB/IGOR MOJZES

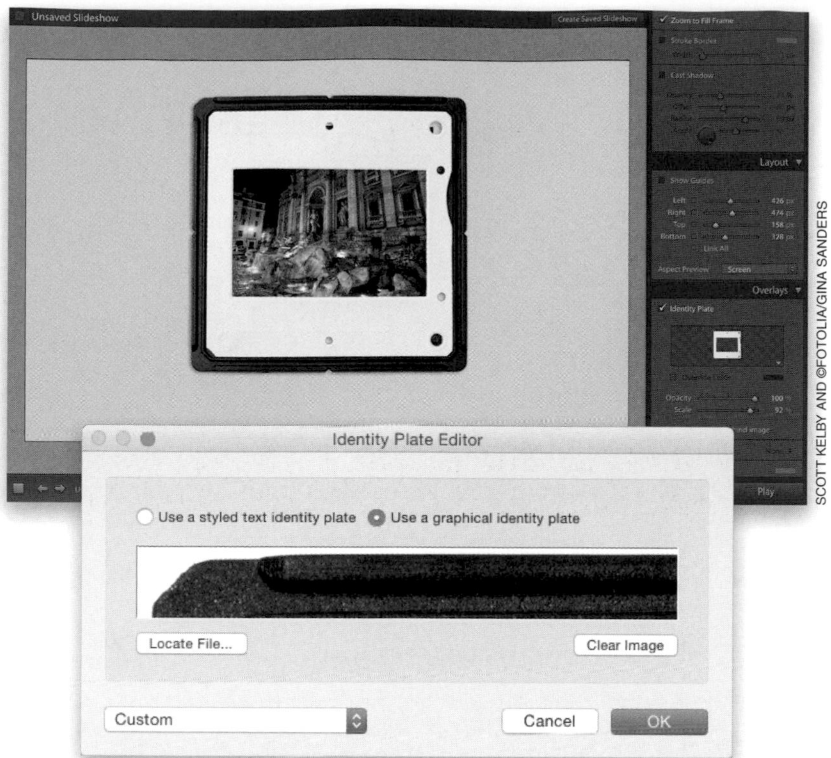

SCOTT KELBY AND ©FOTOLIA/GINA SANDERS

Step Seven:

Here's a workaround background trick that lets you put a photo inside your background (complete with a shadow): instead of using a graphic as a background image, use it as an Identity Plate. That way, you can have the background image appear in front of (or over) your photo rather than behind it. Here's a slide mount image I bought from Fotolia. I took it into Photoshop, selected the slide and put it on its own layer, then selected the box in the center, and deleted it (to make the slide opening see-through). Next, I added a drop shadow in the opening, deleted the Background layer, and saved the file as a PNG to maintain its transparency when I bring it into Lightroom as a graphical Identity Plate. To bring it in, go to the Overlays panel, turn on the Identity Plate checkbox, click on the triangle at the bottom right of the Identity Plate preview, and choose **Edit** from the pop-up menu. When the Identity Plate Editor appears (shown here), click on the Use a Graphical Identity Plate radio button, then click on Locate File to find your slide file, and click OK. Once it appears in the Preview area, resize both the Identity Plate (by dragging the corner points) and the image (by dragging the margin guides). Also, be sure to have the Zoom to Fill Frame checkbox turned on in the Options panel.

BONUS VIDEO:

I did a bonus video for you, to show you step by step how to create Identity Plate graphics with transparency like you see here. You'll find it at **http://kelbyone.com/books/LRCC**.

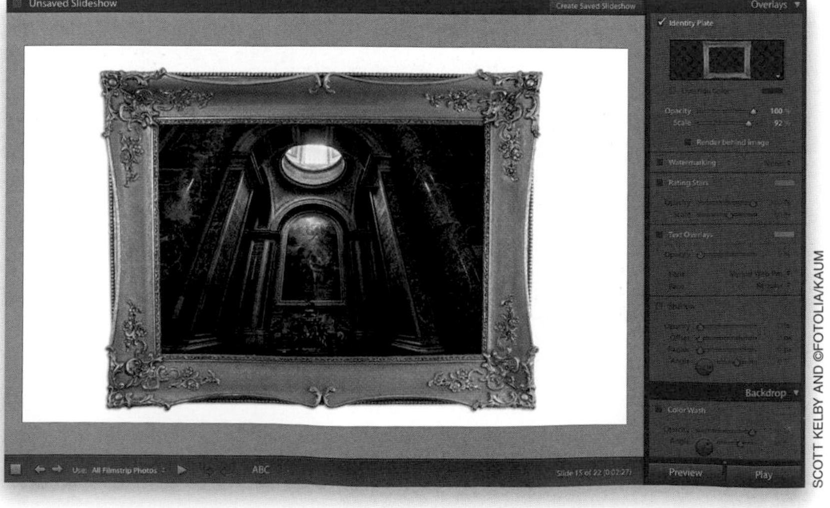

SCOTT KELBY AND ©FOTOLIA/KAUM

Step Eight:

Here's another variation using a picture frame I bought from Fotolia. The only difference is that I changed the Background Color (in the Backdrop panel) from gray to white. Now that you're seeing the potential of these backgrounds and Identity Plates, let's put the two together for some really creative layouts.

Continued

Step Nine:

For this layout, let's start from scratch. Go to the Template Browser and click on the Caption and Rating template, then go to the Overlays panel and turn off the checkboxes for Rating Stars and Text Overlays, and be sure the Identity Plate checkbox is turned off, as well. Go to the Backdrop panel and turn off Color Wash, then go up to the Options panel and turn off the Cast Shadow and Stroke Border checkboxes. Now, use the margin guides to resize your image to give us the simple, clean look you see here.

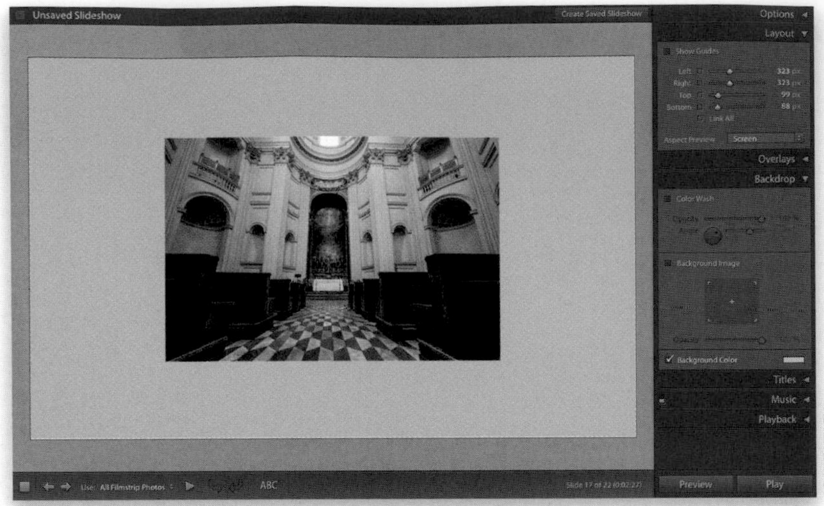

SCOTT KELBY

Step 10:

I went and downloaded an old map from Fotolia (believe it or not, I searched for "old map" and this is what came up as the first result. Perfect!). Import that old map image into Lightroom, then drag it into the collection you're working with. Once it's there, drag that old map image into the Background Image well in the Backdrop panel (as seen here) to make the map the background for the slide. So far, so good.

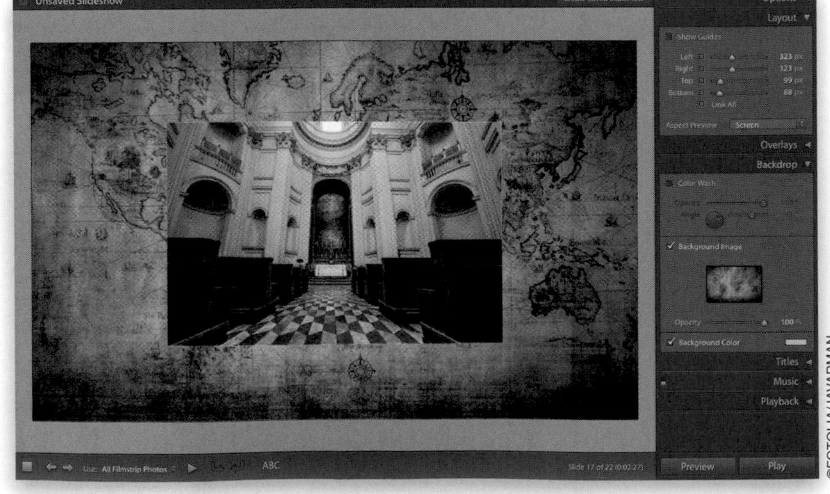

©FOTOLIA/JAVARMAN

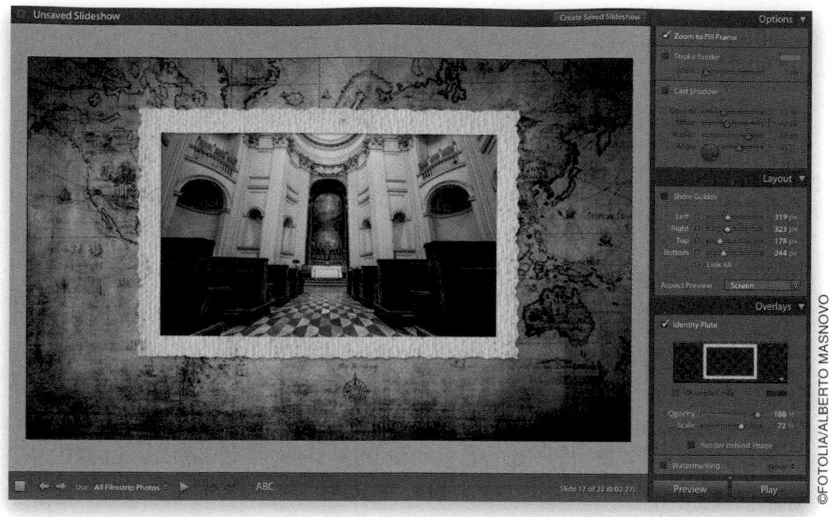

Step 11:

When I searched "photo frame" in Fotolia earlier, I found this antique-looking photo frame. We're going to use this as a graphical Identity Plate, but before we do that, you'll need to use the same Photoshop technique I mentioned in Step Seven (and showed you in the bonus video), to make the center and surrounding area transparent (if we don't do that, you'd see a white box inside and around your frame, instead of the background around the frame, and inside being transparent, so it would totally wreck the look). Also notice how a slight drop shadow appears inside the frame, so it appears the photo is actually inside the frame. Anyway, once you've done the Photoshop transparency trick, go to the Overlays panel, turn on the Identity Plate checkbox, click on the triangle in the bottom-right corner of the Identity Plate preview, and choose Edit from the pop-up menu. When the Identity Plate Editor appears, click on the Use a Graphical Identity Plate radio button, then find your frame file, and click OK. Once it appears in the Preview area, resize both the Identity Plate and the image for the look you see here.

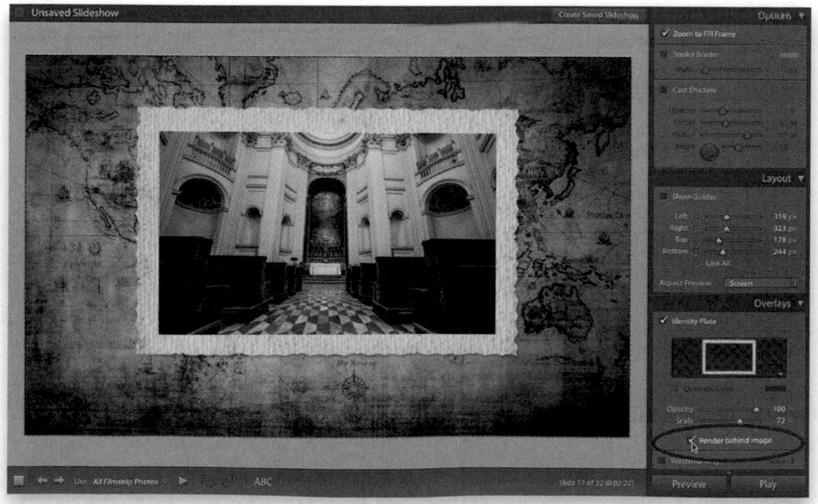

Step 12:

Make sure you have the Render Behind Image checkbox turned off, if you want the photo frame to appear in front of your image (like it does in Step 11), or for a slightly different look, turn it on (as seen here), so the image appears on top of the frame—you won't get the drop shadow appearing on the inside of your image, adding depth. The final layout is shown here (or in Step 11, depending on whether you turned the Render Behind Image checkbox on or off). I hope these few pages spark some ideas for you of what can be done with background images, Identity Plates, and using both together.

Working with Drop Shadows and Strokes

If you're building a slide show on a light background, or on a photo background, you can add a drop shadow behind your image to help it stand out from the background. You also have the option of adding a stroke to your images. While most of the built-in templates already have these features turned on, here we'll look at how to add them and how to make adjustments to both.

Step One:

To add a drop shadow, go the Options panel in the right side Panels area, and turn on the Cast Shadow checkbox. Most of the built-in templates, like Caption and Rating (shown here), already have the drop shadow feature turned on. The two controls you'll probably use the most are Opacity (how dark your drop shadow appears), and Radius (which controls how soft your drop shadow is. Why don't they call it "Softness?" Because that would be too obvious and easy [wink]). The Offset setting controls how far the shadow appears from the photo, so if you want it to look like your photo is higher off the background, increase the Offset amount. The Angle setting determines where the light is coming from, and by default, it positions your shadow down and to the right.

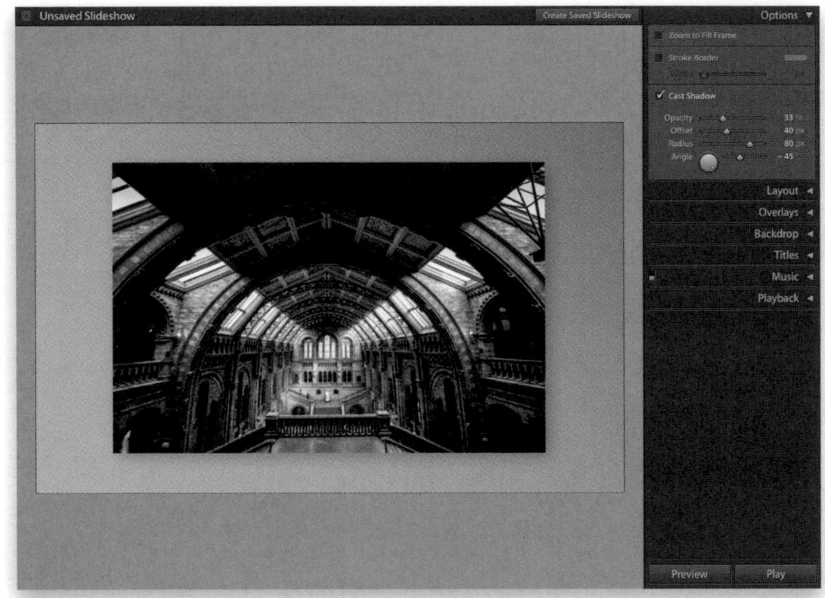

SCOTT KELBY

Step Two:

Let's tweak the drop shadow a bit: lower the Opacity amount to 25%, so it's lighter, then increase the Offset amount to 100%, so it looks like the photo is an inch or two off the background. Next, lower the Radius to 48%, so it's not quite as soft, and lastly, set the Angle to –41°, just to tweak its position a bit. Turning on the Stroke Border checkbox (at the top of the Options panel) puts a color stroke around your image. In this built-in template (and a couple of the others), the stroke is already on, but it's white and only 1-pixel thick, so you can hardly see it. To change the color, click on the color swatch, then choose a new color from the color picker (I chose black here). To make the stroke thicker, drag the Width slider to the right (I dragged mine to 12 px).

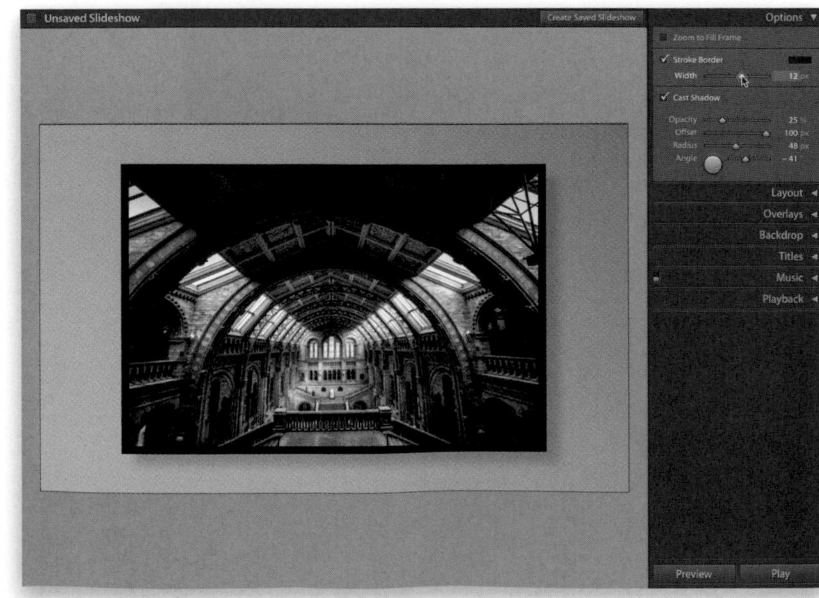

Besides adding text using the Identity Plate, you can add other lines of text to your photo (either custom text that you type in, or info that Lightroom pulls from the photo's EXIF data, or any metadata you added when you imported the photos, like your copyright info). You can also add a watermark to your slide show images, in case you're sending this slide show to a client or posting it on the web.

Adding Additional Lines of Text and Watermarking

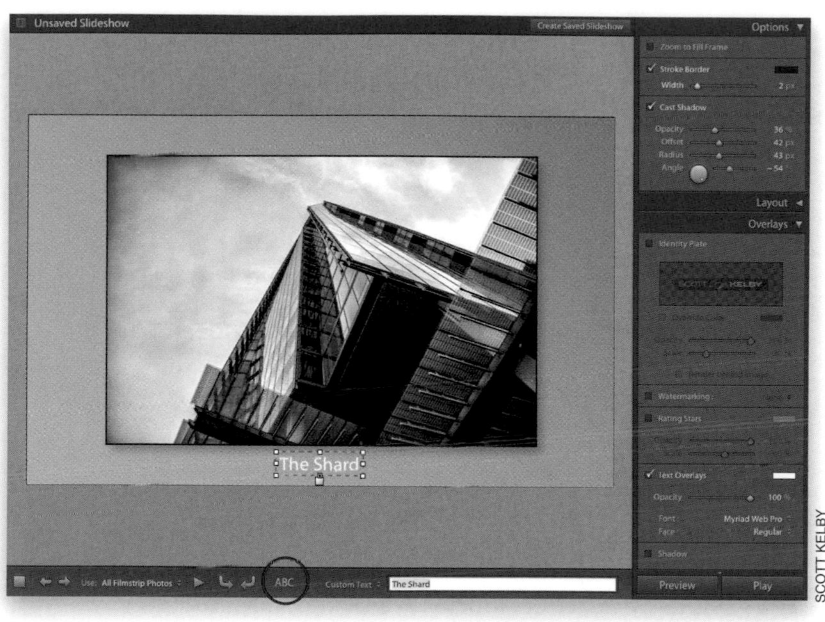

SCOTT KELBY

Step One:

To add text, click on the ABC button down in the toolbar (shown circled here in red), and a pop-up menu and text field will appear to the right of it. The default setting is Custom Text, and you can simply type the text you want in the text field, and then press the Return (PC: Enter) key. Your text appears on your slide with a resizing border around it. To resize your text, click-and-drag on any corner point. To move the text, just click right on it and drag it where you want it. If you click-and-hold on the words Custom Text in the toolbar, a pop-up menu appears that lets you choose text that may be embedded into your photo's metadata. For example, if you choose Date, it displays the date the photo was taken. If you choose any of the other options, it only displays that info if it's in the file (in other words, if you didn't add caption info in the Metadata panel, choosing Caption here won't get you anything).

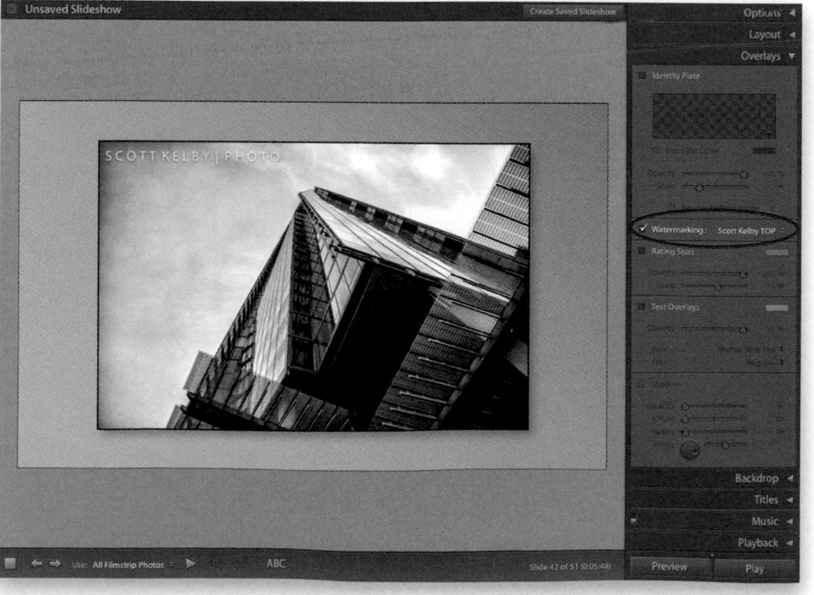

Step Two:

If you set up a watermark (see page 338), you can add that, as well (or instead of the additional text). Go to the Overlays panel and turn on the Watermarking checkbox, and then choose your watermark preset from the pop-up menu (you can see the watermark here at the top left). The advantage of using a watermark (rather than custom text) is that you can use pre-made templates, where you also can lower the opacity so it's see-through, and doesn't fully cover the image behind it.

Adding Opening and Closing Title Slides

One way to customize your slide show is to create your own custom opening and closing title slides (I usually only create an opening slide). Besides just looking nice, having an opening slide serves an important purpose—it conceals the first slide in your presentation, so your client doesn't see the first image until the show actually begins.

Step One:

You create opening/closing slides in the Titles panel (found in the right side Panels area). To turn this feature on, turn on the Intro Screen checkbox and your title screen appears for just a few seconds (as seen here), then the first photo appears again. (Arrrgh!!! It makes working with titles really frustrating, however, here's a cool trick I stumbled upon to make it stick around as long and whenever you want: just click-and-hold directly on the Scale slider [as shown here] and it assumes you're going to use it, so the title screen stays visible until you let go.) The little color swatch to the right lets you choose a background color (by default, the background color is black). To add text, you add your Identity Plate text (or graphic) by turning on the Add Identity Plate checkbox, and your current Identity Plate text appears (as seen here).

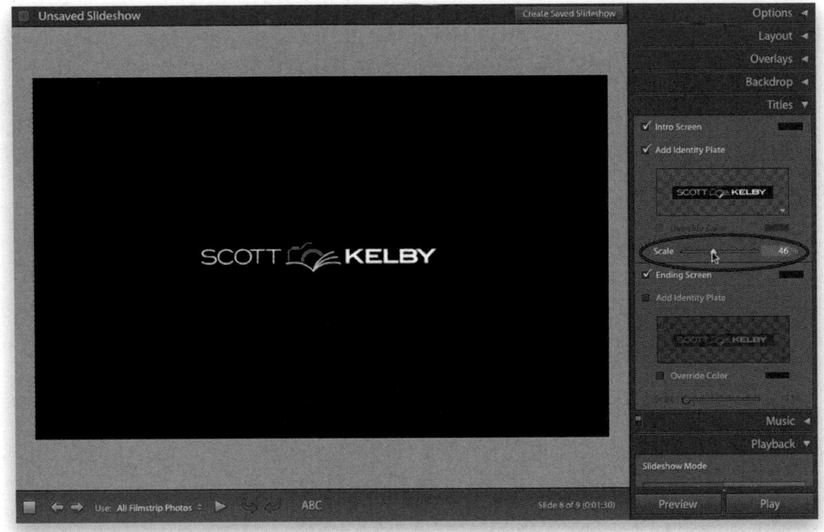

Step Two:

To customize your Identity Plate text, click on the little triangle in the bottom-right corner of the Identity Plate preview and choose **Edit** from the pop-up menu that appears to bring up the Identity Plate Editor, seen here. Now you can highlight the existing text, type in any text you'd like (in this case, I added the bride's and groom's names), and choose a different font from the Font pop-up menu (I used "Al Fresco" from MyFonts [www.myfonts.com]). Click OK to apply this text to your intro slide. *Note:* If you make your text white, it's impossible to see in this dialog, so I highlight it before I start typing and then again when I'm done, as seen here.

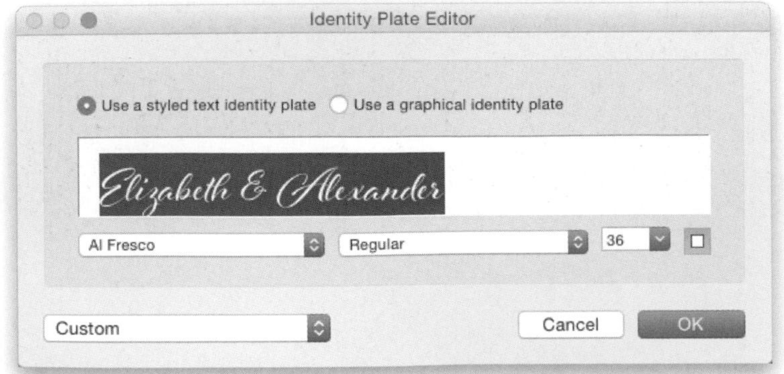

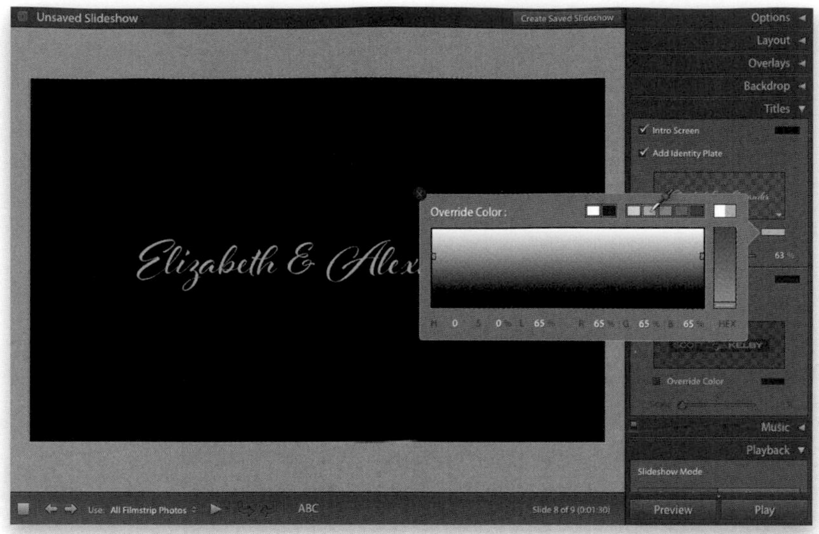

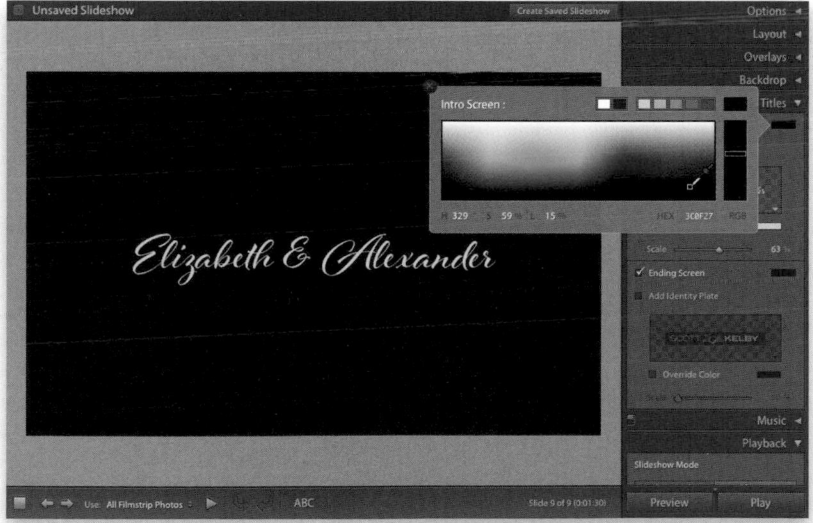

Step Three:

You can control the color of your Identity Plate text by turning on the Override Color checkbox (found under the Identity Plate preview). Once you turn that on, click once on the color swatch to its right and a color picker appears (shown here). At the top are some handy color swatches in white, black, and different shades of gray. You can choose one of those, or drag the bar up/down on the far right to choose a hue, and then you can choose your color's saturation from the large color picker gradient (here, I'm choosing a gray color, and you can see that color instantly reflected in the text). You can also control the size of your Identity Plate text by using the Scale slider at the bottom of the Intro Screen section.

Step Four:

To change the color of the intro screen's background, just click on the color swatch to the right of the Intro Screen checkbox. In this case, I changed the background to a maroon color just to show you what it looks like (I also changed the color of my Identity Plate to match the background). Once all your title text is formatted the way you want it (good luck on that, by the way, because editing text in the Identity Plate Editor is…well…it's clunky as heck, and I didn't want to say heck), you can preview the slide show in the Preview area. The ending screen works the same way: to turn it on, you turn on the Ending Screen checkbox in the Titles panel, and you can choose that screen's background color, Identity Plate size, etc., just like you did with the intro screen.

Adding Background Music

The right background music can make all the difference in a slide show presentation, and if you get a chance to see the pros show their work, you'll find they choose music that creates emotion and supports the images beautifully. Lightroom lets you add background music to your slide shows, and you can even embed that music into your slide shows and save them outside of Lightroom in multiple formats. More on that later, but for now, here's how to add background music to your slide shows.

Step One:

Go to the Music panel, near the bottom of the right side Panels area, and start by clicking on the Turn on Audio switch on the left side of the panel header. Now, click the Add Music button (as shown here), and a standard Open dialog will appear, where you choose which music file you want to play behind your slide show. Find your song and click Choose.

TIP: Add Multiple Music Tracks

In previous versions of Lightroom, you could only use one song, so if you had a long slide show, you had to choose a longer song. But, now, you can have multiple songs, playing back-to-back. After you've added your first song, just go to the Music panel and click the Add Music button again to add more tracks. Lightroom even calculates the total run time of all the songs—just look at the top of the Music panel and you'll see the Duration listed.

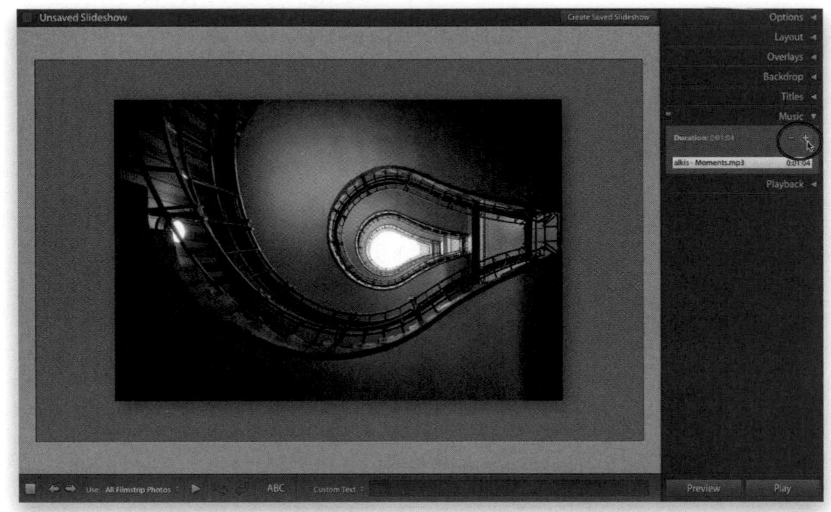

SCOTT KELBY

Note: Lightroom requires that your music file be in MP3 or AAC format, so it won't recognize WAV files. If you have Apple's iTunes, it can convert a music file to AAC format for you. In your Music library, click on My Music at the top, then click on the song you want to convert. Next, go to iTunes' File menu, under Create New Version, and choose **Create AAC Version**, and you'll see the converted version of your song appear directly below the original (these files are located in your iTunes folder in your Music folder).

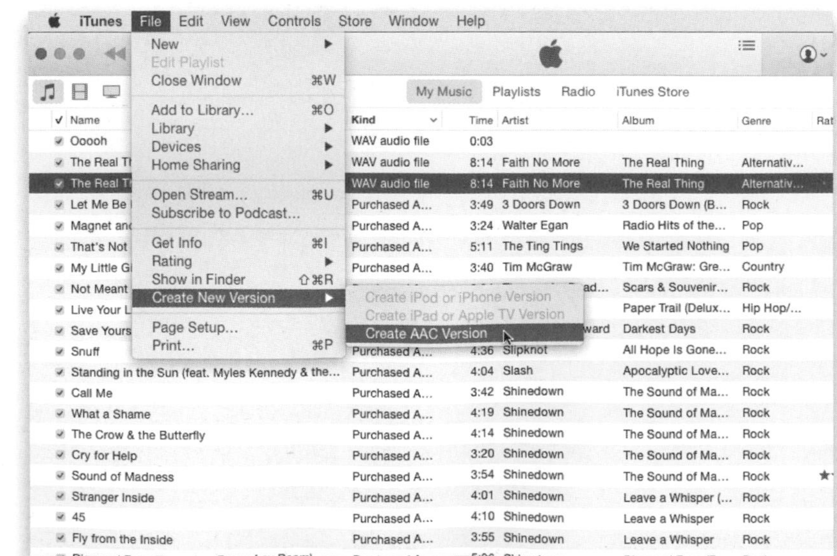

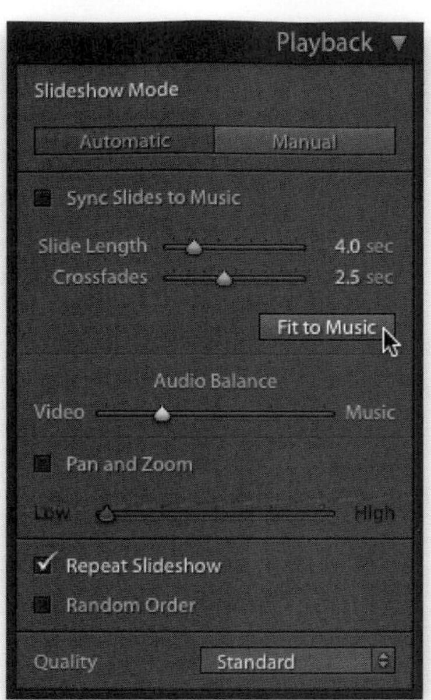

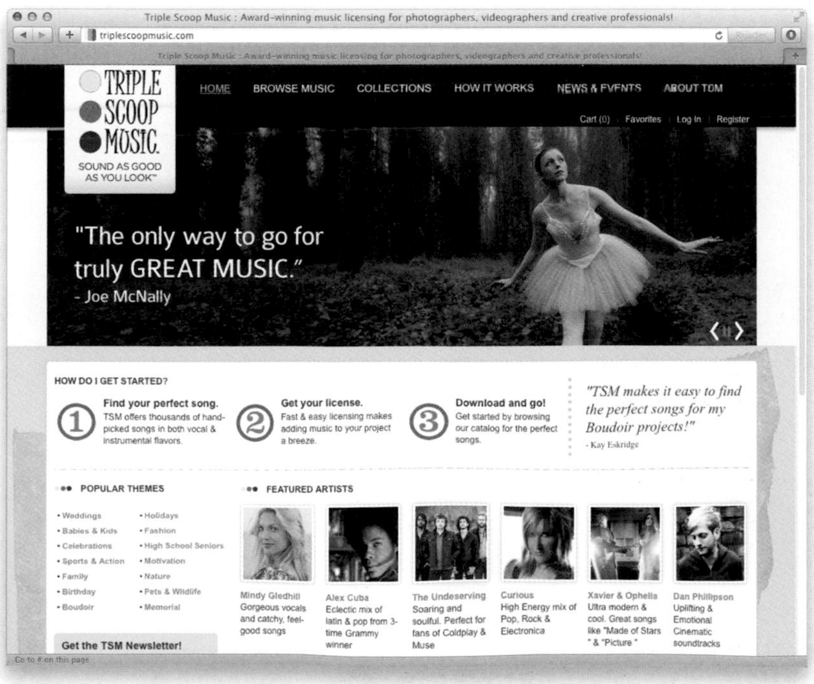

Step Two:

Now when you start your slide show (or even just preview it in the Preview area), the background music will play behind it. If you want to automatically have Lightroom adjust the length of your slide show so it matches the length of the song you chose, just click the Fit to Music button in the Playback panel (as shown here). What this actually does is adjusts the duration and fade time of your slides, based on how long the song is (so basically, it does the math for you).

TIP: Auto Syncing Music

There's a new feature in Lightroom CC that automatically syncs your slide show to the music. In the Playback panel, just turn on the Sync Slides to Music checkbox, and it analyzes the music track and chooses what it thinks is a suitable place to switch to the next slide based on the beat of the music, and son of a gun if every once in a while it actually works the way you want it to. Most of the time, I just sit there shaking my head wishing I could just choose where I want the slide to change by tapping a key or something, but hey, automatic syncing that works occasionally in a best-case scenario is better than none at all, right? Right? Hello? Is anybody there? ;-)

BONUS TIP: Background Music Ideas

I know how hard it is to find great background music. I've been a fan of Triple Scoop Music (www.triplescoopmusic.com) ever since I heard some of the instructors at Photoshop World Conference & Expo using Triple Scoop's royalty-free music tracks in their photo slide show presentations. As a musician myself, I am just so impressed with the quality of their tracks—their stuff is "the real deal." So, check out Triple Scoop Music for some ideas. They make it easy to find and license music for your slide show.

Choosing Your Slide Duration and Fade Length

Besides choosing your music, Lightroom's Playback panel in the Slideshow module is where you choose how long each slide stays onscreen and how long the transition (fade) between slides is. You can choose to play your slides in order or randomly, whether you want your slide show to repeat after your last slide or end at the last slide, and if you want your previews prepared in advance, so that your slide show doesn't get interrupted waiting for image data to render to the display.

Step One:

To choose how long your slides stay onscreen, go to the Playback panel and, in the Automatic settings, choose how many seconds each image should appear onscreen using the Slide Length slider. Then, choose how long the fade transition between images should last using the Crossfades slider. Lightroom uses a dissolve transition—each photo dissolves into the next—but if you want to advance the slides yourself (if you are using them to illustrate a talk or lecture), click on the Manual button at the top of the panel. Then, when you start your slide show, use the **Right Arrow key** to move to the next slide (this will be a hard transition, rather than a dissolve).

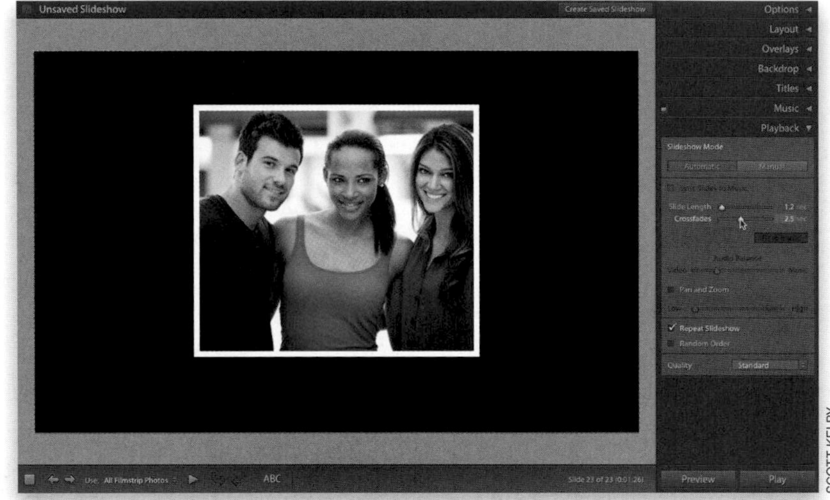

SCOTT KELBY

Step Two:

There are just a few other controls to mention: (1) By default, your slides play in the order they appear in the Filmstrip, unless you turn on the Random Order checkbox. (2) Also by default, when you reach the last slide in the Filmstrip, your slide show will loop around and play the whole thing again (and again, and again), unless you turn off the Repeat Slideshow checkbox. (3) In Lightroom CC, Adobe added their version of what's known as the "Ken Burns Effect, where your images slowly zoom in and pan as they appear onscreen, adding a sense of motion to your slide show. Just use the Pan and Zoom checkbox to toggle the effect on/off, along with the slider below, which is kind of an intensity slider (with Low, the movement is very subtle; High gets things really moving).

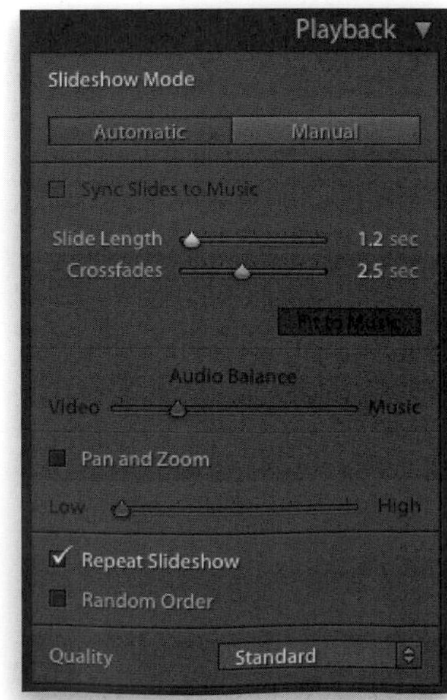

Sharing Your Slide Show

If you want to show someone your slide show and they happen to be nearby, then no sweat—you can show it right within Lightroom. But if they're not standing nearby (perhaps it's a client across town or across the country), you can output your slide show in a number of different formats, like Windows Movie Format, QuickTime, Flash, and H.264, and these'll include your images, layout, background music, and transitions. Sweet! You can also save your slide show in PDF format, but if you do, sadly, it won't include your background music.

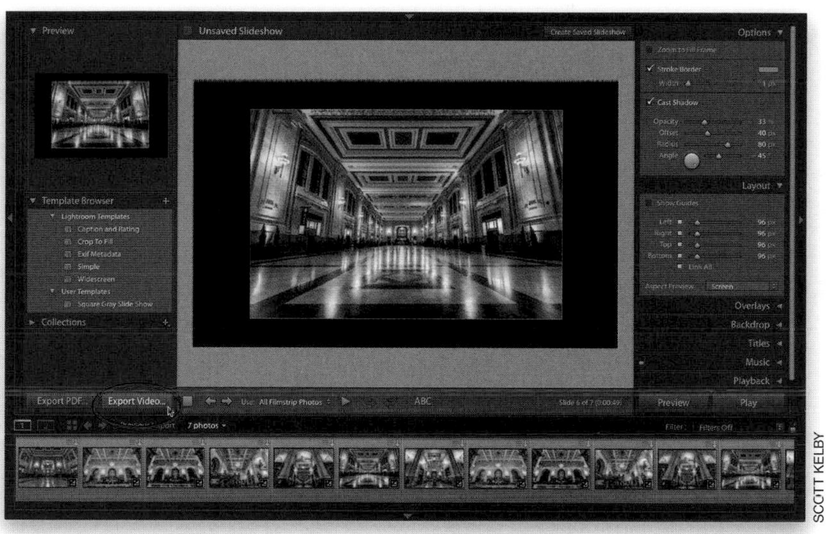

SCOTT KELBY

Step One:

To save your slide show in a video format (with background music), click on the Export Video button at the bottom of the left side Panels area (as shown here).

TIP: See a Preview in Different Screen Sizes

Want to see a preview of how your slide show would look in different output aspect ratios (like 16:9 for viewing on an HDTV, or the standard 4:3 ratio of regular NTSC and PAL monitors)? Just choose these from the Aspect Ratio pop-up menu at the bottom of the Layout panel. The default is Screen, which uses the aspect ratio of the monitor you're currently using for Lightroom.

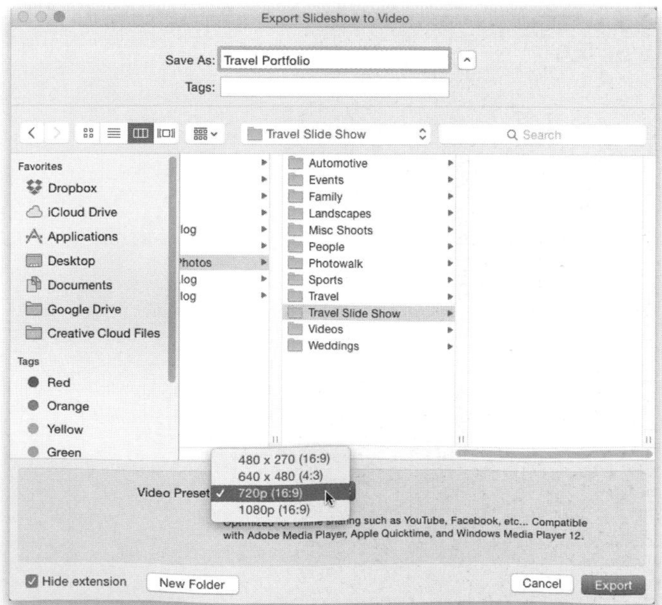

Step Two:

This brings up the Export Slideshow to Video dialog (shown here), where there's a Video Preset pop-up menu listing different sizes for your video. When you choose a preset size, it tells you right below the menu what that size works best for, and what type of devices (or software) will read the file. So, name your slide show, and then just choose the size you want, then click the Export (PC: Save) button and it creates the file for you, in the size you choose, and in a compatible format for that type of video.

Continued

Step Three:

The other export option is to save your slide show in PDF format. PDF is ideal for emailing because it compresses the file size big time, but of course the downside is that it doesn't include any background music you've added, which is a deal breaker for a lot of users. If that's not an issue for you, then it's worth considering. Just click the Export PDF button at the bottom of the left side Panels area, to bring up the Export Slideshow to PDF dialog (shown here). Go ahead and name your slide show, then at the bottom of the dialog, you'll see the Quality slider—the higher the quality, the larger the file size (which is a consideration when emailing). I usually use a Quality setting of 80 and I also always turn on the Automatically Show Full Screen checkbox, so the recipient can see the slide show without any other onscreen distractions. The width and height dimensions are automatically inserted in the Width and Height fields, but if you need the images to be smaller for emailing, you can enter smaller settings and Lightroom will automatically scale the photos down proportionally. When you're done, click the Export (PC: Save) button (as shown here).

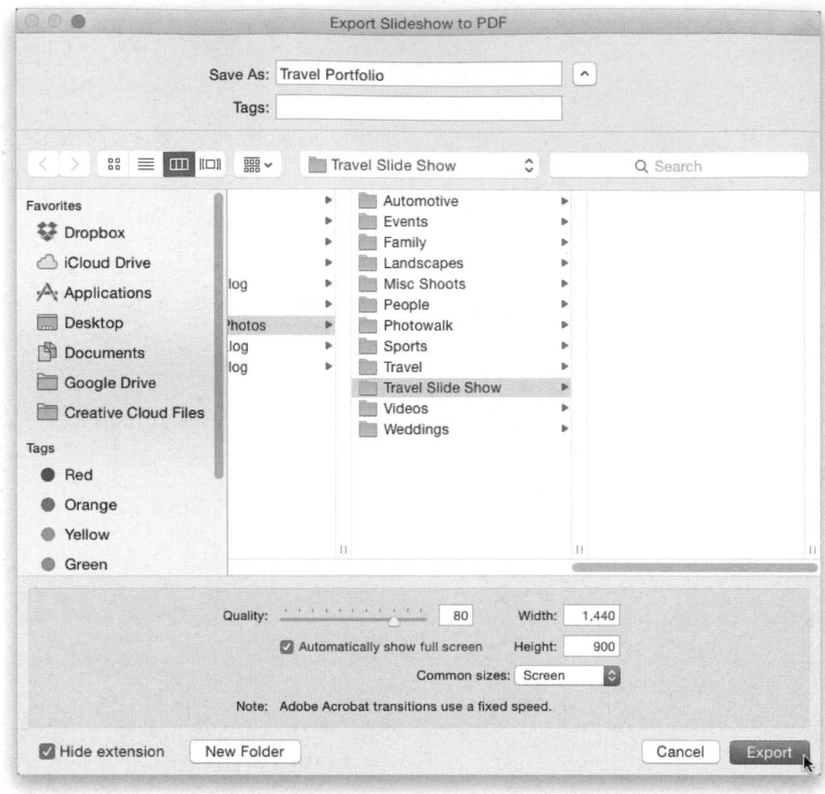

Step Four:

When your client (friend, relative, parole officer, etc.) double-clicks on your PDF, it will launch their Adobe Reader, and when it opens, it will go into full-screen mode and start your slide show, complete with smooth transitions between slides.

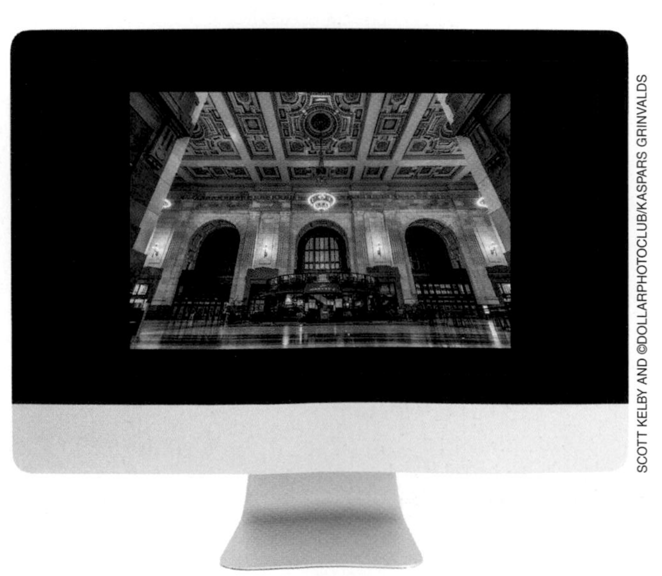

SCOTT KELBY AND ©DOLLARPHOTOCLUB/KASPARS GRINVALDS

TIP: Adding Filenames to a PDF

If you're planning on sending this PDF slide show to a client for proofing purposes, be sure to make the filename text overlay visible before you make the PDF. That way, your client will be able to tell you the name of the photo(s) they've approved.

Lightroom Killer Tips > >

▼ Draft Mode Speeds Things Up

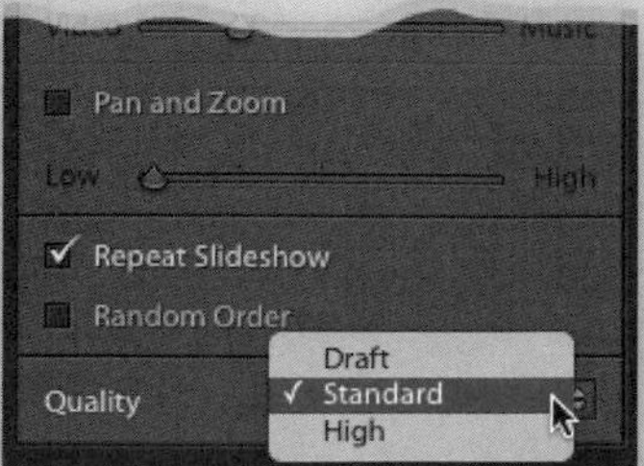

Nothing's worse than sitting there waiting for high-res previews to draw while you're working on your slide show, so Adobe introduced a draft mode that lets you quickly see a preview of your slide show without having to wait for the images to render. Choose this from the Quality pop-up menu at the bottom of the Playback panel. There are three quality choices: Draft (super fast), Standard (regular speed), and High (this might take a minute). Remember, these are just quality settings for while you're previewing the slide show here in Lightroom. When you export the slide show it's always exported using High Quality.

▼ Turn Off the "Effects"

Want to see your slide show without all the fancy stuff (music sync, pan and zoom, random order options)? Just click on Manual (at the top of the Playback panel) and it turns it all off until you click Automatic again.

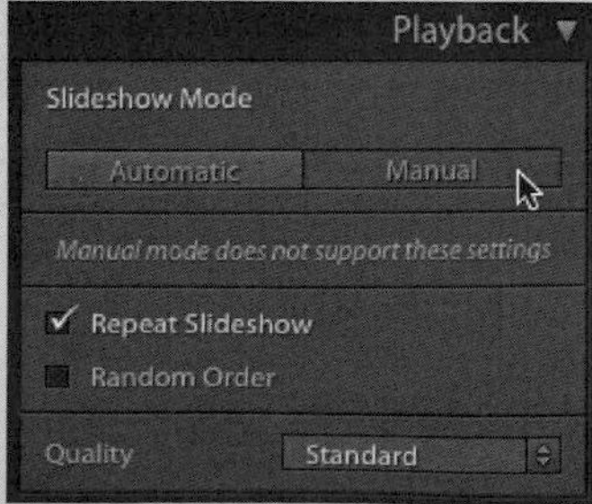

▼ Preview How Photos Will Look in Your Slide Show

On the far-right side of the toolbar that appears under the center Preview area, you'll see some text showing how many photos are in your current collection. If you move your cursor over that text, your

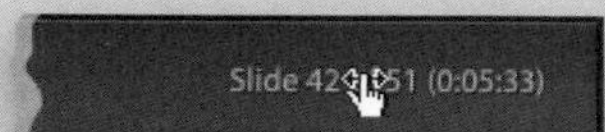

cursor turns into a scrubby slider, and you can click-and-drag left or right to see the other photos in your slide show appear in your current slide show layout (it's one of those things you have to try, and then you'll dig it).

▼ What Those Rotate Arrows Are For

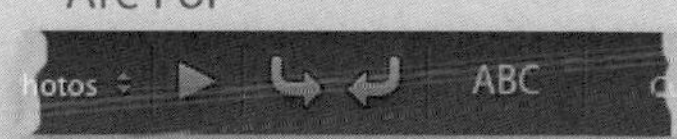

If you look down in the toolbar, you'll see two rotation arrows, but they're always grayed out. That's because they're not for rotating photos, they're for rotating any custom text you create (you add custom text by clicking on the ABC button in the toolbar).

▼ A Better Start to Your Slide Show

When you make a slide show presentation for a client, before the client is in front of your monitor, start the slide show, and as soon as it appears onscreen, press the **Spacebar** to pause it. Now when your client sits in front of the screen, they don't see your first photo—they see a black screen (or your title screen). When you're ready to begin your presentation, press the Spacebar again and your slide show starts.

▼ Detailed Slide Design

Although you can create your slide shows from scratch in Lightroom, there's nothing that says that you have to design your slides in Lightroom. If there are things you want to do that you can't do in Lightroom, just build the slides over in Photoshop, save them as JPEGs, then re-import the finished slides into Lightroom, and drop those into your slide show layout, add your background music, etc.

▼ Collections Remember Which Template You Used Last

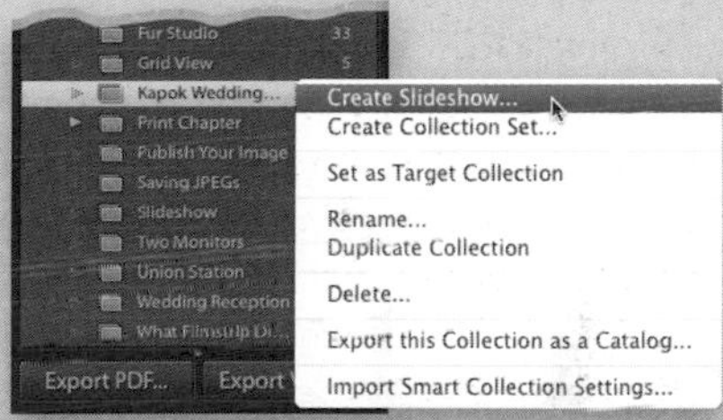

The Collections panel also appears in the Slideshow module (which you learned about in this chapter). If you click on a collection and select just a few photos in that collection for your slide show (and change the Use pop-up menu to Selected Photos in the toolbar at the bottom of the Preview area), and use them to set up a slide show, you probably want to be able to save that slide show so you don't have to go through all that again. Well, you can. Just Right-click on the collection, and choose **Create Slideshow** from the pop-up menu, or click on the Create Saved Slideshow button at the top right of the Preview area. This creates a new collection with just the photos you used in that particular slide show, in the right order, along with the template, so when you want that exact same slide show again (same look, same photos, same order), you're one click away.

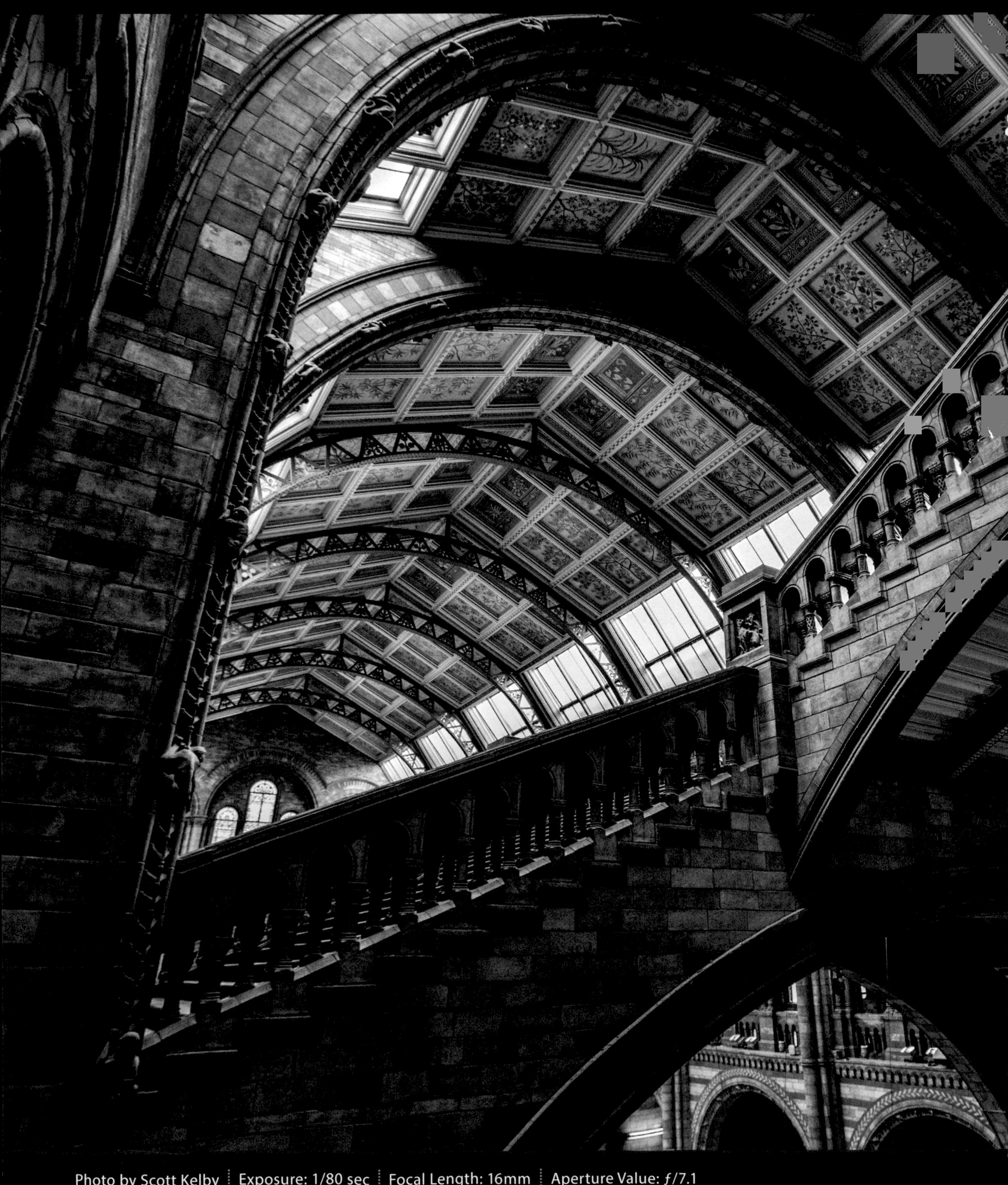

Photo by Scott Kelby | Exposure: 1/80 sec | Focal Length: 16mm | Aperture Value: ƒ/7.1

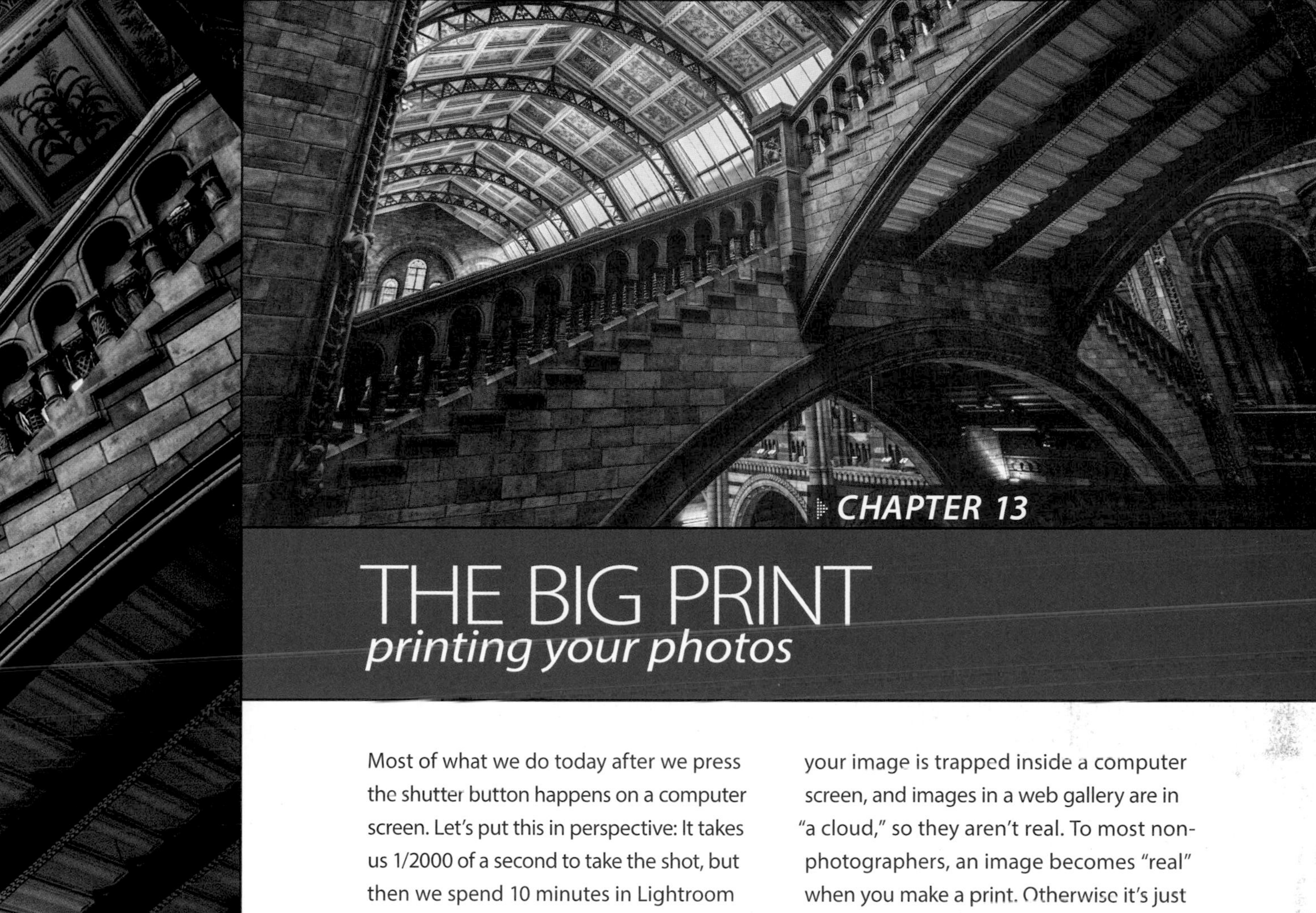

CHAPTER 13

THE BIG PRINT
printing your photos

Most of what we do today after we press the shutter button happens on a computer screen. Let's put this in perspective: It takes us 1/2000 of a second to take the shot, but then we spend 10 minutes in Lightroom processing the image, so the majority of our work takes place after the photo is taken. However, in real life, when we talk about a photo, your average person thinks of the 1/2000 of a second part of the photograph much more than they do the 10 minutes we spent on the computer balancing, sharpening, dodging and burning, etc., part. So, to them, the 1/2000 of a second part is the "real" part and the rest they (thankfully) don't really think that much about. So, when you show them a picture onscreen, it kind of reminds them that this is all software-based, because your image is trapped inside a computer screen, and images in a web gallery are in "a cloud," so they aren't real. To most non-photographers, an image becomes "real" when you make a print. Otherwise it's just some manipulated image on a computer. Think about it. So, you are kind of like a modern-day Dr. Frankenstein, in that you have created this thing, but you need to flip a switch (the printing switch), to give your creation life. Now, when you print, it's not entirely necessary to look toward the heavens, laugh an evil laugh, and yell, "It's alive!" but I can tell you that most of the pro photographers I know do exactly that (but you also should know that they generally wait to do all their printing on a dark, stormy night). Now you know.

Printing Individual Photos

If you really like everything else in Lightroom, it's the Print module where you'll fall deeply in love. It's really brilliantly designed (I've never worked with any program that had a better, easier, and more functional printing feature than this). The built-in templates make the printing process not only easy, but also fun (plus, they make a great starting point for customizing and saving your own templates).

Step One:

Before you do anything in the Print module, click on the Page Setup button at the bottom left, and choose your paper size (so you won't have to resize your layout once it's all in place). Now, start in the Template Browser (in the left side Panels area) by clicking on the Fine Art Mat template. The layout you see here should appear, displaying the first photo in your current collection (unless you have a photo selected—then it shows that one). There's a Collections panel here, too, so if you want to change collections, you can do so in the left side Panels area. A few lines of info appear over the top-left corner of your photo. It doesn't actually print on the photo itself, but if you find it distracting, you can turn this off by pressing the letter **I**, or going under the View menu and choosing **Show Info Overlay**.

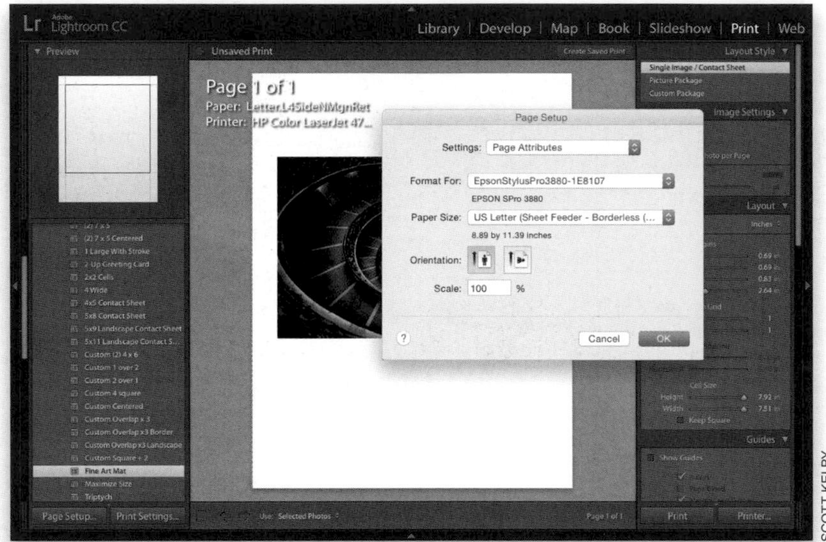

SCOTT KELBY

Step Two:

If you want to print more than one photo using this same template, go down to the Filmstrip and Command-click (PC: Ctrl-click) on the photos you want to print, and it instantly adds as many pages as you need (here, I've only selected one photo, but if I had selected 26, you'd see Page 1 of 26 down in the toolbar). There are three Layout Styles (in the Layout Style panel at the top right), and this first one is called Single Image/Contact Sheet. This works by putting each photo in a cell you can resize. To see this photo's cell, go to the Guides panel and turn on the Show Guides checkbox. Now you can see the page margins (in light gray), and your image cell (outlined in black, as seen here).

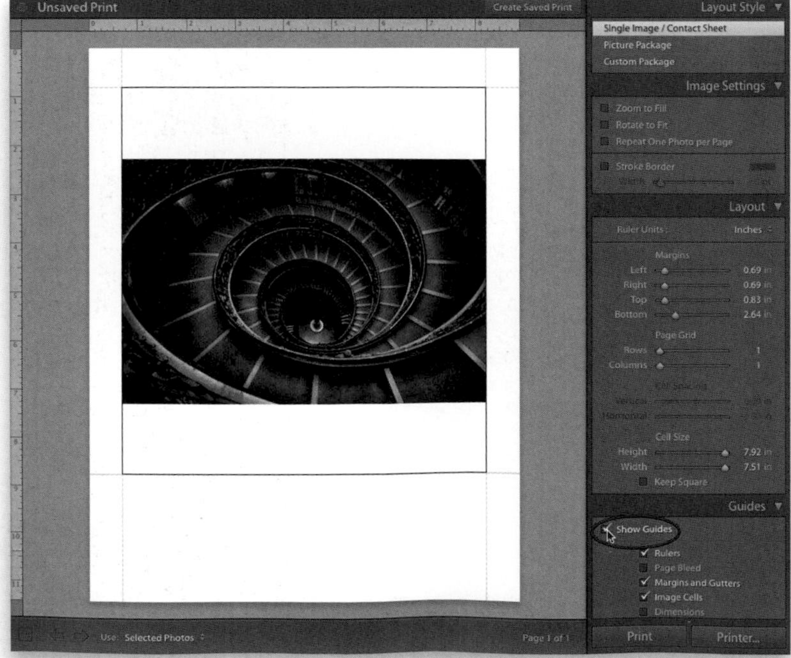

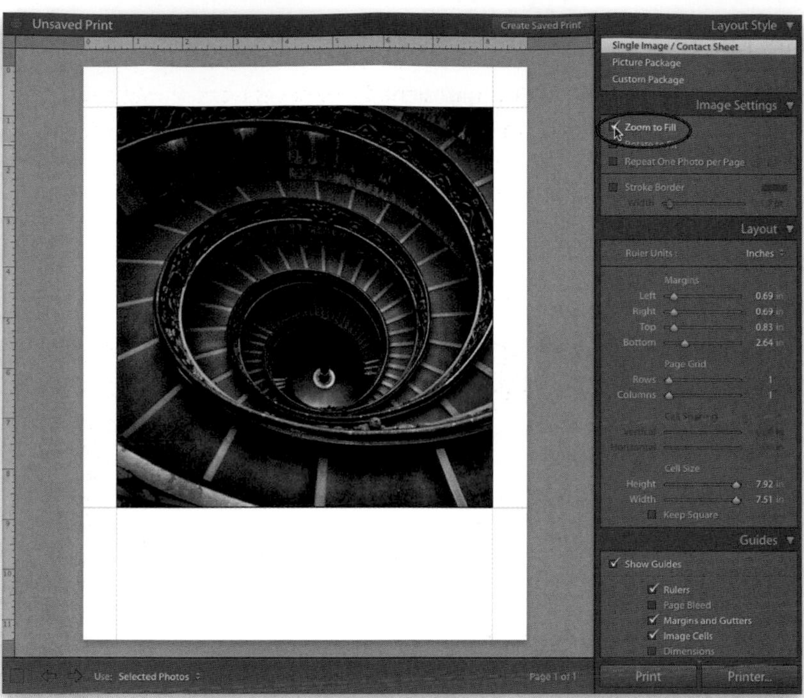

Step Three:

If you look back at the layout in Step Two, did you notice that the image fit the cell side-to-side, but there was a gap on the top and bottom? That's because, by default, it tries to fit your image in that cell so the entire image is visible. If you want to fill the cell with your photo, go to the Image Settings panel and turn on the Zoom to Fill checkbox (as shown here), and now your image fills it up (as seen here). Now, of course, this crops the image a bit, too (well, at least with this layout it did). This Zoom to Fill feature was designed to help you make contact sheets, but as we go through this chapter, I bet you'll totally start to love this little checkbox, because with it you can create some really slick layouts—ones your clients will love. So, even though it does crop the photo a bit, don't dismiss this puppy yet—it's going to get really useful very soon.

Step Four:

Now, let's work on the whole cell concept, because if you "get" this, the rest is easy. First, because your image is inside a cell and you have the Zoom to Fill checkbox turned on, if you change the size of your cell, the size of your photo doesn't change. So, if you make the cell smaller, it crops off part of your image, which is really handy when you're making layouts. To see what I mean, go to the Layout panel, and at the bottom of the panel are the Cell Size sliders. Drag the Height slider to the left (down to 3.87 in), and look at how it starts to shrink the entire image size down right away, until it reaches its original unzoomed width, then the top and bottom of the cell move inward without changing the width further. This kind of gives you a "letter box" view of your image (HD movie buffs will totally get that analogy).

Continued

Step Five:

Now drag the Height slider back to the right, kind of where it was before, then drag the Width slider to the left to shrink the width. This particular photo is wide (in landscape orientation), so while moving the top and bottom of the cell shrunk the image, and then the cell, dragging the Width slider like we are here, just shrinks the cell inward (this will all make sense in a minute). See how the left and right sides of your cell have moved in, creating the tall, thin cell you see here? This tall, thin layout is actually kind of cool on some level (well, it's one you don't see every day, right?), but the problem is that the center of the staircase is off the right side of the frame. We can fix that.

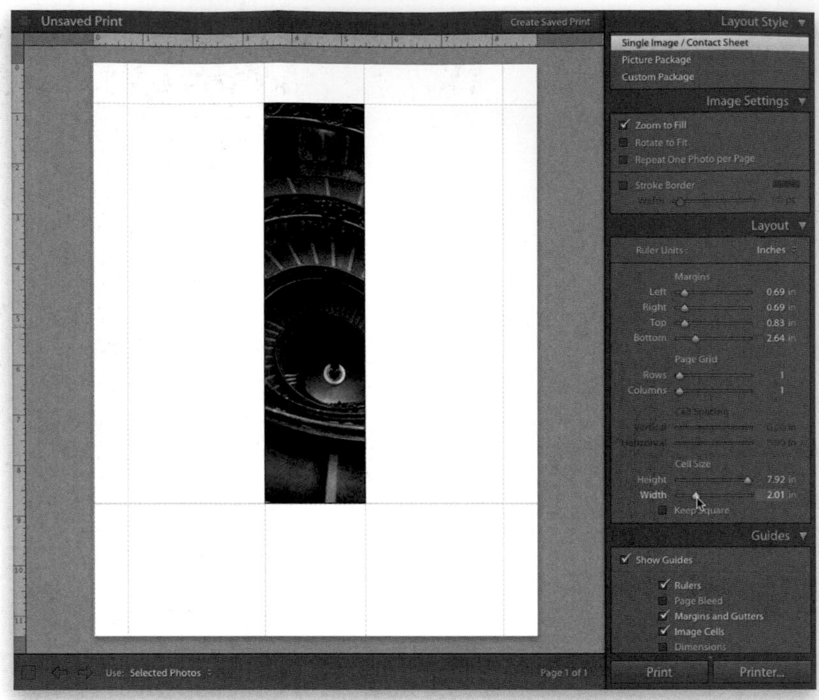

TIP: Print Module Shortcut

When you want to jump over to the Print module, you can use the same keyboard shortcut you do in almost any program that lets you print: it's the standard old **Command-P (PC: Ctrl-P)**.

Step Six:

One of my favorite things about using these cell layouts is that you can reposition your image inside the cell. Just move your cursor over the cell, and your cursor turns into the Hand tool. Now, just click-and-drag the image inside the cell to the position you want it. In this case, I just slid the photo over to the left a bit until the middle of the staircase was in the center.

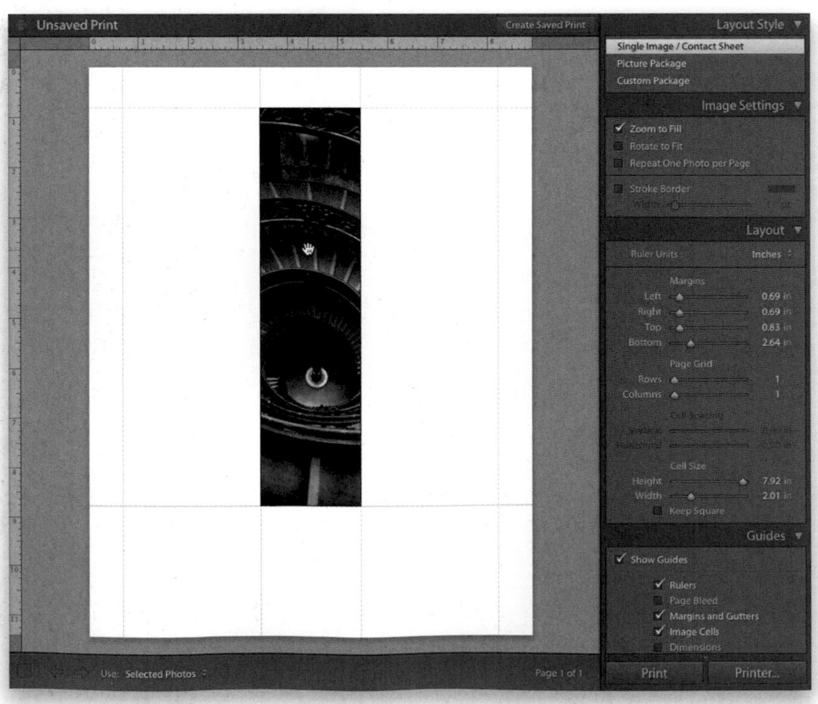

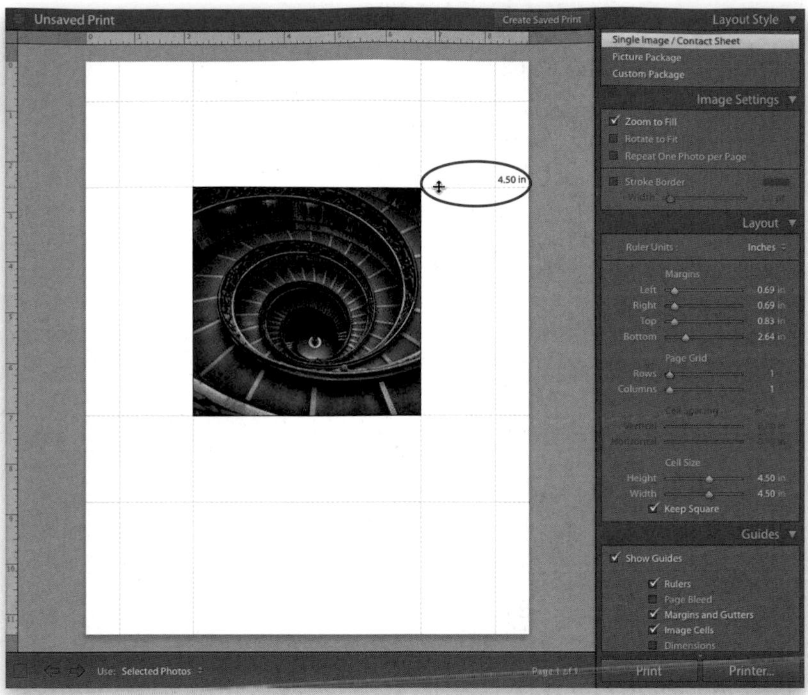

Step Seven:

At the bottom of the Cell Size section is a checkbox called "Keep Square." Go ahead and turn on this checkbox, which sets your Height and Width to the exact same size, and now they move together as one unit (since it's perfectly square). Let's try a different way of resizing the cell: click-and-drag the cell borders themselves, right on the layout in the Preview area. You see those vertical and horizontal lines extending across and up/down the page showing the boundaries of your cell? You can click-and-drag directly on them, so go ahead and give it a try. Here, I'm clicking on the top horizontal guide (shown circled here in red), and dragging outward to enlarge my square cell (and the photo inside it). So, by now you've probably realized that the cell is like a window into your photo.

TIP: Rotating Images

If you have a tall photo in a wide cell (or on a wide page), you can make your photo fill as much of that page as possible by going to the Image Settings panel, and turning on the Rotate to Fit checkbox.

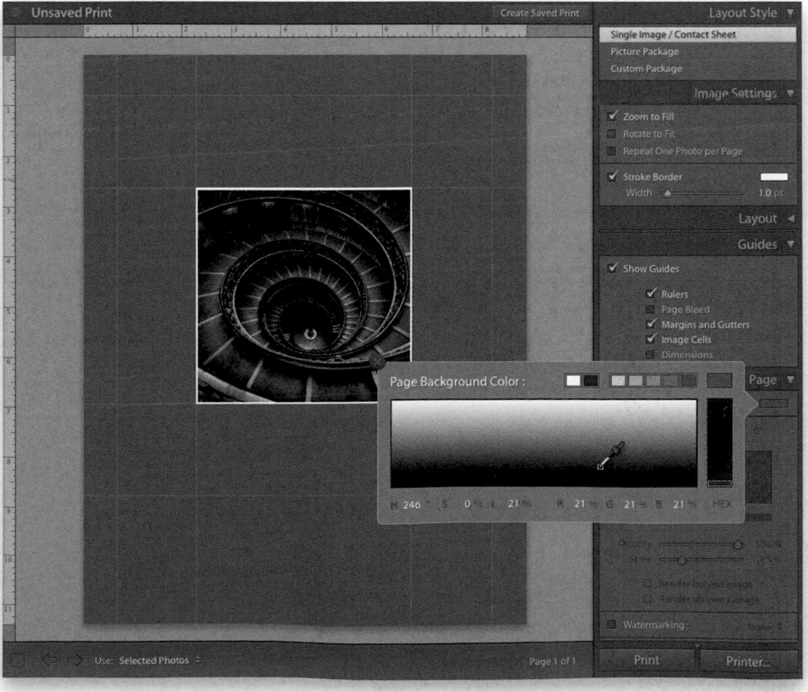

Step Eight:

Let's finish this one off with one of my favorite printing features in Lightroom: the ability to change the color of your page background. To do this, just go to the Page panel, turn on the Page Background Color checkbox, and click the color swatch to the right of it to bring up the Page Background Color picker (seen here). In this case, I'm choosing a dark gray, but you can choose any color you'd like (black, blue, red—you name it), then close the color picker. Also, you can put a stroke around your image cell by going up to the Image Settings panel, turning on the checkbox for Stroke Border, then choosing a color (just click on the color swatch), and choosing how thick you want your stroke using the Width slider.

Creating Multi-Photo Contact Sheets

The reason you jumped through all those hoops just to print one photo was because the whole Single Image/Contact Sheet was really designed for you to have quick access to multi-photo layouts and contact sheets, which is where this all gets really fun. We're picking up here, with another set of photos, to show you how easy it is to create really interesting multi-photo layouts that clients just love!

Step One:

Start by clicking on any of the multi-photo templates that come with Lightroom (if you hover your cursor over any of the templates in the Template Browser, a preview of the layout will appear in the Preview panel at the top of the left side Panels area). For example, click on the 2x2 Cells template, and it puts your selected photos in two columns and two rows (as shown here). Here, I selected 10 photos, and if you look at the right end of the toolbar, you'll see Lightroom will make three prints, although only two will have four photos each—the last print will just have those two leftover photos. The layout you see here doesn't look that good, because they're all horizontal photos in vertical cells, but we can fix that. It would look worse if there were tall photos mixed in.

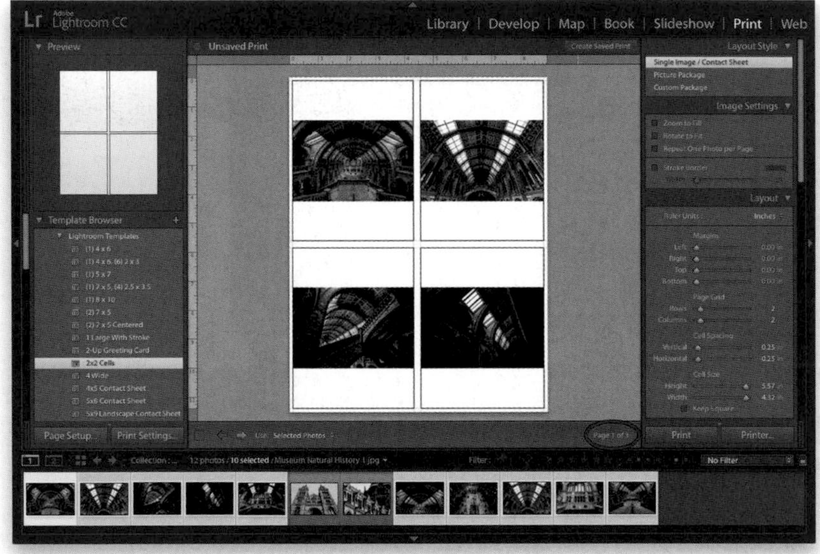

SCOTT KELBY

Step Two:

Of course, just printing all your wide photos on a page with wide cells, and then creating a second template with tall cells, would fix that, but an easier way is to go to the Image Settings panel and turn on the Zoom to Fill checkbox (as shown here). This zooms all the images up to fill the cells, so the wide photos zoom in, and how they fill the cells looks uniform (as seen here). Plus, you can reposition the images in their cells by clicking-and-dragging them. However, turning on Zoom to Fill usually crops a tiny bit off of tall shots, and quite a bit off the wide shots, changing the whole look of the photos (luckily, there is a way around this, too).

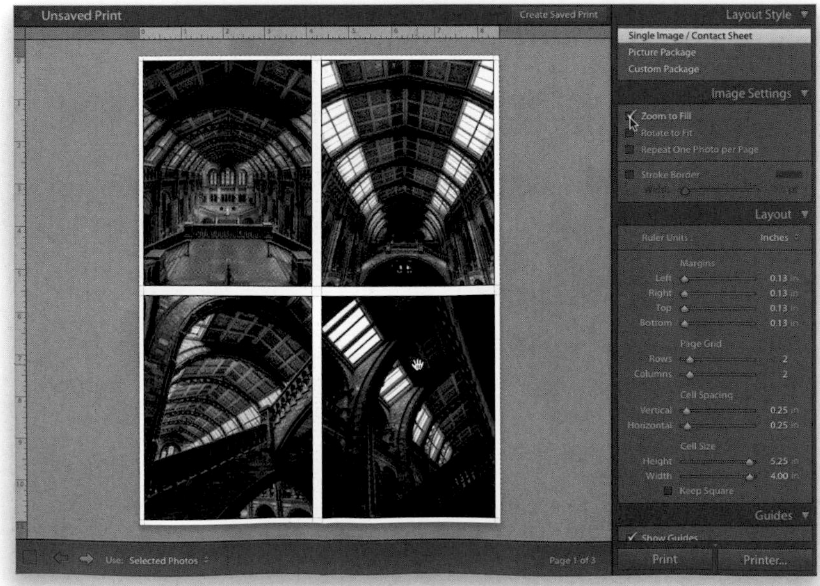

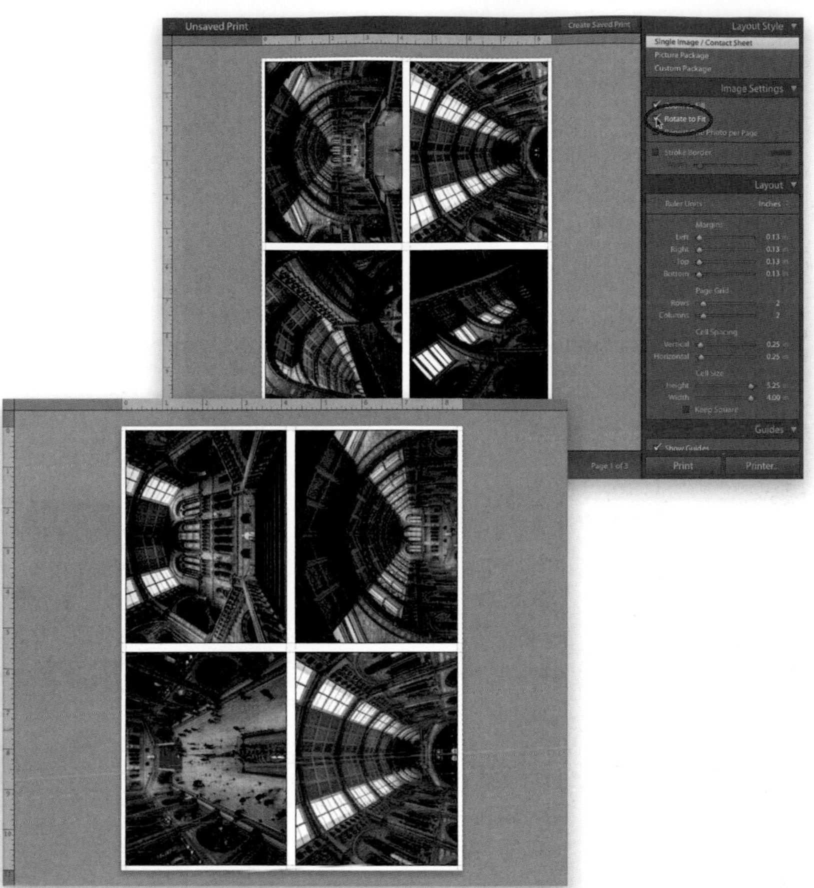

Step Three:

What you need is a way to print tall images and wide images together at nearly full size, without much cropping. The trick is to turn on the Rotate to Fit checkbox (shown circled here in red, in the Image Settings panel), which rotates the wide photos so they best fill the tall cells (as seen here at the top, where the wide photos are now turned sideways to fit in the cells as large as possible). When you turn on Rotate to Fit, it applies that to all your pages, so if you have other wide photos on other pages, it will rotate them, as well (as seen in the bottom graphic here, showing the second page of photos, and they're all rotated sideways. To see your other pages, click on the Right Arrow button on the left side of the toolbar).

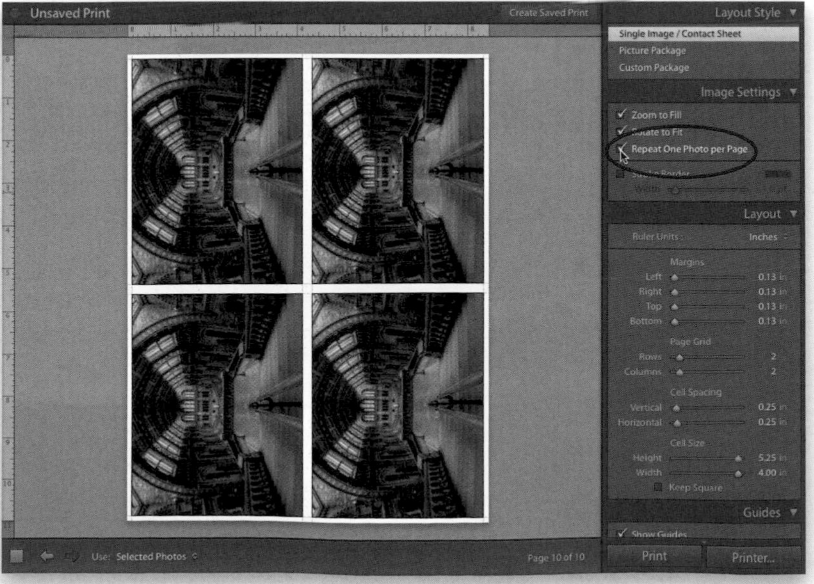

Step Four:

If you want to print the same photo, at the same exact size, multiple times on the same page, then you can go to the Image Settings panel and turn on the checkbox for Repeat One Photo per Page, as shown here. If you want to print the same photo multiple times on the same page, but you want them to be different sizes (like one 5x7" and four wallet-size photos), then turn to page 456 for details on how to set that up.

Continued

Step Five:

If you click on a different multi-photo layout, like the 4x5 Contact Sheet (as shown here; I switched collections for a moment so you can see the layout better), your photos instantly adjust to the new layout. One nice feature of this template is that the names of your images appear directly below each image. If you want to turn this feature off, go to the Page panel and, near the bottom of the panel, turn off the Photo Info checkbox. By the way, when you have this checkbox turned on, you can choose other text to appear under your images from the pop-up menu to the right of the words Photo Info. Here, I turned on the Zoom to Fill checkbox, but of course, that's totally optional—if you don't want your images cropped, then you should leave Zoom to Fill turned off.

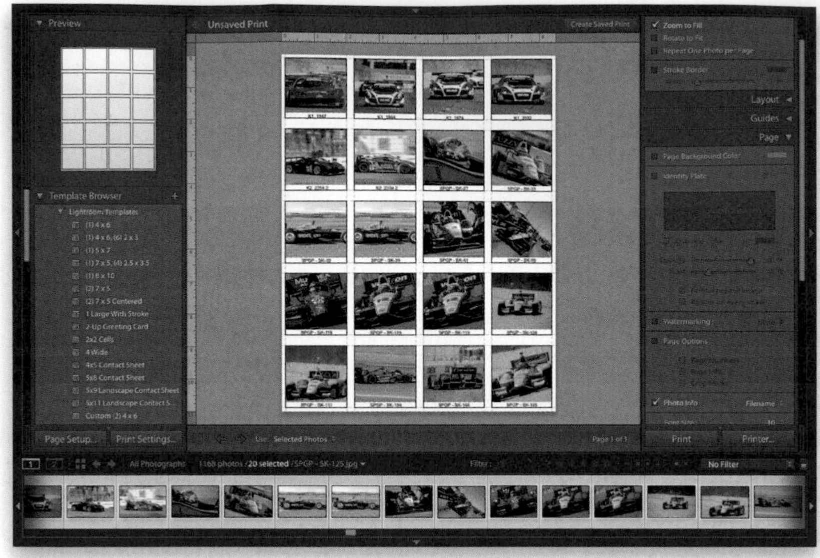

SCOTT KELBY

Step Six:

So far, we've been using Lightroom's built-in templates, but half the fun of this process is building your own, and it's surprisingly easy, as long as you don't mind having all your cells being the same exact size, which is the limitation of using the Single Image/Contact Sheet type of layout. You can't have one photo that's square, and two that are rectangular. They're either all square or all rectangular, but don't worry, we'll tackle how to create multiple photos at any size you want a little later. For now, we'll use this contact sheet power to create some cool layouts. Start by selecting some photos (eight or nine should be fine), then click on the template called "Maximize Size" (shown here; it's a decent starting place for building your own templates). Since we're going to be adding photos, I turned off the Rotate to Fit checkbox (it's on by default in this template) in the Image Settings panel.

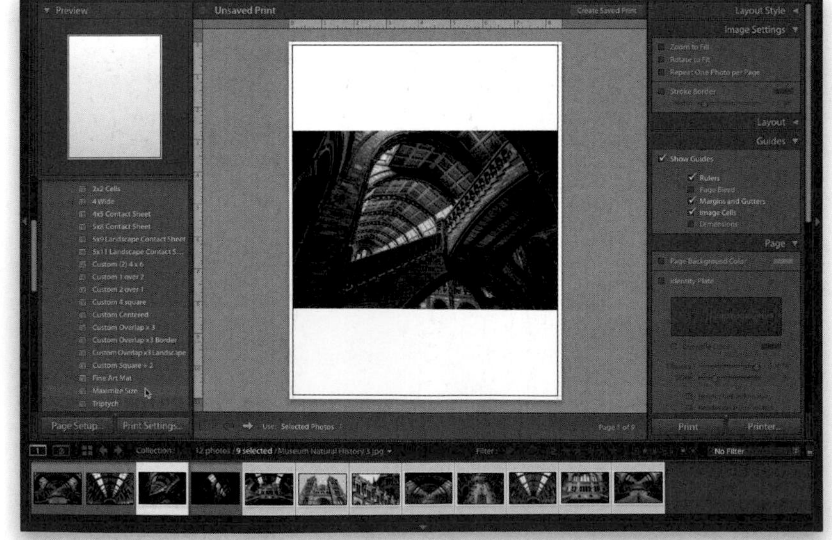

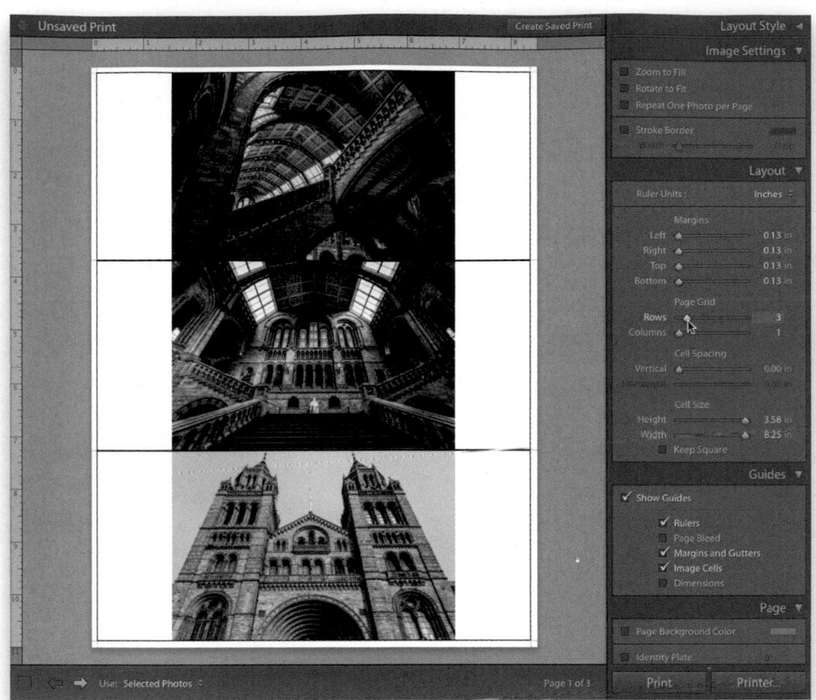

Step Seven:

You create custom multi-photo layouts in the Layout panel. There's a Page Grid section, which is where you pick how many rows and columns you want in your layout, so start by dragging the Rows slider over to 3, so you get three photos in a row (like you see here). You'll notice that the three photos are stacked one on top of another with no space between them. *(Note:* The black lines you see around the cells are just guides, so you can easily see where the cell borders are. You can get rid of these in the Guides panel by turning off the Image Cells checkbox. I usually leave these off, because you can still see the cell borders in light gray, as you'll see in the next step, where I have those black Image Cell borders turned off.)

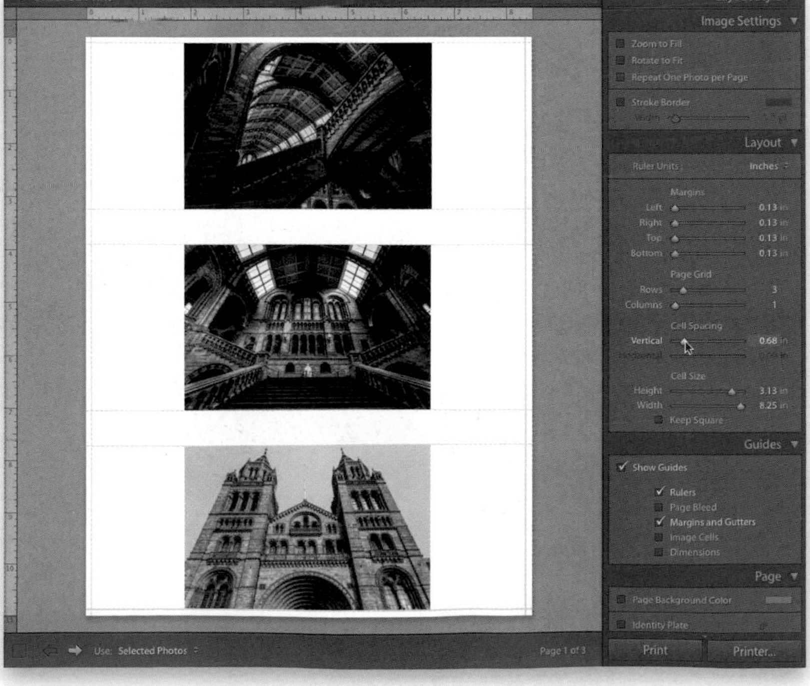

Step Eight:

To create some vertical space between your photos, go to the Cell Spacing section and click-and-drag the Vertical slider to the right (as shown here, where I dragged it over to 0.68 in to put a little more than a half-inch of space between the photos). Now let's take things up a notch.

Continued

Step Nine:

Now go to the Page Grid sliders and increase the Columns to 3, so now you have this layout of three columns wide by three rows deep. Of course, since the default setting is to not have any space between photos, the columns of photos don't have any space between them horizontally.

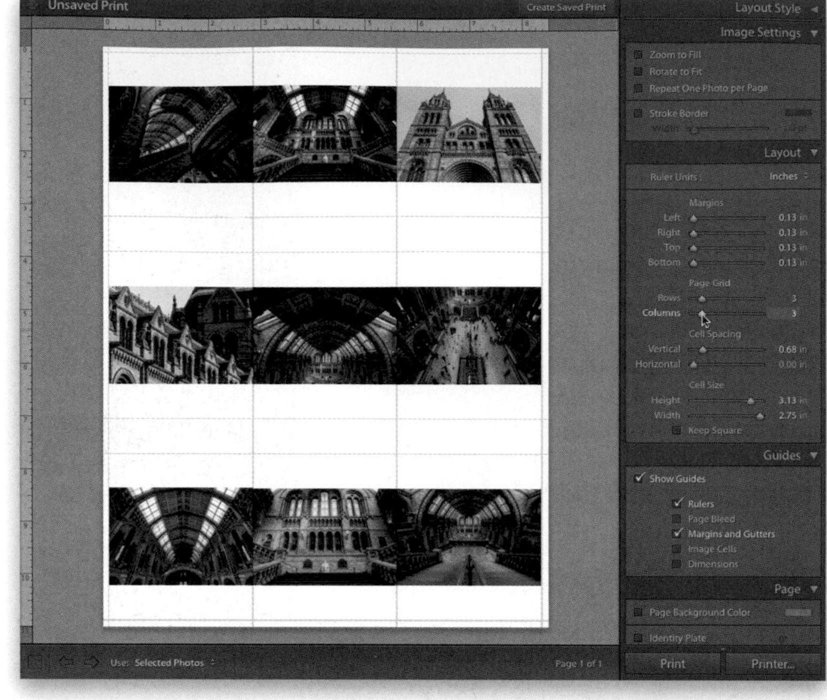

Step 10:

You add space between the photos in columns by going to the Cell Spacing section, and clicking-and-dragging the Horizontal slider to the right (as shown here). Now that you've got space between your columns, take a look at the page margins. There's lots of space at the top and bottom, and just a little bit of space on the sides of the page.

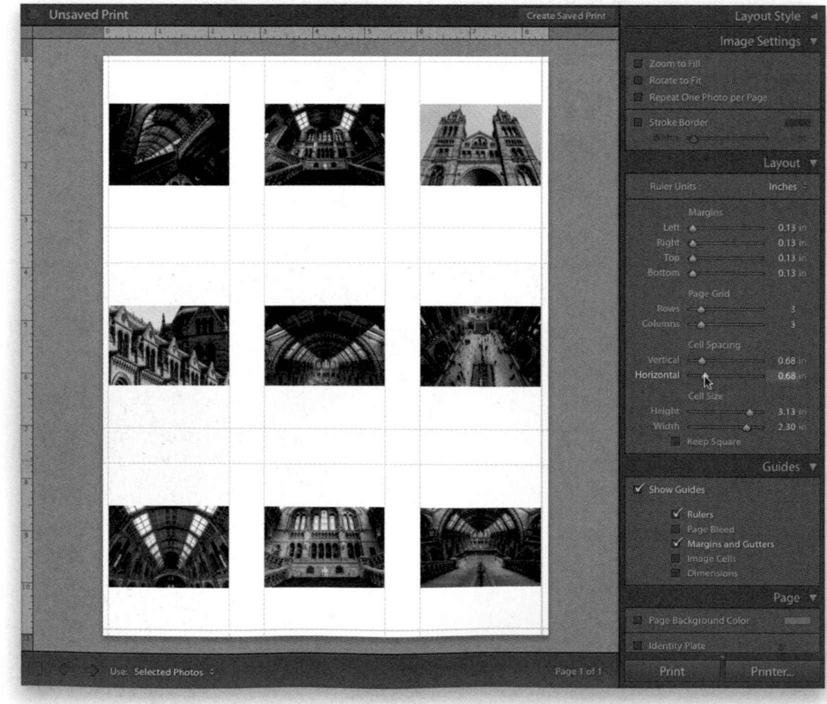

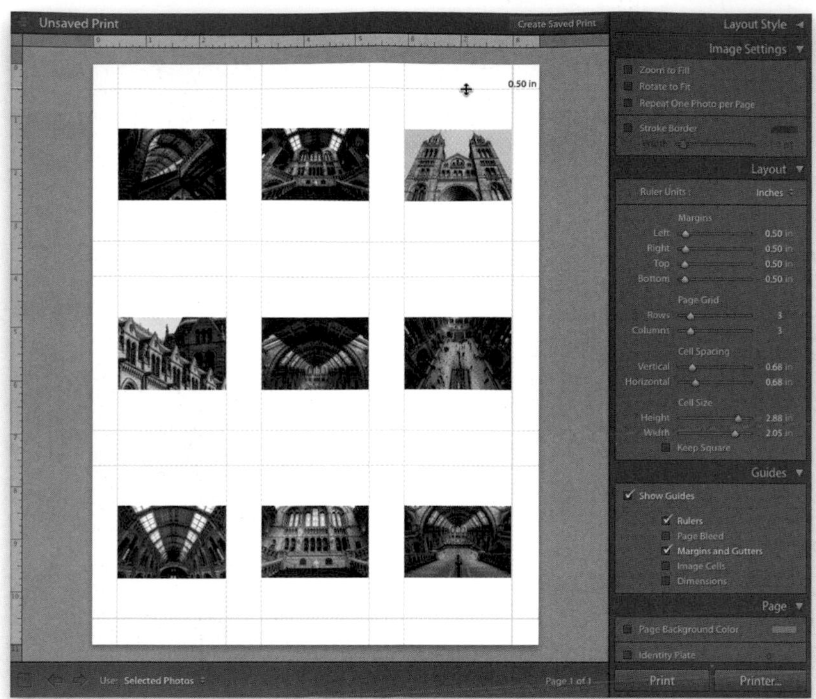

Step 11:

Although you can drag the Margins sliders to adjust the page margins (right there in the Layout panel), you can also just click directly on the margins themselves and drag them (as shown here). Here, I clicked-and-dragged the top, bottom, and side margins in to where they were about a half-inch from the edge of the page.

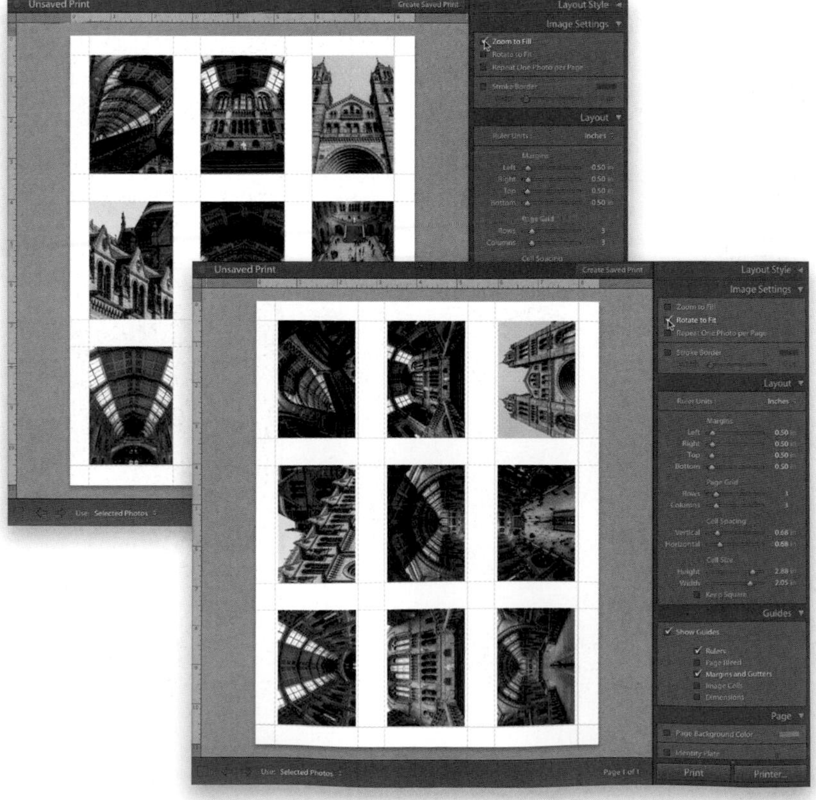

Step 12:

If you look back in the image shown in Step 11, you can see the images are all wide, but they're in tall cells. To get the images larger, you can go back up to the Image Settings panel and either: (a) turn on the Zoom to Fill checkbox (as shown here at the top) to fill the cells with the images (don't forget, you can reposition your images inside those cells by just clicking-and-dragging on them), or (b) turn on the Rotate to Fit checkbox, in which case, all the photos would be turned on their sides so they fit larger in the cells you've created (seen here at the bottom).

Continued

Step 13:

Let's wrap this section up with a few examples of cool layouts you can create using these Contact Sheet style layouts (all based on a borderless 8.5x11" page size, which you can choose by clicking the Page Setup button at the bottom of the left side Panels area). Start by going up to the Image Settings panel and turning on the Zoom to Fill checkbox. Now, go to the Layout panel, under Page Grid, then change the number of Rows to 1 and the number of Columns to 3. Drag the Left, Right, and Top Margins sliders to around 0.75 in, and the Bottom Margins slider to around 2.75 (to leave lots of room for your Identity Plate). Jump down to Cell Spacing and set Horizontal to 0.13. Under Cell Size, for the Height, drag it to around 7.50 in, and set the Width at only around 2.38 in, which gives you very tall, narrow cells (as shown here). Now, select three photos and turn on the Identity Plate feature (in the Page panel), make it larger, and click-and-drag it so it's centered below your images, giving you the look you see here (I also turned off the Show Guides checkbox to get rid of the distracting guides).

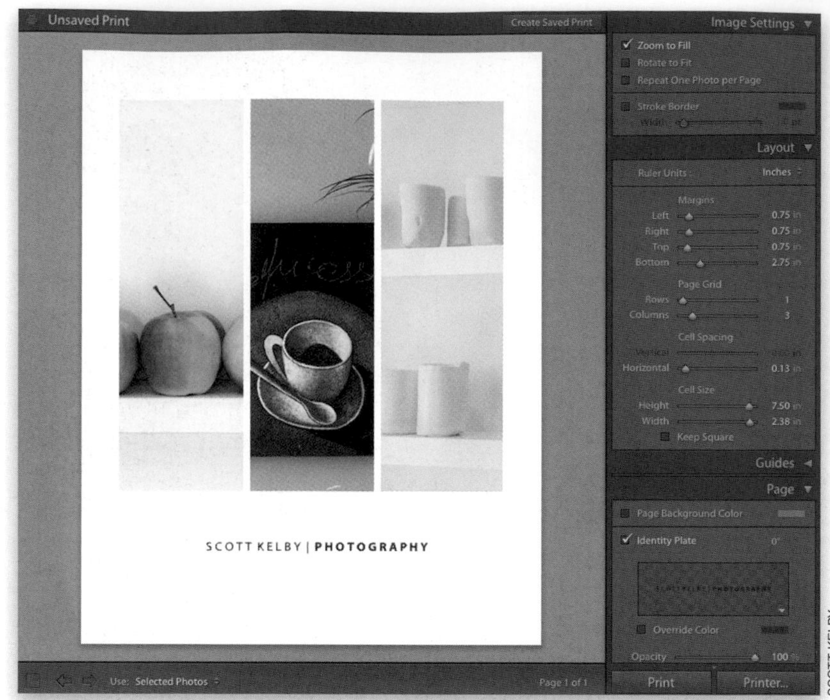

SCOTT KELBY

Step 14:

Now let's create four panorama layouts in one photo (you don't need to use real panos—this creates fake panos instantly from any photo you select). Start by turning on the Zoom to Fill checkbox and setting your Rows to 4 and Columns to 1. Then set your Left and Right Margins to 0.50 in, and set the Top to around 0.75 in or 0.80 in. Set your Bottom margin to 1.50 in. Turn off the Identity Plate checkbox in the Page panel, then increase your Cell Size Width to 7.33 in, and your Cell Size Height to 1.90 in to give you thin, wide cells. Now, set the space between your fake panos using the Vertical slider (set it to around 0.50) to give you the layout you see here. I went and clicked on four travel photos, and got the instant pano layout you see here.

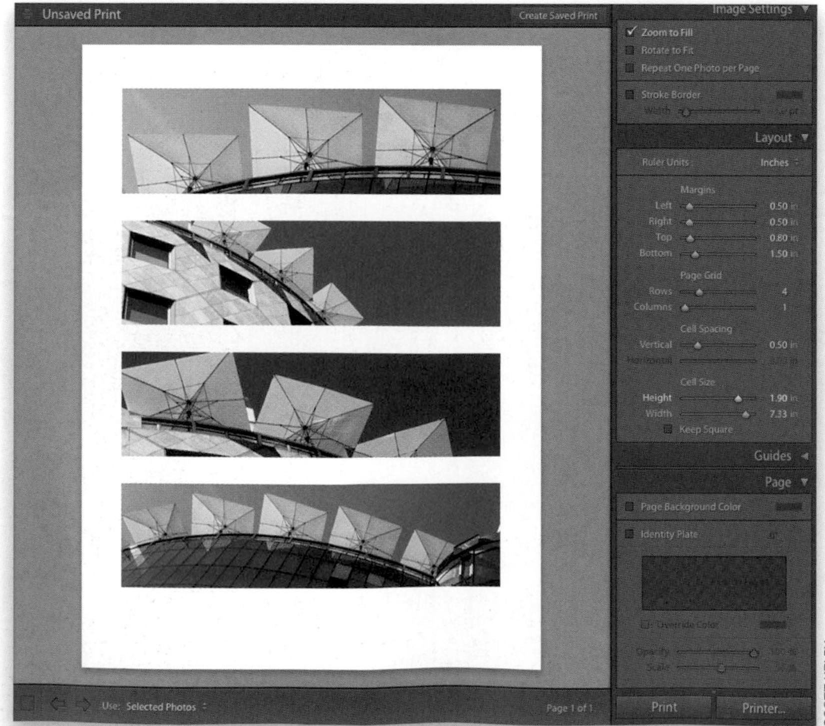

SCOTT KELBY

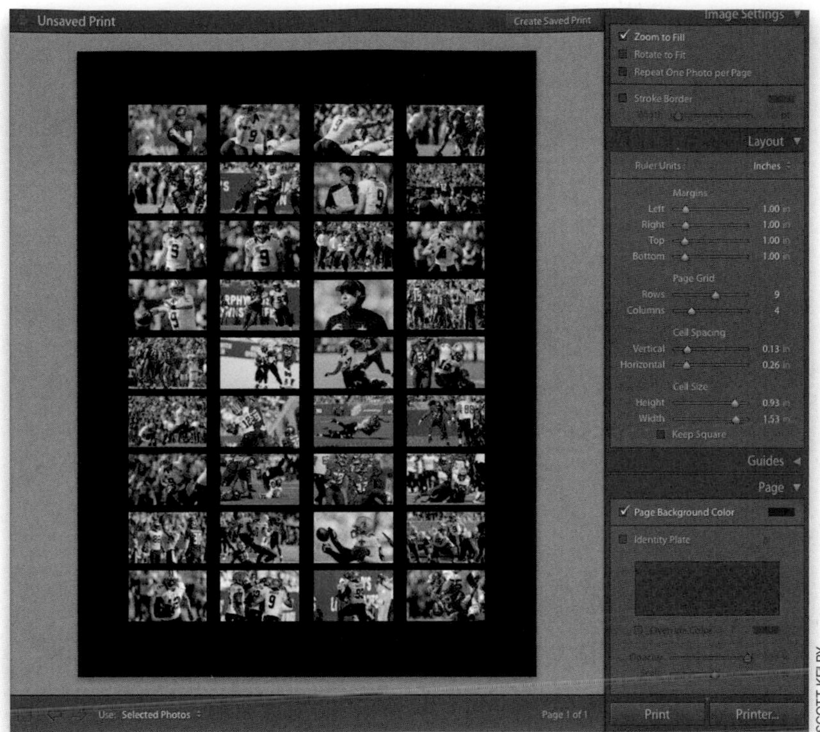

SCOTT KELBY

Step 15:

How about a poster, on black, with 36 wide images? Easy. Start by creating a collection made up of only wide images. Then go to the Image Settings panel and turn on the Zoom to Fill checkbox. Go to the Layout panel and set a 1-inch margin all the way around the page, using the Margins sliders. Now, set your Page Grid to 9 Rows, and 4 Columns. Set your Horizontal Cell Spacing at 0.26 in, then put just enough Vertical Cell Spacing to make the space between the photos about half the size of the horizontal spacing (I set it at 0.13). Lastly, in the Page panel, turn on the Page Background Color checkbox, then click on the color swatch to the right of it, and choose black for your background color. If you have a white border, click on Page Setup and choose borderless printing.

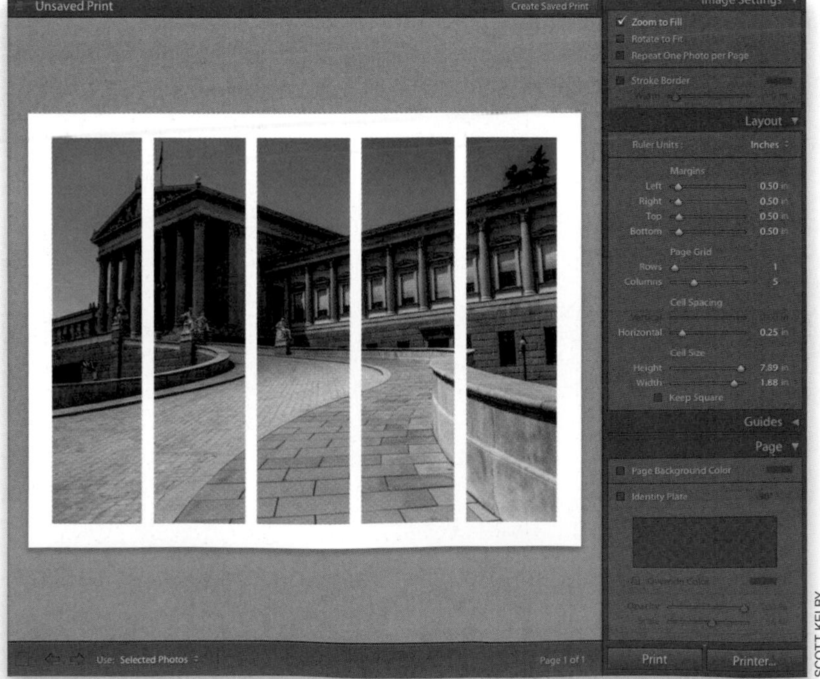

SCOTT KELBY

Step 16:

Okay, this one's kinda wild—one photo split into five separate thin vertical cells. Here's how it's done: You start by clicking the Page Setup button (at the bottom left), and set your page to be Landscape orientation. Then Right-click on a photo in the Filmstrip and choose **Create Virtual Copy**. You need to do this three more times, so you have a total of five copies of your photo. Now, in the Image Settings panel, turn on Zoom to Fill, then in the Layout panel, set your Margins to 0.50 in all the way around the page. For your Page Grid, choose 1 Rows and 5 Columns. Add a little Horizontal Cell Spacing—around 0.25 in. Then drag the Cell Size Height slider all the way to the right (this sets it around 7.89 in and the Width to around 1.88 in). Select all five photos in the Filmstrip, then you'll click-and-drag each of the five images around inside their cells—dragging left and right—until they appear to be one single image (like you see here).

Creating Custom Layouts Any Way You Want Them

In Lightroom, Adobe also gives you the option to break away from the structured cell layouts of earlier versions to create your own custom cell layouts in any size, shape, and placement, using a Print layout style called "Custom Package." Here's where you can create photos in any size and any layout you want, without being tied into a grid.

Step One:

Start in the Layout Style panel by clicking on Custom Package (we want to start from scratch, so if you see any cells already in place, go to the Cells panel and click the Clear Layout button). There are two ways to get photos onto your page: The first is to go down to the Filmstrip and simply to drag-and-drop images right onto your page (as seen here). The image appears inside its own fully resizable cell, so you can just drag one of the corner handles to resize the image (this image came in pretty small, so I resized it to nearly fill the bottom of the page). It will resize proportionally by default, but if you turn off the Lock to Photo Aspect Ratio checkbox (at the bottom of the Cells panel), then it acts like a regular cell with Zoom to Fill turned on, in that you can crop the photo using the cell. More on that in a minute.

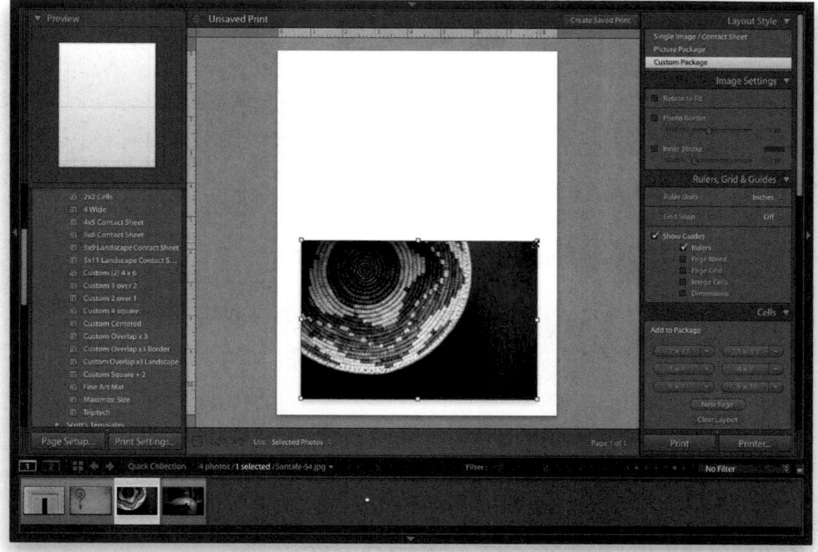

SCOTT KELBY

Step Two:

Go ahead and hit the Clear Layout button, so you can try the other way to get your images into your layout, which is to create the cells first, arrange them where you want, then drag-and-drop your images into those cells. You do this by going to the Cells panel, and in the Add to Package section, just click on the size you want. For example, if you wanted to add a 3x7"cell, you'd just click on the 3x7 button (as shown here) and it creates an empty cell that size on the page. Now you can just click inside the cell and drag it anywhere you'd like on the page. Once it's where you like it, you can drag-and-drop a photo into that cell from the Filmstrip.

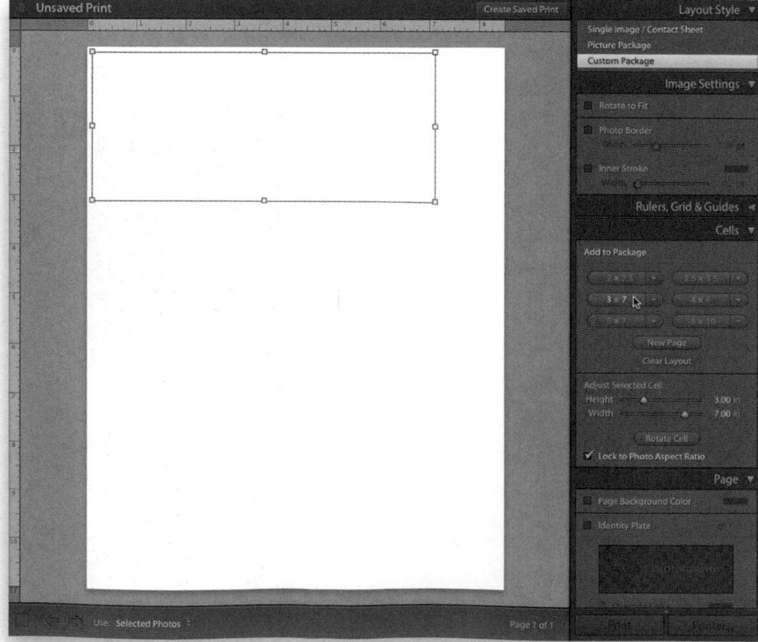

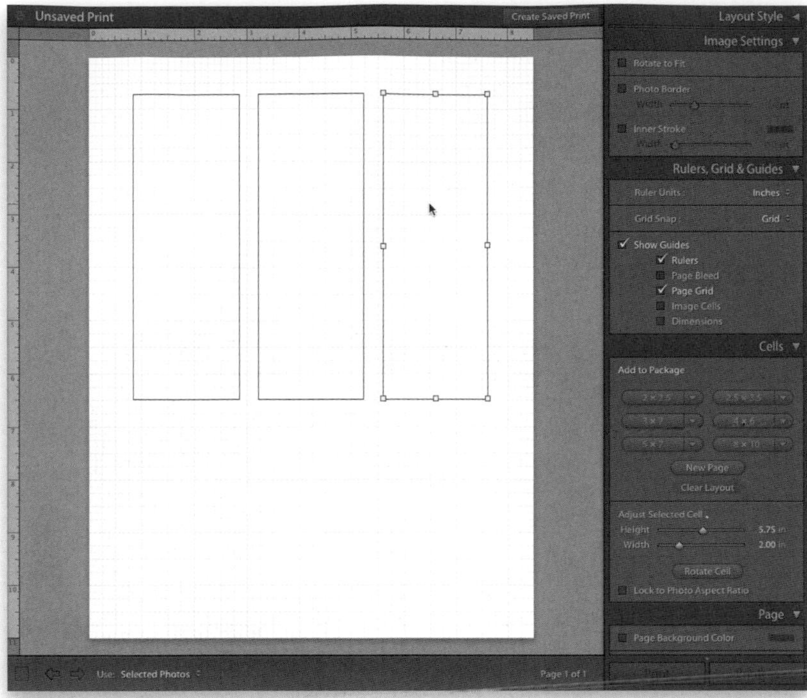

Step Three:

Let's create a layout using these cell buttons, so hit the Clear Layout button to start from scratch again. Click the 3x7 button to add a long, thin cell to your layout, but then click the Rotate Cell button to make this a tall, thin cell. This cell is actually pretty large on the page, but you can resize it by grabbing any of the handles, or using the Adjust Selected Cell sliders to choose any size you'd like (here, shrink your Height to 5.75 in). Now, we need to make two more cells just like this one. The quickest way to do that is to press-and-hold the **Option (PC: Alt) key**, then click inside the cell and drag to the right to make a copy. Do this twice until you have three cells, like you see here, and arrange them side by side, as shown (as you drag these cells, you'll feel a little snap. That's it snapping to an invisible alignment grid that's there to simply help you line things up. You can see the grid by going to the Rulers, Grid & Guides panel and turning on the checkboxes for Show Guides and Page Grid).

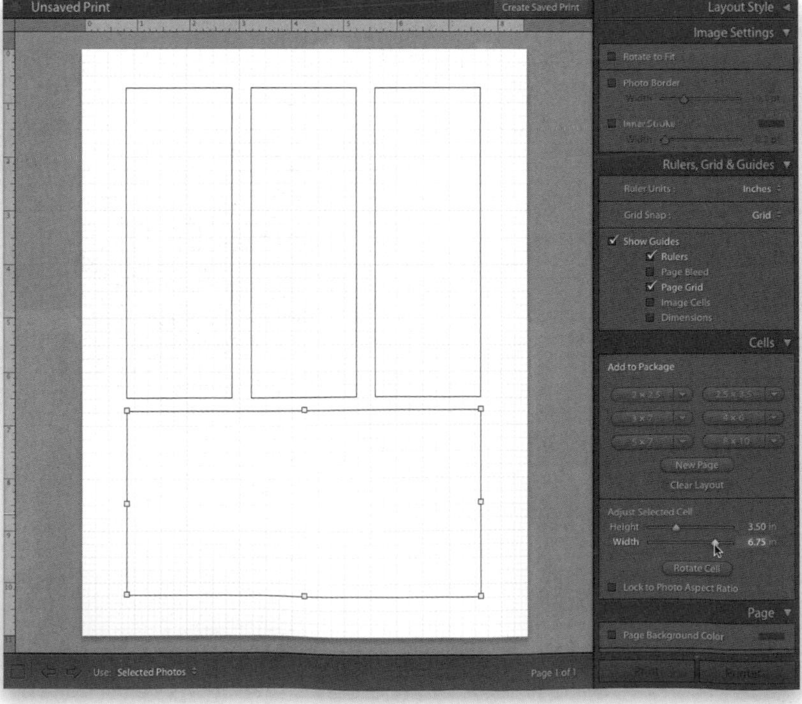

Step Four:

Next, let's add a larger photo to the bottom of our layout. Click the 4x6 button and it adds a larger cell to the layout, but it's taller and not quite as wide as our three thin cells above. You'll need to first turn off the Lock to Photo Aspect Ratio checkbox, and then set the Height to 3.50 in and the Width to 6.75 in (as seen here). The layout's done, but before you start dragging-and-dropping images, there are two things you need to change first: (1) Because the cells at the top are tall and thin, the checkbox for Lock to Photo Aspect Ratio must be off (we already did this). Otherwise, when you drag-and-drop photos into those thin cells, they will just expand to the full size of the photo. (2) You'll also need to make sure the Rotate to Fit checkbox at the top of the Image Settings panel is turned off, so wide images won't rotate to fit the cell.

Continued

Step Five:

Now you're ready to start dragging-and-dropping photos into your layout. If you drag one that doesn't look good in your layout, just drag another right over it. You can reposition your photo inside a smaller cell by pressing-and-holding the Command (PC: Ctrl) key, then just dragging the image left/right (or up/down), so just the part you want is showing.

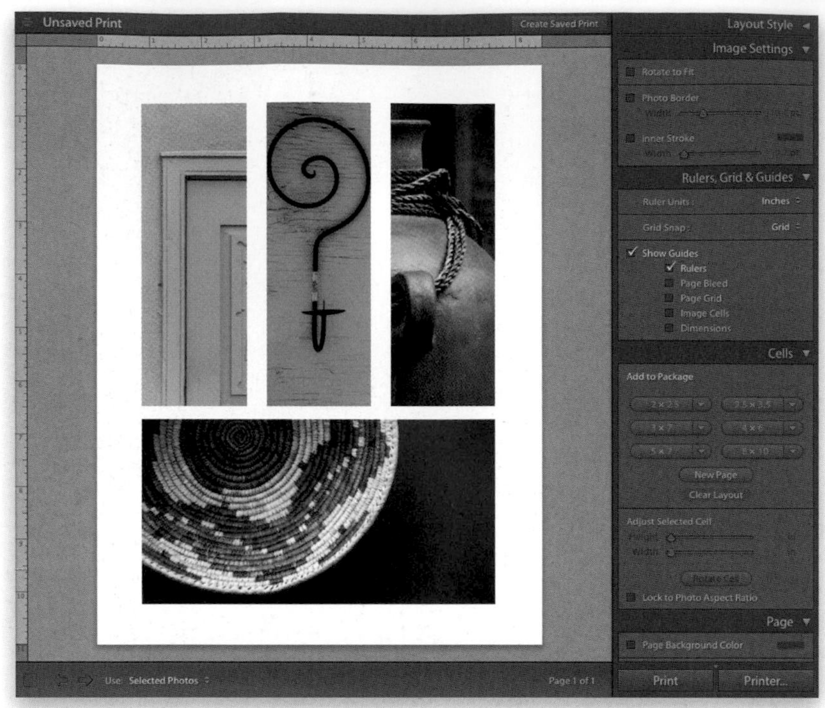

SCOTT KELBY

Step Six:

You can stack images so they overlap, almost like they're Photoshop layers. Let's start from scratch again, but first click the Page Setup button (at the bottom left), and turn your page orientation to Landscape. Now go back to the Cells panel, click the Clear Layout button, then click the 8x10 button, resize it, and position it so it takes up most of the page (as shown here). Now, click the 2x2.5 button three times, make each cell a little wider (like the ones seen here), and position them so they overlap the main photo, as shown. Drag-and-drop photos on each cell. You can move the photos in front or behind each other by Right-clicking on the photo, and from the pop-up menu, choosing to send the photo back/forward one level or all the way to the bottom/top of the stack. To add a white photo border around your images (like I did here), in the Image Settings panel, turn on the Photo Border checkbox (turn on the Guides to see this better). Also, try switching your Page Orientation to Portrait and see how that looks. For example, I thought it might make a good wedding book layout, so I swapped out the photos, rotated the small cells, made the main photo a little wider, turned off the Photo Border, then turned on the Inner Stroke checkbox, and added a 3-pt black stroke (as shown on the bottom left). It only took about 30 seconds. I also tried just rotating the three small cells, making the main photo fill the page, and adding a white stroke (as shown on the bottom right).

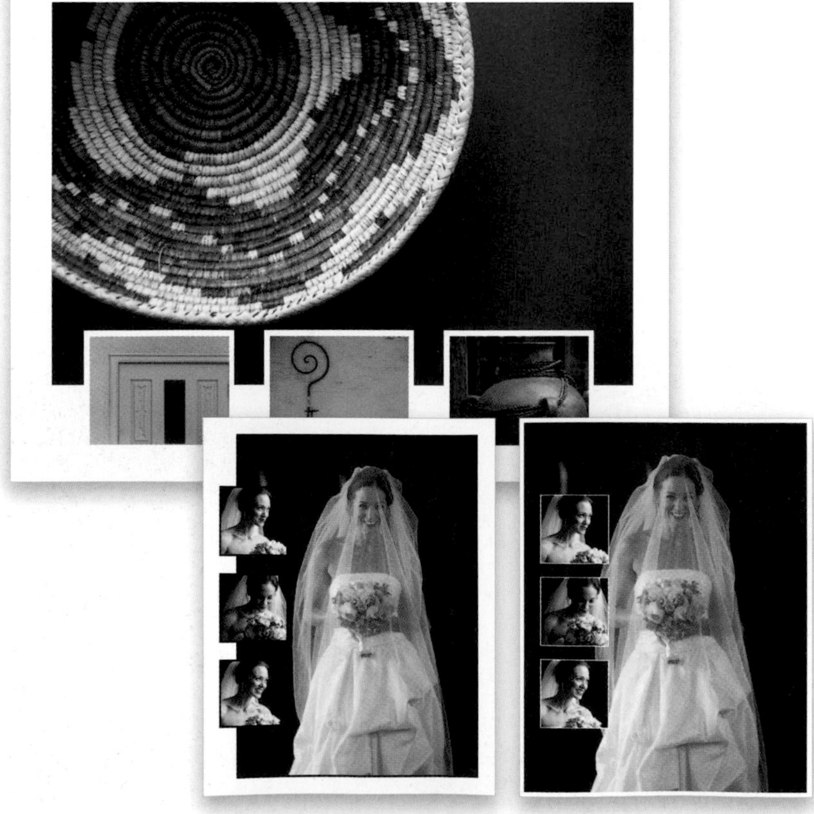

SCOTT KELBY

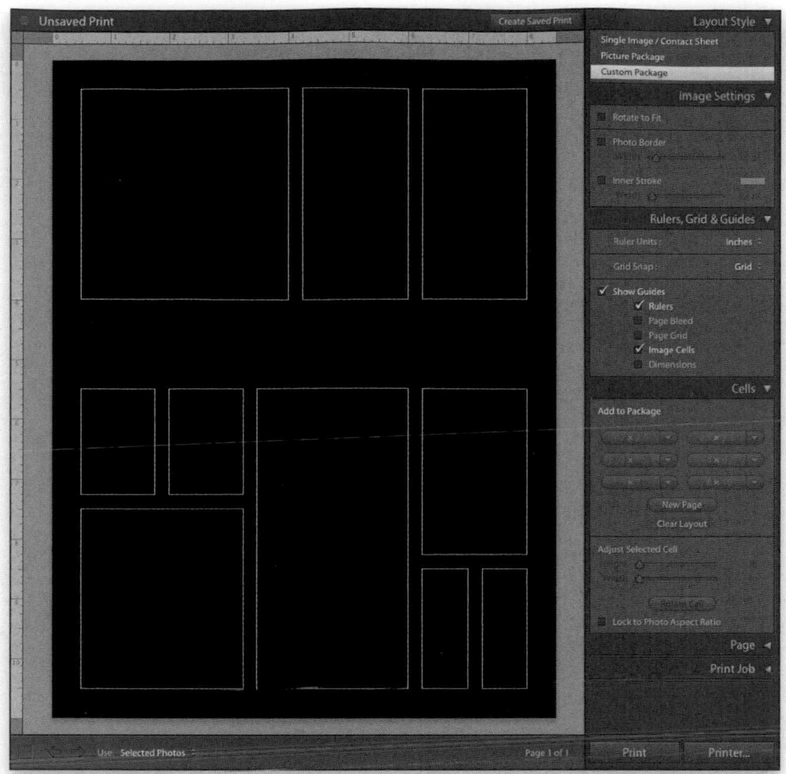

Step Seven:

Okay, let's start from scratch again and shoot for something pretty ambitious (well, as far as layouts go anyway). Clear your layout again, then go to the Page panel, turn on the checkbox for Page Background Color, click on the color swatch, and choose black as your background color. Now, make sure the Lock to Photo Aspect Ratio checkbox is turned off, then just go to the Cells panel and click the buttons to add a bunch of cells, and resize them so your layout looks kinda like what I have here, with a gap between the top and bottom set of images (so you can add your Identity Plate).

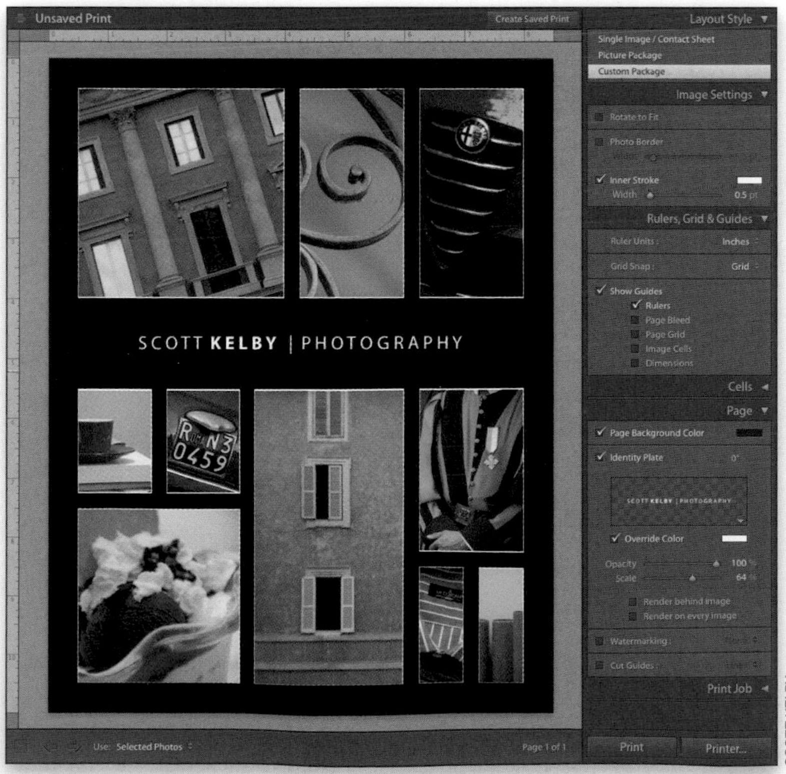

SCOTT KELBY

Step Eight:

Now, go ahead and drag-and-drop your photos into these cells. By the way, the thin white border you see around your cells is just there to show you where the cell borders are—those don't actually print in the final image. If you want a white stroke around your images, go up to the Image Settings panel and turn on the checkbox for Inner Stroke, then click on the color swatch to the right and set the color to white. For the image shown here, I switched to a collection of shots from a trip to Rome, then I dragged some of those images into the cells. Lastly, to have your studio name appear between the images, go to the Page panel and turn on the checkbox for Identity Plate, then turn on the Override Color checkbox, click on the color swatch and choose white as your Identity Plate color. You can drag your Identity Plate anywhere on the page, but for this layout, just drag it to the center and you're done.

Adding Text to Your Print Layouts

If you want to add text to your print layouts, it's pretty easy, as well, and like the Web and Slideshow modules, you can have Lightroom automatically pull metadata info from your photos and have it appear on the photo print, or you can add your own custom text (and/or Identity Plate) just as easily. Here's what you can add, and how you can add it:

Step One:

Select a photo, then choose the Fine Art Mat template in the Template Browser and turn on the Zoom to Fill checkbox. The easiest way to add text is to go to the Page panel and turn on the Identity Plate checkbox (see Chapter 3 for how to set it up). Once it's there, you can click-and-drag it right where you want it (in this case, drag it down and position it in the center of the space below the photo, as shown here). Here's how I got two lines of text with different fonts (Trajan Pro on top; Minion Pro Italic on the bottom): Once you set the top row of text (I hit the spacebar once between each letter), then press Option-Return twice to move down two lines. (*Note:* This doesn't work on a PC, but you can create it in Photoshop as a graphical Identity Plate.) Then, hit the Spacebar about 30 times (to center the text) and type the second line. Then highlight everything under the first line, and change the font. It's a workaround, but it works.

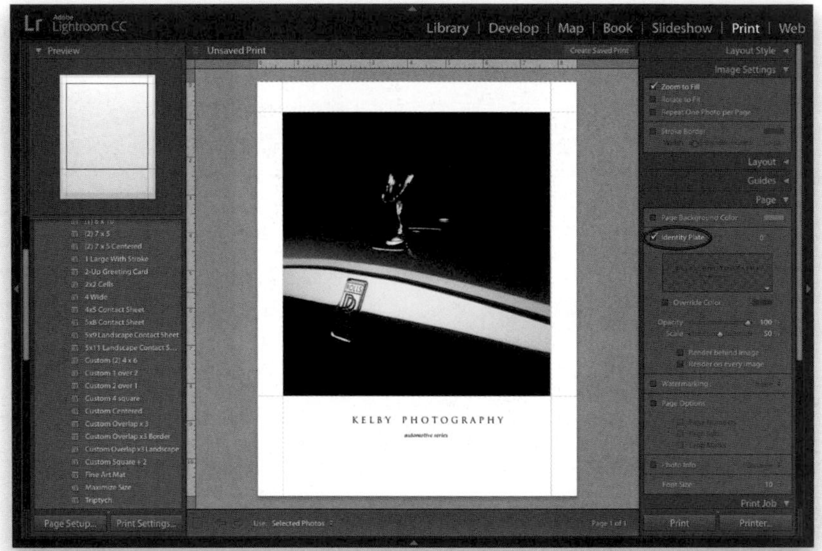

SCOTT KELBY

Step Two:

Besides adding your Identity Plate, Lightroom can also pull text from your metadata (things like exposure settings, camera make and model, filename, or caption info you added in the Library module's Metadata panel). You do this in the Page panel by turning on the Photo Info checkbox and choosing which type of info you want displayed at the bottom of your cell from the pop-up menu on the right (as shown here). You can change the size of your text right below it, but the largest size is 16 points, and on a large print, it's pretty tiny.

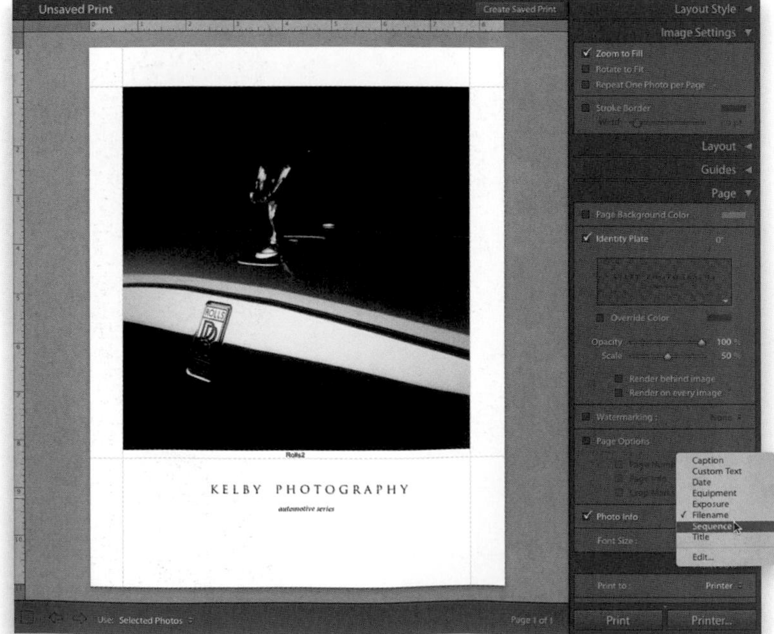

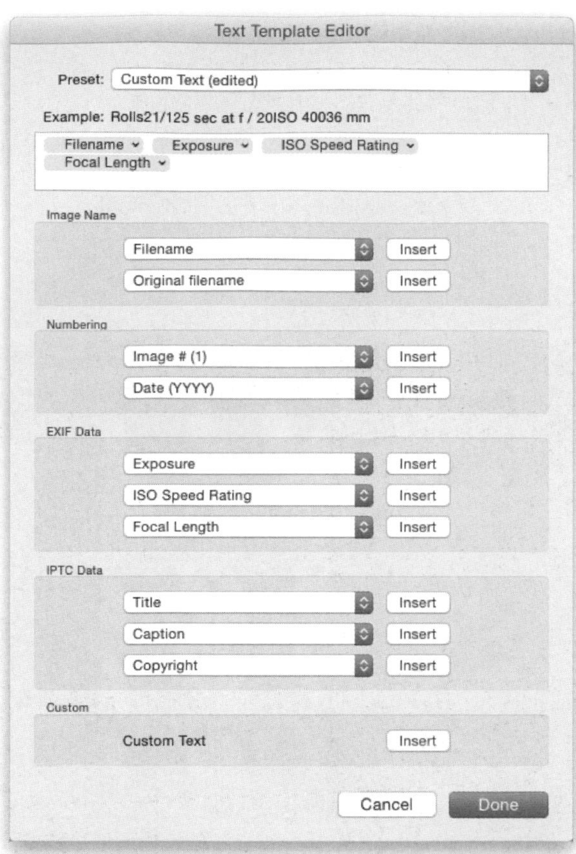

Step Three:

Now, besides just pulling the filename and metadata stuff, you can also create your own custom text (but it's going to show up at the bottom of the cell and this text is stuck there—you can't reposition it like you can the Identity Plate text, which is why I usually use that instead). If you choose Custom Text from the Photo Info pop-up menu, a field appears below it, so you can type in your custom text. You can also choose Edit from that same pop-up menu to bring up the Text Template Editor (shown here), where you can create your own custom list of data that Lightroom will pull from each photo's metadata and print under that photo. In this case, I chose to add text showing the filename, exposure, ISO, and the focal length of the lens by clicking the Insert button beside each of these fields in the Editor or choosing them from the pop-up menus. I can't imagine why anyone would want that type of information printed beneath the photo. But you know, and I know, there's somebody out there right now reading this and thinking, "All right! Now I can put the EXIF camera data right on the print!" The world needs these people.

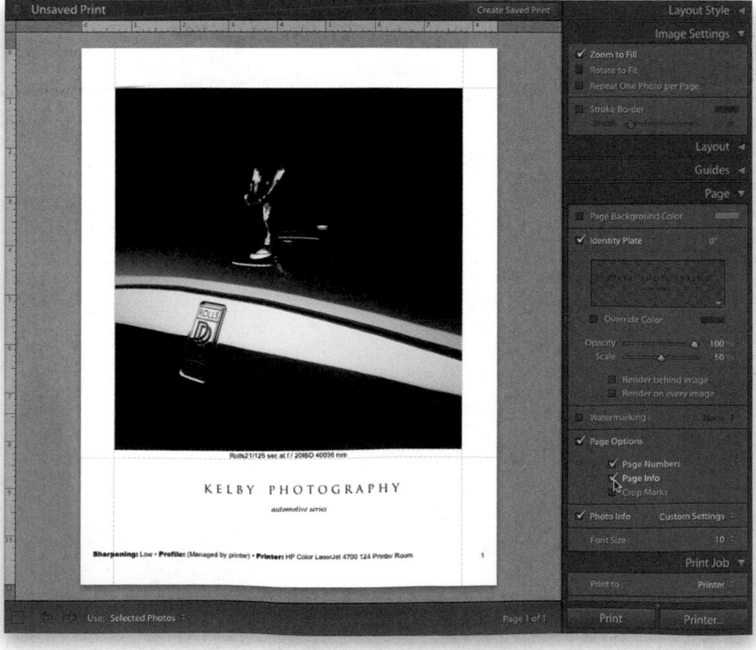

Step Four:

If you're printing pages for a photo book, you can have Lightroom automatically number those pages. In the Page panel, turn on the Page Options checkbox, then turn on the checkbox for Page Numbers. Lastly, if you're doing a series of test prints, you can have your print settings (including your level of sharpening, your color management profile, and your selected printer) appear near the bottom of the print (as seen here) by turning on the Page Info checkbox.

Printing Multiple Photos on One Page

You saw earlier in this chapter how to print the same photo, at the same exact size, multiple times on the same print. But what if you want to print the same photo at different sizes (like a 5x7" and four wallet sizes)? That's when you want to use Lightroom's Picture Package feature.

Step One:

Start by clicking on the photo you want to have appear multiple times, in multiple sizes, on the same page. Go to the Template Browser in the left side Panels area and click on the built-in template named (1) 4x6, (6) 2x3, which gives you the layout you see here. If you look over in the Layout Style panel at the top of the right side Panels area, you'll see that the selected style is Picture Package (as seen circled here in red). *Note:* Here, I made sure the Show Guides checkbox was turned on, along with the Page Grid and Image Cells checkboxes, so you can see how the image fits in the cells, and the cells fit on the page.

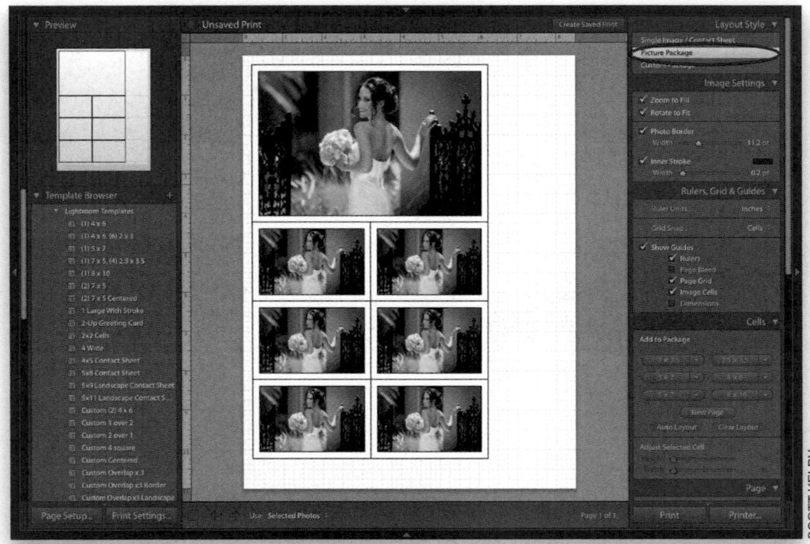

SCOTT KELBY

Step Two:

If you look at the Preview area in Step One, you can see that, by default, it puts a little white border around each photo. If you don't want the white border, go to the Image Settings panel and turn off the Photo Border checkbox (as shown here). Also, by default, the Zoom to Fill checkbox is turned on, so your photo is cropped in a little bit. If you don't want your photo cropped like that, turn the Zoom to Fill checkbox off.

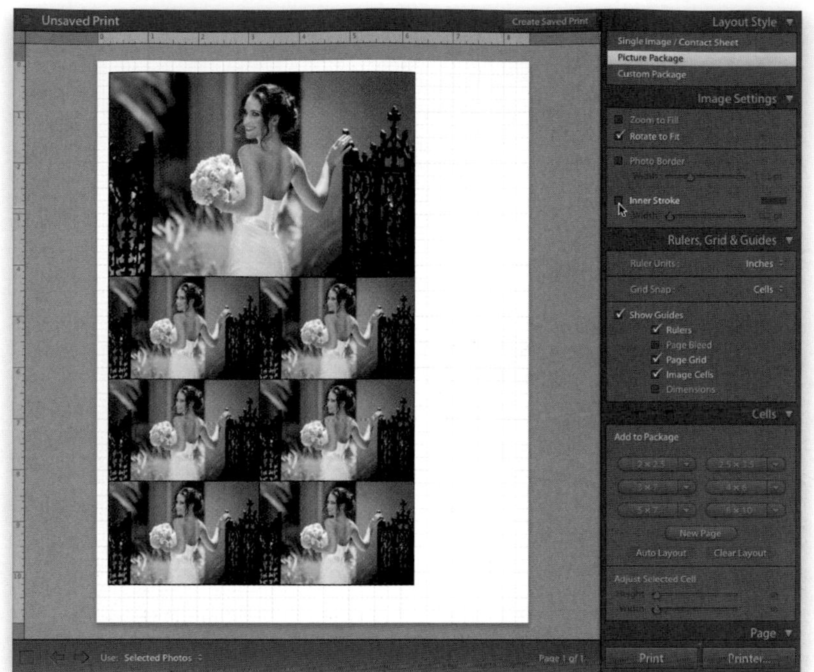

Step Three:

Another option it has on by default is that it puts a black stroke around each image (you can control the size of this stroke, using the Width slider right below the Inner Stroke checkbox). To remove this stroke, turn off the Inner Stroke checkbox (as shown here. You'll still see a thin stroke that separates the images, but does not print). Now your images are back to their original cropping, they're right up against each other (there's no extra white border), and you've removed the black stroke around the photos (by the way, if you like this layout, don't forget to save it as your own custom template by clicking on the + [plus sign] button on the right side of the Template Browser header).

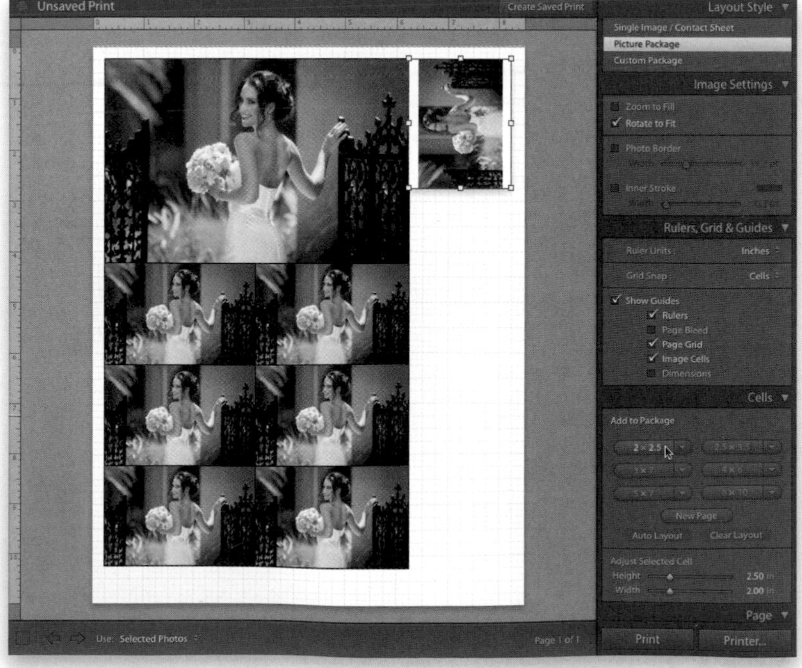

Step Four:

Adding more photos is easy—just go to the Cells panel (in the right side Panels area) and you'll see a number of pill-shaped buttons marked with different sizes. Just click on any one of those to add a photo that size to your layout (I clicked on the 2x2.5 button, and it added the new cell you see selected here). So, that's the routine: you click on those buttons to add more photos to your Picture Package layout. To delete a cell, just click on it, then press the **Delete (PC: Backspace)** key on your keyboard.

Continued

Step Five:
If you want to create your own custom Picture Package layout from scratch, go to the Cells panels and click on the Clear Layout button (as shown here), which removes all the cells, so you can start from scratch.

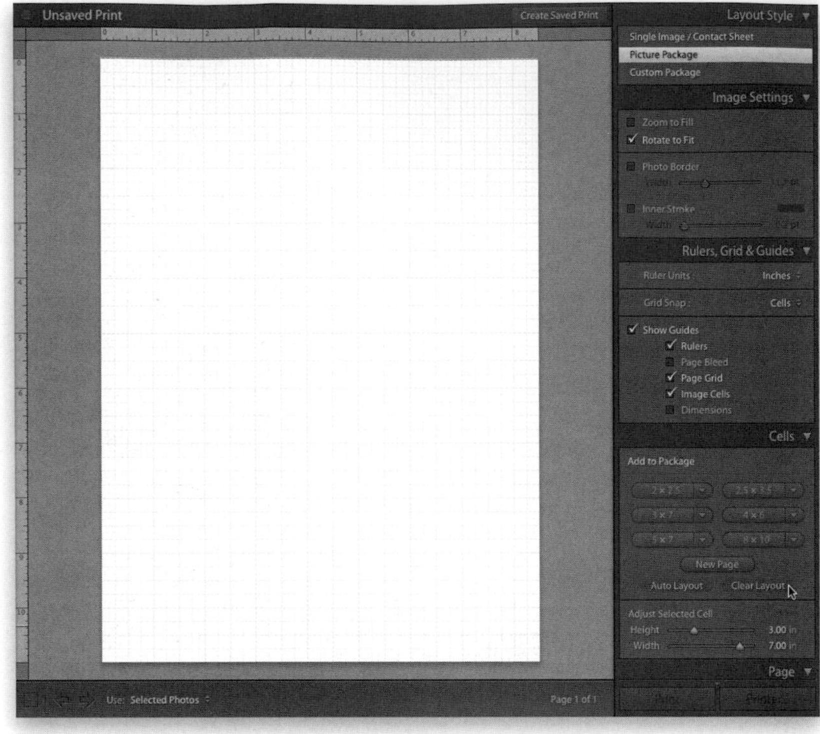

Step Six:
Now you can just start clicking on sizes, and Lightroom will place them on the page each time you click one of those Add to Package buttons (as shown here). As you can see, it doesn't always place the photos in the optimum location for the page dimensions, but Lightroom can actually fix that for you.

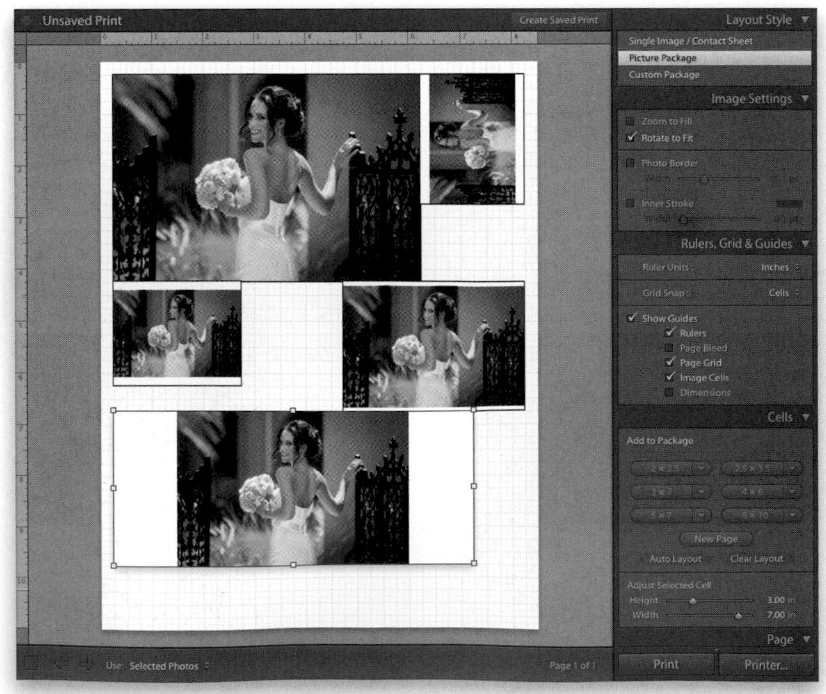

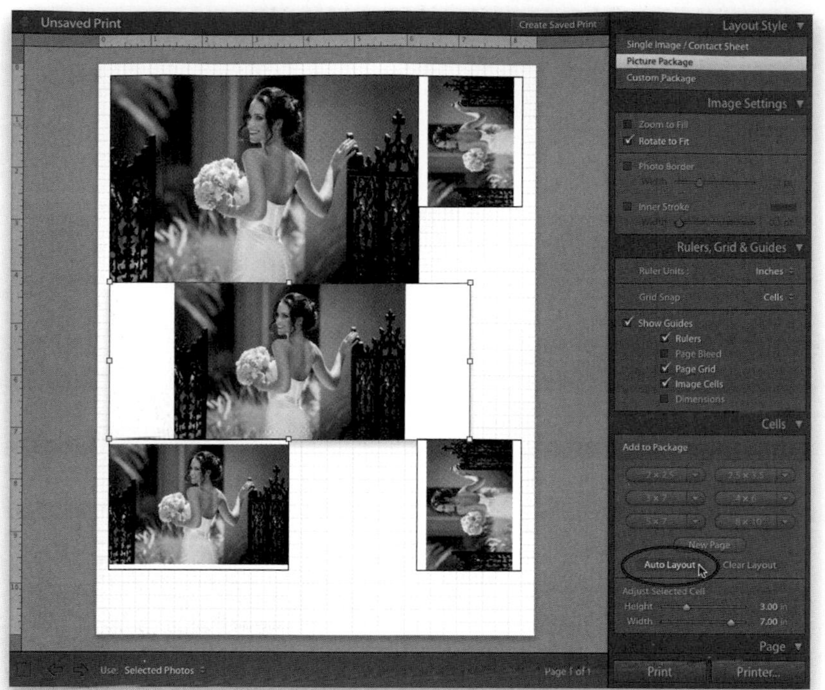

Step Seven:

If you click on the Auto Layout button, at the bottom of the Add to Package section (as shown here), it tries to automatically arrange the photos so they fit more logically, and gives you extra space to add more photos. Okay, hit the Clear Layout button and let's start from scratch again, so I can show you another handy feature.

TIP: Dragging-and-Copying

If you want to duplicate a cell, just press-and-hold the **Option (PC: Alt) key**, click-and-drag yourself a copy, and position it anywhere you'd like. If one of your photos overlaps another photo, you'll get a little warning icon up in the top-right corner of your page.

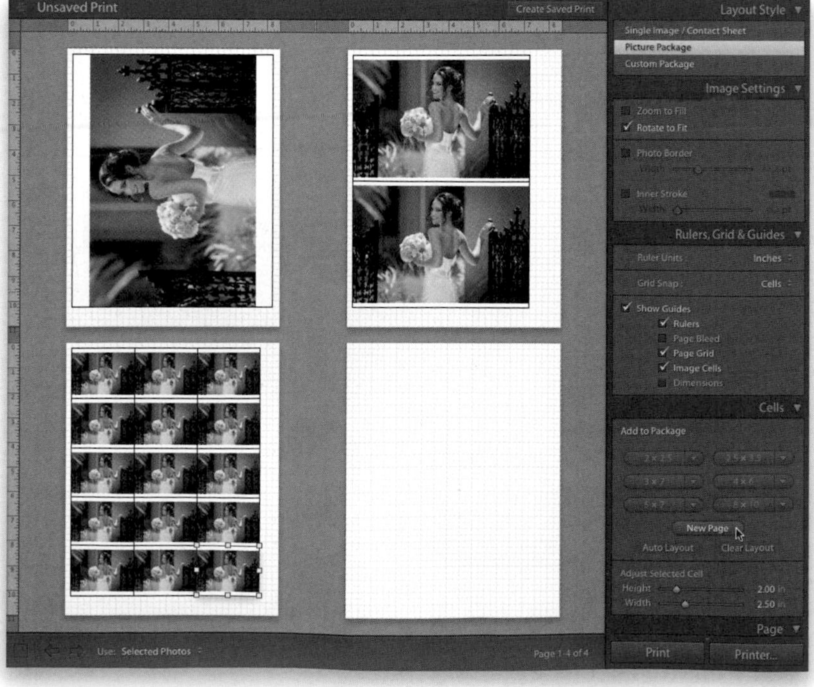

Step Eight:

If you add so many cells that they can't fit on one page, Lightroom automatically adds new pages to accommodate your extra cells. For example, start by adding an 8x10, then add a 5x7 (which can't fit on the same letter-sized page), and it automatically creates a new page for you with the 5x7. Now add another 5x7 (so you have two-up), then a 2x2.5 (which won't fit on the same page), and it will add yet another page. Pretty smart, eh? (By the way, I think this "automatically do the obvious thing" is a big step forward in software development. In the past, if something like this happened, wouldn't you have expected to see a dialog pop up that said, "This cell cannot fit on the page. Would you like to add an additional page?") Also, if you decide you want to add another blank page yourself, just click on the New Page button that appears below the Add to Package buttons.

Continued

Step Nine:

If you want to delete a page, just hover your cursor over the page you want to delete, and a little X appears over the top-left corner (as seen here, on the third page). Click on that X and the page is deleted. Now, on the page with the two 5x7s, click on each of the 5x7s, press the **Delete (PC: Backspace) key** to remove them, and then go and turn on the Zoom to Fill checkbox up in the Image Settings panel.

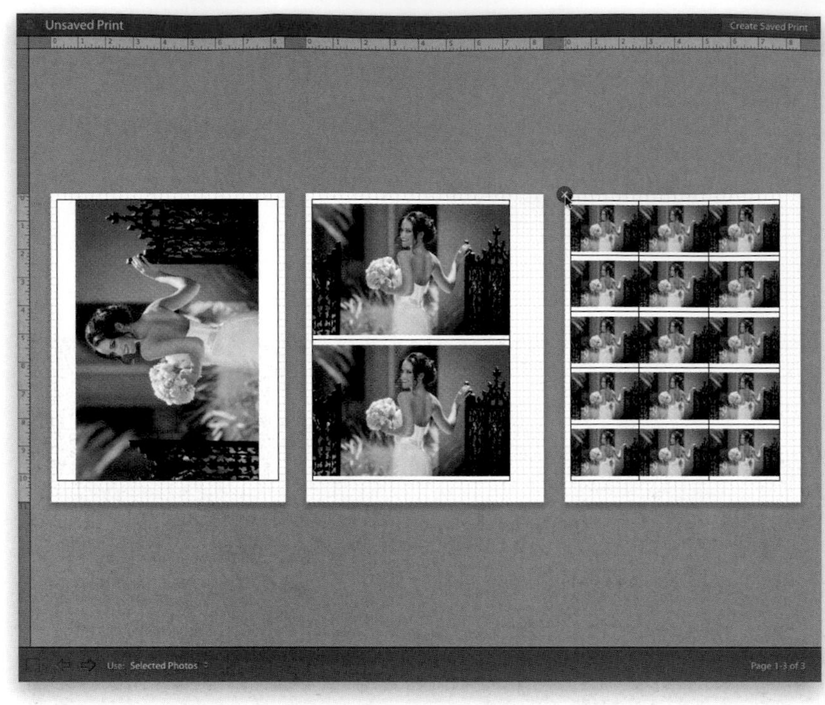

TIP: Zooming In on One Page

Once you have multiple pages like this and you want to work on just one of these pages, you can zoom right in on the page by clicking on it, then clicking on Zoom Page on the right side of the Preview panel header (at the top of the left side Panels area).

Step 10:

You can also manually adjust the size of each cell (which is a handy way to crop your photos on the fly, if you have Zoom to Fill turned on). For example, go ahead and add two 3x7 cells on this second (now empty) page, which gives you a wide, thin, cropped image. Click on the bottom image (to bring up the adjustment handles around the cell), then click-and-drag the bottom handle upward to make the cell thinner (as seen here). You can get the same effect by clicking-and-dragging the Adjust Selected Cell sliders, at the bottom of the Cells panel (there are sliders for both Height and Width). Press the Command (PC: Ctrl) key and click-and-drag on the photo to move it within the cell. There's only one real downside, and that is you can't have different photos at these different sizes—it has to be the same photo repeated for each different size (interestingly enough, this Picture Package feature was borrowed from Photoshop, but Photoshop actually does let you use different photos in your cells, not just one repeated).

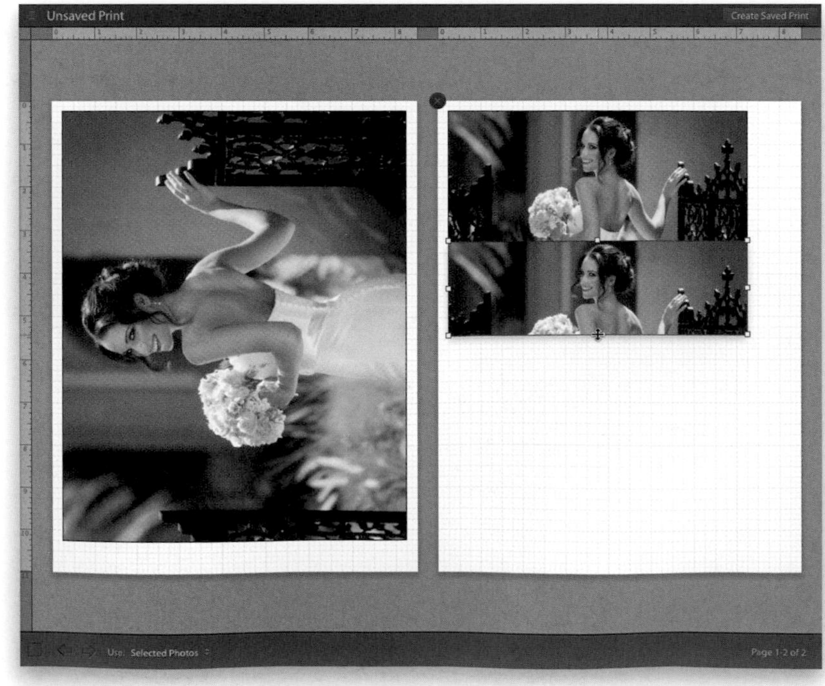

If you've come up with a layout you really like and want to be able to apply it at any time with just one click, you need to save it as a template. But beyond just saving your layout, print templates have extra power, because they can remember everything from your paper size to your printer name, color management settings, the kind of sharpening you want applied—the whole nine yards!

Saving Your Custom Layouts as Templates

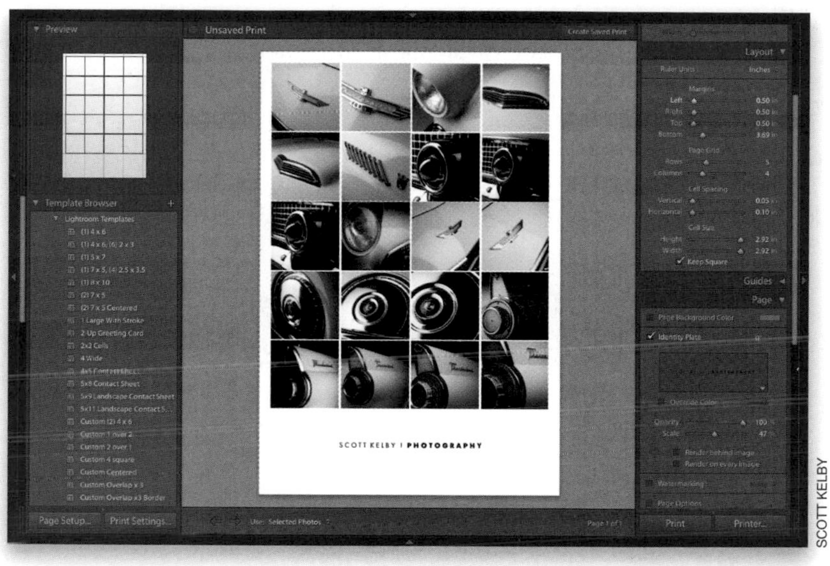

SCOTT KELBY

Step One:

Go ahead and set up a page with a layout you like, so you can save it as a print template. The page layout here is based on a 13x19" page (you choose your page size by clicking the Page Setup button at the bottom of the left side Panels area). The layout uses a Page Grid of 5 Rows and 4 Columns. The cell sizes are square (around 3 inches each), and the page has a ½" margin on the left, right, and top, with a 3.69" margin at the bottom. I turned on the Stroke Border checkbox and changed the color to white, and turned on my Identity Plate. Also, make sure the Zoom to Fill checkbox (in the Image Settings panel) is turned on.

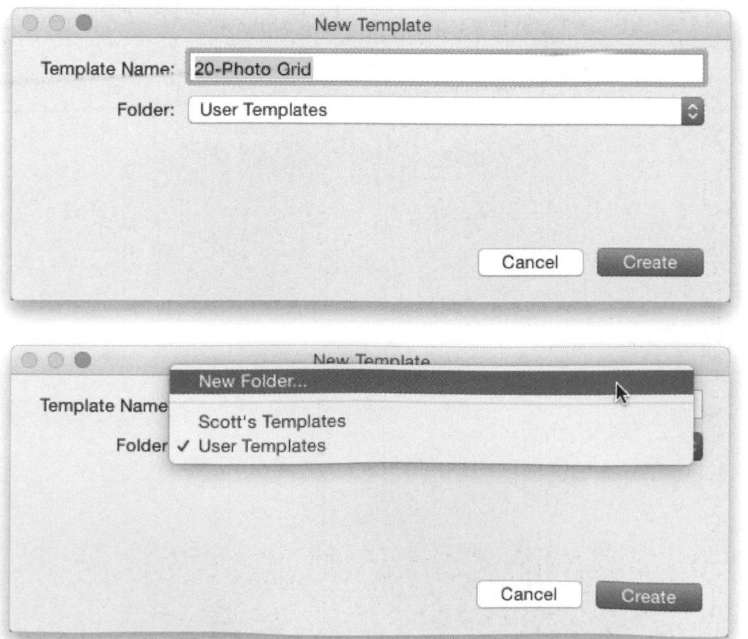

Step Two:

Once it's set up the way you like it, go to the Template Browser and click the plus sign (+) button on the right side of the header to bring up the New Template dialog (shown here). By default, it wants to save any templates you create into a folder called User Templates (you can have as many folders of print templates as you like to help you organize them. For example, you could have one set for letter-sized, one set for 13x19", one set for layouts that work with portraits, etc.). To create a new template folder, click on the Folder pop-up menu (shown here at bottom), and choose **New Folder**. Give your template a name, click Create, and now this template will appear in the folder you chose. When you hover your cursor over the template, a preview of the template will appear up in the Preview panel at the top of the left side Panels area.

Having Lightroom Remember Your Printing Layouts

Once you've gone through the trouble of creating a cool print layout, with the photos right where you want them on the page, you don't want to lose all that when you change collections, right? Right! Luckily, you can create a saved print, which keeps everything intact—from page size, to the exact layout, to which photos in your collection wound up on the page (and which ones didn't) and in which order. Here's how ya do it:

Step One:

Once you make a print, and you're happy with the final layout (and all your output settings and such, which we'll get into in a bit), click on the Create Saved Print button (shown circled here) that appears above the top-right corner of the center Preview area. This brings up the Create Print dialog (shown here). Here, you'll be saving a print collection. The key thing here, though, is to make sure the Include Only Used Photos checkbox is turned on. That way, when you save this new print collection, only the photos that are actually in this print are saved in it. Also, in the dialog, you'll have the option of including this new print collection inside an existing collection—just turn on the Inside checkbox and then choose the collection or collection set you want it to appear within.

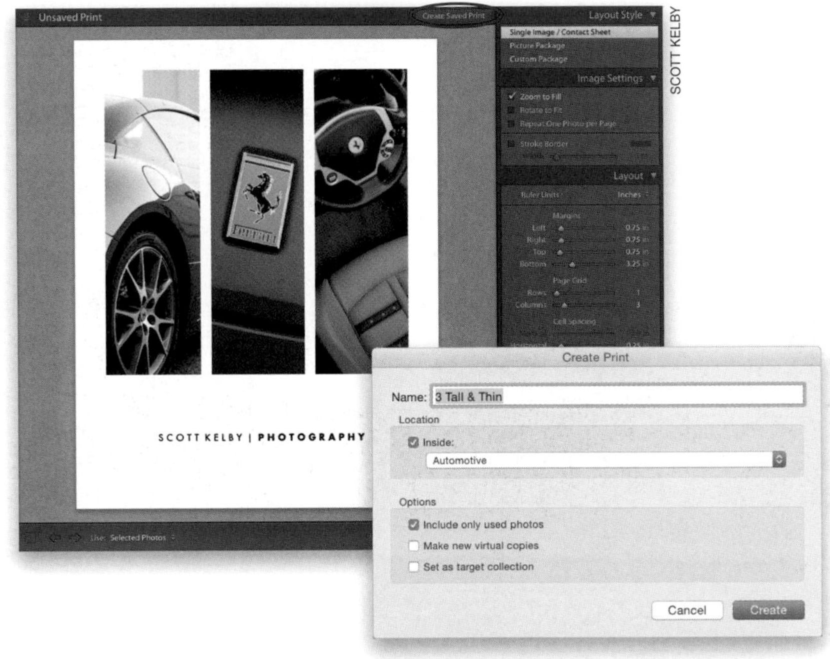

Step Two:

Now click the Create button, and a new print collection is added to the Collections panel (you'll know at a glance that it's a print collection because it will have a printer icon right before the collection's name). Well, that's it! When you click on that print collection and select all the photos in it, you'll see the layout, just the way you designed it, with the images already in order ready to go, including all your output settings (like which printer you printed to, your sharpening and resolution settings—the works!), even if it's a year from now. *Note:* If all your images don't appear in the layout, just go to the Filmstrip and select them all—now they'll appear in your layout.

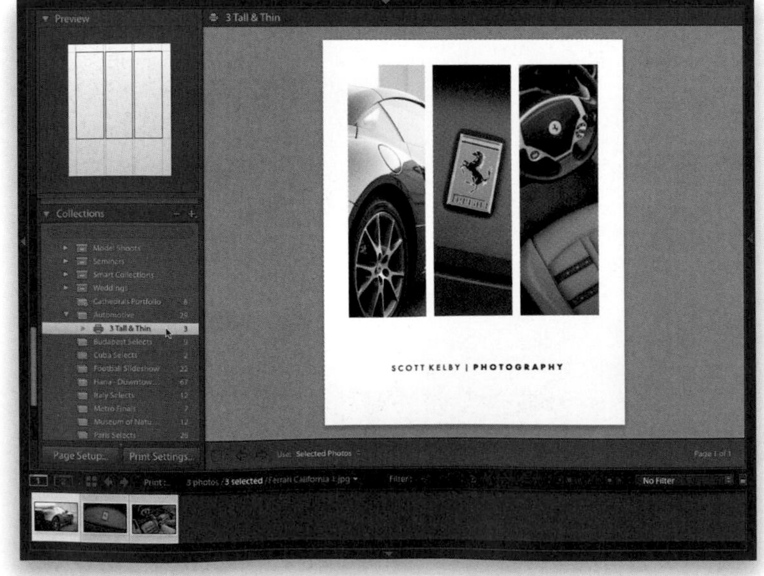

Creating Backscreened Prints

For all the wonderful things Lightroom's Print module does, one feature it doesn't have is one that lets you backscreen a photo (a staple in most wedding albums). So, I came up with a workaround, where we can use a backscreened image as our page background, and then put another non-backscreened image in front of it on the same page. It's easy, but not really obvious.

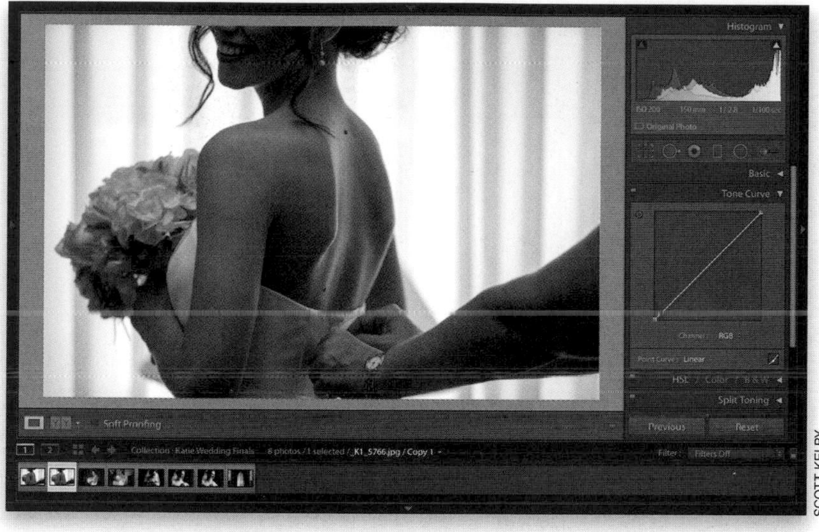
SCOTT KELBY

Step One:
Choose the photo you want to use as your backscreened image, then create a virtual copy of it by pressing **Command-'** (apostrophe; **PC: Ctrl-'**). We'll use this virtual copy to make our backscreened image, so our original stays intact. Once you've created your virtual copy, go to the Develop module's Tone Curve panel. Make sure the Point Curve is visible (if yours has more sliders below it, and doesn't look like the one you see here, just click on the little Point Curve icon at the bottom-right corner of the panel).

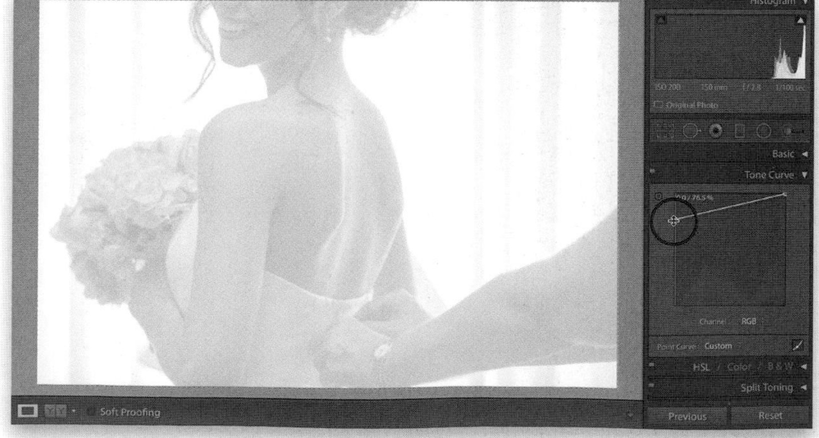

Step Two:
To create the backscreened look, click-and-drag the bottom-left corner point straight up along the left edge until it's about 3/4 or so of the way up to the top (as shown circled here in red).

Continued

Step Three:

This is an optional step, but you see this often enough that you might want to consider converting the image you just backscreened to black and white. The advantage is it creates more contrast with the image you're going to put on top of it. To make it a black-and-white image, just go to the HSL/Color/B&W panel and click directly on B&W (as shown here). That's it—it's black and white. (*Note:* Because the image is backscreened, we can get away with this one-click black-and-white conversion. Otherwise, we'd use the technique for creating high-contrast black and whites found in Chapter 6). I'm going to leave mine in color here, so press **Command-Z (PC: Ctrl-Z)** to undo that switch to black and white. Now switch to the Print module. Click on the Page Setup button and choose a borderless 8.5x11" landscape page.

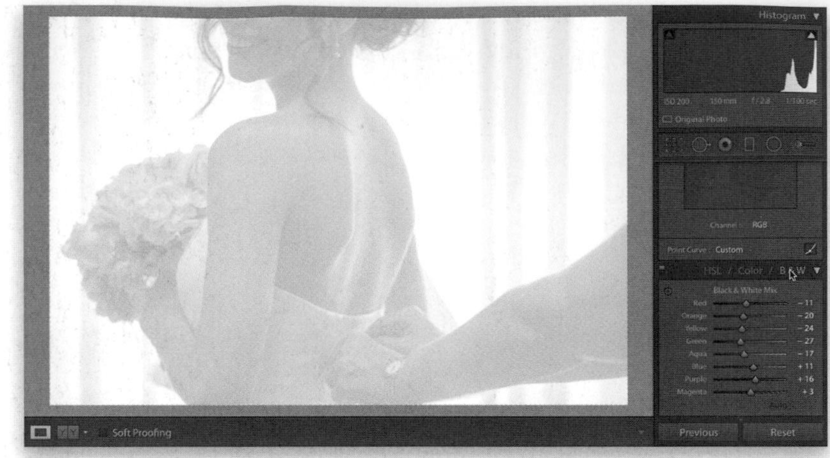

Step Four:

Then, click on Custom Package in the Layout Style panel at the top of the right side Panels area and scroll down to the Cells panel. Click the Clear Layout button, then make sure the Lock to Photo Aspect Ratio checkbox is turned off (turning this off allows you to drag a photo out larger than the page size if necessary). Now, click on your backscreened image, and drag it onto the page. To make your backscreened image fill the page, click-and-drag the image up to the top-left corner of the page, then grab the bottom-right corner point and just drag it out until it fills the entire page, edge to edge (as shown here). If your image won't stretch large enough to extend off the page, that's because you didn't turn off the Lock to Photo Aspect Ratio checkbox at the beginning of this step.

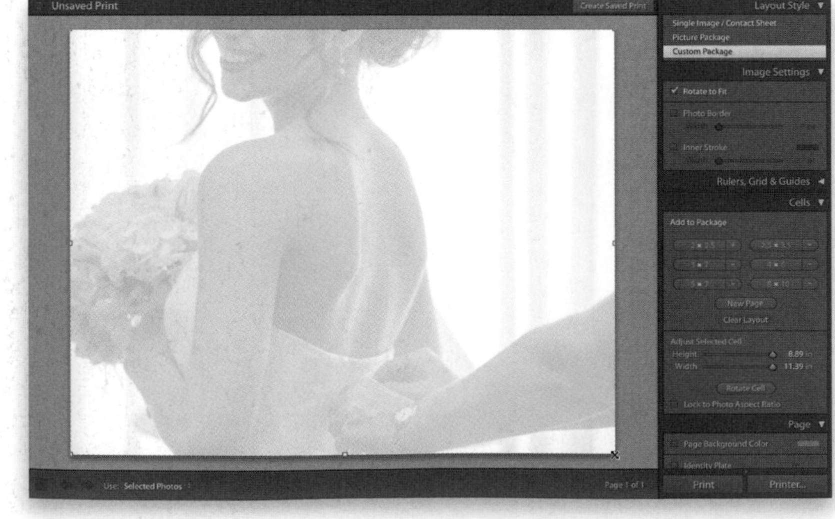

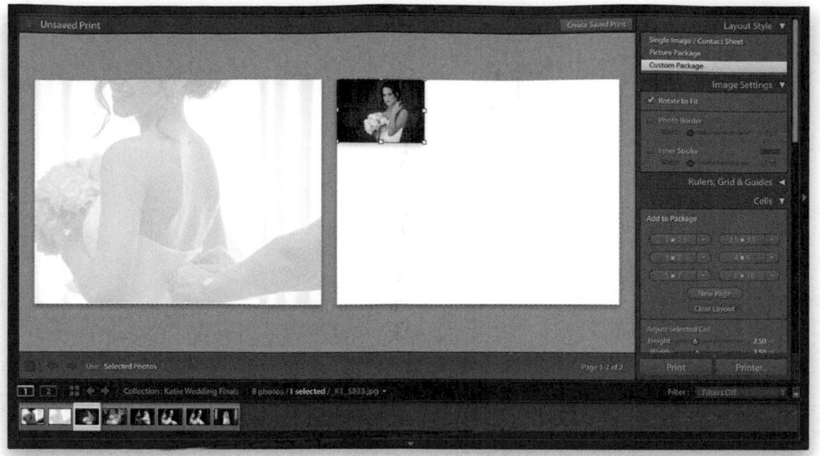

Step Five:

Getting another image to sit on top of this backscreened image is actually easy, but you kind of have to know a trick. The problem is if you add a new cell (like, for example, a 2.5 x 3.5 cell) it doesn't appear on the same page as your backscreened image. Instead, it creates a new page and adds the cell there. So, what you'll need to do is just click-and-drag your full-color photo into that new cell on the extra page (as seen here). Then, click-and-drag the cell onto the first page, and it appears over your backscreened image (as seen in the next step).

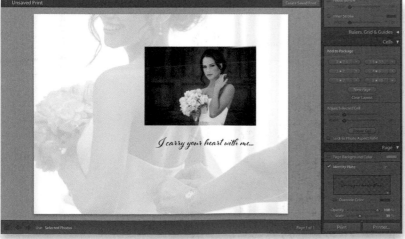

Step Six:

You can now position the image wherever you'd like (you'll see that now-blank additional page is still there, but to get rid of it, just click on the round X button in the top-left corner and it's gone). Here's the final page with the backscreened image and the second image on top of it. I also added a line of text (using the Identity Plate in the Page panel), using my favorite new wedding font, Al Fresco Regular by Laura Worthington (from MyFonts.com for around $39).

The Final Print and Color Management Settings

Once you've got your page set up with the printing layout you want, you just need to make a few choices in the Print Job panel, so your photos look their best when printed. Here are which buttons to click, when, and why:

Step One:

Get your page layout the way you want it to look. In the capture shown here, I clicked on Page Setup at the bottom of the left side Panels area, chose a 17x22" page size, set my page to a wide [landscape] orientation, and then I went to the Template Browser and clicked on the Maximize Size template. I set my Left, Right, and Top Margins sliders to 2.00 in, and my Bottom Margins slider to 6.50 in. I also turned on the Zoom to Fill checkbox. Lastly, I added my Identity Plate below the photo (like the one we created earlier in this chapter). Once that's done, it's time to choose our printing options in the Print Job panel, at the bottom of the right side Panels area.

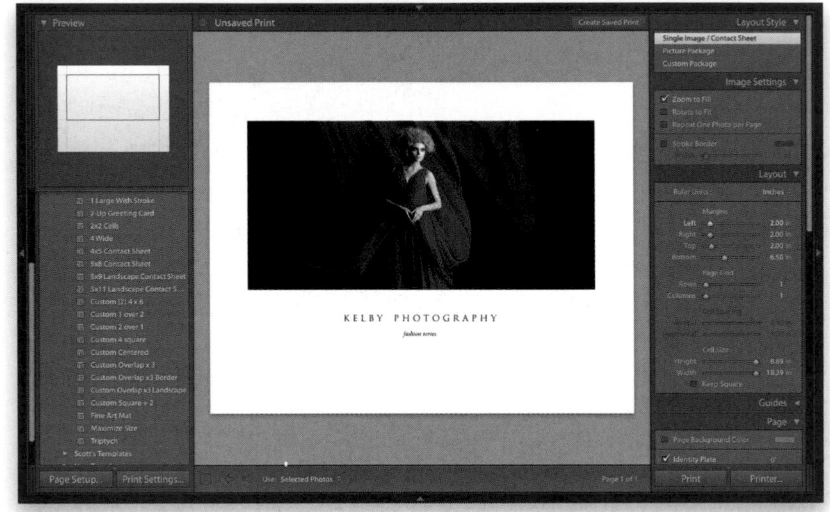

SCOTT KELBY

Step Two:

You have the choice of sending your image to your printer, or just creating a high-resolution JPEG file of your photo layout (that way, you could send this finished page to a photo lab for printing, or email it to a client as a high-res proof, or use the layout on a website, or…whatever). You choose whether it's going to output the image to a printer or save it as a JPEG from the Print To pop-up menu, at the top right of the Print Job panel (as seen here). If you want to choose the Print to JPEG File route, go to the next tutorial in this chapter for details on how to use the JPEG settings and export the file.

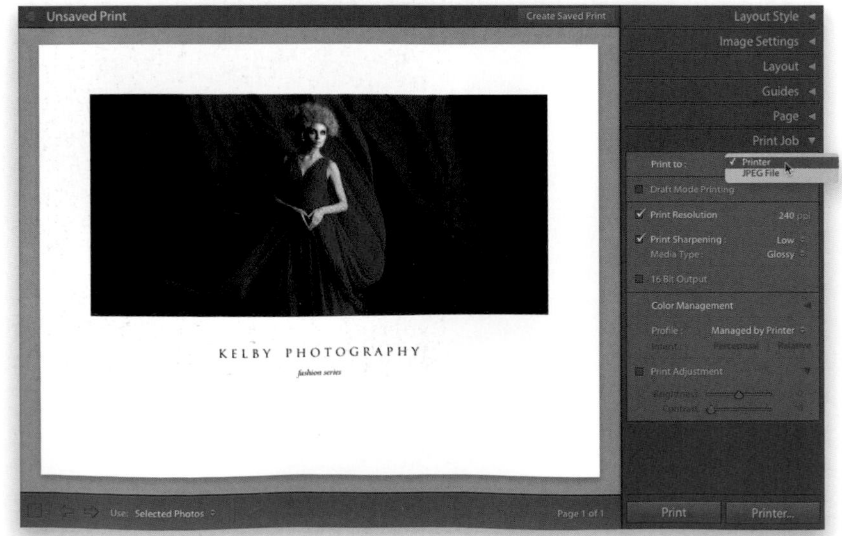

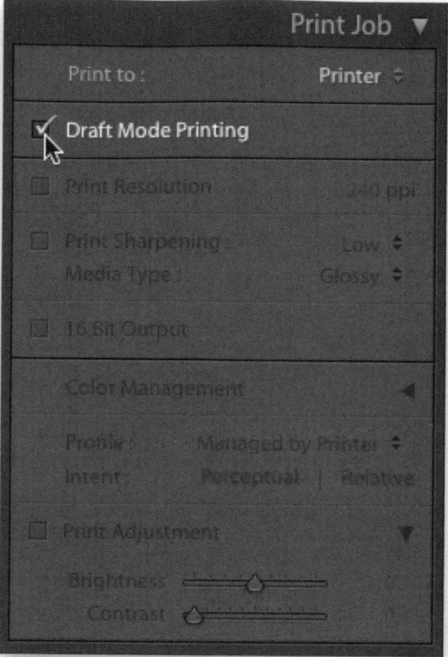

Step Three:

Since we've already started at the top, we'll just kind of work our way down. The next setting down in the panel is a checkbox for Draft Mode Printing, and when you turn this on, you're swapping quality for speed. That's because rather than rendering the full-resolution image, it just prints the low-res JPEG preview image that's embedded in the file, so the print comes out of your printer faster than a greased pig. I would only recommend using this if you're printing multi-photo contact sheets. In fact, I always turn this on when printing contact sheets, because for printing a page of small thumbnail images, it works beautifully—the small images look crisp and clear. Notice, though, that when you turn Draft Mode Printing on, all the other options are grayed out. So, for contact sheets, turn it on. Otherwise, leave this off.

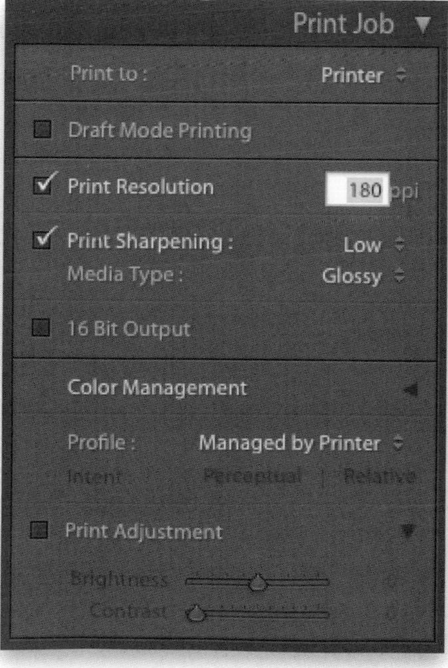

Step Four:

Make sure the Draft Mode Printing checkbox is turned off, and now it's time to choose the resolution of your image. If you want to print at your file's native resolution, then turn the Print Resolution checkbox off. Otherwise, when you turn the checkbox on, the default resolution is 240 ppi (fine for most color inkjet printing). I use Epson printers, and I've found resolutions that work well for them at various sizes. For example, I use 360 ppi for letter-sized or smaller prints, 240 ppi for 13x19" prints, or just 180 ppi for a 16x20" or larger. (The larger the print size, the lower the resolution you can get away with.) In this instance, I'm printing to an Epson Stylus Pro 3880 on a 17x22" sheet, so I would highlight the Print Resolution field and type in 180 (as shown here), then press the Return (PC: Enter) key. *Note:* If printing at 180 ppi freaks you out, just leave it set to the default of 240 ppi, but at least try 180 ppi once on a big print, and see if you can tell a difference.

Continued

Step Five:

Next is the pop-up menu for Print Sharpening, and in Lightroom 2, Adobe really made this a powerful tool (the output sharpening in earlier versions was just too weak for most folks' tastes). Now when you tell Lightroom which type of paper you're printing on and which level of sharpening you'd like, it looks at those, along with the resolution you're printing at, and it applies the right amount of sharpening to give you the best results on that paper media at that resolution (sweet!). So, start by turning on the Print Sharpening checkbox (I always turn this on for every print, and every JPEG file), then choose either Glossy or Matte from the Media Type pop-up menu. Now choose the amount of sharpening you want from the Print Sharpening pop-up menu (I generally use High for glossy and Standard for matte paper, like Epson's Velvet Fine Art). That's all there is to it—Lightroom does all the work for you.

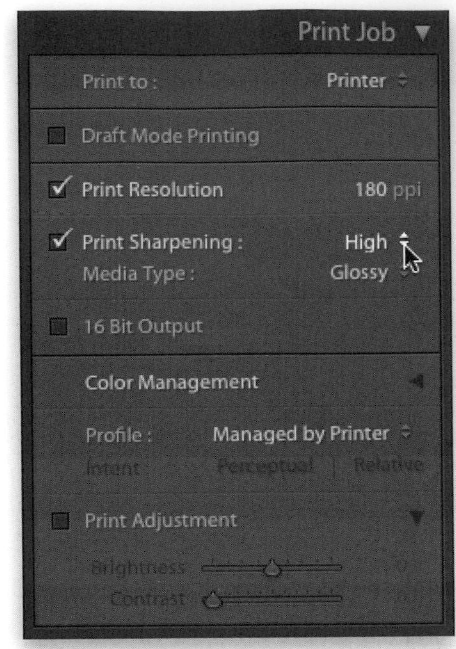

Step Six:

The next checkbox down reveals another feature: 16-bit printing, which gives you an expanded dynamic range on printers that support 16-bit printing. (*Note:* At the time this book was published, 16-bit printing in Lightroom was only available for Mac OS X Leopard or higher users, but, of course, that is subject to change if Adobe releases an update for Windows.) So, if you're running Mac OS X Leopard or higher, and you have a 16-bit-capable printer, like some of the newer Canon printers (or if you've downloaded a 16-bit printer driver, like the ones Epson released in early 2008 that make your current printer 16-bit capable), then you should turn the 16 Bit Output checkbox on (as shown here).

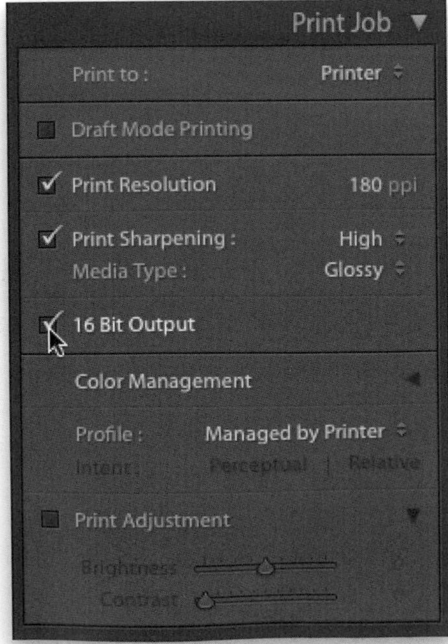

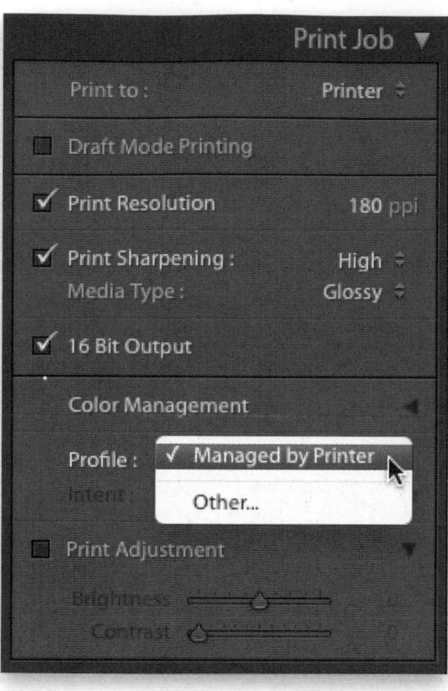

Step Seven:

Now it's time to set the Color Management options, so what you see onscreen and what comes out of the printer both match. (By the way, if you have any hope of this happening, you've first got to use a hardware monitor calibrator to calibrate your monitor. Without a calibrated monitor, all bets are off. More on this in a bit.) There are only two things you have to set here: (1) you have to choose your printer profile, and (2) you have to choose your rendering intent. For Profile, the default setting is Managed by Printer (as shown here), which means your printer is going to color manage your print job for you. This choice used to be out of the question, but today's printers have come so far that you'll actually now get decent results leaving it set to Managed by Printer (but if you want "better than decent," read on).

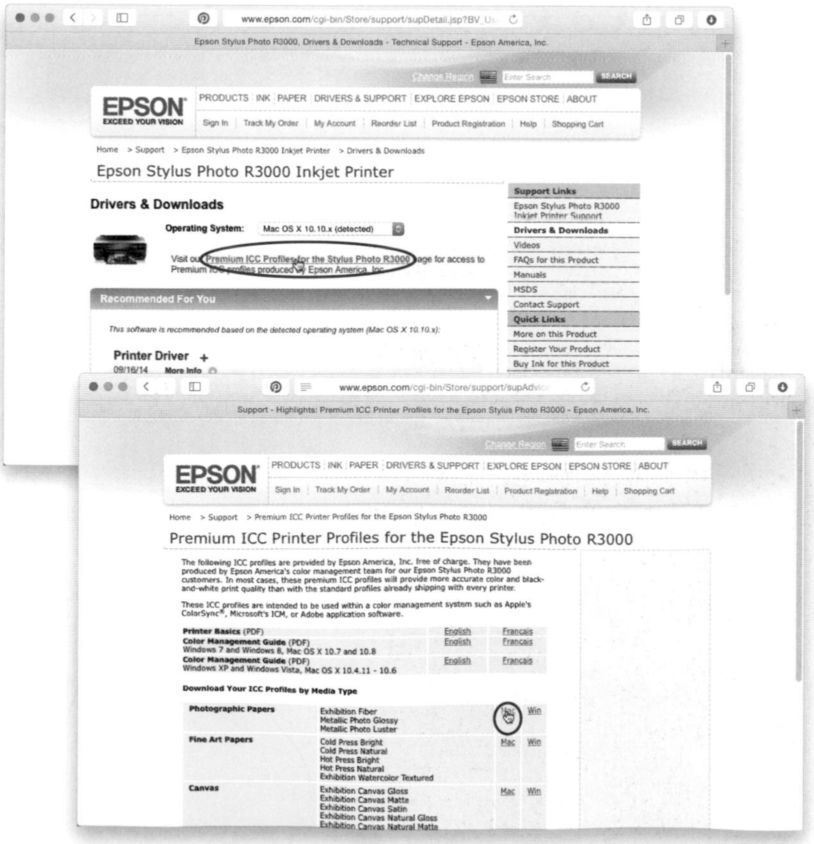

Step Eight:

You'll get better looking prints by assigning a custom printer/paper profile. If the profiles don't come with your printer driver (they do for my Epson Stylus Pro 3880), go to the website of the company that manufactures the paper you're going to be printing on. On their site, find the ICC color profiles they provide for free downloading that exactly match (a) the paper you're going to be printing on, and (b) the exact printer you're going to be printing to. So, if I was printing to an Epson Stylus Photo R3000 printer on Epson's Exhibition Fiber Paper, on Epson's website, under Drivers & Support for Printers & All in Ones, I'd find the R3000 downloads for a Macintosh. At the top of that page, I'd click on the ICC Profile downloads link, then on the download button for Exhibition Fiber Paper, and install the free color profile for my printer. On a Mac, the unzipped file should be placed in your Library/ColorSync/Profiles folder. In Windows Vista or newer, Right-click on the unzipped file and choose Install Profile.

Continued

Step Nine:

Once your color profile is installed, click-and-hold on the Profile pop-up menu (right where it says Managed by Printer), and choose **Other**. This brings up a dialog (shown here) listing all the color profiles installed on your computer. Scroll through the list and find the paper profiles for your printer, then find the profile(s) for the paper(s) you normally print on (in my case, I'm looking for that Epson Exhibition Fiber Paper for the Epson Stylus Pro 3880), and then turn on the checkbox beside that paper (as shown here). Once you've found your profile(s), click OK to add it to your pop-up menu.

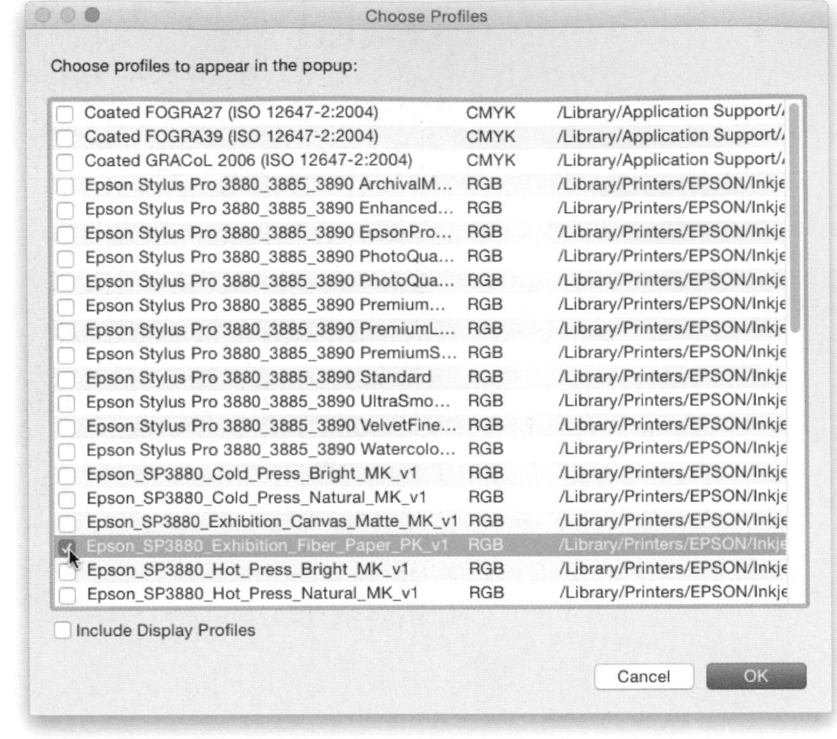

Step 10:

Return to that Profile pop-up menu in the Print Job panel, and you'll see the color profile for your printer is now available as one of the choices in this menu (as seen here). Choose your color profile from this pop-up menu (if it's not already chosen; in my case, I would choose the Epson_SP3880_Exhibition_Fiber_Paper_PK_v1, as shown here). Now you've set up Lightroom so it knows exactly how to handle the color for that printer on that particular type of paper. This step is really key to getting the quality prints we're all aiming for, because at the end of the day, it's all about the print.

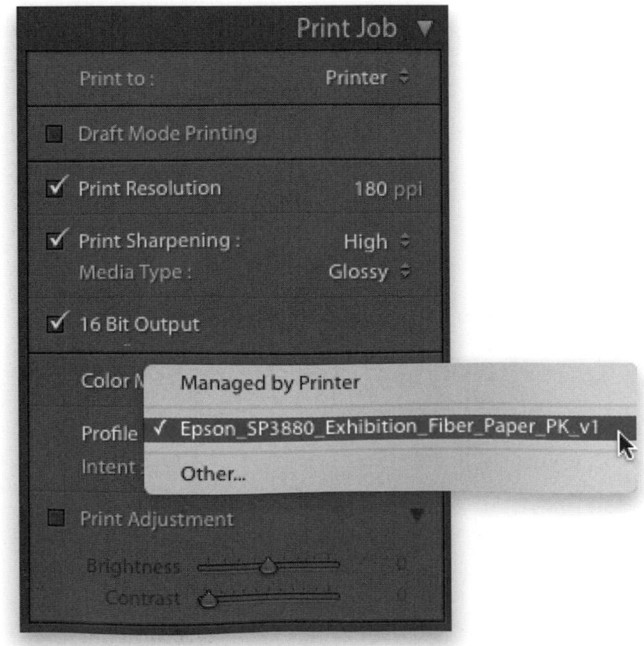

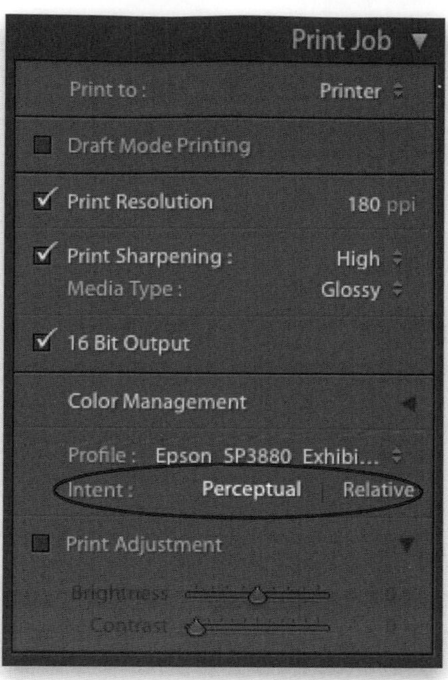

Step 11:

Next to Intent, you have two choices: (a) Perceptual, or (b) Relative. Theoretically, choosing Perceptual may give you a more pleasing print because it tries to maintain color relationships, but it's not necessarily accurate as to what you see tonally on-screen. Choosing Relative may provide a more accurate interpretation of the tone of the photo, but you may not like the final color as much. So, which one is right? The one that looks best on your own printer. Relative is probably the most popular choice, but personally, I usually use Perceptual because my style uses very rich, saturated colors, and it seems that Perceptual gives me better color on my particular printer. So, which one should you choose? The best way to know which one looks best for your printer is to print a few test prints for each photo—try one with Perceptual and one with Relative—when the prints come out, you'll know right away which one works best for your printer. We'll cover the last option, Print Adjustment, after you make your first print.

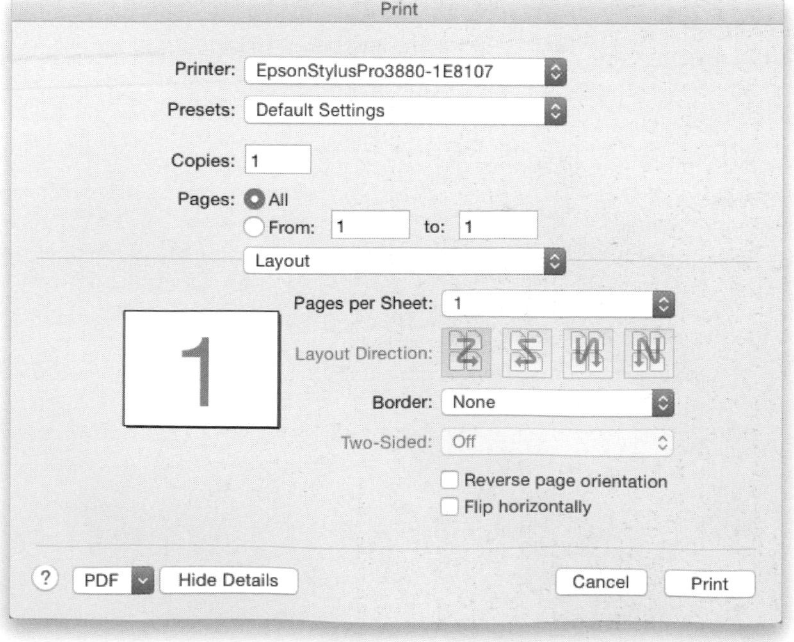

Step 12:

Now it's time to click the Printer button at the bottom of the right side Panels area. This will bring up the Print dialog (shown here. If you're using a Mac, and you see a small dialog with just two pop-up menus, rather than the larger one you see here, click the Show Details button to expand the dialog to its full size, more like the one shown here).

Continued

Step 13:

Click-and-hold on the dialog's main section pop-up menu, and choose **Printer Settings** (as shown here). By the way, the part of this dialog that controls printer color management, and your pop-up menu choices, may be different depending on your printer, so if it doesn't look exactly like this, don't freak out. On a PC, click on the Properties button next to the Printer Name pop-up menu to locate it instead.

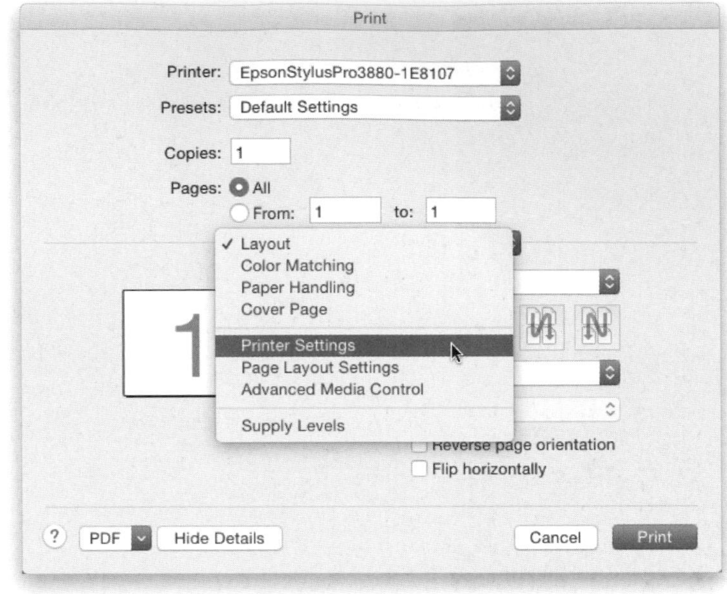

Step 14:

When the Printer Settings options appear, under Color Mode, your printer's color management may be turned on. Since you're having Lightroom manage your color, you don't want the printer also trying to manage your color, because when the two color management systems start both trying to manage your color, nobody wins. So, if it's not already set that way, choose **Off (No Color Management)** from the pop-up menu (as seen here). On a PC (this may be different, depending on your printer), in the Media Settings section, under Mode, click the Custom radio button and choose **Off (No Color Adjustment)** from the pop-up menu. Here, mine was automatically turned off, and grayed out so I couldn't change it.

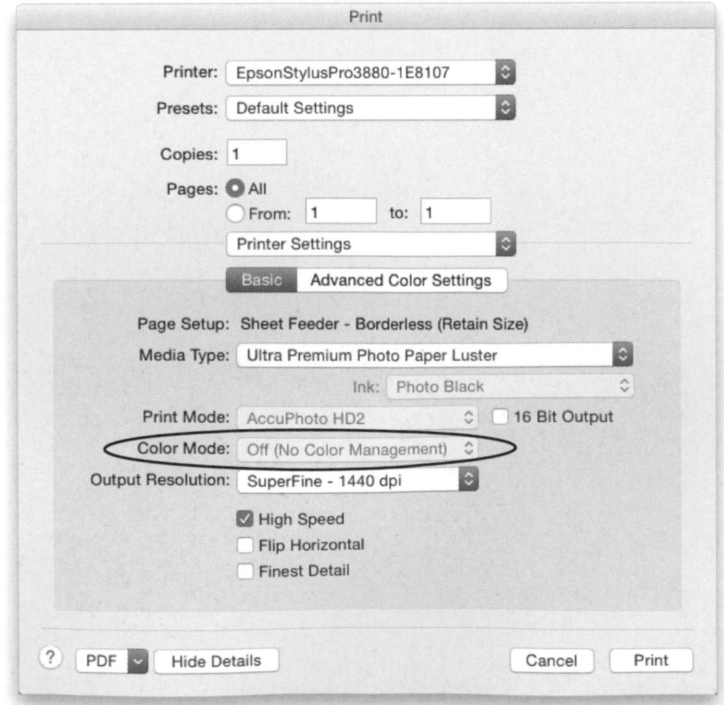

Print

Printer: EpsonStylusPro3880-1E8107
Presets: Default Settings
Copies: 1
Pages: All
From: 1 to: 1
Printer Settings
Basic Advanced Color Settings
Page Setup: Sheet Feeder - Borderless (Retain Size)
Media Type: Exhibition Fiber Paper
Ink: Photo Black
Print Mode: AccuPhoto HD2 16 Bit Output
Color Mode: Off (No Color Management)
Output Resolution: SuperFine - 1440 dpi
High Speed
Flip Horizontal
Finest Detail
? PDF Hide Details Cancel Print

Step 15:

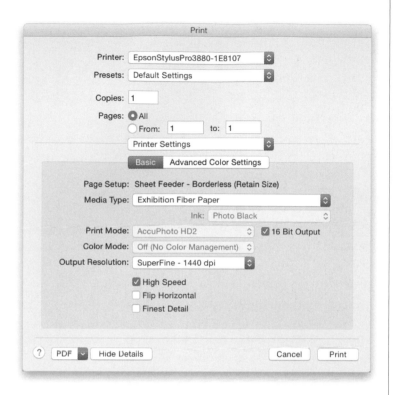

Now, also in the Printer Settings section (or Media Settings on a PC) of the Print dialog (again, your pop-up menus may be different, and on a PC, these will be in the Properties dialog for your printer), for Media Type, choose the exact paper you'll be printing to from the pop-up menu (as seen here, where I chose Exhibition Fiber Paper) and turn on the 16 Bit Output checkbox if your printer supports it.

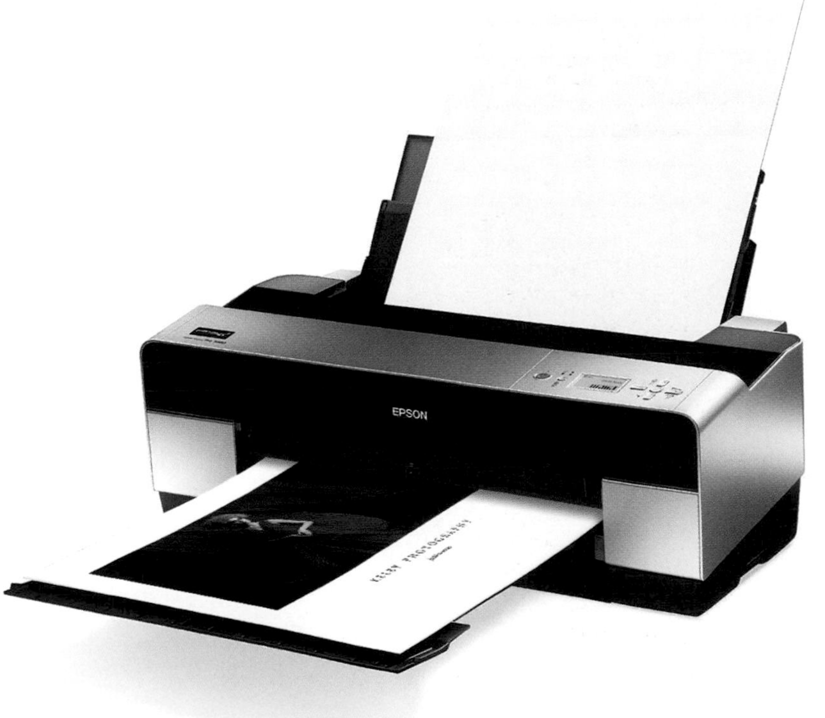

Step 16:

In that same Printer Settings section, for Output Resolution, choose **SuperFine – 1440 dpi** from the pop-up menu, and turn on the High Speed setting checkbox (if it's not already turned on; as seen in the previous step. Again, this is for printing to an Epson printer using Epson paper. If you don't have an Epson printer…why not? Just kidding—if you don't have an Epson printer, you're probably not using Epson paper, so for Print Quality, choose the one that most closely matches the paper you are printing to). On a PC, under Print Quality, choose Quality Options from the pop-up menu. In the resulting Quality Options dialog, you can turn on the High Speed checkbox and choose your Print Quality by setting the Speed slider. Now sit back and watch your glorious print(s) roll gently out of your printer. So far, so good.

Continued

Step 17:
Once your print comes out of the printer, now it's time to take a good look at the print to see if what we're holding in our hands actually matches what we saw onscreen. If you use a hardware-based monitor calibrator, and you followed all the instructions up to this point on downloading printer profiles and all that stuff, the color of your image should be pretty spot on. If your color is way off, my first guess would be you didn't use a hardware-based calibrator. The one I use is the Spyder4 Elite by Datacolor (shown here), and using it is seriously a no-brainer. You put it on your monitor, launch the software, choose "easy-you-do-it-all-automatically-for-me" mode (not it's actual name), and in about four minutes your monitor is calibrated. This is such a critical step in getting your color right that without hardware calibration of some sort, you really have little hope of the colors on your monitor and your print actually matching.

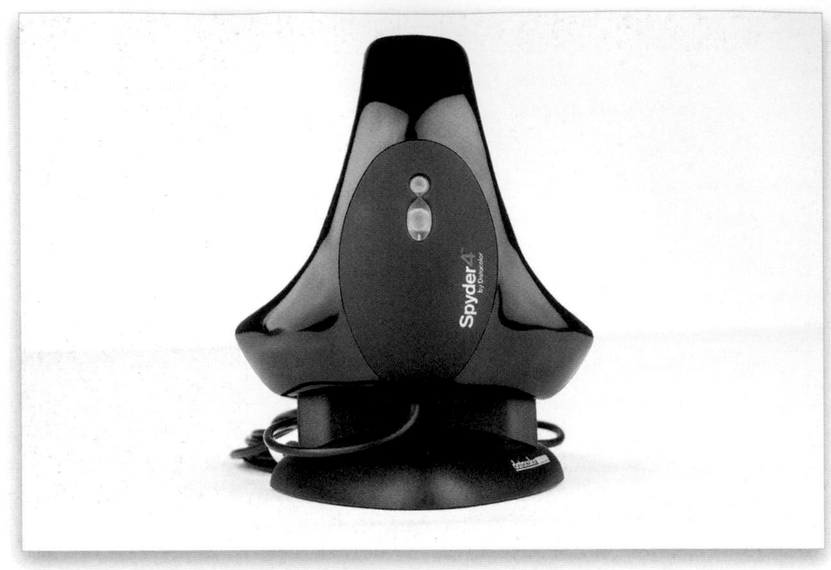

Step 18:
If you've used a hardware calibrator, and followed the instructions in this section of the book, your color should be pretty much spot on, but there's another printing problem you're likely to run up against. Your color probably matches pretty darn well, but my guess is that the print you're holding in your hand right now is quite a bit darker than what you see on your screen. That's mostly because, up to this point, you've been seeing your image on a very bright, backlit monitor, but now your image isn't backlit—it's flat on a printed page (imagine how a backlit sign looks when you turn off the back lighting. Well, that's what you're holding). Luckily, in Lightroom 4, Adobe addressed this problem by adding a Print Adjustment option at the bottom of the Print Job panel (shown here).

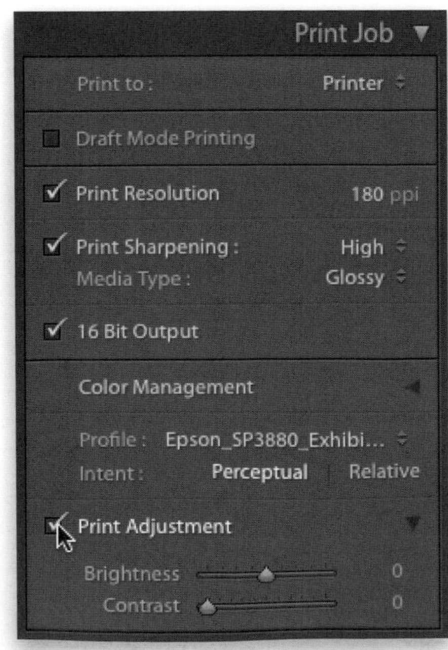

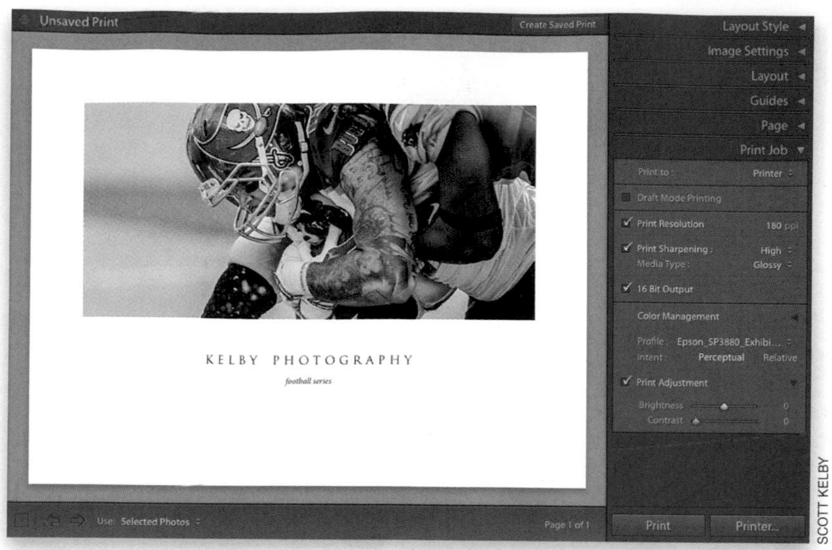

SCOTT KELBY

Step 19:

In earlier versions of Lightroom, we would intentionally bump up the Brightness slider (back when there was a Brightness slider) right before we would make a print, so when it came out, it would actually look as bright as it did on our monitor (I had to bump up mine by around 20% for my Epson printer). The problem with this was it actually made an adjustment to the image, so if you wanted to use the image somewhere else (like in a web gallery, or in a magazine), then you'd have to re-tweak the image every time. Now, if we need a little adjustment to the brightness or contrast at the printing stage, we can leave our image alone (in most cases) and use the new Print Adjustment sliders to have it just print brighter or with more contrast without actually changing our file.

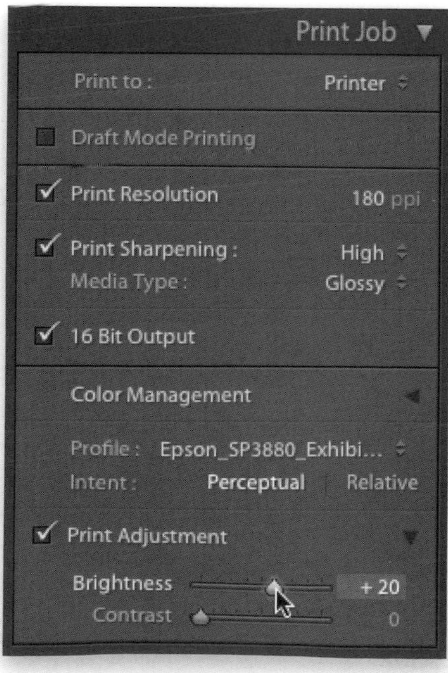

Step 20:

Let's start with the Brightness. How do you know how much to increase it? (I've never had to decrease it. Not once.) You do a test print. In fact, you kind of have to do a test print, since the changes you make with the Brightness and Contrast sliders aren't seen onscreen (they're only applied as the image is printed). Now, the good news is your test print doesn't have to be output on a big expensive 16x20" sheet of paper—it can be a small 4x6" print. Once you have your test print in hand, compare the brightness to what you see on your screen. If the image is too dark (my guess is that it will be), then try bumping up the Brightness slider to maybe +20 and do another test print, then see where you're at.

Continued

Step 21:
By the way, you may have to tweak that Brightness number up or down a little bit, but after just a few quick test prints, you'll know the amount you need for the paper profile and printer you chose, and you'll use that same setting every time when you print on that paper to that printer (unless you change paper types, as I've done here, because different papers display brightness differently, so you'll need to do a test for that paper, too). Luckily, you only have to do this once, because once you know where to set the Brightness…well…ya know.

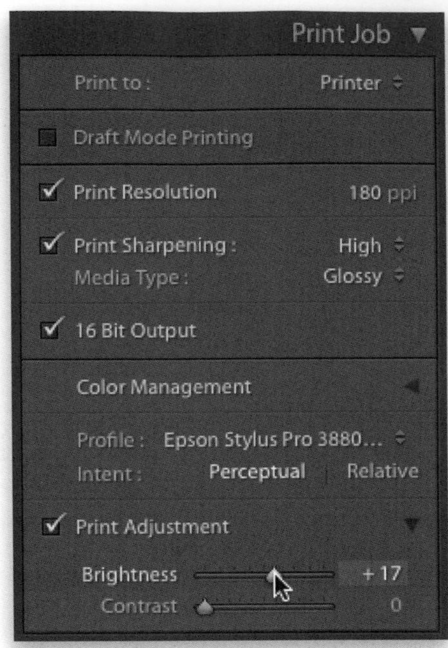

Step 22:
As for the Contrast slider, you use it the same way, but of course only if your image prints kind of flat looking and less contrasty. Drag it to the right to add contrast to the image, but again, you'll need a test print to see and test the effect, since there is no onscreen preview of this slider, either. *Note:* These two sliders are for minor tweaks to just the contrast and brightness.

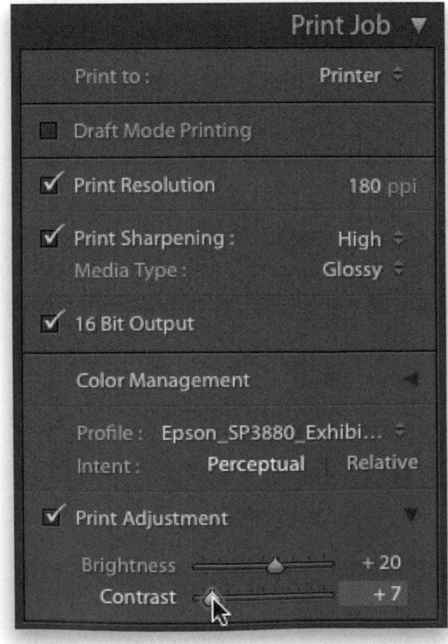

You can save any of these print layouts as JPEG files, so you can send them to a photo lab, or have someone else output your files, or email them to your client, or one of the dozen different things you want JPEGs of your layouts for. Here's how it's done:

Saving Your Page Layout as a JPEG

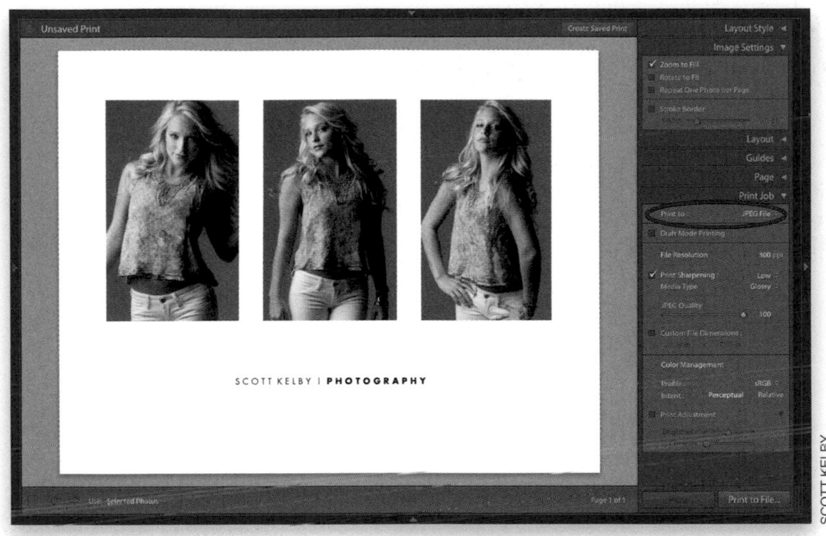

SCOTT KELBY

Step One:

Once your layout is all set, go to the Print Job panel (in the right side Panels area), and from the Print To pop-up menu (at the top right of the panel), choose **JPEG File** (as seen here).

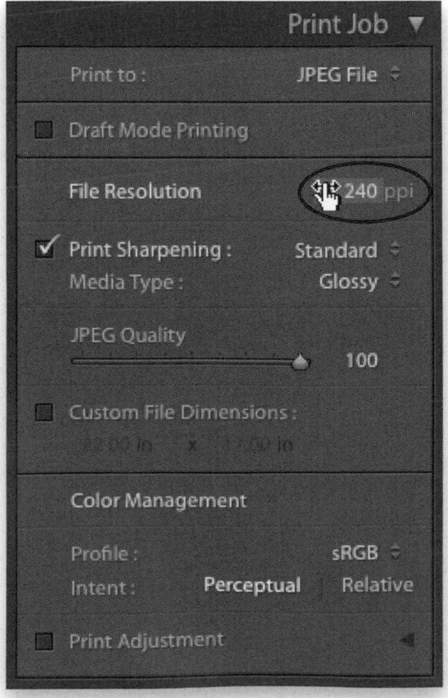

Step Two:

When you choose to print to a JPEG, a new set of features appears. First, ignore the Draft Mode Printing checkbox (it's just for when you're actually printing contact sheets full of small thumbnails). For File Resolution, the default is 300 ppi, but if you want to change it, move your cursor directly over the File Resolution field (the 300), and your cursor will change into a "scrubby slider" (it's that hand with the two arrows, as seen here). Now you can click-and-drag left to lower the resolution amount, or click-and-drag right to increase it.

Continued

Step Three:
Next is the pop-up menu for Print Sharpening. What you do here is tell Lightroom which type of paper you'll be printing on (Matte or Glossy), and which level of sharpening you'd like applied (Low, Standard, or High). Lightroom looks at your choices (including resolution) and comes up with the optimum amount and type of sharpening to match your choices. So, start there (I apply this print sharpening to every photo I print or save as a JPEG). If you don't want this output sharpening applied to your exported JPEG, just turn off the Print Sharpening checkbox.

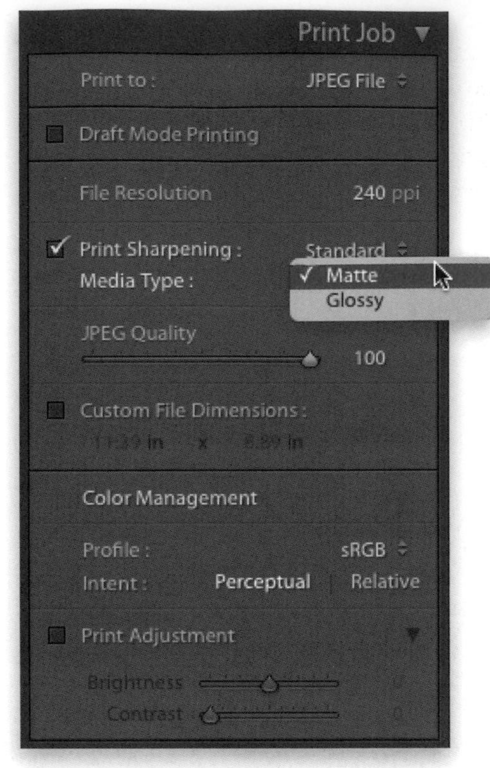

Step Four:
You've got a couple more choices to make before we're done. Next, is JPEG Quality (I usually use 80, because I think it gives a good balance between quality and compression of the file size, but you can choose anything you want, up to 100). Below that is the Custom File Dimensions section. If you leave the checkbox turned off, it will just use whatever page size you had chosen in the Page Setup dialog. If you want to change the size of your JPEG, turn on the Custom File Dimensions checkbox, then move your cursor over the size fields and use the scrubby slider to change sizes (shown here, where I changed it to 11x8½". Depending on the layout, you may have to adjust your margins and cell sizes if you do this). Lastly, you set your Color Management Profile (many labs require that you use sRGB as your profile, so ask your lab). If you want a custom color profile, go back to the last project for info on how to find those, and you can find info on the rendering Intent setting there, too. Now just click the Print to File button at the bottom of the right side Panels area to save your file.

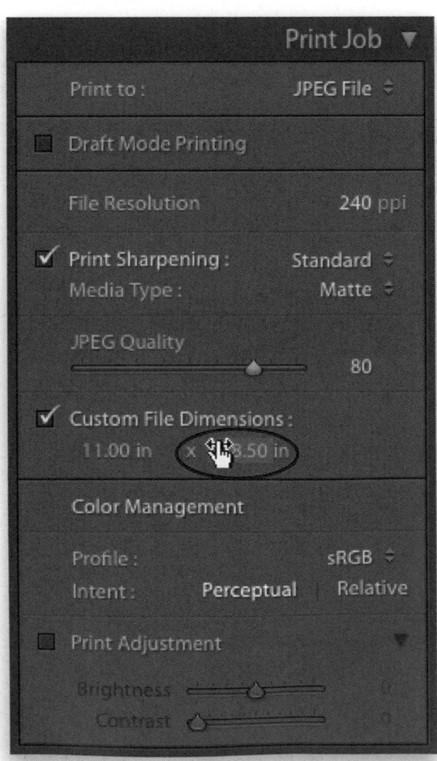

I wish Lightroom had the built-in ability to add custom borders, edges, and frames around your photos, but unfortunately it just doesn't. However, you can do a little workaround that lets you use your Identity Plate, and a special option in the Identity Plate section, to get the same effect right within Lightroom itself. Here's how it's done:

Adding Custom Borders to Your Prints

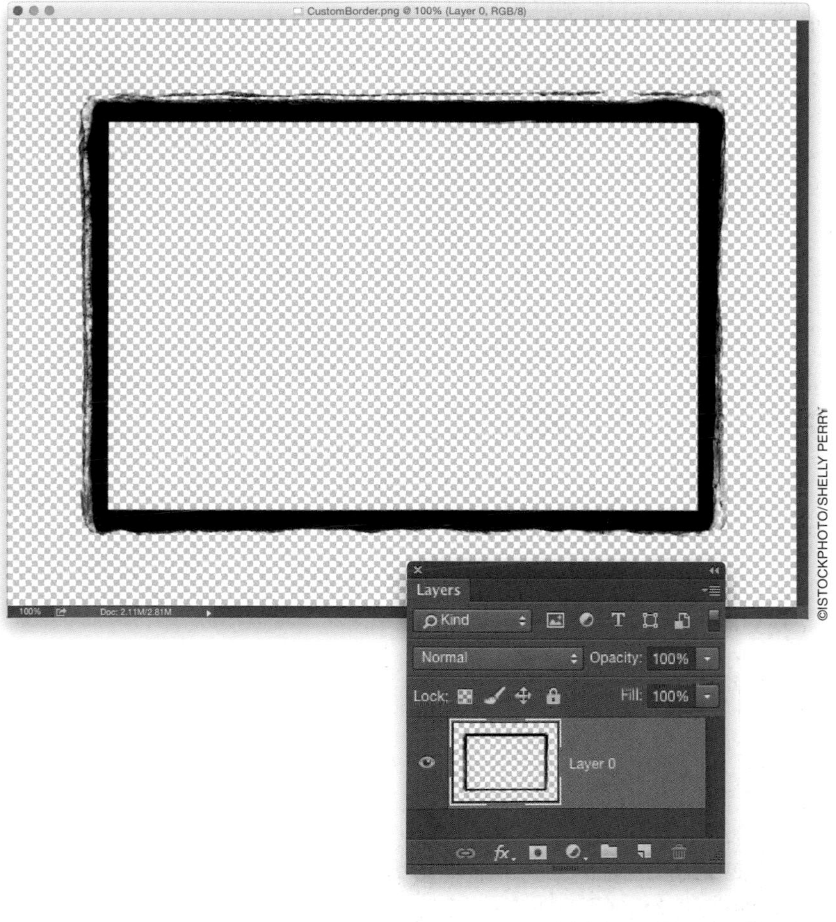

©ISTOCKPHOTO/SHELLY PERRY

Step One:

We'll start in Photoshop with the edge border here (from iStockphoto.com; you can download it for free from this book's website, mentioned in the introduction). The edge comes flattened on the background, so select the entire black area. Then press **Command-Shift-J (PC: Ctrl-Shift-J)** to put it up on its own separate layer. Cut a rectangular hole out of the center (so our photo can show through) using the Rectangular Marquee tool **(M)**, then press the Delete (PC: Backspace) key. Our file can't have a solid white background, or it will cover our photo in Lightroom—instead it has to be transparent. So, go to the Layers panel and click-and-drag the Background layer into the Trash (at the bottom of the panel). Now, save the file in PNG format.

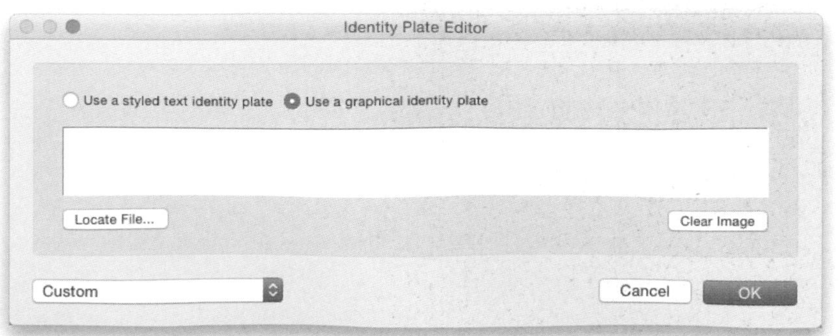

Step Two:

All right, that's all the prep work in Photoshop—back to Lightroom. Click on the photo you want to have an edge frame, then go to the Print module. In the Page panel, turn on the Identity Plate checkbox. Then, in the Identity Plate pop-up menu, choose **Edit** to bring up the Identity Plate Editor seen here. Click on the Use a Graphical Identity Plate radio button (because we're going to import a graphic, rather than using text), then click on the Locate File button, locate your saved PNG frame file, and click Choose to load it into your Identity Plate Editor (you may not be able to see the edge frame graphic in the small preview window, as shown here).

Continued

BONUS VIDEO:
I did a little bonus video for you, to show you step by step how to create Identity Plate graphics with transparency. You'll find it at **http://kelbyone.com/books/lrcc**.

Step Three:

When you click OK, your edge frame will appear, hovering over your print (almost like it's on its own layer). The size and position won't be right, so that's the first thing you'll want to fix (which we'll do in the next step, but while we're here, notice how the center of our frame is transparent—you can see right through it to the photo below it. That's why we had to save this file without the Background layer, and as a PNG—to keep that transparency intact).

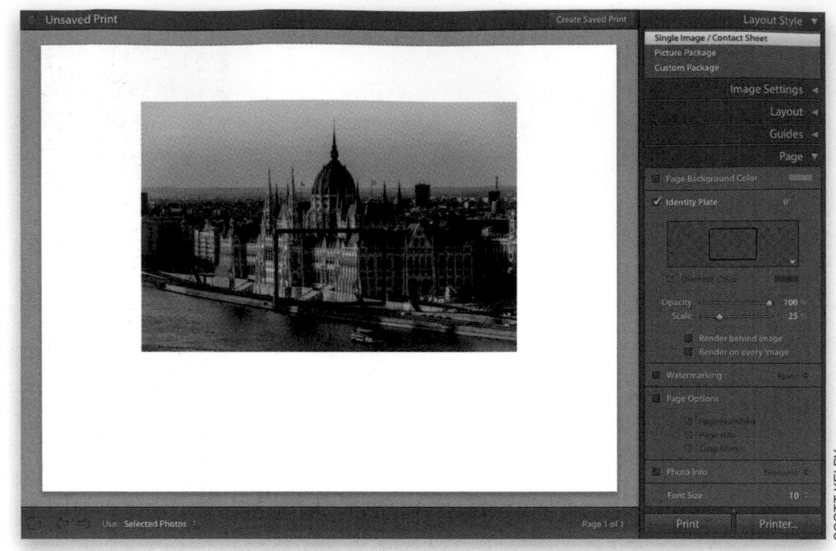

SCOTT KELBY

Step Four:

To resize your border, you can either click-and-drag a corner point outward (as shown here), or use the Scale slider in the Page panel. Once the size looks about right, you can reposition the frame edge by simply clicking-and-dragging inside its borders. You may need to resize your image, as well, using the Margins sliders in the Layout panel.

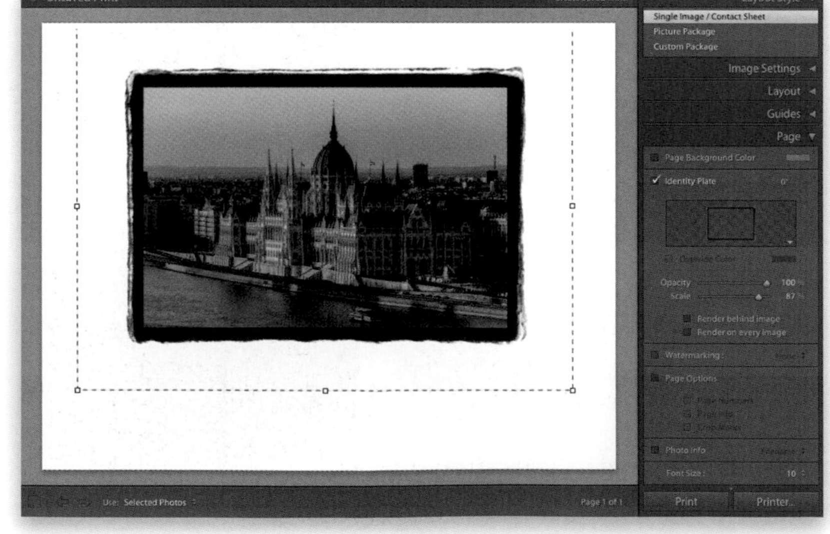

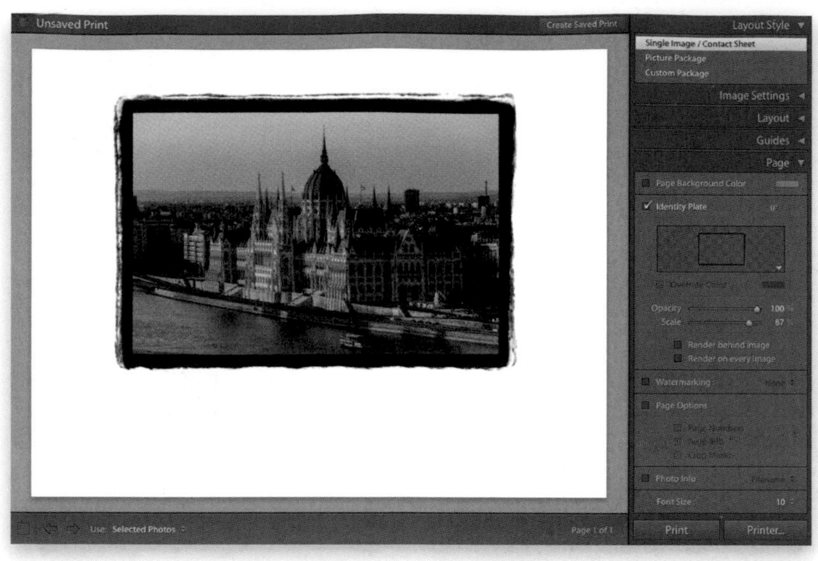

Step Five:

When it's right where you want it, just click your cursor outside the border and it will deselect. The final photo with the edge frame border is shown here. Now, if you decide you want to keep this border and use it in the future, go back to the Identity Plate Editor and from the Custom pop-up menu at the bottom-left corner of the dialog, choose **Save As** to save this frame border as an Identity Plate you can use anytime to add a quick border effect.

TIP: Frames for Multiple Photos

If you have more than one photo on the page, you can have that Identity Plate frame added to all the photos on the page automatically by going to the Page panel and turning on the Render on Every Image checkbox.

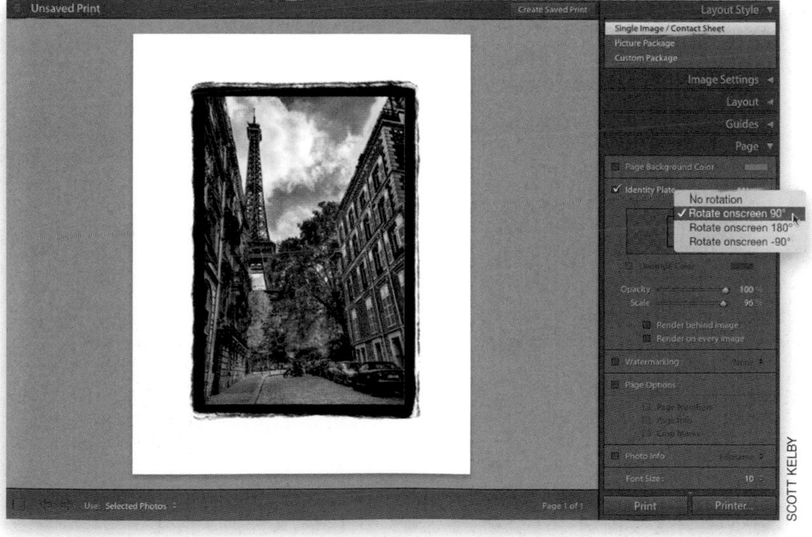

SCOTT KELBY

Step Six:

We created a horizontal frame, but how do you add this frame edge to a vertical photo, like the one shown here? If you change your page setup to Portrait (by clicking on the Page Setup button at the bottom of the left side Panels area), the Identity Plate will rotate automatically. If you are printing a vertical photo in a Landscape setup, you can rotate the Identity Plate by clicking on the degree field that appears to the right of the Identity Plate checkbox in the Page panel and choosing the rotation angle (as shown here). You'll probably have to resize and reposition the frame (as I did here) to make it fit just right, but now your single frame edge is doing double duty.

Lightroom Killer Tips > >

▼ Can't See Your Rulers?

If you're pressing **Command-R (PC: Ctrl-R)** and you can't see your printing rulers (the ones that appear above the top of your photo, and along the left side), it's because you have to make your guides visible first. Press **Command-Shift-G (PC: Ctrl-Shift-G)** or just choose **Show Guides** from the View menu. Now when you use that shortcut, you'll be toggling the rulers on/off.

▼ Changing Your Ruler Units

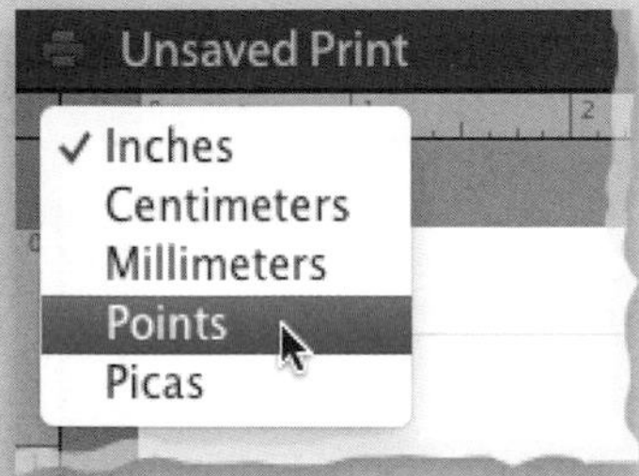

To change the unit of measure for your rulers, just Right-click on either ruler, and a pop-up menu of measurements (Inches, Centimeters, Millimeters, Points, and Picas) will appear, so you can choose the one you'd like.

▼ Adding Photos to Your Printing Queue

Adding more photos to print couldn't be easier—just go to the Filmstrip and Command-click (PC: Ctrl-click) on any photo you want to add to your print queue, and Lightroom instantly creates another page for it in the queue. To remove a photo from the print queue, it's just as easy: go to the Filmstrip and Command-click (PC: Ctrl-click) on any already selected photo to deselect it (Lightroom removes the page from your queue automatically, so you don't print a blank sheet).

▼ Changing the Preview Area Background Color

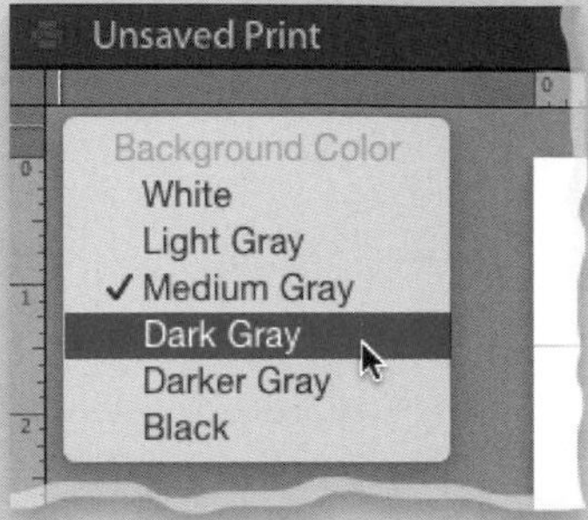

You can change the color of the gray canvas area that surrounds your printed page. Just Right-click anywhere on that gray background area and a pop-up menu will appear where you can choose different colors.

▼ Precise Margins Way Quicker Than Using the Margins Sliders

If you need to reposition your image on the page, you can adjust the Margins or Cell Size sliders. But if your guides are visible, it's easier just to click-and-drag a

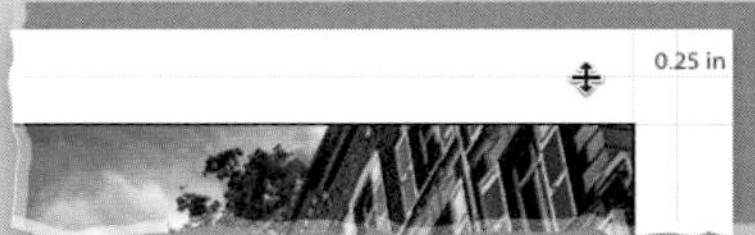

margin guide itself, because as soon as you start dragging, the position of the guide (in inches) appears above the top of the guide, so it's easy to quickly set two side or top and bottom margins to the exact same amount.

▼ Sending Prints to a Lab?

If you use Lightroom's ability to save a page layout to JPEG, so you can send your prints to a lab for final printing, then here's a great tip: make a new template

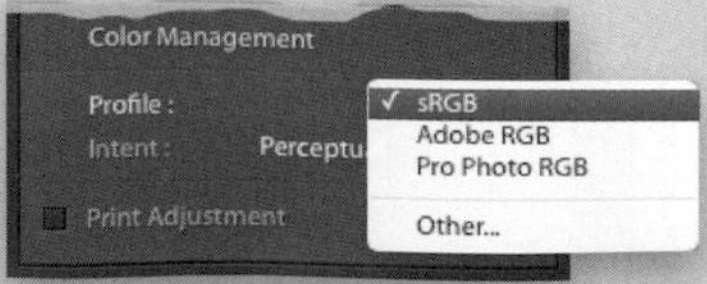

that has your usual page size, layout, etc., but make sure you set your color profile to the color space your lab prefers (which is usually sRGB for color labs). That way, when you save it as a JPEG, you won't forget to embed the right color space.

▼ Enabling 16-Bit Printing

If your inkjet printer was made in the last few years, it probably supports 16-bit printing, but to take advantage of it, make sure you have the latest printer driver (which can be downloaded for free from your printer manufacturer's website). *Note:* 16-bit printing currently only works for Mac users, and only those using Mac OS X Leopard or higher.

▼ Choosing How the Identity Plate Prints

There are two other options for how the Identity Plate is used in multi-photo layouts. If you choose Render on Every Image, it puts your Identity Plate right smack dab in the middle of each photo, in each cell (so if you wanted to use your logo as a watermark by lowering the

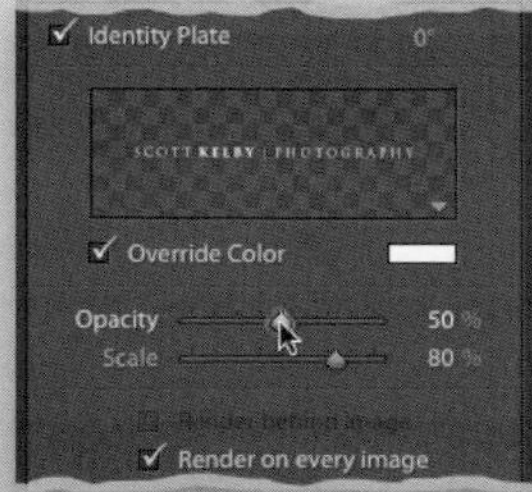

opacity of that Identity Plate, that would work). If you choose Render Behind Image, it prints on the background, as if it was a paper watermark (scale it up so it is slightly larger than your image).

▼ Nudging the Identity Plate

In the Print module, you can move the position of your Identity Plate graphic (or text) by small increments by using the **Arrow keys** on your keyboard.

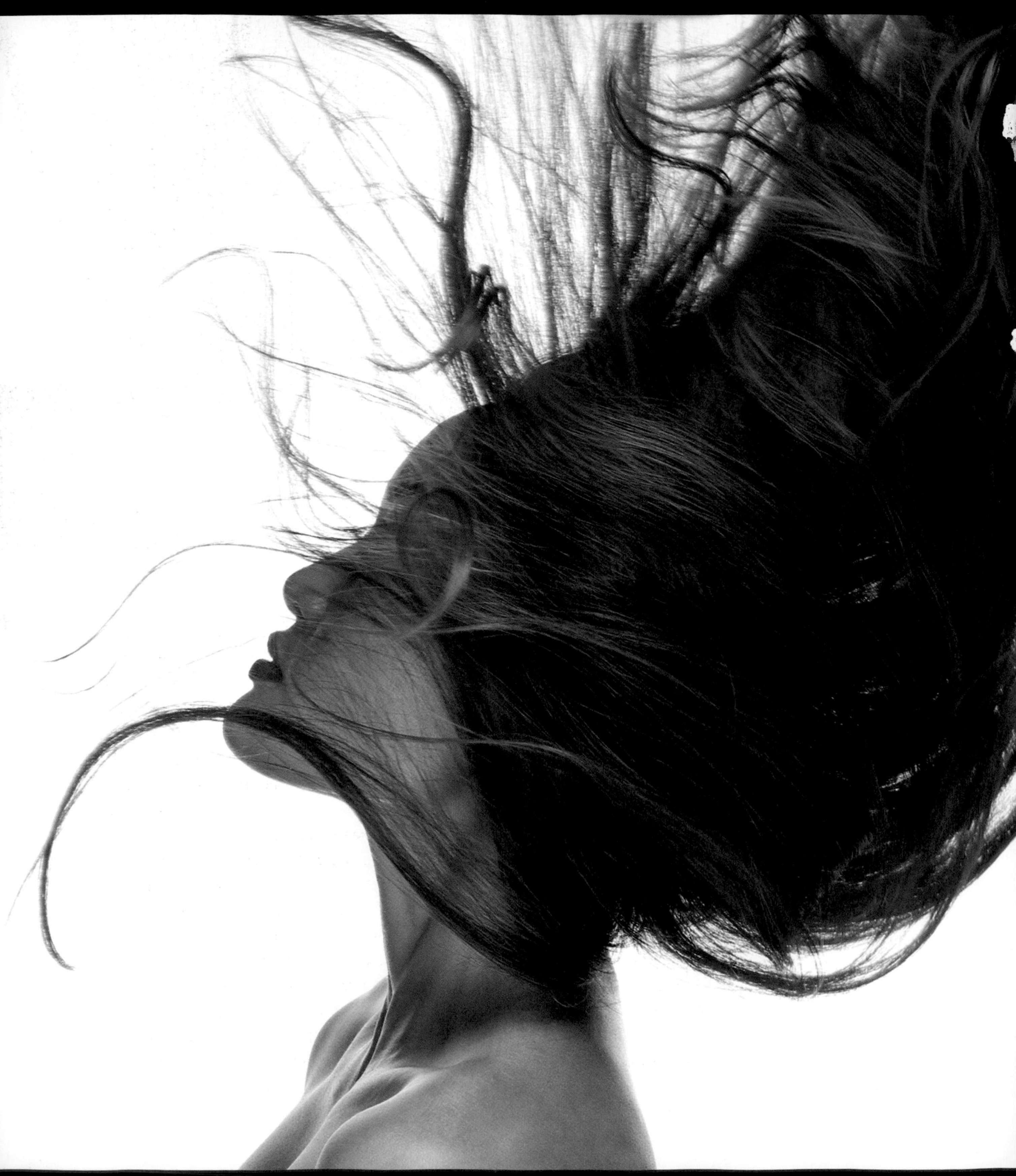

Photo by Scott Kelby | Exposure: 1/125 sec | Focal Length: 110mm | Aperture Value: ƒ/13

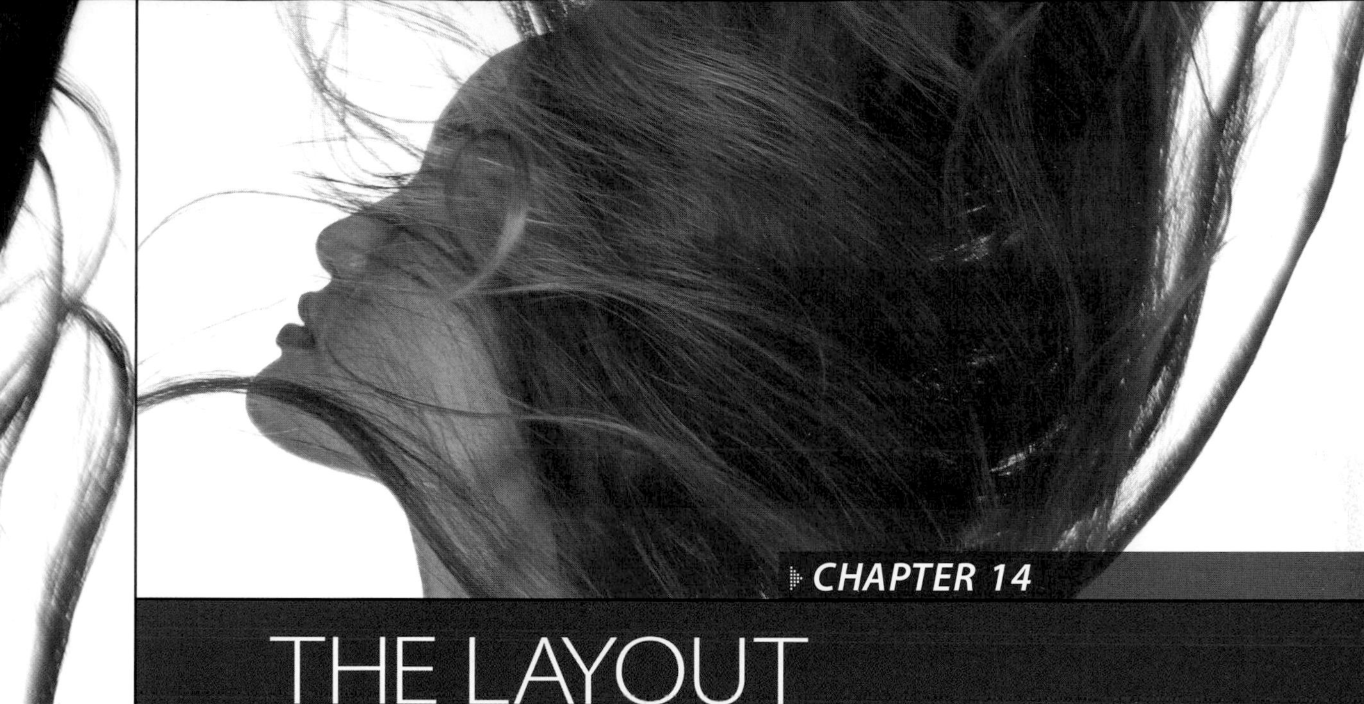

CHAPTER 14

THE LAYOUT

creating cool layouts for web & print

Man, I just love it when you go searching for a song or movie title with the word "layout" in it, and the first album that pops up is "The Layout" by Frankie Jones. That's a lot better luck than I had when I searched for the chapter on Rendering Intents (ya know, if I actually had a chapter on that, and if I did, it would be an incredibly short chapter. About a page or two, and that's if I used a lot of big words, like Rendering and Intents). Anyway, some of these layouts were in the Lightroom 3 version of this book, buried in the Print chapter. I think that was a mistake. Mind you, I'm not saying I made this mistake. I learned long ago that, to be a successful author, a particular skill you need to master is the immediate and indiscriminate assigning of blame to your editor for anything that isn't 100% absolutely perfect. One reason this works so consistently, for authors across all genres of books, is that editors say so many messed up things during the course of producing a book that they honestly have no idea what they really said or when they said it. I talked to my editor Ted Waitt about this, and he admitted what I had always suspected, which is that many editors today are hooked on steroids (that explains why Ted is so freakishly muscular). Anyway, most photographers today don't actually make prints—their images go straight to the web (for the most part), so a lot of readers had no idea I put all these cool layouts in the book that work perfectly for the web, too (I use these on my blog, on Google+, in photo galleries, and at steroid conventions), so by putting these in their own separate chapter (and adding 24 bad @$! Lightroom presets on the book's download site), it distracts Olympic officials from administering their monthly mandatory drug tests for book editors. Well, at least that's what I've been told.

Here Are Some of My Layouts for You to Use

I wanted to share some of my most popular multi-photo print layouts with you (clients love these types of layouts), showing the panels needed for the layout, and an example of each. These all use a 13x19" final page size, so click the Page Setup button and set that first. Unless otherwise shown, they use the Single Image/Contact Sheet layout. Also, for a full-page bleed, set your page to borderless. I did a short video tutorial for you on how I created the Identity Plates I used in these examples at **http://kelbyone.com/books/lrcc**. Enjoy!

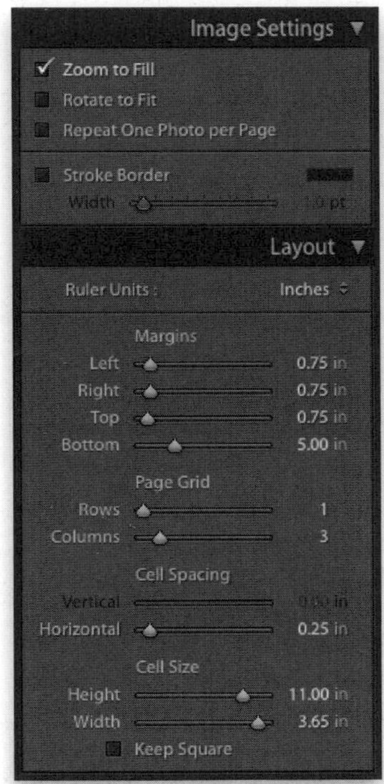

Note: The goal of this section is to teach you how easy it is to create your own layouts for the web or printing, and once you build a few, you'll have a blast building your own, but just so you know, I did save all these layouts as templates (once again, using the standard 13x19" size). So, if you don't want to recreate these layouts yourself, you can download them as templates by going to the book's companion webpage (the address is in that section up front you weren't supposed to skip), and load them into Lightroom.

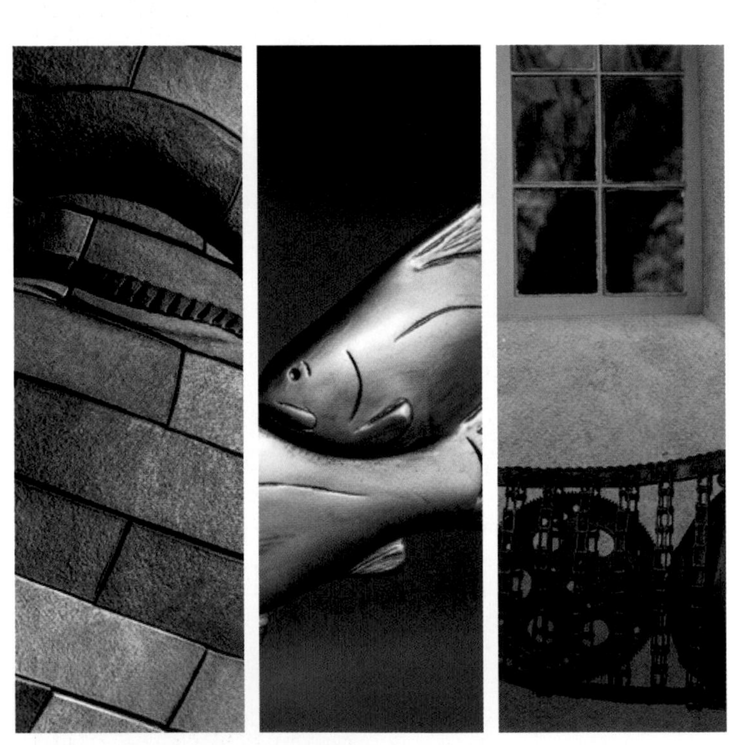

SCOTT KELBY

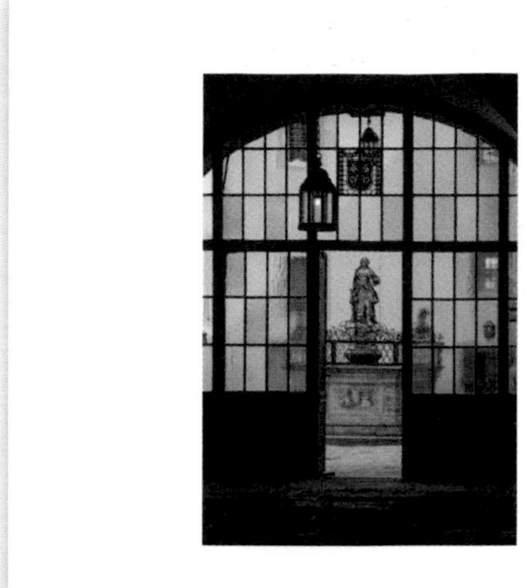

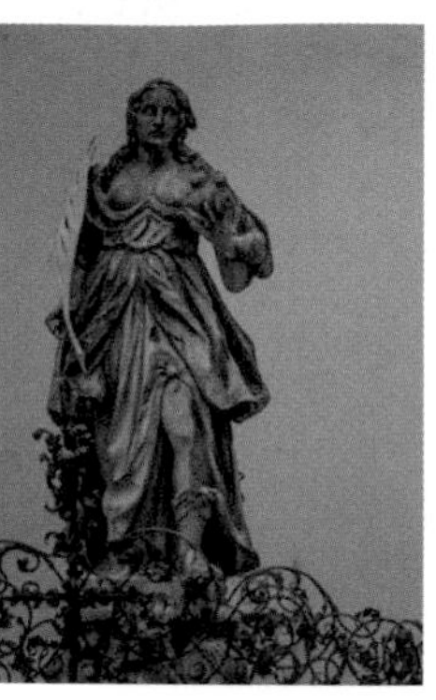

SCOTT KELBY

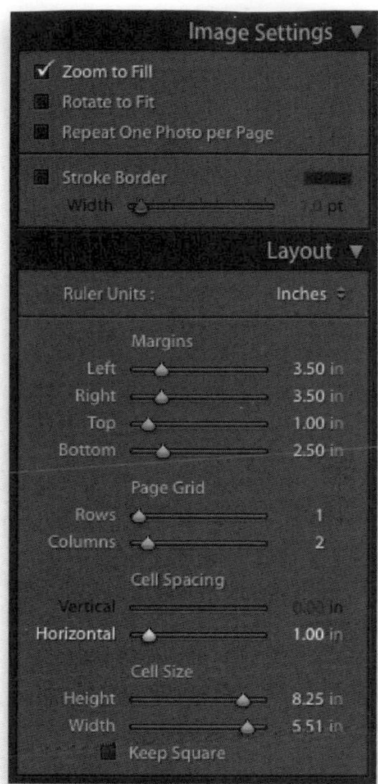

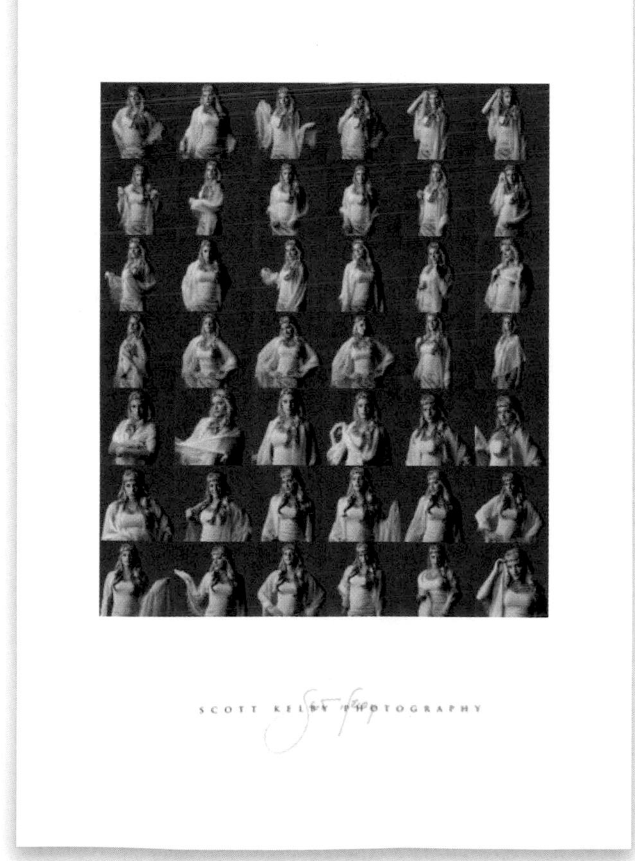

SCOTT KELBY

Image Settings
Zoom to Fill
Rotate to Fit
Repeat One Photo per Page
Stroke Border
Width
Layout
Ruler Units : Inches
Margins
Left 1.75 in
Right 1.75 in
Top 3.00 in
Bottom 4.92 in
Page Grid
Rows 7
Columns 6
Cell Spacing
Vertical 0.00 in
Horizontal 0.00 in
Cell Size
Height 1.58 in
Width 1.58 in
Keep Square

Continued

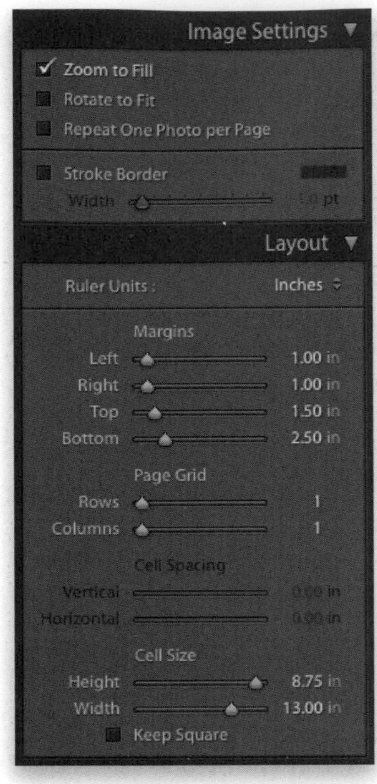
Image Settings
Zoom to Fill
Rotate to Fit
Repeat One Photo per Page
Stroke Border
Width
Layout
Ruler Units :
Inches
Margins
Left 1.00 in
Right 1.00 in
Top 1.50 in
Bottom 2.50 in
Page Grid
Rows 1
Columns 1
Cell Spacing
Vertical
Horizontal
Cell Size
Height 8.75 in
Width 13.00 in
Keep Square

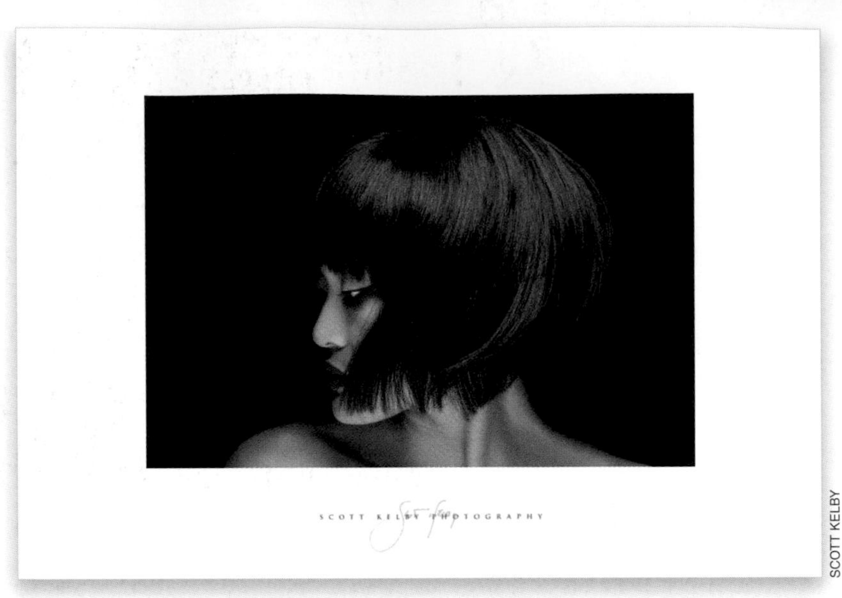
SCOTT KELBY PHOTOGRAPHY
SCOTT KELBY

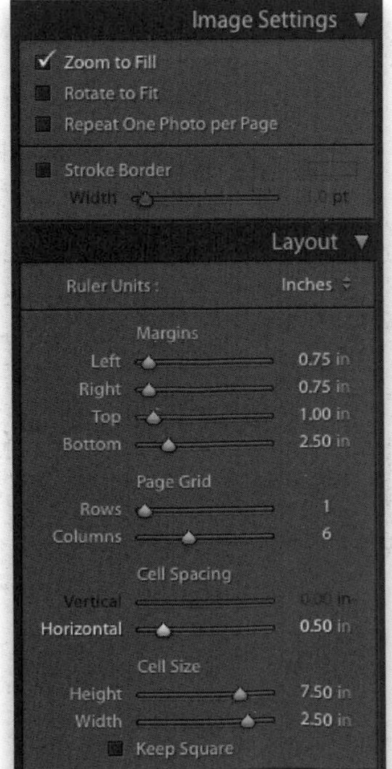
Image Settings
Zoom to Fill
Rotate to Fit
Repeat One Photo per Page
Stroke Border
Width
Layout
Ruler Units :
Inches
Margins
Left 0.75 in
Right 0.75 in
Top 1.00 in
Bottom 2.50 in
Page Grid
Rows 1
Columns 6
Cell Spacing
Vertical
Horizontal 0.50 in
Cell Size
Height 7.50 in
Width 2.50 in
Keep Square

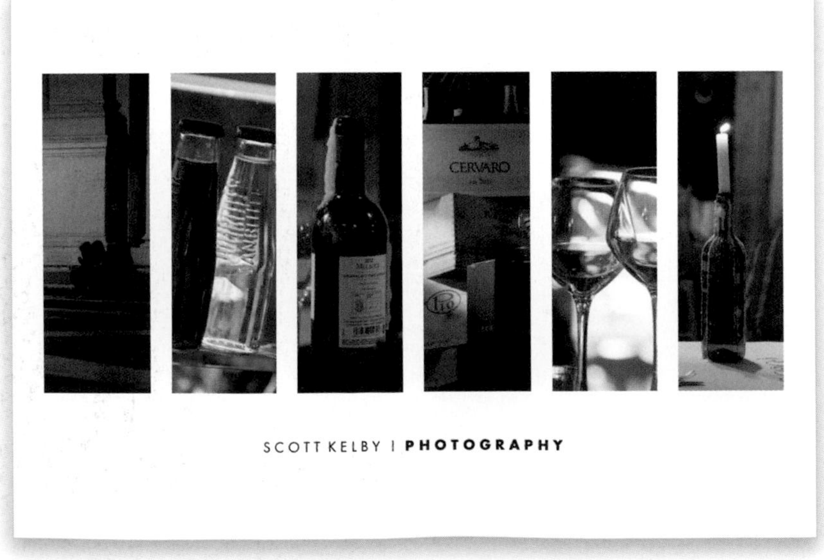
CERVARO
SCOTT KELBY | PHOTOGRAPHY
SCOTT KELBY

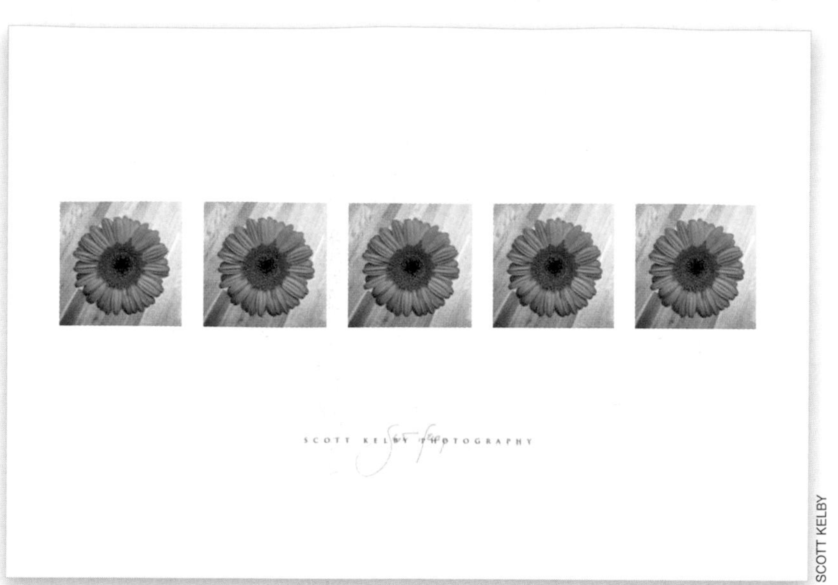

SCOTT KELBY

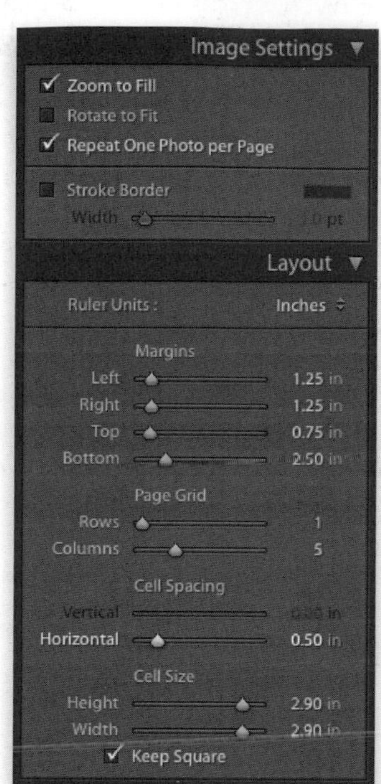

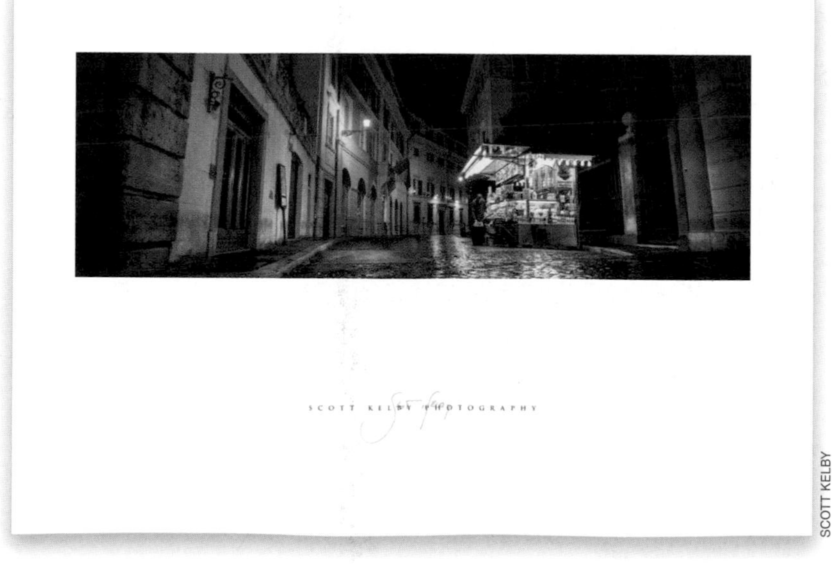

SCOTT KELBY

Image Settings

- Zoom to Fill
- Rotate to Fit
- Repeat One Photo per Page
- Stroke Border
  - Width 1.0 pt

Layout

Ruler Units : Inches

Margins

Left	0.50 in
Right	0.50 in
Top	1.00 in
Bottom	5.50 in

Page Grid

Rows	1
Columns	1

Cell Spacing

Vertical	0.00 in
Horizontal	0.00 in

Cell Size

Height	5.25 in
Width	16.00 in

Keep Square

Continued

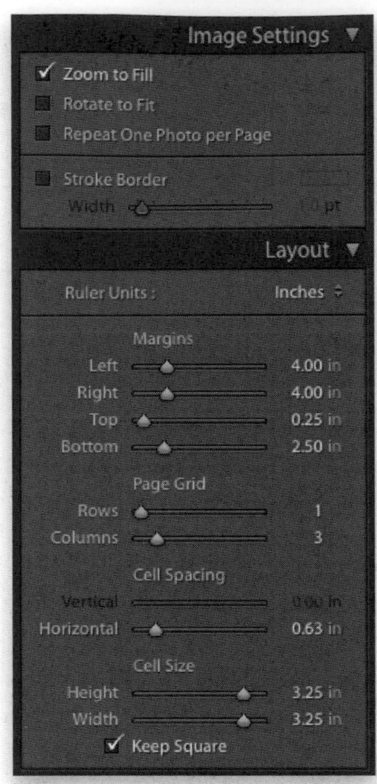

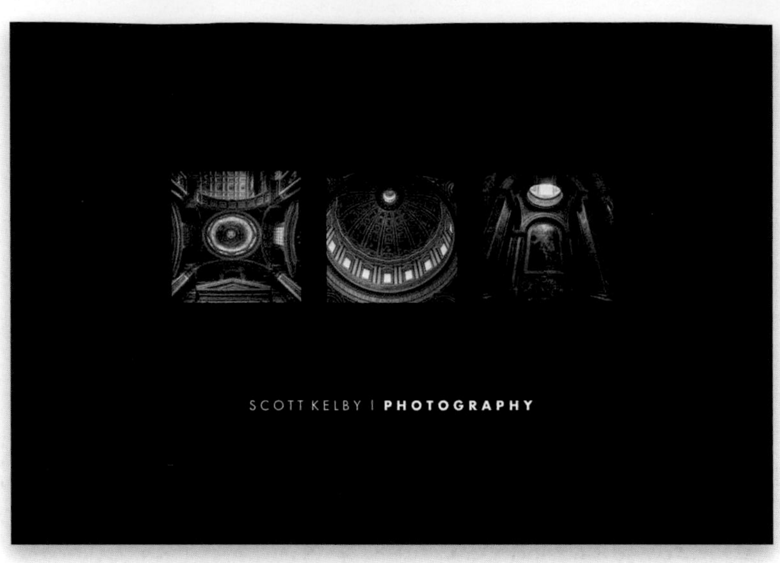

Turn on the Zoom to Fill checkbox in the Image Settings panel. Click on the Page Background Color color swatch and change it to black in the Page panel, then turn on the Override Color checkbox for your Identity Plate and set the color to white

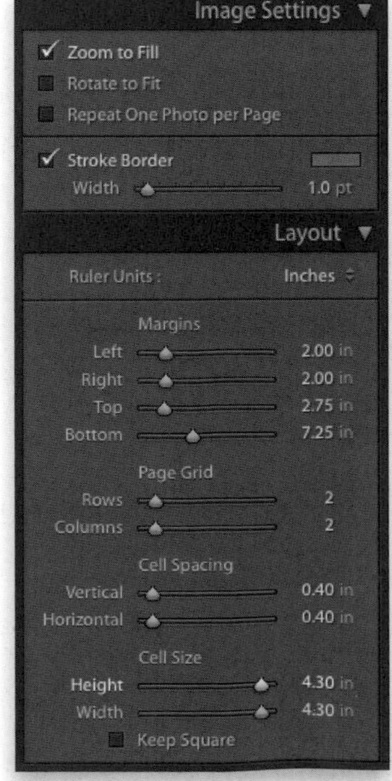

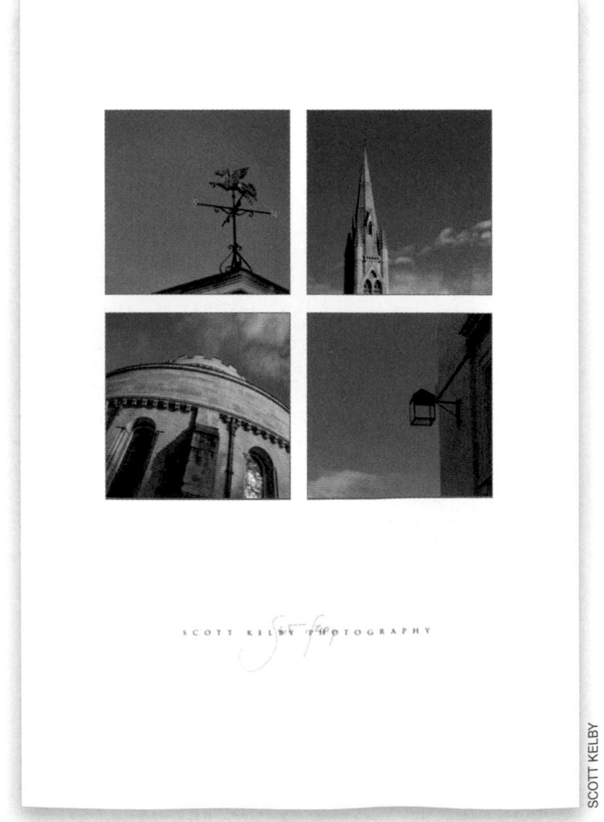

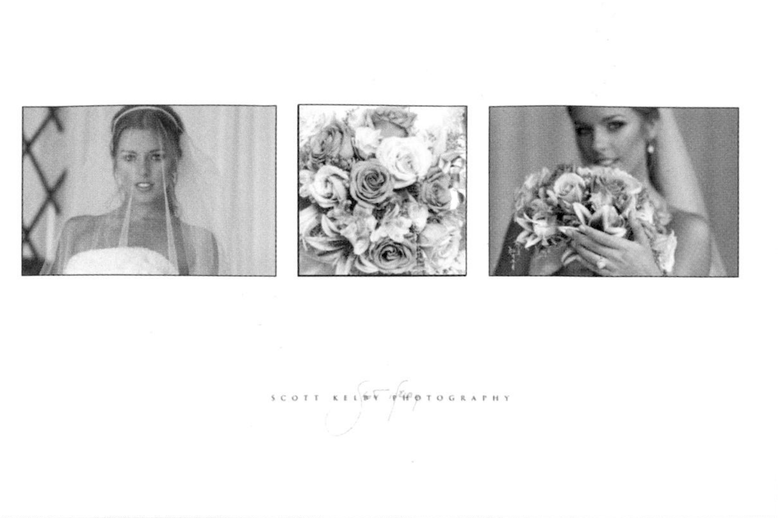

Here, in the Cells panel, you're going to create a 4x6 cell, then grab one side and drag inward until it becomes a square 4x4 cell (turn off the Lock to Photo Aspect Ratio checkbox first). Position that in the middle, above the center of the page. Now, create two more 4x6 cells and put them on either side of the square

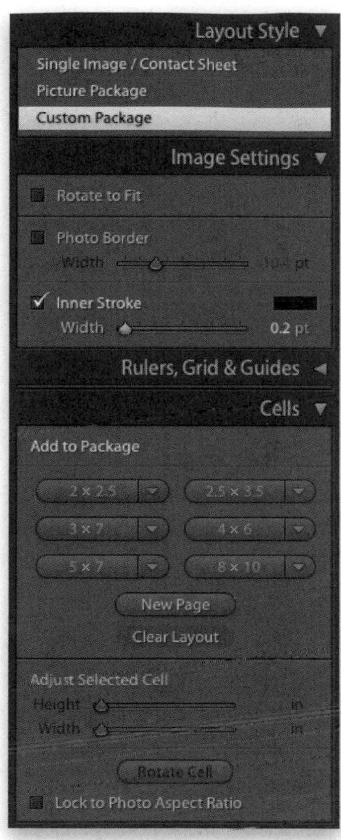

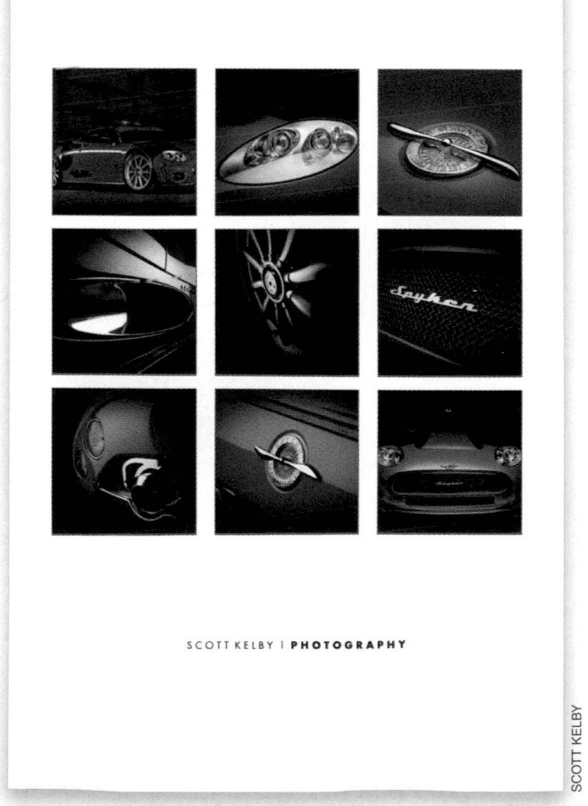

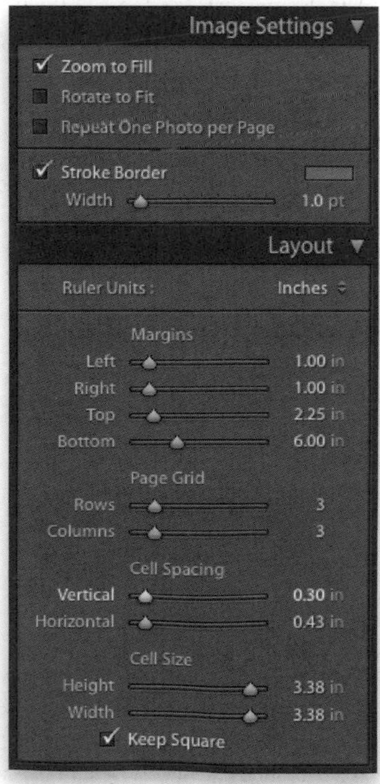

Continued

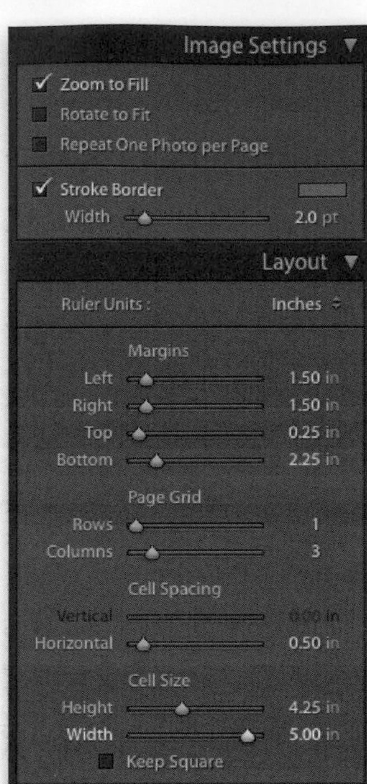

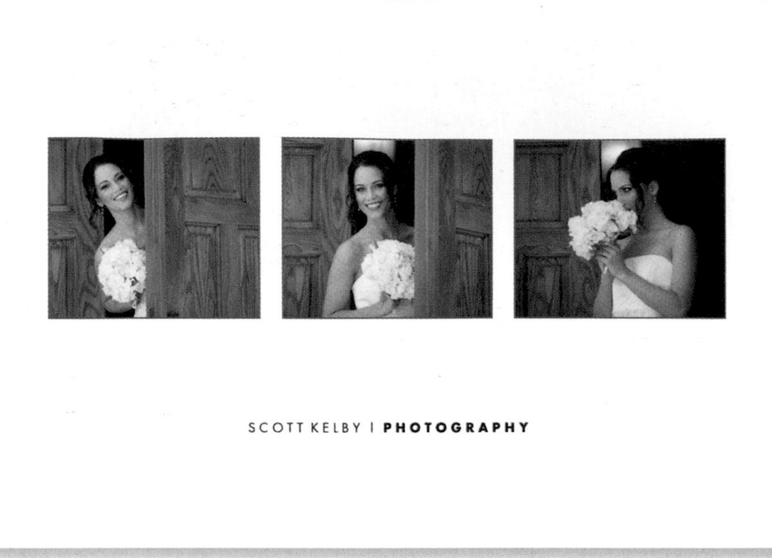

SCOTT KELBY

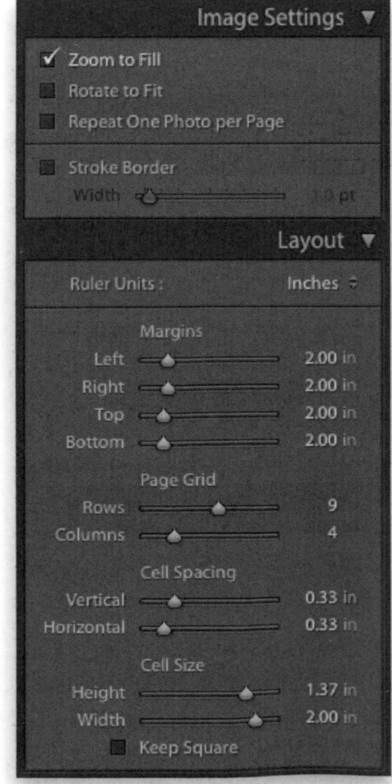

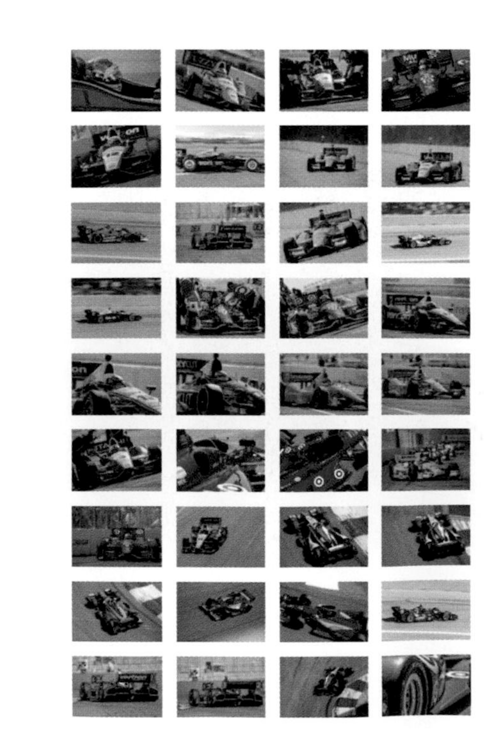

SCOTT KELBY

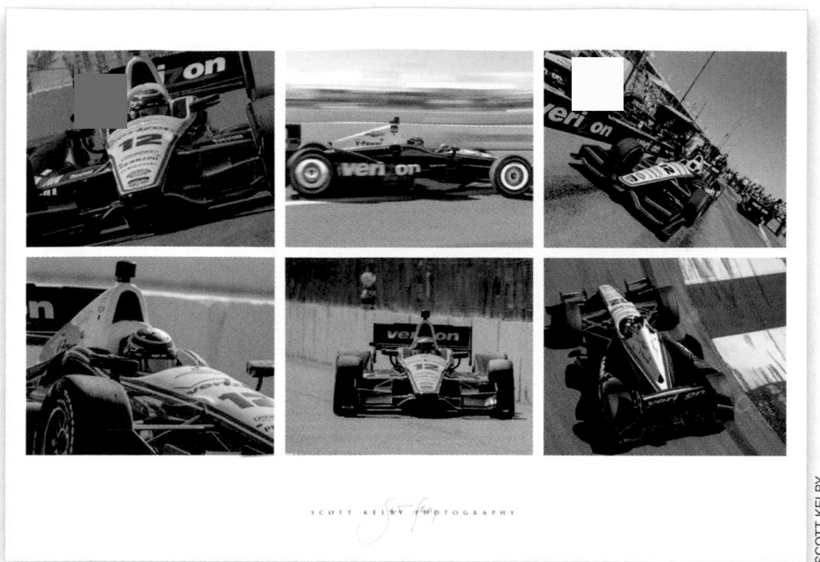

SCOTT KELBY

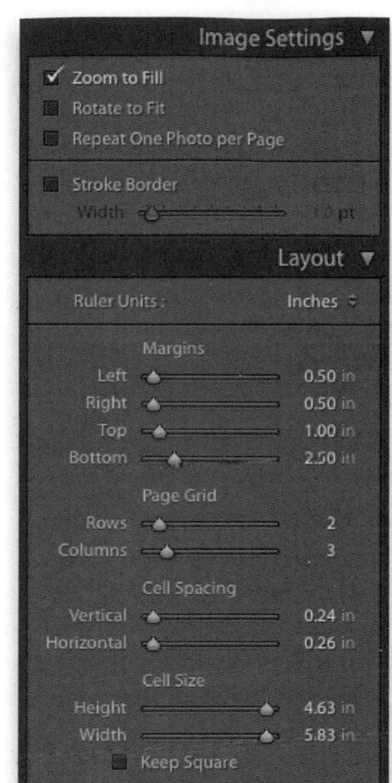

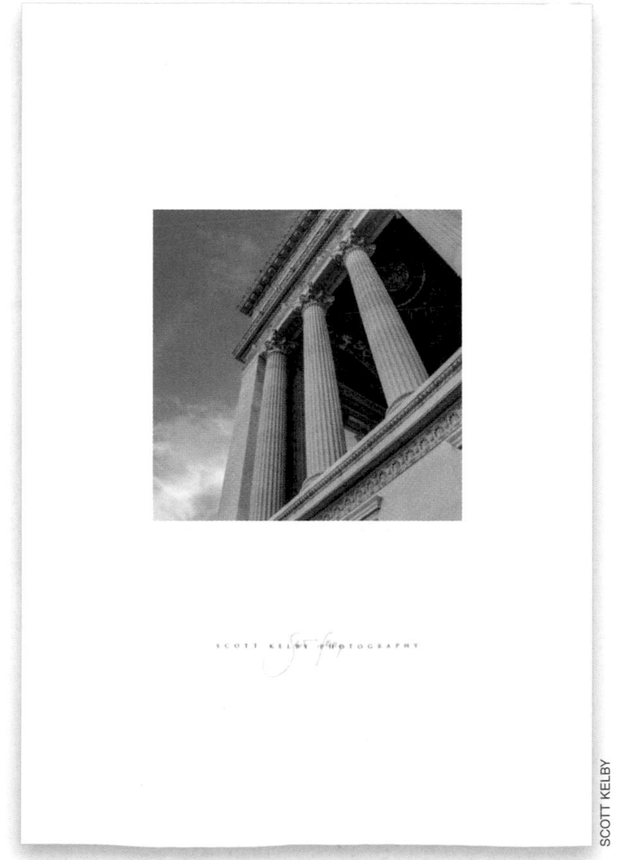

SCOTT KELBY

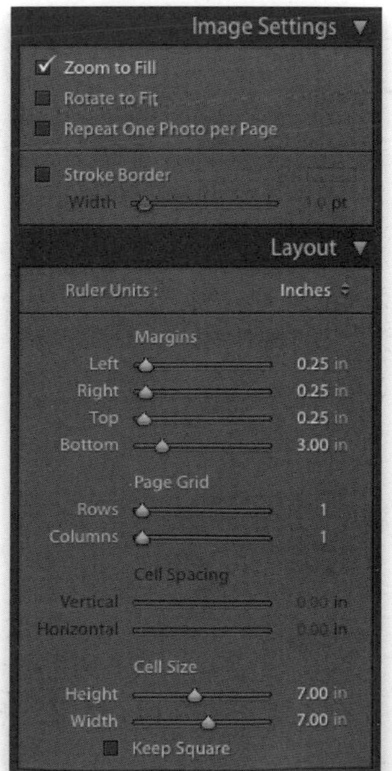

Continued

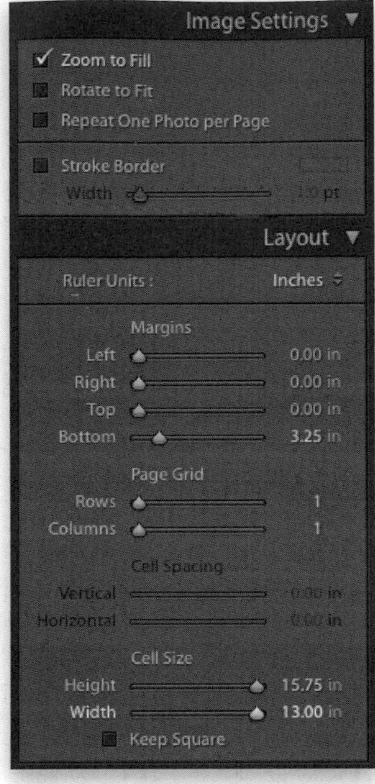

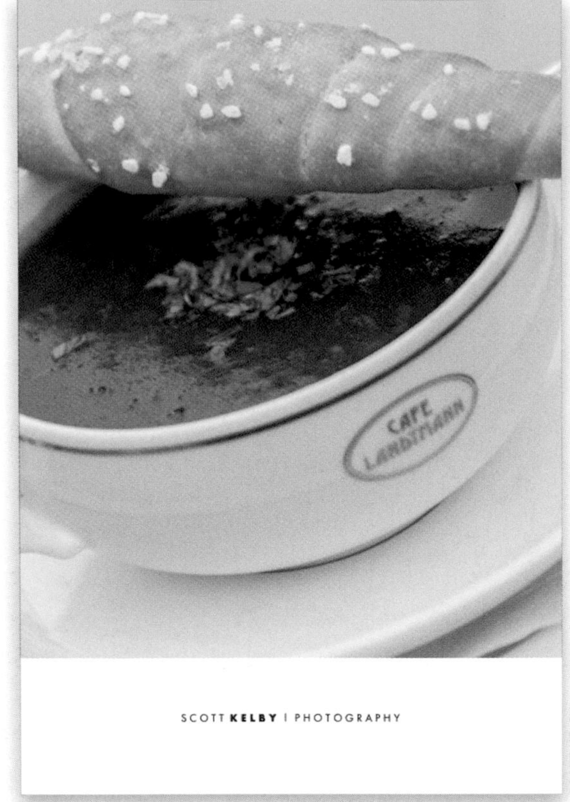

Click the Page Setup button and set your page to borderless so Lightroom will let you set your page margins to 0.00" all the way around for this full-page bleed look

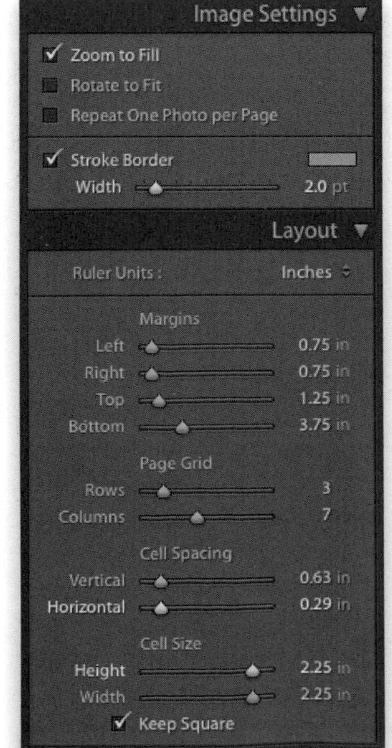

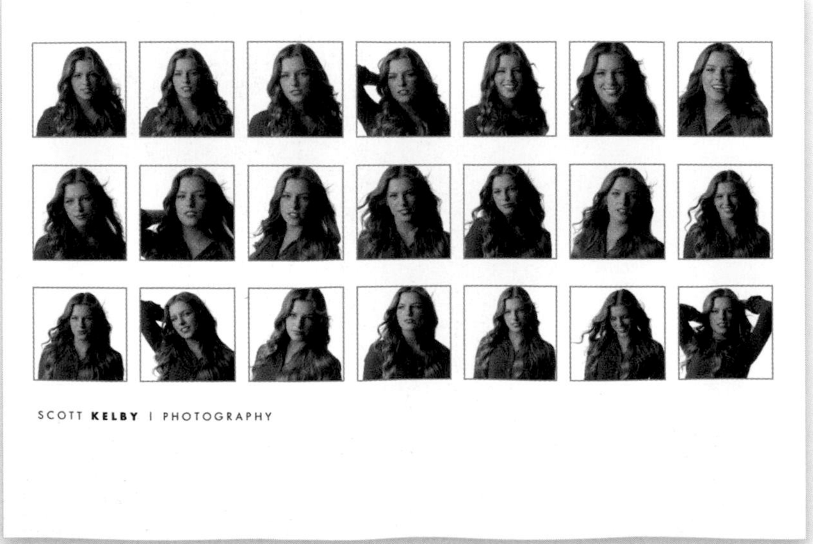

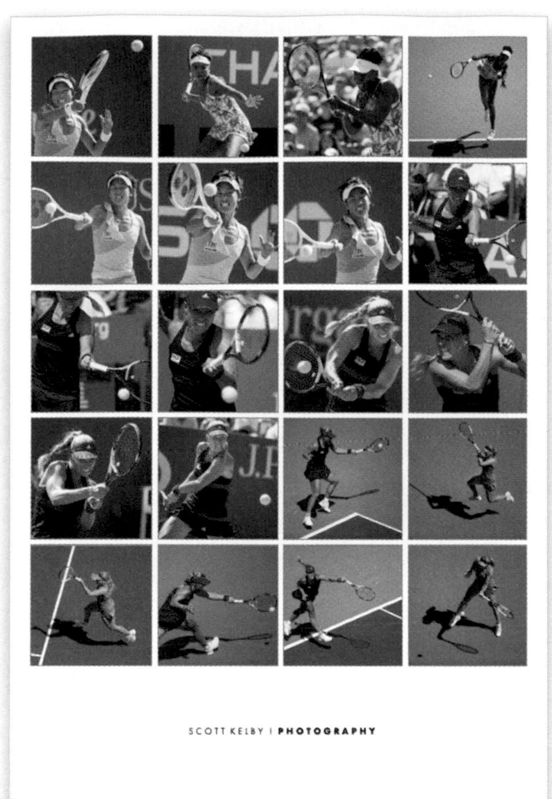

SCOTT KELBY

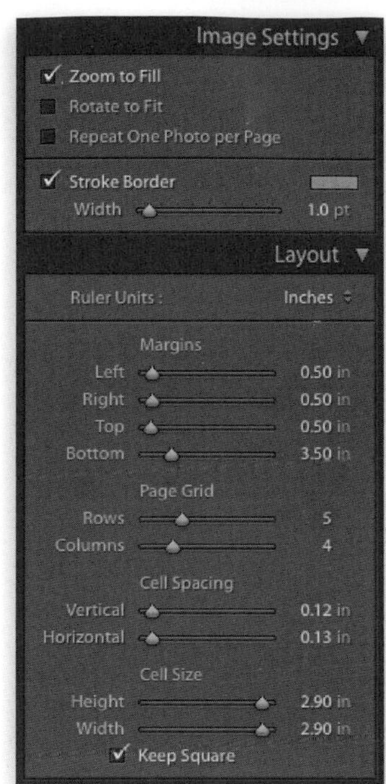

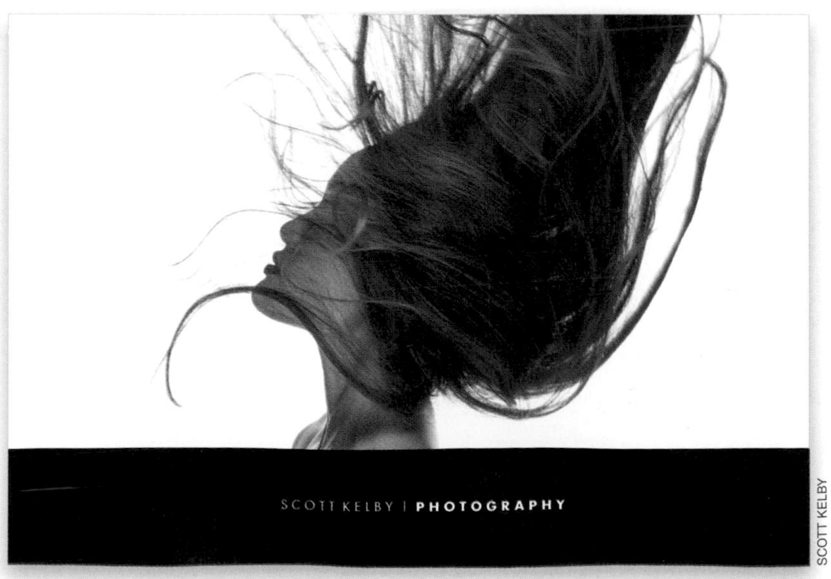

SCOTT KELBY

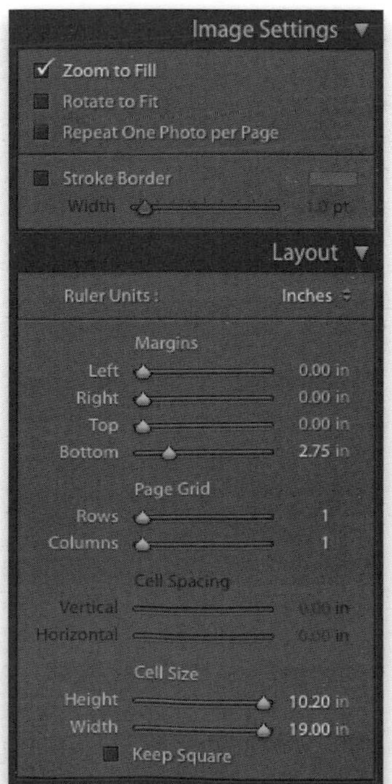

Continued

Image Settings
Zoom to Fill
Rotate to Fit
Repeat One Photo per Page
Stroke Border
Width 1.0 pt
Layout
Ruler Units: Inches
Margins
Left 1.50 in
Right 1.50 in
Top 1.50 in
Bottom 4.75 in
Page Grid
Rows 1
Columns 5
Cell Spacing
Vertical 0.00 in
Horizontal 0.56 in
Cell Size
Height 6.50 in
Width 2.75 in
Keep Square

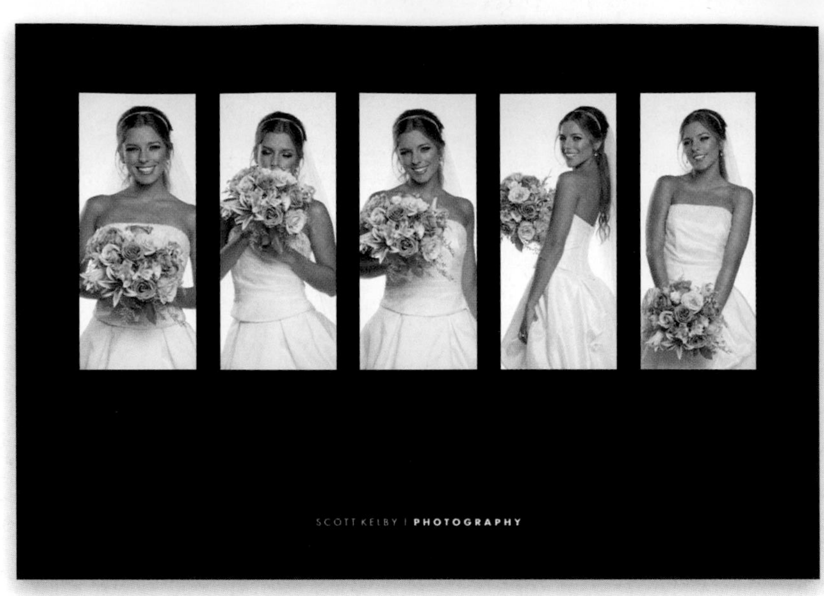

SCOTT KELBY

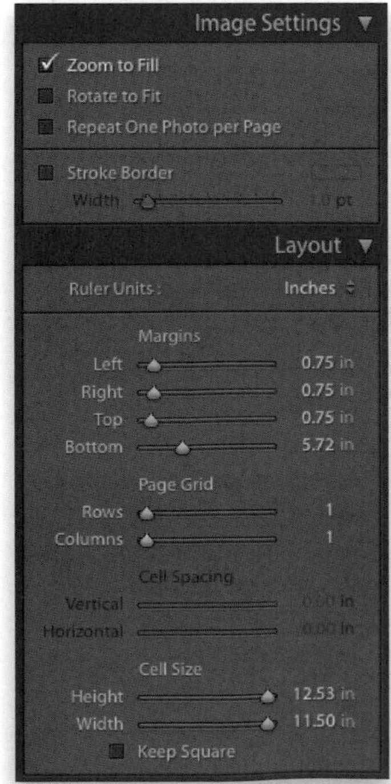

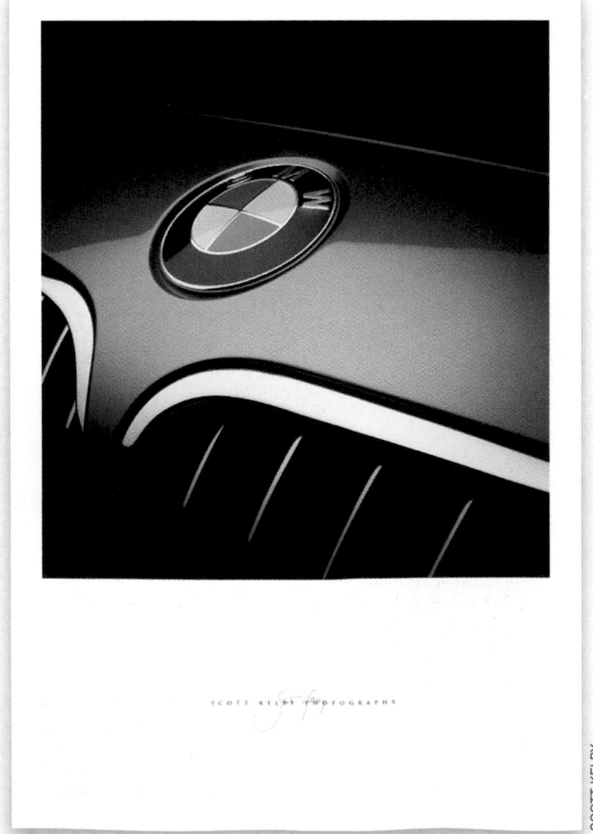

SCOTT KELBY

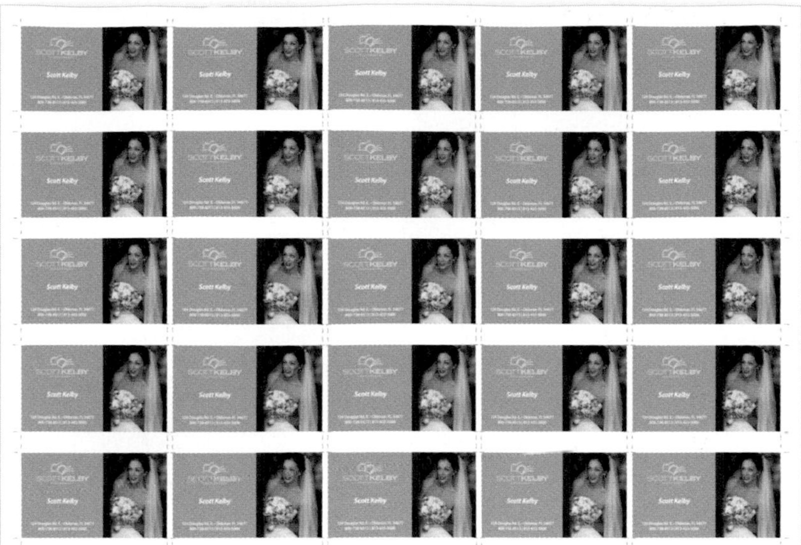
SCOTT KELBY

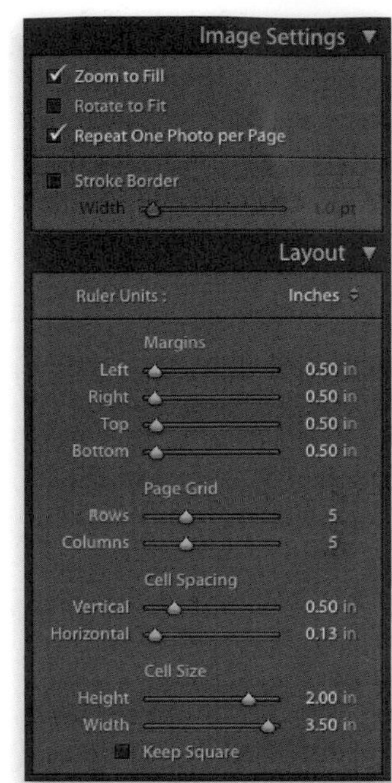

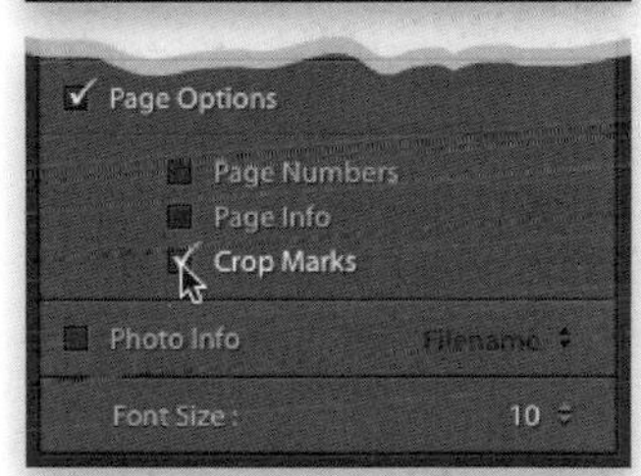

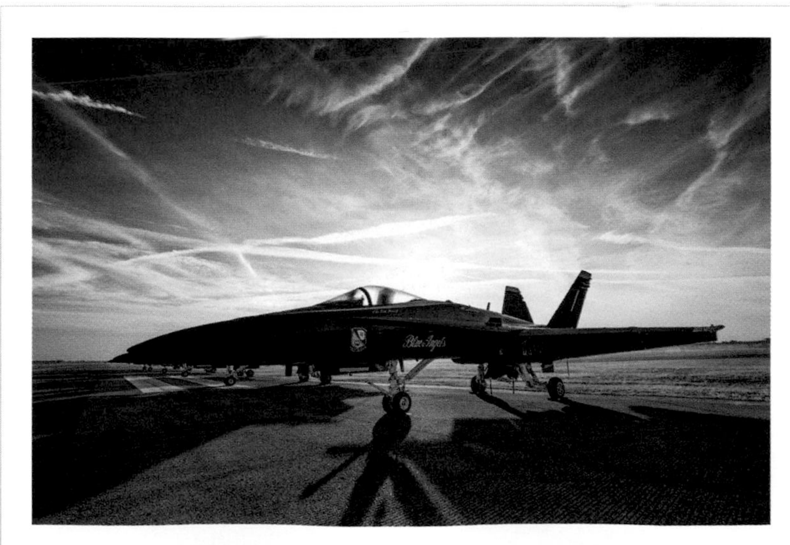
SCOTT KELBY

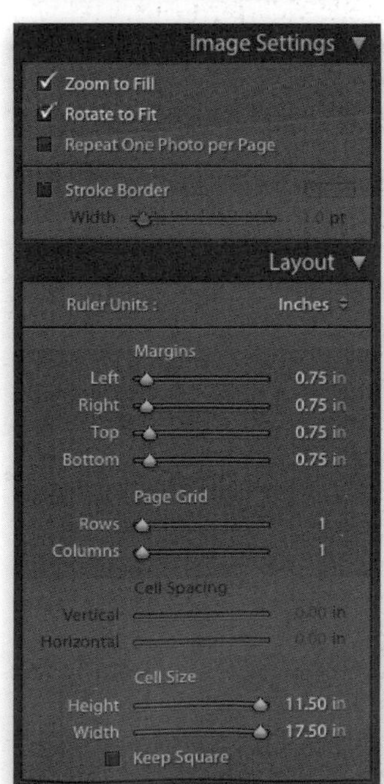

Continued

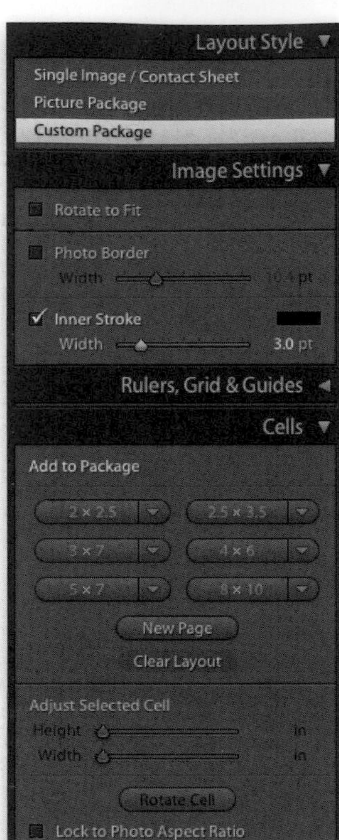

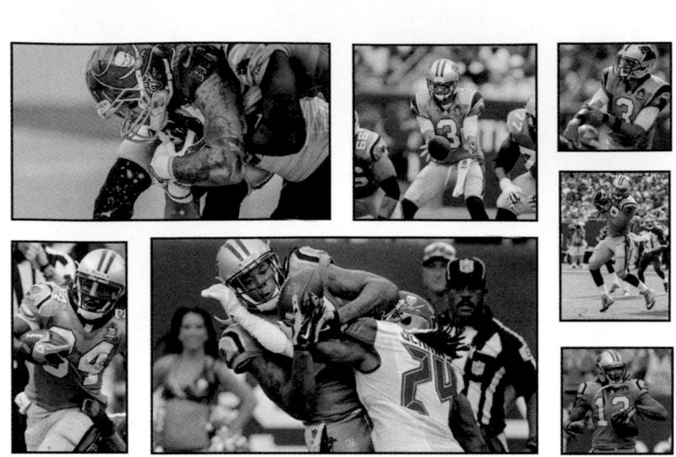

SCOTT KELBY

This is a do-it-yourself project, because you have to basically just start in the left-hand corner, create a series of 4x6 cells, and resize them one by one, until you have the layout you see here. That's the thing about using the Custom Package, it's up to you to create the custom layout yourself

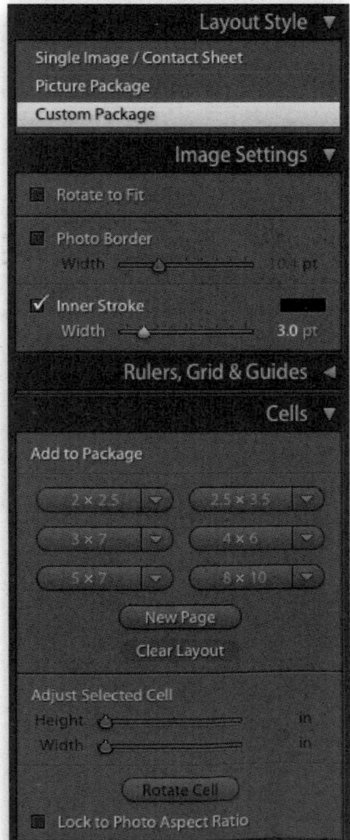

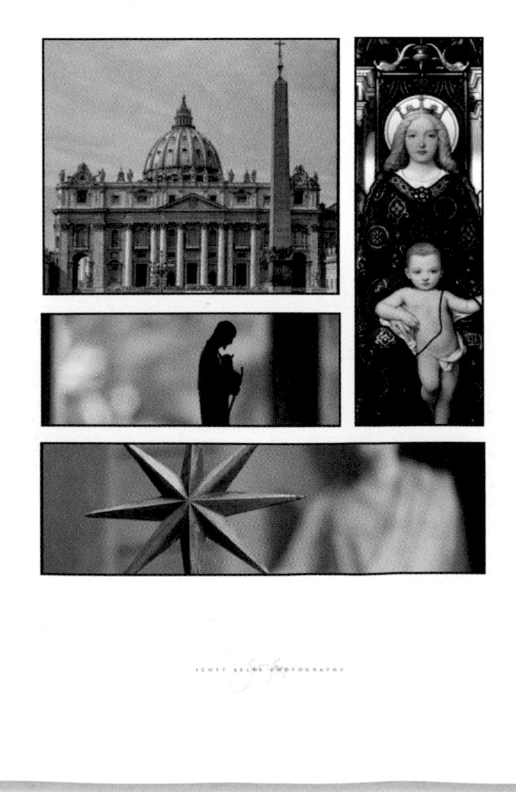

SCOTT KELBY

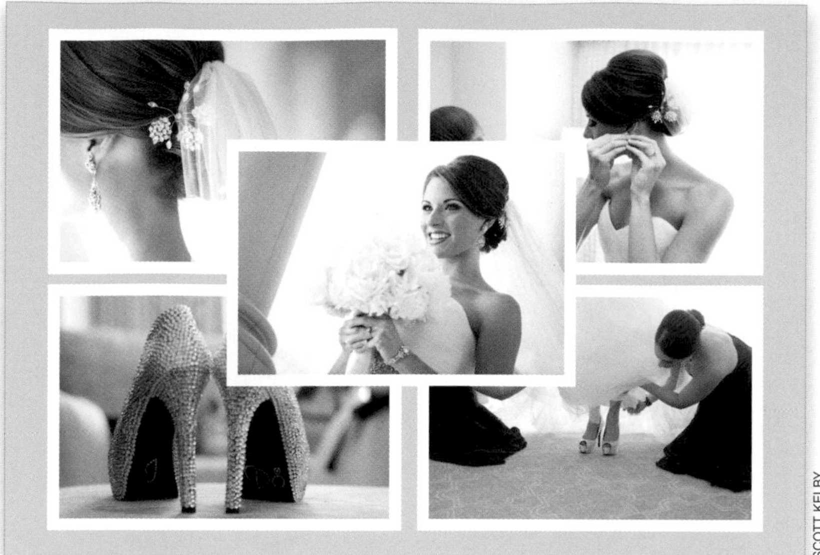

Set your Page Background Color to light gray, then create four 5x7 cells and position them 2 across and 2 down. Then, press-and-hold the Option (PC: Alt) key, and click-and-drag one of the cells to make a copy, which you position in the center, on top of the original four. Then, you turn on Inner Stroke and add about an 18-pt white stroke

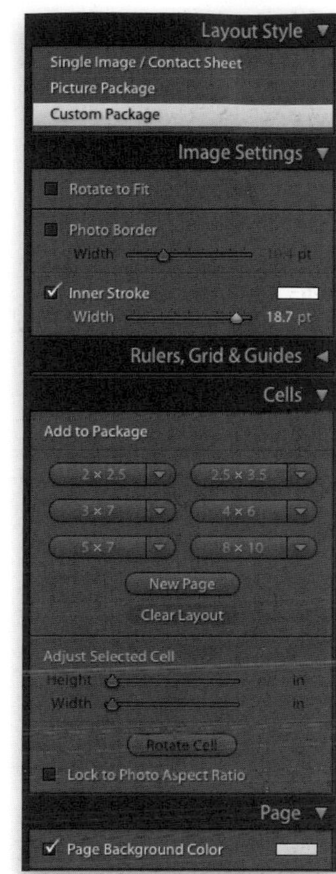

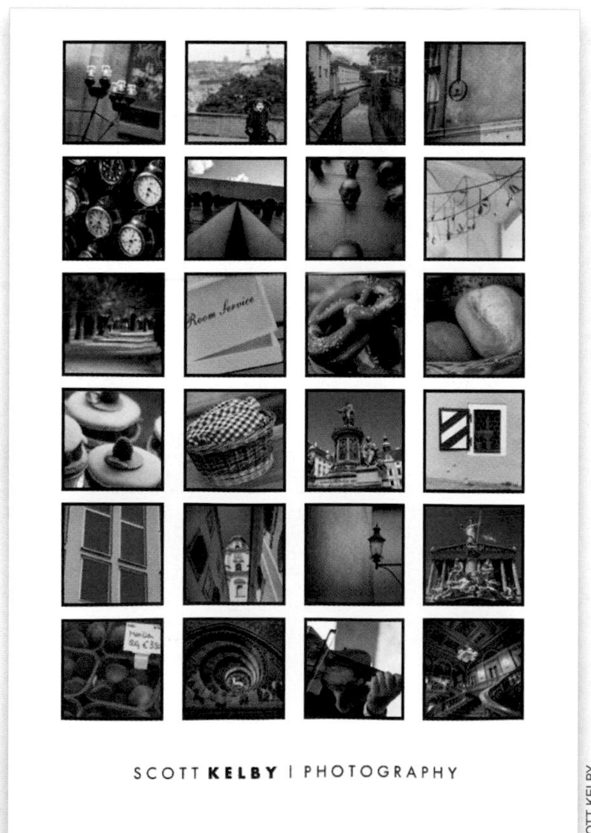

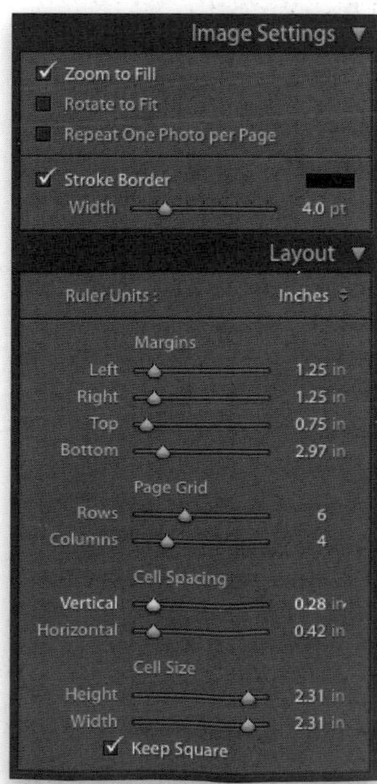

**The last three layouts on these two pages were inspired by layouts used in the Mac OS X App Posterino*

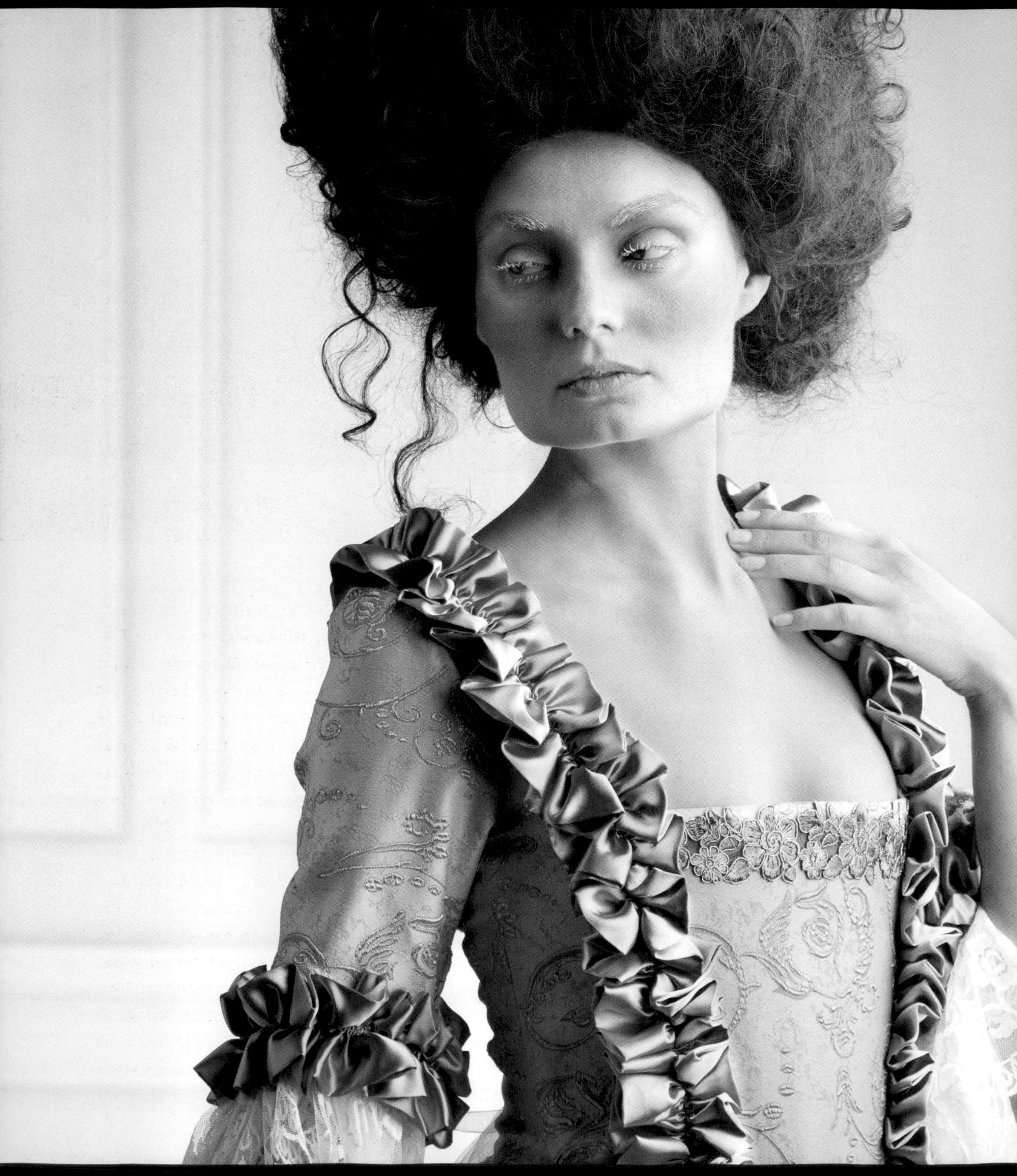

Photo by Scott Kelby | Exposure: 1/125 sec | Focal Length: 175mm | Aperture Value: ƒ/10

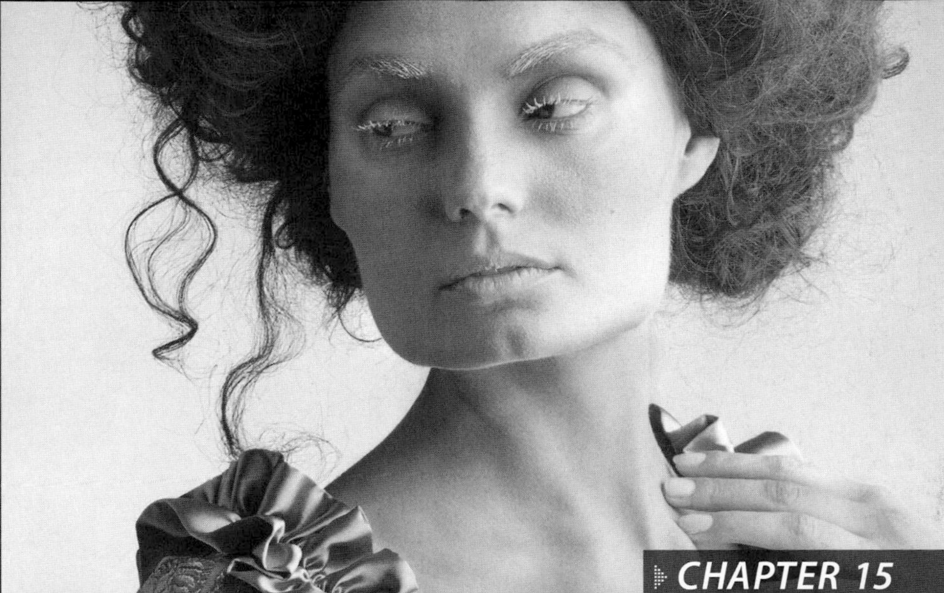

CHAPTER 15

DSLR: THE MOVIE

working with video shot on your DSLR

Here, I went with my longstanding tradition of naming chapter titles after a song title, movie, or TV show, and named this chapter after a movie. Well, sort of. Technically, this chapter title is mostly a movie title. Okay, the "DSLR" part isn't, but do you know how many movies have "The Movie" in their name? Remember *Sex in the City: The Movie* or *Mama Mia: The Movie*? And, believe it or not, there actually is a movie titled simply, *The Movie*. I am not making this up (although, I'm totally capable of doing so, but in this rare case, that movie actually does exist. However, since nobody that any of us knows actually saw *The Movie*, you probably aren't 100% sure that I didn't make it up in the first place, but that's what makes this whole thing so precarious). As it is, these chapter intros are held together by the thinnest thread and things really start to fall apart if you do even 60 seconds of follow-up research on *The Movie*, because you'd find out that it is, in fact, only a 7-minute "movie short" and not really a movie at all (in the sense that a movie is long). But, one of the stars is Fiona Foulkes and, like you, I have no idea who she is, but there was a Princess Fiona in the movie *Shrek*, which was voiced by Cameron Diaz, who used to date Justin Timberlake, who was in the movie *The Social Network*, and it was Timberlake who recommended actor/dancer Kenny Wormald for the remake of the movie *Footloose* to play the lead role, which was originally played by (that's right) Kevin Bacon, which clearly supports the "Six Degrees of Separation" that the word DSLR is from the phrase "The Movie." Wow, this is holding up way better than I thought.

Working with Videos

In earlier versions of Lightroom, you could import video clips from DSLR cameras and...well...that was pretty much it. In Lightroom CC, you can do everything from trim a video to add special effects, like black and white, or split-tone looks, or well, basically, a lot of the stuff you can do to photos, you can now do to video (including applying curves, adding contrast, changing hues, or standard stuff like matching color across multiple videos). Here's whatcha need to do:

Step One:

You import a video into Lightroom just like you would a photo, but you'll know it's a video because you'll see a video camera icon in the lower-left corner of its thumbnail when it appears in the Import window (Lightroom supports most major DSLR video formats, so chances are your video clips will import with no problem). Once it's in Lightroom, you can do all the organizational things you normally do with an image (like put it in a collection, add flags, metadata, and so on). Once the video(s) is imported, you won't see the little camera icon any more, though. Instead, you'll see the length of the video displayed in the bottom-left corner of the thumbnail (as seen here, where the length of the selected video clip is 26 seconds).

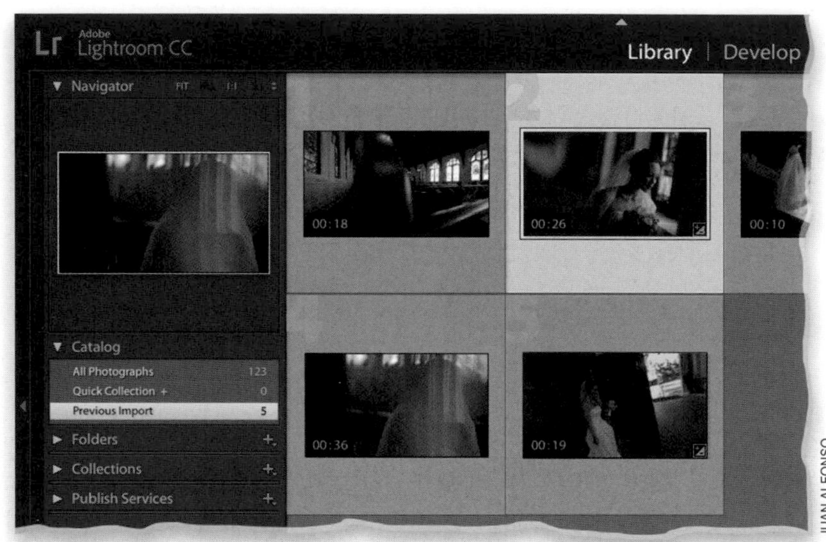

JUAN ALFONSO

Step Two:

You can see a visual preview of what's on the video by moving your cursor over the thumbnail itself and dragging either left or right to quickly "scrub" through the video. Although you're not going to see all the frames in the video by doing this quick scrub, it comes in handy when you have two or three similar clips, and you want to find the one you're looking for. Let's say, for example, you've got a number of short clips of a bride and groom about to cut a wedding cake. Well, to find the one where they actually do the cutting (and not the cutting up), you can quickly scrub through each clip and find what you're looking for without having to actually open the video.

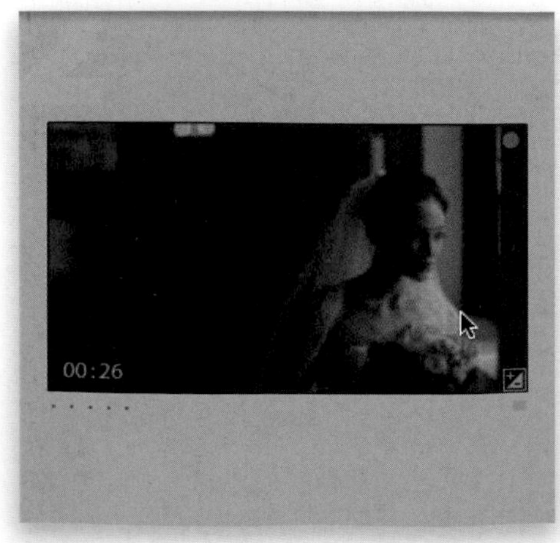

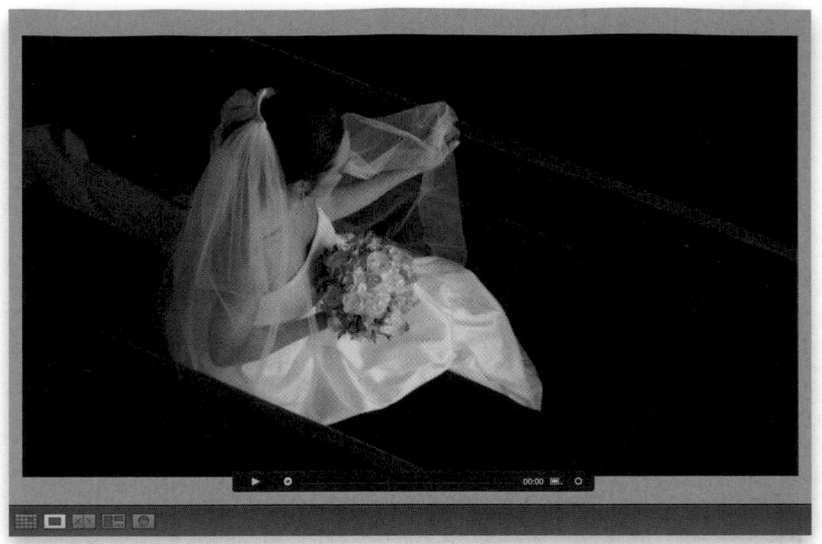

Step Three:

If you want to watch your video clip, just double-click on it and it opens in Loupe view (as seen here). To play the video, you can click the Play button (duh), in the control bar under the video, or just press the **Spacebar** on your keyboard to start/stop it. If, instead, you want to scrub through the video (kind of like manually fast-forwarding or rewinding), you can just drag the playhead in the control bar. When you play the video, it plays both the video and audio, but there's no volume control for the audio within Lightroom itself, so you'll have to control the audio volume using your computer's own volume control.

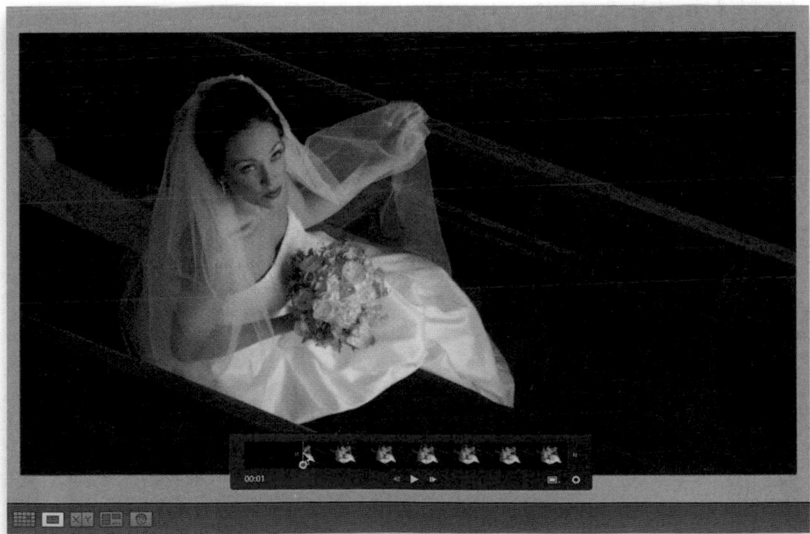

Step Four:

If your video needs to be trimmed down to size (maybe you need to cut off the end a bit, or crop the video so it starts after a few seconds or so), you can click on the Trim Video button (the little gear icon on the far-right side of the control bar) and the trim controls pop up (seen here). There are two ways to trim: One way is to just click on an end marker handle on either side of the video clip (they look like two little vertical bars) and drag inward to trim your clip (as shown here). The other way to trim is to set Trim Start and Trim End points (which basically means "start here" and "end here") by hitting the Spacebar to let the video play, then when you reach the point you want your video to actually start, press **Shift-I** to set the Trim Start point. When you reach the point in the video where you want the rest trimmed away, press **Shift-O** to set your Trim End point. Both methods (dragging the end markers or using the shortcuts) do exactly the same thing, so choose whichever you're most comfortable with.

Continued

Step Five:

There's something very cool you need to know about trimming your video clips: it doesn't permanently trim your video—it's non-destructive, so the original is always protected. The trimming is applied to a copy when you export the file (more on exporting later), so while that exported video will be trimmed (and what you see in Lightroom will be trimmed, as well), you can always come back to the original video clip anytime and pull those trim handles right back out (as shown here).

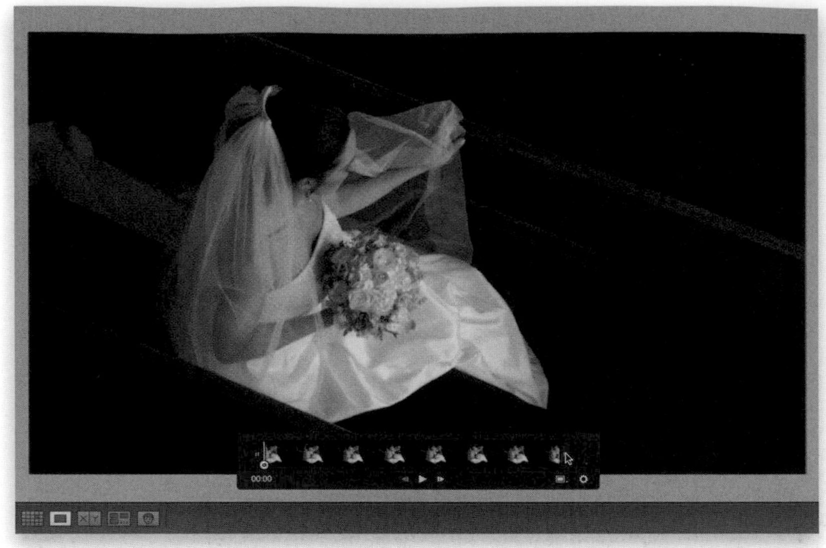

Step Six:

Okay, let's look at another handy feature: Have you ever had a friend upload a video they made to YouTube, and when you see the thumbnail for that video, you see them in mid-sentence with their mouth gaping open? Not the most flattering look, right? That's because the thumbnail is chosen randomly from a frame a few seconds into the video clip itself (if it chose the first frame, and the video faded in from black, the thumbnail would be black, which doesn't help identify the video clip, right?). Well, in Lightroom, you actually get to choose which individual frame becomes your thumbnail (called a "poster frame" in video speak). Being able to choose your poster frame is especially handy if you have four or five similar-looking clips—you can choose thumbnails that show which video has which important part in it (you don't just see it here in Lightroom, that thumbnail goes with it when you export it outside of Lightroom, too). To choose your custom thumbnail, first find the section of the video that has a frame you'd like as your thumbnail, then go to the control bar, click-and-hold on the Frame button (the little rectangle icon to the left of the Trim Video button) and choose **Set Poster Frame** (as shown here) and now your video clip will have that current image as your thumbnail.

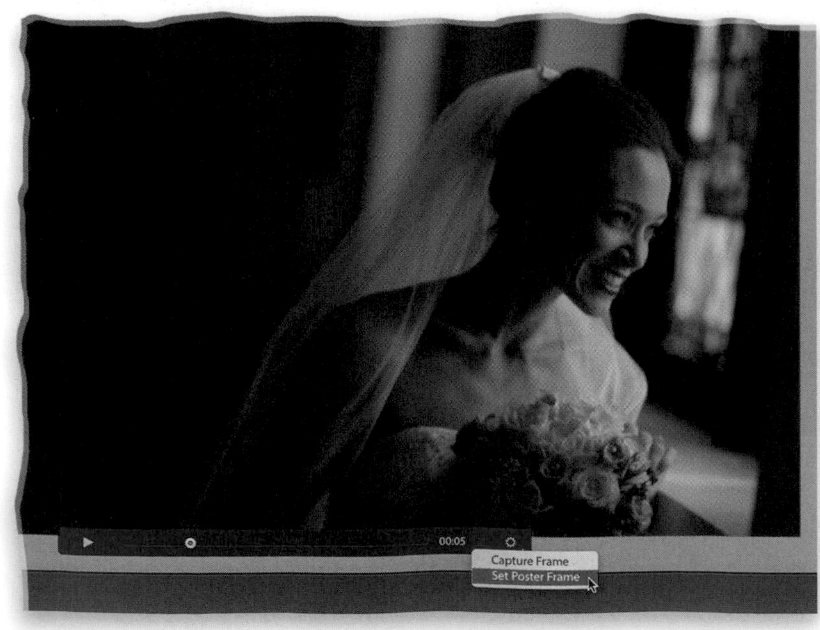

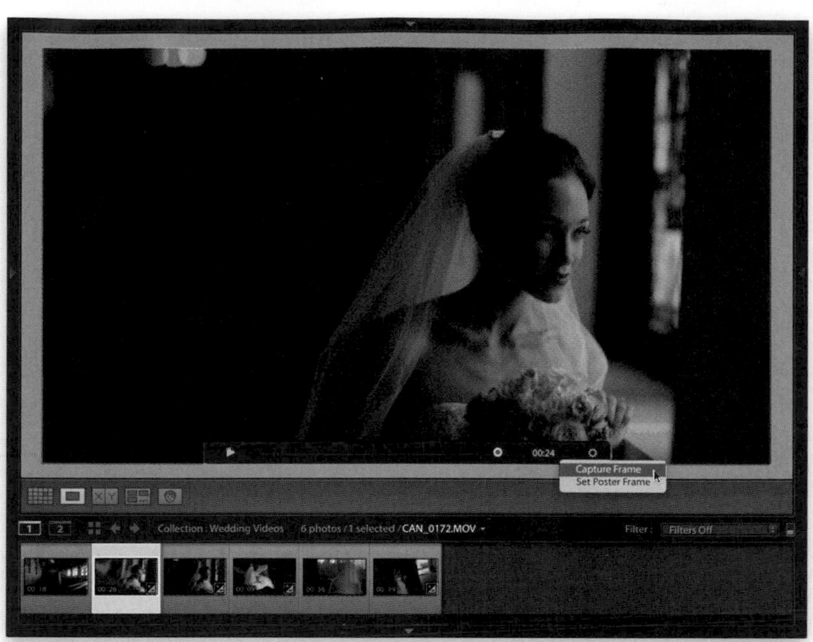

Step Seven:

If you want to pull a single frame out of your video and actually make a still image from it, then you'd do the same thing you did in the previous step: find the part of the video where you'd like to pull a still image from, then click on the Frame button, but this time choose **Capture Frame**. This creates a second file (a JPEG image file just like any other photo) and puts it to the right of your selected video clip in the Filmstrip (as seen here). By the way, if you haven't added this video to a collection yet, instead, the JPEG image gets stacked with your video clip (see Chapter 2 for what stacking is and why it's handy). You'll know it worked if you see a "2" in the upper-left corner of your thumbnail (that's letting you know you have two images in your stack). Again, that's only if your video isn't in a collection (like mine is here).

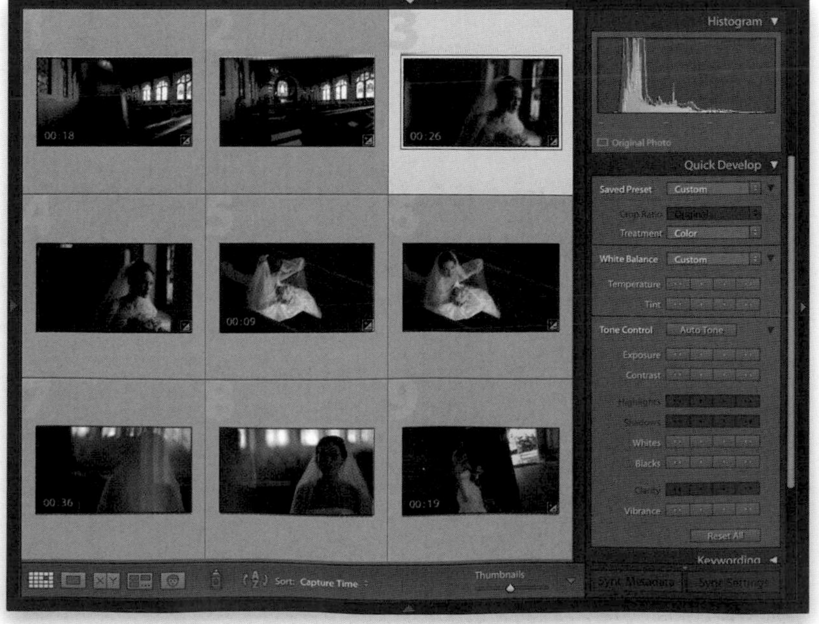

Step Eight:

Knowing how to create a still frame like we just did is really important, because now we're going to use that technique to get into the really fun stuff, which is applying effects to your video clips. Now, just for fun, click on your video clip, then press the letter **D** on your keyboard to jump over to the Develop module. You'll see "Video is not supported in Develop." appear in the center Preview area, but don't worry, you're not out of luck. Press **G** to jump back to the Library module's Grid view, and then look over in the right side Panels area. You see those Quick Develop controls? That's right, baby, we can use 'em on our video (well, not all of them, but some of the most important ones. I'll show you the trick to getting more editing controls in a moment).

Continued

Step Nine:

Let's try it out: double-click on your video clip, then click the Contrast double-right-arrow button three or four times and look at how contrasty the image onscreen looks. That's not just affecting the thumbnail—it applied that to the entire video (cool, right?). You'll also notice that a number of editing controls here are grayed out, and that's because you can't apply all the Quick Develop controls to video (for example, you can't apply Clarity or use the Highlights and Shadows controls), but again, I'll show you in a moment how to get at least some more controls than these.

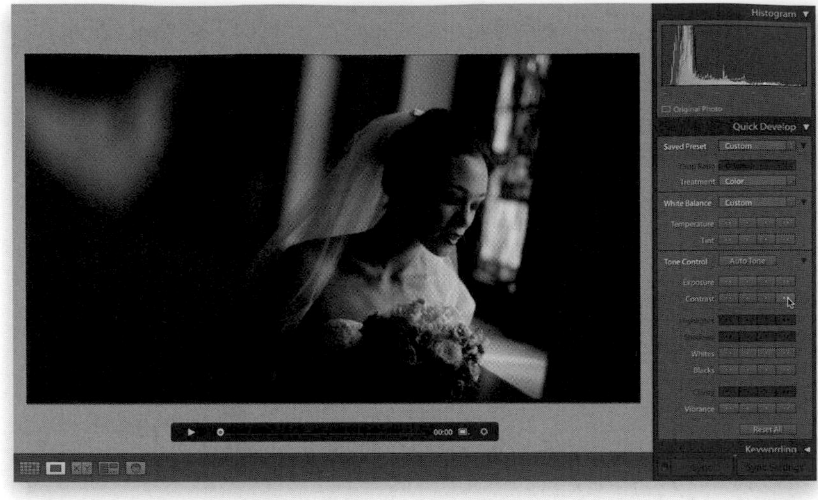

Step 10:

So, while you can apply overall changes like changing the white balance for the entire video (how handy is that?!), or making your whole video clip brighter or darker using Exposure, or more vivid using the Vibrance controls, there probably are still a lot of things you wish you could do that are over in the Develop module, right? Right! But we just learned that the Develop module doesn't support video, right? Right. So what do we do? We cheat. There's a cool workaround that lets you use a lot more (but not all) of the controls in the Develop module by pulling a single frame from the video, taking that over to the Develop module, tweaking it there using everything from the Tone Curve to the HSL panel, and while you're applying these tweaks, the same edits are being applied to your entire video in real time. Totally sick. I know! :) Okay, let's try it: Click the Reset All button at the bottom of the Quick Develop panel, then grab a frame from somewhere inside your video (choose Capture Frame from the Frame pop-up menu), and then when the JPEG image appears next to your video clip in the Filmstrip at the bottom, press **D** to jump over to the Develop module.

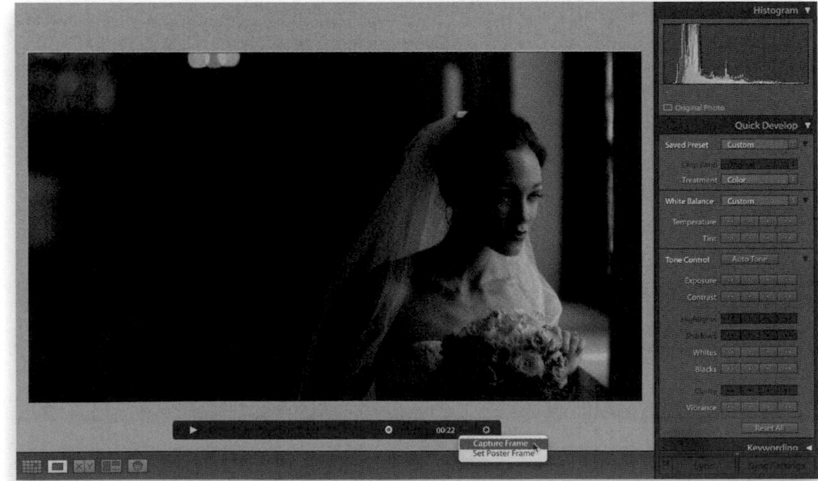

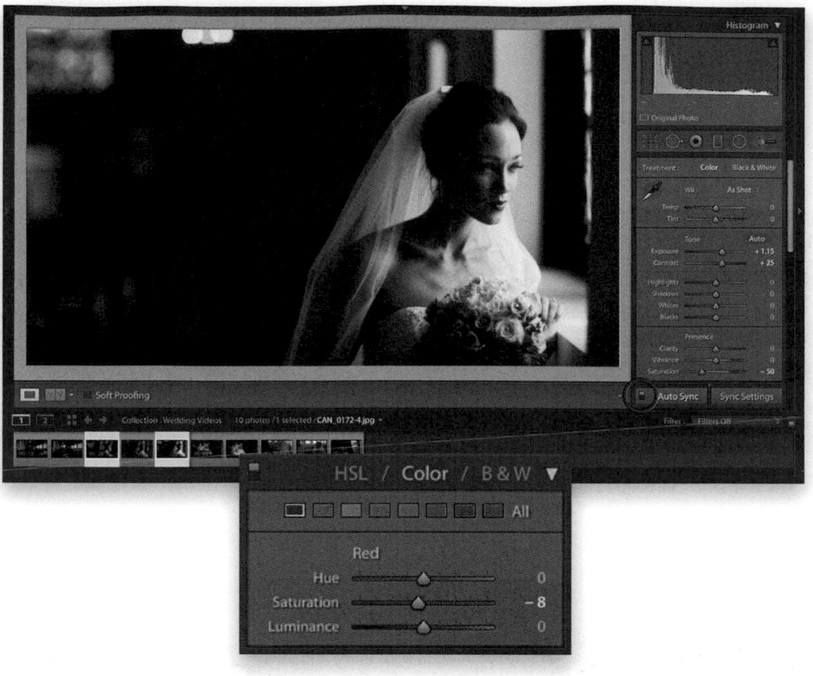

Step 11:

Now, what you're going to do is use Lightroom's Auto Sync feature, which takes whatever effects you apply to one image and applies them to any other selected images (or even a video clip, in our case). Give this is a try: Down in the Filmstrip, click on your still image, then Command-click (PC: Ctrl-click) on your video clip, so they're both selected. At the bottom of the right side Panels area, make sure the Auto Sync switch is turned on (it's shown circled here in red). Now, you can tweak the White Balance, Exposure, Contrast, Vibrance, etc. You can use the Camera Calibration panel, make it black and white, add a duotone or split-tone effect, use the Tone Curve—basically, have a ball—and those changes are automatically applied to your selected video, as well. Not too shabby, eh? Here, I increased the Exposure to +1.15, increased the Contrast to +25, and decreased the Saturation to –50. Then, I went to the Color panel (in the HSL/Color/B&W panel) and decreased the Red Saturation to –8 to get this type of bleach bypass look. (*Note:* It may take a minute or two to see the adjustments reflect in your video thumbnail in the Filmstrip.)

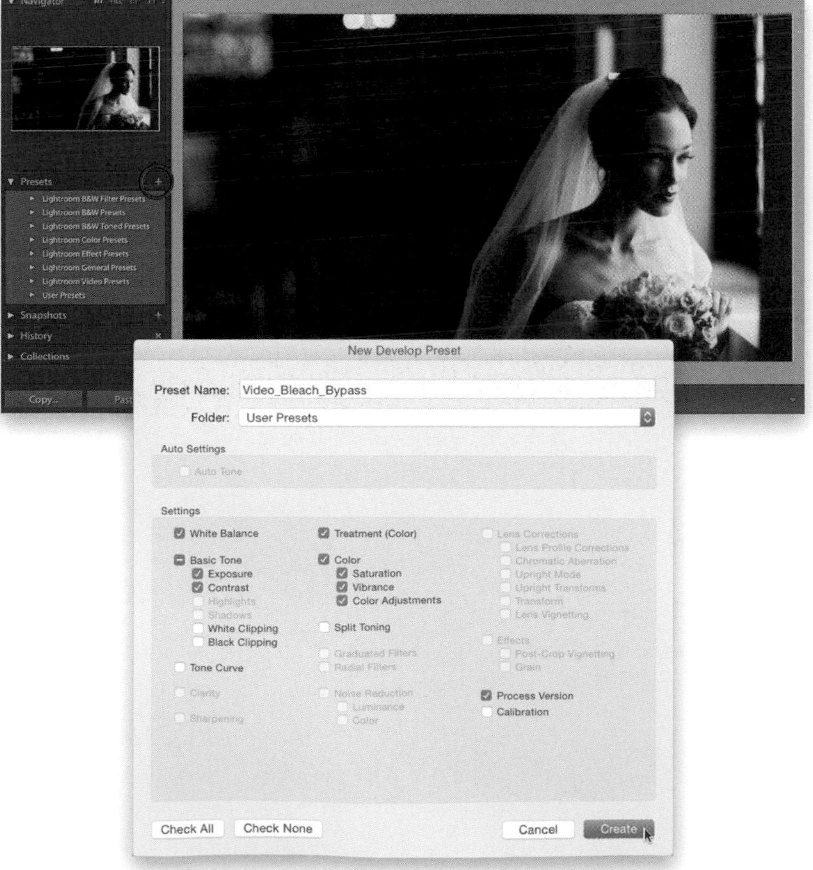

Step 12:

Okay, so what if you create a cool look and think you'll want to use this exact look again on another video clip? Save it as a preset, and then you can apply it with just one click from the Quick Develop panel in the Library module. To save a preset, go to the Presets panel (in the left side Panels area of the Develop module) and click the + (plus sign) button on the right side of the panel header. When the New Develop Preset dialog appears, start by clicking the Check None button, then turn on the checkboxes for the changes you just made, give your preset a descriptive name, and click the Create button (as shown here).

Continued

Step 13:
Okay, now that we've got our preset, let's put it to use. Click the Reset button at the bottom of the right side Panels area, then press **G** to jump back to the Library module's Grid view, and double-click on your video clip. Now, go to the Quick Develop panel's Saved Preset pop-up menu (at the top of the panel), go under User Presets, and you'll see the preset you just saved. Choose that preset and now that effect will be applied to your entire video (if you have the Trim Video bar visible, like I do here, you can see the effect has been applied to the entire video).

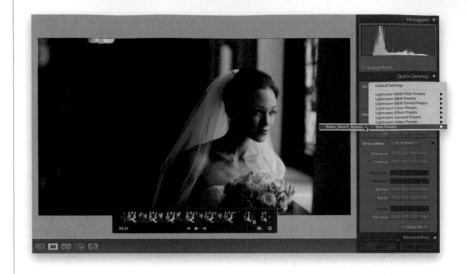

TIP: What You Can't Apply to Video
You can't add Clarity, Highlights, or Shadows from the Basic panel in the Develop module, or anything in the Lens Corrections or Effects panels, and you can't use the Adjustment Brush. What might throw you off is that these sliders aren't grayed out, because at this point you're just working on a still image, so everything's fair game. So, how do you know if what you're doing can be applied to video as a preset or when you sync? One way is to look at your thumbnails down in the Filmstrip while you're editing. If you only see one thumbnail changing (the JPEG image file), then it's not being applied to the video. Another quick way to tell is when you go to save a preset. See all those things that are grayed out in the New Develop Preset dialog in Step 12? Those edits, even if you did them, won't be applied to video.

Step 14:
Remember, these are all "non-destructive" edits you're making here, so if you apply these effects to your video and you decide you don't like them (right now, or a year from now), you can remove all those effects by clicking the Reset All button at the bottom of the Quick Develop panel (shown circled here in red).

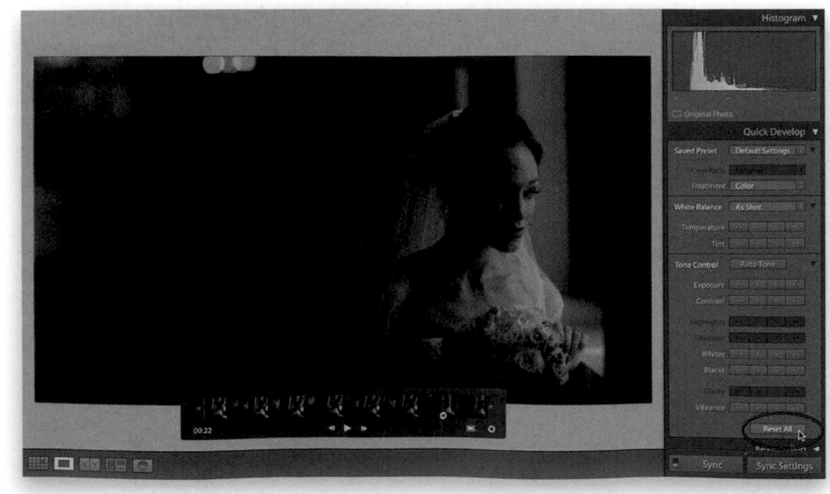

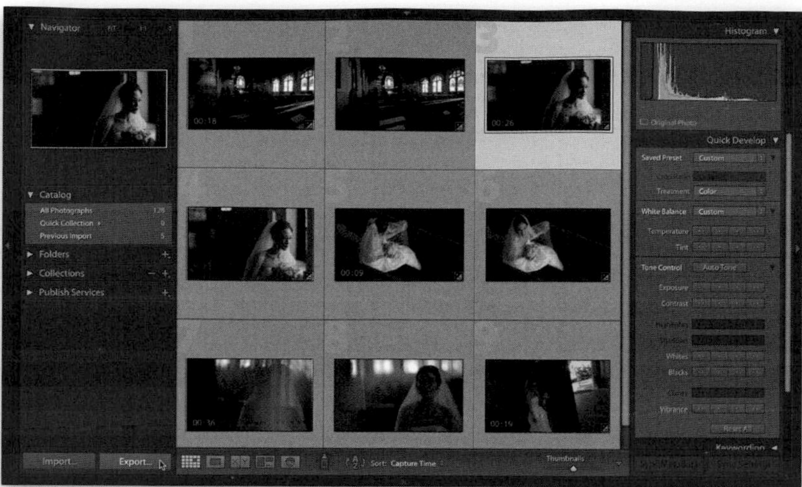

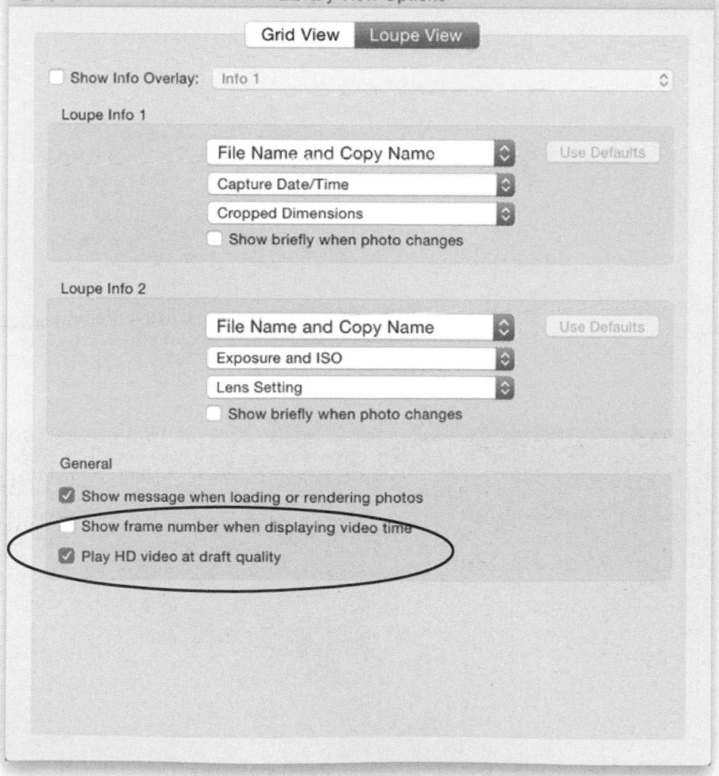

Step 15:

Once you've got your video just the way you want it, you're probably going to want to save it outside of Lightroom, so you can share it somewhere (or open it in a video editing program as part of a bigger video project). Although you can't email your video directly from Lightroom (most likely, the file size would be too large to email anyway), you can post the video directly to Facebook or Flickr using the Export presets or Publish Services (see Chapter 9 for more on how to use both, but I thought you'd want to know they do support posting your video directly from Lightroom). Otherwise, click on the video clip you want to export, then click the Export button at the bottom of the left side Panels area (as shown here).

TIP: Video Preferences

There are really only two video preferences and they're found in the Library View Options (press **Command-J [PC: Ctrl-J]**), on the Loupe View tab. In the General section, at the bottom, Show Frame Number When Displaying Video Time does just what it says—it adds the frame number beside the time (yawn). The option beneath that, Play HD Video at Draft Quality, is there to make sure the playback of your HD video is smooth if you don't have a super-fast computer—the lower-resolution draft-quality video takes less power to display the video in real time than the full HD version does.

Continued

Step 16:

When the Export dialog appears, if you scroll down a bit, you'll see an area dedicated to exporting video (seen here). Since you clicked on your video file to export it, the Include Video Files checkbox should already be turned on, so all you have to do is make two simple choices: (1) Which video format do you want to save your clip in? I use H.264 as it's a widely supported format, and makes the file size smaller without losing much (if any) visible quality (kind of like JPEG does for image files), but of course, how much it's compressed is based on (2) the Quality setting you choose. If you're going to be sharing this somewhere on the web (YouTube, Animoto, etc.), then you'll probably want to consider a lower quality than Max (the physical size and fps will appear to the right when you choose a Quality size from the menu, so you know what each delivers). However, if you're taking this video over to a dedicated video editing application, that's when you'd want to choose Max quality. For the rest of the exporting features, see Chapter 9 (the exporting chapter).

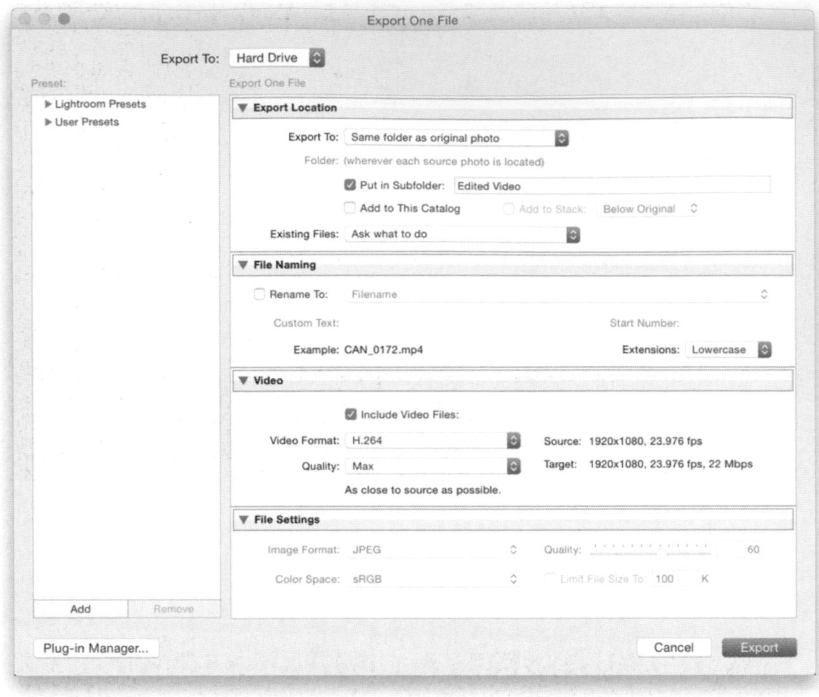

Step 17:

Before you jump to the other sections of the book, I wanted to give you a few great examples of what kinds of things you can use Lightroom's video editing features for that might make your life easier. One I use a lot is to warm up skin tones. Although we set proper white balance for video by using a white card (rather than a gray card for still photos), that white balance, while being technically accurate, is a bit on the cool side, and people generally look better a little warmer. So, by capturing a still frame of the video, taking it into the Develop module, and dragging the Temp slider to the right, toward yellow, you can make the skin tones of people in your video look much more pleasing. Be sure you have Auto Sync turned on and have the video selected in the Filmstrip, along with the still frame.

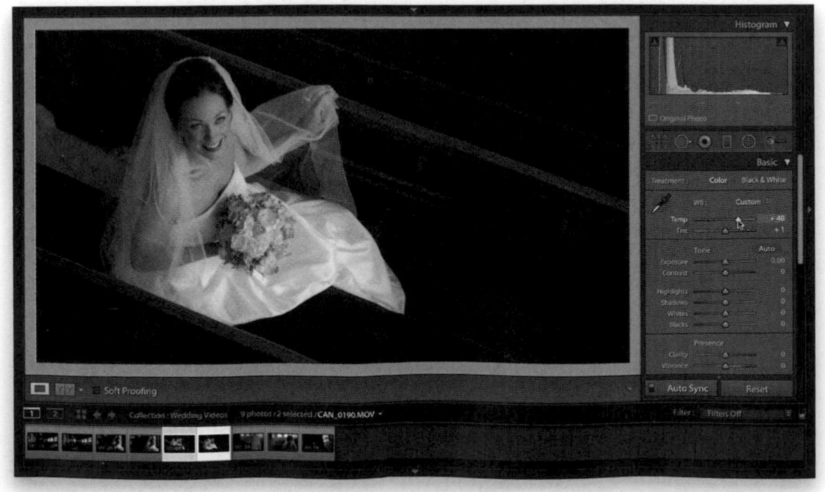

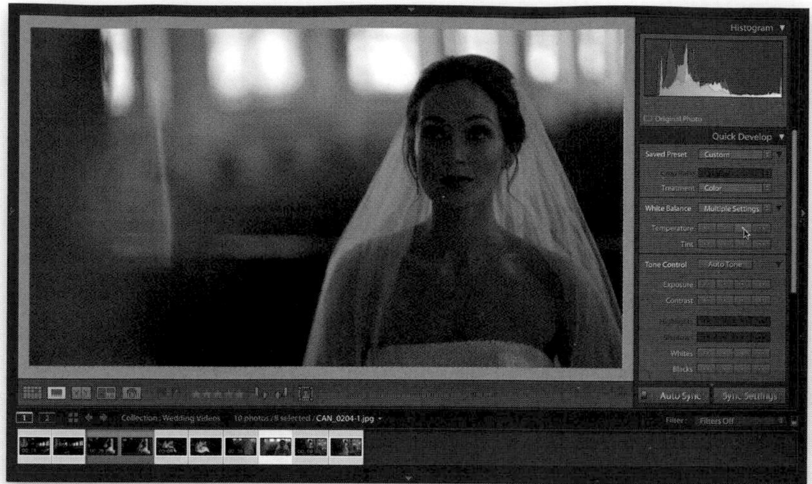

Step 18:

Another very important tweak is making sure the color is the same between multiple video clips—especially important if you're going to be putting these clips together in a video editing application. The quickest way to do this is to capture a still frame from one video, open it in Loupe view, then select that frame, along with all the video clips, and right there in the Library module, use the White Balance controls in the Quick Develop panel to tweak the still frame, and all the other selected video clips will now have the same white balance. Be sure, though, that the Auto Sync switch at the bottom of the right side Panels area is turned on.

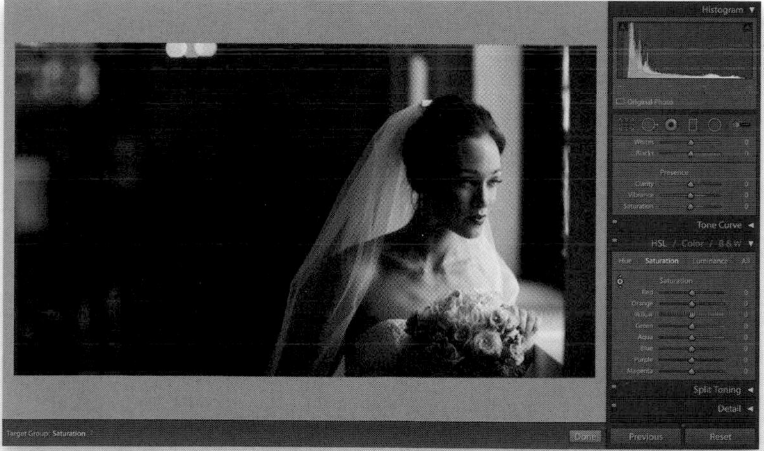

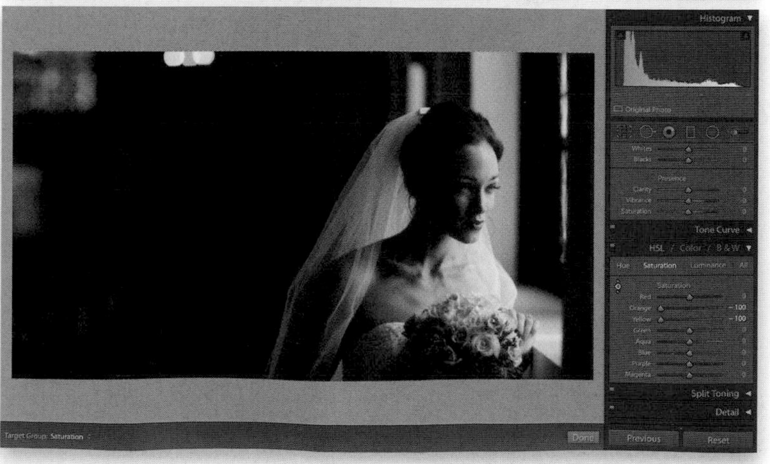

Step 19:

If you want a more film-like look for your videos, you can increase the contrast by going to the Library module, clicking on the video clip, and clicking the Contrast double-right-arrow button once or twice. Do the same thing with the Vibrance to give your video a little more "pop." Those are "every day" types of edits, but of course, there are other things, like special effects, that are easy to do, too. For example, how about having your video look like it's black and white, but have one color that stays in color throughout the entire video. To do that, capture a still frame, then take that frame over to the Develop module. Pick one color to avoid (like red), then go to the HSL panel, click on Saturation at the top, take the Targeted Adjustment tool (near the top left of the panel), and click on any color but the one you want to keep. Now, drag straight down until everything else is black and white (this video isn't the perfect example for this trick, but here I desaturated the colors, and left some of the veil and flowers, her lips, and the stained glass in color). Then, go back and apply those changes to your video.

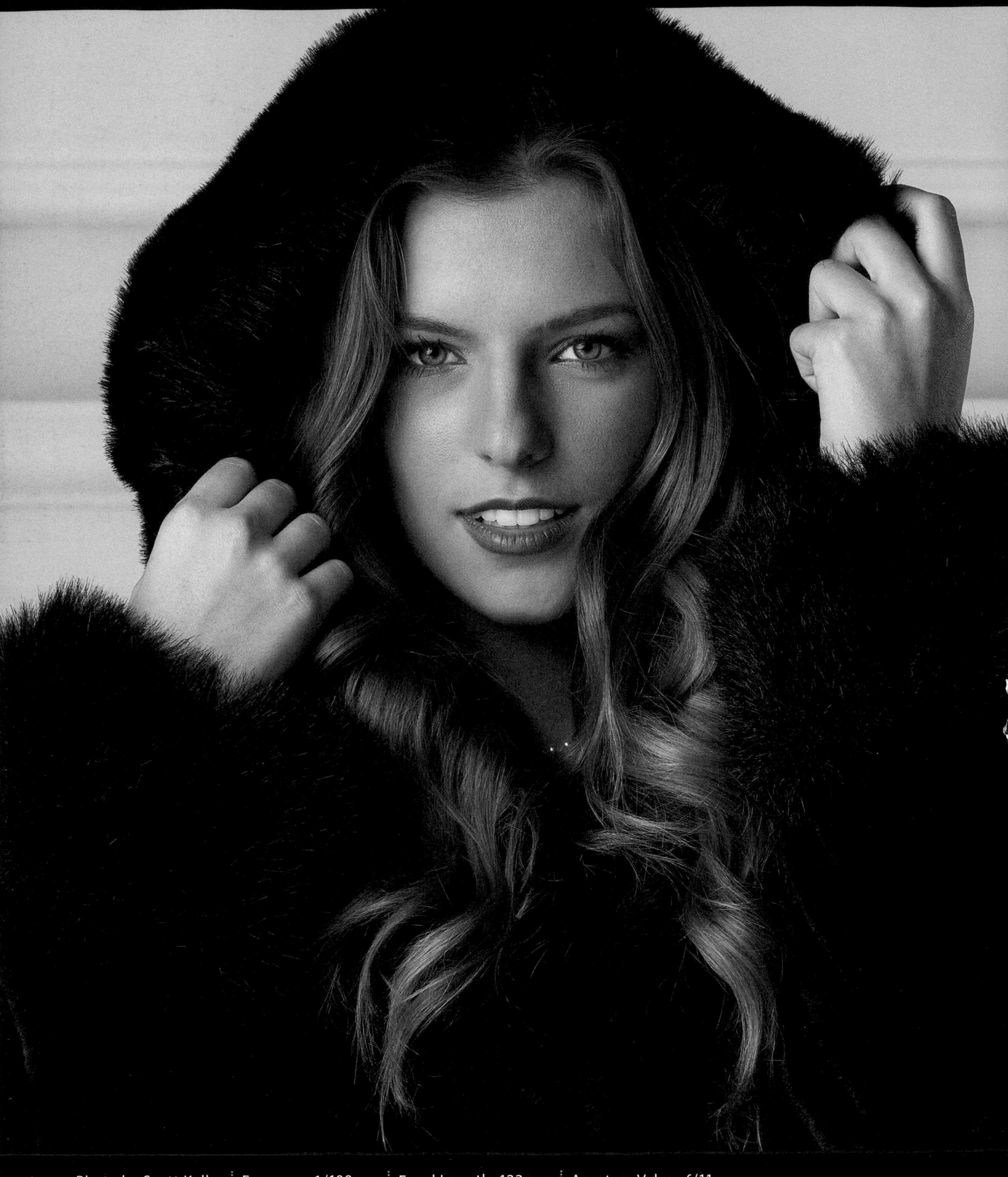

Photo by Scott Kelby | Exposure: 1/100 sec | Focal Length: 123mm | Aperture Value: ƒ/11

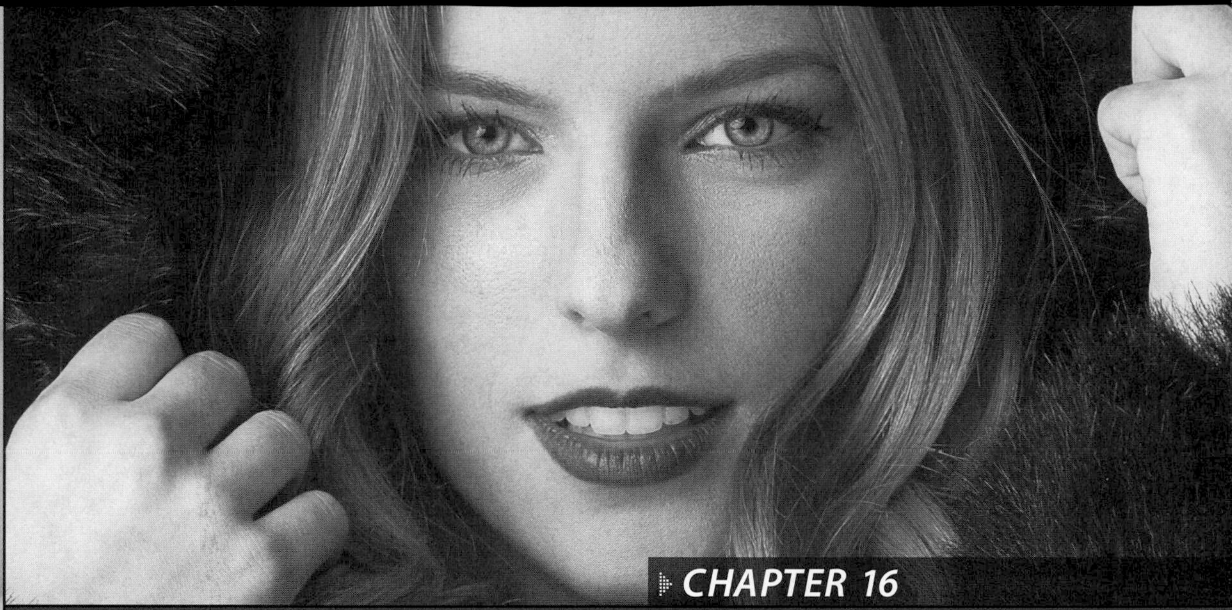

CHAPTER 16

MY PORTRAIT WORKFLOW

my step-by-step process from the shoot to the final print

If you've come to this chapter, you've either already invested a lot of time and energy in learning these techniques, or you just bought the book, and flipped right to this chapter, in which case you're one of those rabble-rousers who flaunt the time-honored tradition of book reading (where you start at Chapter 1 and work your way tirelessly through the book), and instead just jump to where the "good stuff" is hidden in the back. I'm going to assume you're not that person. Instead, I'll pretend you worked hard to get here, and therefore deserve a treat (Who's a good boy? Who's a good boy?). Thus far, the book has been one chapter on this topic, and another on that—one on importing, and another on editing; one on organizing, and another on printing. But I thought it would be helpful for you to see it all come together—to see the entire process from beginning to end—and I thought I would even include the details of the photo shoot. Why? Because it takes up more pages, and publishers love that, because they think what readers want is more pages. In fact, if you tell them, "I'm going to add a page with just random words," they get absolutely giddy. If you tell them you're including a few pages that say "This page intentionally left blank," they black out for a few moments, and have to be revived with smelling salts—this is the Holy Grail of book publishing. Now, I have no idea if, when this book was printed, they added some blank pages, but I can tell you this: if they did, they added page numbers to them, then ran around their offices high-fiving everybody in sight. Welcome to their world.

Workflow Step One: It All Starts with the Shoot

What you're about to learn is my typical day-in, day-out, workflow, and it doesn't matter if I'm doing a landscape shoot, portrait shoot, or a sports shoot, I pretty much use Lightroom the same way in the same order every time. For this particular example, I'm doing a studio shoot, so it actually starts with me shooting tethered, where I connect the camera to my laptop and shoot directly into Lightroom itself (see Chapter 1 for more on tethering). If you're not shooting tethered, I cover my importing workflow two pages from here.

Step One:

Before I set up the lighting, I use the USB cable that came with my camera to connect my Canon DSLR to my laptop. Once connected, I launch Lightroom, then go under the File menu, under Tethered Capture, and choose **Start Tethered Capture**. I enter what I need to in the Tethered Capture Settings dialog (like where I want to save the images on my laptop), click OK, and it brings up the floating window you see here. Now, I'm ready to go (for details on setting up tethered capture, see Chapter 1).

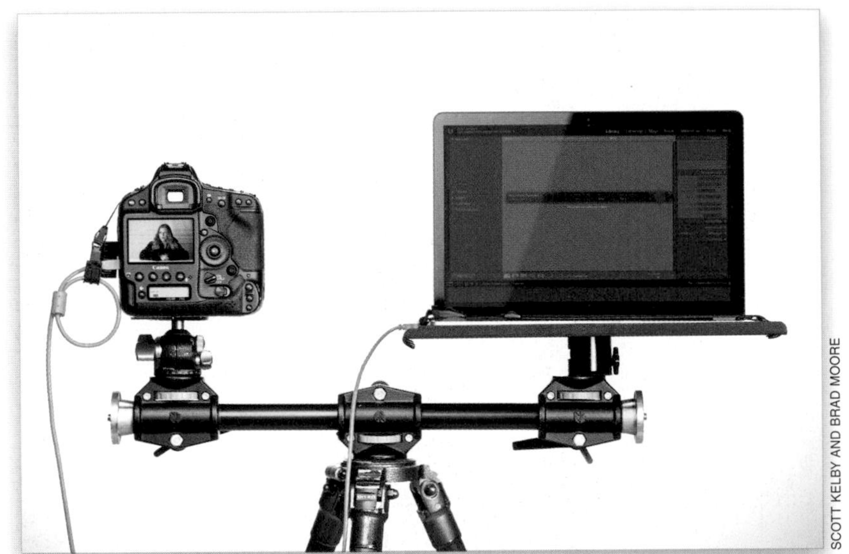

SCOTT KELBY AND BRAD MOORE

Step Two:

The lighting setup I used is really simple: just a two-light setup. The flash heads are Elinchrom BXR 500s (a value-priced 500-watt studio strobe with a built-in wireless receiver). The main light has a 53" Midi Octa softbox attached (pretty much my go-to softbox for portraits) up a little higher than the subject and tilted so it's aiming down. The second flash has a 27x27" softbox used to light the printed fabric background behind her. Camera settings: My lens is a Canon 70–200mm f/2.8 lens. In the studio, I shoot in Manual mode, and leave my shutter speed set at 1/125 of a second, and then I can just adjust my f-stop (which for this shoot was f/11). Also, in the studio, I set my ISO at the lowest native ISO for my camera (which in my case is 100 ISO). She's sitting at a white IKEA work table, and we put a thin sheet of Plexiglass under her arms to create a glassy reflection. That's it: a simple two-light setup.

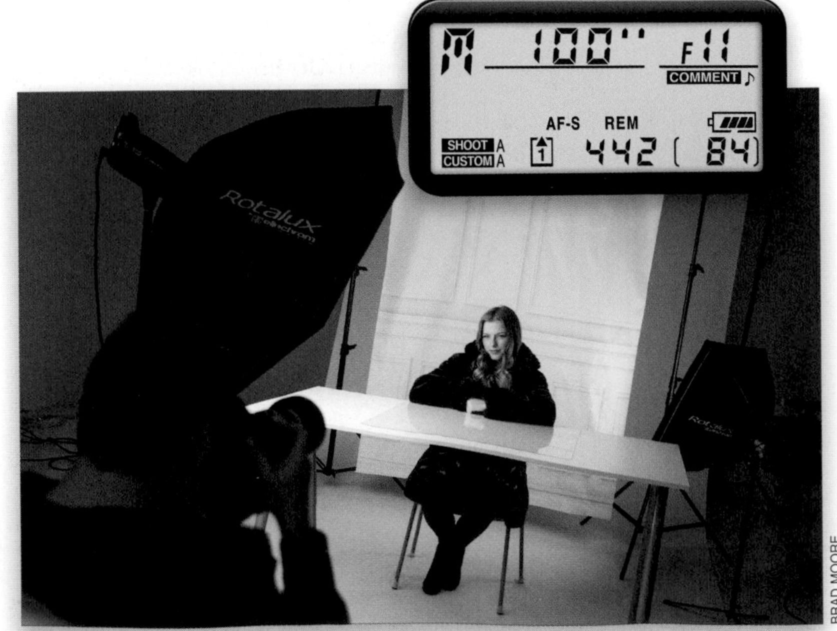

BRAD MOORE

Workflow Step Two: Right After the Shoot, Do This First

Once the shoot is over, before you start the sorting/editing process in Lightroom and Photoshop, you've got some absolutely critical "first-things-first" stuff to do, and that is to back up your photos, right now, before anything else—I actually back up even when I'm on location shoots. Here's the step by step on backing up:

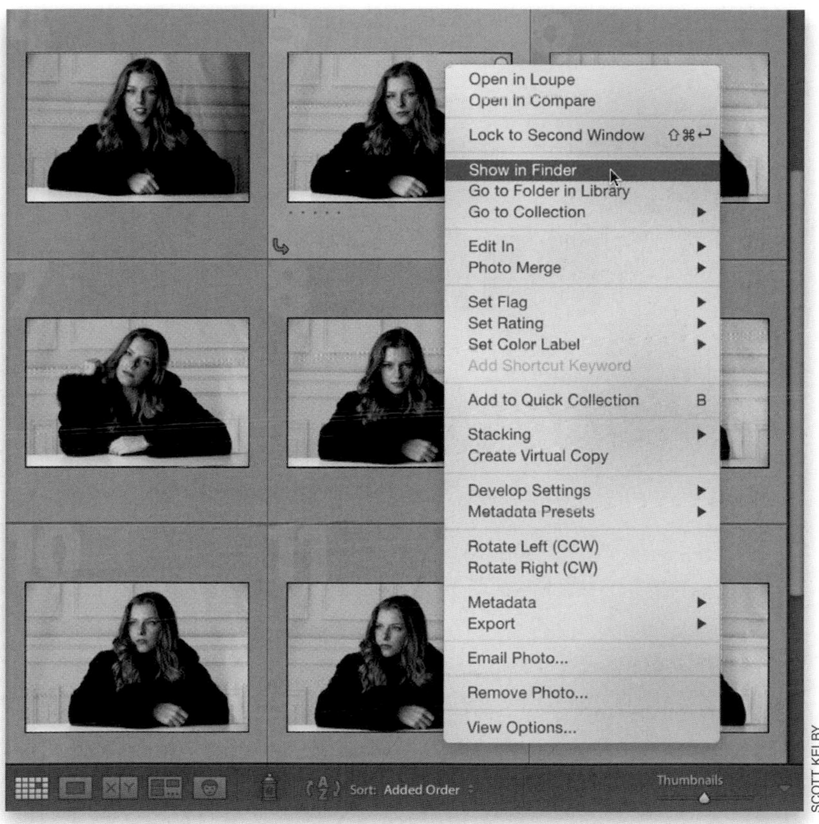

SCOTT KELBY

Step One:

When you shoot tethered (directly from your camera to your laptop, like I did at this shoot), your photos are already in your computer, and they're already in Lightroom, but they're not backed up anywhere yet—the only copies of those photos are on that computer. If anything happens to your laptop, those photos are gone forever. So immediately after the shoot, I back up those photos. Although you can see the photos in Lightroom, you need to back up the photo files themselves. A quick way to find that folder is to go to Lightroom and Right-click on a photo from that shoot and choose **Show in Finder (PC: Show in Explorer)** from the pop-up menu, as shown here.

Step Two:

This opens a Finder (PC: Windows Explorer) window of the folder with your actual photo files inside, so click on that folder and drag the whole thing to your backup hard drive (this has to be a separate external hard drive—not just another partitioned disk on the same computer). If you don't have an external drive with you, then at the very least, burn that folder to a CD or DVD.

If I Didn't Shoot Tethered, Here's Importing from a Memory Card

I try to shoot tethered as much as possible—it's such a big advantage being able to see your images that large as they come in—but, of course, there are times where shooting tethered just doesn't make sense (like when I'm shooting sports, or a wedding, or one of a dozen other shoots where it's just not practical, so I shoot to the memory card in my camera). Here's my importing workflow when I shoot to card instead of tethering:

Step One:

When I'm ready to import the images from my shoot into Lightroom, I plug the memory card into my card reader and it brings up Lightroom's Import window (seen here). At the top, from left to right, you can see I'm importing from my memory card. At the top center, I click on Copy (so I'm copying the images), and on the far right, it shows where I'm copying them (my external hard drive). If I see shots now where the flash didn't fire, or it's a blank frame, or a shot that's so messed up I can see it in the thumbnail, I turn off the checkbox for that thumbnail, since I would just wind up deleting it later anyway.

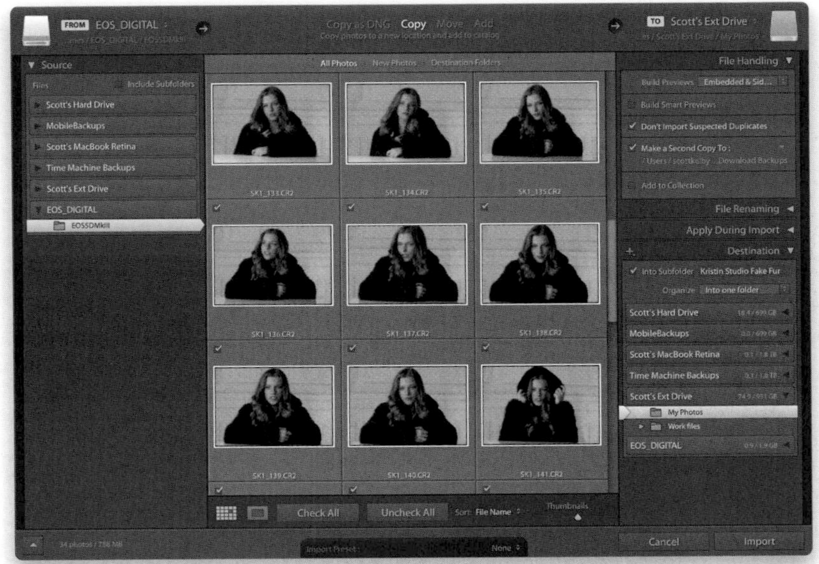

SCOTT KELBY

Step Two:

Over in the right side panels, I turn on the option to make a second copy of these images to my backup drive (so I have two copies of every image, in two different places. Peace of mind for the win!). I pick a fast-loading preview (Embedded & Sidecar) because I want to see my images in the Library as quickly as possible. Next, I never want to import duplicates, so I always leave that checkbox turned on. I also pick a simple descriptive name for the files (like "FakeFurStudioShoot," in this case) and then I have Lightroom sequentially number them, starting with 001. Lastly, in the Apply During Import section, under Metadata, I apply my copyright information to each photo as it's imported (see Chapter 2 for how to create a copyright template). Pretty simple and straightforward. Now I just hit the Import button and in they go!

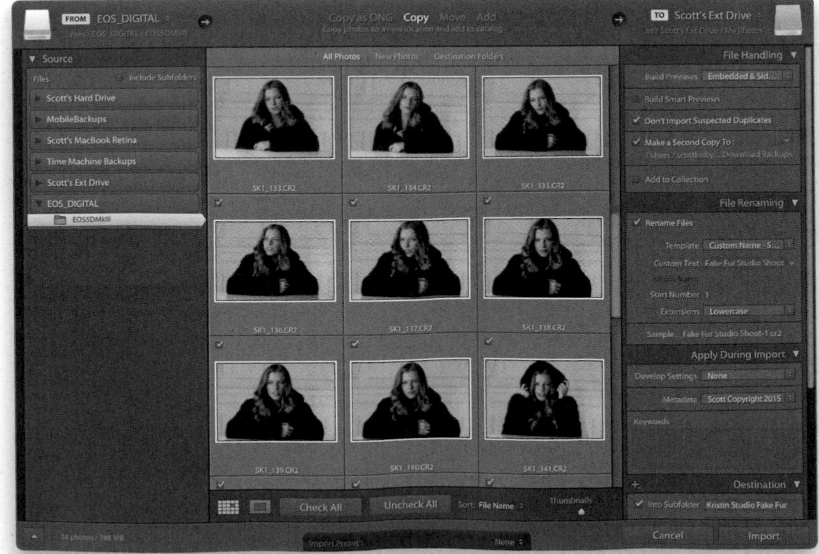

Workflow Step Three: Finding Your Picks & Making a Collection

Okay, your photos are in Lightroom, and they're backed up to a separate hard drive, so now it's time to make a collection of the keepers from the shoot, and get rid of the shots that are out of focus, the flash didn't fire for, or are just generally messed up (the Rejects). We're going to make our lives easy by creating a collection set right off the bat, and then we'll make other collections inside that set for our Picks and Selects (the final images we'll show to the client).

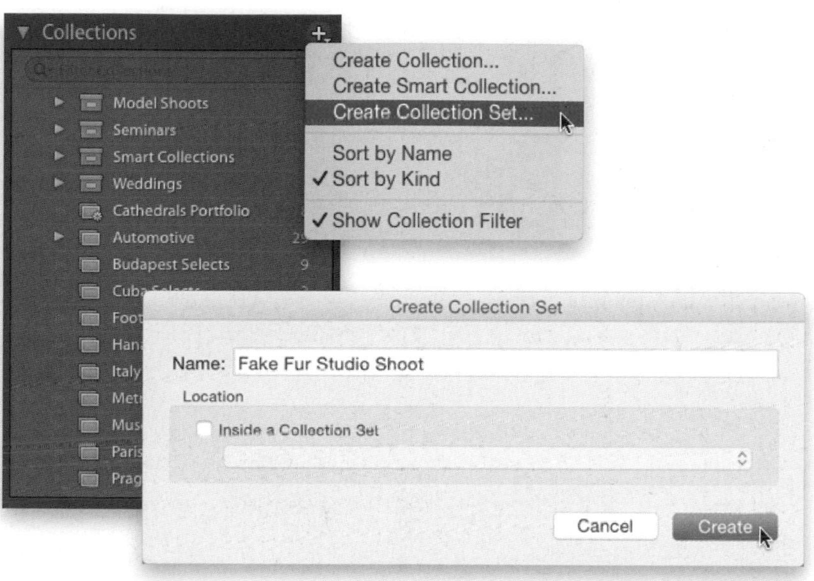

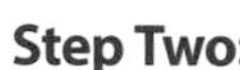

Step One:

In the Library module, go to the Collections panel (in the left side Panels area), click on the + (plus sign) button on the right side of the panel header, and choose **Create Collection Set** from the pop-up menu. When the Create Collection Set dialog appears, name your new collection set "Fake Fur Studio Shoot," and then click the Create button. We've now got a set where we can save our Picks and our final images to show to the client (but we're not actually going to use this set right this minute—we just set it up to use a step or two down the road).

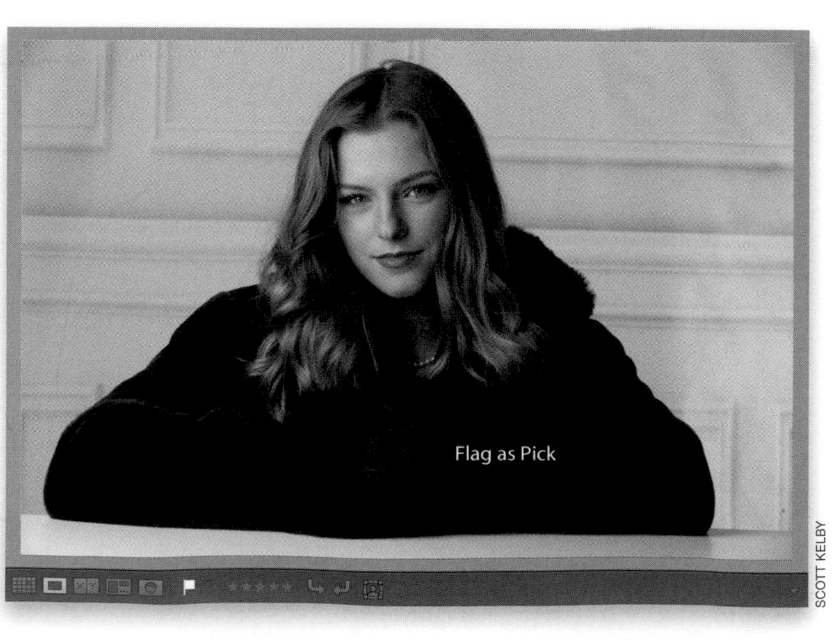

SCOTT KELBY

Step Two:

Now I go through the process of finding just the Picks and the Rejects from the shoot. Press **G** to see your images in Grid view, then scroll up to the very top and double-click on the first photo (so it zooms in to Loupe view). Now use the Left/Right Arrow keys on your keyboard to view each image from the shoot. When you see a really good shot, press the letter **P** on your keyboard to flag it as a Pick, and when you see a Reject (shots that are out of focus, badly composed, messed up, etc.), press the letter **X** (to flag it as a Reject to be deleted). As you move through these images, remember: just Picks and Rejects—no star ratings, etc. If you make a mistake, press **U** to unflag it. For more on Picks and Rejects see page 64 in Chapter 2.

Continued

Step Three:

Once you've chosen your Picks and Rejects, let's get rid of those Rejects for good by choosing **Delete Rejected Photos** from the Photo menu (as shown here). By the way, when you flag an image as a Reject, its thumbnail actually dims to give you another visual cue (besides the black flag) that it's marked as a Reject: look at the first image in the second row and you can see the thumbnail is dimmed.

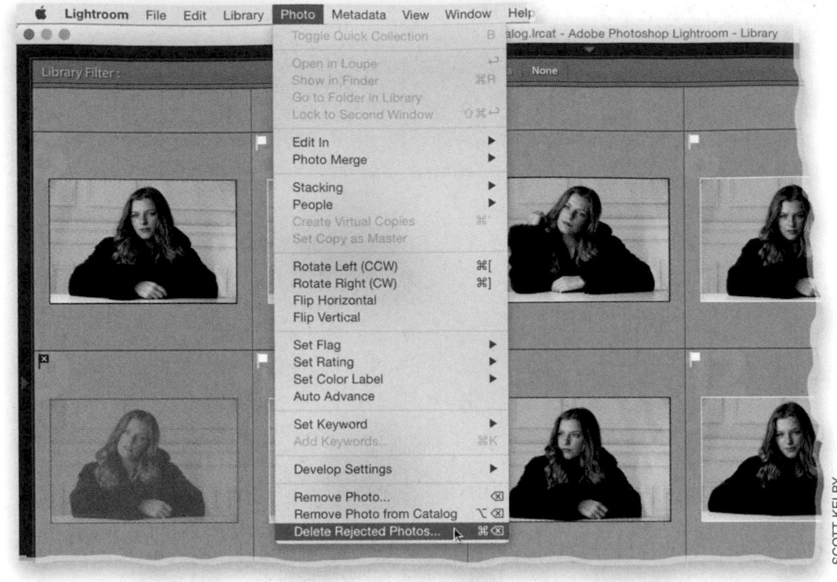

SCOTT KELBY

Step Four:

Now, let's turn on a filter that just shows our Picks (after all, this is what this is all about—separating our Picks from the rest of the shoot). Go up to the Library Filter above the Preview area, click on Attribute, and then click on the white Pick flag to filter your images so only the Picks are showing. *Note:* If you don't see the Library Filter bar at the top of your Preview area, press the backslash key **(\)** on your keyboard to make it visible.

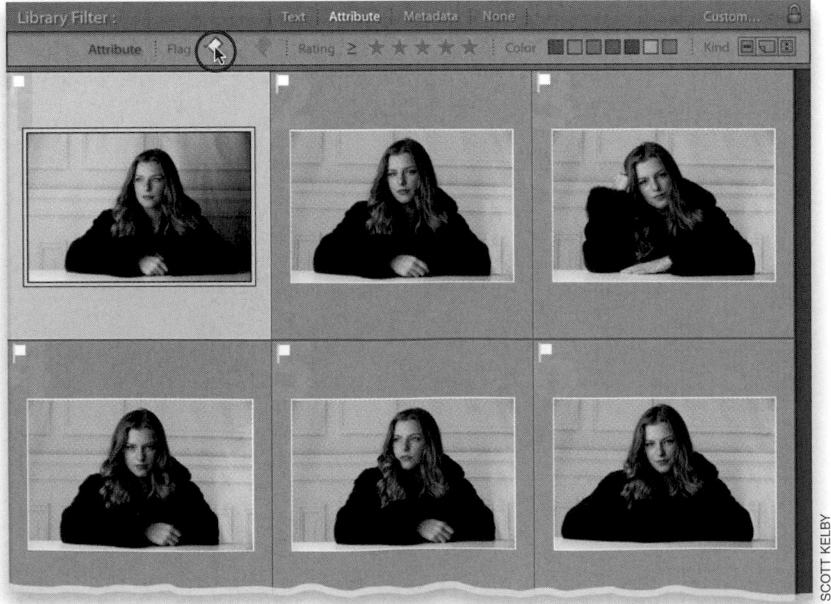

SCOTT KELBY

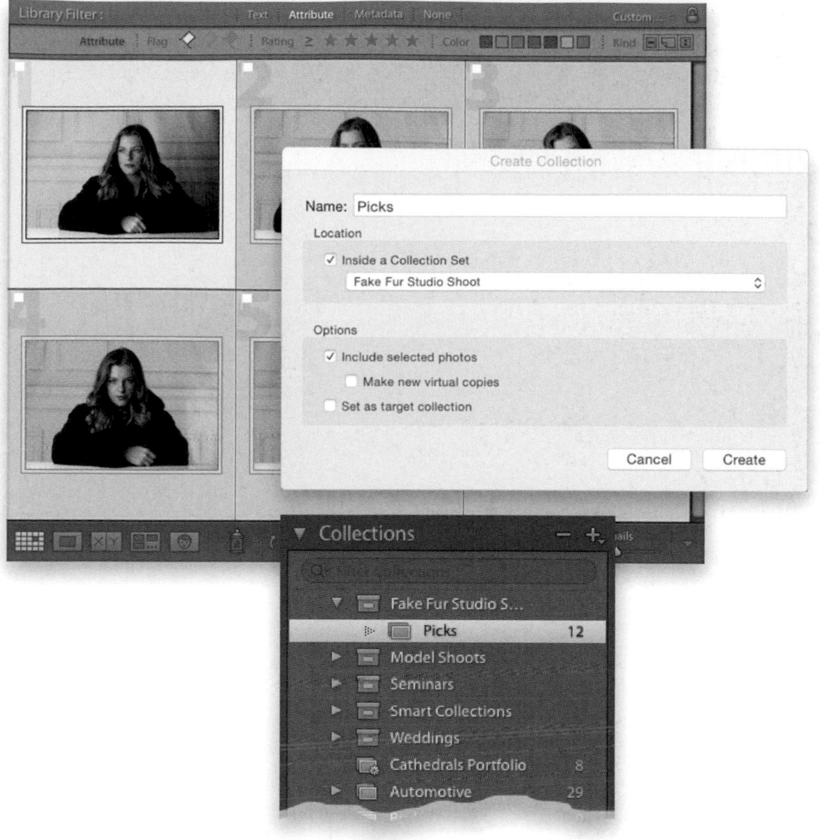

Step Five:

Now, press **Command-A (PC: Ctrl-A)** to select all the Picks, and then press **Command-N (PC: Ctrl-N)** to create a new collection. When the dialog appears, name this collection "Picks," turn on the Inside a Collection Set checkbox, and from the pop-up menu, choose the Fake Fur Studio Shoot set we made back in Step One (see, I told you we'd wind up using this later on). Make sure the Include Selected Photos checkbox is turned on (so these selected photos wind up in this new collection automatically), and click the Create button. This saves your Picks into their own collection inside your Fake Fur Studio Shoot set (shown here at the bottom). At this point, all our Picks are still flagged, but since they're in their own collection now, we need to remove the flags for the next step. So, select them all, then press the letter U to unflag them. (For more on collections, see page 64 in Chapter 2.)

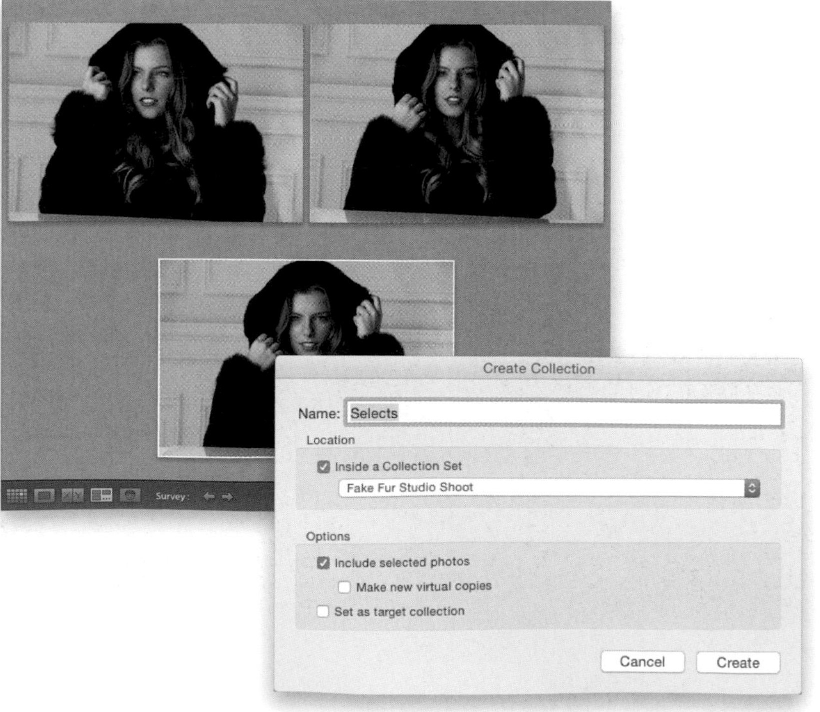

Step Six:

It's time to narrow things down even further—to the images we'll send to the client for approval. To help with this, I select any images in this Picks collection with a similar pose and go into Survey view by pressing the letter **N**. The images show up together onscreen, and I keep removing my least favorite shot until I wind up with just a couple of a pose I like. I click on that image (as seen here, where I clicked on the bottom image), then I flag it as a Pick. Press G to return to the Grid view, select another set of images with the same pose, and narrow things down the same way (I wound up with three photos that are my Selects). Turn on the Pick flag filter up in the Library Filter, select all the images flagged as Picks, create a new collection, name it "Selects," and save it in your Fake Fur Studio Shoot set.

Workflow Step Four: A Quick Retouch for Your Selects

Now that you've whittled things down to the images you're going to show the client, it's decision time: are you going to let your client look at the proofs "as is," or do you want to tweak 'em a bit first in Lightroom's Develop module? If you're leaving them "as is," jump over to page 522. But, if you want to take a couple of minutes and tweak a few things, then stick with me here. By the way, these are just some quick tweaks—we don't want to invest a bunch of editing time now, because the client may only choose one (or none).

Step One:

Let's do some light tweaking on this Select image to get it ready to show the client for approval. Of course, if the white balance or exposure is off, I would fix it in the Develop module before I did any retouching (in this case, both are okay already). We'll start by removing some minor blemishes, so in the Develop module, get the Spot Removal tool **(Q)** and click it once over any blemishes (as seen here). Make your brush size just a little larger than the blemishes you want to remove, using the Size slider at the bottom of the Spot Removal options panel.

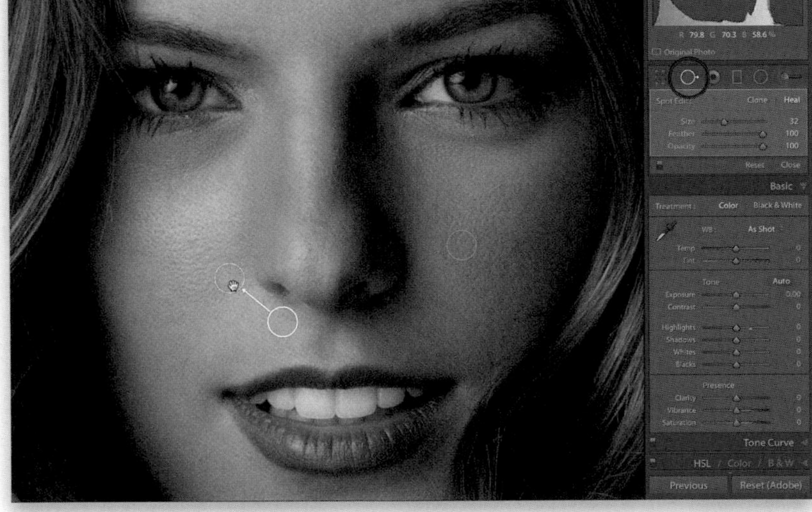

Step Two:

The next thing that stands out to me is that the whites of her eyes and her irises could be a bit brighter. Get the Adjustment Brush **(K)**, double-click on the word "Effect" in the Adjustment Brush options panel (to reset all the sliders to zero) and then increase the exposure a bit by dragging the Exposure slider to the right (here, I dragged to 0.51). Now, paint over the whites of her eyes (as seen here). After you've painted over them, make sure they're not too bright (a dead giveaway of a bad retouch), and if you need to, back off the Exposure amount a bit. Then, let's paint over the irises. I generally just paint a stroke over the bottom half of the iris (almost like you're painting a smile). Again, once you've painted, adjust the Exposure slider to where it all looks good to you.

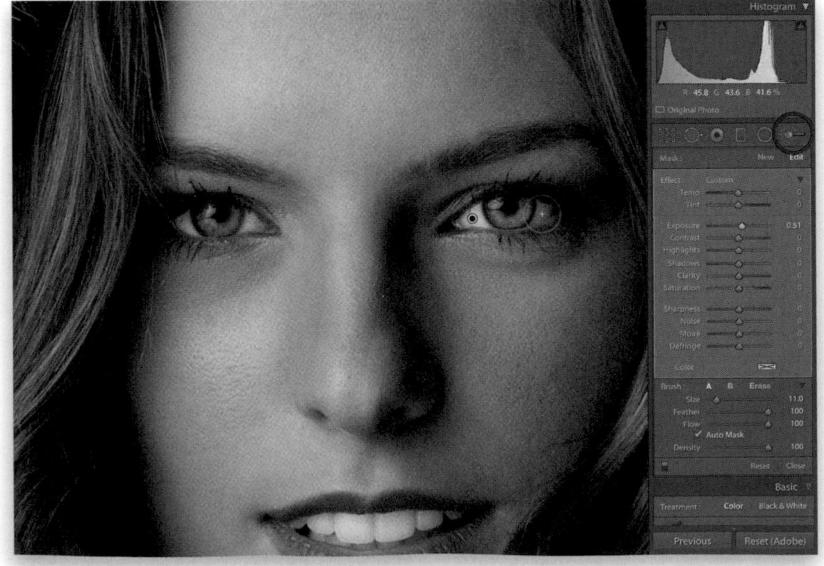

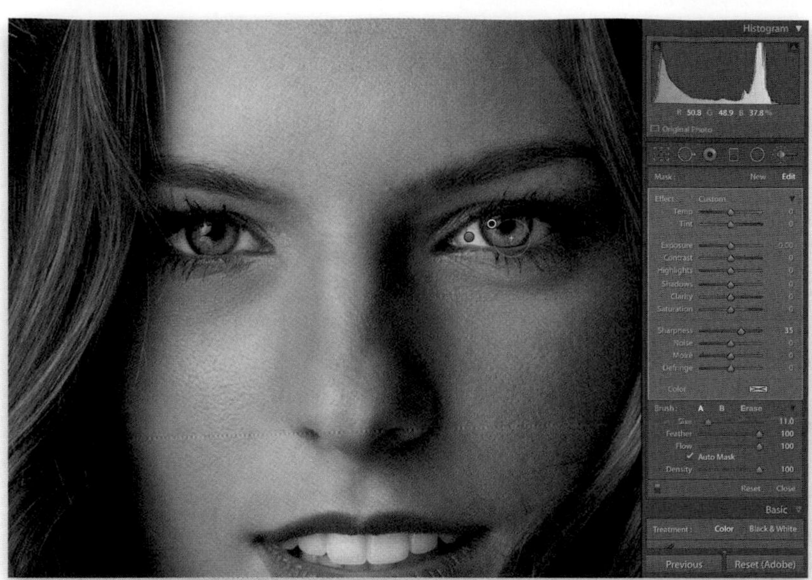

Step Three:

Now let's sharpen her irises. In the Adjustment Brush options panel, click the New button up top (to create a new adjustment, leaving the adjustments we made to her eyes in place). Double-click on the word Effect (to reset all the sliders to 0) and then increase the Sharpness amount and paint a few brush strokes over her irises until they're nice and sharp. If it looks too sharp, you know what to do: back off the Sharpness slider amount.

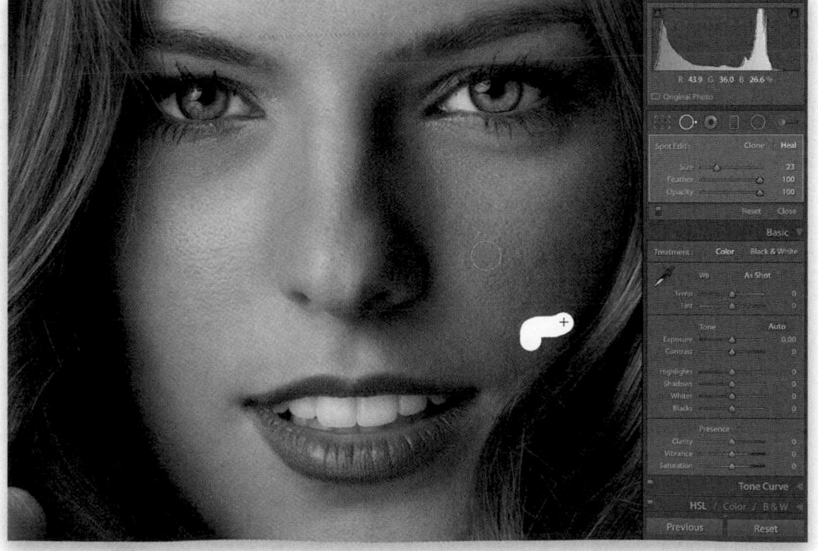

Step Four:

Lastly, there's a stray hair coming into her face on the right side that looks kind of distracting, so let's remove it. Get the Spot Removal tool again and paint over that area to remove it, as shown here (the brush paints in white at first, so you can see where you're healing, and then after a moment, that disappears and it heals the area). Also, don't forget to apply these quick retouches to any other images you're sending to your client for proofing.

Workflow Step Five: Emailing Your Clients the Proofs

At this point, I want to get the proofs to the client as quickly and easily as possible, and for a small number of images like this, that means emailing them directly from Lightroom straight to the client. If I had a large number of images to send (15, 20, or more), at that point I'd create a web proofing page, and you can find out how to do exactly that in the bonus web chapter I included on this book's companion webpage (the address is in the intro of this book).

Step One:

Press **G** to jump back to the Grid view and click on your Selects collection. Select the three images you just gave the quick retouch to, as they're the one's we're going to send to the client. Now, go under the Library menu and choose **Rename Photos** (as shown here). When the Rename Photos dialog appears, change the name to something simple the client will be able to work with (I use the person's name or something specific to the shoot, then Proof, then a sequential number, so in this case, all the images will be renamed FurProof-1, FurProof-2, and so on).

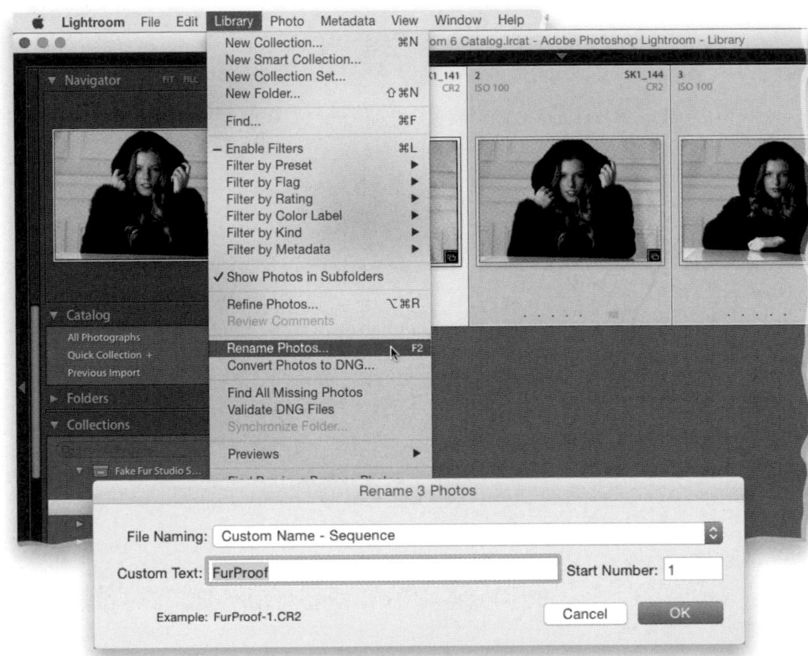

Step Two:

Now, while your three Selects are still selected, go under the File menu and choose **Email Photos** (as shown here).

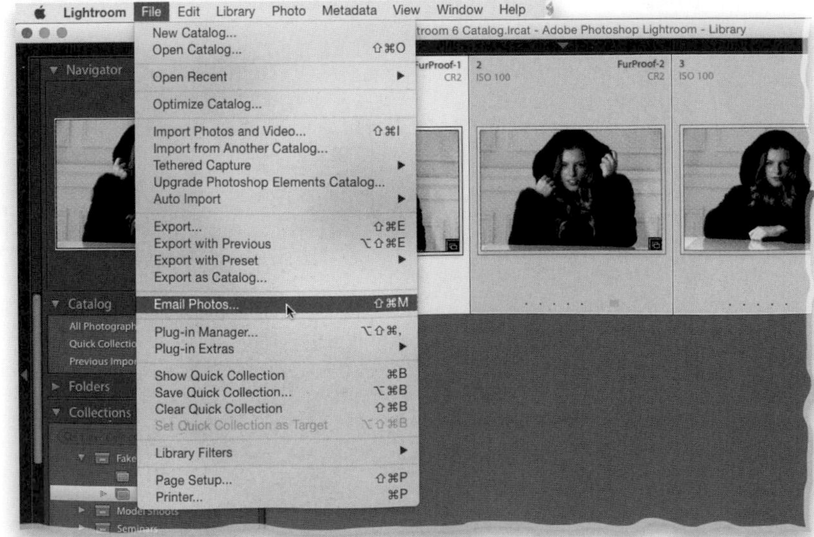

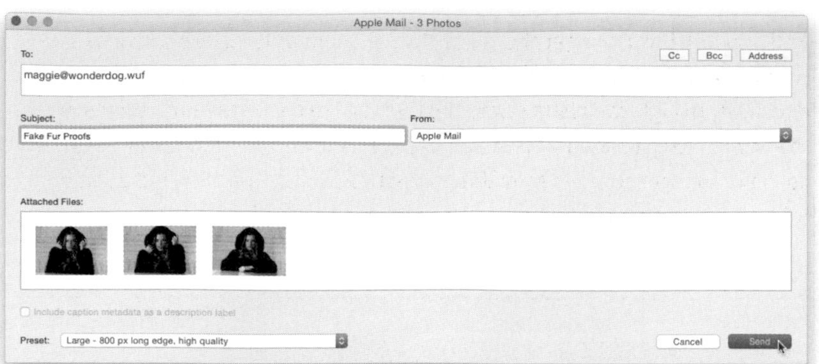

Step Three:

This brings up Lightroom's email message dialog (shown here), where you enter your client's email address, the subject line of your email, and so on (more on emailing back on page 342). The one thing I do want to point out is the size you'll be sending these. You might want to send very small proofs if you're concerned about the client using the images before they're finished (or before you've been paid), in which case, not only should you send a smaller size (choose **Small** from the Preset pop-up menu in the bottom-left corner), but you also might want to add a visible watermark (see page 338 for how to do that). Once you've added your client's address, just click the Send button in the lower-right corner.

Step Four:

This opens your email application, creates a blank email, fills in all the info you just added, and attaches your photos. If you take a look here, I sent pretty decent-sized proofs to the client. I left the preset set to Large, so the long edge is 800 pixels long, and the quality was set to High, but even at that, these three JPEG files combined only added up to 283 KB. So, you can see that you could actually send quite a few via email (if each one is approximately just 94 KB in file size, with these settings, you could send around 50 JPEG proofs like this via email and still be under even the most conservative email attachment limit of 5 MB). Hit the Send button and off they go to the client. Now, we just keep our fingers crossed and hope they like 'em (don't worry, they'll like 'em).

Workflow Step Six: Making the Final Tweaks & Working with Photoshop

Once the client gets back to me with their pick(s), then I start working on the final image(s)—first in Lightroom, and then, if necessary, I jump over to Photoshop. In this case, the Plexiglas doesn't reach all the way to the left side of the image and we need to fix the background on the right side of the image, so we'll jump over to Photoshop for that stuff, but the process always starts here in Lightroom.

Step One:

Once the client emails me their pick(s), I go back to the Selects collection in the Library module and I label it as Red by pressing the number **6** on my keyboard (I don't usually do this, but you could even make a separate collection with just their final picks and name it "Client Selects," but that's totally up to you). In this case, the client only chose one shot (which I marked with a Red label, as seen here). We need to fix the Plexiglas on the left and the background on the right, in addition to straightening the photo. Go ahead and straighten it in the Develop module (see Chapter 8 for how to do this). The rest is a job for Photoshop, so press **Command-E (PC: Ctrl-E)** to send the red-labeled image over to Photoshop. When the Edit Photo dialog appears, choose Edit a Copy with Lightroom Adjustments (as seen here), then click Edit to open it in Photoshop.

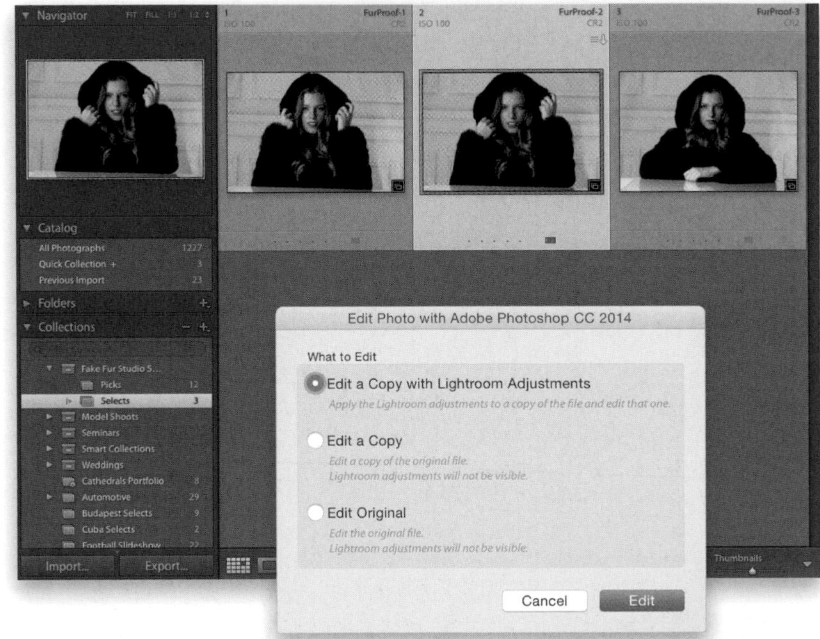

Step Two:

Once the image opens in Photoshop, zoom in tight (press **Command–+ [PC: Ctrl–+]**). Now get the Rectangular Marquee tool **(M)** from the Toolbox and drag out a rectangular selection over the end of the Plexiglas, where it's sticking up (as seen here). By doing this before we start retouching, it kind of puts a protective "fence" around that area so we don't accidentally retouch any of the table we want to keep—it keeps our retouching within that rectangle and we can't paint or clone outside of it.

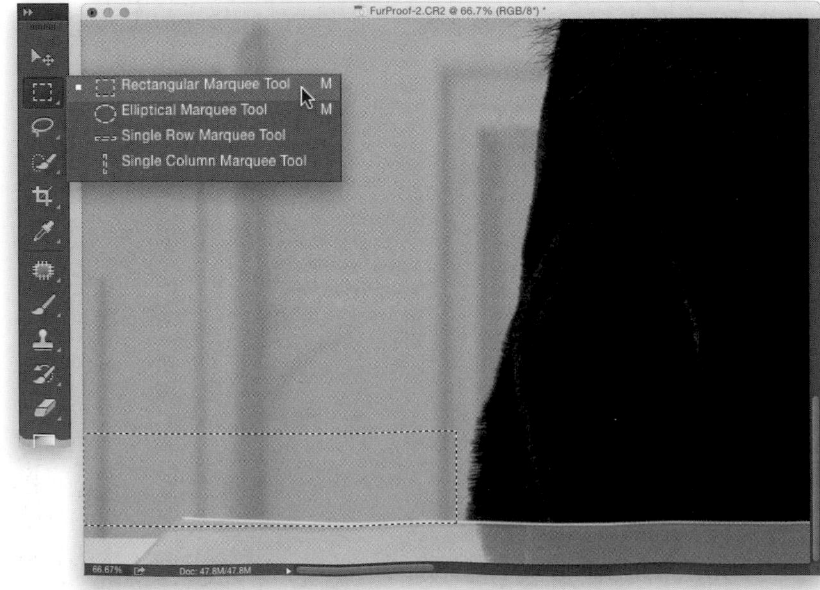

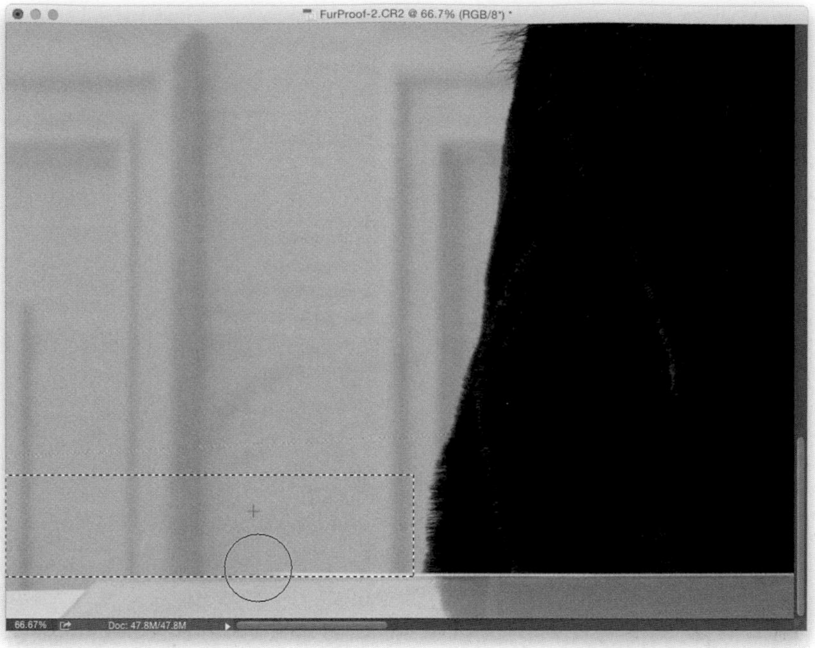

Step Three:

Get the Clone Stamp tool (**S**; its icon looks like a rubber stamp). We're going to use it to clone (copy) the area right above where the Plexiglas bends up, and clone right over that bend. The way the Clone tool works is: you press-and-hold the Option (PC: Alt) key and click on the clean area you want to use to clone over the bad area (this is called "sampling"). Once you've done that, you just move your cursor over the bad area and start painting (well, cloning) over that area, and it copies from that area you sampled right over the bad stuff. So, let's do that here. Option-click (PC: Alt-click) once right along that gray edge of the background and then move straight down and start painting. The + (plus sign) cursor you see shows where you're cloning from (where you're sampling) and the circle shows where you're cloning to. Paint all along that edge to clone over that part that's sticking up.

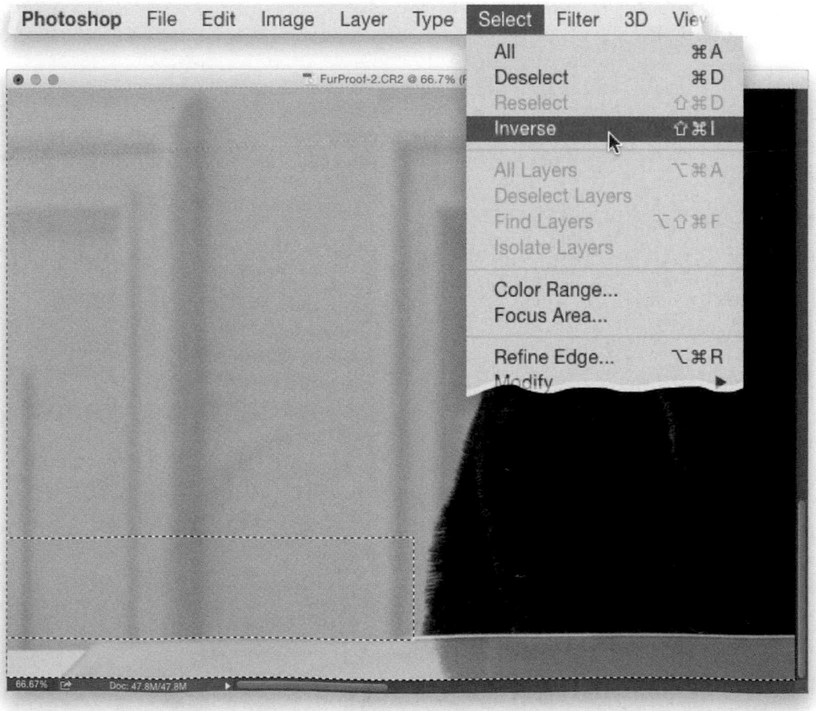

Step Four:

Once that's cloned over (as seen here), we need to work on extending the Plexiglas to the edge of the image. Right now, anything we do will only affect what's inside that rectangular selected area, right? So, we need the opposite—we need to protect the area inside that rectangle and paint over the area outside of (below) it. We need to protect the inverse of the selection, so go under the Select menu and choose **Inverse** (as shown here). Now, everything is selected *but* that rectangular area where we cloned (this way, we don't have to worry about accidentally cloning over the area we just fixed). See that bottom-left corner? See how there's a gap there where the Plexiglas stopped short? That's what we've got to fix. We've got to clone over that spot by sampling in the existing Plexiglas and painting over that gap.

Continued

Step Five:

Take the Clone Stamp tool, Option-click (PC: Alt-click) once to the right of the gap to sample that area of Plexiglas (see where that plus-sign cursor is? That's the spot), and then just clone right over that gap until it looks like the Plexiglas goes all the way to the edge. If you mess up, just press **Command-Z (PC: Ctrl-Z)** to Undo and try again. Okay, that fixes the left side. Press **Command-D (PC: Ctrl-D)** to Deselect. Now, on to fixing the wall behind her on the right side, which has some weird lighting problems.

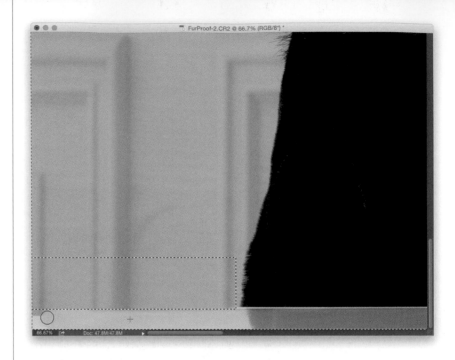

Step Six:

See that weird area in the bottom-right corner, where you see the shadow hitting the wall, but then suddenly it's much brighter? It's pretty distracting, so we'll have to deal with that. One trick I try to use in situations like this is to use a different part of the wall (the wall on the other side) and make a copy of it so I can use it cover the mistake, but it'll take a little doing to get it match the color and tone. Start by making a rectangular selection of the left side of the wall in about the size you think would cover the problem over on the far right side (as seen here). Don't select down to the table—just select the wall. Once your selection is in place, press **Command-J (PC: Ctrl-J)** to put that selected area up on its own separate layer above the background.

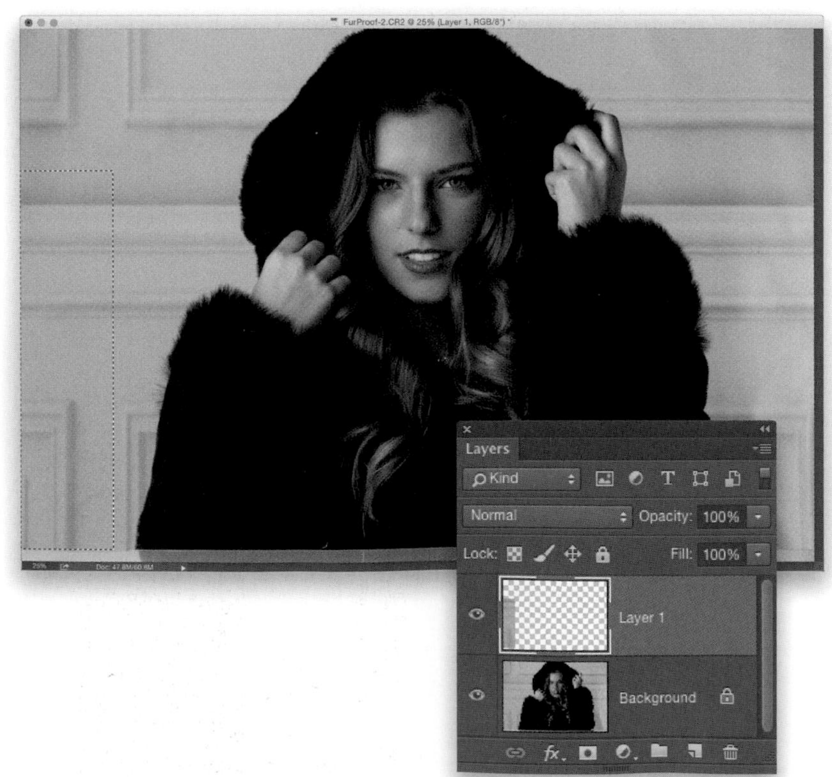

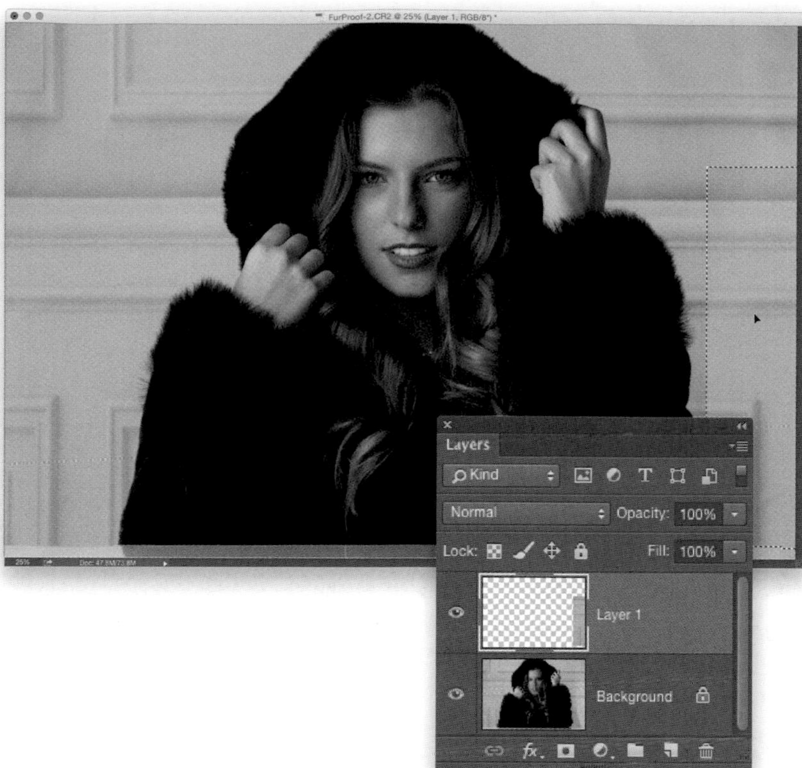

Step Seven:

Now that we have that selected area up on its own separate layer, let's move it into position on the other side. Press **V** on your keyboard to switch to the Move tool, then click-and-drag that tall rectangular area over to the other side (the right side of the image) and line it up with existing lines as best you can (as seen here). The lighting and color are very different on the right side than on the left, so even through our layer looks bluish against this more yellowish background, just go ahead and do the best you can to line it up and we'll deal with the weird color problem and the fact that you can see all the hard edges, in just a moment. Now, press-and-hold the Command (PC: Ctrl) key and, in the Layers panel, click once directly on the thumbnail for your top layer to put a selection around just that area (as seen here, where you can now see a selection around it again).

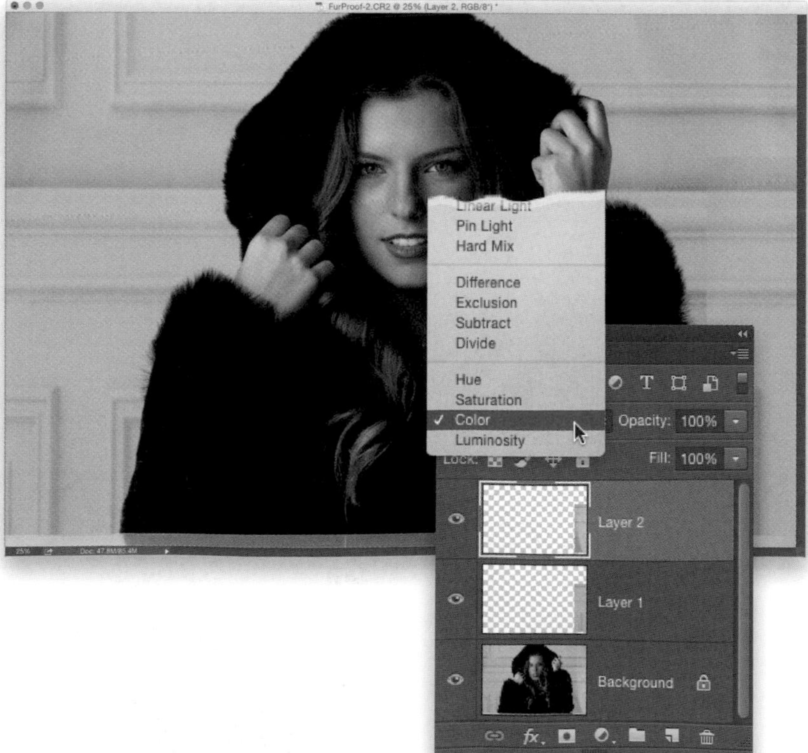

Step Eight:

Here's what we're going to do to fix our color problem and get rid of that bluish look to our repair: we're going to copy part of the bad wall up to its own separate layer, then we're going to change to a layer blend mode that will just bring over the color of the original wall, and not the detail. You do this in the Layers panel by, first, clicking on the Background layer to make it active, so the selection is now on the Background layer. Now, press Command-J again to put that selected area up onto its own separate layer, then drag this new layer to the top of the layer stack. At the top of the panel, you'll see a pop-up menu that says Normal. Click-and-hold on that pop-up menu and choose **Color**, and now the color matches better. We still see the hard edge, but at least the color is pretty good now.

Continued

Step Nine:

Now we're going to hide those hard edges by masking them away. But, before we do that, we need to make these two layers (the fix from the left side, and the Color mode layer on top of it that we used to match up the color), into just one layer. Click on the top layer (the Color layer) and press **Command-E (PC: Ctrl-E)** to merge these two layers while leaving the look intact. Now, to mask away that hard edge. First, click the Add Layer Mask icon at the bottom of the Layers panel (it's the third icon from the left). Next, press **D**, then **X**, to set your Foreground color to black, get the Brush tool **(B)** from the Toolbox, choose a nice soft-edged brush from the Brush picker up the Options Bar, and just paint along that edge and, as you do, it softens the edge (as seen here) to complete the repair.

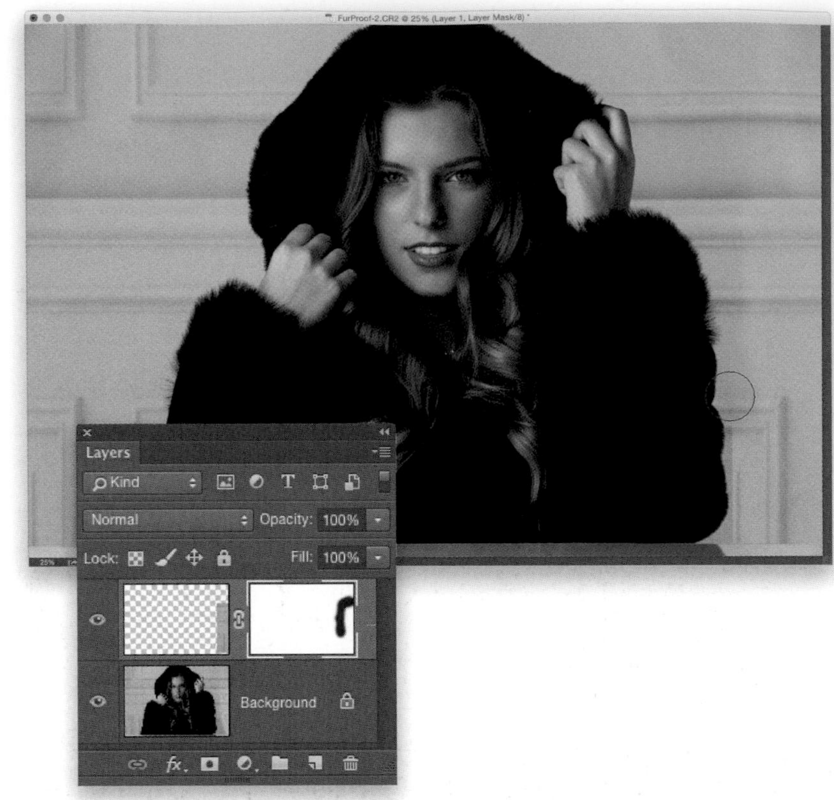

Step 10:

When you're done in Photoshop, you know the routine to send this edited image back to Lightroom: simply Save (press **Command-S [PC: Ctrl-S]**) and close the image window. That's it. When you switch back over to Lightroom, you'll see your edited image appear right next to the original in your collection, as seen here.

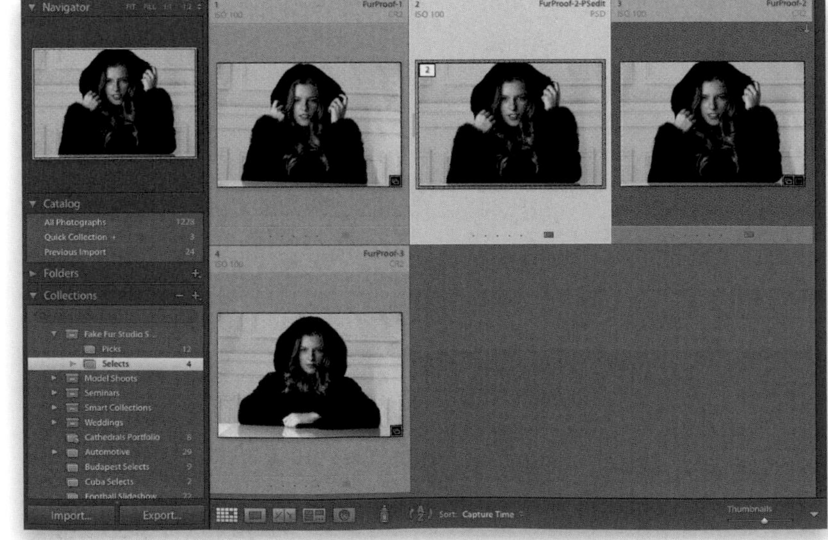

Once your image(s) has been retouched, it's time to deliver the final image(s) to the client, either via email or by delivering prints. The email part is the same as the emailing proofs part, so I won't put you through that again, but I do want to take you through making a print for the client.

Workflow Step Seven: Delivering the Finished Image(s)

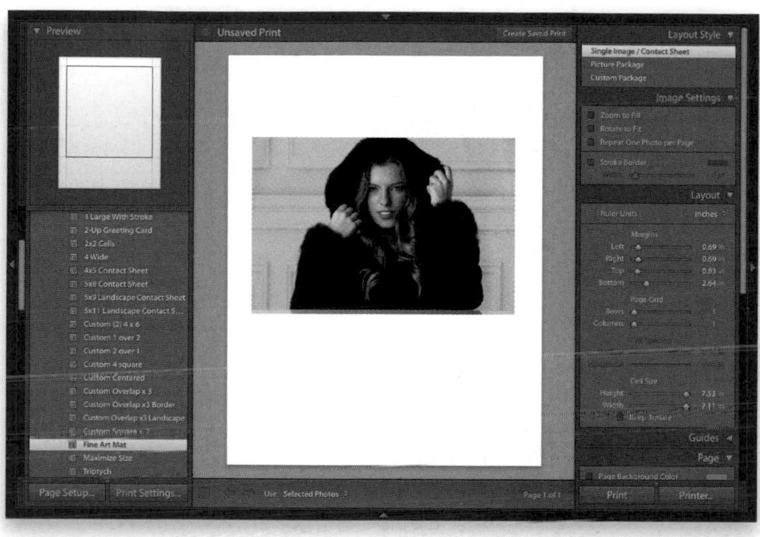

Step One:

Click on the image you've fully retouched, then go to the Print module and, in the Template Browser, click on whichever template you want to use (I chose the Fine Art Mat template for the image you see here). The default page setup for this template is US Letter (8x11"), so if you need a different size, click the Page Setup button (at the bottom of the left side Panels area) and choose your size there. When the dialog appears, choose the printer, paper size, and orientation, then click OK to apply these settings. You might need to tweak the margins a bit after choosing a new page size, since it doesn't automatically adjust everything.

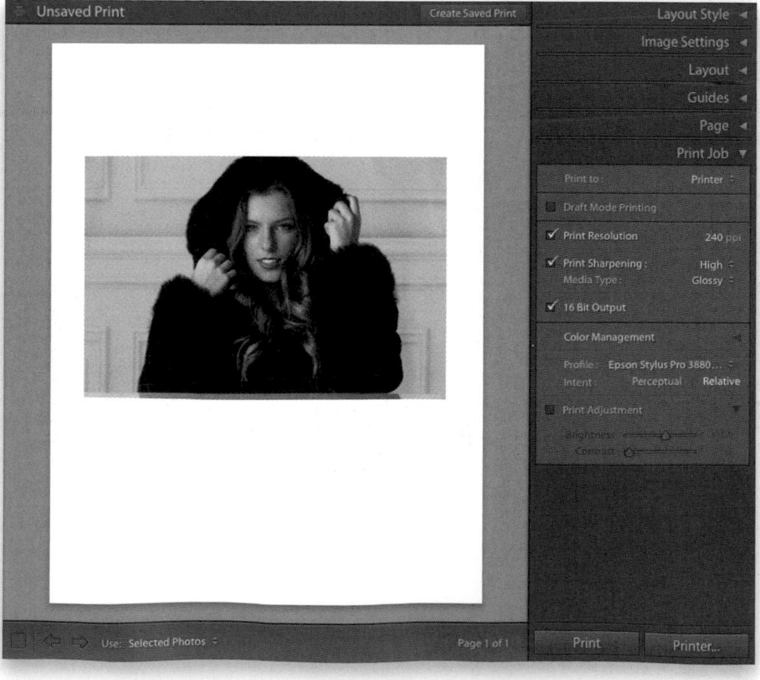

Step Two:

Now it's time to print the image (this is covered in-depth starting back in Chapter 13). Scroll down to the Print Job panel (in the right side Panels area), and from the Print To pop-up menu at the top, choose **Printer**. Then, for Print Resolution, since I'm printing to a color inkjet printer, I can leave it at 240 ppi. Make sure the Print Sharpening checkbox is turned on, choose the amount of sharpening from the pop-up menu on the right (I generally choose High), and then choose the type of paper you'll be printing on from the Media Type pop-up menu (I chose Glossy here). If your printer supports 16-bit printing, then you can turn on the 16 Bit Output checkbox. Then, in the Color Management section, choose your Profile and set your rendering Intent (again, covered in Chapter 13). I chose Relative here.

Continued

Step Three:

Now, click the Printer button at the bottom of the right side Panels area, and the Print dialog appears (the one shown here is from a Mac, but the Windows print dialog has the same basic features, just in a different layout). Your options will vary depending on your printer, but you'll want to choose the type of paper you're printing to from the Media Type pop-up menu, then under Output Resolution, I use SuperFine-1440dpi with the High Speed checkbox turned on.

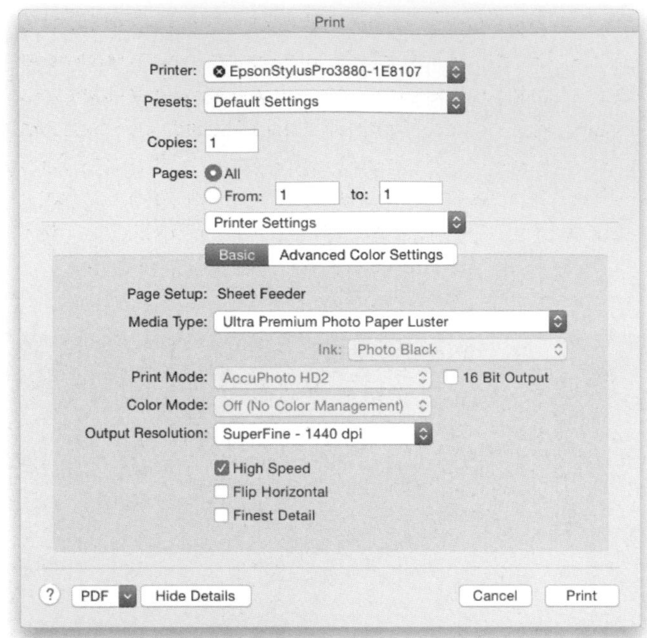

Step Four:

Let's print a proof: click the Print button, sit back, and wait for that puppy to roll out of the printer. Chances are your print is going to be darker than what you see on your super-bright, backlit computer screen. If so, turn on the Print Adjustment checkbox (at the bottom of the Print Job panel) and drag the Brightness slider to the right a bit, and then make another test print to compare to your screen. It might take a couple of test prints to get it right, but once you know how much brighter to make it, remember that setting for other prints on the same type of paper (you can adjust the contrast the same way). However, if there's a color problem, like the image looks too red, or too blue, etc., then you'll need to jump back to the Develop module, go to the HSL panel, and lower the Saturation for that color, then make another test print. There you have it: my workflow, from beginning to end. Remember, this workflow stuff is at the very end of the book for a reason: because it only makes sense after you've read the rest of the book. So, if anything didn't make sense, make sure you go back and reference the chapters I gave you here, so you can learn about anything you might have skipped over or didn't think you'd need.

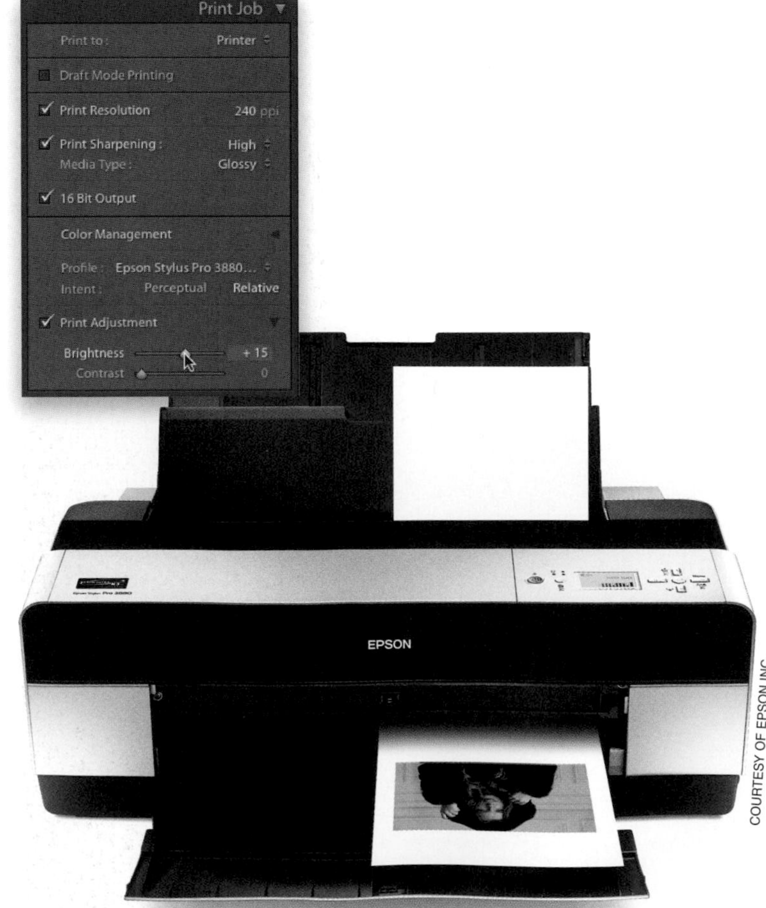

COURTESY OF EPSON INC.

10 Important Bits of Advice for New Lightroom Users

Here are 10 things I wish somebody had told me when I first started using Lightroom. Of course, at this point, you might be wondering why I'm giving you this important advice this late in the book. It's because if you are a new Lightroom user, you needed to learn some of these Lightroom terms, features, and concepts first, so this advice would actually make sense. If you're reading this and thinking, "But Scott, I already knew these terms and features!" then you're probably not a beginner, now, are you? :) Anyway, here they are (in no particular order):

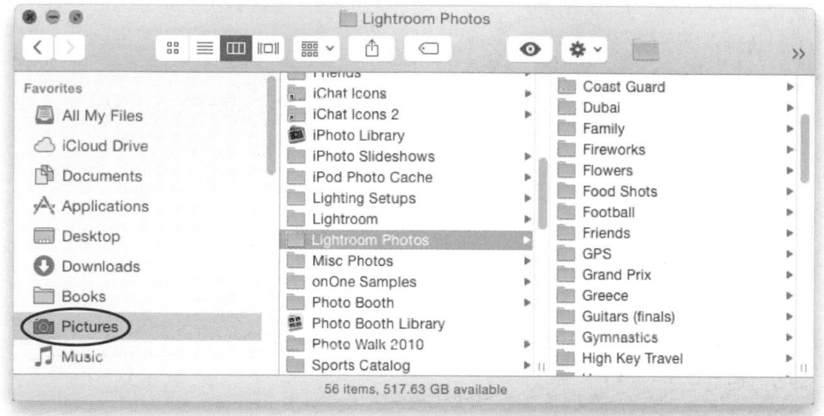

(1) Store all your photos inside one main folder.

You can have as many subfolders inside that one main folder as you want, but if you want to have peace, calm, and order in your Lightroom workflow, the key is not to import photos from all different locations on your computer (or on an external hard drive). Choose one main folder (like we talked about in Chapter 1), and put all your folders of photos inside that one main folder. *Then*, import them into Lightroom (or if you're importing from a memory card, have those images copied from the card into a folder within your main folder). Plus, this makes backing up your image library a breeze. Every time I run into someone whose Lightroom life is a mess, it's because they didn't follow this one simple rule. Also, if you're working on a laptop, it's totally fine to store your photos on an external drive, rather than on your laptop ('cause your laptop's drive is going to get full really quickly)!

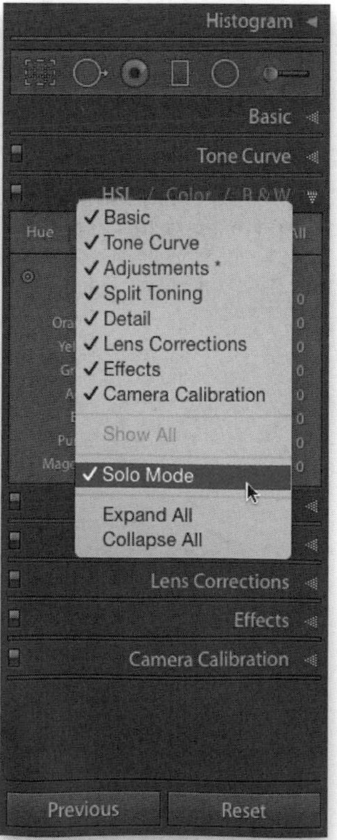

(2) Use Solo Mode to make navigation easier and to cut clutter.

If you're tired of scrolling up and down the long list of open panels in Lightroom, I highly recommend turning on Solo Mode. That way, the only panel you'll see is the one you're working in (and the rest all automatically collapse). This not only cuts clutter, but it saves time and makes it easier to focus on just what you're working with. Turn this on by Right-clicking on the title of any panel and choosing **Solo Mode**. You will so love working like this.

Continued

(3) Use collections instead of folders.

Folders are where all the actual photos you imported from a particular shoot are stored on your computer, or on an external hard drive. But once we import all those photos, all most of us really care about are the good ones, and that's why collections were invented. We always joke that "folders are where we go when we want to see our bad shots from a shoot," because we put all our good shots—our "keepers"—in a collection right away. It's kind of like we used to do with traditional film—we printed the good ones and put them in a photo album, and we kept the rest in the processing sleeve we got from the lab. Collections are like photo albums (in fact, I wish they had just called them albums). Plus, collections are safer because they'll help keep you from accidentally erasing images from your computer or hard drive.

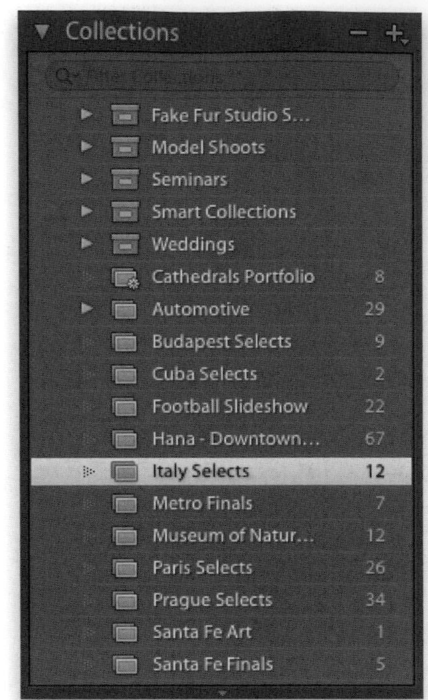

(4) Do as much work in Lightroom as possible.

I do about 85% of my work in Lightroom itself, and I only go over to Photoshop to do something that Lightroom just can't do (like compositing images with layers, or creating professional-level type, or using the Pen tool, or advanced portrait retouching, etc.). You can do an amazing amount of your everyday work within Lightroom's Develop module (especially since the addition of a regular "Healing Brush" in Lightroom 5). So, take the time to learn these tools, and you will speed your workflow (and simplify your life) in ways you can't imagine, by staying in Lightroom as much as possible.

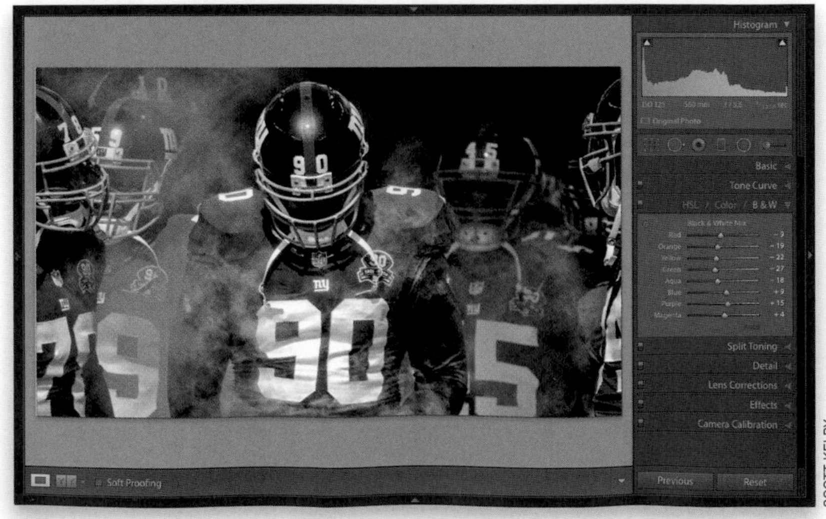

SCOTT KELBY

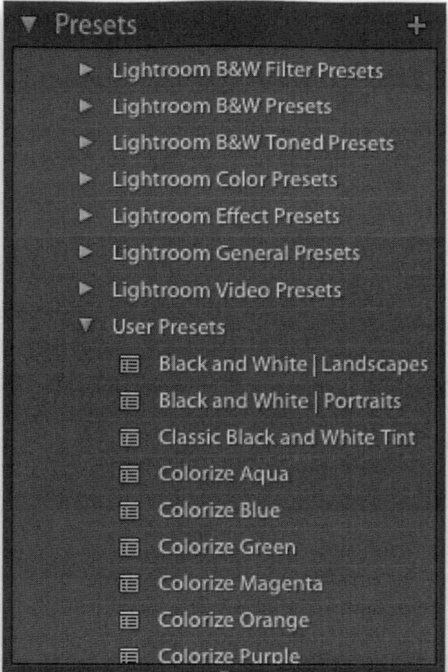

(5) Want to work really fast? Create presets and templates.
The key to working efficiently in Lightroom is to make presets and templates for the things you do every day (even though a lot of users never take the few seconds it takes to create even one). If you find yourself making a particular edit more than just a couple of times, make a Develop module preset for it, so it's always just one click away. Have a printing setup you use pretty often? Save it as a printing template. How about when you're exporting files as JPEGs or TIFFs? Make an Export preset and save time. Or even an Import preset to save time there. The ability to make and use presets and templates is one of the big advantages of Lightroom, and once you start using them, your efficiency will go through the roof.

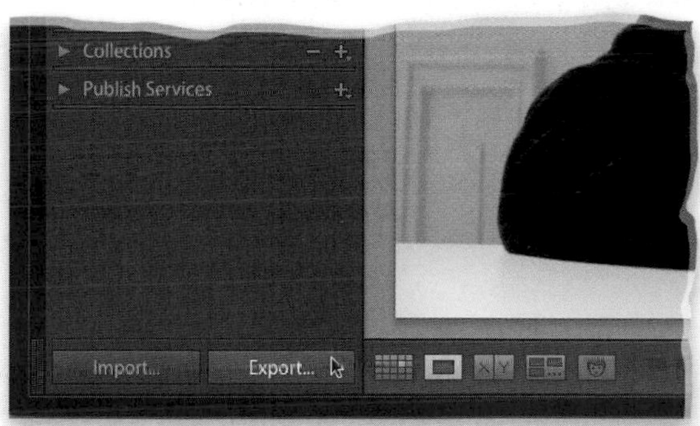

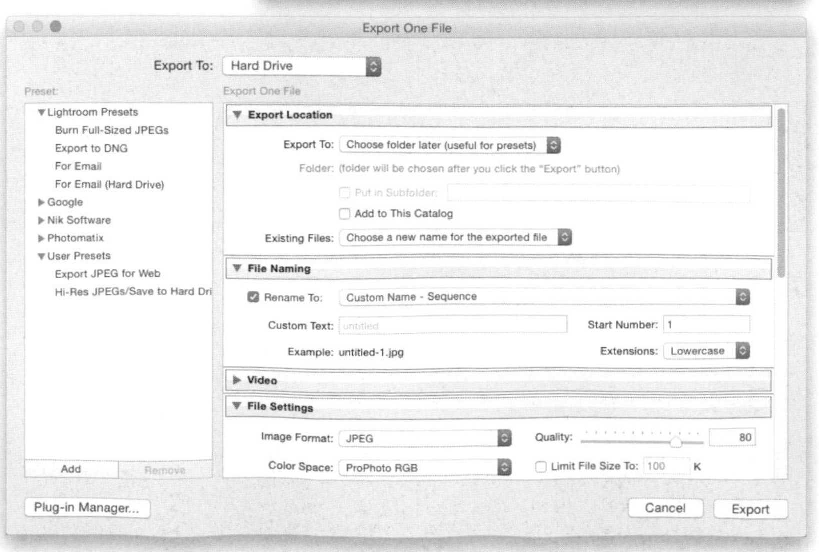

(6) Saving your images as JPEGs.
I get asked this question again and again at my Lightroom seminars. It's because it's not totally obvious how to do it, because there is no "Save As" or even just a "Save" command under the File menu (like almost every other application on earth). If you do go under the File menu, you'll find four different Export commands, but none of them say "Export as JPEG," so again, it's not really obvious. However, you can just choose Export, and when the Export dialog appears, you'll have the option to save your selected image (or images) as a JPEG. By the way, since saving JPEGs is something you'll probably be doing a lot, you might as well create an Export preset, so you don't have to fill everything in every time. I'm just sayin'.

Continued

(7) Turn off Auto Hide & Show for panels.

I get more emails from new Lightroom users asking if there's a way to turn off this feature than you can shake a stick at. I have users literally begging me, "Please tell me there's a way to stop the panels from popping in and out on me all day long!" Thankfully, there is: Right-click on the little arrow on the center edge of each panel and a pop-up menu will appear, where you can just choose **Manual** and now the panels will only open when you actually click on that little arrow (or if you press the F-key keyboard shortcuts—**F5** to show/hide the top Navigation panel; **F6** for the Filmstrip at the bottom; **F7** for the left side Panels area; and **F8** for the right side Panels area—or if you press the **Tab key**, which will hide all the panels).

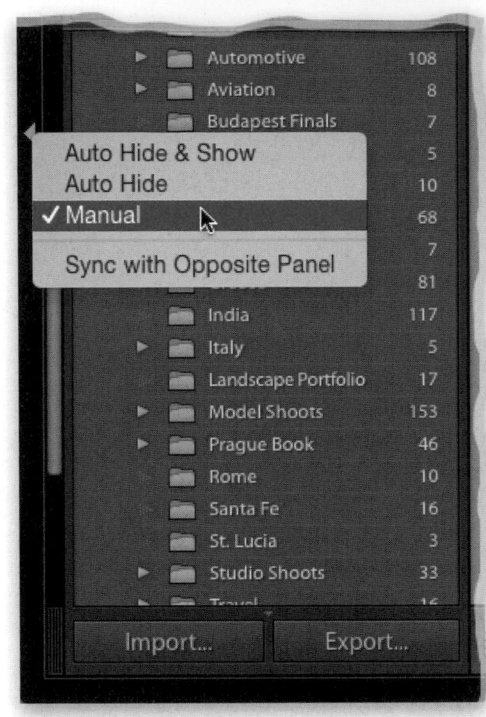

(8) Throw away your old backups.

If you back up your catalogs on a regular basis (once a day or weekly), before long, you're going to have a whole bunch of backups stored on your computer. After a short while, if you've got a lot of photos, those old, outdated backups are going to start eating up a lot of space on your hard disk. So, go to your backups folder and delete the ones that are more than a couple of weeks old. After all, if your catalog got messed up, would you want to go back months in time, or to last week's backup? Right—those old ones are pretty much useless. Also, if you already back up your entire computer on a regular basis (like to the Cloud, or a wireless hard drive like Time Capsule, or Crash Plan, or whatever), you might not need to back up your catalog at all because you've already got a recent backup in those places.

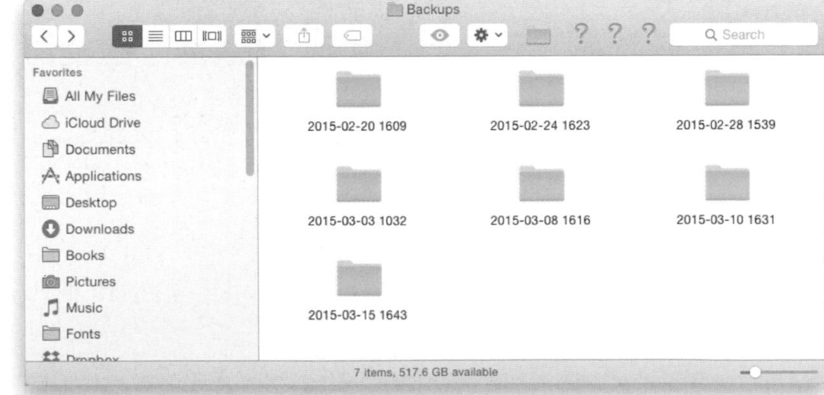

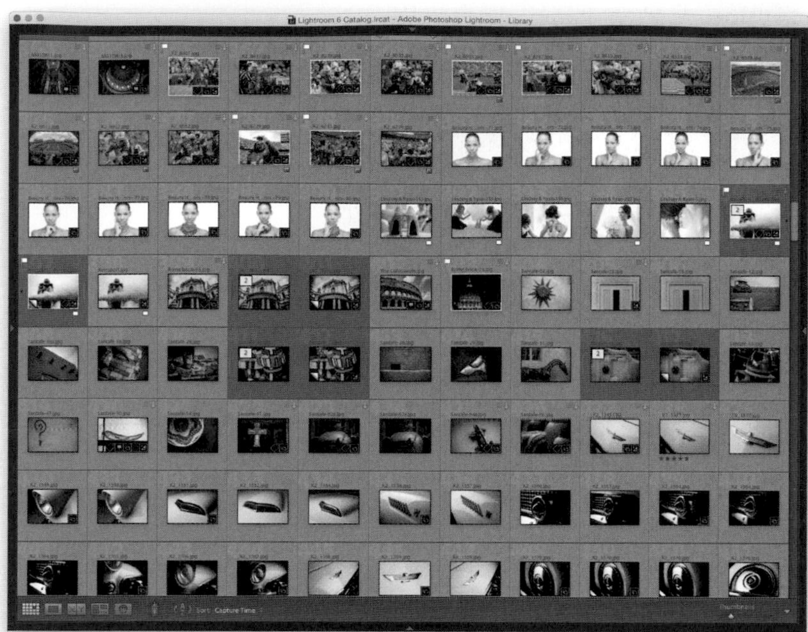

Lightroom File Edit Library Photo Metadata

- New Catalog...
- Open Catalog... ⇧⌘O
- Open Recent ▶
- Optimize Catalog...
- Import Photos and Video... ⇧⌘I
- Import from Another Catalog...
- Tethered Capture ▶
- Upgrade Photoshop Elements Catalog...
- Auto Import ▶
- Export... ⇧⌘E
- Export with Previous ⌥⇧⌘E
- Export with Preset ▶
- Export as Catalog...
- Email Photos... ⇧⌘M
- Plug-in Manager... ⌥⇧⌘,
- Plug-in Extras ▶
- Show Quick Collection ⌘B
- Save Quick Collection... ⌥⌘B
- Clear Quick Collection ⇧⌘B
- Set Quick Collection as Target ⌥⇧⌘B
- Library Filters ▶
- Page Setup... ⇧⌘P
- Printer... ⌘P

(9) Stick with one single catalog as long as you can.

While you certainly can have multiple catalogs (it's a Lightroom feature), my advice to you would be to try to stick with just one single catalog as long as you possibly can. That's a long time these days, because Lightroom can now handle up to around 150,000 images with no problem (although, if things start to move slowly when you have over 100,000 or so images, make sure you run Optimize Catalog from the File menu). Having just one catalog will make your life so much easier, and you'll have all your images right in front of you without having to reload different catalogs to search through your personal image library. I hear the same advice from Adobe's Lightroom Product Manager, Tom Hogarty, when people ask him about multiple catalogs. His answer? Stick with one catalog. It's sage advice.

Continued

(10) Ask yourself if you really need to be adding keywords or not. We were all originally taught to invest a reasonable amount of time adding global and specific keywords (search terms) to all the photos we import. If you're selling stock photography, or if you're a journalist, this is an absolute must, and if you have a client base that might call you up and ask, "Send me all your photos of red cars, and they need to all be in vertical orientation, and I only need ones where you can see the driver, and the driver has to be female," then you'll want to keyword like a pro. However, if you're just keeping track of the photos from your vacation to Paris last year, you might not need to go through all your photos and assign keywords. Ask yourself this question: "When was the last time I couldn't find the photos I needed by just going to my Collections panel?" For example, if I needed to find my photos from a family trip I took to Italy two years ago, I'd just go to my Collections panel, look under 2013, under Travel, and scroll down to Italy. If I went to Italy twice, I'd see two collections: one called "Italy" and one called "Italy 2." How hard is that? It's a no-brainer, right? So, if you're not having problems getting your hands on the photos you need in just a few seconds using collections with simple descriptive names (like Italy), you might be able to skip all the keywording stuff altogether (like I usually do). I'm not telling you not to keyword—I'm just asking you to consider whether you really need to spend the time adding a bunch of keywords or not, because most users probably don't need many (or any).

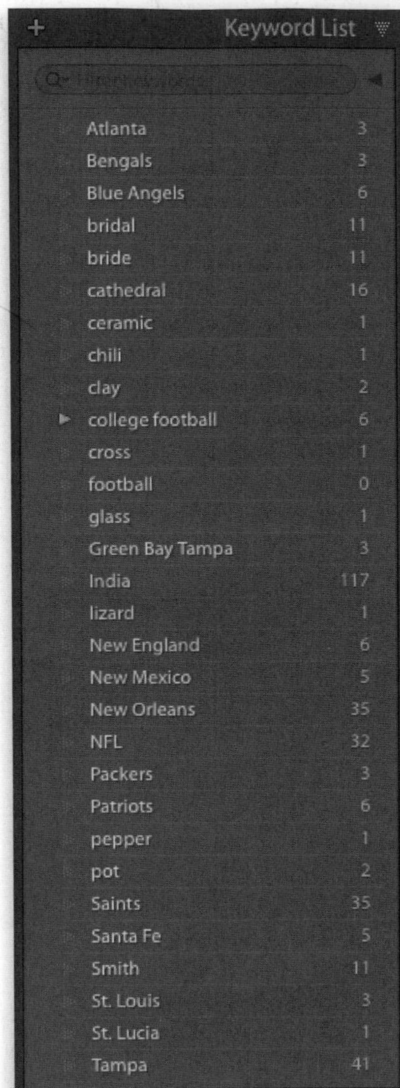

If this way of learning Lightroom resonated with you, and now you want to learn more about Lightroom (or Photoshop), or even just how to take better photos, I've got you totally covered! Here's a little bit about another book that I've written, using the same style and feel that I've written this book in, as well as some other cool resources. Hope you find these helpful.

Want to Learn More?

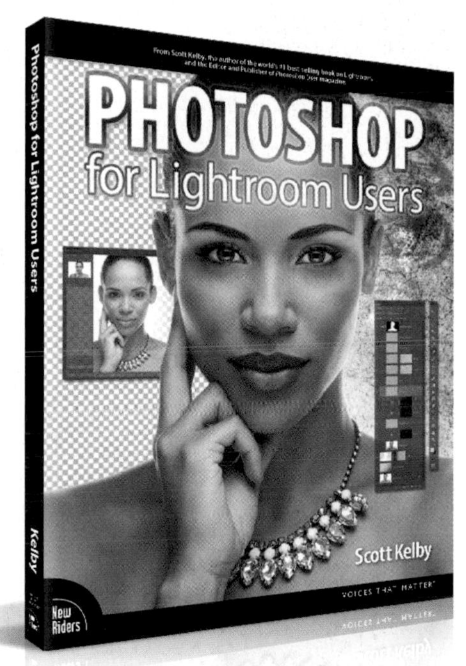

Photoshop for Lightroom Users

As you saw a couple times here in the book, there are things that Lightroom still can't do and times where you'll need to jump over to Photoshop, so I created a book for Lightroom users to teach just those things photographers need to do over in Photoshop, without duplicating things we can already do in Lightroom. So, you're not going to learn all of Photoshop, just the stuff for photographers that you can't do here in Lightroom.

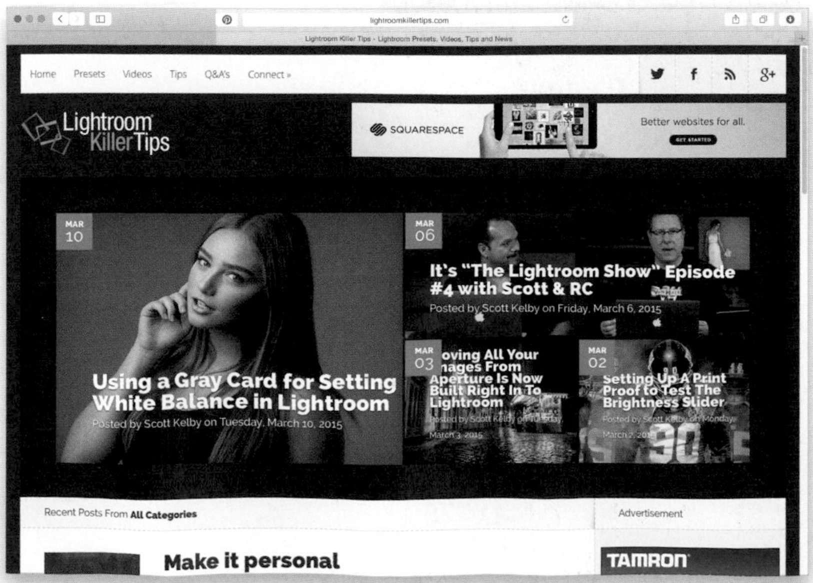

My Site: LightroomKillerTips.com

My buddy, RC Concepcion, and I post free tips and tutorials about Lightroom there every weekday, and we've got free preset downloads, and we answer a lot of questions, and do fun giveaways and contests, and it's just a really great community of Lightroom users. We'd love to have you join in. Just go to LightroomKillerTips.com and bookmark it (or follow the RSS feed, if you like). There's nothing to sign up for or register—just come and be a part of it all. You'll dig it.

Continued

My Full-Length Online Training Classes on Lightroom

Well, it's not just my Lightroom classes—we've got lots of full-length, in-depth online classes from some of the best-known Lightroom instructors in the world over at KelbyOne.com (that's the home of our online education for photographers). While you're there, we've got literally hundreds of classes on everything from lighting to Photoshop, from posing to landscape photography, and everything in between from instructors you know and trust (like Joe McNally, Jay Maisel, Joel Grimes, Moose Peterson, Zack Arias, Peter Hurley, and many more). It's super-affordable, you can be a monthly member or annual, but either way, you get full access to our complete library of classes. The full scoop is at KelbyOne.com.

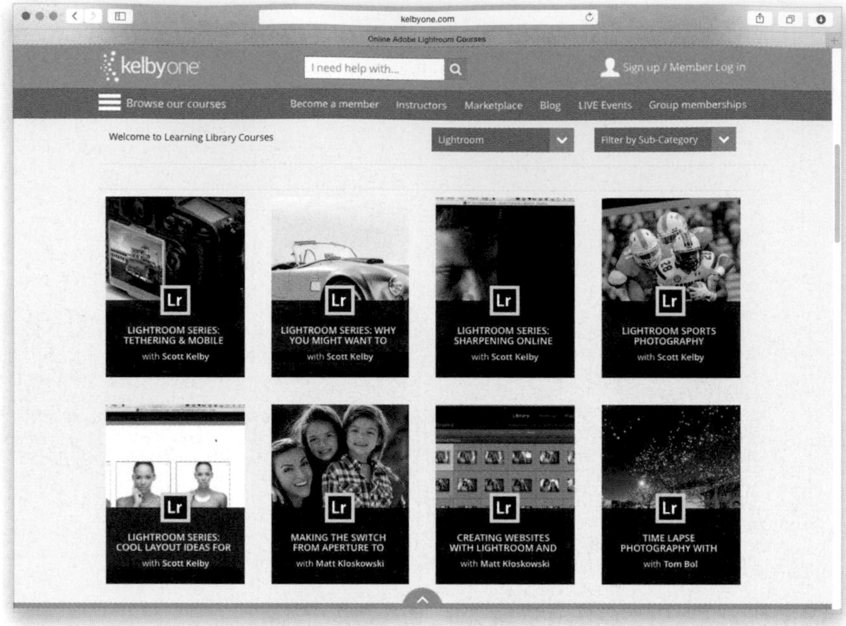

Come Learn from Us Live

I'm out on the road doing live full-day seminars all over the U.S., Canada, and in the UK (and hopefully, this year in Europe again). During my Shoot Like a Pro Tour: Reloaded, I do quite a bit of Lightroom training, including a class on my "Seven-Point System for Lightroom," so if you get a chance, I hope you'll come out and spend the day with me. RC Concepcion is on tour, as well, with our Lightroom LIVE! tour, which is a full day dedicated to taking your Lightroom skills to the next level. Also out there for KelbyOne Live is Ben Willmore, and he's doing a tour for us on using Lightroom & Photoshop together. Ben is just an awesome teacher—one of the best. You can find out about all our live seminar tours at kelbyonelive.com. Hope to meet you in person at one this year!

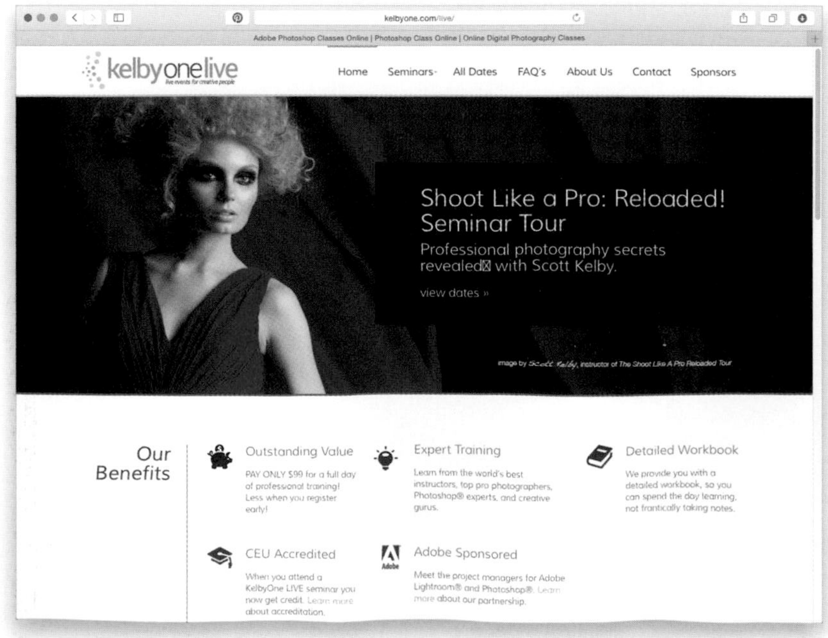

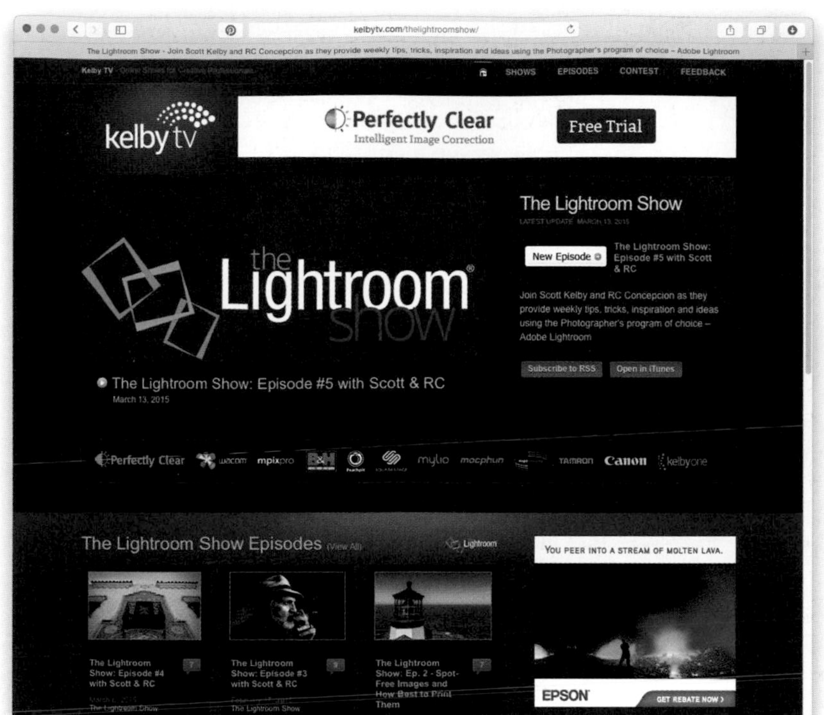

Learn Awesome Tips Every Week from *The Lightroom Show*

Each week, I co-host a show (with my buddy RC Concepcion) called *The Lightroom Show*. It's around 12 to 15 minutes long, but we pack it start to finish with Lightroom tips and techniques, and we take viewer images from start to finish, so folks can see how we would edit the images. The show is free (we post a new episode every Friday), and you can watch it at **kelbytv.com/thelightroomshow**. We also post the show each week at LightroomKillerTips.com.

Index

D

E

N

O

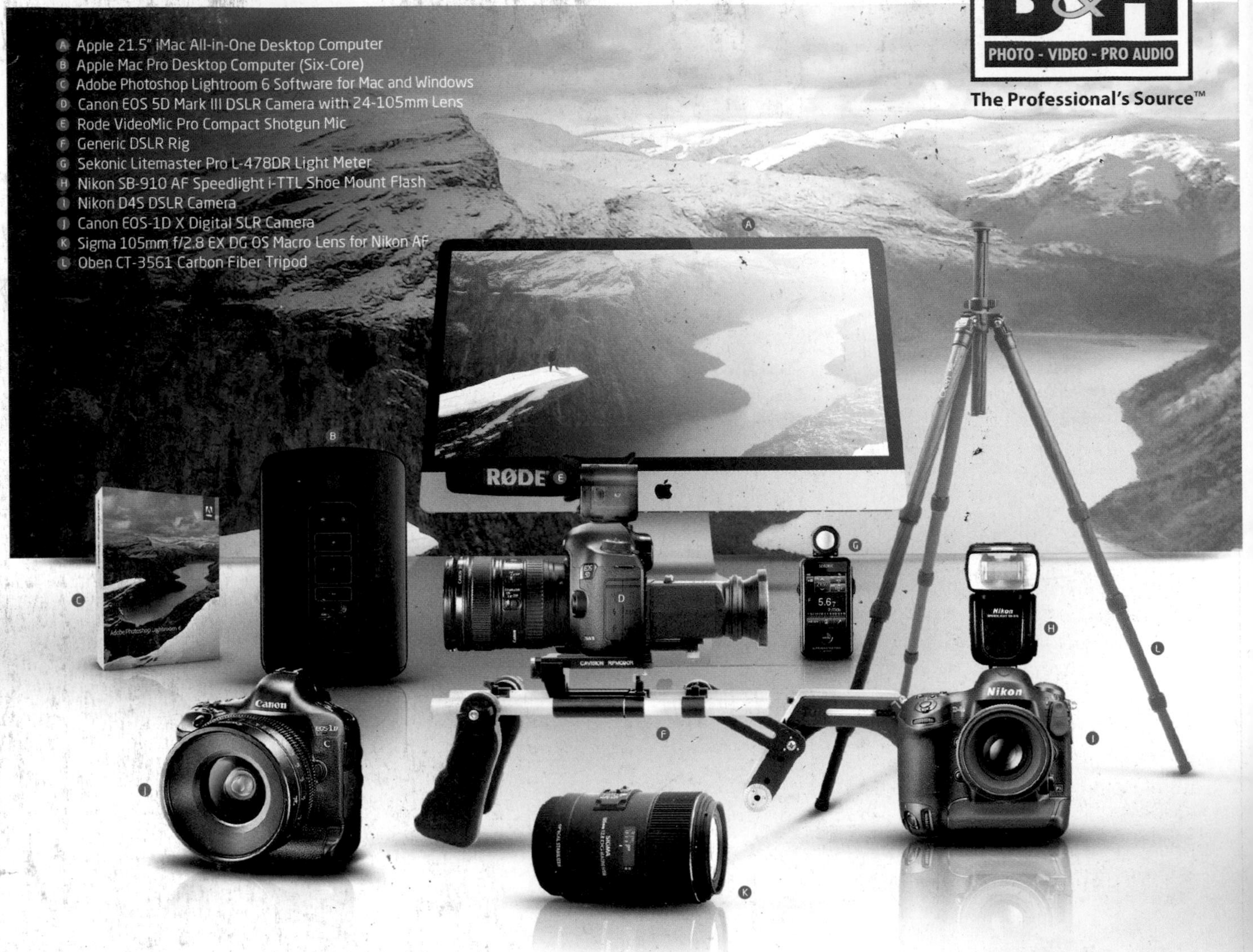

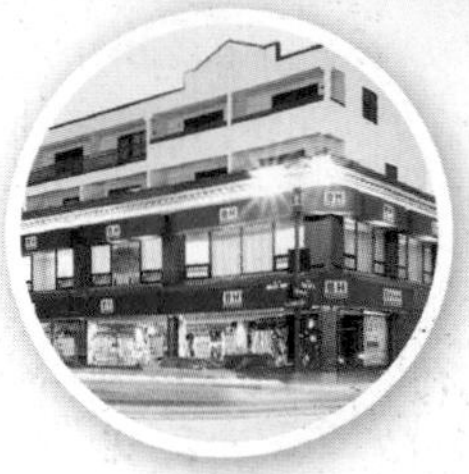

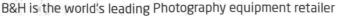